MASTER VISUALLY™ Windows® XP

From
maranGraphics®

&

Hungry Minds™

Best-Selling Books • Digital Downloads • e-books • Answer Networks •
e-Newsletters • Branded Web Sites • e-learning

New York, NY • Cleveland, OH • Indianapolis, IN

Master VISUALLY™ Windows® XP

Published by
Hungry Minds, Inc.
909 Third Avenue
New York, NY 10022
www.hungryminds.com

Library of Congress Control Number: 2001099506
ISBN: 0-7645-3621-4
Printed in the United States of America
10 9 8 7 6 5 4 3 2

1V/QU/QS/QS/MG

Distributed in the United States by Hungry Minds, Inc.
Distributed by CDG Books Canada Inc. for Canada; by Transworld Publishers Limited in the United Kingdom; by IDG Norge Books for Norway; by IDG Sweden Books for Sweden; by IDG Books Australia Publishing Corporation Pty. Ltd. for Australia and New Zealand; by TransQuest Publishers Pte Ltd. for Singapore, Malaysia, Thailand, Indonesia, and Hong Kong; by Gotop Information Inc. for Taiwan; by ICG Muse, Inc. for Japan; by Intersoft for South Africa; by Eyrolles for France; by International Thomson Publishing for Germany, Austria and Switzerland; by Distribuidora Cuspide for Argentina; by LR International for Brazil; by Galileo Libros for Chile; by Ediciones ZETA S.C.R. Ltda. for Peru; by WS Computer Publishing Corporation, Inc. for the Philippines; by Contemporanea de Ediciones for Venezuela; by Express Computer Distributors for the Caribbean and West Indies; by Micronesia Media Distributor, Inc. for Micronesia; by Chips Computadoras S.A. de C.V. for Mexico; by Editorial Norma de Panama S.A. for Panama; by American Bookshops for Finland.
For corporate orders, please call maranGraphics at 800-469-6616 or fax 905-890-9434.
For general information on Hungry Minds' products and services, please contact our Customer Care Department within the U.S. at 800-762-2974, outside the U.S. at 317-572-3993 or fax 317-572-4002.
For sales inquiries and reseller information, including discounts, premium and bulk quantity sales, and foreign-language translations, please contact our Customer Care Department at 800-434-3422, fax 317-572-4002, or write to Hungry Minds, Inc., Attn: Customer Care Department, 10475 Crosspoint Boulevard, Indianapolis, IN 46256.
For information on licensing foreign or domestic rights, please contact our Sub-Rights Customer Care Department at 212-844-5000.
For information on using Hungry Minds' products and services in the classroom or for ordering examination copies, please contact our Educational Sales Department at 800-434-2086 or fax 317-572-4005.
For press review copies, author interviews, or other publicity information, please contact our Public Relations department at 317-572-3168 or fax 317-572-4168.
For authorization to photocopy items for corporate, personal, or educational use, please contact maranGraphics at the address above.

Trademark Acknowledgments

Permissions

U.S. Corporate Sales

Contact maranGraphics at (800) 469-6616 or fax (905) 890-9434.

U.S. Trade Sales

Contact Hungry Minds at (800) 434-3422 or fax (317) 572-4002.

Praise for Visual books...

"If you have to see it to believe it, this is the book for you!"
–PC World

"I would like to take this time to compliment maranGraphics on creating such great books. I work for a leading manufacturer of office products, and sometimes they tend to NOT give you the meat and potatoes of certain subjects, which causes great confusion. Thank you for making it clear. Keep up the good work."
–Kirk Santoro (Burbank, CA)

"I write to extend my thanks and appreciation for your books. They are clear, easy to follow, and straight to the point. Keep up the good work! I bought several of your books and they are just right! No regrets! I will always buy your books because they are the best."
–Seward Kollie (Dakar, Senegal)

"What fantastic teaching books you have produced! Congratulations to you and your staff."
–Bruno Tonon (Melbourne, Australia)

"Compliments To The Chef!! Your books are extraordinary! Or, simply put, Extra-Ordinary, meaning way above the rest! THANK YOU THANK YOU THANK YOU! for creating these. They have saved me from serious mistakes, and showed me a right and simple way to do things. I buy them for friends, family, and colleagues."
–Christine J. Manfrin (Castle Rock, CO)

"A master tutorial/reference — from the leaders in visual learning!"
–Infoworld

"Your books are superior! An avid reader since childhood, I've consumed literally tens of thousands of books, a significant quantity in the learning/teaching category. Your series is the most precise, visually appealing and compelling to peruse. Kudos!"
–Margaret Rose Chmilar (Edmonton, Alberta, Canada)

"You're marvelous! I am greatly in your debt."
–Patrick Baird (Lacey, WA)

"Just wanted to say THANK YOU to your company for providing books which make learning fast, easy, and exciting! I learn visually so your books have helped me greatly–from Windows instruction to Web page development. I'm looking forward to using more of your Master Books series in the future as I am now a computer support specialist. Best wishes for continued success."
–Angela J. Barker (Springfield, MO)

"A publishing concept whose time has come!"
–The Globe and Mail

"I have over the last 10-15 years purchased $1000's worth of computer books but find your books the most easily read, best set out and most helpful and easily understood books on software and computers I have ever read. You produce the best computer books money can buy. Please keep up the good work."
–John Gatt (Adamstown Heights, Australia)

"The Greatest. This whole series is the best computer learning tool of any kind I've ever seen."
–Joe Orr (Brooklyn, NY)

maranGraphics is a family-run business
located near Toronto, Canada.

At maranGraphics, we believe in producing great computer books—one book at a time.

Each maranGraphics book uses the award-winning communication process that we have been developing over the last 25 years. Using this process, we organize screen shots, text and illustrations in a way that makes it easy for you to learn new concepts and tasks.

We spend hours deciding the best way to perform each task, so you don't have to! Our clear, easy-to-follow screen shots and instructions walk you through each task from beginning to end.

We want to thank you for purchasing what we feel are the best computer books money can buy. We hope you enjoy using this book as much as we enjoyed creating it!

Sincerely,

The Maran Family

Please visit us on the Web at:
www.maran.com

CREDITS

Authors:
Ruth Maran & Paul Whitehead

Director of Copy Development:
Kelleigh Johnson

Copy Development and Editing:
Raquel Scott
Cathy Lo
Roderick Anatalio

Screen Captures:
Jill Maran
Wanda Lawrie

Project Manager:
Judy Maran

Editors:
Wanda Lawrie
Roxanne Van Damme
Norm Schumacher
Megan Kirby

Layout Designers:
Treena Lees
Steven Schaerer

Illustrator:
Russ Marini

Screen Artist:
Darryl Grossi

Screen Shot Permissions:
Jennifer Amaral

Indexer:
Kelleigh Johnson

Senior Vice President and Publisher, Hungry Minds Technology Publishing Group:
Richard Swadley

Publishing Director, Hungry Minds Technology Publishing Group:
Barry Pruett

Editorial Support, Hungry Minds Technology Publishing Group:
Martine Edwards
Lindsay Sandman
Sandy Rodrigues

Post Production:
Robert Maran

ACKNOWLEDGMENTS

Thanks to the dedicated staff of maranGraphics, including Jennifer Amaral, Roderick Anatalio, Darryl Grossi, Kelleigh Johnson, Megan Kirby, Wanda Lawrie, Treena Lees, Cathy Lo, Jill Maran, Judy Maran, Robert Maran, Ruth Maran, Russ Marini, Steven Schaerer, Norm Schumacher, Raquel Scott, Roxanne Van Damme and Paul Whitehead.

Finally, to Richard Maran who originated the easy-to-use graphic format of this guide. Thank you for your inspiration and guidance.

1 GETTING STARTED

1) WINDOWS XP BASICS

2) VIEWING FILES

TABLE OF CONTENTS

3) WORK WITH FILES

4) PRINTING

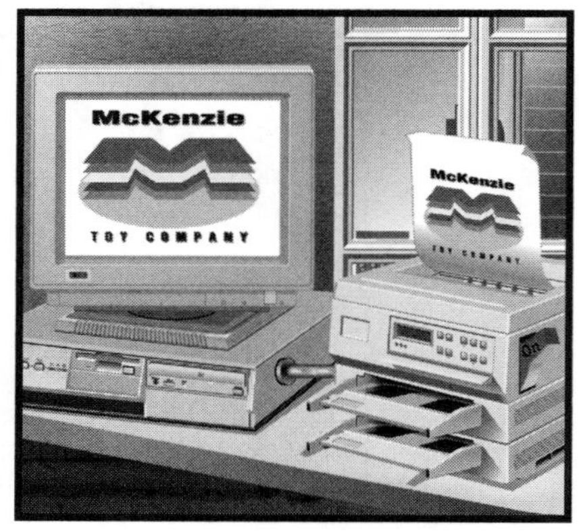

2 WINDOWS XP ACCESSORIES

5) USING WORDPAD

6) USING PAINT

TABLE OF CONTENTS

7) MORE ACCESSORIES

3 CUSTOMIZE WINDOWS XP

8) MANAGE MULTIPLE USERS

9) CUSTOMIZE YOUR COMPUTER

9) CUSTOMIZE YOUR COMPUTER (Continued)

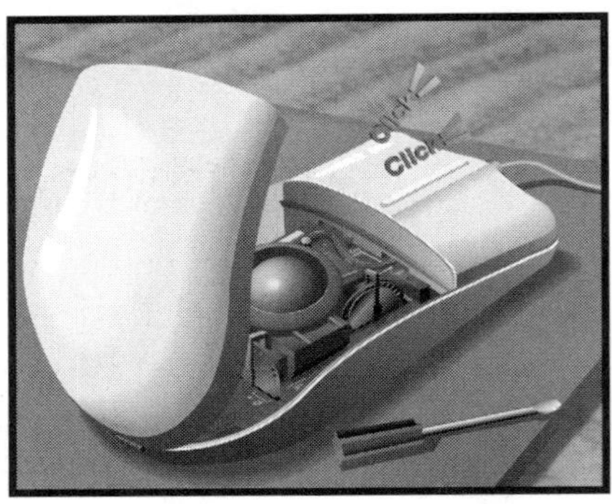

10) CUSTOMIZE THE TASKBAR AND START MENU

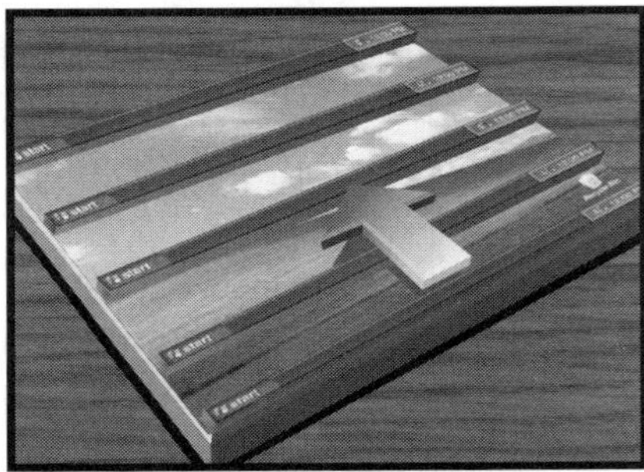

TABLE OF CONTENTS

11) USING THE ACCESSIBILITY FEATURES

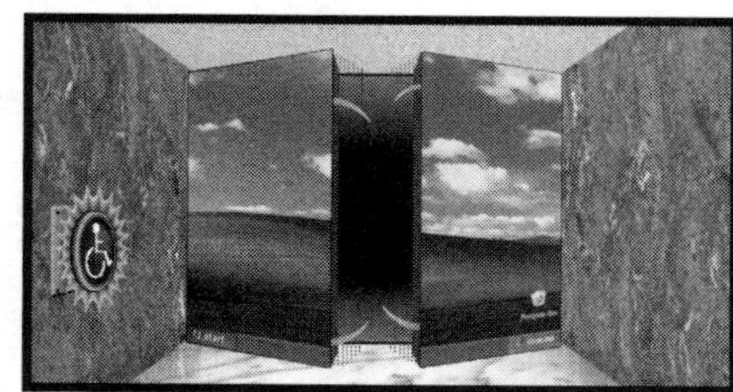

4 WINDOWS XP AND MULTIMEDIA

12) WORK WITH MULTIMEDIA

13) USING WINDOWS MEDIA PLAYER

14) CREATE MOVIES

5 CONNECT TO OTHER COMPUTERS

15) WORK WITH MODEMS

16) WORK WITH DIAL-UP CONNECTIONS

TABLE OF CONTENTS

17) MORE CONNECTION METHODS

6 NETWORKING

18) SET UP AND MONITOR A NETWORK

19) WORK ON A NETWORK

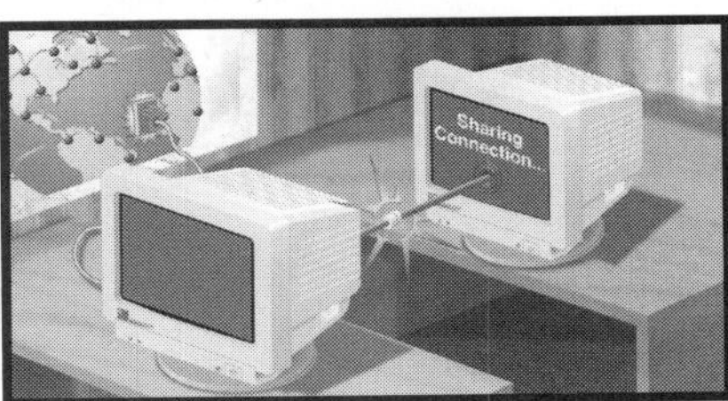

7 WINDOWS XP AND THE INTERNET

20) GET CONNECTED TO THE INTERNET

21) BROWSE THE WEB

TABLE OF CONTENTS

22) EXCHANGE E-MAIL MESSAGES

23) USING WINDOWS MESSENGER

24) WORK WITH NEWSGROUPS

8 MANAGE HARDWARE AND SOFTWARE

25) DISK MANAGEMENT

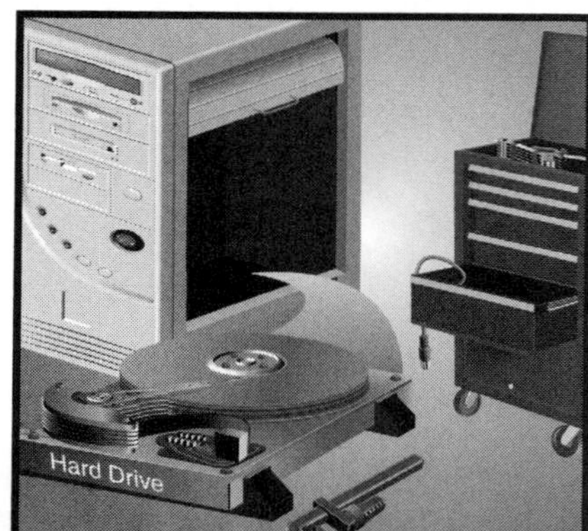

26) INSTALL SOFTWARE AND HARDWARE

TABLE OF CONTENTS

27) INSTALL AND UPDATE WINDOWS XP

28) MANAGE COMPUTER AND TROUBLESHOOT PROBLEMS

SECTION I

1) WINDOWS XP BASICS

2) VIEWING FILES

3) WORK WITH FILES

4) PRINTING

INTRODUCTION TO WINDOWS XP

Windows XP (Experience) is an operating system which ensures that all parts of your computer work together smoothly and efficiently. Windows XP controls the hardware on your computer and starts and operates your programs. Windows XP allows you to easily use your computer for work or entertainment.

Work With Files

When you create and save a document, Windows stores the document as a file. You can open, sort, move, copy, rename, print, search for and delete your files. If you accidentally delete a file, you can usually restore the file from the Recycle Bin. You can create folders to organize your files and you can place shortcuts on your desktop to help you easily access your favorite files and folders. You can also copy files to a CD and copy pictures from a digital camera. If you want to share files with friends and family, you can e-mail files and publish files to the Web.

Accessory Programs

Windows includes several programs you can use to perform tasks. You can use WordPad to compose simple documents or use Paint to create and work with pictures. You can also perform calculations using the on-screen Calculator.

Customization and Personalization

You can change the appearance and behavior of Windows to suit your needs. You can display a different picture on your desktop or change the style and colors used to display screen elements. Changing the screen resolution allows you to display more or less information on the screen. You can also have a screen saver appear when you are not using your computer. If you share your computer with other people, you can create a personalized user account for each person. You can also have programs start automatically each time you start Windows. The Accessibility features can help make the computer easier to use for people with special needs.

Entertaining Features

When you need a break from your work, you can play games such as Solitaire and Pinball. You can also make Windows more entertaining by assigning sounds to program events. Windows Media Player allows you to play video and sound files, listen to music CDs, play DVD movies and listen to radio stations that broadcast on the Internet. You can also use Windows Media Player to copy songs from music CDs and copy songs to a CD or a portable device such as an MP3 player. Windows Movie Maker allows you to transfer, organize and edit home movies on your computer before sharing them with friends and family.

Connect to Other Computers

You can use a dial-up connection to connect to your computer at work when you are traveling. You can also use Remote Desktop Connection to connect to another computer on your network or the Internet so you can remotely control the computer. The Briefcase feature allows you to work with your files on your home or portable computer when you are away from the office. When you return to the office, Briefcase can automatically update the files on your office computer.

Networking

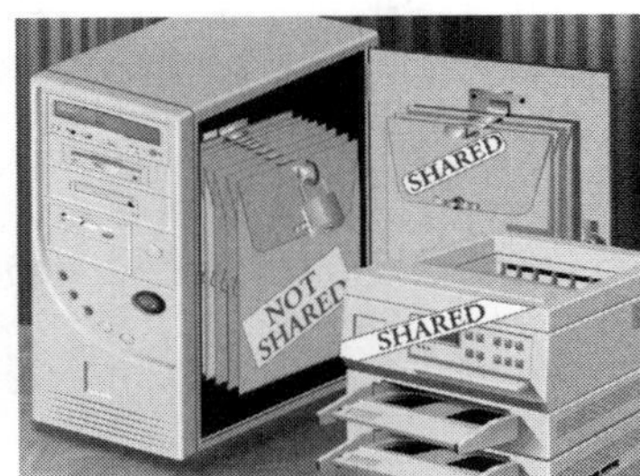

You can share your files and printer with people on your network. My Network Places allows you to view the shared resources on your network. Windows also provides a wizard that helps you quickly set up a home or small office network.

Access the Internet

Windows includes Internet Explorer, which allows you to browse through information on the Web. You can display, search for and print Web pages of interest and create a list of your favorite Web pages. Outlook Express allows you to exchange e-mail messages with people around the world. You can read, send and manage e-mail messages. Outlook Express also allows you to read and send newsgroup messages. You can use Windows Messenger to see when your friends are online, send instant messages, exchange files, have voice and video conversations and share programs.

Disk Management

Windows allows you to optimize the performance of your computer. You can view the amount of used and free space on your hard drive. You can also have Windows locate and repair any errors on your hard drive. Disk Cleanup allows you to remove unneeded files from your computer to free up disk space, while Disk Defragmenter better organizes the files on your hard drive.

Install Hardware and Software

You can use the wizards included with Windows to install a new hardware device or program. The wizards guide you step by step through the installation process. You can set up Windows to automatically get the latest Windows updates available on the Internet. This ensures that your computer is always up to date.

Solve Computer Problems

If you are experiencing problems with your computer, you can use System Restore to return your computer to a time before the problems occurred. You can allow a person at another computer to view your computer screen and chat with you to help you solve a computer problem. With your permission, the other person can even control your computer to help you fix the problem. If you are having problems running an older program on Windows XP, the Program Compatibility Wizard can help you find the proper compatibility settings for the program to run properly.

WHAT'S NEW IN WINDOWS XP

Windows XP is the next generation of the Windows operating system. Windows XP allows users to work more efficiently and is more secure and robust than older versions of Windows. Many programs will run faster on Windows XP than on older versions of Windows.

New Visual Design

Windows XP features a cleaner and more streamlined display. The Start menu automatically moves programs you have recently worked with to make them easy to access in the future. The new taskbar allows you to manage multiple programs and documents. The new ClearType text display makes text displayed on the screen easier to read, particularly on newer flat screen and LCD monitors. The Desktop Cleanup Wizard can automatically remove rarely used items from your desktop to ensure the desktop stays free of clutter.

File Management

Windows XP can automatically display options on a shortcut menu and display a list of common tasks on the left side of a window that correspond to the type of files you are working with. Windows XP allows you to group items together in a window to organize the information. The Search Companion allows you to easily search for files, folders, computers and more. When working with music files, you can copy files from a CD and then sort, organize and place the files in the My Music folder. The Web Publishing Wizard allows you to publish files to the Web. If you have a CD-recordable drive, you can also copy files to a CD. If you store large amounts of information on your computer, you can create more storage space by using zipped compressed folders.

Work With Pictures

When you are working with a folder containing pictures in Windows XP, the folder's icon can display miniature versions of up to four pictures stored within the folder to make finding pictures easier. You can use the Windows Picture and Fax Viewer to view your pictures without opening an image editing program. Windows XP also allows you to publish your pictures to the Web, attach them to e-mail messages or order prints of your pictures from an online printing service. The Scanner and Camera Wizard allows you to transfer images from a camera or scan pictures into your computer.

Multiple User Accounts

Windows XP makes sharing a computer with multiple users easier. Each user can have their own password-protected account that can help keep personal files and information private. You can, however, share information with other users by placing the information in the Shared Documents folder. Each user can also have their own .NET Passport to quickly access information at Web sites that support Passports. A new Welcome screen allows users to access their user accounts quickly and easily.

Windows Media Player

The new Windows Media Player allows you to access a wide range of media, including music CDs, MP3 files, video files, DVD movies and radio stations. You can also download or copy music files and then create your own music CDs. Using the Media Library, you can efficiently organize all your multimedia content.

Windows Movie Maker

You can use Windows Movie Maker to record videos directly to your computer using a wide range of video cameras and video capture cards. You can then use Windows Movie Maker to assemble the video clips and add audio, narration and special transition effects to create professional-looking videos.

Internet Explorer

The latest version of Internet Explorer makes it easier than ever to surf the World Wide Web. The new Media bar makes it easy to locate and access multimedia files on the Web. The new Related Links feature can help you quickly locate other Web pages that contain information related to the Web page you are currently viewing.

Windows Messenger

Windows Messenger lets you communicate with your friends and colleagues while you are connected to the Internet. You can exchange instant messages, have voice or video conversations, share programs and exchange files with other people.

Connect Computers

Windows XP's built-in network support allows you to connect multiple computers together to create a home or small office network. Windows XP provides easy-to-use wizards you can use to set up your network connections, share devices such as printers and connect your network to the Internet. Windows XP's Internet Connection Firewall helps prevent unauthorized access to your network. You can use the new Remote Desktop Connection feature to connect to your computer from another computer on the Internet or your local area network.

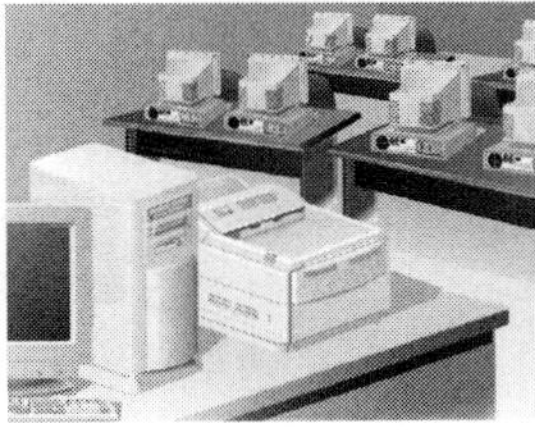

Assistance and Troubleshooting

Windows XP's Remote Assistance feature allows you to turn over control of your computer to a colleague or support personnel to help troubleshoot and solve any computer problems you may have. You can also use the System Restore feature to return your computer to a time before the problems occurred. Windows XP has an expanded and enhanced help feature that now allows you to access online support groups and information. The Program Compatibility Wizard can help you run older applications that may have problems working on Windows XP. The enhanced Task Manager lets you identify and close misbehaving programs.

PARTS OF THE WINDOWS XP SCREEN

The Windows XP screen displays various items that allow you to perform tasks in Windows. If you upgraded to Windows XP from a previous version of Windows, your screen may display different items than a computer that has a completely new installation of Windows XP. The preferences set on your computer will also affect the items that appear on your screen.

Menu Bar

Provides access to lists of commands available in a window.

Title Bar

Displays the name of an open window. The title bar of the window you are currently using has a darker color than other open windows.

Desktop

The background area of your screen.

Window

Displays the contents of a folder, document or other information. A window can be moved and sized.

Toolbar

Contains buttons that provide quick access to frequently used commands.

Icon

An item on the desktop or in a window. An icon can represent an item such as a file or a program.

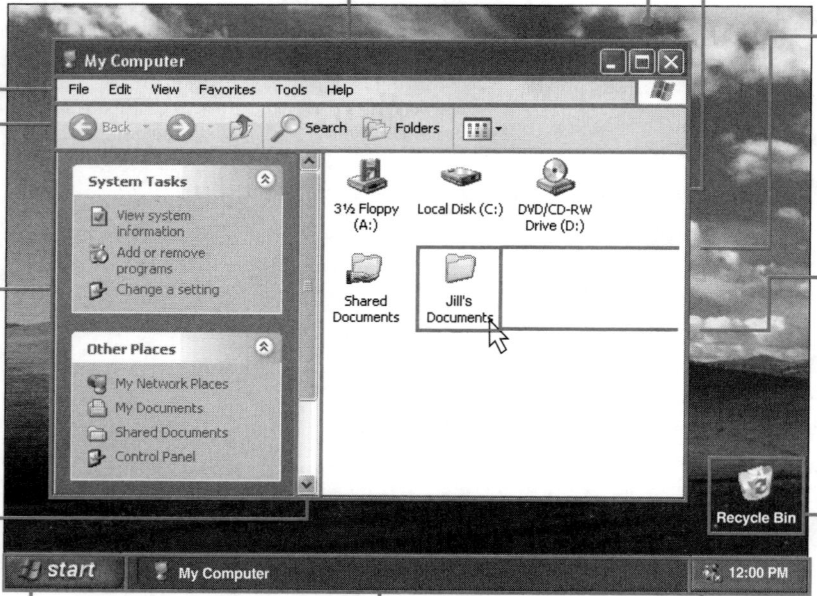

Task Pane

Provides quick access to common tasks and locations on your computer. The available options depend on the selected item.

Mouse Pointer

Indicates the position of the mouse on your screen. The mouse pointer moves when you move the mouse on your desk.

Recycle Bin

Stores deleted files and allows you to recover them later.

Scroll Bar

Allows you to scroll through a window.

Start Button

Gives you quick access to programs, files, computer settings, help and support and other Windows features.

Taskbar

Displays a button for each open window on your screen. You can use these buttons to switch between open windows.

Notification Area

Displays the current time and notification icons. Notification icons usually appear when events occur on your computer, such as when you print a file or receive an e-mail message.

USING THE MOUSE

A mouse is a handheld device that allows you to select and move items on your screen. When you move the mouse on your desk, the mouse pointer on your screen moves in the same direction.

The mouse pointer assumes different shapes, such as ⇖ or I, depending on its location on the screen and the task you are performing.

Click

Press and release the left mouse button. A click is usually used to select an item on the screen.

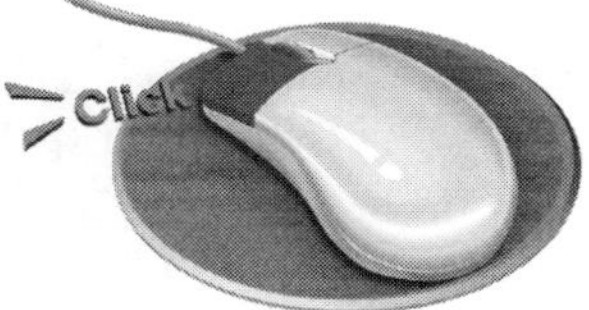

Right-click

Press and release the right mouse button. A right-click is usually used to display a list of frequently used commands for an item.

Mouse Wheel

Many mice have a wheel between the left and right mouse buttons that you can use to perform functions such as scrolling through a window or zooming in or out of a document.

Cleaning the Mouse

If the mouse has a moving ball, you should occasionally remove the small cover on the bottom of the mouse and clean the ball inside the mouse. Make sure you also remove dust and dirt from the inside of the mouse to help ensure smooth motion of the mouse.

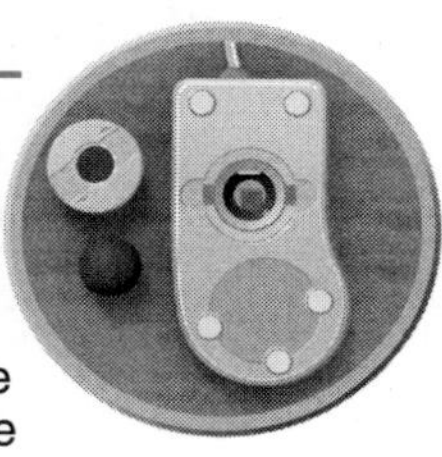

Double-click

Quickly press and release the left mouse button twice. A double-click is usually used to open a file or start a program.

Drag and Drop

Position the mouse pointer over an item on the screen and then press and hold down the left mouse button as you move the mouse to where you want to place the item. Then release the button. Dragging and dropping allows you to easily move an item to a new location. You can also drag and drop an item using the right mouse button. When you release the mouse button, a menu appears, allowing you to choose an option.

Mouse Pads

A mouse pad provides a smooth surface for moving the mouse on your desk. A mouse pad also reduces the amount of dirt that enters the mouse and protects your desk from scratches. Hard plastic mouse pads attract less dirt and provide a smoother surface than fabric mouse pads.

USING THE START MENU

You can use the Start menu to quickly access programs and Windows features on your computer.

The Start menu provides quick access to programs such as your Web browser, e-mail program and programs you have most recently used. The Start menu also provides access to commonly used locations, such as the My Documents and My Computer folders. You can also use the Start menu to quickly access Windows features, such as Windows help and the Search feature.

The Start menu contains the All Programs menu, which allows you to access all the programs installed on your computer. You can browse through the All Programs menu to find a program you want to use.

You can access the Start menu while you are working in any program. This is useful if you want to quickly start a new program without having to close or minimize the current program. For example, you may want to open a spreadsheet program while working with WordPad to compare data in the two programs.

USING THE START MENU

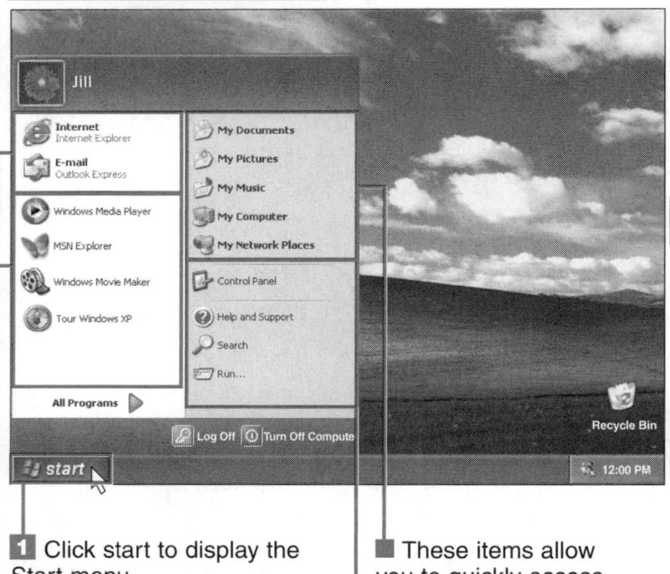

1 Click start to display the Start menu.

■ These items start your Web browser and e-mail program.

■ These items allow you to quickly start the programs you have most recently used.

■ These items allow you to quickly access commonly used locations.

■ These items allow you to change your computer's settings, get help, search for information and run programs.

■ If the Start menu displays the item you want to use, click the item.

2 If the item you want to use is not displayed on the Start menu, click All Programs.

■ A list of the programs on your computer appears. A menu item with an arrow (▶) will display another menu.

3 To display another menu, position the mouse over the menu item with an arrow (▶).

How can I find a program that does not appear on the Start menu?

✔ Try to locate the program using either My Computer, Windows Explorer or the Search feature. For information about the Search feature, see page 84.

Can I add an item to the Start menu?

✔ You can add any program or file to the Start menu. Find the item you want to add and then drag the item to the start button. Do not release the mouse button and the Start menu will appear. Continue dragging the item to the location on the Start menu or All Programs menu where you want the item to appear.

Can I rearrange the items on the Start menu?

✔ You can move an item on the Start menu by dragging the item to a new location.

Can I display the Start menu using my keyboard?

✔ Yes. You can press and hold down the Ctrl key and then press the Esc key to display the Start menu. If the Windows key (⊞) is available on your keyboard, you can also press this key to display the Start menu.

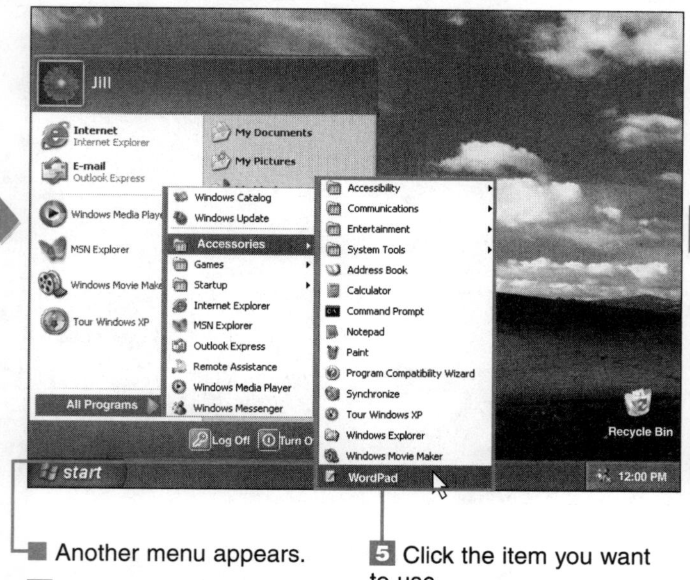

■ Another menu appears.

4 You can repeat step 3 until the item you want to use appears.

5 Click the item you want to use.

Note: To close the Start menu without selecting an item, click outside the menu area or press the Alt key.

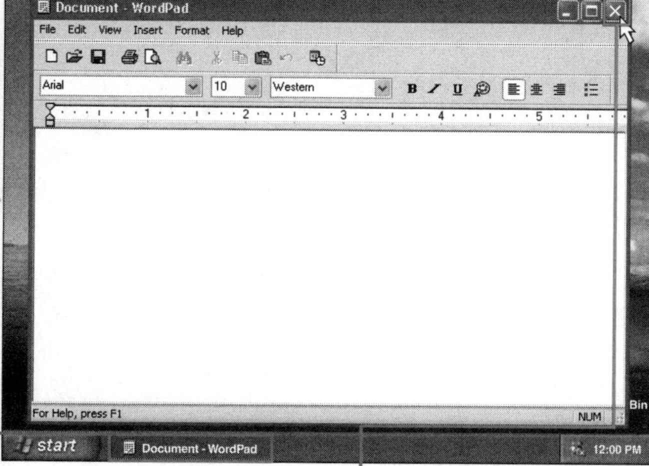

■ In this example, the WordPad window appears.

■ A button for the open window appears on the taskbar.

6 When you finish working with the window, click ☒ to close the window.

USING RUN TO START A PROGRAM

You can use the Run feature to quickly start a program. The Run feature is especially useful for programs that do not appear on the Start menu.

There are many programs that Windows does not display on the Start menu, such as programs that can be used to change the settings on your computer. This helps to avoid the accidental misuse of these programs. For example, if you type regedit in the Run dialog box, the Registry Editor starts. The Registry Editor allows you to change your system registry settings. Incorrect use of this program may cause serious damage to your computer.

You may also have MS-DOS and older Windows programs, such as games, that are not displayed on the Start menu. You can use the Run feature to start these types of programs.

When you begin typing the name of a program you want to start using the Run feature, Windows may display a list of matching programs that you can choose from. You can also display a list of programs you have recently started using the Run feature and then choose a program from the list.

USING RUN TO START A PROGRAM

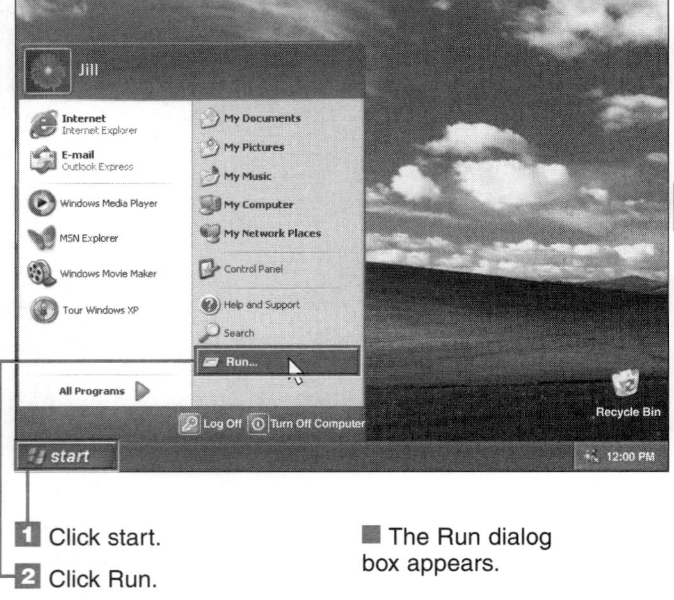

1 Click start.

2 Click Run.

■ The Run dialog box appears.

3 Type the name of the program you want to start.

■ You can click ⌄ to display a list of programs you recently used the Run feature to start. You can then select the program you want to start from the list.

What if I do not know the name of the program I want to start?

✔ You can click the Browse button in the Run dialog box to find a program you want to start.

Can I use the Run feature to open items other than programs?

✔ The Run feature can open many types of items. For example, you can open a Web page by typing the Web page address, such as www.maran.com. Typing the location and name of a file or folder, such as c:\Documents and Settings\Jill\My Documents\notes.txt, allows you to open the file or folder. You can also type the location of a shared computer, such as \\Wanda, to connect to the computer.

Is there another way to quickly start a program?

✔ You can add the program to the Start menu. Drag the program from your desktop or an open window to the start button. When you want to start the program, click the start button and then select the program.

Windows cannot find the program I want to start. What should I do?

✔ Some programs do not register the program location with Windows. You should type the location and program name, such as c:\Program Files\hockey.exe, to start these programs.

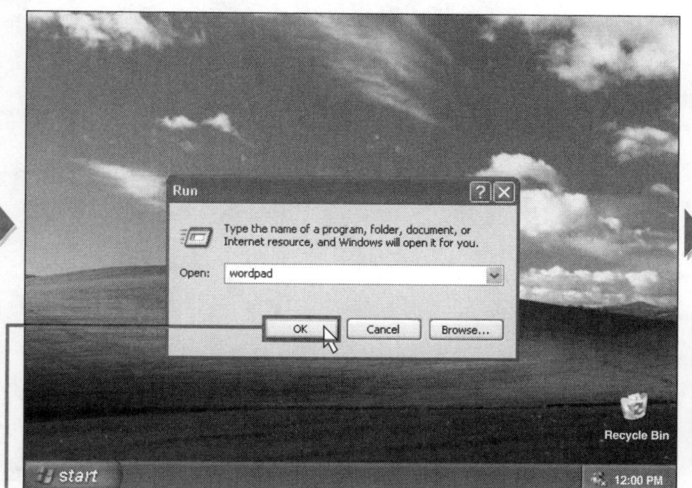

4 Click OK to start the program.

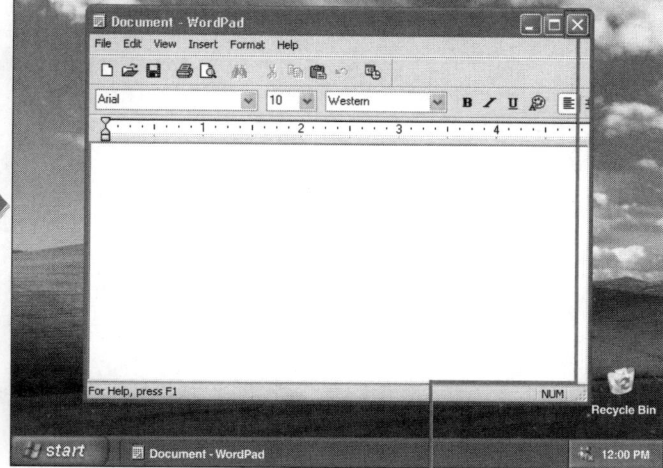

■ The program starts.

■ When you finish working with the program, click ☒ to close the program.

MAXIMIZE OR MINIMIZE A WINDOW

You may want to maximize a window to fill your screen so you can see more of the information in the window. You can also minimize a window to put the window aside so you can concentrate on other tasks.

Maximizing a window enlarges the window to fill your screen. This allows you to view more of the contents of the window.

When you are not using a window, you can minimize the window to remove it from your screen. Minimizing a window reduces the window to a button on your taskbar that displays all or part of the name of the window.

When you are ready to once again use a minimized window, you can restore the window. Restoring a minimized window displays the window in its original size and location.

If you have many open windows on your screen, you can save time by minimizing all the windows at once so you can clearly view your desktop.

MAXIMIZE A WINDOW

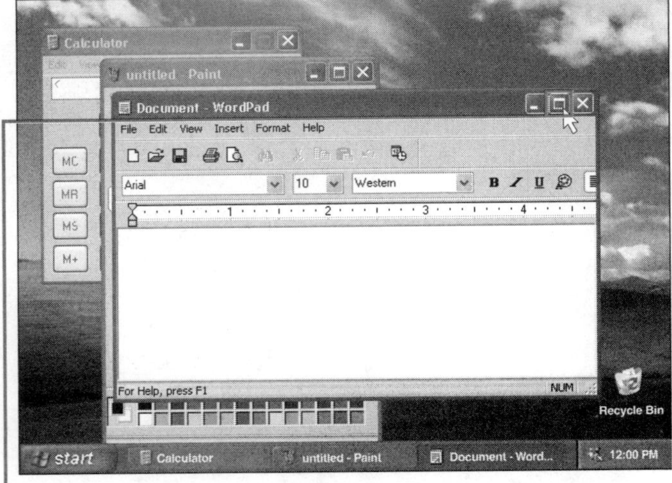

1 Click ▣ in the window you want to maximize.

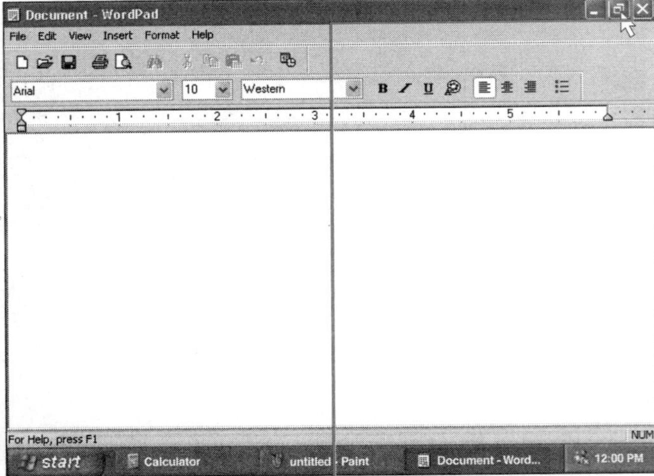

■ The window fills your screen.

RESTORE A WINDOW

1 To return the window to its previous size, click ▣.

I keep clicking the wrong button when I try to maximize a window. Is there an easier way to maximize a window?

✔ You can double-click the title bar of a window to maximize the window. Double-clicking the title bar again returns the window to its original size. You can also increase the size of the buttons at the top right corner of windows to make the buttons more visible. Right-click a blank area on your desktop and then select Properties. In the dialog box that appears, choose the Appearance tab. Click the Font size area and then select Large Fonts or Extra Large Fonts.

How do I close a minimized window?

✔ If you no longer need a window that is minimized on your screen, right-click the button for the window on the taskbar and then select Close.

Why does a menu appear when I click a button on the taskbar?

✔ If you have many windows open, all the buttons for one program may appear as a single button on the taskbar. When you click the button, a menu appears, displaying the names of the open windows for the program. Select the name of the window you want to redisplay.

MINIMIZE A WINDOW

1 Click ▬ in the window you want to minimize.

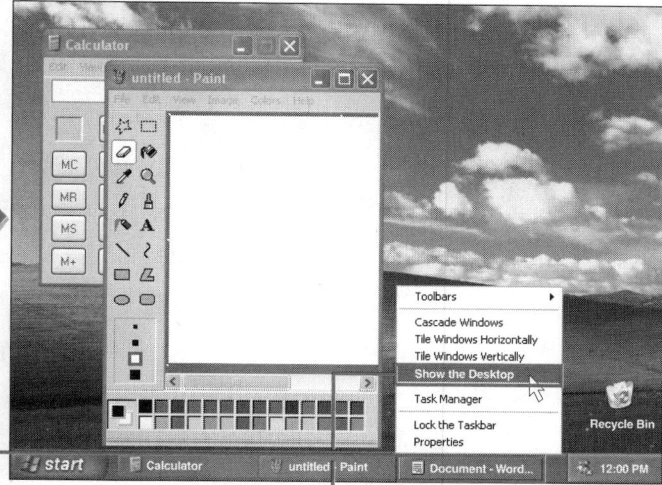

■ The window reduces to a button on the taskbar. To redisplay the window, click its button.

MINIMIZE ALL WINDOWS

1 To minimize all windows displayed on your screen, right-click an empty area on the taskbar. A menu appears.

2 Click Show the Desktop.

MOVE OR SIZE A WINDOW

You can have many windows open on your desktop at one time. Adjusting the location and size of windows can help you work with their contents more easily.

You can move a window to a new location if it covers important items on your screen. If you have more than one window open, you can adjust the position of the windows to ensure that you can view the contents of each window. You can click on any open window to bring it to the front so you can clearly view its contents.

You can increase the size of a window to see more of its contents or reduce the size of a window to view items covered by the window. To change only the width of a window, you can adjust the left or right edge of the window. To change only the height of a window, adjust the top or bottom edge of the window. You can use any corner of a window to change both the width and height of the window at once.

Just as you can move and size windows on your desktop, you can also move and size windows in open programs.

MOVE A WINDOW

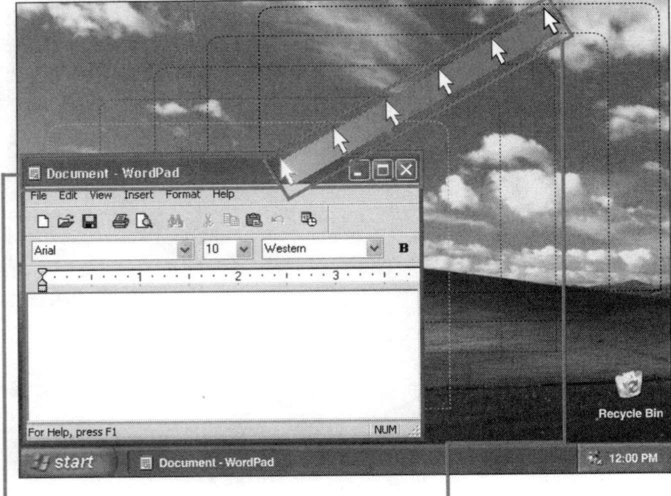

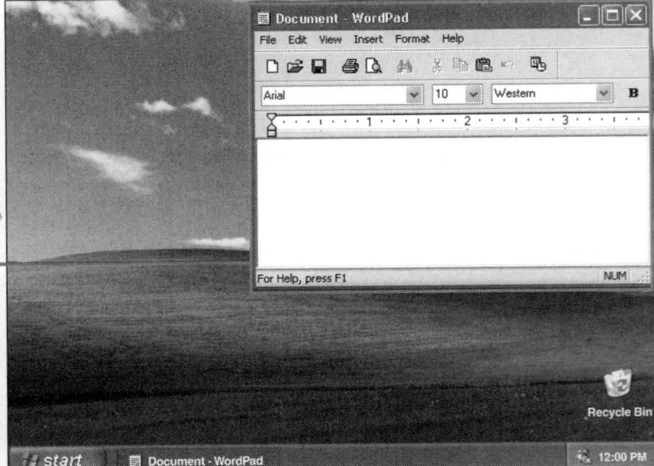

1 Position the mouse over the title bar of the window you want to move.

2 Drag the mouse to where you want to place the window.

■ The window moves to the new location.

How can I see the outline of a window as I move or size the window?

✔ Right-click a blank area on your desktop. On the menu that appears, select Properties. Choose the Appearance tab and then click the Effects button. In the dialog box that appears, click the Show window contents while dragging option (☑ changes to ☐).

Can I move or size a maximized window?

✔ You will not be able to move or size a window that has been maximized. You must restore the window before you can move or size it. To restore a window, see page 14.

Can I move a window entirely off the screen?

✔ You can move most of a window off the screen but some of the window will still be visible. This allows you to put a document aside, as you might on a real desk.

Can all program windows be sized?

✔ Some programs, like Calculator, have windows that cannot be sized.

SIZE A WINDOW

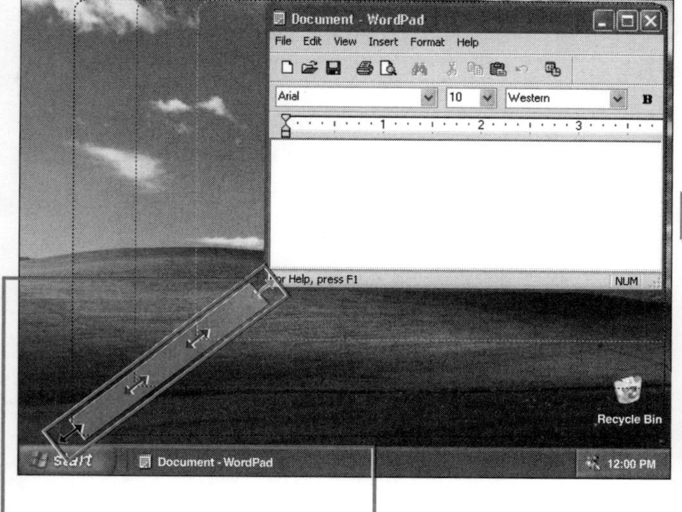

1 Position the mouse over an edge of the window you want to size (changes to ↗, ↘, ↕ or ↔).

2 Drag the mouse ↗ until the window displays the size you want.

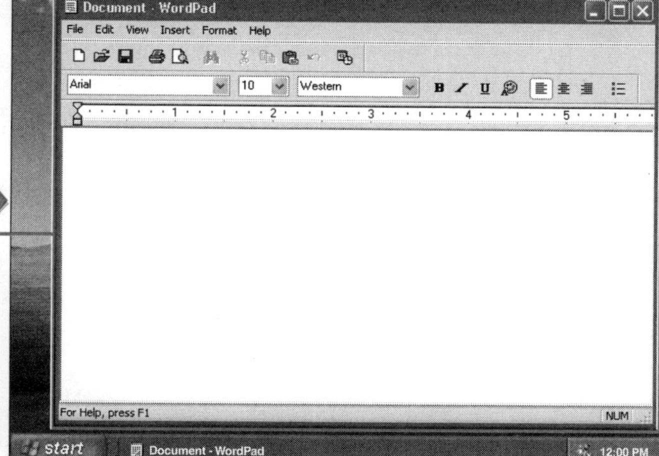

■ The window changes to the new size.

SWITCH BETWEEN WINDOWS

When you have more than one window open on your screen, you can switch between the windows.

Although you are able to have several windows open, you can work in only one window at a time. This window is called the active window and appears in front of all the other windows. The title bar of the active window is darker than the title bar of the other open windows.

The taskbar displays a button for each open window on your screen. If you have many windows open, Windows may group some buttons to help reduce clutter on the taskbar. When Windows groups buttons, all the buttons for a program may appear as a single button on the taskbar.

You can make a window active by clicking its button on the taskbar. A button that displays a small triangle represents several buttons that have been grouped together. You can click a button with a triangle to display a list of windows you can choose from. You can also use your keyboard to switch between open windows.

Switching between windows allows you to perform several tasks at once, such as consulting a report while you answer your e-mail and prepare a presentation.

SWITCH BETWEEN WINDOWS

■ The taskbar displays a button for each open window. If you have many windows open, all the buttons for a program may appear as a single button on the taskbar.

1 To display the window you want to work with, click its button on the taskbar.

■ A menu may appear, displaying the name of each open window in the program.

2 Click the name of the window you want to display.

The taskbar is not displayed on my screen. How do I get the taskbar to appear?

✔ If you have turned on the Auto-hide feature, you can display the taskbar by moving the mouse pointer to where the taskbar was last seen. You can also press and hold down the Ctrl key and then press the Esc key to display the taskbar and the Start menu. For more information about the Auto-hide feature, see page 256.

How can I stop Windows from grouping buttons on the taskbar?

✔ Right-click the taskbar and select Properties from the menu that appears. Select the Taskbar tab in the dialog box that appears and then click the Group similar taskbar buttons option (☑ changes to ☐).

The text on the button for a window is cut off. How can I see all the text?

✔ Each taskbar button displays all or part of the name of the window it represents. A button displays three dots (...) if it is too small to display the entire name. You can position the mouse pointer over a button to display all the information for the button. A yellow box will appear, displaying the information.

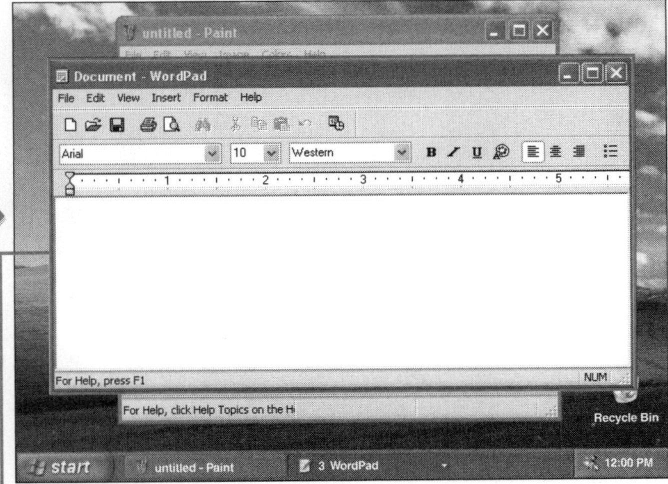

■ The window appears in front of all other windows. You can now clearly view the contents of the window.

Note: You can also click anywhere inside a window to display the window in front of all other windows.

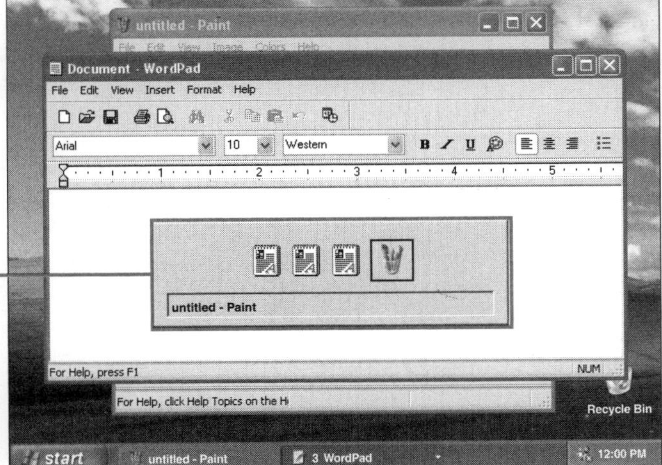

USING THE KEYBOARD

1 Press and hold down the Alt key and then press the Tab key.

■ A box appears, displaying an icon for each open window.

2 Still holding down the Alt key, press the Tab key until the box displays the name of the window you want to work with. Then release the Alt key.

ARRANGE WINDOWS

You can arrange the open windows on your desktop to make them easier to work with or to display more of their contents.

You can have several windows open at the same time. Similar to a real desk, you can have many items, such as an agenda, a letter and a budget, all open on your desktop at once. Windows allows you to arrange and organize these items so they are easier to use.

You can choose to cascade your open windows. The Cascade Windows command displays windows one on top of the other so you can see the title bar of each window. You can move between the open windows by clicking the title bar of the window you want to view.

You can use the Tile Windows Horizontally or Tile Windows Vertically commands to arrange open windows one above the other or side by side. Tiling windows allows you to easily compare the contents of your windows and drag information from one window to another.

ARRANGE WINDOWS

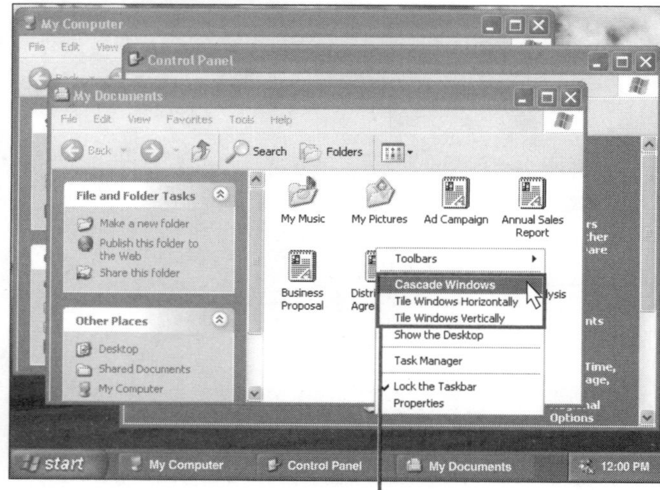

1 Right-click an empty area on the taskbar. A menu appears.

2 Click the way you want to arrange the open windows on your screen.

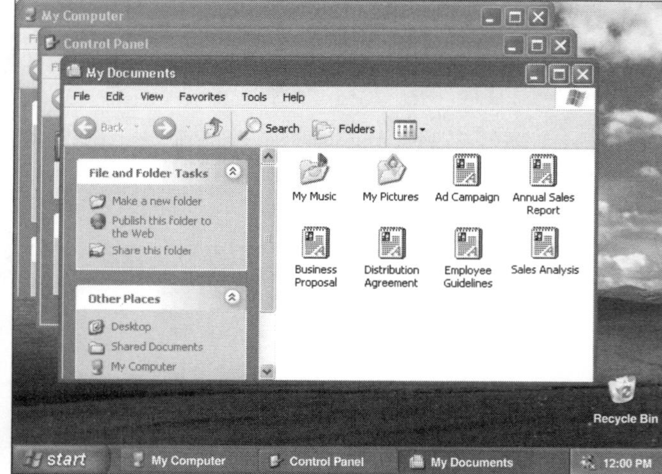

CASCADE

■ The windows neatly overlap each other. You can clearly see the title bar of each window.

■ You can click the title bar of the window you want to work with to make that window active. The window will appear in front of all other windows.

How do I change back to the previous window arrangement?

✔ To immediately change back to the previous window arrangement, right-click an empty area on the taskbar and then select Undo.

Why are some of my program windows not tiling correctly?

✔ Some programs with a fixed window size, such as Calculator, cannot be tiled correctly.

Why can't I see a difference between horizontally and vertically tiled windows?

✔ Horizontally and vertically tiled windows are displayed the same way on your screen when there are four or more windows open.

How do I cascade or tile only some of the windows I have open?

✔ Minimize the windows you do not want to cascade or tile before you use the Cascade Windows or Tile commands. To minimize a window, click in the window.

How can I quickly minimize all the open windows on my screen so I can clearly see the desktop?

✔ Right-click an empty area on the taskbar and then select Show the Desktop from the menu that appears.

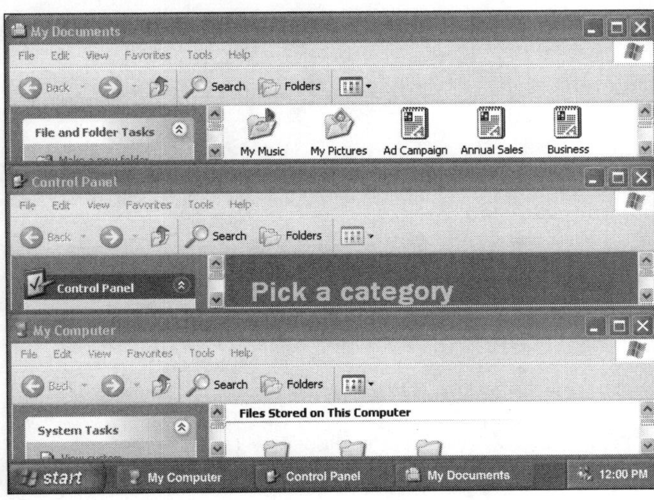

TILE HORIZONTALLY

■ The windows appear one above the other. You can view the contents of each window.

■ You can easily compare the contents of the windows and exchange information between the windows.

■ You can click anywhere in the window you want to work with to make that window active.

TILE VERTICALLY

■ The windows appear side by side. You can view the contents of each window.

■ You can easily compare the contents of the windows and exchange information between the windows.

■ You can click anywhere in the window you want to work with to make that window active.

GETTING HELP

If you do not know how to perform a task in Windows, you can use the Windows Help feature to find information about the task.

You can use the Help and Support home page to browse through help topics, common tasks and other resources. The home page appears automatically each time you open the Help and Support Center window and is a good starting point for finding help information.

You can select an item of interest on the home page to browse through help topics for the item. When you select an item of interest, a list of related help topics appears. You can continue selecting topics of interest to find the help information you need. For example, the What's new in Windows XP topic contains help topics you may find useful if you are upgrading from a previous version of Windows.

The Customizing your computer topic contains help topics that teach you how to customize Windows.

When you are connected to the Internet, the Did you know? area in the Help and Support Center window displays links to regularly updated help information on the Web.

USING THE HELP AND SUPPORT HOME PAGE

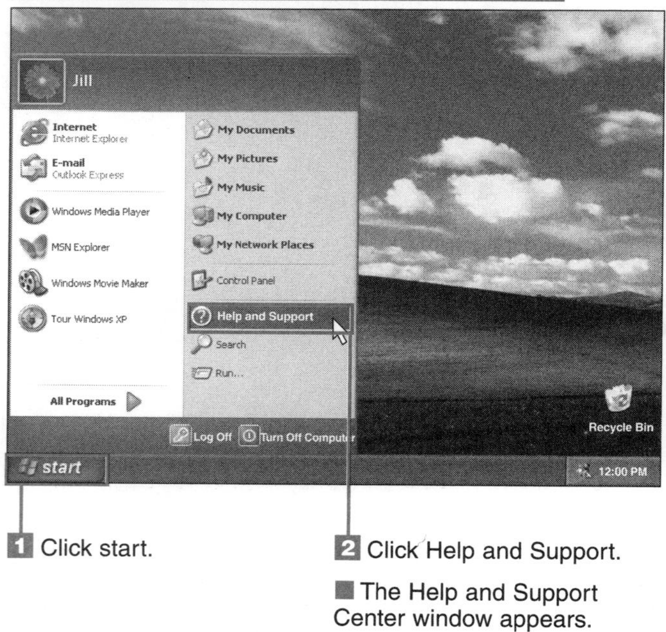

1 Click start.

2 Click Help and Support.

■ The Help and Support Center window appears.

■ The Help and Support home page appears each time you open the Help and Support Center window.

■ This area displays a list of common help topics, ways that you can ask for assistance and tasks you can perform.

3 Click an item of interest.

Note: The following screens depend on the item you select in step 3.

How do I return to the home page?

✔ Click [home] in the Help and Support Center window to return to the home page at any time.

How can I quickly display help information?

✔ When working in a folder window, press the F1 key to quickly open the Help and Support Center window. When you are working in a program, pressing the F1 key will usually open the help feature provided by the program.

Why do some help topics display green text?

✔ You can click a word or phrase that appears in green to have Windows display a definition of the word or phrase. To hide the definition, click anywhere on the screen.

Why do some help topics display blue text?

✔ You can click a word or phrase that appears in blue to have Windows open the window or dialog box needed to perform the task or to display another help topic.

How can I find a help topic related to the currently displayed information?

✔ Many help topics display a Related Topics link at the end of the help information. You can click the link to view a list of related help topics and then select the topic you want to display.

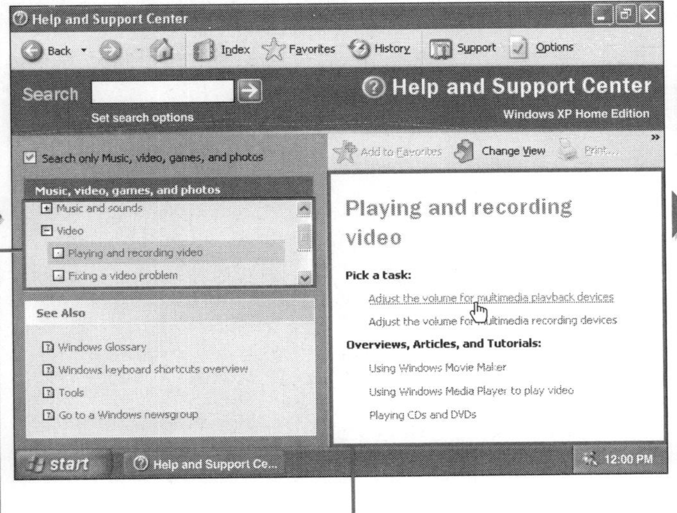

■ This area lists the help topics for the item you selected.

4 Click a help topic of interest. A list of subtopics may appear.

5 If a list of subtopics appears, click a subtopic of interest.

■ This area displays a list of topics for the subtopic you selected.

6 Click a topic of interest.

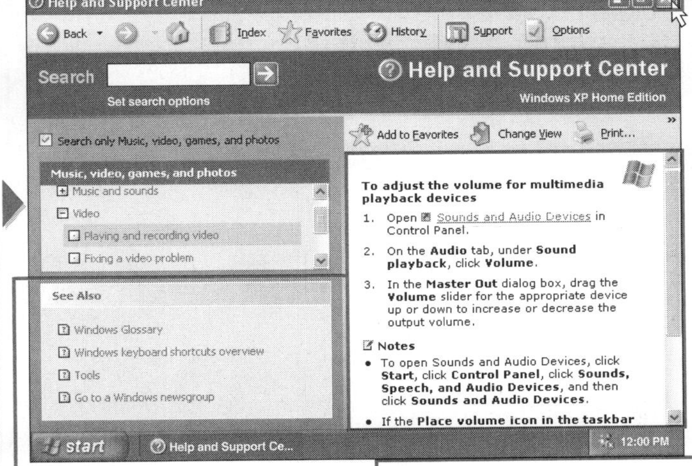

■ This area displays information about the topic you selected.

Note: You can repeat steps 4 to 6 to display information for another help topic.

7 When you finish reviewing help information, click [X] to close the Help and Support Center window.

CONTINUED

GETTING HELP (CONTINUED)

The search tool provided by Windows Help allows you to find help information for specific topics. You can type a word or phrase and have Windows display help topics that contain the information.

To help focus your search, enter only the words you want to find. For example, if you want information about saving files, type "save files" instead of "I need information on saving files."

When the search is complete, Windows displays a list of matching help topics. Windows organizes the search results under different headings. Suggested Topics usually displays the most relevant search results, since the keywords, or main ideas, in the help information are matched with the words you type. Full-text Search Matches displays help topics that contain the words you typed, even if the words do not relate directly to the main idea of the topic. If you are connected to the Internet, you can use the Microsoft Knowledge Base heading to display relevant articles from the Microsoft Knowledge Base Web site.

If Windows displays many help topics, you can narrow your search by adding another word or by searching for a more specific word.

After you find the help topic you want, you can display the help information for the topic.

SEARCH FOR HELP INFORMATION

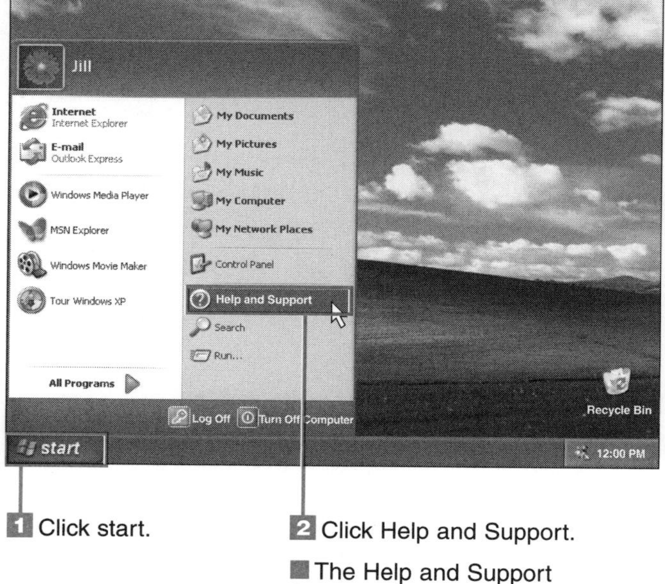

1 Click start.

2 Click Help and Support.

■ The Help and Support Center window appears.

3 To search for specific help information, click this area and then type a word or phrase that describes the topic of interest.

4 Click ➔ or press the Enter key to start the search.

Are there other ways to narrow my search?

✔ If you have previously performed a search, you can click the box (☐) beside Search within previous results (☐ changes to ☑) to have Windows search for information only within the help topics displayed in your previous search. You can also use the AND, OR, NOT or NEAR operator to narrow your search. For example, if you want to find help topics about sharing resources but do not want information about sharing printers, you can type **share NOT printers**. To search for a specific phrase, enclose the phrase in quotation marks.

How do I find definitions for the terms used in Windows?

✔ You can type **glossary** in the Search area and then press the Enter key to find the Windows Glossary help topic. After you select the topic, you can click a letter to display definitions for terms that begin with that letter.

Can I specify the options Windows should use to perform a search?

✔ Yes. Click the Set search options link below the Search area to display a list of search options. You can specify the maximum number of topics each search result category should display or whether you want Windows to highlight every occurrence of your search words in the help information. You can also specify which categories you want to include in the search results.

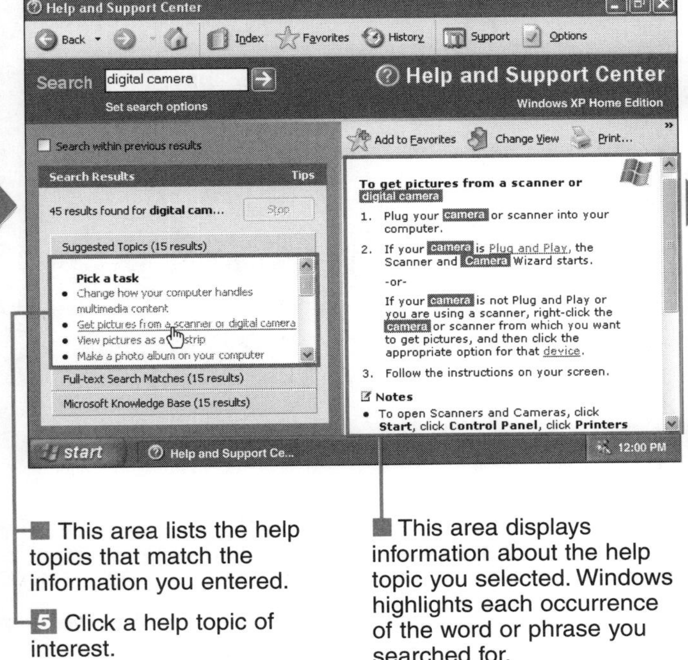

■ This area lists the help topics that match the information you entered.

5 Click a help topic of interest.

■ This area displays information about the help topic you selected. Windows highlights each occurrence of the word or phrase you searched for.

Note: You can repeat step 5 to display information for another help topic.

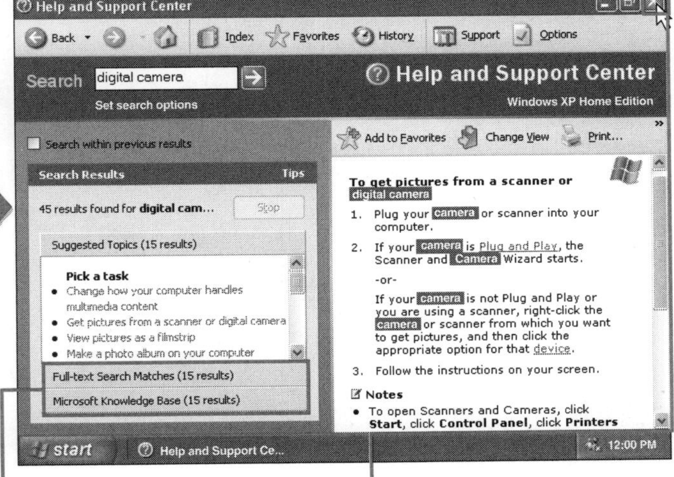

■ If you want to view a list of help topics under a different heading, click the heading of interest.

6 When you finish reviewing help information, click ☒ to close the Help and Support Center window.

CONTINUED

GETTING HELP (CONTINUED)

The Windows help feature includes an index that displays an alphabetical list of all the Windows help topics. You can use the index to find information the same way you would use the index in a book.

You can use the scroll bar to browse through the index to locate a help topic of interest.

If you want to quickly find a specific help topic, you can type the first few letters of the help topic you want to find. Windows will immediately take you to the location in the index that displays topics beginning with the letters you typed.

Windows categorizes topics in the index so you can quickly find the information you need.

For example, if you want to add an item to your computer, you can type the word "adding." Listed under "adding," you will find help topics for adding fonts, hardware, programs and users to your computer.

After you find the help topic you want, you can display the help information for the topic.

USING THE INDEX

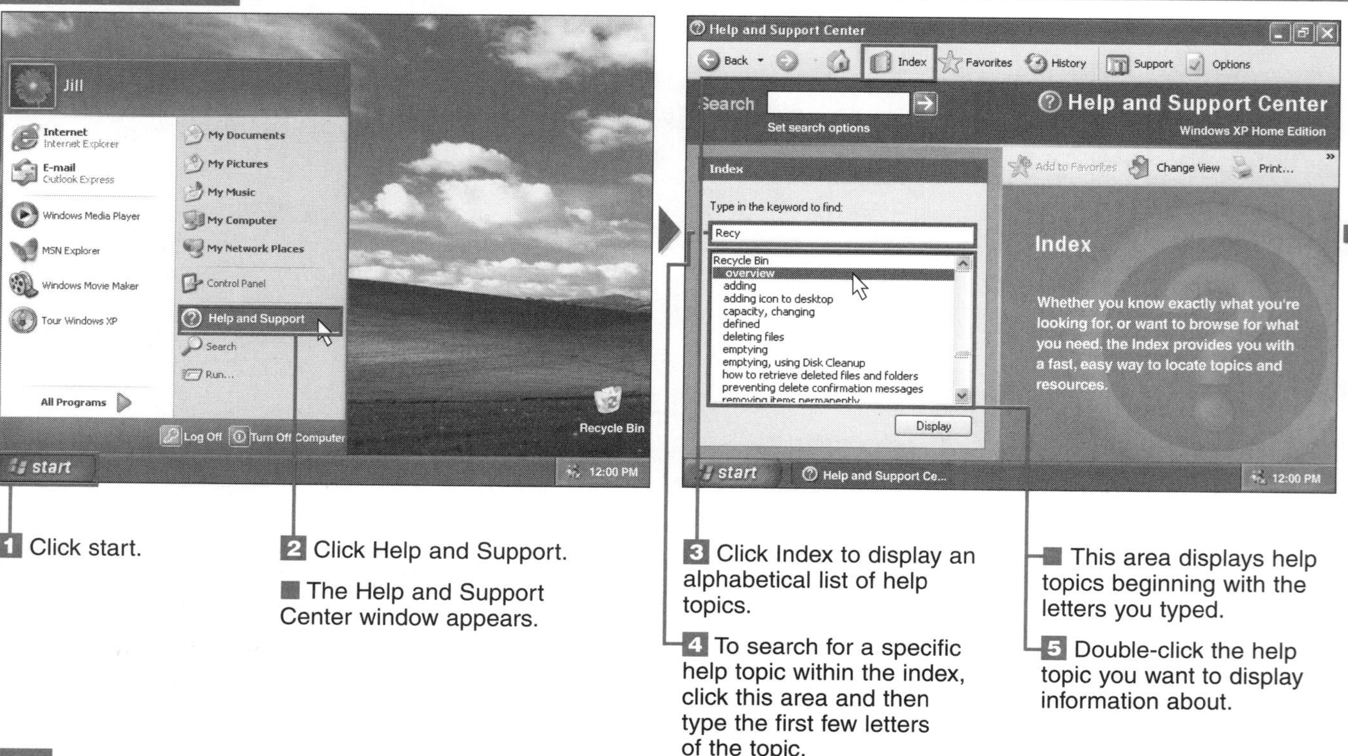

1 Click start.

2 Click Help and Support.

■ The Help and Support Center window appears.

3 Click Index to display an alphabetical list of help topics.

4 To search for a specific help topic within the index, click this area and then type the first few letters of the topic.

■ This area displays help topics beginning with the letters you typed.

5 Double-click the help topic you want to display information about.

Can I reduce the size of the Help and Support Center window?

✔ You can hide parts of the Help and Support Center window to reduce the size of the window. This is useful if you need access to your desktop while viewing help information. Click Change View to hide parts of the Help and Support Center window. Click Change View to once again display the entire window. If the Change View button is not displayed, click » on the toolbar to display the button.

How can I display help information in a larger area of the Help and Support Center window?

✔ Position the mouse pointer over the left edge of the area displaying the help information (↖ changes to ↔). Then drag the mouse until the area displays the size you want.

How do I return to a help topic I have already viewed?

✔ You can click the Back or ➔ button in the window to quickly return to a help topic you have viewed. You can also click the History button to view a list of help topics you have previously read. To redisplay a topic in the History list, double-click the topic.

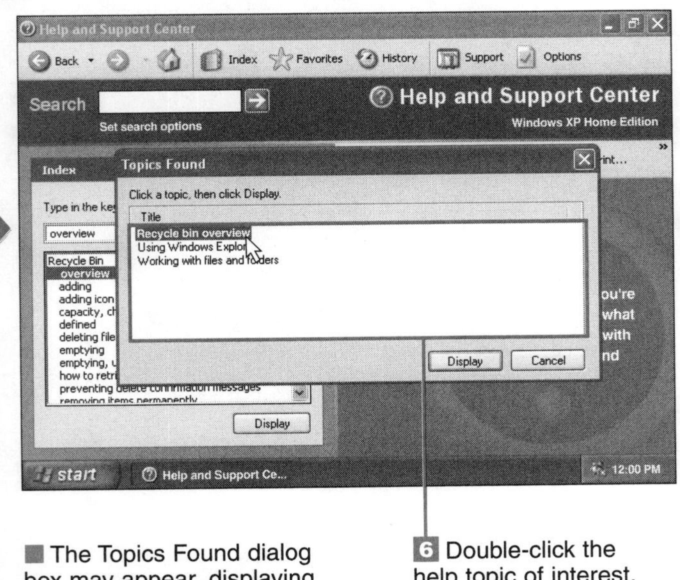

■ The Topics Found dialog box may appear, displaying a list of related help topics.

6 Double-click the help topic of interest.

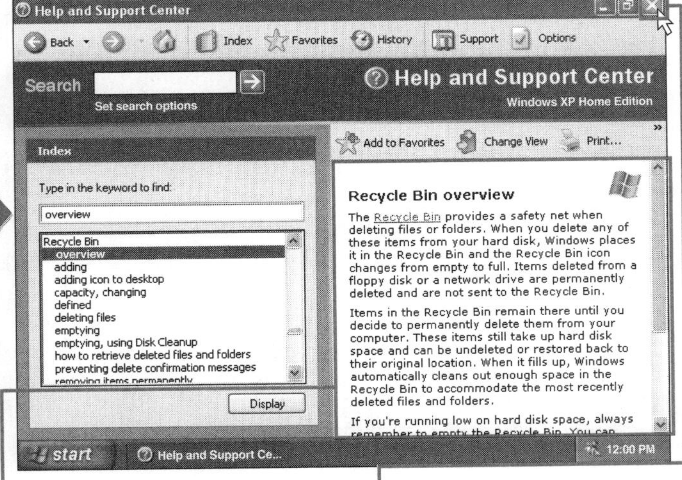

■ This area displays information for the help topic you selected.

7 When you finish reviewing help information, click ☒ to close the Help and Support Center window.

CONTINUED

GETTING HELP (CONTINUED)

You can produce a paper copy of the help topic displayed on your screen. Printing a help topic can be useful because it is often difficult to remember all the information for a help topic.

If you are not able to view help information on the screen while performing a task, a printed copy of the information will help you complete the task. For example, if you are completing a task that requires you to restart your computer, you can refer to the printed help information while the computer is restarting.

A printed reference of a help topic can also help you learn about Windows features. For example, you can use a printed reference to help you memorize all the Windows keyboard shortcuts.

When you are working in Windows, if you are unfamiliar with a dialog box, you can use the Help button (?) to display help information. When you click the Help button and then click an item in the dialog box, a box containing help information appears. The help information explains what the item you selected does and how you can use the item. Help information may not be available for some items.

You must click the Help button each time you want to display help information for an item in a dialog box.

PRINT A HELP TOPIC

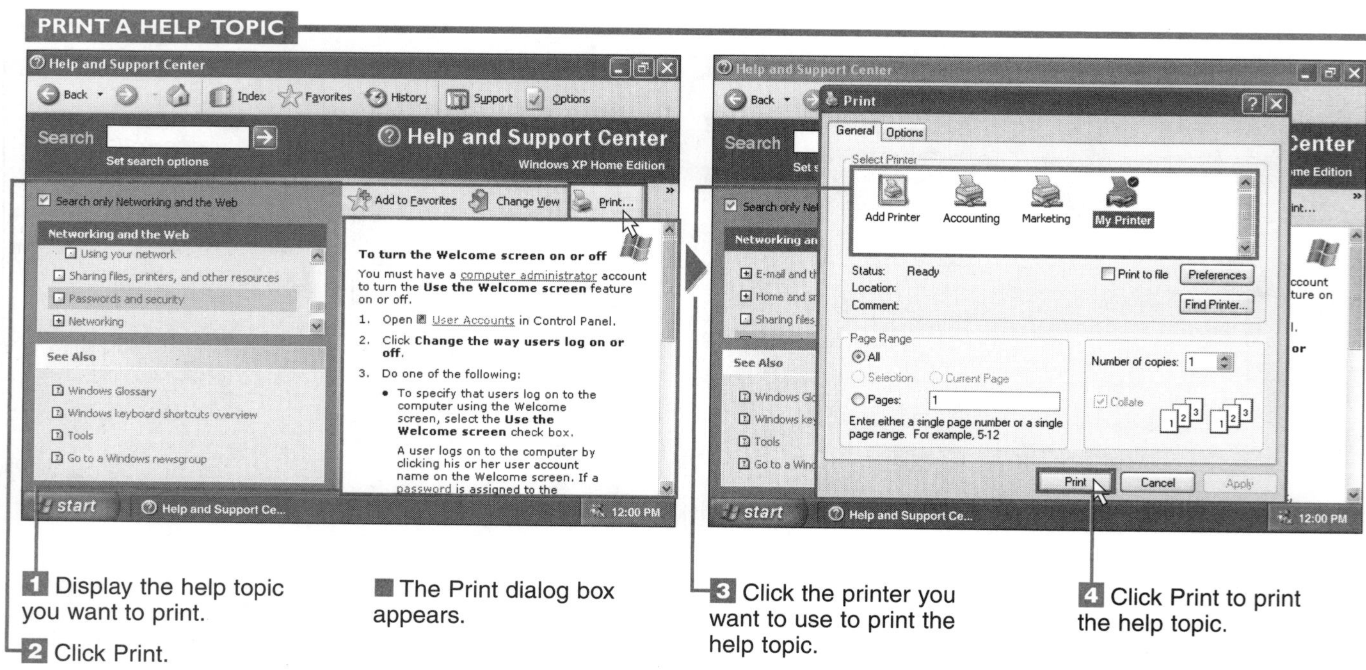

1 Display the help topic you want to print.

2 Click Print.

■ The Print dialog box appears.

3 Click the printer you want to use to print the help topic.

4 Click Print to print the help topic.

The Help button does not appear in a dialog box. What can I do?

✔ You may be able to right-click an item in a dialog box and then click What's This? to display help information.

What other ways can I get help?

✔ You can use the Internet to contact people who can help you with Windows. Click the Support button in the Help and Support Center window. You can then ask a friend for help using Remote Assistance, get help from a Microsoft support professional or join a Windows XP newsgroup to share information with other Windows XP users.

Can I save a help topic I view?

✔ When viewing a help topic, you can click the Add to Favorites button in the Help and Support Center window to save the topic to your list of favorite help topics. To later view your list of favorites, click the Favorites button. You can double-click a topic in the list to redisplay the topic.

How can I customize the Help and Support Center window?

✔ In the Help and Support Center window, click the Options button and then click the Change Help and Support Center options link. You can display or hide the History or Favorites button on the Navigation bar, change the text size of help information or choose whether you want to show the text labels for buttons on the Navigation bar.

GETTING HELP IN A DIALOG BOX

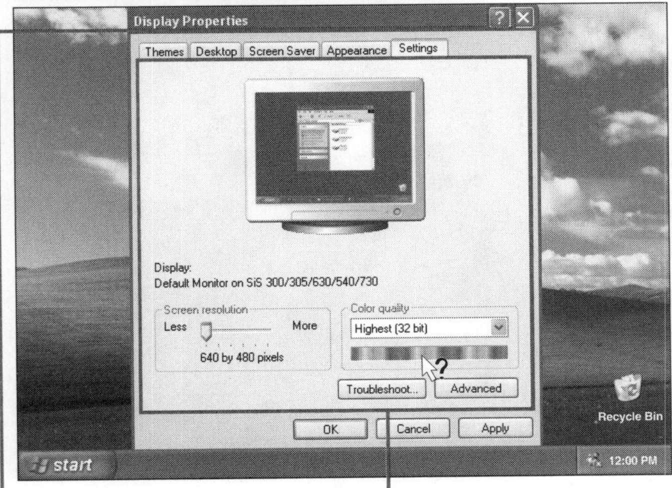

1 Click ? in a dialog box to get help information for an item (↖ changes to ↖?).

2 Click an item of interest in the dialog box.

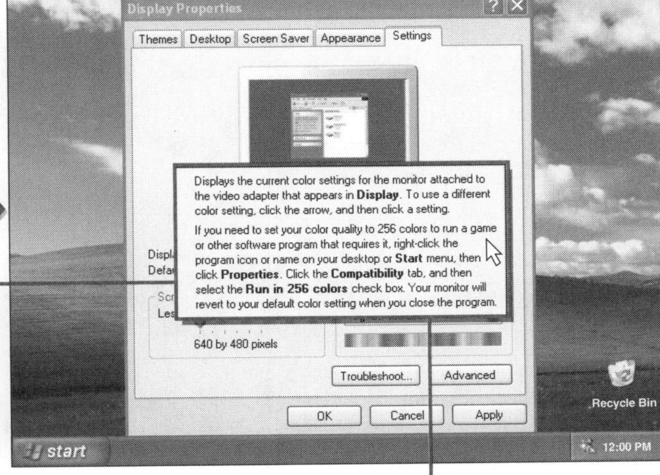

■ A yellow box appears, displaying help information for the item you selected.

3 When you finish reviewing the help information, click the yellow box to remove the information from your screen.

SHUT DOWN WINDOWS

You should always shut down Windows before turning off your computer. Shutting down properly allows Windows to save settings you have changed, disconnect from the network and warn you about users on the network who may be accessing your files. Turning off your computer without shutting down properly may cause you to lose data.

There are several shut down options from which you can choose. The Turn Off option shuts down Windows so you can turn off the power. After making changes to your computer, such as installing software or a new device, you may need to use the Restart option to restart your computer. Before shutting down Windows or restarting your computer, you should close all open programs and make sure no other users are logged on to the computer.

The Stand By option places the computer in a low-power mode. Standby mode is useful if you do not need to use your computer for a short period of time. You should save all your open documents before choosing standby mode. If a power outage occurs while your computer is on standby, you will lose any unsaved information.

SHUT DOWN WINDOWS

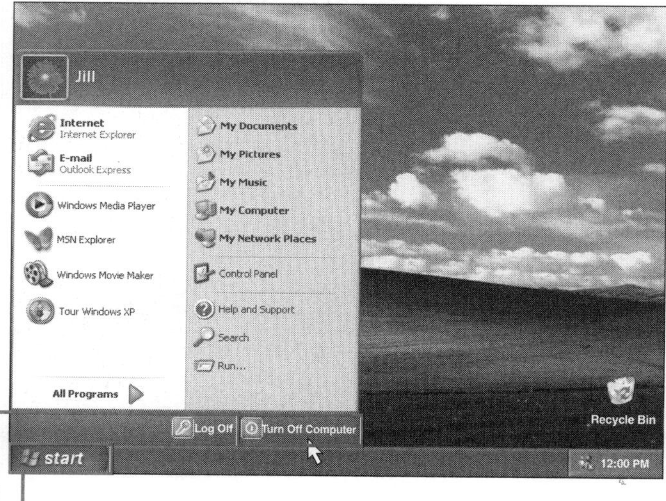

1 Click start.

2 Click Turn Off Computer.

■ The Turn off computer dialog box appears.

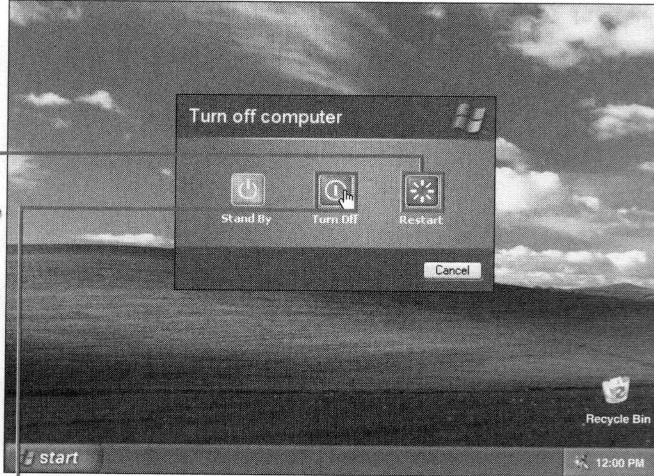

3 To shut down Windows, click Turn Off.

■ To restart your computer, click Restart.

■ If you selected to shut down Windows, do not turn off your computer until a message appears, stating that you can safely turn off the computer. Many computers will not display the message and will turn off automatically.

Why isn't the Stand By option available on my computer?

✔ Your computer may not have power management capabilities or the power management feature may be turned off. You can consult the documentation that came with your computer to determine if your computer supports power management features.

Can I put my computer into hibernation?

✔ You can put your computer into hibernation only if the computer supports the hibernation feature and hibernation is enabled. To ensure hibernation is enabled, you can check your power settings. For more information, see page 534. To put your computer into hibernation, perform steps 1 and 2 below to display the Turn off computer dialog box. Then press and hold down the Shift key. When the Stand By option changes to Hibernate, click Hibernate.

When would I use the Hibernate option?

✔ The Hibernate option is useful when you need to turn off the computer for an extended period of time but wish to continue your work from where you stopped. When you select the Hibernate option, the current settings are saved before the computer is turned off. When you turn on your computer again, your desktop will look exactly as it did when the computer was turned off.

PUT COMPUTER ON STANDBY

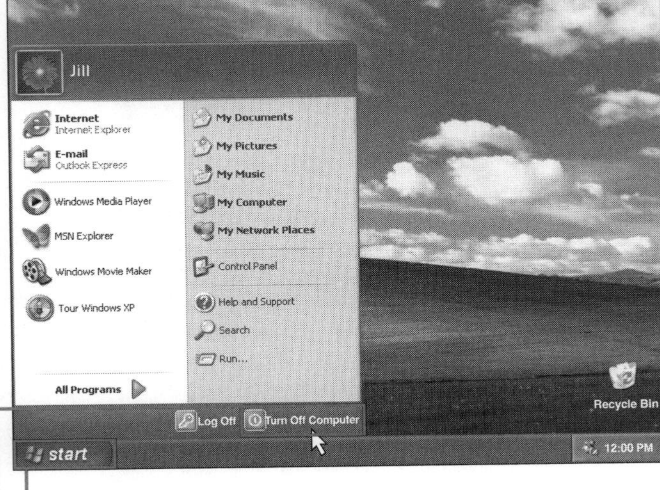

1 Click start.

2 Click Turn Off Computer.

■ The Turn off computer dialog box appears.

3 To put your computer on standby, click Stand By.

■ Your computer enters a low-power mode.

■ To resume using your computer, press the power button on your computer.

Note: You may also be able to move your mouse or press a key on your keyboard to resume using your computer.

COMPUTER HARDWARE

Devices You Attach to a Computer

Monitor

A monitor displays text and images generated by a computer. The size of a monitor is measured diagonally across the screen. Common monitor sizes range from 15 to 21 inches.

Keyboard

A keyboard is used to enter information and instructions into a computer. Many keyboards have buttons that you can press to perform tasks on your computer, such as adjusting the sound volume or accessing the Internet.

Mouse

A mouse is a handheld device that allows you to select and move items on your screen. There are many alternatives to the mouse, including trackballs, touch-sensitive pads and tablets that use pens. Most new mice have a wheel between the mouse buttons that you can use to scroll through information or zoom in or out of information in a window.

Speakers and Headphones

Speakers and headphones are used to listen to sounds created by a computer. Many computer speakers include an amplifier that can improve the sound quality. Headphones allow you to listen to sounds privately.

Microphone

A microphone plugs into a computer to allow you to record speech and other sounds onto your computer.

Game Controller

A game controller is a device, such as a joystick, gamepad or steering wheel, that connects to a computer and allows you to interact with a game. Some game controllers offer enhanced features. For example, you can obtain a game controller that will vibrate in response to actions in a game or one that offers extra controls.

Printer

A printer produces a paper copy of documents created on a computer. Laser printers produce high-quality printouts that are most suitable for office use. Ink jet printers produce medium-quality printouts that are most suitable for home use and make color printing affordable.

Scanner

A scanner converts paper documents into a format your computer can use. The resolution used by a scanner determines the amount of detail the scanner can detect. Scanner resolution is measured in dots per inch (dpi).

Web Camera

A Web camera is used to create video files or for videoconferencing. Videoconferencing allows you to have face-to-face conversations with other people on a network or over the Internet.

Removable Drive

A removable drive stores and retrieves large amounts of data on removable disks. The disks you use with a removable drive can typically contain from 100 MB to 2 GB of information. You can use a removable drive to store information, back up information on your computer or transfer large amounts of information between computers. A Zip drive is one of the most popular types of removable drives.

Modem

A modem allows computers to exchange information through telephone lines. You can use a modem to connect to the Internet or connect to a computer at work. There are two types of modems. Internal modems are expansion cards that fit inside your computer. External modems plug into your computer. The speed of a modem determines how fast it can send and receive information through telephone lines. The most common modem speed is 56 Kbps.

High-Speed Internet Connection Devices

You can use a cable modem, Integrated Services Digital Network (ISDN) line or Digital Subscriber Line (DSL) to obtain a high-speed connection to the Internet. A cable modem uses the same type of cable as your television. An ISDN line connects to a dedicated telephone line, while a DSL line uses a regular telephone line. Some regions do not offer some or all of the high-speed Internet connection methods.

Port

A port is a connector on a computer where you plug in an external device, such as a printer or modem. A port allows instructions and data to flow between the computer and the device. A parallel port has 25 pins and connects devices such as a printer or removable drive. The computer uses the letters LPT, followed by a number, to identify a parallel port. A serial port has either 9 or 25 pins and is used to connect many types of devices, such as a mouse or modem. The computer uses the letters COM, followed by a number, to identify a serial port. Your computer also has additional ports to connect devices such as your monitor, keyboard or joystick. Universal Serial Bus (USB) and FireWire ports provide a way to easily connect and automatically install a wide range of devices. Devices that connect to a USB or FireWire port are generally high-speed devices. Infrared ports let a computer communicate with devices by using infrared light instead of cables.

CONTINUED

COMPUTER HARDWARE (CONTINUED)

Inside a Computer

Hard Drive

A hard drive is the primary device that a computer uses to store information. Most computers have one hard drive, named drive C. Most new hard drives have 40 GB or more of storage space.

Floppy Drive

A floppy drive stores and retrieves information on floppy disks. You can use floppy disks to store a small amount of information. A floppy disk can typically store 1.44 MB of information.

CD Drive

A Compact Disc (CD) drive reads information stored on compact discs. There are several types of CD drives available. You can use a CD drive to install programs, play games directly from CDs and listen to music CDs. CDs can typically store up to 700 MB of information. You cannot record information on a CD using a CD-Read-Only Memory (CD-ROM) drive. To record information on a disc, you can use a CD-Recordable (CD-R) drive with a CD-R disc. You cannot erase information on a CD-R disc. To be able to record and erase information on a disc, you can use a CD-ReWritable (CD-RW) drive with a CD-RW disc.

DVD Drive

A Digital Versatile Disc (DVD) drive reads information stored on DVDs or CDs. A DVD is identical in size and shape to a CD but can store a lot more information. DVDs can store up to 17 GB of information and are often used for storing and playing video files such as movies. To record information on a DVD, you can use a recordable DVD drive.

Bytes

Bytes are used to measure the amount of information a device can store. One byte represents one character. One kilobyte (KB) is 1,024 characters. One megabyte (MB) is 1,048,576 characters. One gigabyte (GB) is 1,073,741,824 characters.

Motherboard

A motherboard is the main circuit board of a computer. All the computer's electronic components plug into the motherboard. A motherboard often includes additional components such as video, sound or networking components. The motherboard is also known as the system board.

Expansion Slot

An expansion slot is a socket on the motherboard where you plug in an expansion card, which is a circuit board that lets you add new features to a computer. For example, expansion slots allow you to add a network interface card or a sound card to your computer. The number of expansion slots inside your computer determines how many expansion cards you can add to the computer.

Central Processing Unit (CPU)

The Central Processing Unit (CPU) is the main chip in a computer. The CPU processes instructions, performs calculations and manages the flow of information through a computer system. The most popular CPU chips available in new computers are the Pentium 4 made by Intel and the Athlon processor made by AMD. Each type of processor is available in several speeds. The faster the speed, the faster the computer operates. Processor speed is measured in megahertz (MHz).

Memory

Memory, also known as Random Access Memory (RAM), temporarily stores information inside a computer. The information stored in RAM is lost when you turn off your computer. The amount of memory a computer has impacts on how fast programs will operate. Most new computers have at least 128 MB of RAM.

Bus

The bus is the electronic pathway that carries information between devices in a computer. Common bus types include ISA (Industry Standard Architecture), SCSI (Small Computer Systems Interface), PCI (Peripheral Component Interconnect) and AGP (Accelerated Graphics Port). AGP is a bus type used to provide faster video speeds.

Video Card

A video card translates instructions from a computer into information a monitor can display. Some computers have video capabilities built into the motherboard.

Video Capture Card

A video capture card is used to transfer video from a Web camera, video camera or VCR into files that can be used on a computer. Some video capture cards also have TV capabilities that allow you to watch television on a computer.

Network Interface Card

A Network Interface Card (NIC) can physically connect each computer to a network to allow the computers to communicate. A NIC is also often used to connect a high-speed communication device, such as a cable modem, to a computer.

Sound Card

A sound card allows a computer to play and record sounds. A sound card is used to play music CDs as well as music and sound effects during games. Sound cards also allow you to record from a microphone, stereo or other audio device. Some computers have sound capabilities built into the motherboard.

USING MY COMPUTER

My Computer provides access to all the drives, folders and files on your computer. Each item in a My Computer window displays an icon to help you distinguish between the different types of items, such as a folder or text file.

If multiple users are set up on your computer, the My Computer window displays the Shared Documents folder, which contains files users have chosen to share with other users on the computer. The My Computer window also displays a folder for each user, containing the user's personal files. In most cases, you can view the contents of every user's folder. If your computer uses the NTFS file system, you cannot view another user's folder if you have a limited user account or if a user has made their personal folders private.

You can use My Computer to browse through the files and folders on your computer and open files and folders of interest. A folder can contain items such as documents, programs and other folders. Folders keep items organized so they are easy to find and use.

My Computer can help you manage and organize your files and folders. You can create, rename, copy, move or delete files and folders in a My Computer window.

USING MY COMPUTER

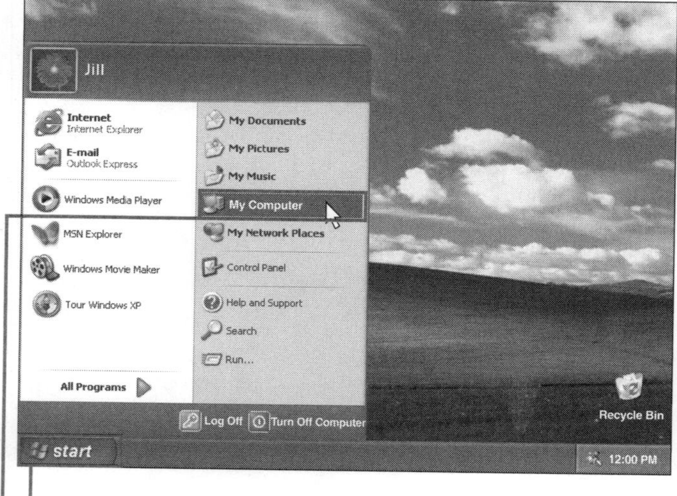

1 Click start.

2 Click My Computer.

■ The My Computer window appears.

Note: To view the contents of a floppy or CD-ROM drive, make sure you insert the floppy disk or CD-ROM disc into the appropriate drive before continuing.

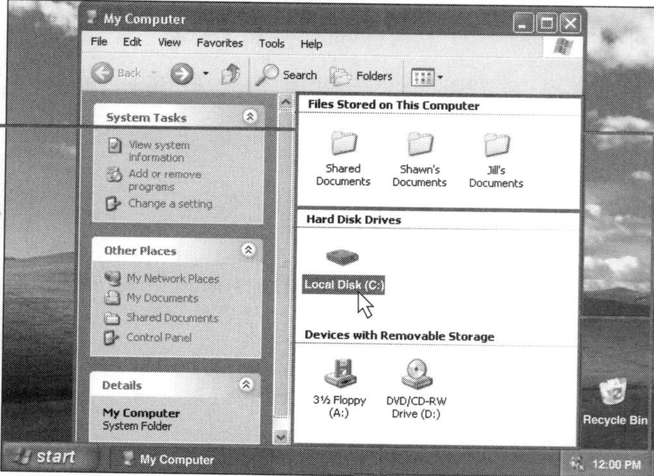

■ If multiple user accounts are set up on your computer, this area displays folders that contain shared documents and the personal files of each user.

■ The items in this area represent your hard drive, floppy drive, CD-ROM drive and any other drives on your computer.

3 To display the contents of a drive or folder, double-click the item.

Why don't the contents of some folders appear when I double-click the folder?

✔ Some folders contain important files that help keep your computer working properly. Windows does not automatically display the contents of these folders to prevent you from accidentally changing or deleting the files. To view the contents of the folder, click the Show the contents of this folder link.

Can Windows display the contents of each folder I open in its own window?

✔ Yes. To have each folder open in its own window, click the start button, click Control Panel and then click Appearance and Themes. Click Folder Options and then click the Open each folder in its own window option.

How can I open an item if I have trouble double-clicking?

✔ Right-click the item and then select Open from the menu that appears. If you right-click a file and the Open option is not available, click Open With and then select the program you want to use to open the file.

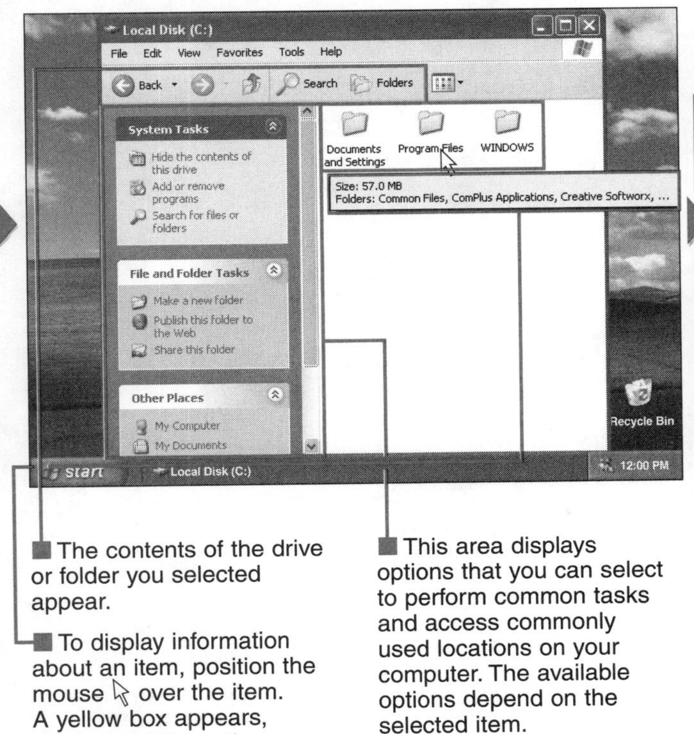

■ The contents of the drive or folder you selected appear.

■ To display information about an item, position the mouse over the item. A yellow box appears, displaying information about the item.

■ This area displays options that you can select to perform common tasks and access commonly used locations on your computer. The available options depend on the selected item.

4 To continue browsing through the contents of your computer, you can double-click a folder to display its contents.

■ You can click Back or ➔ to move through the drives and folders you have previously viewed.

5 When you finish browsing, click ☒ to close the window.

VIEW YOUR PERSONAL FOLDERS

Windows provides personal folders that offer a convenient place for you to store and manage your files. You can view the contents of your personal folders at any time.

The My Documents folder is useful for storing documents such as letters, reports and memos. You can use the My Pictures and My Music folders to store your pictures and music files, respectively. The My Pictures and My Music folders are subfolders of the My Documents folder.

When you view the contents of a personal folder, Windows displays a list of options you can select to work with the files in the folder. The available options depend on the folder you are viewing and the files you have selected.

Many programs automatically store files in your personal folders. For example, WordPad stores your documents in the My Documents folder, while Paint stores your pictures in the My Pictures folder. When you copy songs to your computer from a music CD, Windows Media Player automatically creates folders within the My Music folder to store the files.

Your My Documents folder may also contain other personal folders, depending on the programs you use. For example, Windows Movie Maker creates a subfolder called My Videos to store your movies.

VIEW THE MY DOCUMENTS FOLDER

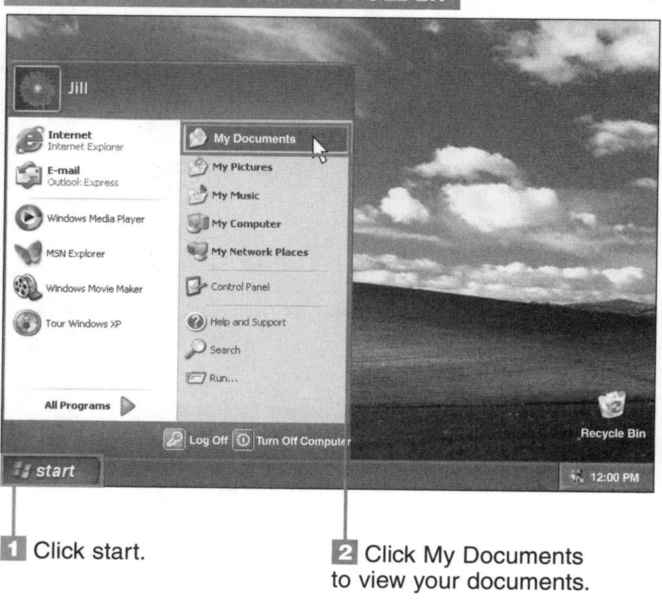

1 Click start.

2 Click My Documents to view your documents.

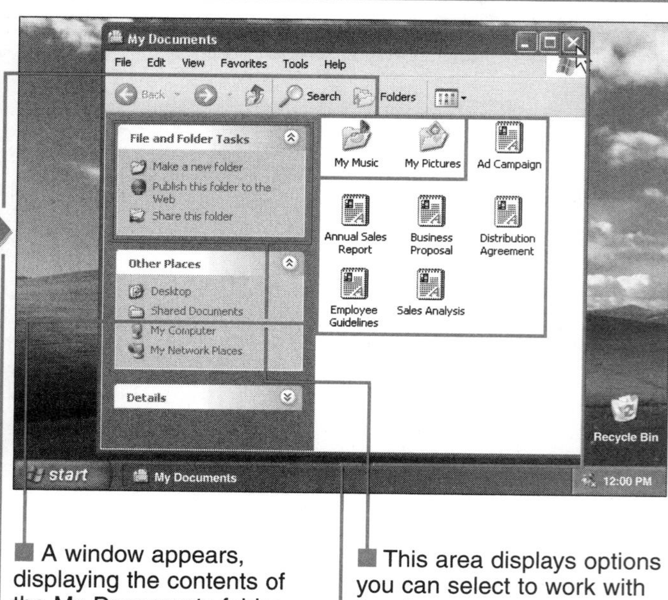

■ A window appears, displaying the contents of the My Documents folder.

■ The My Documents folder contains the My Music and My Pictures folders.

■ This area displays options you can select to work with the documents in the folder.

3 When you finish viewing the contents of the My Documents folder, click ☒ to close the folder.

Will other users on my computer be able to view the contents of my personal folders?

✔ Users with computer administrator accounts on your computer will be able to view your personal folders unless you make the folders private. To make a personal folder private, see page 192.

What are some options I can select to work with my pictures and music files?

✔ In the My Pictures folder, the View as a slide show option lets you display your pictures as a full-screen slide show, while the Order prints online option allows you to order prints of your pictures from a Web site. In the My Music folder, the Play all option lets you play all the music files in the folder, while the Shop for music online option connects you to a Web site where you can listen to and purchase music.

Can I change the location of the My Documents folder?

✔ Yes. This is useful when you want to move the My Documents folder to a network or removable drive. Click start and then right-click My Documents. In the menu that appears, select Properties. Click the Target tab and then click the Move button to select a new location for the folder.

VIEW THE MY PICTURES OR MY MUSIC FOLDER

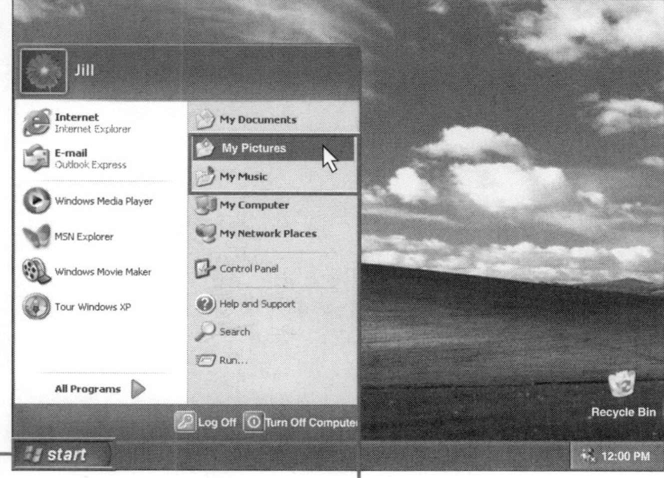

1 Click start.

2 Click My Pictures or My Music to view your pictures or music files.

■ A window appears, displaying the contents of the folder you selected.

■ In this example, the contents of the My Pictures folder appear. This folder displays a miniature version of each picture in the folder.

■ This area displays options you can select to work with the files in the folder.

3 When you finish viewing the contents of the folder, click ☒ to close the folder.

USING WINDOWS EXPLORER

Like a map, Windows Explorer shows you the location of every file and folder on your computer. Windows Explorer helps you understand how your files and folders are organized.

The Windows Explorer window has two panes. The left pane shows the structure of the drives and folders on your computer. You can expand the information in the left pane to show drives and folders that are hidden from view. You can also reduce the information in the left pane to provide an overview of the items available on your computer.

When you select a drive or folder in the left pane, Windows Explorer displays the contents of the drive or folder in the right pane.

To change the size of the left and right panes, you move the vertical bar that separates the two panes. You may want to make the right pane larger to clearly view the contents of a folder.

You can work with the files in Windows Explorer as you would work with the files in any window. For example, you can easily move, rename, delete and open files in Windows Explorer.

USING WINDOWS EXPLORER

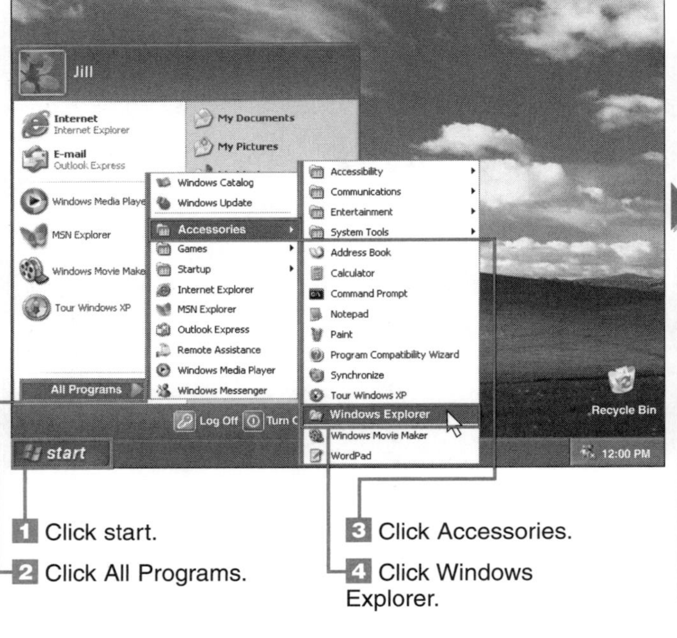

1 Click start.

2 Click All Programs.

3 Click Accessories.

4 Click Windows Explorer.

■ A Windows Explorer window appears.

■ This area displays the organization of the folders on your computer.

5 A folder displaying a plus sign (+) contains folders hidden from view. Click the plus sign (+) to display the hidden folders.

Why don't the contents of some folders appear when I click the name of the folder?

✔ Windows does not automatically display the contents of folders that contain files your computer needs to work properly. This helps prevent you from accidentally deleting or modifying the files. For example, the first time you click the WINDOWS folder, no files or folders are displayed. To view the contents of the folder, click the Show the contents of this folder link.

How do I open a file or folder using Windows Explorer?

✔ You can double-click a file or folder in the right pane.

How can I quickly perform tasks with the files and folders in Windows Explorer?

✔ You can click the Folders button to display a list of options that allow you to perform tasks. The options that appear depend on the file or folder that is currently selected. To return to the organization of the folders, click the Folders button again.

How can I quickly display all the hidden folders within a folder?

✔ Select the folder and then press the asterisk (*) key on the numeric keypad. To once again hide all the folders, click the minus sign (⊟) beside the top folder.

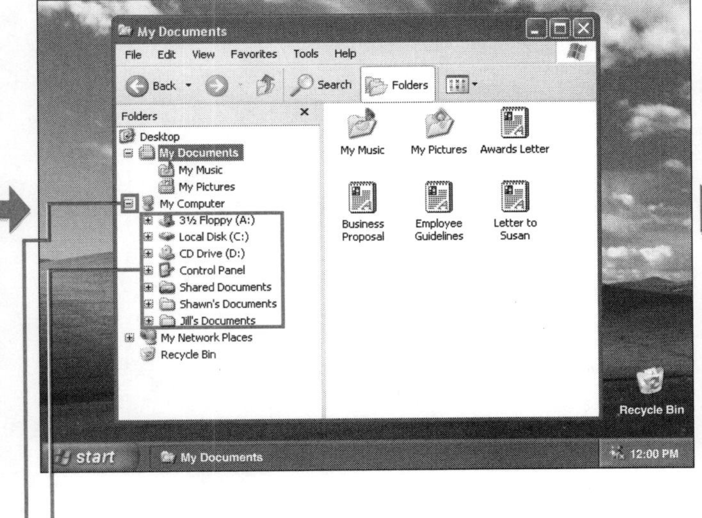

■ The hidden folders appear.

■ The plus sign (⊞) beside the folder changes to a minus sign (⊟). This indicates that the hidden folders within the folder are displayed.

Note: You can click the minus sign (⊟) to once again hide the folders within the folder.

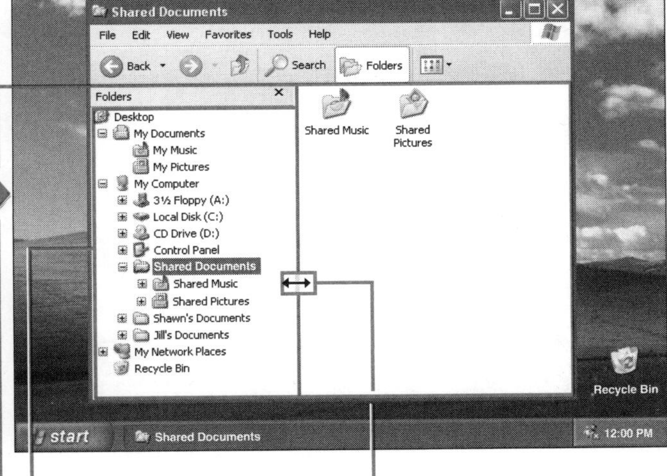

6 To display the contents of a folder, click the name of the folder.

■ This area displays the contents of the folder.

7 To change the size of the left and right panes in the window, position the mouse ⇖ over the vertical bar that separates the two panes (⇖ changes to ↔). Then drag the bar to a new location.

CHANGE VIEW OF ITEMS

You can change the view of items in a window. The view you select determines the information you will see in the window.

Windows displays a picture, or icon, to represent each type of item in a window. For example, the 📁 icon indicates the item is a folder.

When you first use Windows, items are displayed in the Tiles view. Information about each item is displayed under the file or folder name.

You can choose the Icons view or List view to see more items in a window.

The Details view displays item information in columns. You can change the width of the columns in the Details view to make the information easier to view.

The Thumbnails view displays a miniature version of each picture and some other types of files in the window. In this view, miniature versions of up to four pictures within a folder are shown on the folder's icon.

Changing the view of items affects only the open window. Each window remembers the view you selected and displays the items in that view the next time you open the window.

CHANGE VIEW OF ITEMS

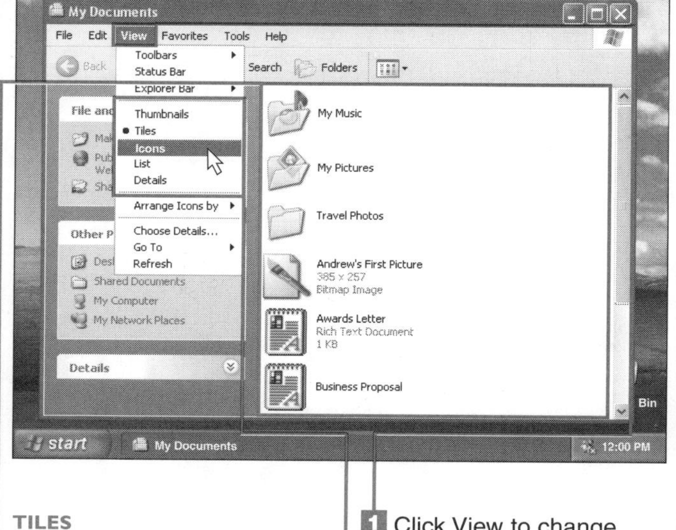

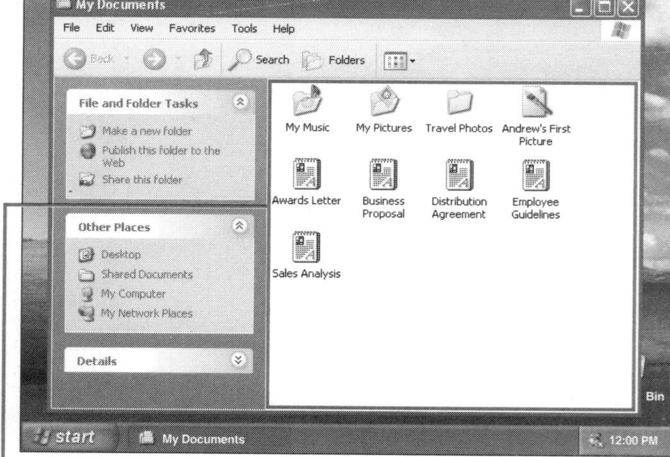

TILES

- When you first start using Windows, items are displayed in the Tiles view.
- The Tiles view displays items as large icons and displays information about each item below the item's name.

1. Click View to change the view of items.
- A bullet (●) appears beside the current view.
2. Click the way you want to view the items.

ICONS

- Items are displayed as small icons, from left to right, with the name appearing below each icon.

LIST

- Items are displayed as small icons in a list. Items are displayed from top to bottom.

Why does the View menu sometimes offer a Filmstrip view?

✔ The Filmstrip view is only available in some windows, such as the My Pictures window. This view displays pictures in a single row that you can scroll through. You can click a picture to display a larger version of the picture above the other pictures.

How do I change the information that each item displays in the Tiles view?

✔ You can sort the items in the Tiles view to change the information that each item displays. To sort items, see page 44.

Is there another way to change the view?

✔ To quickly change the view of items, click ▦▾ in the window and then select the way you want to view the items. If you cannot see ▦▾, you may have to increase the size of the window. To size a window, see page 16.

How can I add additional column headings to the Details view?

✔ Right-click a column heading and then select the name of the column you want to add. You can click the More option to view additional column headings you can add.

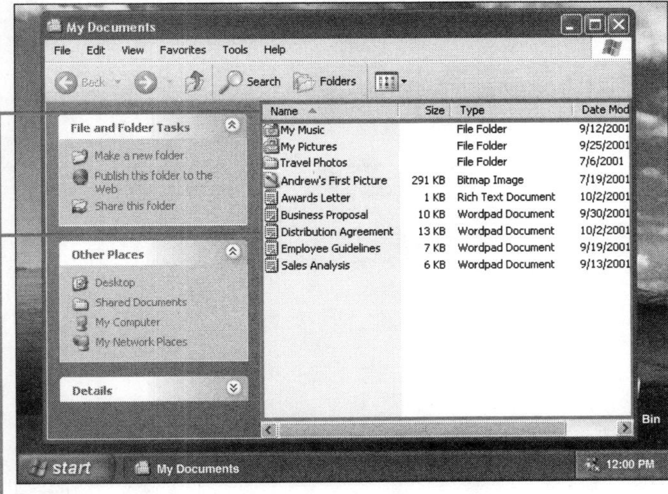

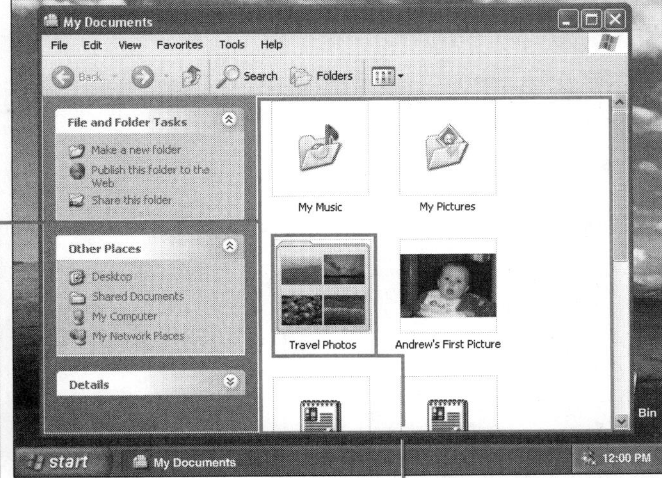

DETAILS

■ Information about each item is displayed, such as the name, size and type of item.

■ To change the width of a column, position the mouse ↖ over the right edge of a column heading (↖ changes to ✛) and then drag the column to a new width.

Note: To resize a column to fit the longest item, double-click the right edge of the column heading.

THUMBNAILS

■ A miniature version of each picture and some other types of files are displayed. If a miniature version of a file cannot be shown, an icon is displayed to indicate the type of file.

■ A folder's icon displays a miniature version of a few pictures within the folder.

SORT ITEMS

You can sort the items displayed in a window to help you find files and folders more easily.

Windows allows you to sort items by name, size, type or the date the items were last modified. Windows sorts files and folders separately.

Sorting by name displays items alphabetically, from A to Z. If you know the name of the item you want to find, try sorting by name.

Sorting by size displays items by their size, from smallest to largest. To find a large file, try sorting by size.

Sorting by type displays items alphabetically according to the file type. If you are looking for a file of a specific type, try sorting by type.

Sorting by the date items were last modified displays items according to when they were last changed, from oldest to newest. This is useful when you know the date you last worked with a file.

Some windows allow you to sort items in other ways. For example, the My Music window allows you to sort items by artist and track number.

If a window displays items in the Details view, you can use the column headings in the window to sort items.

SORT ITEMS

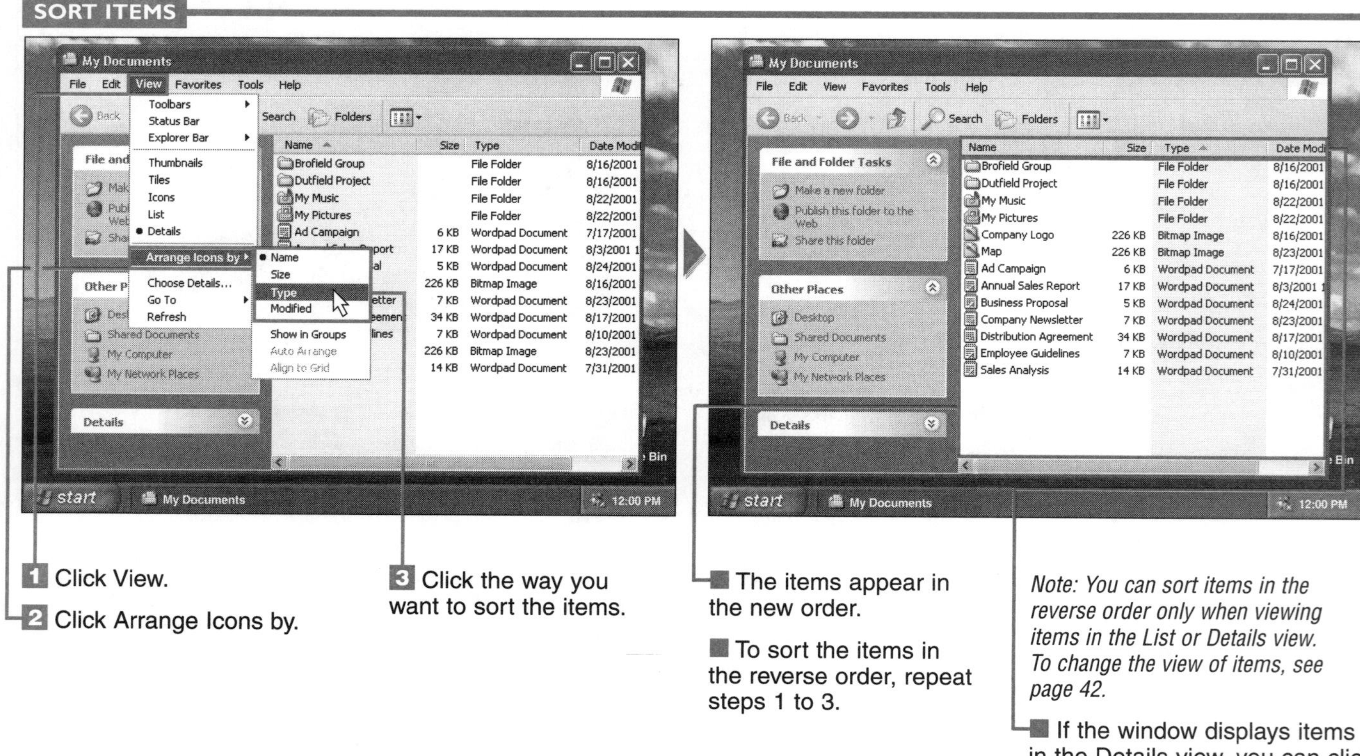

1 Click View.

2 Click Arrange Icons by.

3 Click the way you want to sort the items.

■ The items appear in the new order.

■ To sort the items in the reverse order, repeat steps 1 to 3.

Note: You can sort items in the reverse order only when viewing items in the List or Details view. To change the view of items, see page 42.

■ If the window displays items in the Details view, you can click a column heading to sort the items.

GROUP ITEMS

You can group items to better organize the files and folders in a window. Grouping items can make it easier to find files and folders of interest in a window that contains many items.

When you group items, Windows will usually organize the items in the window alphabetically by name.

After grouping items, you can change the way the items are grouped by sorting the items.

For example, you can sort items by name, size, type or the date the items were last modified. The items will be grouped according to the way you sort the items. For more information about sorting items, see page 44.

You cannot group items in a window that displays its contents in the List or Filmstrip view. For information about changing the view of items in a window, see page 42.

Grouping items in a window will not affect the way items are displayed in other windows. Each window remembers the way its items are arranged and displays the items in that arrangement the next time you open the window.

GROUP ITEMS

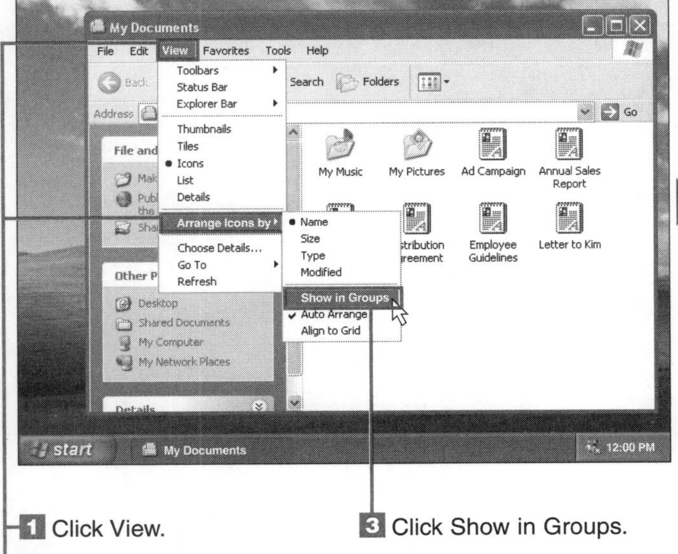

1 Click View.

2 Click Arrange Icons by.

3 Click Show in Groups.

Note: The Show in Groups option is not available when viewing items in the List or Filmstrip view. To change the view of items, see page 42.

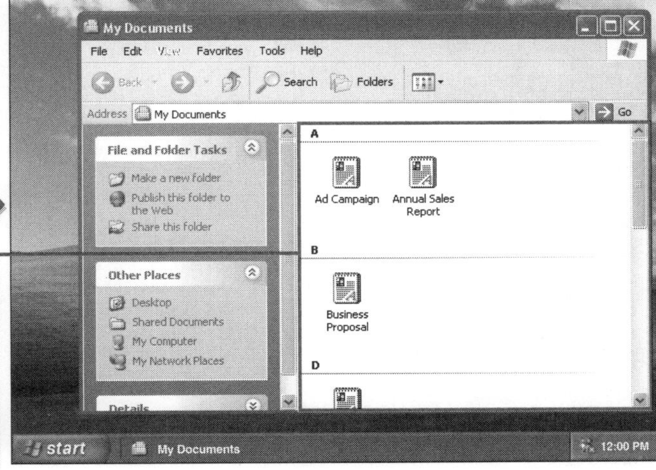

■ Windows groups the items in the window.

■ If you no longer want to group the items in a window, repeat steps 1 to 3.

SCROLL THROUGH A WINDOW

A scroll bar allows you to browse through information in a window. This is useful when a window is not large enough to display all the information it contains. Some dialog boxes also display scroll bars that you can use to view all the items in a list.

A window can display a vertical scroll bar, a horizontal scroll bar or both. A vertical scroll bar allows you to scroll up and down through information. A horizontal scroll bar allows you to scroll left and right through information.

The location of the scroll box on the scroll bar indicates which part of the window you are viewing. For example, when the scroll box is halfway down the scroll bar, you are viewing information in the middle of the window. The size of the scroll box varies, depending on the amount of information the window contains and the size of the window.

You can purchase a mouse that has a wheel between the left and right mouse buttons. Moving this wheel also allows you to scroll through information in a window.

SCROLL THROUGH A WINDOW

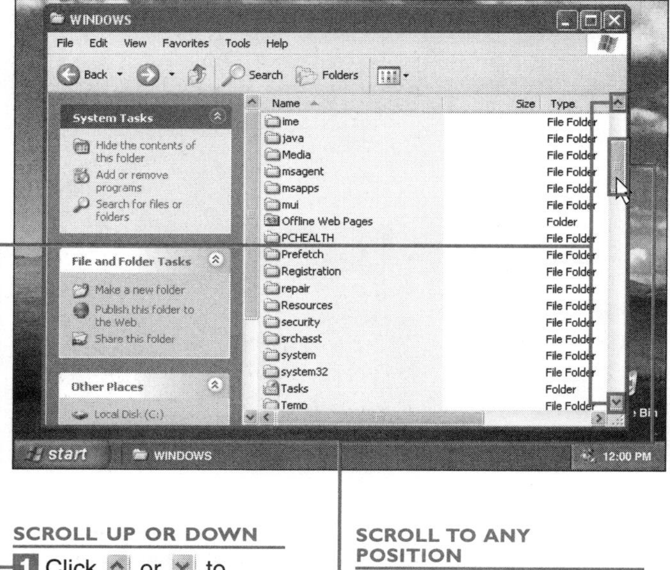

SCROLL UP OR DOWN

1 Click ^ or v to scroll up or down through the information in a window.

SCROLL TO ANY POSITION

1 Position the mouse over the scroll box.

2 Drag the scroll box up or down the scroll bar until the information you want to view appears.

SCROLL LEFT OR RIGHT

1 Click < or > to scroll left or right through the information in a window.

SCROLL TO ANY POSITION

1 Position the mouse over the scroll box.

2 Drag the scroll box left or right along the scroll bar until the information you want to view appears.

AUTOMATICALLY ARRANGE DESKTOP ITEMS

You can use the Auto Arrange feature to have Windows automatically arrange items to fit neatly on the desktop. If your desktop items are scattered, arranging the items will make the contents of your desktop more organized and easier to view.

When you arrange items on your desktop, Windows arranges the items in columns, starting at the left edge of your screen.

When the Auto Arrange feature is turned on, you cannot move an item to a blank area away from the other items, but you can move an item to a new location within the columns of items. The other items will shift to make room for the item and will remain neatly arranged.

Is there another way to arrange items on the desktop?

✔ You can arrange the items on the desktop by name, size, type or the date the items were last modified. Right-click a blank area on the desktop, click Arrange Icons By and then click the option you want to use to arrange the items.

AUTOMATICALLY ARRANGE DESKTOP ITEMS

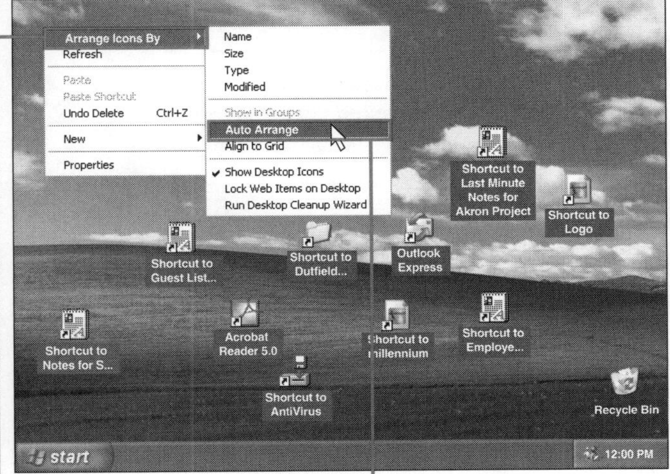

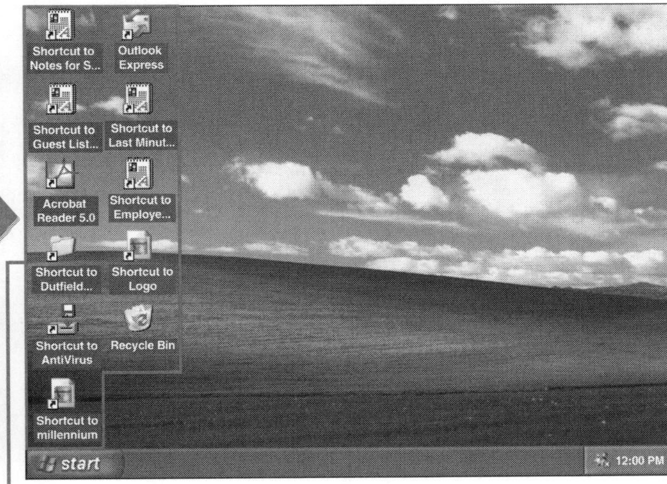

1 Right-click a blank area on your desktop. A menu appears.

2 Click Arrange Icons By.

3 Click Auto Arrange to turn on this feature.

■ A check mark (✔) appears beside Auto Arrange when this feature is on.

■ The items on the desktop are automatically arranged.

■ To turn off the Auto Arrange feature, repeat steps 1 to 3 to remove the check mark (✔).

DISPLAY OR HIDE A TOOLBAR OR THE STATUS BAR

Toolbars allow you to quickly access commonly used commands and features. The status bar provides information about the items displayed in a window. You can display or hide these bars to suit your needs.

Toolbars appear at the top of a window. The Standard Buttons toolbar contains buttons that allow you to quickly perform common tasks, such as searching for files and changing the view of items. You can use the Address Bar toolbar to quickly access another drive or folder on your computer. You can also type a Web page address in the Address Bar toolbar to display a Web page without first starting your Web browser. The Links toolbar contains links you can select to quickly access useful Web pages. If all the items on a toolbar are not displayed, the right edge of the toolbar may display an arrow that you can click to display the hidden items.

The status bar appears at the bottom of a window and displays information about all the items in the window or the selected item. For example, when you select a file, the status bar displays the type and size of the file.

DISPLAY OR HIDE A TOOLBAR

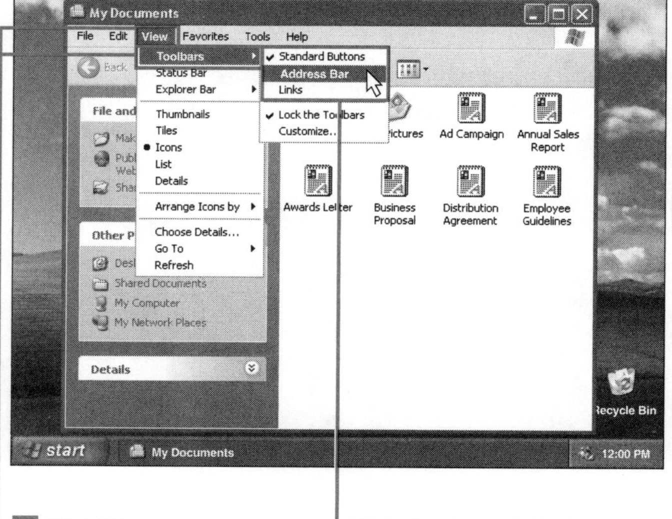

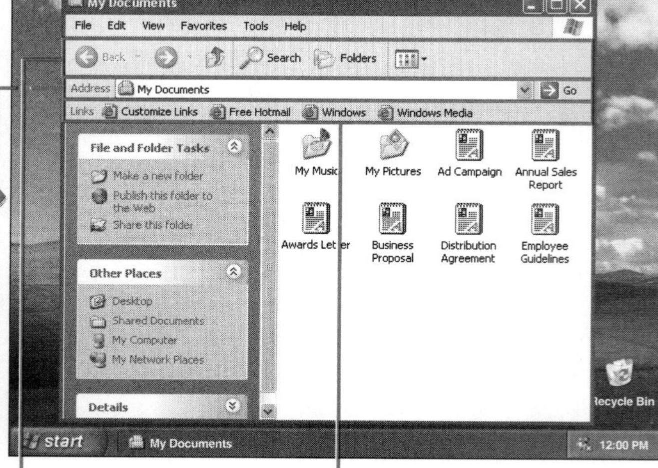

1 Click View.

2 Click Toolbars.

■ A check mark (✔) appears beside the name of each toolbar that is currently displayed.

3 Click the toolbar you want to display or hide.

■ The Standard Buttons toolbar displays buttons for commonly used commands.

■ The Address Bar toolbar displays the location of the open folder and allows you to quickly access another drive or folder.

Note: To access another drive or folder, you can click ⌄ on the Address Bar toolbar and then select a drive or folder.

■ The Links toolbar allows you to quickly access useful Web pages.

Can I customize the Standard Buttons toolbar?

✔ Yes. Select the View menu, choose Toolbars and then click Customize. To add a button, double-click the button in the Available toolbar buttons area. To remove or change the location of the button labels, click the Text options area and then select the text option you want to use. To remove a button, double-click the button in the Current toolbar buttons area.

Why is the address area of the Address Bar toolbar not displayed?

✔ You may need to unlock the toolbar. Click the View menu, click Toolbars and select Lock the Toolbars. Then double-click Address to display the entire toolbar.

Can I change the size of toolbars that appear on the same line?

✔ Yes. You must first unlock the toolbars. Click the View menu, click Toolbars and select Lock the Toolbars. Then position the mouse over the dotted line at the left edge of a toolbar (⇖ changes to ↔). Drag the dotted line until the toolbars display the size you want.

How can I move a toolbar?

✔ You must first unlock the toolbar. Click the View menu, click Toolbars and select Lock the Toolbars. Then position the mouse over the dotted line at the left edge of the toolbar (⇖ changes to ↔) and drag the toolbar to a new location.

DISPLAY OR HIDE THE STATUS BAR

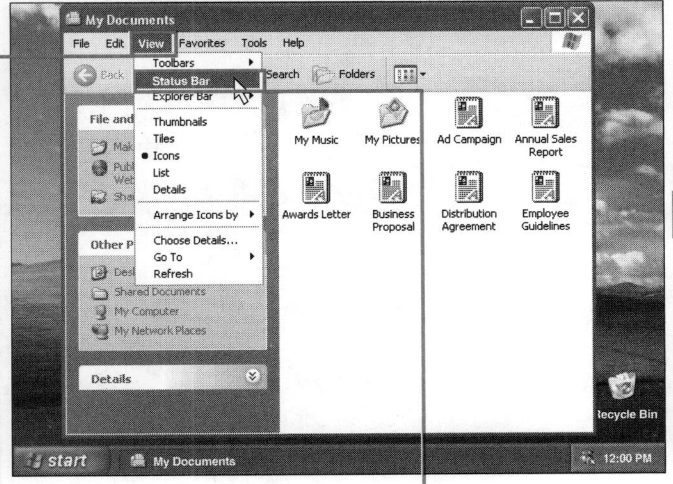

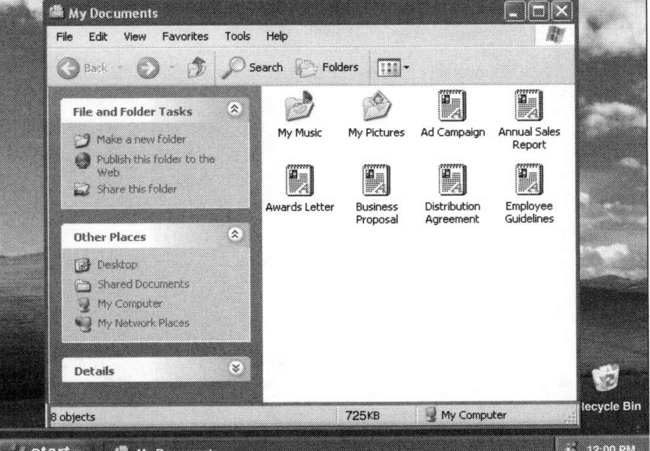

1 Click View.

■ A check mark (✔) appears beside Status Bar if the bar is currently displayed.

2 Click Status Bar to display or hide the bar.

■ In this example, the status bar appears.

■ The status bar usually displays the number of items and the total size of the files in the window.

Note: When you select a file in the window, the status bar usually displays the type and size of the file.

CHANGE FOLDER VIEW OPTIONS

You can customize the way Windows displays the contents of folders.

You can have Windows regularly search your network for shared folders and printers and place the items in My Network Places. You can also change the way Windows displays the contents and subfolders of a folder in Windows Explorer.

Windows can hide or show the contents of system folders and protected operating system files. Windows can also hide or show hidden files and folders or file name extensions.

You can have Windows display the location of folders in the Address bar and title bar of a window or have each folder open in a separate part of your computer's memory. Windows can remember the way you display items in each folder and redisplay the items the same way the next time you open the folders. Windows can also remember which folders were left open when you logged off and reopen those folders when you log on again.

Windows can store thumbnail images in cache files to allow folders containing thumbnails to open faster.

You can choose to display the Control Panel in the My Computer folder. You can also have Windows display compressed files in a different color to make them easy to recognize.

When you position the mouse pointer over a file, folder or desktop item, Windows can display a description of the item in a small box. You can also have Windows show the size of a folder and the names of a few files and subfolders within the folder.

CHANGE FOLDER VIEW OPTIONS

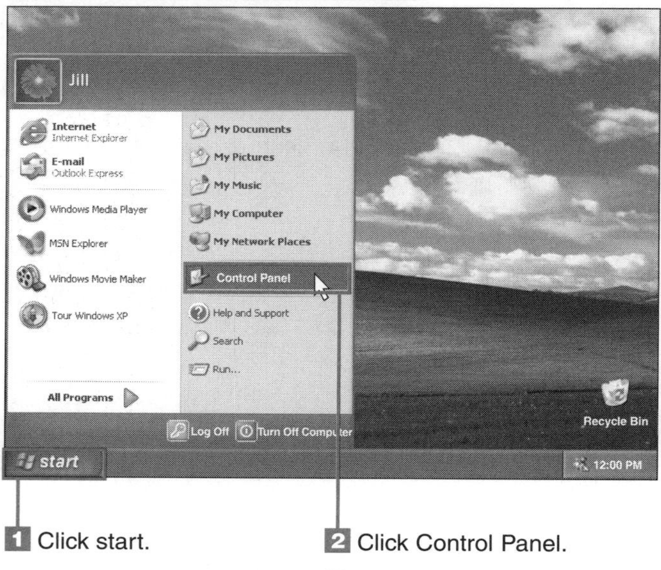

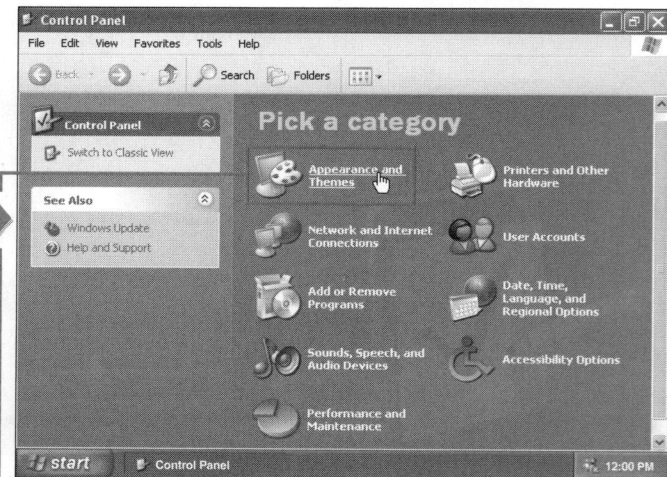

1 Click start.

2 Click Control Panel.

■ The Control Panel window appears.

3 Click Appearance and Themes.

■ The Appearance and Themes window appears.

Can I return to the original folder view options?

✔ Yes. In the Folder Options dialog box, choose the View tab and then click the Restore Defaults button.

Can I make the view of items the same in all folders?

✔ Yes. Open the folder that displays the view you like. For information about changing the view of items, see page 42. On the Tools menu, click Folder Options. Select the View tab and click the Apply to All Folders button. To return all folders on your computer to the default view, click the Reset All Folders button.

Should I hide or show file extensions?

✔ You can have Windows hide file extensions when you want to reduce clutter in windows. Showing file extensions can help you identify the type of files you are viewing. For example, viewing file extensions would help you realize that a Windows Media File you thought was a movie is actually a sound file (.wav).

Why would I want to hide operating system files and hidden files?

✔ Operating system files and hidden files are files that Windows and your programs need to run. If you change or delete operating system files or hidden files, your computer may no longer operate properly.

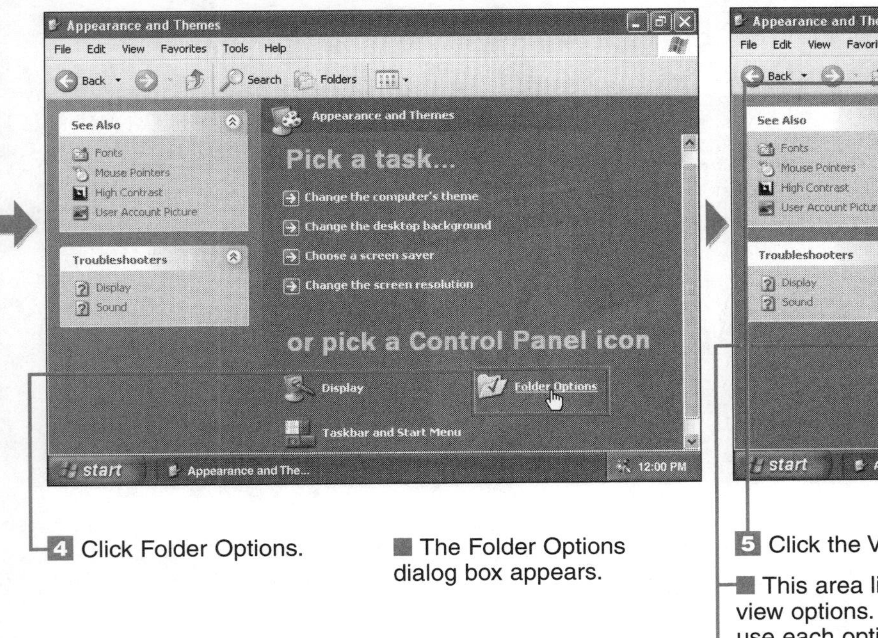

4 Click Folder Options.

■ The Folder Options dialog box appears.

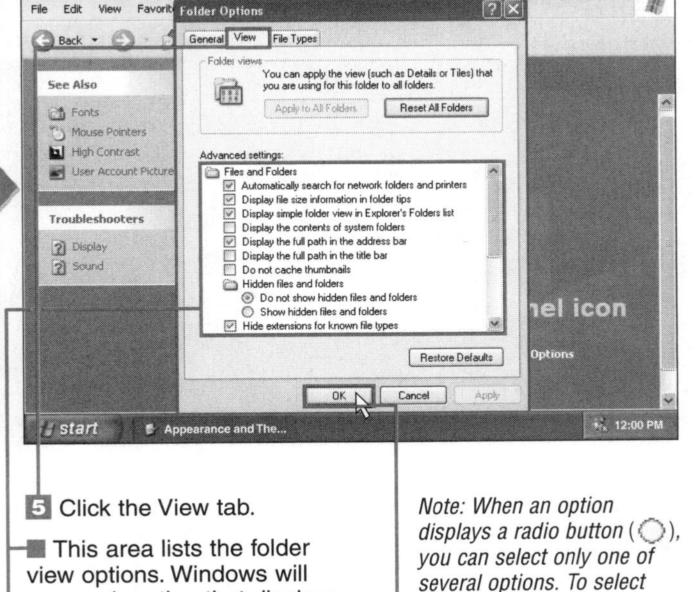

5 Click the View tab.

■ This area lists the folder view options. Windows will use each option that displays a check mark (✔).

6 To turn an option on (☑) or off (☐), click the option.

Note: When an option displays a radio button (○), you can select only one of several options. To select an option, click the option (○ changes to ◉).

7 Click OK to confirm your changes.

SELECT FILES

Before you can work with a file or folder, you often need to select the item. For example, you must first select a file or folder you want to copy, move, delete or open.

When you select a file or folder, Windows highlights the item. When you select a folder, all the items contained in the folder are automatically selected.

You can display the Details area in the left side of the window to view information about an item you select. The information displayed for a selected file includes the file type, the date and time the file was last modified and the size of the file. If you select an image or Web page, a small preview of the image or Web page may appear in the Details area.

You can select and work with multiple files and folders. This lets you perform the same procedure on several items at the same time. When you select multiple files in a window, you can view the number of selected files and the total size of the selected files in the Details area.

SELECT FILES

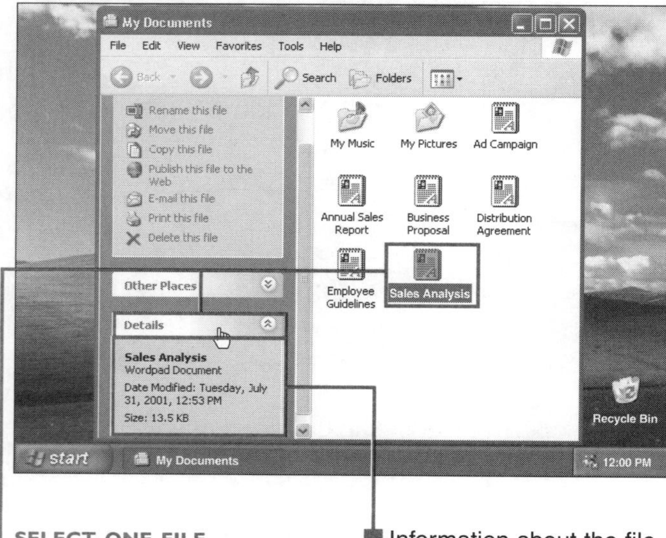

SELECT ONE FILE

1 Click the file you want to select. The file is highlighted.

2 If you want to display information about the file, click Details.

■ Information about the file appears, including the file type and the date and time the file was last changed.

Note: To hide the information, click Details again.

SELECT RANDOM FILES

1 Click a file you want to select.

2 Press and hold down the Ctrl key as you click each additional file you want to select.

How do I deselect files and folders?

✔ To deselect all the files and folders in a window, click a blank area in the window. To deselect one file or folder from a group of selected items, hold down the Ctrl key as you click the file or folder you want to deselect.

Is there an easy way to select all but a few files in a window?

✔ Select all the files in the window and then hold down the Ctrl key as you click the files you do not want to select. You can also select the files you do not want and then choose the Edit menu and select Invert Selection.

When I select all the files in a window, a dialog box appears, indicating that the folder contains hidden files. How do I display hidden files?

✔ In the window, click the Tools menu and then select Folder Options. In the dialog box that appears, choose the View tab and then click the Show hidden files and folders option (◯ changes to ◉).

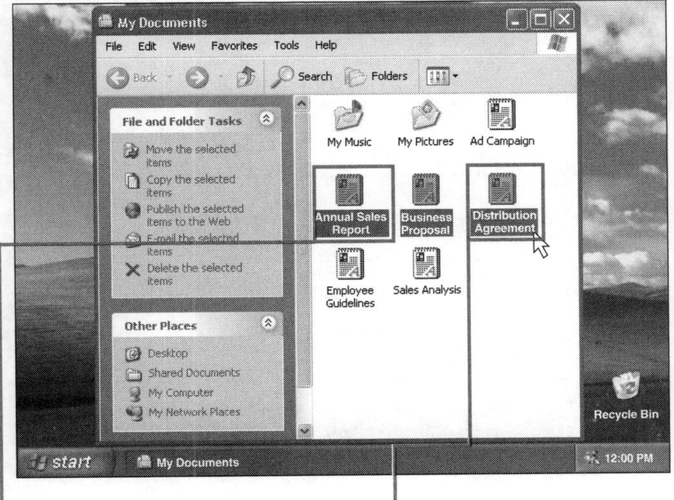

SELECT GROUP OF FILES

1 Click the first file you want to select.

2 Press and hold down the Shift key as you click the last file you want to select.

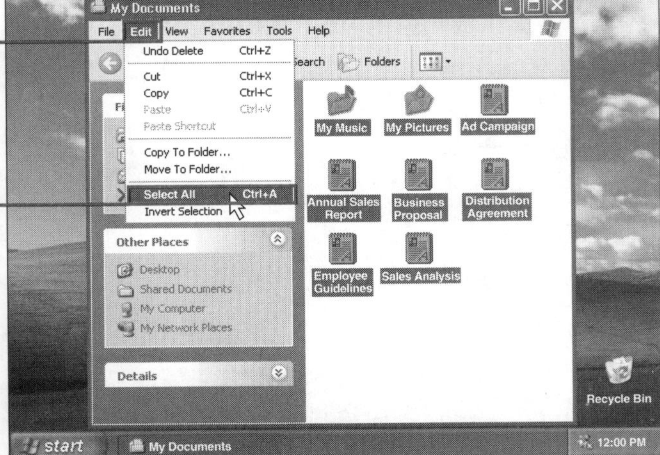

SELECT ALL FILES

1 Click Edit.

2 Click Select All to select all the files and folders in a window.

Note: The Select All dialog box appears if the window contains hidden files. Click OK to select only the displayed files.

OPEN FILES

You can open a file directly from any window or the desktop to display its contents on the screen. Opening a file allows you to review and make changes to the file.

Each file on your computer is associated with a specific program. When you open a file, the associated program starts automatically. For example, text files are associated with the Notepad program. When you open a text file, the Notepad program starts and the file is opened.

You can select a different program to open a file. For example, Windows automatically opens a picture in the Windows Picture and Fax Viewer window, which allows you to view the picture. To make changes to the picture, you will need to open the picture within the program you used to create the picture or in another image editing program.

You can use the Open With feature to specify which program you want to use to open a file. You can also specify if the program you select should always be used to open the file and every file of that type.

OPEN FILES

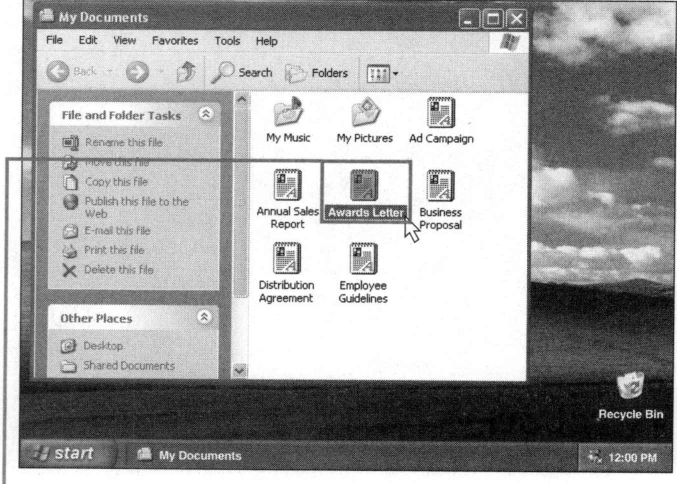

1 Double-click the file you want to open.

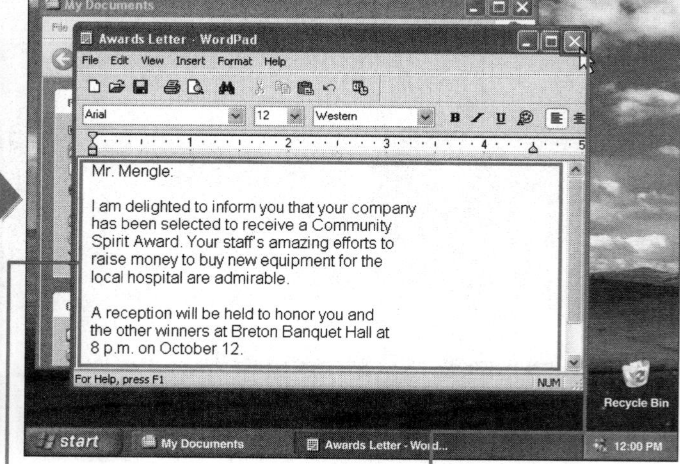

■ The contents of the file appear. You can review and make changes to the file.

Note: If you opened a picture, the picture appears in the Windows Picture and Fax Viewer window.

2 When you finish working with the file, click ☒ to close the file.

When I double-click a file, why does a dialog box appear?

✔ A dialog box appears when Windows does not know which program to use to open the file. You can open the file by selecting a program from a list of programs available on your computer or visit a Web site that can help find a program you can use to open the file.

I can't open a file using any of the programs on my computer. What can I do?

✔ You can click the "look for the appropriate program on the Web" link in the Open With dialog box to search the Internet for a program you can use to open the file.

How can I quickly access the files I most recently used?

✔ You can have the Start menu display the My Recent Documents folder, which provides quick access to the files you used most recently. Right-click the start button and then select Properties. In the dialog box that appears, choose the Start Menu tab, select the Start menu option (○ changes to ◉) and then click the Customize button. In the dialog box that appears, choose the Advanced tab and then select List my most recently opened documents (☐ changes to ☑).

OPEN FILES IN A DIFFERENT PROGRAM

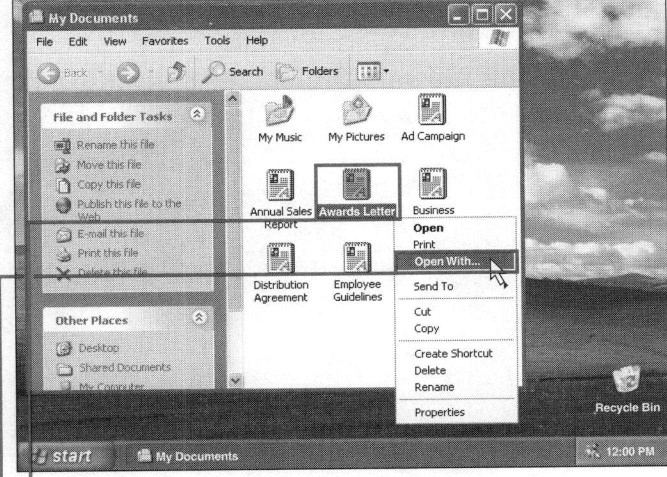

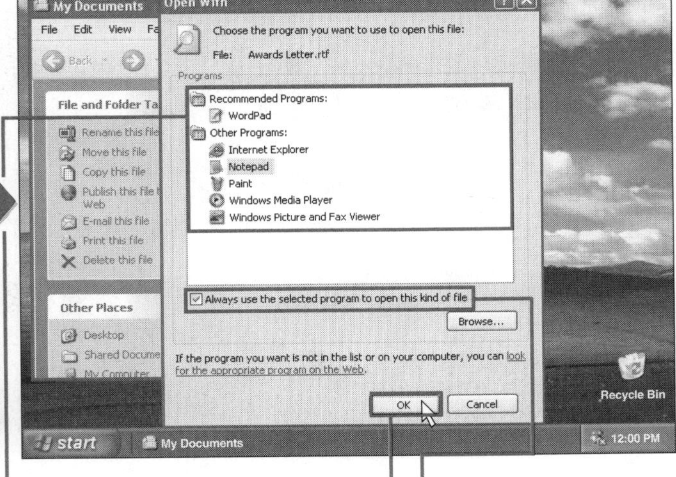

1 Right-click the file you want to open in a different program. A menu appears.

2 Click Open With.

■ If another menu appears, click the program you want to use to open the file. If the program you want to use does not appear on the menu, click Choose Program.

■ The Open With dialog box appears.

3 Click the program you want to use to open the file.

4 To always use the program you selected to open this type of file, click this option (☐ changes to ☑).

5 Click OK to open the file.

VIEW PICTURES

You can use the Windows Picture and Fax Viewer window to view your pictures without opening an image editing program.

By default, most pictures on your computer are stored in the My Pictures folder, which is located in the My Documents folder. The My Pictures folder automatically displays a miniature version of each picture in the folder. Displaying a picture in the Windows Picture and Fax Viewer window allows you to preview the picture in more detail.

In the Windows Picture and Fax Viewer window, you can quickly display other pictures stored in the same folder as the displayed picture. If you want to preview how a picture will look when printed, you can choose to display the picture at its actual size. You can also view the picture in the size that fits best in the Windows Picture and Fax Viewer window.

You can zoom into a part of the picture to view more detail or zoom out to see more of the picture. You can also rotate the picture clockwise or counterclockwise in the window. This is useful if you want to turn the picture on its side or view the picture upside down.

If you want to make changes to the picture, you can open the picture in an image editing program.

VIEW PICTURES

1 Double-click a picture you want to view.

■ The Windows Picture and Fax Viewer window appears, displaying the picture you selected.

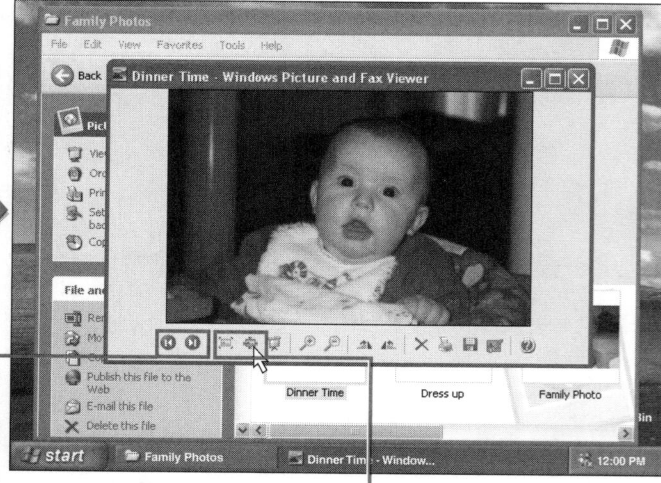

2 To display other pictures in the same folder, click Previous Image ( ) or Next Image ( ).

3 To display the picture in a size that fits best in the window or at its actual size, click Best Fit ( ) or Actual Size ( ).

Why do additional options appear when I view some pictures?

✔ The options displayed in the Windows Picture and Fax Viewer window depend on the type of picture you are viewing. For example, if you are viewing a fax document or TIFF picture, options appear that allow you to perform tasks such as adding notes to a picture, highlighting a section of a picture or moving through the pages in a multi-page fax document.

How do I print the picture displayed in the Windows Picture and Fax Viewer window?

✔ Click [print icon] in the Windows Picture and Fax Viewer window to start the Photo Printing Wizard. Follow the instructions in the wizard to print the picture. For information about the Photo Printing Wizard, see page 116.

Can I delete a picture in the Windows Picture and Fax Viewer window?

✔ Yes. Click [X] to delete the displayed picture from your computer. Windows will display the next picture stored in the folder.

How can I display all the pictures in a folder automatically?

✔ When viewing a picture, you can click [slide show icon] to display a slide show of all the pictures in the same folder.

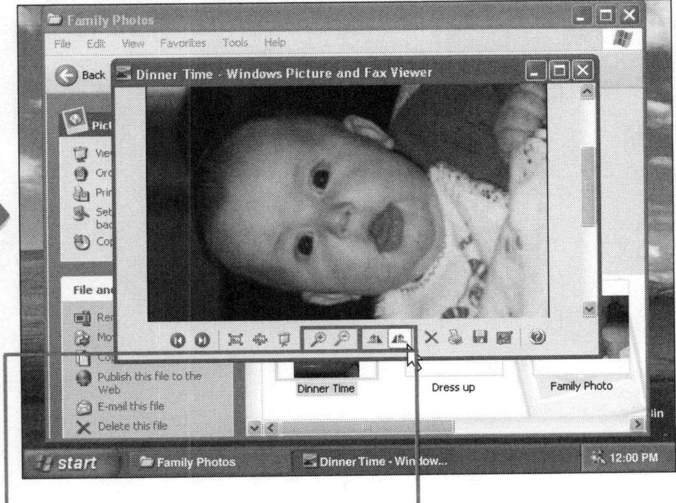

4 To magnify or reduce the size of the picture, click Zoom In ([zoom in icon]) or Zoom Out ([zoom out icon]).

Note: You can also click the area of the picture you want to magnify or reduce.

5 To rotate the picture 90 degrees, click Rotate Clockwise ([rotate clockwise icon]) or Rotate Counterclockwise ([rotate counterclockwise icon]).

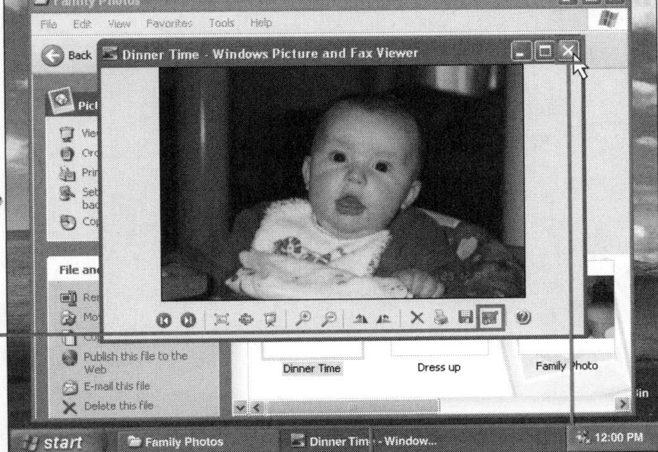

6 To close the Windows Picture and Fax Viewer window and open the picture in an image editing program, click [edit icon].

7 To close the Windows Picture and Fax Viewer window when you finish viewing the picture, click [X].

MOVE FILES

You can move files when you want to reorganize files on your hard drive. When you move a file, you delete the file from its original location.

You may want to move a file to a different folder to keep files of the same type in one location on your computer. For example, you can move all your documents to the My Documents folder provided by Windows. Windows also includes the My Pictures and My Music folders that you can use to store your pictures and music files.

You can use the drag and drop method to move files from one location to another. Before using this method, make sure you can clearly see the location where you want to move the files. You may want to use this method in the Windows Explorer window to simplify the task of dragging files from one location to another. For information about using Windows Explorer, see page 40.

You can move a folder the same way you move a file. When you move a folder, all the files in the folder are also moved.

MOVE FILES

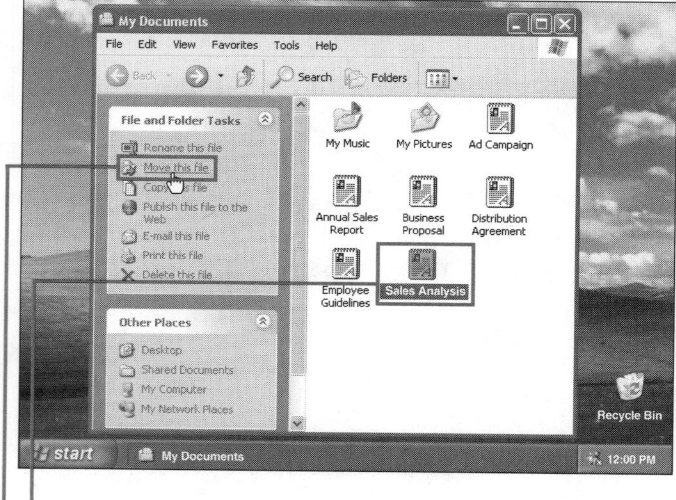

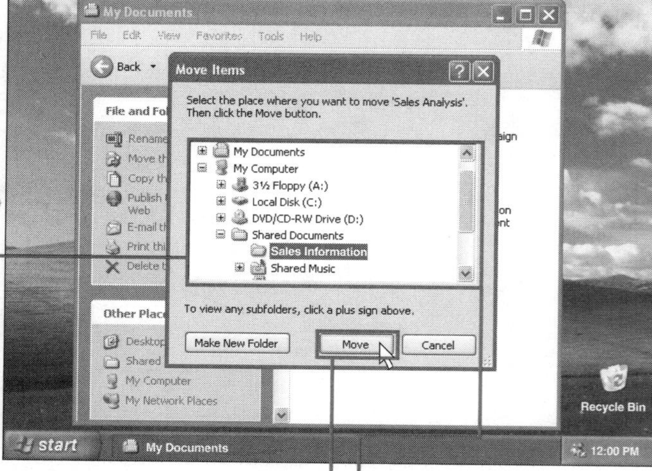

1 Select the file(s) you want to move. To select multiple files, see page 52.

2 Click Move this file.

Note: If you selected multiple files, click Move the selected items in step 2.

■ The Move Items dialog box appears.

■ This area displays the locations where you can move the file. A location displaying a plus sign (⊞) contains hidden items.

3 To display the hidden items within a location, click the plus sign (⊞) beside the location (⊞ changes to ⊟).

4 Click the location where you want to move the file.

5 Click Move to move the file.

How do I use the drag and drop method to move a file to a different drive?

✔ By default, when you drag a file to a different drive, a copy of the file is placed on the drive. To move a file to a different drive, you must hold down the Shift key while dragging the file.

Why does a dialog box appear when I try to move a file?

✔ If you try to move a file to a folder that contains a file with the same name, a dialog box appears, confirming the move. Click Yes or No to specify if you want to replace the existing file with the file you are moving.

Are there other ways to move files?

✔ Using the right mouse button, drag the files to the new location. From the menu that appears, select Move Here. You can also select the files you want to move and then right-click one of the selected files. On the menu that appears, click Cut. Open the folder where you want to place the files. Right-click a blank area in the folder and then click Paste.

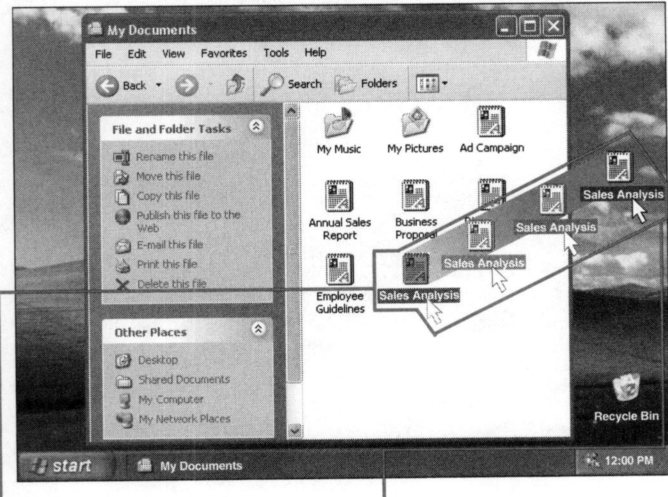

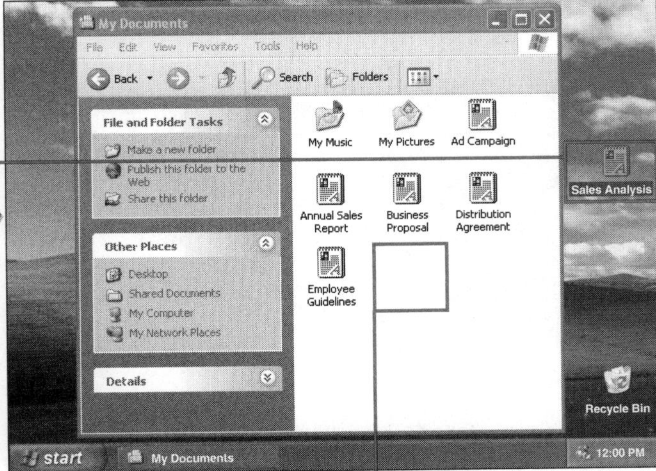

USING DRAG AND DROP

1 Select the file(s) you want to move. To select multiple files, see page 52.

2 Position the mouse over the file you selected.

Note: If you selected multiple files, position the mouse over one of the selected files.

3 Drag the file to a new location.

■ The file moves to the new location.

■ The file disappears from its original location.

COPY FILES

You can copy files when you want to share documents with a colleague, take work home on a floppy disk or make backup copies of your files. When you copy a file, you create a second file that is exactly the same as the first.

You can place a copy of a file in another location on your computer, on a network or on removable media. You can also copy a file to the same folder that contains the file. This is useful if you plan to make major changes to a file but want to keep the original file. When you create a copy of a file in the same folder, Windows adds "Copy of" to the new file name.

You can use the drag and drop method to copy files. Before using this method, make sure you can clearly see the location where you want to copy the files. When copying files using the drag and drop method, the mouse pointer displays a plus sign (⊞).

You can copy a folder the same way you copy a file. When you copy a folder, all the files in the folder are also copied.

COPY FILES

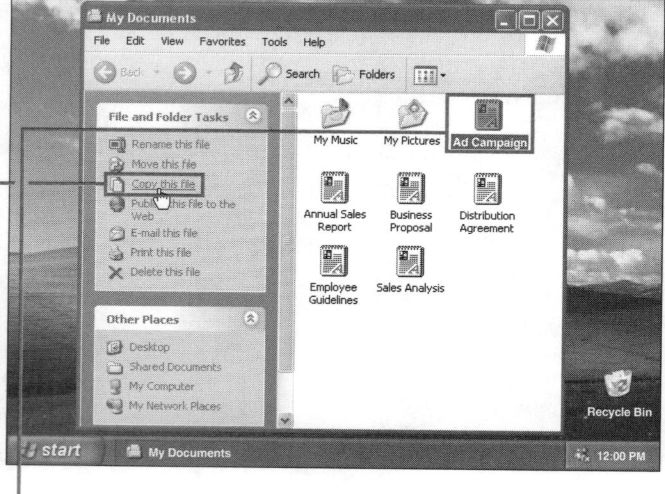

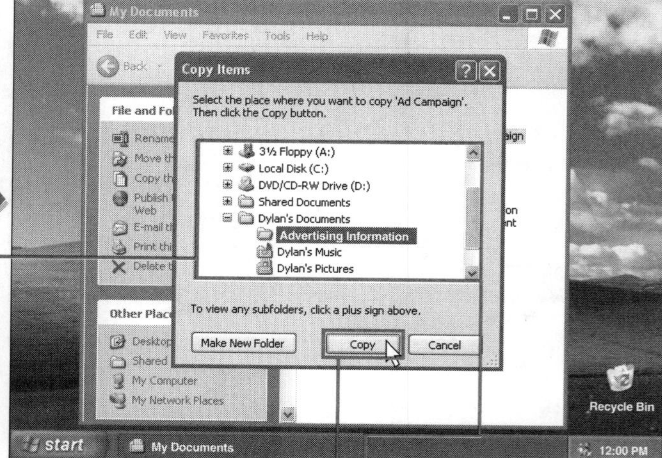

1 Select the file(s) you want to copy. To select multiple files, see page 52.

2 Click Copy this file.

Note: If you selected multiple files, click Copy the selected items in step 2.

■ The Copy Items dialog box appears.

■ This area displays the locations where you can copy the file. A location displaying a plus sign (⊞) contains hidden items.

3 To display the hidden items within a location, click the plus sign (⊞) beside the location (⊞ changes to ⊟).

4 Click the location where you want to copy the file.

5 Click Copy to copy the file.

I frequently copy files to the same folder. How can I simplify this task?

✔ You can add the folder to the Send To menu. For information about adding destinations to the Send To menu, see page 112. You can also place a shortcut to the folder on your desktop. For information about creating shortcuts, see page 96.

How can I quickly copy files to a floppy disk?

✔ Select the files you want to copy to a floppy disk and then right-click one of the selected files. In the menu that appears, select Send To and then click the drive that contains the floppy disk.

Are there other ways to copy files?

✔ Using the right mouse button, drag the files to the new location. From the menu that appears, select Copy Here. You can also select the files you want to copy and then right-click one of the selected files. On the menu that appears, click Copy. Open the folder where you want to place the files. Right-click a blank area in the folder and then click Paste.

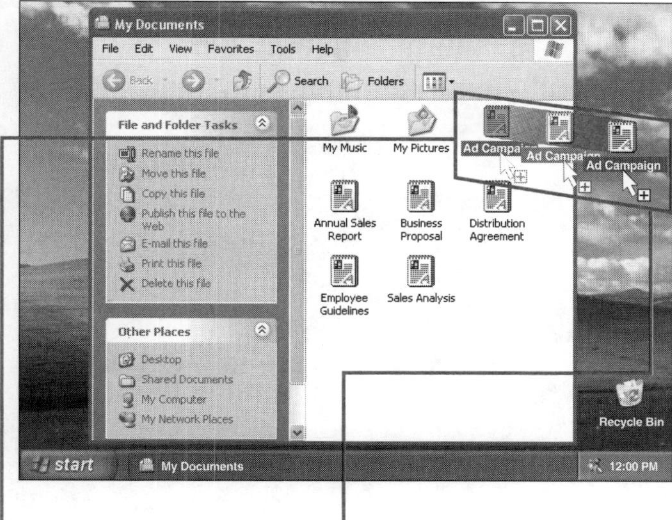

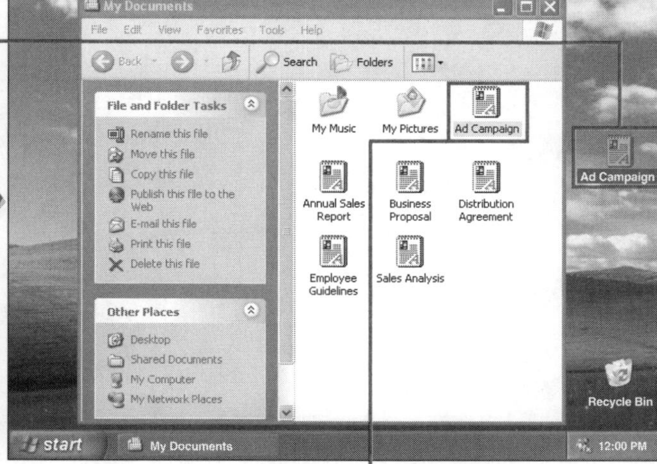

USING DRAG AND DROP

1 Select the file(s) you want to copy. To select multiple files, see page 52.

2 Position the mouse over the file you selected.

Note: If you selected multiple files, position the mouse over one of the selected files.

3 Press and hold down the Ctrl key as you drag the file to a new location.

■ The copy of the file appears in the new location.

■ The original file remains in its original location.

COPY FILES TO A CD

You can copy files, such as documents and pictures, from your computer to a CD. If you only want to copy songs to a CD, see page 326 for more information.

You will need a recordable CD drive to copy files to a CD. There are several types of recordable CD drives you can use. A CD-R (Compact Disc-Recordable) drive allows you to permanently record data on CD-R discs. You cannot erase the contents of a CD-R disc. A CD-RW (Compact Disc-ReWritable) drive allows you to record data on CD-RW or CD-R discs. You can erase the contents of a CD-RW disc in order to copy new data to the disc.

When selecting the files you want to copy to a CD, make sure you do not select more files than the CD can hold. A CD can typically store 650 MB of information.

Windows places a copy of each file you select in a temporary storage area before copying the files to a CD. You must have enough free space on your hard drive to store the copies. A 650 MB CD can require up to 700 MB of hard drive space.

COPY FILES TO A CD

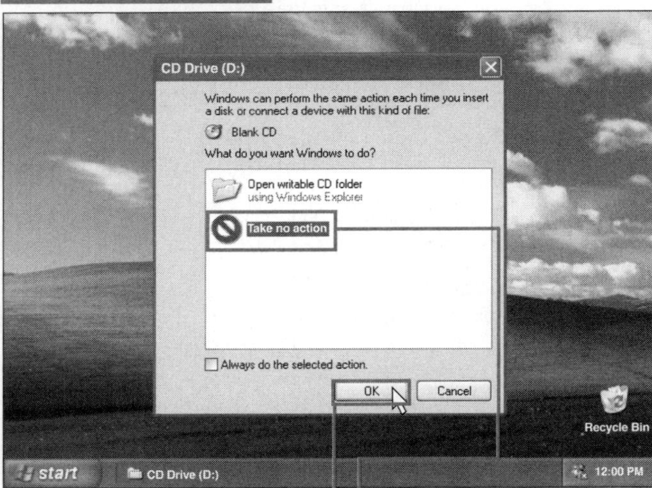

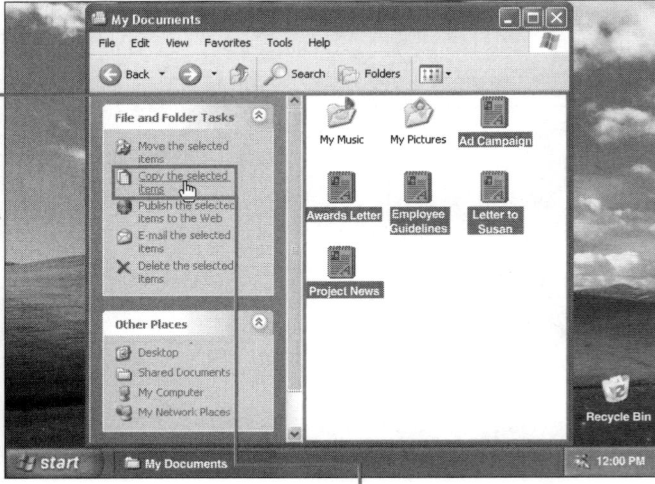

SELECT FILES TO COPY

1 Insert a CD into your recordable CD drive.

■ A dialog box may appear, asking what you want Windows to do.

2 Click Take no action.

3 Click OK.

Note: A window displaying the contents of the CD may appear instead of the dialog box. You can click ☒ in the window to close the window.

4 Select the file(s) you want to copy to the CD. To select multiple files, see page 52.

5 Click Copy the selected items.

Note: If you selected only one file, click Copy this file in step 5.

Why would I copy files to a CD?

✔ You can copy files to a CD to transfer large amounts of information between computers or make backup copies of the files stored on your computer. Making backup copies of your files will provide you with extra copies of the files in case you accidentally erase the files or your computer fails.

Can I copy a folder to a CD?

✔ Yes. You can copy a folder to a CD the same way you copy files to a CD. When you copy a folder to a CD, Windows will copy all the files in the folder. To copy a folder to a CD, perform steps 1 to 7 starting on page 62, except select Copy this folder in step 5. Then perform steps 1 to 8 starting on page 63.

How do I copy pictures stored in the My Pictures folder to a CD?

✔ To copy all the pictures in the My Pictures folder to a CD, display the contents of the folder and then click Copy all items to CD. To copy only some of the pictures, select the pictures you want and then click Copy to CD. Then perform steps 1 to 8 starting on page 63.

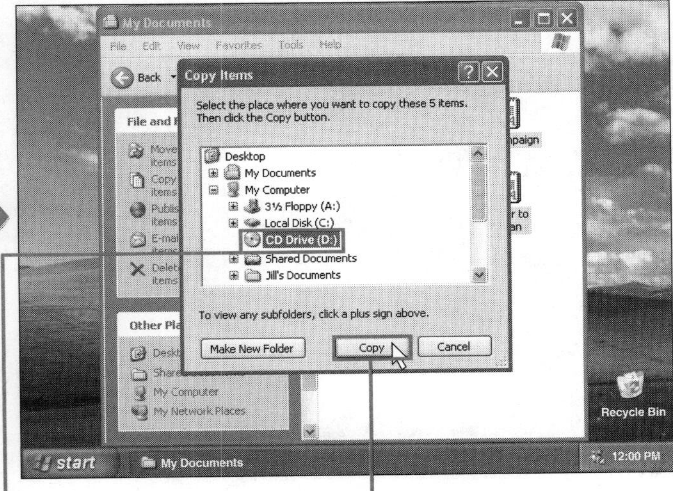

■ The Copy Items dialog box appears.

6 Click the recordable CD drive that contains the CD you want to copy the files to.

7 Click Copy to place a copy of the files in a temporary storage area on your computer where the files will be held until you copy them to the CD.

■ You can repeat steps 4 to 7 for each set of files you want to copy to the CD.

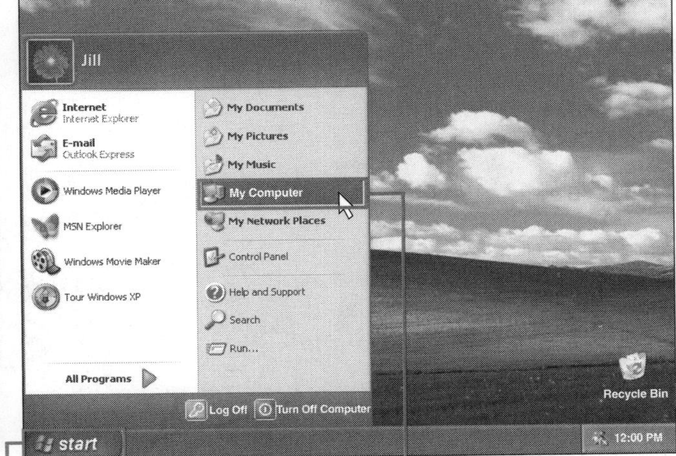

COPY SELECTED FILES TO A CD

1 Click start.

2 Click My Computer.

CONTINUED

COPY FILES TO A CD (CONTINUED)

You can view the contents of the temporary storage area that contains the files you selected to copy to a CD. This allows you to review the files before copying them to a CD.

The CD Writing Wizard automatically names a CD using the current date. You can specify a different name for the CD.

The name you use will appear in the My Computer window when the CD is in a CD drive.

It is important that no interruptions occur while files are being copied to a CD, since this may cause the CD to become unreadable. As a precaution, you should avoid running other programs and screen savers while copying files to a CD.

Although you can copy files to a CD at different times, approximately 20 MB of extra information is stored on a CD each time you copy files to the CD. To make the most efficient use of the storage space on a CD, you may want to copy all the files to the CD at once.

COPY FILES TO A CD (CONTINUED)

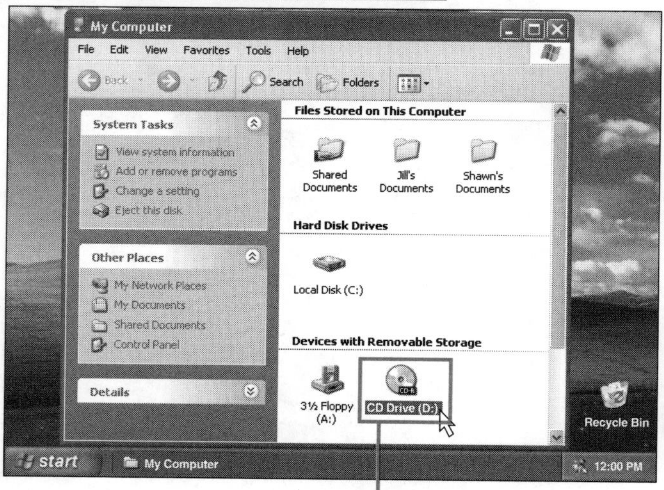

■ The My Computer window appears.

3 Double-click the recordable CD drive that contains the CD you want to copy the files to.

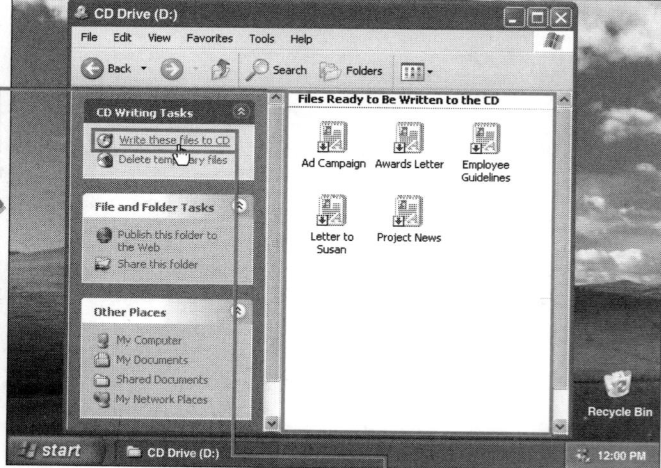

■ A window appears, displaying the files being held in a temporary storage area on your computer and any files currently stored on the CD.

4 Click Write these files to CD to copy the files to the CD.

How do I remove files I no longer want to copy to a CD from the temporary storage area?

✔ To display the contents of the temporary storage area, click start, select My Computer and then double-click the recordable CD drive. You can then click Delete temporary files to remove all the files from the temporary storage area. To remove only some of the files, select the files you want to remove and then press the Delete key.

How do I erase a CD-RW disc?

✔ To permanently delete all the files on a CD-RW disc, click start, select My Computer and then double-click the CD drive to display the contents of the disc. Then click Erase this CD-RW and follow the instructions in the CD Writing Wizard to erase the disc. You cannot erase a CD-R disc.

How can I confirm that the files I selected were copied to a CD?

✔ You can display the contents of the CD to confirm that the files were copied to the CD. The contents of the CD may automatically appear when you insert the CD into your CD drive. If the contents of the CD do not appear, click start, select My Computer and then double-click the CD drive to display the contents of the CD.

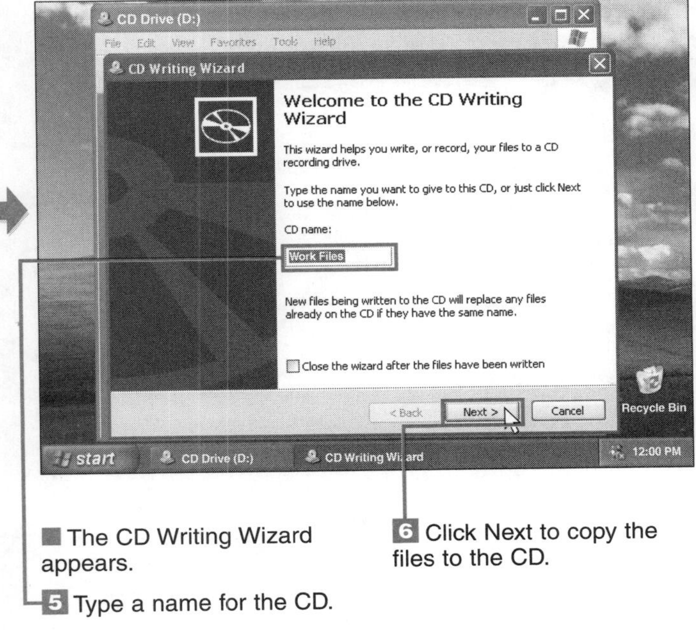

■ The CD Writing Wizard appears.

5 Type a name for the CD.

6 Click Next to copy the files to the CD.

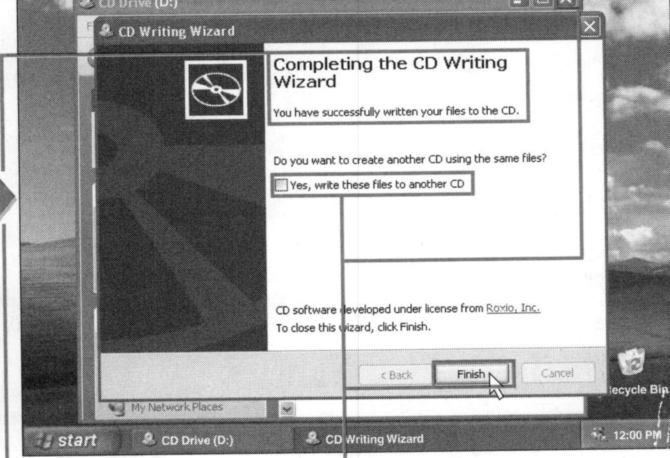

■ This message appears when Windows has successfully copied the files to the CD.

Note: Windows will automatically eject the CD from your recordable CD drive when the copy is complete.

■ To immediately copy the files to another CD, you can click this option (☐ changes to ☑) and then click Next.

7 Click Finish to close the wizard.

8 Click ☒ to close the window for the recordable CD drive.

COPY PICTURES FROM A DIGITAL CAMERA

You can take pictures using a digital camera and then use the Scanner and Camera Wizard to copy the pictures from the camera to your computer. This allows you to edit and print the pictures, as well as add the pictures to documents or e-mail messages.

You need a Windows Image Acquisition (WIA) compatible digital camera to use the Scanner and Camera Wizard. Check the documentation that came with your camera to determine if it is WIA compatible. If your digital camera is not WIA compatible, you can use the software that came with the camera to copy pictures to your computer.

To copy pictures from a digital camera, the camera must be installed, connected to your computer and turned on. You may also need to set the camera to a specific mode, such as the Connect mode, before you can copy pictures to your computer.

By default, the Scanner and Camera Wizard will copy all the pictures on your digital camera to your computer. If you want to copy only specific pictures, you can select the pictures.

COPY PICTURES FROM A DIGITAL CAMERA

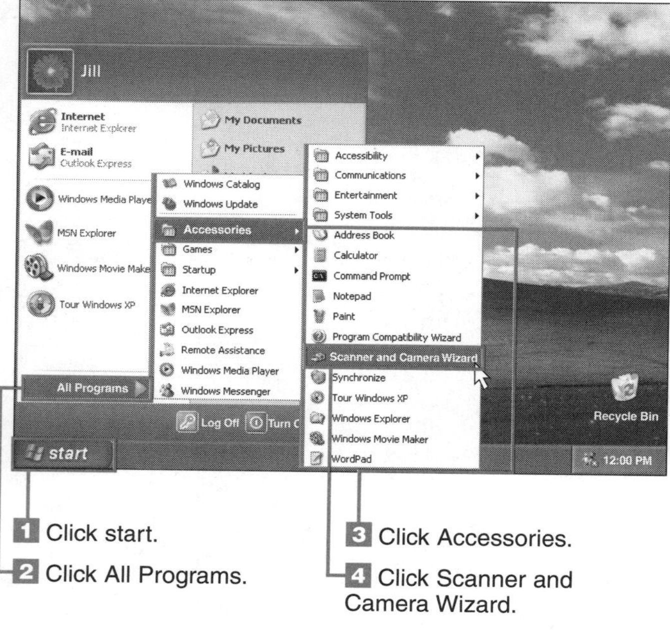

1 Click start.

2 Click All Programs.

3 Click Accessories.

4 Click Scanner and Camera Wizard.

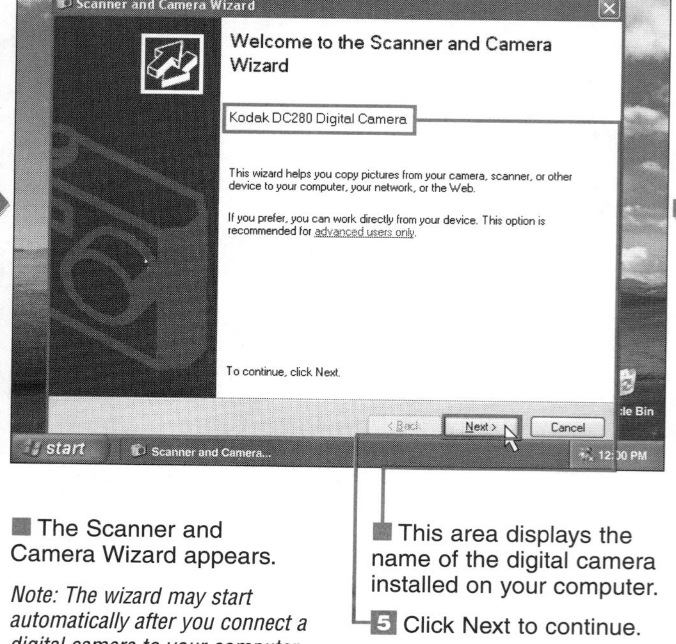

■ The Scanner and Camera Wizard appears.

Note: The wizard may start automatically after you connect a digital camera to your computer.

■ This area displays the name of the digital camera installed on your computer.

5 Click Next to continue.

How do I install a digital camera on my computer?

✔ Connect the digital camera to your computer. Windows can automatically detect and install a Plug and Play camera for you when you turn on the computer. If Windows does not automatically install your camera, click start, select Control Panel, click Printers and Other Hardware and then click Scanners and Cameras. In the Scanners and Cameras window, click Add an imaging device and then follow the instructions in the Scanner and Camera Installation Wizard.

Why did the Select Device dialog box appear when I started the Scanner and Camera Wizard?

✔ The Select Device dialog box appears if you have more than one imaging device connected to your computer, such as a scanner and a digital camera. Select your digital camera in the dialog box and click OK.

Can I work with pictures directly on a digital camera?

✔ Yes. In the Scanner and Camera Wizard, click the "advanced users only" link to display all the pictures stored on the camera. You can click a picture to display a list of links you can use to work with the picture. For example, you can copy the picture to your computer or delete the picture from the camera.

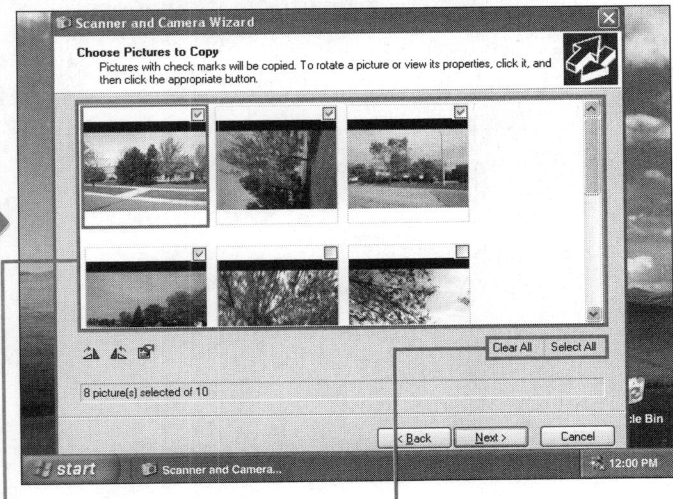

■ This area displays the pictures stored on your digital camera. Windows will copy each picture that displays a check mark (✔).

6 To add (☑) or remove (☐) a check mark from a picture, click the check box (☐) for the picture.

■ To quickly deselect or select all the pictures, click Clear All or Select All.

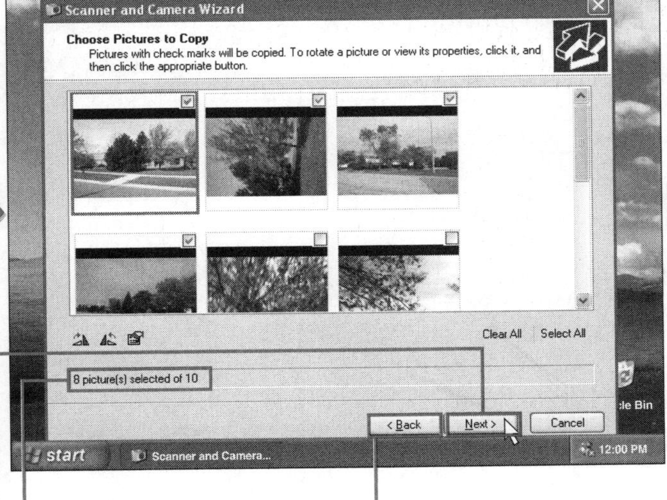

■ This area indicates the number of selected pictures and the total number of pictures.

7 Click Next to continue.

■ You can click Back to return to a previous step and change your selections.

CONTINUED

COPY PICTURES FROM A DIGITAL CAMERA (CONTINUED)

When you copy pictures from a digital camera, you can specify the name you want to use to save the pictures on your computer.

Windows allows you to select the folder on your computer where you want to store the pictures. You can store the pictures in a subfolder Windows creates in the My Pictures folder or directly in the My Pictures folder. You can also save the pictures in the Shared Pictures folder, which is stored in the Shared Documents folder on your computer. For more information about the Shared Documents folder, see page 190.

You can also specify if you want to delete the pictures from the digital camera once the pictures have been copied to your computer. Pictures you delete from the camera cannot be recovered.

Once the pictures have been copied, you can specify whether you want to publish the pictures to a Web site, order prints of the pictures from a photo printing Web site or finish working with the pictures.

When you close the wizard, Windows automatically displays the contents of the folder that contains the pictures. Each picture in the folder displays the name you specified for the pictures. Windows also sequentially numbers the pictures so that each picture is saved in a separate file with a unique name.

COPY PICTURES FROM A DIGITAL CAMERA (CONTINUED)

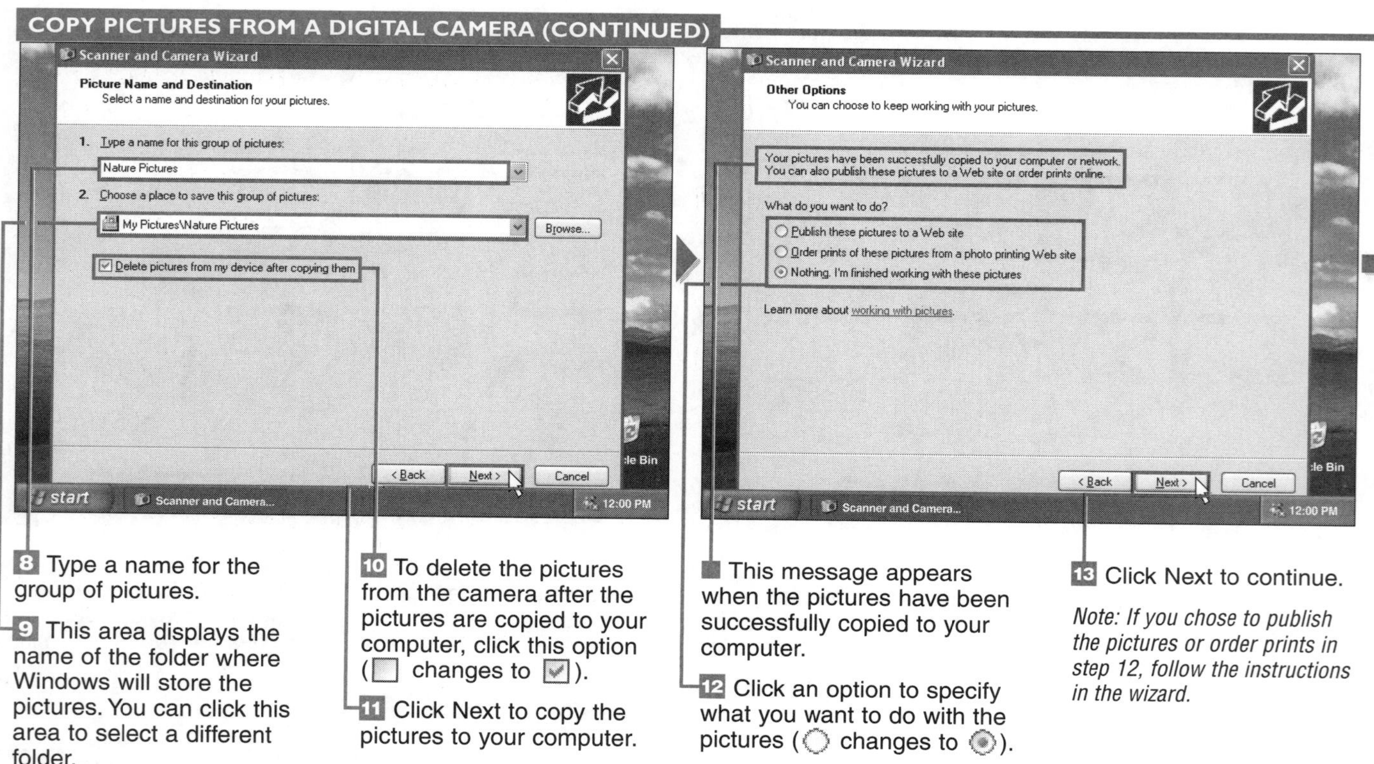

8 Type a name for the group of pictures.

9 This area displays the name of the folder where Windows will store the pictures. You can click this area to select a different folder.

10 To delete the pictures from the camera after the pictures are copied to your computer, click this option (☐ changes to ☑).

11 Click Next to copy the pictures to your computer.

■ This message appears when the pictures have been successfully copied to your computer.

12 Click an option to specify what you want to do with the pictures (○ changes to ◉).

13 Click Next to continue.

Note: If you chose to publish the pictures or order prints in step 12, follow the instructions in the wizard.

Can I specify another location to save my pictures?

✔ Yes. If your computer has a recordable CD drive, the CD Burning option appears in the list of locations in the Scanner and Camera Wizard. You can click this option to save the pictures on a recordable CD. To choose a location that does not appear in the list of options, click the Browse button. In the Browse For Folder dialog box, select the location where you want to save the pictures.

Can I use the pictures I copied from my digital camera as a screen saver?

✔ If you saved your pictures in the My Pictures folder or one of its subfolders, you can use the My Pictures Slideshow screen saver, which displays a slideshow of all the pictures stored in the My Pictures folder and its subfolders. To change the screen saver, see page 204.

How can I work with the pictures I copied from my digital camera?

✔ The folder where you stored your pictures may provide options that allow you to work with the pictures. For example, the View as a slide show option lets you display your pictures as a full-screen slide show. You can also order prints of your pictures online, set a picture as your desktop background, print the pictures or publish the pictures to the Web.

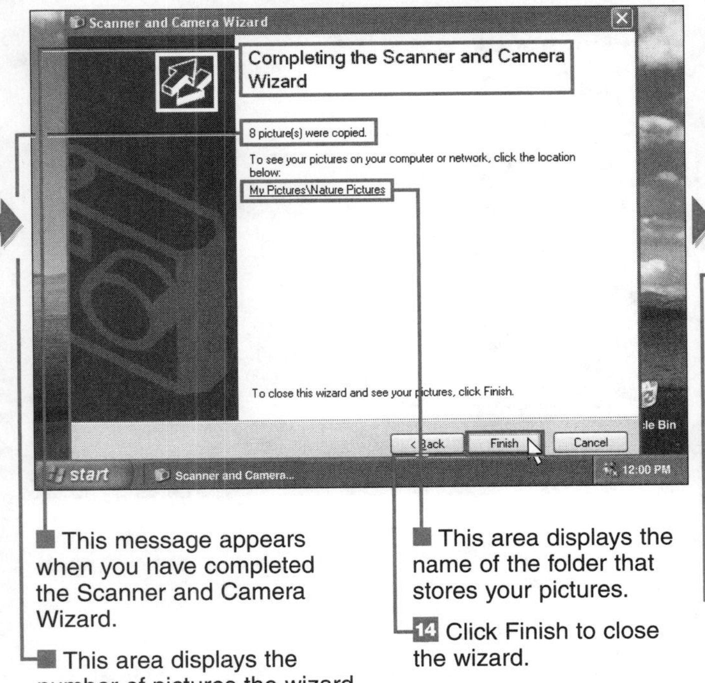

■ This message appears when you have completed the Scanner and Camera Wizard.

■ This area displays the number of pictures the wizard copied to your computer.

■ This area displays the name of the folder that stores your pictures.

14 Click Finish to close the wizard.

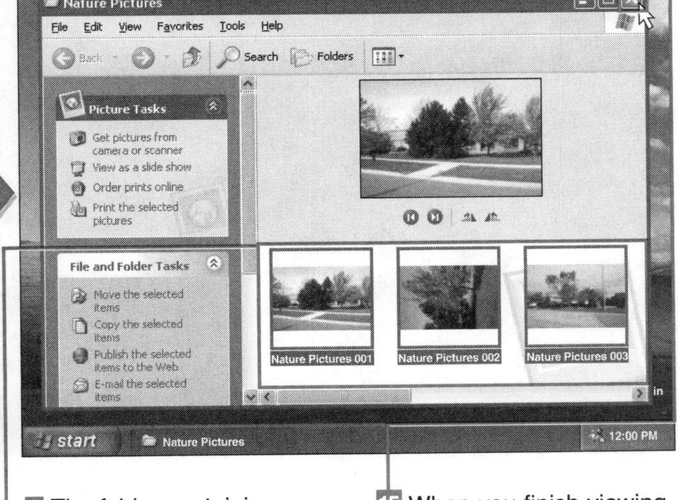

■ The folder containing your pictures appears.

■ Each picture displays the name you specified in step 8 and is sequentially numbered.

15 When you finish viewing the pictures, click ☒ to close the folder.

SCAN A DOCUMENT

The Scanner and Camera Wizard allows you to use a scanner to turn paper documents, such as forms and newspaper clippings, into pictures you can use on your computer.

You need a Windows Image Acquisition (WIA) compatible scanner to scan a document using the Scanner and Camera Wizard. You can check the documentation that came with your scanner to determine if it is WIA compatible.

To scan documents with a scanner that is not WIA compatible, use the software that came with the scanner.

Before scanning a document, the Scanner and Camera Wizard asks you to specify whether you are scanning a color, grayscale, black and white or text document. Specifying the type of document helps the wizard efficiently scan the document.

The Scanner and Camera Wizard can display a preview of the scanned document. You can use the preview to adjust the area the wizard will scan.

You can save a scanned document in the Bitmap, JPEG, TIF or PNG file format. The file format you should choose depends on how you plan to use the document. For example, the JPEG and PNG file formats are useful for pictures you intend to publish to the Web.

SCAN A DOCUMENT

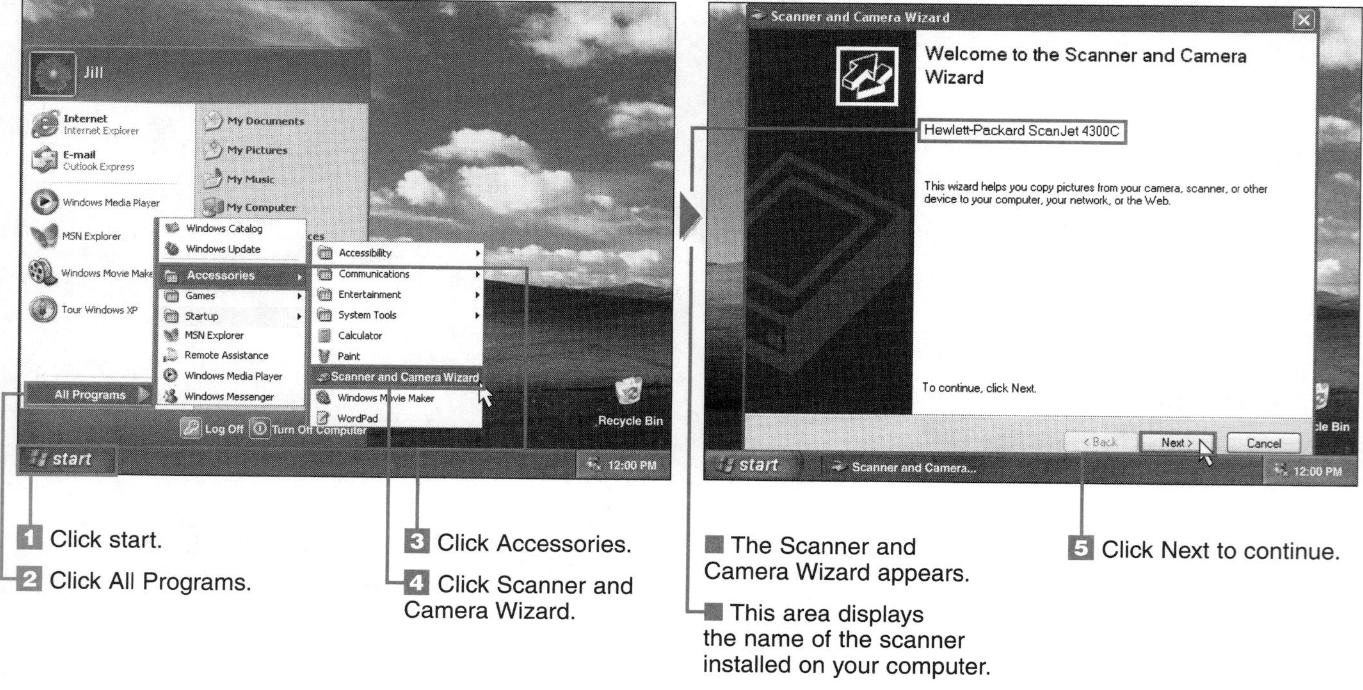

1 Click start.

2 Click All Programs.

3 Click Accessories.

4 Click Scanner and Camera Wizard.

■ The Scanner and Camera Wizard appears.

■ This area displays the name of the scanner installed on your computer.

5 Click Next to continue.

How do I install a scanner on my computer?

✔ Connect the scanner to your computer. Windows can automatically detect and install a Plug and Play scanner for you when you turn on the computer. If Windows does not automatically install your scanner, click start, select Control Panel, click Printers and Other Hardware and then click Scanners and Cameras. In the Scanners and Cameras window, click Add an imaging device and then follow the instructions in the Scanner and Camera Installation Wizard.

I selected to scan a small area of a document. Can I magnify the area?

✔ Yes. In the Scanner and Camera Wizard, click [magnify icon] below the preview area to magnify the area of the document you selected to scan. You can click [full view icon] to once again display the entire document.

How do I specify custom settings for a document I want to scan?

✔ Perform steps 1 to 5 below to start the Scanner and Camera Wizard. Select the Custom option and then click the Custom settings button. The Properties dialog box appears, displaying settings you can customize, such as the brightness and contrast. When you are finished adjusting the settings, click OK to return to the Scanner and Camera Wizard.

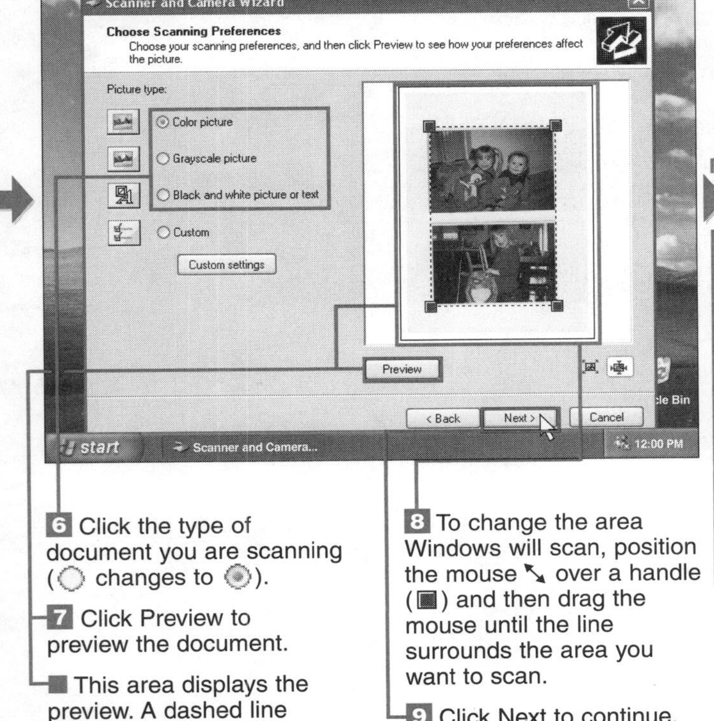

6 Click the type of document you are scanning (○ changes to ◉).

7 Click Preview to preview the document.

■ This area displays the preview. A dashed line appears around the area Windows will scan.

8 To change the area Windows will scan, position the mouse ↖ over a handle (■) and then drag the mouse until the line surrounds the area you want to scan.

9 Click Next to continue.

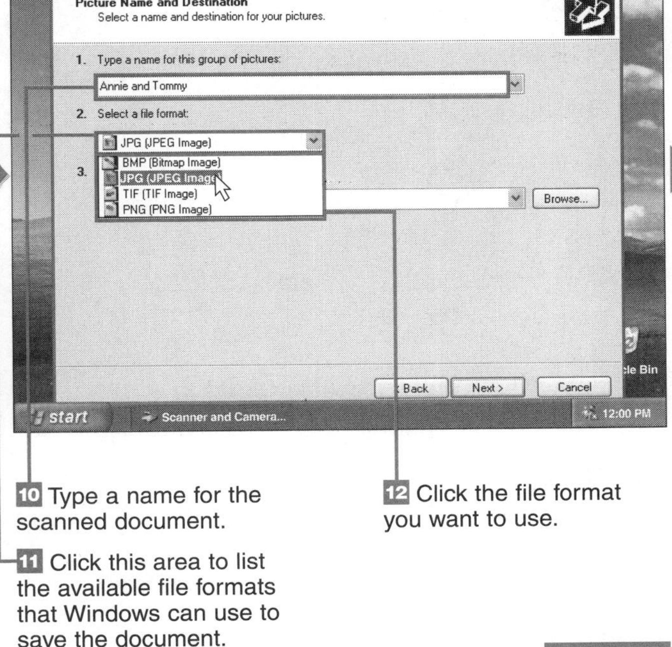

10 Type a name for the scanned document.

11 Click this area to list the available file formats that Windows can use to save the document.

12 Click the file format you want to use.

CONTINUED

SCAN A DOCUMENT (CONTINUED)

Windows allows you to select the folder on your computer where you want to store the scanned document. Windows will save the document as a picture on your computer. You can store the document in a subfolder Windows creates in the My Pictures folder or directly in the My Pictures folder. You can also save the document in the Shared Pictures folder, which is stored in the Shared Documents folder on your computer. For more information about the Shared Documents folder, see page 190.

After the scan is complete, you can specify whether you want to publish the scanned document to a Web site, order prints of the document from a photo printing Web site or finish working with the document. If you choose to finish working with the document, you will still be able to later publish the document to the Web or order prints from a photo printing Web site.

When the wizard closes, Windows automatically displays the contents of the folder that contains the scanned document on your screen. The document in the folder displays the name you specified in the wizard.

SCAN A DOCUMENT (CONTINUED)

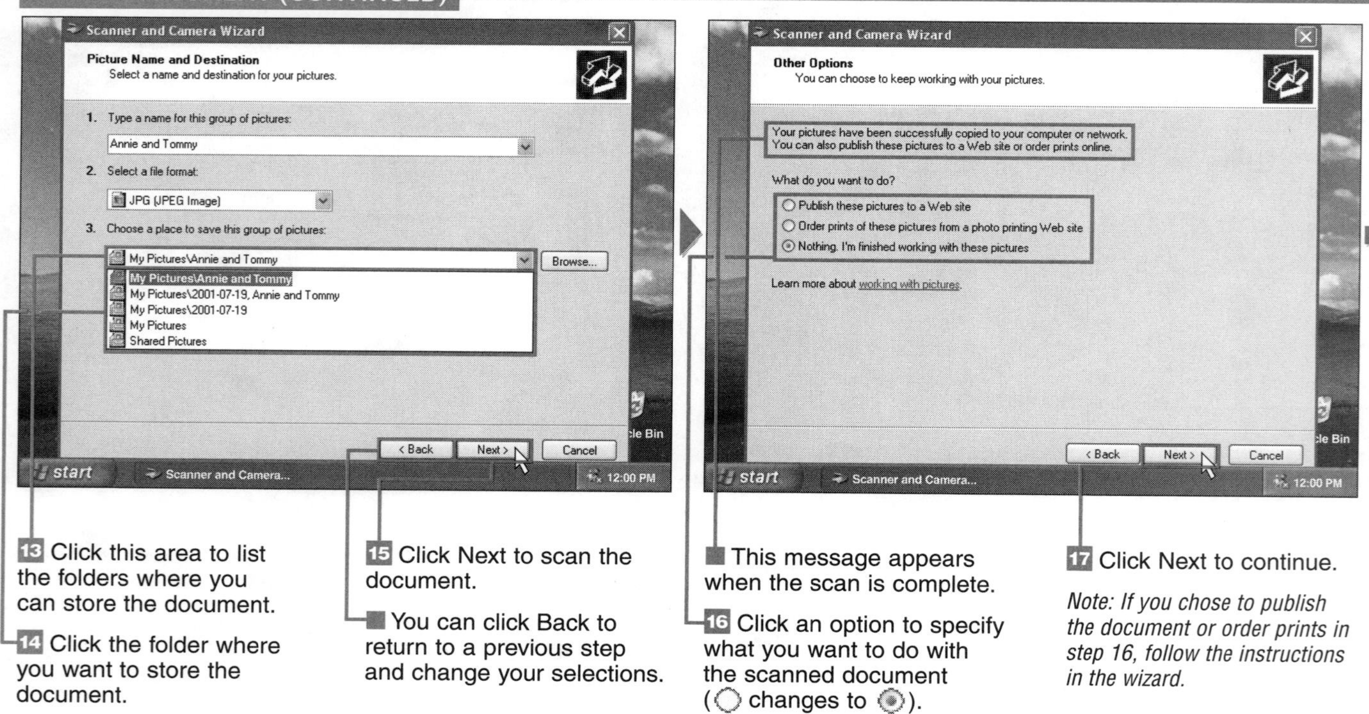

13 Click this area to list the folders where you can store the document.

14 Click the folder where you want to store the document.

15 Click Next to scan the document.

■ You can click Back to return to a previous step and change your selections.

■ This message appears when the scan is complete.

16 Click an option to specify what you want to do with the scanned document (○ changes to ◉).

17 Click Next to continue.

Note: If you chose to publish the document or order prints in step 16, follow the instructions in the wizard.

Can I specify another location to save the scanned document?

✔ Yes. If your computer has a recordable CD drive, the CD Burning option appears in the list of locations in the Scanner and Camera Wizard. You can click this option to save the document to a recordable CD. To choose a location that does not appear in the list of options, click the Browse button. In the Browse For Folder dialog box, select the location where you want to store the document.

How can I work with a scanned document after saving the document on my computer?

✔ The folder where you stored your scanned document provides options that allow you to work with the document. For example, the E-mail this file option lets you send the document in an e-mail message and the Set as desktop background option lets you display the document on your desktop. If you did not choose to publish the document to a Web site or order prints from a photo printing Web site in step 16 below, the window may also provide links that allow you to perform these tasks.

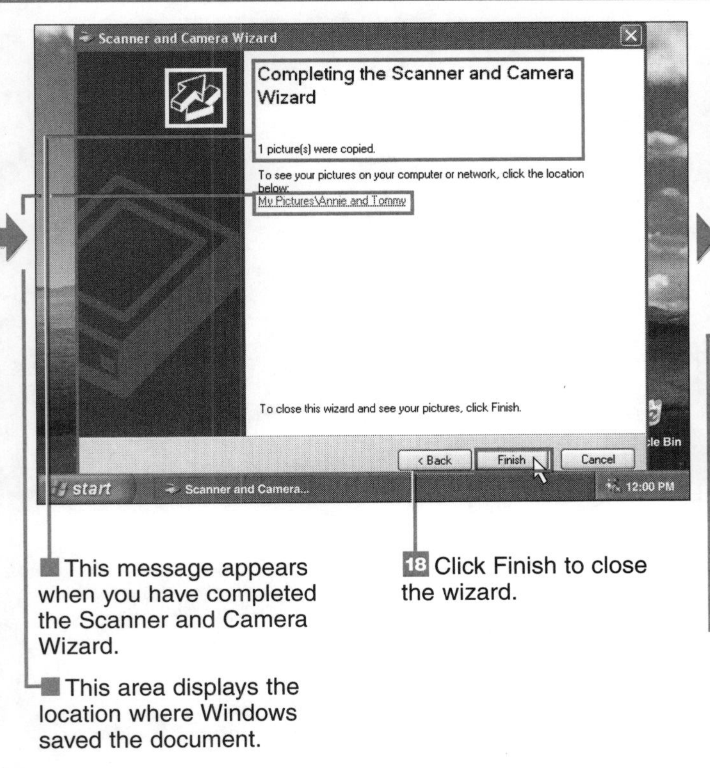

■ This message appears when you have completed the Scanner and Camera Wizard.

■ This area displays the location where Windows saved the document.

18 Click Finish to close the wizard.

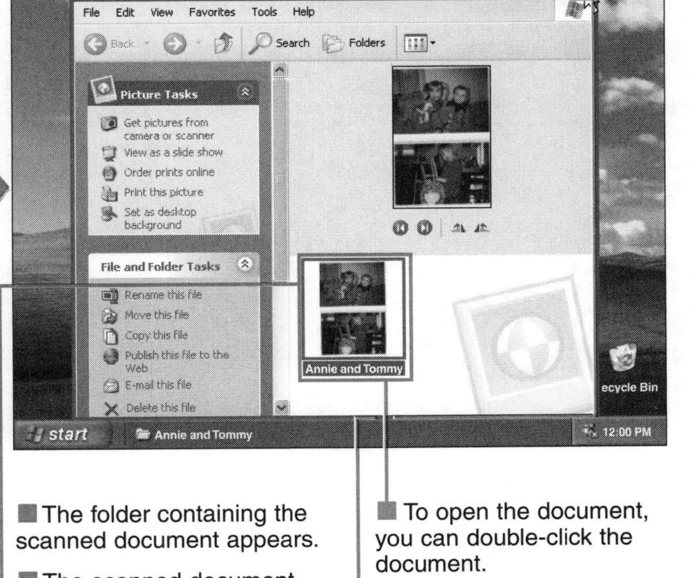

■ The folder containing the scanned document appears.

■ The scanned document is selected. The document displays the name you specified in step 10 on page 71.

■ To open the document, you can double-click the document.

19 When you finish viewing the scanned document, click ☒ to close the folder.

RENAME FILES

You can change the name of a file to better describe the contents of the file. You should only rename files that you have created.

When renaming your files, choose a name that will identify the file, such as the name of a project or event. Renaming a file can help make the file easier to find.

In Windows, you can use up to 215 characters to name a file, including spaces and periods. The only characters you cannot use to name a file are the symbols \ / : * ? | " < or >.

If you are working with older programs, you should keep your file names relatively short since the programs may not be able to work with long file names. For example, MS-DOS and Windows 3.1 programs do not support long file names. If you use these programs, you should use file names with no more than eight characters followed by a three-character extension, such as report.txt.

Windows does not recognize the difference between upper and lower case letters in file names. For example, Windows sees readme, ReadMe and README as the same file name.

RENAME FILES

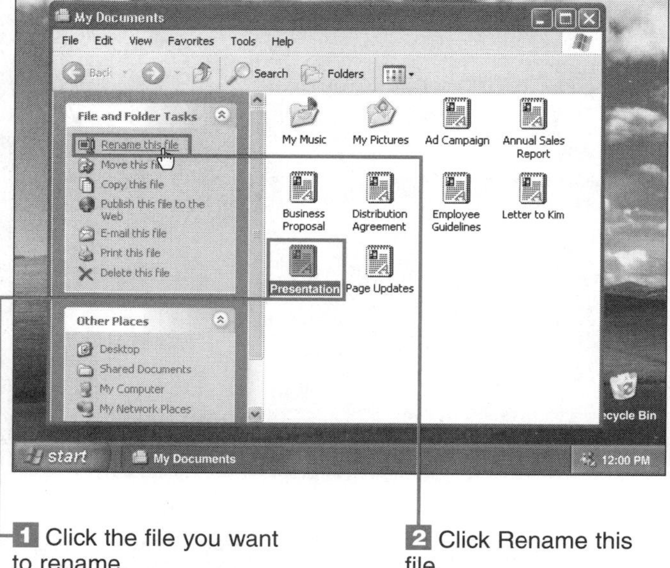

1 Click the file you want to rename.

2 Click Rename this file.

■ A box appears around the file name.

3 Type a new name for the file and then press the Enter key.

Note: You can edit the file name instead of replacing the entire name. In step 3, click the file name where you want to edit the name and make the change.

■ If you change your mind while typing a new file name, press the Esc key to cancel your change.

Are there any other ways to rename a file?

✔ Yes. Click the name of the file you want to rename. Wait a moment and click the name again. Then type a new name for the file. You can also rename a file by right-clicking the file and selecting Rename from the menu that appears.

Can I use the same file name for two different files?

✔ You can use the same file name for the files if they are located in different folders or are different file types, such as a document and an image file.

Can I rename folders?

✔ You can rename folders the same way you rename files. You should only rename folders that you have created so you do not change the names of folders that Windows or other programs require to operate.

How can I quickly rename a group of related files?

✔ Select the files you want to rename. In the window containing the files, choose the File menu and click Rename. Type a new file name and then press the Enter key. Windows will rename the files using the file name you specify, such as SalesReport, SalesReport (1) and SalesReport (2).

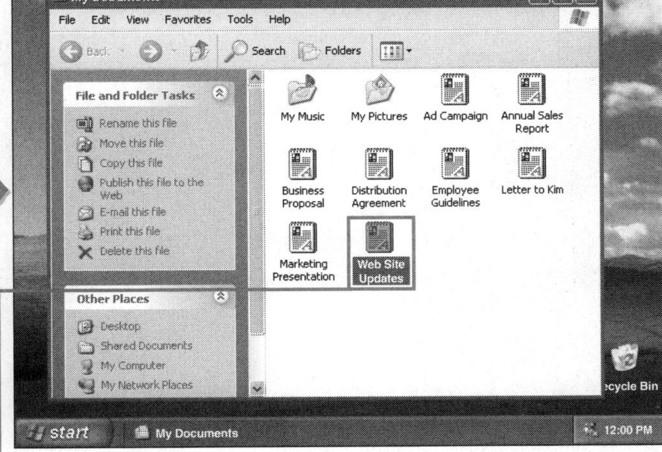

RENAME FILES USING THE F2 KEY

1 Click the file you want to rename.

2 Press the F2 key to select the current file name.

■ A box appears around the file name.

3 Type a new name for the file and then press the Enter key.

DELETE FILES

You can remove files and folders you no longer need to free up space on your computer. If you delete a folder, Windows will erase all the files and folders within the folder. To protect you from accidentally erasing important files, Windows stores deleted files in the Recycle Bin.

As a precaution, Windows asks you to confirm the files you are deleting. Do not delete any file unless you are certain you no longer need the file. You should delete only files that you have created to avoid removing system files that Windows or other programs require to operate. If you want to delete other files to free up space on your hard drive, you can use the Disk Cleanup tool. For more information about Disk Cleanup, see page 520.

Before you delete files, consider the value of the files. You may want to save copies of files on a removable disk such as a CD-R disc or Zip disk in case you need the files later. The cost of removable disks is small compared to the time and effort of recreating a file.

DELETE FILES

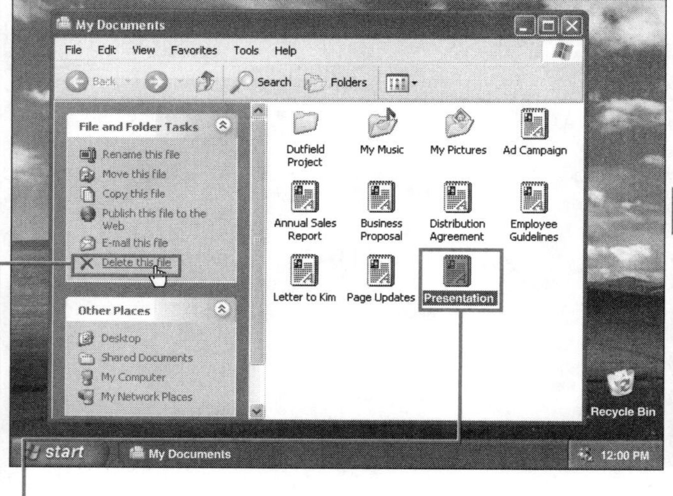

1 Select the file(s) you want to delete. To select multiple files, see page 52.

2 Click Delete this file or press the Delete key.

Note: If you selected multiple files, click Delete the selected items in step 2.

■ A dialog box appears, confirming the deletion.

3 Click Yes to delete the file.

How do I delete a confidential file so it cannot be recovered?

✔ Select the file and then press the Shift and Delete keys. The file will be deleted from your computer and will not appear in the Recycle Bin.

Are there any other ways to delete a file?

✔ You can drag and drop a file onto the Recycle Bin to delete the file. You can also delete a file by right-clicking the file and selecting Delete from the menu that appears.

Are all deleted files placed in the Recycle Bin?

✔ Files deleted from your network, from removable storage media such as floppy disks and files that are larger than the storage capacity of the Recycle Bin are not placed in the Recycle Bin and cannot be recovered.

How can I prevent the Confirm File Delete dialog box from appearing each time I delete a file?

✔ Right-click the Recycle Bin and then select Properties. On the Global tab, click the Display delete confirmation dialog option (☑ changes to ☐).

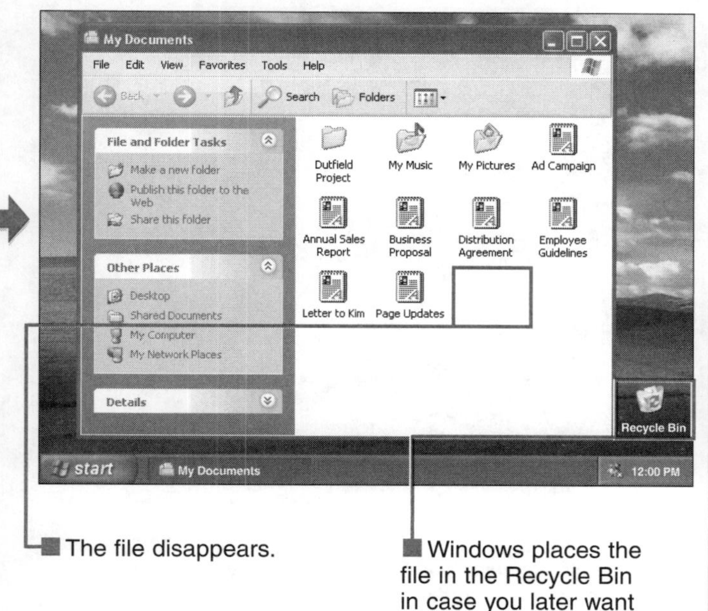

■ The file disappears.

■ Windows places the file in the Recycle Bin in case you later want to restore the file. To restore a deleted file, see page 78.

DELETE A FOLDER

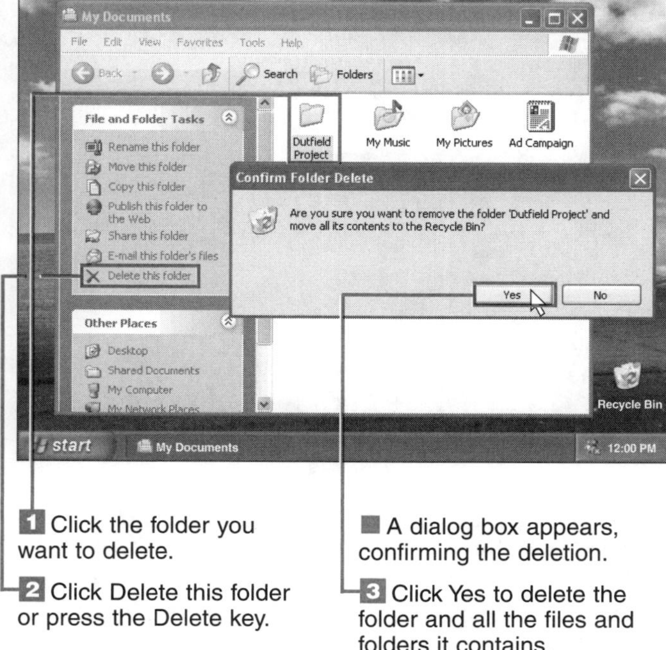

1 Click the folder you want to delete.

2 Click Delete this folder or press the Delete key.

■ A dialog box appears, confirming the deletion.

3 Click Yes to delete the folder and all the files and folders it contains.

RESTORE DELETED FILES

The Recycle Bin is a special folder that stores the files you have deleted. If you have accidentally deleted a file, you will probably find the file in the Recycle Bin. You can then restore the file to its original location on your computer. If you restore a file that was originally located in a folder that has also been deleted, Windows will recreate the folder and restore the file in the folder.

You cannot restore files deleted from your network, from removable storage media such as floppy disks or files that were larger than the storage capacity of the Recycle Bin. These files are permanently deleted.

When you are certain that you no longer need the files in the Recycle Bin, you can empty the Recycle Bin to remove all the deleted files and increase the available disk space on your computer. When you empty the Recycle Bin, all the files are permanently removed from your computer.

When the Recycle Bin fills up with deleted files, Windows will permanently remove older files to make room for recently deleted files.

RESTORE DELETED FILES

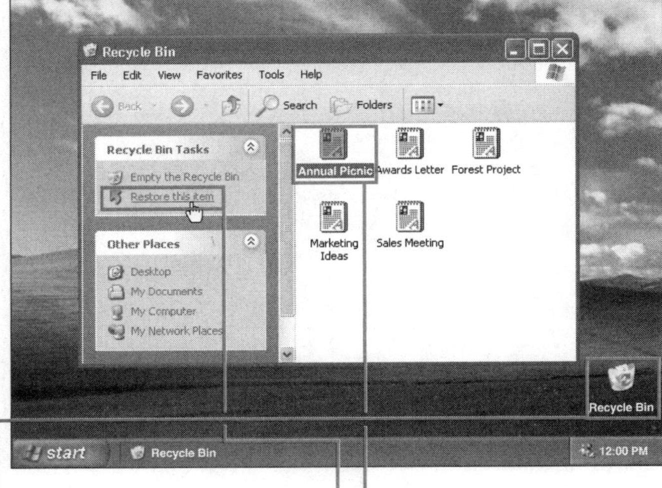

1 Double-click Recycle Bin to display the files you have deleted.

■ The Recycle Bin window appears.

2 Select the file(s) you want to restore. To select multiple files, see page 52.

3 Click Restore this item.

Note: If you selected multiple files, click Restore the selected items in step 3.

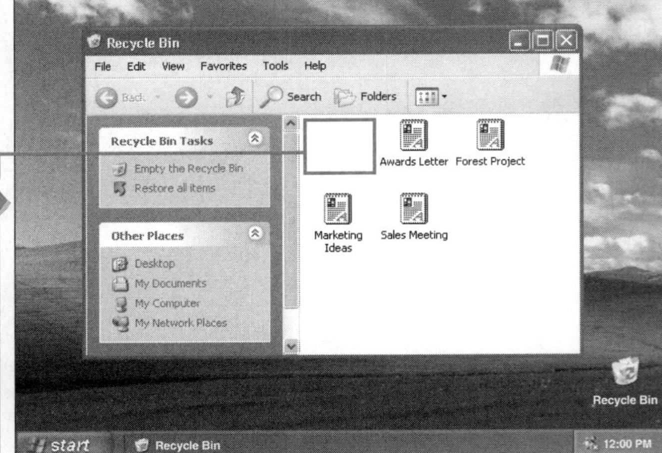

■ The file disappears from the Recycle Bin window. Windows restores the file to its original location.

Note: You can restore a deleted folder the same way you restore a deleted file. When you restore a folder, Windows also restores all the files in the folder.

The Recycle Bin window does not display the Restore this item command. What is wrong?

✔ The Recycle Bin window may be too small to display the commands for working with deleted files. You can increase the size of the window to display the commands. To size a window, see page 16.

Can I view the contents of a file located in the Recycle Bin?

✔ To view the contents of a deleted file, drag the file from the Recycle Bin window to the desktop and then double-click the file to display its contents.

Can I restore all the files in the Recycle Bin at once?

✔ Yes. Click a blank area in the Recycle Bin window and then click Restore all items on the left side of the window.

How can I quickly empty the Recycle Bin?

✔ Right-click the Recycle Bin icon on the desktop. From the menu that appears, select Empty Recycle Bin.

Can I permanently delete only some of the files in the Recycle Bin?

✔ Yes. Select each file you want to delete in the Recycle Bin window and then press the Delete key.

EMPTY THE RECYCLE BIN

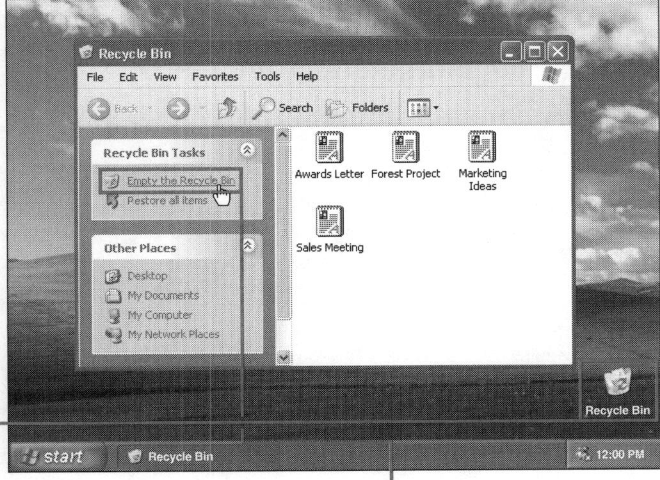

1 Double-click Recycle Bin to display the files you have deleted.

■ The Recycle Bin window appears.

2 Click Empty the Recycle Bin.

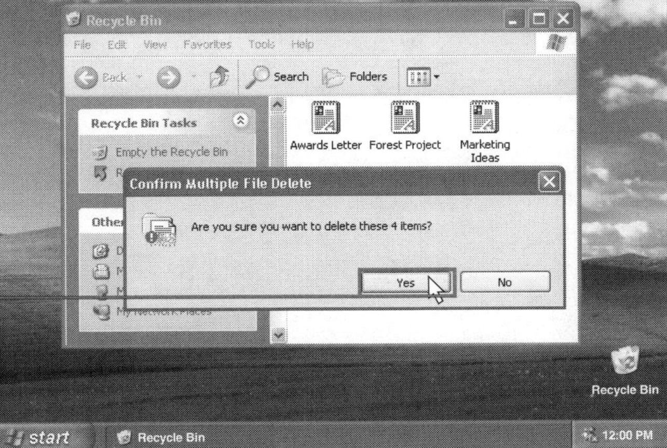

■ A dialog box appears, confirming the deletion.

3 Click Yes to permanently remove all the files from the Recycle Bin.

■ The files disappear and are permanently removed from your computer.

CHANGE RECYCLE BIN PROPERTIES

The Recycle Bin protects your files by temporarily storing the files you delete. You can change the properties of the Recycle Bin to specify the kind of protection you want.

If you have more than one drive on your computer, you can specify the same or different Recycle Bin settings for each drive.

The Recycle Bin normally uses up to 10% of a hard drive's space to store deleted files. For example, on a 20 GB drive, the Recycle Bin may use up as much as 2 GB. Reducing the storage size of the Recycle Bin can help conserve disk space on a drive.

You can choose to permanently delete files from your computer rather than send them to the Recycle Bin. Permanently deleted files cannot be restored.

Windows normally displays a confirmation dialog box when you delete a file. To delete files more quickly, you can change the Recycle Bin properties so the dialog box will no longer appear.

CHANGE RECYCLE BIN PROPERTIES

1 Right-click the Recycle Bin. A menu appears.

2 Click Properties.

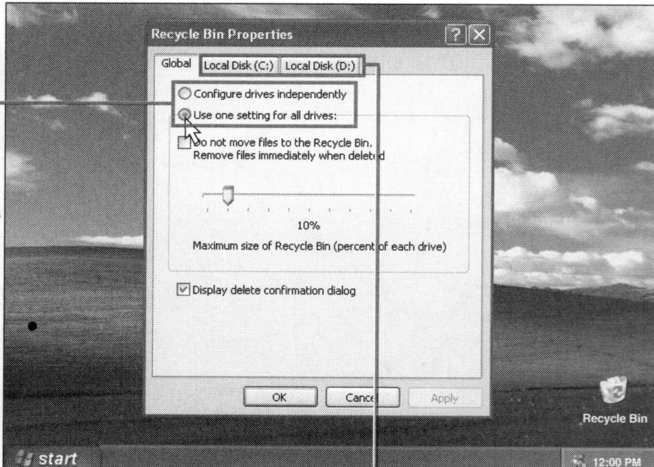

■ The Recycle Bin Properties dialog box appears.

3 Click an option to specify if you want to use different Recycle Bin settings for each drive or the same settings for all of your drives (○ changes to ◉).

■ If you chose to use different settings for each drive, you can use these tabs to change the settings for the drives.

How can I view the amount of space reserved for the Recycle Bin on a drive?

✔ In the Recycle Bin Properties dialog box, click the tab for the drive whose Recycle Bin properties you want to view. Windows displays the space reserved on the drive for the Recycle Bin.

How can I determine the amount of storage space I need for my Recycle Bin?

✔ Checking the status of files in the Recycle Bin for a week or two allows you to estimate how much space is needed to safeguard a day's, week's or month's worth of work. You can then adjust the storage size of the Recycle Bin accordingly.

Can I permanently delete a file without changing the Recycle Bin settings for all files?

✔ To delete a file or group of files permanently, select the file(s) and then hold down the Shift key while you press the Delete key. In the dialog box that appears, click Yes to confirm your deletion.

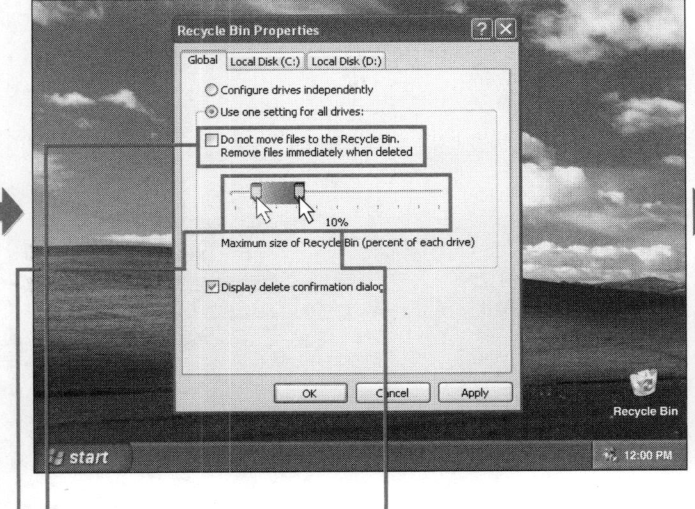

4 Click this option if you want to permanently remove files you delete rather than send them to the Recycle Bin (☐ changes to ☑).

5 To change the storage size of the Recycle Bin, drag the slider (▯) to a new location.

Note: The slider is not available if you chose to permanently remove files in step 4.

■ This area displays the percentage of the drive the Recycle Bin uses.

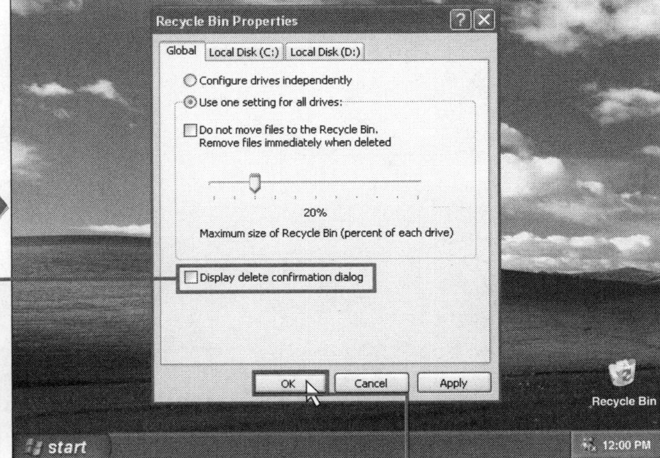

6 Click this option if you do not want a warning message to appear when you delete files (☑ changes to ☐).

7 Click OK to confirm all your changes.

CREATE A NEW FILE

You can create, name and store a new file in the location you want without having to start any programs. This allows you to focus on the organization of your work, rather than the programs you need to accomplish your tasks.

Before writing a letter or creating a new picture, you can first determine where you want to store the new file. By selecting the location of the file first, you can organize your work and later find the file more easily.

Once you decide on the location of a new file, you can create and name the file. A file name can contain up to 215 characters and can include spaces. File names cannot contain the \ / : * ? " < > or | characters.

The types of new files you can create depend on the programs installed on your computer. By default, you can create a briefcase, bitmap image, WordPad document, rich text document, text document, wave sound and compressed folder.

CREATE A NEW FILE

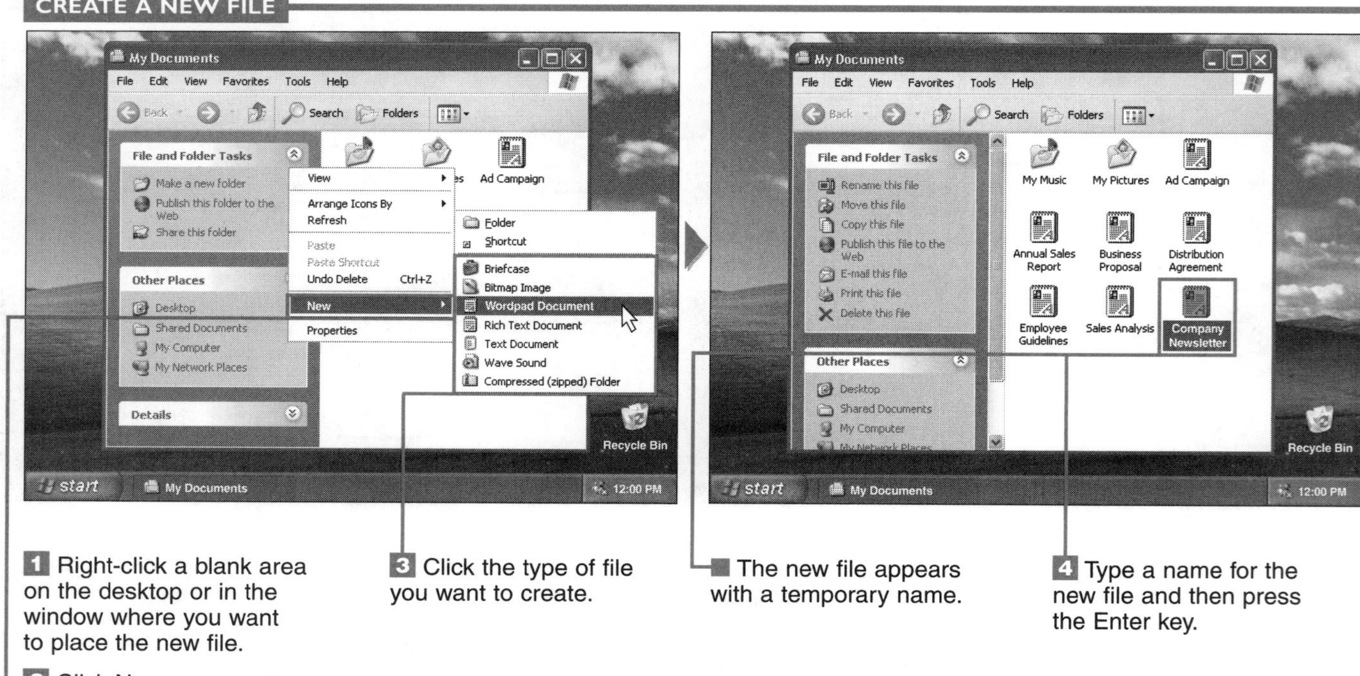

1 Right-click a blank area on the desktop or in the window where you want to place the new file.

2 Click New.

3 Click the type of file you want to create.

■ The new file appears with a temporary name.

4 Type a name for the new file and then press the Enter key.

CREATE A NEW FOLDER

You can create a new folder to better organize the information stored on your computer.

When you begin using your computer, you can create new folders to store your work. For example, you can create a new folder to store files for a particular project. Storing files in folders that have descriptive names helps you keep related files together and helps you quickly locate your files.

You can create folders within other folders you have created to help further organize information. For example, you can create a folder named "letters." This folder can store other folders named "clients," "colleagues" and "personal." You may also want to create folders on your desktop to organize any shortcuts that you have created on the desktop.

You can create as many folders as you need to organize your files by date, project or type. Use a system that makes sense to you and will help you find your files.

A folder name can contain up to 215 characters and can include spaces. Folder names cannot contain the \ / : * ? " < > or | characters.

CREATE A NEW FOLDER

1 Display the contents of the folder you want to contain a new folder.

2 Click Make a new folder.

Note: If the Make a new folder option is not available, click a blank area in the window to display the option.

■ The new folder appears, displaying a temporary name.

3 Type a name for the new folder and then press the Enter key.

Note: To create a new folder on the desktop, right-click an empty area on your desktop. In the menu that appears, click New and then click Folder. Type a name for the new folder and then press the Enter key.

SEARCH FOR FILES

If you cannot remember the name or location of a file you want to work with, you can have Windows search for the file. You can search for all files and folders on your computer. You can also search for media files, such as pictures, music or videos, or search for documents, such as spreadsheets and word processing documents.

Besides files, Windows also allows you to search for a computer on a network, a person in your address book, information in the Help and Support Center or Web pages of interest on the Internet.

Searching for a file by name is an effective way of finding a file when you know all or part of the file name. For example, searching for a file named "report" will find every file or folder with a name that contains the word "report."

If you know a word or phrase that a file contains, you can have Windows search for the file using this information. Searching by file content will slow down your search.

You can specify which location on your computer you want Windows to search. If you cannot remember where a file is located, you can select My Computer to have Windows search all the drives and folders on your computer.

SEARCH FOR FILES

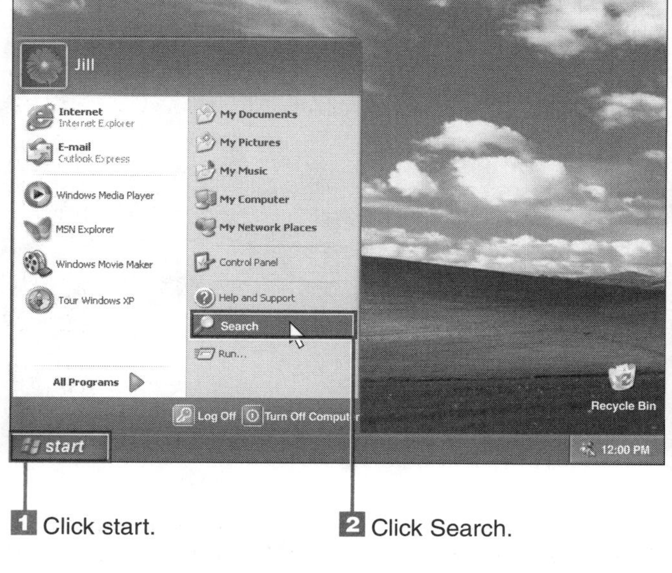

1 Click start.

2 Click Search.

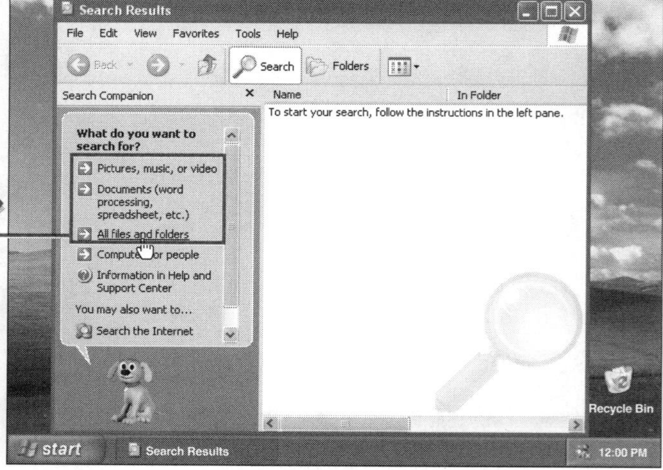

■ The Search Results window appears.

3 Click the type of file you want to search for.

Note: The following options depend on the type of file you select.

Can I customize the way I search for files?

✔ Yes. Before beginning a search, you can click Change preferences to display options you can select to customize the way you search for files. For example, you can turn off the animated screen character, make searches faster by enabling Indexing Service or change the files and folders search behavior.

What options can I specify when I search for a media file or document?

✔ When you search for a media file, you can specify whether the file is a picture, music or video file and all or part of the file name. When you search for a document, you can specify when the document was last modified and all or part of the document name.

Can I use wildcard characters to find files?

✔ You can use an asterisk (*) or a question mark (?) to find files by name. The asterisk (*) represents one or more characters. The question mark (?) represents a single character.

How do I search for a file on my network?

✔ Click ▾ in the Look in area and then select Browse. In the dialog box that appears, you can use the My Network Places item to select the network location you want to search.

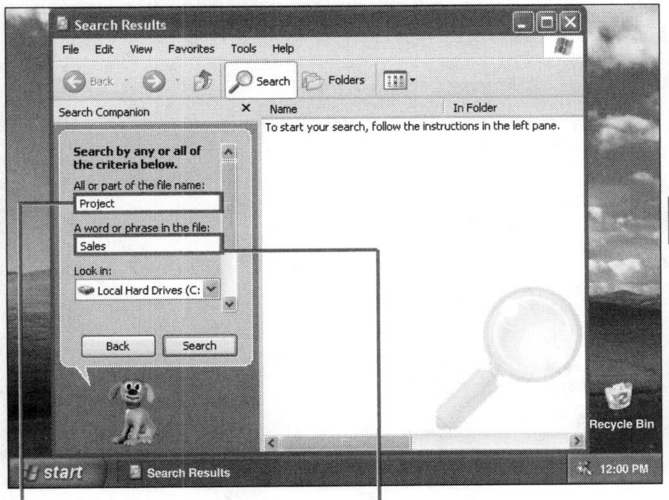

4 To specify the name of the file you want to find, click this area and type all or part of the file name.

5 To specify a word or phrase that appears in the file you want to find, click this area and type the word or phrase.

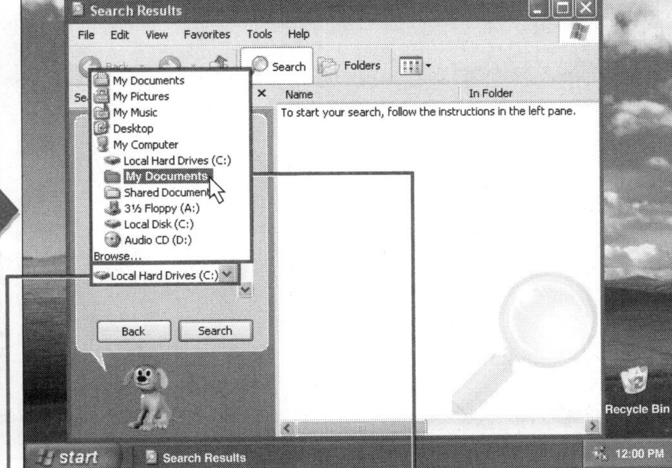

■ This area displays the location Windows will search.

6 To specify a different location, click ▾ in this area.

7 Click the location you want Windows to search.

CONTINUED

SEARCH FOR FILES (CONTINUED)

The search options provided by Windows allow you to narrow your search for a file. You can use all, some or just one of the search options.

You can search for a file based on the date the file was last modified. This is useful if you know the file was last worked on during a specific time period. You can specify whether a file was modified within the last week, month or year or you can specify an exact range of dates when the file was last modified.

You can also search for a file based on its size. You can indicate whether the file you want to find is less than 100 KB, less than 1 MB or more than 1 MB. You can also search for a file that is larger or smaller than a size you specify.

When the search is complete, Windows displays all the matching files and information about each file, such as location and size. You can open and work with a file Windows finds as you would open and work with a file in any window.

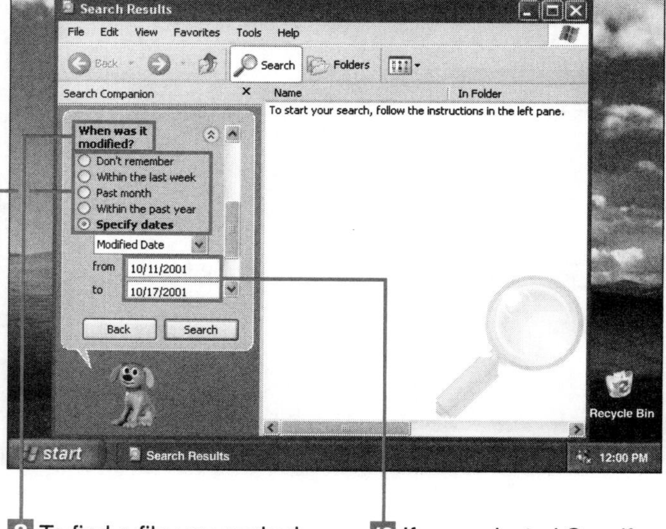

8 To find a file you worked with during a specific time period, click this option.

9 Click an option to specify when you last worked with the file (○ changes to ◉).

10 If you selected Specify dates in step 9, you can click these areas to specify the beginning and end dates.

11 To specify the size of the file you want to find, click this option.

12 Click an option to specify the size of the file (○ changes to ◉).

13 If you selected Specify size in step 12, double-click this area and type the file size in kilobytes (KB).

■ Windows will search for files that are at least the size you specify. You can click this area to select a different option.

Can I search for files based on the date the files were created or last accessed?

✔ Yes. After selecting what you want to search for, click "When was it modified?" and select the Specify dates option (◯ changes to ◉). Click the box below the Specify dates options and then choose Created Date or Accessed Date.

How can I stop a search once Windows has found the file I am looking for?

✔ Click the Stop button at any time to end a search.

How do I start a new search?

✔ Click the Start a new search option.

Can I save a search so I can perform the same search again?

✔ Yes. From the File menu, select Save Search. Type a name for the search and then click the Save button. By default, Windows saves the search as a file in the My Documents folder. To once again perform the search, double-click the file and then click the Search button.

How can I further refine my search?

✔ You can click "More advanced options" to further refine your search. You can choose to search for a specific type of file or to include system folders, subfolders and hidden files and folders in your search. You can also choose to perform a case-sensitive search or to search backup tapes.

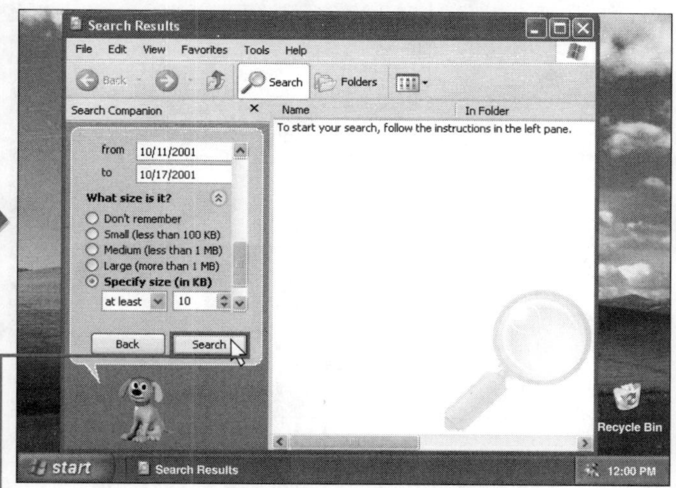

14 Click Search to start the search.

■ Windows searches for files that match the information you specified.

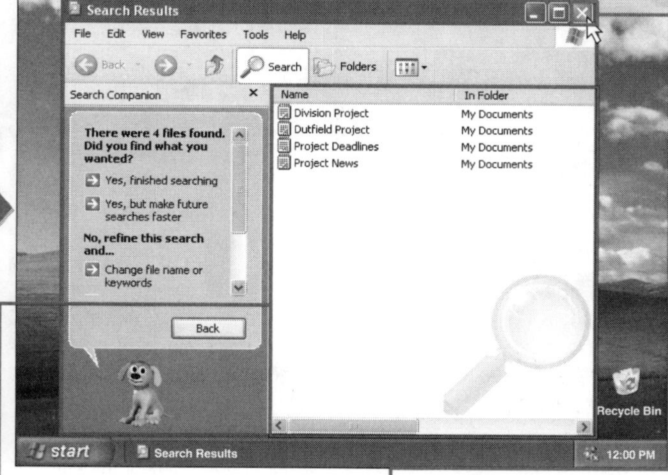

■ This area lists the matching files that Windows found.

■ To open a file that Windows found, double-click the name of the file.

15 When you finish viewing the results of your search, click ☒ to close the Search Results window.

E-MAIL FILES

You can e-mail a file, such as a document, picture, sound or video, to a friend, colleague or family member. You must have an e-mail account set up on your computer and be connected to the Internet to be able to e-mail a file. The computer receiving the file must have the necessary hardware and software installed to display or play the file.

When e-mailing a picture, you can have Windows change the file size and dimensions of the picture so it will transfer faster over the Internet and fit better on a recipient's computer screen. Reducing the file size of a picture is useful when you are e-mailing a large picture, since most companies that provide e-mail accounts do not allow you to send messages larger than 2 MB.

When you e-mail a file, Windows provides sample text for your message and attaches the file you selected to the message. You can replace the sample text Windows provides with the text you want the message to display.

To prevent the accidental spreading of viruses, you should scan your files with virus scanning software before e-mailing the files.

E-MAIL FILES

1 Select the file(s) you want to send in an e-mail message. To select multiple files, see page 52.

2 Click E-mail this file.

Note: If you selected multiple files, click E-mail the selected items in step 2.

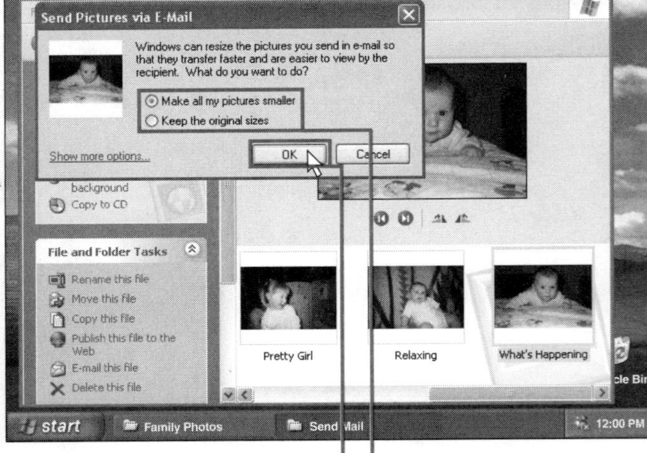

■ If you selected a picture in step 1, the Send Pictures via E-Mail dialog box appears, indicating that Windows can resize the picture so it will transfer faster over the Internet and be easier to view on the recipient's computer screen.

3 Click an option to make the picture smaller or keep the original size of the picture (○ changes to ◉).

4 Click OK.

Is there another way to e-mail a file?

✔ Yes. Right-click the file you want to e-mail and select Send To in the menu that appears. Then click Mail Recipient. You can then perform steps 5 to 9 below to compose and send the message. This method is useful when you want to e-mail a file located on the desktop.

How can I quickly e-mail all the files in a folder?

✔ To e-mail all the files in a folder, click the folder and then perform steps 2 to 9 below, selecting E-mail this folder's files in step 2.

When changing the file size and dimensions of a picture, can I specify the size I want Windows to make the picture?

✔ Windows allows you to choose whether you want your picture to be small, medium or large. To choose a size in the Send Pictures via E-Mail dialog box, click the Show more options link and then click the option for the size you want to use (○ changes to ◉).

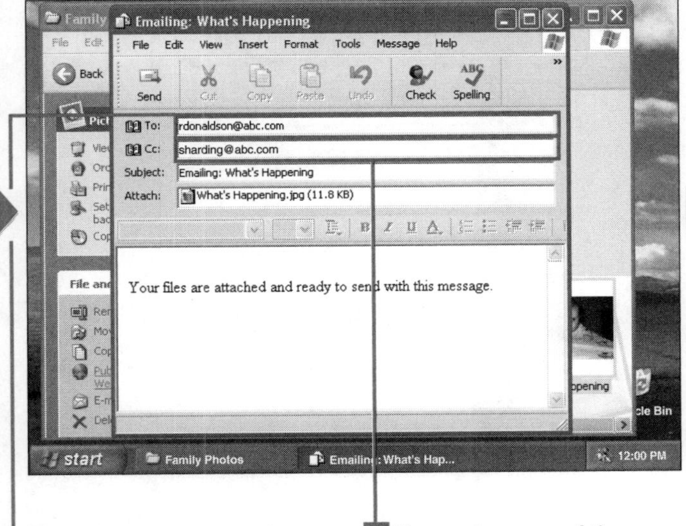

■ A window appears that allows you to compose a message.

5 Type the e-mail address of the person you want to receive the message.

6 To send a copy of the message to a person who is not directly involved but would be interested in the message, click this area and then type the person's e-mail address.

Note: To send the message to more than one person, separate each e-mail address with a semicolon (;) or comma (,).

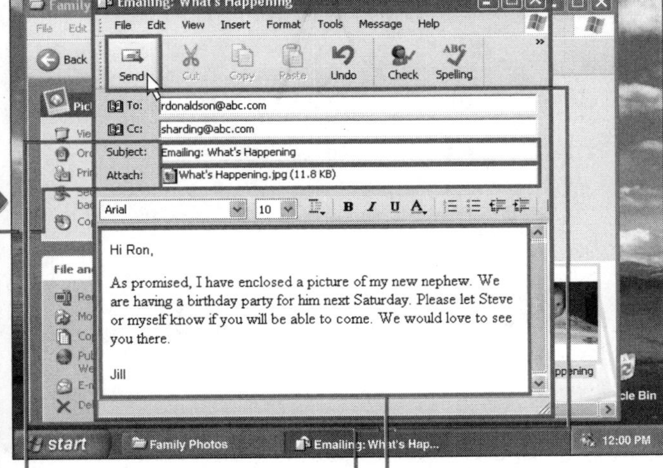

7 Windows uses the name of the file as the subject. To specify a different subject, drag the mouse I over the subject and then type a new subject.

■ This area displays the name and size of the file you selected.

8 Windows includes a message indicating that your files are attached. To use a different message, drag the mouse I over the message and then type a new message.

9 Click Send.

PUBLISH A FILE TO THE WEB

You can publish files, such as documents and pictures, to the Web to allow friends, family and colleagues to view the files.

Publishing a file to the Web also allows you to transfer files that may be too large to send in an e-mail message. Most companies that provide e-mail accounts will not allow you to send e-mail messages larger than 2 MB. For more information about sending files in an e-mail message, see page 88.

When publishing a file, the Web Publishing Wizard asks you to choose from a list of service providers that allow you to store files on the Web. The wizard retrieves an updated list of service providers from the Internet each time you want to publish a file. The steps you must perform to publish a file to the Web depend on the service provider you select.

You can publish one or more files to the Web. You can also publish a folder to the Web the same way you publish a file. When you publish a folder to the Web, all the files in the folder are published.

PUBLISH A FILE TO THE WEB

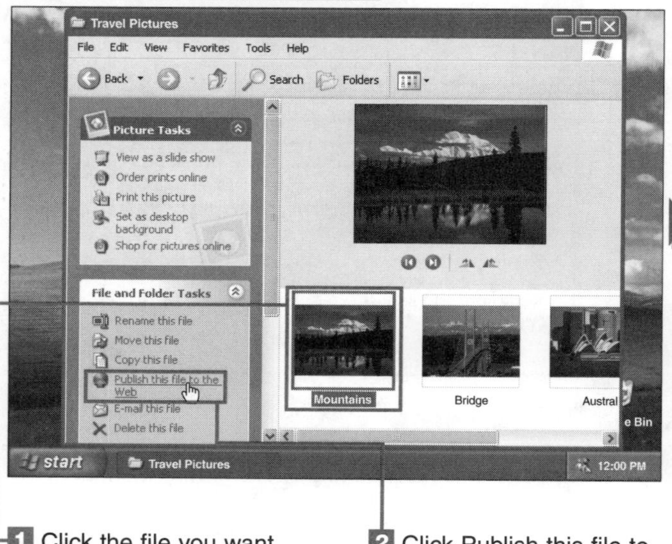

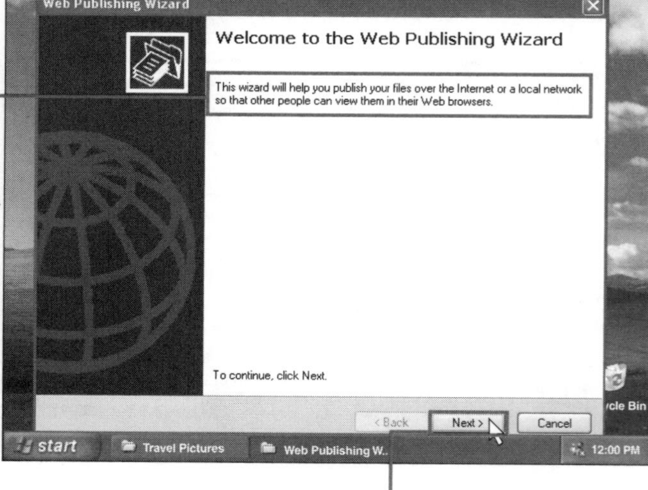

1 Click the file you want to publish to the Web.

■ To publish more than one file, select all the files you want to publish. To select multiple files, see page 52.

2 Click Publish this file to the Web.

Note: If you selected multiple files, click Publish the selected items to the Web in step 2.

■ The Web Publishing Wizard appears.

■ This area describes the wizard.

3 Click Next to continue.

How do I publish a file stored on my desktop?

✔ You can display the contents of the desktop in Windows Explorer to publish a file stored on the desktop. Click start, select All Programs, choose Accessories and select Windows Explorer. Click Desktop in the left pane of the Windows Explorer window to display the contents of the desktop. Click the Folders button to display the task pane and then perform steps 1 to 26 starting on page 90 to publish the file.

Can I quickly select all the files displayed in the Web Publishing Wizard?

✔ You can click the Select All button to select all the displayed files. To quickly deselect all the files, click the Clear All button.

Why does the Web Publishing Wizard ask me to set up an account after I choose a service provider?

✔ You need to set up an account with a service provider before publishing files to the Web. Follow the instructions on your screen to set up an account. When you set up an account, you may be required to obtain a .NET Passport, which allows you to access many services on the Internet using a single user name and password. For information about creating a .NET Passport, see page 184. If you have previously set up an account, you may be asked to log in to your account or enter additional information, such as your date of birth, to continue.

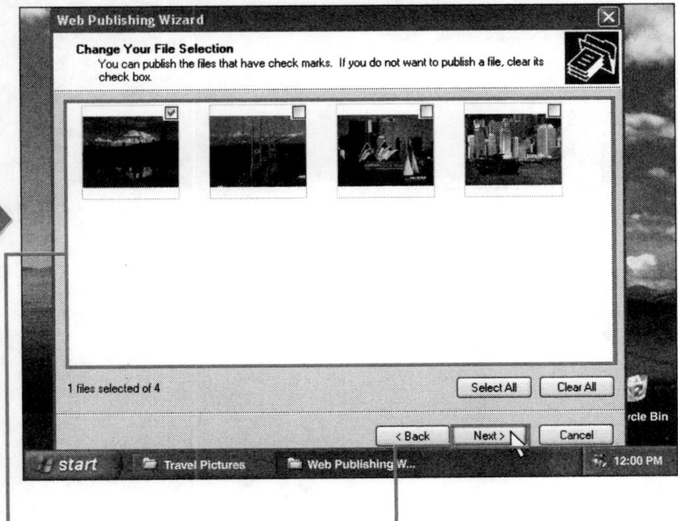

■ This area displays the contents of the folder that stores the file you selected to publish. Windows will publish each file that displays a check mark (✔).

4 To add (☑) or remove (☐) a check mark from a file, click the check box for the file.

5 Click Next to continue.

Note: If you are not currently connected to the Internet, a dialog box will appear, allowing you to connect.

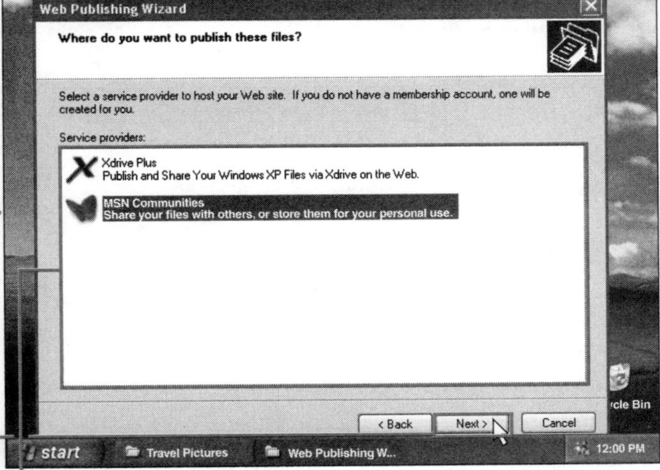

6 Click the service provider you want to publish the file.

7 Click Next to continue.

Note: The following screens depend on the service provider you selected. A service provider may occasionally change the options displayed in the screens to make the wizard easier to use or to provide different options.

CONTINUED

PUBLISH A FILE TO THE WEB (CONTINUED)

Depending on the service provider you choose, the Web Publishing Wizard may ask you to set up a Web site where you can publish your files.

If you chose the MSN communities service provider, you can create a new MSN community to store the file or publish the file to a community you previously created. MSN communities are Web sites that allow you to use interactive tools such as message boards and chat rooms to share information and communicate with friends and family.

You can specify whether you want other people to be able to view the file you publish or if you want to publish the file for your own use.

When creating an MSN community, you must specify a name for the community and verify your e-mail address. You must also read and accept MSN's code of conduct, which specifies guidelines for using the MSN communities.

You can include a description of your community, which will appear when people search for the community on the Web. You can also select a language for the community and specify whether you want the community to be listed in the MSN directory. Listing your community in a directory allows people to easily find your community.

PUBLISH A FILE TO THE WEB (CONTINUED)

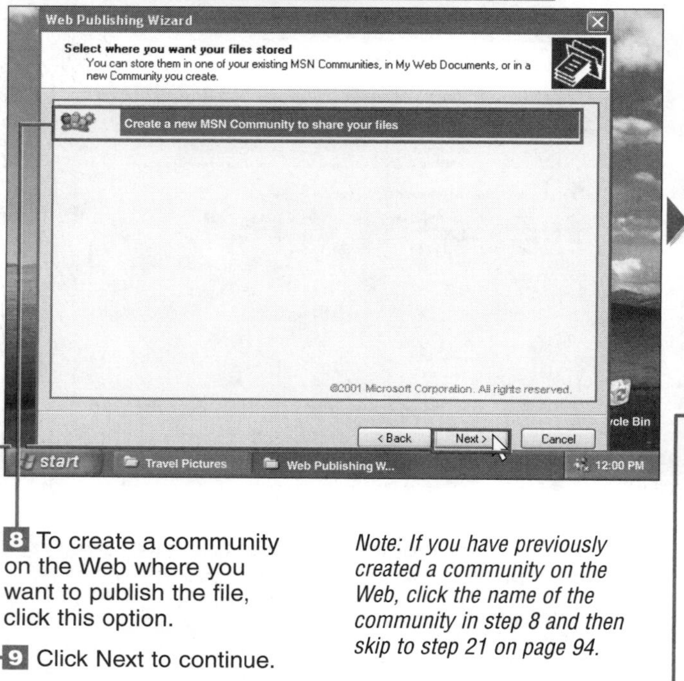

8 To create a community on the Web where you want to publish the file, click this option.

9 Click Next to continue.

Note: If you have previously created a community on the Web, click the name of the community in step 8 and then skip to step 21 on page 94.

10 Click an option to specify if you want to publish the file for other people to view or for your own private use (○ changes to ◉).

11 Click Next to continue.

■ You can click Back to return to a previous step and change your selections.

Note: If you selected Personal in step 10, skip to step 13.

Why would I publish a file for my own private use?

✔ Publishing a file for your own private use is helpful for storing a backup copy of an important file in case your computer fails or you accidentally erase the file. You can also publish a file to the Web so you can access the file from many locations. For example, you can publish a presentation that you plan to deliver so you can access the presentation from any computer connected to the Internet.

If I publish files for my own use, will my information be kept private?

✔ When you publish files for your own use, other people will not be able to access the information you publish. Keep in mind that no service provider can guarantee the confidentiality of your information. You should never publish information you want to keep private to the Web.

Are there restrictions on the type of information I can publish?

✔ All service providers have rules and regulations that determine the type of information you can publish and how that information can be used. For example, most service providers will not allow you to publish material that belongs to other people. Make sure you read and understand the service provider's guidelines before publishing your files.

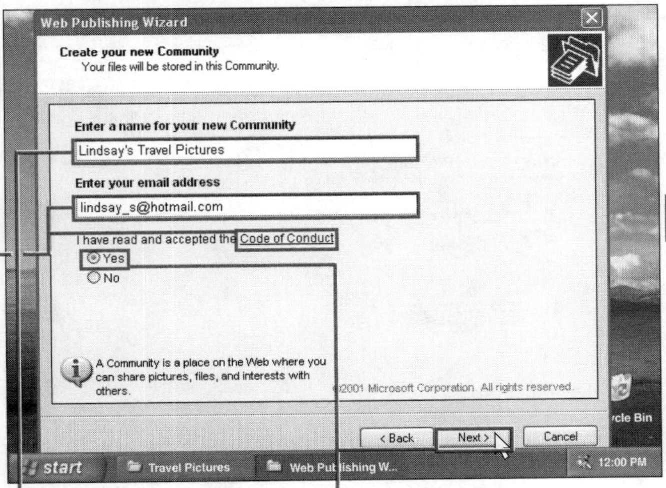

12 Type a name for the community you want to create.

■ This area displays your e-mail address.

13 To display the code of conduct for MSN communities, click Code of Conduct.

Note: When you finish reviewing the code of conduct, click ☒ to close the Code of Conduct window.

14 Click Yes to accept the code of conduct (○ changes to ◉).

15 Click Next to continue.

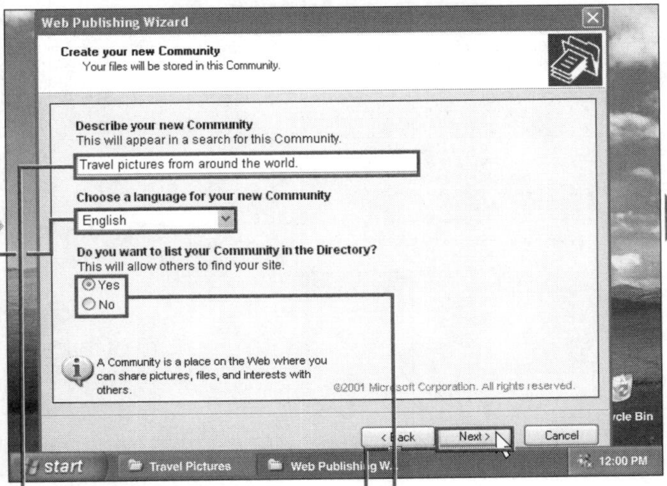

16 Type a description for your community.

17 This area displays the language for your community. To change the language, click this area to select a different language.

18 Click an option to specify if you want to list your community in the directory so other people can find your community (○ changes to ◉).

19 Click Next to continue.

CONTINUED

PUBLISH A FILE TO THE WEB (CONTINUED)

The Web Publishing Wizard displays the address of the Web community where you selected to publish the file. You can have your list of favorite Web pages display a link to the Web site. You can use this link to quickly display your published files.

MSN creates two folders to store files you publish to the Web—one for documents and one for pictures.

You can specify the folder in the Web community where you want to publish the files.

If you are publishing a picture, the Web Publishing Wizard can adjust the size of a large picture so it will transfer faster and be easier to view on a computer screen. Resizing a picture will not change the proportions of the picture when it is displayed on the Web.

Once the file is published, the Internet Explorer window appears, displaying the Web site where you published the file. This allows you to quickly check to make sure your file was published successfully.

After you publish files to the Web, the My Network Places window may contain a folder that stores links to the files you have published.

PUBLISH A FILE TO THE WEB (CONTINUED)

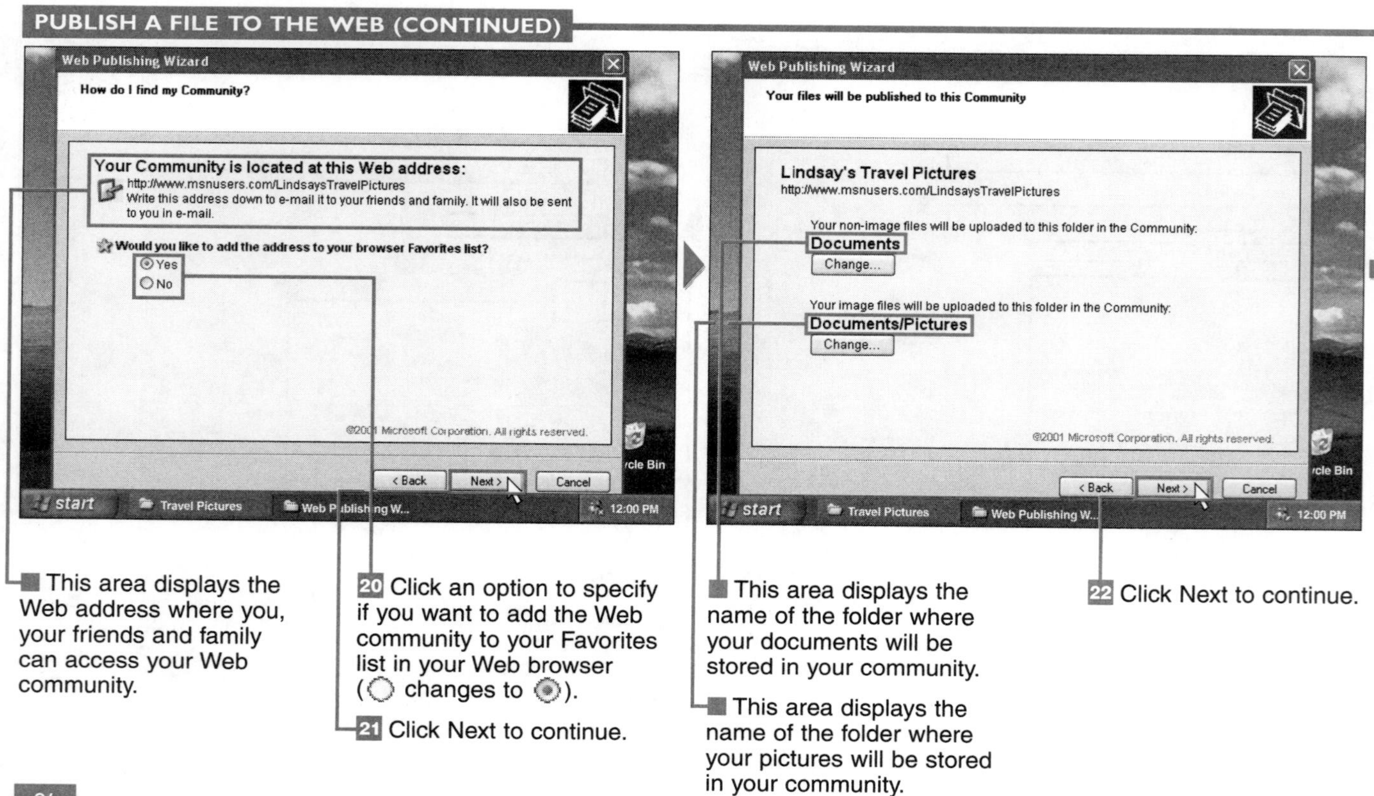

■ This area displays the Web address where you, your friends and family can access your Web community.

20 Click an option to specify if you want to add the Web community to your Favorites list in your Web browser (○ changes to ◉).

21 Click Next to continue.

■ This area displays the name of the folder where your documents will be stored in your community.

■ This area displays the name of the folder where your pictures will be stored in your community.

22 Click Next to continue.

How long will it take to publish my files?

✔ The speed of your computer's Internet connection, the size of the files you are publishing and whether you have chosen to resize the pictures being published all determine how long it will take to publish your files. The Web Publishing Wizard displays a progress area to give you an estimate of how long the files will take to publish.

How can other people access my published files?

✔ If your service provider allows other people to access the files you publish, you can give other people the Web page address where you published the files. Some services require you to use a login name and password in order to access the published files. The computer accessing the files must have the necessary software installed to view or play the files.

How can I manage the files I published to the Web?

✔ If the My Network Places window contains a folder that stores links to the files you have published to the Web, you can use the links to manage the files. To open the My Network Places window, see page 406. When you are connected to the Internet, you can add and delete the links in the My Network Places window to add and delete the same files on the Web. Most services also allow you to manage your files directly on the Web site.

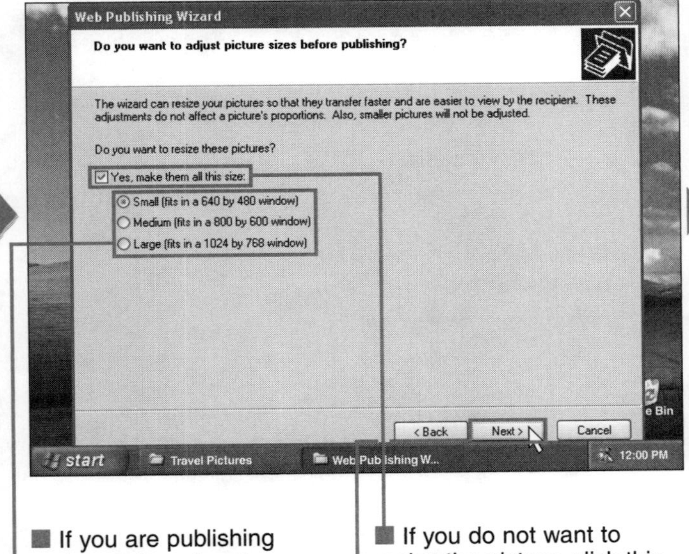

■ If you are publishing a picture, the wizard can resize the picture.

Note: If this message does not appear, skip to step 25.

23 Click the size you want to use for the picture (○ changes to ◉).

■ If you do not want to resize the picture, click this option (☑ changes to ☐).

24 Click Next to publish the file to the Web.

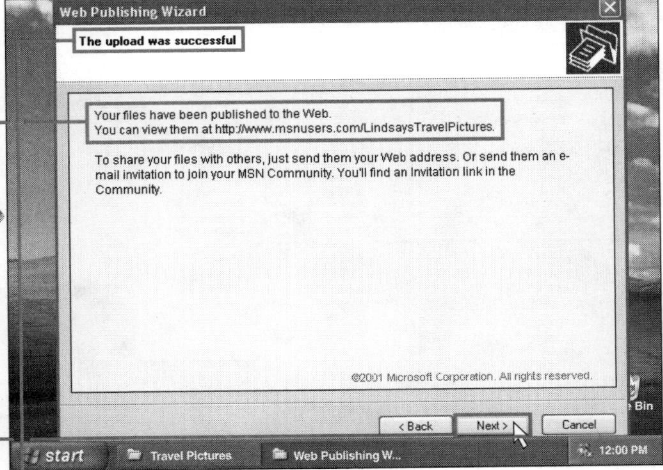

■ This message appears when you have successfully published the file to the Web.

■ This area displays the Web address where the file can be accessed.

25 Click Next to continue.

26 In the dialog box that appears, click Finish to close the wizard.

■ The Microsoft Internet Explorer window will appear, displaying the Web site where you published the file.

CREATE A SHORTCUT

You can create a shortcut to provide a quick way of opening an item you use regularly.

A shortcut icon resembles the original item, but displays an arrow (↗) in the bottom left corner. A shortcut is a link that contains the information needed to locate the original item, but does not contain the item itself.

You can place a shortcut on the desktop, inside a folder or on the Start menu. A shortcut allows you to access an item on your computer, such as a program, file, folder, drive, printer or other Control Panel item, without having to search for the item's actual location.

Creating a shortcut to a folder gives you quick access to all the files in the folder.

Creating shortcuts to files makes working with the files easier. For example, you can use shortcuts to access all the files for a project from one folder, without having to move the original files. This is particularly useful if some of the files are stored on other computers on a network.

CREATE A SHORTCUT

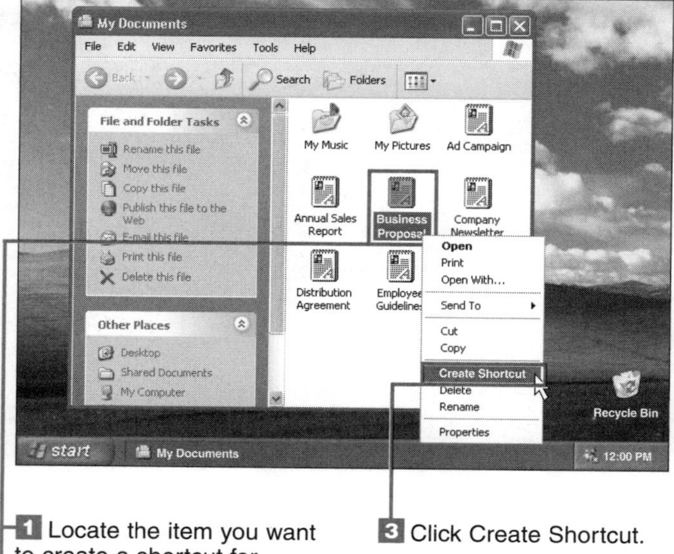

1 Locate the item you want to create a shortcut for.

2 Right-click the item. A menu appears.

3 Click Create Shortcut.

■ A shortcut for the item appears.

■ You can tell the difference between the shortcut and the original item because the shortcut icon displays an arrow (↗).

Are there other ways to create a shortcut?

✔ To place a shortcut for an item on the desktop, right-click the item. On the menu that appears, click Send To and then select Desktop (create shortcut). You can also use the right mouse button to drag an item to the location where you want to place a shortcut for the item. From the menu that appears, select Create Shortcuts Here.

Can I rename a shortcut?

✔ Yes. Click the shortcut and then press the F2 key. Type a new name for the shortcut and then press the Enter key. Renaming a shortcut will not affect the original item.

How do I delete a shortcut?

✔ Click the shortcut and then press the Delete key. Deleting a shortcut will not remove the original item from your computer.

What will happen if I try to use a shortcut for a file that has been deleted?

✔ Windows will display a dialog box that indicates there is a problem with the shortcut. Windows may also display the name of a file that best matches the missing file. You can change the shortcut to refer to this file or delete the shortcut.

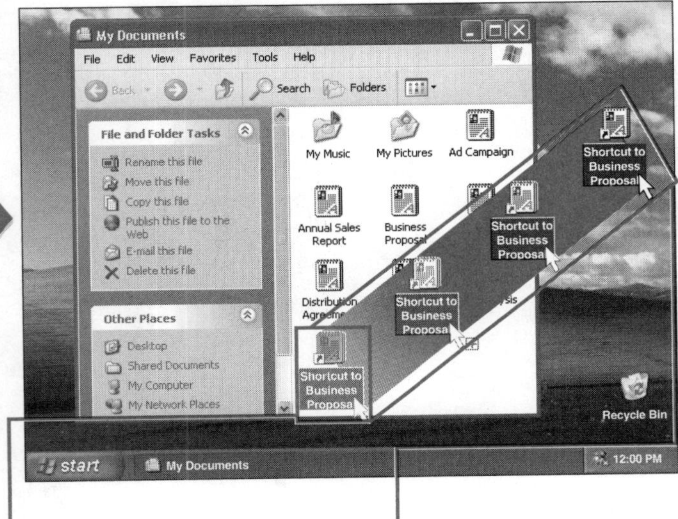

4 Position the mouse over the shortcut you created.

5 Drag the shortcut to the location where you want the shortcut to appear.

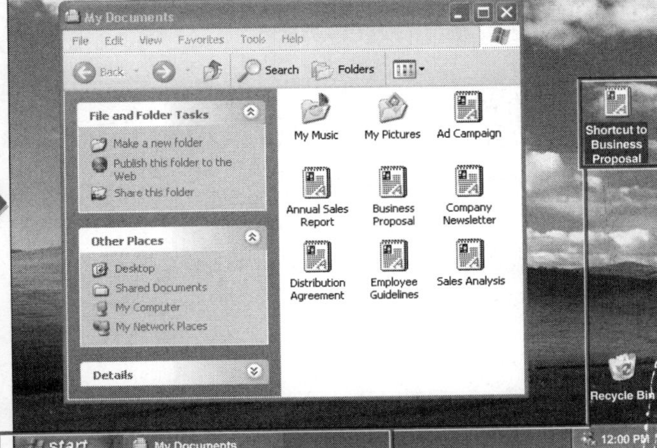

■ The shortcut appears in the new location.

■ You can double-click the shortcut to open the item.

CHANGE SHORTCUT PROPERTIES

Windows allows you to view and change the properties of a shortcut.

You can change the name of the shortcut. Changing the name of a shortcut will not change the name of the original item.

You can view information about the shortcut, such as the size of the shortcut and the date and time the shortcut was created.

The item the shortcut refers to is displayed in the Properties dialog box. The default folder that contains the files required to start the program associated with the shortcut is also displayed.

You can specify a keyboard shortcut that allows you to press a single key or a combination of keys to open the item the shortcut refers to. You can assign a function key, such as F9, or a combination of the Ctrl and Alt keys and a letter or number, such as Ctrl+Alt+Y.

When changing the properties of a shortcut, you can choose how you want the item to appear when you use the shortcut to open the item. You can have the item open in a normal window, minimized as a button on the taskbar or maximized to fill your screen. You can also add a comment that describes the shortcut. The comment will appear when you position the mouse pointer over the icon for the shortcut.

CHANGE SHORTCUT PROPERTIES

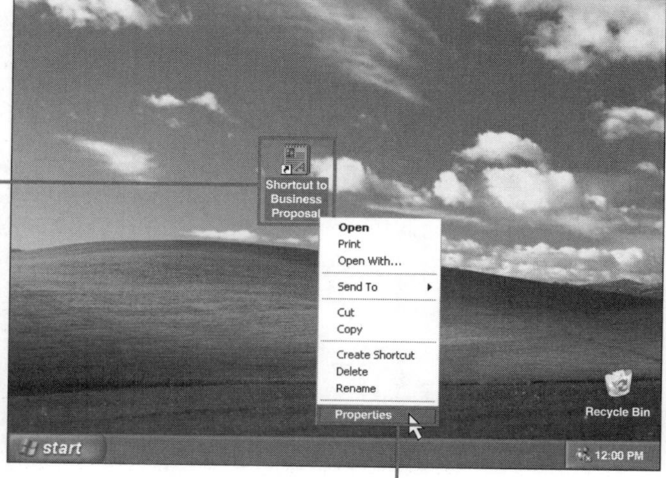

1 Right-click the shortcut whose properties you want to change. A menu appears.

2 Click Properties.

■ The Properties dialog box appears.

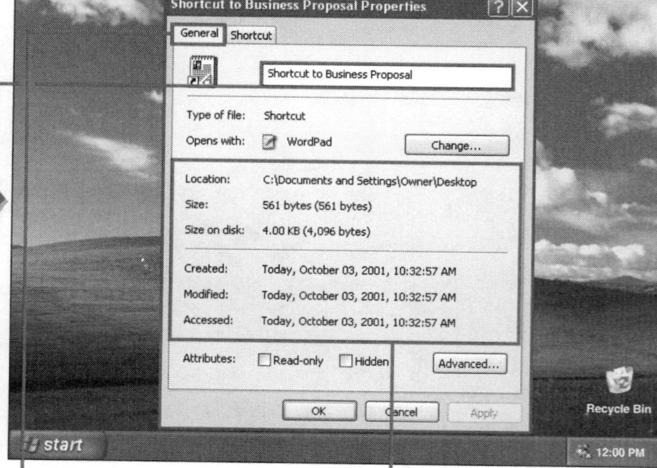

3 Click the General tab.

4 This area displays the name of the shortcut. To change the name of the shortcut, select the current name and then type a new name.

■ This area displays information about the shortcut, including the location and size of the shortcut and the date and time you created the shortcut.

How can I quickly find the original item a shortcut refers to?

✔ In the Properties dialog box for the shortcut, select the Shortcut tab and then click the Find Target button.

Can I specify a new default folder for the program associated with a shortcut?

✔ Specifying a different folder is useful when the files needed to start the program are not saved in the current default folder. To specify a new folder, click the Shortcut tab in the Properties dialog box. Select the text in the Start in area and then type a new folder location and name.

How can I change the icon for a shortcut?

✔ In the Properties dialog box, select the Shortcut tab and click the Change Icon button. Click the icon you want to use for the shortcut and then click OK.

How can I use a program shortcut when logged on as a different user?

✔ In the Properties dialog box, select the Shortcut tab and click the Advanced button. Then select the Run with different credentials option (☐ changes to ☑). When you double-click the shortcut, Windows will allow you to choose which user account you want to use to run the program. This is useful for running administrative programs when you are not logged on as an administrator.

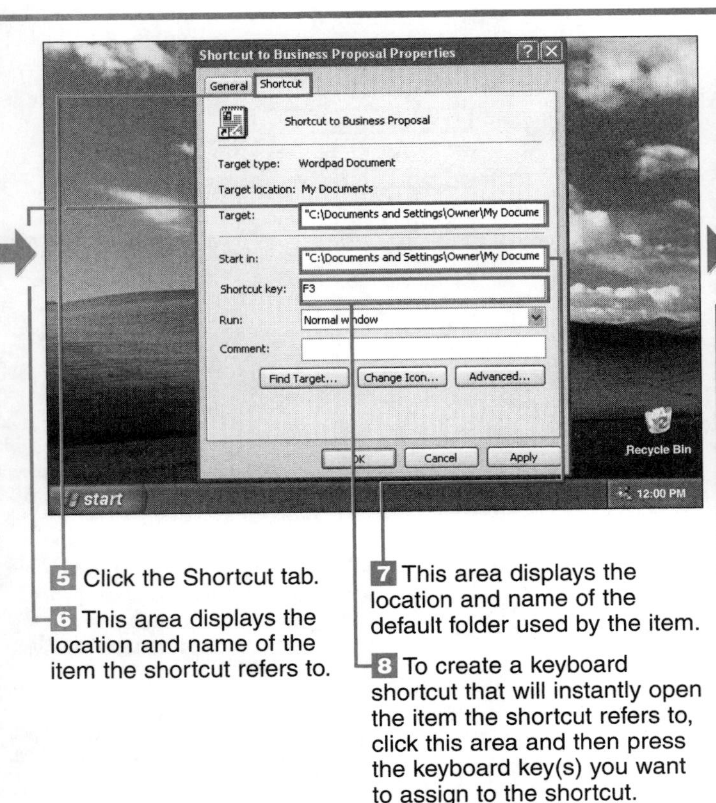

5 Click the Shortcut tab.

6 This area displays the location and name of the item the shortcut refers to.

7 This area displays the location and name of the default folder used by the item.

8 To create a keyboard shortcut that will instantly open the item the shortcut refers to, click this area and then press the keyboard key(s) you want to assign to the shortcut.

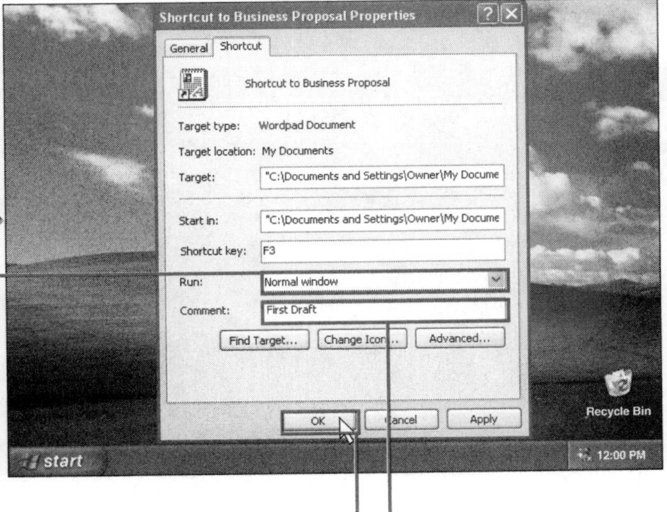

9 This area displays the way the window for the item will appear when you use the shortcut to open the item. You can click this area to select a different option.

10 To add a comment that describes the shortcut, click this area and type the comment.

11 Click OK to confirm all your changes.

DISPLAY AND CHANGE FILE PROPERTIES

You can find information about a file or folder by reviewing its properties. When viewing the properties of a file, you can change the name of the file. You can also see the file's type and the program Windows will use to open the file.

You can view where the file is stored on your computer, the size of the file and the amount of disk space required to store the file.

You can also find the date and time the file was created, last changed and last opened.

Each file has attributes that you can verify and change. The Read-only attribute prevents you from saving changes you make to a file. The Hidden attribute is used to hide and protect the files Windows requires to operate. The Archive attribute appears if your computer uses the FAT file system. This attribute is used by some programs to determine if a file needs to be backed up.

The Properties dialog box may display additional tabs that show additional information about a file. For example, when you view the properties for a Notepad document, you can use the Summary tab to find out the document's title, subject and author.

DISPLAY AND CHANGE FILE PROPERTIES

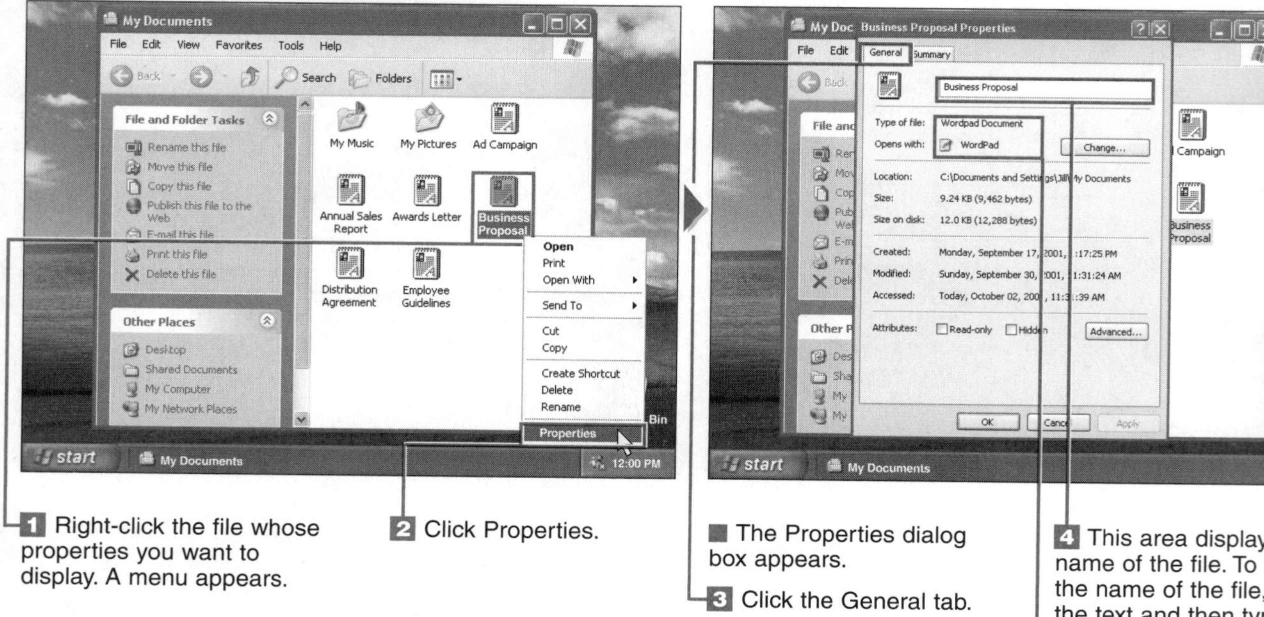

1 Right-click the file whose properties you want to display. A menu appears.

2 Click Properties.

■ The Properties dialog box appears.

3 Click the General tab.

4 This area displays the name of the file. To change the name of the file, select the text and then type a new name.

■ This area displays the type of file and the name of the program that opens the file.

Why is the amount of disk space required to store a file larger than the actual size of the file?

✔ The amount of disk space required to store a file is based on the number of clusters in which the file is stored. A cluster is the smallest amount of space on a hard drive that can be used to store a file. If the size of a file is smaller than a cluster, the entire cluster is still used to store the file.

Are there other attributes I can change?

✔ If your computer uses the NTFS file system, display the Properties dialog box and then click the Advanced button. The dialog box that appears displays options you can use to turn on or off the Archive, Index and Compress attributes.

How do I display hidden files?

✔ Click the start button and then choose Control Panel. Click Appearance and Themes and then select Folder Options. In the dialog box that appears, choose the View tab and then click the Show hidden files and folders option (○ changes to ◉).

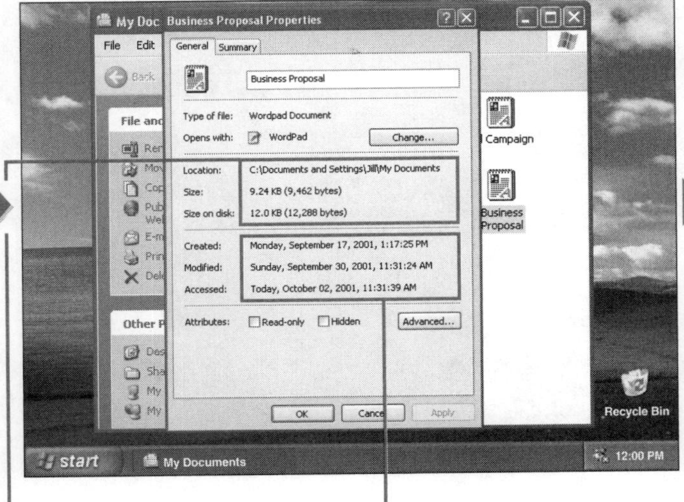

■ This area displays the location of the file on your computer, the size of the file and the amount of disk space required to store the file.

■ This area displays the date and time you created, last changed and last opened the file.

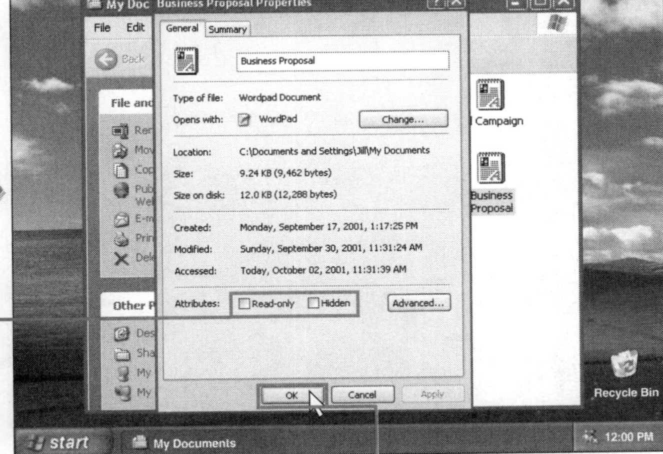

■ This area displays the attributes for the file.

5 Click an attribute to turn the attribute on (☑) or off (☐).

6 Click OK to confirm your changes.

PUT PART OF A FILE ON THE DESKTOP

You can place frequently used information on your desktop. Information you place on the desktop is called a scrap. Scraps give you quick access to information and are useful if you frequently add the same information to documents.

Document scraps save you time since you do not have to retype the information over and over. For example, you can create a scrap containing your name, address and phone number. You can then drag the scrap into a document whenever you need the information. You can also create a scrap for images, such as your company logo.

When creating a scrap, make sure the file that contains the information is not maximized. If the file is maximized, you will not be able to drag the information to the desktop.

Scraps are available only for programs that allow you to drag and drop information to other programs. For example, you cannot create scraps using a Microsoft Notepad document.

You can work with a scrap the same way you work with any file on your computer. For example, you can rename, edit or delete a scrap at any time.

PUT PART OF A FILE ON THE DESKTOP

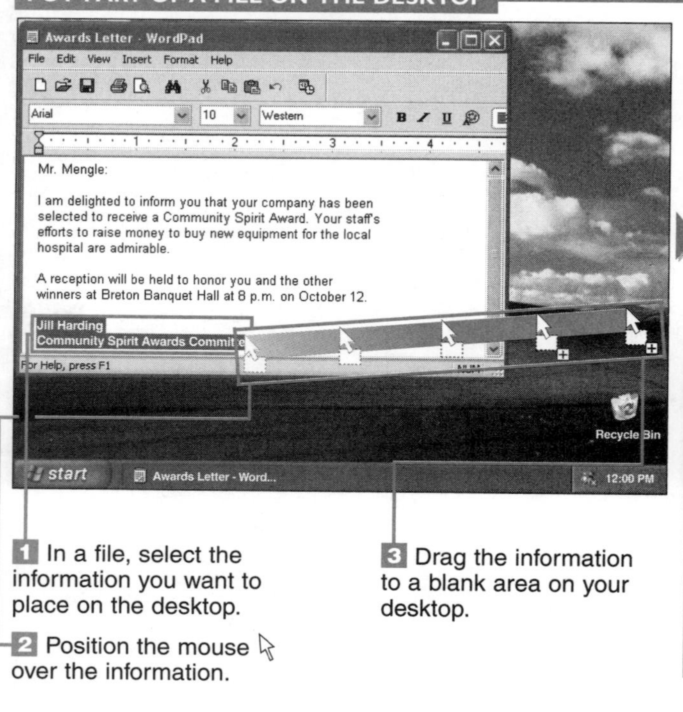

1 In a file, select the information you want to place on the desktop.

2 Position the mouse over the information.

3 Drag the information to a blank area on your desktop.

■ Windows creates a file called a scrap. The scrap stores the information you selected.

■ The information remains in the original file.

■ To place the information in another file, drag the scrap to the location in the file where you want to place the information.

COPY SCREEN OR WINDOW CONTENTS

You can create a copy of all or part of your screen. This is useful if you are trying to explain a computer problem or procedure and you want a visual example to illustrate what you are trying to explain. Copying the contents of the screen is also useful for keeping records of program settings and for printing information that cannot be easily printed using regular printing methods.

You can take a picture of the entire screen or just the active window or dialog box. When you copy the entire screen, active window or active dialog box, the image is stored on the Clipboard. You can place the image in a program such as Paint or WordPad and then print the image or e-mail the image to another person.

You can buy programs, often called screen capture programs, that provide options the Print Screen key does not offer. For example, some screen capture programs allow you to select an exact region of your screen that you want to copy, such as a menu in a program, or allow you to record a series of movements on your screen. SnagIt by TechSmith Corporation is a popular example of screen capture software. You can download a trial version of SnagIt from the www.techsmith.com Web site.

COPY SCREEN OR WINDOW CONTENTS

1 Press the Print Screen key to copy the entire screen.

■ To copy just the active window or dialog box, press and hold down the Alt key as you press the Print Screen key.

■ Windows places a copy of the image on the Clipboard.

2 Open the document you want to display the copy of the image.

3 Click Edit.

4 Click Paste.

■ The image appears in the document.

UNDO YOUR LAST ACTION

When you change your mind or make a mistake, Windows can help you undo your last action.

Windows can undo actions such as renaming, deleting, copying or moving a file. The word that appears beside the Undo command indicates which action is available to undo. You may be able to undo up to the last 10 actions.

If the Undo command is not available, you cannot undo your last action. For example, you cannot undo the deletion of a file after you empty the Recycle Bin. You also cannot undo a save or an undo action you performed. If you move a file to a folder that already has a file with the same name, Windows asks if you want to replace the file located in the folder. If you replace the file, you will not be able to undo the action to restore the original file.

Many applications, such as Microsoft Word and Excel, also offer the Undo command.

UNDO YOUR LAST ACTION

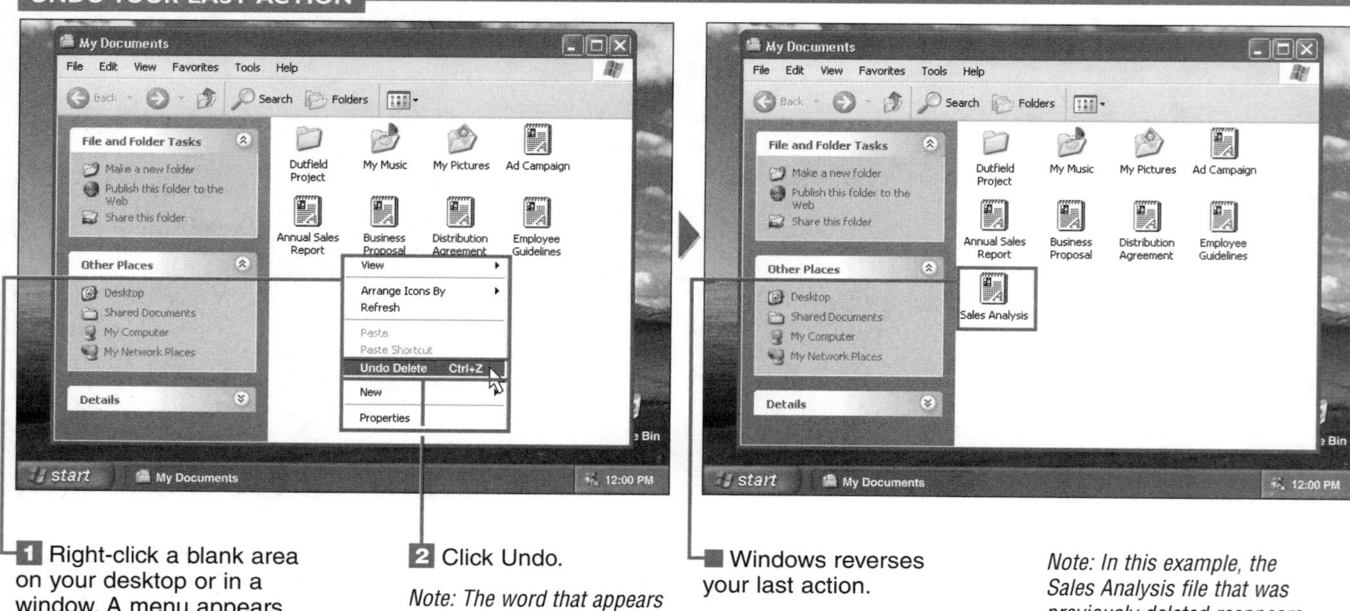

1 Right-click a blank area on your desktop or in a window. A menu appears.

2 Click Undo.

Note: The word that appears beside Undo indicates which action you can undo.

■ Windows reverses your last action.

Note: In this example, the Sales Analysis file that was previously deleted reappears.

CLOSE MISBEHAVING PROGRAMS

You can view the status of the programs running on your computer and close a program that is no longer working properly without shutting down Windows or other programs. You can close a misbehaving program even when you do not have access to the program's menus or commands.

When a program fails to respond to mouse or keyboard actions, Windows identifies the program as not responding. Windows may detect that a program is not responding before you do and display a warning message. You may also discover, while using a program, that it is not behaving as it should.

When you close a program that is not responding, you lose all the unsaved information in the program. Closing a misbehaving program should not affect the operation of your other open programs or Windows.

CLOSE MISBEHAVING PROGRAMS

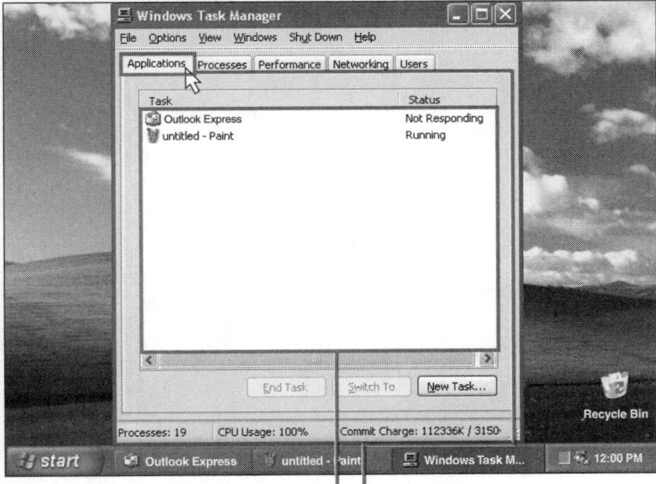

1 To close a misbehaving program, press and hold down the Ctrl and Alt keys as you press the Delete key.

■ The Windows Task Manager window appears.

2 Click the Applications tab.

■ This area lists the programs that are currently running. The phrase Not Responding appears beside the name of a misbehaving program.

3 Click the program that is misbehaving.

4 Click End Task.

■ The End Program dialog box appears, stating that the program is not responding.

5 Click End Now to close the program.

6 Click ☒ to close the Windows Task Manager window.

CREATE A ZIPPED COMPRESSED FOLDER

You can create a zipped compressed folder that you can use to store files and folders. Creating compressed folders can help you save storage space on your computer and on removable storage media, such as floppy disks. Compressed folders also transfer quickly over the Internet. The amount of space a compressed folder saves depends on the types of files you add to the folder. For example, text files will compress significantly more than pictures.

Windows allows you to assign a password to the files in a compressed folder. Assigning a password ensures that only those who know the password will be able to open files in the folder.

Before assigning a password to the files in a compressed folder, you should make sure the folder contains all the files you want the folder to store. Files added to the compressed folder after you assign a password will not be password protected.

You cannot make changes to the files in a compressed folder. Some programs may also require you to extract, or decompress, the program files from a compressed folder before running the program. To extract files from a compressed folder, see page 108.

CREATE A ZIPPED COMPRESSED FOLDER

1 Right-click a blank area on the desktop or in the window where you want to place a compressed folder.
A menu appears.

2 Click New.

3 Click Compressed (zipped) Folder.

■ A compressed folder appears with a temporary name. Compressed folders display the ( ) icon.

4 Type a name for the folder and then press the Enter key.

5 To add a file to the compressed folder, position the mouse over the file and then drag the file to the folder.

■ Windows will add a compressed copy of the file to the folder.

How can I view information about the files in a compressed folder?

✔ You can view information about each file, such as whether a file is password protected or the percentage of compression for the file. To display information for each file in the compressed folder, double-click the folder to display its contents. Click the View menu and then select Details.

Can I remove the password from a compressed folder?

✔ Yes. Double-click the folder to open the folder. Then click the File menu and select Remove Password. Type the password you assigned to the folder and then press the Enter key.

Can other people work with my compressed folders?

✔ Other people can work with compressed folders on their computers if they have a program that can work with compressed folders. Windows XP includes software that can work with compressed folders. People who do not have the appropriate software can obtain a program, such as WinZip, that allows them to work with compressed folders. WinZip is available at the www.winzip.com Web site.

PROTECT FILES IN A ZIPPED COMPRESSED FOLDER

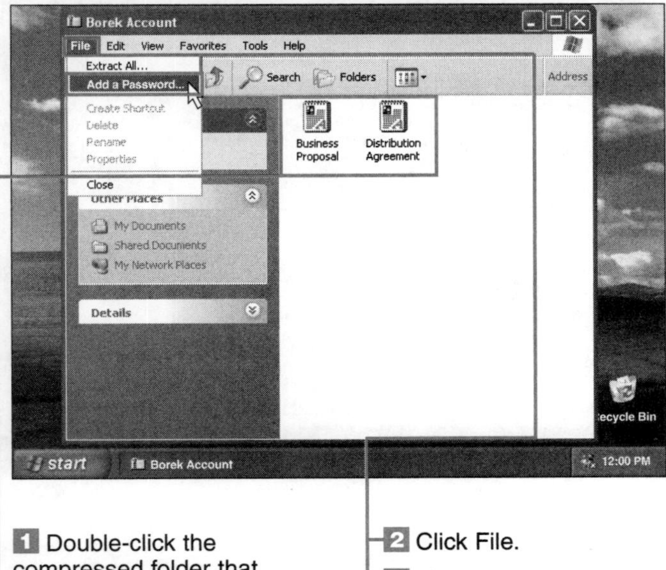

1 Double-click the compressed folder that contains the files you want to protect with a password.

■ The contents of the folder appear.

2 Click File.

3 Click Add a Password.

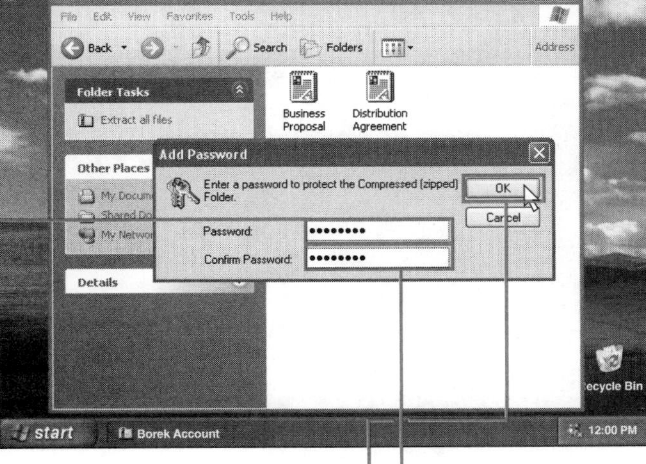

■ The Add Password dialog box appears.

4 Type the password you want to use to prevent unauthorized people from opening the files in the compressed folder.

5 Click this area and type the password again.

6 Click OK.

EXTRACT FILES FROM A ZIPPED COMPRESSED FOLDER

You can use the Extraction Wizard to extract all the files and folders from a compressed folder at once. You need to extract files from a compressed folder before you can save changes you make to the files. When you extract files from a compressed folder, Windows creates uncompressed copies of the files that you can work with as you would work with any file on your computer.

You can also use the Extraction Wizard to extract compressed files you have downloaded from the Internet. Files offered on the Internet are often compressed to allow them to transfer over the Internet more quickly.

Windows will create a new folder to store the compressed files you extract. The wizard indicates where the new folder is stored.

If you assigned a password to the files in the compressed folder, Windows will ask you to enter the password before you can extract the files. The extracted files in the new folder will no longer be password protected, but the files in the original compressed folder will remain password protected.

EXTRACT FILES FROM A ZIPPED COMPRESSED FOLDER

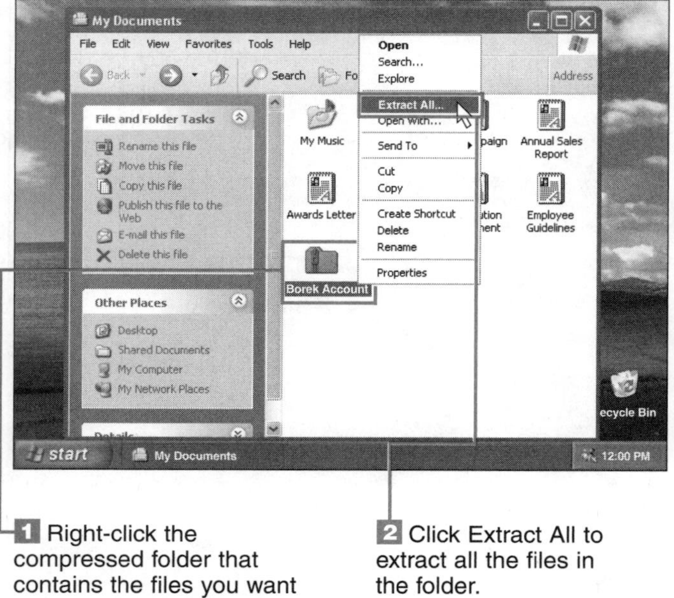

1 Right-click the compressed folder that contains the files you want to extract. A menu appears.

2 Click Extract All to extract all the files in the folder.

■ The Extraction Wizard appears.

■ This area describes the wizard.

3 Click Next to continue.

How do I extract a single file or folder from a compressed folder?

✔ Drag the file or folder from the compressed folder to a new location outside the folder. A compressed version of the file or folder will remain in the compressed folder.

Can I specify a different location to store extracted files?

✔ Yes. In the Extraction Wizard, click the Browse button. A dialog box appears, allowing you to select another location to store the extracted files.

How do I delete a compressed folder?

✔ Click the folder you want to delete and then press the Delete key. All the files and folders within the compressed folder will be deleted. To delete a single file or folder within a compressed folder, click the file or folder and then press the Delete key.

Can I stop the wizard from automatically displaying the contents of the new folder after I extract files?

✔ Yes. In the Extraction Wizard, click the Show extracted files option to turn the option off (☑ changes to ☐).

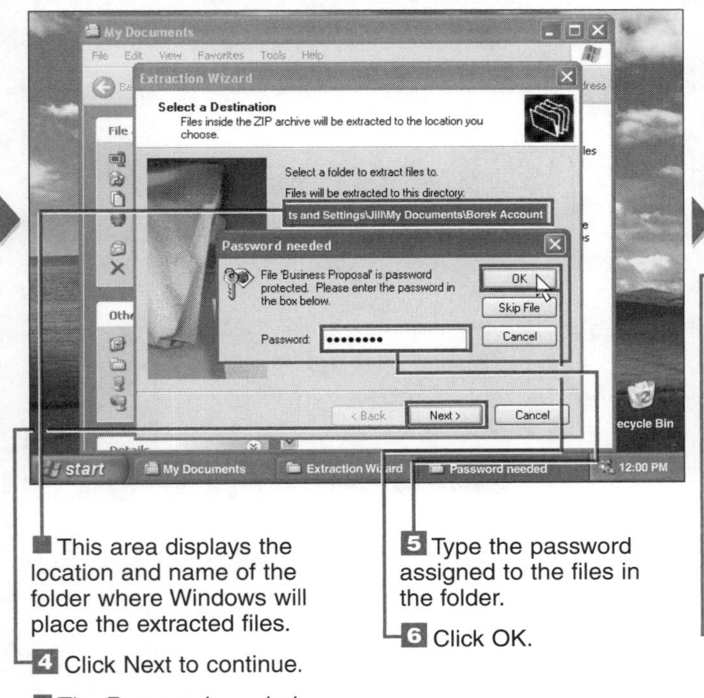

■ This area displays the location and name of the folder where Windows will place the extracted files.

4 Click Next to continue.

■ The Password needed dialog box appears if you assigned a password to files in the folder.

5 Type the password assigned to the files in the folder.

6 Click OK.

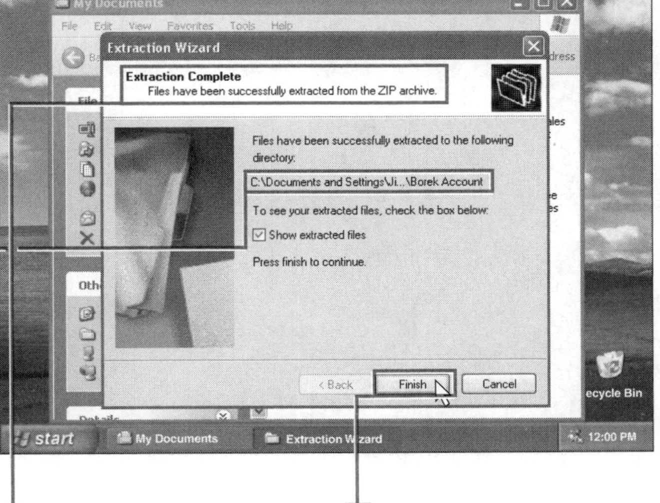

■ This message appears when the files have been successfully extracted.

■ This area indicates the location and name of the folder that contains the extracted files.

7 Click Finish to close the Extraction Wizard.

■ The new folder containing the extracted files will appear. The original compressed folder will remain on your computer.

COMPRESS A FOLDER ON AN NTFS DRIVE

If your computer's hard drive uses the NTFS file system, you can compress a folder stored on the hard drive to decrease the amount of space that the folder takes up.

When you compress a folder, you can choose to compress only the folder or to also compress all the files and folders stored in the folder.

Compressed folders can store any type of file, such as documents, program files and multimedia files. You can open a compressed file as you would open any file. Windows will automatically uncompress the file when you open the file and will recompress the file when you close it. When working with large files, you may notice a slight decrease in your computer's performance as Windows uncompresses and compresses the files.

Windows displays the names of compressed files and folders in a different color than regular files and folders. This can help you distinguish between compressed and non-compressed items.

When you move or copy a file from a folder on your hard drive to a compressed folder on the hard drive, Windows will not automatically compress the file for you. You must compress the file in the new location. You can compress an individual file on your computer as you would compress a folder.

COMPRESS A FOLDER ON AN NTFS DRIVE

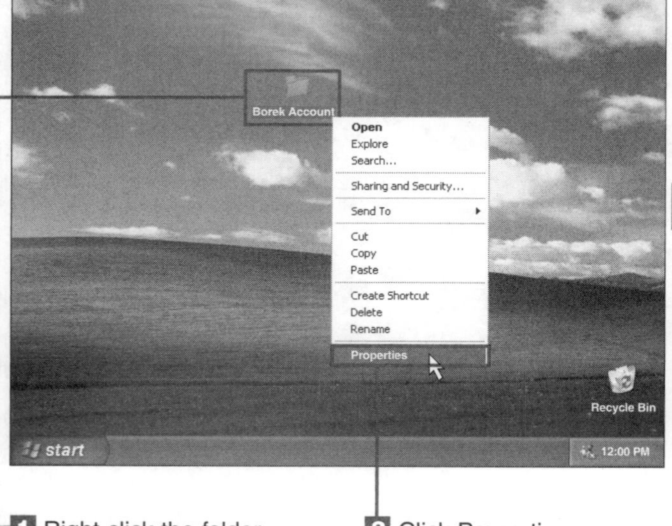

1 Right-click the folder you want to compress. A menu appears.

2 Click Properties.

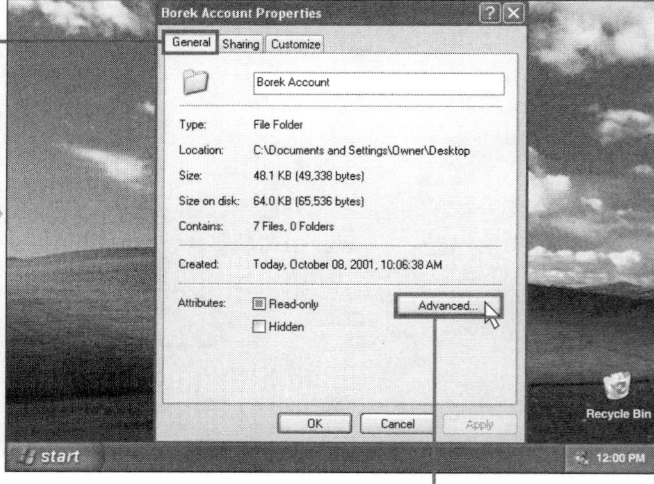

■ The Properties dialog box appears.

3 Click the General tab.

4 Click Advanced.

How can I tell if my hard drive uses the NTFS file system?

✔ Click start and select My Computer. Right-click the hard drive for your computer and then select Properties. In the dialog box that appears, click the General tab. The file system your computer uses appears in the File System area. If your hard drive does not use the NTFS file system, you can convert the drive to NTFS. For information, see page 538.

Can I compress an entire drive?

✔ Yes. Click start and then select My Computer. Right-click the drive you want to compress and then choose Properties. Select the General tab, click the Compress drive to save disk space option and then click OK. You must be logged on as a computer administrator to compress an entire drive.

Can I have Windows display compressed files and folders in the same color as uncompressed files and folders?

✔ Yes. Click start, select Control Panel and choose Appearance and Themes. Select Folder Options and then choose the View tab in the dialog box that appears. In the Advanced settings area, click the Show encrypted or compressed NTFS files in color option (☑ changes to ☐).

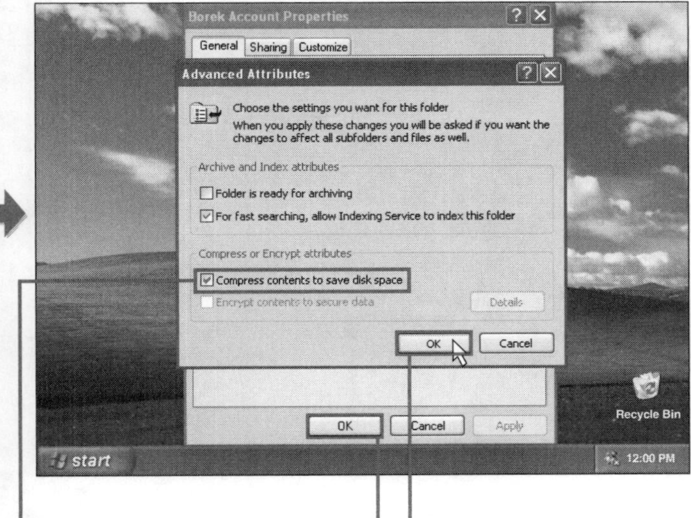

■ The Advanced Attributes dialog box appears.

5 Click this option to compress the folder (☐ changes to ☑).

6 Click OK to confirm your change.

7 Click OK to close the Properties dialog box.

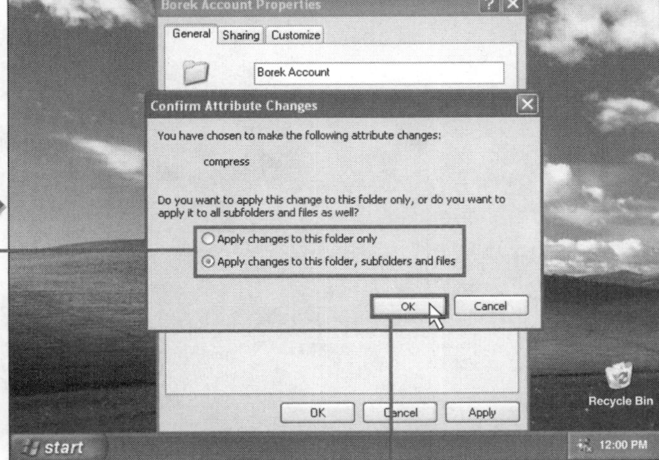

■ The Confirm Attribute Changes dialog box appears.

8 Click an option to specify if you want to compress only the folder or to compress the folder and all the files and subfolders within the folder (○ changes to ◉).

9 Click OK to compress the folder.

Note: To uncompress a folder, repeat steps 1 to 9 (☑ changes to ☐ in step 5).

ADD DESTINATIONS TO SEND TO MENU

The Send To menu allows you to send copies of files to another location. You can customize the Send To menu to include the programs, folders and devices to which you most often send files.

Windows automatically displays your floppy drive, the desktop and the My Documents folder on the Send To menu. The menu also displays the Mail Recipient item, which allows you to quickly send a file in an e-mail message. The Compressed (zipped) Folder item is also displayed, allowing you to create a compressed folder where you can store files to save space on your computer.

You can place a shortcut for a folder or a device, such as a printer, on the Send To menu. This allows you to send a file directly to the specific folder or device.

You may also want to add a program to the Send To menu so you can quickly open files in the program. For example, if you frequently use WordPad to open files created in other programs, you can place a shortcut for the WordPad program on the Send To menu. You can then use the menu to quickly open files in WordPad.

You must add a shortcut for an item to the SendTo folder in order to have the item appear on the Send To menu.

ADD DESTINATIONS TO SEND TO MENU

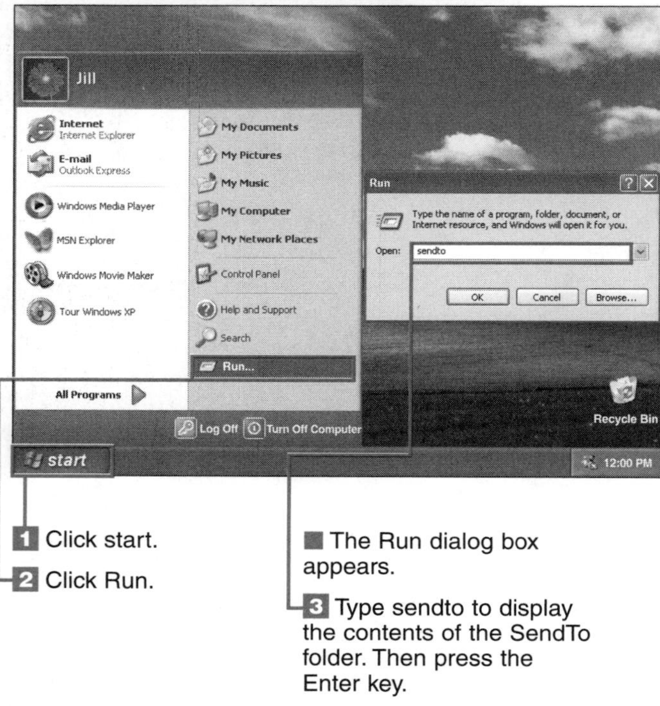

1 Click start.

2 Click Run.

■ The Run dialog box appears.

3 Type sendto to display the contents of the SendTo folder. Then press the Enter key.

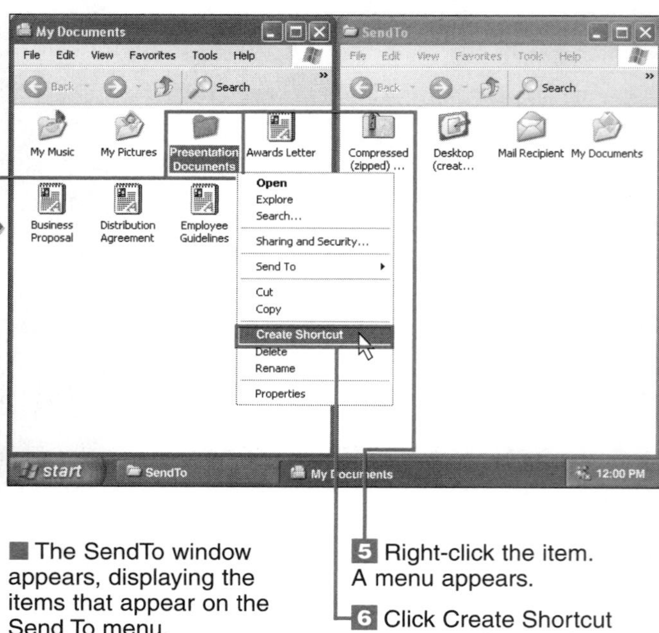

■ The SendTo window appears, displaying the items that appear on the Send To menu.

4 Locate the item you want to add to the Send To menu.

5 Right-click the item. A menu appears.

6 Click Create Shortcut to create a shortcut for the item.

Where is the SendTo folder located on my computer?

✔ The SendTo folder is located within the folder that displays your user name in the Documents and Settings folder on your hard drive (C:). The SendTo folder is a hidden folder. You may need to show hidden folders before you can see the SendTo folder. To show hidden folders, see page 50.

Can I use folders to organize the items on the Send To menu?

✔ Yes. You can create a folder in the SendTo folder and then move items to the new folder. To create a folder, see page 83. The folder will appear on the Send To menu with an arrow (▸) indicating there are more choices. You can click the folder to display the choices.

Can I add shared folders on the network to the Send To menu?

✔ Yes. From the Start menu, select My Computer and click the My Network Places link in the window. Then locate the folder you want to add to the Send To menu and perform steps 5 to 8 below.

How do I delete an item from the Send To menu?

✔ In the SendTo window, click the item and then press the Delete key.

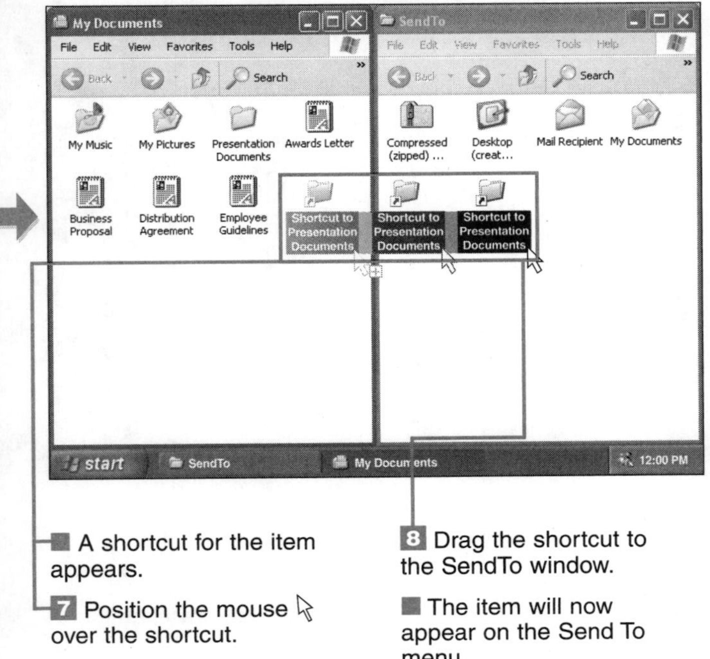

■ A shortcut for the item appears.

7 Position the mouse over the shortcut.

8 Drag the shortcut to the SendTo window.

■ The item will now appear on the Send To menu.

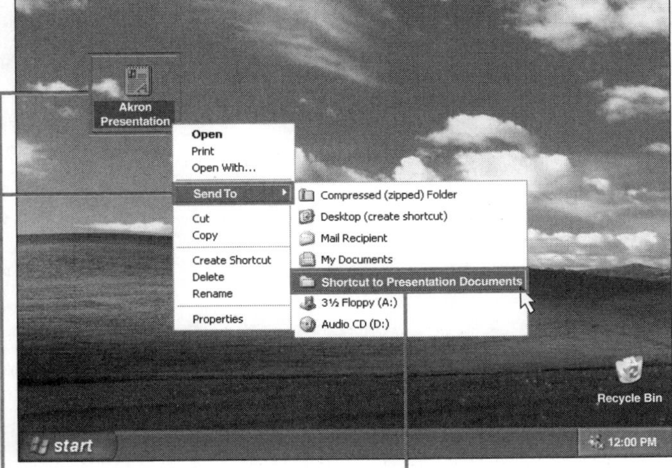

USING THE SEND TO MENU

1 Right-click the file you want to send to another location. A menu appears.

2 Click Send To.

3 Click the location where you want to send a copy of the file.

PRINT FILES

You can produce a paper copy of a file without having to open the program that created the file. This allows you to quickly print a file from a window or the desktop.

You can print a single file or you can select many different types of files and print them all at the same time. For example, you can print a document, a spreadsheet and a presentation at once.

When you print a file, Windows starts the program associated with the file and briefly opens the file on your screen. Windows closes the program when the file has been sent to the printer.

When you print files, Windows sends the files to your default printer. You can print files to a different printer by changing the default printer. To change the default printer, see page 126.

Before printing a file, you should make sure your printer is turned on and contains paper.

When you print a picture, the Photo Printing Wizard appears, helping you get the best results when printing your pictures. For information about the Photo Printing Wizard, see page 116.

PRINT FILES

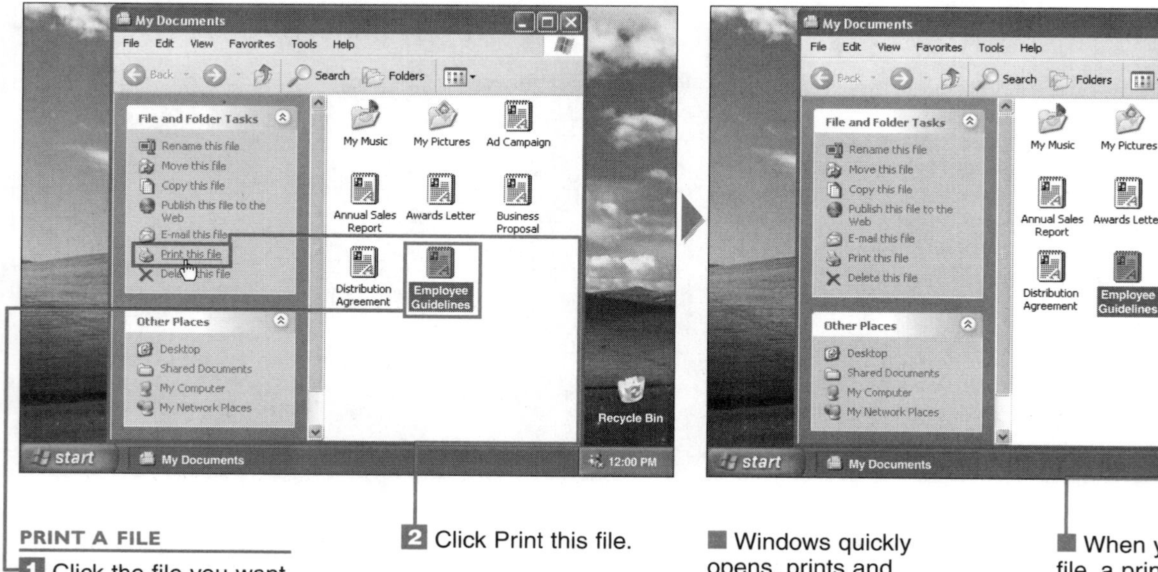

PRINT A FILE

1 Click the file you want to print.

2 Click Print this file.

■ Windows quickly opens, prints and then closes the file.

■ When you print a file, a printer icon ( ) appears in this area. The icon disappears when the file has finished printing.

Why is the Print this file command not available when I select a file?

✔ Windows does not recognize the type of file and does not know which program to use to open and print the file. If you have a program on your computer that you can use to open the file, open the file in the program. Then in the window for the program, click the File menu and select Print.

Is there another way to quickly print a document?

✔ Yes. You can drag the icon for a document you want to print to a printer shortcut on the desktop. To create a printer shortcut on the desktop, click start, select Control Panel, click Printers and Other Hardware and then click View installed printers or fax printers. Using the right mouse button, drag the icon for the printer you want to use from the Printers and Faxes window to the desktop. Then click Create Shortcuts Here on the menu that appears.

My file is not printing properly. What can I do?

✔ You can use the Printing Troubleshooter to help you determine and fix the problem. Click start, select Control Panel, click Printers and Other Hardware and then click View installed printers or fax printers. Then click the Troubleshoot printing link and follow the instructions on your screen.

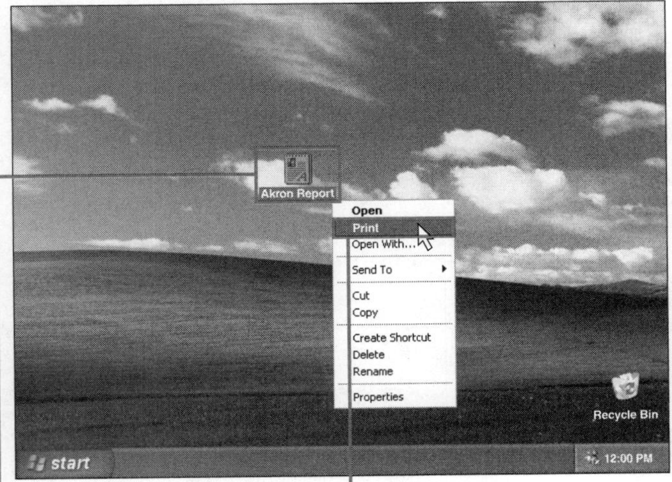

PRINT A FILE ON THE DESKTOP

1 Right-click the file you want to print. A menu appears.

2 Click Print.

■ Windows quickly opens, prints and then closes the file.

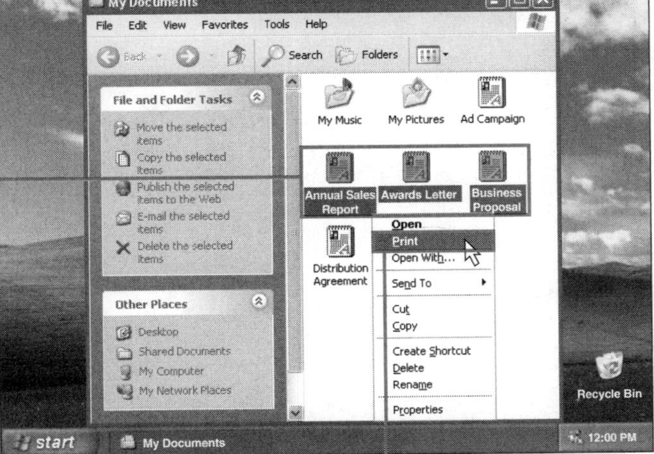

PRINT MULTIPLE FILES

1 Select all the files you want to print. To select multiple files, see page 52.

2 Right-click one of the files. A menu appears.

3 Click Print to print the files.

■ Windows quickly opens, prints and then closes each file.

PRINT PICTURES

You can use the Photo Printing Wizard to print pictures stored on your computer. The Photo Printing Wizard guides you step by step through the process of printing pictures.

You can obtain pictures on the Internet, purchase pictures at computer stores or use a drawing program, such as Paint, to create your own pictures. You can also use a digital camera to take pictures that you can copy to your computer or use a scanner to scan pictures into your computer. Windows also includes a few sample pictures.

Windows provides the My Pictures folder which is a convenient place to store your pictures. To keep your files organized, you should store all your pictures in the My Pictures folder. The My Pictures folder also provides options that make it easy to perform tasks with pictures.

When printing pictures, the Photo Printing Wizard displays a small version of each picture in the My Pictures folder and allows you to select each picture you want to print. You can also quickly select all the pictures in the folder.

PRINT PICTURES

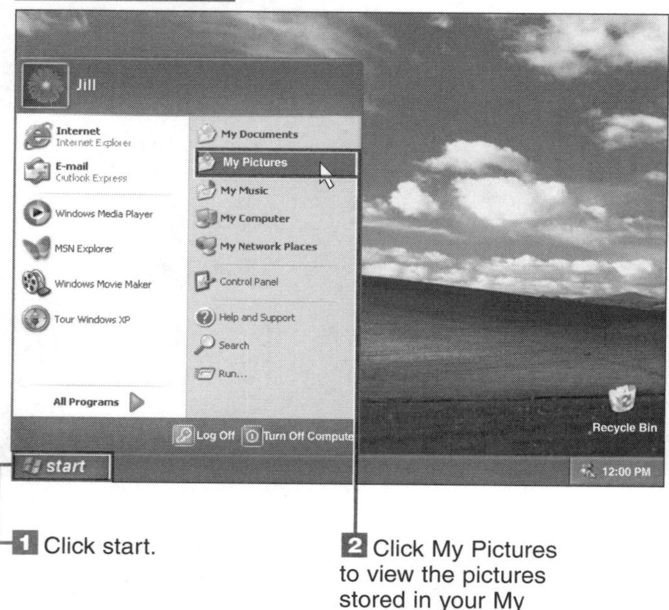

1 Click start.

2 Click My Pictures to view the pictures stored in your My Pictures folder.

■ The contents of the My Pictures folder appear.

3 Click Print pictures to print the pictures in the folder.

Note: To print the pictures in a subfolder within the My Pictures folder, click the subfolder before performing step 3.

What type of paper should I use to get the best results when printing pictures?

✔ If your printer allows, you should use high-quality, glossy paper that is specifically designed for printing pictures. This type of paper will produce the best results when printing pictures.

How should I set my printer's resolution to achieve the best results?

✔ You should make sure your printer is set to print at a resolution that is the same or higher than the resolution of the picture you are printing. A higher resolution will usually result in higher-quality pictures, but the pictures may take longer to print.

Can I use the Photo Printing Wizard to print pictures that are not stored in the My Pictures folder?

✔ Yes. When you print a picture stored in another location on your computer, the Photo Printing Wizard will automatically appear to help you print the picture. You can print a picture stored in another location on your computer as you would print any file. For information about printing a file, see page 114.

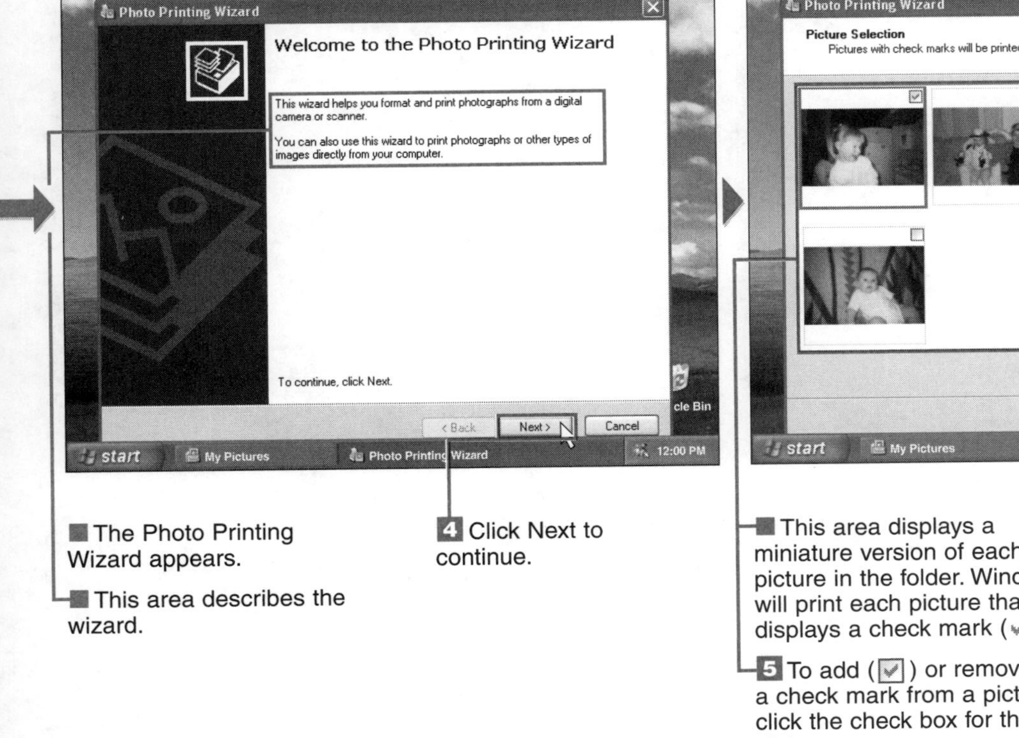

■ The Photo Printing Wizard appears.

■ This area describes the wizard.

4 Click Next to continue.

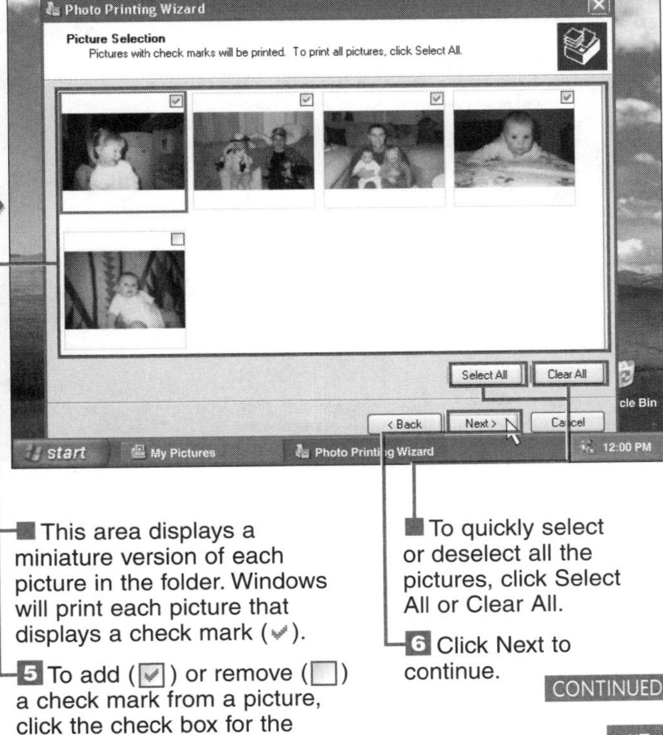

■ This area displays a miniature version of each picture in the folder. Windows will print each picture that displays a check mark (✔).

5 To add (☑) or remove (☐) a check mark from a picture, click the check box for the picture.

■ To quickly select or deselect all the pictures, click Select All or Clear All.

6 Click Next to continue.

CONTINUED

PRINT PICTURES (CONTINUED)

Once you have selected the pictures you want to print, the Photo Printing Wizard asks you to choose the printer you want to use.

You can change the settings for your printer before printing pictures. For example, you can specify the type of paper you are using and where the paper is located in the printer. The settings you can change depend on the printer you are using.

Before printing pictures, you should ensure that the printer has an adequate supply of ink or toner, since printing pictures will consume more of these materials than printing text.

The Photo Printing Wizard allows you to select the layout you want to use for your printed pictures. There are several layouts you can choose from to specify the size you want the pictures to print. For example, you can choose a layout that prints pictures in the 8x10, 5x7 or 4x6 size. There are also layouts that allow you to print wallet size pictures or pictures that are the size of a full sheet of printed paper. Some layouts may crop part of a large picture so the picture will fit better on a page.

PRINT PICTURES (CONTINUED)

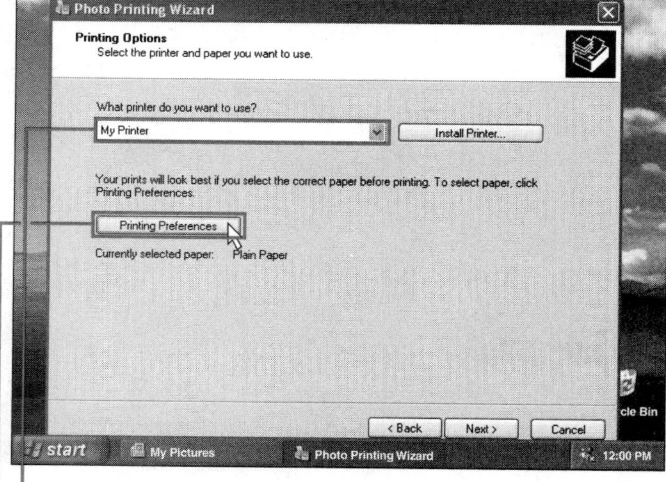

■ This area displays the printer you will use to print the pictures. You can click this area to select a different printer.

7 Click Printing Preferences to select the paper you want to use to print the pictures.

■ A Properties dialog box for the printer appears.

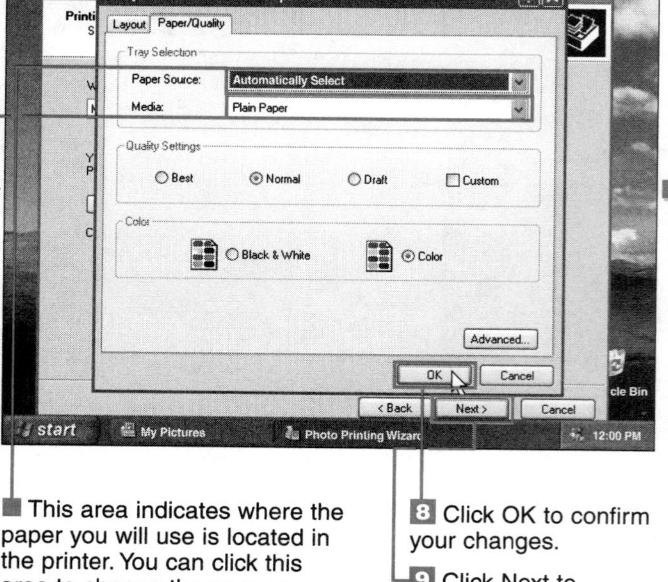

■ This area indicates where the paper you will use is located in the printer. You can click this area to change the paper source.

■ This area displays the type of paper you will use to print your pictures. You can click this area to change the type of paper.

Note: The available settings depend on your printer.

8 Click OK to confirm your changes.

9 Click Next to continue.

How can I print more than one version of each picture?

✔ After selecting the layout you want to use for your pictures in step 10 below, double-click the Number of times to use each picture area and then type the number of times you want to print each picture.

How can I improve the appearance of a picture that appears unclear when printed?

✔ Try choosing a layout that prints a smaller version of the picture. Printing a smaller version can help reduce distortion in an unclear picture.

What other tasks can I perform with my pictures?

✔ The My Pictures folder offers several options you can select to perform tasks with your pictures. The View as a slide show option lets you view a full-screen slide show of each picture in the My Pictures folder. You can use the Order prints online option to order prints of your pictures from a Web site. The Set as desktop background option allows you to use a picture as your desktop background. For information about changing the desktop background, see page 196.

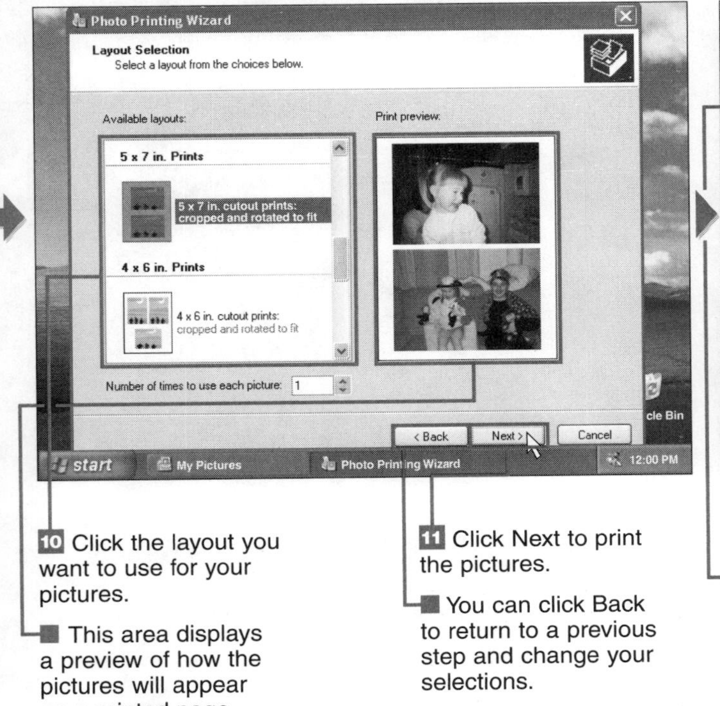

10 Click the layout you want to use for your pictures.

■ This area displays a preview of how the pictures will appear on a printed page.

11 Click Next to print the pictures.

■ You can click Back to return to a previous step and change your selections.

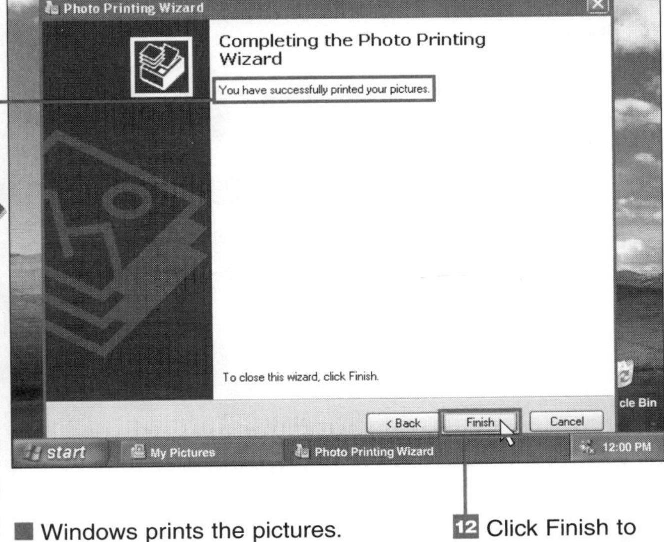

■ Windows prints the pictures.

■ This area indicates that you have successfully completed the Photo Printing Wizard.

12 Click Finish to close the wizard.

VIEW FILES WAITING TO PRINT

You can view information about the files you have sent to a printer.

You can display a print queue window for each printer available for you to use. A print queue window displays information about the current status of the printer and the files waiting to print. The title bar for a print queue window displays the name of the printer.

Each file that is printing or waiting to print is listed in the print queue window. The columns in the window list information about each print job, including the name and status of the file and the name of the person who is printing the file. You can also view the number of pages, the size of the file, the time and date each file was sent to the printer and the port to which the printer is connected.

While a file is printing, a printer icon appears on the taskbar. You can use this icon to quickly view the files waiting to print. The icon disappears when the file has finished printing.

VIEW FILES WAITING TO PRINT

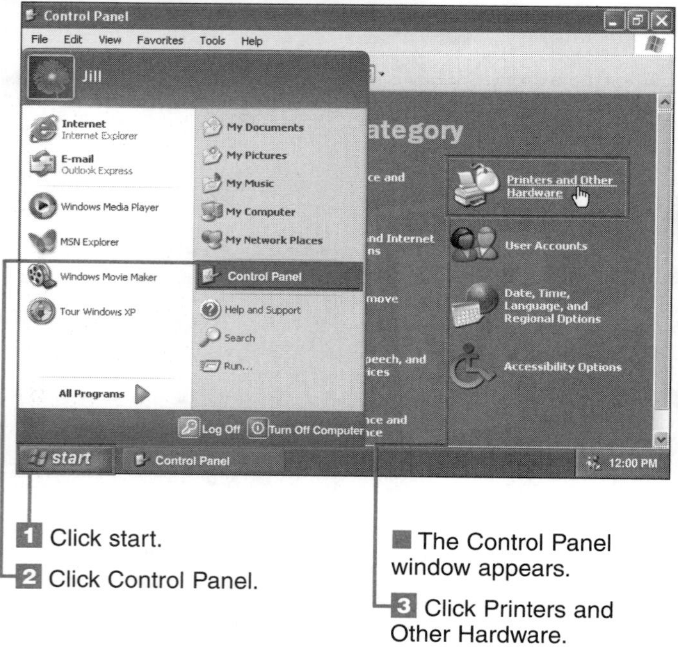

1 Click start.

2 Click Control Panel.

■ The Control Panel window appears.

3 Click Printers and Other Hardware.

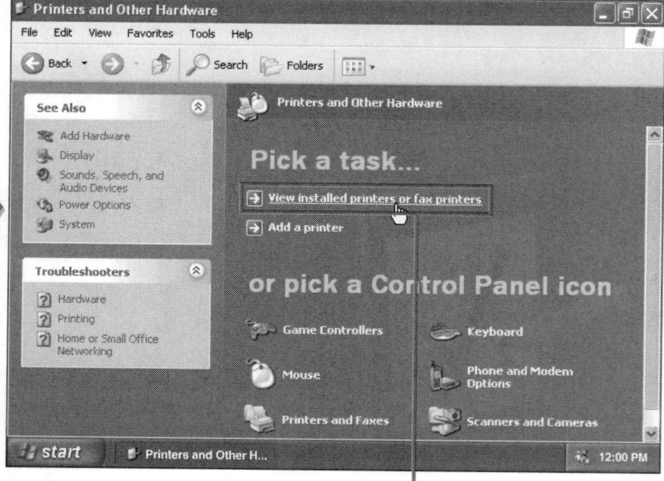

■ The Printers and Other Hardware window appears.

4 Click View installed printers or fax printers.

How can I change the order in which files will print?

✔ You may be able to change the print order by changing the priority of a file. In the print queue window, right-click the file you want to change the print order of and click Properties on the menu that appears. Then drag the priority slider ( ) right or left to increase or decrease the priority of the file. The file will print according to the new priority, but the print queue window may not reflect the changes. The file that is currently being printed will not be affected.

What happens when I close the print queue window?

✔ Closing the print queue window does not affect the files waiting to print. The printer icon ( ) remains on the taskbar until the files are finished printing.

How can I view information about all available printers at once?

✔ In the Printers and Faxes window, choose the View menu and then select Details. Windows displays information about the number of files waiting to print and the printer status for each printer. Viewing information about all the printers at once can help you decide which printer you should use to print files.

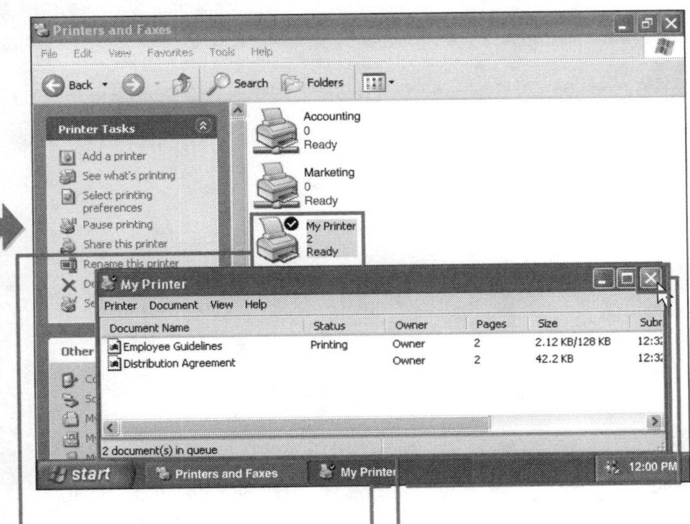

■ The Printers and Faxes window appears, displaying each printer you can use.

5 To view the files waiting to print on a printer, double-click the printer.

■ A print queue window appears, displaying information about each file waiting to print. The file at the top of the list will print first.

6 When you finish viewing the information, click ✕ to close the window.

QUICKLY VIEW FILES WAITING TO PRINT

■ When you print files, the printer icon ( ) appears in this area. The printer icon disappears when the files have finished printing.

1 To see how many files are waiting to print, position the mouse over the printer icon ( ).

■ A yellow box appears, displaying the number of files.

2 To view information about the files, double-click the printer icon ( ).

PAUSE PRINTING

You can pause the printer connected to your computer to temporarily stop all print jobs. Pausing the printer is useful when you want to change the toner or add more paper to the printer.

When you pause printing, the document that is currently printing will finish before the printer pauses. The other documents waiting to print will remain in the print queue. The order of the documents in the print queue is not affected when printing is paused.

If you have shared your printer with other users, pausing the printer will stop the documents you are printing and the documents that other users have sent to the printer. You cannot usually pause a printer connected to another computer on a network.

When you pause a printer, the word "Paused" appears at the top of the window for the printer and beside the printer's icon in the Printers and Faxes window. This allows you to easily see when a printer has been paused. When you no longer want to pause a printer, you can resume printing to print the rest of the documents in the print queue.

PAUSE PRINTING

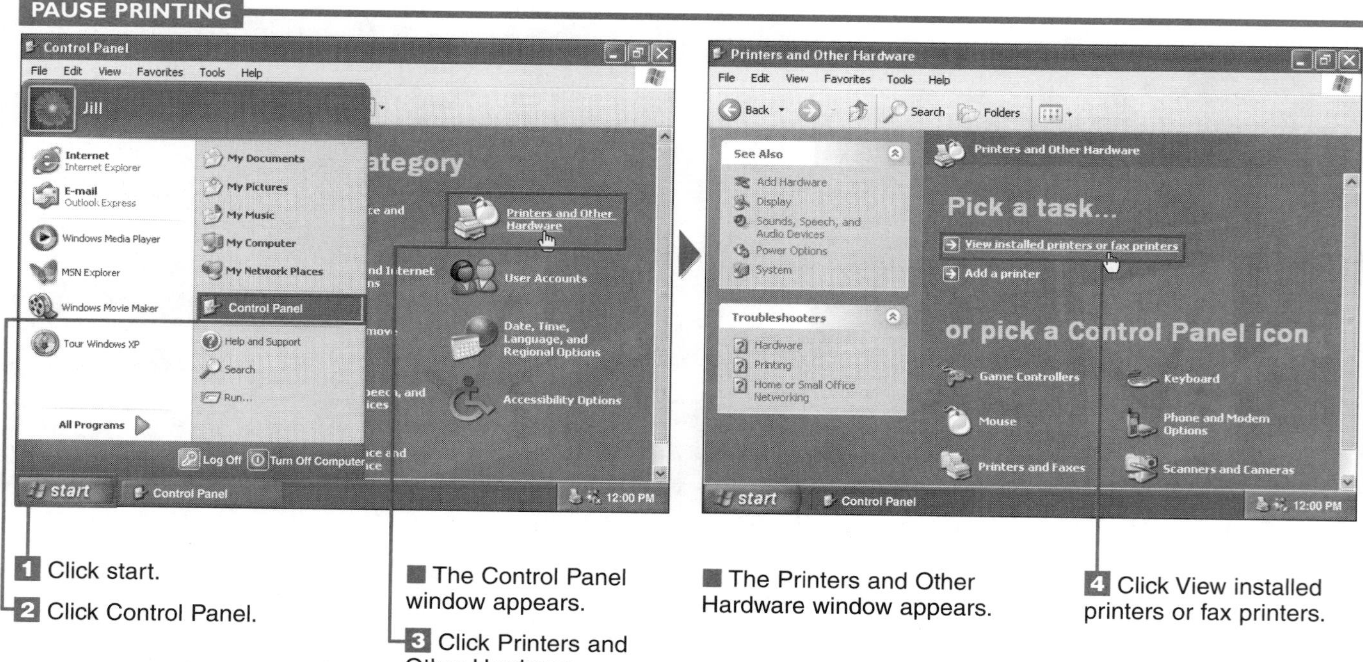

1 Click start.

2 Click Control Panel.

■ The Control Panel window appears.

3 Click Printers and Other Hardware.

■ The Printers and Other Hardware window appears.

4 Click View installed printers or fax printers.

Is there another way to pause a printer?

✔ In the Printers and Faxes window, you can click the printer you want to pause and then click Pause printing to quickly pause the printer. When you are ready to continue printing, click the printer and then click Resume printing.

Can I pause the printing of a single document?

✔ Yes. Pausing a specific document is useful when you want to allow more important documents to print first. Perform steps 1 to 5 below and then click the document you want to pause. Click the Document menu and then choose Pause. To resume printing the document, click the document, select the Document menu and then choose Resume.

How can I quickly display the list of documents waiting to print on a printer?

✔ When you print documents, a printer icon (🖨) appears on the taskbar. You can double-click the printer icon to quickly open a window displaying information about each document waiting to print.

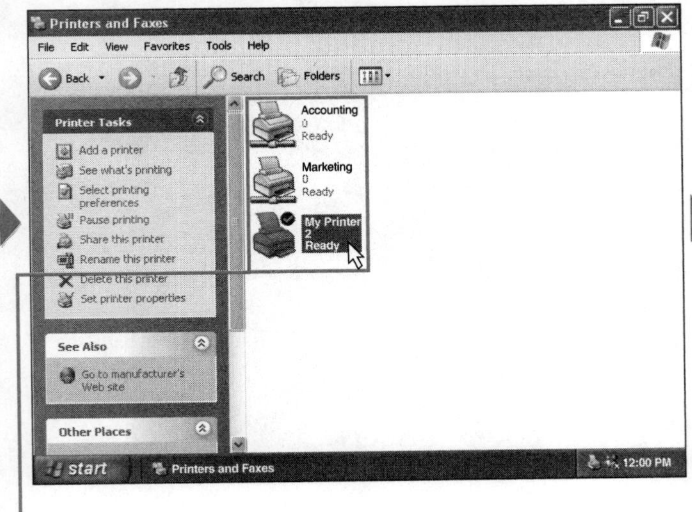

■ The Printers and Faxes window appears, displaying an icon for each printer you can use.

5 Double-click the printer you want to pause.

■ A window appears, displaying information about each document waiting to print.

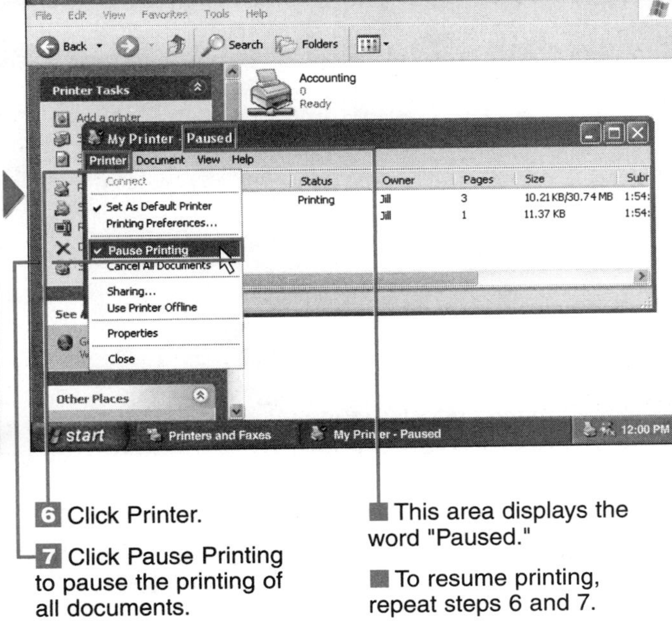

6 Click Printer.

7 Click Pause Printing to pause the printing of all documents.

■ This area displays the word "Paused."

■ To resume printing, repeat steps 6 and 7.

CANCEL PRINTING

You can stop a document from printing if you have made a mistake and need to make a correction. You may also want to cancel the printing of a document if the wrong file was sent to the printer or if a document is taking too long to print. When you cancel the printing of a document, the file disappears from the list of files waiting to print.

You can cancel the printing of documents you have sent to your own printer or to a network printer. If you have shared your printer with other users, you can also cancel the printing of documents that others have sent to your printer. You cannot cancel the printing of documents that other users have sent to a network printer.

When you cancel the printing of a document, Windows displays a warning message. Do not cancel any print jobs unless you are sure you do not want to print the documents. You may want to pause the printer first, before deciding if you want to cancel the printing of a document. For information about pausing a printer, see page 122.

CANCEL PRINTING

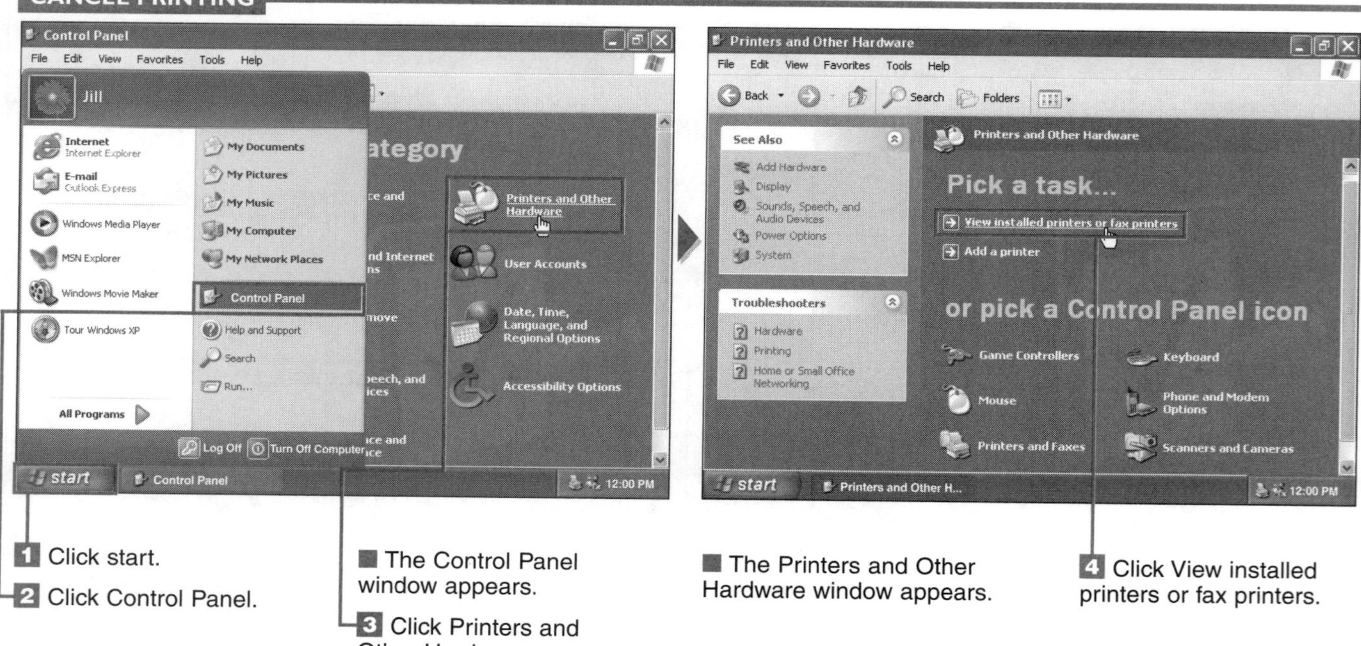

1 Click start.

2 Click Control Panel.

■ The Control Panel window appears.

3 Click Printers and Other Hardware.

■ The Printers and Other Hardware window appears.

4 Click View installed printers or fax printers.

Can I cancel a document while it is printing?

✔ Yes. You can cancel the printing of a document even if the document has already started printing, but this may cause problems with the next document waiting to print. If you are using an older printer, the printer may have to be reset.

How can I cancel the printing of all documents?

✔ Right-click the icon for the printer in the Printers and Faxes window and select Cancel All Documents from the menu that appears. The printer may finish printing the current document before all the other documents waiting to print are cancelled.

How can I get quick access to the list of files waiting to print?

✔ You can create a shortcut icon to the printer on your desktop. Using the right mouse button, drag the icon for the printer from the Printers and Faxes window to your desktop. Select Create Shortcuts Here from the menu that appears. You can now double-click the shortcut icon to quickly access the list of files waiting to print at any time. You can also double-click the printer icon ( ) that appears in the taskbar to view the list of files waiting to print.

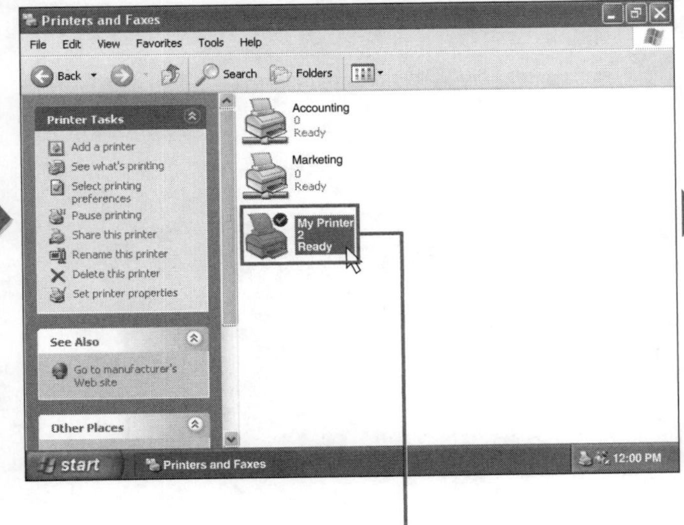

■ The Printers and Faxes window appears, displaying an icon for each printer you can use.

5 Double-click the printer you are using.

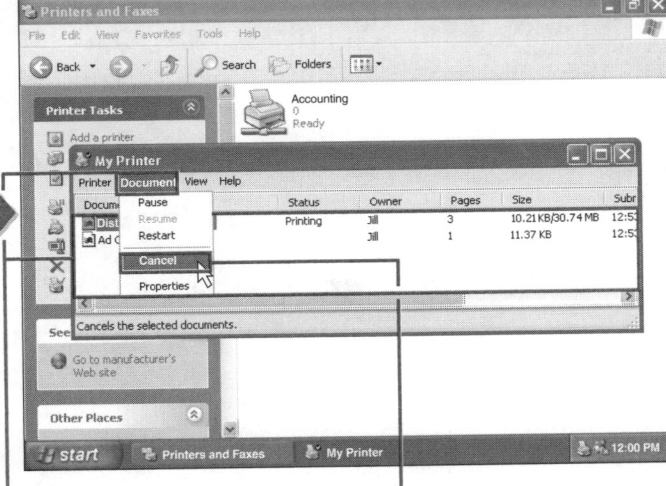

■ A window appears, displaying information about each document waiting to print.

6 Click the document you no longer want to print.

7 Click Document.

8 Click Cancel.

Note: You can also press the Delete key instead of performing steps 7 and 8.

■ A confirmation dialog box will appear. Click Yes to cancel the printing of the document.

CHANGE THE DEFAULT PRINTER

If you have access to more than one printer, you can select which printer you want to automatically print your documents. The printer you select is referred to as the default printer.

When selecting a default printer, you should select the printer that you use most often and that offers the capabilities you need.

Windows will automatically use the default printer to print your files unless you specify that you want to use a different printer. You may occasionally want to print a document on another printer, such as when your default printer is not working properly or when you need to use a printer that offers different capabilities. When you print a document, most programs will display a Print dialog box that allows you to select the printer you want to use.

In some situations, a Print dialog box will not be available and your document will be sent directly to the default printer. For example, a Print dialog box is not available when you right-click a file and select the Print command. In such cases, changing the default printer is the only way to choose a different printer.

CHANGE THE DEFAULT PRINTER

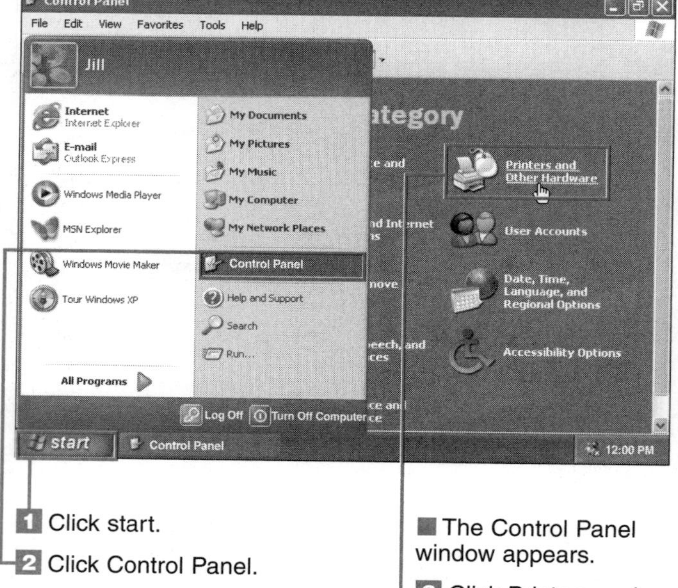

1 Click start.

2 Click Control Panel.

■ The Control Panel window appears.

3 Click Printers and Other Hardware.

■ The Printers and Other Hardware window appears.

4 Click View installed printers or fax printers.

Are there any other ways to change the default printer?

✔ Yes. In the Printers and Faxes window, you can right-click a printer you want to make the default printer and then select Set as Default Printer from the menu that appears. You can also set a new printer as the default printer while installing the printer. For information about installing a printer, see page 130.

What happens if I delete the default printer?

✔ When you delete the default printer, Windows will display a warning message. If you have other printers available on your computer, Windows will automatically make one of these printers the new default printer. If you do not have another printer available on your computer, Windows will indicate this in the warning message.

My documents stopped printing correctly after I changed the default printer. What is wrong?

✔ The program you are using to print your documents may offer settings that can be customized for the default printer. For example, you may be able to specify a paper size or type for the printer. After changing the default printer, you may need to adjust the program's printer settings for the new default printer. Consult the program's documentation for more information.

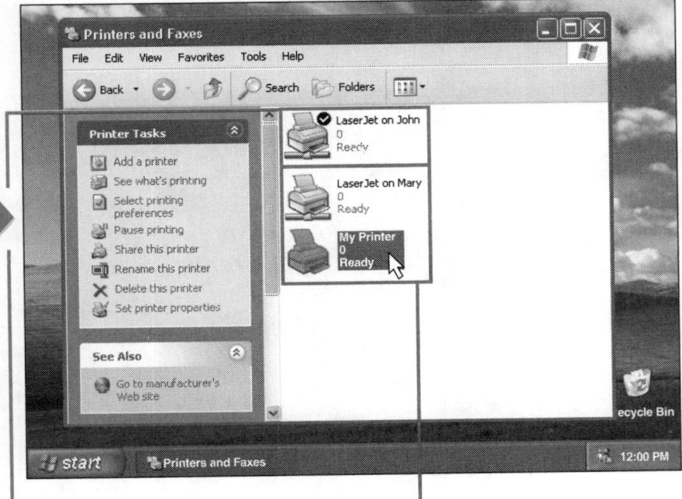

■ The Printers and Faxes window appears, displaying an icon for each printer you can use.

■ The default printer displays a check mark (✔) in its icon.

5 Click the printer you want to set as your new default printer.

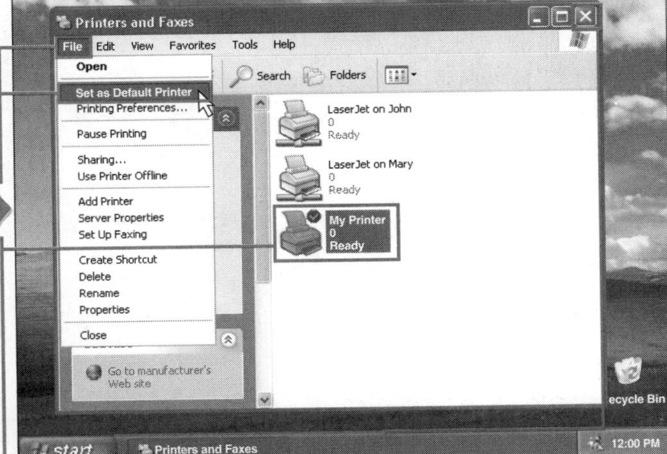

6 Click File.

7 Click Set as Default Printer.

■ The new default printer displays a check mark (✔) in its icon.

■ Your documents will now automatically print to the new default printer.

8 Click ✕ to close the Printers and Faxes window.

RENAME OR DELETE A PRINTER

You can change the name of a printer to help you better identify the printer. This is useful when you have access to more than one printer.

The Printers and Faxes window displays an icon for each printer available on your computer. The name of each printer appears beside its icon in the window.

Printer names can include letters, numbers, spaces and some special characters. A printer name cannot contain the \ ! or , characters.

When you rename a printer, the new name will appear in the Print dialog boxes in all your programs. This helps you select the printer when printing a document. You should use a descriptive name, such as "Kim's color printer in room 204", to make it easy to identify the printer.

Renaming a printer does not affect any documents currently waiting to print.

If you no longer use a printer, you should delete the printer from your computer. Deleting a printer removes the software that runs the printer from your computer. The icon for the printer will disappear from the Printers and Faxes window and Windows will no longer display the printer in the Print dialog boxes of your programs.

RENAME OR DELETE A PRINTER

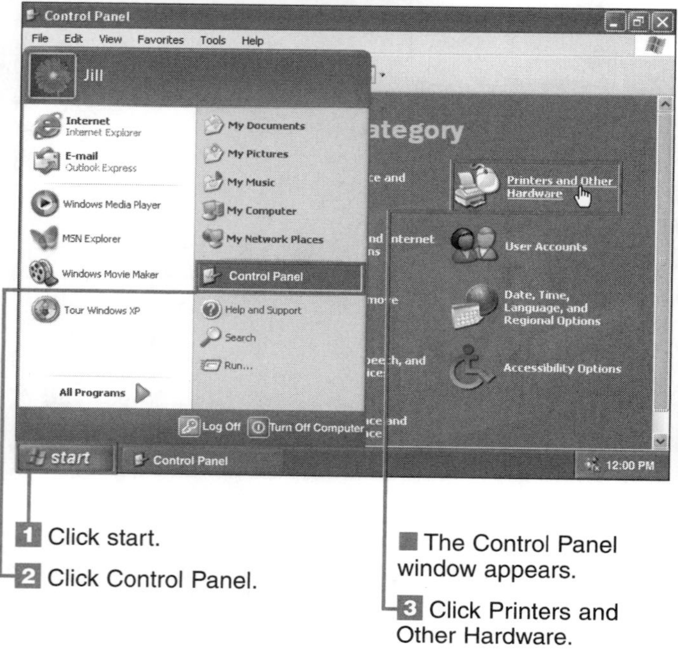

1 Click start.

2 Click Control Panel.

■ The Control Panel window appears.

3 Click Printers and Other Hardware.

■ The Printers and Other Hardware window appears.

4 Click View installed printers or fax printers.

■ The Printers and Faxes window appears, displaying an icon for each printer you can use.

Why is the Rename this printer command not available?

✔ The Rename this printer command is not available for printers you cannot rename. For example, you may not be able to rename some printers on your network. The ability to rename a network printer depends on the setup of your network and the access permissions for the printer.

I cannot delete a printer from my computer. What is wrong?

✔ You cannot delete a printer from your computer while there are documents waiting to print on the printer. You must wait for all the print jobs in the print queue to finish printing before you can delete the printer.

Why did a warning message appear when I deleted a printer?

✔ Windows displays a warning message when you delete your default printer. The default printer is the printer that automatically prints your documents. If you have another printer available on your computer, Windows will make this printer the new default printer. If you do not have another printer available on your computer, Windows will indicate this in the warning message. For information about setting the default printer, see page 126.

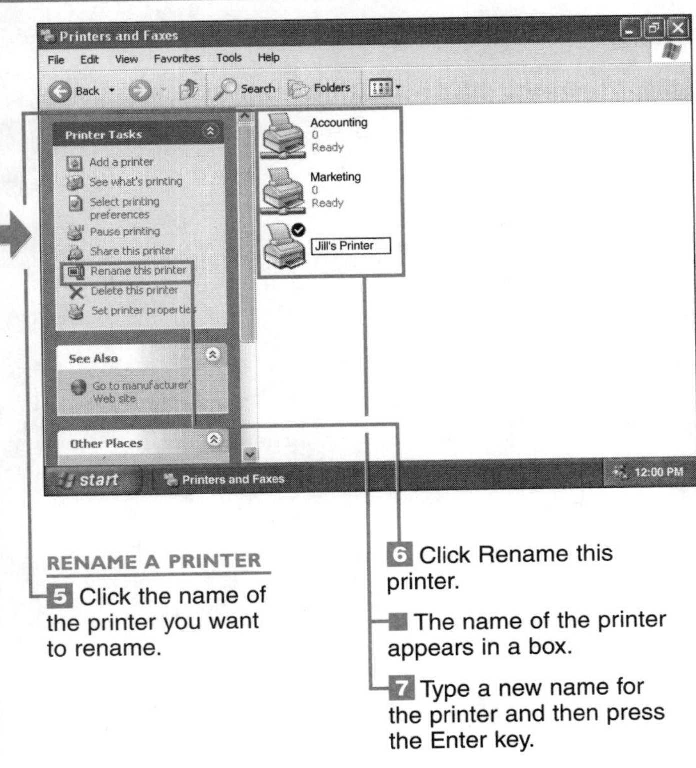

RENAME A PRINTER

5 Click the name of the printer you want to rename.

6 Click Rename this printer.

■ The name of the printer appears in a box.

7 Type a new name for the printer and then press the Enter key.

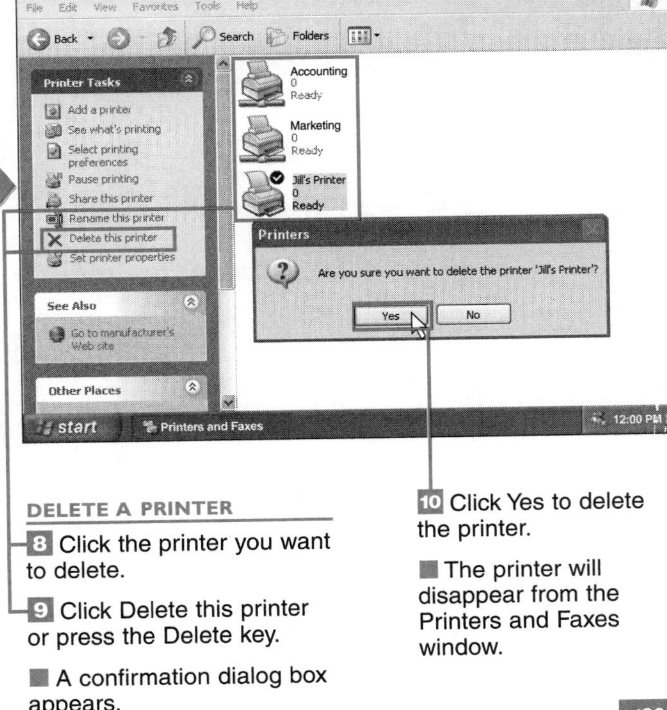

DELETE A PRINTER

8 Click the printer you want to delete.

9 Click Delete this printer or press the Delete key.

■ A confirmation dialog box appears.

10 Click Yes to delete the printer.

■ The printer will disappear from the Printers and Faxes window.

INSTALL A PRINTER

Before you can use a printer attached to your computer, you need to install the printer on your computer. A printer connected directly to your computer is called a local printer.

Installing a printer allows you to install the printer driver that Windows needs to work with the printer. A printer driver is special software that enables Windows to communicate with a printer.

Before installing a printer, make sure you connect the printer to your computer and turn on the printer.

Windows provides the Add Printer Wizard, which guides you step by step through the process of installing a printer. The Add Printer Wizard helps ensure that your new printer is installed correctly and works properly. The wizard asks a series of questions and then sets up the printer according to the information you provide.

You must be logged on as a computer administrator to install a printer. You need to install a printer only once.

INSTALL A PRINTER

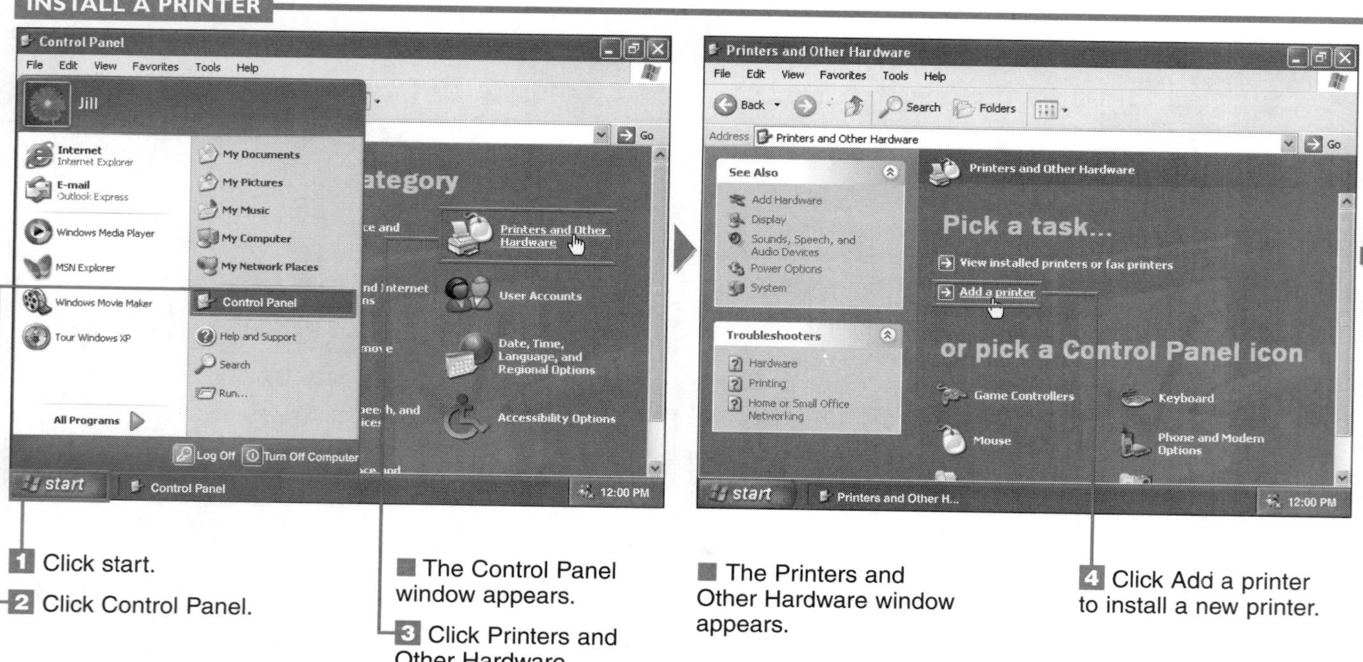

1 Click start.

2 Click Control Panel.

■ The Control Panel window appears.

3 Click Printers and Other Hardware.

■ The Printers and Other Hardware window appears.

4 Click Add a printer to install a new printer.

How do I install a Plug and Play printer?

✔ A Plug and Play printer is a printer that Windows can automatically detect and install. The first time you connect a Plug and Play printer to your computer and turn on the printer, Windows will usually install the printer without requiring you to make any selections. In some cases, the Found New Hardware Wizard appears, displaying instructions you can follow to install the printer. If Windows does not automatically detect your Plug and Play printer, you can perform the steps below to try installing the printer using the Add Printer Wizard.

How do I connect to a shared printer on my network?

✔ Windows can automatically detect and connect to printers on your network. To display the printers you are connected to, click start, select Control Panel and choose Printers and Other Hardware. Then click View installed printers or fax printers. If the network printer you want to use is not displayed in the Printers and Faxes window, perform steps 1 to 6 below, except select the A network printer, or a printer attached to another computer option in step 6. Then click Next and follow the instructions in the wizard to connect to the network printer.

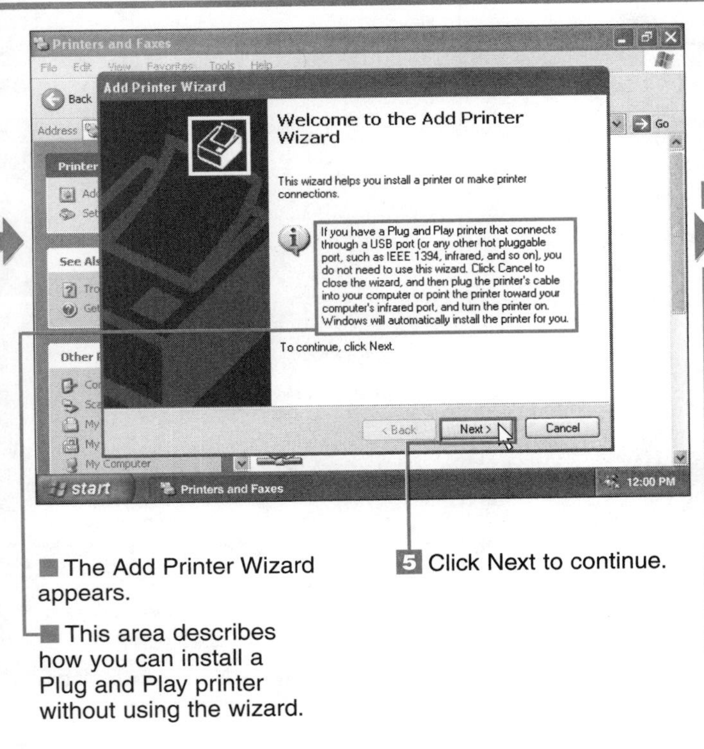

■ The Add Printer Wizard appears.

■ This area describes how you can install a Plug and Play printer without using the wizard.

5 Click Next to continue.

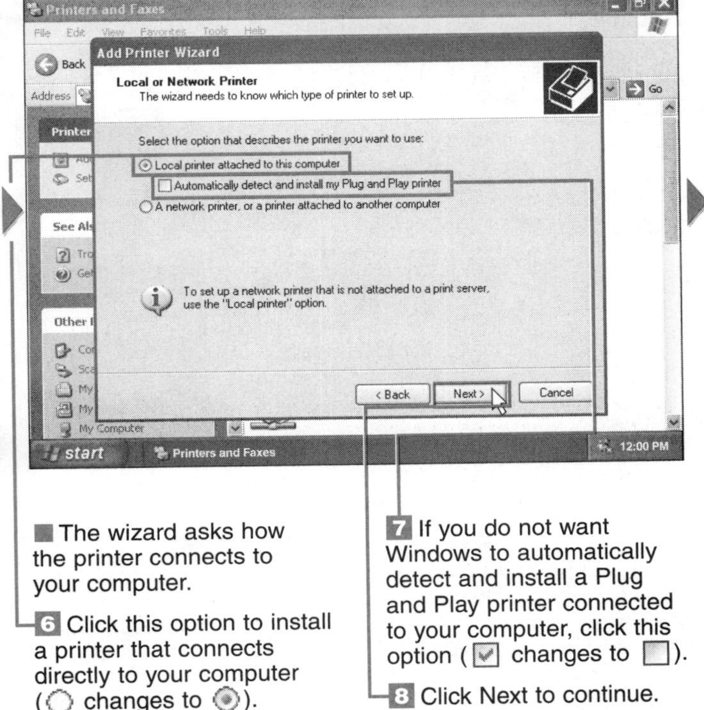

■ The wizard asks how the printer connects to your computer.

6 Click this option to install a printer that connects directly to your computer (○ changes to ◉).

7 If you do not want Windows to automatically detect and install a Plug and Play printer connected to your computer, click this option (☑ changes to ☐).

8 Click Next to continue.

CONTINUED

INSTALL A PRINTER (CONTINUED)

When installing a printer, you need to specify which port you want the printer to use. A port is a socket where you plug a device into a computer. Ports are usually located at the back of a computer and allow a computer to communicate with the connected devices. In most cases, printers are attached to a computer's parallel port, called LPT1.

You must specify the manufacturer and model of the printer you are installing. Windows supports hundreds of printer models from over 70 manufacturers, including Hewlett-Packard, Epson and Canon.

The wizard allows you to name your printer to help identify the printer. The printer name you choose should not be longer than 31 characters, since some programs do not support longer printer names.

If you have more than one printer installed on your computer, you can specify whether you want the printer to be your default printer. Windows automatically sends files you print to the default printer. If you have only one printer installed on your computer, it is automatically set as the default printer.

INSTALL A PRINTER (CONTINUED)

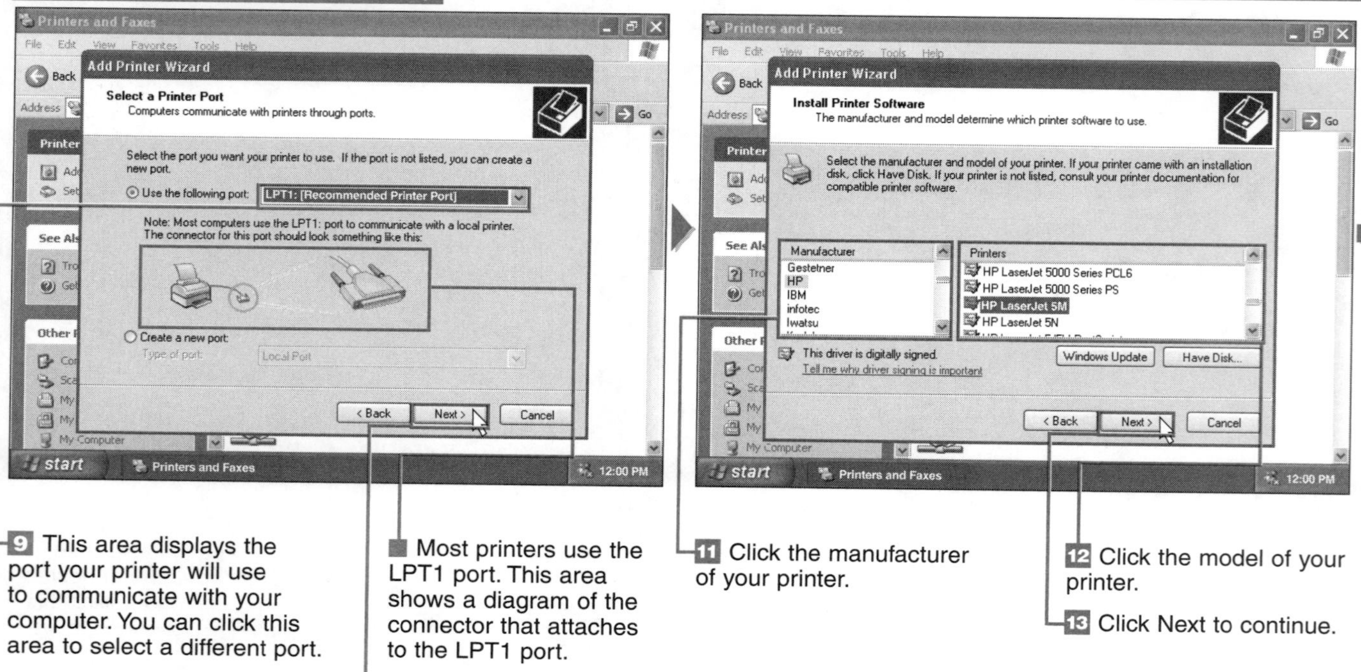

9 This area displays the port your printer will use to communicate with your computer. You can click this area to select a different port.

■ Most printers use the LPT1 port. This area shows a diagram of the connector that attaches to the LPT1 port.

10 Click Next to continue.

11 Click the manufacturer of your printer.

12 Click the model of your printer.

13 Click Next to continue.

The printer I want to install does not appear in the list. What should I do?

✔ You can use the installation disk that came with the printer to install the printer. Insert the installation disk into a drive. Click the Have Disk button in the Add Printer Wizard, select the drive that contains the disk and then press the Enter key.

I do not have an installation disk and my printer does not appear in the list. What should I do?

✔ You can select a printer that closely resembles your printer. For example, select a similar model made by the same manufacturer or select the Generic printer. Keep in mind that choosing one of these options may limit the features available for your printer.

Do I need to use the installation disk that came with my printer if my printer appears in the list?

✔ If you purchased a printer after the release of Windows XP, the installation disk may contain a more up-to-date printer driver than the driver included with Windows XP. Insert the installation disk into a drive. Click the Have Disk button in the Add Printer Wizard, select the drive that contains the disk and then press the Enter key.

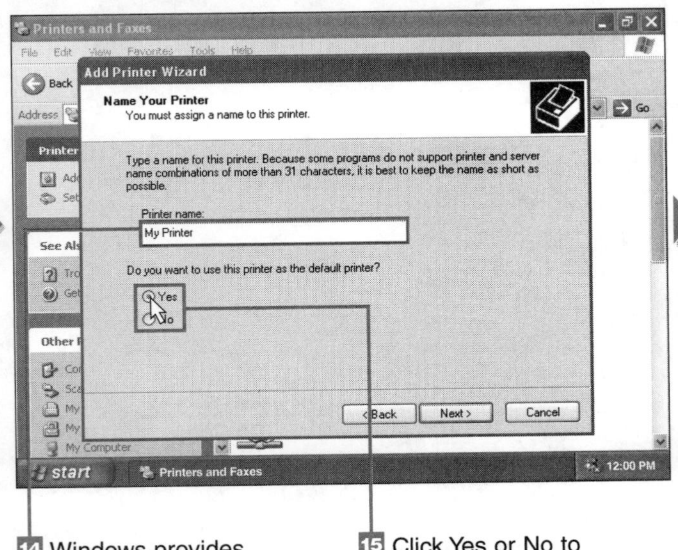

14 Windows provides a name for your printer. To use a different name, type a new name.

15 Click Yes or No to specify if you want to use the printer as your default printer (◯ changes to ◉). Files will automatically print to the default printer.

Note: If you are installing your first printer, you will not need to perform step 15.

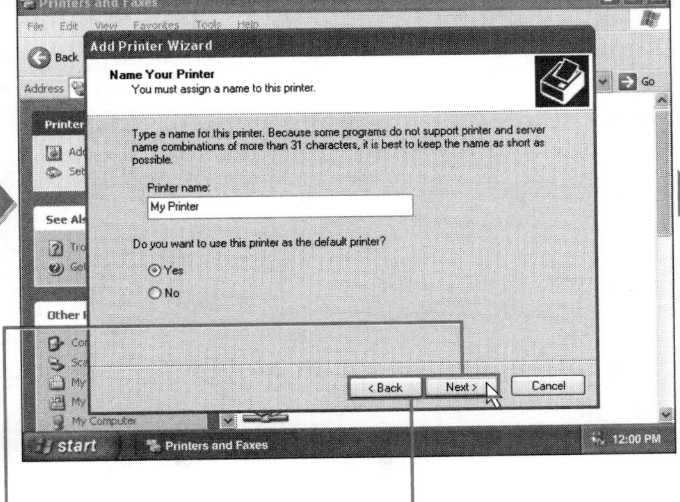

16 Click Next to continue.

■ You can click Back at any time to return to a previous step and change your selections.

CONTINUED

INSTALL A PRINTER (CONTINUED)

If your computer is set up on a network, you can share your printer with other people on the network. Sharing a printer allows other people to use your printer to print documents. This can help individuals and companies save money, since several people on a network can use the same printer.

If you choose to share your printer on your network, you can provide a share name for the printer. Assigning a descriptive share name to a printer can help other people using the printer easily identify the printer. When giving a printer a share name, keep in mind that some computers may not be able to access printers that have names with spaces or names longer than 12 characters.

The Add Printer Wizard also allows you to specify a location and comment for a printer you are sharing on a network. You can use a comment to describe the capabilities of your printer, such as "Color Printer."

Windows allows you to print a test page to confirm that your printer is working properly. The test page contains information about the printer. You may want to keep the page for future reference.

INSTALL A PRINTER (CONTINUED)

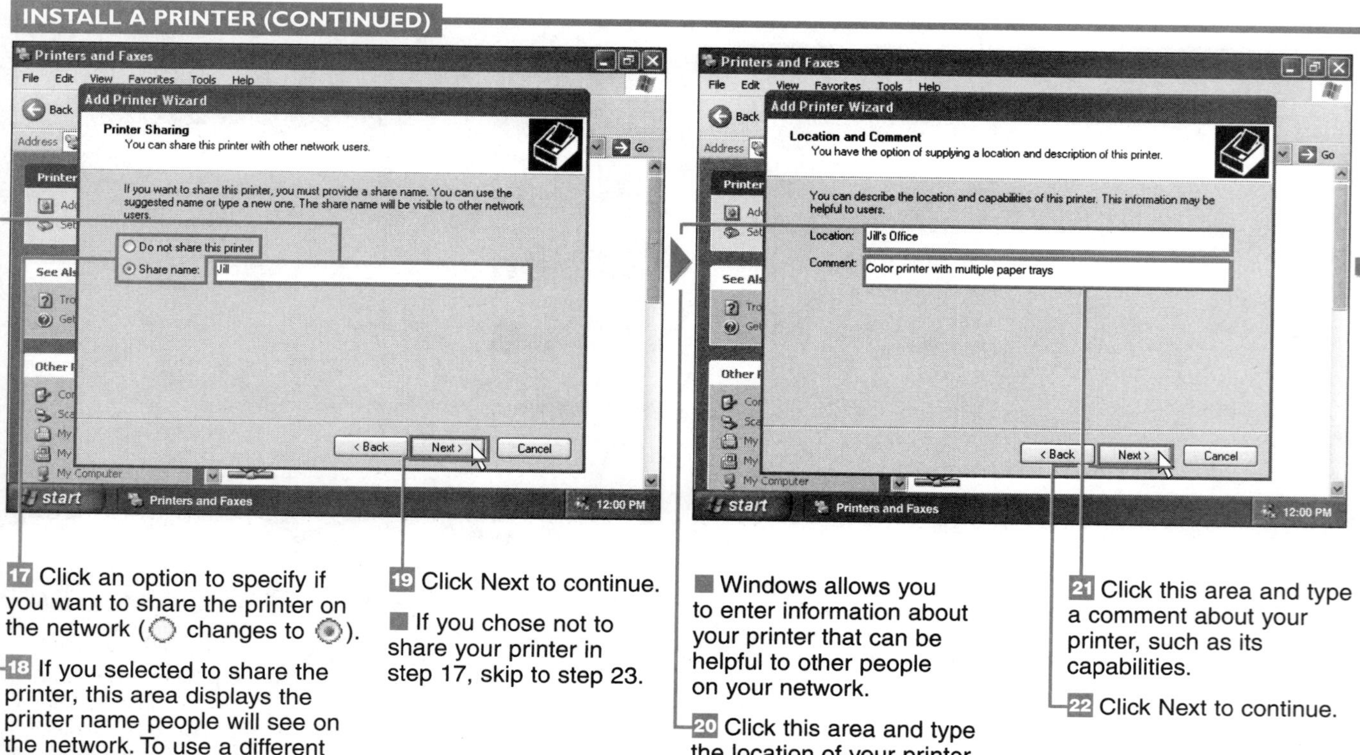

17 Click an option to specify if you want to share the printer on the network (○ changes to ◉).

18 If you selected to share the printer, this area displays the printer name people will see on the network. To use a different printer name, type a new name.

19 Click Next to continue.

■ If you chose not to share your printer in step 17, skip to step 23.

■ Windows allows you to enter information about your printer that can be helpful to other people on your network.

20 Click this area and type the location of your printer.

21 Click this area and type a comment about your printer, such as its capabilities.

22 Click Next to continue.

How can I view the printer I installed on my computer?

✔ The Printers and Faxes window displays an icon for each printer available on your computer. To open the Printers and Faxes window, click start, select Control Panel, choose Printers and Other Hardware and then click View installed printers or fax printers. If you chose to share your printer on your network, a hand ( ) appears in the printer's icon. If you chose to make the printer the default printer, the printer's icon displays a check mark ( ).

How can I later print another test page?

✔ You can print another test page at any time. Click start, select Control Panel, choose Printers and Other Hardware and then click View installed printers or fax printers. Right-click the printer you want to print a test page for and then click Properties. In the dialog box that appears, click the Print Test Page button.

I am having printer problems. Where can I get help?

✔ Windows includes a Printing Troubleshooter that can help you with many common printer problems. To start the Printing Troubleshooter, click start and select Help and Support. Click Printing and faxing and select Fixing a printer problem. Click Printing Troubleshooter and then follow the instructions that appear on your screen.

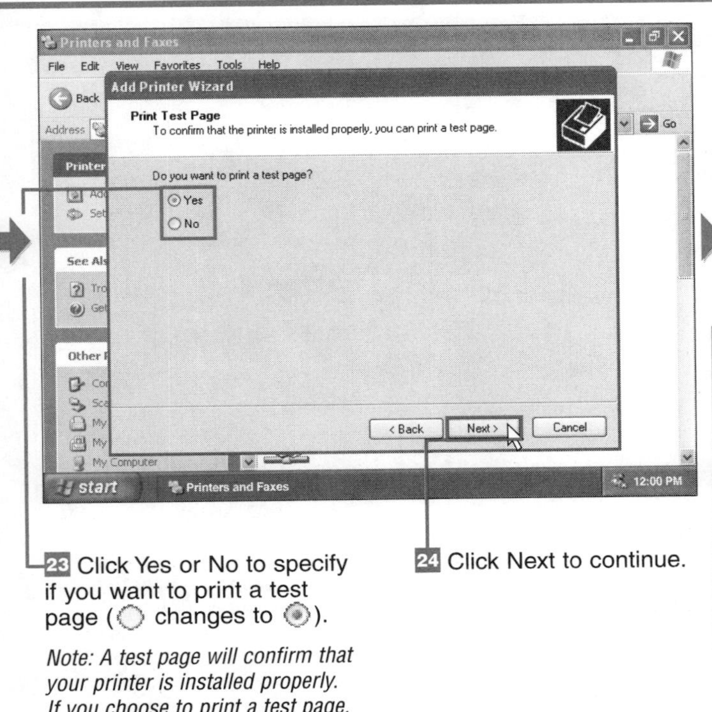

23 Click Yes or No to specify if you want to print a test page (◯ changes to ◉).

Note: A test page will confirm that your printer is installed properly. If you choose to print a test page, make sure your printer is turned on and contains paper.

24 Click Next to continue.

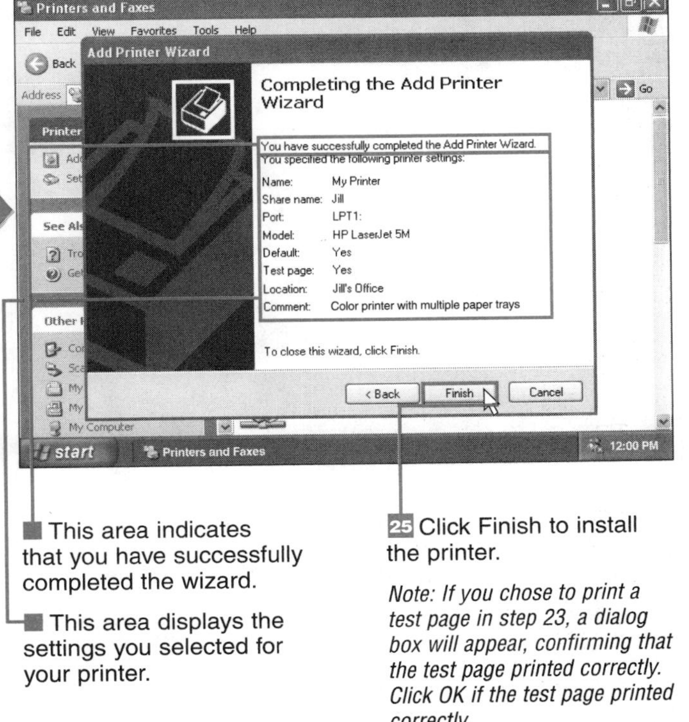

■ This area indicates that you have successfully completed the wizard.

■ This area displays the settings you selected for your printer.

25 Click Finish to install the printer.

Note: If you chose to print a test page in step 23, a dialog box will appear, confirming that the test page printed correctly. Click OK if the test page printed correctly.

CHANGE PRINTER PROPERTIES

You can change the properties of your printer to suit your needs. The properties you can change depend on the printer. You must be logged on as a computer administrator to change printer properties.

You can change the name of a printer to a more descriptive name that will help you easily identify the printer. You can also specify the location of a printer, such as "Sales Department" and add a comment about the printer, such as a phrase describing the printer's purpose. Specifying a location and comment for a printer is useful when the printer is shared with other people on a network. For information about sharing a printer, see page 412.

You can view the model of the printer. You can also view features of the printer, such as the color capabilities, speed and maximum resolution. The speed indicates the maximum number of pages per minute (ppm) the printer can print. Color documents and documents that contain pictures may print slower than the maximum speed. The maximum resolution indicates the maximum number of dots per inch (dpi) the printer can print on a page. A high resolution, such as 600 dpi or higher, produces better quality pictures but documents will take longer to print.

CHANGE PRINTER PROPERTIES

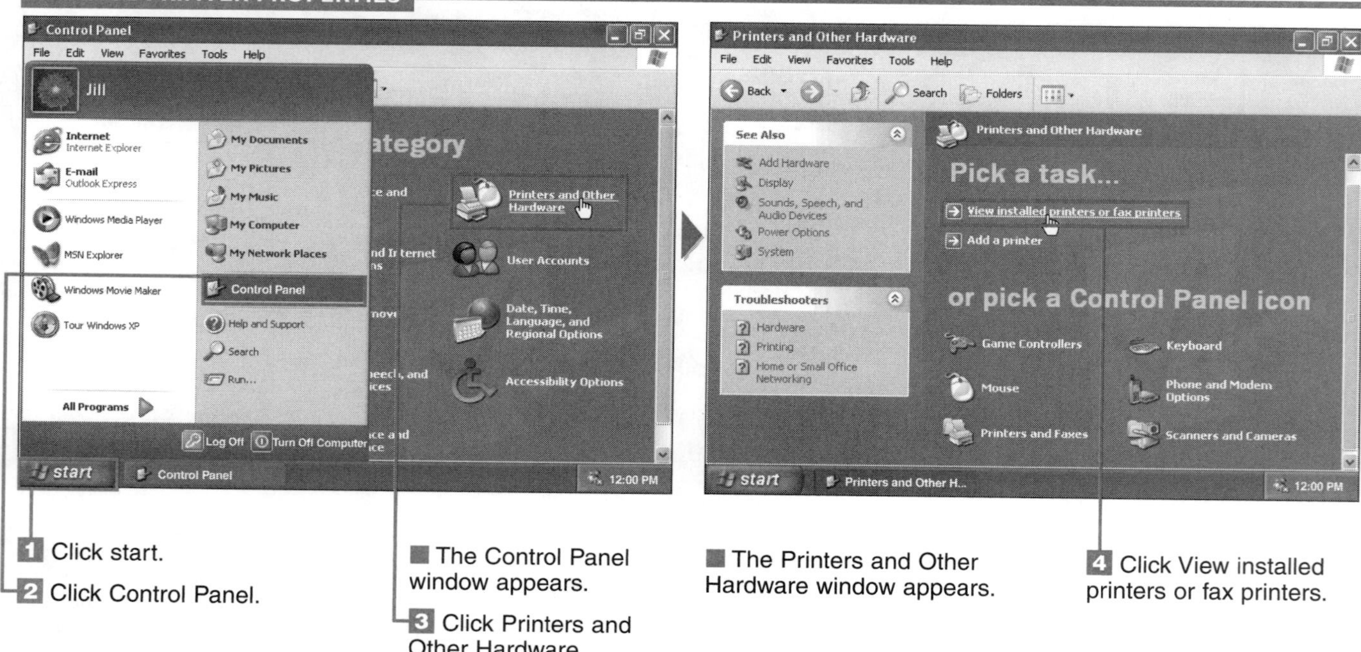

1 Click start.

2 Click Control Panel.

■ The Control Panel window appears.

3 Click Printers and Other Hardware.

■ The Printers and Other Hardware window appears.

4 Click View installed printers or fax printers.

What other features are displayed for my printer?

✔ In the Properties dialog box on the General tab, the Features area may indicate whether your printer can print on both sides of a sheet of paper and if the printer can staple documents you print. The area may also indicate the type of paper that is currently available for printing in the printer.

How can I test whether the printer is working properly?

✔ You can have the printer print a test page. In the Properties dialog box, select the General tab and click the Print Test Page button. If the test page printed properly, click OK in the dialog box that appears. If the test page did not print properly, click the Troubleshoot button in the dialog box. Then follow the instructions in the Help and Support Center window to try to fix the problem.

Are there additional printer settings I can change?

✔ Yes. You can specify the settings you want the printer to use to print all your documents. In the Properties dialog box, select the General tab and click the Printing Preferences button. For more information about changing printing preferences for your printer, see page 142.

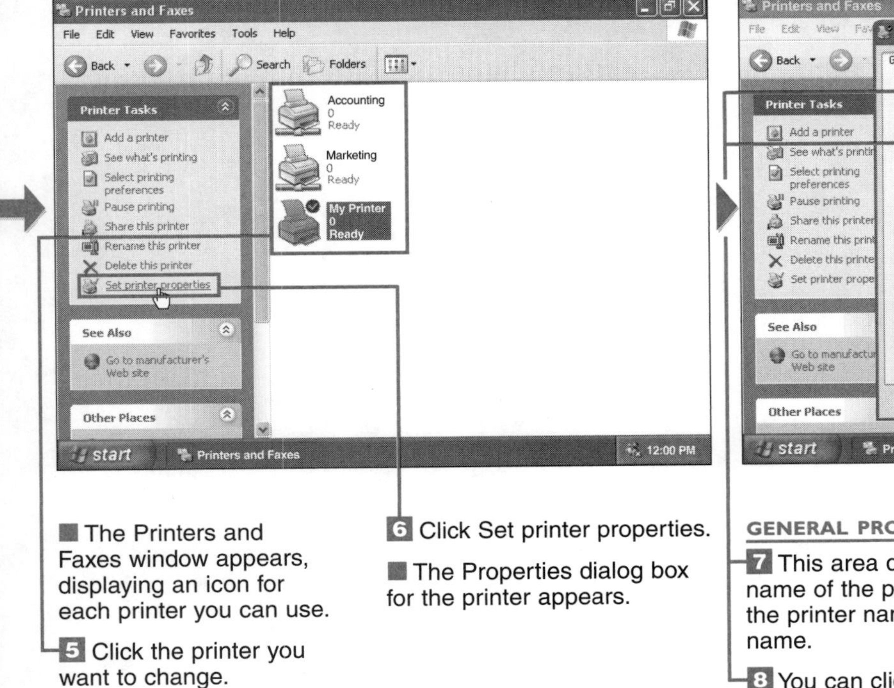

■ The Printers and Faxes window appears, displaying an icon for each printer you can use.

5 Click the printer you want to change.

6 Click Set printer properties.

■ The Properties dialog box for the printer appears.

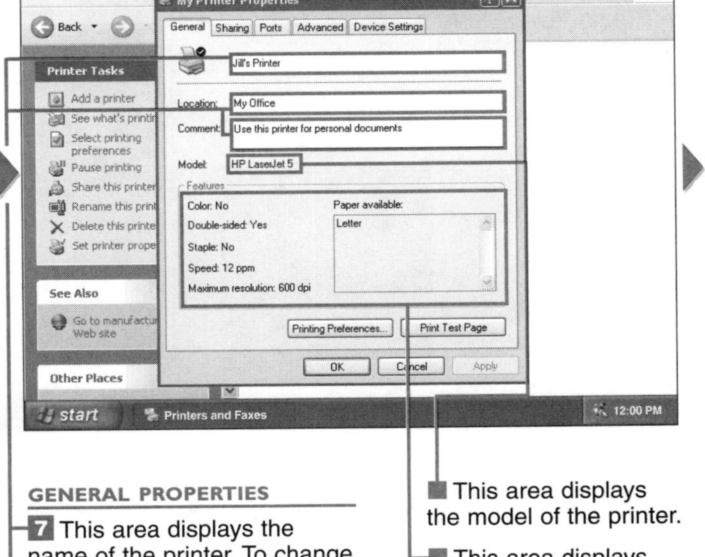

GENERAL PROPERTIES

7 This area displays the name of the printer. To change the printer name, type a new name.

8 You can click these areas and type the location of the printer and a comment about the printer.

■ This area displays the model of the printer.

■ This area displays the features of the printer.

CONTINUED

CHANGE PRINTER PROPERTIES (CONTINUED)

Windows allows you to change the device settings for the printer. For example, you can tell the printer what size of paper each tray holds. You may want to specify that the upper tray will hold letter-sized paper and the lower tray will hold legal-sized paper. Changing the printer's device settings will affect all the documents you print.

Windows also allows you to change advanced properties for your printer. You can choose whether you want the printer to always be available or if you want the printer to be available only during a period you specify. If the printer is not available when you print a document, Windows will hold the document until the printer becomes available. You can also specify the priority of documents sent to the printer. The priority determines the order in which documents will print. The highest priority is 99.

The name of the driver your printer uses is also displayed in the Properties dialog box. A driver is software that allows your computer to communicate with the printer.

CHANGE PRINTER PROPERTIES (CONTINUED)

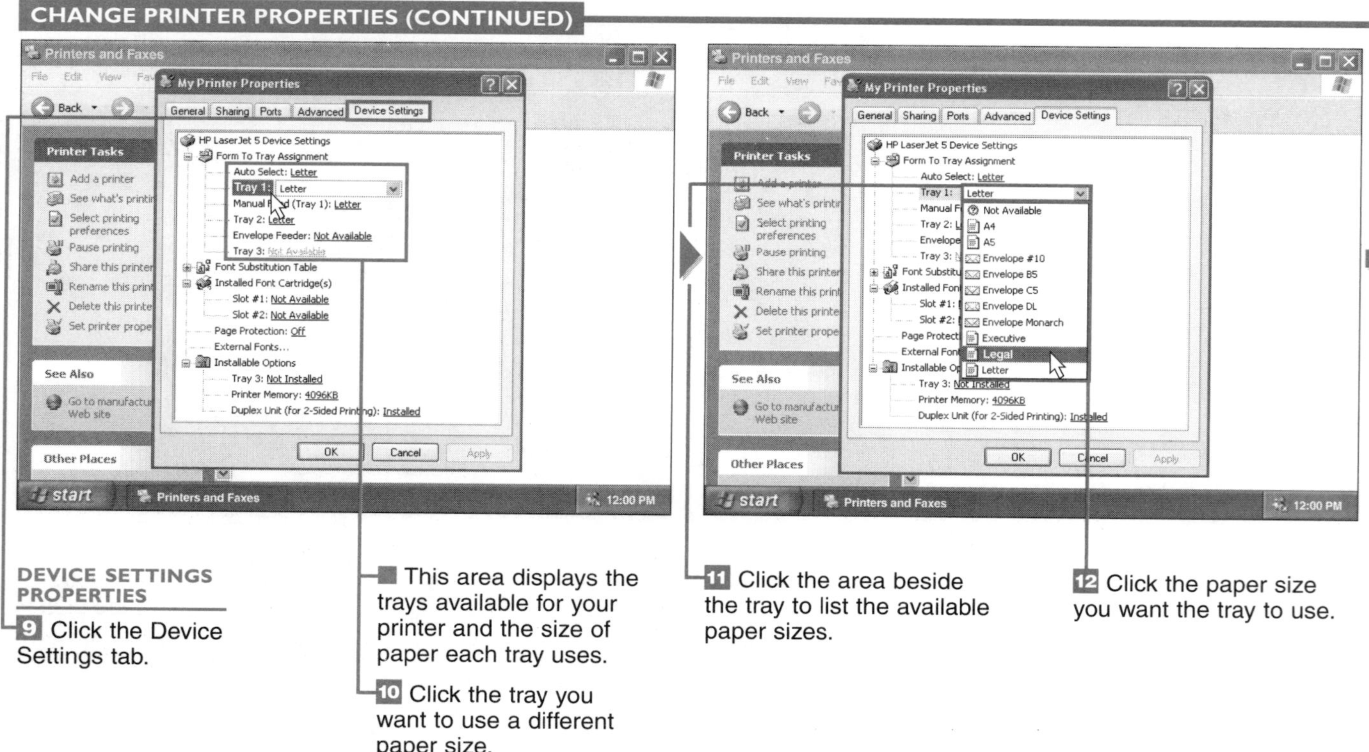

DEVICE SETTINGS PROPERTIES

9 Click the Device Settings tab.

■ This area displays the trays available for your printer and the size of paper each tray uses.

10 Click the tray you want to use a different paper size.

11 Click the area beside the tray to list the available paper sizes.

12 Click the paper size you want the tray to use.

Can I update my printer driver?

✔ If you printed a test page, you can compare the driver information on the test page to the driver information provided by the manufacturer of the printer to determine if a more up-to-date printer driver is available. To update a driver, display the Properties dialog box, select the Advanced tab and click the New Driver button. Then follow the instructions in the Add Printer Driver Wizard.

What information does the Sharing tab contain?

✔ If you are connected to a network, the Sharing tab allows you to share your printer with other people on the network. For information about sharing a printer, see page 412.

How can I identify the documents each person prints on a shared printer?

✔ You can have the printer insert a separator page between each printed document. A separator page can display the date and time the document was printed and the name of the person who printed the document. In the Properties dialog box, select the Advanced tab and click the Separator Page button. Then type the name and location of the separator page you want to use or click the Browse button to locate the separator page. Separator pages display the .sep extension.

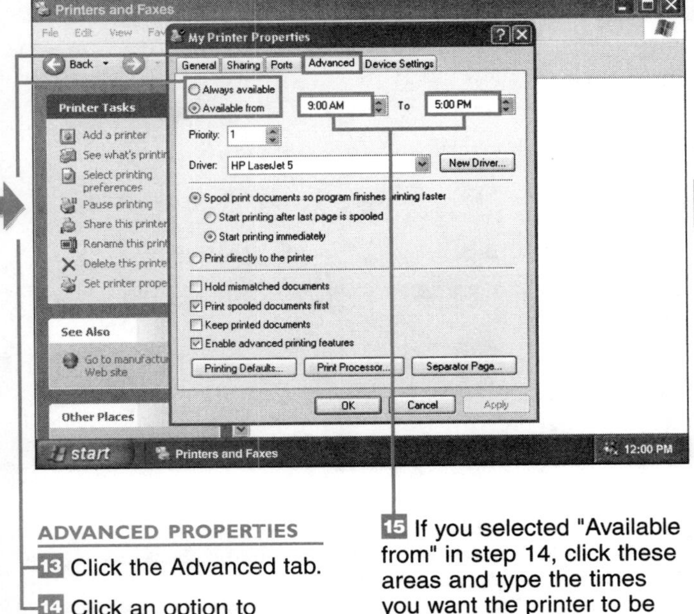

ADVANCED PROPERTIES

13 Click the Advanced tab.

14 Click an option to specify when you want the printer to be available (◯ changes to ◉).

15 If you selected "Available from" in step 14, click these areas and type the times you want the printer to be available.

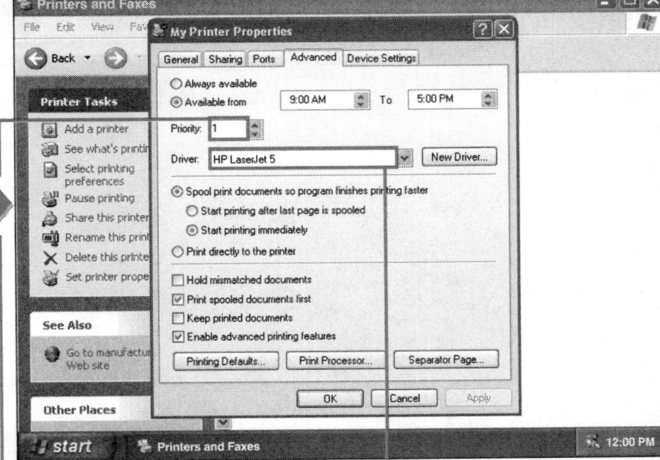

16 To specify the priority of documents sent to the printer, double-click this area and type a number. The highest priority is 99.

■ This area displays the name of the driver that allows your computer to communicate with the printer.

CONTINUED

CHANGE PRINTER PROPERTIES (CONTINUED)

The spool options control how and when information is sent to the printer. When you spool printed documents, the program you are working in creates a file on your hard drive to store the document until the printer is ready. When the printer is ready, Windows sends the file from your hard drive to the printer. This process is called spooling.

You can choose to spool documents you print or send the documents directly to the printer. If you choose to spool documents, you can also specify when you want the printer to start printing the documents.

You can have Windows prevent documents from printing when the printing preferences of the documents do not match the printing preferences of the printer.

To increase the efficiency of your printer, you can specify that documents that have finished spooling should be printed first, even if other documents have a higher priority.

You can have Windows keep documents in the spooler after the documents have finished printing. This allows you to quickly resubmit documents from the spooler to the printer.

The Enable advanced printing features option allows you to use advanced printing features for the printer, such as specifying the order in which pages will print.

CHANGE PRINTER PROPERTIES (CONTINUED)

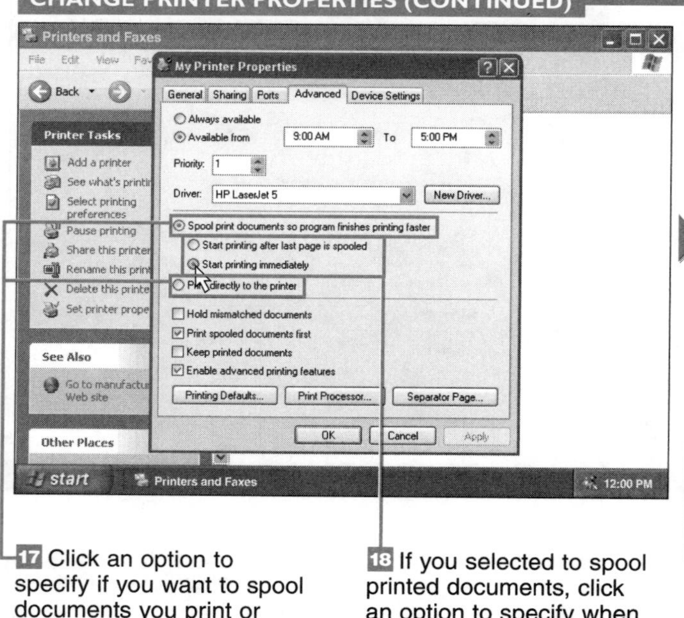

17 Click an option to specify if you want to spool documents you print or print directly to the printer (○ changes to ◉).

18 If you selected to spool printed documents, click an option to specify when you want the printer to start printing your documents (○ changes to ◉).

■ This option prevents documents from printing when the printing preferences of the documents do not match the printing preferences of the printer. You can click the option to turn the option on (☑) or off (☐).

■ This option prints documents that have completed spooling before documents that are still spooling. You can click the option to turn the option on (☑) or off (☐).

Should I spool documents I print?

✔ If you want to be able to use your computer soon after printing, you should spool documents you print. Spooling allows you to perform other tasks on your computer without having to wait for the printer to print your documents. If your printer is having trouble spooling, you can choose not to spool your documents and print directly to the printer.

Can I set the same document properties for all users of a shared printer?

✔ Yes. In the Properties dialog box, select the Advanced tab and click the Printing Defaults button. You can then set default document properties for all users of your shared printer. For more information, see page 142.

How can I resubmit a document I previously printed?

✔ In the Properties dialog box, click the Advanced tab and select the Keep printed documents option to keep documents you print in the spooler. To resubmit a document to the printer, perform steps 1 to 4 on page 136 to display the Printers and Faxes window. Then double-click the printer to which you want to resubmit the document. In the window that appears, click the name of the document you want to resubmit. Then select the Document menu and click Restart.

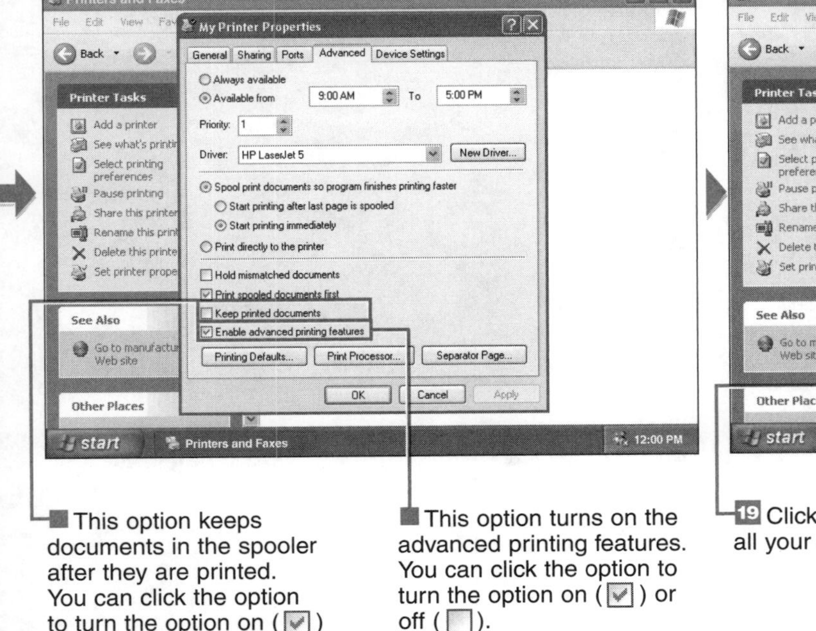

■ This option keeps documents in the spooler after they are printed. You can click the option to turn the option on (☑) or off (☐).

■ This option turns on the advanced printing features. You can click the option to turn the option on (☑) or off (☐).

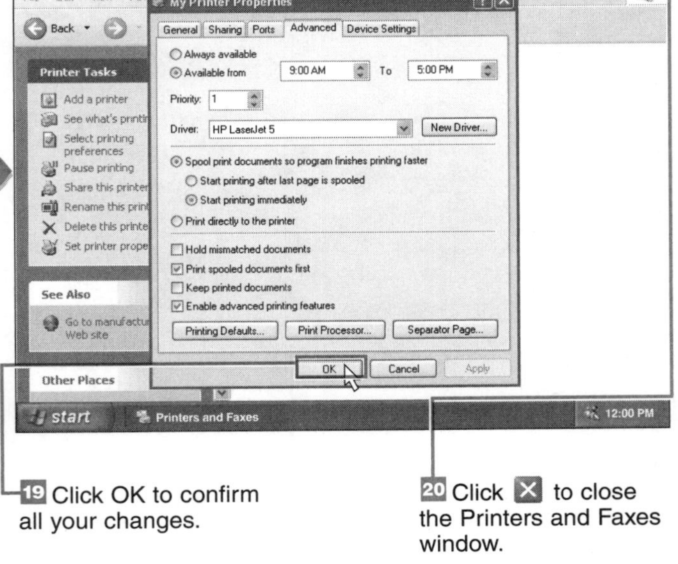

19 Click OK to confirm all your changes.

20 Click ☒ to close the Printers and Faxes window.

CHANGE PRINTING PREFERENCES

You can change the printing preferences for a printer to specify how you want the printer to print all your documents. The available printing preferences depend on the printer. Before changing printing preferences, you may want to consult the documentation that came with your printer to help you determine which options relate to the tasks you want to perform.

Windows allows you to specify the orientation of pages you print. The page orientation determines how a document is positioned on a page. The Portrait orientation positions a document vertically on the page and is the standard orientation. The Landscape orientation positions a document horizontally on the page and is often used to print certificates and tables.

You can specify the order in which the pages in your documents will print. Windows can print each document starting with the first or last page.

You can also specify how many pages of a document you want to print on each sheet of paper. For example, you can have a two-page document print on one side of a sheet of paper.

CHANGE PRINTING PREFERENCES

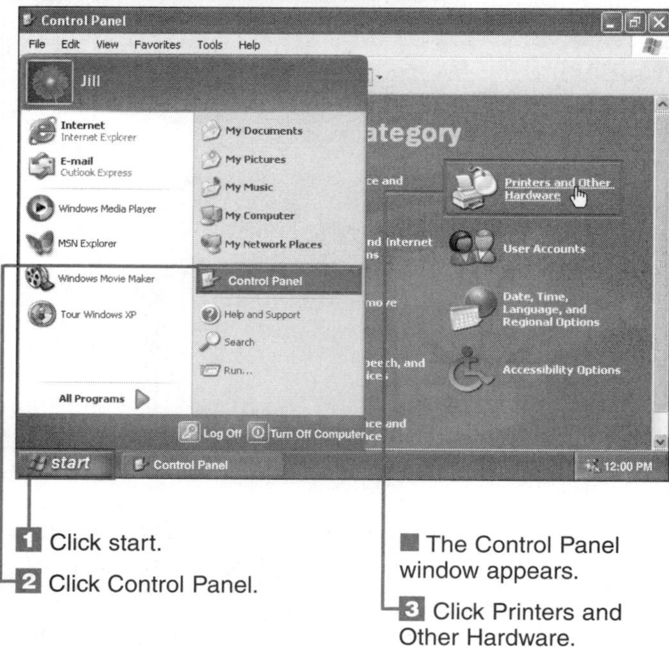

1 Click start.

2 Click Control Panel.

■ The Control Panel window appears.

3 Click Printers and Other Hardware.

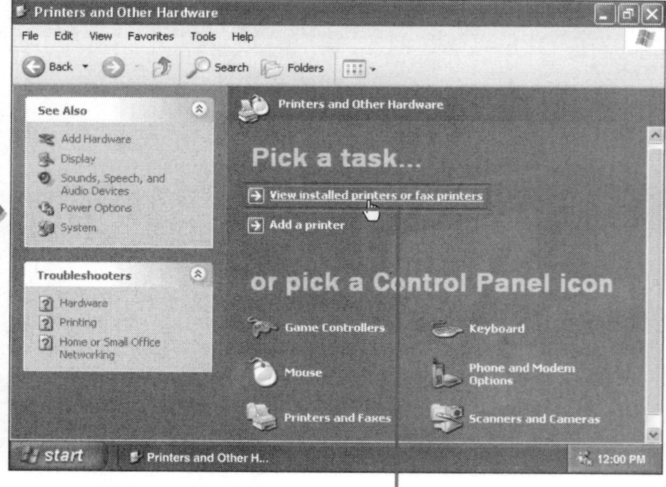

■ The Printers and Other Hardware window appears.

4 Click View installed printers or fax printers.

Can I change printing preferences for a specific document?

✔ You can usually change the printing preferences in the program you used to create a document. When the document is displayed on your screen, select the File menu and then click Page Setup to access the printing preferences for the document.

Can I set printing preferences for a printer I shared?

✔ Yes. If you want to set default printing preferences for all the users of the printer at once, right-click the printer in the Printers and Faxes window and click Properties on the menu that appears. Click the Advanced tab, click the Printing Defaults button and then set the preferences. Users can also set their own printing preferences for your shared printer.

How can I have my documents print on both sides of a sheet of paper?

✔ If your printer can print on both sides of your paper, the Layout tab in the Printing Preferences dialog box displays the Print on Both Sides area. The Flip on Long Edge option is useful for documents that will be bound on the left edge, like a book. The Flip on Short Edge option is useful for documents that will be bound on the top edge, like a notepad. Select the option you want to use (○ changes to ◉).

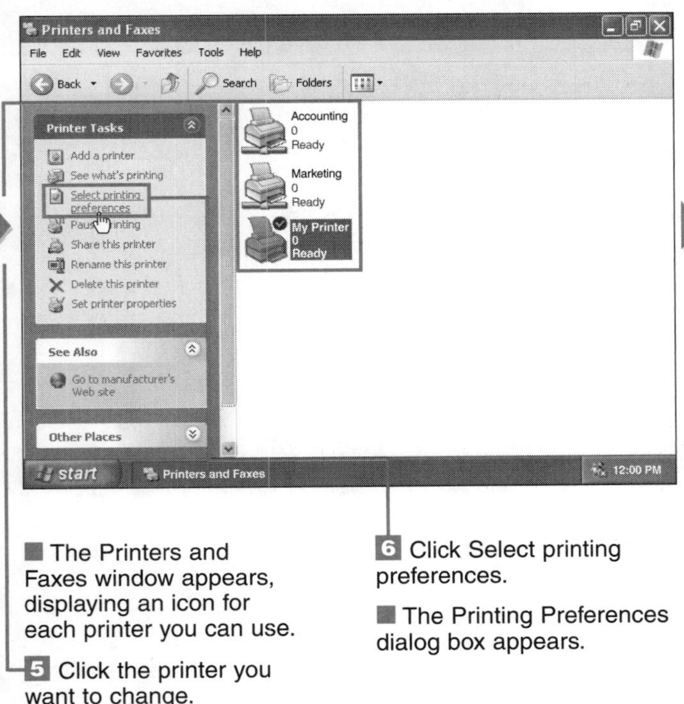

■ The Printers and Faxes window appears, displaying an icon for each printer you can use.

5 Click the printer you want to change.

6 Click Select printing preferences.

■ The Printing Preferences dialog box appears.

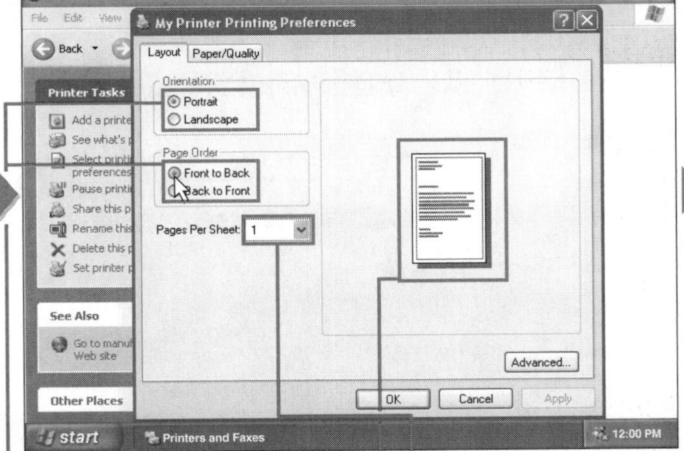

LAYOUT PREFERENCES

7 Click the page orientation you want to use (○ changes to ◉).

8 Click the order in which you want pages to print (○ changes to ◉).

9 This area displays the number of pages that will print on a sheet of paper. You can click this area to select a different number of pages.

■ This area displays the way a printed page will appear.

CONTINUED

CHANGE PRINTING PREFERENCES (CONTINUED)

Windows allows you to specify where the paper you want to use is located in your printer, such as the upper or lower tray. You may want to have Windows automatically select the appropriate paper source for the documents you print.

You can use the advanced printing preferences to specify additional instructions for printing your documents. The available advanced printing preferences depend on the printer.

You can specify the size of paper you want to use to print your documents. For example, you may want to set up your printer to always print on legal-size paper or on envelopes.

You can also specify how many copies of each document you want to print. This is useful if you always need more than one copy of the documents you print.

Windows allows you to specify the print quality of your documents.

Print quality depends on the resolution you select and the capabilities of your printer. Resolution is measured by the number of dots printed per inch on a page. To produce sharper and more detailed images, select a higher resolution. To print documents faster or print rough drafts, select a lower resolution.

CHANGE PRINTING PREFERENCES (CONTINUED)

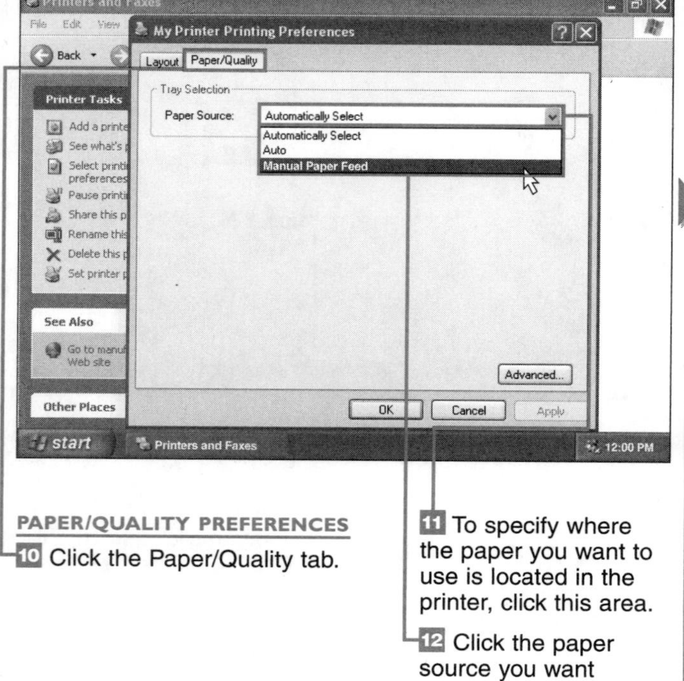

PAPER/QUALITY PREFERENCES

10 Click the Paper/Quality tab.

11 To specify where the paper you want to use is located in the printer, click this area.

12 Click the paper source you want to use.

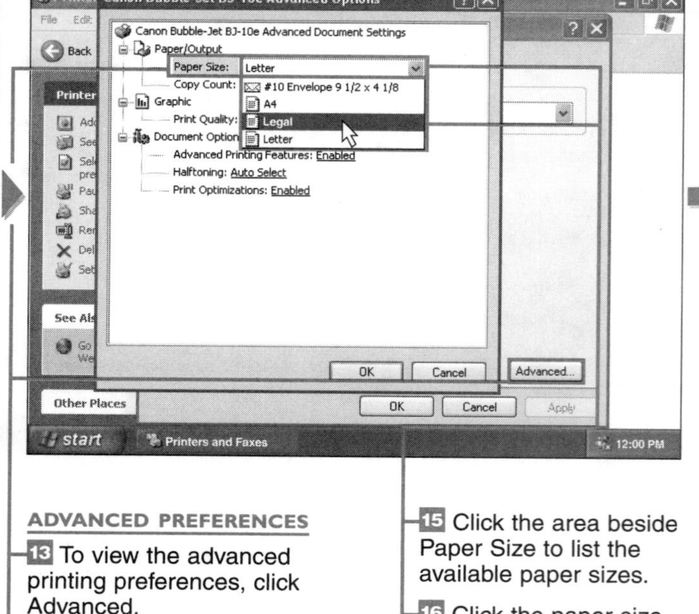

ADVANCED PREFERENCES

13 To view the advanced printing preferences, click Advanced.

■ The Advanced Options dialog box appears.

14 To change the paper size, click Paper Size.

15 Click the area beside Paper Size to list the available paper sizes.

16 Click the paper size you want to use.

What is the purpose of the Collated option in the Advanced Options dialog box?

✔ When you choose to print more than one copy of a document that contains multiple pages, this option prints the pages in each copy in order. This option is on by default. To turn off the option in order to print copies of each page together, click Collated (☑ changes to ☐).

How can I have my color printer print documents in black and white?

✔ In the Printing Preferences dialog box, select the Paper/Quality tab. Then click the Black & White option in the Color area (○ changes to ◉).

Can I specify a special type of paper I want to use to print documents?

✔ If your printer can print documents using specialty papers, such as high resolution or glossy paper, the Paper/Quality tab in the Printing Preferences dialog box displays the Media option. You can click the area beside this option and select the type of paper you will use to print your documents. The printer will automatically adjust the quality settings to produce the best results when printing on the type of paper you select.

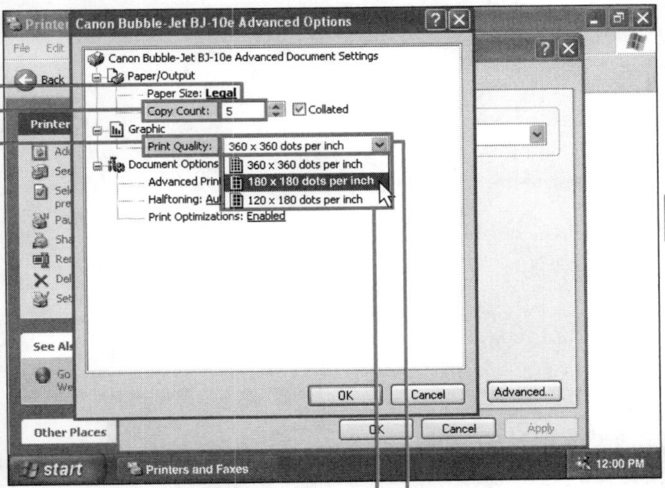

17 To change the number of copies you want to print, click Copy Count.

18 Click this area and type the number of copies you want to print.

19 To change the print quality, click Print Quality.

20 Click the area beside Print Quality to list the available print qualities.

21 Click the print quality you want to use.

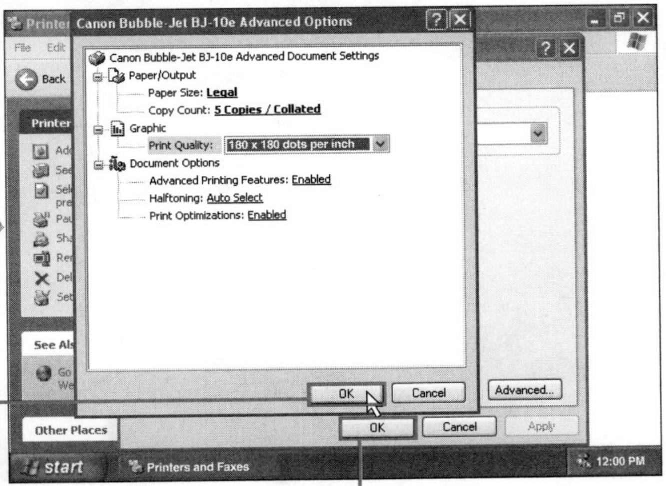

22 Click OK to confirm all your changes.

23 Click OK to close the Printing Preferences dialog box.

SECTION II

5) USING WORDPAD

6) USING PAINT

7) MORE ACCESSORIES

WINDOWS XP ACCESSORIES

START WORDPAD

WordPad is a word processing program included with Windows. You can use WordPad to create documents, such as letters and memos. You can also use WordPad to review and edit files created in other word processing programs, such as Microsoft Word.

WordPad allows you to insert, delete and reorganize the text in your document without having to retype the entire document. When you add new text to a document, the existing text will shift to make room for the text you add. You can delete text you no longer need from a document and the remaining text will shift to fill any empty spaces.

Moving text allows you to try out different ways of organizing the text in a document. You can find the most effective structure for a document by experimenting with different placements of sentences and paragraphs. You can also place a copy of text in a different location in your document. This will save you time since you can repeat information without having to retype the text.

If you need more advanced features than those offered in WordPad, you can purchase a more powerful word processor, such as Microsoft Word or Corel WordPerfect. These programs include features such as tables, graphics, a spell checker and a thesaurus.

START WORDPAD

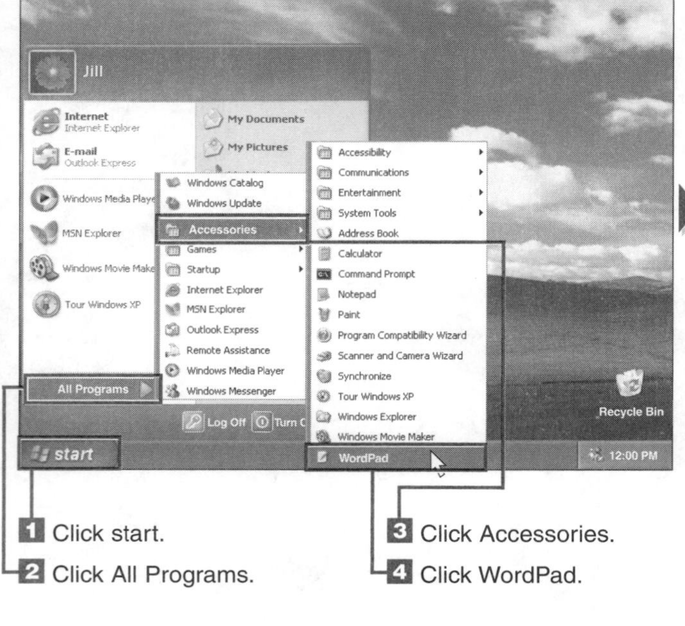

1 Click start.

2 Click All Programs.

3 Click Accessories.

4 Click WordPad.

■ The WordPad window appears, displaying a blank document.

■ The flashing insertion point indicates where text you type will appear.

5 Type the text for your document.

Note: In this example, the size of text was changed to make the text easier to read. To change the size of text, see page 150.

How do I select text?

✔ To select a word, double-click the word. To select one line of text, click in the left margin beside the line you want to select. To select a paragraph, double-click in the left margin beside the paragraph you want to select. To select all the text in a document, choose the Edit menu and then click Select All. To select any amount of text, drag the mouse pointer until you highlight all the text you want to select.

Can I cancel a change I made?

✔ WordPad remembers the last changes you made. Click the Undo button ( ) to cancel the last change you made. You can click the Undo button again to cancel previous changes.

How can I find or change every occurrence of a word or phrase in a document?

✔ To find every occurrence of a word or phrase in your document, click the Find button ( ) and then type the text you want to find. To change every occurrence of a word or phrase in your document, click the Edit menu and choose Replace. Then type the text you want to find and the replacement text.

EDIT TEXT

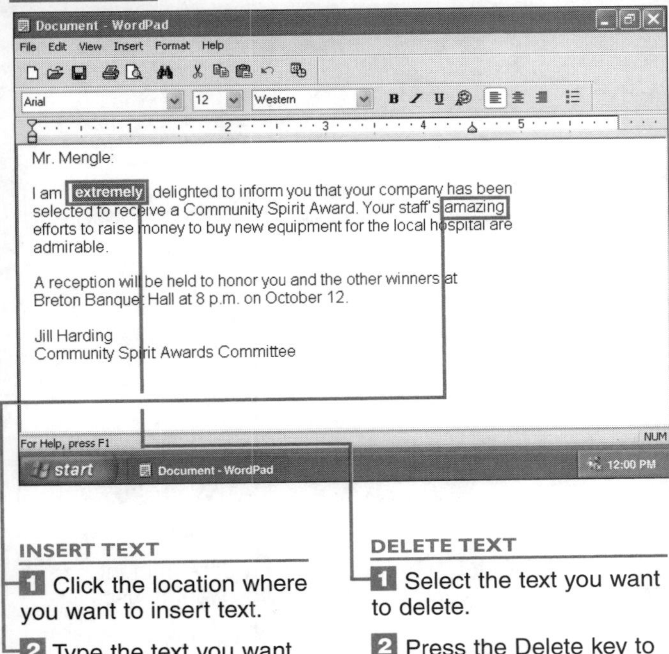

INSERT TEXT

1 Click the location where you want to insert text.

2 Type the text you want to insert.

DELETE TEXT

1 Select the text you want to delete.

2 Press the Delete key to remove the text.

■ To delete one character, click to the left of the character. Then press the Delete key.

MOVE TEXT

1 Select the text you want to move.

2 Position the mouse I over the text (I changes to).

3 Drag the mouse to where you want to place the text.

■ The text will appear where you position the insertion point on your screen.

Note: To copy text, perform steps 1 to 3, except press and hold down the Ctrl key as you perform step 3.

FORMAT CHARACTERS

You can make text in your document look more attractive by using various fonts, sizes, styles and colors.

When you first enter text in WordPad, the text appears in the Arial font. The default size for text is 10 points and the default color is black.

Several other fonts are also installed with Windows, including Courier New and Times New Roman. The fonts available in WordPad depend on the programs installed on your computer.

WordPad allows you to change the size of text. Larger text is easier to read, while smaller text allows you to fit more information on a page. WordPad measures the size of text in points. There are approximately 72 points in one inch. Due to differences in design, two fonts may appear to be different sizes even though they are displayed using the same point size.

You can change the style of text using the Bold, Italic and Underline features. These features are often used to emphasize text, such as titles.

You can change the color of text to draw attention to headings or important information in your document.

FORMAT CHARACTERS

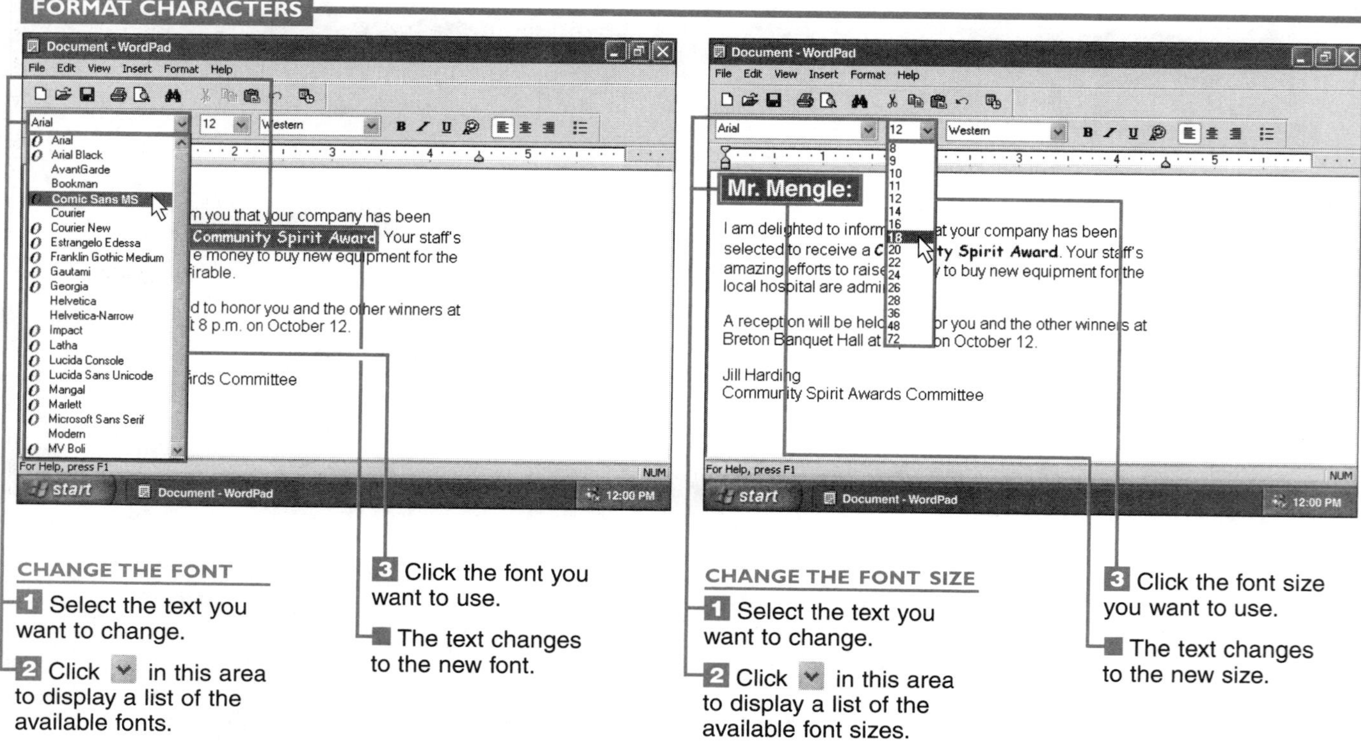

CHANGE THE FONT

1 Select the text you want to change.

2 Click ▾ in this area to display a list of the available fonts.

3 Click the font you want to use.

■ The text changes to the new font.

CHANGE THE FONT SIZE

1 Select the text you want to change.

2 Click ▾ in this area to display a list of the available font sizes.

3 Click the font size you want to use.

■ The text changes to the new size.

How can I change the format of text before I type the text?

✔ Before you begin typing the text you want to format differently, select the format you want to use. The new text you type will display the new format.

Is there another way that I can format selected text?

✔ Choose the Format menu and select Font. The Font dialog box appears, allowing you to change the formatting of the selected text. The dialog box also displays an area where you can preview the font settings you choose.

Can I add fonts to my computer?

✔ You can purchase fonts at most computer stores and obtain fonts on the Internet. To install fonts on your computer, see page 230. If you have installed other programs on your computer, WordPad can usually use the fonts provided with these programs.

Can I use colored text if I do not have a color printer?

✔ You can add color to your text, but any colors you add will appear as shades of gray when printed on a black-and-white printer. You can use color effectively in documents that you will only view on the screen.

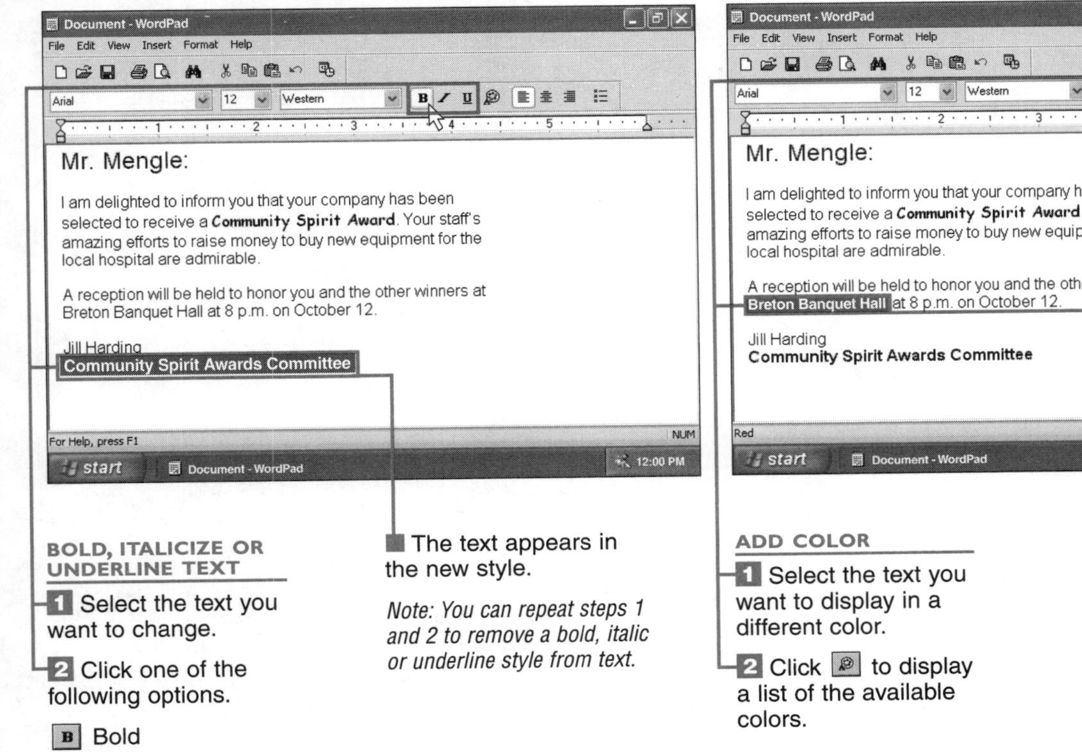

BOLD, ITALICIZE OR UNDERLINE TEXT

1 Select the text you want to change.

2 Click one of the following options.

- B Bold
- I Italic
- U Underline

■ The text appears in the new style.

Note: You can repeat steps 1 and 2 to remove a bold, italic or underline style from text.

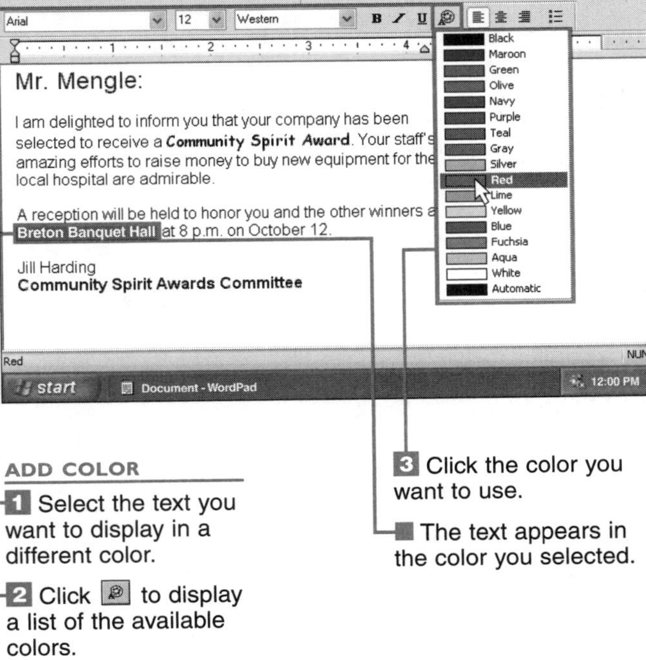

ADD COLOR

1 Select the text you want to display in a different color.

2 Click to display a list of the available colors.

3 Click the color you want to use.

■ The text appears in the color you selected.

FORMAT PARAGRAPHS AND PAGES

You can format the paragraphs and pages in your document to make the information easier to read and determine how the document will print on a page.

The text in most documents is left aligned so the edge of each paragraph lines up along the left margin. You can right align text to line up dates or addresses along the right margin. You can also center text between the left and right margins. Centering text is most effective for headings and titles.

You can indent a paragraph from the left, right or both margins. Indenting paragraphs is often used to set apart quotations.

You can change the orientation of pages in your document. The portrait orientation prints across the short side of a page and is used for most documents. You can use the landscape orientation to print documents, such as certificates, across the long side of a page.

You can also change the margins in your document. A margin is the amount of space between text and the edge of your paper. Changing margins lets you accommodate letterhead and other specialty paper. Changing margins also allows you to fit more or less information on a page.

FORMAT PARAGRAPHS

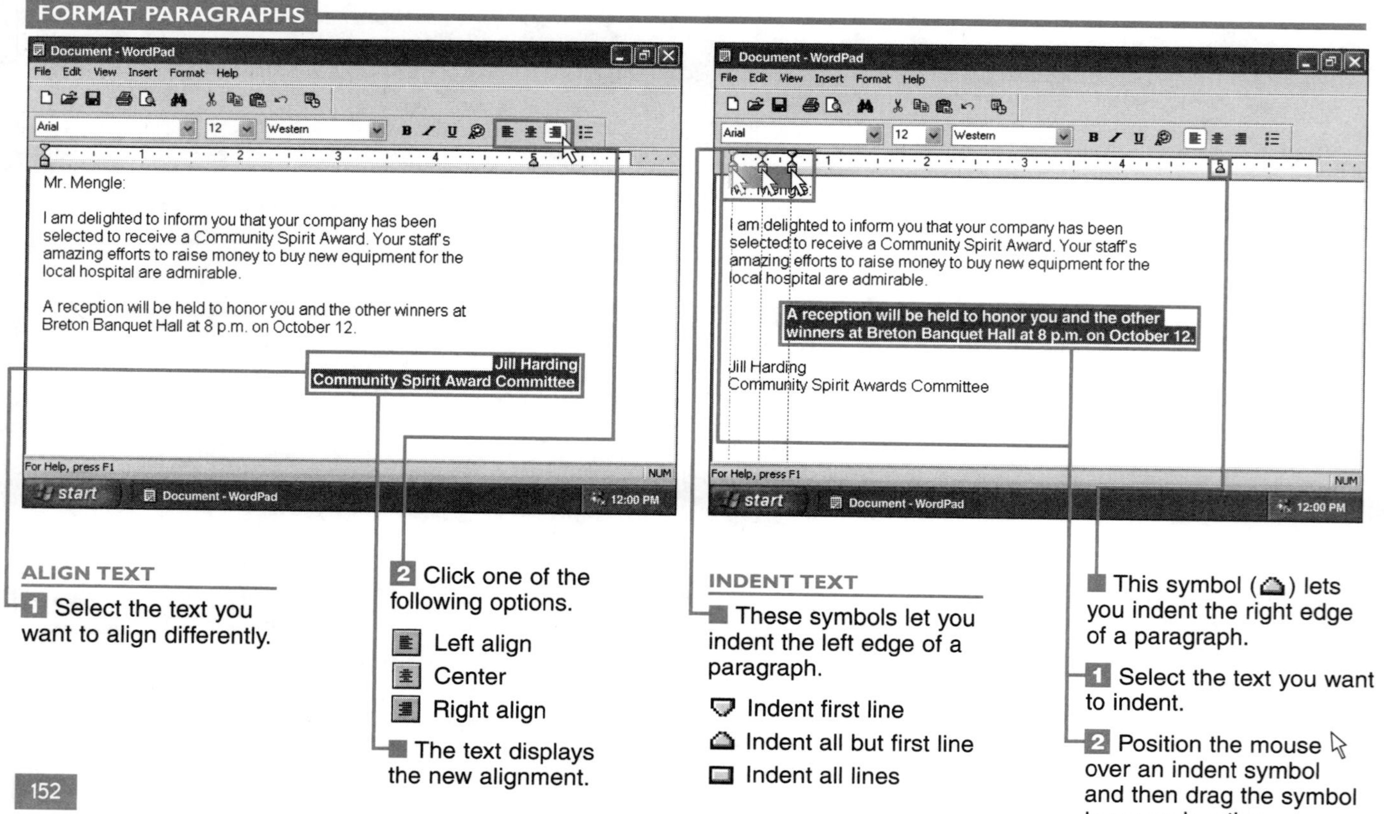

ALIGN TEXT

1 Select the text you want to align differently.

2 Click one of the following options.

- Left align
- Center
- Right align

■ The text displays the new alignment.

INDENT TEXT

■ These symbols let you indent the left edge of a paragraph.

- Indent first line
- Indent all but first line
- Indent all lines

■ This symbol (△) lets you indent the right edge of a paragraph.

1 Select the text you want to indent.

2 Position the mouse over an indent symbol and then drag the symbol to a new location.

How do I set a tab in my document?

✔ Select the text you want to use the tab. Click the location on the ruler where you want to add a tab. A tab (∟) appears on the ruler. To move a line of text to the tab, click the beginning of the line and then press the Tab key.

Can I create a bulleted list?

✔ Yes. Select the paragraphs you want to display as a bulleted list and then click ☰.

How do I display or hide the ruler on my screen?

✔ From the View menu, select Ruler to display or hide the ruler. When the ruler is displayed, a check mark appears beside Ruler in the View menu.

How do I change the size of the paper or envelope I want to use?

✔ In the Page Setup dialog box, click the area beside Size and then select the paper or envelope size you want to use.

Can I change how WordPad measures the margins?

✔ From the View menu, select Options. Click the Options tab and select the preferred unit of measure. You can choose from inches, centimeters, points and picas. There are approximately 72 points in one inch and 6 picas in one inch. The unit of measure you select will be used throughout WordPad.

FORMAT PAGES

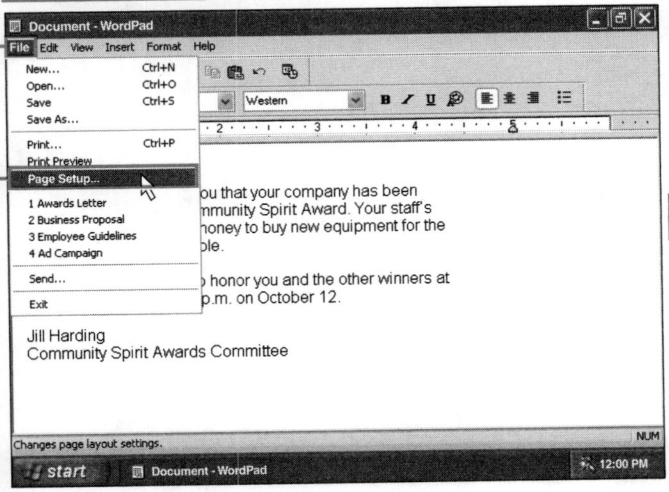

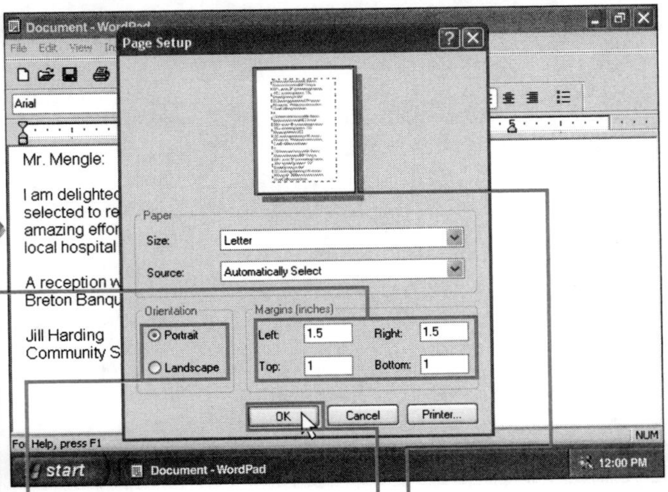

1 Click File.

2 Click Page Setup.

■ The Page Setup dialog box appears.

3 Click the page orientation you want to use (○ changes to ◉).

4 To change a margin, double-click the margin you want to change. Then type a new margin.

■ This area displays how your document will appear.

5 Click OK to confirm your changes.

SAVE AND OPEN A DOCUMENT

You can save your document to store it for future use. This allows you to later review and edit the document. When you save a document, you should use a descriptive name that will help you find the document later.

You may want to save a document as soon as you create the document and then regularly save your changes. If there is an equipment failure or power loss, you will lose the work you have completed since the last time you saved the document.

By default, Windows stores WordPad documents you save in the My Documents folder. You can choose to save your document in another location. For example, you may want to save a document you frequently work with on the desktop for easier access.

You can open a saved document to review and make changes to the document.

WordPad allows you to work with only one document at a time, so make sure you save the document you are working with before opening another. You can work with several documents at once by starting WordPad several times and opening a document in each window.

SAVE A DOCUMENT

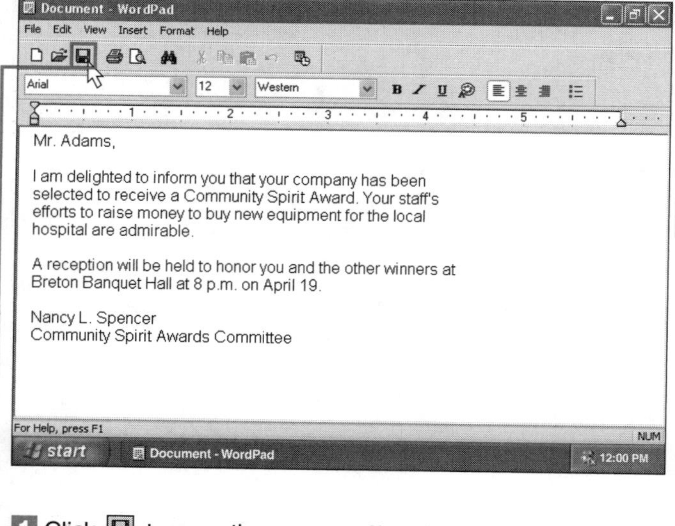

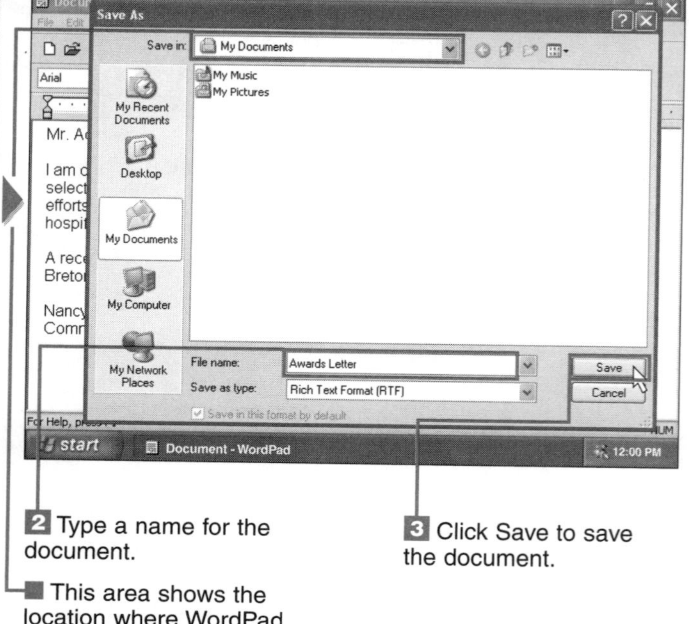

1 Click 💾 to save the document.

■ The Save As dialog box appears.

Note: If you previously saved the document, the Save As dialog box will not appear since you have already named the document.

2 Type a name for the document.

■ This area shows the location where WordPad will save the document. You can click this area to change the location.

3 Click Save to save the document.

Can I save my document in a different format?

✔ WordPad automatically saves your document in the Rich Text format. To save your document in a different format, click the Save as type area in the Save As dialog box and then select the way you want to save the document.

Is there a faster way to open a document?

✔ The names of the last four documents you worked with in WordPad appear on the File menu. To open one of these documents, click the name of the document on the File menu.

How do I create a new document?

✔ Click 🗋 to start a new document. In the dialog box that appears, select the type of document you want to create.

How do I print a document?

✔ Select the File menu and then click Print. In the Print dialog box, choose a printer, select the options for the pages you want to print and then click Print. You can also click the Print button (🖨) to quickly print an entire document. To preview a document before printing, click the Print Preview button (🔍).

OPEN A DOCUMENT

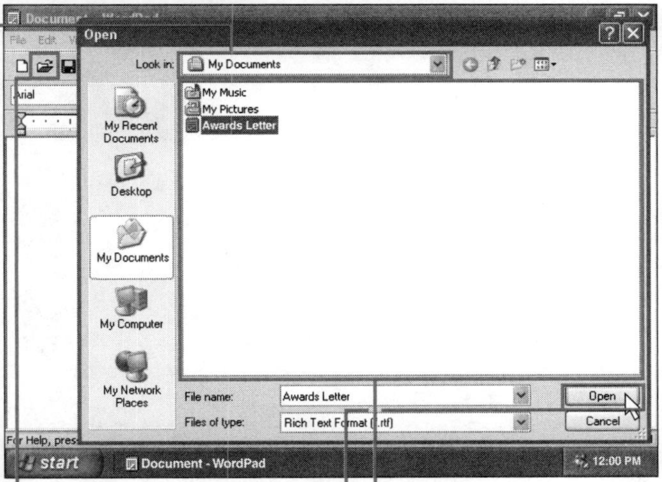

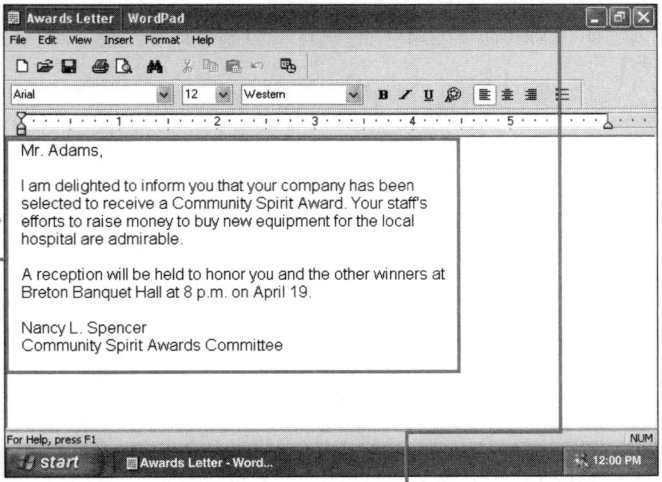

1 Click 📂 to open a saved document.

■ The Open dialog box appears.

■ This area shows the location of the displayed documents. You can click this area to change the location.

2 Click the name of the document you want to open.

3 Click Open to open the document.

■ The document opens and appears on your screen. You can now review and make changes to the document.

■ This area displays the name of the document.

START PAINT AND DRAW SHAPES

Paint is a simple drawing program included with Windows that you can use to create and edit pictures. Pictures you create in Paint can be printed, inserted into other programs or set as a desktop background.

You can use Paint's tools to draw shapes such as squares, rectangles, rounded rectangles, circles, ellipses and polygons.

You can use the Polygon tool to draw many different kinds of multi-sided shapes, ranging from simple triangles to complex objects.

Before you draw a shape, you can specify whether you want to outline the shape, fill the shape with a color or both. You can also specify the colors you want to use for the outline and the inside of the shape.

Although Paint offers many features to help you create pictures, you may want to obtain a more sophisticated image editing program, such as Jasc Paint Shop Pro or Adobe Photoshop. You can obtain Paint Shop Pro at the www.jasc.com Web site and Photoshop at the www.adobe.com Web site.

START PAINT

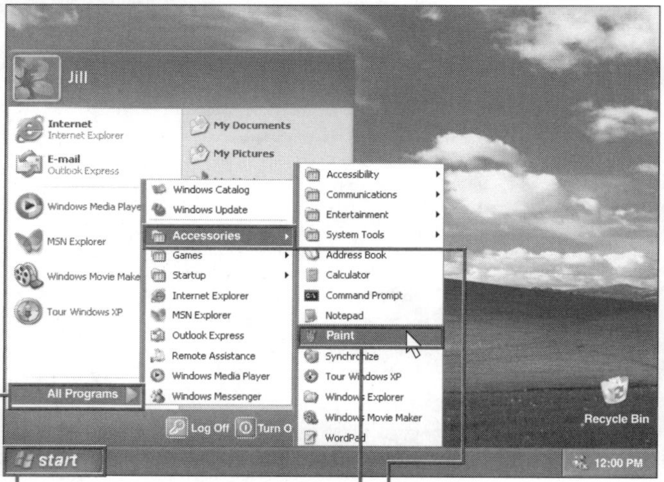

1 Click start.

2 Click All Programs.

3 Click Accessories.

4 Click Paint.

■ The Paint window appears.

■ This area displays the tools you can use to create pictures.

5 To display a description of a tool, position the mouse over the tool. The name of the tool appears.

■ This area displays a description of the tool.

■ To increase the size of the white drawing area, position the mouse over the bottom right corner of the drawing area (changes to ↘) and then drag the mouse ↘ until the area is the size you want.

How do I draw a circle or a square?

✔ To draw a circle, select the Ellipse tool ( ). To draw a square, select the Rectangle tool ( ). Then press and hold down the Shift key as you draw the shape.

Can I change the border thickness of a shape?

✔ When you draw a shape, the border thickness is the same as the thickness currently selected for the Line or Curve tool. To change the border thickness, click the Line ( ) or Curve ( ) tool and then select the thickness you want in the area below the toolbox before creating the shape.

How do I fill an area with color?

✔ Select the Fill With Color tool ( ), choose the color you want to use and then click the area you want to fill with color. Keep in mind that if there are gaps in the border of the object you are filling, the color will leak out into the surrounding area.

How do I use a picture as a desktop background?

✔ Click the File menu and then select Set As Background (Tiled) or Set As Background (Centered). Before you can use a picture as your desktop background, you must save the picture. To save a picture, see page 162.

DRAW SHAPES

1 Click the tool for the type of shape you want to draw.

2 Click an option to draw the shape with an outline, an inside color or both.

3 To select a color for the outline of the shape, click the color.

4 To select a color for the inside of the shape, right-click the color.

5 Position the mouse where you want to begin drawing the shape.

6 Drag the mouse until the shape is the size you want.

7 If you selected in step 1, repeat steps 5 and 6 until you finish drawing all the lines for the shape. Then immediately double-click the mouse to complete the shape.

DRAW LINES AND USE BRUSHES

You can draw three different types of lines in your pictures. You can draw pencil lines, straight lines and curved lines. You can also use brushes to paint brush strokes or spray areas of a picture.

The Pencil tool draws a thin line and allows you to draw lines and curves more freely than the Line or Curve tool.

The Line tool allows you to draw a perfectly straight line when you drag the mouse from one point to another.

When you use the Curve tool, the line begins as a perfectly straight line. You can then bend or twist the line to create the curve you want.

The Brush tool is similar to the Pencil tool, but it has many different brush styles that you can choose from, including some that work like a calligraphy pen.

You can use the Airbrush tool to spray areas of color onto a picture and create shading effects. When using the Airbrush tool, the slower you drag the mouse, the darker the color appears in your picture.

DRAW LINES

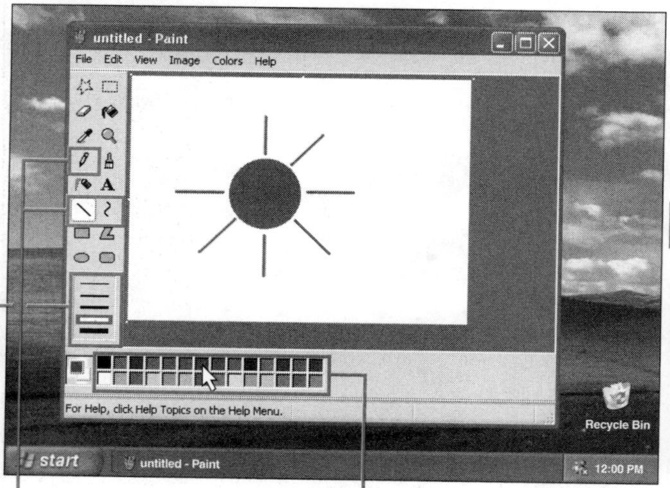

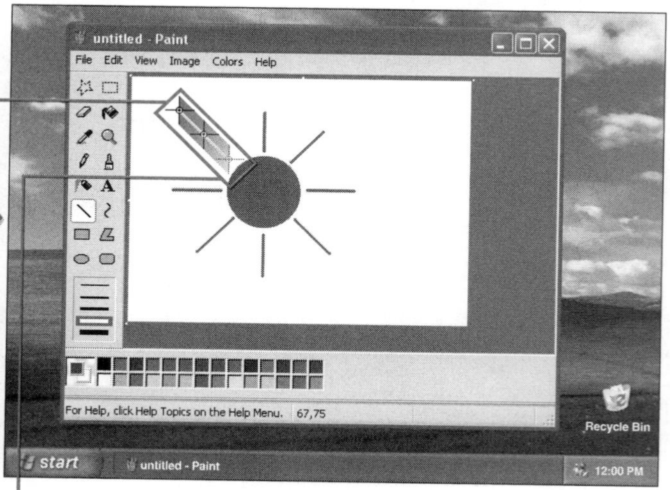

1 Click the Pencil ( ), Line ( ) or Curve ( ) tool to select the type of line you want to draw.

2 Click the thickness you want to use for the line.

Note: The tool does not provide any line thickness options.

3 Click the color you want to use for the line.

4 Position the mouse (or) where you want to begin drawing the line.

5 Drag the mouse (or) until the line is the length you want.

6 If you selected the tool in step 1, position the mouse over the line and then drag the mouse until the line curves the way you want. Then immediately click the mouse to complete the curved line.

How do I draw a perfectly horizontal line?

✔ You can draw a perfectly horizontal, vertical or 45-degree diagonal line by holding down the Shift key while you draw the line.

How can I zoom in to draw precise lines?

✔ Click the View menu, choose Zoom and then select Large Size. To access more zoom levels, click the View menu, choose Zoom and then select Custom. When you are finished, you can return to the normal zoom level. Click the View menu, choose Zoom and then select Normal Size.

How do I move an item in a picture?

✔ To move an item in a picture, click . Choose an option in the area below the toolbox to move the item with () or without () the background. To select the item, drag the mouse over the item until a dashed line surrounds the item. Right-click the color you want to use to fill the space left after you move the item. Then position the mouse over the item and drag it to a new location.

USE BRUSHES

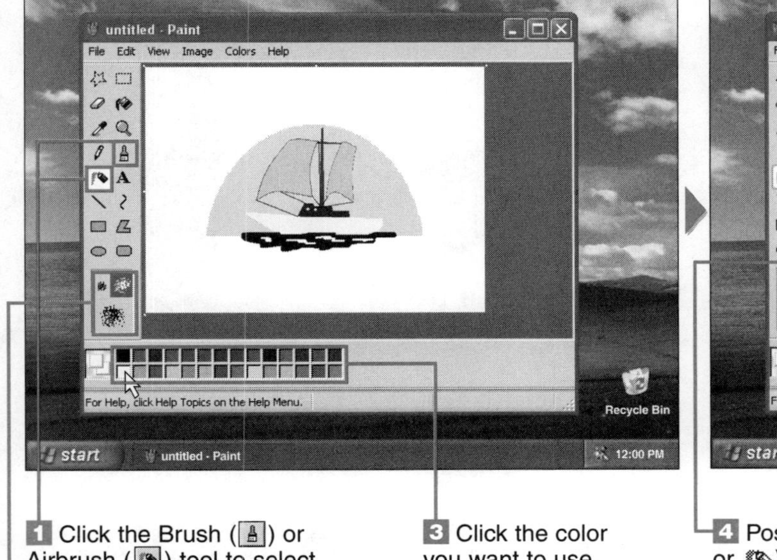

1 Click the Brush () or Airbrush () tool to select the type of brush you want to use.

2 Click the brush shape or spray size you want to use.

3 Click the color you want to use.

4 Position the mouse (or) where you want to start painting.

5 Drag the mouse (or) over the area you want to brush with color.

ERASE PART OF A PICTURE

You can remove an area from your picture. Paint offers four different eraser sizes that you can use. Choose the small eraser size when you want to be precise in your erasing. The large eraser size is useful when you want to erase a larger area of your picture.

You can use any color to erase an area of your picture. The color you select should match the background color of your picture. For example, use a white eraser when the area you want to erase has a white background and a colored eraser when the area you want to erase has a colored background.

Is there a fast way to erase a large area of my picture?

✔ To select the area you want to erase, click the Select tool (⬚) and then drag the mouse over the area you want to erase until a dashed line surrounds the area. Right-click the color you want to use to erase the area and then press the Delete key.

How can I quickly clear the entire drawing area?

✔ Right-click the color you want to use as the new background of the drawing area, select the Image menu and then choose Clear Image.

ERASE PART OF A PICTURE

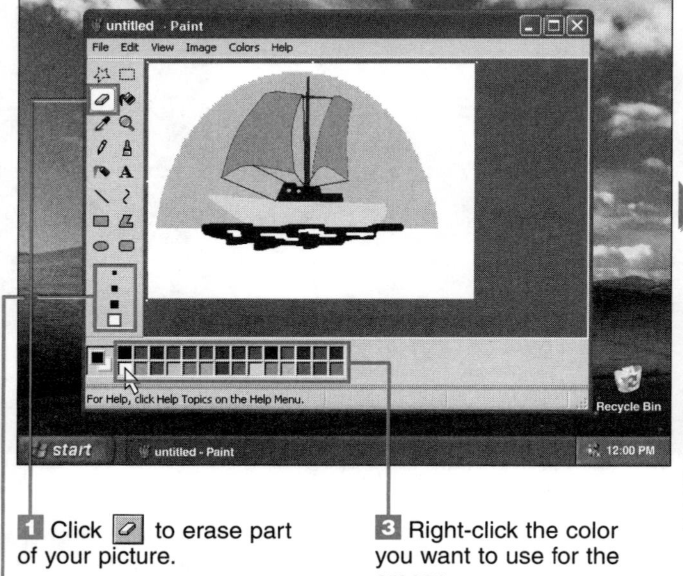

1 Click ⌫ to erase part of your picture.

2 Click the size of eraser you want to use.

3 Right-click the color you want to use for the eraser.

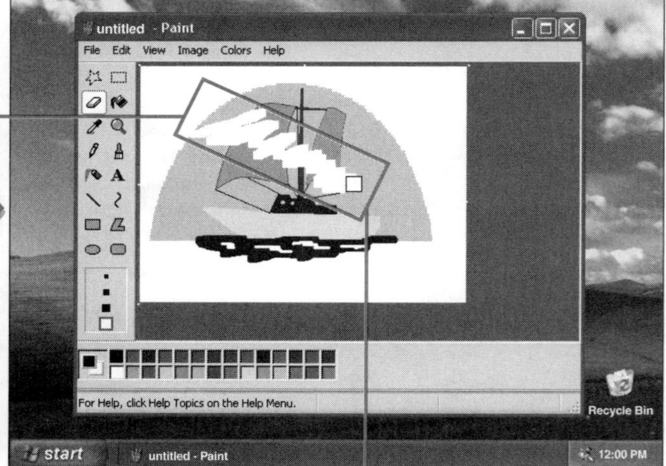

4 Position the mouse □ where you want to begin erasing.

5 Drag the mouse □ over the area you want to erase.

ADD TEXT

You can add text to your picture to provide written information or explanations.

When adding text to a picture, you first need to create a text box that will hold the text. Text you type will automatically wrap to fit within the text box.

Paint does not have a spell-checker, so you should check the spelling of your text as you type the text. You will not be able to make changes to the text after you select another tool or click outside the text box.

Can I use text from another document?

✔ Yes. Open the document that contains the text and then select and copy the text. Display the Paint window and create a text box large enough to fit the text. Click the Edit menu and select Paste to place the text in the text box.

How can I format text?

✔ The Fonts toolbar appears when you add text to a picture. You can use the options on the toolbar to change the font, size and style of the text. If the Fonts toolbar does not appear, click the View menu and then select Text Toolbar.

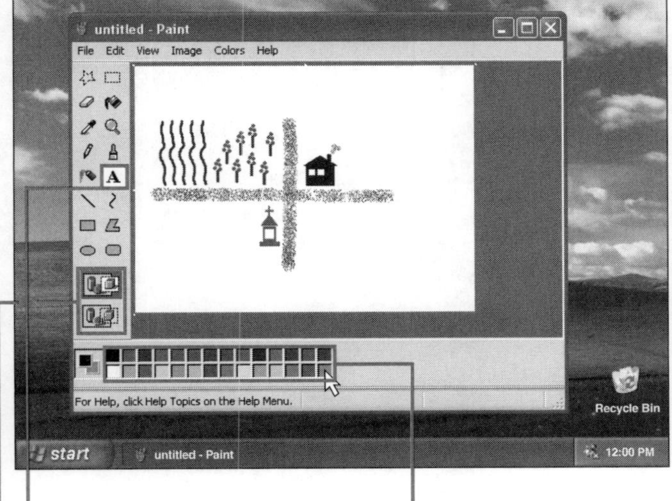

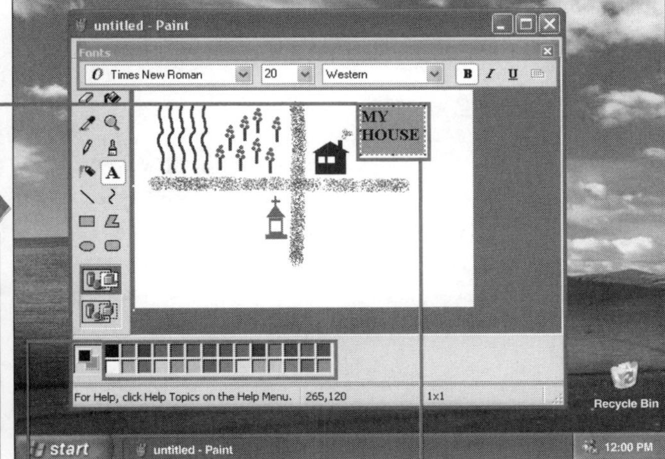

1 Click A to add text to your picture.

2 Click an option to specify if you want to place the text on a colored background (▣) or directly on the picture (▣).

3 If you selected to place the text on a colored background, right-click the color you want to use for the background.

4 Click the color you want to use for the text.

5 Position the mouse ✛ where you want the top left corner of the text box to appear and then drag the mouse ✛ until the text box is the size you want.

6 Type the text.

7 Click outside the text box when you finish typing the text.

SAVE AND OPEN A PICTURE

You can save your picture to store it for future use. This allows you to later review and make changes to the picture. You should regularly save changes you make to a picture to avoid losing your work due to a computer problem or power failure.

Paint saves pictures you create in the Bitmap format. Pictures stored in the Bitmap format usually have the .bmp extension.

You should store your pictures in a location on your computer that will be easy to find. By default, Paint stores pictures you create in the My Pictures folder.

You can open a saved picture to display the picture on your screen. This allows you to review and make changes to the picture. In the Open dialog box, Windows displays a miniature version of each picture stored in the My Pictures folder. You can open many different types of pictures, such as those in the Bitmap, JPEG, GIF, TIFF, PNG and ICO formats.

Paint allows you to work with only one picture at a time. Make sure you save the picture you are currently working with before opening another picture. You can work with many pictures at the same time by starting the Paint program several times and opening a picture in each window.

SAVE A PICTURE

1 Click File.

2 Click Save.

■ The Save As dialog box appears.

Note: If you previously saved the picture, the Save As dialog box will not appear since you have already named the picture.

3 Type a name for your picture.

■ This area shows the location where Paint will store the picture. You can click this area to change the location.

4 Click Save to save your picture.

Is there a faster way to open a picture?

✔ The names of the last four pictures you opened in Paint appear on the File menu. Click the name of the picture you want to open on the File menu.

Can I open a picture from a window or the desktop?

✔ You can open a picture from a window or the desktop by double-clicking the icon for the picture. Windows will display the picture in the Windows Picture and Fax Viewer window, which allows you to preview the picture. To make changes to the picture, you must open the picture in Paint.

Can I change the format used to save a picture?

✔ You can select the format used to save a picture from the Save as type area in the Save As dialog box. If you are saving a picture in the Bitmap format, you can also select the number of colors used to save the picture. Saving a Bitmap picture with fewer colors results in a smaller file size.

How do I print a picture displayed on my screen?

✔ Select the File menu and then click Print. In the Print dialog box, select the printer you want to use and then click the Print button. To preview the picture before printing, select the File menu and then click Print Preview.

OPEN A PICTURE

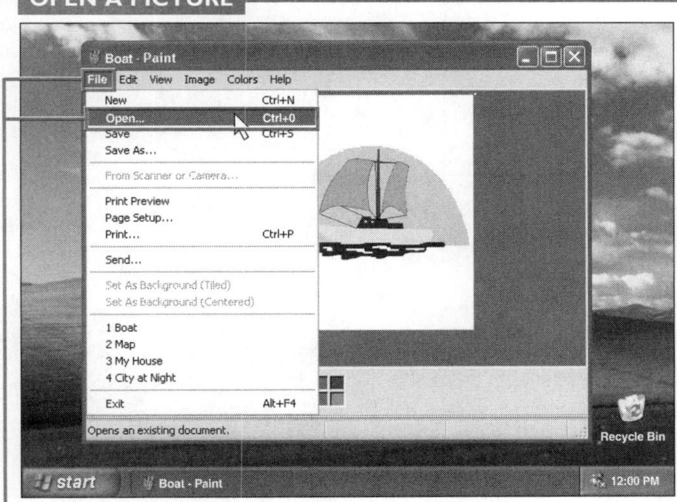

1 Click File.

2 Click Open.

■ The Open dialog box appears.

■ This area shows the location of the displayed pictures. You can click this area to change the location.

3 Click the picture you want to open.

4 Click Open to open the picture.

■ The picture opens and appears on your screen.

USING CALCULATOR

Windows provides a calculator to help you perform calculations. You can work with the Calculator in either the Standard or Scientific view.

The Calculator's Standard view allows you to perform basic mathematical calculations. In this view, the Calculator resembles a small handheld calculator.

You can use the Scientific view to perform more complex mathematical calculations. This view lets you calculate factorial numbers, numbers raised to an exponent, sines, cosines or tangents of numbers and much more.

You can enter information into the Calculator by using your mouse to click the Calculator buttons or by using the keys on your keyboard, including the keys on the numeric keypad. To be able to enter numbers using the numeric keypad, the Num Lock setting must be on. A status light on the keyboard indicates that this setting is on. You may need to press the Num Lock key on your keyboard to turn on the setting.

The result of each calculation you perform appears at the top of the Calculator window.

USING CALCULATOR

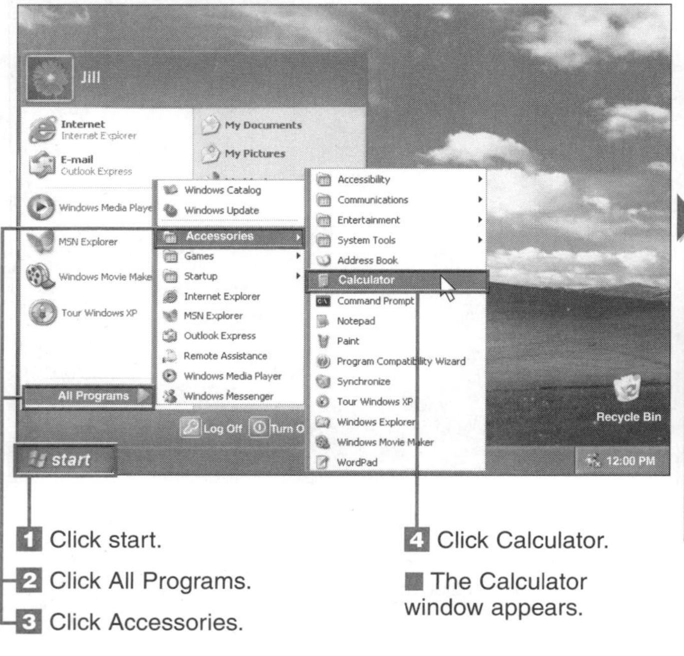

1 Click start.

2 Click All Programs.

3 Click Accessories.

4 Click Calculator.

■ The Calculator window appears.

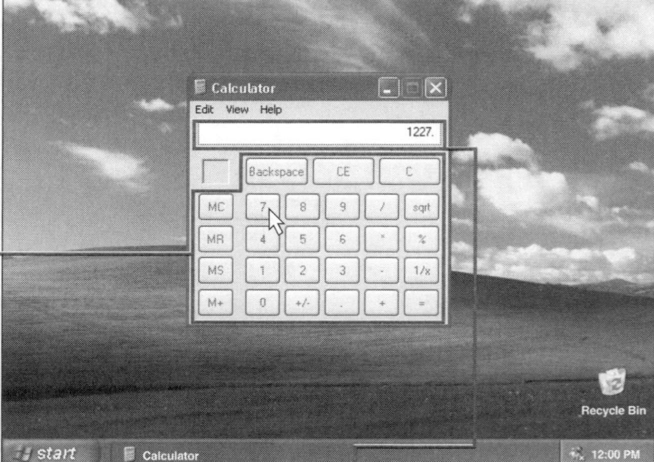

5 To enter information into the Calculator, click each button as you would press the buttons on a handheld calculator.

Note: You can also use the keys on your keyboard to enter information.

■ This area displays the numbers you enter and the result of each calculation.

■ You can click C to start a new calculation at any time.

How can I determine what a button on the Calculator does?

✔ Right-click a button of interest. A box containing the text "What's This?" appears. Click this box to display information about the button. You can click a blank area on your screen to remove the information.

Can I have the Calculator display commas in large numbers?

✔ Yes. Using commas can help make the numbers displayed in the Calculator window easier to read. To display commas, choose the View menu and select Digit grouping.

How can I copy the result of a calculation into another program?

✔ To copy the result of a calculation, press the Ctrl and C keys. In the other program, position the insertion point where you want to paste the result and then press the Ctrl and V keys. You can also use this technique to copy a number you have selected from another program into the Calculator.

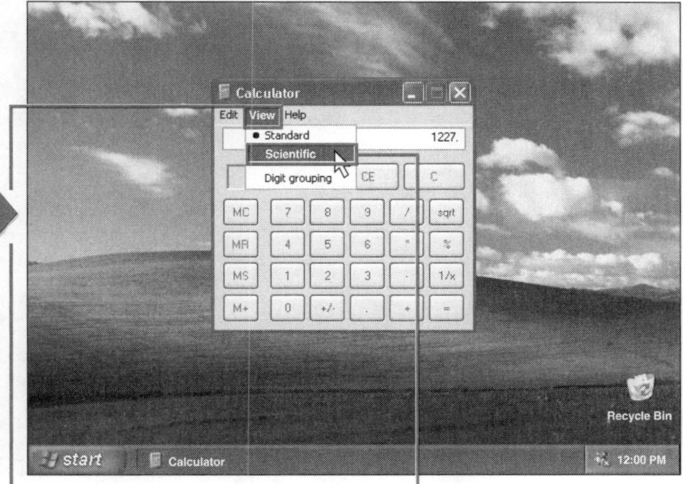

6 To change to the Scientific view of the Calculator, click View.

7 Click Scientific.

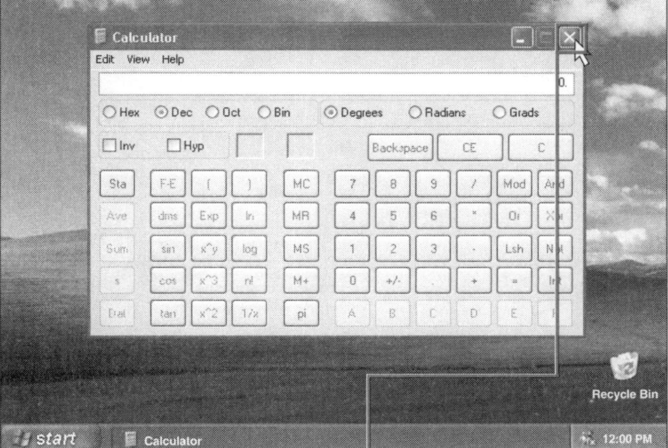

■ The Scientific view of the Calculator appears. This view offers additional features that allow you to perform advanced scientific and statistical calculations.

Note: To return to the Standard view, perform steps 6 and 7, selecting Standard in step 7.

8 When you finish using the Calculator, click ☒ to close the Calculator window.

USING NOTEPAD

Notepad is a fast and easy-to-use text editor that can help you accomplish many tasks. Notepad does not require a lot of your computer's resources to run.

Notepad is useful for creating small text documents that do not require formatting or graphics. Notepad is also useful for creating and editing Web pages and viewing files with the .log or .ini extension.

Most word processors and desktop publishing programs can open documents created in Notepad. This makes Notepad useful for creating documents you plan to exchange with people who use a different operating system, such as a Macintosh or UNIX operating system.

By default, Notepad displays each paragraph in a document on one line. To read an entire line, you have to scroll from left to right in the window. You can use Notepad's Word Wrap feature to wrap the text to fit in the window. Wrapping text can make the document easier to read.

You can have Notepad enter the current time and date set in your computer into a document. This is useful if you use Notepad to create documents such as logs and want to quickly record when each document was created.

USING NOTEPAD

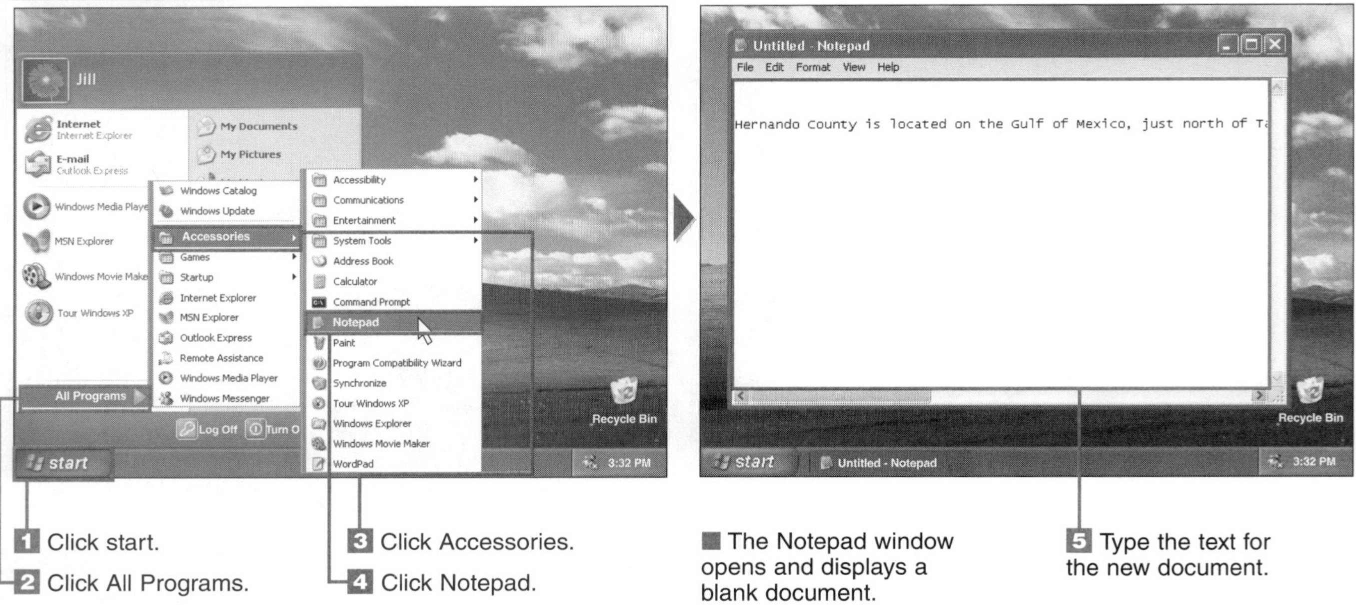

1 Click start.

2 Click All Programs.

3 Click Accessories.

4 Click Notepad.

■ The Notepad window opens and displays a blank document.

5 Type the text for the new document.

How do I save a document in Notepad?

✔ Choose the File menu and then select Save. The first time you save a document, the Save As dialog box appears, allowing you to name the document.

How do I open a document I previously saved?

✔ Choose the File menu, select Open and then double-click the document you want to open. Notepad lets you work with only one document at a time. If you are currently working with a document, save the document before opening another.

Is there a way to have Notepad automatically enter the time and date into my document?

✔ If you type .LOG on the first line of a document, Notepad will add the current time and date to the end of the document each time you open the document.

How can I make the text I type in Notepad easier to read?

✔ You can change the font that Notepad uses to display the text. To change the font, choose the Format menu and then click Font to display the Font dialog box. You can then choose the font, style and size you want to use.

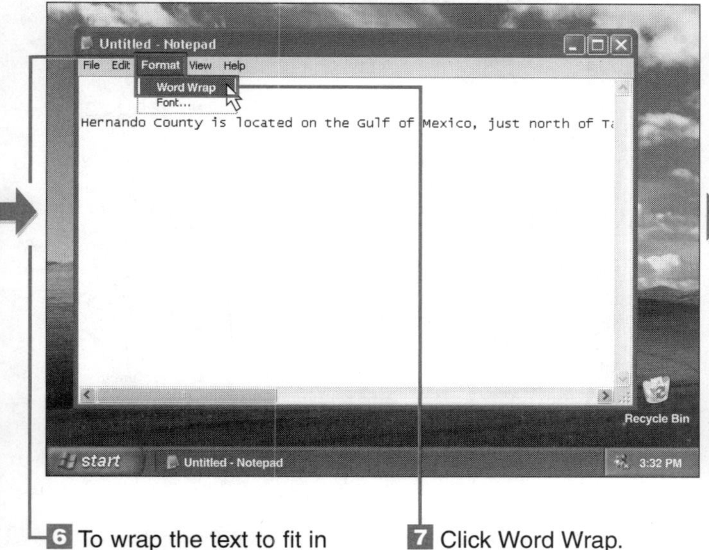

6 To wrap the text to fit in the window, click Format.

7 Click Word Wrap.

■ Notepad wraps the text to fit in the window.

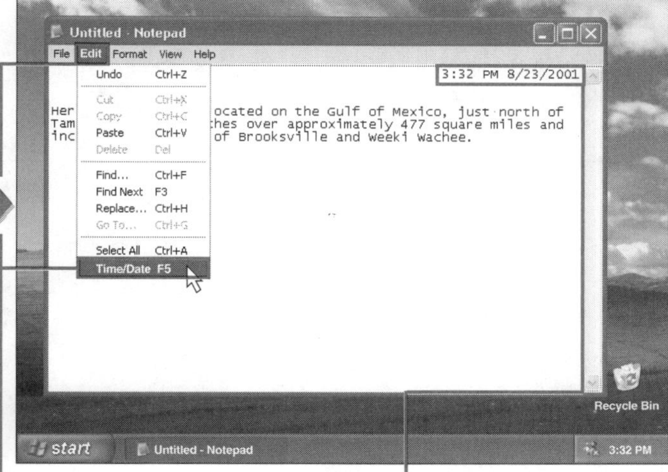

8 To insert the current time and date at the location of the flashing insertion point, click Edit.

9 Click Time/Date.

■ Notepad inserts the current time and date into your document.

Note: You can also press the F5 key to insert the current time and date.

USING CHARACTER MAP

You can use Character Map to include special characters in your documents that are not available on your keyboard. Special characters can include upper and lower case accented letters such as é, graphical characters such as ✎, one character fractions such as ¼ and symbols such as ©.

There are many sets of characters, or fonts, that you can choose from.

The Character Map window displays all the characters for each font. Many fonts contain regular numbers and letters in addition to the special characters, while some fonts contain only special characters. For example, the Wingdings font contains a variety of bullet characters and arrows.

You can view an enlarged version of each character a font offers.

This can help you select the characters you want to add to your documents.

Once you have selected the special characters you want to use, you can copy the special characters from Character Map and paste them into your documents. Keep in mind that you can only paste characters into documents created in Windows-based programs.

USING CHARACTER MAP

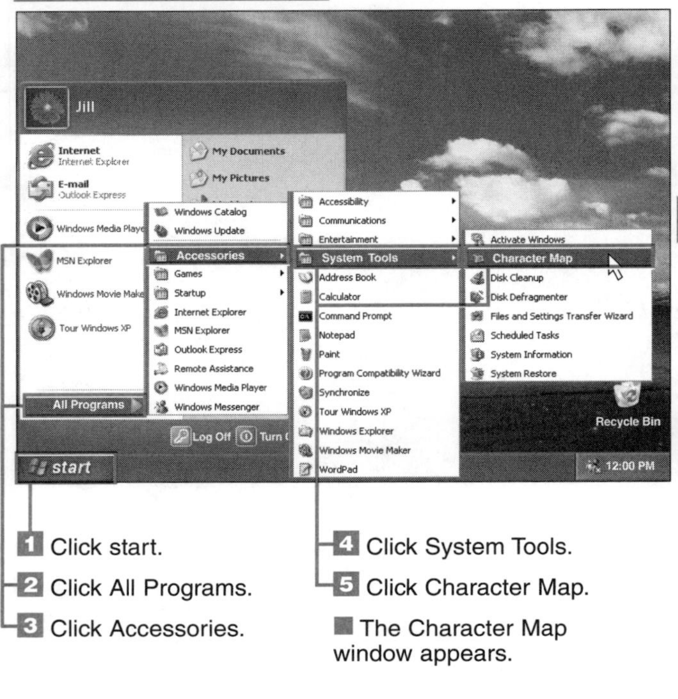

1 Click start.

2 Click All Programs.

3 Click Accessories.

4 Click System Tools.

5 Click Character Map.

■ The Character Map window appears.

6 Click this area to display a list of the available fonts.

7 Click the font that contains the set of characters you want to display.

■ This area displays the characters for the font you selected.

8 To display an enlarged version of a character, click the character.

How do I search for a character of interest?

✔ In the Character Map window, select Advanced view (☐ changes to ☑). Click the box beside Search for. Then type a name or description of the character you want to find and press the Enter key. This search feature is not available for all fonts.

Is there another way of copying a character into a document?

✔ If you are working with a document in a program that supports drag and drop, you can click the character you want to copy in the Character Map window and then drag the character directly into the document.

Can I add special characters to a document without opening Character Map?

✔ Many special characters have a keystroke combination you can use to quickly add the characters to a document. For example, to enter the copyright symbol ©, hold down the Alt key as you enter 0169. When you click a character in the Character Map window, the keystroke combination for the character appears in the bottom right corner of the window. When using a keystroke combination, make sure you use the numeric keypad on your keyboard to enter numbers. Also, make sure the fonts selected in Character Map and in the document you are entering the character into are the same.

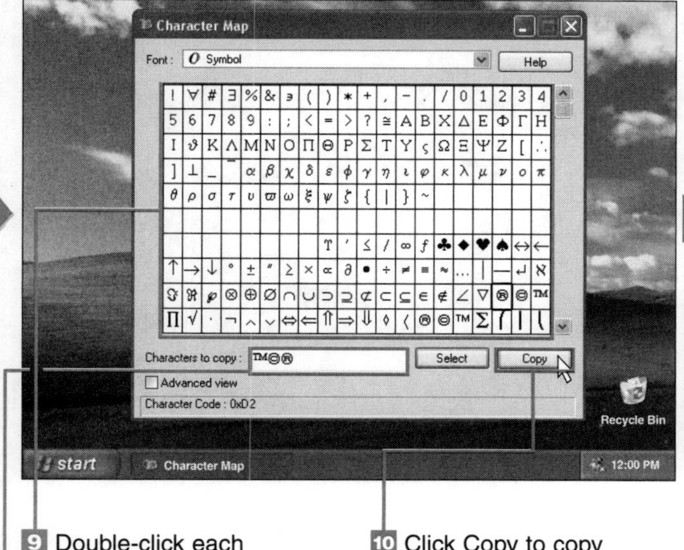

9 Double-click each character you want to select.

■ This area displays each character you select.

10 Click Copy to copy all the characters you selected.

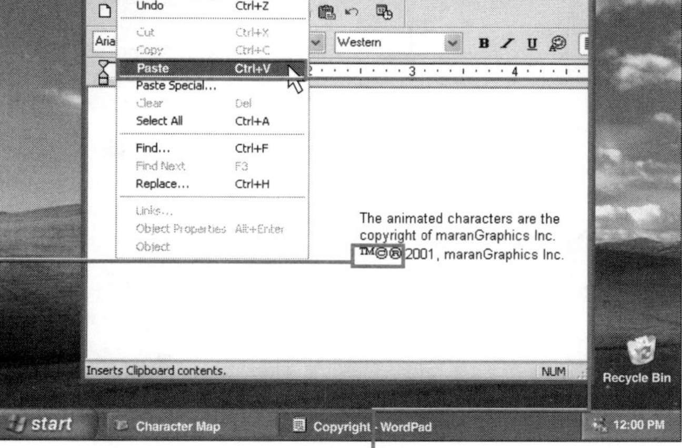

11 Open the document you want to receive a copy of the characters.

12 Position the insertion point where you want the characters to appear.

13 Click Edit.

14 Click Paste.

■ The characters appear in the document.

USING THE COMMAND PROMPT

You can use the Command Prompt window to work with commands in Windows. For example, you can use the Command Prompt window to display the contents of a directory or to copy a list of files from one directory to another.

You can also use the Command Prompt window to run MS-DOS programs in Windows. Windows can run many MS-DOS games and programs without any problems. If Windows cannot run an MS-DOS program, a message may appear indicating that the program is not suitable for use with Windows.

To make the contents of the Command Prompt window easier to read, you can enlarge the window to fill the entire screen. Some MS-DOS programs, especially games, can run only in full-screen mode. You can also change the size of the Command Prompt window as you would change the size of any window.

Although you can have several Command Prompt windows open at the same time, they require some of your computer's resources. Running programs in several Command Prompt windows at once may slow down your computer's performance.

USING THE COMMAND PROMPT

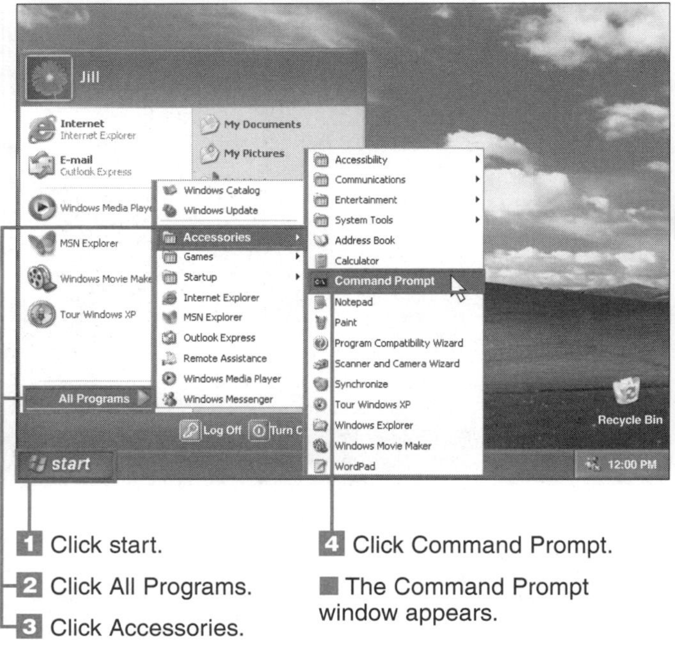

1 Click start.

2 Click All Programs.

3 Click Accessories.

4 Click Command Prompt.

■ The Command Prompt window appears.

■ You can enter commands and start programs in the window. In this example, we enter the **dir** command to list the contents of the current directory.

5 To fill the entire screen with the Command Prompt window, press and hold down the Alt key as you press the Enter key.

How do I find out how to use a command in the Command Prompt window?

✔ To find out which commands you can use, type **help** in the Command Prompt window and then press Enter. To find out how to use a command, type the name of the command followed by a space and /? and then press Enter. For example, type **move /?** to find out how to use the move command.

Can I copy text from the Command Prompt window?

✔ Yes. Right-click the title bar of the Command Prompt window, select Edit and then choose Mark. Drag the mouse pointer over the text you want to copy to highlight the text and then press Enter. Then open the program you want to receive the copy, click the Edit menu and select Paste.

How can I change the font and colors displayed in the Command Prompt window?

✔ Right-click the title bar of the Command Prompt window and then select Properties to display the "Command Prompt" Properties dialog box. To change the font of text, choose the Font tab and then select the size and font you want to use. To change the colors, choose the Colors tab, click an item you want to change (○ changes to ⊙) and then select a color for the item. Click OK and then click OK in the dialog box that appears.

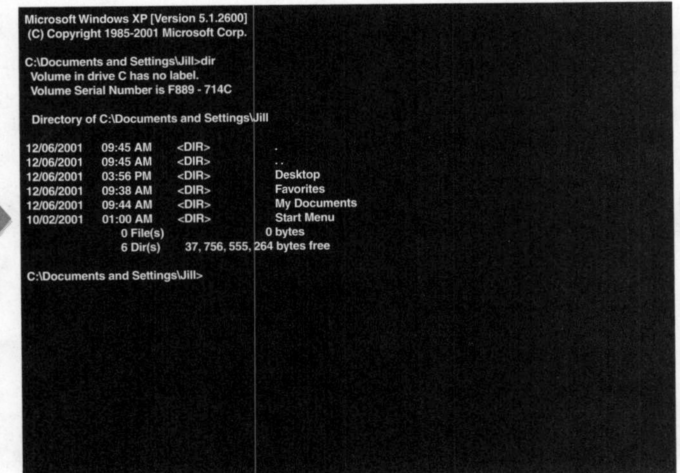

■ The Command Prompt window fills the entire screen.

6 To return the screen to a window, press and hold down the Alt key as you press the Enter key.

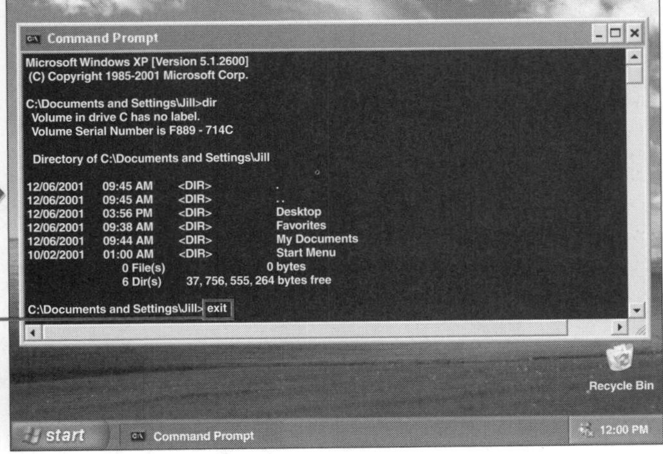

7 When you finish using the Command Prompt window, type **exit** and then press the Enter key to close the window.

SECTION III

8) MANAGE MULTIPLE USERS

9) CUSTOMIZE YOUR COMPUTER

CUSTOMIZE WINDOWS XP

10) CUSTOMIZE THE TASKBAR AND START MENU

11) USING THE ACCESSIBILITY FEATURES

CREATE A USER ACCOUNT

If you share your computer with other people, you can create a personalized user account for each person. Each user account must have a unique name. Windows will keep the personal files and settings, such as screen savers and desktop backgrounds, separate for each account.

You must be logged in as a computer administrator in order to create a user account.

When you create a user account, you must select the type of account you want to create. There are two account types you can choose from—computer administrator and limited.

A user with a computer administrator account can perform any task on the computer. For example, the user can create and change all user accounts as well as install programs and hardware.

A user with a limited account can perform only certain tasks on the computer. For example, the user can create and change their own password and change some computer settings but cannot delete important files or create user accounts.

Windows automatically creates the Guest account on your computer. The Guest account allows a person without a user account to use the computer.

CREATE A USER ACCOUNT

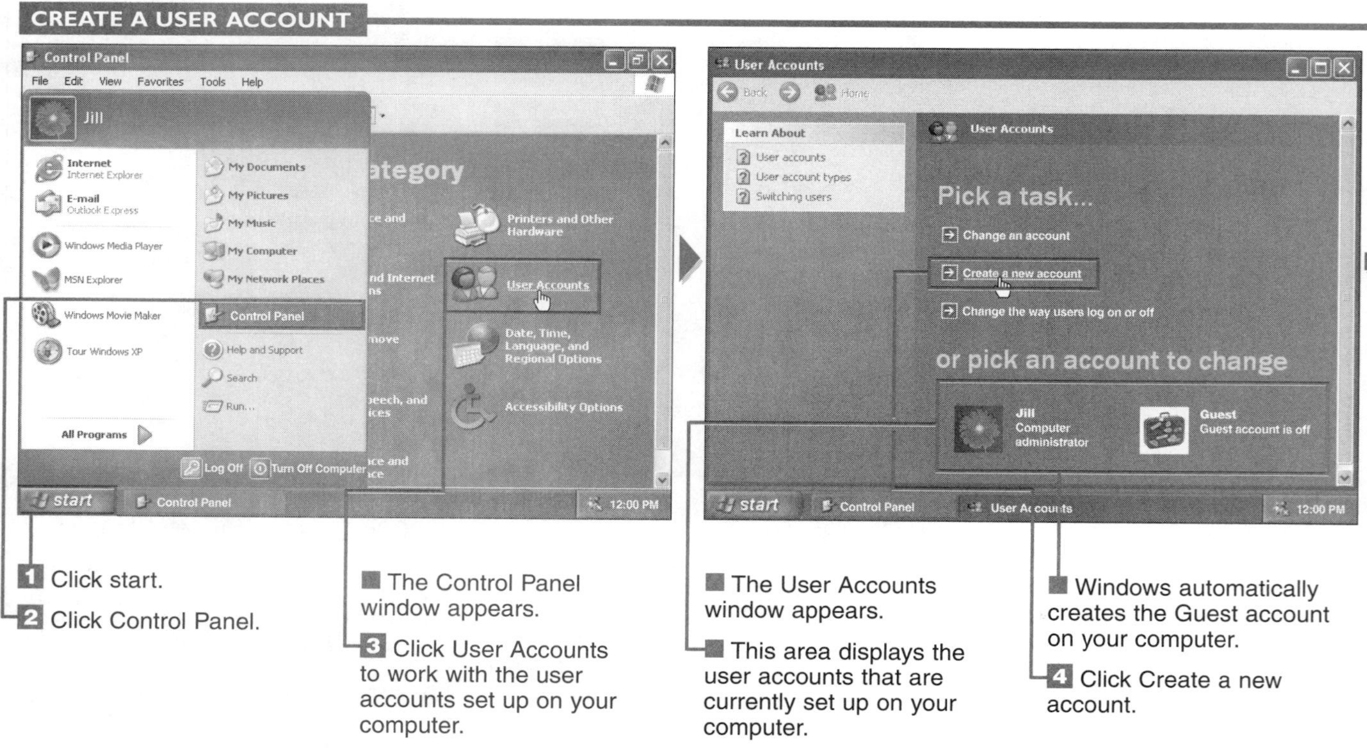

1 Click start.

2 Click Control Panel.

■ The Control Panel window appears.

3 Click User Accounts to work with the user accounts set up on your computer.

■ The User Accounts window appears.

■ This area displays the user accounts that are currently set up on your computer.

■ Windows automatically creates the Guest account on your computer.

4 Click Create a new account.

How can I change the type of user account I created?

✔ Perform steps 1 to 3 below to display the User Accounts window and then click the user account you want to change. Click Change the account type or Change my account type and choose a new type of account. Then click Change Account Type. You must always have at least one computer administrator account set up on the computer.

Can I change the name of a user account?

✔ If you have a computer administrator account, you can change the name of any user account set up on your computer. Perform steps 1 to 3 below to display the User Accounts window and then click the user account you want to change. Click Change the name or Change my name and type a new name for the account. Then click Change Name.

How do I change the picture that appears for an account I created?

✔ To change the picture for a user account, perform steps 1 to 3 below and then click the user account you want to change. Click Change the picture or Change my picture to display a list of pictures you can choose from. Click the picture you want to use and then click Change Picture.

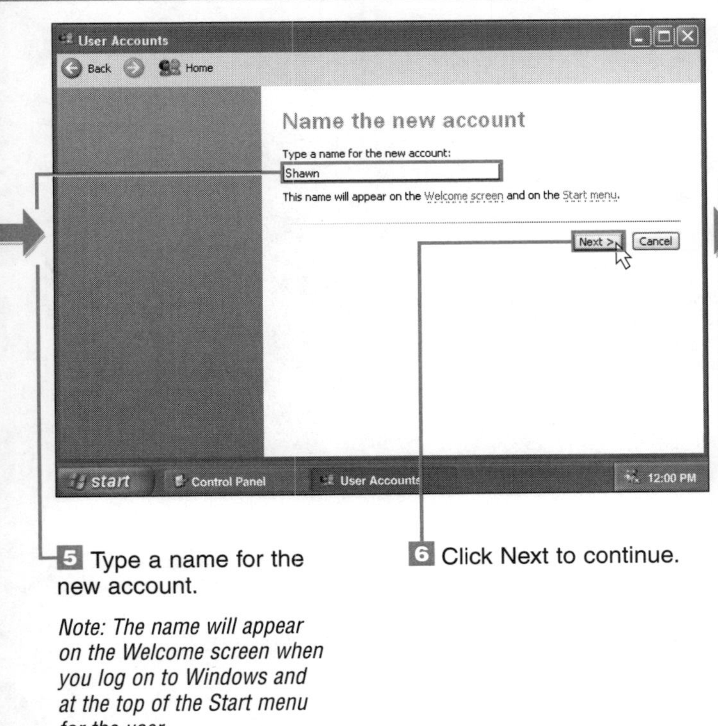

5 Type a name for the new account.

Note: The name will appear on the Welcome screen when you log on to Windows and at the top of the Start menu for the user.

6 Click Next to continue.

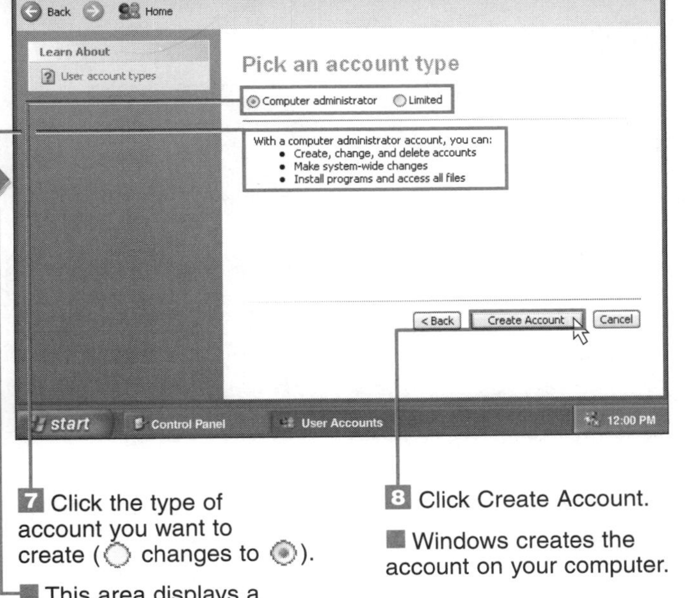

7 Click the type of account you want to create (○ changes to ◉).

■ This area displays a description of the account type you selected.

8 Click Create Account.

■ Windows creates the account on your computer.

ASSIGN A PASSWORD TO A USER ACCOUNT

You can assign a password to your user account to prevent other people from accessing the account. You will need to enter the password each time you want to log on to Windows.

Assigning a password to your user account is useful when you want to keep your customized settings and programs secure from other users set up on your computer.

To make it harder for other people to guess your password, you should choose a password that is at least seven characters long and contains a random combination of letters, numbers and symbols. Do not use words that people can easily associate with you, such as your name.

To protect your password, you should take care not to reveal the password to anyone. Avoid writing your password down and try to change your password on a regular basis.

If you have a computer administrator account, you can assign passwords to other accounts set up on your computer. If you have a limited account, you can assign a password only to your own account. For more information about the types of accounts, see page 174.

ASSIGN A PASSWORD TO A USER ACCOUNT

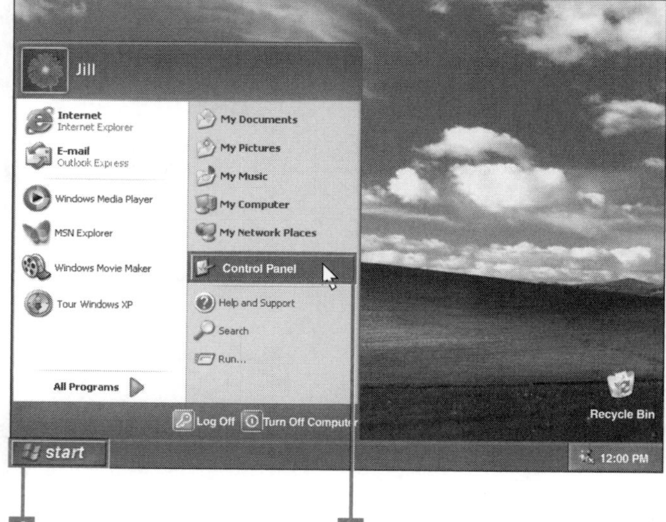

1 Click start.

2 Click Control Panel.

■ The Control Panel window appears.

3 Click User Accounts to work with the user accounts set up on your computer.

Will assigning a password to my user account prevent other users from viewing my files?

✔ If your computer uses the NTFS file system, other users with computer administrator accounts set up on your computer will be able to view the files in your personal folders. You must make the folders private to prevent users from viewing the files. For information about making your personal folders private, see page 192. For information about viewing the personal files of other users set up on your computer, see page 190.

Can I use the User Accounts window to change any of my other passwords?

✔ Yes. You can change the password for any network locations or Web sites Windows stores your login information for. For example, you can change the password for the Passport account you use to log in to Windows Messenger. Click the user account you want to change a password for and then click the Manage my network passwords link. The dialog box that appears lists the network and Internet locations Windows currently stores login information for. Click the location you want to change your password for and then click Properties to change your password.

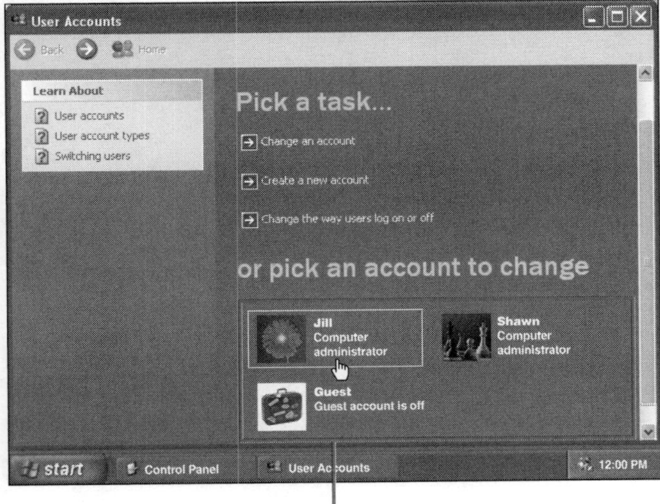

■ The User Accounts window appears.

■ If you have a limited account, skip to step 5.

■ If you have a computer administrator account, this area displays the accounts set up on your computer.

4 Click the account you want to assign a password to.

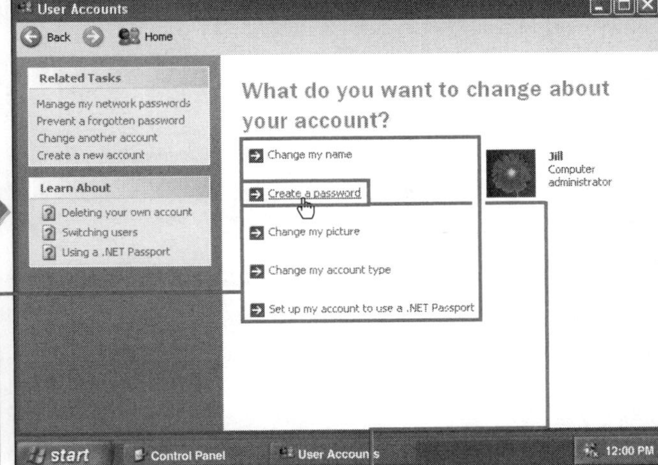

■ A list of tasks that you can perform to change the account appears.

5 Click Create a password to assign a password to the account.

CONTINUED

ASSIGN A PASSWORD TO A USER ACCOUNT (CONTINUED)

When assigning a password to a user account, you must enter the password twice to confirm the password. Keep in mind that passwords are case sensitive. This means that you will need to enter the same combination of upper and lower case letters each time you use the password.

You can create a password hint that will help you remember your password should you forget it. The password hint will be available on the Welcome screen each time you log on to Windows. Every user set up on your computer will be able to view the password hint, so you should choose a hint that is understandable to you, but not to other users.

After creating your password, Windows may ask if you want to make your files and folders private to prevent other people from accessing the files and folders. For more information, see page 192.

You can change the existing password for your user account. If you have a computer administrator account, you can also change the passwords for other user accounts set up on your computer. When you change the password for another user's account, any stored passwords and security certificates associated with the account will be lost.

ASSIGN A PASSWORD TO A USER ACCOUNT (CONTINUED)

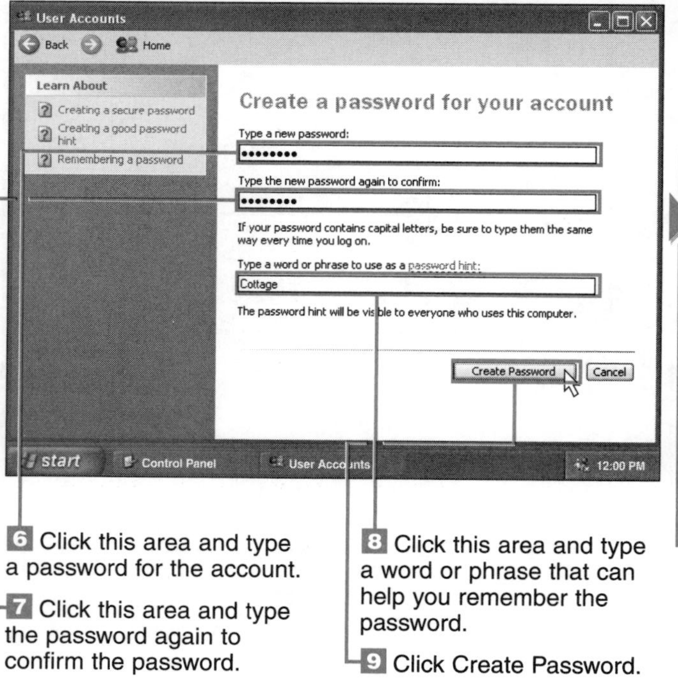

6 Click this area and type a password for the account.

7 Click this area and type the password again to confirm the password.

8 Click this area and type a word or phrase that can help you remember the password.

9 Click Create Password.

■ Windows may ask if you want to make your files and folders private to prevent other people from accessing the files and folders.

Note: This message appears only if your computer uses the NTFS file system and you are assigning a password to your own computer administrator account.

10 Click an option to specify if you want to make your files and folders private.

What should I do if I forget my password?

✔ You can display your password hint on the Welcome screen by clicking the question mark beside the password area for your account. If the password hint does not remind you of the password, you can have a user with a computer administrator account change your password.

Is there any way I can protect myself against forgetting my password?

✔ You can create a password reset disk that will allow you to reset your password yourself if you forget the password. Perform steps 1 to 4 starting on page 176 and then click Prevent a forgotten password. Then follow the instructions on your screen. Make sure you store the password reset disk in a safe place, since anyone will be able to reset your password using the disk.

How do I remove a password from a user account?

✔ Perform steps 1 to 4 starting on page 176 and then click Remove my password or Remove the password. Type the current password for the user account and then click Remove Password. You must have a computer administrator account to remove another user's password.

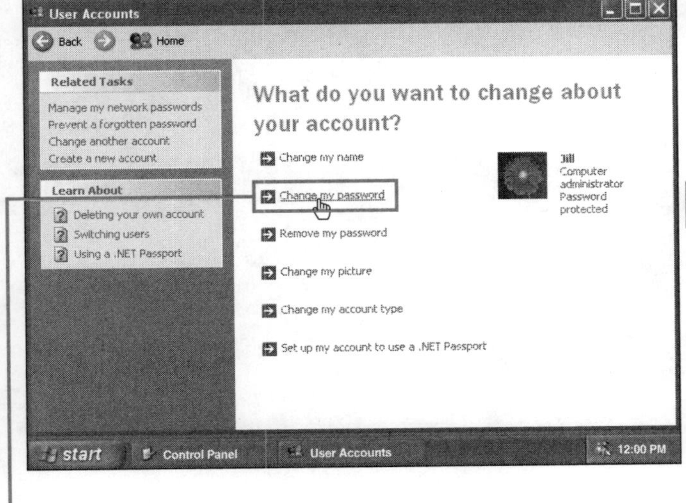

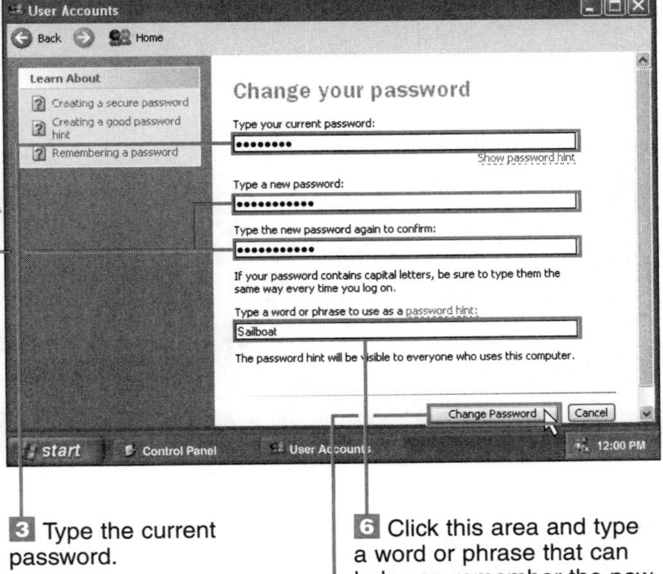

CHANGE A PASSWORD

1 To select the account you want to change the password for, perform steps 1 to 4 starting on page 176.

2 Click Change my password.

Note: If you have a computer administrator account and you are changing the password for another account, click Change the password in step 2. Then skip to step 4.

3 Type the current password.

4 Click this area and type a new password.

5 Click this area and type the new password again to confirm the password.

6 Click this area and type a word or phrase that can help you remember the new password.

7 Click Change Password.

DELETE A USER ACCOUNT

If a person no longer uses your computer, you can delete the person's user account from your computer. You must be logged in as a computer administrator to delete a user account. For information about the types of user accounts, see page 174.

As a security precaution, you should always delete user accounts that will no longer be used. Deleting user accounts also helps free up space on your computer's hard drive.

When you delete a user account, you can choose to keep or delete the user's personal files.

If you choose to keep the personal files, Windows will save the files on your desktop in a new folder that has the same name as the deleted user account. If you choose to delete the personal files, Windows will remove all the files in the user account. If possible, you should check with the person before deleting the files to ensure that the user account does not contain important files that the person may need later.

You cannot delete the guest account from your computer. For information about the guest account, see page 182.

DELETE A USER ACCOUNT

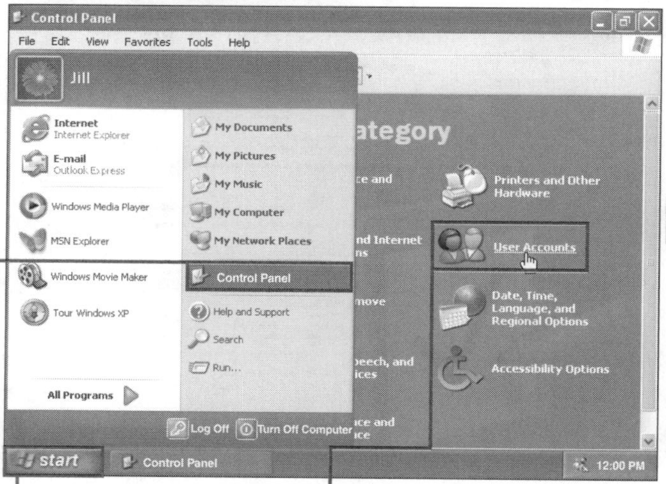

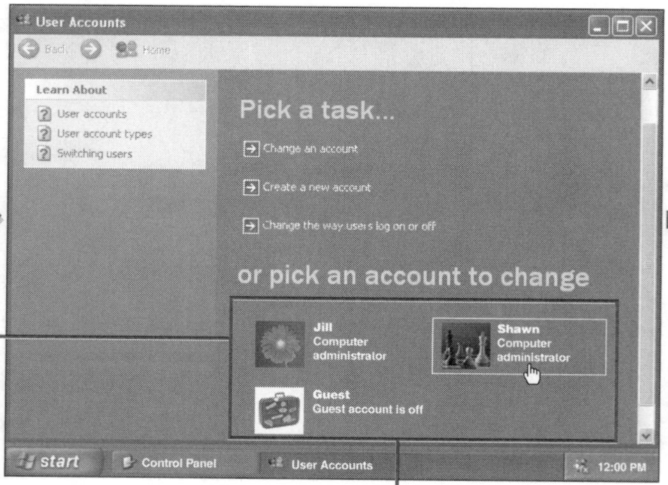

1 Click start.

2 Click Control Panel.

■ The Control Panel window appears.

3 Click User Accounts to work with the user accounts set up on your computer.

■ The User Accounts window appears.

■ This area displays the accounts that are set up on your computer.

4 Click the account you want to delete.

If I choose to keep the personal files for a deleted user account, which files will Windows save?

✔ Windows will save the user's personal files that are displayed on the desktop and stored in the My Documents folder and its subfolders. Windows will not save the user's e-mail messages, list of favorite Web pages and other computer settings.

Can I delete a computer administrator account?

✔ Yes. If you have a computer administrator account, you can delete other computer administrator accounts. Windows will not allow you to delete the last computer administrator account on your computer. This ensures that one computer administrator account always exists on the computer.

Is there any way to restore an account I deleted?

✔ If you regret deleting an account, you can use the System Restore feature to return your computer to a time before you deleted the account. For more information about the System Restore feature, see page 584.

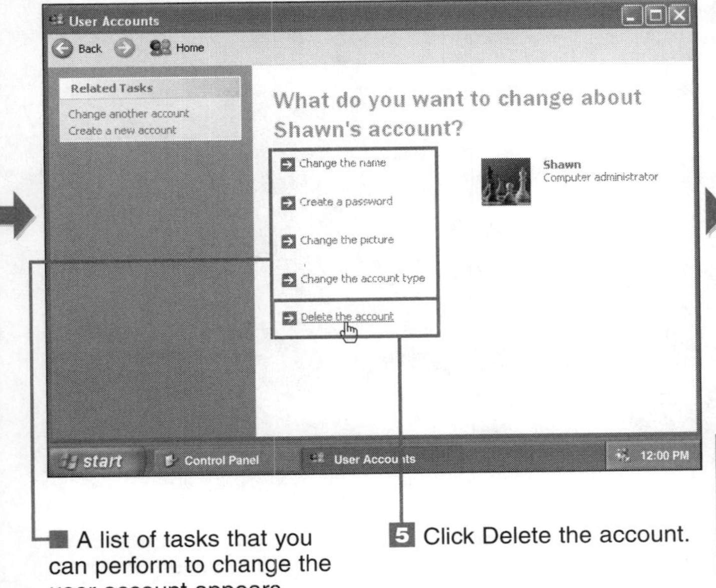

■ A list of tasks that you can perform to change the user account appears.

5 Click Delete the account.

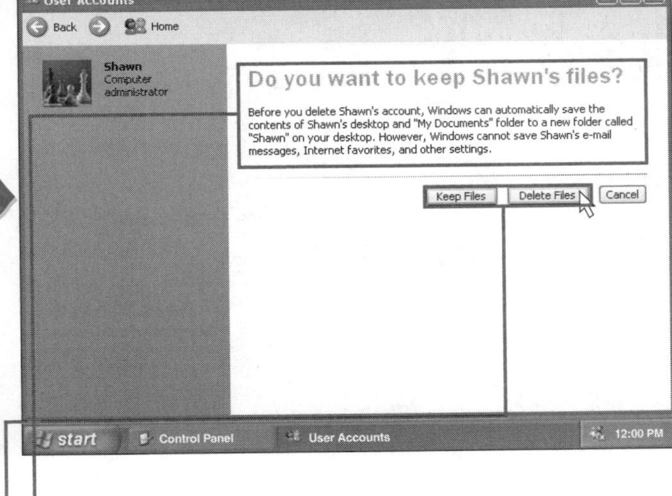

■ Windows asks if you want to keep the user's personal files.

6 Click an option to specify if you want to keep or delete the user's personal files.

7 Windows will display a message, asking you to confirm that you want to delete the account. Click Delete Account to permanently delete the account.

TURN ON THE GUEST ACCOUNT

You can turn on the Guest account to allow a person who does not have a user account set up on your computer to use the computer. Windows automatically creates the Guest account on your computer. As a security precaution, the Guest account is initially turned off.

You must be logged in as a computer administrator to turn on the Guest account.

When the Guest account is turned on, anyone can log on to your computer using the account. You cannot protect the Guest account with a password.

For security reasons, a person who logs on to your computer using the Guest account can perform only certain tasks on the computer. For example, the person can run programs that have already been installed on the computer, but cannot install any new programs. A person logged in as a guest also cannot create new user accounts or modify existing user accounts.

There is only one Guest account available. Every person who logs on to your computer as a guest must use the same Guest account. You cannot change the name of the Guest account.

TURN ON THE GUEST ACCOUNT

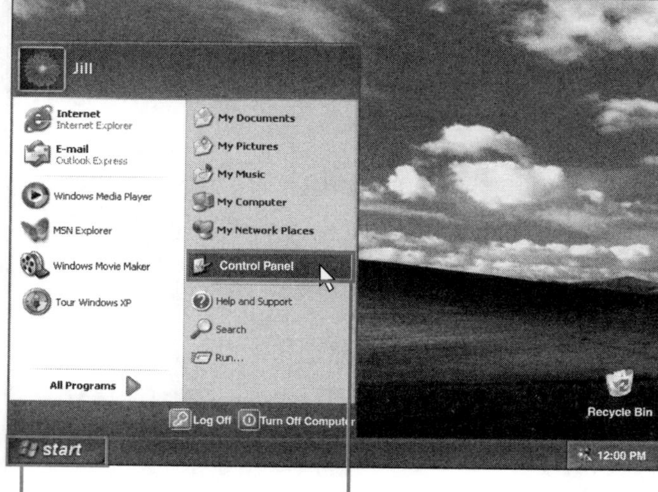

1 Click start.

2 Click Control Panel.

■ The Control Panel window appears.

3 Click User Accounts to work with the user accounts set up on your computer.

How do I turn off the Guest account?

✔ You must be logged in as a computer administrator to turn off the Guest account. In the User Accounts window, click Guest and then choose Turn off the guest account. As a security precaution, you should always turn off the Guest account when the account is not being used.

Can I change the picture that appears for the Guest account?

✔ You can change the picture for the Guest account when logged in as a computer administrator or as a guest. In the User Accounts window, click Guest and then choose Change the picture or Change my picture to display a list of pictures you can choose from. Click the picture you want to use and then click Change Picture.

Will a person who is logged in as a guest be able to view my personal files?

✔ If your computer uses the NTFS file system, a guest will not be able to access the personal files of any users set up on your computer. A guest will be able to view the personal files of other users if your computer uses the FAT file system.

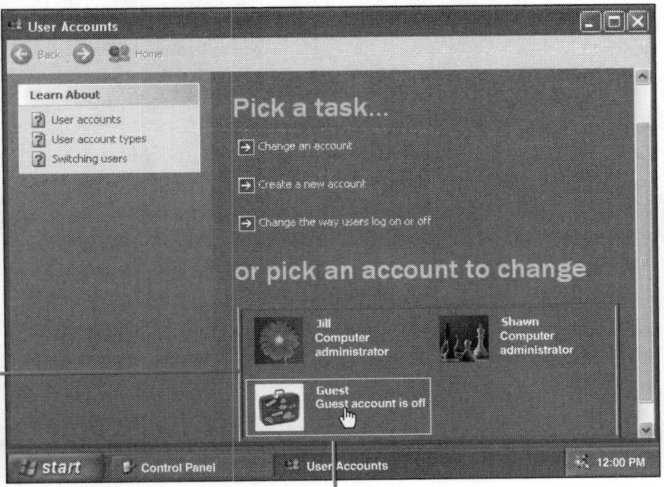

■ The User Accounts window appears.

■ This area displays the user accounts that are currently set up on your computer.

■ Windows automatically creates the Guest account on your computer.

4 Click Guest to turn on the Guest account.

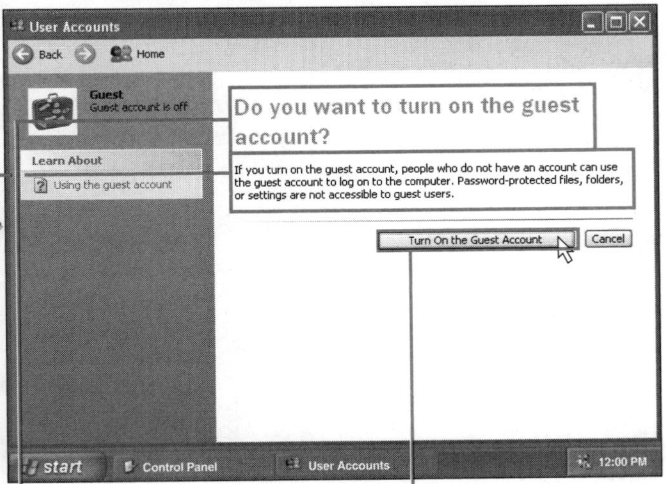

■ Windows asks if you want to turn on the Guest account.

■ This area displays information about the Guest account.

5 Click Turn On the Guest Account.

ADD A .NET PASSPORT TO A USER ACCOUNT

You can add a .NET Passport to your user account to save the information for the Passport with your user account. A .NET Passport allows you to access many features and services on the Internet using a single e-mail address and password. The .NET Passport Wizard guides you step by step through the process of adding a .NET Passport to your user account.

Adding a .NET Passport to your user account allows Windows to automatically sign you in to services that use .NET Passports, such as Windows Messenger. This saves you from having to enter your e-mail address and password for the Passport each time you want to use the services. For information about Windows Messenger, see pages 484 to 501.

If you have a Hotmail or MSN.com e-mail account, you already have a .NET Passport that you can add to your user account. If you do not already have a .NET Passport, you can use the .NET Passport Wizard to create a Passport. You can also obtain a Passport at the www.passport.com Web site.

You must be connected to the Internet to add a .NET Passport to your user account.

ADD A .NET PASSPORT TO A USER ACCOUNT

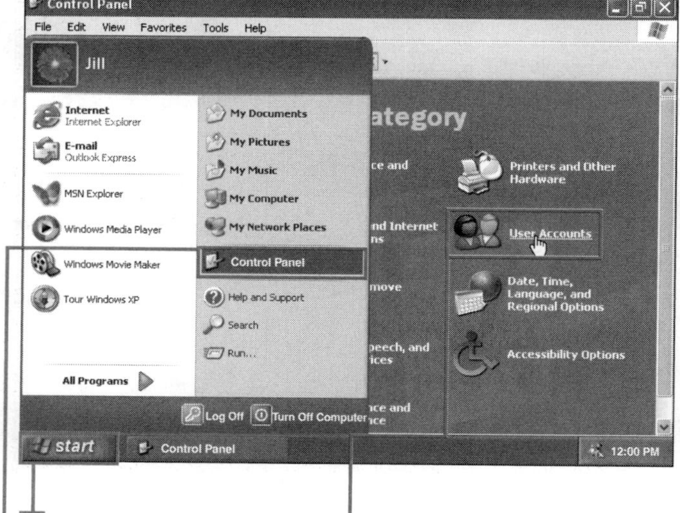

1 Click start.

2 Click Control Panel.

■ The Control Panel window appears.

3 Click User Accounts to work with the user accounts set up on your computer.

■ The User Accounts window appears.

■ If you have a limited account, skip to step 5.

■ If you have a computer administrator account, this area displays the accounts set up on your computer.

4 Click your user account.

The Set up my account to use a .NET Passport option is not available. What is wrong?

✔ If you have used Windows Messenger, you may have already added a .NET Passport to your user account. The .NET Passport Wizard starts automatically the first time you start Windows Messenger. For more information, see page 484.

Can I use my .NET Passport on other computers?

✔ You can use your .NET Passport on any computer that is connected to the Internet. If you have a user account on another computer running Windows XP, you can add your Passport to the user account. You can also sign in to .NET Passport Web sites and services from any computer by entering the e-mail address and password for the Passport.

Can I have more than one .NET Passport?

✔ You can have multiple .NET Passports, but you can add only one of the Passports to your user account using the .NET Passport Wizard. If you want to change the Passport for your account, perform steps 1 to 4 below and then click Change my .NET Passport. Click the Use a Different Passport button and then enter the information for the new Passport in the wizard.

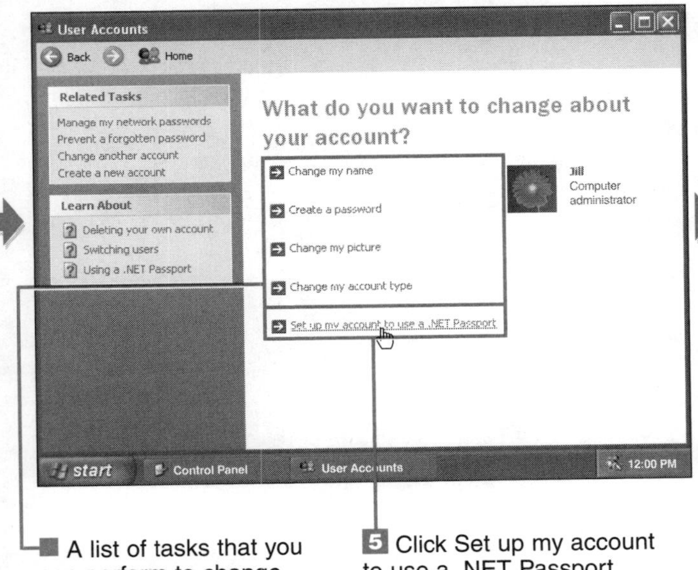

■ A list of tasks that you can perform to change your account appears.

5 Click Set up my account to use a .NET Passport.

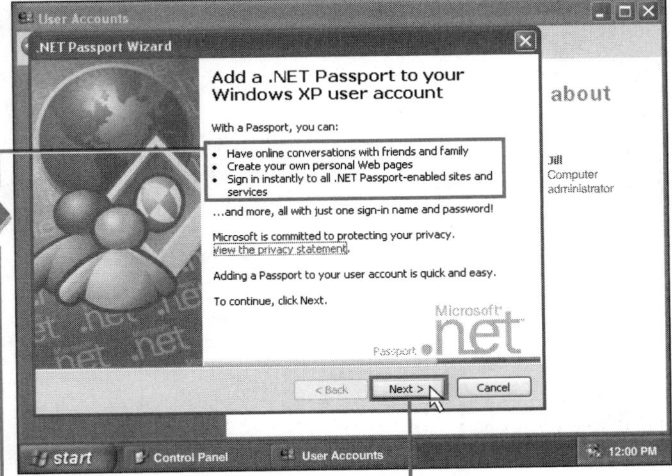

■ The .NET Passport Wizard appears.

■ This area describes tasks that you can perform with a Passport.

6 Click Next to continue.

Note: If you are not currently connected to the Internet, a dialog box will appear, allowing you to connect.

CONTINUED

ADD A .NET PASSPORT TO A USER ACCOUNT (CONTINUED)

When adding a .NET Passport to your user account, the .NET Passport Wizard asks you to enter the e-mail address for the Passport you want to add. You must have an e-mail address to add a .NET Passport to your user account.

The .NET Passport Wizard checks the e-mail address you enter to see if the address is a Passport. If the e-mail address is a Passport, you can enter the password for the Passport to have the wizard add the Passport to your user account.

Once you have completed the .NET Passport Wizard, Windows can quickly enter your Passport information at Web sites that use .NET Passports. For example, Web sites such as www.msn.com and www.ebay.com display Sign In buttons you can click to quickly sign in. Windows will retrieve your information from the Passport stored in your user account and will automatically enter the information for you. You can find a list of Web sites that use Passports at the www.passport.com/Directory Web site.

ADD A .NET PASSPORT TO A USER ACCOUNT (CONTINUED)

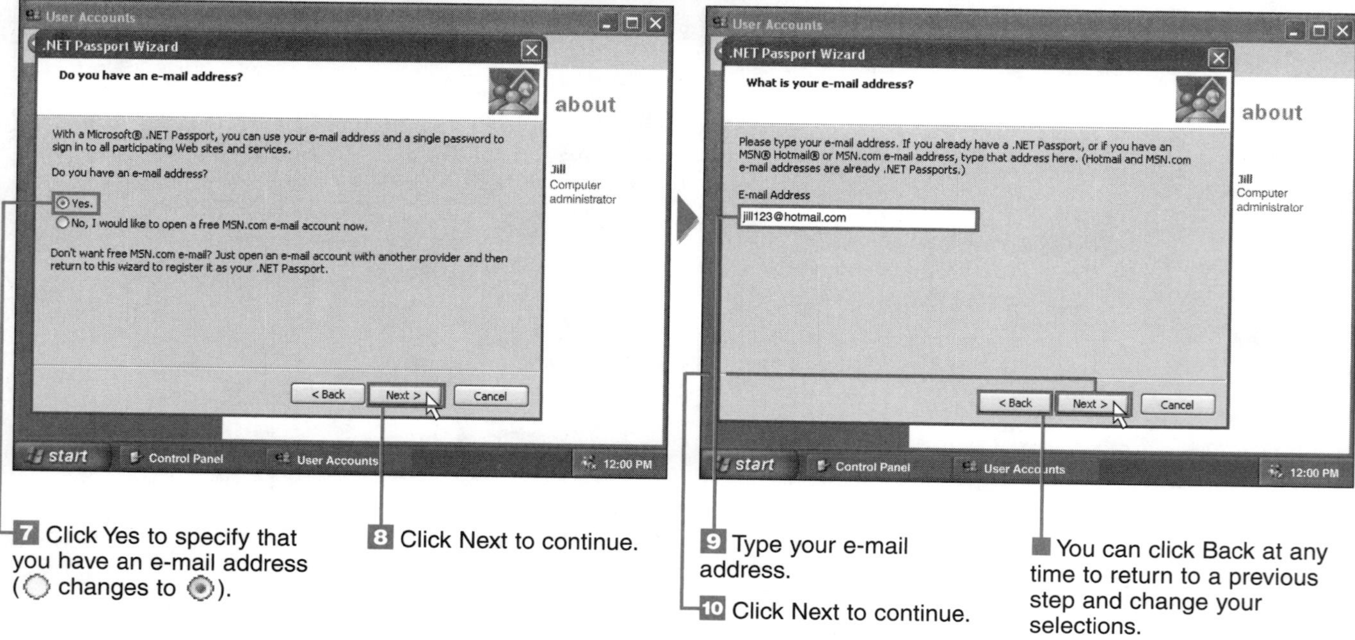

7 Click Yes to specify that you have an e-mail address (○ changes to ◉).

8 Click Next to continue.

9 Type your e-mail address.

10 Click Next to continue.

■ You can click Back at any time to return to a previous step and change your selections.

I do not have an e-mail address. What should I do?

✔ You can sign up for a free MSN.com e-mail account using the .NET Passport Wizard. Click No in step 7 below and then click Next. You can then follow the instructions in the wizard to set up the e-mail account and the Passport.

What should I do if the e-mail address I entered is not a Passport?

✔ The .NET Passport Wizard allows you to create a Passport using any e-mail address. Type a password for the Passport in the areas provided and then click Next. You can then follow the instructions in the wizard to set up the Passport.

How can I change the information for my .NET Passport?

✔ To change the information stored in your .NET Passport, such as your name, address and birth date, click start, select Control Panel and choose User Accounts. Click your user account and select Change my .NET Passport. Then click the Change Passport Attributes button to connect to a Web page that displays the information for your Passport. You can make changes to the information and then click Update. People on the Internet will not be able to view the information for your .NET Passport.

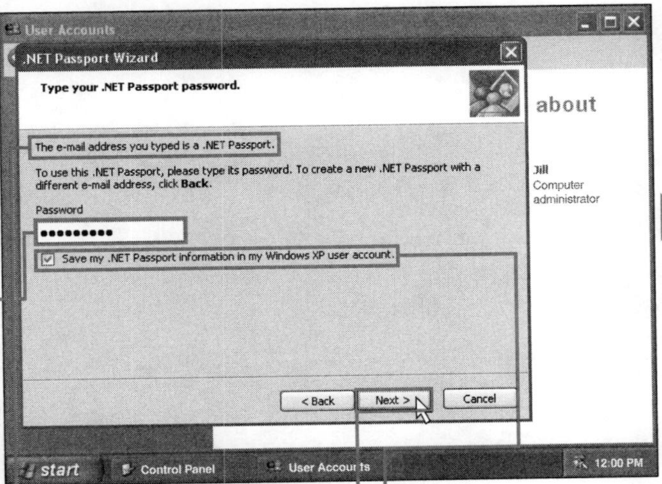

■ If the e-mail address you typed in step 9 is a .NET Passport, this message appears.

11 Type the password for your .NET Passport.

■ This option saves your .NET Passport information in your user account.

12 Click Next to continue.

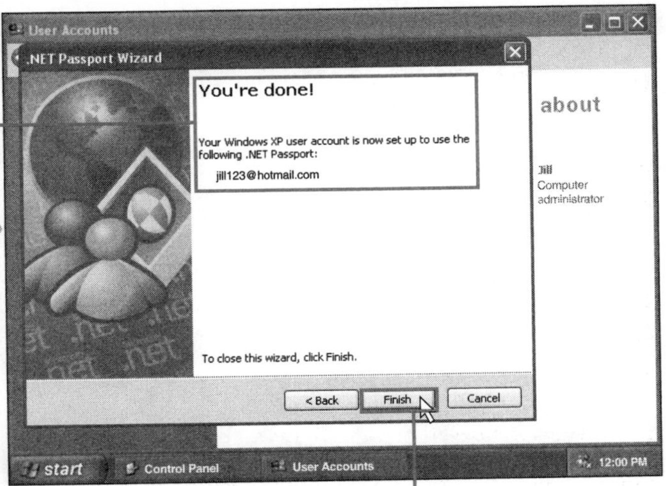

■ This message appears when the .NET Passport you specified has been added to your user account.

13 Click Finish to close the wizard.

LOG ON OR OFF WINDOWS

If multiple user accounts are set up on your computer, you will need to log on to Windows to use the computer. You must log on to Windows each time you turn on your computer or log off Windows to switch between user accounts.

If you have assigned a password to your user account, you must type the password each time you log on to Windows. If you cannot remember your password, you can display the password hint you entered when you created the password. For information about creating user passwords and password hints, see page 176.

You can log off Windows so another person can log on to Windows to use the computer. When you log off Windows, you can choose whether you want to keep your programs and files open or close the programs and files.

Keeping your programs and files open while another person uses the computer allows you to quickly return to your work when the other person finishes using the computer. Closing your open programs and files can free up some of your computer's resources, improving the performance of the computer for the other user.

LOG ON TO WINDOWS

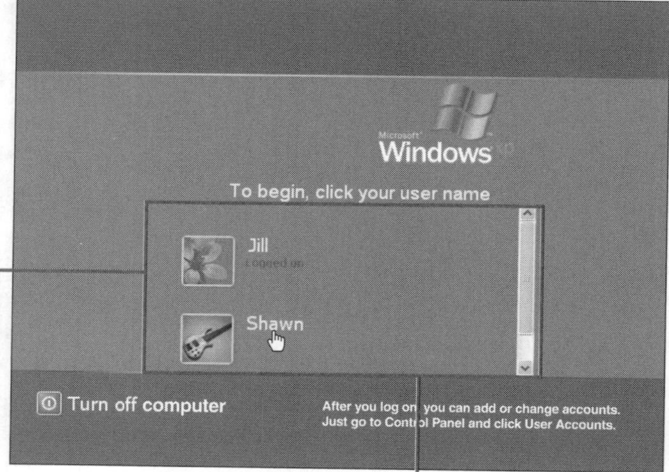

■ When you turn on your computer or log off Windows to switch between user accounts, the Welcome screen appears.

■ This area displays the user accounts set up on your computer.

1 Click the name of your user account.

■ If you assigned a password to your user account, a box appears that allows you to enter your password.

2 If you cannot remember your password, click ? to display the password hint you entered when you created the password.

3 Click this area and type your password. Then press the Enter key to log on to Windows.

■ Windows starts, displaying your own personalized files and computer settings.

Can I prevent people from keeping their programs and files open when they log off Windows?

✔ If you are logged on as a computer administrator, you can turn off the Fast User Switching option to prevent people from keeping their programs and files open while another person uses the computer. Click start, select Control Panel and then click User Accounts. Click Change the way users log on or off, click Use Fast User Switching (☑ changes to ☐) and then click Apply Options. If any other users are logged on to Windows, they will need to log off before you can turn off the Fast User Switching option.

Can I change the way people log on to Windows?

✔ If you want people to log on to Windows using a dialog box similar to the one used in previous versions of Windows, you can turn off the Welcome screen. Click start, select Control Panel and then click User Accounts. Click Change the way users log on or off, click Use the Welcome screen (☑ changes to ☐) and then click Apply Options. You must be logged on as a computer administrator to turn off the Welcome screen.

LOG OFF WINDOWS

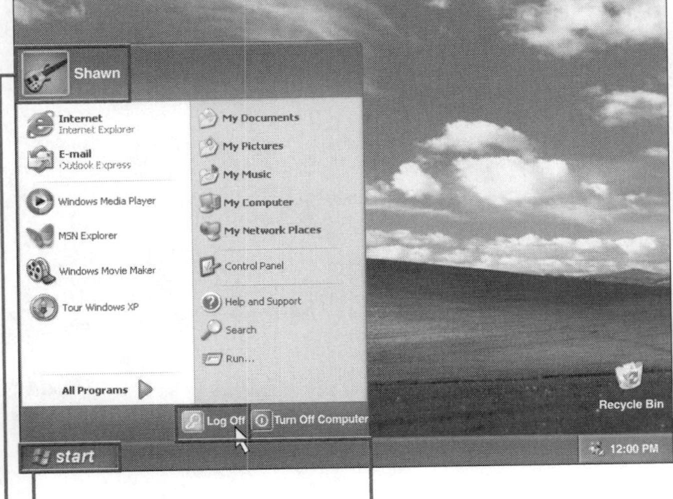

1 Click start.

■ This area displays the name of the current user account.

2 Click Log Off to log off Windows.

■ The Log Off Windows dialog box appears.

3 Click an option to specify how you want to log off Windows.

Note: The Switch User option keeps your programs and files open. The Log Off option closes your open programs and files.

■ The Welcome screen appears, allowing another person to log on to Windows to use the computer.

SHARE FILES WITH OTHER USERS

You can view the personal files of users who have accounts set up on your computer. Windows creates a folder for each user, containing copies of the files stored in the user's My Documents folder and its subfolders.

In most cases, the personal files of every user are available to other users set up on the computer. If your computer uses the NTFS file system, you cannot view the files of other users if you have a limited user account or if a user has made their personal folders private.

If you want to share files with every user set up on your computer, you can copy the files to the Shared Documents folder. This is useful when you want to share files that are not stored in the My Documents folder or if your computer uses the NTFS file system and other users are restricted from viewing the contents of your personal folders.

The Shared Documents folder contains the Shared Music and Shared Pictures subfolders, where you can place copies of music files and pictures you want to share with other users. When you store a file in the Shared Documents folder or one of its subfolders, the file will always be available to other users on your computer.

VIEW SHARED FILES

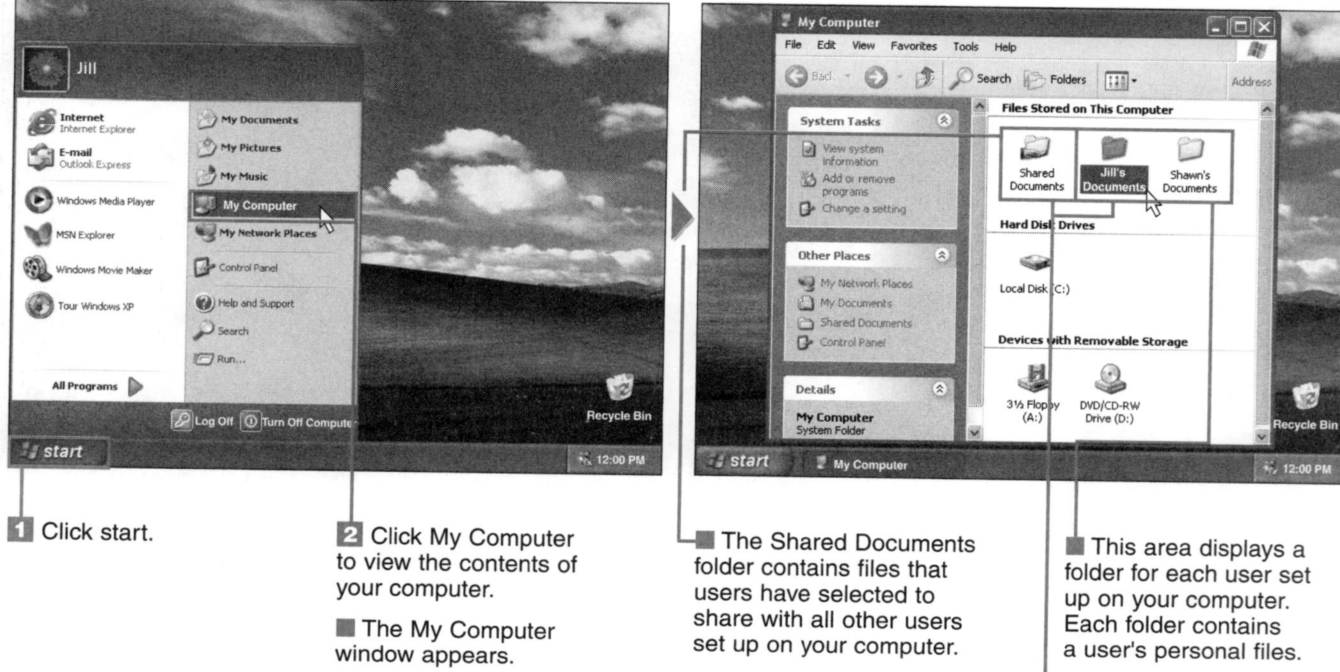

1 Click start.

2 Click My Computer to view the contents of your computer.

■ The My Computer window appears.

■ The Shared Documents folder contains files that users have selected to share with all other users set up on your computer.

■ This area displays a folder for each user set up on your computer. Each folder contains a user's personal files.

3 To display the contents of a folder, double-click the folder.

How can I prevent other users from viewing my personal files?

✔ If your computer uses the NTFS file system, you can prevent other users from viewing the files in your personal folders by making the folders private. To make your personal folders private, see page 192. If your computer uses the FAT file system, you cannot prevent other users from viewing your personal files.

How do I stop sharing a file?

✔ If you no longer want to share a file you copied to the Shared Documents folder, you can delete the file from the folder. Click start, choose My Computer and then double-click the Shared Documents folder. Click the file you want to stop sharing and then click Delete this file.

How can I tell if my hard drive uses the FAT or NTFS file system?

✔ You can determine which file system your computer uses by viewing the properties for your hard drive. Click start and select My Computer. Right-click the hard drive for your computer and then select Properties. In the dialog box that appears, click the General tab. The file system your computer uses appears in the File System area.

SHARE FILES

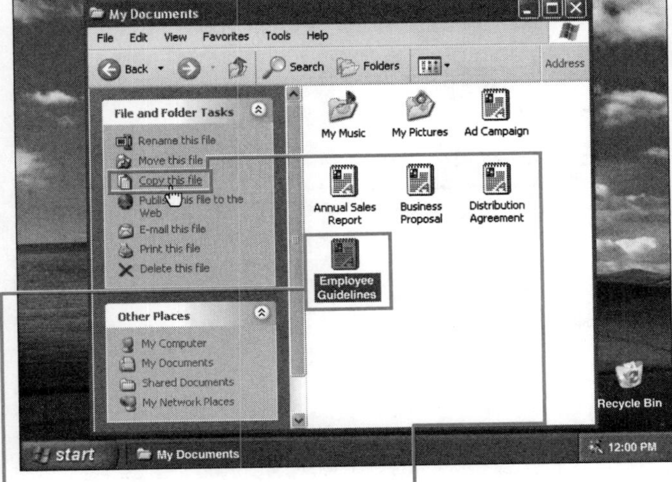

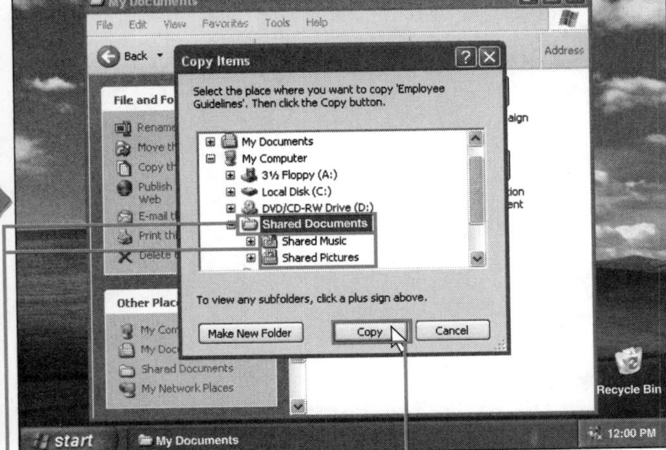

1 Select the file(s) you want to share with every user set up on your computer. To select multiple files, see page 52.

2 Click Copy this file.

Note: If you selected multiple files, click Copy the selected items in step 2.

■ The Copy Items dialog box appears.

3 Click Shared Documents.

■ If you are sharing a music file or picture, you can click the Shared Music or Shared Pictures folder to place a copy of the file in one of these subfolders.

4 Click Copy to place a copy of the file in the Shared Documents folder.

MAKE YOUR PERSONAL FOLDERS PRIVATE

You can make the contents of your personal folders private so that only you can access the files within the folders. Your computer must use the NTFS file system in order for you to make your personal folders private. The file system your computer uses is typically determined when you install Windows. For more information about file systems, see page 538.

On a computer using the NTFS file system, your personal folders are initially available to every user with a computer administrator account set up on the computer.

Your personal folders include the Cookies folder, which stores small text files created by Web pages you visit, the Desktop folder, which contains items you have saved on your desktop, and the Favorites folder, which stores links to Web pages you have added to your list of favorites. Your My Documents and Start Menu folders are also personal folders you can make private.

You can only make the personal folders private for the user account you are logged on to. To make the folders for another user account private, you must first log on to the other account.

Making your personal folders private does not affect the performance of your computer.

MAKE YOUR PERSONAL FOLDERS PRIVATE

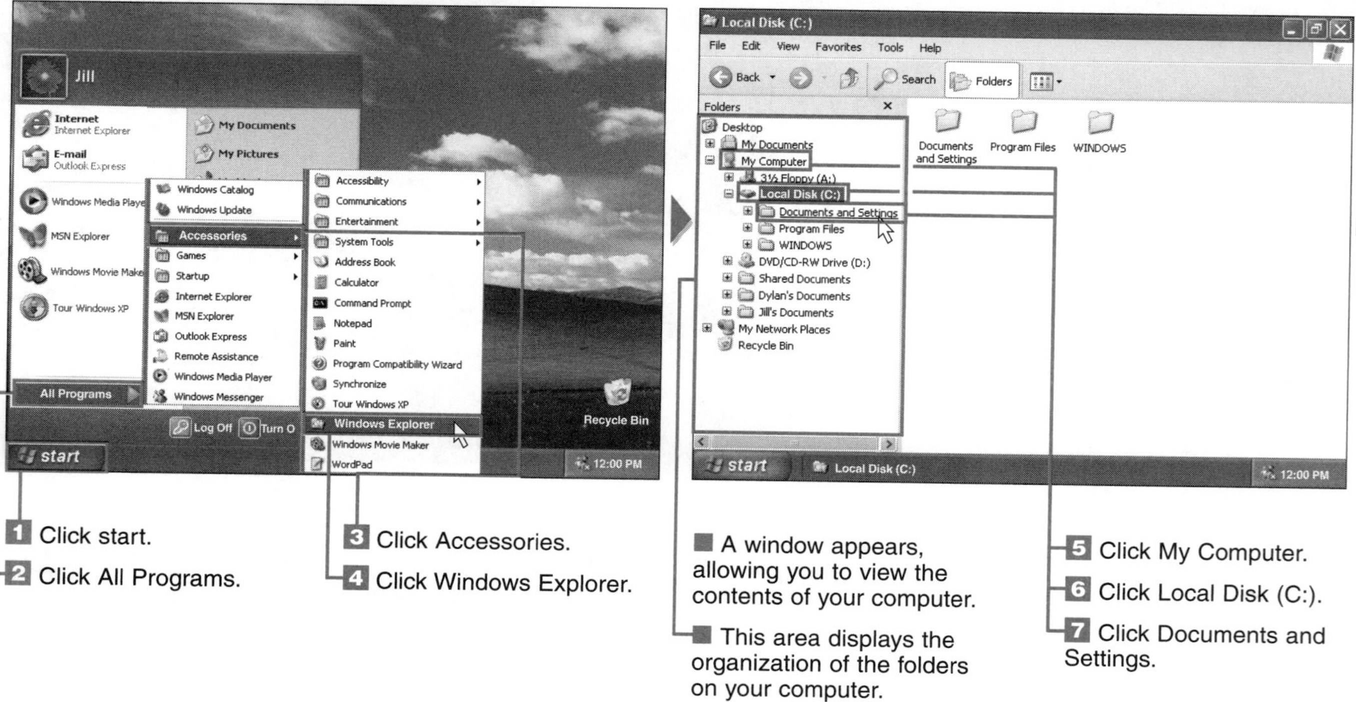

1 Click start.

2 Click All Programs.

3 Click Accessories.

4 Click Windows Explorer.

■ A window appears, allowing you to view the contents of your computer.

■ This area displays the organization of the folders on your computer.

5 Click My Computer.

6 Click Local Disk (C:).

7 Click Documents and Settings.

Why does a dialog box appear asking if I want to create a password?

✔ This dialog box appears if you have not assigned a password to your user account. If your user account does not have a password, anyone will be able to log on to your account and view the contents of your personal folders even if you have made the folders private. For information about assigning a password to your user account, see page 176.

After making a personal folder private, can I share a file in the folder?

✔ Yes. To share a specific file with every user set up on your computer, you must place a copy of the file in the Shared Documents folder. The Shared Documents folder contains files that every user set up on your computer can access. For information on the Shared Documents folder, see page 190.

Can I make just one subfolder within a personal folder private?

✔ Yes. Perform steps 1 to 8 below to display the personal folders for your user account. Then double-click the personal folder containing the subfolder you want to make private. Right-click the subfolder and then perform steps 10 to 14.

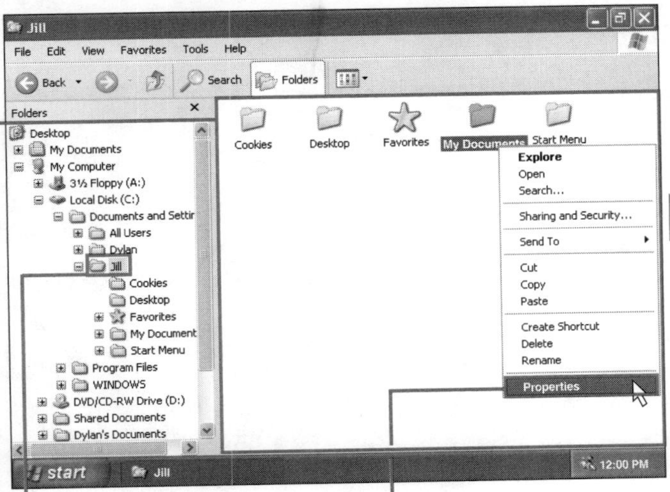

8 Click the name of your user account.

■ This area displays the folders that store your personal information.

9 Right-click the folder you want to make private. A menu appears.

10 Click Properties.

■ A Properties dialog box appears.

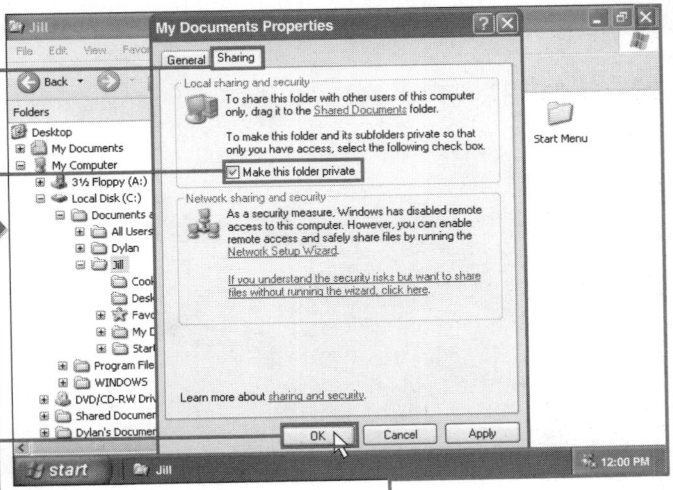

11 Click the Sharing tab.

12 Click Make this folder private (☐ changes to ☑).

13 Click OK to confirm your change.

14 Click ☒ to close the Windows Explorer window.

■ If you no longer want to make your personal folders private, perform steps 1 to 14 (☑ changes to ☐ in step 12).

CHANGE THE DATE AND TIME

You can change the date and time set in your computer. Setting the correct date and time is important because Windows uses this information to identify when you create and update files. If your computer's calendar and clock are accurate, you will be able to find your files more easily.

The correct date and time are also important for many time management programs, such as Microsoft Outlook. Time management programs use the date and time set in your computer to keep track of your appointments for you.

Your computer maintains the date and time even when you turn off the computer. Windows also adjusts the time automatically to compensate for daylight saving time. When you turn on your computer after daylight saving time occurs, Windows will have automatically changed the time.

Windows automatically synchronizes your computer's clock with a time server on the Internet approximately once a week. You must be connected to the Internet for the synchronization to occur. If you are on a network that uses a firewall to protect against unauthorized access, Windows will not be able to synchronize your computer's clock.

CHANGE THE DATE AND TIME

■ This area displays the time set in your computer.

1 To display the date set in your computer, position the mouse over this area. After a moment, the date appears.

2 Double-click this area to change the date or time.

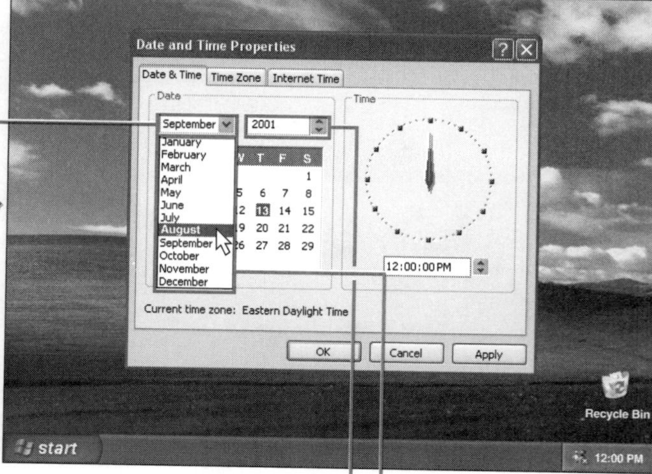

■ The Date and Time Properties dialog box appears.

3 This area displays the month set in your computer. To change the month, click this area.

4 Click the correct month.

5 This area displays the year set in your computer. To change the year, click ▲ or ▼ until the correct year appears.

How can I remove the clock from my taskbar?

✔ Right-click an empty area of the taskbar. From the menu that appears, click Properties. In the Taskbar and Start Menu Properties dialog box, click the Show the clock option (☑ changes to ☐).

How do I change the time zone set in my computer?

✔ In the Date and Time Properties dialog box, select the Time Zone tab. Click the current time zone to display a list of time zones and then choose the time zone you want to use.

Can I change the format Windows uses to display the date and time?

✔ Yes. You can have Windows display a shorter version of the date or use a 24-hour clock format to display the time. Click start, select Control Panel and then choose Date, Time, Language, and Regional Options. Click the Change the format of numbers, dates, and times option. In the dialog box that appears, select Customize and then use the options on the Date and Time tabs to change the format of the date and time. For more information, see page 226.

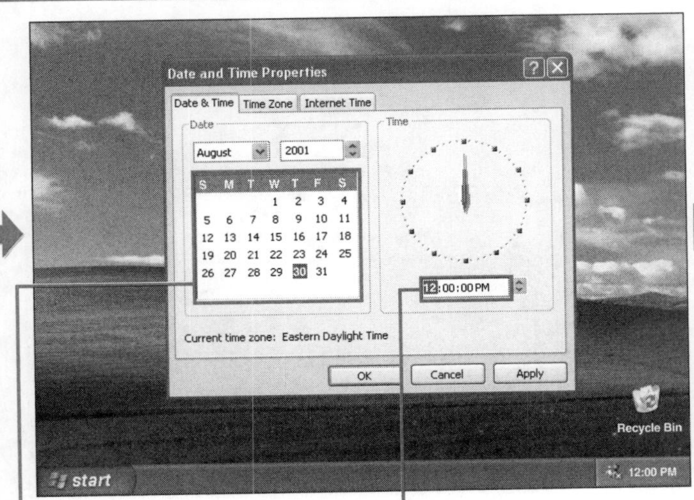

6 This area displays the days in the month. The day set in your computer is highlighted. To change the day, click the correct day.

7 This area displays the time set in your computer. To change the time, double-click the part of the time you want to change.

8 Type the correct information.

■ This area visually displays the time set in your computer.

■ This area displays the time zone set in your computer.

9 Click OK to confirm your changes.

CHANGE THE DESKTOP BACKGROUND

Like hanging posters on your walls or placing photographs on your desk, you can customize the Windows desktop to create a friendly and personalized working environment. You can use a picture, a color or both as a desktop background.

When using a picture as your desktop background, you can center a large picture on your desktop or tile a small picture so it repeats over the entire desktop. You can also stretch a picture to cover your desktop.

Windows provides several background pictures you can use. You can also search the Internet for sites providing images you can use as a desktop background or purchase collections of clip art and photographs from computer stores to use as a desktop background.

Using a scanner, you can turn personal photographs or your own artwork into pictures that you can use as a desktop background. You can also use pictures created using the Paint program included with Windows. Windows automatically adds any image stored in your My Pictures folder to the list of available background pictures.

CHANGE THE DESKTOP BACKGROUND

1 Right-click a blank area on your desktop.

A menu appears.

2 Click Properties.

■ The Display Properties dialog box appears.

3 Click the Desktop tab.

4 Click the picture you want to use.

5 Click this area to select how you want to display the picture on your desktop.

6 Click the way you want to display the picture.

Center - Places the picture in the middle of your desktop.

Tile - Repeats the picture until it covers your entire desktop.

Stretch - Stretches the picture to cover your entire desktop.

How do I use pictures that are not stored in the My Pictures folder as a desktop background?

✔ In the Display Properties dialog box, click the Browse button to locate the picture you want to use. You can use many different types of pictures, including pictures with the .bmp, .gif, .jpg, .jpeg, .dib or .png extension. In addition to picture files, you can also use this method to set HTML documents with the .htm or .html extension as your desktop background.

How can I use a picture displayed on a Web page as my desktop background?

✔ When viewing a page on the Web, right-click the picture you want to use as your background. On the menu that appears, click Set as Background.

Is there another way to set a picture as a desktop background?

✔ Display the contents of the folder that contains the picture you want to use. Click the picture and then select Set as desktop background from the Picture Tasks area in the window. The Set as desktop background option is not available in all folders.

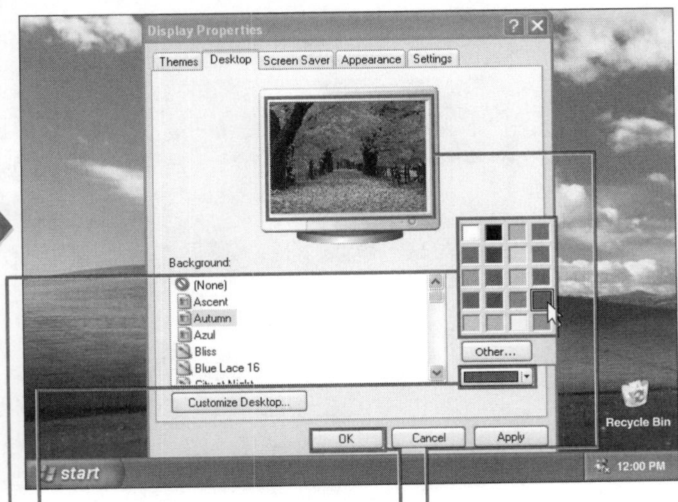

7 To select a color for your desktop, click this area to display a list of the available colors.

8 Click the color you want to use.

Note: If you selected a picture in step 4, the color you select will fill any space not covered by the picture.

■ This area displays how the picture and/or color will appear on your desktop.

9 Click OK to add the picture and/or color to your desktop.

■ The picture and/or color appear on your desktop.

■ To remove a picture from your desktop, perform steps 1 to 4, selecting (None) in step 4. Then perform step 9.

CHANGE THE SCREEN APPEARANCE

You can change the style and colors that Windows uses to display windows and other items on your screen.

By default, you can choose between the Windows XP style, which is the default style of Windows XP, and the Windows Classic style, which is the style used in previous versions of Windows.

You can change the colors used in items such as windows, dialog boxes and the Start menu. The available color schemes depend on the style you select. The Windows XP style offers 3 color schemes—Default (blue), Olive Green and Silver. The Windows Classic style offers 22 different color schemes.

You can change the size of text shown in items such as menus, icons and the title bars of windows. Changing the font size will also change the size of some buttons on the screen. Increasing the font size is useful if you have trouble reading the text on your screen or clicking small buttons. The available font sizes depend on the color scheme you select. In some cases, you may have only one font size option.

CHANGE THE SCREEN APPEARANCE

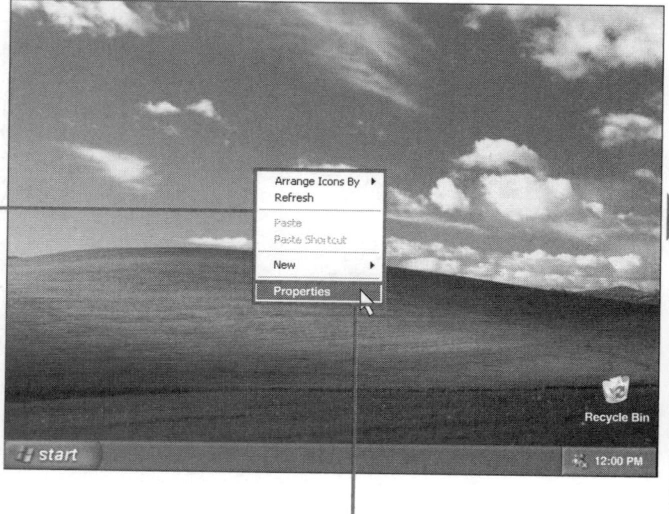

1 Right-click a blank area on your desktop. A menu appears.

2 Click Properties.

■ The Display Properties dialog box appears.

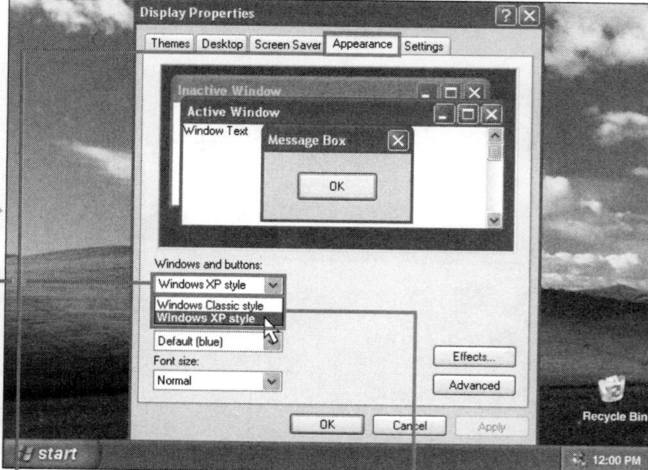

3 Click the Appearance tab.

4 Click this area to display the available styles.

5 Click the style you want to use.

Note: The available styles depend on the current theme. For information on themes, see page 206.

How do I change my screen back to its original appearance?

✔ In the Display Properties dialog box, choose the Appearance tab and then select the Windows XP style, the Default (blue) color scheme and the Normal font size to return the screen to its original appearance. You can also change the screen back to its original appearance by selecting the Windows XP desktop theme. To change the desktop theme, see page 206.

What special color schemes are available for the Windows Classic style?

✔ The Windows Classic style provides High Contrast schemes, which are designed for people with vision impairments. High color schemes designed for computers displaying more than 256 colors are also available. If your computer is limited to 16 colors, you may want to choose one of the VGA schemes.

Can I change the size, color and font settings of specific Windows items?

✔ Yes. In the Display Properties dialog box, choose the Appearance tab and click the Advanced button. In the dialog box that appears, click the Item area to display a list of Windows items. Select the item you want to change and then select the size, color or font settings you want to use. Windows may not apply all your changes to some items.

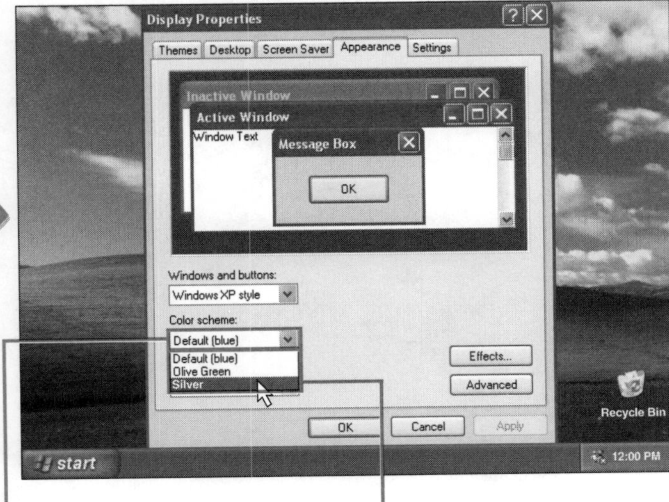

6 Click this area to display the available color schemes.

7 Click the color scheme you want to use.

Note: The available color schemes depend on the style you selected in step 5.

8 Click this area to display the available font sizes.

9 Click the font size you want to use.

Note: The available font sizes depend on the color scheme you selected in step 7.

■ This area displays a preview of how your screen will appear.

10 Click OK to change the appearance of your screen.

CHANGE THE SCREEN RESOLUTION

You can change the screen resolution to adjust the amount of information that can fit on your screen. Your monitor and video adapter determine which screen resolutions you can use.

Screen resolution is measured by the number of horizontal and vertical pixels on a screen. A pixel is the smallest point on a screen. The most common screen resolutions are 800 by 600 pixels and 1024 by 768 pixels.

Lower screen resolutions display larger images so you can see the information on your screen more clearly. Some games are designed to run at a specific screen resolution. You may need to use a lower resolution to have a game fill your entire screen.

Higher screen resolutions display smaller images so you can display more information on your screen at once. A higher resolution allows you to see more of a word processing document or more cells in a spreadsheet without scrolling.

If you have multiple users set up on your computer, Windows will change the resolution for each user.

CHANGE THE SCREEN RESOLUTION

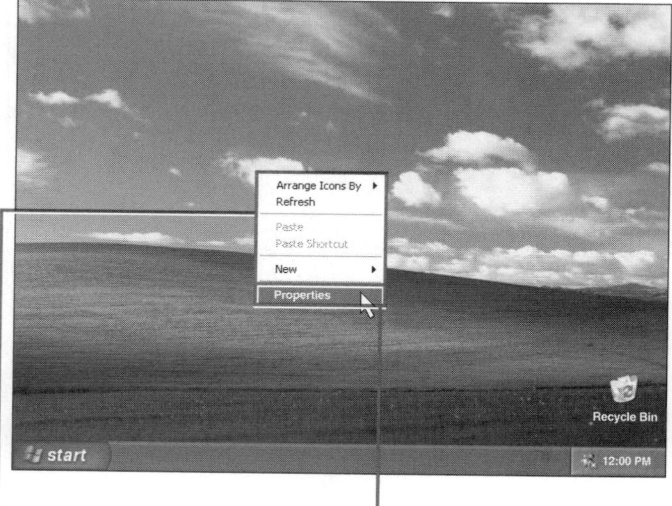

1 Right-click a blank area on your desktop.
A menu appears.

2 Click Properties.

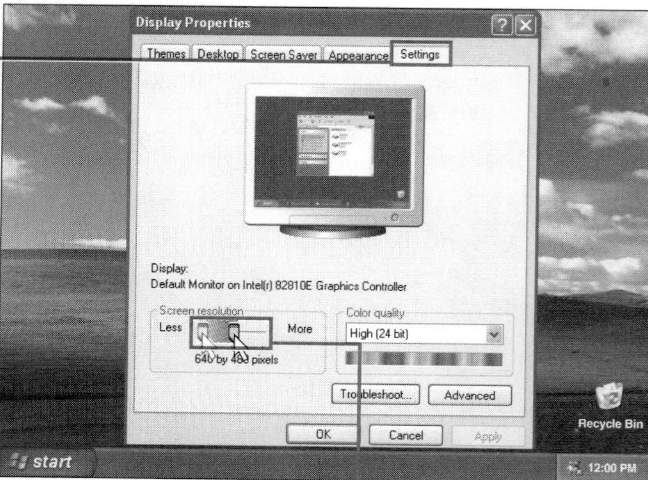

■ The Display Properties dialog box appears.

3 Click the Settings tab.

4 To change the screen resolution, drag the slider ( ) to select the resolution you want to use.

The screen resolution I want to use is not available. What can I do?

✔ Windows lists only the recommended screen resolutions in the Display Properties dialog box. To use a screen resolution that is not listed, select the Settings tab and click the Advanced button. In the dialog box that appears, click the Adapter tab and then click the List All Modes button. You can then select the screen resolution you want to use from the list that appears.

I find it difficult to read screen items after I change to a higher resolution. What can I do?

✔ You can increase the size of text in menus and other screen items to make the text easier to read. In the Display Properties dialog box, click the Appearance tab. In the Font size area, select Large Fonts.

Why do I have wide black borders around the edge of my screen or lose part of the desktop after I change the screen resolution?

✔ You may need to make adjustments to your monitor after changing the screen resolution. Consult the manual included with your monitor for information about the monitor controls you can use to make the necessary adjustments.

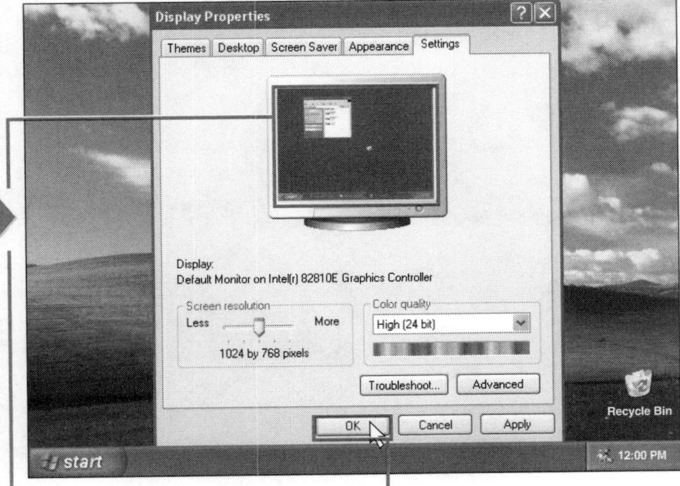

■ This area displays how your screen will look at the new screen resolution.

5 Click OK to confirm your change.

■ Your screen will turn black for a moment.

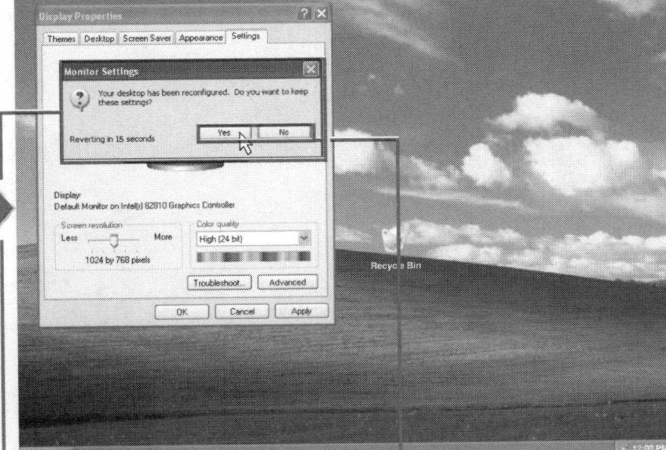

■ Windows resizes the information on your screen.

■ The Monitor Settings dialog box may appear, asking if you want to keep the new screen resolution.

6 Click Yes or No to specify if you want to keep the screen resolution.

Note: If you do not perform step 6 within 15 seconds, Windows will automatically restore your original screen resolution.

CHANGE THE COLOR SETTING

You can change the color setting on your computer. The color setting determines the number of colors Windows can display on your screen. Changing the color setting will affect the quality of images on your computer and the general appearance of your screen.

The available color settings depend on the capabilities of your computer's video adapter and monitor. Windows usually offers two color settings. The Medium (16 bit) setting allows Windows to display more than 65,000 colors on your screen. You may also be able to choose the High (24 bit) setting, which can display more than 16 million colors or the Highest (32 bit) setting, which can display more than 4 billion colors on your screen.

You may want to display more colors on your screen when viewing photographs, playing videos or playing games on your computer. Some programs, particularly games, require you to use a specific color setting.

After you change the color setting, you should restart your computer. Some programs may not operate properly if you do not restart your computer.

Changes you make to the color setting will affect all the users set up on your computer.

CHANGE THE COLOR SETTING

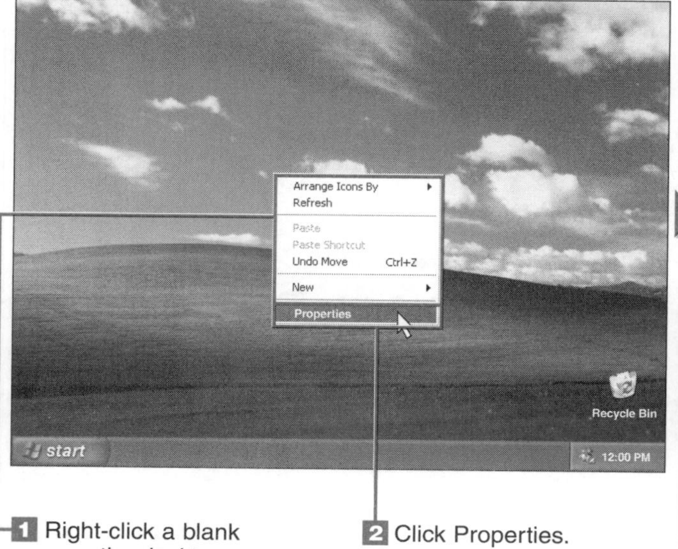

1 Right-click a blank area on the desktop. A menu appears.

2 Click Properties.

■ The Display Properties dialog box appears.

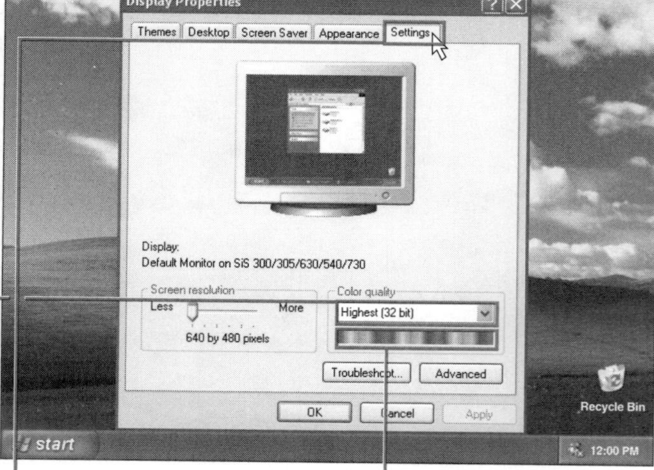

3 Click the Settings tab.

■ This area displays the current color setting.

■ This area displays the range of colors that the color setting allows Windows to display.

The color setting I want to use is not available. What can I do?

✔ The Settings tab in the Display Properties dialog box lists only the recommended color settings. To use a color setting that is not listed, click the Advanced button. In the dialog box that appears, click the Adapter tab and then click the List All Modes button. You can then select the color setting you want to use from the list that appears.

Will a high color setting affect my computer's performance?

✔ Although your computer may work slightly faster at a lower color setting compared to a higher color setting, the difference in speed is minor.

Can I change the color setting for only some programs?

✔ If you need to change the color setting to 256 colors for a program, such as a game, you can have Windows temporarily switch your color setting to 256 colors when you run the program. Right-click the program file and select Properties on the menu that appears. Click the Compatibility tab and select the Run in 256 colors option (☐ changes to ☑). Your screen will return to the previous color setting when you close the program.

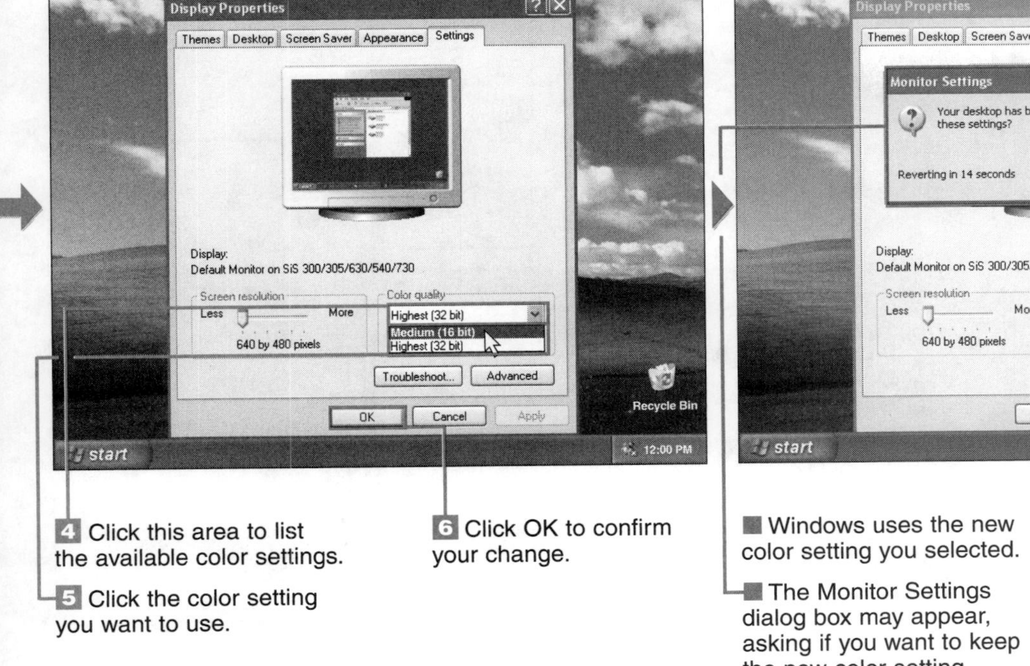

4 Click this area to list the available color settings.

5 Click the color setting you want to use.

6 Click OK to confirm your change.

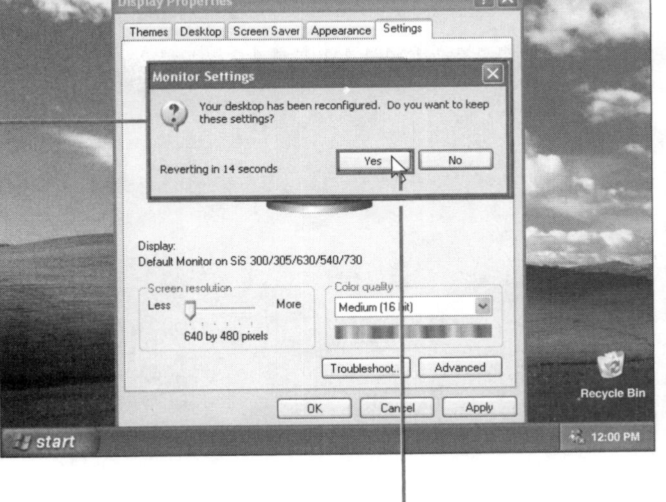

■ Windows uses the new color setting you selected.

■ The Monitor Settings dialog box may appear, asking if you want to keep the new color setting.

7 Click Yes to keep the new color setting.

CHANGE THE SCREEN SAVER

A screen saver is a moving picture or pattern that appears on your screen when you do not use your computer for a period of time. You can use a screen saver to hide your work while you are away from your desk. Windows provides several interesting screen savers that you can use.

By default, Windows will display a screen saver when you do not use your computer for ten minutes. You can change the number of minutes the computer must be inactive before the screen saver appears. Adjusting the time period before a screen saver starts can help prevent the screen saver from disrupting your work while you are reviewing information on your screen.

Windows provides a security feature to prevent unauthorized people from using your computer after the screen saver appears. You can have Windows require you to log on to the computer to remove the screen saver. If your account is the only user account set up on the computer and you have assigned a password to your account, you must enter the password when you log on. If multiple users are set up on the computer, the Welcome screen will appear when the screen saver is removed so you can log on and return to your work.

CHANGE THE SCREEN SAVER

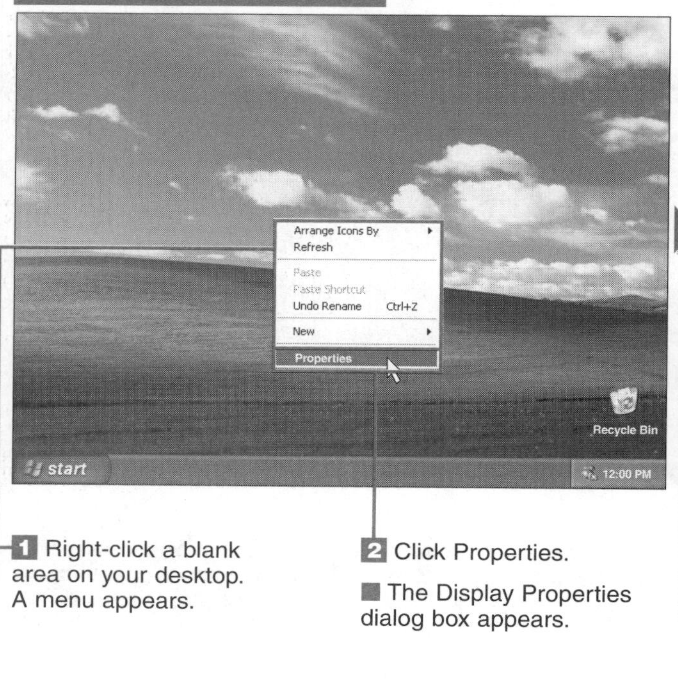

1 Right-click a blank area on your desktop.
- A menu appears.

2 Click Properties.
- The Display Properties dialog box appears.

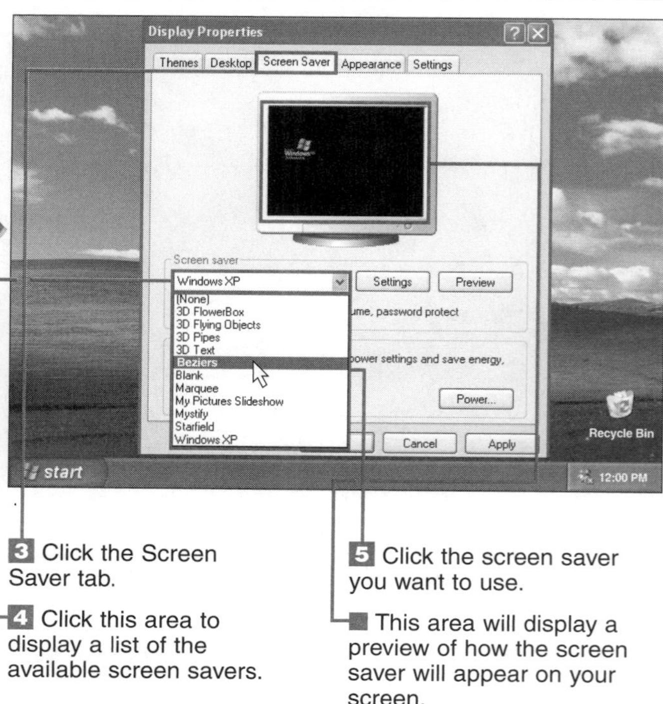

3 Click the Screen Saver tab.

4 Click this area to display a list of the available screen savers.

5 Click the screen saver you want to use.
- This area will display a preview of how the screen saver will appear on your screen.

What does the My Pictures Slideshow screen saver do?

✔ The My Pictures Slideshow screen saver uses the pictures stored in your My Pictures folder as your screen saver. Windows will rotate through all the pictures in the folder, displaying each picture on your screen for six seconds at a time. To view the contents of your My Pictures folder, see page 38.

Can I customize my screen savers?

✔ After you select a screen saver, you can click the Settings button to customize the screen saver. Most screen savers offer options that you can change.

How can I preview a screen saver?

✔ When choosing a screen saver, you can click the Preview button to see how the screen saver will appear on your screen. To end the preview, move the mouse or press a key on your keyboard.

What impact does a screen saver have on my computer?

✔ A screen saver can use a lot of your computer's resources when displayed on your screen, especially if the screen saver contains detailed graphics. You should turn off the screen saver if your computer will be performing unattended tasks that require a lot of processing power, such as copying files to a recordable CD.

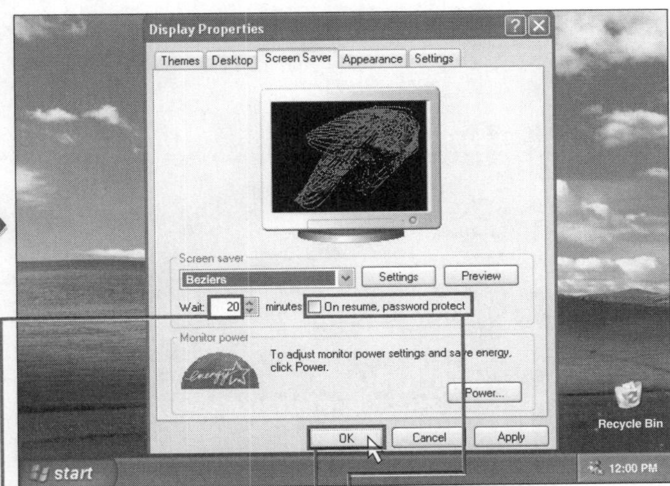

6 To specify the number of minutes your computer must be inactive before the screen saver will appear, double-click this area. Then type the number of minutes.

7 This option requires you to log on to Windows each time you remove the screen saver. You can click this option to turn the option on (☑) or off (☐).

Note: The name of the option is different if multiple users are set up on your computer.

8 Click OK.

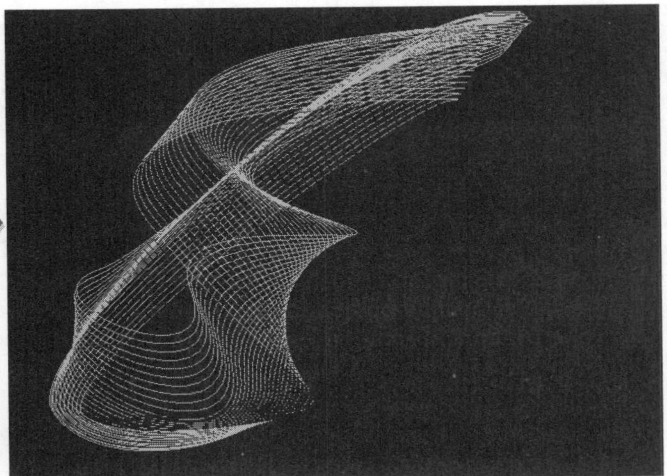

■ The screen saver appears when you do not use your computer for the number of minutes you specified.

■ You can move the mouse or press a key on the keyboard to remove the screen saver from your screen.

■ To stop a screen saver from appearing, perform steps 1 to 5, selecting (None) in step 5. Then perform step 8.

CHANGE THE DESKTOP THEME

You can use a desktop theme to personalize the overall appearance of Windows. Each desktop theme contains several coordinated items, including a desktop background, screen saver, colors, sounds, mouse pointers, icons and fonts.

Windows provides several desktop themes you can choose from. The Windows XP theme is the theme that is initially displayed on Windows XP, while the Windows Classic theme resembles the style used in previous versions of Windows.

In the list of themes Windows offers, the My Current Theme option indicates the theme you are currently using. When you make changes to a theme, such as changing the desktop background, a new theme appears in the list with the word Modified in its name.

If multiple people have user accounts set up on your computer, each person can choose a different desktop theme. Changing the desktop theme for one user account will not affect the themes used by other user accounts.

CHANGE THE DESKTOP THEME

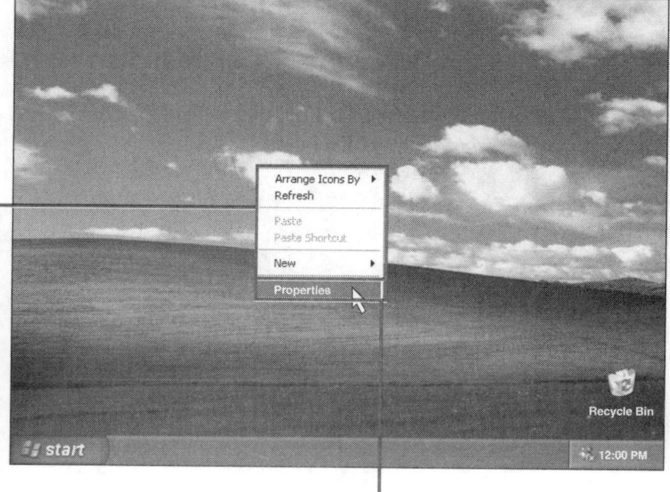

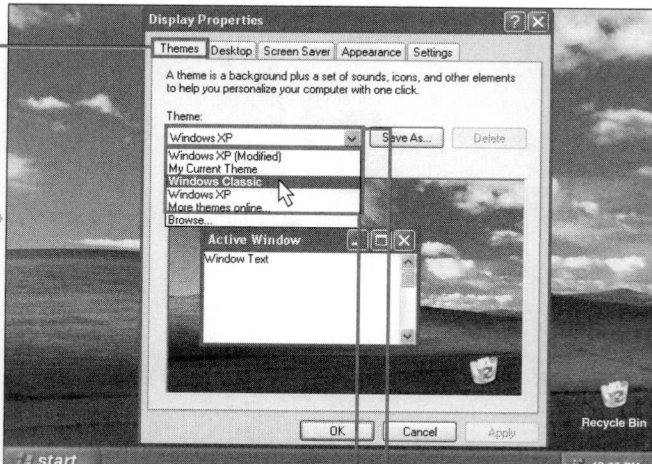

1 Right-click a blank area on your desktop. A menu appears.

2 Click Properties.

■ The Display Properties dialog box appears.

3 Click the Themes tab.

4 Click this area to display a list of the available desktop themes.

5 Click the desktop theme you want to use.

Where can I get more themes?

✔ You can find more themes on the Internet. Perform steps 1 to 4 below and then click More themes online to connect to a Web page that offers new themes that you can download and install.

How can I create my own custom theme?

✔ You can save changes you make to an existing theme to create a new custom theme. After making changes to the theme you are currently using, such as selecting a different screen saver or changing the desktop background, perform steps 1 to 3 below and then click Save As. Type a name for the new theme and click Save. Windows will save the new theme in your My Documents folder.

Can I delete a theme?

✔ You can delete custom themes you have created and themes that you have downloaded from the Internet, but you cannot delete the Windows XP or Windows Classic themes. To delete a theme, perform steps 1 to 4 below, select the theme you want to delete and then click Delete.

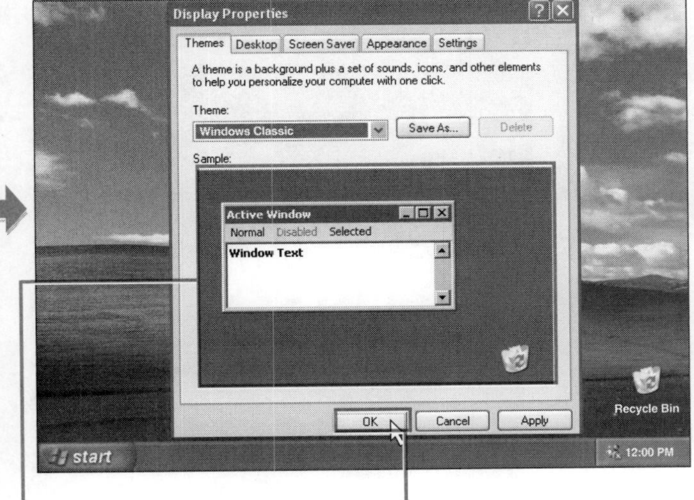

■ This area displays a preview of the desktop theme you selected.

6 Click OK to confirm your change.

■ Windows applies the desktop theme you selected.

■ To return to the original desktop theme, perform steps 1 to 6, selecting Windows XP in step 5.

CHANGE VISUAL EFFECTS

You can customize Windows by changing the visual effects that Windows uses to display items on your screen. Windows provides several ways you can customize visual effects. Using the Display Properties dialog box allows you to change the visual effects Windows uses to display menus, tooltips, fonts and icons.

Transition effects enhance the way menus and tooltips appear and disappear on the screen.

You can turn transition effects on or off and specify the type of transition effect you want to use.

You can have Windows smooth the edges of fonts to make the text on your screen easier to read. You can also have Windows display large icons for the items on your desktop.

If you want to give menus a three-dimensional appearance, you can choose to display shadows under the menus.

By default, Windows shows the contents of a window when the window is moved or resized. You can choose to display just the outline of a window when you move or resize the window. You can also choose to hide the underlined letters used for keyboard navigation in menus and controls until the Alt key is pressed or display the underlined letters at all times.

CHANGE VISUAL EFFECTS USING DISPLAY PROPERTIES

1 Right-click a blank area on your desktop. A menu appears.

2 Click Properties.

■ The Display Properties dialog box appears.

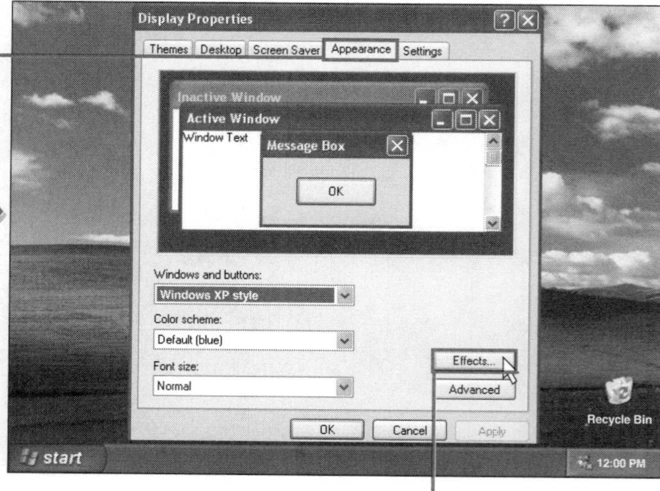

3 Click the Appearance tab.

4 Click Effects.

■ The Effects dialog box appears.

What transition effects can I use for menus and tooltips?

✔ Windows offers two transition effects—Fade and Scroll. The Fade effect will fade-in menus and tooltips when they are displayed and dissolve them when they are closed. The Scroll effect will slide menus and tooltips in and out.

When smoothing the edges of fonts, should I use Standard or ClearType?

✔ The option you should choose depends on the type of computer you are using. The Standard option is used for desktop monitors, while ClearType is used for most portable computers and flat screen monitors. Using the ClearType option on a desktop monitor may make the fonts appear blurry.

When would I use large icons for items on my desktop?

✔ Displaying large icons is useful when you are using a high screen resolution, such as 1024x768 or higher. To change the screen resolution, see page 200.

Will using visual effects make my computer operate slower?

✔ Some visual effects may affect your computer's performance. If you want to have Windows help you choose the visual effects you should use, you can change the visual effects using the Performance Options dialog box. For more information, see page 210.

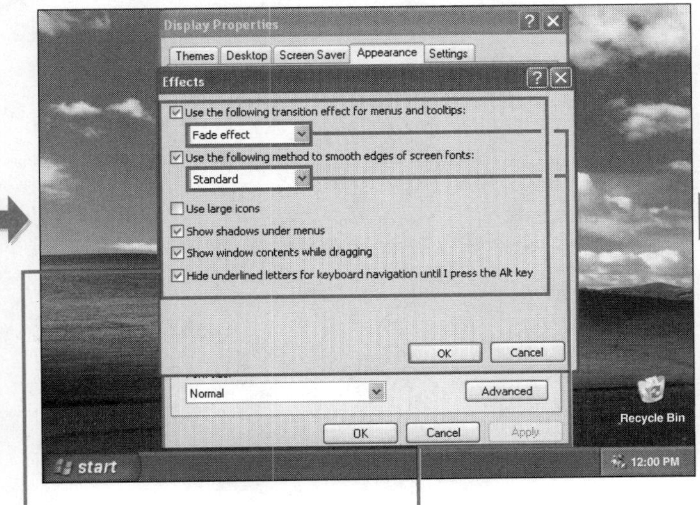

■ This area lists the visual effects that you can use.

5 To turn a visual effect on (☑) or off (☐), click the effect.

6 If you selected to use a transition effect or to smooth the edges of screen fonts, you can click an area to select the option you want to use.

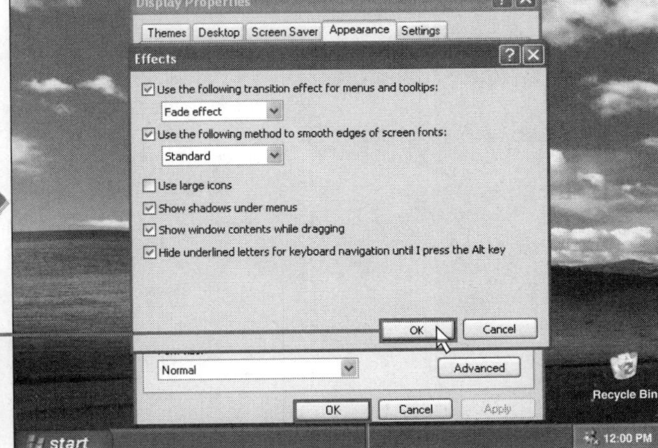

7 Click OK to confirm your changes.

8 Click OK in the Display Properties dialog box.

CONTINUED

CHANGE VISUAL EFFECTS (CONTINUED)

While visual effects improve the appearance of Windows, they can affect the performance of your computer. You can have Windows help you adjust the visual effects for your computer by using the Performance Options dialog box.

You can select an option in the Performance Options dialog box to specify how you want to change visual effects. For example, you can have Windows choose the visual effects that are best suited for your computer. You can also specify that you want to set the visual effects for the best appearance of Windows or for the best performance of your computer.

The Performance Options dialog box displays a list of the available visual effects. Once you select the way you want to adjust the visual effects, a check mark (✔) will appear beside each effect that Windows will use. When you choose to adjust the visual effects for the best appearance, Windows will automatically turn on all the visual effects. Adjusting the visual effects for best performance will turn off all the effects.

If you want to change the visual effects without Windows' help, you can choose the Custom option. This option allows you to select each visual effect you want Windows to use.

CHANGE VISUAL EFFECTS USING PERFORMANCE OPTIONS

1 Click start.

2 Click Control Panel.

■ The Control Panel window appears.

3 Click Performance and Maintenance.

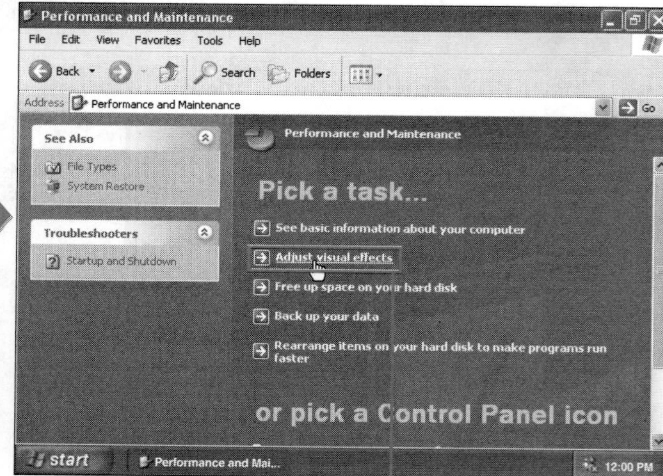

■ The Performance and Maintenance window appears.

4 Click Adjust visual effects.

What are some of the visual effects I can change using the Performance Options dialog box?

✔ You can use the Performance Options dialog box to turn transition effects on or off for menus and tooltips, display shadows under menus or mouse pointers and have Windows smooth the edges of fonts displayed on your screen. You can also change visual effects that animate windows when they are minimized and maximized, display background images in folders and more.

How can I quickly restore the visual effects to their original settings?

✔ By default, Windows is set to choose the visual effects that are best suited to your computer. To return to the default settings, click the Let Windows choose what's best for my computer option on the Visual Effects tab of the Performance Options dialog box.

Why have some visual effects stopped working?

✔ The visual effects that Windows uses can be affected by changes you make to your computer's settings. For example, when you use a new desktop theme, the display settings for the theme may override the visual effects you previously selected. For information about using desktop themes, see page 206.

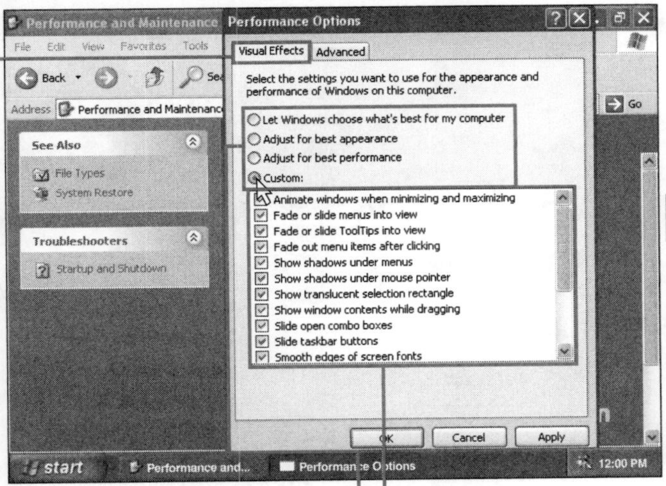

■ The Performance Options dialog box appears.

5 Click the Visual Effects tab.

■ This area lists the visual effects that Windows can apply to your computer.

6 Click an option to specify how you want to adjust the visual effects for your computer (○ changes to ◉).

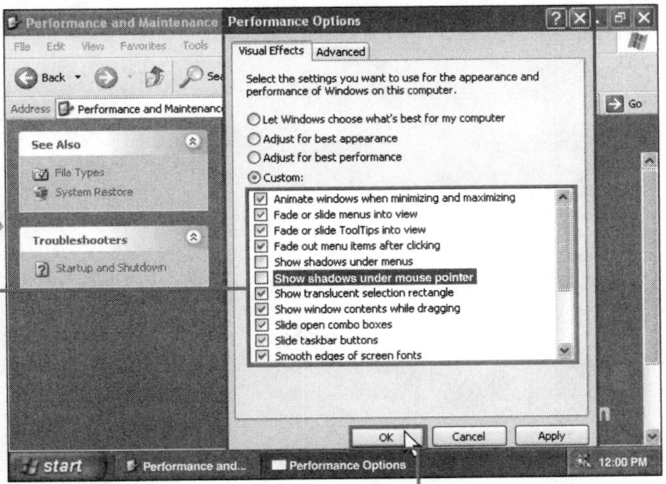

■ Windows will apply each visual effect that displays a check mark (✔).

7 If you selected Custom in step 6, you can select the visual effects you want to apply to your computer. To turn a visual effect on (☑) or off (☐), click the effect.

8 Click OK to confirm your changes.

ADD OR CHANGE DESKTOP ICONS

You can add icons to your desktop to help you work more efficiently. You can add the icons for the My Documents, My Computer and My Network Places folders to the desktop so you can quickly access the contents of the folders. You can also place an icon for Internet Explorer on the desktop to allow you to quickly open the Web browser.

The My Documents folder provides a convenient place to store your documents. The My Computer folder lets you view all the folders and files stored on your computer. The My Network Places folder allows you to view all the folders and files available on the network.

You can also change the icons displayed for the My Computer, My Documents and My Network Places folders on your computer. There are many different icons available for you to choose from. Windows also allows you to change the icons for the full and empty Recycle Bin on your desktop.

ADD OR CHANGE DESKTOP ICONS

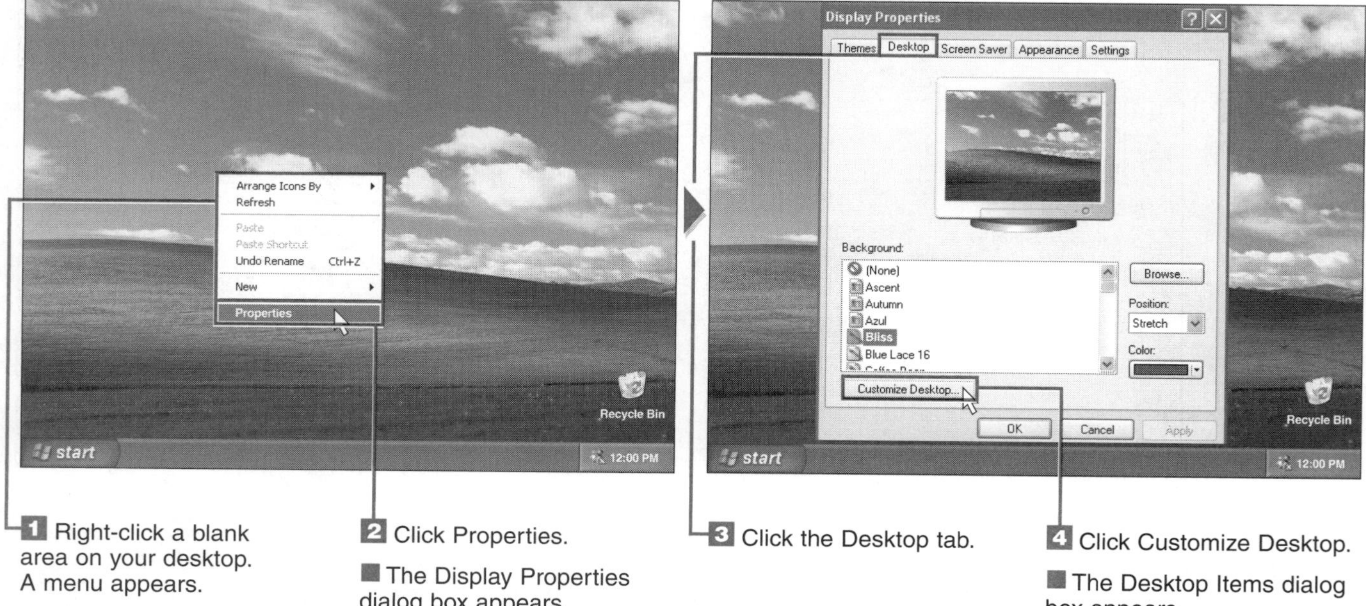

1 Right-click a blank area on your desktop. A menu appears.

2 Click Properties.

■ The Display Properties dialog box appears.

3 Click the Desktop tab.

4 Click Customize Desktop.

■ The Desktop Items dialog box appears.

Are there other icons I can use?

✔ Yes. There are many icons available for you to download on the Internet. After downloading an icon you want to use, you can click the Browse button in the Change Icon dialog box to locate the file for the icon on your computer. Icon files use the .ico extension.

How can I change an icon on my desktop back to its original icon?

✔ In the Desktop Items dialog box, select the icon you want to change back to the original icon and then click the Restore Default button.

My desktop is cluttered with shortcut icons. How can I clean up my desktop?

✔ You can use the Desktop Cleanup Wizard to remove unused shortcuts from your desktop and place the shortcuts on your desktop in a folder called Unused Desktop Shortcuts. Perform steps 1 to 4 below to display the Desktop Items dialog box and then click the Clean Desktop Now button to start the Desktop Cleanup Wizard. Follow the instructions in the wizard to clean up the desktop. By default, Windows will automatically run the wizard for you every 60 days.

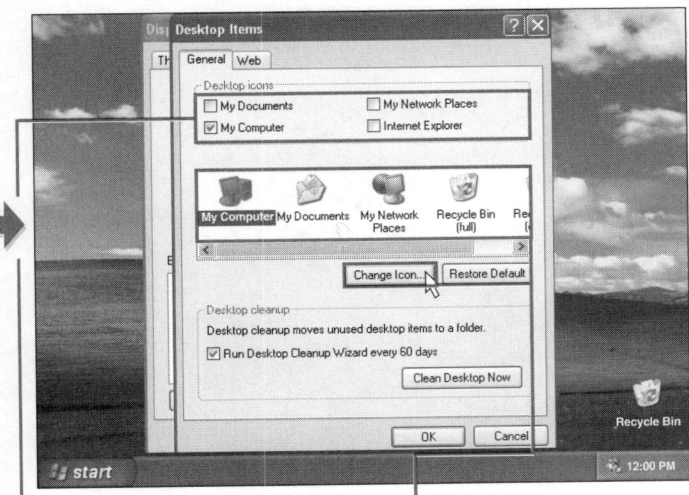

■ Windows can display these items on your desktop. Each item that displays a check mark (✔) will appear on your desktop.

5 To add (☑) or remove (☐) a check mark from an item, click the item.

■ This area displays the icons used to represent items on your desktop.

6 To change the icon for an item, click the item.

7 Click Change Icon.

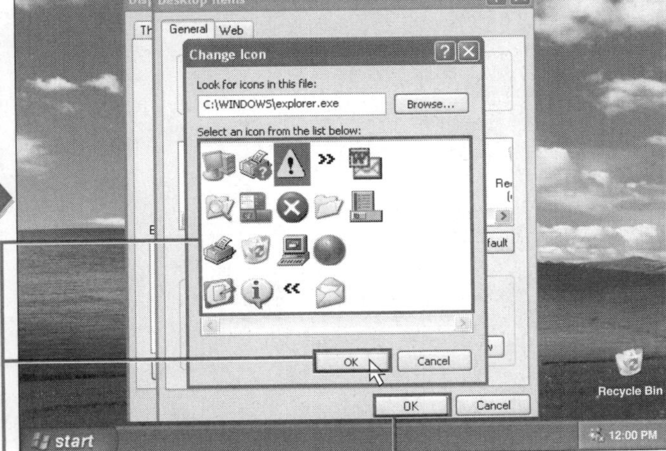

■ The Change Icon dialog box appears.

8 Click the icon you want to use.

9 Click OK to confirm your change.

10 Click OK in the Desktop Items dialog box.

11 Click OK in the Display Properties dialog box.

■ The changes are displayed on your desktop.

ADD WEB CONTENT TO THE DESKTOP

You can customize your desktop to include content from the Web, such as a Web page. You must be connected to the Internet to add Web content to your desktop.

Adding Web content to your desktop allows you to display Web pages you frequently use in a location you can quickly access.

For example, you may want to add a search tool such as Yahoo! or Google to your desktop so you can quickly search for topics of interest on the Web. This is also useful for Web pages, such as MSN.com, that allow you to personalize the Web page to display specific information of interest, such as your horoscope or a local weather report.

When adding a Web page to your desktop, you can choose to add your current home page or you can specify the address of another Web page. Your current home page is the first page that appears when you start your Web browser. For more information about your home page, see page 439.

ADD WEB CONTENT TO THE DESKTOP

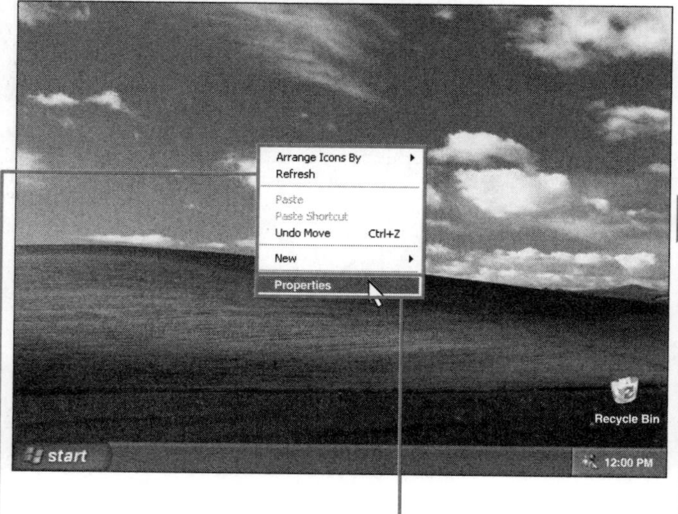

1 Right-click a blank area on your desktop. A menu appears.

2 Click Properties.

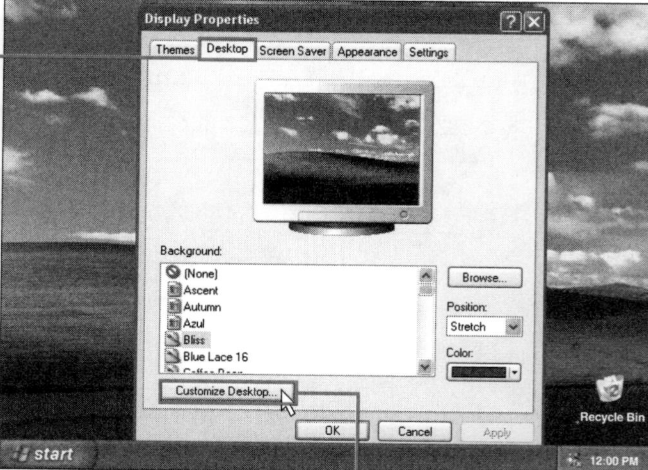

■ The Display Properties dialog box appears.

3 Click the Desktop tab.

4 Click Customize Desktop.

Is there another way to add a Web page to my desktop?

✔ When viewing a Web page in Internet Explorer, use the right mouse button to drag the icon (e) that appears beside the address of the page in the Address bar to your desktop. Then select Create Active Desktop items Here from the menu that appears.

Can I add a picture or Web page stored on my computer to my desktop?

✔ Yes. In the New Desktop Item wizard, click the Browse button to locate the picture or Web page on your computer. Click the picture or Web page you want to add and then click the Open button.

How can I add an animated picture from the Internet to my desktop?

✔ In the Location area of the New Desktop Item wizard, type the Internet address of the picture you want to add.

Where can I find other items that I can add to my desktop?

✔ The Internet Explorer 4.0 Desktop Gallery Web site provides items, such as a stock ticker or a weather map, that you can add to your desktop. In the New Desktop Item wizard, click the Visit Gallery button to display the Web site.

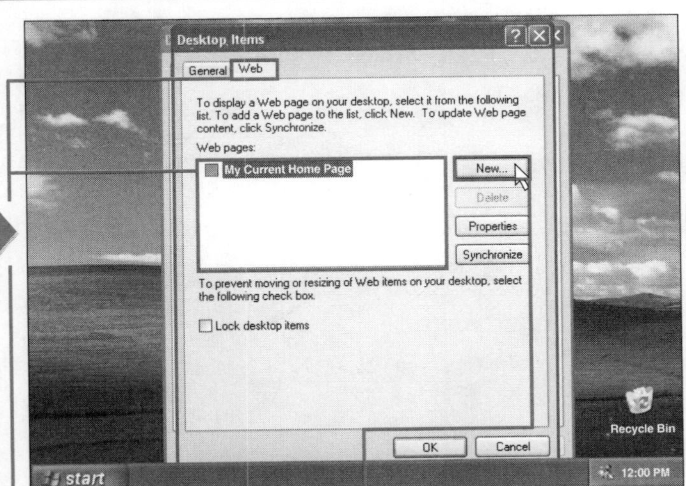

■ The Desktop Items dialog box appears.

5 Click the Web tab.

■ This area lists the Web pages you can display on your desktop.

Note: My Current Home Page is the first page that appears when you start your Web browser. To display this Web page on your desktop, see step 10 on page 216.

6 To add a Web page to the list of Web pages, click New.

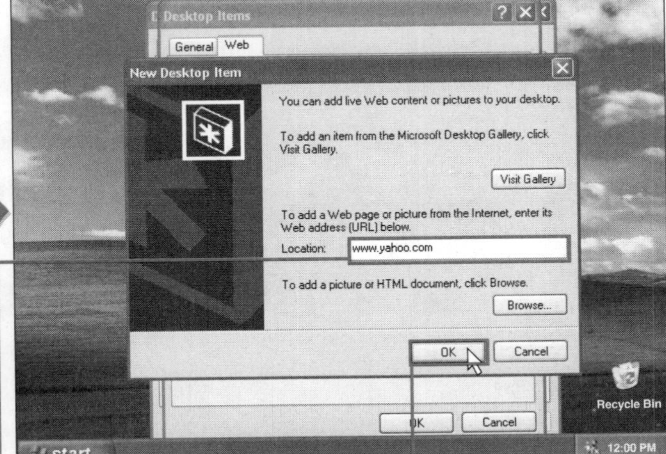

■ The New Desktop Item wizard appears.

7 Click this area and type the address of the Web page you want to add.

8 Click OK.

Note: If you are not currently connected to the Internet, a dialog box will appear, allowing you to connect.

CONTINUED

ADD WEB CONTENT TO THE DESKTOP (CONTINUED)

When you add a Web page to your desktop, the Web page is copied to your computer and automatically appears on your desktop. Windows makes the Web page available offline so the page will be displayed even when you are not connected to the Internet.

A Web page you add to your desktop will usually be updated on the Web on a regular basis.

Many Web pages, such as Web pages that report the news, contain information that must be updated in order to continue being useful. If the Web page does not update automatically on your computer, you can manually refresh the information on the Web page. Keep in mind that Web pages on your computer will update only when you are connected to the Internet.

When you add a Web page to your desktop, Windows may automatically change the background of the text for the icons on your desktop to make the text easier to read against the Web page background.

You can move a Web page to another position on your desktop to allow you to work more easily with other items on your desktop.

ADD WEB CONTENT TO THE DESKTOP (CONTINUED)

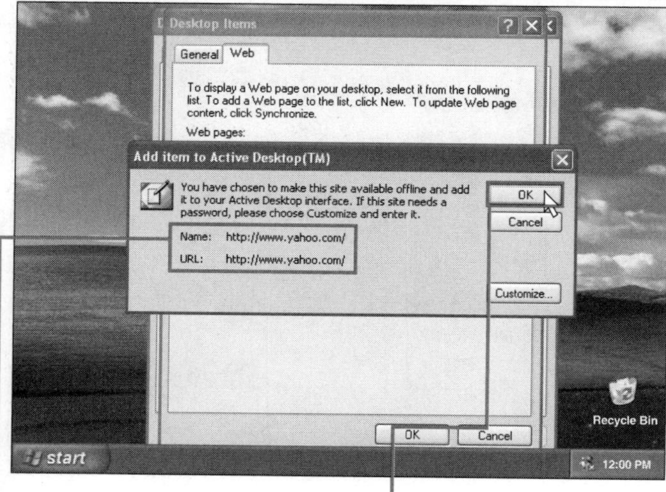

■ The Add item to Active Desktop dialog box appears.

■ This area displays the name and address of the Web page you specified.

9 Click OK to continue.

■ Windows copies the Web page to your computer.

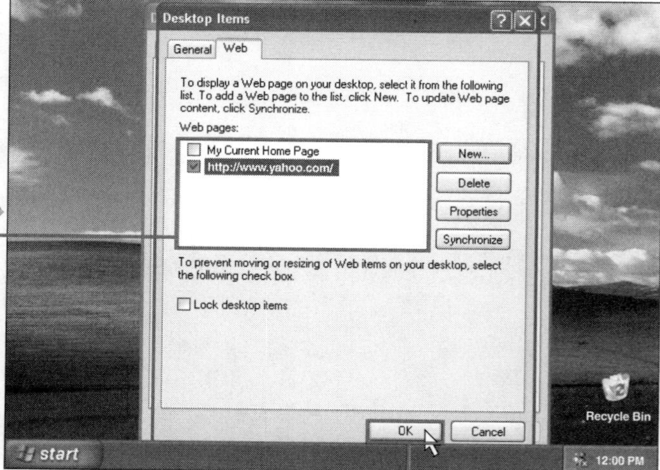

■ The Web page appears in the list of Web pages.

10 Each Web page that displays a check mark (✔) will appear on your desktop. To add (☑) or remove (☐) a check mark, click the box beside the Web page.

11 Click OK to confirm your changes.

12 Click OK to close the Display Properties dialog box.

Can I change the size of a Web page on my desktop?

✔ Yes. Position the mouse pointer over an edge of the Web page (↖ changes to ↕, ↔, ⤢ or ⤡) and then drag the Web page to a new size.

How do I remove a Web page from my desktop?

✔ To remove a Web page from your desktop, position the mouse pointer over the top edge of the Web page. On the gray bar that appears, click ☒. To permanently delete a Web page from your computer, display the Desktop Items dialog box and select the Web tab. Select the Web page and then click the Delete button. You cannot delete the My Current Home Page item.

Can a Web page fill the screen?

✔ Yes. Position the mouse pointer over the top of the Web page. On the gray bar that appears, click ☐. To return the Web page to its original size, click ▣.

How can I change the properties for a Web page on my desktop?

✔ Display the Desktop Items dialog box and select the Web tab. Click the Web page you want to change and then click the Properties button. You can specify properties such as the Web page content you want to make available offline and the user name and password required to display the Web page.

■ The Web page you selected appears on your desktop.

■ Windows will update the Web page only when you are connected to the Internet.

Note: To immediately update the contents of the Web page, click a blank area on your desktop and then press the F5 key.

MOVE A WEB PAGE ON THE DESKTOP

1 Position the mouse ↖ over the top edge of the Web page. A gray bar appears.

2 Drag the Web page to a new location on your desktop.

CLEAN UP YOUR DESKTOP

You can use the Desktop Cleanup Wizard to identify desktop shortcuts you use infrequently and move the shortcuts to a special folder, called the Unused Desktop Shortcuts folder. This can help reduce clutter on your desktop.

Over time, shortcuts can accumulate on your desktop as you install new programs on your computer and download information from the Internet.

You may also have created desktop shortcuts to files and folders you no longer need.

The Desktop Cleanup Wizard displays a list of the shortcuts on your desktop and the date you last used each shortcut to help you identify shortcuts that are no longer useful. You can choose each shortcut you no longer want to appear on the desktop. The wizard will automatically create the Unused Desktop Shortcuts folder on your desktop for you and move each shortcut you chose to the folder.

Moving an item's shortcut to the Unused Desktop Shortcuts folder will not affect the original item on your computer.

The Desktop Cleanup Wizard can move only shortcuts to the Unused Desktop Shortcuts folder. The wizard will not move items you have stored on the desktop, such as files and folders.

CLEAN UP YOUR DESKTOP

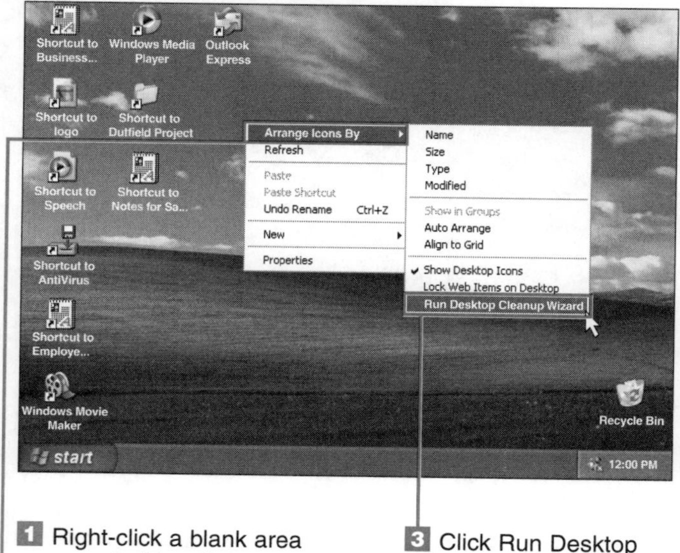

1 Right-click a blank area on your desktop. A menu appears.

2 Click Arrange Icons By.

3 Click Run Desktop Cleanup Wizard.

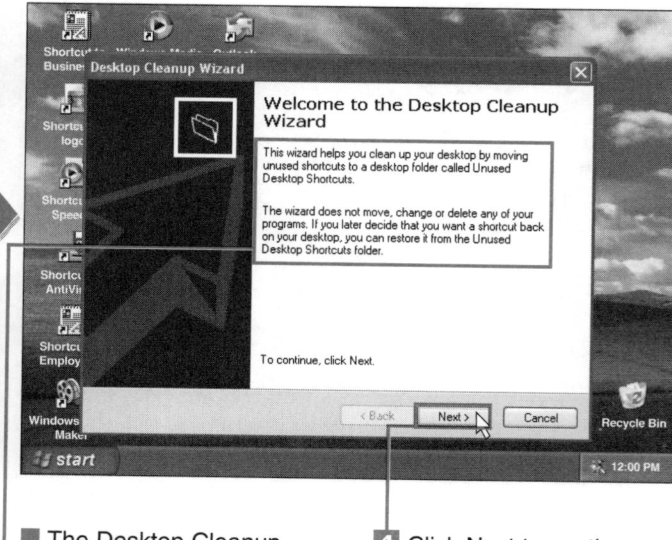

■ The Desktop Cleanup Wizard appears.

■ This area describes the wizard.

4 Click Next to continue.

Can I restore a shortcut to the desktop?

✔ If you regret moving a shortcut to the Unused Desktop Shortcuts folder, you can move the shortcut back to the desktop. Double-click the Unused Desktop Shortcuts folder to display its contents and then drag the shortcut to the desktop.

Why did the Desktop Cleanup Wizard start automatically?

✔ The Desktop Cleanup Wizard automatically runs every 60 days. If you do not want the wizard to run automatically, you can disable this feature. Right-click a blank area on your desktop and select Properties. Choose the Desktop tab and then click Customize Desktop. In the dialog box that appears, click the Run Desktop Cleanup Wizard every 60 days option (☑ changes to ☐).

Can I temporarily hide all the items on my desktop?

✔ Yes. Right-click a blank area on your desktop, select Arrange Items By and then click Show Desktop Items. To once again display the items, you can repeat these steps.

How can I delete unused desktop shortcuts?

✔ After running the Desktop Cleanup Wizard, you can delete the Unused Desktop Shortcuts folder to remove the folder and all the shortcuts it contains from your desktop. The next time you run the Desktop Cleanup Wizard, it will create a new Unused Desktop Shortcuts folder.

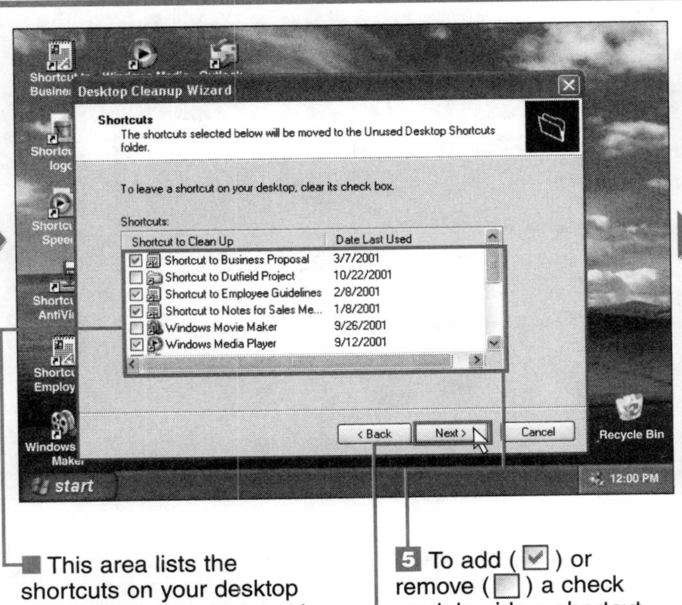

■ This area lists the shortcuts on your desktop and the date you last used each shortcut. A check mark (✔) appears beside each shortcut that Windows will move to the Unused Desktop Shortcuts folder.

5 To add (☑) or remove (☐) a check mark beside a shortcut, click the box beside the shortcut.

6 Click Next to continue.

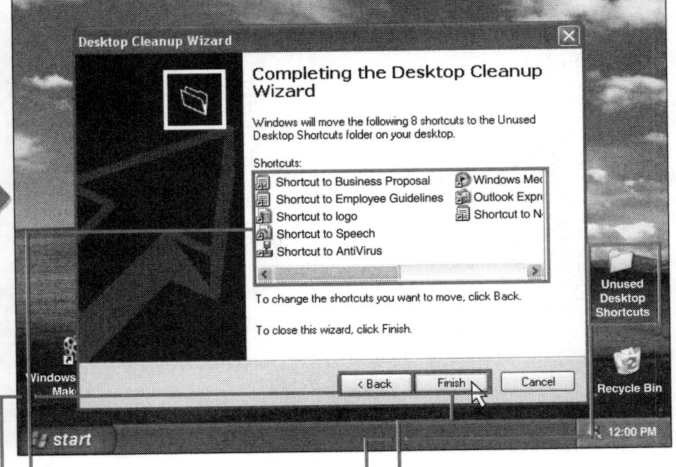

■ This area lists the shortcuts that Windows will move to the Unused Desktop Shortcuts folder.

■ You can click Back to return to the previous screen and change the shortcuts you selected to move.

7 Click Finish to close the wizard.

■ Windows creates the Unused Desktop Shortcuts folder on your desktop and moves the shortcuts you selected to this folder.

START A PROGRAM AUTOMATICALLY

You can have a program start automatically each time you turn on your computer.

Having a program start automatically is useful for programs you use every day and for programs you want to be able to access immediately.

To have a program start automatically, you need to place a shortcut for the program in the Startup folder. A shortcut is a link to the program. For information about shortcuts, see page 96. The Start menu contains shortcuts for the programs on your computer. You can easily copy a program's shortcut from the Start menu to the Startup folder. Each program in the Startup folder will start automatically each time you turn on your computer.

Your Startup folder may already contain several programs. Some programs, such as virus checkers, are automatically added to the Startup folder when they are installed.

You can also have a file open automatically by placing a shortcut for the file in the Startup folder. This is useful for files you frequently use, such as an order form.

START A PROGRAM AUTOMATICALLY

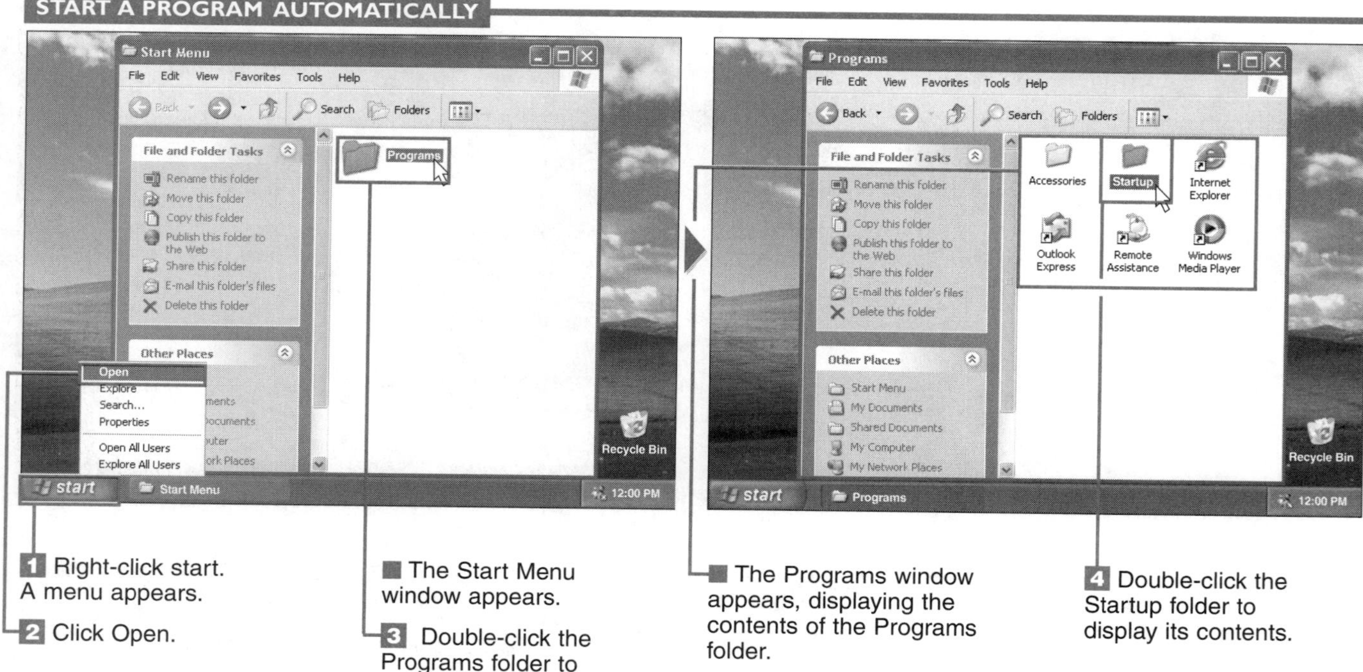

1 Right-click start. A menu appears.

2 Click Open.

■ The Start Menu window appears.

3 Double-click the Programs folder to display its contents.

■ The Programs window appears, displaying the contents of the Programs folder.

4 Double-click the Startup folder to display its contents.

How can I have a program start automatically if it does not appear on the Start menu?

✔ Locate the program you want to start automatically. Then create a shortcut for the program and drag the shortcut to the Startup window. To create a shortcut, see page 96.

How do I stop a program from starting automatically?

✔ You can delete the shortcut for the program from the Startup folder. Display the Startup window, click the shortcut you want to delete and then press the Delete key.

How do I quickly display a list of all the programs that will start automatically?

✔ Click the start button to display the Start menu. Click All Programs and then select Startup. A list of all the programs that will start automatically appears.

Can I have a program appear minimized as a button on the taskbar when the program starts automatically?

✔ Yes. Display the Startup window, right-click the shortcut for the program and then click Properties. In the dialog box that appears, select the Shortcut tab, click the Run area and then choose the Minimized option.

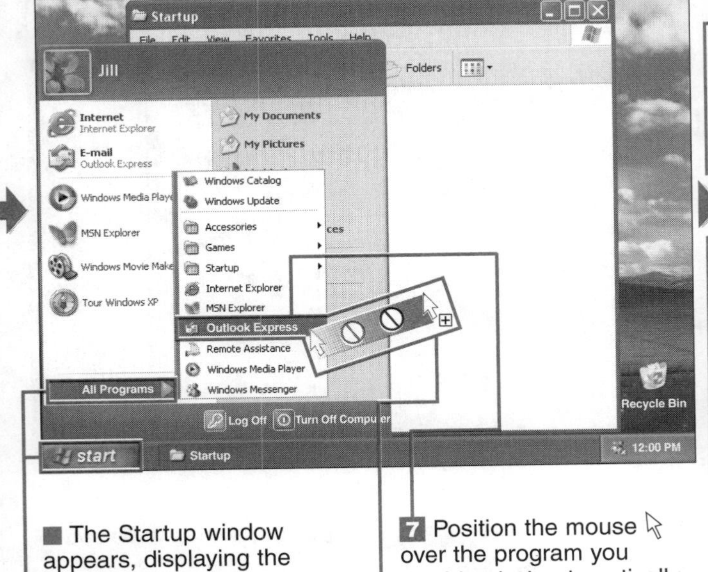

■ The Startup window appears, displaying the contents of the Startup folder.

5 Click start.

6 Click All Programs to view a list of the programs on your computer.

7 Position the mouse over the program you want to start automatically.

8 Press and hold down the Ctrl key as you drag the program to a blank area in the Startup window.

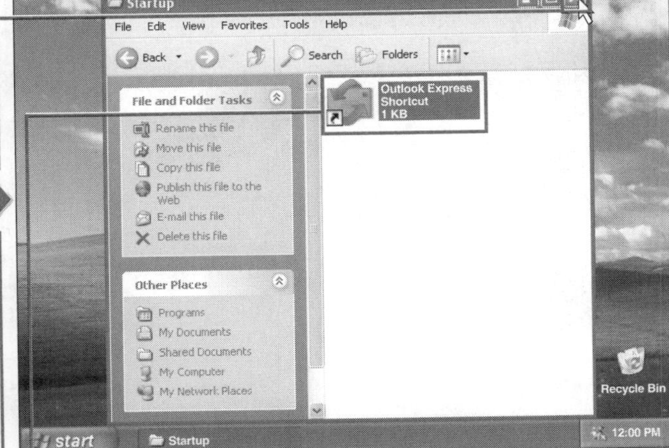

■ A shortcut for the program appears in the Startup window. A shortcut displays an arrow (↗) in its icon.

9 Click ☒ to close the Startup window.

■ The program will now start automatically each time you turn on your computer.

CHANGE FOLDER APPEARANCE

You can change the folder template and picture for a folder to customize the appearance of the folder.

Windows offers several folder templates you can choose from. Each template provides settings that are specialized for the type of files a folder contains, such as documents, pictures, music files or videos. Applying a folder template to a folder changes the task links that appear in the folder and the way the contents of the folder are displayed. For example, the Pictures template displays task links such as Print pictures and displays folder contents as thumbnail images.

When applying a template to a folder, you can specify if you want to also apply the template to all the subfolders within the folder.

You can specify a picture that you want to appear on the icon for a folder when the folder is displayed in the Thumbnails view. For information about the Thumbnails view, see page 42.

When a folder contains pictures, the icon for the folder will automatically display up to four of the pictures. You can choose a specific picture to change the appearance of the icon.

You cannot change the appearance of the My Documents, My Pictures or My Music folders, although you can change the subfolders they contain.

CHANGE FOLDER APPEARANCE

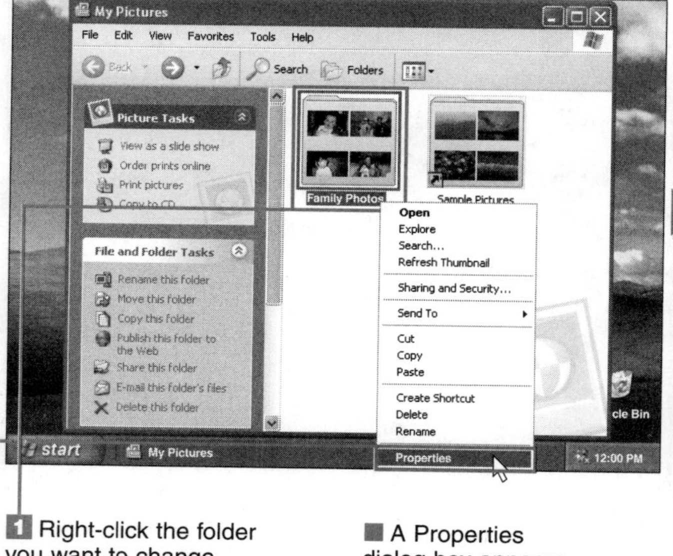

1 Right-click the folder you want to change. A menu appears.

2 Click Properties.

■ A Properties dialog box appears.

3 Click the Customize tab.

4 Click this area to list the available templates you can select for the folder.

5 Click the template you want to use for the folder.

Which folder template should I choose for my folder?

✔ The folder template you should choose depends on the type of files the folder contains. The name of a folder template indicates the type of file it is suited for. Windows also displays a description in parentheses beside most folder template names to help you determine which template will best suit your needs.

How do I remove a picture I specified for a folder?

✔ Perform steps 1 to 3 below and then click the Restore Default button to return the folder to its default appearance. If the folder contains no pictures, the folder icon will be blank. If the folder contains pictures, the icon for the folder will display up to four of the pictures.

Can I use a different icon for my folder?

✔ If you do not want to use the standard folder icon for a folder, you can choose a different icon. Perform steps 1 to 3 below and then click the Change Icon button. Select a new icon for the folder and click OK. The icon will appear in all views except the Thumbnails view. For information about the different views, see page 42.

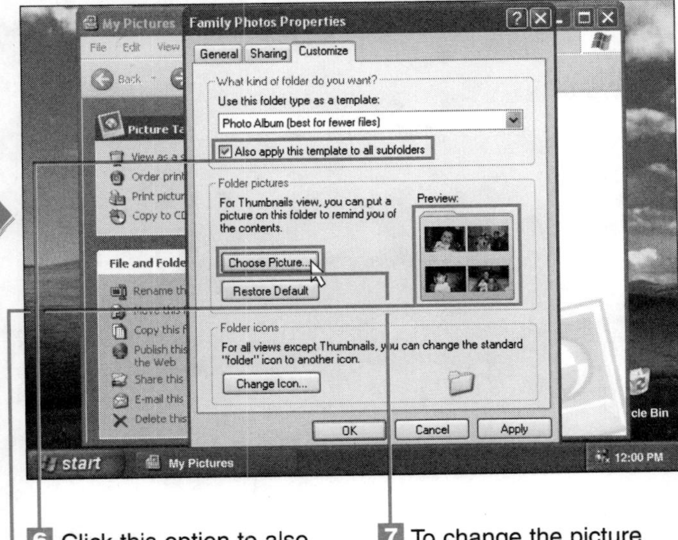

6 Click this option to also apply the template to all subfolders within the folder (☐ changes to ☑).

■ This area displays the current appearance of the folder.

7 To change the picture that appears on the folder, click Choose Picture.

■ The Browse dialog box appears.

8 Click the picture you want to appear on the folder.

9 Click Open to select the picture.

10 Click OK to confirm your changes.

CHANGE FOLDER OPTIONS

Windows provides several options you can use to change the way your folders look and act.

You can have your folders display links for common tasks or display the classic Windows style. When you choose to show common tasks in folders, the left side of open windows will display links that allow you to perform common tasks and quickly access other locations on your computer, such as the desktop and My Computer. When you use Windows classic folders, open windows will display only the icons for the items in the folder, as in earlier versions of Windows.

When opening folders, you can have each folder you open appear in the same window or in a different window. Opening folders in the same window reduces clutter on your desktop. Opening folders in different windows allows you to view the contents of several folders at once.

Windows also allows you to change the way you open items on your computer. You can choose to open items using a single-click or a double-click. If you choose the Single-click option, you can specify when you want items to display an underline.

CHANGE FOLDER OPTIONS

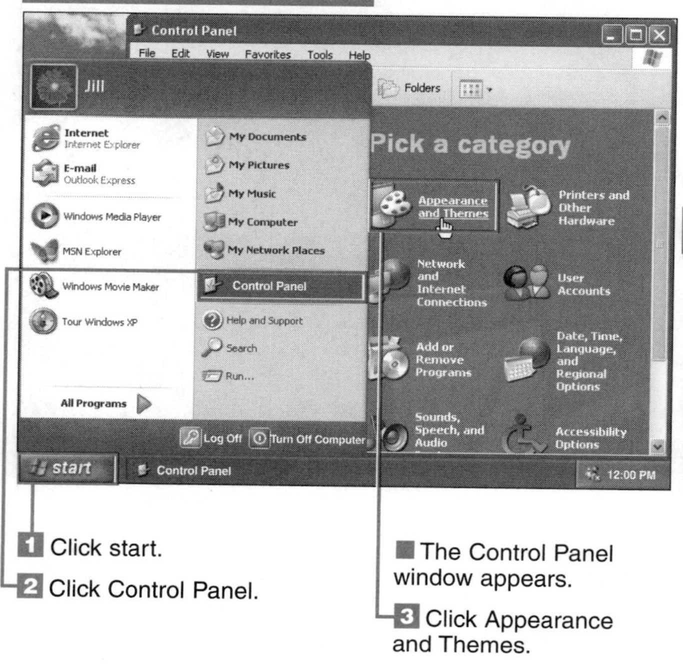

1 Click start.

2 Click Control Panel.

■ The Control Panel window appears.

3 Click Appearance and Themes.

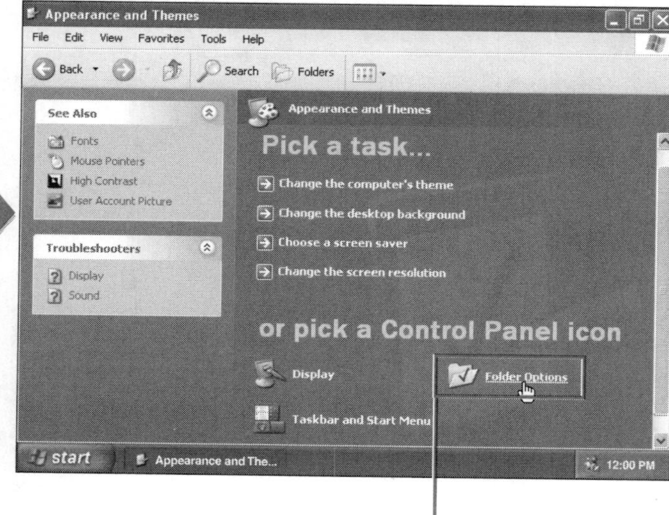

■ The Appearance and Themes window appears.

4 Click Folder Options.

How can I quickly return to the original folder settings?

✔ If you do not like the changes you made, you can click the Restore Defaults button in the Folder Options dialog box to quickly return to the original folder settings.

How do I select items when using the Single-click option?

✔ To select an item, position the mouse pointer over the item. To select a group of items, position the mouse pointer over the first item. Hold down the Shift key and then position the mouse pointer over the last item. To select random items, hold down the Ctrl key and position the mouse pointer over each item you want to select.

Why don't icon titles appear underlined after I select the Underline icon titles consistent with my browser option?

✔ You should make sure your Web browser is set to always underline links. To set up Internet Explorer to always underline links, click start, click All Programs and select Internet Explorer. In the Internet Explorer window, select the Tools menu and choose Internet Options. Click the Advanced tab and under the Underline links option, select Always (○ changes to ◉).

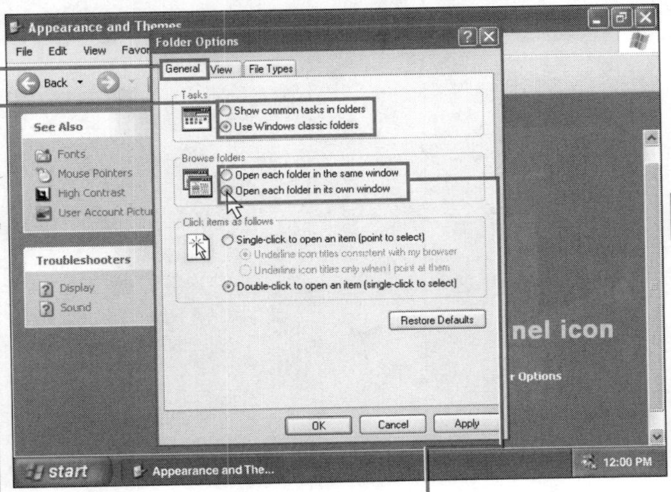

■ The Folder Options dialog box appears.

5 Click the General tab.

6 Click an option to display links for common tasks in folders or use Windows classic folders (○ changes to ◉).

7 Click an option to have each folder you open appear in the same window or in a new window (○ changes to ◉).

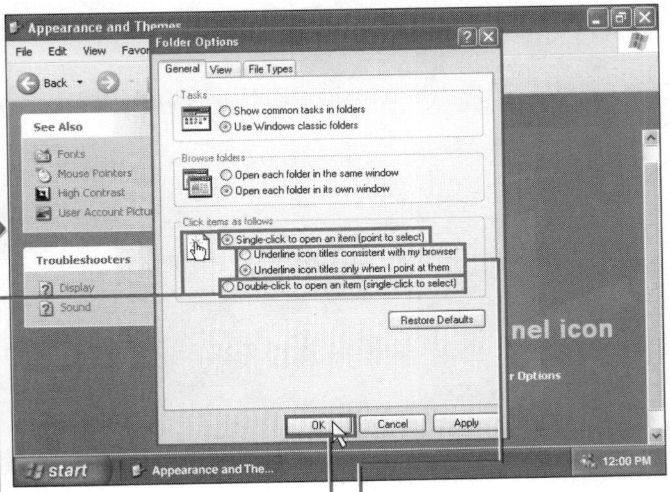

8 Click an option to open items using a single-click or a double-click (○ changes to ◉).

9 If you selected Single-click in step 8, click an option to have icon titles always appear underlined or appear underlined only when you position the mouse 👆 over an icon (○ changes to ◉).

10 Click OK to confirm your changes.

CHANGE THE FORMAT OF NUMBERS, DATES AND TIMES

You can change the way numbers, currency, dates and times are displayed on your computer. This allows you to use the settings common to your language and region of the world.

When you select a new language and region for your computer, Windows displays a preview of how the new settings will affect numbers, currency, dates and times. The new settings may also affect how these items are sorted in some programs.

Most North Americans use a period (.) to indicate the decimal point and a comma (,) to separate large numbers. These settings are not universal. In fact, in many regions, these settings are reversed.

When you receive a document from a computer set to a different language or region, Windows may adjust some of the numbers, currency, dates and times in the document to the language and region you have selected.

You can change your location setting to customize local content, such as news and weather, that you receive through your Web browser. You can choose a location that is different from the region you selected for the format of numbers, currency, dates and times. Not all Web sites can customize local content for your location.

CHANGE THE FORMAT OF NUMBERS, DATES AND TIMES

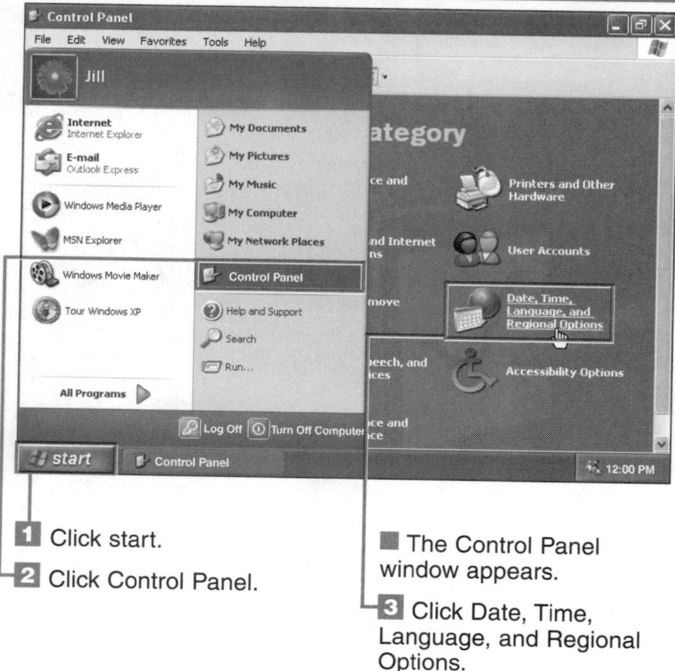

1 Click start.

2 Click Control Panel.

■ The Control Panel window appears.

3 Click Date, Time, Language, and Regional Options.

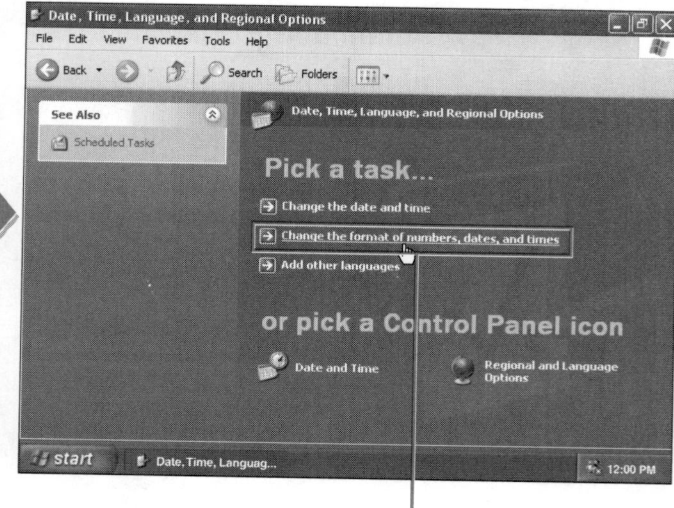

■ The Date, Time, Language, and Regional Options window appears.

4 Click Change the format of numbers, dates, and times.

Can I change an individual number, currency, date or time setting?

✔ Yes. You can customize an individual number, currency, date or time setting to your own preference. In the Regional and Language Options dialog box, choose the Regional Options tab and then click the Customize button in the Standards and formats area. In the dialog box that appears, click the tab for the type of information you want to change and then select the settings you want to use. For example, to change the clock to a 24-hour clock, choose the Time tab and then select a time format where the hours are represented by the capital letter H.

Can I enter text in a different language?

✔ Yes. To enter text in a different language, you must add the appropriate input language. In the Regional and Language Options dialog box, choose the Languages tab and then click the Details button in the Text services and input languages area. In the dialog box that appears, select the Add button in the Installed services area to display a dialog box that allows you to choose the input language you want to add. Once you have added the appropriate input language, a language icon (EN) appears on the taskbar. Click the language icon and then select the input language you want to use from the menu that appears.

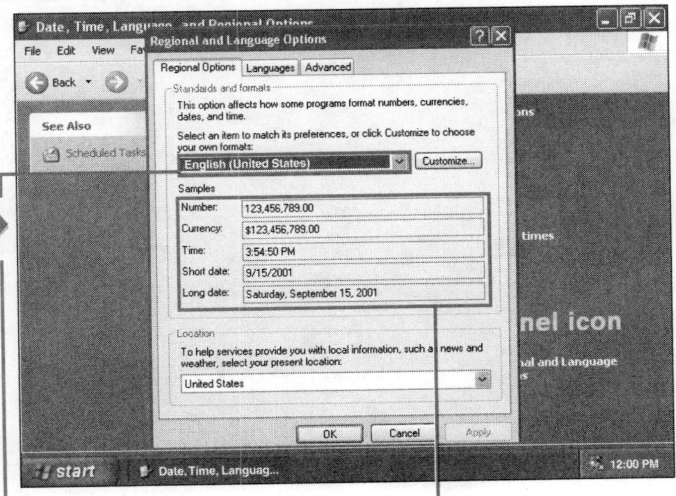

■ The Regional and Language Options dialog box appears.

5 This area displays the current language and regional setting, which controls how some programs display numbers, currency, dates and times. You can click this area to select a different language and regional setting.

■ This area displays samples of the way numbers, currency, dates and times currently appear.

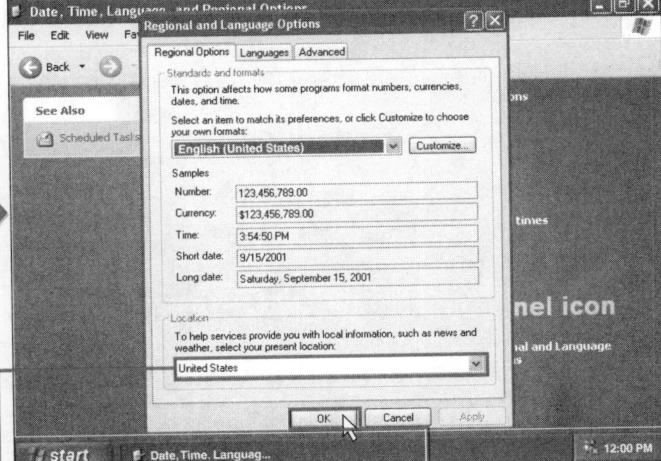

6 This area displays your location, which helps services typically found on the Web to provide you with local information, such as news and weather. You can click this area to select a different location.

7 Click OK to confirm your changes.

VIEW FONTS ON YOUR COMPUTER

You can view the fonts on your computer to see what they look like before using the fonts in your documents.

A font is a set of characters with a particular design. There are a wide variety of fonts you can use. Fonts can be serious and corporate or fancy and funny.

Most of the fonts included with Windows are OpenType fonts. In the Fonts window, the icon for an OpenType font displays the letter O. An OpenType font generates characters using mathematical formulas so you can change the size of an OpenType font without distorting the font. An OpenType font will print exactly as it appears on the screen.

The Fonts window may also contain TrueType fonts, which display an icon with two letter Ts and are similar to OpenType fonts.

Windows uses system fonts to display text in menus and dialog boxes. In the Fonts window, the icon for a system font displays a red A. These fonts are available only in specific sizes. Although system fonts may appear in a program's font list, they may not be suitable for some printing tasks.

Windows offers information about each font on your computer as well as samples of each font in various sizes.

VIEW FONTS ON YOUR COMPUTER

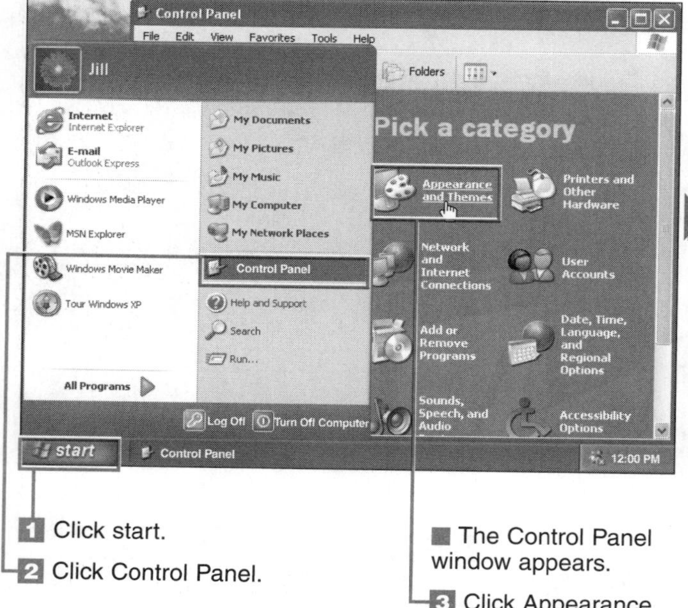

1 Click start.

2 Click Control Panel.

■ The Control Panel window appears.

3 Click Appearance and Themes.

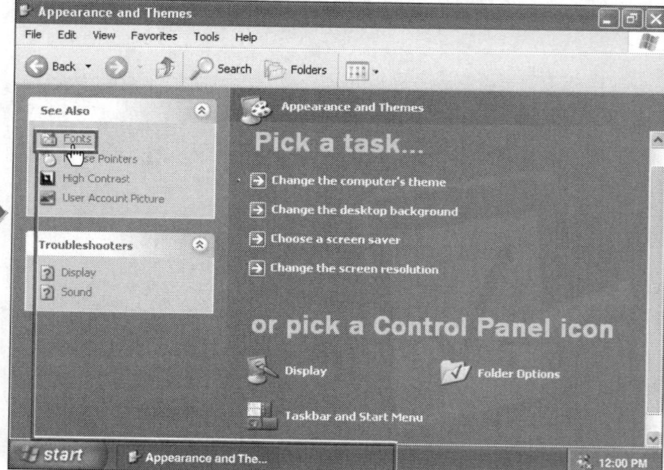

■ The Appearance and Themes window appears.

4 Click Fonts to view the fonts available on your computer.

Why do many font names appear more than once in the Fonts window?

✔ Windows displays variations of many fonts, such as bold and italic versions. In the View menu, click Hide Variations to remove the variations and display only the basic style for each font.

How can I change the way Windows displays items in the Fonts window?

✔ Click to display items as large icons. Click to display items as small icons in a list. Click to have Windows display how similar each font is to a font you select. Then click the area beside List fonts by similarity to and select the font you want to compare to other fonts. Click to view file information for each item in the Fonts window.

What are printer fonts?

✔ Printer fonts are fonts that are stored in a printer's memory. Nearly all printers include printer fonts. Printer fonts do not appear in the Fonts window and may not be accurately represented on your screen. This type of font may appear in a program's font list and is indicated by a printer icon ( ).

Can I print a sample of a font?

✔ Yes. In the Fonts window, double-click the font. Then click the Print button in the window that displays the font information to print the font samples.

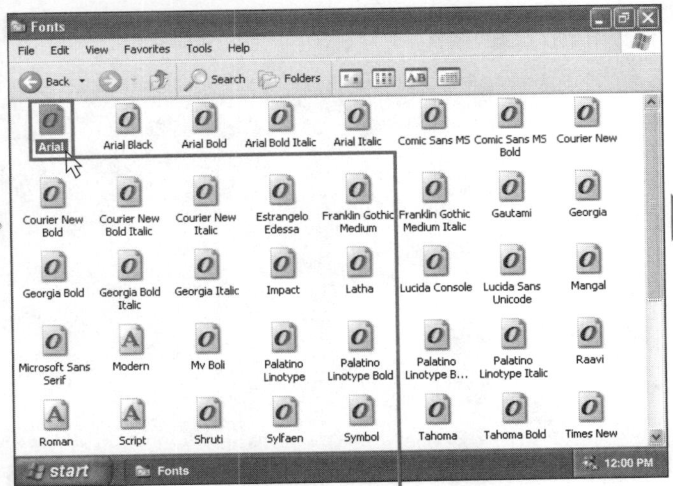

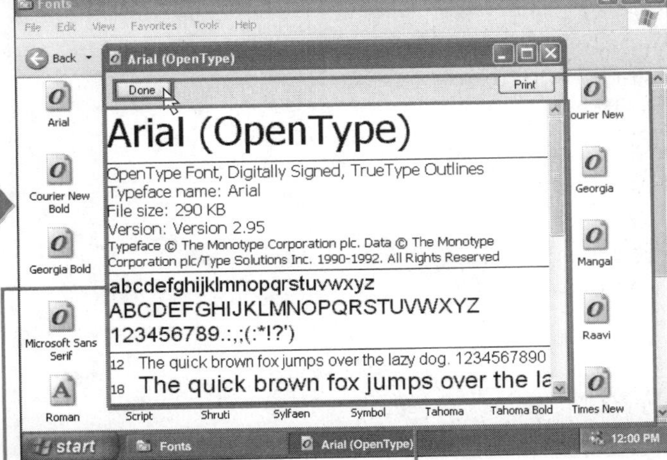

■ The Fonts window appears.

■ Each icon in the Fonts window represents a font installed on your computer. OpenType fonts display an O, TrueType fonts display two Ts and system fonts display a red A.

5 Double-click a font of interest to view information about the font.

■ A window appears, displaying information about the font you selected and samples of the font in various sizes.

6 When you finish reviewing the information, click Done to close the window.

ADD AND DELETE FONTS

You can add fonts to your computer to give you more choices when creating documents.

Windows includes several standard fonts. The fonts included with Windows and any other fonts you add are available in all Windows-based programs on your computer.

There are thousands of fonts available that you can add to your computer. When obtaining fonts, look for OpenType and TrueType fonts, since they are the most commonly used fonts in Windows. OpenType and TrueType fonts generate characters using mathematical formulas. These types of fonts will print exactly as they appear on your screen.

You can typically buy fonts wherever software is sold. You can also obtain fonts on the Internet.

To find fonts on the Internet, simply search for "OpenType fonts" or "TrueType fonts." To search the Web, see page 436.

There are fonts available for many different types of operating systems. When you buy fonts or obtain fonts on the Internet, make sure you choose the Windows version of the fonts.

ADD FONTS

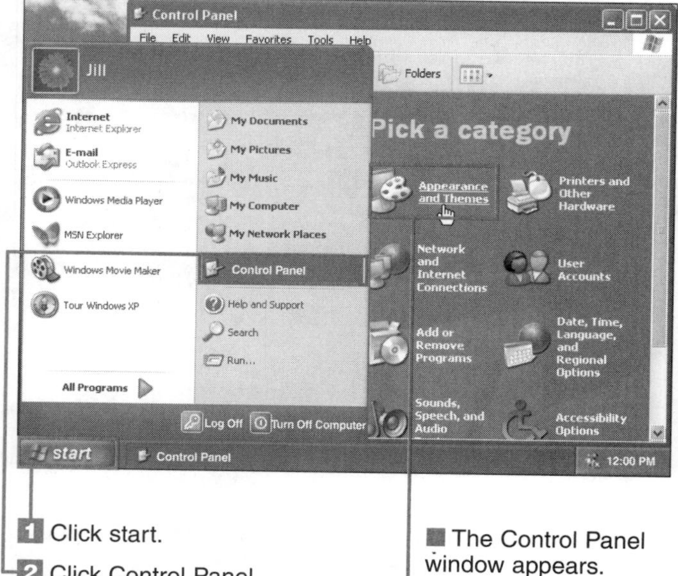

1 Click start.

2 Click Control Panel.

■ The Control Panel window appears.

3 Click Appearance and Themes.

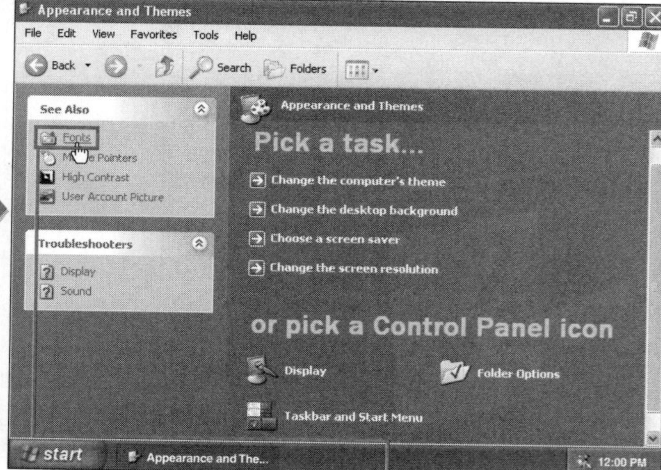

■ The Appearance and Themes window appears.

4 Click Fonts to add new fonts to your computer.

How many fonts can I install?

✔ There is no limit to the number of fonts you can install, but keep in mind that fonts take up storage space on your computer. You may also find that a long list of fonts becomes cluttered and difficult to use.

Is there an easy way to manage fonts?

✔ There are several programs, such as Adobe Type Manager, that can arrange fonts into groups. You can then select the group of fonts with which you want to work. You may want to group fonts that you use for a specific task, such as word processing or desktop publishing.

Is there a faster way to install a font?

✔ When the Fonts window is open on your screen, you can drag and drop the icon for a new font into the Fonts window. An icon for the font will appear in the window, but the original font file will remain in its original location on your computer. You can place only font files in the Fonts window. If you try to place another type of file in the Fonts window, Windows may display an error message.

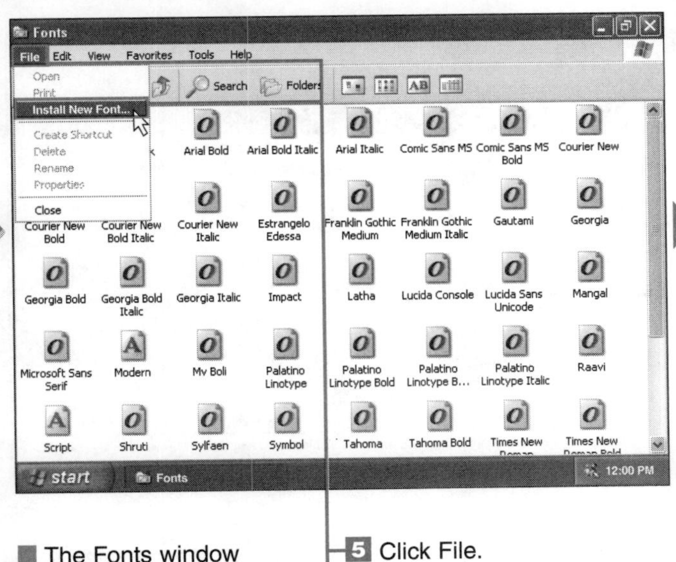

■ The Fonts window appears, displaying the fonts available on your computer.

5 Click File.

6 Click Install New Font.

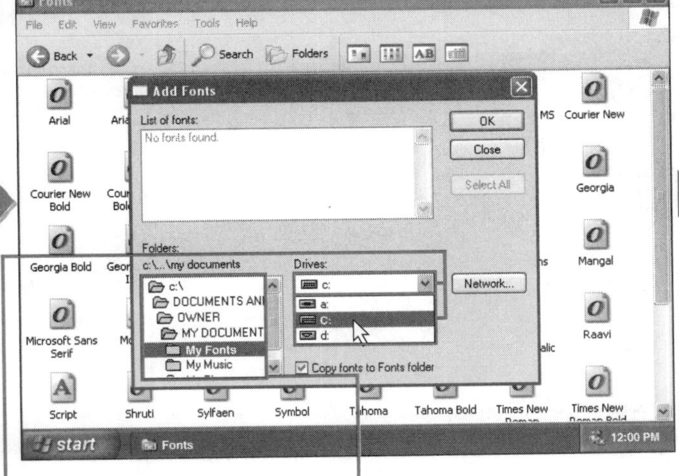

■ The Add Fonts dialog box appears.

7 Click this area to select the drive containing the fonts you want to add.

8 Click the drive containing the fonts.

■ This area lists the folders on the drive you selected.

9 Double-click the folder containing the fonts you want to add.

CONTINUED

ADD AND DELETE FONTS (CONTINUED)

When adding fonts, you can select one font, several fonts or all of the available fonts in the folder. Windows copies the new fonts to the Fonts folder so you can use the fonts in your documents.

You can also remove fonts you no longer use from your computer. You can select several fonts and delete them at the same time.

Fonts that display a red A in the Fonts window are required by Windows. Many other programs also install their own special fonts. Before you delete a font you did not add, make sure the font is not required by a program.

If you delete a font that is used by Windows or a Windows program, a different font will be used to replace the one you deleted. You may not like the substitution Windows makes.

Deleted fonts are sent to your Recycle Bin. To be safe, you may want to make a backup copy of a font before you delete the font.

ADD FONTS (CONTINUED)

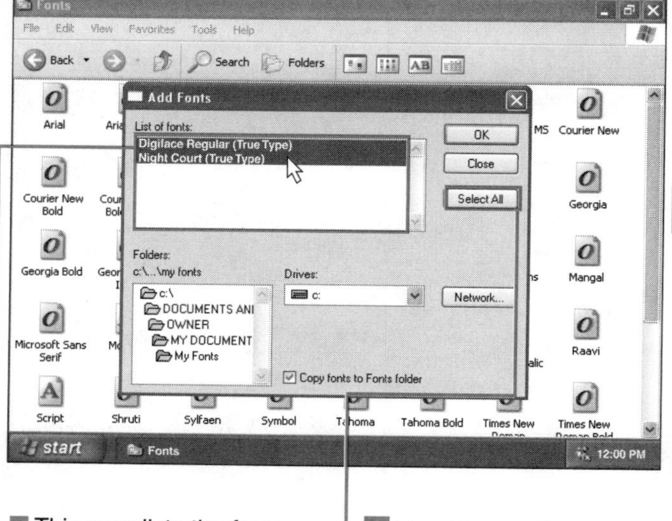

- This area lists the fonts stored in the folder you selected.

10 Click the font you want to add to your computer.

11 To add more than one font, press and hold down the Ctrl key as you click each font you want to add.

- To quickly select all the fonts in the current folder, click Select All.

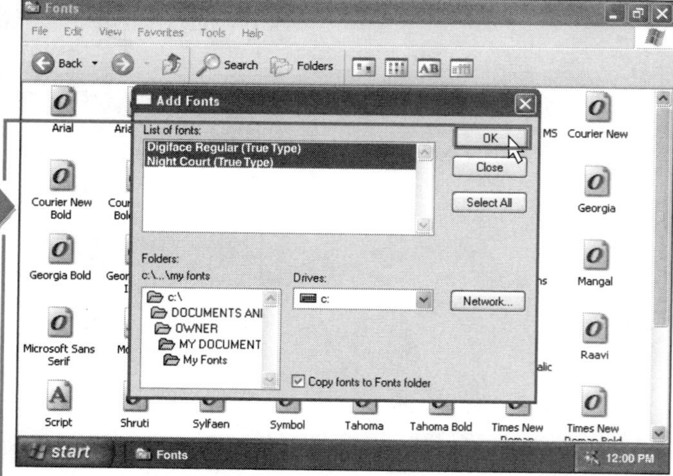

12 Click OK to add the fonts you selected to your computer.

- The fonts appear in the Fonts window.

Can I prevent Windows from copying fonts I add to the Fonts folder?

✔ Yes. You can have Windows add shortcuts to the fonts instead. This allows you to use the fonts directly from their current location. Adding shortcuts to fonts is useful when you want to add fonts from a network drive without using disk space on your computer. If the fonts are changed on the network, you can access the updated fonts automatically. In the Add Fonts dialog box, select the Copy fonts to Fonts folder option (☑ changes to ☐).

Why is my network drive not displayed in the list of drives in the Add Fonts dialog box?

✔ You may need to map the drive to have it appear in the Add Fonts dialog box. For information about mapping a network drive, see page 414.

Is there another way to delete fonts?

✔ In the Fonts window, position the mouse pointer over the font you want to delete. Then drag the font onto the Recycle Bin icon on the desktop.

How can I restore a font I accidentally deleted?

✔ Double-click Recycle Bin on the desktop to open the Recycle Bin window. Then right-click the font you want to retrieve and choose Restore from the menu that appears.

DELETE FONTS

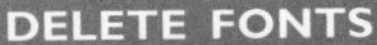

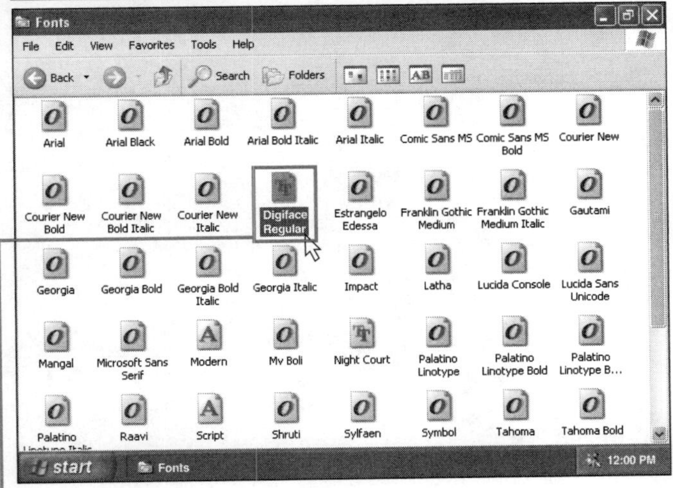

1 Click the font you want to delete.

■ To delete more than one font, press and hold down the Ctrl key as you click each font you want to delete.

2 Press the Delete key.

■ A confirmation dialog box appears.

3 Click Yes to delete the font.

■ The font disappears from the Fonts window. Windows places the font in the Recycle Bin.

CHANGE MOUSE SETTINGS

You can change the way your mouse works to make it easier to use. The Mouse Properties dialog box offers many options you can adjust to suit your needs.

The left mouse button is used to select and drag items. The right mouse button is used to display a list of commands for a selected item. If you are left-handed, you can switch the functions of the left and right mouse buttons to make the mouse easier to use.

You can change the amount of time that can pass between two clicks of the mouse button for Windows to recognize a double-click. Double-clicking is most often used to open an item. If you are a new mouse user or you have difficulty double-clicking, you may find a slower speed easier to use. You can try out the double-click speed to find the setting you prefer.

You can also turn on the ClickLock option to allow you to drag items or select text without having to continuously hold down the mouse button.

When you change most settings in the Mouse Properties dialog box, Windows immediately changes the way your mouse works.

CHANGE MOUSE SETTINGS

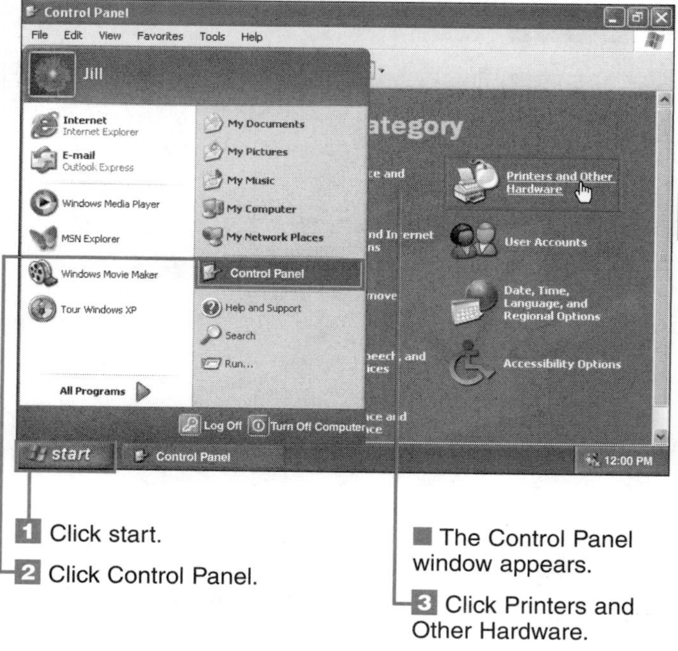

1 Click start.

2 Click Control Panel.

■ The Control Panel window appears.

3 Click Printers and Other Hardware.

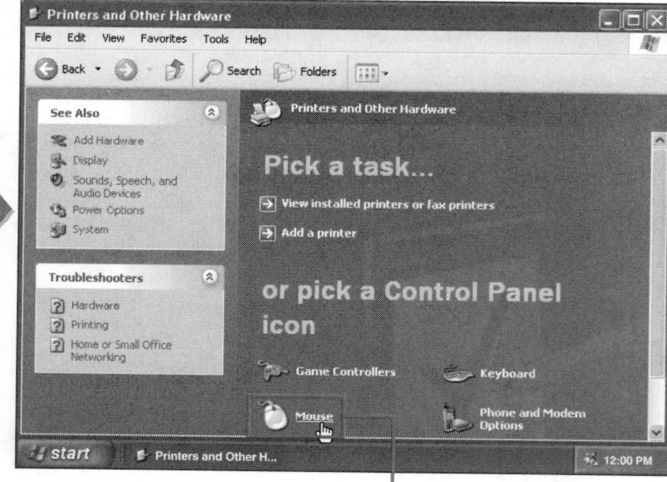

■ The Printers and Other Hardware window appears.

4 Click Mouse to change your mouse settings.

My mouse pointer does not move smoothly on my screen. What can I do?

✔ You may need to clean your mouse. Turn the mouse over and remove and clean the roller ball. Then use a cotton swab to remove the dirt from the rollers inside the mouse.

Should I use a mouse pad?

✔ A mouse pad provides a smooth surface for moving the mouse on your desk. You should use a mouse pad to reduce the amount of dirt that enters the mouse and protect your desk from scratches. Hard plastic mouse pads attract less dirt and provide a smoother surface than fabric mouse pads.

How can I use the ClickLock mouse setting to work with text and items on my screen?

✔ To select text, position the mouse pointer to the left of the text you want to select and briefly hold down the mouse button. Then click at the end of the text. To drag items, position the mouse pointer over the item you want to move and briefly hold down the mouse button. Then click where you want to place the item.

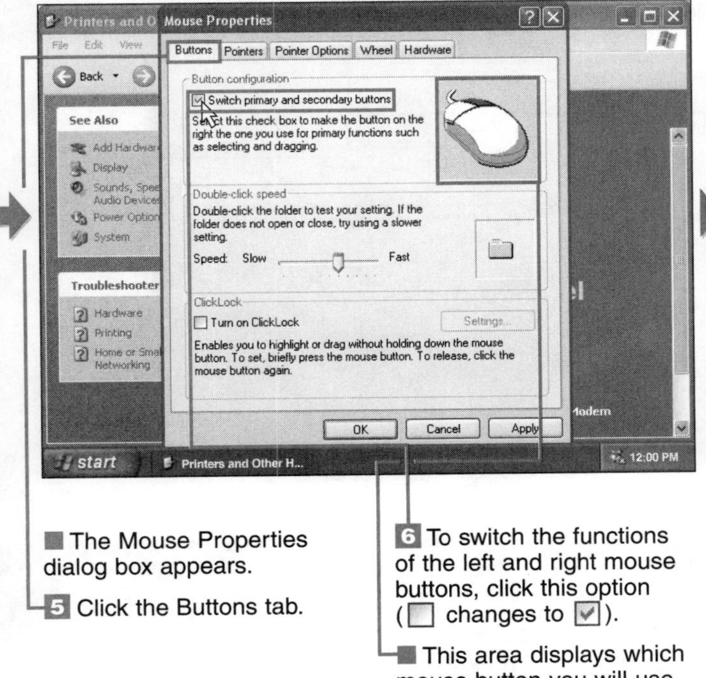

■ The Mouse Properties dialog box appears.

5 Click the Buttons tab.

6 To switch the functions of the left and right mouse buttons, click this option (☐ changes to ☑).

■ This area displays which mouse button you will use to perform most tasks.

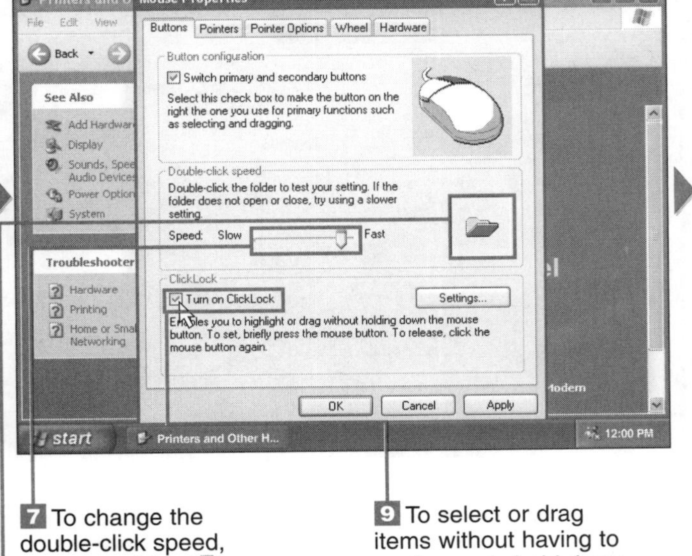

7 To change the double-click speed, drag this slider (▯) to a new position.

8 Double-click the folder in this area to test the double-click speed. The folder opens or closes when you double-click at the correct speed.

9 To select or drag items without having to continuously hold down the mouse button, click this option (☐ changes to ☑).

CONTINUED

CHANGE MOUSE SETTINGS (CONTINUED)

You can personalize your mouse by changing the look of the mouse pointers and the way the pointer moves on your screen.

Windows includes several sets of mouse pointers, including colored and large pointers. You can choose to display a different set of mouse pointers. You can also choose whether you want pointers to display a shadow, giving the pointers a 3-D effect.

You can change how fast the mouse pointer moves on your screen and specify whether you want to use enhanced pointer precision, which provides finer control of the mouse pointer. You can also have the mouse pointer automatically appear over the default button in most dialog boxes. The default button in most dialog boxes is the OK button.

You can leave a trail of mouse pointers as you move the mouse on your screen to help you follow the movement of the pointer. You can also specify the length of the mouse pointer trails.

Windows also lets you specify whether you want to temporarily hide the mouse pointer while you type.

If you need help locating the mouse pointer on your screen, you can have Windows display moving circles around the mouse pointer when you press the Ctrl key.

CHANGE MOUSE SETTINGS (CONTINUED)

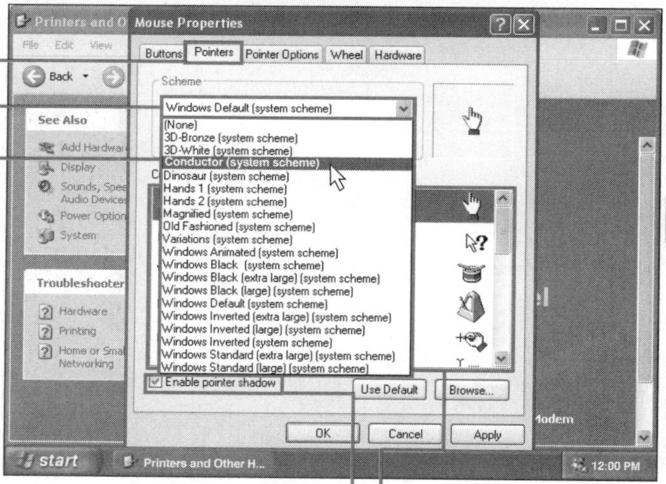

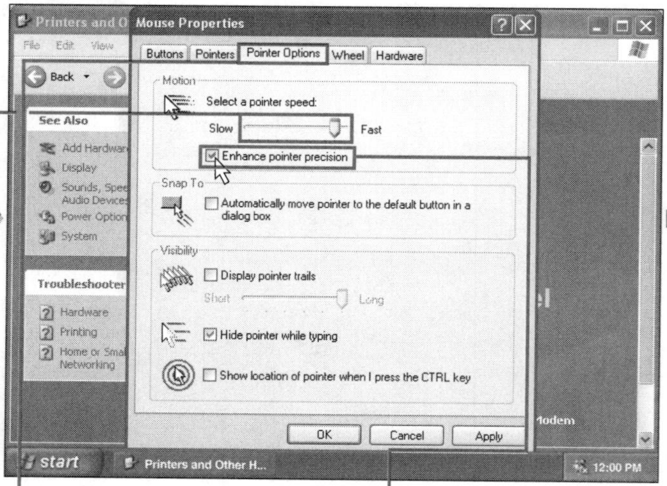

10 Click the Pointers tab to change the appearance of the mouse pointers.

11 Click this area to display a list of mouse pointer sets.

12 Click the mouse pointer set you want to use.

■ This area lists the mouse pointers in the set you selected.

13 This option activates pointer shadows. You can click this option to turn the option on (☑) or off (☐).

14 Click the Pointer Options tab to specify additional mouse pointer options.

15 To change how fast the mouse pointer moves on your screen, drag this slider (▯) to a new position.

16 This option provides finer control of the mouse pointer. You can click this option to turn the option on (☑) or off (☐).

Why does my Mouse Properties dialog box have additional options?

✔ If you installed software that came with your mouse, you may find additional options in the Mouse Properties dialog box.

Why does each set of mouse pointers contain so many shapes?

✔ The mouse pointer assumes different shapes depending on its location on your screen and the task you are performing. For example, the standard mouse pointer turns into an hourglass when your computer is busy, or changes to a double-headed arrow when you are adjusting the size of a window.

How can I change the appearance of individual pointers in a set of mouse pointers?

✔ In the Mouse Properties dialog box, display the Pointers tab and then double-click the mouse pointer you want to change. In the Browse dialog box that appears, double-click the mouse pointer you want to use. After you have customized a set of mouse pointers, you can click the Save As button to name and save the set.

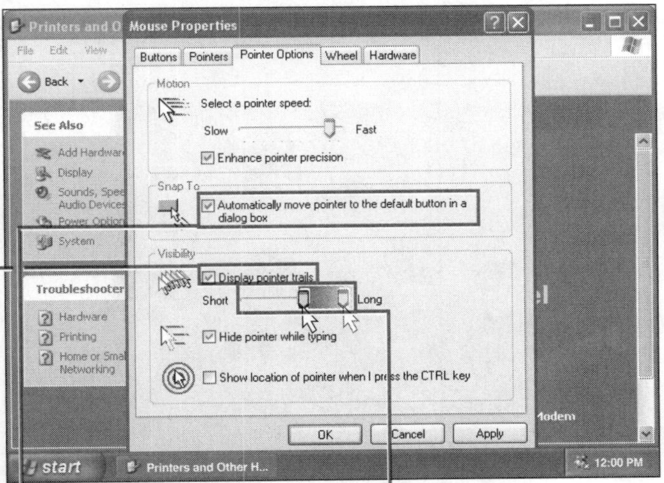

17 To have the mouse pointer automatically appear over the default button in most dialog boxes, click this option (☐ changes to ☑).

18 To leave a trail of mouse pointers as you move the mouse pointer on your screen, click this option (☐ changes to ☑).

19 To change the length of the mouse pointer trail, drag this slider (⬚) to a new position.

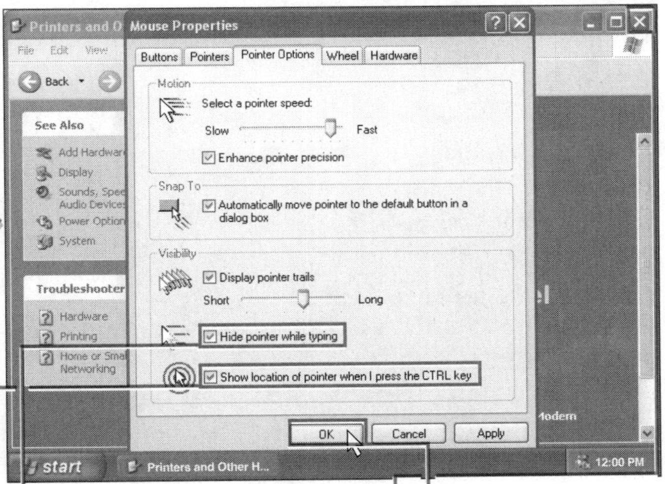

20 This option hides the mouse pointer when you type. You can click this option to turn the option on (☑) or off (☐).

21 To show the location of the mouse pointer when you press the Ctrl key, click this option (☐ changes to ☑).

22 Click OK when you finish selecting all the mouse settings you want to change.

23 Click ☒ to close the Printers and Other Hardware window.

CHANGE KEYBOARD SETTINGS

You can change the way your keyboard responds to your commands. For example, you can change the way a character repeats when you hold down a key on your keyboard. This is useful if you often use repeated characters to underline, separate or emphasize text.

The Repeat delay setting adjusts the length of time a key must be held down before the character starts to repeat. The Repeat rate setting determines how quickly characters appear on your screen when you hold down a key. You can test the settings while making adjustments.

You can also change the speed at which the cursor blinks. The cursor, or insertion point, indicates where the text you type will appear in a document. The cursor should blink fast enough so it is easy to find, but slow enough so it is not distracting. You can preview your cursor blink rate to find a setting you prefer.

CHANGE KEYBOARD SETTINGS

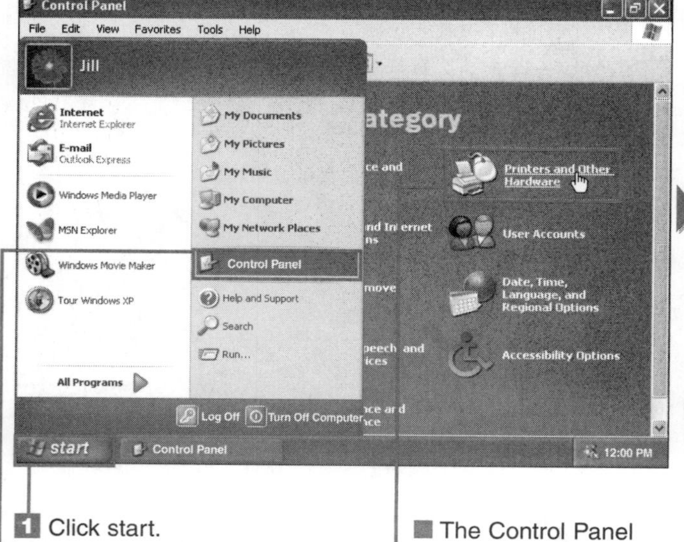

1 Click start.

2 Click Control Panel.

■ The Control Panel window appears.

3 Click Printers and Other Hardware.

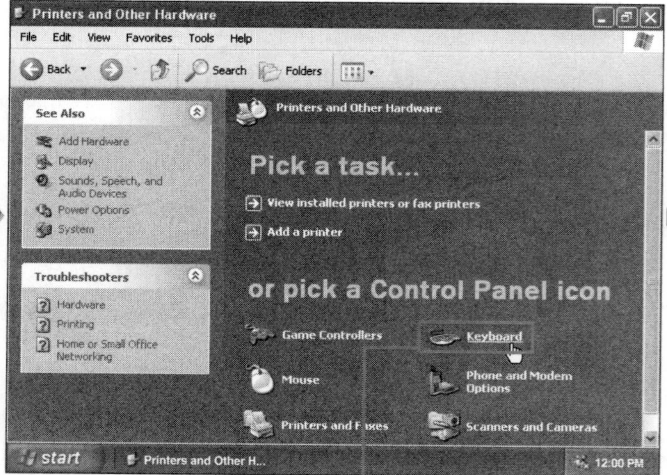

■ The Printers and Other Hardware window appears.

4 Click Keyboard.

■ The Keyboard Properties dialog box appears.

Can I make my keyboard easier to use?

✔ Windows offers various accessibility options that you can select to make your keyboard easier to use. For example, you can have Windows ignore repeated keystrokes or play tones when you press the Caps Lock, Num Lock or Scroll Lock keys. For more information, see page 274.

I have trouble using my keyboard to type my documents. What can I do?

✔ You can use the On-Screen Keyboard. The On-Screen Keyboard allows you to use your mouse to select characters you want to enter in a document. For more information, see page 270.

What is the correct typing position to help avoid wrist strain?

✔ You should keep your elbows level with the keyboard. Always keep your wrists straight and higher than your fingers while working on the keyboard. You can use a wrist rest to elevate your wrists and ensure they remain straight at all times. If you start to experience any pain, tingling or numbness while working, take a break. If the sensation continues, you should see a doctor.

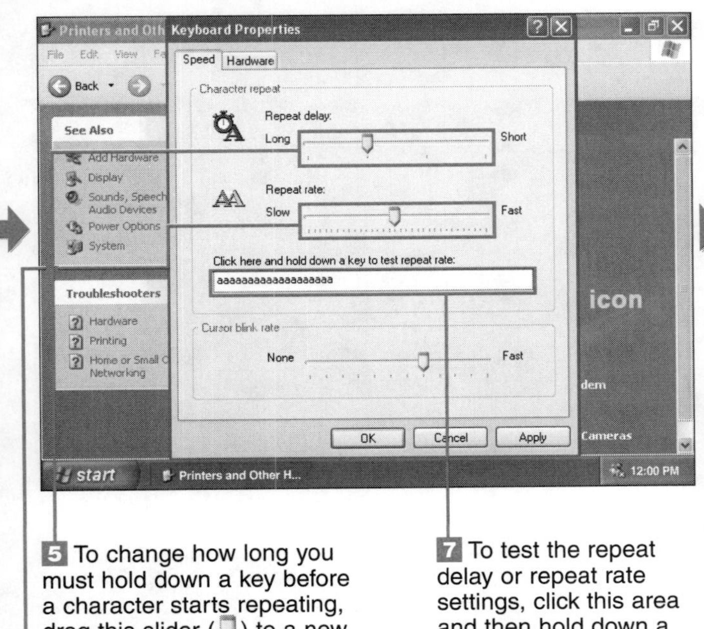

5 To change how long you must hold down a key before a character starts repeating, drag this slider (▽) to a new position.

6 To change how quickly characters repeat when you hold down a key, drag this slider (▽) to a new position.

7 To test the repeat delay or repeat rate settings, click this area and then hold down a key on your keyboard.

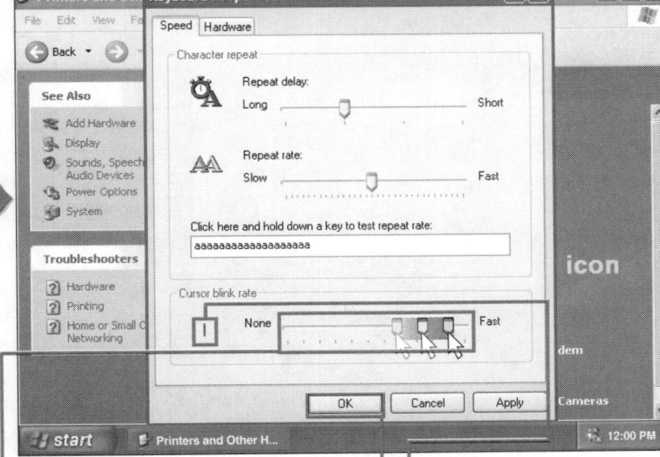

8 To change how quickly the cursor blinks, drag this slider (▽) to a new position.

Note: If you want the cursor to stop blinking and remain visible at all times, drag the slider to the left end of the bar.

■ This area displays the cursor blink rate.

9 Click OK to confirm all your changes.

CHANGE SPEECH SETTINGS

Windows allows you to change settings on your computer for programs that have speech capabilities, such as Microsoft Office XP programs. Changing speech settings allows you to customize the speech capabilities of a program to suit your needs.

Speech capabilities in a program can include Text-To-Speech (TTS), which is the ability to have Windows read text in a document aloud, or Speech Recognition (SR), which is the ability to convert spoken words to text. TTS capabilities are installed on Windows by default. Normally, you must install a program with speech capabilities to make SR capabilities available in Windows.

Programs that include text-to-speech capabilities contain an internal driver, called a TTS engine, which recognizes the text in a document and uses a synthesized voice to read the text aloud.

If you have more than one voice available on your computer, you can choose the voice you want Windows to use to read text. You can play a preview of the voice by having the voice read sample text that Windows provides or text you type. You can also change how quickly the voice will read text.

You must have a program with speech capabilities installed on your computer to use the speech settings you specify. You may also need to adjust the speech settings within the program.

CHANGE SPEECH SETTINGS

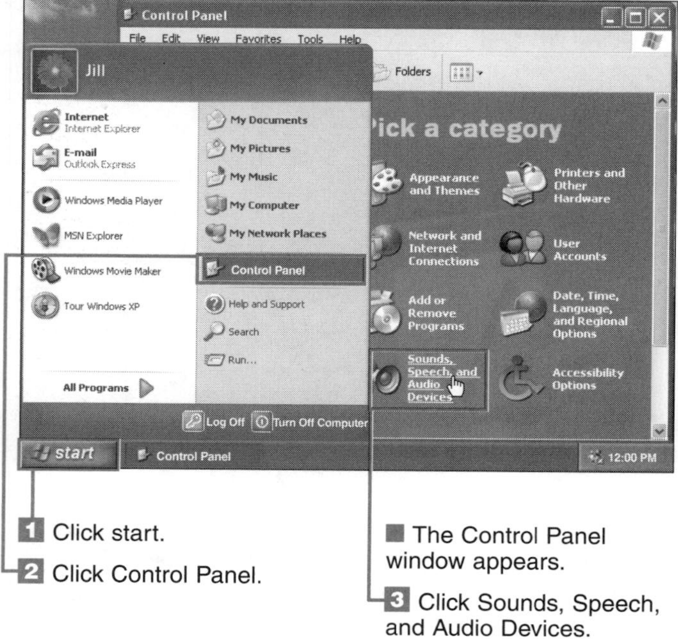

1 Click start.

2 Click Control Panel.

■ The Control Panel window appears.

3 Click Sounds, Speech, and Audio Devices.

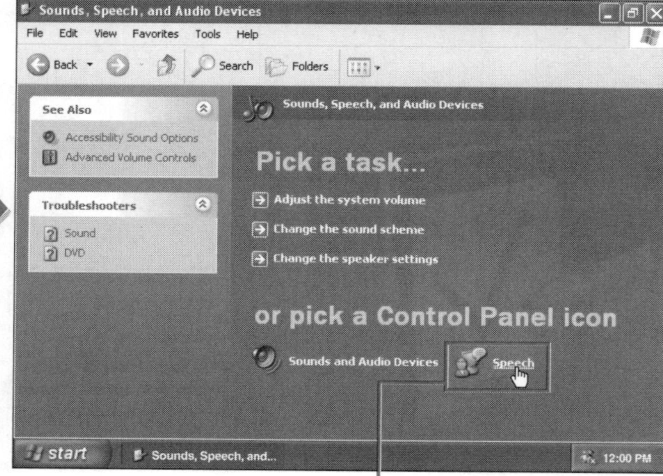

■ The Sounds, Speech, and Audio Devices window appears.

4 Click Speech to change the speech settings for your computer.

Where can I get programs that include text-to-speech capabilities?

✔ Most speech recognition programs include text-to-speech capabilities. Two popular speech recognition programs are ViaVoice, which is available at the www-4.ibm.com/software/speech Web site and Dragon NaturallySpeaking, which is available at the www.lhsl.com/naturallyspeaking Web site.

How can I change settings for speech recognition?

✔ If you have a program with speech recognition capabilities installed on your computer, the Speech Properties dialog box displays a Speech Recognition tab. You can click the tab to change settings such as pronunciation sensitivity and response time, which can help the computer better recognize your voice. If your computer has multiple input devices connected, you can also select which input device you want to use, such as a microphone or tape recorder.

Can I have a program recognize my handwriting?

✔ Some programs, such as Microsoft Office XP programs, include handwriting recognition capabilities. Handwriting recognition allows you to use an input device, such as a digital pen and tablet or your mouse, to write text on your computer as you would use a pen. Windows will convert the handwritten text to typed characters on your computer. To install handwriting recognition for a program, refer to the documentation included with the program.

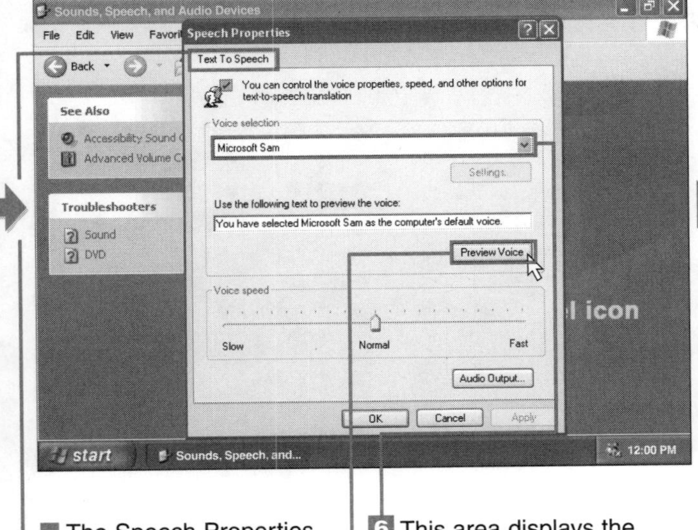

■ The Speech Properties dialog box appears.

5 Click the Text To Speech tab.

6 This area displays the voice Windows will use to read text. If more than one voice is available on your computer, you can click this area to select a different voice.

7 To preview the currently selected voice, click Preview Voice.

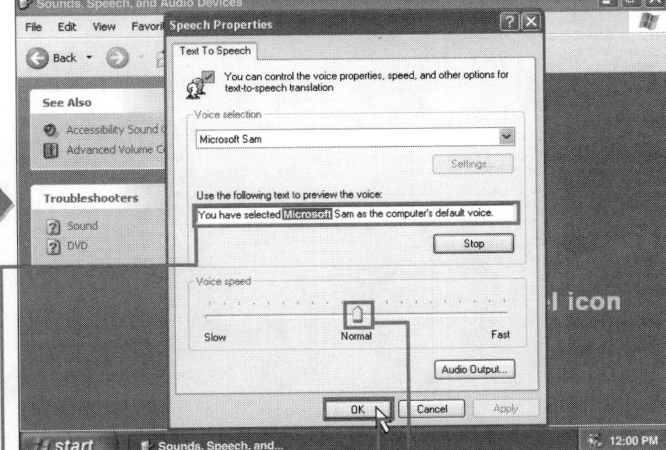

■ Windows reads the text shown in this area.

Note: If you want Windows to read different text, you can select the text in the area and type the new text.

8 To change the speed of the voice, drag this slider (⌂) to the left or right.

9 Click OK to confirm your changes.

DISPLAY AND CREATE FILE TYPES

Most files on your computer are associated with a certain program. Windows uses a file name extension to associate each file type with the program that Windows will use to open the file. File name extensions are usually three letters that appear after the period at the end of a file name, such as .doc or .txt. For example, the file name extension for a file called report.txt indicates that the file is a Text Document type of file and is associated with the Notepad program.

Windows automatically recognizes over 200 types of files, such as text, sound, picture and video files.

You can create a new file type to tell Windows how you want to work with a certain type of file. For example, you can create a file type with the .let extension for letters you create and associate the file type with the WordPad program. Before creating a new file type, you can view a list of all the extensions and associated file types that are currently registered with Windows. Any new file types you create will be added to this list.

DISPLAY AND CREATE FILE TYPES

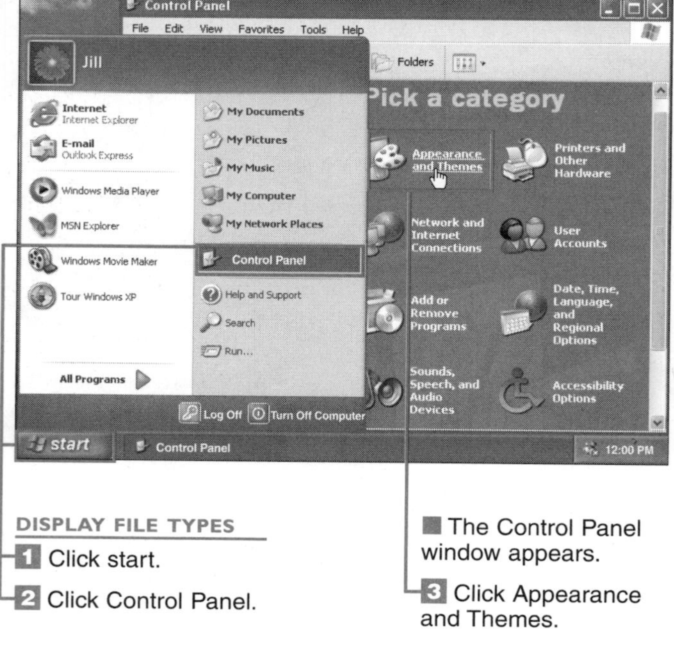

DISPLAY FILE TYPES

1 Click start.

2 Click Control Panel.

■ The Control Panel window appears.

3 Click Appearance and Themes.

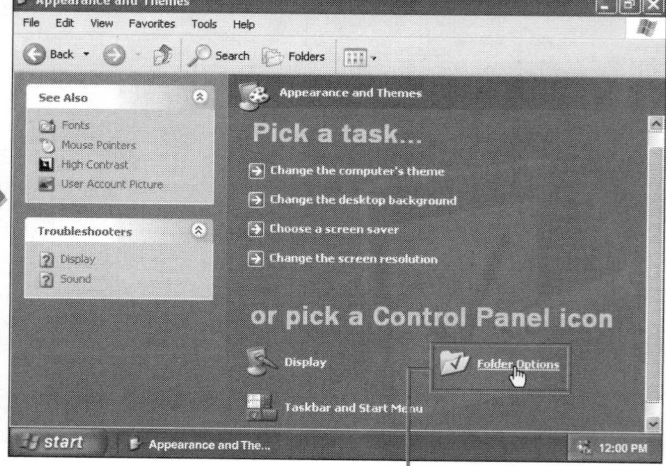

■ The Appearance and Themes window appears.

4 Click Folder Options.

Why can't I see the file name extensions in my folders?

✔ By default, Windows does not display the file name extensions for registered file types. To display the file name extensions for all files, display the Folder Options dialog box, select the View tab and click the Hide extensions for known file types option (☑ changes to ☐).

How do I quickly find a file type in the Folder Options dialog box?

✔ You can click in the list of file types and type the first letter of the file name extension for the file type you want to find. Windows will display the section of the list that contains file types with extensions that start with the letter you typed. You can also click the File Types column heading to sort the file types alphabetically in the list.

Can I change the file type that is associated with an existing file name extension?

✔ Yes. In the Folder Options dialog box, select the File Types tab and then click the New button to display the Create New Extension dialog box. In the File Extension area, type the file name extension you want to change. Click the Advanced button to display the Associated File Type area and then click the area to select the new file type you want to associate with the extension.

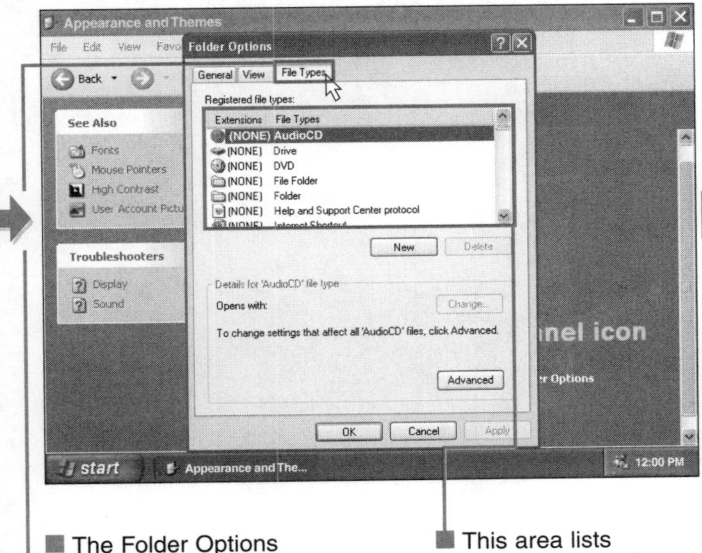

■ The Folder Options dialog box appears.

5 Click the File Types tab.

■ This area lists the extensions and associated file types that are registered with Windows.

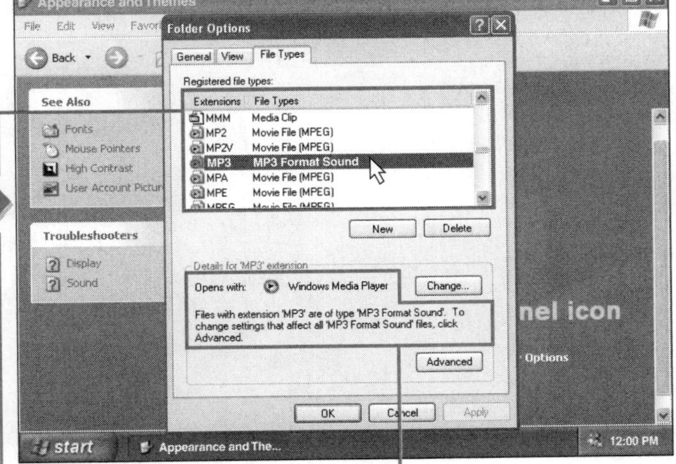

6 To display information about a file type, click the file type.

■ This area displays information about the file type, including the program that opens files of this type.

CONTINUED

DISPLAY AND CREATE FILE TYPES (CONTINUED)

When creating a new file type, you must provide an extension for the file type. You can create file name extensions longer than three characters, such as .budget, but make sure your extensions do not contain any spaces or periods. If you share files with people who use older programs, these programs may not be able to work with files that have long file name extensions.

You can associate a new file type with an existing file type or create a completely new file type. If you associate the new file type with an existing file type, Windows will copy the characteristics of the existing file type to the new file type. For example, if you associate the .let extension with the Wordpad Document file type, Windows will handle the new file type the same way it handles WordPad files.

If you create a completely new file type, you will have to select the program that will open files of that type.

After you create a file type, you can edit the file type. For example, you can specify an action you want Windows to display on the menu that appears when you right-click files of that type. To edit a file type, see page 246.

DISPLAY AND CREATE FILE TYPES (CONTINUED)

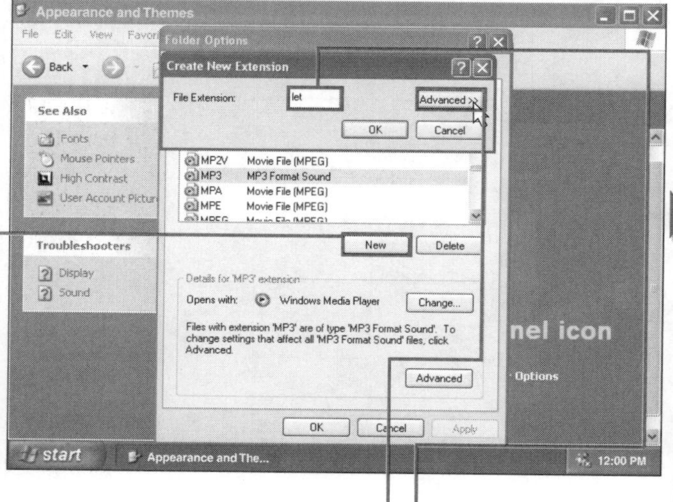

CREATE A NEW FILE TYPE

7 Click New to create a new file type.

■ The Create New Extension dialog box appears.

8 Click this area and then type an extension for the new file type.

9 Click Advanced to select the file type you want to associate with the new extension.

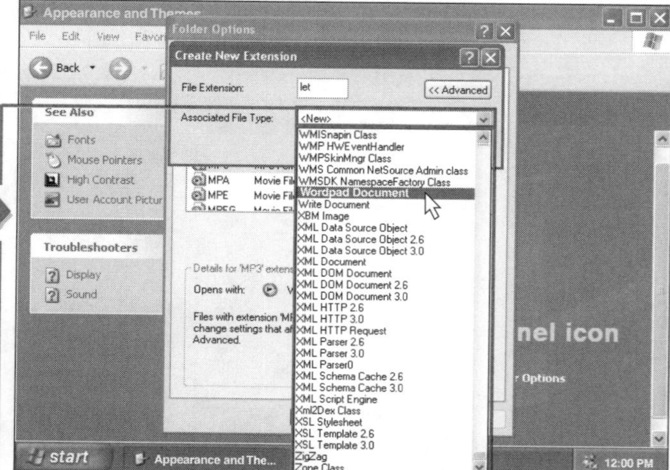

10 Click this area to display a list of file types that you can associate with the extension.

11 Click the file type you want to associate with the extension.

Note: To create a new file type, select <New>.

Is there another way to create a new file type?

✔ Yes. When you double-click a file type Windows does not recognize, a dialog box appears, stating that Windows cannot open the file. Click the Select the program from a list option (◯ changes to ◉) and click OK. Click the program you want to use to open the file type and then click the Always use the selected program to open this kind of file option (☐ changes to ☑). Windows will create a new file type using the extension of the file. The next time you double-click a file of this type, the file will open in the program you selected.

How can I delete a file type I created?

✔ In the Folder Options dialog box, select the File Types tab. Click the file type you want to delete and then click the Delete button. When you delete a file type, Windows will no longer be able to open files of that type when you double-click the files.

Can I later change the program that opens a file type I created?

✔ Yes. In the Folder Options dialog box, select the File Types tab. Click the file type you want to change and then click the Change button to select the program you want to use to open files of that type.

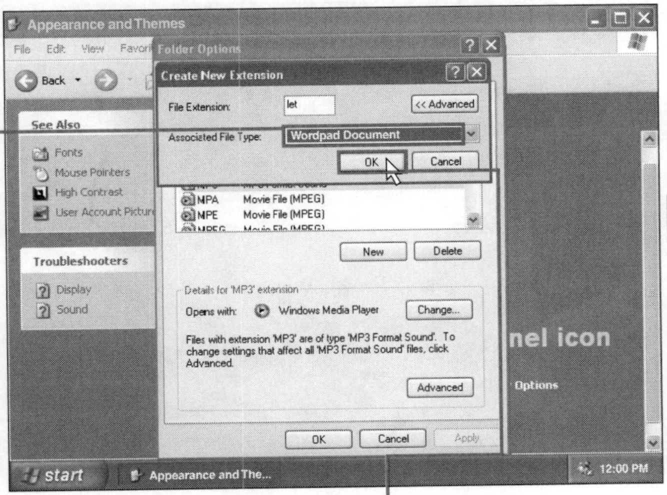

■ This area displays the file type you selected.

12 Click OK to confirm your changes.

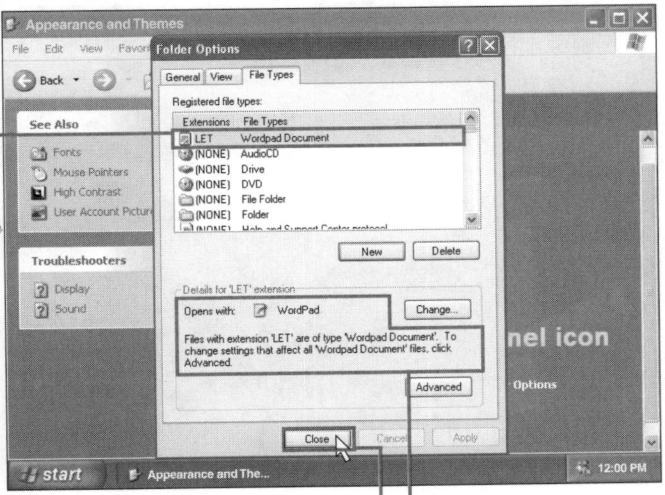

■ The file type you created appears in the list of file types that are registered with Windows.

■ This area displays information about the file type.

13 Click Close to close the Folder Options dialog box.

EDIT A FILE TYPE

You can make changes to a file type. You should be careful when making changes to a file type, since this can affect the way files of that type work.

If a file type you created has not yet been associated with a program, you can specify a short description for the file type, such as Business Letter. You should make sure the description you specify for the file type clearly indicates the purpose of the files of that type. When you view items in a window using the Details view, Windows displays the description. To change the view of items in a window, see page 42.

Most file types have one or more actions. An action of a file type is a command that allows you to work with files of that type. Common actions include Open and Print. When you right-click a file, the actions available for the files of that type appear on the shortcut menu. You can specify the name for an action that appears on the shortcut menu. You can also specify which program will perform an action.

EDIT A FILE TYPE

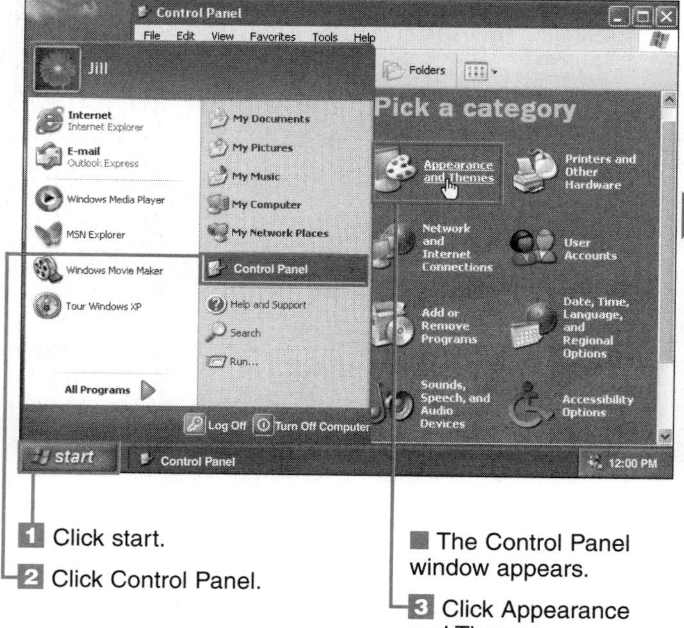

1 Click start.

2 Click Control Panel.

■ The Control Panel window appears.

3 Click Appearance and Themes.

■ The Appearance and Themes window appears.

4 Click Folder Options.

Can I edit an action?

✔ In the Edit File Type dialog box for the file type you want to change, click the action you want to change and then click the Edit button. You can type a new name for the action or click the Browse button to select the program you want to perform the action.

How do I remove an action I no longer want a file type to use?

✔ In the Edit File Type dialog box for the file type, select the action you want to remove and then click the Remove button.

How can I tell Windows which action I want to make the default action?

✔ The default action for a file type is performed when you double-click a file. When you right-click a file, the default action appears in bold on the shortcut menu. The default action for most file types is Open. To change the default action, display the Edit File Type dialog box for the file type and select the action you want to make the default action. Then click the Set Default button.

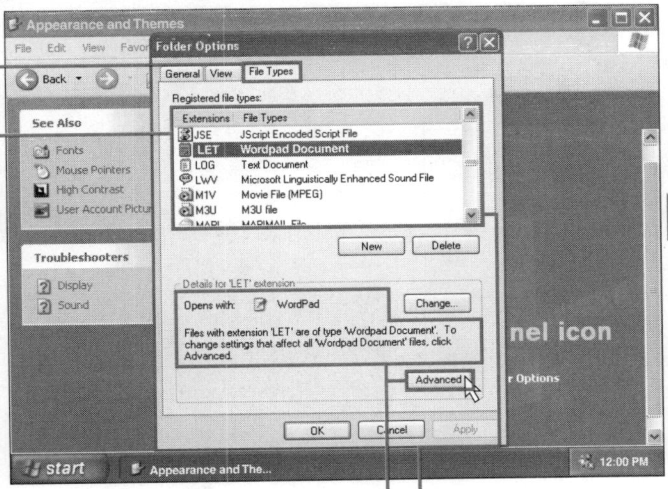

■ The Folder Options dialog box appears.

5 Click the File Types tab.

■ This area lists the extensions and associated file types that are registered with Windows.

6 Click the file type you want to change.

■ This area displays information about the file type you selected.

7 Click Advanced to make changes to the file type.

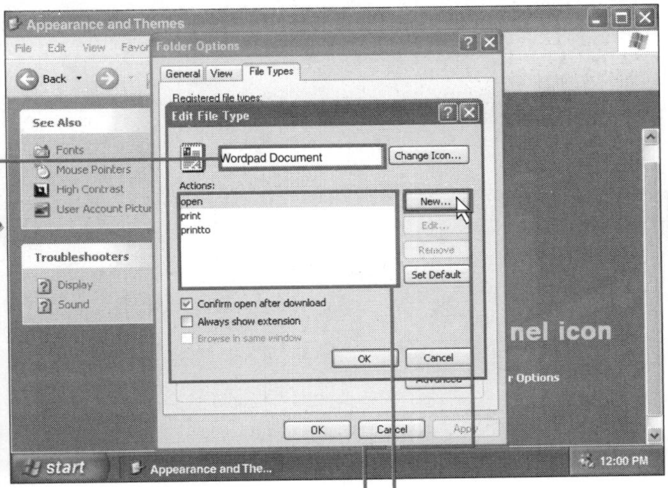

■ The Edit File Type dialog box appears.

8 This area displays the description of the file type. To change the description, type a new description.

■ This area lists the available actions for the file type.

9 To add a new action for the file type, click New.

CONTINUED

EDIT A FILE TYPE (CONTINUED)

When editing a file type, you can specify a new action you want to appear on the menu that appears when you right-click a file of that type. For example, if WordPad currently opens a file, you can specify another program, such as Notepad, to also open files of that type. Both actions will appear on the shortcut menu for the item.

You can specify whether you want Windows to ask you before opening files of a certain type after the files are downloaded to your computer or whether Windows should automatically open the downloaded files. Files downloaded from other computers on the Internet may contain viruses which can damage the information on your computer. You may want to have Windows always ask before opening downloaded files so you can save the files to your computer and perform a virus check on the files before opening them.

You can also choose to display the file name extension for files of a certain type. Displaying file name extensions can help you identify the types of files you are viewing.

Changes you make to a file type will affect all files of that type.

EDIT A FILE TYPE (CONTINUED)

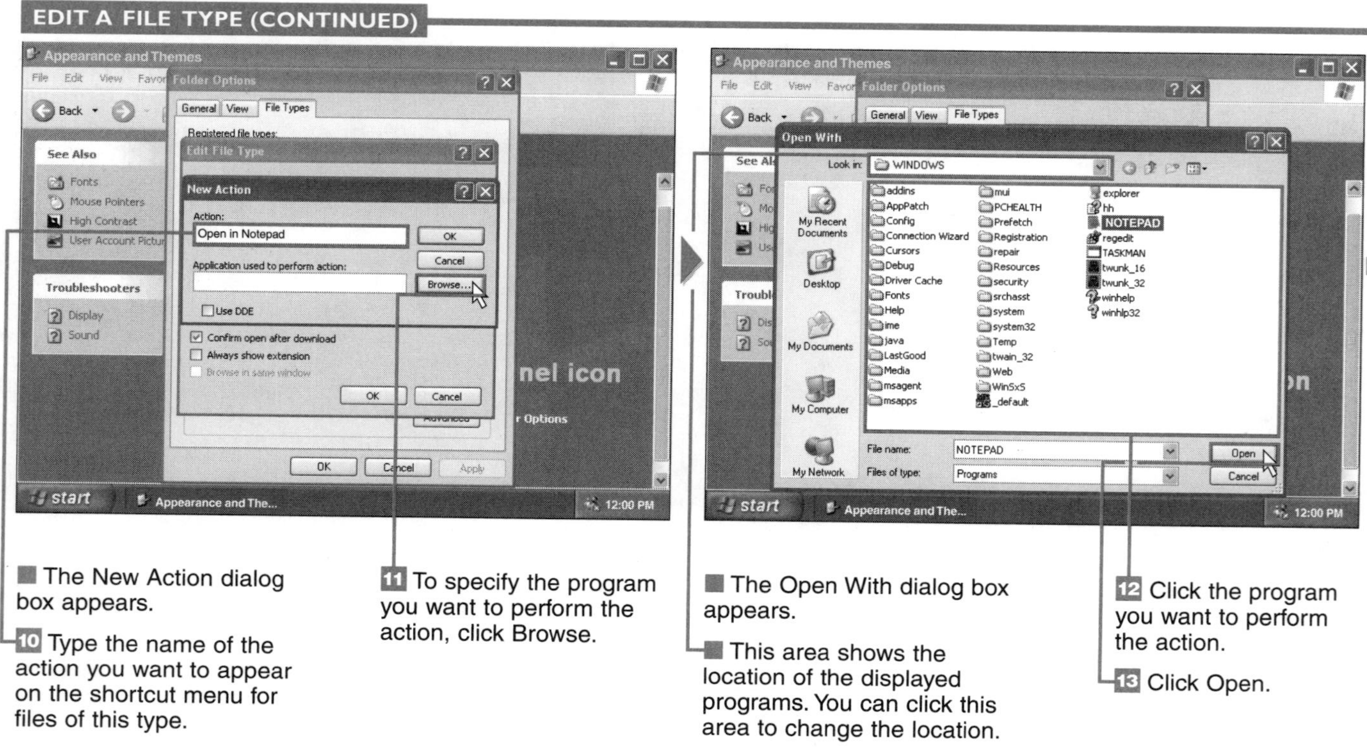

■ The New Action dialog box appears.

10 Type the name of the action you want to appear on the shortcut menu for files of this type.

11 To specify the program you want to perform the action, click Browse.

■ The Open With dialog box appears.

■ This area shows the location of the displayed programs. You can click this area to change the location.

12 Click the program you want to perform the action.

13 Click Open.

After I select a program I want to perform an action, why does Windows state it cannot find the program?

✔ You may have selected the program's shortcut. Shortcuts display an arrow (↗) in their icon and contain only the information needed to find a program. When specifying the program that performs an action, you must select the program file.

Can I change the icon for a file type?

✔ Yes. In the Edit File Type dialog box, click the Change Icon button. Then select the new icon you want to use for the file type.

Why won't Windows perform an action I specified for a file type?

✔ Some programs may require certain settings, or parameters, to perform the action you want. To find parameters for a program, click start, select All Programs, choose Accessories and then click Command Prompt. At the command prompt, type the program's name followed by a space and /?, such as **xcopy /?**. To specify the parameters for the program, display the Edit File Type dialog box. Select the action for which you want to specify parameters and click the Edit button. Then type the parameters for the program in the Application used to perform action area.

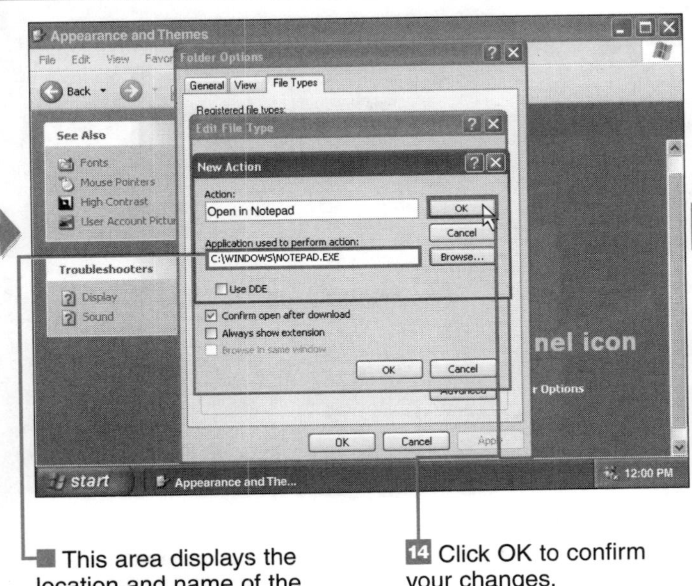

■ This area displays the location and name of the program you selected.

14 Click OK to confirm your changes.

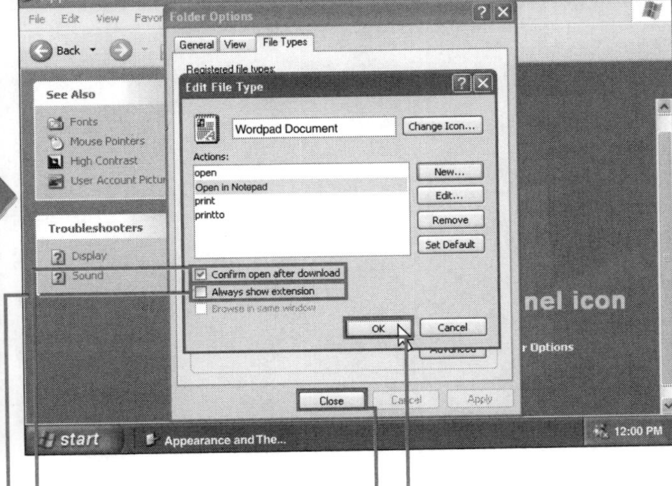

■ This option displays a message before Windows opens downloaded files of this type.

■ This option shows the file extension for files of this type.

15 You can click an option to turn the option on (☑) or off (☐).

16 Click OK to save the changes you made to the file type.

17 Click Close to close the Folder Options dialog box.

USING MULTIPLE MONITORS

Windows allows you to use more than one monitor to expand your desktop area. For example, graphic artists often use multiple monitors to display an image on one monitor and their tools on another monitor. You can also use multiple monitors to display several documents at once or stretch a document across more than one monitor to view more of the document without scrolling.

You can connect up to 10 separate monitors to your computer. Each monitor you use requires its own video adapter and each video adapter must support the ability to work with multiple monitors.

When using multiple monitors, one monitor will be the primary monitor. The primary monitor displays the Welcome screen that appears each time you start Windows. The windows for most programs will also appear on the primary monitor when you open the programs.

You can change the arrangement of the monitor icons in the Display Properties dialog box to match the physical arrangement of your monitors. The position of the monitor icons determines how you move items from one monitor to another.

Although all the monitors display the same background and screen saver, you can specify a different screen resolution and color setting for each monitor.

USING MULTIPLE MONITORS

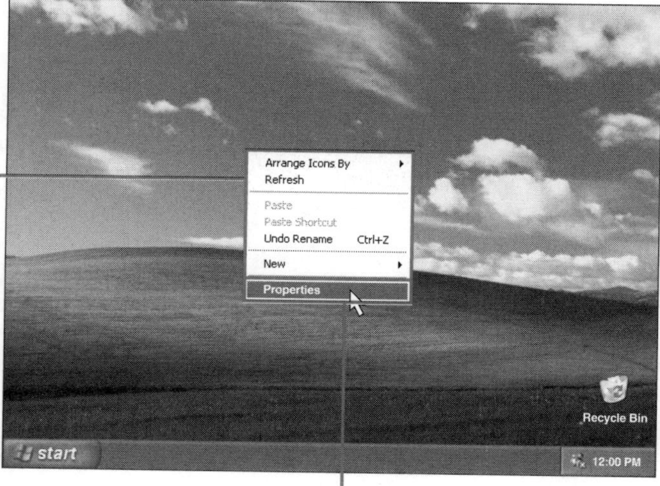

1 Right-click a blank area on the desktop. A menu appears.

2 Click Properties.

■ The Display Properties dialog box appears.

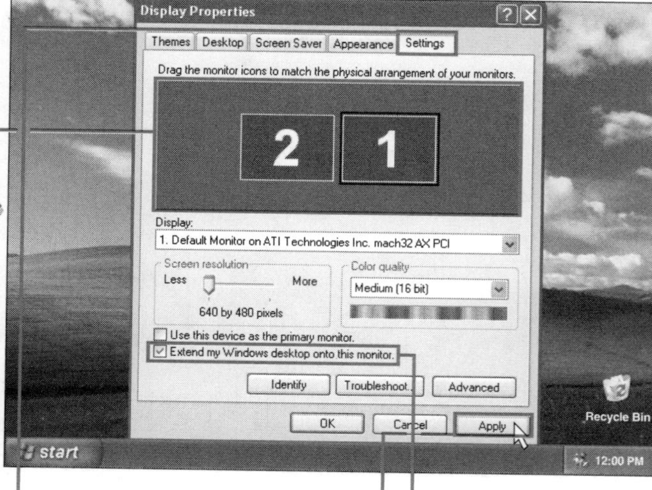

3 Click the Settings tab.

■ This area displays an icon for each monitor available on your computer.

4 Click the dimmed icon for the additional monitor you want to use.

5 Click Extend my Windows desktop onto this monitor (☐ changes to ☑).

6 Click Apply to apply your change.

How do I install a second monitor?

✔ Follow the manufacturer's instructions to add the video adapter for the second monitor to your computer. When you turn on your computer, Windows will usually detect the new video adapter and automatically install the appropriate software. If Windows does not detect the video adapter, see page 548 for information about installing hardware.

Can I change which monitor is the primary monitor?

✔ Yes. In the Display Properties dialog box, select the Settings tab. Click the icon for the monitor you want to use as the primary monitor and then select the Use this device as the primary monitor option (☐ changes to ☑).

How do I determine which icon in the Display Properties dialog box represents each monitor?

✔ In the Display Properties dialog box, click the Settings tab and select Identify. Each monitor will display the number of the icon to which it corresponds.

How do I stop using a secondary monitor?

✔ In the Display Properties dialog box, click the Settings tab and then click the secondary monitor you want to stop using. Click the Extend my Windows desktop onto this monitor option (☑ changes to ☐).

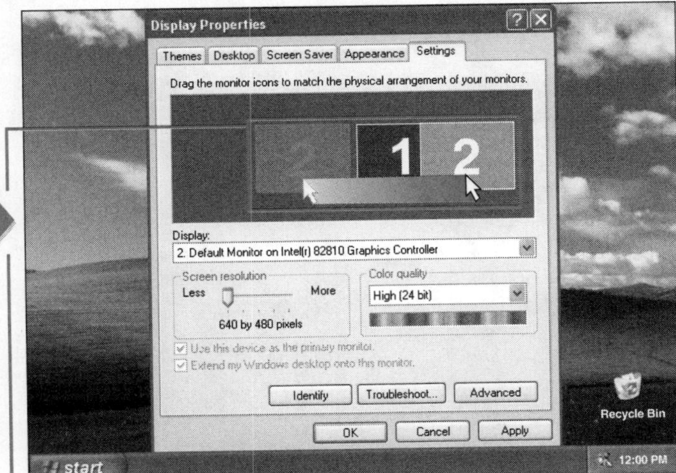

7 To change the arrangement of the icons to match the physical arrangement of your monitors, position the mouse over an icon and then drag the icon to a new position.

Note: The position of the icons determines how you will move items between the monitors.

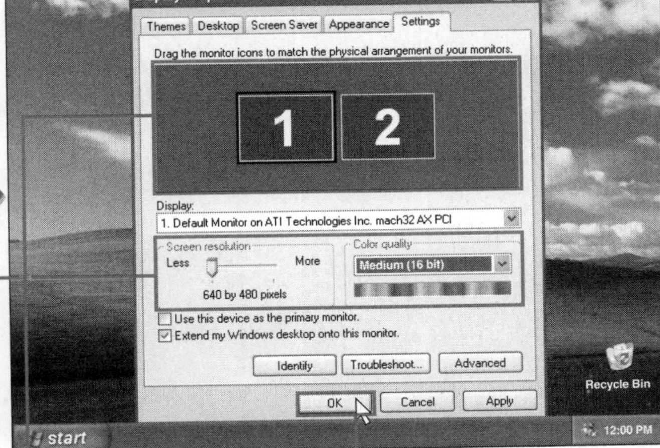

8 To display the settings for a monitor, click the icon for the monitor.

■ This area displays the screen resolution and color setting for the monitor you selected.

Note: To change the screen resolution for a monitor, see page 200. To change the color setting for a monitor, see page 202.

9 Click OK to confirm your changes.

MOVE OR SIZE THE TASKBAR

You can move or size the taskbar to accommodate your preferences. The taskbar is the starting point for most of the tasks you perform in Windows. The taskbar contains the start button and displays the name of each open window on your screen as well as the current time. The area beside the current time on the taskbar displays notification icons, which usually appear when events occur on your computer, such as when you print a file or receive an e-mail message.

Windows initially displays the taskbar at the bottom edge of your screen. By default, the taskbar is locked into this position and cannot be moved or sized. You must unlock the taskbar before you can move or size the taskbar.

You may want to move the taskbar to a different edge of your screen. Since many software programs display their menus at the top of the screen, you may prefer to have the taskbar also appear at the top of your screen.

You can adjust the size of the taskbar. Increasing the size of the taskbar provides more space to display information, such as the buttons for open windows.

MOVE OR SIZE THE TASKBAR

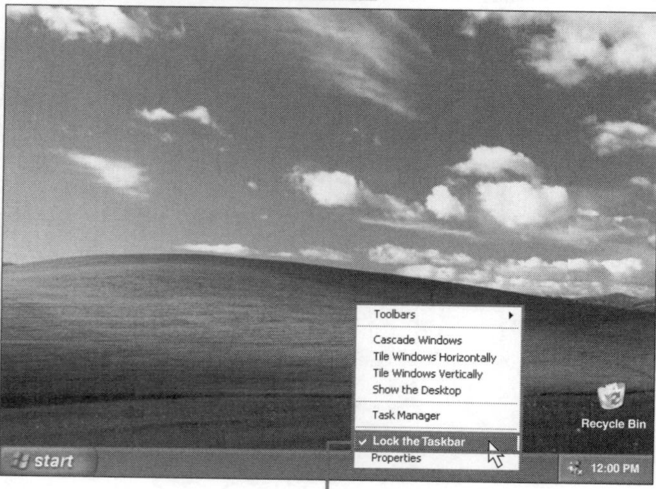

UNLOCK THE TASKBAR

■ The taskbar must be unlocked before you can move or size the taskbar.

1 Right-click an empty area on the taskbar. A menu appears.

■ A check mark (✔) appears beside Lock the Taskbar when the taskbar is locked.

2 Click Lock the Taskbar to unlock the taskbar.

Note: To once again lock the taskbar, repeat steps 1 and 2.

MOVE THE TASKBAR

1 Position the mouse over an empty area on the taskbar.

2 Drag the taskbar to the top, bottom, left or right edge of the screen.

■ The taskbar moves to the new location.

How can I use the taskbar to display the current date?

✔ Position the mouse pointer over the time displayed on the taskbar. After a few seconds, Windows displays the current date. When you move the taskbar to the right or left edge of your screen or increase the taskbar size, the current date may appear with the time on the taskbar.

Can I have Windows hide the taskbar automatically when I am not using the taskbar?

✔ Yes. Right-click an empty area on the taskbar and select Properties. Then click the Auto-hide the taskbar option (☐ changes to ☑). The taskbar will disappear when you are not using it. To redisplay the taskbar at any time, position the mouse over the area where you last saw the taskbar.

Why has my taskbar disappeared?

✔ You may have accidentally sized the taskbar to a thin line at the edge of your screen. Position the mouse pointer over the edge of the screen where you last saw the taskbar. When the pointer changes to ↕ or ↔, you can drag the mouse to increase the size of the taskbar.

How can I see more information about a button on the taskbar?

✔ Position the mouse pointer over the button. After a few seconds, a box appears displaying the full name of the window the button represents.

SIZE THE TASKBAR

1 Position the mouse over the edge of the taskbar (pointer changes to ↕ or ↔).

2 Drag the mouse ↕ until the taskbar displays the size you want.

■ The taskbar changes to the new size.

ADD A TOOLBAR TO THE TASKBAR

Windows includes several ready-made toolbars that you can add to the taskbar. Toolbars contain buttons to provide easy access to files, programs and Web pages.

The Address and Links toolbars allow you to access the Web without first starting your Web browser. You can type a Web page address in the Address toolbar to access the Web page from your desktop. You can click an option in the Links toolbar to access a useful Web page.

The Desktop toolbar contains all the items on your desktop and also provides easy access to common locations on your computer. The Quick Launch toolbar allows you to quickly access Internet Explorer, the desktop and Windows Media Player.

You can create a new toolbar from any folder on your computer and place the toolbar on the taskbar. For example, you can create toolbars from the Control Panel and My Documents folders to quickly access the items in the folders. If all the documents you frequently use are stored in one folder, you can create a toolbar from the folder to be able to quickly open the documents. When you create a new toolbar, the original folder remains in the same location on your computer.

ADD A TOOLBAR TO THE TASKBAR

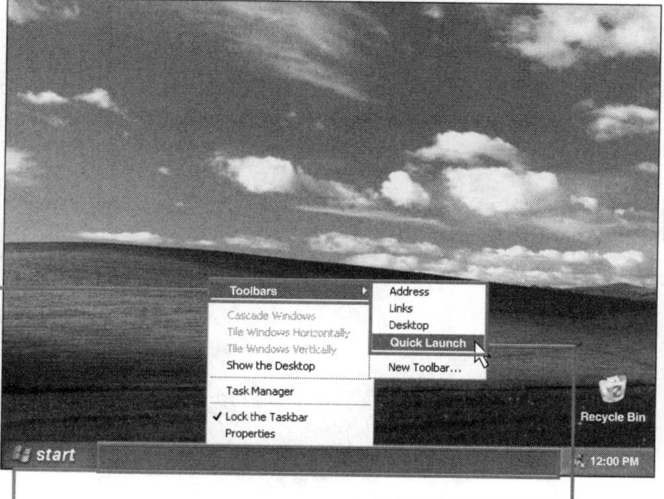

1 Right-click an empty area on the taskbar. A menu appears.

2 Click Toolbars.

3 Click the toolbar you want to display.

Note: A toolbar with a check mark (✔) is currently displayed on the taskbar.

■ The toolbar you selected appears on the taskbar. The Quick Launch toolbar appears in this example.

■ If you selected the Address toolbar, you can double-click Address to display the toolbar.

■ If you selected the Links or Desktop toolbars, you can click » to display the toolbar items.

When I double-click Address on the taskbar, why doesn't the toolbar appear?

✔ You must unlock the taskbar before you can use the Address toolbar. Right-click an empty area on the taskbar and then select Lock the Taskbar.

Can I move a toolbar?

✔ Yes. You must first unlock the taskbar. Right-click an empty area on the taskbar and then select Lock the Taskbar. Then position the mouse over the button for the toolbar you want to move and drag the toolbar to any edge of your screen or to the middle of your screen to create a floating toolbar.

Can I add an item to the Quick Launch toolbar?

✔ Yes. You can place a shortcut to an item such as a program, document or folder on the Quick Launch toolbar. To do so, drag the item to the Quick Launch toolbar.

How do I remove a toolbar from the taskbar?

✔ Right-click an empty area on the taskbar. Choose Toolbars and then select the name of the toolbar you want to remove. If you remove a toolbar you created, the toolbar will no longer appear in the list of available toolbars.

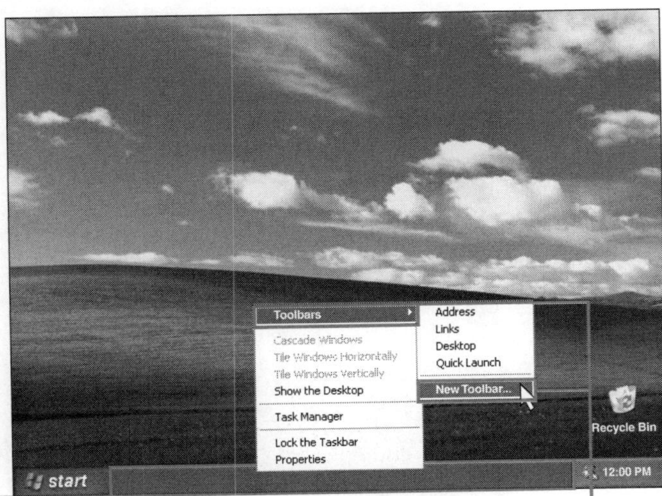

CREATE A NEW TOOLBAR

1 Right-click an empty area on the taskbar.
A menu appears.

2 Click Toolbars.

3 Click New Toolbar.

■ The New Toolbar dialog box appears.

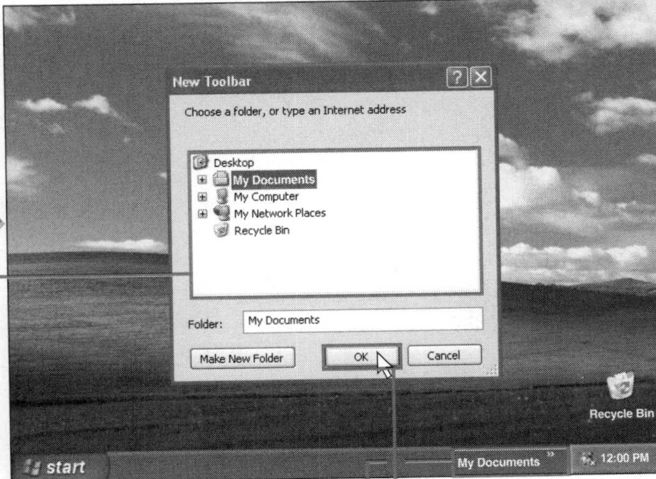

■ This area displays the organization of the folders on your computer.

Note: You can click the plus sign (⊞) beside a folder to display the hidden folders within the folder (⊞ changes to ⊟).

4 Click the folder you want to appear as a toolbar on the taskbar.

5 Click OK.

■ A button for the toolbar appears on the taskbar. You can click » to display the toolbar items.

CHANGE THE TASKBAR SETTINGS

You can change the taskbar settings to suit your needs.

The Lock the taskbar option freezes the taskbar at its current position. You must turn off this option before you can move or resize the taskbar or any toolbars displayed on the taskbar.

You can use the Auto-hide the taskbar option to automatically hide the taskbar when you are not using the taskbar. Hiding the taskbar provides more working space on your desktop.

The Keep the taskbar on top of other windows option ensures that the taskbar is always visible, even when a window fills the entire screen. You can turn off this option to provide more working space in windows.

The Group similar taskbar buttons option keeps buttons for the same program together on the taskbar. If the taskbar becomes crowded, Windows will display all the buttons for a program as a single button.

You can use the Show Quick Launch option to display the Quick Launch toolbar, which gives you quick access to the desktop and other items.

The Show the clock option displays the current time on the taskbar.

The Hide inactive icons option keeps the notification area of the taskbar uncluttered by hiding icons you have not recently used.

CHANGE THE TASKBAR SETTINGS

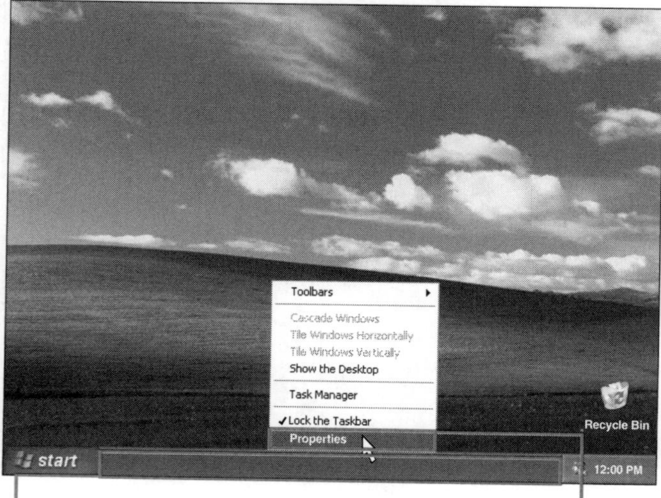

1 Right-click an empty area on the taskbar.
A menu appears.

2 Click Properties.

■ The Taskbar and Start Menu Properties dialog box appears.

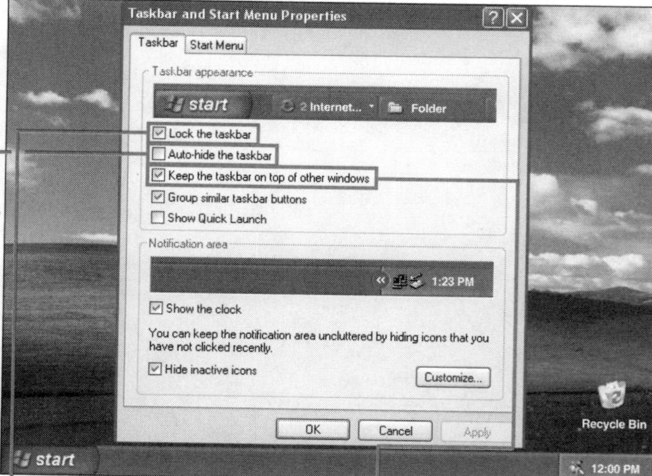

■ This option locks the taskbar so you cannot move or resize the taskbar.

■ This option hides the taskbar when you are not using the taskbar.

■ This option ensures the taskbar is always visible, even when a window fills the entire screen.

3 You can click an option to turn the option on (☑) or off (☐).

How can I prevent Windows from hiding inactive notification icons on the taskbar?

✔ In the Taskbar and Start Menu Properties dialog box, click the Customize button. Click the notification icon you want to change and then click ▾ in the behavior area beside the icon. You can then click an option to always show the icon, always hide the icon or hide the icon when it is inactive.

How can I make the taskbar appear when the Auto-hide option is on?

✔ Position the mouse over the area where you last saw the taskbar. You can also press Ctrl+Esc to display the taskbar and Start menu.

What happens when the number of buttons on the taskbar exceeds the available space?

✔ Two small arrows (▴ and ▾) appear to the right of the taskbar buttons. You can click these arrows to scroll through buttons not currently displayed on the taskbar.

How can I change the time displayed on the taskbar?

✔ The taskbar displays the time set in your computer. To change the time, double-click the time to display the Date and Time Properties dialog box, which allows you to change the time and date set in your computer. For more information, see page 194.

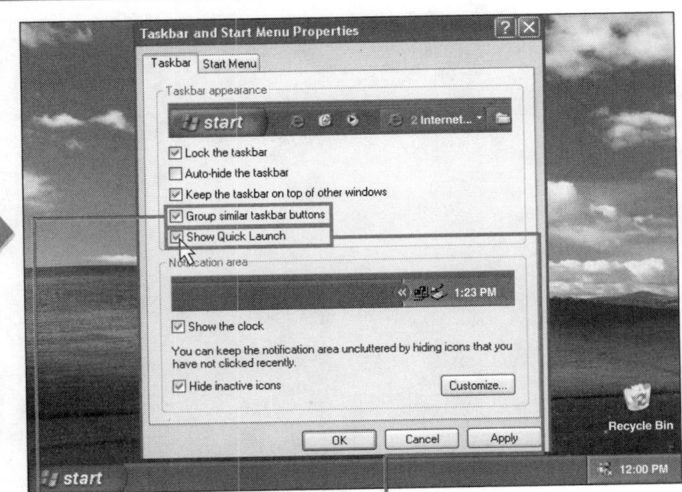

■ This option groups similar taskbar buttons. If the taskbar becomes crowded, this option will display all the buttons for a program as a single button.

■ This option displays the Quick Launch toolbar on the taskbar, which gives you quick access to Internet Explorer, your desktop and Windows Media Player.

4 You can click an option to turn the option on (☑) or off (☐).

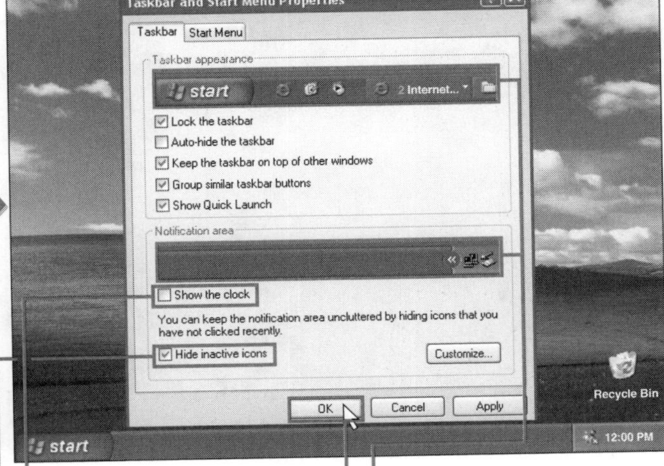

■ This option displays the time on the taskbar.

■ This option hides notification icons on the taskbar that you have not recently used.

5 You can click an option to turn the option on (☑) or off (☐).

■ These areas display a preview of the changes you have made.

6 Click OK to confirm your changes.

ADD OR REMOVE A PROGRAM ON THE START MENU

You can add programs to the Start menu so you can quickly open them. Having programs you frequently use on the Start menu saves you time, since you do not have to search for the programs on your computer.

Most programs designed for Windows will place a shortcut on the Start menu when you install the program. If a program does not appear on the Start menu, you can add the program yourself.

When you add a program to the Start menu, Windows creates a shortcut to the program and adds the shortcut to the Start menu. The original program remains in the same location on your computer.

You can also add files to the Start menu in the same way you add programs to the Start menu.

You can remove programs you no longer want to appear on the Start menu. Removing programs you do not need or rarely use reduces clutter on the Start menu. When you remove a program from the Start menu, Windows does not delete the program from your computer.

The shortcuts to some programs may remain on the Start menu even after the programs have been deleted from your computer. You can also easily remove these shortcuts from the Start menu.

ADD A PROGRAM TO THE START MENU

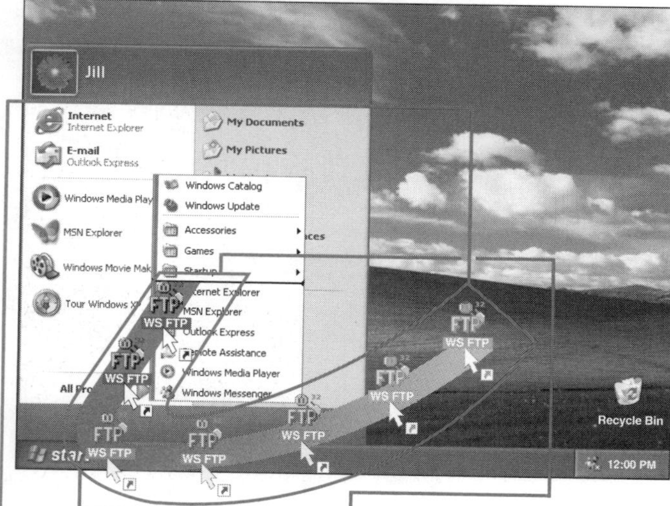

1 Locate the program that you want to add to the Start menu on your computer.

2 Position the mouse over the program.

3 Drag the program to the start button.

4 Still holding down the mouse button, drag the program to the location on the Start menu where you want the program to appear.

Note: A black line indicates where the program will appear.

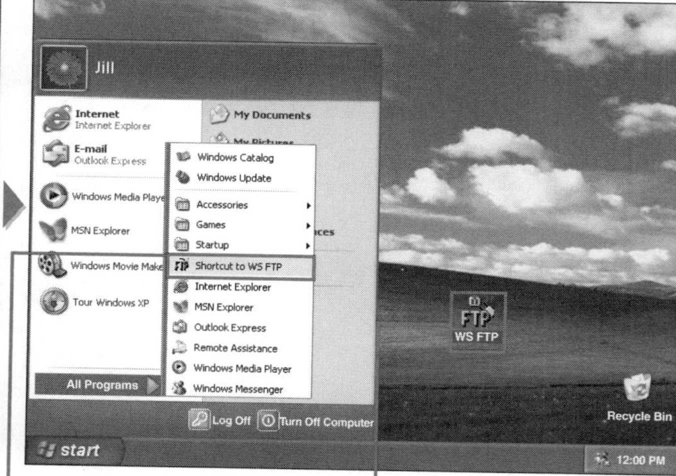

■ Windows places a shortcut to the program on the Start menu.

■ The program remains in its original location on your computer.

How do I add or remove items, such as the My Recent Documents folder, on the Start menu?

✔ To customize the items displayed on the Start menu, perform steps 1 to 5 on page 264 to display the Customize Start Menu dialog box. Choose the Advanced tab and then select the options you want to use to customize the Start menu.

Can I rename a program I added to the Start menu?

✔ Yes. Display the Start menu, right-click the program you want to rename and then select Rename from the menu that appears. In the dialog box that appears, type a new name.

How do I restore a program I accidentally removed from the Start menu?

✔ You can use the Recycle Bin to restore a program you accidentally removed from the Start menu. To restore a deleted program from the Recycle Bin, see page 78. If the program is not in the Recycle Bin, you can add the program to the Start menu again.

Is there an easy way to reorganize programs on the Start menu?

✔ Yes. You can easily sort the programs on the Start menu. Display the menu that contains the programs you want to sort and then right-click the menu. Click Sort by Name to arrange the programs on the menu alphabetically.

REMOVE A PROGRAM FROM THE START MENU

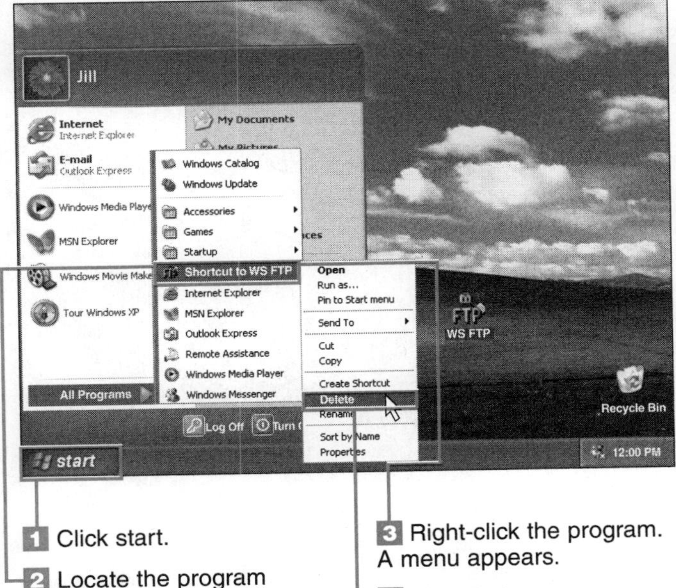

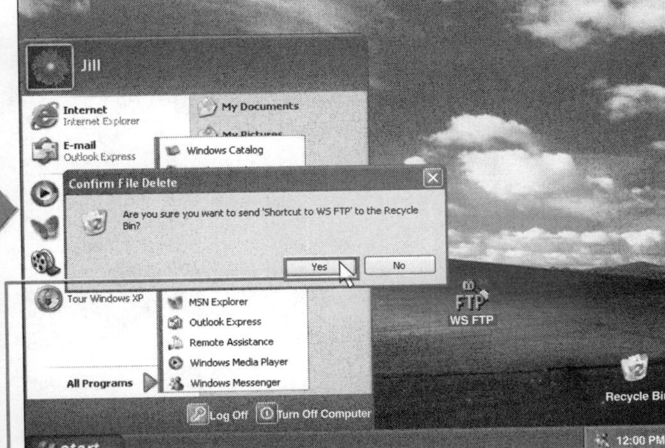

1 Click start.

2 Locate the program you want to remove from the Start menu.

3 Right-click the program. A menu appears.

4 Click Delete.

■ A confirmation dialog box appears.

5 Click Yes to delete the shortcut to the program from the Start menu.

■ Windows places the shortcut in the Recycle Bin in case you later want to restore the shortcut.

REARRANGE PROGRAMS ON THE START MENU

You can move a program on your Start menu to a new location to rearrange the programs on the Start menu. This allows you to customize your Start menu and reorganize programs to suit your preferences.

Rearranging programs on the Start menu is useful when you want to place programs you frequently use in a convenient location, such as at the top of the All Programs menu.

Rearranging programs is also useful for placing programs in submenus you have created on the Start menu. For information about creating submenus, see page 262.

There are some Start menu areas that you cannot rearrange. For example, you cannot change the order of the Help and Support, Search and Run features on the Start menu.

When rearranging programs on your Start menu, keep in mind that the Help and Support feature describes how to locate and use Windows programs based on the default location of the programs. You should avoid rearranging programs that you are not familiar with, since this can make the programs difficult to find later.

REARRANGE PROGRAMS ON THE START MENU

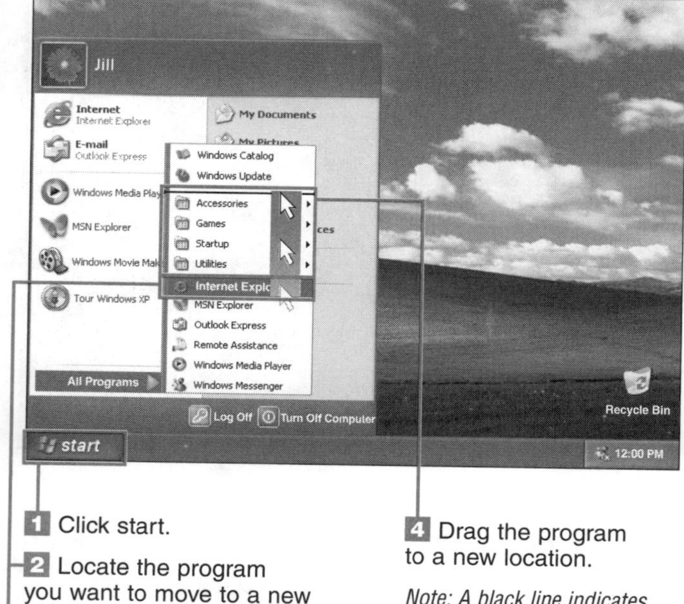

1 Click start.

2 Locate the program you want to move to a new location on the Start menu.

3 Position the mouse over the program.

4 Drag the program to a new location.

Note: A black line indicates where the program will appear.

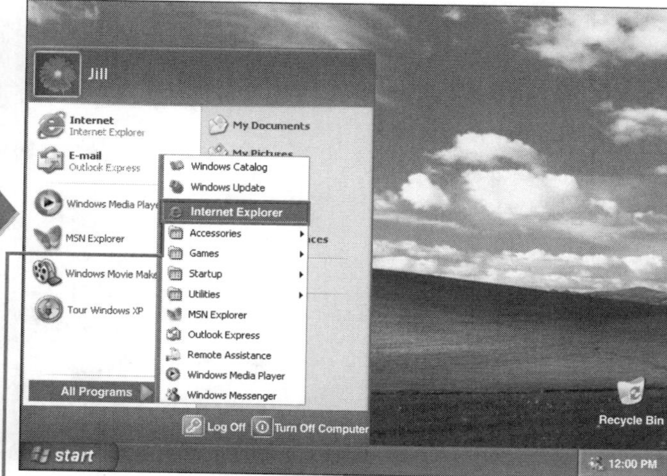

■ The program appears in the new location on the Start menu.

■ The program disappears from its original location on the Start menu.

PIN A PROGRAM TO THE TOP OF THE START MENU

You can pin a program to the top of the Start menu to provide a quick way of opening a program you use regularly.

When you pin a program to the top of the Start menu, a shortcut to the program appears above the separator line in the left column of the Start menu. You can use the shortcut to quickly access the program at any time.

Before you can pin a program to the Start menu, you must locate the program you want to use. You can locate programs using Windows Explorer, the My Computer window or the Start menu. You can also pin programs on your desktop to the Start menu.

Pinning a program to the Start menu does not move the program from its original location.

After pinning a program to the top of the Start menu, you can move the program to rearrange the order of items at the top of the Start menu. For information about rearranging programs on the Start menu, see page 260.

If you no longer want to pin a program to the top of the Start menu, you can unpin the program.

PIN A PROGRAM TO THE TOP OF THE START MENU

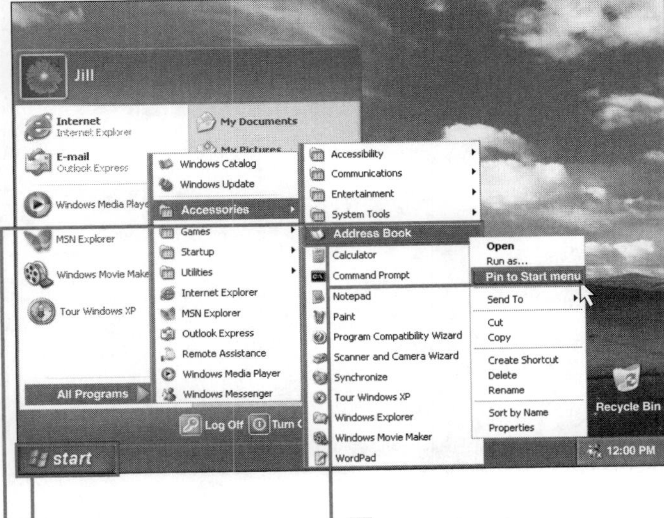

1 Click start.

2 Locate the program you want to pin to the top of the Start menu.

3 Right-click the program. A menu appears.

4 Click Pin to Start menu.

■ The program appears at the top of the Start menu.

■ The program also remains in its original location.

Note: To unpin a program from the top of the Start menu, click start and then right-click the program you want to unpin. From the menu that appears, click Unpin from Start menu.

ADD A SUBMENU TO THE START MENU

You can create folders to organize the items on the Start menu. Each new folder you create will appear as a submenu on the Start menu.

When you install a new program, a shortcut for the program usually appears on the Start menu to give you quick access to the program. Eventually, the Start menu may become cluttered. You can create folders to organize the programs into logical groups. Programs organized into folders are easier to find. For example, you can create a new folder named Utilities that will contain the utility programs you frequently use.

When creating a new folder on the Start menu, you should give the folder a descriptive name that clearly indicates what items the folder contains. The Start menu will expand to display the name of the folder you add. Try to use a short folder name so the Start menu will not take up too much space when displayed on your screen.

ADD A SUBMENU TO THE START MENU

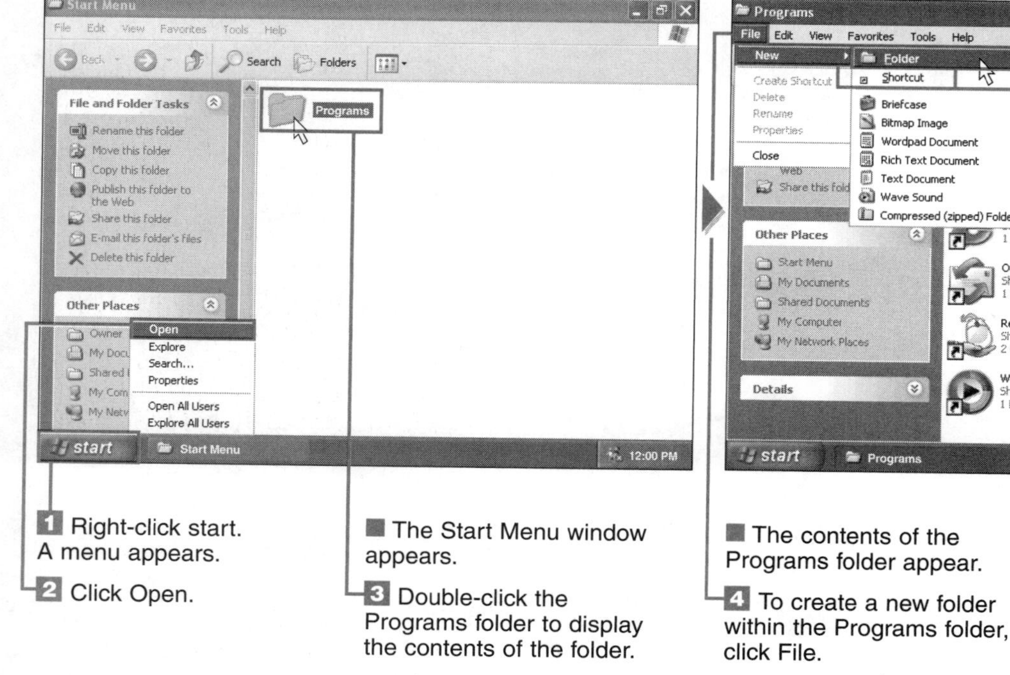

1 Right-click start. A menu appears.

2 Click Open.

■ The Start Menu window appears.

3 Double-click the Programs folder to display the contents of the folder.

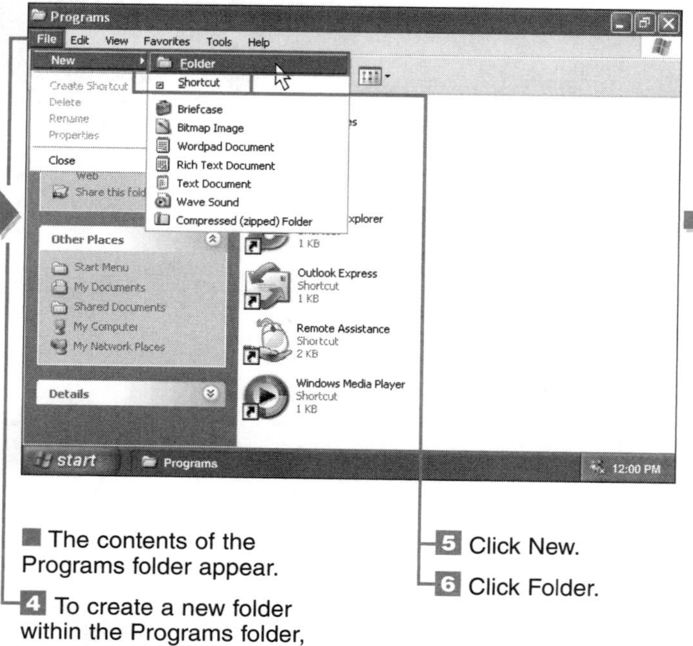

■ The contents of the Programs folder appear.

4 To create a new folder within the Programs folder, click File.

5 Click New.

6 Click Folder.

How do I add programs and files to the new submenu I created?

✔ You can drag programs and files from other Start menu locations to the new submenu. To add a program or file that is not already located on the Start menu to the submenu, drag the item to the start button to open the Start menu. Then drag the item to the new submenu.

How do I remove a submenu I created from my Start menu?

✔ On the Start menu, right-click the submenu you want to delete and then click Delete.

Can I quickly add a submenu to the Start menus of every user set up on my computer?

✔ To add a submenu to the Start menus of every user account set up on your computer, right-click the start button, click Open All Users and then perform steps 3 to 8 below. You must be logged on as a computer administrator to add a submenu to the Start menus of every user. For information about creating user accounts on your computer, see page 174.

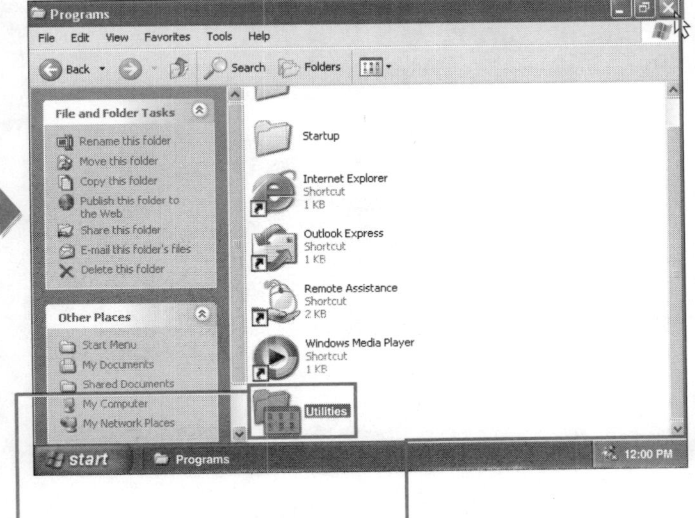

■ The new folder appears, displaying a temporary name.

7 Type a name for the new folder and then press the Enter key.

■ The folder will now appear as a submenu on the Start menu.

8 Click ☒ to close the Programs window.

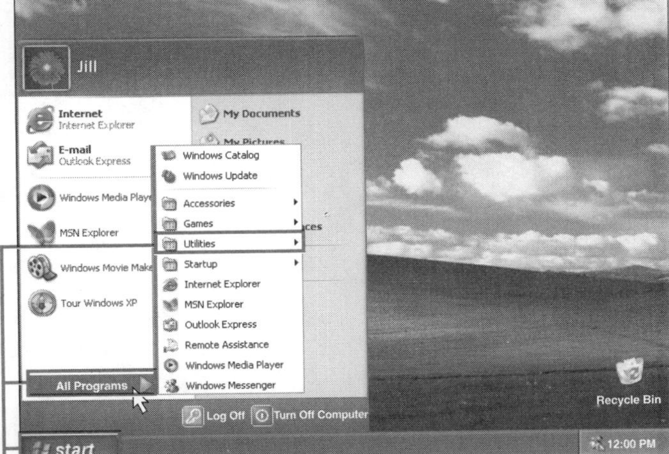

DISPLAY THE NEW SUBMENU

1 Click start.

2 Click All Programs.

■ The submenu you created appears on the All Programs menu.

■ You can add programs and files to the new submenu.

Note: To close the Start menu without selecting an item, click outside the menu area.

CUSTOMIZE THE START MENU

The Start menu gives you quick access to items on your computer, such as programs, documents, pictures and music files. You can customize the Start menu to change the appearance of the Start menu and the way the Start menu works.

Windows displays an icon beside each item on the Start menu. You can change the size of the icons for items that appear in the left column of the Start menu by specifying whether you want to use large or small icons for the items.

The Start menu gives you quick access to programs you have recently used by displaying shortcuts to the programs in the left column of the Start menu. By default, up to six recently-used programs will appear on the Start menu. You can specify a new maximum number of programs you want the Start menu to display.

The top of the Start menu automatically displays shortcuts you can use to browse the Web and access your e-mail. If you do not want to display the shortcuts on your Start menu, you can remove the shortcuts. You can also change the Web browser and e-mail programs Windows will use for the shortcuts.

CUSTOMIZE THE START MENU

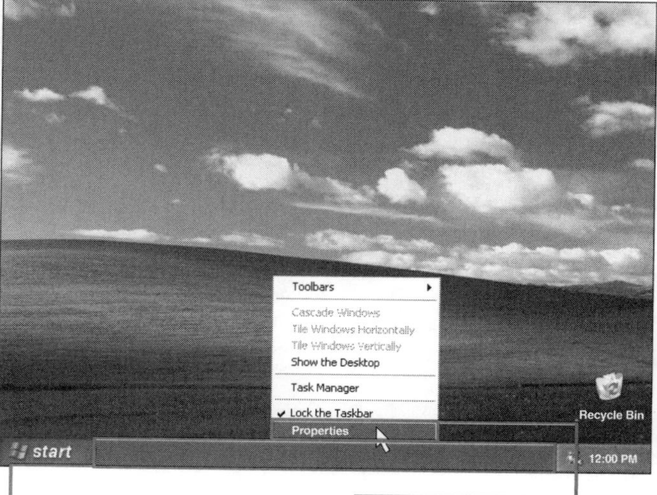

1 Right-click an empty area on the taskbar.
A menu appears.

2 Click Properties.

■ The Taskbar and Start Menu Properties dialog box appears.

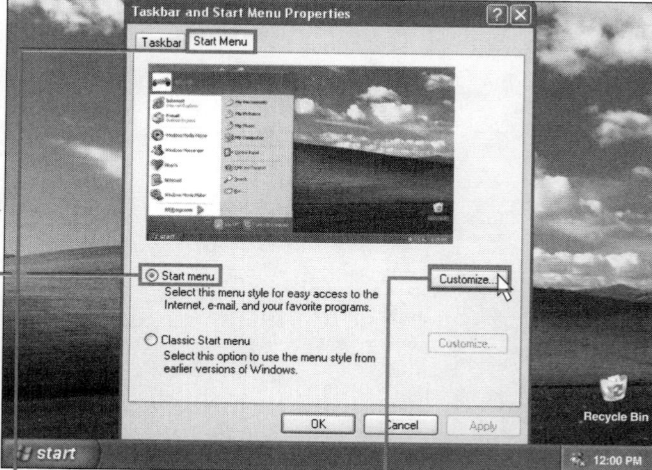

3 Click the Start Menu tab.

4 Click Start menu to use the Start menu designed for Windows XP (○ changes to ◉).

5 Click Customize to personalize the Start menu.

■ The Customize Start Menu dialog box appears.

Can I have my Start menu resemble the style used in previous versions of Windows?

✔ If you are more comfortable with the Start menu used in previous versions of Windows, you can have Windows use this style of Start menu. Perform steps 1 to 3 below, select the Classic Start menu option (○ changes to ◉) and then click OK.

How can I clear the list of recently-used programs?

✔ In the Customize Start Menu dialog box, on the General tab, click the Clear List button. Clearing the list of recently-used programs will remove the shortcuts to the programs from the left column of the Start menu, but will not remove the programs from your computer.

How do I access my Web browser and e-mail program if I have removed the shortcuts from the top of the Start menu?

✔ The All Programs menu on the Start menu gives you access to all the programs installed on your computer. To access your Web browser or e-mail program, click start, select All Programs and then click your Web browser or e-mail program in the list of programs that appears.

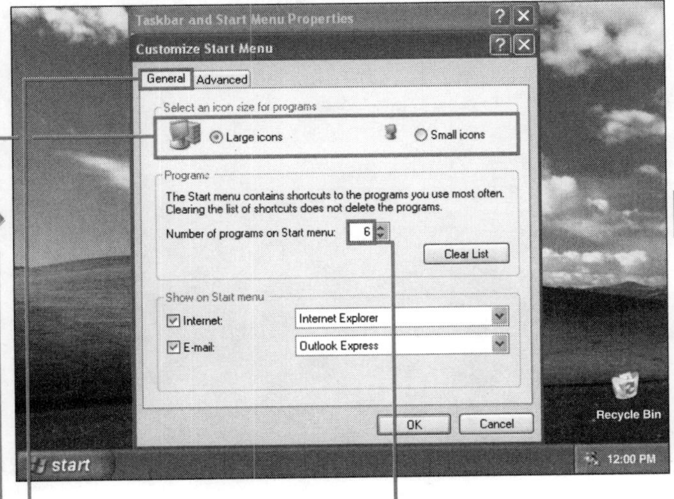

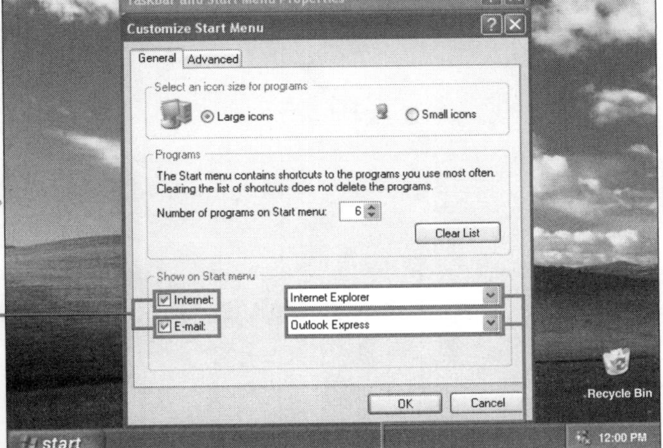

6 Click the General tab.

7 Click an option to specify if you want to display large or small icons for programs on the Start menu (○ changes to ◉).

8 This area displays the number of recently used programs that can appear on the Start menu. To change the maximum number of programs that can appear, double-click this area and type a new number.

9 These options display your Web browser and e-mail program on the Start menu. You can click an option to turn the option on (☑) or off (☐).

10 These areas display the Web browser and e-mail program Windows will use. You can click an area to change the program.

CONTINUED

CUSTOMIZE THE START MENU (CONTINUED)

Some items on the Start menu contain submenus. When customizing the Start menu, you can specify how you want submenus to appear. You can have submenus appear automatically when you position the mouse over an item or have submenus appear only after you click an item.

You can specify whether you want new programs you install on your computer to appear highlighted on the Start menu. This can help you locate and identify the programs.

Windows allows you to add, remove and change items that appear on the Start menu. For example, you can add a menu to display the contents of your Favorites or Printers and Faxes folder or remove the Run or Search command. You can also specify whether you want to display items such as Control Panel, My Computer and My Documents as links or as menus. An item displayed as a link will open a window displaying its contents.

An item displayed as a menu will display its contents in a submenu.

If you want to be able to quickly access documents you have recently opened, you can choose to list the documents on the Start menu. The documents will appear as a submenu of a new Start menu item called My Recent Documents.

CUSTOMIZE THE START MENU (CONTINUED)

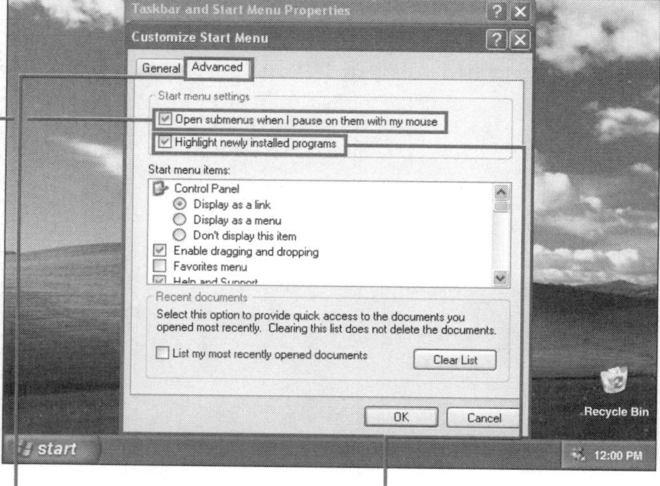

11 Click the Advanced tab.

12 This option displays a menu's submenu when you position the mouse pointer over the menu. You can click the option to turn the option on (☑) or off (☐).

13 This option highlights newly installed programs on the Start menu. You can click the option to turn the option on (☑) or off (☐).

■ This area allows you to add, remove or change items that appear on the Start menu.

14 To select an item that displays a check box (☐), click the item to turn the item on (☑) or off (☐).

15 If an item displays radio buttons (○), click the radio button beside the appropriate option (○ changes to ◉).

Can I prevent items from being moved on the Start menu?

✔ If you do not want to be able to rearrange items on the Start menu by dragging the items to a new location, you can disable dragging and dropping on the Start menu. In the Customize Start Menu dialog box, on the Advanced tab, click the Enable dragging and dropping option in the Start menu items area (☑ changes to ☐).

How do I clear the list of recently-opened documents?

✔ In the Customize Start Menu dialog box, on the Advanced tab, click the Clear List button. This will remove the documents from the My Recent Documents submenu, but will not remove the documents from your computer.

How can I change the appearance of submenus on the Start menu?

✔ By default, long submenus display items in several columns. To reduce the amount of space that the Start menu takes up on your screen, you can have items appear in a single column that you can scroll through. In the Customize Start Menu dialog box, on the Advanced tab, click the Scroll Programs option in the Start menu items area (☐ changes to ☑).

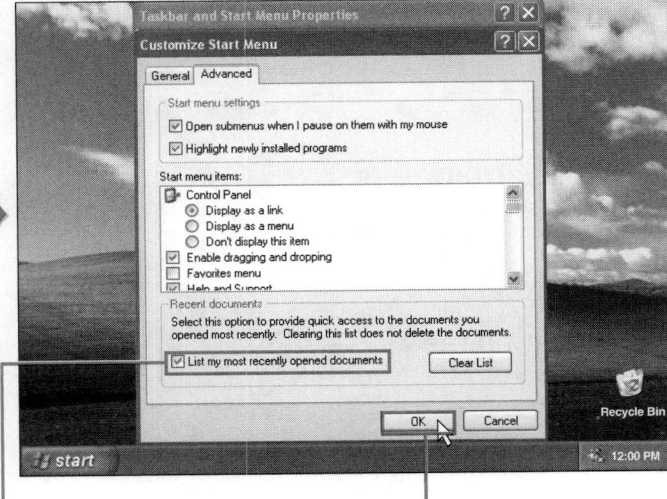

16 This option lists documents you have recently opened on the Start menu to give you quick access to the documents. You can click the option to turn the option on (☑) or off (☐).

17 Click OK to confirm your changes.

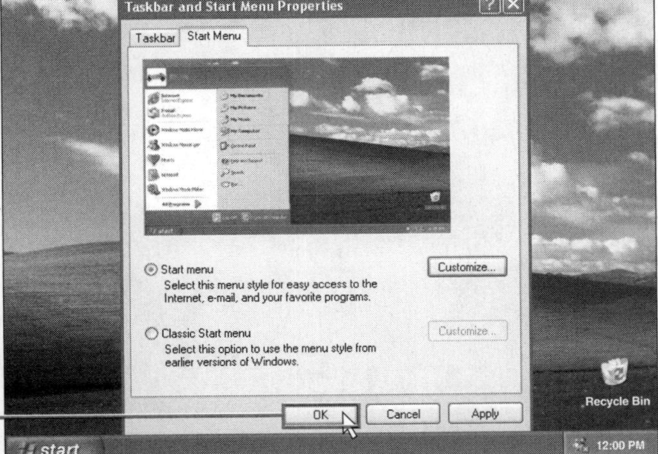

18 Click OK to close the Taskbar and Start Menu Properties dialog box.

■ Your Start menu will now display the changes you specified.

USING MAGNIFIER

If you have difficulty reading the information displayed on your screen, you can use Magnifier to display an enlarged area of the screen. The enlarged area appears in a window at the top of your screen.

You can customize Magnifier's settings to suit your needs. Magnifier is initially set to double the size of the area displayed on your screen. You can increase or decrease the amount of magnification.

By default, Magnifier displays an enlarged view of the area surrounding the mouse pointer. Magnifier also follows keyboard commands and the insertion point while you type. You can turn off one or more of these options to have Magnifier work the way you want.

You can change the colors displayed in the magnifier window to their complementary colors. For example, white changes to black.

You can have the Magnifier Settings window automatically minimize to a button on the taskbar when you start Magnifier and you can hide the magnifier window at any time.

USING MAGNIFIER

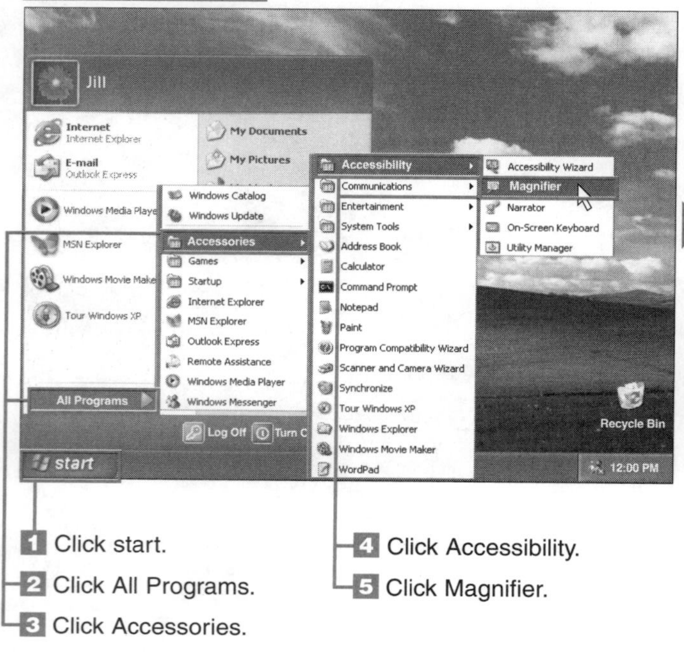

1 Click start.

2 Click All Programs.

3 Click Accessories.

4 Click Accessibility.

5 Click Magnifier.

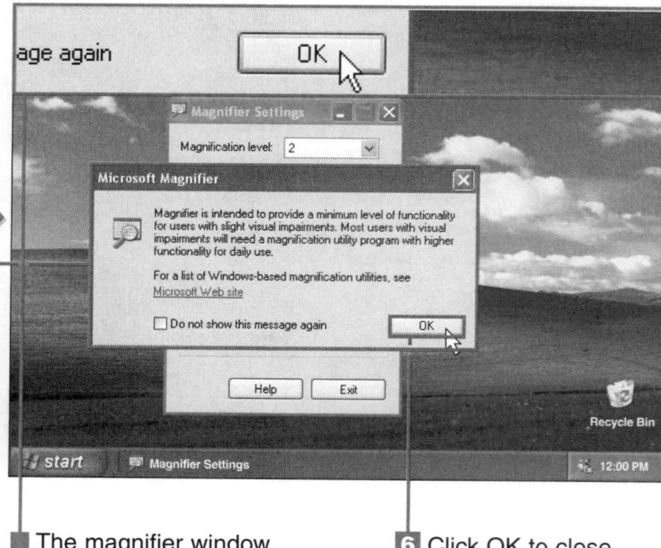

■ The magnifier window displays an enlarged view of the screen surrounding the mouse.

■ The Microsoft Magnifier dialog box indicates that Magnifier may help people with minor visual impairments.

6 Click OK to close the dialog box.

How can I change the size of the magnifier window?

✔ Position the mouse pointer over the bottom edge of the window (pointer changes to ↕). Drag the edge of the window until the window is the size you want.

How can I move the magnifier window?

✔ Position the mouse pointer inside the window (pointer changes to hand). Drag the window to any edge of your screen. You can also create a floating window by dragging the window to the middle of your screen.

Can I use the keyboard to change the amount of magnification?

✔ Yes. If your keyboard has a Windows key (Windows key), you can use the keyboard to change the amount of magnification. Hold down the Windows key as you press the up or down arrow keys to increase or decrease the magnification.

Where can I find magnification utility programs with more functionality than Magnifier?

✔ You can visit the Microsoft Accessibility Web site (www.microsoft.com/enable) to find a list of Windows-based magnification utility programs. You can click the link displayed in the Microsoft Magnifier dialog box to visit the Web site.

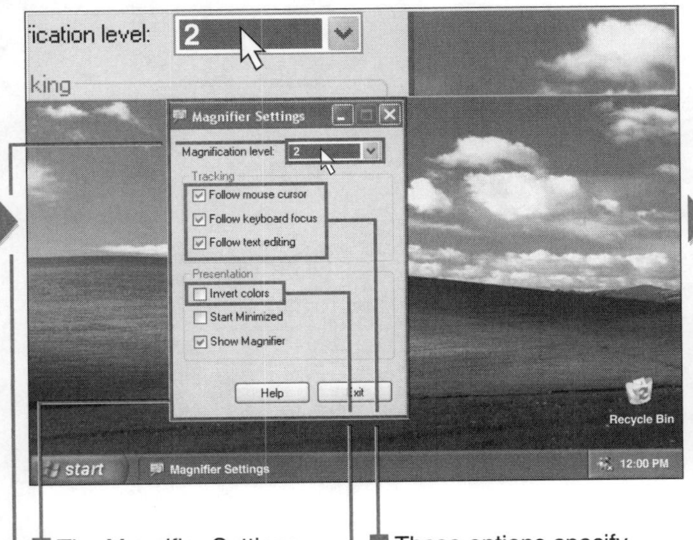

■ The Magnifier Settings window allows you to change the settings for Magnifier.

7 This area shows the amount of magnification. You can click this area to select a different magnification.

■ These options specify if Magnifier will follow the mouse pointer, keyboard commands or the insertion point while typing.

■ This option changes colors to their complementary colors in the magnifier window.

■ This option minimizes the Magnifier Settings window to a button on the taskbar when you start Magnifier.

■ This option displays the magnifier window.

8 You can click an option to turn the option on (☑) or off (☐).

9 Click Exit when you finish using Magnifier.

USING ON-SCREEN KEYBOARD

If you have limited mobility, you can display a keyboard on your screen. This keyboard allows you to type when you have difficulty using a conventional keyboard.

When using On-Screen Keyboard, the clicking mode is turned on by default, but you can choose the way you want to type. In clicking mode, you can use a mouse or joystick to click the keyboard characters you want to type. In hovering mode, you can use a mouse or joystick to position the mouse pointer over a key until Windows types the character for you. You can specify the length of time you must position the mouse pointer over a key.

In scanning mode, Windows scans the keyboard and highlights each row of keys. When Windows highlights the row containing the key you want, you can use a joystick, keyboard key or mouse to select the row. Windows then scans the row and highlights individual keys so you can select the character you want to type. You can specify the amount of time keys are highlighted during a scan.

You can visit the Microsoft Accessibility Web page at www.microsoft.com/enable to find information about utility programs with more functionality than On-Screen Keyboard for mobility-impaired users.

USING ON-SCREEN KEYBOARD

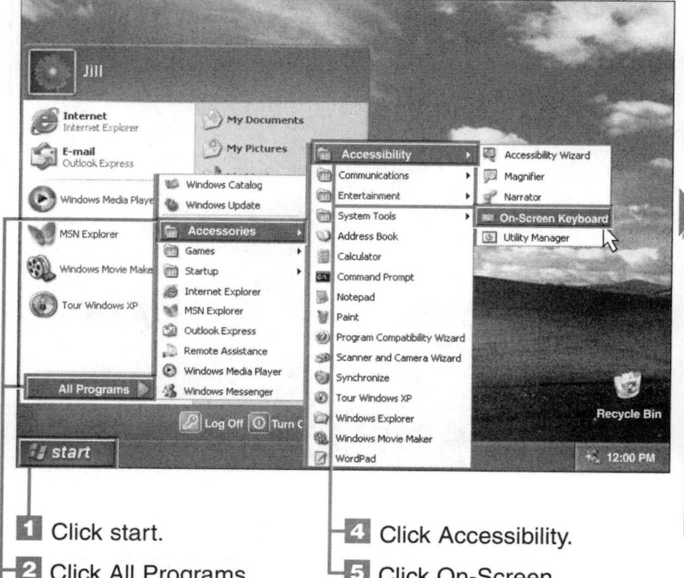

1 Click start.

2 Click All Programs.

3 Click Accessories.

4 Click Accessibility.

5 Click On-Screen Keyboard.

■ The On-Screen Keyboard dialog box appears, stating that the keyboard provides minimal help for people with mobility impairments.

6 Click OK to close the dialog box.

■ The On-Screen Keyboard window also appears.

7 Open the program you want to use with On-Screen Keyboard. In this example, WordPad is opened.

Can I change the font of the keyboard characters?

✔ Yes. This is useful if you find the keyboard characters difficult to see. Choose the Settings menu and click Font. Then select the font, font style and size you want to use. Changing the font of the keyboard characters does not change the font of the characters you type.

When using scanning mode, how do I change the keyboard key used to start the scan and make a selection?

✔ In the Typing Mode dialog box, click the Advanced button. In the dialog box that appears, click ▾ beside Keyboard key and then choose the keyboard key you want to use.

Can I change the appearance of the keyboard?

✔ Yes. Select the Keyboard menu and then click the way you want to display the keyboard. A dot (•) appears beside the currently selected options. If you do not want to display a numeric keypad, you can choose the Standard Keyboard. To group the keys together in the window, choose the Block Layout. Block layout is especially useful in scanning mode. Most keyboards have 101 keys, but you can display a 102-key universal keyboard or a 106-key keyboard that has additional Japanese characters.

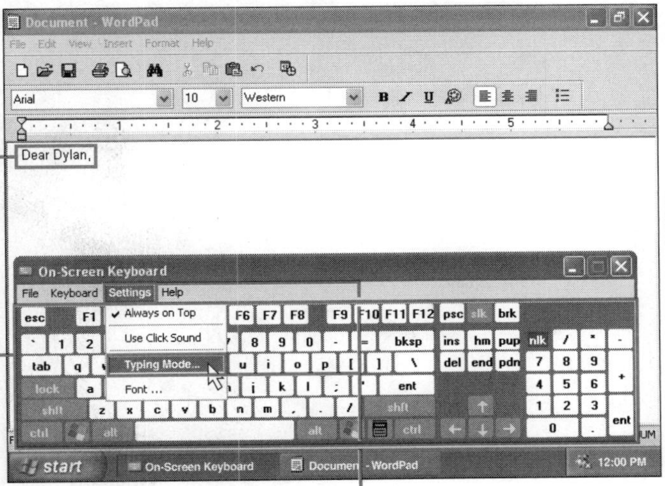

8 Click the location in the program window where you want to enter text.

9 Click each keyboard character you want to enter.

SELECT A TYPING MODE

1 Click Settings.

2 Click Typing Mode.

■ The Typing Mode dialog box appears.

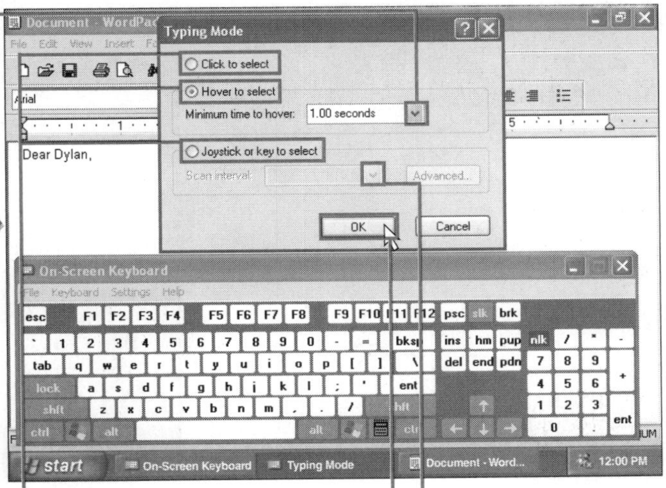

3 Click the way you want to select characters on the keyboard (○ changes to ◉).

4 If you selected Hover, click ▾ in this area to specify the number of seconds the mouse pointer must remain over a key to select the character.

5 If you selected Joystick or key, click ▾ in this area to specify the number of seconds keys are highlighted during a scan.

6 Click OK.

USING NARRATOR

If you have difficulty seeing the information displayed on your screen, you can have Narrator read aloud the items on the screen. To use Narrator, your computer must have sound capabilities.

Narrator will read aloud when you use Notepad, WordPad, Internet Explorer and items in the Control Panel or on the desktop. Narrator may not function properly with some programs and can read only in English.

You can customize Narrator to suit your needs. By default, Narrator will read aloud all the contents of active windows and dialog boxes. You may want to have Narrator only read aloud the items you select in windows, dialog boxes and menus.

Narrator can read aloud each character you type. For example, narrator will read aloud alphanumeric characters and any special keys you type, such as the Ctrl, Tab, Esc and Num Lock keys.

Narrator provides an option that automatically moves the mouse pointer to each item you select using the keyboard. This can help you select an option without having to move the mouse to the option.

You can also have the Narrator window automatically open as a minimized button on the taskbar when you start Narrator.

USING NARRATOR

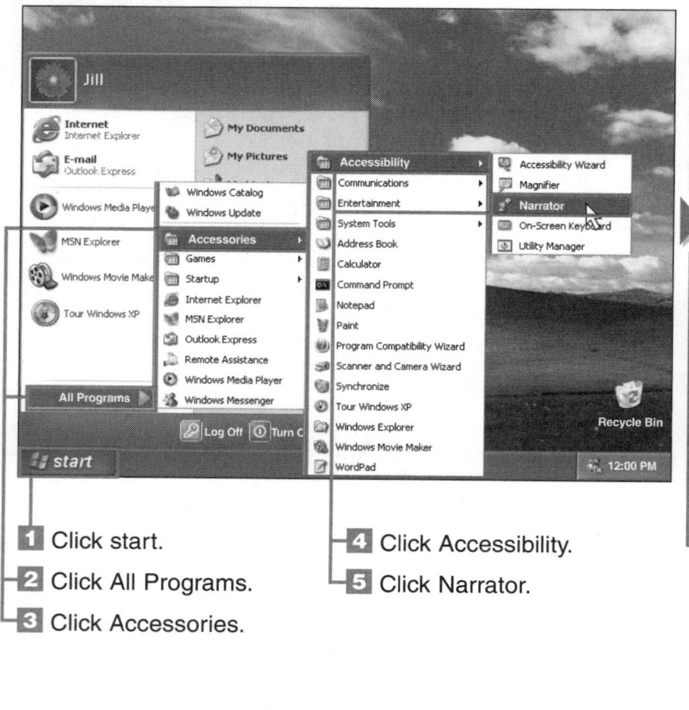

1 Click start.

2 Click All Programs.

3 Click Accessories.

4 Click Accessibility.

5 Click Narrator.

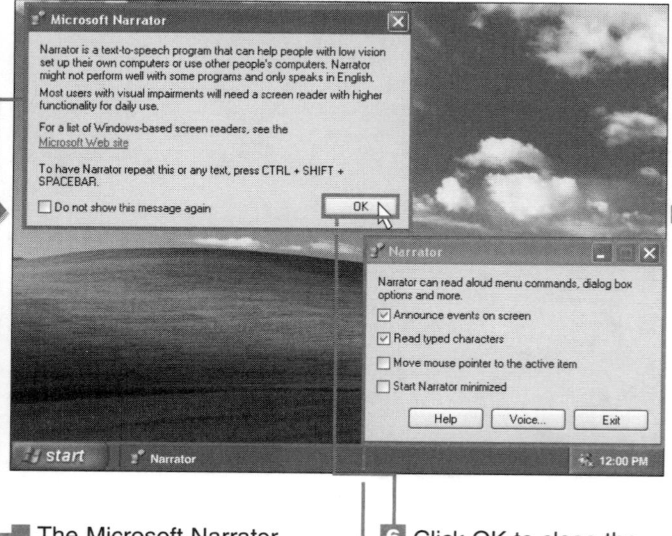

■ The Microsoft Narrator dialog box appears, displaying a description of Microsoft Narrator.

Note: Narrator immediately begins describing the contents of the dialog box.

6 Click OK to close the dialog box.

■ The Narrator window also opens.

How can I have Narrator repeat information?

✔ To have Narrator repeat the contents of the active window or dialog box, press the Ctrl+Shift+Spacebar keys. To have Narrator repeat a selected item, press the Ctrl+Shift+Enter keys.

Can I make Narrator read the title bar or status bar of a window?

✔ Yes. To have Narrator read the title bar of a window, press the Alt+Home keys. To have Narrator read the status bar of a window, press the Alt+End keys.

How can I make Narrator stop speaking?

✔ Press the Ctrl key to temporarily stop Narrator.

I am having trouble understanding the narrator's voice. What can I do?

✔ In the Narrator window, click the Voice button. The Voice Settings dialog box appears, allowing you to increase or decrease the speed, volume and pitch of the narrator's voice. Click ⌄ in the Speed, Volume or Pitch area to select a different setting.

Where can I find screen readers with more functionality than Narrator?

✔ You can visit the Microsoft Accessibility Web site at www.microsoft.com/enable to find a list of Windows-based screen readers. You can also click the link displayed in the Microsoft Narrator dialog box to visit the Web site.

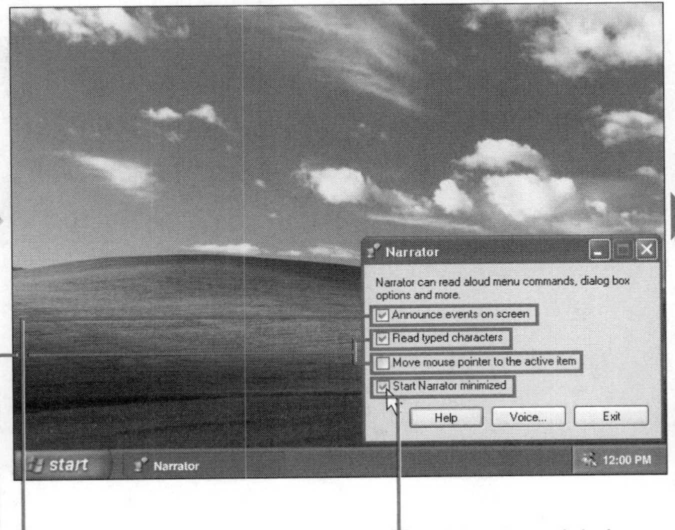

■ This option reads aloud the contents of active windows and dialog boxes.

■ This option reads aloud characters you type.

■ This option moves the mouse to the items you select using the keyboard.

■ This option minimizes the Narrator window to a button on a taskbar when you start Narrator.

7 To turn an option on (☑) or off (☐), click the option.

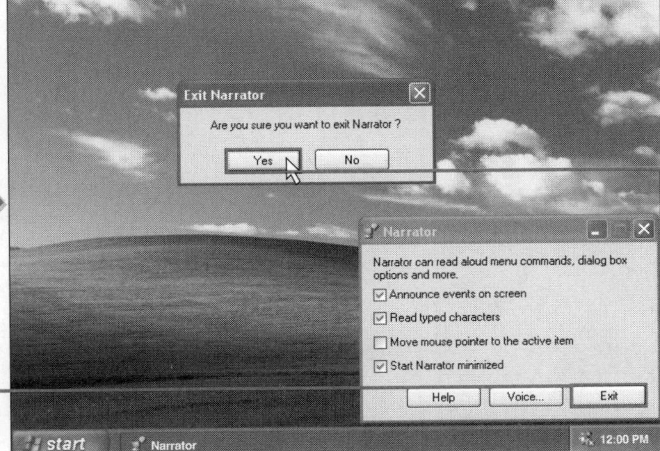

8 When you finish using Narrator, click Exit.

■ A dialog box appears, confirming that you want to exit Narrator.

9 Click Yes to exit Narrator.

USING THE ACCESSIBILITY OPTIONS

You can customize the way your computer operates to accommodate special needs and situations. The Windows accessibility options allow you to make a computer easier to use if you have physical or visual restrictions.

Windows offers several options designed to make your keyboard easier to use. StickyKeys helps users who have difficulty pressing two keys at the same time. After you press the Shift, Ctrl, Alt or Windows logo key on your keyboard, the key will remain active while you press another key.

FilterKeys reduces the keyboard's sensitivity to brief or repeated keystrokes and plays a sound every time you press a key.

ToggleKeys plays a sound when you press the Caps Lock, Num Lock or Scroll Lock key.

Windows also allows you to replace sound cues with visual ones. SoundSentry flashes a part of your screen when your computer makes a sound. ShowSounds provides captions for speech and sound events in some programs.

USING THE ACCESSIBILITY OPTIONS

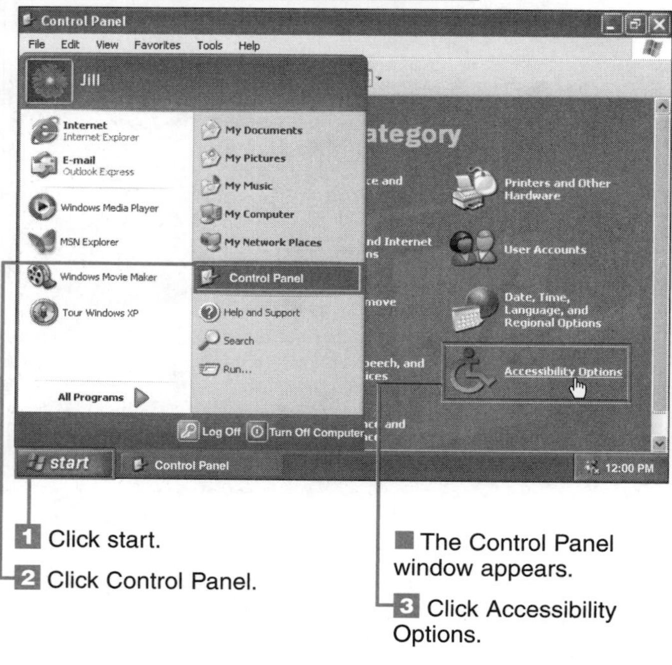

1 Click start.

2 Click Control Panel.

■ The Control Panel window appears.

3 Click Accessibility Options.

■ The Accessibility Options window appears.

4 Click Accessibility Options.

■ The Accessibility Options dialog box appears.

Why did StickyKeys stop working?

✔ Windows automatically turns off StickyKeys when you press two keys at once. To have StickyKeys remain on even when you press two keys at once, choose the Keyboard tab in the Accessibility Options dialog box and then click the Settings button in the StickyKeys area. In the dialog box that appears, select the Turn StickyKeys off if two keys are pressed at once option (☑ changes to ☐).

How can I have a program provide additional help information for the keyboard?

✔ In the Accessibility Options dialog box, choose the Keyboard tab and then select the Show extra keyboard help in programs option (☐ changes to ☑). Some programs may not provide additional help information for the keyboard.

Can I use keyboard shortcuts to enable accessibility features?

✔ Yes. You can use keyboard shortcuts to enable most accessibility features. To determine the keyboard shortcut used to enable a specific accessibility feature, display the Accessibility Options dialog box and click the Settings button for the feature. In the dialog box that appears, the information under the Keyboard shortcut area indicates the keyboard shortcut you can use to enable the accessibility feature.

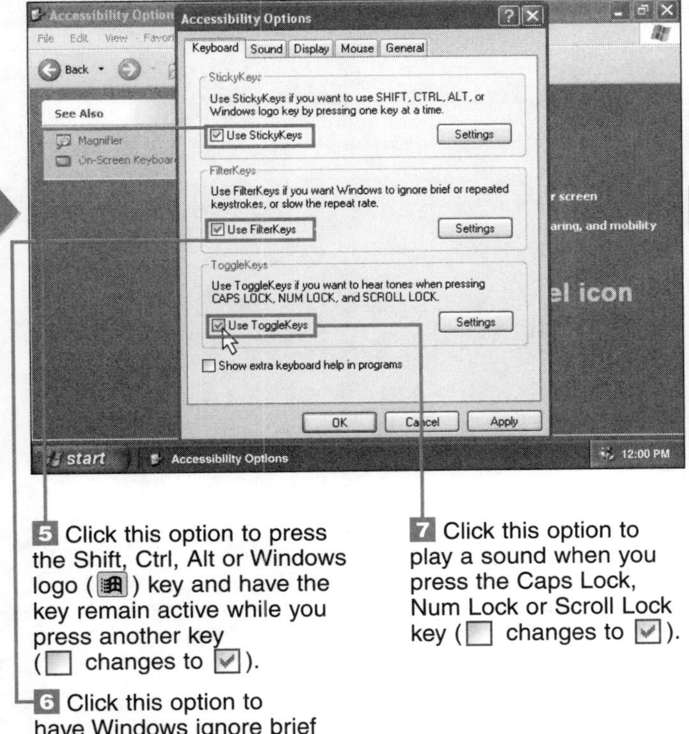

5 Click this option to press the Shift, Ctrl, Alt or Windows logo (⊞) key and have the key remain active while you press another key (☐ changes to ☑).

6 Click this option to have Windows ignore brief or repeated keystrokes (☐ changes to ☑).

7 Click this option to play a sound when you press the Caps Lock, Num Lock or Scroll Lock key (☐ changes to ☑).

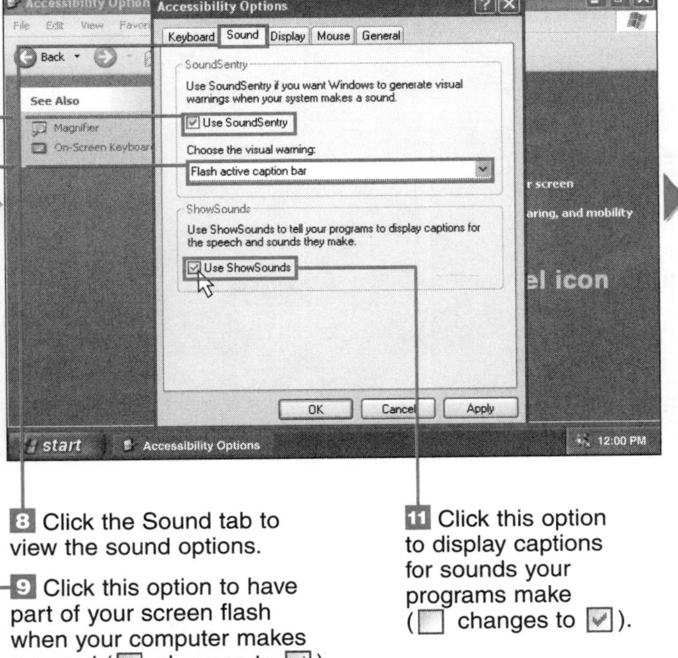

8 Click the Sound tab to view the sound options.

9 Click this option to have part of your screen flash when your computer makes a sound (☐ changes to ☑).

10 This area displays the part of the screen that Windows will flash. You can click this area to select a different part.

11 Click this option to display captions for sounds your programs make (☐ changes to ☑).

CONTINUED

USING THE ACCESSIBILITY OPTIONS (CONTINUED)

If you find the screen difficult to read, you can use the accessibility options to change to the High Contrast screen display. Windows will change the color and size of text and other items to make the screen easier to read.

You can change the speed at which the cursor blinks and the width of the cursor. The cursor indicates where the text you type will appear in a document.

MouseKeys allows you to control the mouse pointer using the numeric keypad on your keyboard instead of the mouse.

If you share a computer with other users who do not want to use the accessibility options, you can have Windows automatically turn off these features when your computer has been idle for a specified time. You can also choose to use visual and sound cues to indicate when an accessibility option is turned on or off using a keyboard shortcut.

SerialKey allows you to connect an alternative input device, such as a foot pedal, to your computer's serial port. This enables you to communicate with your computer when you cannot use the mouse or keyboard. You must be logged on as a computer administrator to turn on the SerialKey feature.

USING THE ACCESSIBILITY OPTIONS (CONTINUED)

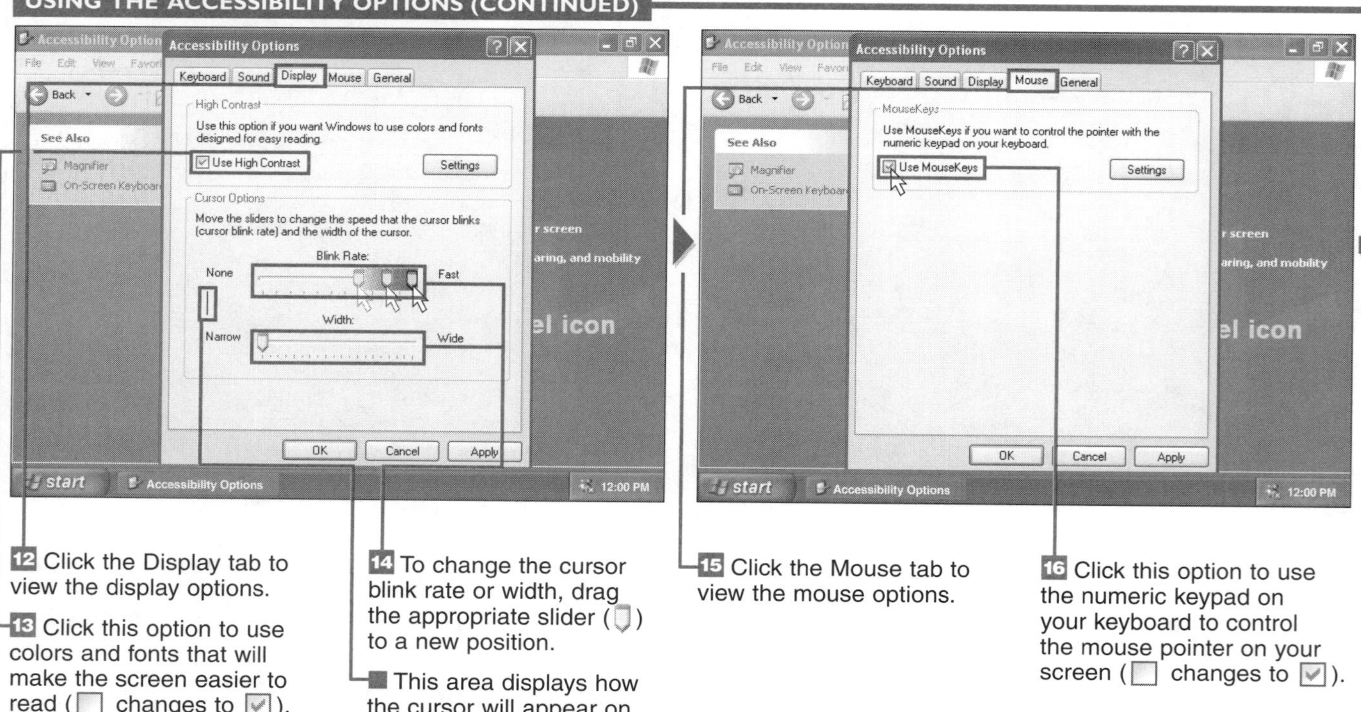

12 Click the Display tab to view the display options.

13 Click this option to use colors and fonts that will make the screen easier to read (☐ changes to ☑).

14 To change the cursor blink rate or width, drag the appropriate slider (▯) to a new position.

■ This area displays how the cursor will appear on your screen.

15 Click the Mouse tab to view the mouse options.

16 Click this option to use the numeric keypad on your keyboard to control the mouse pointer on your screen (☐ changes to ☑).

After I turn on the MouseKeys feature, what keys can I use to control the mouse pointer?

✔ The Num Lock key must be on to use the MouseKeys feature. A light on your keyboard indicates the status of the Num Lock key.

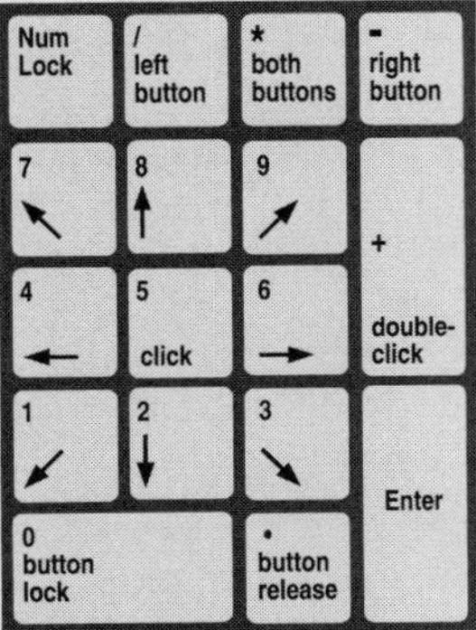

Can I allow all users to use accessibility features to log on to the computer?

✔ Yes. In the Accessibility Options dialog box, choose the General tab. In the Administrative options area, select the Apply all settings to logon desktop option (☐ changes to ☑). You can also choose the Apply all settings to defaults for new users option to apply the accessibility options you have set as the default for all new user accounts created on your computer. You must be logged on as a computer administrator to access these options.

I selected SerialKey, but my input device is not working. Why?

✔ You must turn off the Fast User Switching feature in order to use SerialKey. Click start, select Control Panel and then choose User Accounts. In the window that appears, click Change the way users log on or off and then select the Use Fast User Switching option (☑ changes to ☐).

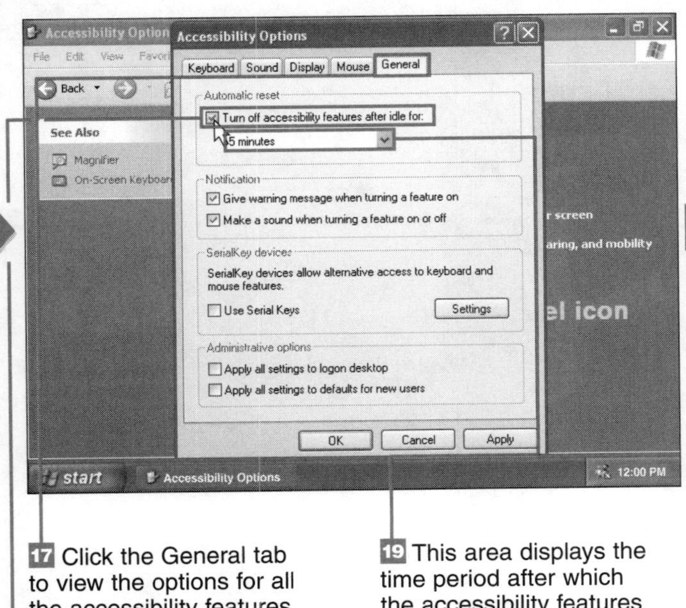

17 Click the General tab to view the options for all the accessibility features.

18 Click this option to automatically turn off the accessibility features after your computer has been idle for a period of time (☐ changes to ☑).

19 This area displays the time period after which the accessibility features will automatically turn off. You can click this area to select a different time.

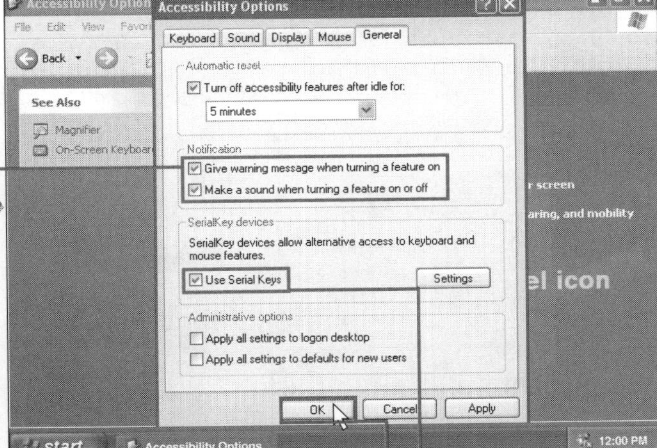

20 These options display a message or make a sound when you use a keyboard shortcut to turn an accessibility feature on or off. You can click an option to turn the option on (☑) or off (☐).

21 Click this option to be able to attach an alternative input device to your computer (☐ changes to ☑).

22 Click OK to confirm your changes.

USING THE ACCESSIBILITY WIZARD

The Accessibility Wizard can help you set up Windows to meet your vision, hearing and mobility needs. Although the accessibility options were designed to help people with special needs operate a computer, there are some options that may be of interest to all users.

The wizard asks you to select the smallest text you can read. The text size option you select affects your screen immediately.

If you select the largest text size, Windows automatically starts Microsoft Magnifier. Magnifier displays an enlarged view of the area surrounding the mouse pointer at the top of your screen.

The wizard allows you to choose the way you want text and items to appear on your screen. You can increase the font size used in title bars, menus and other features. If you are currently using a high screen resolution, you can select a lower screen resolution, which will increase the size of text and items so you can see the information on your screen more clearly. If Magnifier is not already displayed, you can choose to display Magnifier. If you use the Classic style Start menu, you can disable the Personalized Menus feature to ensure Windows does not hide any items on the Programs menu. For information about the Classic Start menu, see the top of page 265.

USING THE ACCESSIBILITY WIZARD

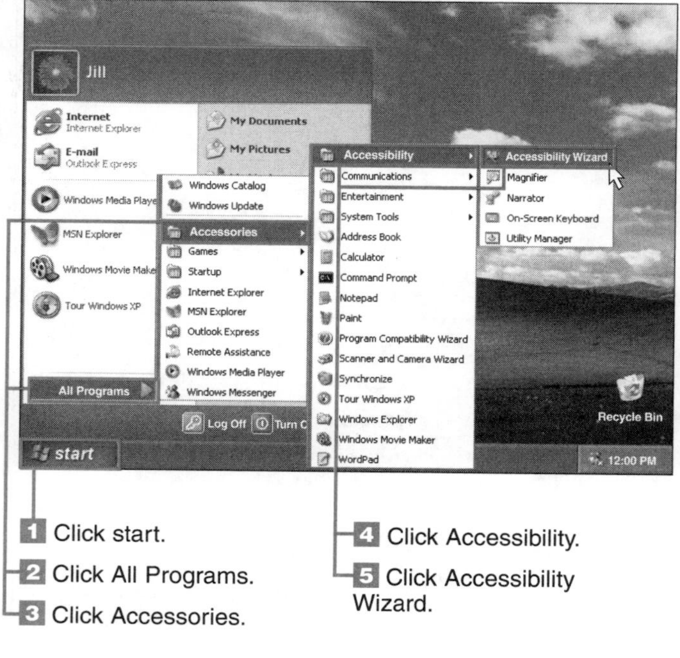

1 Click start.

2 Click All Programs.

3 Click Accessories.

4 Click Accessibility.

5 Click Accessibility Wizard.

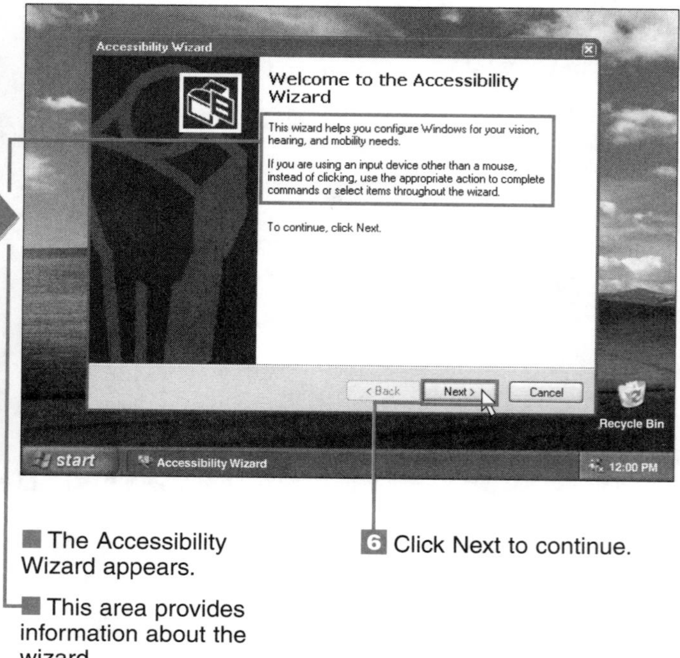

■ The Accessibility Wizard appears.

■ This area provides information about the wizard.

6 Click Next to continue.

Why do additional windows appear on my screen when Magnifier starts?

✔ When Magnifier starts, the Microsoft Magnifier dialog box and Magnifier Settings window appear on your screen. Click OK to close the Microsoft Magnifier dialog box so you can clearly view the Magnifier Settings window. For information about changing the available Magnifier settings, see page 268. To keep Magnifier open but remove the Magnifier Settings window from your screen, click ▬ in the window. If you do not want to use Magnifier, click the Exit button in the Magnifier Settings window.

Can I turn on Magnifier without starting the wizard?

✔ Yes. Click the start button, select All Programs, choose Accessories, click Accessibility and then select Magnifier. For more information about Magnifier, see page 268.

Why is the Switch to a lower screen resolution option unavailable?

✔ This option is only available if your screen displays a resolution of 1024x768 or higher. For more information about changing the screen resolution, see page 200.

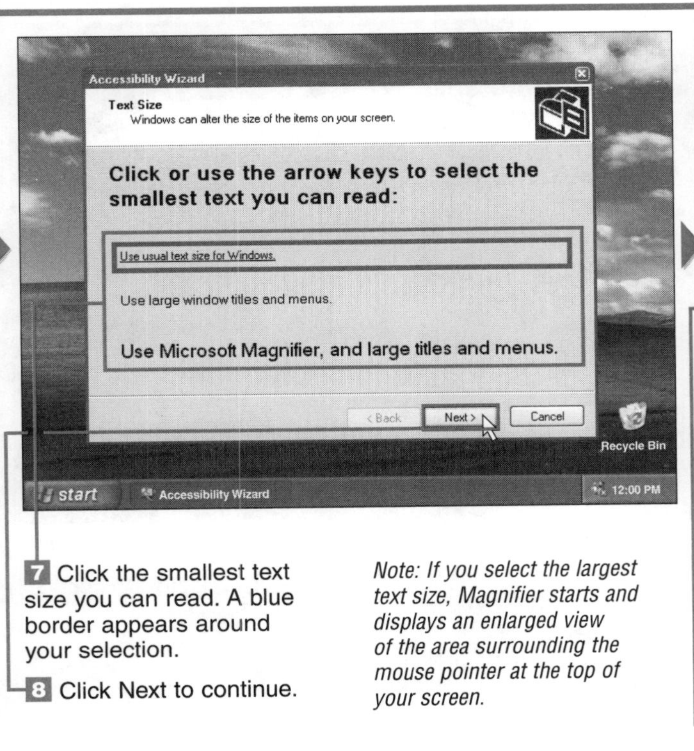

7 Click the smallest text size you can read. A blue border appears around your selection.

8 Click Next to continue.

Note: If you select the largest text size, Magnifier starts and displays an enlarged view of the area surrounding the mouse pointer at the top of your screen.

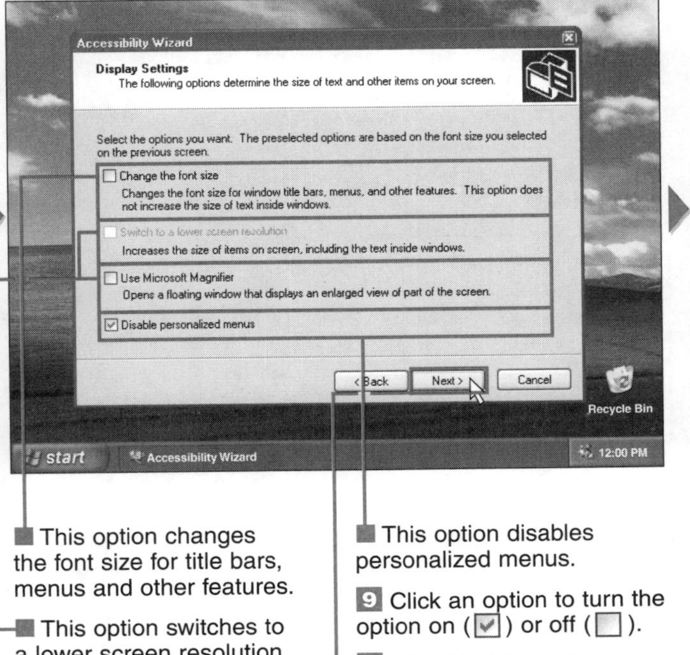

■ This option changes the font size for title bars, menus and other features.

■ This option switches to a lower screen resolution.

■ This option displays an enlarged view of the area surrounding the mouse pointer.

■ This option disables personalized menus.

9 Click an option to turn the option on (☑) or off (☐).

10 Click Next to continue.

CONTINUED

USING THE ACCESSIBILITY WIZARD (CONTINUED)

The Accessibility Wizard displays a list of statements and asks you to select each statement that applies to you. The statements you select help the wizard decide which accessibility options will benefit you the most when using Windows.

If you have difficulty seeing, you can select options that will make viewing information on your screen easier. You can increase the size of scroll bars, window borders and icons. You can also select a high contrast color scheme.

If you have difficulty hearing, you can have Windows display visual warnings when sound events occur on your computer. Windows can also display captions for sounds in some programs.

There are many options you can select to make the keyboard and mouse easier to use. For example, you can have Windows ignore repeated keystrokes or you can use the numeric keypad instead of the mouse to move the pointer on your screen.

The administrative options are useful if more than one person uses your computer. For example, you can have Windows automatically turn off accessibility options after the computer is idle for a certain number of minutes.

When you complete the Accessibility Wizard, the wizard displays a list of the accessibility options you changed.

USING THE ACCESSIBILITY WIZARD (CONTINUED)

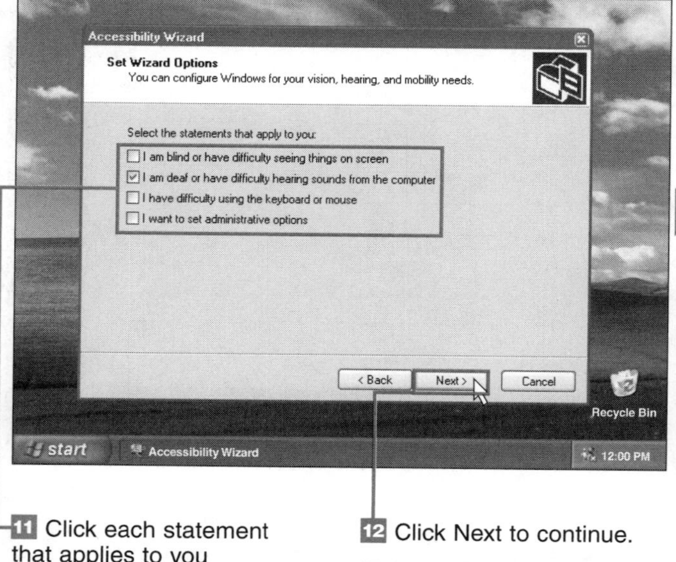

11 Click each statement that applies to you (☐ changes to ☑).

12 Click Next to continue.

■ The options available in the next screens depend on the statement(s) you selected in step 11.

13 Click Yes or No to specify if you want Windows to generate visual warnings when your system makes a sound (○ changes to ◉).

14 Click Next to continue.

Is there another way to set accessibility options?

✔ Yes. You can customize the way your computer operates to accommodate special needs and situations by adjusting specific accessibility options. See page 274 for more information about changing the accessibility options in Windows.

Where can I find more information about the accessibility options Windows offers?

✔ The Windows help feature provides more information about the accessibility options that Windows offers. Click the start button and then select Help and Support. In the Help and Support Center window, click the Accessibility link and then choose the link for the accessibility option of interest. For more information about using the Windows help feature, see page 22.

Are there more advanced accessibility features available?

✔ The accessibility features that come with Windows provide a minimum level of functionality for people with special needs. There are programs available that offer more support. For information about these programs, visit the Microsoft Accessibility Web site at www.microsoft.com/enable.

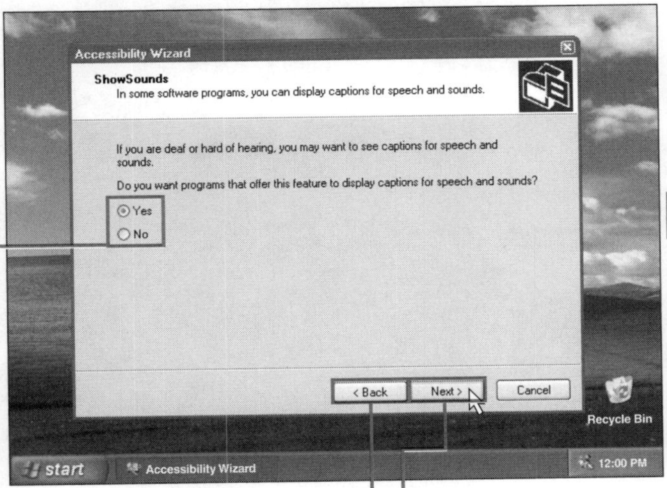

15 Click Yes or No to specify if you want programs to display captions for speech and sounds (◯ changes to ◉).

16 Click Next to continue.

■ You can click Back to return to a previous step and change your selections.

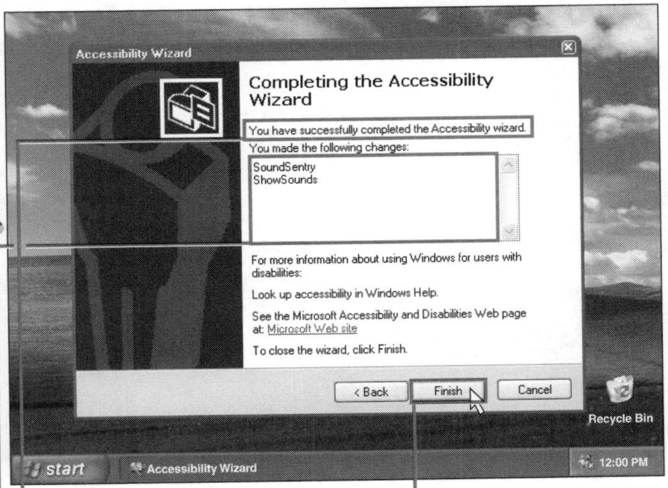

■ The wizard indicates that you have successfully completed the wizard.

■ This area displays the changes you have made.

17 Click Finish to close the wizard and use the accessibility options you selected.

USING UTILITY MANAGER

Utility Manager allows you to control the accessibility programs that come with Windows, including Magnifier, Narrator and On-Screen Keyboard.

Magnifier and Narrator are useful for people with visual impairments. Magnifier shows an enlarged area of the screen that surrounds the mouse pointer. For information about Magnifier, see page 268. Narrator reads aloud the contents of active windows and dialog boxes. For information about Narrator, see page 272.

On-Screen Keyboard displays a keyboard on the screen and is useful for people with limited mobility. See page 270 for information about On-Screen Keyboard.

You can check the status of an accessibility program to see if the program is running, not running or not responding. You can also start or stop an accessibility program using Utility Manager.

You can have an accessibility program start automatically each time you log on to your computer, lock your desktop or start Utility Manager. Starting a program automatically saves you time and allows you to access the program immediately.

You must be logged on as a computer administrator to have access to some of the options in Utility Manager.

USING UTILITY MANAGER

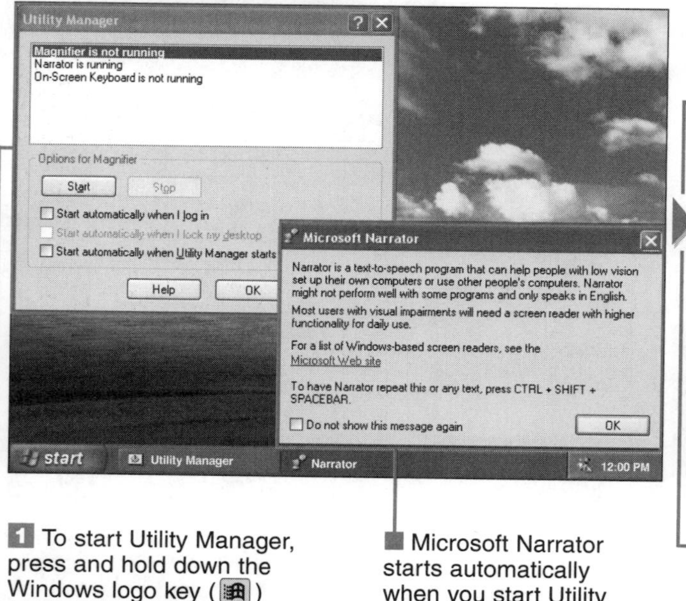

1 To start Utility Manager, press and hold down the Windows logo key (⊞) as you press the U key.

■ The Utility Manager dialog box appears.

■ Microsoft Narrator starts automatically when you start Utility Manager.

■ This area displays the name and status of each accessibility program.

■ This area displays the options for the currently selected accessibility program.

Is there another way to start Utility Manager?

✔ Yes. You can start Utility Manager using the Start menu. Click start, select All Programs, choose Accessories, select Accessibility and then click Utility Manager. When you start Utility Manager using the Start menu, the options that allow you to start accessibility programs automatically may not be available.

Can I use Utility Manager before logging on to Windows?

✔ Yes. In the Welcome screen, press and hold down the Windows logo key (⊞) as you press the U key to start Utility Manager.

Why isn't the option to start accessibility programs automatically when I lock my desktop available?

✔ You can lock your desktop only when your computer belongs to a domain. A domain is a group of computers that are administered together on a network. If the option is not available in Utility Manager, your computer does not belong to a domain.

Where can I get information about other accessibility programs?

✔ The accessibility programs included with Windows provide a minimum level of support for users with special needs. You can visit the Microsoft Accessibility Web site at www.microsoft.com/enable to obtain information about programs that can provide more support.

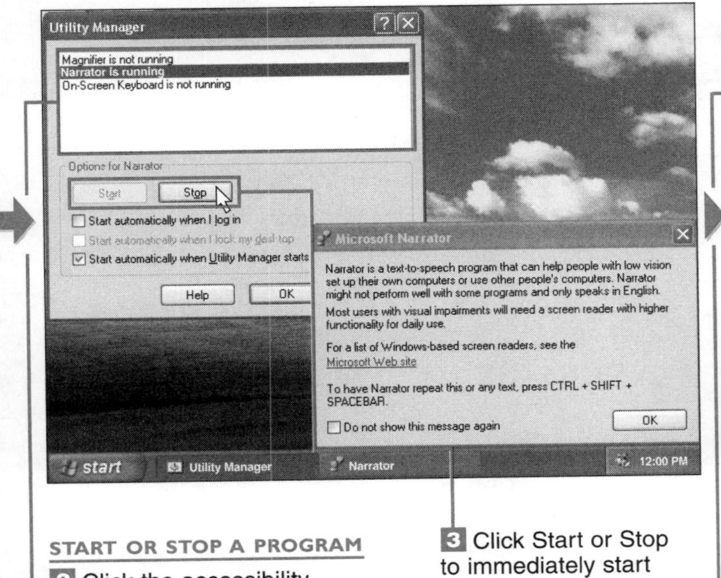

START OR STOP A PROGRAM

2 Click the accessibility program you want to start or stop.

3 Click Start or Stop to immediately start or stop the program.

START A PROGRAM AUTOMATICALLY

4 Click the accessibility program you want to start automatically.

■ This area displays options that allow you to start the program automatically when you log on to your computer, lock your desktop or start Utility Manager.

5 Click an option to turn the option on (☑) or off (☐).

6 Click OK to confirm your changes.

SECTION IV

12) WORK WITH MULTIMEDIA

13) USING WINDOWS MEDIA PLAYER

14) CREATE MOVIES

WINDOWS XP AND MULTIMEDIA

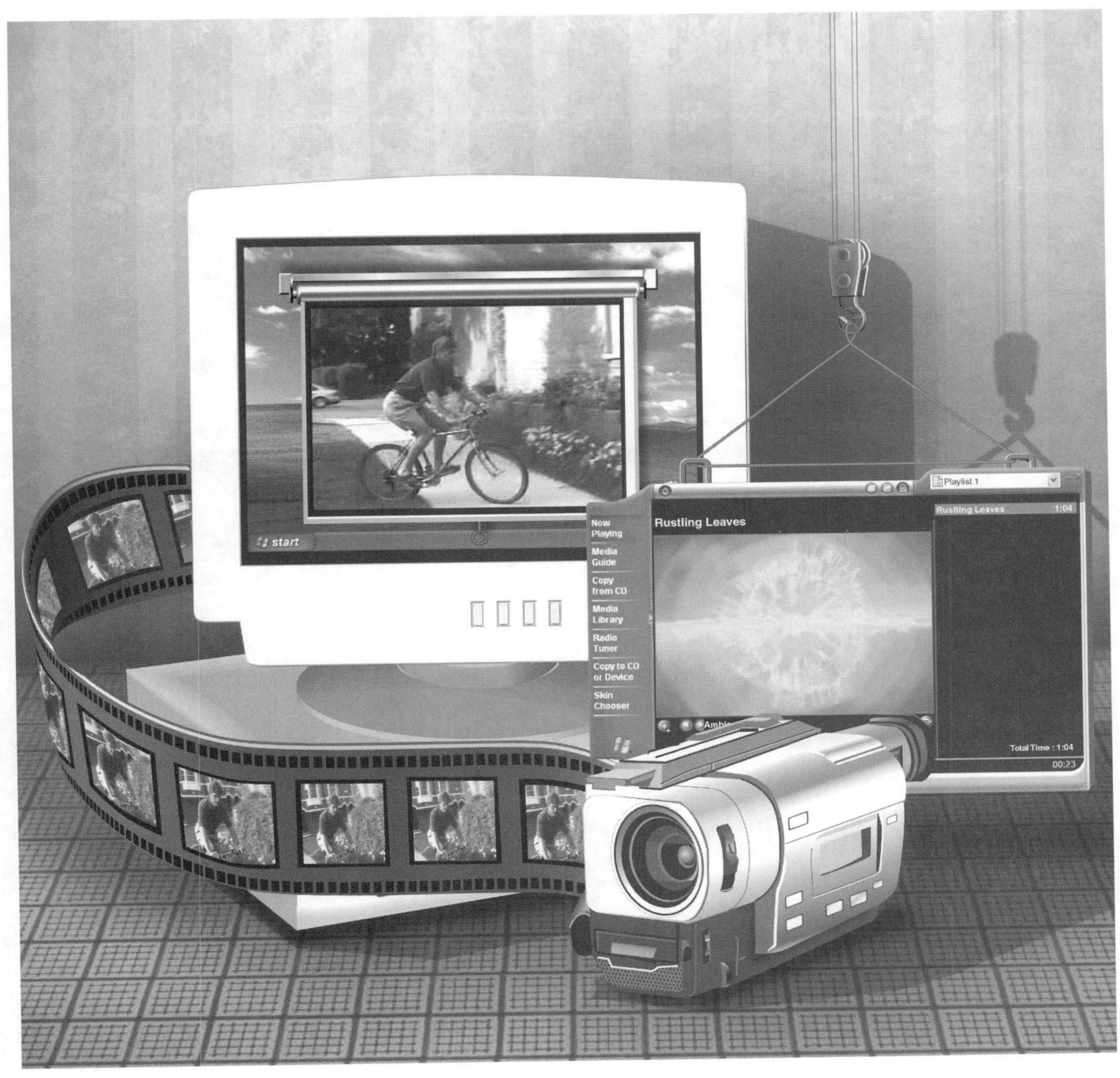

CHANGE THE VOLUME

You can change the overall volume of sound on your computer, referred to as the system volume. Changing the overall volume of sound on your computer allows you to change the volume of all devices on the computer at once.

You can increase or decrease the volume of sound on your computer. You can also turn off, or mute, the sound on your computer and turn on the sound again at any time.

If you frequently make changes to the volume, you can display a speaker icon in the notification area on the taskbar. The speaker icon will allow you to quickly access controls you can use to increase or decrease the volume of sound on the computer or turn off the sound for the computer.

When you change the volume in the Sounds and Audio Devices Properties dialog box, the volume level indicated in the Master Volume area of the volume control window is automatically updated to show the same volume level. For more information about the volume control window, see page 288.

CHANGE THE COMPUTER VOLUME

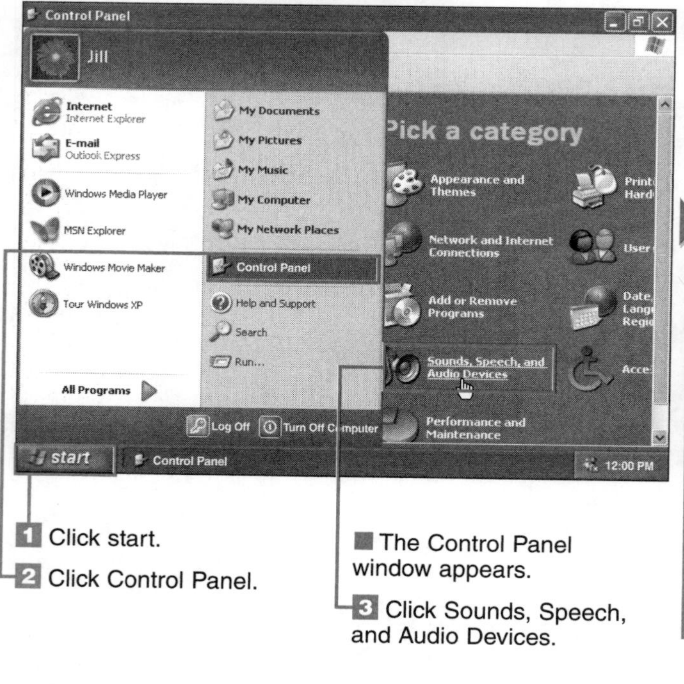

1 Click start.

2 Click Control Panel.

■ The Control Panel window appears.

3 Click Sounds, Speech, and Audio Devices.

■ The Sounds, Speech, and Audio Devices window appears.

4 Click Adjust the system volume.

■ The Sounds and Audio Devices Properties dialog box appears.

How do I change the system volume using the speaker icon?

✔ Click the speaker icon ( ) in the notification area on the taskbar. In the volume control box that appears, move the volume slider ( ) up or down to increase or decrease the system volume. To turn off the sound, select the Mute option in the volume control box (changes to).

Can I adjust the volume for each speaker separately?

✔ Yes. In the Sounds and Audio Devices Properties dialog box, select the Volume tab and click the Speaker Volume button. You can drag the volume slider ( ) for a speaker to change the volume of the speaker. To return the volume of the speakers to the default levels, click the Restore Defaults button.

How can I improve the sound quality of my speakers?

✔ Windows customizes your computer's sound configuration to optimize the sound quality based on the setup of your speakers. You can ensure that the speaker setup specified on your computer corresponds to the physical setup of your speakers. In the Sounds and Audio Devices Properties dialog box, select the Volume tab and click the Advanced button in the Speaker settings area. If the option displayed in the Speaker setup area does not match your speaker setup, you can click the area and select a more appropriate option.

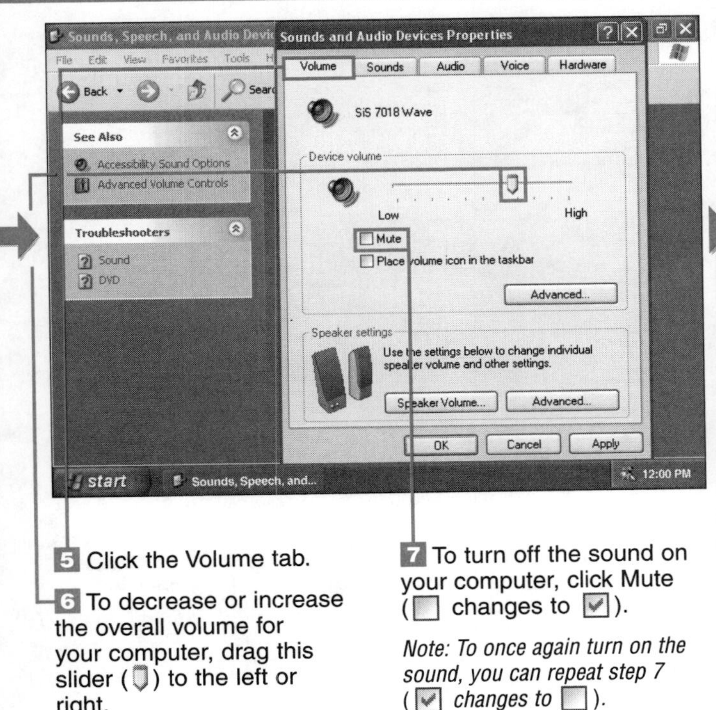

5 Click the Volume tab.

6 To decrease or increase the overall volume for your computer, drag this slider ( ) to the left or right.

7 To turn off the sound on your computer, click Mute (changes to).

Note: To once again turn on the sound, you can repeat step 7 (changes to).

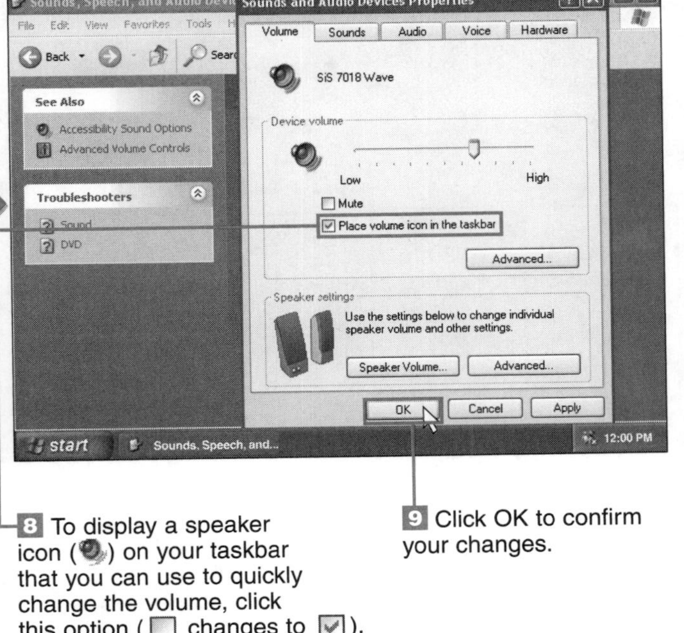

8 To display a speaker icon ( ) on your taskbar that you can use to quickly change the volume, click this option (changes to).

9 Click OK to confirm your changes.

CONTINUED

CHANGE THE VOLUME (CONTINUED)

When playing sounds, such as music CDs or videos, on your computer, you may need to adjust the volume of sound on your computer.

You can adjust the volume of all the devices on your computer at once. You can also adjust the volume of specific devices without affecting the volume of other devices. For example, if your CDs play too loudly, you can lower the volume of the CD player without affecting the volume of other devices.

If you want to turn off the sound, you can mute all the devices on your computer or mute the sound of specific devices. You can also change the balance between the left and right speakers for each device on your computer. For example, if one speaker is farther away than the other, you can make that speaker louder.

In the window that allows you to change the volume on your computer, you can choose to display devices that are used for playing back or recording sounds and then specify which playback or recording devices you want to display. For example, you can have Windows display the microphone and CD Audio devices. The available devices depend on the sound capabilities of your computer.

CHANGE THE VOLUME OF SPECIFIC DEVICES

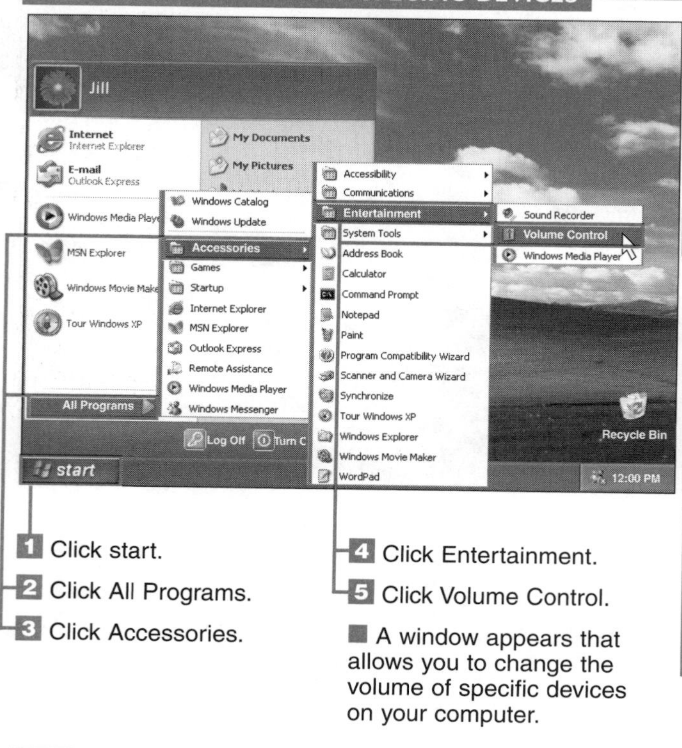

1 Click start.

2 Click All Programs.

3 Click Accessories.

4 Click Entertainment.

5 Click Volume Control.

■ A window appears that allows you to change the volume of specific devices on your computer.

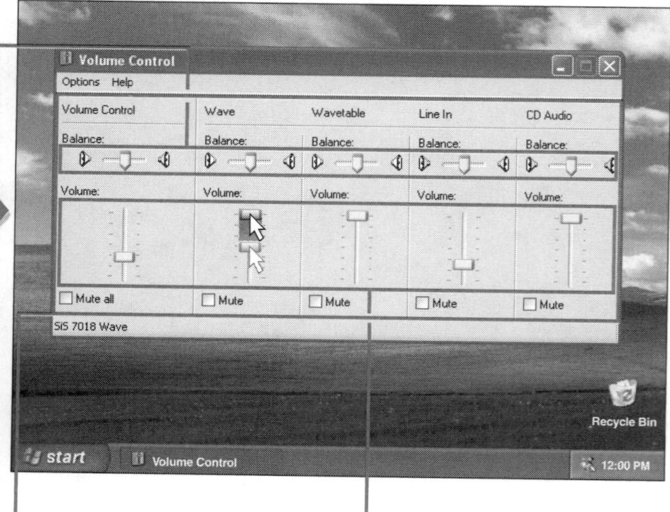

■ This area displays the master volume control and each device that you can control the volume for.

6 To change the balance between the left and right speakers for a device, drag the balance slider ( ) for the device.

7 To increase or decrease the volume for a device, drag the volume slider ( ) for the device.

What are some of the common devices I can adjust the volume for?

✔ Microphone controls the recording volume when using a microphone to record sounds. Line In controls the recording volume of devices, such as a CD player, that connect to the Line In port. CD Audio controls the playback volume of audio CDs. MIDI controls the playback volume of MIDI sounds and Wave controls the playback volume of Wave sounds.

Can I control the amount of bass and treble?

✔ Yes. Perform steps 1 to 5 below. In the window that appears, choose the Options menu, select Advanced Controls and then click the Advanced button. Drag the slider ( ) for the bass or treble setting to change the amount of bass or treble. This feature is not available on all computers.

Why is the sound low even after I increase the volume of a device?

✔ Many speakers have built-in volume dials that control the speaker volume. If your speaker volume is set at a low level, changing the volume for a device may not achieve the volume level you want. You can use the volume dials on your speakers to adjust the volume to an acceptable level. Your speakers may also have a power button that you can use to turn the sound on or off.

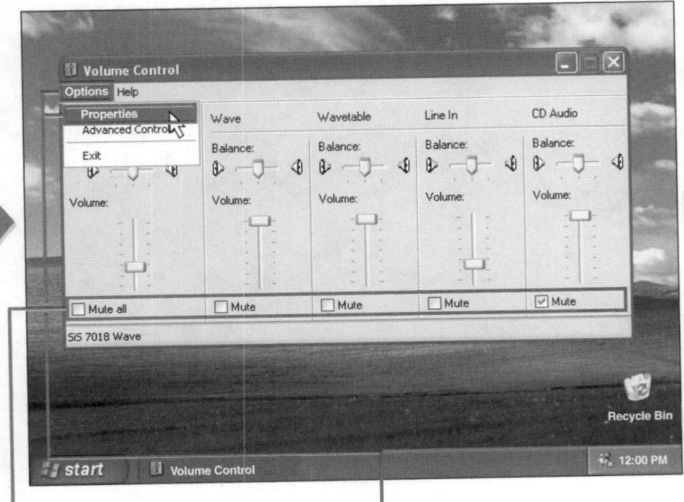

8 To turn off the sound for a device, click Mute for the device (changes to).

■ To once again turn on the sound for a device, repeat step 8.

Note: The Mute option may be labeled Select on some computers.

9 To specify which devices you want to appear in the window, click Options.

10 Click Properties.

■ The Properties dialog box appears.

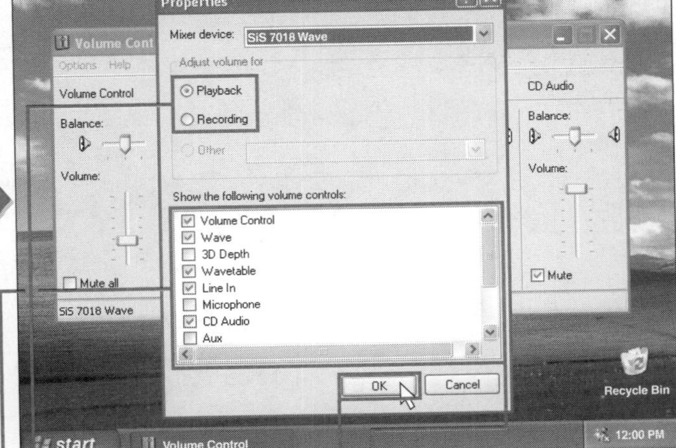

11 Click an option to specify if you want to display playback devices or recording devices (changes to).

■ This area displays the devices for the option you selected.

12 Each device that displays a check mark (✔) will appear in the window. You can click the box beside a device to add ( ) or remove ( ) a check mark.

13 Click OK to confirm your changes.

ASSIGN SOUNDS TO PROGRAM EVENTS

You can have Windows play sounds when you perform certain tasks on your computer. Assigning sounds to tasks can make working with Windows more fun and interesting.

You need a computer with sound capabilities to hear sounds on your computer. If your computer has sound capabilities, you will hear a short musical introduction each time Windows starts.

The sounds on your computer can alert you to an error that has occurred or notify you of specific program events. For example, a sound may play each time you exit Windows, empty the Recycle Bin or receive a new e-mail message.

You can add or change the sounds for many events on your computer at once by choosing a sound scheme, which is a set of related sounds. When selecting a sound scheme, you can also choose not to play sounds for any events.

When assigning sounds to events, you can preview the sound that will play for each event.

ASSIGN SOUNDS TO PROGRAM EVENTS

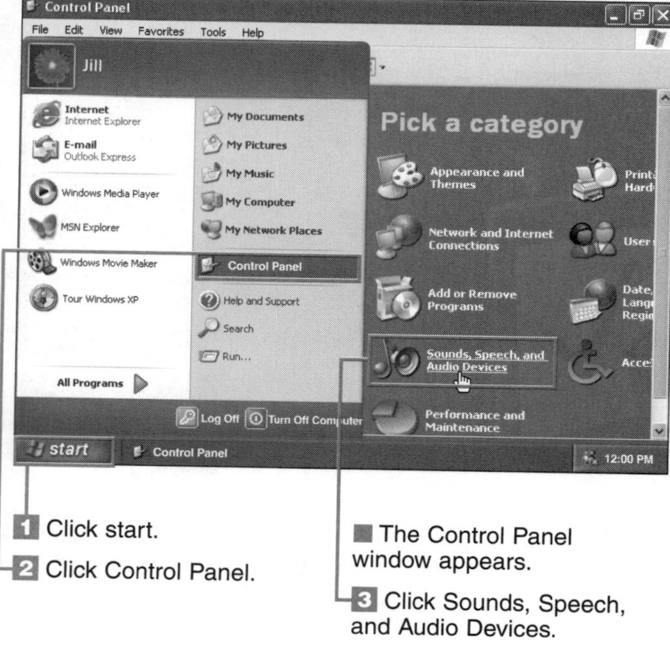

1 Click start.

2 Click Control Panel.

■ The Control Panel window appears.

3 Click Sounds, Speech, and Audio Devices.

■ The Sounds, Speech, and Audio Devices window appears.

4 Click Change the sound scheme to assign sounds to program events on your computer.

Why does the Save Scheme dialog box appear after I select a sound scheme?

✔ If you did not save your previous sound scheme, the Save Scheme dialog box appears and allows you to save the sound scheme for future use. Click Yes to save your previous sound scheme. In the dialog box that appears, type a name for the sound scheme and then click OK. You can also save a sound scheme at any time by clicking the Save As button on the Sounds tab in the Sounds and Audio Devices Properties dialog box.

How do I delete a sound scheme I created?

✔ In the Sounds and Audio Devices Properties dialog box, choose the Sounds tab and then click the Sound scheme area to display the list of available sound schemes. Select the sound scheme you want to delete and then click the Delete button.

How do I adjust the volume of the sounds?

✔ In the Sounds and Audio Devices Properties dialog box, click the Volume tab and then drag the Device volume slider (▯) left or right to decrease or increase the volume. Changing the volume in this dialog box will adjust the volume for all sounds on your computer, such as sound from a music CD or video.

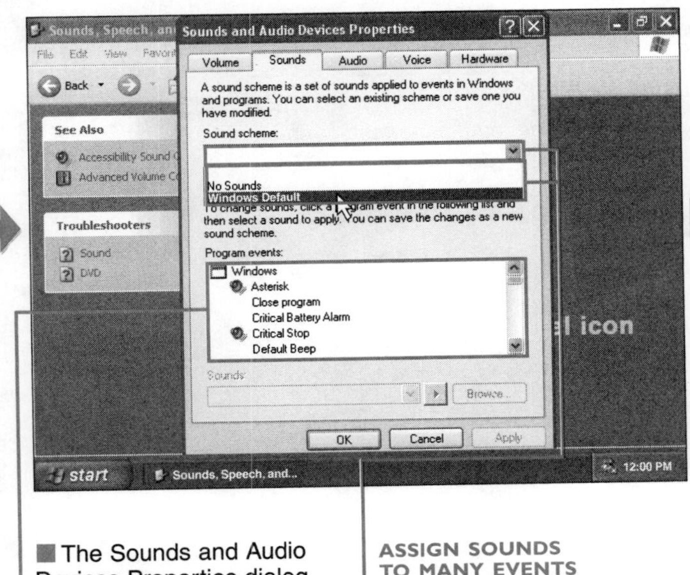

■ The Sounds and Audio Devices Properties dialog box appears.

■ This area lists the events that you can assign sounds to.

ASSIGN SOUNDS TO MANY EVENTS

5 Click this area to display a list of the available sound schemes.

6 Click the sound scheme you want to use.

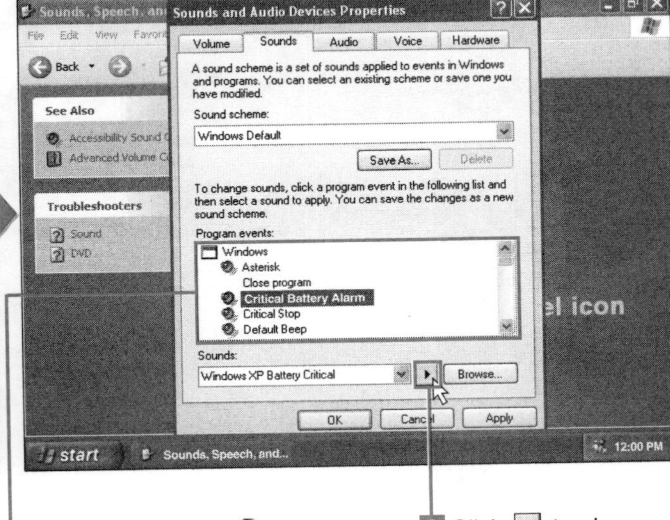

■ A speaker icon (🔊) appears beside each event that will play a sound.

7 To play the sound for an event, click the event.

8 Click ▸ to play the sound.

CONTINUED

ASSIGN SOUNDS TO PROGRAM EVENTS (CONTINUED)

You can assign a sound to a specific event. There are over 30 events to which you can assign sounds on your computer. You may want to play familiar music from a cartoon when Windows closes or hear a sigh of relief when you restore a window. You can mix and match sound files to create a personalized sound scheme for your computer.

You can use sound files included with Windows, purchase collections of sound files from computer stores or use sound files you download from Web sites, such as www.favewavs.com and www.wavlist.com.

You can also use sound files you have created. The sound files you use must be saved in the Wave format. Wave files have the .wav extension, such as chimes.wav. Windows does not include a tool that allows you to convert other types of sound files to the Wave format.

When assigning a sound to an event, you can listen to a preview of the sound.

ASSIGN SOUNDS TO PROGRAM EVENTS (CONTINUED)

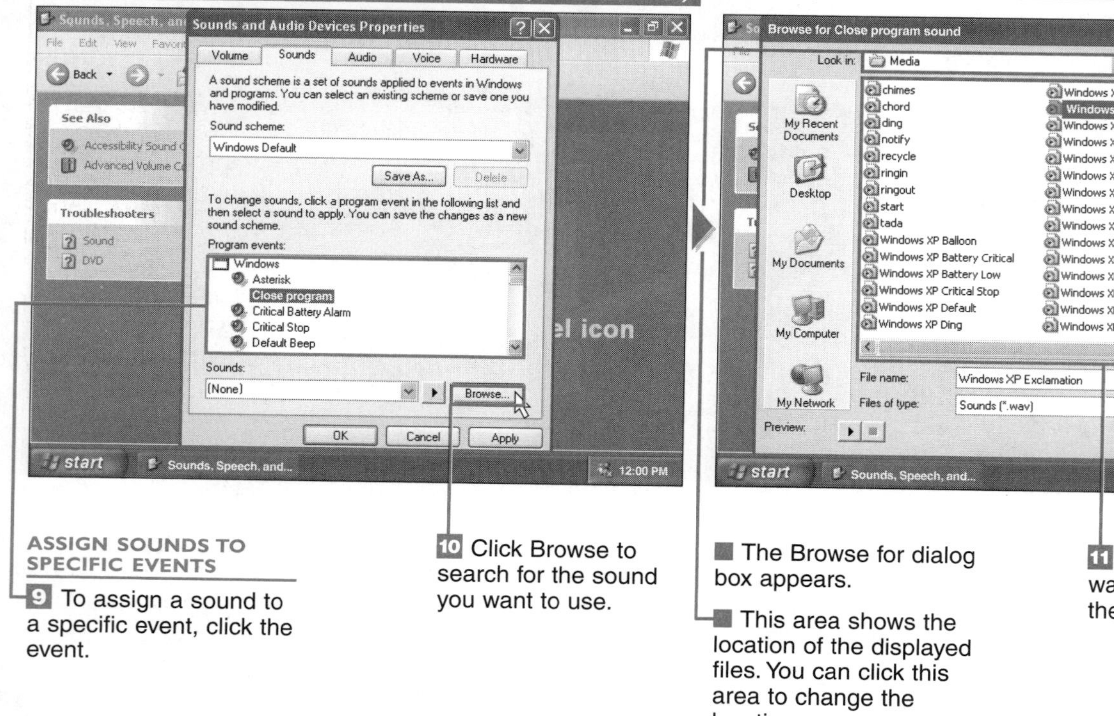

ASSIGN SOUNDS TO SPECIFIC EVENTS

9 To assign a sound to a specific event, click the event.

10 Click Browse to search for the sound you want to use.

■ The Browse for dialog box appears.

■ This area shows the location of the displayed files. You can click this area to change the location.

11 Click the sound you want to play each time the event occurs.

Are there other ways to assign a sound to an event?

✔ You can choose the event in the Program events area of the Sounds and Audio Devices Properties dialog box. Click ▾ below Sounds and then select the sound you want to assign from the list of available sounds. You can also assign a sound to an event by locating the sound file that you want to play when the event occurs and then dragging the sound file onto the event in the Sounds and Audio Devices Properties dialog box.

How do I remove a sound assigned to an event?

✔ In the Sounds and Audio Devices Properties dialog box, select the Sounds tab and then choose the event you no longer want to play a sound in the Program events area. Click ▾ below Sounds and select (None) from the list that appears.

How do I create my own sound files?

✔ You can use a sound recording program to record sounds from a microphone, CD player or stereo onto your computer. Windows includes the Sound Recorder program. For information about using Sound Recorder, see page 294.

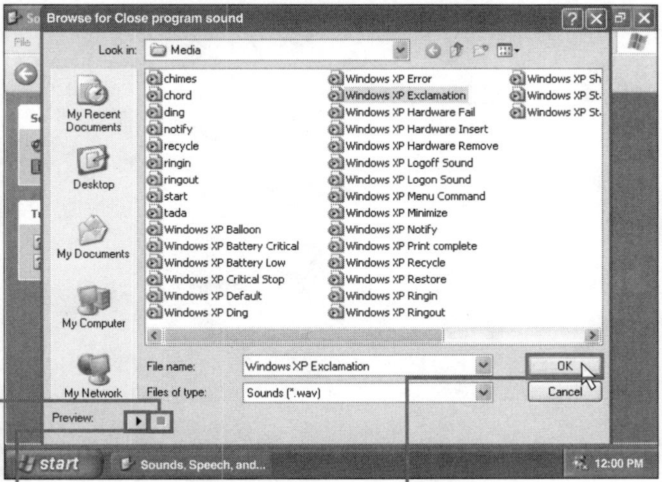

12 Click ▶ to play the sound.

■ To immediately stop playing the sound, click ■.

13 Click OK to confirm your selection.

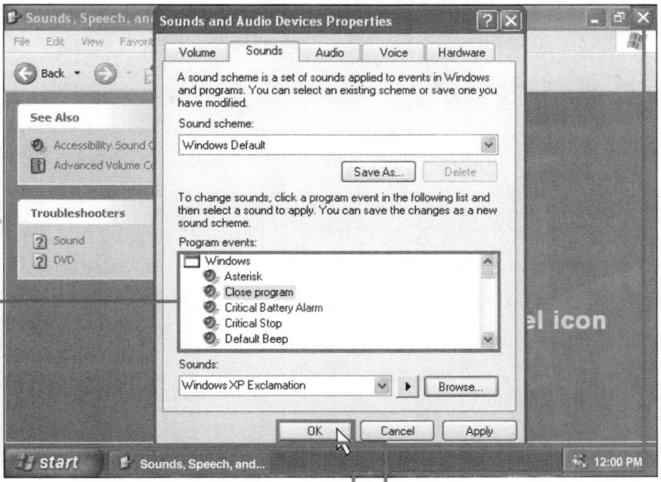

■ A speaker icon ( ) appears beside the event.

14 To assign sounds to other events, repeat steps 9 to 13 for each event.

15 Click OK to confirm all your changes.

16 Click ✕ to close the Sounds, Speech, and Audio Devices window.

USING SOUND RECORDER

You can use Sound Recorder to record, play and edit sounds on your computer. You can record sounds from a microphone, CD player, stereo, VCR or any other sound device you can connect to your computer. You need a computer with sound capabilities to record and play sounds.

You can add recorded sounds to a document to supply additional information or to provide entertainment. For example, a sales report could include a voice recording of a speech given by the company president.

You can also record sounds, effects or comments and have them play when specific events occur on your computer, such as when you close a program. This can help personalize your computer. To assign sounds to program events, see page 290.

When playing a recording in Sound Recorder, you can move to the beginning or end of the recording. You can also move to a specific location in a recording.

Sound Recorder allows you to perform basic sound recording and editing tasks. There are many other more sophisticated sound recording and editing programs that you can obtain on the Internet and at computer stores.

USING SOUND RECORDER

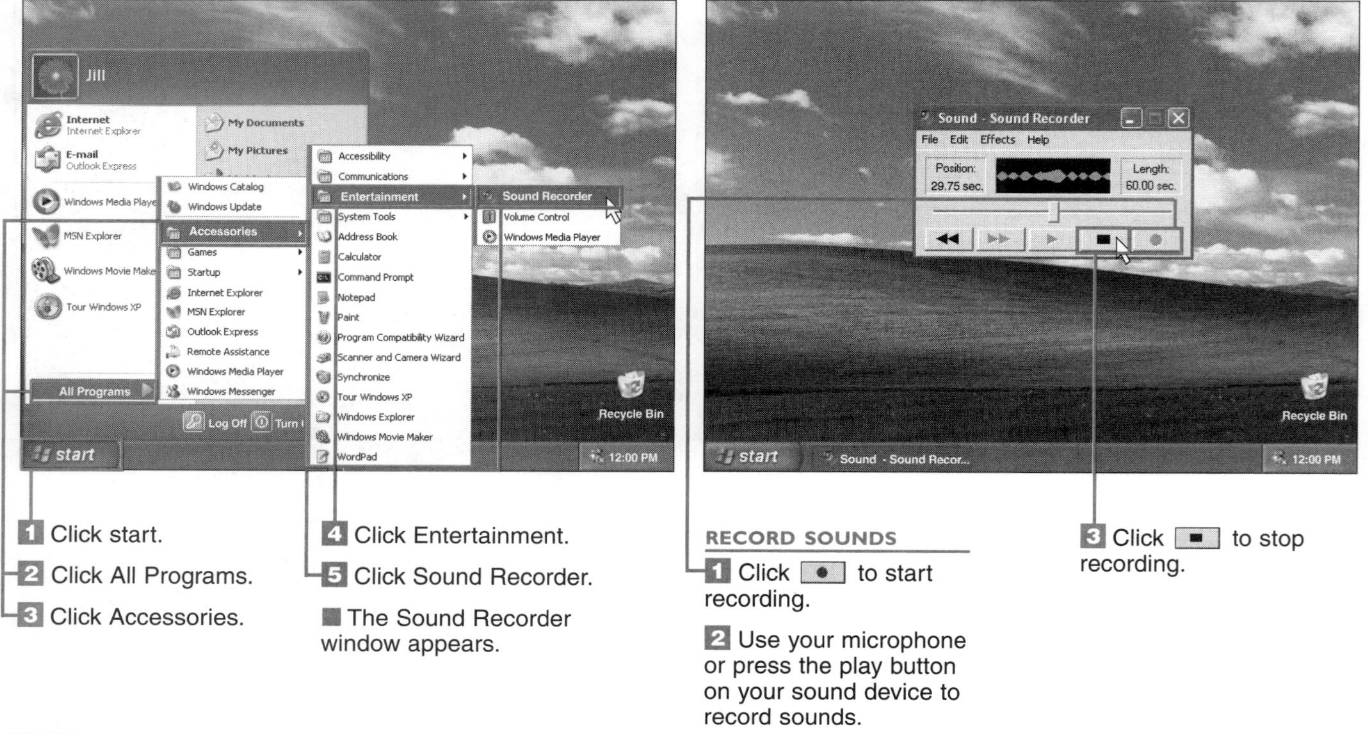

1 Click start.

2 Click All Programs.

3 Click Accessories.

4 Click Entertainment.

5 Click Sound Recorder.

■ The Sound Recorder window appears.

RECORD SOUNDS

1 Click ● to start recording.

2 Use your microphone or press the play button on your sound device to record sounds.

3 Click ■ to stop recording.

How do I save my recording?

✔ In the Sound Recorder window, click the File menu and select Save As to save your recording as a file on your computer. Type a name for the recording and click the Save button. To open a saved recording, select the File menu and click Open. Then select the recording you want to open and click the Open button.

How can I begin a new recording?

✔ In the Sound Recorder window, choose the File menu and then select New.

Can I change the playback volume?

✔ Yes. See page 286 for information about adjusting the volume on your computer.

Can I change the recording volume?

✔ In the Sound Recorder window, the green line shows the volume level of your recording. If the green line barely moves, you should increase the recording volume. If the green line reaches the top and bottom of the box, you can decrease the recording volume. To adjust the recording volume, click the Edit menu and then select Audio Properties. In the Sound recording area, click the Volume button. Then adjust the volume slider for the sound device you are recording from.

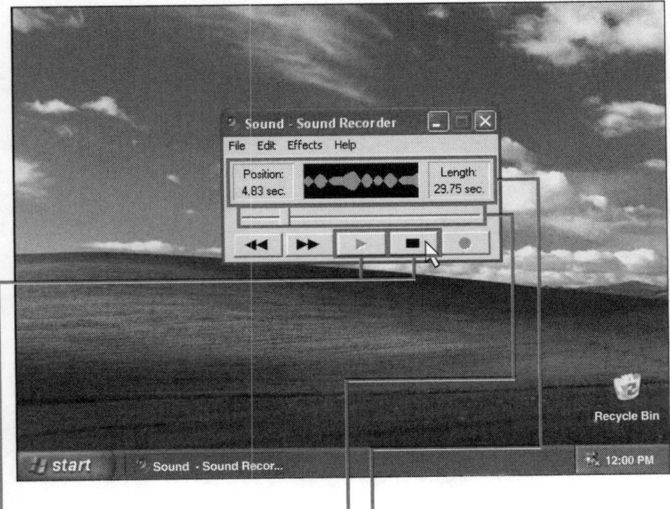

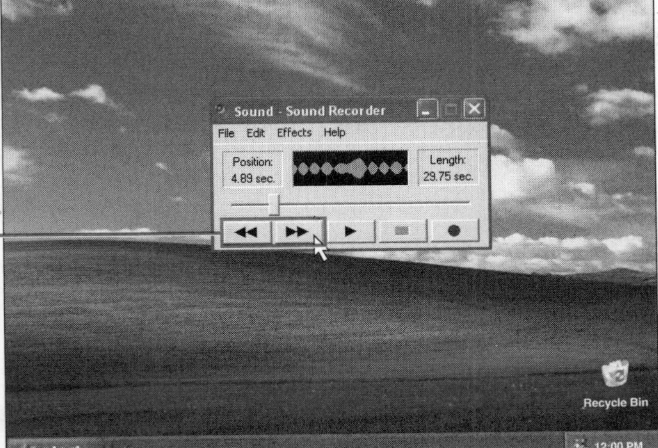

PLAY A RECORDING

1 Click ▶ to play a recording.

2 Click ■ to stop playing the recording at any time.

■ This area indicates the current position in the recording and the total length of the recording.

■ The slider (▯) displays the current position in the recording.

3 Click one of these buttons to move to the beginning or end of the recording.

◀◀ Move to beginning

▶▶ Move to end

Note: You can drag the slider (▯) to move to a specific position in the recording.

CONTINUED

USING SOUND RECORDER (CONTINUED)

Sound Recorder has several sound effects you can use to change your recording. You can adjust the volume of your recording to make it louder or softer. You can also speed up your recording to create a chipmunk effect or slow down the recording to create a spooky and mysterious effect. You may also want to add an echo to your recording or play the recording backwards.

Sound Recorder allows you to insert another sound file into an existing recording. You can choose the exact position in a recording where you want to insert the other sound file. The sound file you insert will not replace any part of the original recording.

Inserting a sound file into an existing recording lets you create one sound file containing your favorite sounds. For example, you can create a Halloween sound file by inserting howls and screams into a recording of spooky music.

There are many sound files available on the Internet that you can insert into another recording. Sound Recorder can only work with files in the Wave format. Wave files have the .wav file extension.

USING SOUND RECORDER (CONTINUED)

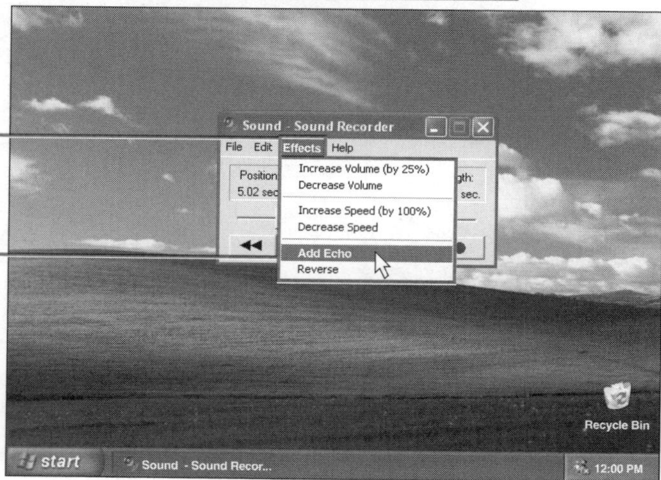

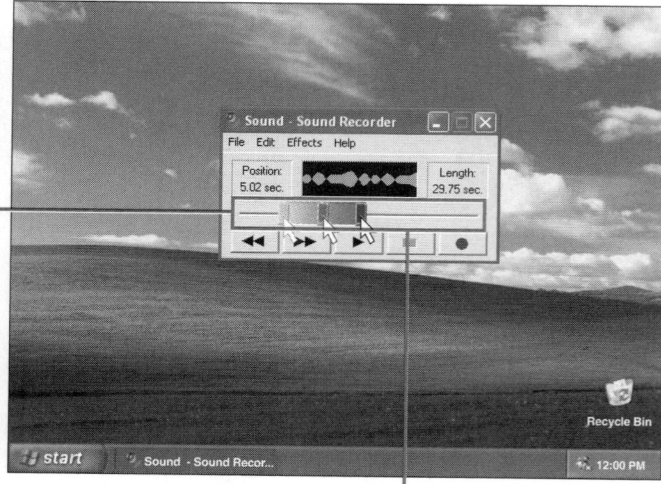

ADD SOUND EFFECTS

1 Click Effects to add a sound effect to a recording.

2 Click the sound effect you want to use.

■ You can repeat steps 1 and 2 for each sound effect you want to use.

INSERT A SOUND FILE

1 To specify where you want to insert a sound file into the current recording, position the mouse over the slider.

2 Drag the slider to where you want to insert a sound file.

How do I undo a mistake?

✔ In the Sound Recorder window, click the File menu and then select Revert. This command will undo all the changes you made since you last saved the recording. You should save your recording every time you make a successful change.

How can I mix two sound files together so both sounds play at the same time?

✔ Mixing two sound files together is useful if you are adding a music background to a voice recording. Position the slider (▯) in one sound file where you want the second sound file to start playing. On the Edit menu, click Mix with File. Select the sound file you want to mix with your current recording and then click the Open button.

Can I change the quality of a recording?

✔ Sound Recorder normally records sounds in Radio Quality. You may want to record sounds in CD Quality to improve the recording quality or in Telephone Quality to reduce the file size. To record sounds using a different quality, click the File menu and then select Properties. Then click the Convert Now button. Click the Name area and then select the quality you want to use.

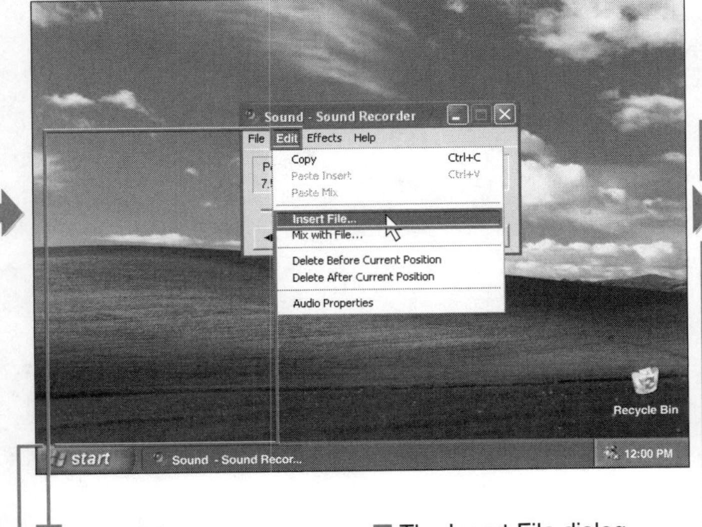

3 Click Edit.

4 Click Insert File.

■ The Insert File dialog box appears.

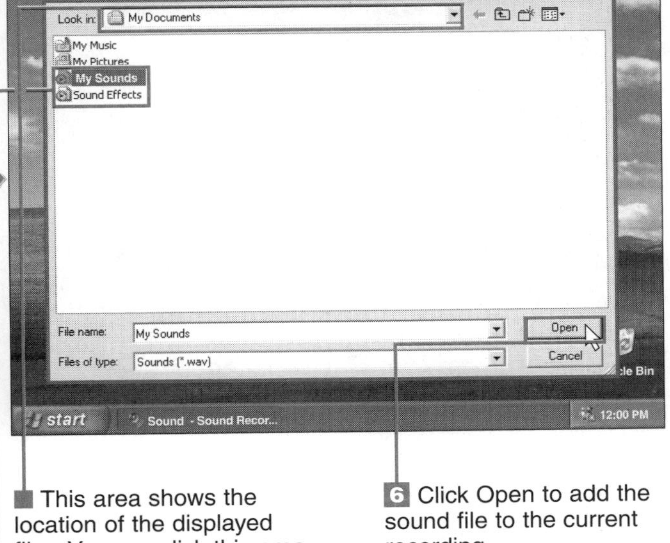

■ This area shows the location of the displayed files. You can click this area to change the location.

5 Click the sound file you want to insert.

6 Click Open to add the sound file to the current recording.

PLAY GAMES

Windows includes several games that you can play on your own or with people on the Internet. Games are a fun way to improve your mouse skills and hand-eye coordination.

You can play single-player card games, including Solitaire, Spider Solitaire and FreeCell. Minesweeper, Hearts and Pinball are other games you can play on your own.

Windows also offers games, such as Backgammon, Checkers, Reversi and Spades, which you can play on the Internet. When you select an Internet game, a dialog box appears, displaying information about playing games on the Internet. Windows automatically sends your computer ID and information about your system to the MSN Gaming Zone Web site to help administer the game.

When playing a game on the Internet, Windows matches you with other players. You can chat with the other players by sending messages such as "It's your turn" or "Play again?".

The games included with Windows are an introduction to the types of games you can play in Windows. You can obtain additional games at computer stores or on the Internet.

PLAY GAMES

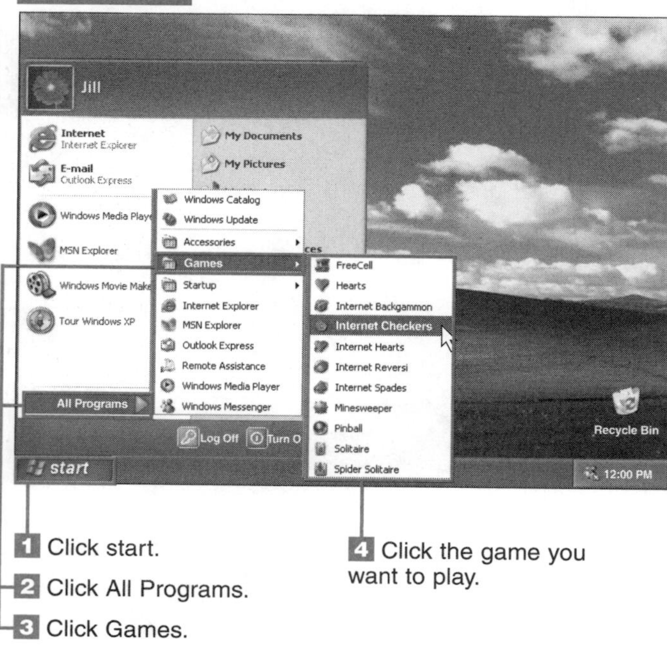

1 Click start.

2 Click All Programs.

3 Click Games.

4 Click the game you want to play.

■ If you selected an Internet game, a dialog box appears that displays information about playing games on the Internet.

Note: If you selected a non-Internet game, the game appears. Skip to step 8.

5 Click Play to have Windows match you with other players from around the world and start the game.

Note: If you are not currently connected to the Internet, a dialog box appears that allows you to connect.

The Games option does not appear on the All Programs menu. What is wrong?

✔ The Games component may not have been installed when you installed Windows on your computer. You can add the Games component as you would add any Windows component to your computer. To add Windows components, see page 540.

How can I learn how to play a game?

✔ You can press the F1 key to display help information in a game.

How do I start a new game?

✔ When playing most games on your own, you can press the F2 key to start a new session. When you finish playing a session of Hearts, a new session starts automatically. When playing an Internet game, you can select the Game menu and then click Find New Opponent(s) to start a new session.

Where can I find other games to play on the Internet?

✔ The MSN Gaming Zone Web site at zone.msn.com provides many games you can play on the Internet.

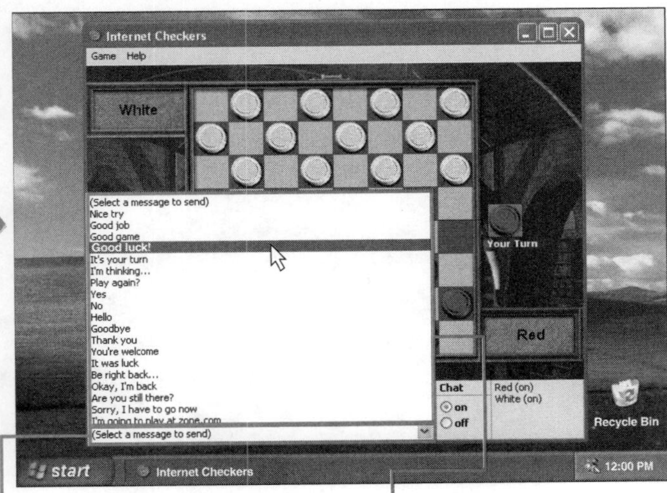

■ A window appears, displaying the game. In this example, the Internet Checkers window appears.

6 To send a message to your opponent, click this area to display a list of messages that you can send.

7 Click the message you want to send.

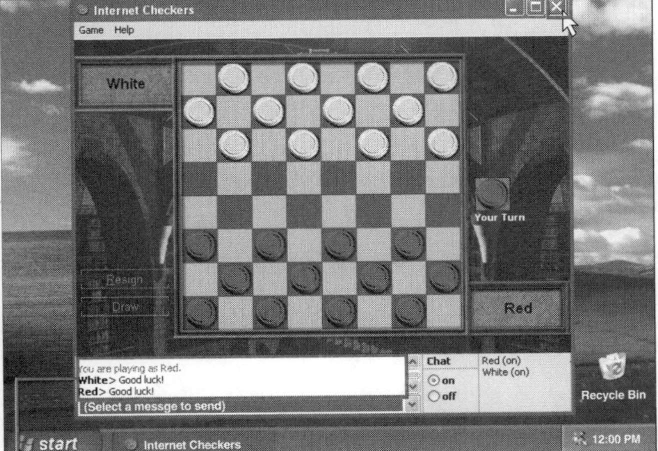

■ This area displays the message you sent, the ongoing conversation and information about the current game.

8 When you finish playing the game, click ☒ to close the window.

■ A message may appear, confirming that you want to leave the game. Click Yes to leave the game.

INSTALL A GAME CONTROLLER

You can install a game controller on your computer. A game controller is a device, such as a joystick or gamepad, that allows you to interact with a game.

A game controller allows you to easily control the direction of movement in a game, such as forward, backward or at an angle. You can use a mouse instead of a game controller in many games, but the greater control that a game controller offers can enhance games such as flight simulators.

Before installing a game controller, you should connect the controller to your computer. A game controller can connect to a game port or a USB port on your computer.

Windows provides a list of popular types of game controllers. You can select your game controller from this list. Windows then chooses the appropriate driver for the controller you select. A driver is software that allows Windows to communicate with your game controller.

If your game controller has a rudder or pedals, you should activate the rudder or pedals so you can use them when playing games. Rudders and pedals are devices that add more features to the controller.

INSTALL A GAME CONTROLLER

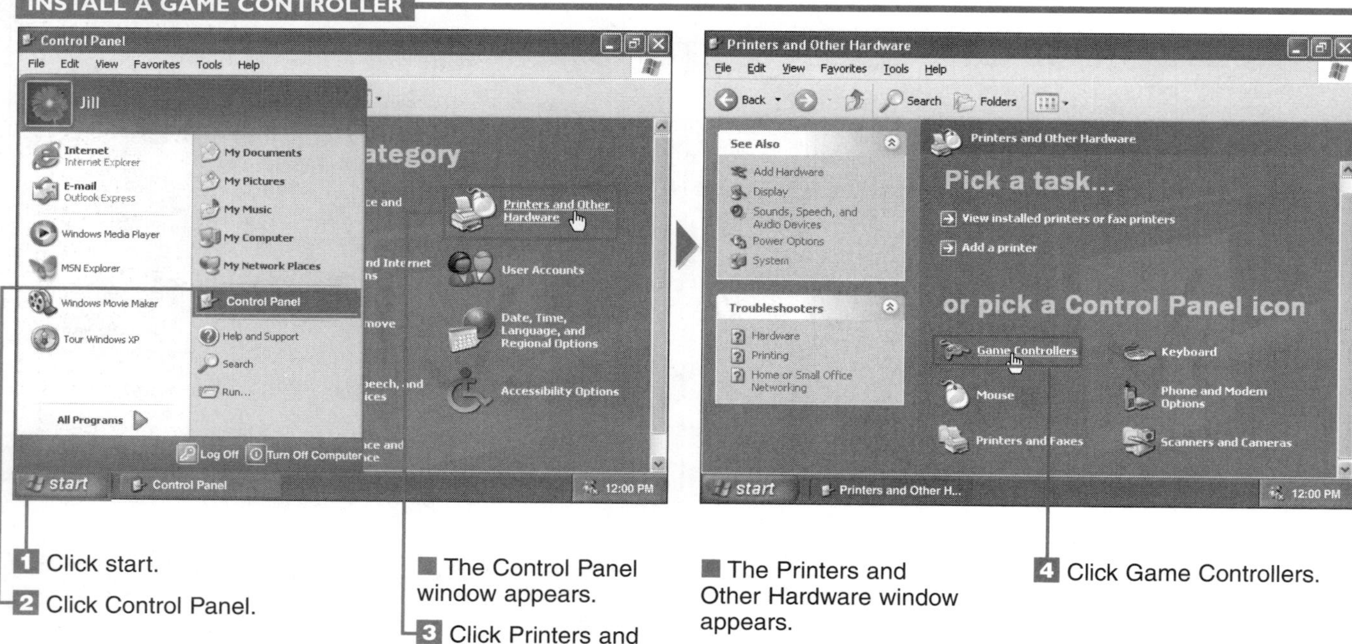

1 Click start.

2 Click Control Panel.

■ The Control Panel window appears.

3 Click Printers and Other Hardware.

■ The Printers and Other Hardware window appears.

4 Click Game Controllers.

My game controller does not appear in the list. What should I do?

✔ You can use the installation disk that came with the game controller to install the controller. Consult the manufacturer's instructions for information on how to install the controller using the disk.

Can I install a game controller that does not appear in the list if I do not have an installation disk?

✔ You can try choosing a game controller in the list that closely resembles your controller. You can also click the Custom button in the Add Game Controller dialog box to specify the features of your controller. The name you specify for the controller will appear in the list of available game controllers.

Do I have to install a Plug and Play game controller?

✔ No. After you physically connect a Plug and Play game controller to your computer, Windows will usually automatically detect and install the game controller for you. Windows will ask you for any information required to install the game controller.

How do I test my game controller?

✔ In the Game Controllers dialog box, click the controller and then click the Properties button. A dialog box appears, allowing you to test the controller. If the controller does not function properly during the test, click the Settings tab and then click the Calibrate button to adjust the controller's settings.

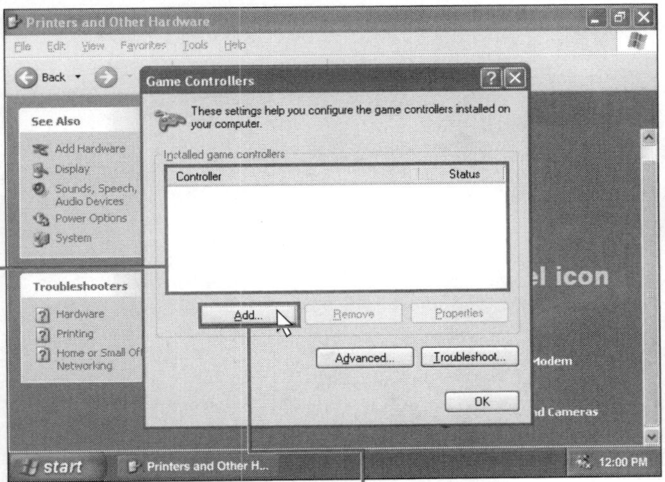

■ The Game Controllers dialog box appears.

■ This area displays any game controllers installed on your computer.

5 Click Add to install a new game controller.

■ The Add Game Controller dialog box appears.

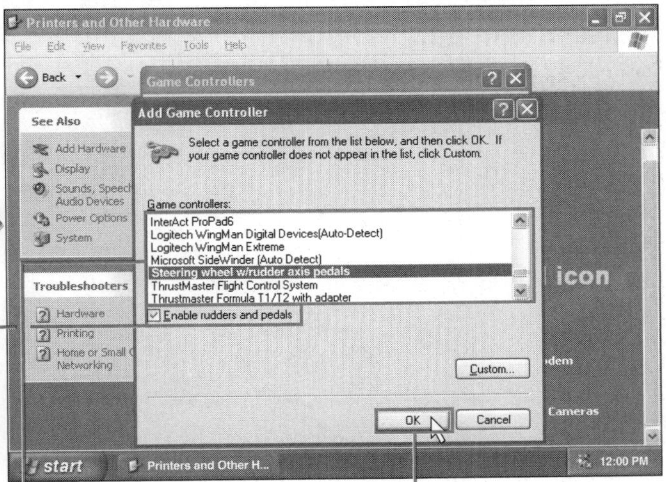

6 Click the game controller you want to install.

7 If your game controller has a rudder or pedals, click this option to activate the rudder or pedals (☐ changes to ☑).

8 Click OK to install the game controller.

■ The game controller will appear in the Game Controllers dialog box.

CHANGE THE AUTOPLAY PROPERTIES OF A CD OR DVD DRIVE

You can change the AutoPlay properties of a CD or DVD drive to specify an action you want Windows to take when you insert a disc into the drive.

When changing the AutoPlay properties of a CD or DVD drive, you must first select a content type. This allows you to specify the type of disc you want Windows to handle differently, such as a disc that contains pictures, music files or a DVD movie.

Once you have selected a content type, you can specify whether you want Windows to perform a specific action or prompt you to choose an action each time you insert a disc containing the content type.

If you choose to have Windows perform a specific action, you can select the action from a list. The available actions depend on the content type you selected. For example, the Music files content type displays options that allow you to have Windows automatically play music files in Media Player or open a folder so you can view the files.

If you choose to have Windows prompt you to select an action, a dialog box will appear displaying the available actions each time you insert a disc containing the content type.

CHANGE THE AUTOPLAY PROPERTIES OF A CD OR DVD DRIVE

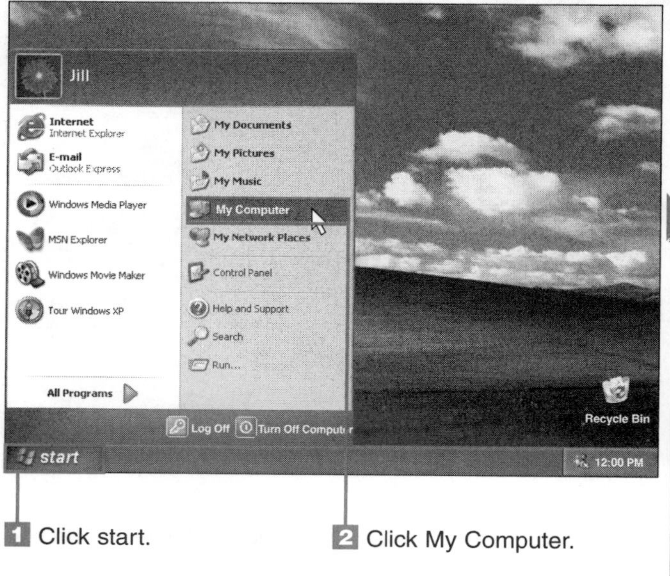

1 Click start.

2 Click My Computer.

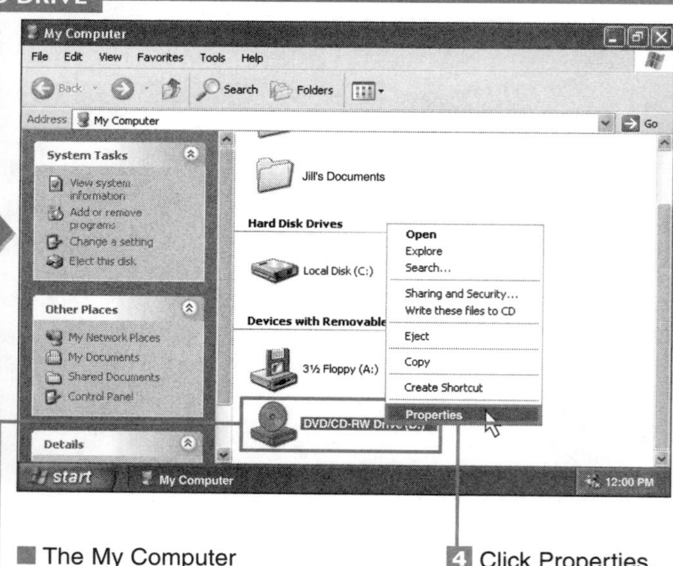

■ The My Computer window appears.

3 Right-click the CD or DVD drive you want to change the AutoPlay properties for. A menu appears.

4 Click Properties.

How can I quickly reset the AutoPlay properties for a content type?

✔ You can click the Restore Defaults button to quickly return to the default AutoPlay settings for the current content type. If the Restore Defaults button is not available, the content type already uses the default settings.

Can I stop Windows from performing an action for a specific disc?

✔ If you do not want Windows to take any action for a specific disc, you can hold down the Shift key while you insert the disc into the CD or DVD drive.

Why did a new AutoPlay action appear in the list?

✔ When you install a new program that allows you to work with a specific content type, such as a program that plays music CDs, Windows may add a new action for the program to the list of AutoPlay actions.

I specified that I wanted Windows to prompt me to choose an action, but my disc started playing automatically. What is wrong?

✔ Some discs, such as program installation discs, contain programs that may start automatically when you insert the discs into a CD or DVD drive, regardless of the AutoPlay properties of the drive.

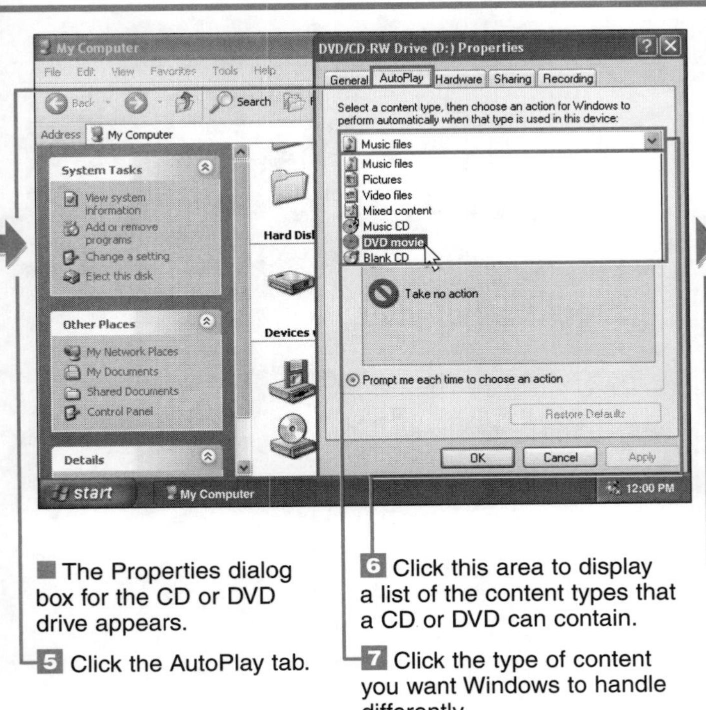

■ The Properties dialog box for the CD or DVD drive appears.

5 Click the AutoPlay tab.

6 Click this area to display a list of the content types that a CD or DVD can contain.

7 Click the type of content you want Windows to handle differently.

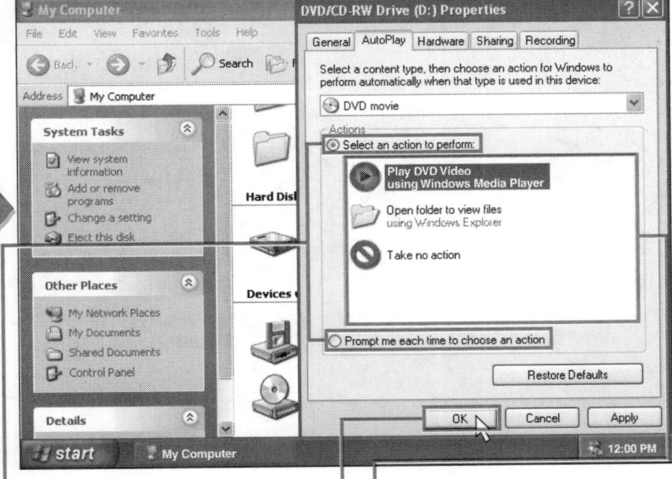

8 Click an option to specify if you want Windows to perform a specific action or prompt you to choose an action when you insert a CD or DVD containing the content type you selected (○ changes to ◉).

9 If you chose to have Windows perform a specific action, click the action you want Windows to perform.

Note: To customize another content type, repeat steps 6 to 9.

10 Click OK.

PLAY MEDIA FILES

Windows Media Player allows you to play many types of sound and video files on your computer. You can obtain sound and video files on the Internet and purchase sound and video files at computer stores. You need a computer with sound capabilities to play sound on your computer.

You can play sound and video files stored anywhere on your computer or listed in the Media Library. The Media Library organizes your sound and video files into categories. You can browse through the categories in the Media Library to locate the media file you want to play.

When you play a video file, the video automatically appears on the Now Playing tab in the Windows Media Player window. When you play a sound file, you can listen to the sound while you view a graphical representation of the sound on the Now Playing tab. While a media file is playing, Windows Media Player indicates how much of the file is left to play.

Windows Media Player lets you control how a file plays. You can play, pause and stop a file. You can also turn off the sound or adjust the volume of a file.

PLAY MEDIA FILES

1 Double-click the sound or video file you want to play.

Note: You can play sound or video files listed in the Media Library or stored on your desktop or in another folder. To locate a file in the Media Library, see page 314.

■ If you selected a video file, the video appears on the Now Playing tab.

Note: If you selected a sound file, the sound plays. You can click the Now Playing tab to display a graphical representation for the sound.

■ The name of the file and the amount of time the file will play are highlighted in this area.

Can I change the audio and video settings used to play media files?

✔ Yes. Select the Now Playing tab and then click . An area appears in the bottom left corner of the Now Playing tab. Click to select the type of audio and video settings you want to change. To hide the area, click again.

I changed the volume using the volume slider ( ). Why didn't I get the result I expected?

✔ The volume used in Windows Media Player also depends on the computer's master volume setting. For information about changing the computer's master volume setting, see page 286.

How do I view a video using the entire screen?

✔ To use the entire screen to view a video that is currently playing, click . To once again display the video in a window, press the Esc key.

Can I display Windows Media Player in a smaller size?

✔ Yes. You can change the size and appearance of Windows Media Player by switching from the full mode to the skin mode. The full mode allows you to access all the features that Windows Media Player provides. You can click to switch to the skin mode. The skin mode takes up less room on your screen, but offers fewer features. You can click to return to the full mode at any time.

■ This slider ( ) indicates the progress of the file.

2 Click one of these buttons to pause ( ) or stop ( ) the play of the file. When you pause or stop the play of a file, changes to .

3 Click to resume the play of the file.

4 Click to turn off the sound (changes to).

■ You can click to once again turn on the sound.

5 To adjust the volume, drag this slider ( ) left or right to decrease or increase the volume.

6 When you finish playing sound or video files, click ✕ to close the Windows Media Player window.

PLAY A MUSIC CD

You can use your computer to play music CDs while you work. You need a computer with sound capabilities and a CD-ROM drive to play music CDs.

If you are connected to the Internet when you play a music CD, Windows Media Player attempts to download information about the CD from the Internet, such as the name of the artist and the name of each song. If you are not connected to the Internet or the information is unavailable, Windows Media Player displays the track number of each song instead. After the information is downloaded, Windows will recognize the CD each time it is inserted and display the information for the CD.

Windows Media Player has many of the same controls as a standard CD player. You can use controls to play, pause and stop a CD. You can also use controls to play the previous or next song on the CD.

Once a CD starts playing, you can continue to work with other programs on your computer. Playing a CD should have very little effect on the performance of your other programs.

PLAY A MUSIC CD

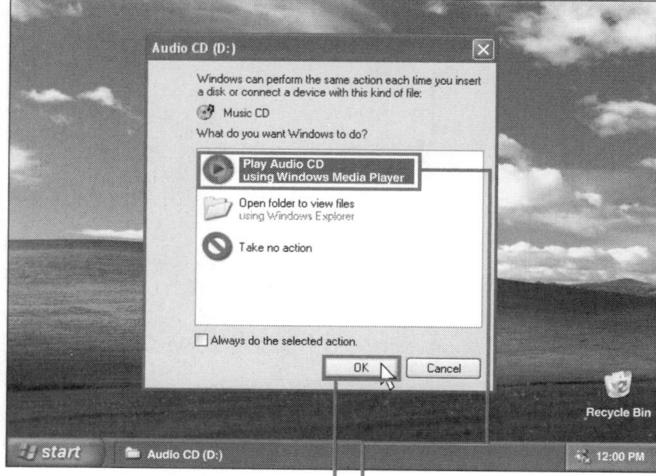

1 Insert a music CD into your CD-ROM drive.

■ The Audio CD dialog box appears, asking what you want Windows to do.

2 Click this option to play the music CD.

3 Click OK.

■ The Windows Media Player window appears and the CD begins to play.

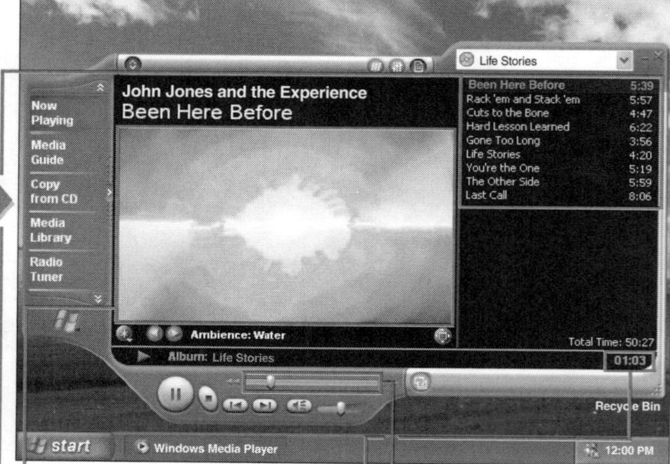

■ This area displays a graphical representation of the song that is currently playing.

■ This area displays a list of songs on the CD and the amount of time each song will play. The song that is currently playing is highlighted.

■ This slider (slider icon) indicates the progress of the current song.

■ This area displays the amount of time the current song has been playing.

Is there another way to start Windows Media Player?

✔ Click start, choose All Programs and then select Windows Media Player.

Can I change the displayed graphical representation for a song?

✔ Yes. Position the mouse over the top of the Windows Media Player window, click View and then select Visualizations. Choose a type of graphical representation and then click the graphical representation you want to display.

How do I hide the playlist displayed on the Now Playing tab?

✔ Click (playlist button) to hide the playlist. To redisplay the playlist, click (playlist button) again.

How can I listen to a music CD privately?

✔ You can listen to a music CD privately by plugging headphones into the jack at the front of your CD-ROM drive or into your speakers. If your CD-ROM drive or speakers do not have a headphone jack, you can plug the headphones into the back of your computer where the speakers plug in.

I am not connected to the Internet. How can I have the playlist display song titles?

✔ Right-click a song in the playlist and select Edit from the menu that appears. Then type the title of the song and press the Enter key to save the information.

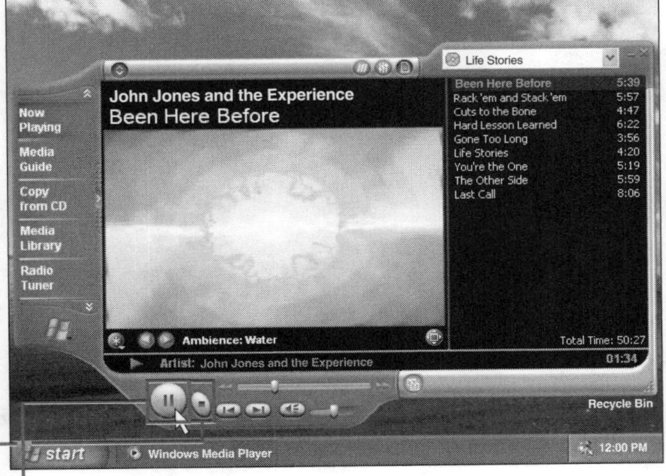

4 Click (pause) to pause the play of the CD ((pause) changes to (play)).

5 Click (stop) to stop the play of the CD.

■ You can click (play) to resume the play of the CD.

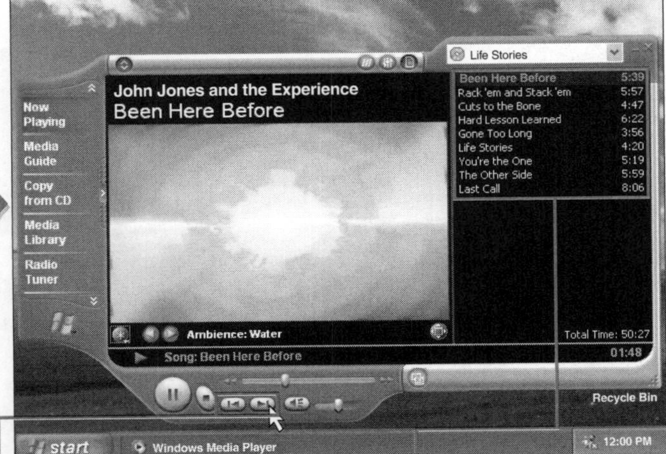

6 Click one of the following options to move through the songs on the CD.

(previous) Play the previous song

(next) Play the next song

7 To play a specific song in the list, double-click the song.

CONTINUED

PLAY A MUSIC CD (CONTINUED)

When playing a music CD, Windows will automatically play the songs in the order in which they appear on the CD. You can choose to have Windows play the songs in random order.

You can also choose to temporarily mute the sound or adjust the volume of the sound to suit your needs. If you are using headphones that are plugged into your computer or speakers, your CD-ROM drive or speakers may have a volume control that allows you to adjust the volume. The volume also depends on the computer's volume setting. For more information about adjusting the volume on your computer, see page 286.

You can view additional information about the CD you are playing by viewing the contents of the Copy from CD tab in the Windows Media Player window. This tab also allows you to copy songs from a music CD to your computer so you can play the songs at any time without having to insert the CD into your computer. For information about copying songs from a music CD, see page 324.

PLAY A MUSIC CD (CONTINUED)

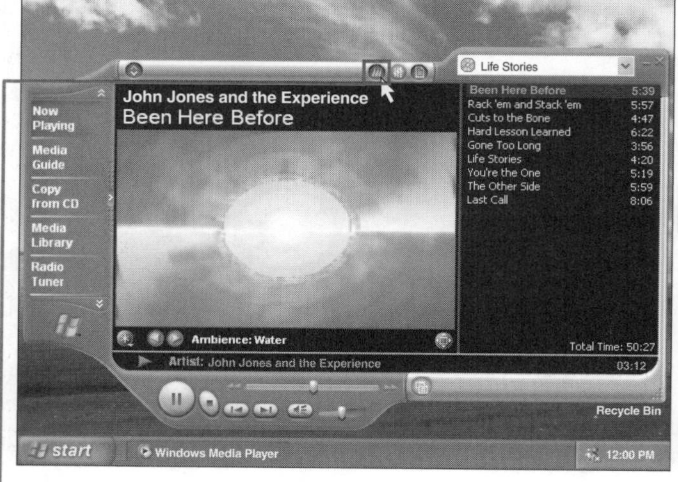

8 Click to play the songs on the CD in random order.

■ You can click to once again play the songs on the CD in order.

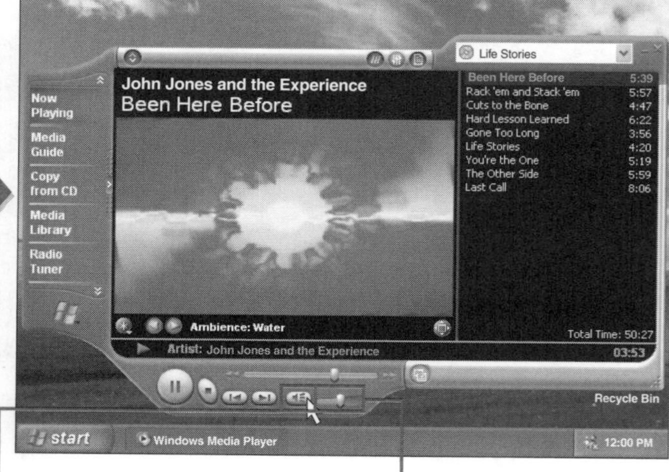

9 Click to turn off the sound (changes to).

■ You can click to once again turn on the sound.

10 To adjust the volume of the sound, drag this slider ( ) left or right to decrease or increase the volume.

Can I stop a song from playing when I play a CD?

✔ Yes. Right-click the song you do not want to play and select Disable Selected Tracks from the menu that appears. To once again play the song when the CD plays, right-click the song and choose Enable Selected Tracks.

Can I have a CD play continuously?

✔ Yes. Position the mouse over the top of the Windows Media Player window, click Play and then select Repeat. Windows will remember this setting each time you play a CD. You can click the Play menu and select Repeat again to turn off the option.

How can I find more information about the current CD?

✔ If you are connected to the Internet, select the Copy from CD tab and then click the Album Details button to display information such as a review of the CD and a biography of the artist. You may need to resize the area to view the information. To do so, position the mouse over the border (↖ changes to ↕) and then drag the border. You can click the Hide Details button to hide the information.

11 Click the Copy from CD tab to view more information about the songs on the CD.

■ This area displays information about the songs on the CD, including the name of each song and the name of the artist.

■ To once again display the graphical representation of the current song, click the Now Playing tab.

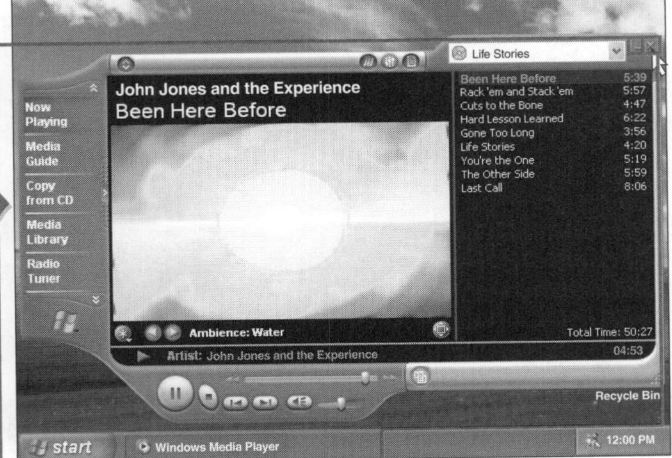

■ To perform other tasks on your computer while you are playing the CD, you can click ▬ to minimize the Windows Media Player window.

Note: To redisplay the Windows Media Player window, click the button for the window on the taskbar.

12 When you finish listening to the CD, click ✖ to close the Windows Media Player window.

PLAY A DVD MOVIE

Windows Media Player allows you to play DVD movies on your computer. You need a computer with sound capabilities and a DVD drive to play DVD movies.

Before you can play a DVD movie, you must have a software or hardware decoder that is compatible with Windows XP installed on your computer. If you do not already have a decoder, you can purchase a decoder from a third-party manufacturer. You can find decoders that work with Windows Media Player at www.intervideo.com and www.gocyberlink.com.

When you play a DVD movie, Windows Media Player displays a list of the titles stored on the DVD. Each title on a DVD represents a section of content, such as the movie or a special feature. Each title can contain one or more chapters. A chapter is usually a scene or sequence. You may be able to use the list of titles and chapters to browse through the contents of a DVD.

Windows Media Player has many of the same controls as a standard DVD player. You can use the controls to play, pause and stop a movie. You can also use controls to play the previous or next chapter in a title and adjust the volume.

PLAY A DVD MOVIE

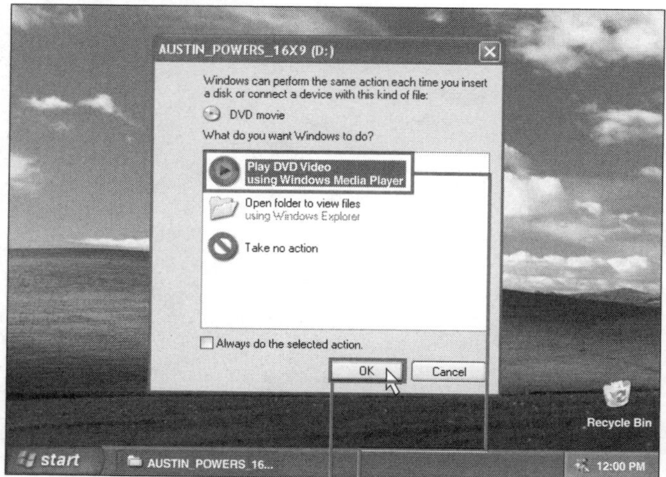

1 Insert a DVD into your DVD drive.

■ A dialog box appears, asking what you want Windows to do.

2 Click this option to play the DVD using Windows Media Player.

3 Click OK.

■ The Windows Media Player window appears.

■ The DVD begins to play in this area. A main menu may appear, displaying links you can click to play the movie or access special features.

■ This area displays a list of titles on the DVD. To display the chapters in a title, click the plus sign (+) beside the title.

4 To play the movie, double-click the title that will play the movie.

Note: The title that will play the movie is often Title 1.

When I inserted a DVD, the dialog box that lets me play the DVD did not appear. What should I do?

✔ You can start Windows Media Player to watch the DVD. Click start, select All Programs and then click Windows Media Player. To start the movie, click ▾ in the top right corner of the Windows Media Player window and then select the DVD option from the list.

How can I redisplay the main menu for a DVD?

✔ Position the mouse over the top of the Windows Media Player window and select the View menu. Click DVD Features and then choose Top Menu or Title Menu. Redisplaying the main menu is useful when you want to access the special features included on the DVD.

How can I view a DVD movie using the entire screen?

✔ To use the entire screen to view a DVD movie that is currently playing, click ▣ below the movie area. To once again display the movie in the Windows Media Player window, press the Esc key.

How can I display subtitles or closed captioning for a DVD?

✔ Position the mouse over the top of the Windows Media Player window and select the View menu. Click DVD Features, select Subtitles and Captions and then click the option you want to display. Some DVDs do not support these features.

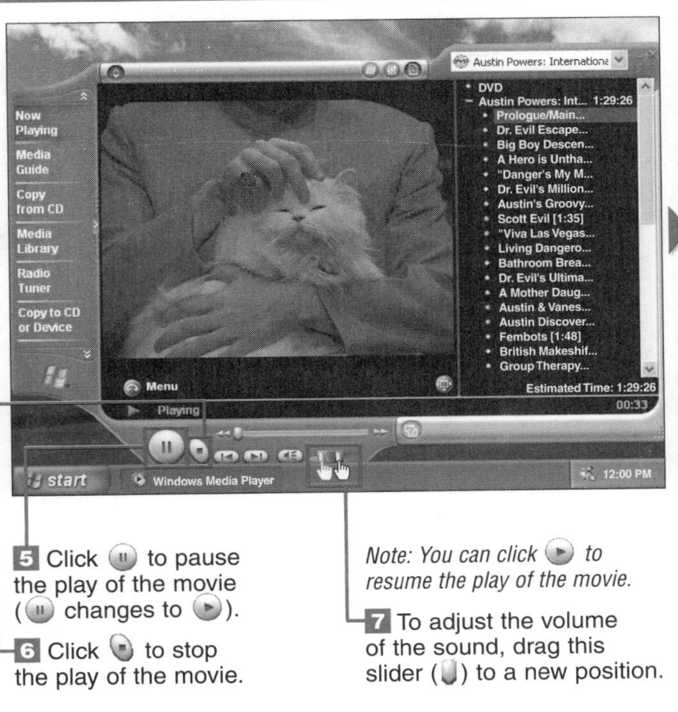

5 Click ⏸ to pause the play of the movie (⏸ changes to ▶).

6 Click ■ to stop the play of the movie.

Note: You can click ▶ to resume the play of the movie.

7 To adjust the volume of the sound, drag this slider (▯) to a new position.

■ The title or chapter that is currently playing is highlighted.

8 To move through the chapters in the current title, click a button to play the previous (⏮) or next (⏭) chapter.

■ To quickly play a specific chapter, you can also double-click the chapter.

9 When you finish playing the DVD, click ✖ to close the Windows Media Player window.

USING THE MEDIA GUIDE

The Media Guide is a Web page that is updated daily to provide you with access to the latest music, movies and videos on the Internet. You must have a connection to the Internet to use the Media Guide.

The Media Guide organizes information into various categories such as Music, Entertainment, Business, News and Sports to help you quickly find information of interest.

The Media Guide includes links that you can select to display information on various topics. Selecting a link may display additional information in the Media Guide, open a Web page in your Web browser or play media files such as movie clips or music videos. You can play all media files accessed through the Media Guide in Windows Media Player.

Keep in mind that the information the Media Guide contains is hosted by the WindowsMedia.com Web site and changes daily. This means that the Media Guide shown below may look different than the Media Guide displayed on your screen.

USING THE MEDIA GUIDE

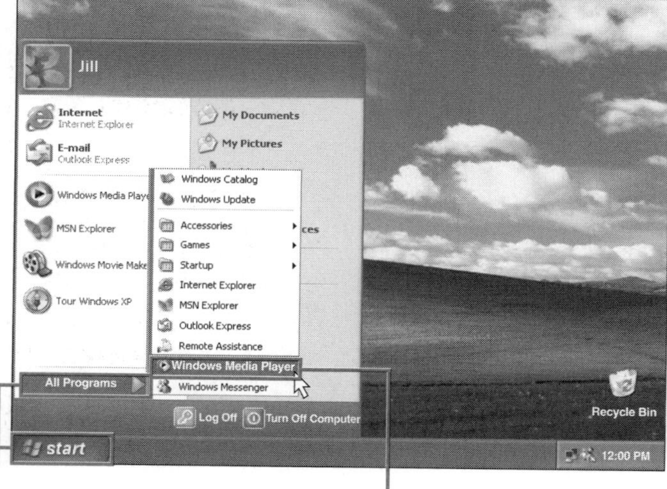

■ You must be connected to the Internet to use the Media Guide. To connect to the Internet, see page 430.

1 Click start.

2 Click All Programs.

3 Click Windows Media Player.

■ The Windows Media Player window appears.

4 Click the Media Guide tab.

■ This area displays the Media Guide, which is a Web page that is updated daily to provide access to the latest music, movies and information on the Internet.

Why does the Media Guide appear each time I start Windows Media Player?

✔ If you are connected to the Internet when you start Windows Media Player, the Media Guide automatically appears. To avoid having to wait for the Media Guide to load each time you start Windows Media Player, select the Tools menu and click Options. In the Options dialog box, click the Player tab and then select the Start player in Media Guide option (☑ changes to ☐).

Can I search for specific information in the Media Guide?

✔ Yes. In the Web Search box, type the information you want to find, such as the name of an artist, and then click Go. A window will appear, displaying links to Web pages that provide information about the topic you specified in your search.

Why are different speeds listed next to a media file in the Media Guide?

✔ These are the connection speeds that you can select to download and play the media file. If you have a high-speed Internet connection, such as a cable modem, you can select a higher speed. If you have a slower Internet connection or if you are not concerned about the playback quality, you can select a slower speed.

■ The Media Guide contains links that you can click to display information or play media files such as music videos or movie clips. The mouse ↖ changes to 👆 when over a link.

5 Click a link of interest.

■ In this example, information on the topic you selected appears.

■ You can repeat step 5 to browse through additional information or play other media files.

6 When you finish using the Media Guide, click ✕ to close the Windows Media Player window.

USING THE MEDIA LIBRARY

You can use the Media Library to organize and work with media files, including sound and video files. The Media Library displays the names of media files on your computer and links to featured radio stations. For information about listening to a radio station on the Internet, see page 318.

The Media Library allows you to search your computer for media files. By default, Windows will search all the available drives, but you can select a specific drive to search. If you want to search for files stored on a network drive, you can assign a drive letter to the drive to have it appear in the list of options. For information about assigning a drive letter to a network drive, see page 414. The length of the search depends on the number of files stored in the location you are searching.

You can obtain media files from many sources. The Media Guide provides access to the latest music, movies and videos on the Internet. For more information about the Media Guide, see page 312. There are also Web sites that offer sound and video files, such as earthstation1.com and www.themez.co.uk. Many computer stores offer collections of media files that you can purchase.

USING THE MEDIA LIBRARY

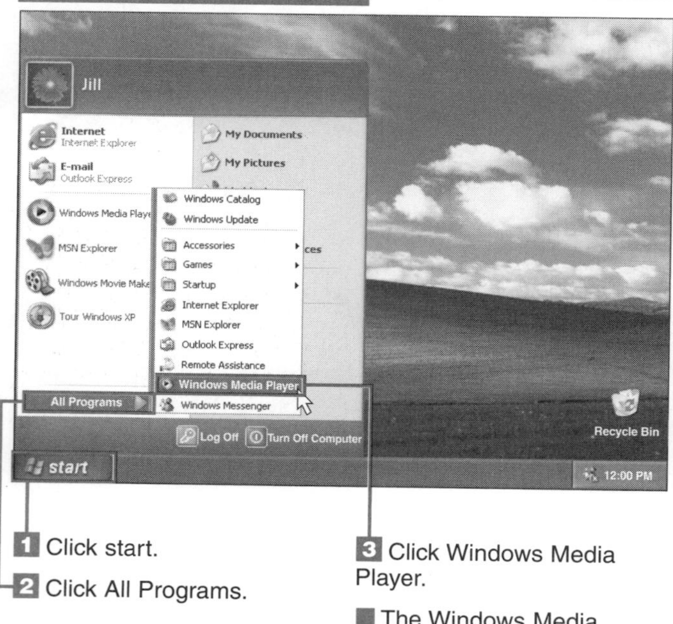

1 Click start.

2 Click All Programs.

3 Click Windows Media Player.

■ The Windows Media Player window appears.

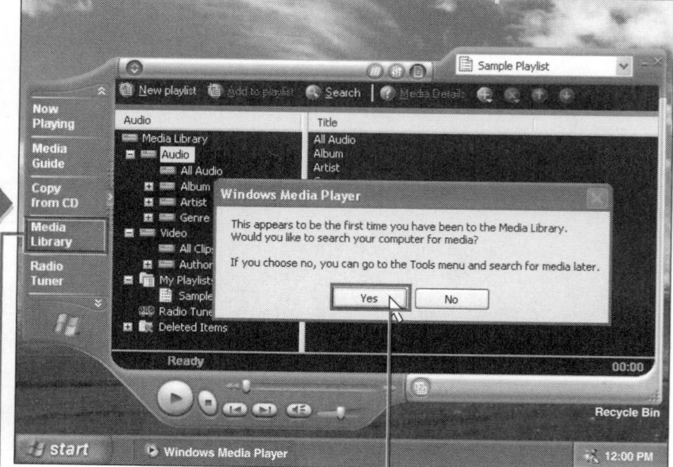

4 Click the Media Library tab.

■ The first time you visit the Media Library, a dialog box appears, asking if you want to search your computer for media files.

SEARCH COMPUTER FOR MEDIA FILES

5 Click Yes to search your computer for media files.

Note: If the dialog box does not appear, press the F3 key to search for media files.

Can I add a file or radio station that is currently playing to the Media Library?

✔ You may be able to add the file or radio station that is currently playing to the Media Library. Position the mouse over the top of the Windows Media Player window, click File, select Add to Media Library and then click Add Currently Playing Track.

How can I have Windows automatically add files I play to the Media Library?

✔ Position the mouse over the top of the Windows Media Player window, click Tools and choose Options. Select the Player tab and then click the Add items to Media Library when played option (☐ changes to ☑).

Can I add a song from a music CD to the Media Library?

✔ To add a song from a music CD to the Media Library, you must copy the song from the CD to your computer. For more information, see page 324.

Are there additional options I can use to search for media files?

✔ Yes. In the Search for Media Files dialog box, click the Advanced button to display an area that provides additional search options. For example, you can choose to have Windows skip small media files during the search or include system folders when searching.

■ The Search for Media Files dialog box appears.

■ This area indicates the drive that Windows will search for media files. You can click this area to change the drive.

■ To search a specific folder, you can click Browse to specify the folder.

6 Click Search to start the search.

■ Windows searches your computer for media files.

■ This area shows the progress of the search.

7 When the search is complete, click Close to close the dialog box.

8 Click Close to close the Search for Media Files dialog box.

CONTINUED

USING THE MEDIA LIBRARY (CONTINUED)

The Media Library organizes your media files into several categories. For example, sound files can be found in the All Audio, Album, Artist and Genre categories. The Radio Tuner Presets category displays radio stations that appear in the Featured Stations list on the Radio Tuner tab. Some categories contain subcategories. For example, the Artist category contains the names of artists. You can browse through categories to find the media file you want to play.

You can play a media file directly from the Media Library. To listen to a radio station that broadcasts over the Internet, you must first connect to the Internet.

The Media Library includes a category called My Playlists. You can add a new playlist to the My Playlists category. This is useful if you want to create a personalized playlist that contains media files you frequently play or if you want to group together sound and video files.

There is no limit to the number of media files you can add to a playlist, but you can only add files that are listed in the Media Library.

You can play all the media files in a playlist. The files play in the order they appear in the playlist.

USING THE MEDIA LIBRARY (CONTINUED)

VIEW MEDIA FILES

■ The Media Library organizes your media files into categories.

1 A category displaying a plus sign (⊞) contains hidden items. You can click the plus sign (⊞) beside a category to display its hidden items (⊞ changes to ⊟).

Note: To once again hide the items in a category, click the minus sign (⊟) beside the category.

2 Click a category that contains the media files of interest.

■ This area displays the media files in the category you selected.

3 To play a media file, double-click the file.

Note: For more information about playing media files, see page 304.

How can I search for a specific media file in the Media Library?

✔ On the Media Library tab, click the Search button. In the Search Media Library dialog box, type a word you want to search for and then click the Search button. When the search is complete, click the View Results button to close the dialog box and view a playlist that contains the results of the search.

Can I change the order in which media files play in a playlist?

✔ Yes. Click the playlist you want to change. Select a media file in the playlist and then click the up or down button to move the file up or down in the list.

How do I delete a playlist from the Media Library?

✔ Select the playlist you want to delete and then press the Delete key. Deleting a playlist will not remove the media files from the Media Library. Deleted playlists are stored in the Deleted Items category.

How do I delete a file from a playlist or the Media Library?

✔ Click the category or playlist that contains the file you want to delete. Then click the name of the file and press the Delete key. Deleting a file from a playlist or the Media Library does not delete the file from your computer.

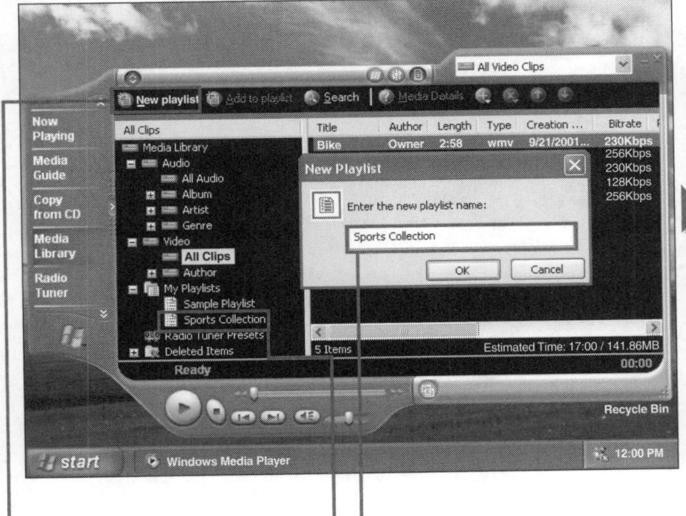

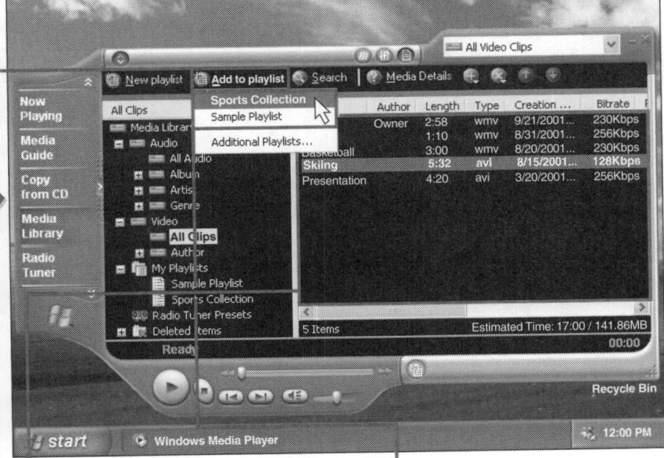

CREATE A PLAYLIST

1 Click New playlist.

■ The New Playlist dialog box appears.

2 Type a name for the playlist and then press the Enter key.

■ The new playlist appears in the My Playlists category.

3 To add a media file to a playlist, locate the file in Media Library and then click the file in this area.

4 Click Add to playlist.

5 Click the playlist to which you want to add the media file.

■ Windows adds the media file to the playlist.

Note: To play all the media files in a playlist, double-click the playlist.

LISTEN TO RADIO STATIONS ON THE INTERNET

You can use Windows Media Player to listen to radio stations from around the world that broadcast on the Internet. You need a computer with sound capabilities and an Internet connection to listen to radio stations on the Internet.

Before Windows Media Player plays a radio station on the Internet, the information from the radio station is partially transferred and temporarily stored in a section of memory on your computer, called a buffer. While the radio station plays, the information is continuously transferred from the Internet and is temporarily stored in the buffer. The buffer minimizes the interruptions to the broadcast playing on your computer. Interruptions are caused when the information transferring to your computer slows down or is disrupted.

When you play a radio station in Windows Media Player, the Microsoft Internet Explorer window opens behind Windows Media Player, displaying the Web page for the radio station. You may need to visit a radio station's Web site to play the radio station.

When listening to a radio station in Windows Media Player, you can adjust the radio station's volume or stop playing the radio station at any time.

LISTEN TO RADIO STATIONS ON THE INTERNET

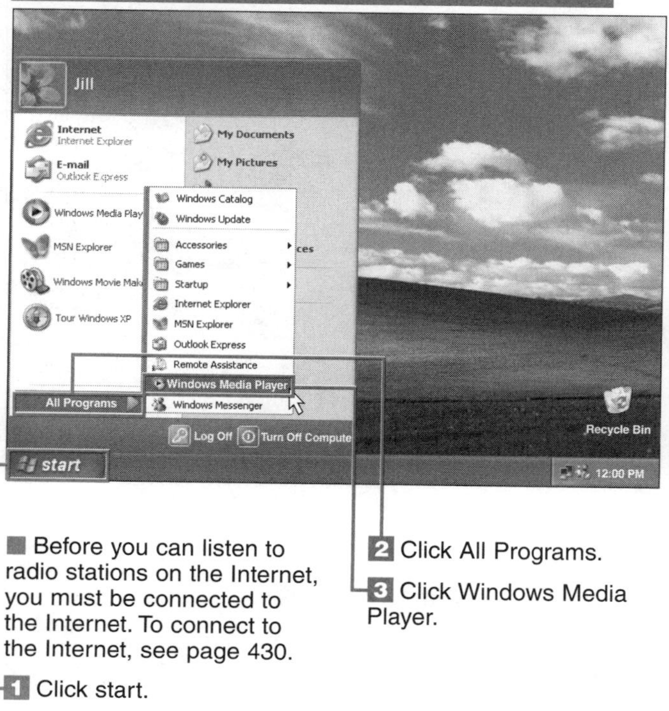

■ Before you can listen to radio stations on the Internet, you must be connected to the Internet. To connect to the Internet, see page 430.

1 Click start.

2 Click All Programs.

3 Click Windows Media Player.

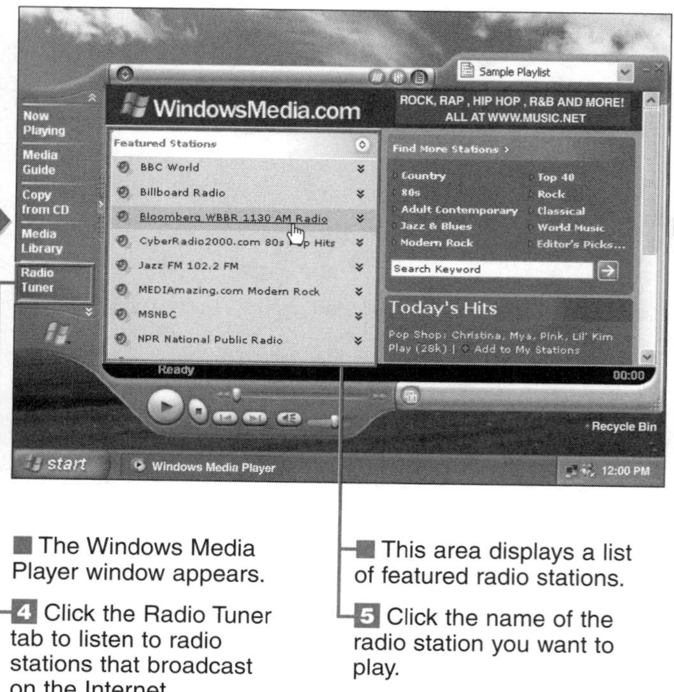

■ The Windows Media Player window appears.

4 Click the Radio Tuner tab to listen to radio stations that broadcast on the Internet.

■ This area displays a list of featured radio stations.

5 Click the name of the radio station you want to play.

How can I quickly return to a radio station I recently played?

✔ Click Recently Played Stations below the Featured Stations area to display a list of radio stations you recently played. To play a radio station in the list, click the radio station and then click Play. If the Play option is unavailable, click Visit Website to Play.

Can I browse the Web while listening to a radio station?

✔ Yes. You can use your Web browser to view Web pages while Windows Media Player plays a radio station. To browse the Web without losing the Web page for the radio station you are playing, you can open a new Web browser window. Click the File menu in the Web browser window, select New and then click Window.

Does the Radio Tuner tab display any other featured items?

✔ The Today's Hits area displays a list of featured radio programs. You can click Play below a program name to listen to the program.

Is there another way to adjust the volume of a radio station?

✔ Click start, select All Programs and choose Accessories. Select Entertainment and then click Volume Control to adjust your computer's volume setting. This setting affects how loud you can play the radio station using the volume slider on the Radio Tuner tab. For more information about your computer's volume setting, see page 286.

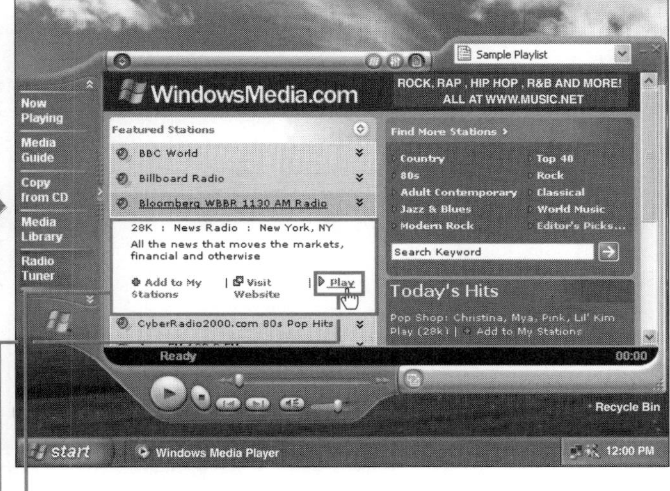

■ Information about the radio station you selected appears.

6 To listen to the radio station, click Play.

Note: If the Play option is not available, you can click Visit Website to Play to display the radio station's Web page and play the radio station.

■ After a moment, the radio station begins to play.

■ The Microsoft Internet Explorer window opens behind Windows Media Player, displaying the Web page for the radio station. To view the Web page, click the window's button on the taskbar.

7 To adjust the volume, drag the slider (▯) to decrease or increase the volume.

8 To stop playing the radio station at any time, click ▪.

CONTINUED

LISTEN TO RADIO STATIONS ON THE INTERNET (CONTINUED)

Windows Media Player allows you to search for specific radio stations that broadcast on the Internet.

There are several methods you can use to search for radio stations. Windows Media Player organizes radio stations into different music categories. You can choose a category of interest, such as modern rock or country.

You can also specify information about the radio station you want to find. For example, you can type a language, such as Spanish, to find a radio station that broadcasts in another language, or specify a location, such as Canada, to find a radio station in another country. You can also specify a call sign, such as CNN, or a frequency, such as 102.3.

When you find a radio station of interest, you can play the radio station. The Web page for the currently playing radio station appears behind the Windows Media Player window.

Keep in mind that the information the Radio Tuner tab contains is hosted by the WindowsMedia.com Web site and is frequently updated. This means the Radio Tuner tab shown below may look different than the Radio Tuner tab displayed on your screen.

LISTEN TO RADIO STATIONS ON THE INTERNET (CONTINUED)

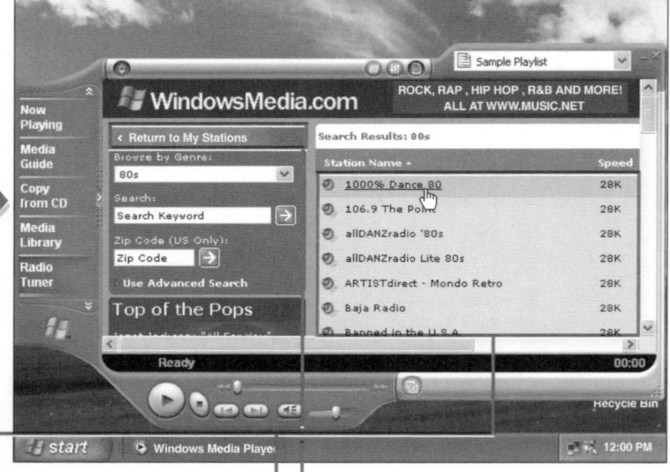

FIND RADIO STATIONS

■ This area displays categories of radio stations that you can listen to.

1 To display the radio stations in a category, click the category of interest.

■ To search for a specific radio station, select the text in this area and then type information about a radio station of interest, such as a station name or call sign. Then press the Enter key.

■ A list of radio stations appears.

■ To redisplay the list of categories at any time, you can click Return to My Stations.

2 Click the name of the radio station you want to listen to.

How can I keep track of my favorite radio stations?

✔ You can add your favorite radio stations to the My Stations list on the Radio Tuner tab. Adding radio stations to the My Stations list allows you to create a personalized list of radio stations that you can quickly access at any time. When you find a radio station you want to add to the My Stations list, click Add to My Stations below the radio station. To display the My Stations list, click My Stations below the Featured Stations area.

Can I sort the radio stations in the results of a search?

✔ You can click a heading displayed in the results of a search to sort the radio stations. For example, sorting by the Station Name column displays names alphabetically from Z to A. To reverse the sort order, click the heading again.

How can I narrow my search?

✔ After selecting a category or performing a search, a search area appears that allows you to specify additional information. You can choose a genre, type a keyword or search by U.S. Zip code. Enter the information you want to use to narrow your search and then click ➔.

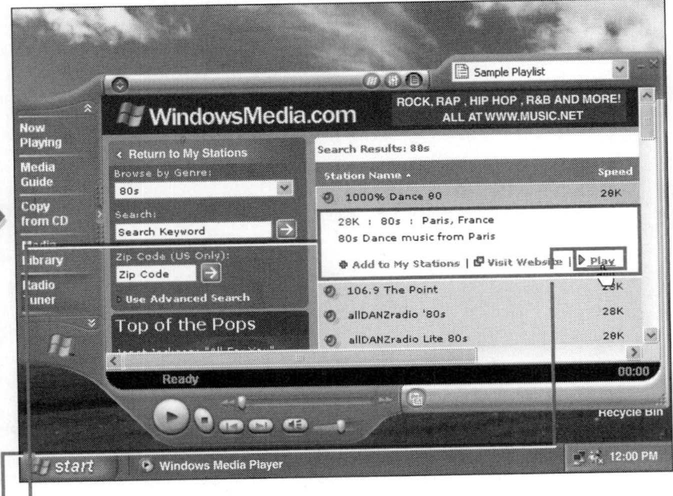

■ Information about the radio station you selected appears.

3 To listen to the radio station, click Play.

Note: If the Play option is not available, you can click Visit Website to Play to display the radio station's Web page and play the radio station.

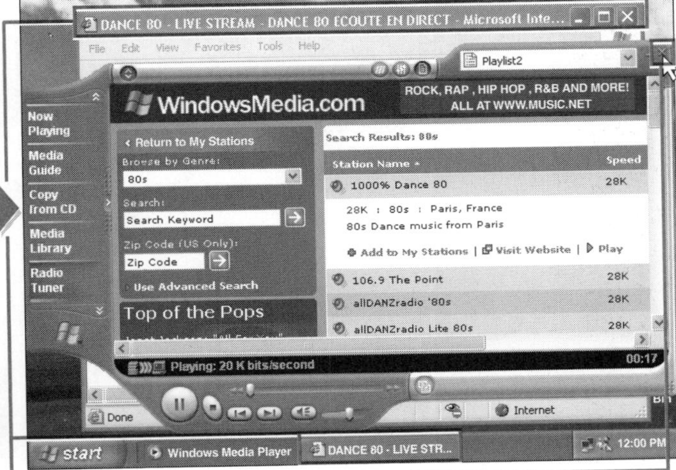

■ After a moment, the radio station begins to play.

■ The Microsoft Internet Explorer window opens behind Windows Media Player, displaying the Web page for the radio station. To view the Web page, click the window's button on the taskbar.

4 When you finish listening to radio stations, click ✖ to close the Windows Media Player window.

CHANGE THE SKIN OF WINDOWS MEDIA PLAYER

You can change the skin of Windows Media Player to customize how the player looks and functions. Windows Media Player allows you to play media files, such as sounds and videos, listen to radio stations that broadcast over the Internet, and play music CDs.

Windows Media Player includes several skins from which you can choose, including Headspace, Rusty and Toothy. Windows Media Player can display a skin only in skin mode. When you apply a skin, Windows Media Player automatically switches to skin mode to display the new skin.

Skin mode displays a smaller player window, which provides more room on your screen for using other programs. In skin mode, however, you do not have access to all the features available in Windows Media Player. For example, you cannot change the skin of Windows Media Player. The number of features available in skin mode depends on the skin you select. You can switch to full mode at any time to access all the Windows Media Player features.

CHANGE THE SKIN OF WINDOWS MEDIA PLAYER

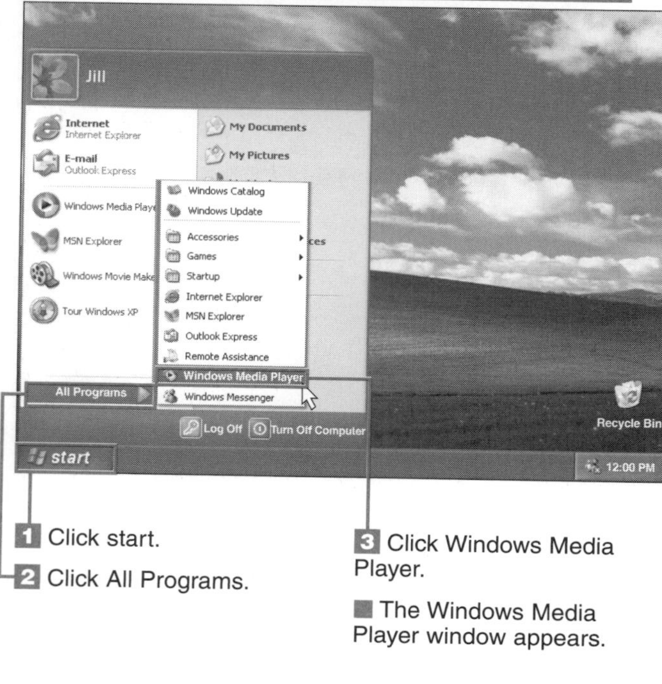

1 Click start.

2 Click All Programs.

3 Click Windows Media Player.

■ The Windows Media Player window appears.

4 Click the Skin Chooser tab to change the skin of Windows Media Player.

■ If the Skin Chooser tab is not displayed, click this arrow (⋎) until the tab appears.

■ This area lists the available skins that you can use with Windows Media Player.

5 Click the skin you want to use.

Where can I obtain more skins for Windows Media Player?

✔ You can obtain more skins for Windows Media Player on the Internet. On the Skin Chooser tab, click the More Skins button to display a Web page that offers skins you can use. When you select the skin you want to use, the skin transfers to your computer and appears in your list of available skins.

How do I delete a skin?

✔ On the Skin Chooser tab, select the skin you want to delete and then click (✖).

Can I change back to the original Windows Media Player skin?

✔ Yes. On the Skin Chooser tab, select the Windows XP skin and then click the Apply Skin button.

How can I quickly switch from full mode to skin mode?

✔ Click ⧉ at the bottom of the Windows Media Player window. The last skin you selected will be displayed.

Can I access additional features when in skin mode?

✔ You can press Shift+F10 to display a shortcut menu, which provides access to more Windows Media Player features.

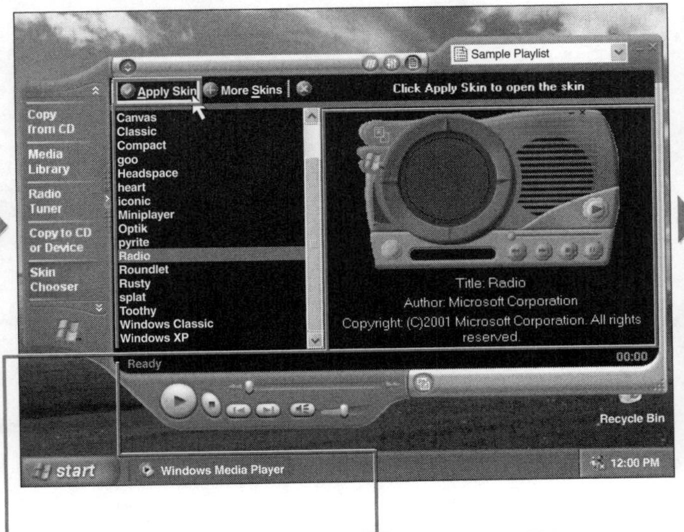

■ This area displays a preview of the skin you selected.

6 Click Apply Skin to apply the skin to Windows Media Player.

■ Windows Media Player changes to skin mode and displays the skin you selected.

■ To once again display Windows Media Player in full mode, click ⧉.

Note: The appearance and location of ⧉ depends on the skin you selected.

COPY SONGS FROM A MUSIC CD

You can copy songs from a music CD onto your computer. Copying songs from a music CD allows you to play the songs at any time without having to insert the CD into your computer. Copying songs from a music CD also allows you to later copy the songs to a recordable CD or portable device. To copy songs to a recordable CD, see page 326.

Depending on your CD-ROM drive and the speakers you use, you may be able to listen to a music CD while you copy songs from the CD.

You can select the songs on a CD that you want to copy to your computer. If you do not select any songs, all the songs on the CD will be copied to your computer.

The first time you copy songs from a music CD, Windows displays a message indicating that it will protect the copies from unauthorized access by preventing the songs from being played on other computers. Protecting the songs in this manner will help ensure that copyright laws protecting the songs are obeyed. If you want to be able to play the songs on another computer, you can stop Windows from protecting the songs.

COPY SONGS FROM A MUSIC CD

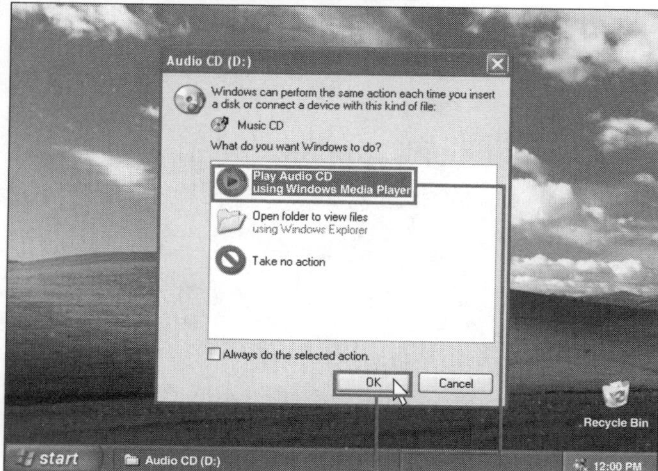

1 Insert the music CD that contains the songs you want to copy into your CD-ROM drive.

■ The Audio CD dialog box appears, asking what you want Windows to do.

2 Click this option to play the music CD.

3 Click OK.

■ The Windows Media Player window appears and the CD begins to play.

4 Click the Copy from CD tab.

■ This area displays information about each song on the CD. Windows Media Player will copy each song that displays a check mark (✔) to your computer.

5 To add (☑) or remove (☐) a check mark beside a song, click the box beside the song.

6 Click Copy Music to start copying the selected songs to your computer.

How can I specify whether I want Windows to protect songs if the dialog box does not appear?

✔ Position the mouse over the top of the Windows Media Player window and then click Tools. Select Options, choose the Copy Music tab and then click the Protect content option to turn the option on (☑) or off (☐).

How can I play a song I copied from a music CD?

✔ Songs you copy from a music CD are stored in the My Music folder. This folder contains a subfolder for each artist whose CDs you have copied songs from. To open the My Music folder, click start and then click My Music. You can double-click a song in a folder to play the song. You can also play a song in the Media Library. For more information about the Media Library, see page 314.

How can I adjust the quality of songs I copy to my computer?

✔ Position the mouse over the top of the Media Player window and then click Tools. Select Options and choose the Copy Music tab. In the Copy settings area, drag the slider (slider icon) to the left or right to decrease or increase the quality. Songs copied using a lower quality take up less storage space on your computer.

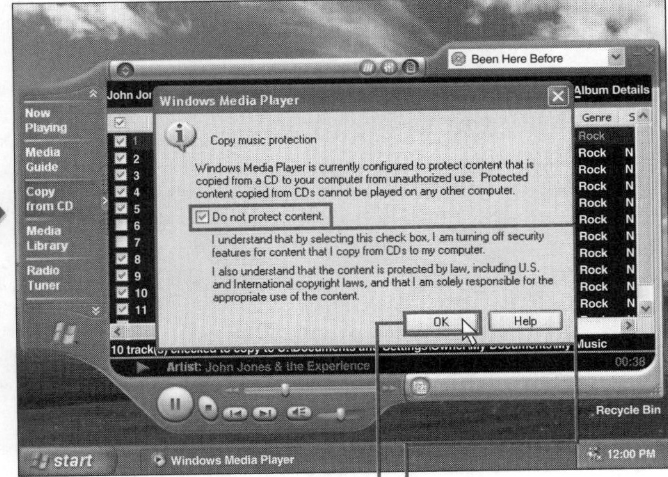

■ The first time you copy songs from a music CD, a dialog box appears, stating that Windows Media Player will protect the songs from unauthorized use. Protected songs cannot be played on another computer.

7 If you want to be able to play the songs on another computer, click this option (☐ changes to ☑).

8 Click OK to continue.

■ This column indicates the progress of the copy.

■ To stop the copy at any time, click Stop Copy.

9 When you finish copying songs from the music CD, click ✖ to close the Windows Media Player window.

COPY SONGS TO A CD OR PORTABLE DEVICE

Windows Media Player allows you to copy audio files from the Media Library to a recordable CD or a portable device such as an MP3 player. This allows you to create your own music CDs and copy songs from your computer that you want to take with you on a portable music player.

Before copying files to your CD or portable device, you must first add the files to the Media Library. For information about using the Media Library, see page 314. You can transfer any audio files stored in the Media Library to your CD or portable device, including files you downloaded from the Internet or copied from a music CD. To copy files to the Media Library from a music CD, see page 324.

You can copy audio files with the .wma, .wav and .mp3 extensions to a CD or portable device. Windows allows you to choose the sound category that contains the files you want to copy. You can choose a category set up by Windows or a playlist you created yourself.

When copying songs to a CD, you should not perform other tasks on your computer, since Windows Media player may stop working.

COPY SONGS TO A CD OR PORTABLE DEVICE

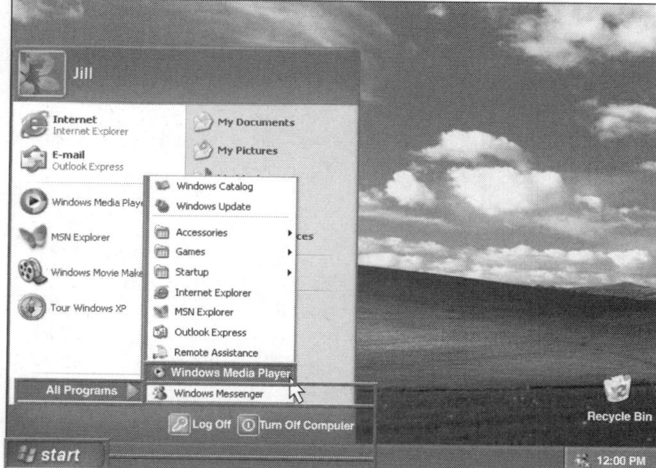

1 To copy songs to a CD, insert a blank CD into your recordable CD drive.

Note: When you insert a blank CD, a dialog box appears, asking what you want Windows to do. Click Cancel to close the dialog box.

2 Click start.

3 Click All Programs.

4 Click Windows Media Player.

■ The Windows Media Player window appears.

5 Click the Copy to CD or Device tab.

■ If the Copy to CD or Device tab is not displayed, click this arrow (⩔) until the tab appears.

6 Click this area to display a list of the categories in the Media Library.

7 Click the category that contains the songs you want to copy.

What hardware do I need to copy songs to a CD?

✔ You need a recordable CD drive, such as a CD-R or CD-RW drive, to copy files to a CD. A CD-R (Compact Disc-Recordable) drive allows you to permanently record data on CD-R discs. You cannot erase a CD-R disc. A CD-RW (Compact Disc-ReWritable) drive allows you to record data on CD-RW or CD-R discs. You can erase a CD-RW disc in order to copy new data to the disc.

How do I erase a CD-RW disc?

✔ Click start, select My Computer and then double-click the CD drive to display the disc's contents. Then click Erase this CD-RW and follow the instructions in the CD Writing Wizard.

Can I copy songs to a CD at different times?

✔ You can copy songs to a CD only once using Windows Media Player. Since you must copy all the songs to a CD at the same time, make sure you carefully select all the songs you want to copy.

Can I quickly select only a few songs to copy?

✔ Click the check mark icon (✔) at the top of the Music to Copy list to remove the check marks from all the songs. Then click the box beside each song you want to copy (☐ changes to ☑).

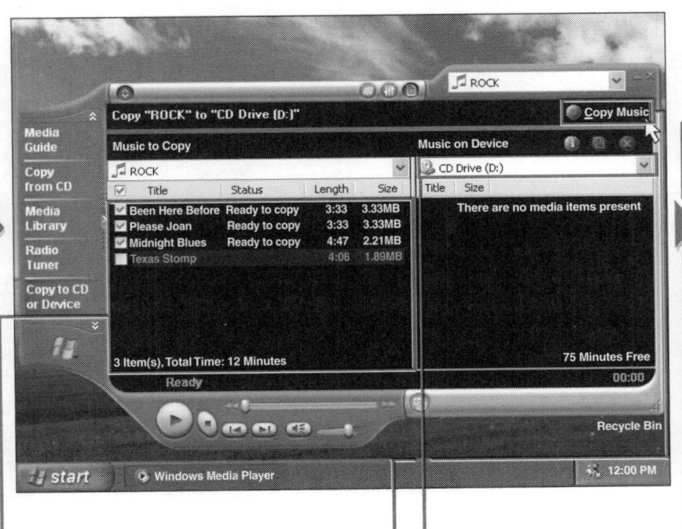

■ This area displays the songs in the selected category. Windows Media Player will copy each song that displays a check mark (✔).

8 To add (☑) or remove (☐) a check mark, click the box beside the song.

9 This area displays the device to which you will copy the songs. You can click this area to select a different device.

10 Click Copy Music to start copying.

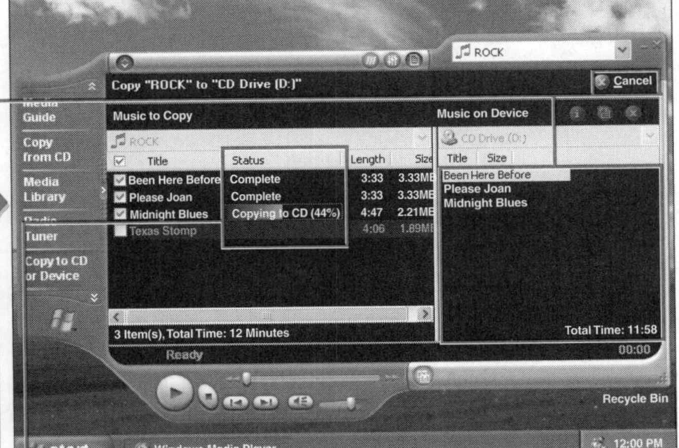

■ This column indicates the progress of the copy.

■ To cancel the copy at any time, click Cancel.

■ When the copy is complete, this area displays all the songs you copied to the device.

Note: When you copy songs to a CD, Windows automatically ejects the CD from the recordable CD drive when the copy is complete.

RECORD A VIDEO

You can use Windows Movie Maker to transfer video files to your computer. You can then organize and edit the files to create movies.

For Windows Movie Maker to work properly, your computer must have a 300 MHz Pentium II processor or equivalent, at least 64 MB of RAM and 2 GB of free hard disk space. If you are recording from a digital video device, your computer requires a 600 MHz Pentium III processor or equivalent, 128 MB of RAM and 2 GB of free hard disk space.

Before using Windows Movie Maker, you need to connect and install the equipment needed to transfer video content to your computer. When recording from a video camera, make sure the camera is in Playback mode, not Standby mode.

Before you start recording, you can specify the length of time you want Windows Movie Maker to record video. You can also specify whether you want Windows Movie Maker to automatically break the video into smaller segments, called clips. If you choose not to create clips, Windows Movie Maker creates one clip for the entire video.

You can also choose a quality setting for your recording. Keep in mind that a high quality setting improves the video quality, but produces a large file, which takes up more space on your computer.

START WINDOWS MOVIE MAKER

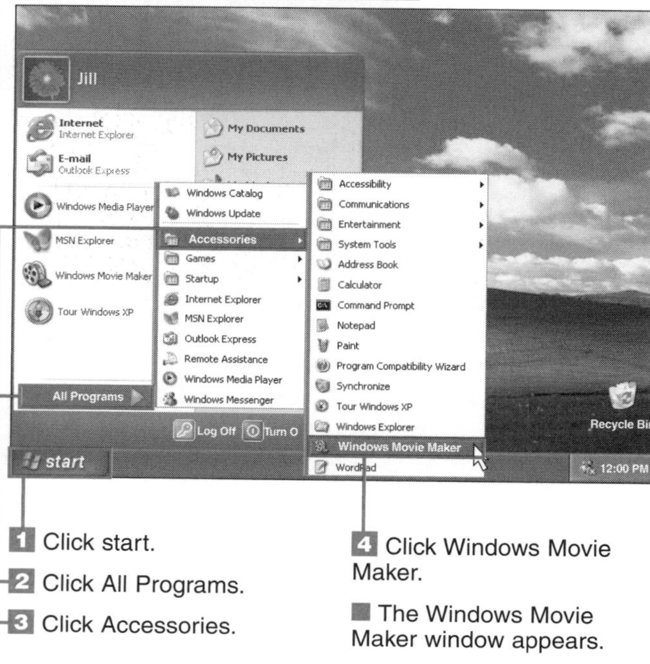

1 Click start.

2 Click All Programs.

3 Click Accessories.

4 Click Windows Movie Maker.

■ The Windows Movie Maker window appears.

RECORD A VIDEO

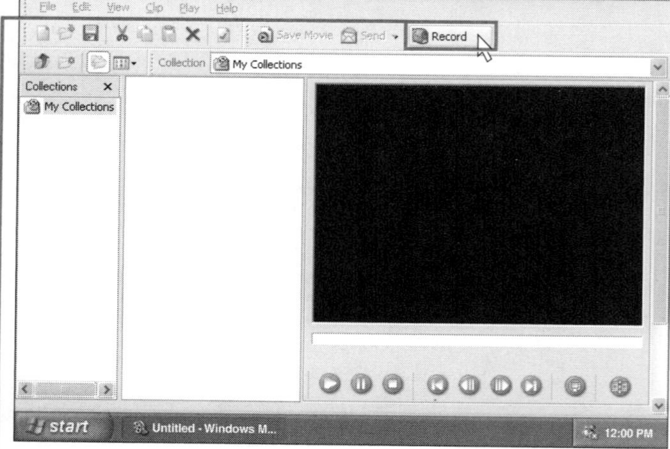

1 Click Record to record video onto your computer.

Note: A dialog box appears if your computer may not provide acceptable performance when recording from a high-speed device such as a digital video camera. Click Yes to record video using the device.

■ The Record dialog box appears.

What equipment will I need to transfer video to my computer?

✔ You can transfer video from a video camera, Web camera, television broadcast, VCR or DVD player. To connect a video source to your computer, you will need cables and a specific type of connector. A digital video camera requires a FireWire port or FireWire card, while an analog video camera requires a video capture card. A Web camera requires a USB port or USB card, while a television broadcast, VCR or DVD requires a TV tuner card. You can purchase cables and connectors at a computer store.

How can I import a video saved on my computer into Windows Movie Maker?

✔ In the Windows Movie Maker window, click File and select Import. Locate and select the file you want and then click Open. Windows Movie Maker will create a new collection to store clips for the video file you import.

Can I capture a photo from the video I am recording?

✔ Yes. When the video in the Record dialog box displays the picture you want to capture, pause the video and then click [camera]. Type a name for the photo and click the Save button to save the photo in the My Pictures folder. The photo will also appear in the clips area in Windows Movie Maker.

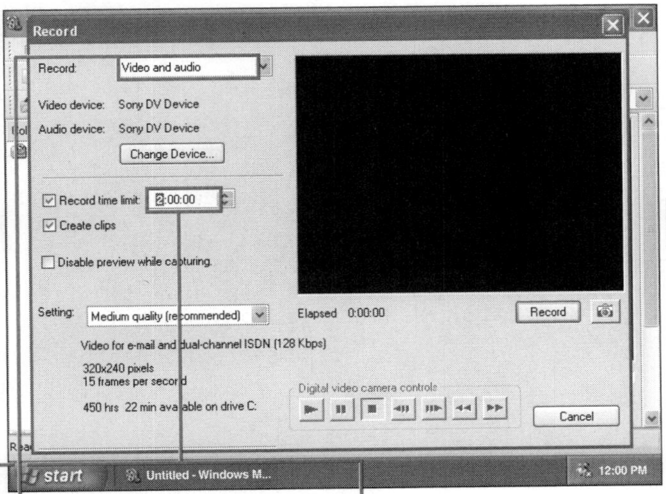

■ This area displays the type of material you will record.

■ This area indicates the length of time Windows Movie Maker will record video.

2 To change the length of time, click the part of the time you want to change and then type a new number.

Note: If you do not want to have a time limit, click Record time limit (☑ changes to ☐).

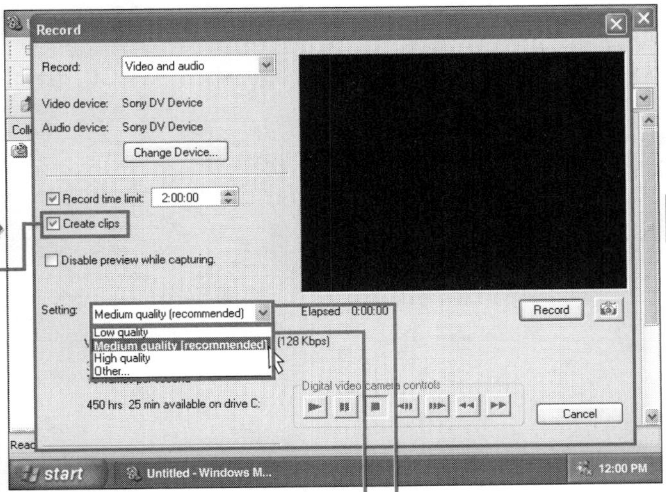

3 This option automatically breaks up video you record into smaller segments, called clips. If you do not want to create clips, click this option to turn off the option (☑ changes to ☐).

4 Click this area to display a list of quality settings that you can use to record the video.

5 Click the quality setting you want to use.

CONTINUED

RECORD A VIDEO (CONTINUED)

Windows automatically stores each video you record in the My Videos folder, which is located in the My Documents folder on your computer. Windows creates the My Videos folder the first time you start Windows Movie Maker. You can choose to save your video in a different location.

When you save your video, Windows Movie Maker stores all the clips for the video in one folder, called a collection. The collection appears in the left pane of the Windows Movie Maker window, displaying the name you specified when saving the video.

The clips in the collection appear in the right pane of the Windows Movie Maker window. A clip is created each time Windows Movie Maker detects a different sequence in a video, such as when you switch from pause to resume recording. Each video clip consists of a number of still images, called frames. To help you identify the clips, Windows Movie Maker displays the first frame of each video clip.

After recording a video, you can organize and edit your collection of clips to create a movie. After creating a movie, you can view the movie on your computer, save it on a recordable CD, send it to people in e-mail messages or publish the movie to the Web.

RECORD A VIDEO (CONTINUED)

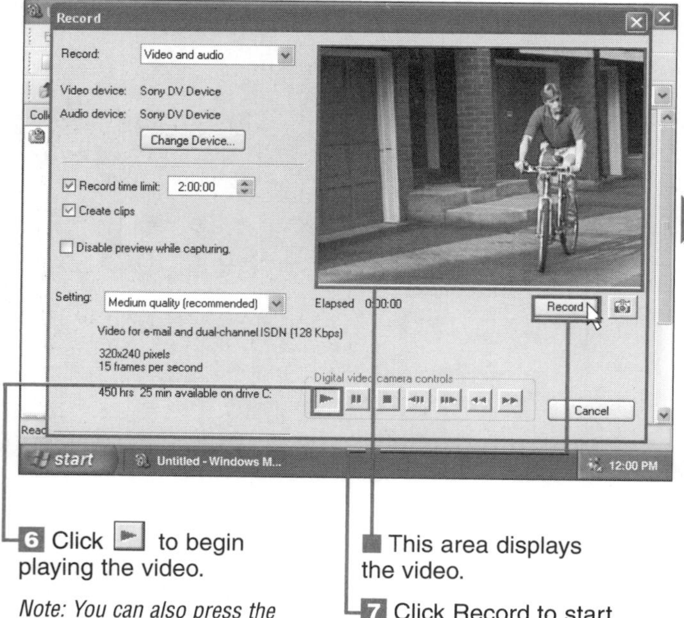

6 Click ▶ to begin playing the video.

Note: You can also press the play button on your video camera or other video source to begin playing the video.

■ This area displays the video.

7 Click Record to start recording.

■ The word "Recording" blinks in this area when Windows Movie Maker is recording.

■ This area displays the time that has passed since you started recording the video.

8 Click Stop when you want to stop recording the video.

Note: You may have to press the stop button on your video camera or other video source to stop the video.

Can I change the way clips are displayed?

✔ When viewing clips, click ▦ and select the way you want to view the clips. The Thumbnails view displays a miniature version of the first frame of each clip. The List view displays the titles of the clips in a list. The Details view displays additional information about the clips, including the date the clips were recorded and the length of each clip.

How do I rename a collection or a clip?

✔ Click the collection you want to rename. To rename a clip, click the clip within the collection. Then click the Edit menu and choose Rename. Type a new name for the collection or clip and then press the Enter key.

How do I delete a collection or a clip?

✔ Click the collection you want to delete. To delete a clip, click the clip within the collection. Then click ☒.

How do I organize a collection of clips?

✔ You can create folders within a collection to help you organize the clips. Click the collection you want to organize and select ▭. Type a name for the new folder and press the Enter key. To move clips to the new folder, drag the clips to the new folder.

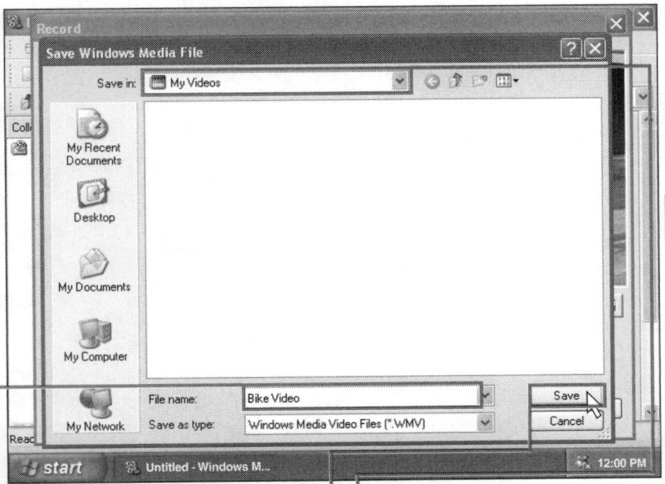

■ The Save Windows Media File dialog box appears.

9 Type a name for your video.

■ This area shows the location where Windows will store your video. You can click this area to change the location.

10 Click Save to save the video.

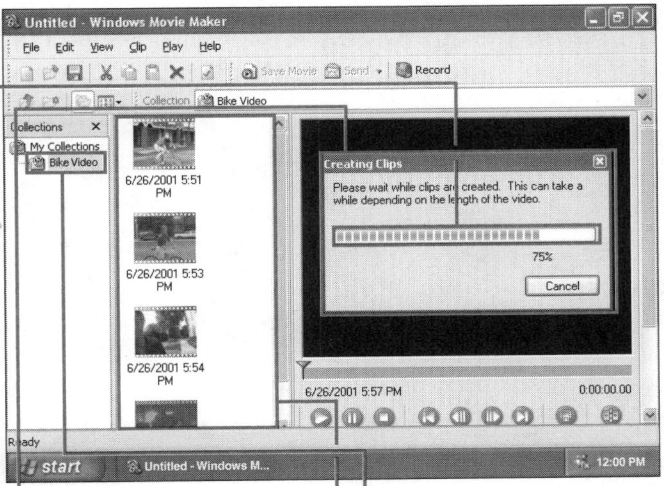

■ The Creating Clips dialog box appears while Windows Movie Maker creates the clips for your video.

■ This area shows the progress of the creation of the clips.

■ When Windows Movie Maker has finished creating the clips for your video, this area displays a folder that stores the collection of video clips.

■ This area displays the video clips within the collection.

PLAY A VIDEO CLIP

You can play each video clip you have recorded on your computer. Playing video clips can help you determine which clips you want to include in your movie.

Each time you record a video, Windows Movie Maker creates a collection to store all the clips for the video. To play a video clip, you must first select the collection that contains the clip you want to play.

The area in the Windows Movie Maker window where the video clip plays is called the monitor. While a video clip is playing, an arrow (Y) on the monitor indicates how much of the video clip is left to play. The monitor also displays buttons that let you control the play of the video clip.

You can play, pause and stop a video clip.

The monitor also has buttons you can use to move to a frame in a video clip. You can move backward or forward through a video clip, frame by frame.

PLAY A VIDEO CLIP

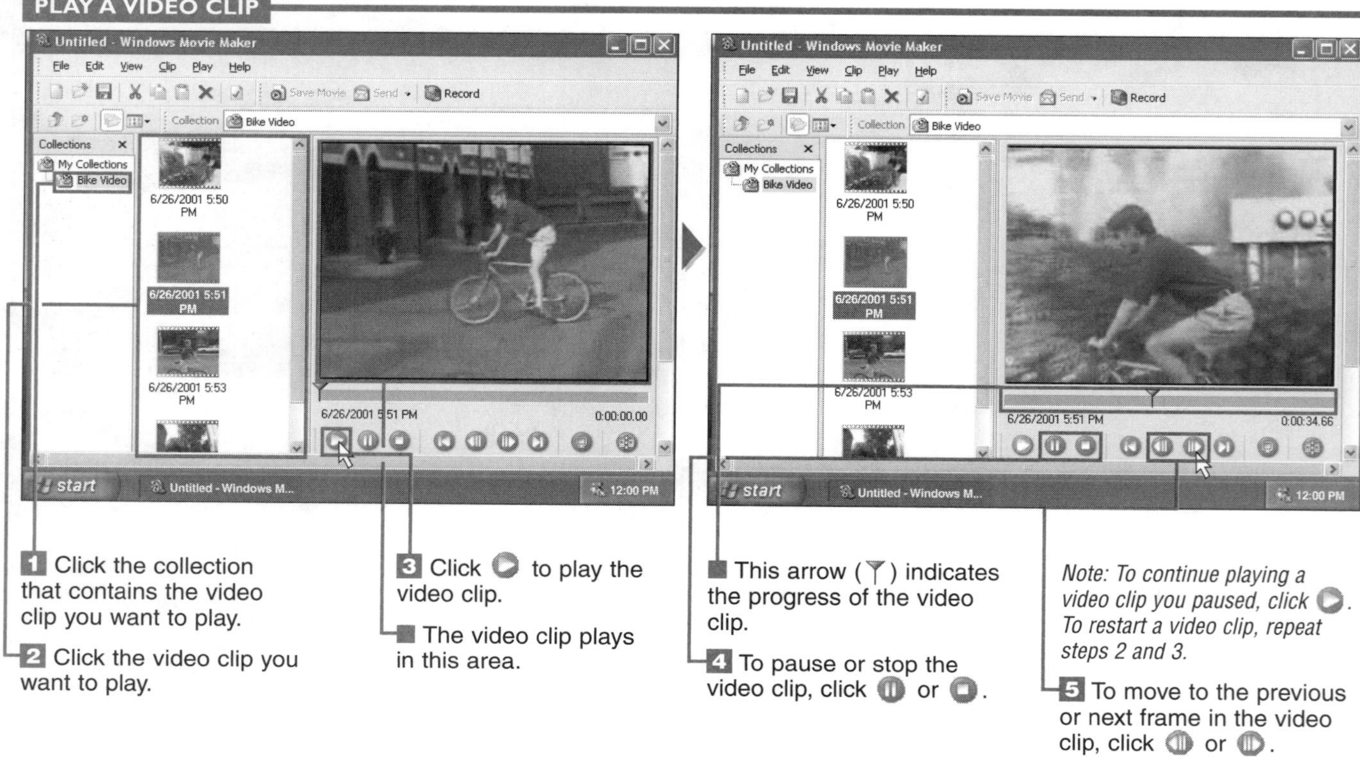

1 Click the collection that contains the video clip you want to play.

2 Click the video clip you want to play.

3 Click ▶ to play the video clip.

■ The video clip plays in this area.

■ This arrow (Y) indicates the progress of the video clip.

4 To pause or stop the video clip, click ⏸ or ⏹.

Note: To continue playing a video clip you paused, click ▶. To restart a video clip, repeat steps 2 and 3.

5 To move to the previous or next frame in the video clip, click ◀ or ▶.

ADD A VIDEO CLIP TO THE STORYBOARD

You can add each video clip that you want to include in your movie to the storyboard. The storyboard displays the order in which video clips will appear in your movie.

Depending on the resolution of your screen, the storyboard may not be displayed on your screen. You can use the scroll bar to view the storyboard or you can increase the resolution of your screen to show more information on the screen at once. For information about changing the screen resolution, see page 200.

In addition to the method shown below, you can add a video clip to the storyboard by dragging the video clip to the location on the storyboard where you want to add the clip. A vertical bar on the storyboard indicates the location where the video clip will appear. You cannot leave empty spaces between clips on the storyboard.

ADD A VIDEO CLIP TO THE STORYBOARD

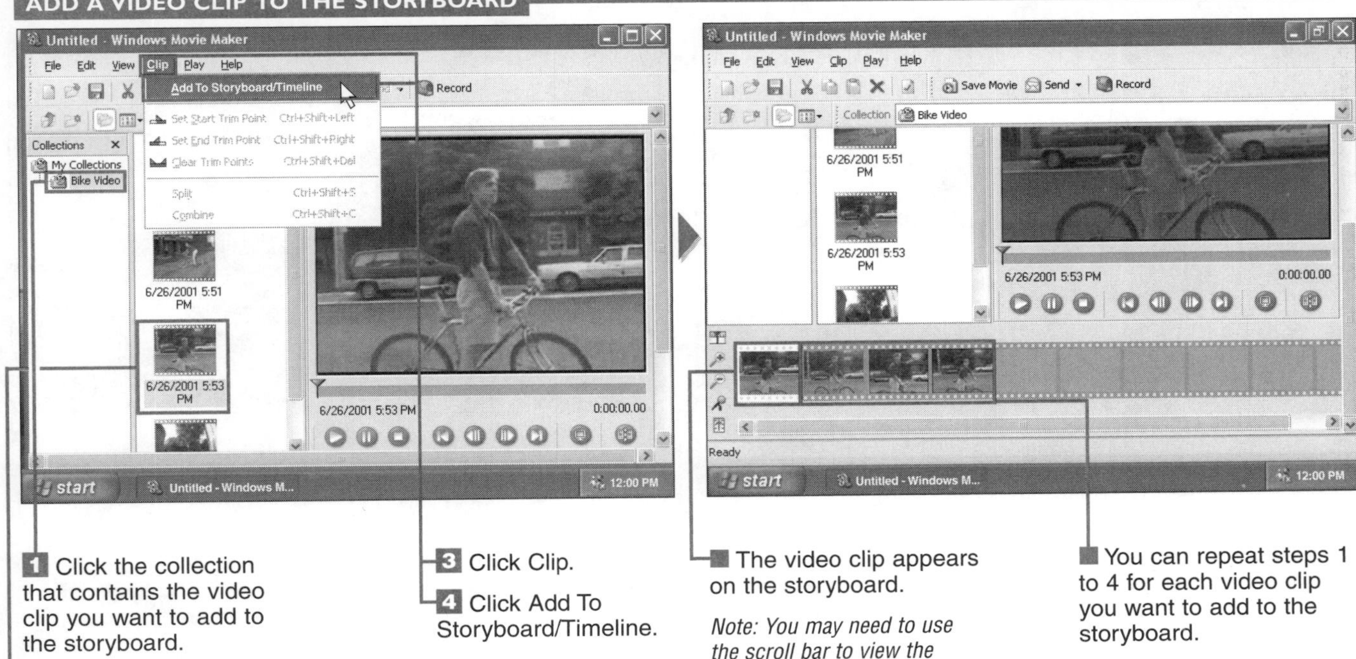

1 Click the collection that contains the video clip you want to add to the storyboard.

2 Click the video clip you want to add.

3 Click Clip.

4 Click Add To Storyboard/Timeline.

■ The video clip appears on the storyboard.

Note: You may need to use the scroll bar to view the storyboard.

■ You can repeat steps 1 to 4 for each video clip you want to add to the storyboard.

REARRANGE VIDEO CLIPS

After adding the video clips you want to use to the storyboard, you can rearrange the clips to change the order in which they will play in your movie. For example, you may want to rearrange video clips so that the clips of the landscaping of a building appear in the movie before the clips of the interior of the building.

When you move a video clip, any surrounding video clips shift to make room for the clip. You cannot move a video clip to a blank area on the storyboard when rearranging video clips.

After rearranging the video clips in a movie, you may want to preview the movie to ensure that the new order of the video clips makes sense. For information about previewing a movie, see page 335.

How do I copy a video clip on the storyboard to another location in my movie?

✔ Position the mouse over the video clip you want to copy on the storyboard. Press and hold down the Ctrl key as you drag the video clip to the position in the movie where you want the copy of the clip to appear.

REARRANGE VIDEO CLIPS

1 Position the mouse over the video clip you want to move to a different location on the storyboard.

Note: You may need to use the scroll bar to view the storyboard.

2 Drag the video clip to a new location on the storyboard. A vertical bar indicates where the video clip will appear.

■ The video clip appears in the new location.

■ The surrounding video clips automatically move to make room for the video clip.

PREVIEW A MOVIE

You can preview all the video clips you added to the storyboard as a movie. Previewing a movie is useful if you want to see what the video clips look like when played together before you save the movie on your computer.

The entire movie will play on the monitor in the Windows Movie Maker window. The slider () in the monitor area indicates the progress of the movie. You can pause or stop the preview of a movie at any time. You can also move to a specific video clip in the movie at any time.

Can I have the movie I am previewing fill the screen?

✔ Yes. This is useful when you want to see the overall effect of the movie when played on a full screen. When you are previewing a movie, click the Full Screen button ( ) in the monitor area to have the movie fill the entire screen. When you are finished viewing the movie on a full screen, click the screen to return to the Windows Movie Maker window.

PREVIEW A MOVIE

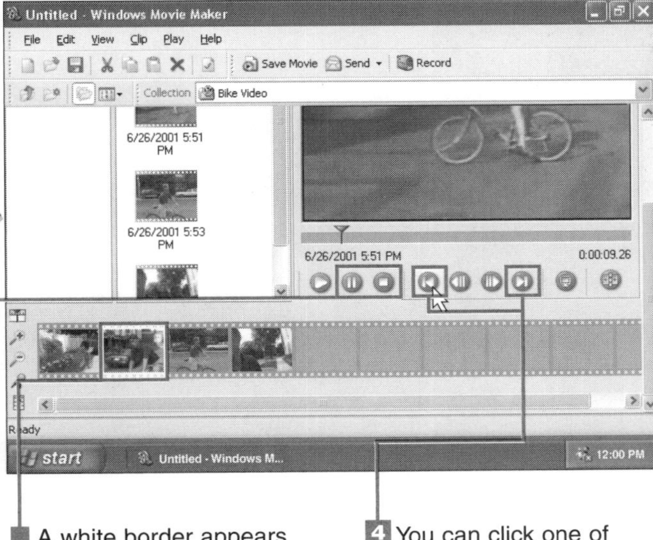

1 Click a blank area on the storyboard.

Note: You may need to use the scroll bar to view the storyboard.

2 Click ( ) to preview all the video clips you added to the storyboard as a movie.

■ The movie plays in this area.

■ A white border appears around the video clip that is currently playing.

3 You can click one of these buttons to pause ( ) or stop ( ) the movie at any time.

Note: To once again play the movie, click ( ).

4 You can click one of these buttons to move to the previous video clip ( ) or next video clip ( ) in the movie.

SAVE AND OPEN A PROJECT

A project is a rough draft of your movie that contains all the video clips you added to the storyboard. You can save your project to store it for future use.

Saving a project allows you to later review and make changes to the project. You should regularly save changes you make to a project to avoid losing your work due to a computer problem or power failure. Windows Movie Maker saves project files with the .mswmm extension.

You should store your projects in a location on your computer that will be easy to find. By default, Windows Movie Maker stores projects you create in the My Videos folder, which is located in the My Documents folder.

You can open a saved project to display the video clips on the storyboard. This allows you to review and make changes to the project, such as adding, removing or rearranging the video clips. For information about working with video clips, see page 338.

SAVE A PROJECT

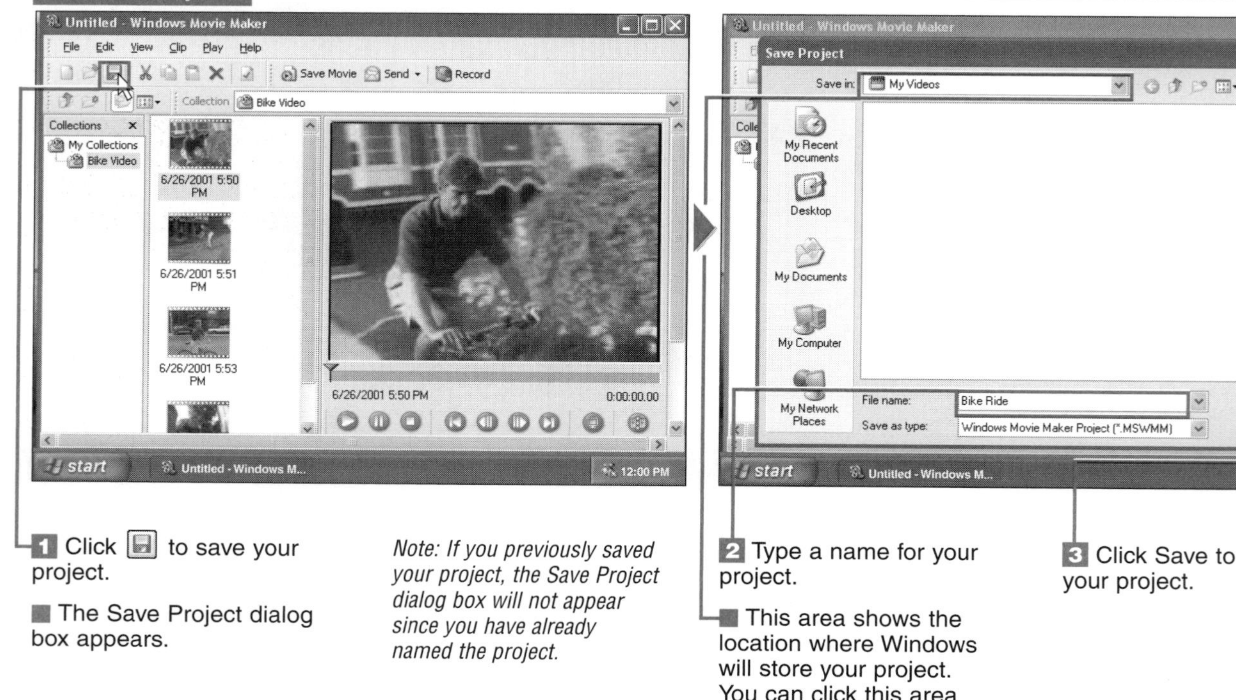

1 Click 💾 to save your project.

■ The Save Project dialog box appears.

Note: If you previously saved your project, the Save Project dialog box will not appear since you have already named the project.

2 Type a name for your project.

■ This area shows the location where Windows will store your project. You can click this area to change the location.

3 Click Save to save your project.

Can I have more than one project open at a time?

✔ No. You can work with only one project at a time. Windows Movie Maker will close a project displayed on your screen when you open another project. Make sure you save the project you are currently working with before opening another project.

How do I create a new project in Windows Movie Maker?

✔ You can click [new project icon] to create a new project. You should make sure you save your current project before creating a new one.

Can I save a project with a new name?

✔ Yes. If you plan to make major changes to a project, you may want to save the project with a new name. This gives you two copies of the project—the original project and a project with all the changes. To save a project with a new name, click the File menu and select Save Project As. In the Save Project dialog box that appears, type a new name for the project and then click Save.

OPEN A PROJECT

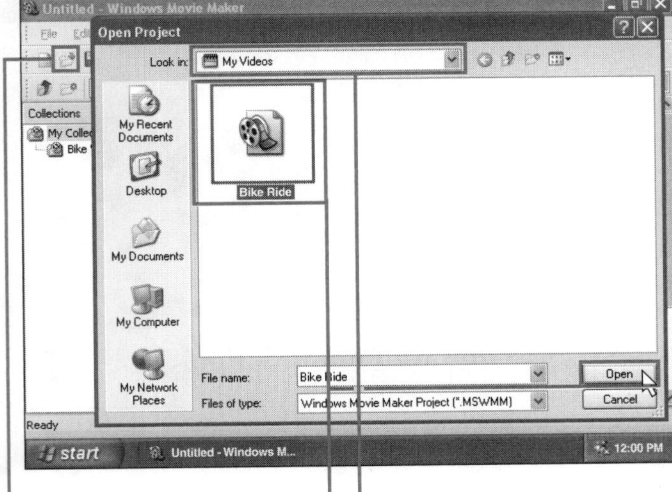

1 Click [open icon] to open a project.

■ The Open Project dialog box appears.

■ This area shows the location of the displayed projects. You can click this area to change the location.

2 Click the name of the project you want to open.

3 Click Open to open the project.

■ The project opens and the video clips in the project appear on the storyboard. You can now review and make changes to the video clips in the project.

Note: You may need to use the scroll bar to view the storyboard.

WORK WITH VIDEO CLIPS

Windows Movie Maker allows you to work with video clips to make changes to a movie on your computer.

You can trim a video clip on the storyboard to remove parts of the clip that you do not want to play in your movie. To trim a video clip, you can set a start trim point, an end trim point or both. A start trim point specifies where a video clip will start playing, while an end trim point specifies where a video clip will stop playing.

Trimming video clips will reduce the length and file size of your movie. A movie with a smaller file size will take up less storage space on your computer and transfer more quickly over the Internet.

You can create a smooth transition from one video clip to another in your movie by overlapping the clips so that the frames in the first video clip fade out as the frames in the following video clip fade in. To create or view a transition, the workspace must be displayed in the timeline view. The workspace is the area at the bottom of the Windows Movie Maker window that allows you to make changes.

Any changes you make to a video clip in the workspace will not affect the video clip stored in Windows Movie Maker.

TRIM A VIDEO CLIP

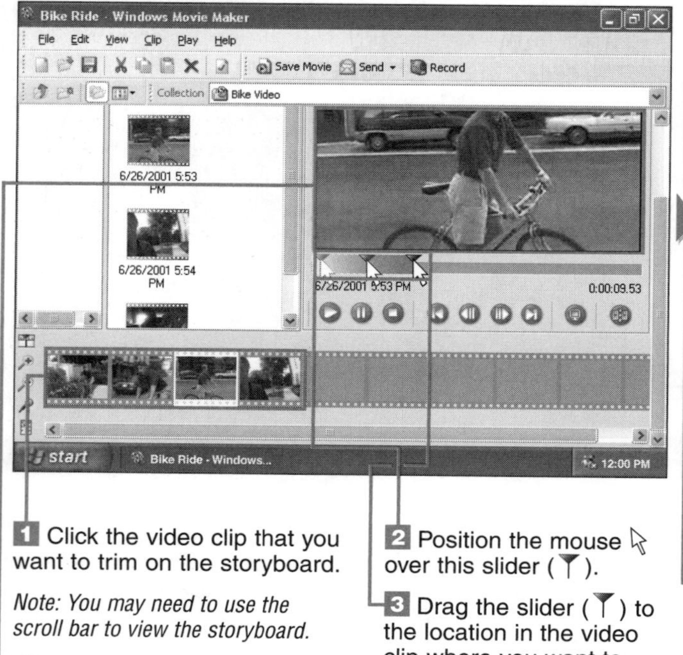

1 Click the video clip that you want to trim on the storyboard.

Note: You may need to use the scroll bar to view the storyboard.

■ The first frame of the video clip appears in this area.

2 Position the mouse over this slider.

3 Drag the slider to the location in the video clip where you want to trim the video.

4 Click Clip.

5 Click one of these options.

Set Start Trim Point
Remove the video before the slider.

Set End Trim Point
Remove the video after the slider.

How do I trim a video clip in the timeline view?

✔ Click [icon] to display the workspace in the timeline view and then click the video clip you want to trim on the timeline. Handles ([icon] and [icon]) appear on the video clip. Position the mouse pointer over a handle and then drag the mouse ↔ to a new position to set the trim point.

How do I remove a video clip from the storyboard?

✔ Click the video clip you no longer want to include on the storyboard and then press the Delete key. This will not remove the video clip from Windows Movie Maker.

How do I remove the trim points I set for a video clip?

✔ Click the video clip you trimmed on the storyboard. Choose the Clip menu and then select Clear Trim Points. Clearing trim points may cause clips to overlap in the movie.

How can I use the [icon] and [icon] buttons that appear to the left of the timeline?

✔ These buttons allow you to zoom in and out of the timeline. You can click the Zoom In button ([icon]) to view a more detailed timeline. If you want to see less detail, you can click the Zoom Out button ([icon]).

CREATE A TRANSITION

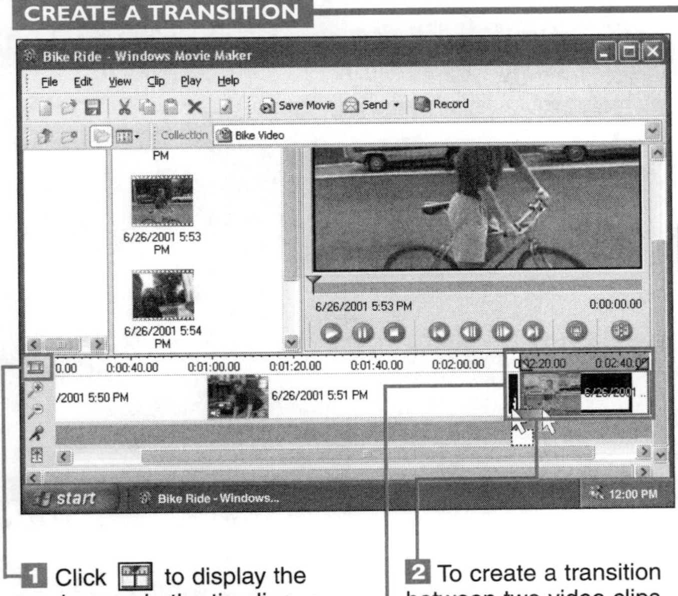

1 Click [icon] to display the workspace in the timeline view ([icon] changes to [icon]).

■ The workspace appears in the timeline view.

2 To create a transition between two video clips, position the mouse [pointer] over the second video clip.

3 Drag the video clip so it overlaps the first video clip.

■ The amount of overlap between the two video clips determines the length of the transition.

Note: To delete a transition, position the mouse [pointer] over the video clip to the right of the transition. Then drag the video clip to the right until the video clips no longer overlap.

■ To once again display the workspace in the storyboard view, click [icon].

RECORD NARRATION

Windows Movie Maker allows you to record voice narration for a movie. This is ideal for narrating a presentation or a home video. You need a computer with sound capabilities and a microphone connected to your computer to record narration.

You can record narration only when the clips for your movie are displayed in the timeline view. If the movie for which you want to record narration already contains sound, you can turn off the existing sound while you record your narration. You can also change the volume of your narration.

When recording narration, you can watch the movie and view the amount of time that has passed since you started recording.

Once the narration is complete, Windows Movie Maker allows you to save the narration as a sound file with the .wav extension on your computer. The sound file will appear as a sound clip below the video clips on the timeline and will also appear as a sound clip in the current collection in the Windows Movie Maker window.

RECORD NARRATION

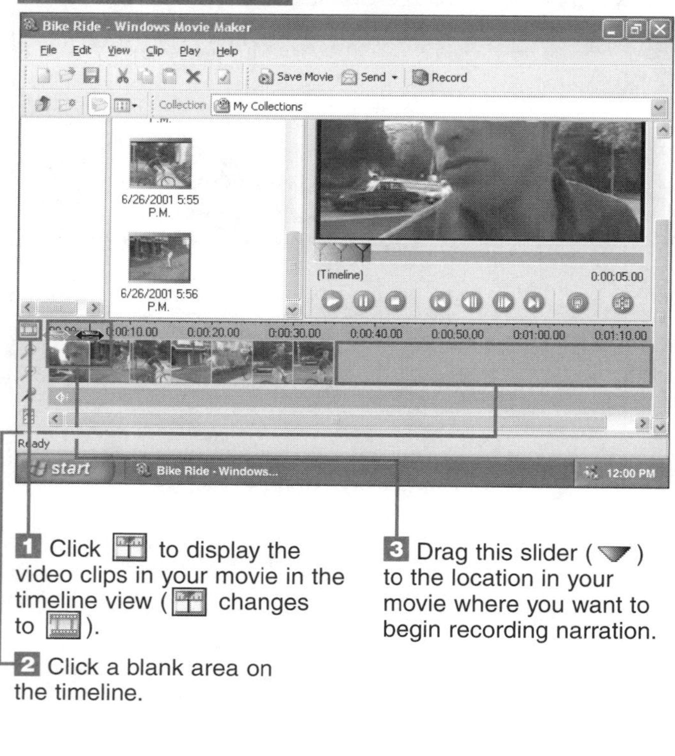

1 Click [icon] to display the video clips in your movie in the timeline view ([icon] changes to [icon]).

2 Click a blank area on the timeline.

3 Drag this slider (▼) to the location in your movie where you want to begin recording narration.

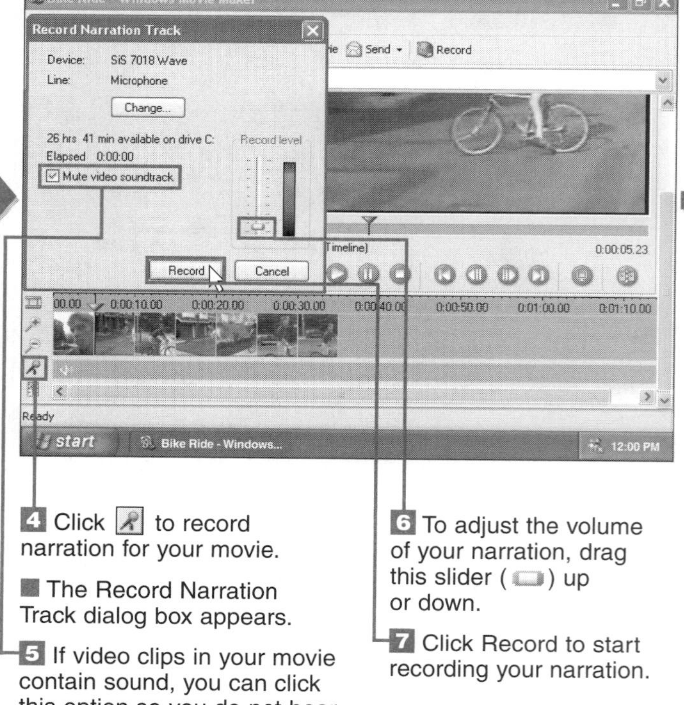

4 Click [icon] to record narration for your movie.

■ The Record Narration Track dialog box appears.

5 If video clips in your movie contain sound, you can click this option so you do not hear the sound while recording your narration (☐ changes to ☑).

6 To adjust the volume of your narration, drag this slider ([icon]) up or down.

7 Click Record to start recording your narration.

How do I remove narration from a movie?

✔ Click the sound clip below the timeline and then press the Delete key. The sound clip will not be removed from the collection in the Windows Movie Maker window.

How can I make the narration I recorded louder than the sound currently in the movie?

✔ Click [icon] to the left of the timeline. In the Audio Levels dialog box that appears, drag the slider ([icon]) to the right to increase the volume of the narration you recorded.

Can I change when the narration will start playing?

✔ Yes. You can drag the sound clip to a new position below the timeline to change when the narration will start playing.

Can I record narration for a movie using a device other than a microphone?

✔ Yes. In the Record Narration Track dialog box, click the Change button. The Configure Audio dialog box appears. Click the Input line area and then select the device you want to use.

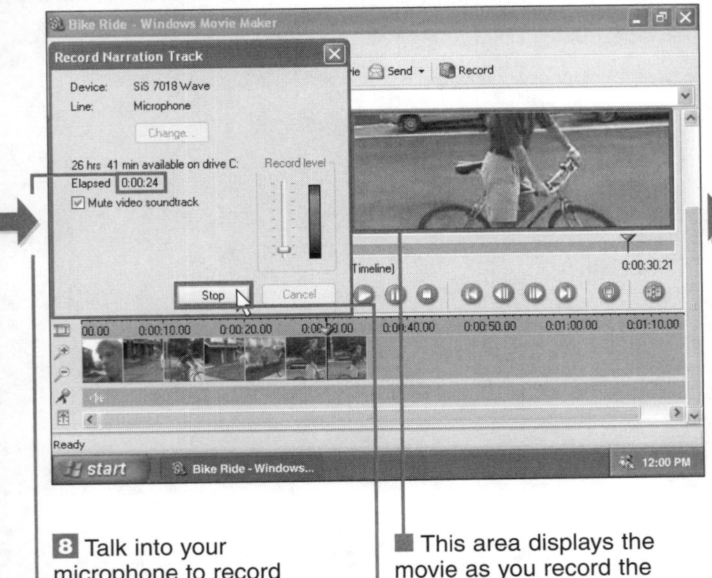

8 Talk into your microphone to record your narration.

■ This area displays the time that has passed since you started recording the narration.

■ This area displays the movie as you record the narration.

9 Click Stop when you want to stop recording the narration.

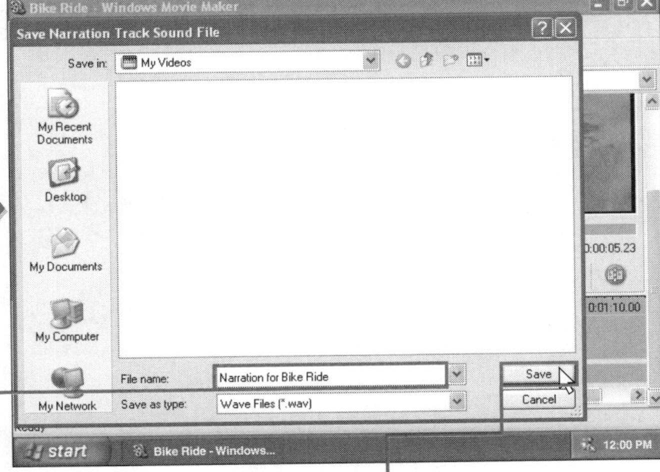

■ The Save Narration Track Sound File dialog box appears.

10 Type a name for the sound file.

11 Click Save to save the sound file.

■ The sound file will appear as a sound clip below the timeline and in the current collection.

ADD MUSIC

You can add music to a movie you are creating. If your movie already contains sound, the music will not replace the sound but will play in the background of the movie.

To add music to a movie, you must first import a music file into your project. Windows Movie Maker allows you to import music files with several types of extensions, including .wma and .mp3. You can create your own music files, copy songs from a music CD or download music from the Internet.

Windows Movie Maker also allows you to add other types of sound files to your movies. For example, you can import sound files with the .wav, .snd or .au extension to add sound effects to your movie.

When you import a music file into your project, Windows Movie Maker converts the file to a sound clip and places the clip in the current collection. Importing a music file does not move the file from its original location on your computer or network.

Once you have imported a music file, you can add the sound clip for the file to your movie. You must display the clips for your movie in the timeline view before you can add a sound clip to the movie.

ADD MUSIC

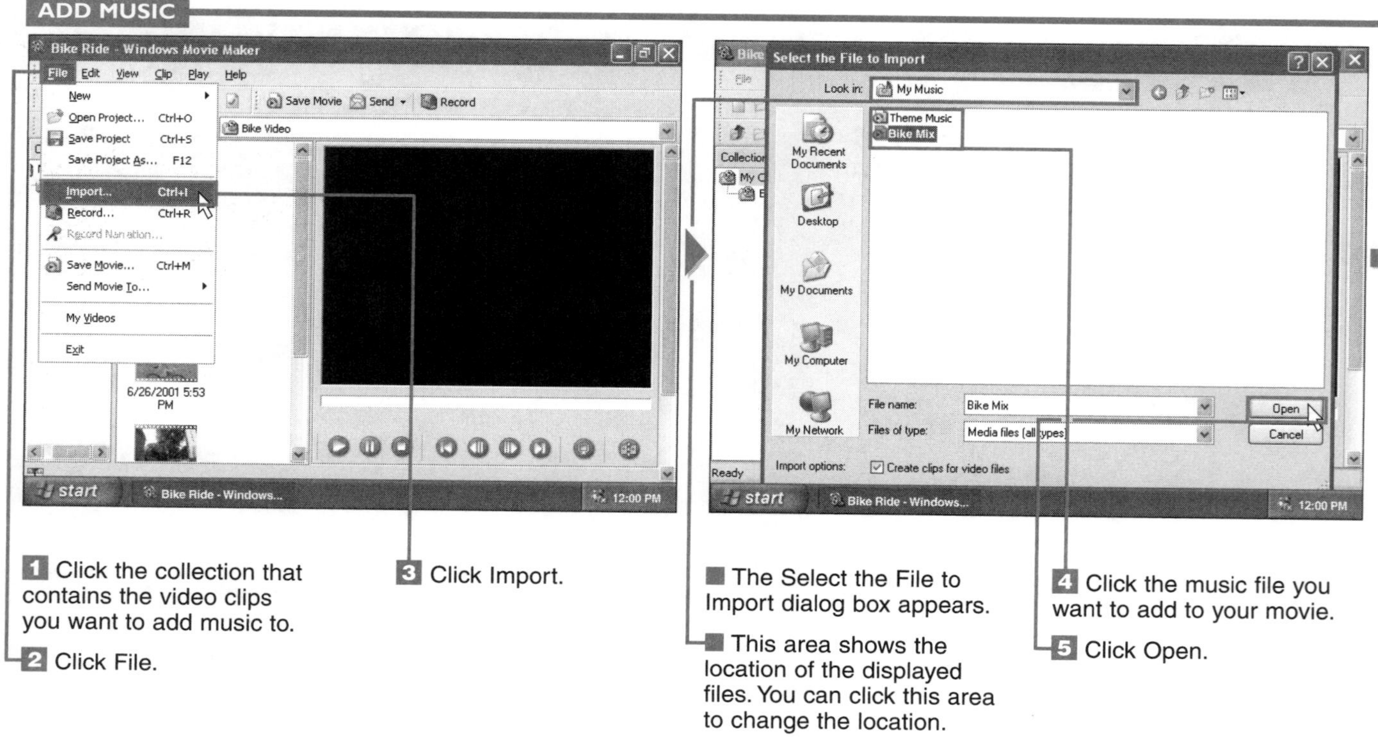

1 Click the collection that contains the video clips you want to add music to.

2 Click File.

3 Click Import.

■ The Select the File to Import dialog box appears.

■ This area shows the location of the displayed files. You can click this area to change the location.

4 Click the music file you want to add to your movie.

5 Click Open.

How can I change when the music will start playing?

✔ You can drag the sound clip for the music to a new location below the timeline to change when the music will begin playing.

Can I trim a sound clip for music I added to my movie?

✔ Yes. This is useful when you want music to play for only part of your movie. Trimming a sound clip is similar to trimming a video clip. Perform steps 1 to 5 on page 338, except click the sound clip you want to trim below the timeline in step 1.

Can I increase the volume of music I added to a movie?

✔ Yes. Click the Set audio levels button( ) located to the left of the timeline. In the dialog box that appears, drag the slider to the right to increase the volume of the music.

How do I remove music I added to my movie?

✔ Click the sound clip for the music below the timeline and then press the Delete key. Removing the sound clip from the timeline will not remove the clip from the collection in the Windows Movie Maker window.

■ The music file appears as a sound clip in the current collection.

6 Click to display the video clips in your movie in the timeline view (changes to).

7 Click the sound clip you want to add to your movie.

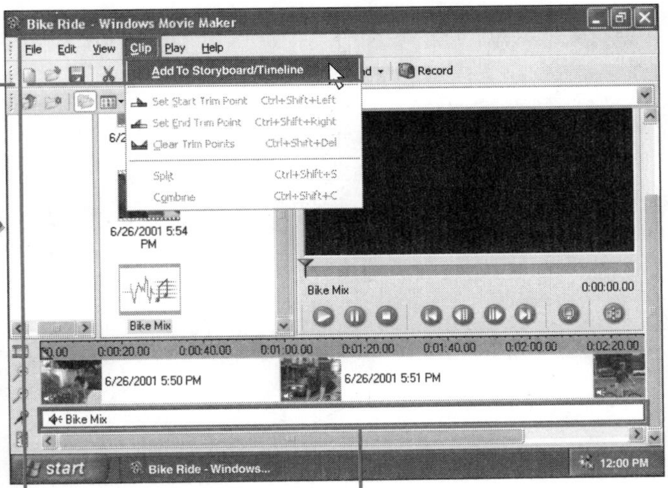

8 Click Clip.

9 Click Add To Storyboard/Timeline.

■ The music file appears as a sound clip below the timeline.

SAVE A MOVIE

After you add all the video clips that you want to include in your movie to the storyboard, you can save the movie on your computer. Saving a movie allows you to play the movie at any time and share the movie with friends and family.

Once you save a movie, you can send the movie in an e-mail to friends and family. The computer receiving the movie must have the necessary software to play the movie, such as Windows Media Player. You should try to keep your movies under 2 MB (2,000 KB) since most companies that provide e-mail accounts limit the size of the messages you can send or receive. You can also publish a movie to the Web to make the movie available to many people.

You can specify the quality setting you want to use for the movie. Higher quality settings result in larger movie file sizes. Make sure you do not select a higher quality setting than you used to record your video.

You can include information about the movie, such as the title and description of the movie. People who view your movie may see the information you enter.

By default, Windows saves your movies in the My Videos folder, which is located within the My Documents folder.

SAVE A MOVIE

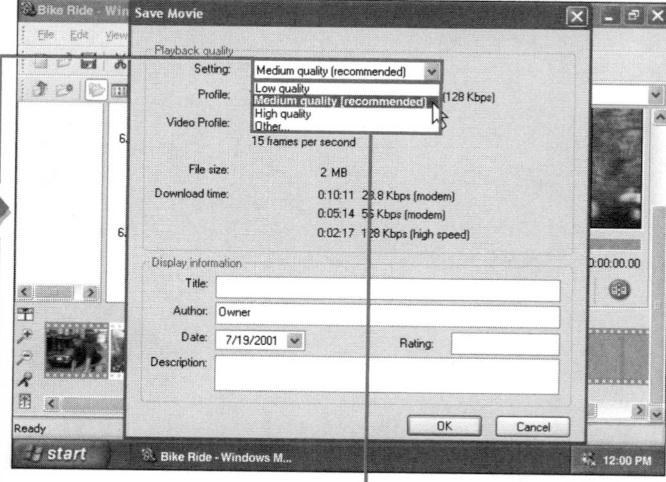

1 Click Save Movie to save the video clips on the storyboard as a movie.

■ The Save Movie dialog box appears.

2 Click this area to display a list of quality settings you can use for the movie.

3 Click the quality setting you want to use.

How do I e-mail a movie?

✔ Open the My Videos folder, select the movie you want to e-mail and click E-mail this file. For more information about e-mailing a file, see page 88.

Can I e-mail a movie from within Windows Movie Maker?

✔ Yes. In the Windows Movie Maker window, click Send and then select E-mail. In the dialog box that appears, select a quality setting, enter the information about the movie and then click OK. Enter a name for the movie and click OK. Then select the e-mail program you want to use to send the movie and click OK. Type the e-mail address of the person you want to receive the movie and click Send.

How do I publish a movie to the Web?

✔ Open the My Videos folder and select the movie you want to publish to the Web. Click Publish this file to the Web and then follow the instructions in the wizard that appears.

Can I publish a movie to the Web from within Windows Movie Maker?

✔ Yes. In the Windows Movie Maker window, click Send and then select Web Server. In the dialog box that appears, select a quality setting, enter the information about the movie and then click OK. Enter a name for the movie and click OK. Then select the name of the Web site host you want to send the movie to, enter your user name and password and click OK. If you need to sign up with a host, you can click Sign me up.

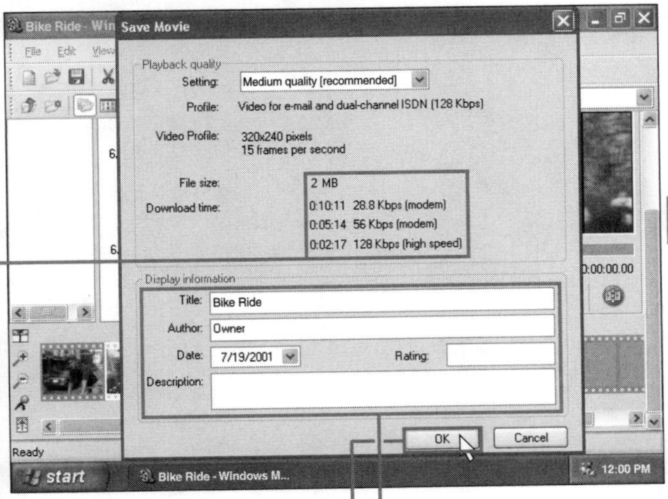

■ This area displays information about the movie, including the file size of the movie and the estimated download time for three different types of Internet connections.

4 These areas display information about the movie. You can click each area and type the appropriate information.

5 Click OK to save the movie.

■ The Save As dialog box appears.

6 Type a name for the movie.

■ This area shows the location where Windows will store the movie. You can click this area to change the location.

7 Click Save.

CONTINUED

SAVE A MOVIE (CONTINUED)

After you save a movie on your computer, you can view the movie in Windows Media Player. If you do not want to view the movie immediately after you create the movie, you can play the movie at a later time.

While a movie is playing in Windows Media Player, a slider (▮) indicates how much of the movie is left to play. Windows Media Player lets you control how a movie plays.

You can pause or stop the playing of a movie. You can also resume the playing of a movie after it has been paused or stopped. For more information about using Windows Media Player to control how a movie plays, see page 304.

Windows Media Player allows you to play only one movie at a time. Once a movie is finished playing, you can select another movie you want to play.

After you finish using Windows Movie Maker to save your movie, you can exit the program. You should always exit Windows Movie Maker and all other programs before turning off your computer.

SAVE A MOVIE (CONTINUED)

■ The Creating Movie dialog box appears while Windows Movie Maker creates your movie.

■ This area shows the progress of the creation of the movie.

■ A dialog box appears when Windows Movie Maker has finished creating and saving your movie.

8 Click Yes to watch the movie now.

Note: If you do not want to watch the movie now, click No.

How can I later play a movie I have saved?

✔ Open the My Videos folder and then double-click the movie you want to play. Windows Media Player appears and plays the movie.

Can I make changes to a movie I have saved?

✔ No. You cannot make changes to a movie you have saved. Windows Movie Maker only allows you to make changes to a project, which is a rough draft of a movie. To open a project, see page 336.

Can I copy a movie to a CD?

✔ If you have a CD-recordable drive, you can copy a movie from your computer to a CD. To copy a movie to a CD, see page 62.

Why does a dialog box appear when I exit Windows Movie Maker?

✔ When you exit Windows Movie Maker, a dialog box may appear, asking if you want to make a backup of your collections file. The collections file stores information about your video clips. If your collections file becomes damaged or you accidentally delete a collection or video clip, you can use the backup to restore the collections file. To save a backup of your collections file, click Yes.

■ The Windows Media Player window appears.

■ The movie plays in this area.

9 You can click a button to pause (⏸) or stop (⏹) the movie at any time.

Note: The pause button changes to ▶ after you pause or stop the movie. To play the movie again, click ▶.

10 When you finish viewing the movie, click ✖ to close the Windows Media Player window.

EXIT WINDOWS MOVIE MAKER

■ Before exiting Windows Movie Maker, make sure you save the project displayed on your screen. To save a project, see page 336.

1 Click File.

2 Click Exit.

SECTION V

15) WORK WITH MODEMS

16) WORK WITH DIAL-UP CONNECTIONS

17) MORE CONNECTION METHODS

CONNECT TO OTHER COMPUTERS

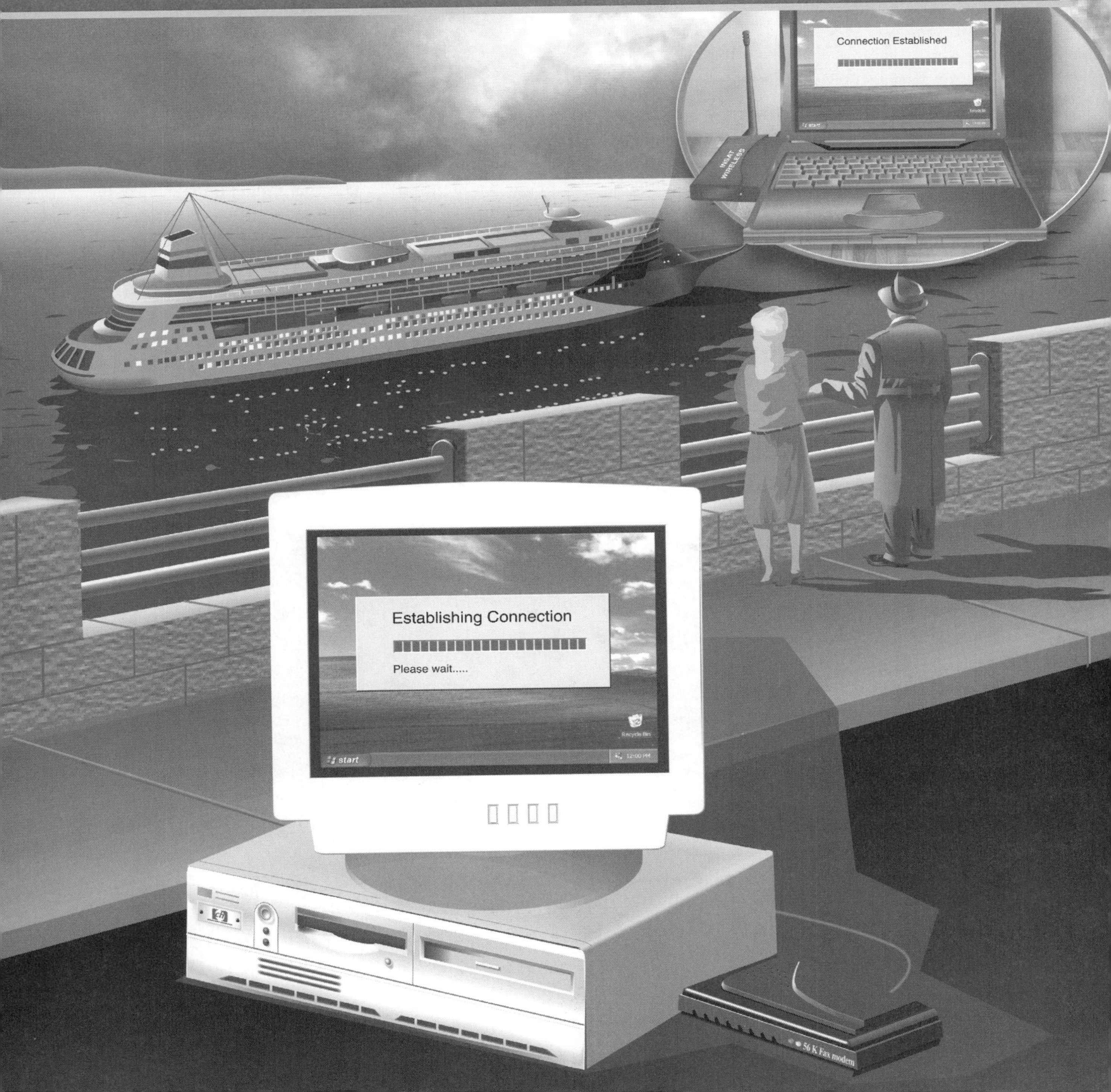

INSTALL A MODEM

You can install a modem on your computer. The Add Hardware Wizard guides you step by step through the installation process.

A modem is a device that allows computers to exchange information using telephone lines. A modem allows you to connect to the Internet or to another computer, such as a computer at work.

There are two types of modems. An external modem attaches to a computer using a cable. External modems are portable and easy to fix if a problem arises. An internal modem is located inside a computer and is less expensive than an external modem. Both types of modems provide the same features.

When you install a modem, Windows installs the necessary software, called a driver, for the modem. A driver allows your computer to communicate with the modem.

Before installing a modem, you should close all programs on your computer and if installing an external modem, make sure the modem is turned on. Windows will try to automatically detect the new modem on your computer.

You must be logged on to the computer as a computer administrator in order to install a modem.

INSTALL A MODEM

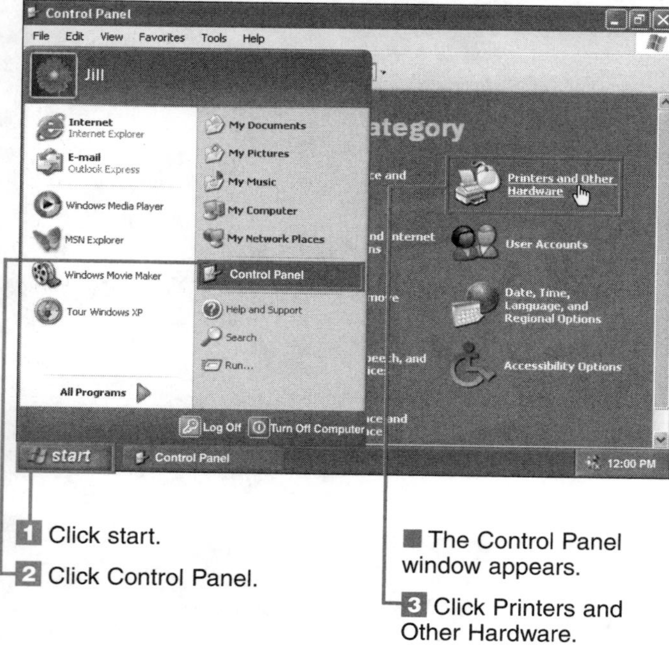

1 Click start.

2 Click Control Panel.

■ The Control Panel window appears.

3 Click Printers and Other Hardware.

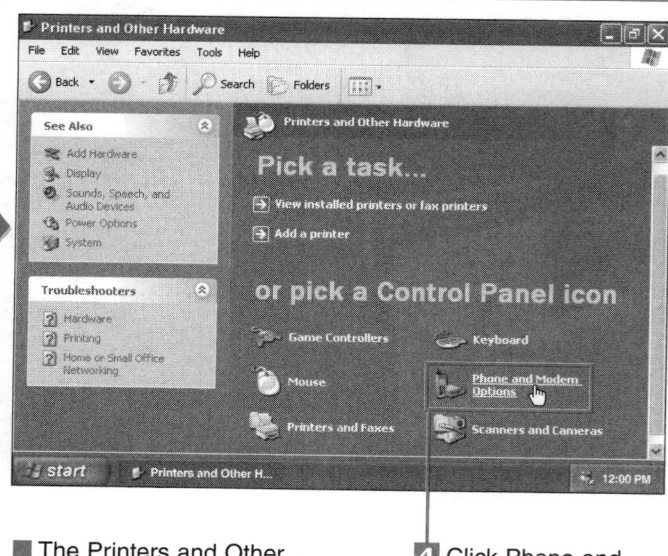

■ The Printers and Other Hardware window appears.

4 Click Phone and Modem Options.

Do I have to use the Add Hardware Wizard to install a new modem?

✔ No. When you physically connect a Plug and Play modem to your computer, Windows will usually automatically detect and install the modem for you.

My external modem does not have a cable to connect it to my computer. What can I do?

✔ Check the manufacturer's instructions to determine what type of cable is required. You can then purchase the required cable at a computer store. Most serial cables should also work with your modem.

Why does a dialog box appear after I click Phone and Modem Options?

✔ If you are installing a modem for the first time, a dialog box may appear, requiring information about the telephone connection at your location. You can specify the required information and then click OK.

Can I install more than one modem?

✔ Yes. Installing multiple modems on your computer is useful if you want to be able to simultaneously perform different tasks that require a modem. For example, you can use one modem to connect to the Internet while using another modem to send or receive faxes. You can repeat steps 1 to 14 below to install another modem.

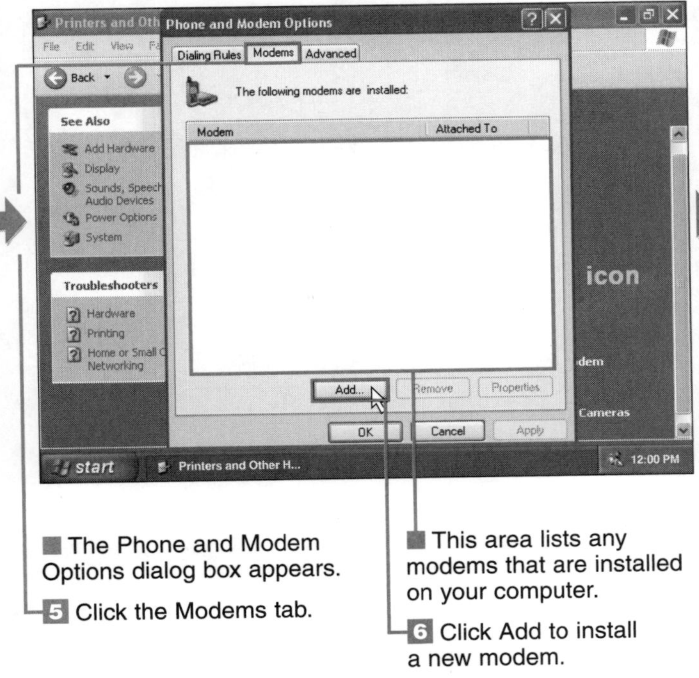

■ The Phone and Modem Options dialog box appears.

5 Click the Modems tab.

■ This area lists any modems that are installed on your computer.

6 Click Add to install a new modem.

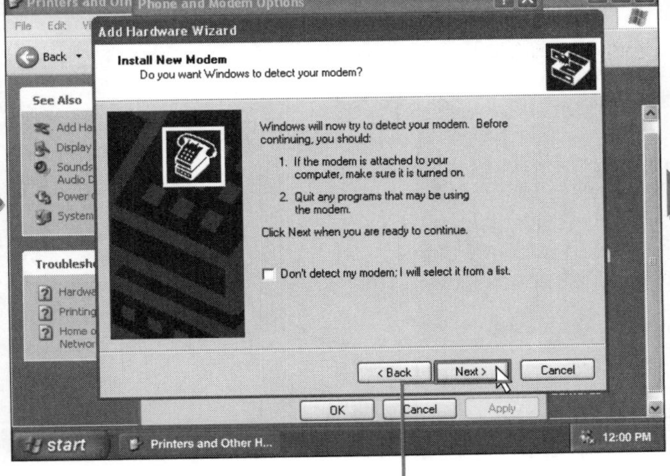

■ The Add Hardware Wizard appears.

■ If your modem is attached to your computer, make sure the modem is turned on. You should also close any open programs before installing the modem.

7 Click Next to continue.

■ Windows will try to detect your modem.

CONTINUED

INSTALL A MODEM (CONTINUED)

If Windows cannot detect a new modem, you will need to select the modem from a list. You can select the modem model that best matches your modem.

When installing a modem, you may need to specify which port the modem should use. A port is a connector that allows instructions and data to flow between the computer and a device. Most modems use a serial, or COM, port. If Windows detected your modem, you do not need to specify a port.

You must also ensure that the settings Windows uses for the modem match the settings on the modem. You can use the Device Manager to view the settings Windows uses for the modem.

For information about Device Manager, see page 580.

You may have to adjust the settings on the modem to correspond with the settings used by Windows. You can adjust the settings on the modem by using the software that came with the modem or by manually adjusting the jumpers or switches on the modem. Consult the modem's documentation before making any adjustments.

INSTALL A MODEM (CONTINUED)

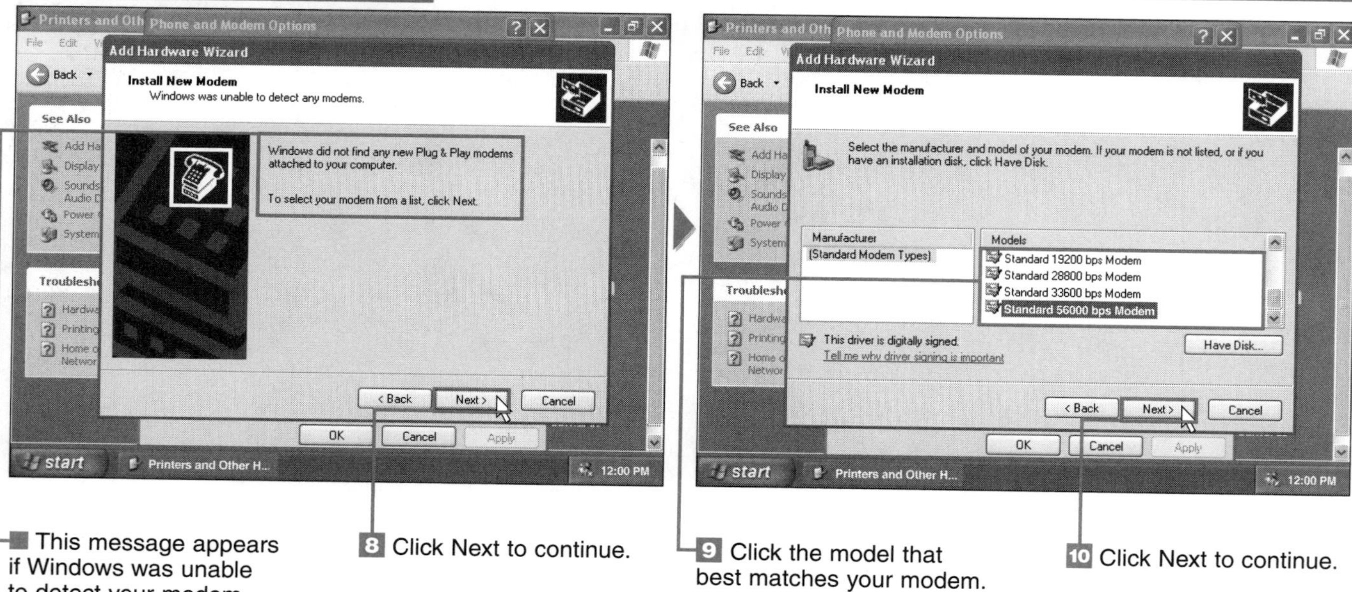

■ This message appears if Windows was unable to detect your modem.

Note: If the message "Your modem has been set up successfully" appears, skip to step 13.

8 Click Next to continue.

9 Click the model that best matches your modem.

10 Click Next to continue.

Should I install a modem using the installation disk that came with the modem?

✔ If your modem came with an installation disk, you should use the disk to install the modem. The software on the installation disk may be more updated than the software Windows might use. To use the installation disk, insert the disk into the drive, click the Have Disk button in the Add Hardware Wizard, select the appropriate drive and then press the Enter key. You may also be able to obtain a more recent version of the installation software from the modem manufacturer's Web site.

What can I do if the modem does not work after it is installed?

✔ You can use the Modem Troubleshooter to help you solve common modem problems. Click the start button and select Help and Support. In the Search area, type **modem troubleshooter** and then press the Enter key.

How do I remove a modem I no longer use?

✔ Perform steps 1 to 5 starting on page 350 to display the Phone and Modem Options dialog box. Select the modem you want to remove and then click Remove.

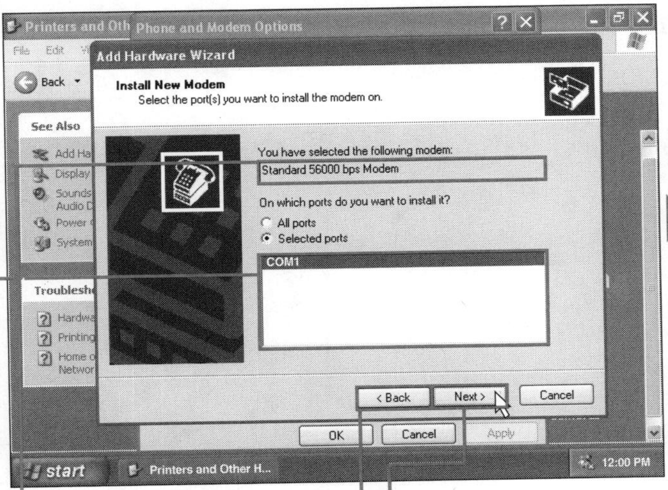

■ This area displays the modem you selected to install.

11 Click the port you want the modem to use.

12 Click Next to install the modem.

■ You can click Back to return to a previous step and change your selections.

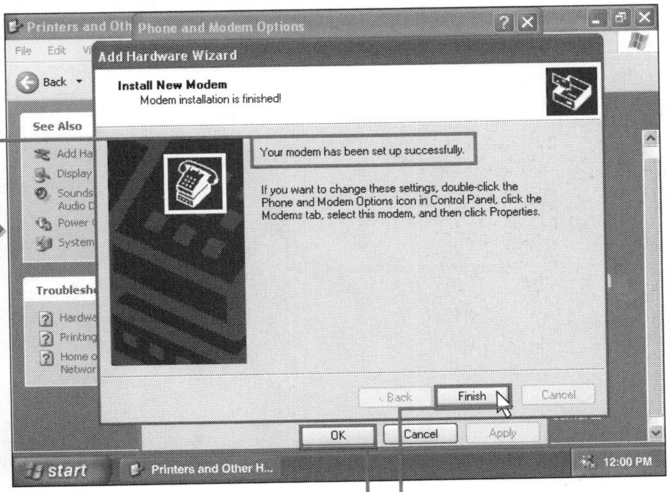

■ This message appears when Windows has successfully set up your modem.

13 Click Finish to close the wizard.

14 Click OK to close the Phone and Modem Options dialog box.

CHANGE THE MODEM DIALING PROPERTIES

You can change the dialing properties for your modem. Dialing properties are settings that determine how your modem will dial phone numbers. Changing the dialing properties may be helpful when you are having problems connecting to another computer. You may also need to change the dialing properties depending on the location where you are using your computer. For example, using your computer at the office requires different dialing properties than using your computer in a hotel room.

When you installed your modem, Windows set up a dialing location called "New Location" and specified basic dialing properties for the location. You can use a more descriptive name to better identify where you are dialing from, such as "Office."

When changing the modem dialing properties, you can tell Windows which country and area code you are calling from. Your modem will use this information to determine if a call will be local or long-distance.

CHANGE THE MODEM DIALING PROPERTIES

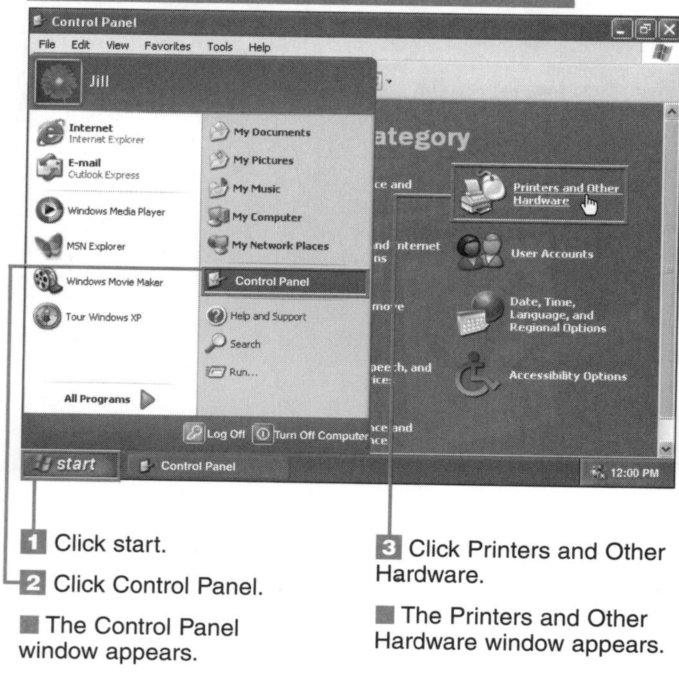

1 Click start.

2 Click Control Panel.

■ The Control Panel window appears.

3 Click Printers and Other Hardware.

■ The Printers and Other Hardware window appears.

4 Click Phone and Modem Options.

■ The Phone and Modem Options dialog box appears.

Can I set dialing properties for different locations?

✔ Windows allows you to specify different dialing properties for each location where you plan to use your computer. For example, you can have one set of dialing properties for your office and another for dialing from a hotel room. To create a new location in the Phone and Modem Options dialog box, select the Dialing Rules tab and then click the New button. Type a name for the new location. You can now enter the properties for the new location.

I have set up different dialing properties for different locations. How do I select a different location when using my modem?

✔ When you use your modem to connect to another computer, a dialog box usually appears, allowing you to select the location you want to use.

How do I remove a dialing location I no longer use from my computer?

✔ In the Phone and Modem Options dialog box, click the Dialing Rules tab, select the dialing location you want to delete and then click Delete. Windows will not allow you to delete the last dialing location set up on your computer.

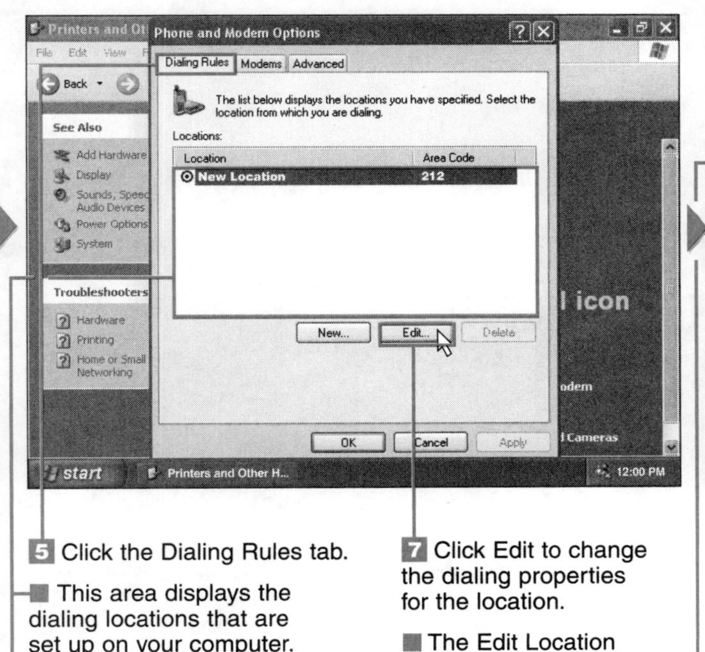

5 Click the Dialing Rules tab.

■ This area displays the dialing locations that are set up on your computer.

6 Click the location you want to change.

7 Click Edit to change the dialing properties for the location.

■ The Edit Location dialog box appears.

8 This area displays the name of the location. To change the name of the location, type a new name.

9 This area displays the country or region for the location. To specify a different country or region, click this area.

10 This area displays the area code for the location. To specify a different area code, double-click this area and type a new area code.

CONTINUED

CHANGE THE MODEM DIALING PROPERTIES (CONTINUED)

When changing the modem dialing properties, you can specify any special numbers you need to enter. For example, some companies require you to dial a special number to access an outside line for local or long-distance calls. If you will be making long-distance or international calls, you can also specify the carrier numbers you must dial for the calls.

Windows allows you to specify whether you want to use tone or pulse dialing. Tone dialing is the most common type of dialing used by phone companies.

If you have the call waiting feature, you can have Windows automatically disable the feature when you use your modem. This prevents call waiting from disrupting the modem connection. The call waiting feature will be automatically restored when you end the modem connection.

You can create area code rules to specify how you want to dial numbers to other area codes and within your own area code. When creating an area code rule, you must specify the area code you want the rule to apply to and whether you want the rule to include all the prefixes within the area code. A prefix is the first three digits of a seven-digit phone number.

CHANGE THE MODEM DIALING PROPERTIES (CONTINUED)

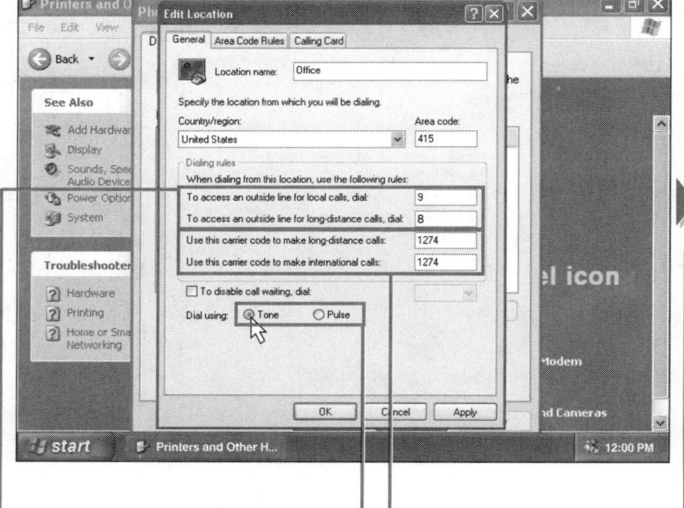

11 If you need to dial a number to access an outside line for local or long-distance calls, click the appropriate area and type the number.

12 To use a carrier code to make long-distance or international calls, click the appropriate area and type the code.

13 Click Tone or Pulse to specify the type of dialing to use (○ changes to ◉).

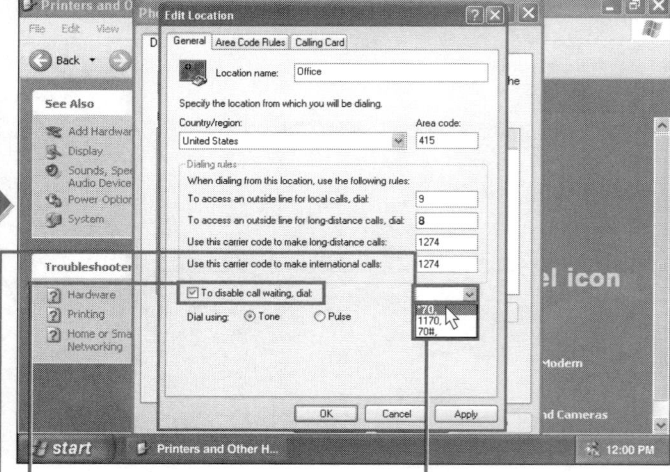

14 To disable call waiting when using the modem, click this option (☐ changes to ☑).

15 Click ▾ in this area to display a list of codes that can disable call waiting.

16 Click the code that disables call waiting for your phone company.

Note: If the code does not appear in the list, type the code in the area provided.

Which code should I choose to disable call waiting?

✔ The code you should choose varies depending on your local phone company. The most common code is *70, but you should check with your local phone company to determine which code to use.

What will happen if I do not create any area code rules?

✔ If you do not create any area code rules, Windows will usually dial numbers that have a different area code than your dialing location as long-distance phone calls. Numbers that have the same area code as your dialing location will be treated as local phone calls.

Can I apply an area code rule I am creating to only some prefixes in an area code?

✔ Yes. This is useful when some prefixes are treated differently than others. For example, only some prefixes in an area code may be long-distance phone calls for your dialing location. In step 20 below, select the Include only the prefixes in the list below option (○ changes to ◉) and then click Add. In the dialog box that appears, enter the prefixes you want the area code rule to apply to, separating each prefix with a space or comma. Then click OK.

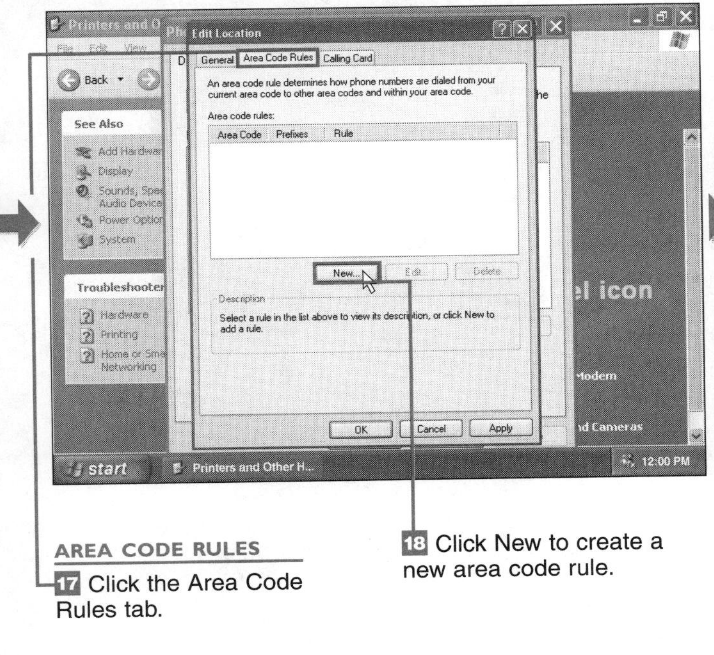

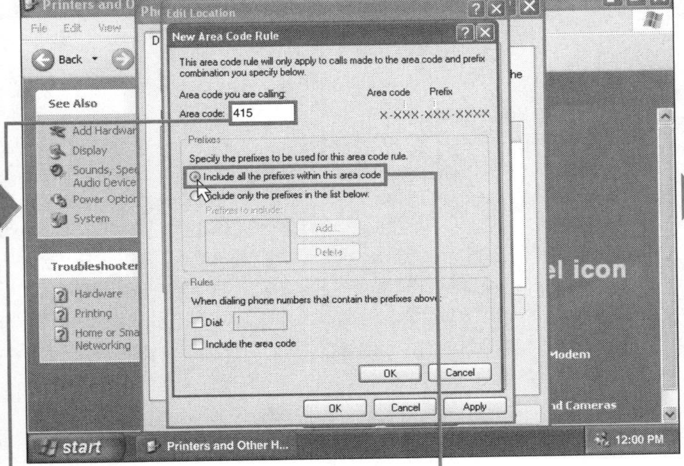

AREA CODE RULES

17 Click the Area Code Rules tab.

18 Click New to create a new area code rule.

■ The New Area Code Rule dialog box appears.

19 Click this area and type the area code the rule will apply to.

20 Click this option to apply the rule to all prefixes within the area code you specified (○ changes to ◉).

CONTINUED

CHANGE THE MODEM DIALING PROPERTIES (CONTINUED)

After entering the area code and prefixes you want an area code rule to apply to, you can specify the actions you want Windows to perform for the rule. For example, you can have Windows always dial a number, such as 1, before dialing phone numbers the rule applies to. This is useful for phone numbers that are long-distance calls.

You can also have Windows always dial the area code for the phone numbers an area code rule applies to. This is useful for local calls in areas that use 10-digit dialing.

You can set up your modem to use a calling card. A calling card allows you to make long-distance calls and have the charges billed to the owner of the calling card. Calling cards are useful when you are dialing from a location where long-distance calls are not permitted.

Before you can set up your modem to use a calling card, you must know the type of calling card you use and the account number for the card. If your calling card uses a Personal Identification Number (PIN), you must also know this number.

CHANGE THE MODEM DIALING PROPERTIES (CONTINUED)

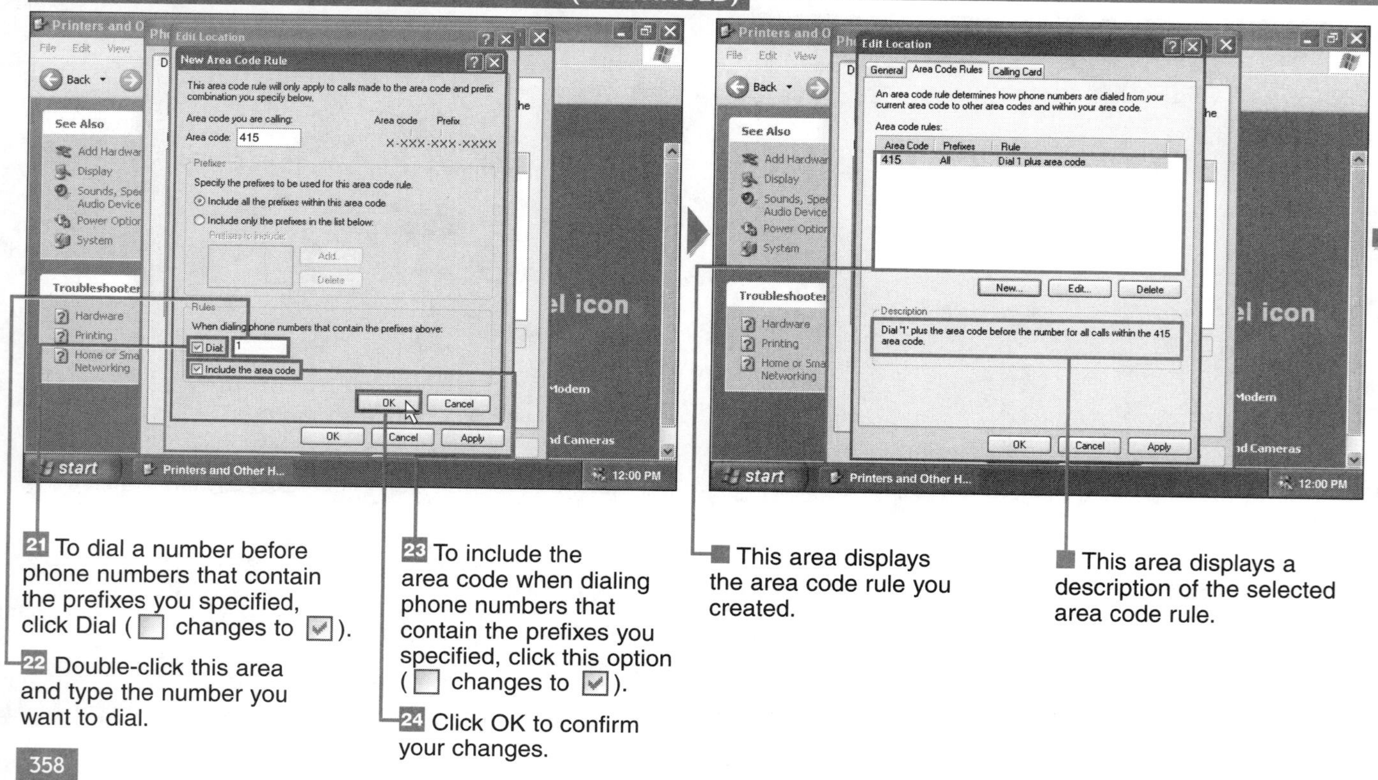

21 To dial a number before phone numbers that contain the prefixes you specified, click Dial (☐ changes to ☑).

22 Double-click this area and type the number you want to dial.

23 To include the area code when dialing phone numbers that contain the prefixes you specified, click this option (☐ changes to ☑).

24 Click OK to confirm your changes.

■ This area displays the area code rule you created.

■ This area displays a description of the selected area code rule.

How can I delete an area code rule I no longer want to use?

✔ In the Area code rules area, click the area code rule you want to delete and then click Delete.

Where can I get a calling card?

✔ Most phone companies offer calling cards to their customers. There are many types of calling cards available. Some cards offer incentives, such as discount rates. Many businesses and organizations use calling cards to track long-distance calls.

What should I do if my calling card is not listed?

✔ You can add your calling card to the list. Before performing step 26 below, click the New button below the Card Types area to display a dialog box where you can enter information about your calling card. On the General tab, enter the name of your calling card, the account number and your PIN in the appropriate areas. You can then use the Long Distance, International and Local Calls tabs to enter the access numbers Windows must dial and the dialing steps Windows must follow for each type of call. When you finish entering the information for your calling card, click OK.

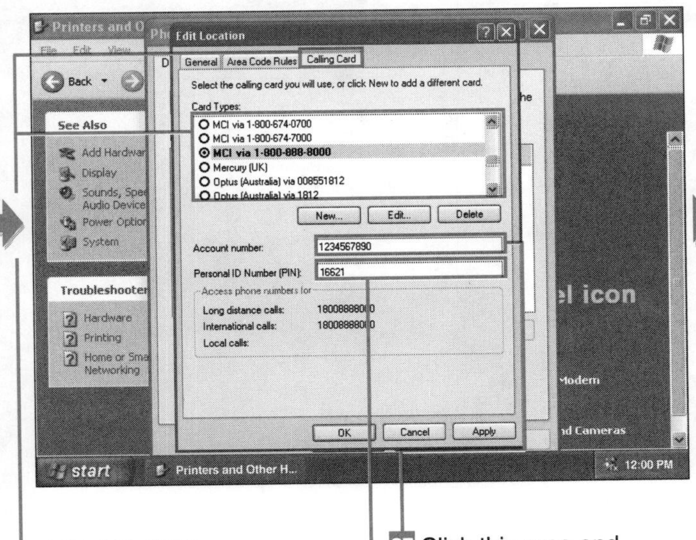

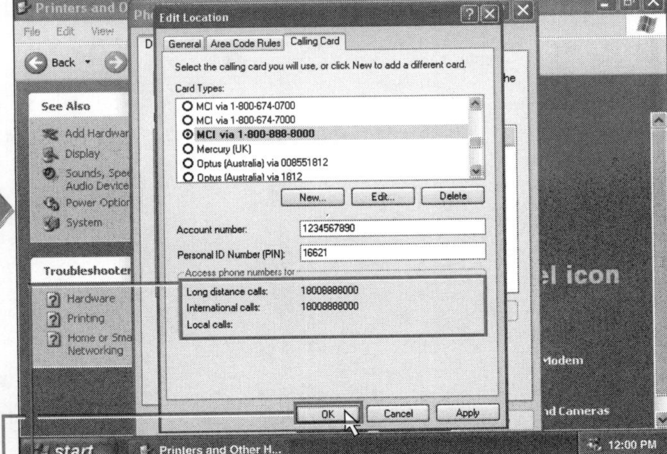

CALLING CARD

25 Click the Calling Card tab to use a calling card.

26 Click the calling card you use (○ changes to ⊙).

27 Click this area and type your account number for the calling card.

28 Click this area and type your Personal Identification Number (PIN) for the calling card.

■ This area displays the access numbers Windows will dial for long-distance, international and local calls.

29 Click OK to confirm all your changes.

30 Click OK to close the Phone and Modem Options dialog box.

CHANGE THE MODEM SETTINGS

You can change the settings for a modem installed on your computer to help the modem operate more effectively. You must be logged on as a computer administrator to change the modem settings.

The settings you can change depend on the type of modem you are using. Also, some settings may not be available if the correct modem driver is not installed on your computer. A driver is software that allows your computer to communicate with the modem. Most modems are already set up correctly so you may not need to change the settings for the modem.

In the Properties dialog box, you can view information about your modem, such as the manufacturer of the modem and the physical location of the modem on your computer.

You can also see whether the modem is working properly. If the modem has a problem, Windows will indicate the problem and display a suggestion for how to fix the problem. Windows may also display a problem code number that can help a support technician diagnose the problem.

CHANGE THE MODEM SETTINGS

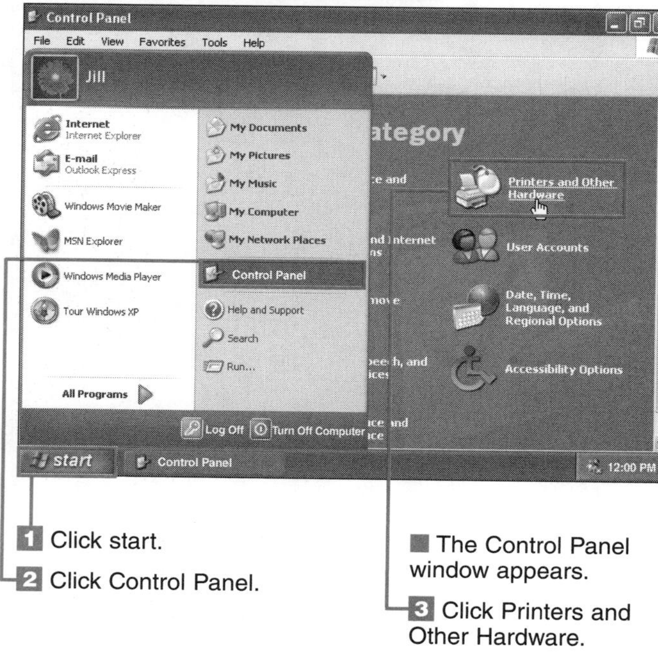

1 Click start.

2 Click Control Panel.

■ The Control Panel window appears.

3 Click Printers and Other Hardware.

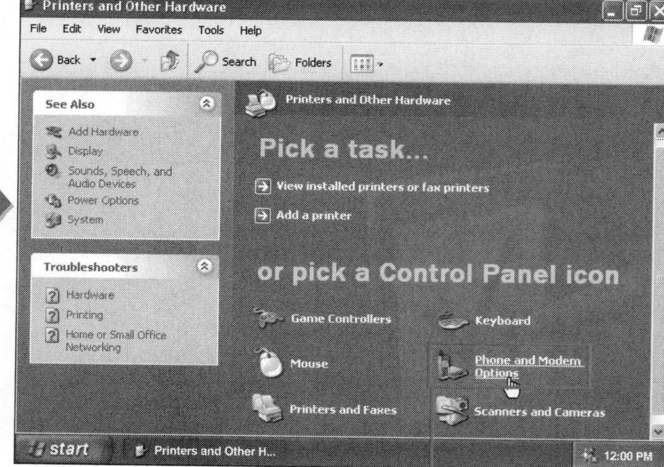

■ The Printers and Other Hardware window appears.

4 Click Phone and Modem Options.

I am having trouble with my modem. What can I do?

✔ In the Properties dialog box, select the General tab and click the Troubleshoot button. The Help and Support Center window appears, displaying the Modem Troubleshooter. Follow the instructions on your screen to try and fix the problem.

How can I disable my modem?

✔ In the Properties dialog box, select the General tab. Click the Device usage area and select the Do not use this device (disable) option. You should disable a modem only if the modem is causing a problem with your computer. You can also uninstall a modem to try to fix a problem. For information about uninstalling a modem, see page 558.

What are the additional tabs that appear in the Properties dialog box?

✔ Depending on the capabilities of your modem, the Properties dialog box may display additional tabs that you can use to change the modem settings. For example, the Power Management tab allows you to change the power options for the modem. You can use the Resources tab to view the computer resources assigned to the modem and the settings for each assigned resource.

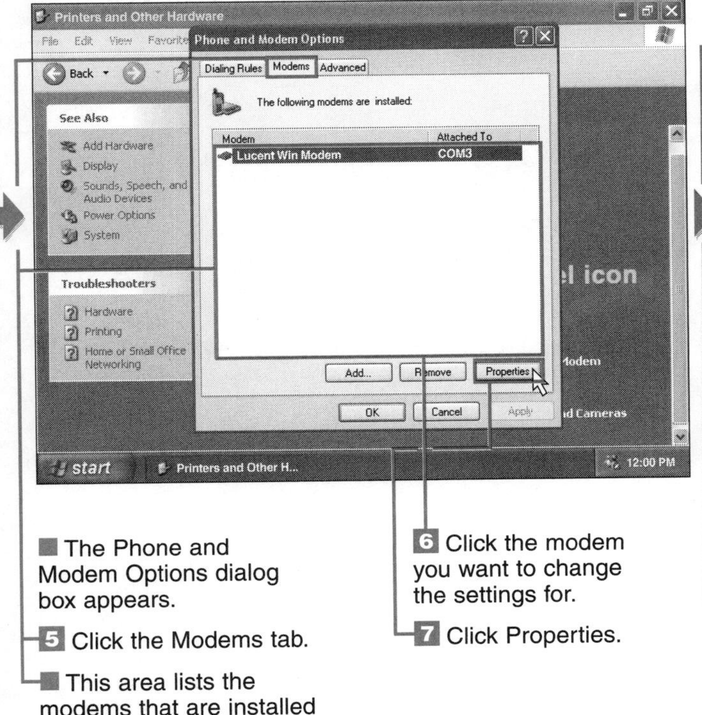

■ The Phone and Modem Options dialog box appears.

5 Click the Modems tab.

■ This area lists the modems that are installed on your computer.

6 Click the modem you want to change the settings for.

7 Click Properties.

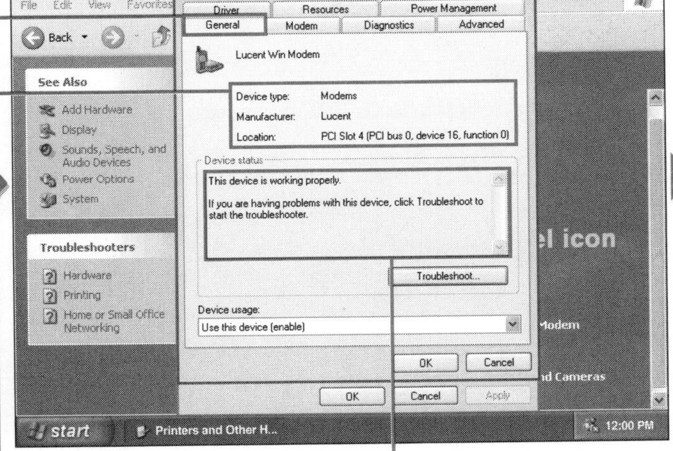

■ The Properties dialog box appears.

8 Click the General tab.

■ This area displays general information about the modem, such as the manufacturer of the modem.

■ This area indicates whether the modem is working properly. If there is a problem with the modem, Windows will indicate the type of problem and a possible solution.

CONTINUED

CHANGE THE MODEM SETTINGS (CONTINUED)

Most modems have a speaker that lets you hear the modem as it dials and connects to another modem. If your modem has a speaker, you may be able to use the modem settings to adjust the speaker volume.

The maximum port speed setting, measured in bits per second (bps), determines the speed at which your modem can exchange information with your computer. You can adjust this setting for the modem.

A modem may not receive a dial tone as soon as it connects to some phone systems. You can choose whether you want to have the modem wait for a dial tone before dialing.

You can view identification information about the modem and determine if the modem is communicating properly with the computer. Windows will display commands sent to the modem and responses from the modem. An error message appears if your computer cannot communicate with the modem.

Windows allows you to use extra settings to send special commands to your modem before it starts communicating with another modem. For example, you may be able to type ATM0 to turn off the modem speaker. These extra settings are often called an initialization string.

You can also display information about the driver the modem uses to communicate with the computer.

CHANGE THE MODEM SETTINGS (CONTINUED)

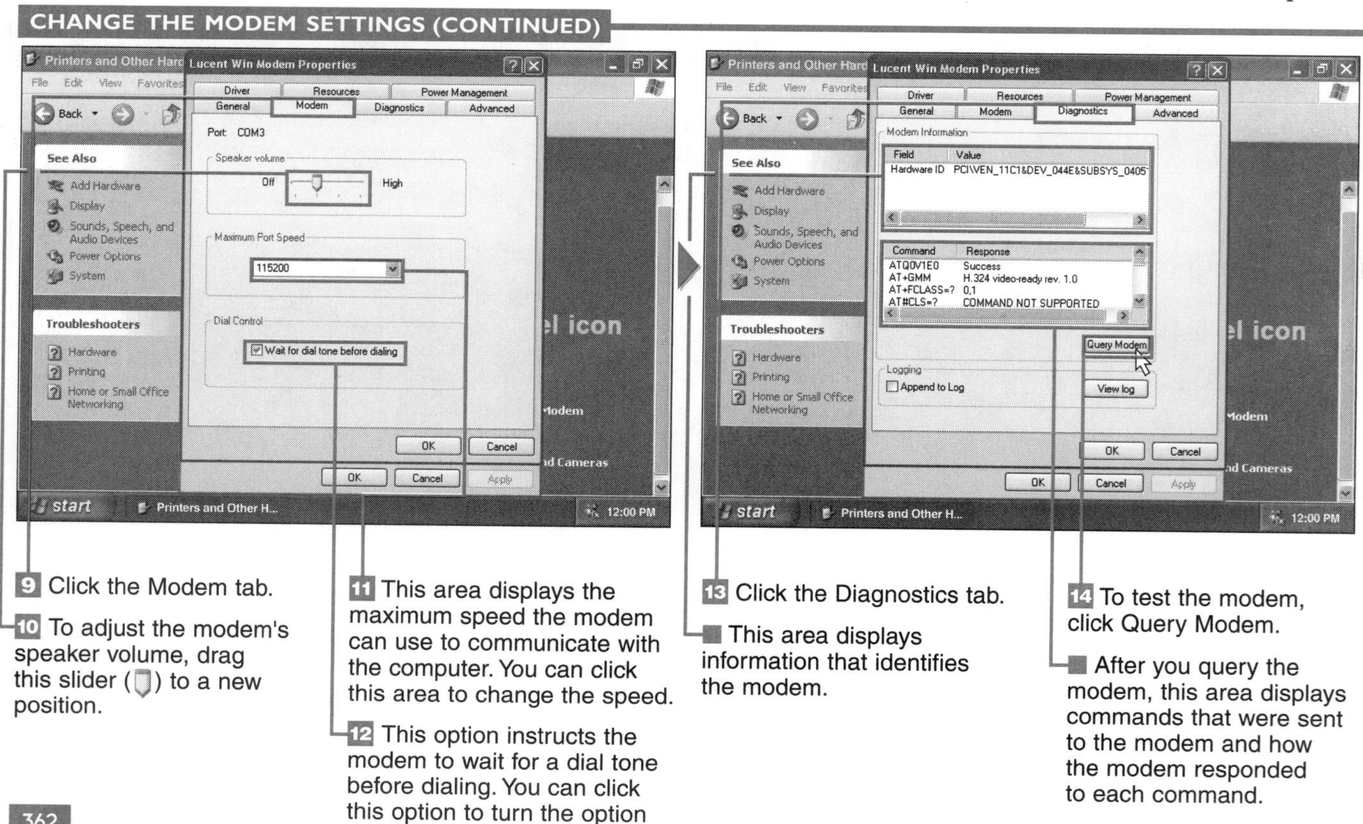

9 Click the Modem tab.

10 To adjust the modem's speaker volume, drag this slider (▯) to a new position.

11 This area displays the maximum speed the modem can use to communicate with the computer. You can click this area to change the speed.

12 This option instructs the modem to wait for a dial tone before dialing. You can click this option to turn the option on (☑) or off (☐).

13 Click the Diagnostics tab.

■ This area displays information that identifies the modem.

14 To test the modem, click Query Modem.

■ After you query the modem, this area displays commands that were sent to the modem and how the modem responded to each command.

Can I view a log file for my modem?

✔ By default, Windows keeps track of the modem activities for the most recent session in a log file. In the Properties dialog box, select the Diagnostics tab and click the View log button. Notepad will open, displaying a record of the modem activities.

Can I have Windows keep track of all the modem activities?

✔ Yes. In the Properties dialog box, select the Diagnostics tab and click the Append to Log option (☐ changes to ☑). Keeping a record of all the modem activities can help you keep track of the time you spend connected to other computers. A more detailed log file can also help you solve problems with your modem by showing which commands are causing errors to occur.

Are there additional modem settings I can change?

✔ Yes. In the Properties dialog box, select the Advanced tab and click the Change Default Preferences button. You can specify additional modem settings such as call preferences, which determine how the modem will handle idle and unresponsive calls, as well as data connection and hardware preferences.

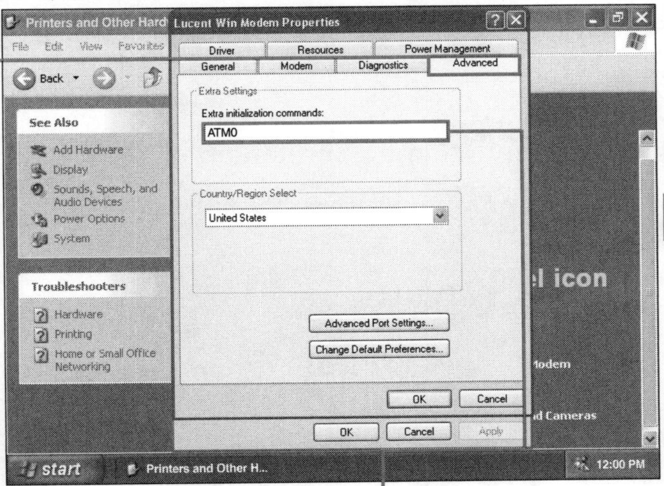

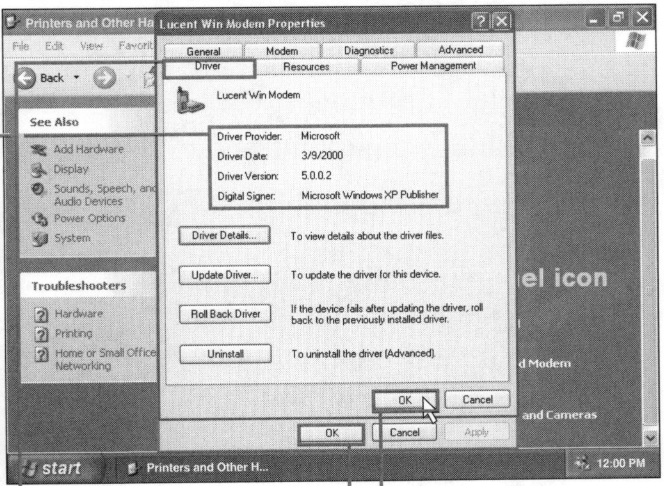

15 Click the Advanced tab.

16 To apply additional settings to the modem before it attempts to connect to another modem, click this area and type the commands.

17 Click the Driver tab.

■ This area displays information about the driver the modem uses to communicate with the computer.

18 Click OK to confirm any changes you made.

19 Click OK to close the Phone and Modem Options dialog box.

SET UP A DIAL-UP CONNECTION

You can use the New Connection Wizard to set up a dial-up connection that will allow you to use a modem to connect to another computer or to a network. When you are connected to the other computer or network, you will be able to work with files on the computer or network as if the files were stored on your own computer.

The dial-up connection you set up can use a modem with a regular phone line or an ISDN phone line. An ISDN line is a digital phone line offered by many telephone companies. An ISDN line transfers information faster than a regular phone line and does not tie up your telephone line.

Connecting to another computer or a network is useful when you are at home or traveling and you need to access information stored on a computer or network at work.

You only need to set up a dial-up connection to a computer or network once. After the connection is set up, Windows will display an icon for the connection in the Network Connections window.

SET UP A DIAL-UP CONNECTION

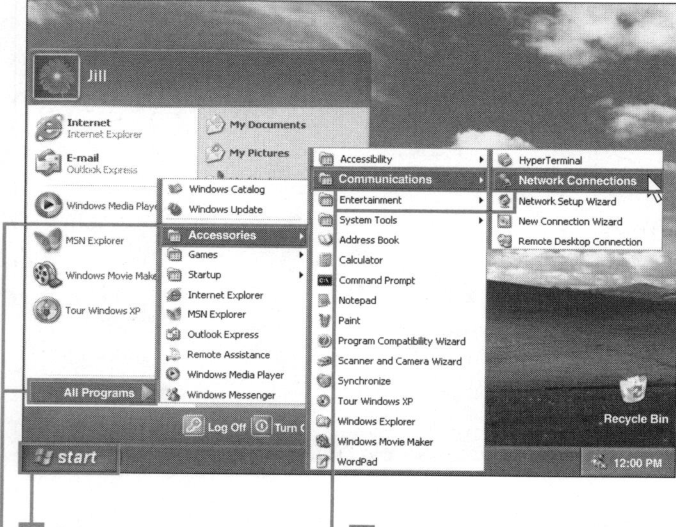

1 Click start.

2 Click All Programs.

3 Click Accessories.

4 Click Communications.

5 Click Network Connections.

■ The Network Connections window appears, displaying any connections that are currently set up on your computer.

6 Click Create a new connection.

Is there another way to start the New Connection Wizard?

✔ Yes. Click start, select All Programs and choose Accessories. Click Communications and then select New Connection Wizard.

How can I quickly display the Network Connections window?

✔ To quickly display the Network Connections window so you can view the connections you have set up on your computer, click start, select Connect To and then click Show all connections.

Can I set up a dial-up connection to the Internet?

✔ You can use the New Connection Wizard to set up a dial-up connection to your Internet Service Provider (ISP) so you can access the Internet. Perform steps 1 to 7 below. When the wizard asks you what you want to do, click Connect to the Internet. Once you connect to your ISP, you will be able to access the resources available on the Internet. See page 424 for more information about setting up an Internet connection.

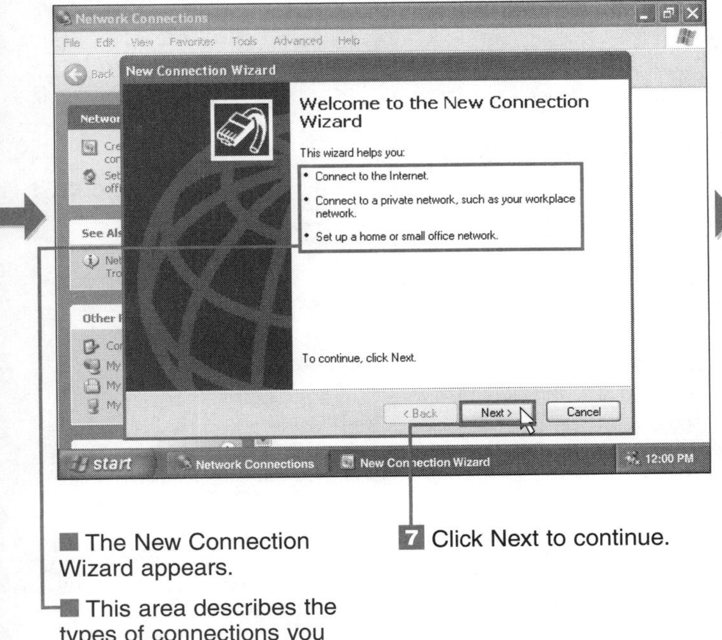

■ The New Connection Wizard appears.

■ This area describes the types of connections you can set up.

7 Click Next to continue.

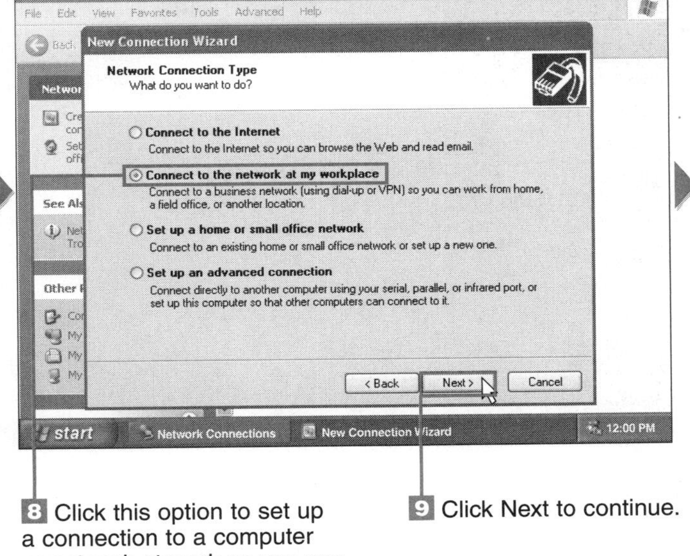

8 Click this option to set up a connection to a computer or network at work so you can work from home or another location (◯ changes to ◉).

9 Click Next to continue.

CONTINUED

SET UP A DIAL-UP CONNECTION (CONTINUED)

You can assign a name to the dial-up connection you are setting up. An icon displaying the name for the connection will appear in the New Connections window.

When setting up a dial-up connection to a computer or network, you must specify the phone number you will use to connect to the computer or network. When connecting to a network, you specify the phone number of the network server you must contact to access the network. You may need to include a 1, the area code or both when entering the phone number for a computer or network.

You can have Windows place a shortcut to the dial-up connection on your desktop. This will allow you to quickly use the dial-up connection to contact a computer or network.

Before you can use a dial-up connection to contact another computer or a network, the computer or network server you want to connect to must be set up to accept incoming connections. For information about setting up a computer to accept incoming connections, see page 374.

SET UP A DIAL-UP CONNECTION (CONTINUED)

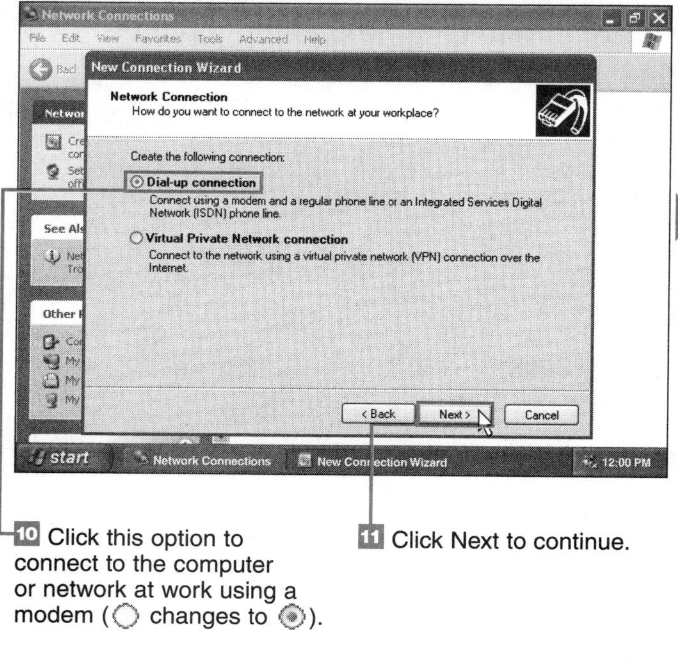

10 Click this option to connect to the computer or network at work using a modem (○ changes to ◉).

11 Click Next to continue.

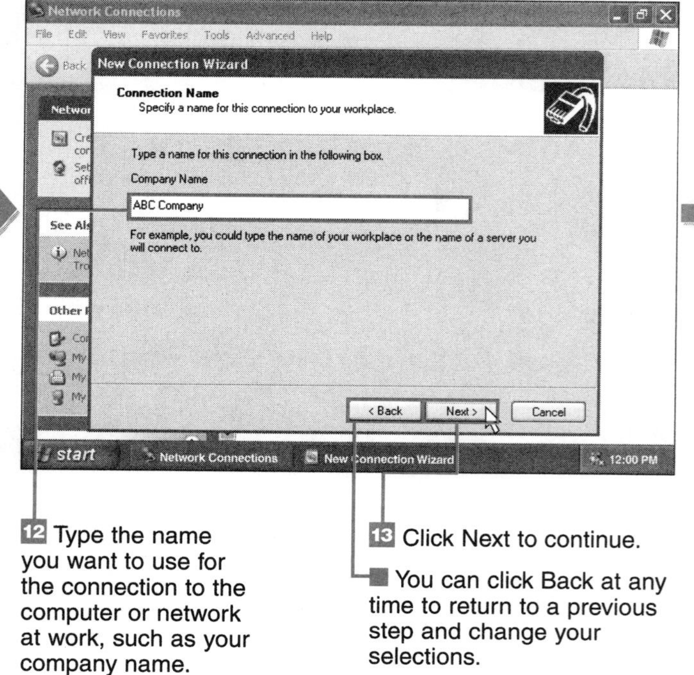

12 Type the name you want to use for the connection to the computer or network at work, such as your company name.

13 Click Next to continue.

■ You can click Back at any time to return to a previous step and change your selections.

Why did a Connect dialog box appear after I set up a connection?

✔ Each time you set up a connection on your computer using the New Connection Wizard, the Connect dialog box appears, allowing you to immediately use the connection. For information about using the Connect dialog box to dial in to a computer or network, see page 368.

How do I rename a connection I set up?

✔ In the Network Connections window, click the connection you want to rename and then click Rename this connection. Type a new name for the connection and then press the Enter key.

How do I securely connect to a network over the Internet?

✔ You can create a Virtual Private Network (VPN) connection to connect to a network using the Internet. The network you want to connect to must support Virtual Private Network connections. To set up a VPN connection, click the Virtual Private Network connection option in step 10, click Next and then follow the instructions on your screen. When the wizard asks for the host name or IP address of the computer you want to connect to, type the name or IP address of the VPN server.

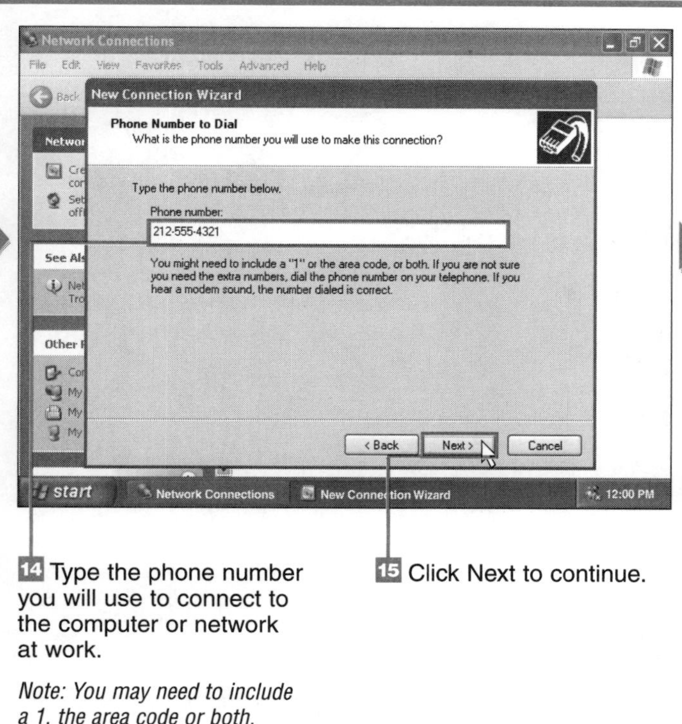

14 Type the phone number you will use to connect to the computer or network at work.

Note: You may need to include a 1, the area code or both.

15 Click Next to continue.

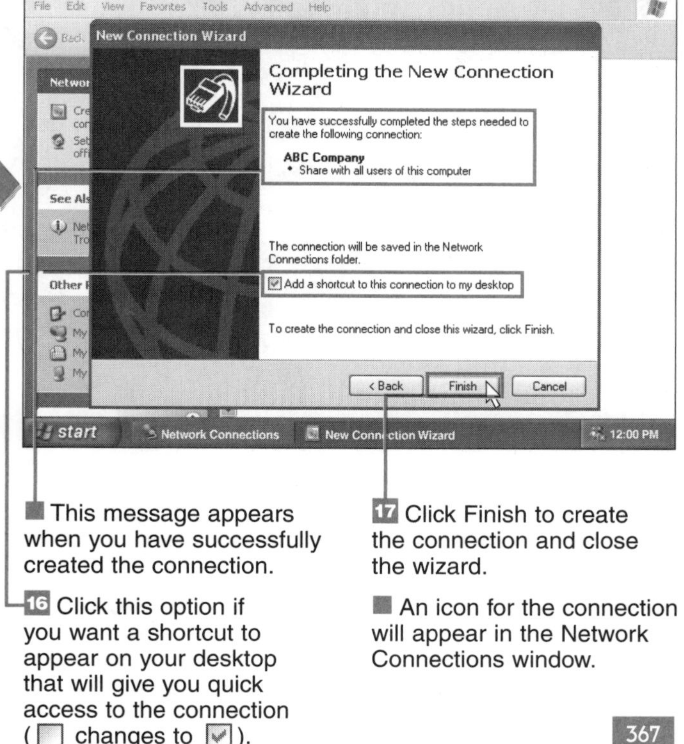

■ This message appears when you have successfully created the connection.

16 Click this option if you want a shortcut to appear on your desktop that will give you quick access to the connection (☐ changes to ☑).

17 Click Finish to create the connection and close the wizard.

■ An icon for the connection will appear in the Network Connections window.

DIAL IN TO ANOTHER COMPUTER

After you set up a connection to another computer, you can dial in to the computer to access information on the computer. For example, while you are away from the office, you can dial in to a computer at work to access files you need. If the computer you dial in to is connected to a network, you may also be able to access information on the network.

The Start menu displays the name of each dial-up connection you have set up. To set up a dial-up connection to another computer, see page 364.

Before connecting to another computer, you need to enter the user name and password that allows you to log on to the computer. You can view and change the telephone number Windows will dial to connect to the other computer.

When you are connected, Windows displays a connection icon in the notification area on your taskbar. You can use the icon to display information about the connection, such as the speed of the connection and the length of time you have been connected.

When you finish using the connection to the other computer, you can end the connection.

DIAL IN TO ANOTHER COMPUTER

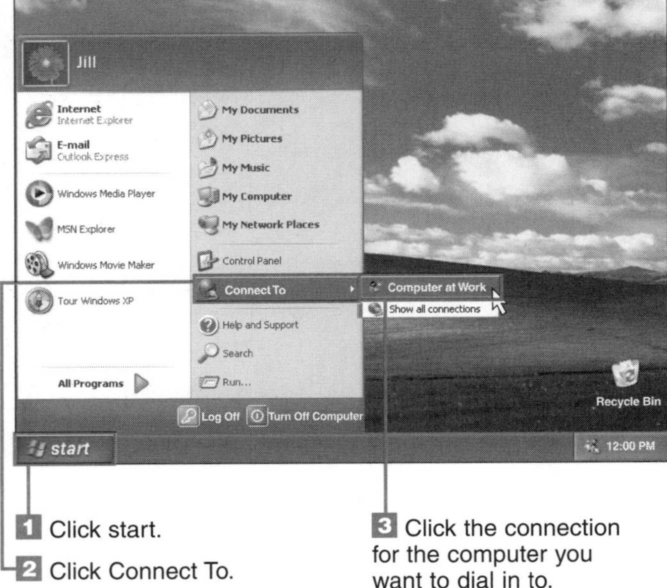

1 Click start.

2 Click Connect To.

3 Click the connection for the computer you want to dial in to.

■ The Connect dialog box appears.

4 Click this area and type the user name that allows you to log on to the other computer.

5 Click this area and type your password.

6 This area displays the phone number Windows will dial. To change the number, select the current number and then type a new number.

7 Click Dial to connect to the computer.

Will I need to enter my user name and password each time I connect?

✔ No. Windows will save the user name and password you type in the Connect dialog box for all users set up on your computer. If you do not want the information to be available to all users, click the Me only option (◯ changes to ◉) in the Connect dialog box. If you do not want Windows to save the user name and password, click the Save this user name and password for the following users option (☑ changes to ☐).

How can I access shared information on the other computer?

✔ You may need to first search for the computer on the network. To search for a computer on your network, see page 408. After you access a shared folder on the computer, the folder will appear in the My Network Places window. For information about using My Network Places, see page 406.

Why did my modem disconnect from the other computer?

✔ There may be interference on the phone line. Try connecting again to get a better phone line connection. Your modem may also disconnect from another computer if you do not use your computer for a period of time or if the computer you are connected to is turned off.

■ When you are connected to the other computer, this message and icon (🖧) appear.

■ You can now access information on the other computer.

8 To view information about the connection or to end the connection, click 🖧.

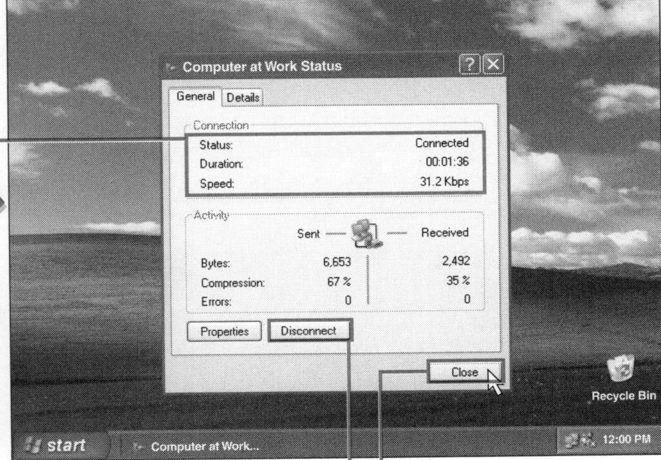

■ The Status dialog box appears.

■ This area displays information about the connection, such as the length of time you have been connected to the other computer and the speed of the connection.

9 To close the dialog box while staying connected, click Close.

■ To end the connection, click Disconnect.

CHANGE THE SETTINGS FOR A DIAL-UP CONNECTION

You can change the settings for a dial-up connection to specify how your computer dials in to another computer. When you change the settings for a dial-up connection, the new settings will affect only that connection. Your other dial-up connections remain unchanged. For accurate information about the settings you should select, you should contact the owner of the computer you are connecting to.

You must be logged on as a computer administrator to change some settings for a dial-up connection.

You can change the phone number Windows uses to contact another computer.

By default, Windows does not use dialing rules for a dial-up connection, but you can choose to use dialing rules to change how your computer dials in to another computer. If you choose to use dialing rules, you can select the area code and the country or region where the computer you want to connect to is located. The country or region you select helps Windows determine the country code it should use to contact the other computer.

When you are connected to another computer, an icon ( ) automatically appears on the taskbar and allows you to view the status of the connection. You can choose not to display the icon.

CHANGE THE SETTINGS FOR A DIAL-UP CONNECTION

1 Click start.

2 Click All Programs.

3 Click Accessories.

4 Click Communications.

5 Click Network Connections.

■ The Network Connections window appears, displaying any connections that are set up on your computer.

6 Click the icon for the dial-up connection you want to change.

7 Click Change settings of this connection.

■ A Properties dialog box for the dial-up connection appears.

How can I tell Windows to use another phone number if the first number fails to make a connection?

✔ In the Properties dialog box for the dial-up connection, select the General tab and then click the Alternates button. Click the Add button, type an alternate phone number and then click OK. When a number fails to make a connection, Windows will dial the next number in the list.

How can I access the dialing rules I have set for my modem while changing the settings for a dial-up connection?

✔ In the Properties dialog box for the dial-up connection, choose the General tab, select the Use dialing rules option (☐ changes to ☑) and click the Dialing Rules button. Then select the dialing rules you want to use and click OK. To create dialing rules, see page 354.

My modem is constantly connecting at a low speed. What can I do?

✔ You should check the maximum speed setting for your modem. Consult your modem's documentation to determine the maximum speed your modem is capable of. Then display the Properties dialog box for the dial-up connection, select the General tab and click the Configure button. Click ⌄ beside Maximum speed (bps) and select the maximum speed for your modem.

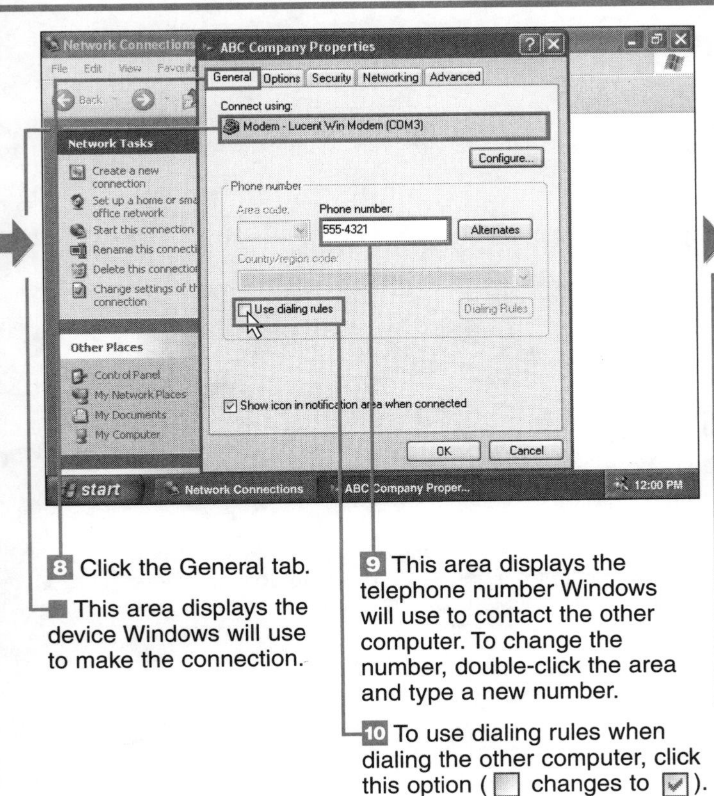

8 Click the General tab.

■ This area displays the device Windows will use to make the connection.

9 This area displays the telephone number Windows will use to contact the other computer. To change the number, double-click the area and type a new number.

10 To use dialing rules when dialing the other computer, click this option (☐ changes to ☑).

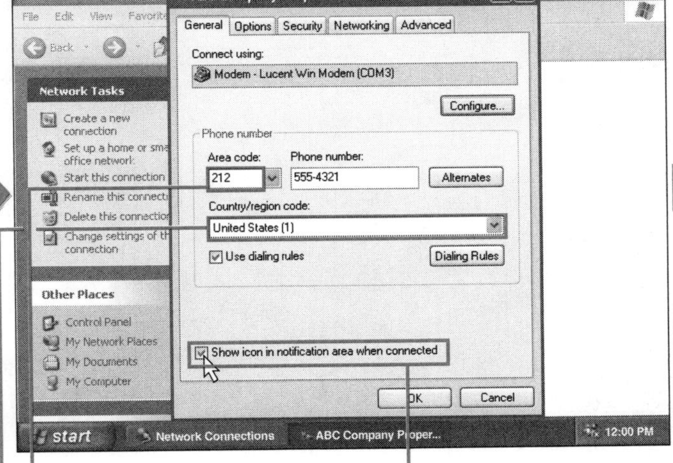

11 If you selected to use dialing rules in step 10, you can click this area to specify the area code you need to dial.

12 This area displays the location of the computer you are connecting to. You can click this area to change the location.

13 This option displays an icon on the taskbar when the connection is made. You can click this option to turn the option on (☑) or off (☐).

CONTINUED

CHANGE THE SETTINGS FOR A DIAL-UP CONNECTION (CONTINUED)

You can specify whether you want Windows to display the progress of a connection.

You can have Windows ask for a user name and password before connecting to another computer and have Windows ask for a domain name when you attempt to dial in to another computer.

If you want to be able to make last minute changes to a number you are dialing, you can have Windows display the number before you connect to the other computer.

You can also change the redial settings for a dial-up connection. When a connection is not made on the first attempt, you can specify the number of times you want Windows to redial the phone number. You can also specify the amount of time in minutes or seconds you want Windows to wait before redialing a phone number when the first attempt to make a connection is unsuccessful.

You can change the amount of time Windows will wait before hanging up when your computer is idle. Your computer is idle when connected to another computer but not in use.

You can specify the type of computer you want to connect to. You can also enable or disable network components for a dial-up connection.

CHANGE THE SETTINGS FOR A DIAL-UP CONNECTION (CONTINUED)

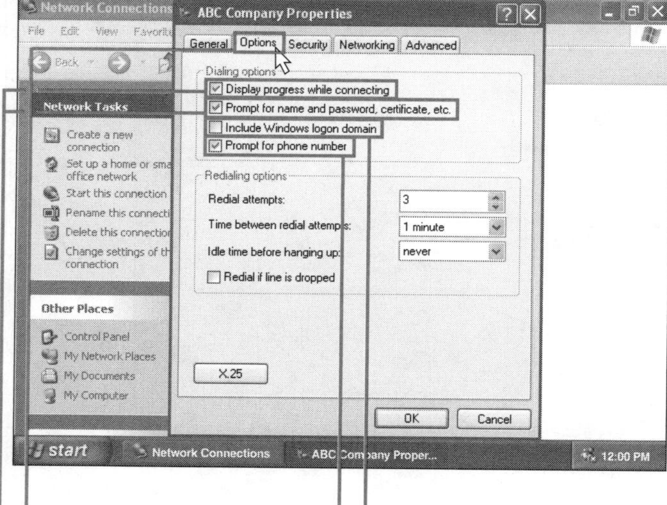

14 Click the Options tab.

■ This option displays the progress of the connection while dialing.

■ This option requests user information before contacting the other computer.

■ This option requests information required to log on to a domain before contacting a computer.

■ This option allows you to view and change the phone number before dialing.

15 You can click an option to turn the option on (☑) or off (☐).

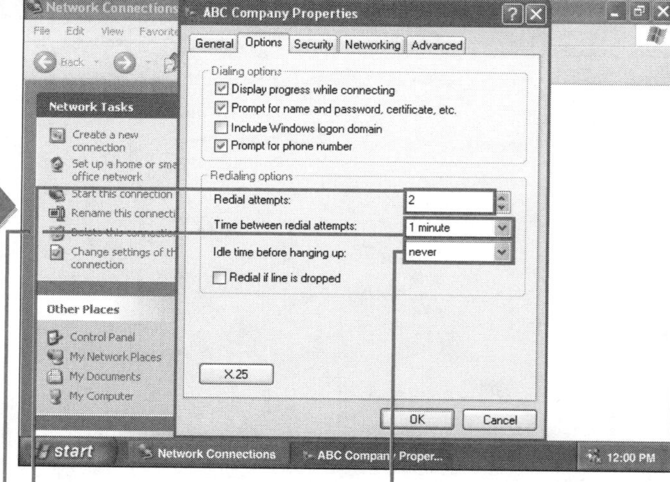

16 To specify the number of times you want to redial the phone number if a connection is not made, double-click this area and type a number.

17 You can click this area to select the number of seconds or minutes you want to wait between redial attempts.

18 You can click this area to select the time period you want to wait before automatically disconnecting an idle connection.

How many times should I have Windows redial?

✔ By default, Windows redials a phone number 3 times. You may want to set this option to a large number so Windows will keep redialing until a connection is made.

I need to change the TCP/IP settings for the dial-up connection I use to connect to my Internet service provider. What should I do?

✔ In the Properties dialog box for the dial-up connection, select the Networking tab. Choose the Internet Protocol (TCP/IP) component and then click the Properties button. You can then make the changes your Internet service provider requires, such as specifying an IP address or a DNS server address.

How long should I have Windows wait before each redial attempt?

✔ You may want to set the time between redial attempts as low as possible. Windows will continuously redial until a connection is made or the specified number of redials is reached.

Can I have Windows redial the other computer if the line is disconnected?

✔ Yes. Display the Properties dialog box for the dial-up connection and select the Options tab. In the Redialing options area, click the Redial if line is dropped option (☐ changes to ☑).

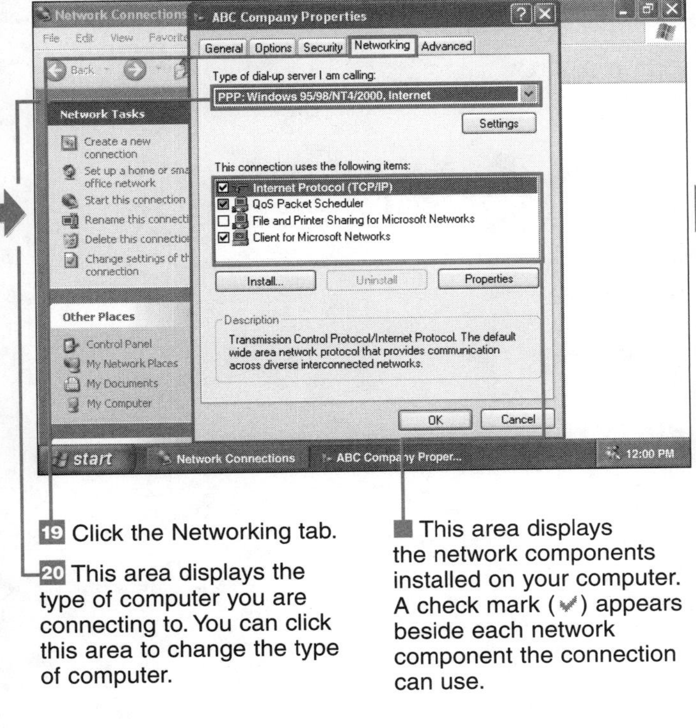

19 Click the Networking tab.

20 This area displays the type of computer you are connecting to. You can click this area to change the type of computer.

■ This area displays the network components installed on your computer. A check mark (✔) appears beside each network component the connection can use.

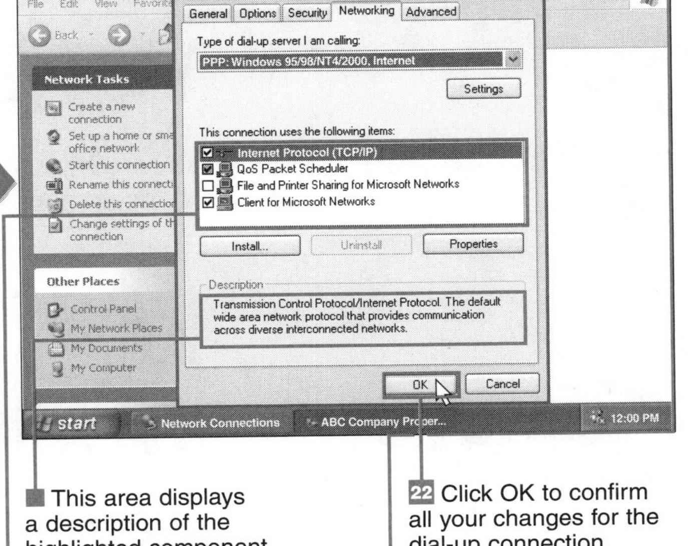

■ This area displays a description of the highlighted component.

Note: To display a description of another network component, click the name of the component.

21 To enable (☑) or disable (☐) a network component for the connection, click the box beside the component.

22 Click OK to confirm all your changes for the dial-up connection.

23 Click ☒ to close the Network Connections window.

SET UP AN INCOMING CONNECTION

You can set up an incoming connection on a computer so you can connect to the computer from another location. Setting up an incoming connection is ideal for someone who uses a laptop computer or home computer and wants to access information stored on a desktop computer at the office.

You must be logged on as a computer administrator to set up an incoming connection.

An incoming connection allows you to connect to the computer to access the information stored on the computer. If the computer is attached to a network, connecting to the computer may allow you to access the information found on the network. Connecting to the computer will also allow you to print documents on printers attached to the computer.

Many large networks have a dedicated computer that is set up to accept incoming calls from computers that require access to the network. These dedicated computers are often called dial-up servers or remote access servers.

SET UP AN INCOMING CONNECTION

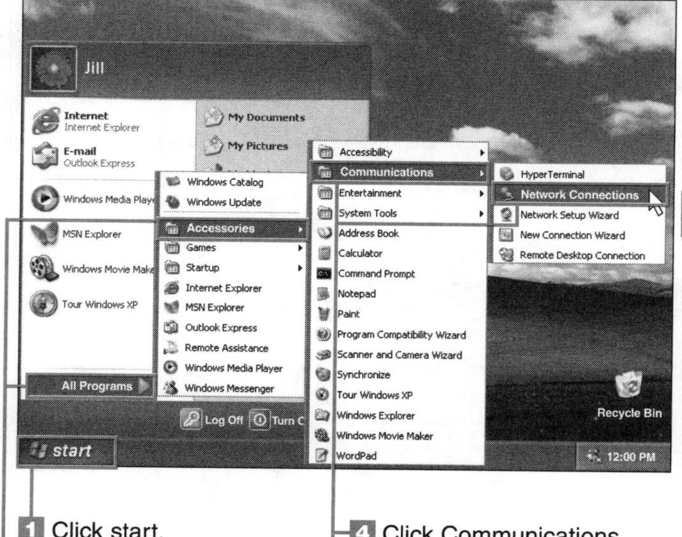

1 Click start.

2 Click All Programs.

3 Click Accessories.

4 Click Communications.

5 Click Network Connections.

■ The Network Connections window appears, displaying any connections that are currently set up on your computer.

6 Click Create a new connection.

Is there a faster way to start the New Connection Wizard?

✔ Yes. Click the start button, select All Programs, choose Accessories, point to Communications and then click New Connection Wizard.

What information will be available on the computer set up to receive incoming connections?

✔ Users will be able to access shared information on the computer. Shared items can include folders and printers. Users can use My Network Places to access the shared information. For information about using My Network Places, see page 406. To share a folder, see page 410. To share a printer, see page 412.

Can more than one user connect to a computer?

✔ Yes. Up to three users can connect to the computer at a time, but each user must use a different type of connection. For example, one user can connect to the computer using a dial-up connection, while another user can connect to the computer using a virtual private network connection. For more information about allowing a virtual private network connection, see page 376.

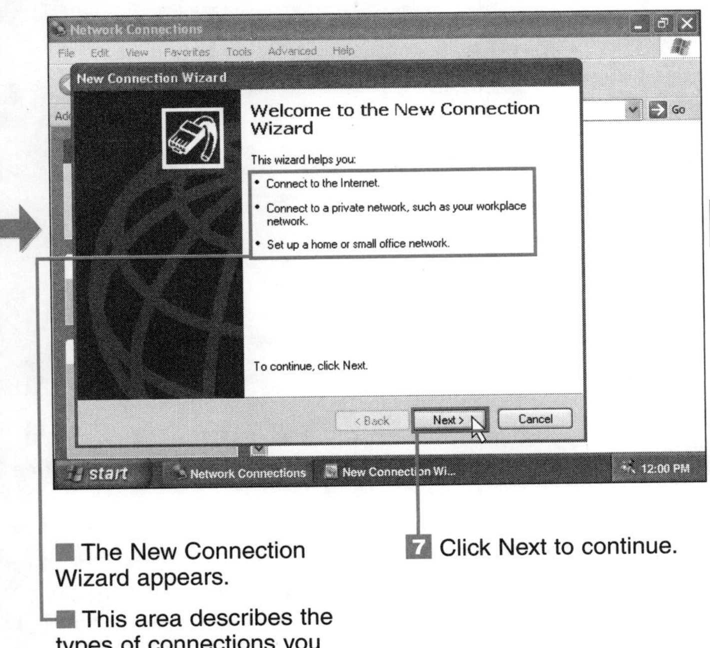

■ The New Connection Wizard appears.

■ This area describes the types of connections you can set up.

7 Click Next to continue.

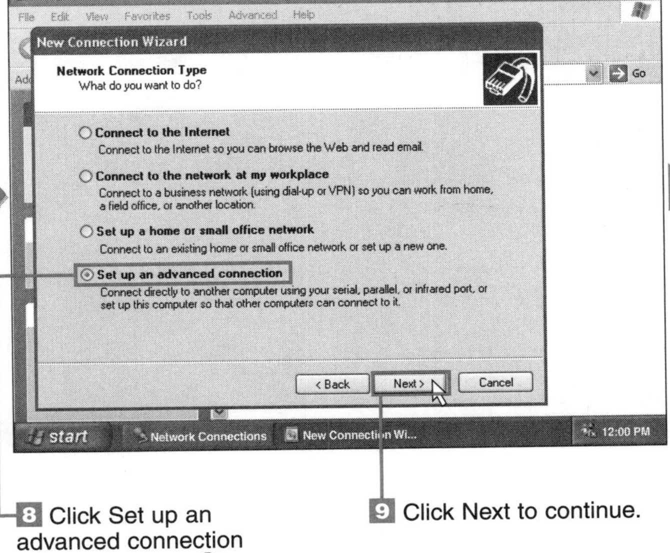

8 Click Set up an advanced connection (○ changes to ◉).

9 Click Next to continue.

SET UP AN INCOMING CONNECTION (CONTINUED)

When you set up an incoming connection, Windows allows you to select each device you want to allow other computers to use to connect to the computer. For example, if you have more than one modem installed on the computer, you can select the modem you want other computers to use to connect to the computer.

You can specify whether you will allow a Virtual Private Network (VPN) connection to the computer. A VPN connection allows people to securely access your computer through an Internet connection. A VPN connection allows you to save on long distance phone charges and helps ensure network security. If you allow a VPN connection, you should note that Windows will modify the Internet Connection Firewall settings to allow Windows to send and receive data through the VPN connection.

You can select the users you want to be able to connect to your computer. The users you select will have to enter their user name and password to connect to the computer. The wizard may also display user accounts that Windows uses as system accounts in the Help feature for troubleshooting and support purposes.

SET UP AN INCOMING CONNECTION (CONTINUED)

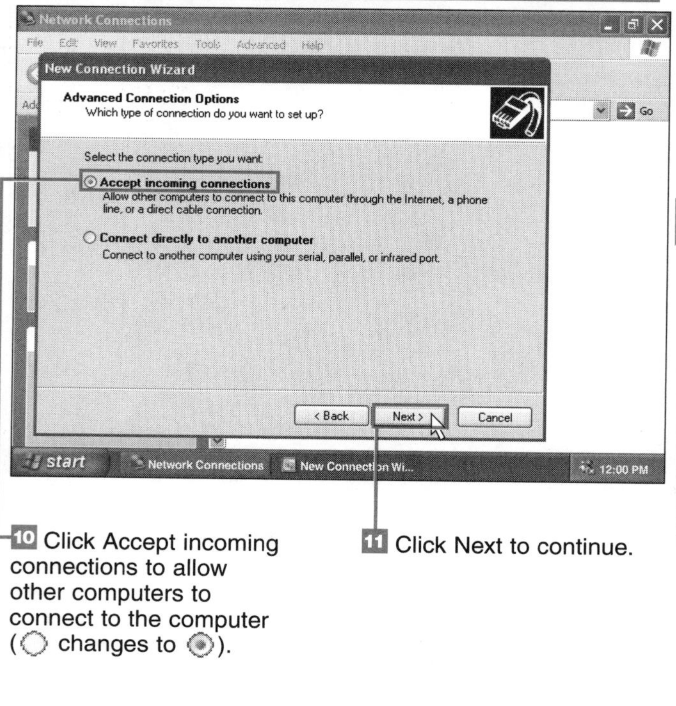

10 Click Accept incoming connections to allow other computers to connect to the computer (○ changes to ◉).

11 Click Next to continue.

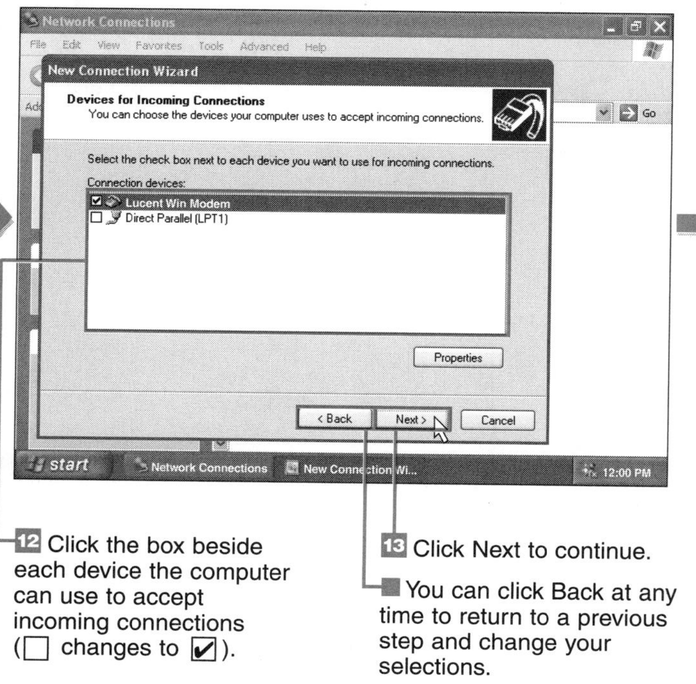

12 Click the box beside each device the computer can use to accept incoming connections (☐ changes to ☑).

13 Click Next to continue.

■ You can click Back at any time to return to a previous step and change your selections.

Can I change the modem settings for an incoming connection?

✔ Yes. After you choose the modem you want to use in the wizard, you can click the modem and then select the Properties button to adjust the settings for the modem. For example, you can have the modem automatically disconnect a call that has been idle for a period of time.

Can I allow other users to connect that are not displayed in the wizard?

✔ Yes. Click the Add button in the wizard and then enter the name and password for the user you want to be able to connect.

How do I change the password a user must enter to connect to the computer?

✔ In the wizard, select the user you want to add or change a password for and then click the Properties button. In the dialog box that appears, enter a new password. Changing a user's password for connecting to the computer also changes the password the user must enter to log on to the computer locally.

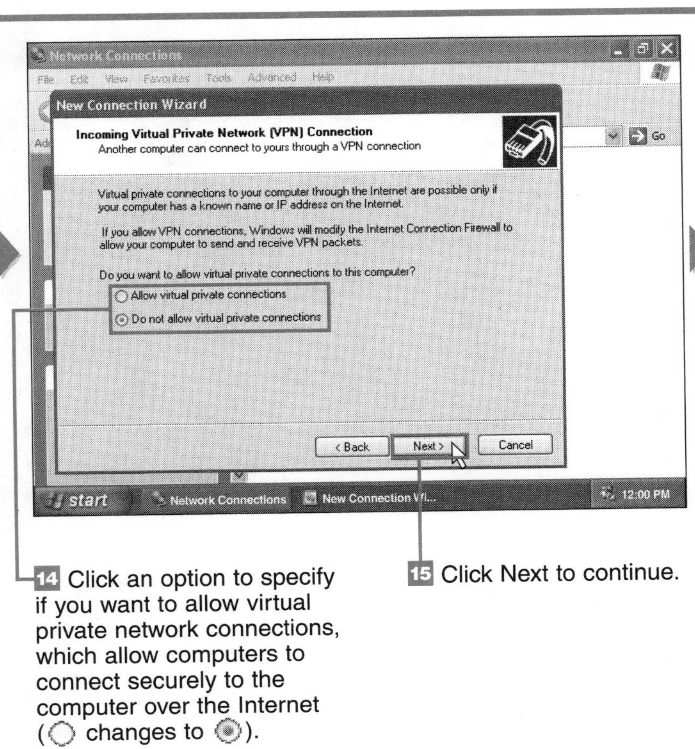

14 Click an option to specify if you want to allow virtual private network connections, which allow computers to connect securely to the computer over the Internet (◯ changes to ◉).

15 Click Next to continue.

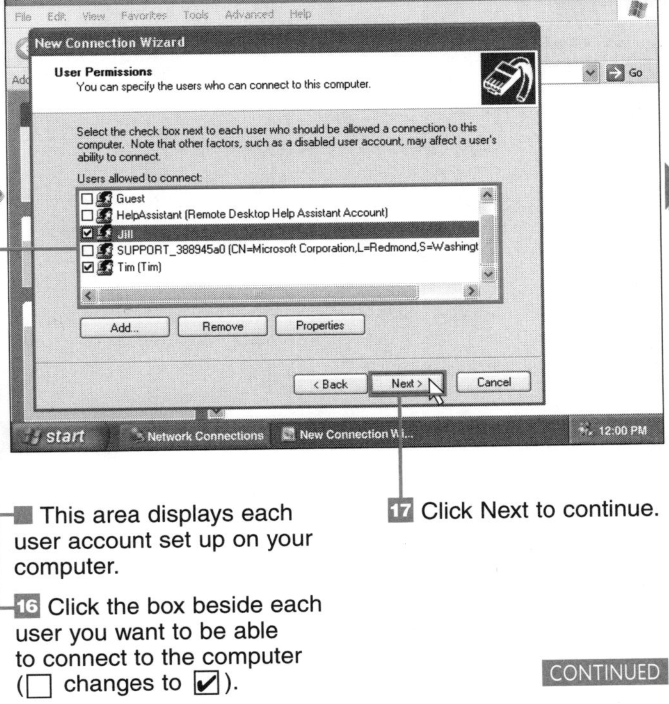

■ This area displays each user account set up on your computer.

16 Click the box beside each user you want to be able to connect to the computer (☐ changes to ☑).

17 Click Next to continue.

CONTINUED

SET UP AN INCOMING CONNECTION (CONTINUED)

Windows allows you to select the types of networking software, such as Internet Protocol (TCP/IP) and Client for Microsoft Networks, you want the computer to use for incoming connections. You should select the types of networking software other computers will use to connect to your computer.

After you set up an incoming connection, an icon for the incoming connection appears in the Network Connections window.

Windows allows you to set up only one incoming connection. If you use the New Connection Wizard again, the wizard will simply modify the incoming connection you have already set up.

You need to set up a dial-up connection on your laptop or home computer to dial in to the other computer. For information about setting up a dial-up connection, see page 364.

The computer that is set up to receive incoming connections must be turned on before you can connect to the computer from another location.

SET UP AN INCOMING CONNECTION (CONTINUED)

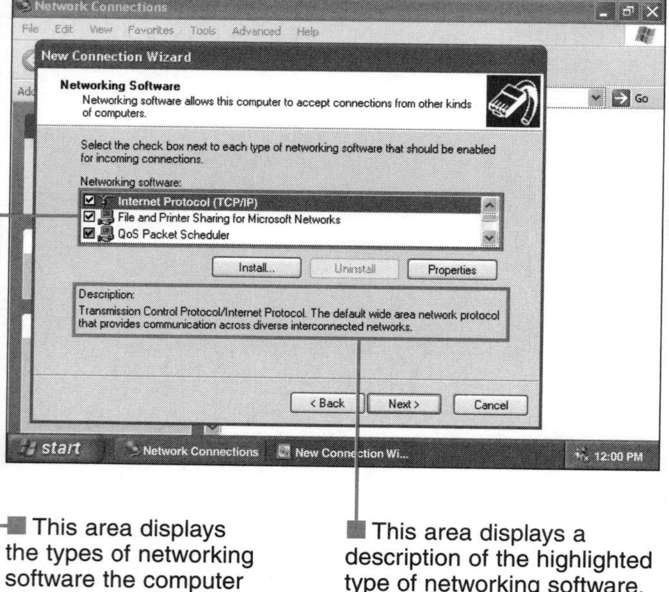

■ This area displays the types of networking software the computer can use to communicate with other computers.

■ This area displays a description of the highlighted type of networking software.

Note: To display a description for another type of networking software, click the software.

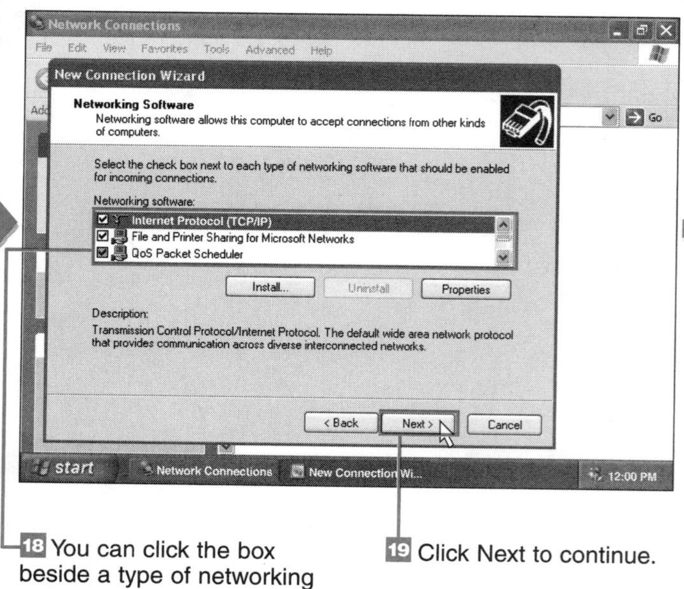

18 You can click the box beside a type of networking software to enable (☑) or disable (☐) the software.

19 Click Next to continue.

Can I make changes to Internet Protocol (TCP/IP)?

✔ Yes. Select Internet Protocol (TCP/IP) in the wizard and then click the Properties button. You can make changes to TCP/IP such as allowing access to your local network or specifying how to assign an IP address to a calling computer.

How do I know when a user is connected to my computer?

✔ An icon ( ) appears on the taskbar when a user connects to your computer. Position the mouse pointer over the icon to view information about the connection, such as the name of the user and the speed of the connection. If you want to disconnect a user, right-click the icon ( ) and then select Disconnect.

How do I later change the settings for an incoming connection?

✔ In the Network Connections window, right-click the icon for the incoming connection and then select Properties. On the General tab, you can change the devices the computer can use to receive incoming connections. The Users tab allows you to select the users that can connect to the computer and set user passwords. On the Networking tab, you can change the networking software you want the computer to use.

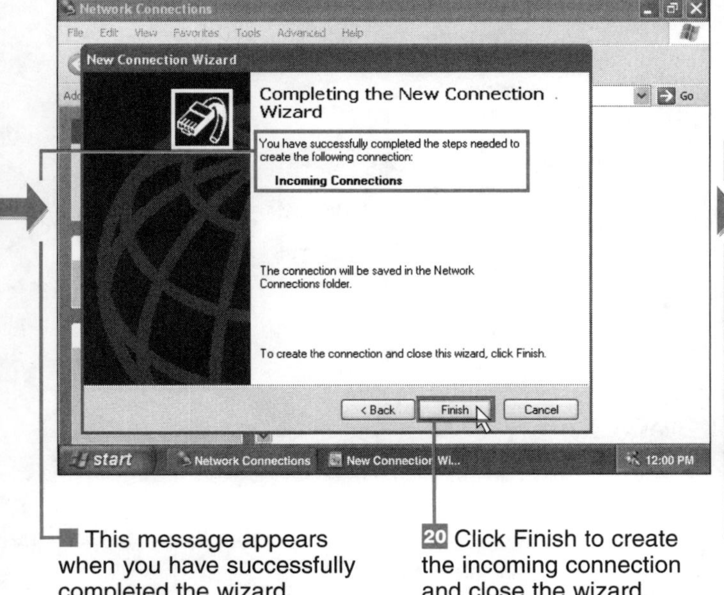

■ This message appears when you have successfully completed the wizard.

20 Click Finish to create the incoming connection and close the wizard.

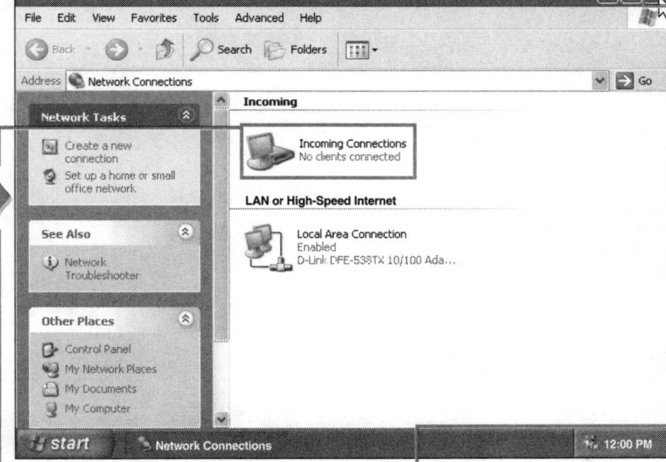

■ An icon for the incoming connection appears in the Network Connections window.

Note: To delete the incoming connection, click the connection and then press the Delete key.

21 Click ☒ to close the Network Connections window.

USING BRIEFCASE

The computer in your office may be the computer you use most often to work with files, but you may also use a home or portable computer. When you place a file in a Briefcase, you can easily transport the file between computers. Briefcase ensures that you are always working with the most up-to-date version of a file, regardless of the computer you use to edit the file.

When you place a folder in a Briefcase, all the files in the folder are added to the Briefcase. The Briefcase contains a copy of your files. The original files remain on your main computer.

You can move a Briefcase to a floppy disk or other type of removable disk so you can work with the files on another computer.

When at home or traveling, you can work with Briefcase files as you would work with any files. When you are ready to return to your main computer, make sure you save and close all Briefcase files you edited and close the Briefcase window before removing the disk containing the Briefcase from the computer's drive.

USING BRIEFCASE

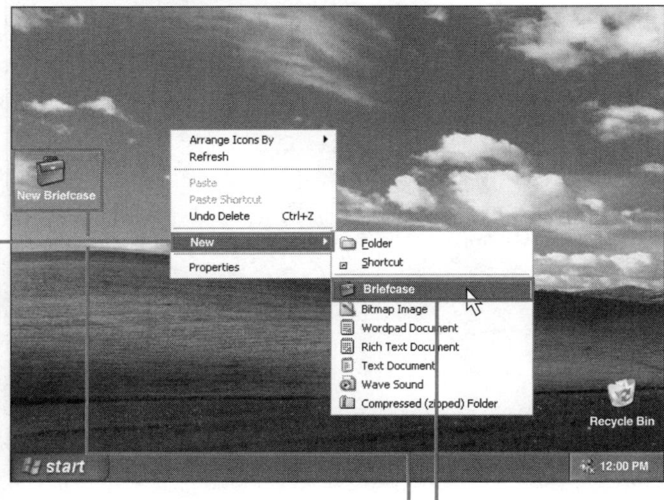

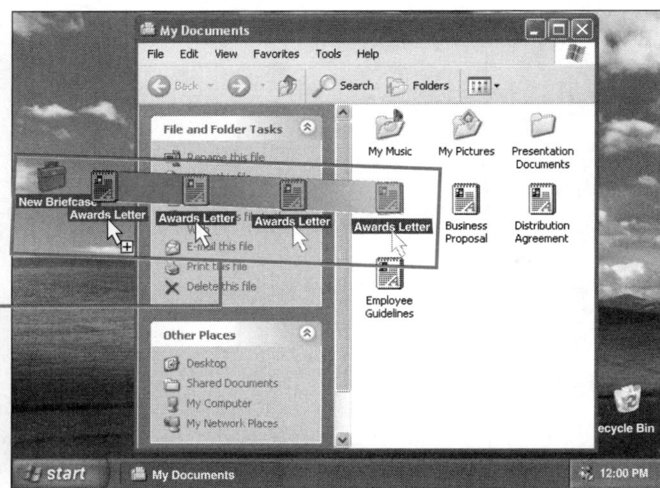

CREATE A NEW BRIEFCASE

1 To create a new Briefcase, right-click a blank area on your desktop or in a window. A menu appears.

2 Click New.

3 Click Briefcase.

■ A new Briefcase appears.

WORK WITH BRIEFCASE FILES

1 Drag each file or folder to the Briefcase that you want to work with while away from your main computer.

2 Insert a floppy disk or other removable disk into a drive on your computer.

Why does a dialog box appear when I open a Briefcase?

✔ A dialog box appears when you open a Briefcase for the first time. The dialog box displays a welcome message that explains how you can use Briefcase to organize your documents and keep your documents up to date when using multiple computers. To close the dialog box, click Finish.

I can't use a Briefcase on another computer. What is wrong?

✔ If a computer is running an older version of Windows, you may need to install the Briefcase component on the computer to work with Briefcase files. To install the Briefcase component in an older version of Windows, you can check the help information for the version of Windows the computer uses.

Can I create more than one Briefcase?

✔ Yes. You can create as many Briefcases as you need. If you create more than one Briefcase, you may want to rename each Briefcase so you can easily tell them apart. You can rename a Briefcase the same way you rename a file. To rename a file, see page 74.

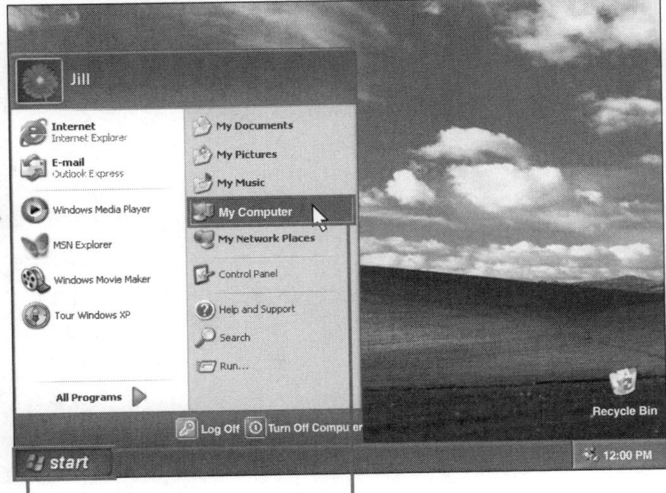

3 Click start.

4 Click My Computer.

■ The My Computer window appears.

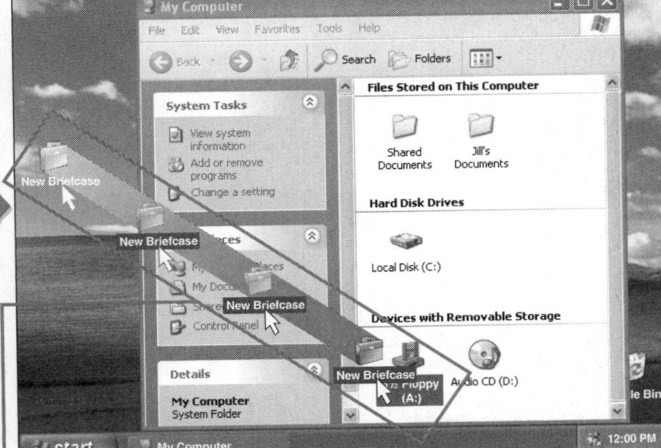

5 Drag the Briefcase to the drive that contains the disk.

■ Windows moves the Briefcase to the disk. You can now use the disk to transfer the Briefcase to another computer.

■ You can open and edit the files in the Briefcase on another computer as you would open and edit any files.

CONTINUED

USING BRIEFCASE (CONTINUED)

Briefcase lets you work with files while you are away from your main computer. When you change a file in the Briefcase, the original file on your main computer becomes out of date. Briefcase can update the files you changed. You can update all files or only specific files.

The update process ensures that the original files and the Briefcase copies are the same. Briefcase compares the files it contains with the files on your main computer and shows you which files need to be updated. You can replace the original file with the Briefcase file, replace the Briefcase file with the original file or skip replacing the file completely.

By default, Briefcase replaces the older version of the file with the newer version of the file. If both the original and Briefcase copies have been changed, Briefcase will indicate this and will not update the file.

Do not rename or move the original files on your main computer and do not rename the files in the Briefcase. If you do, Briefcase will not be able to update the files.

USING BRIEFCASE (CONTINUED)

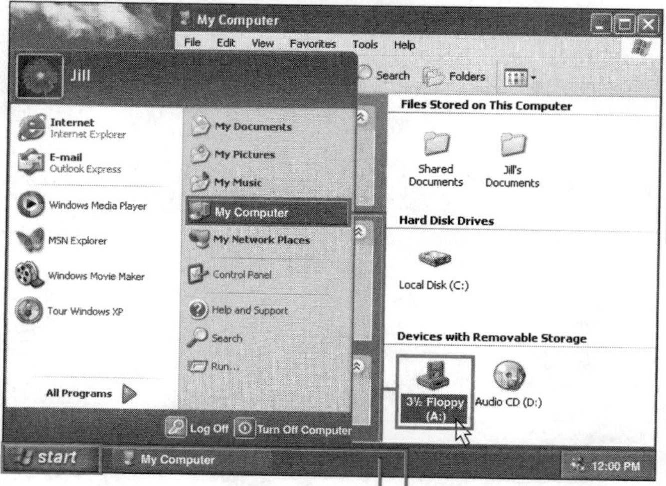

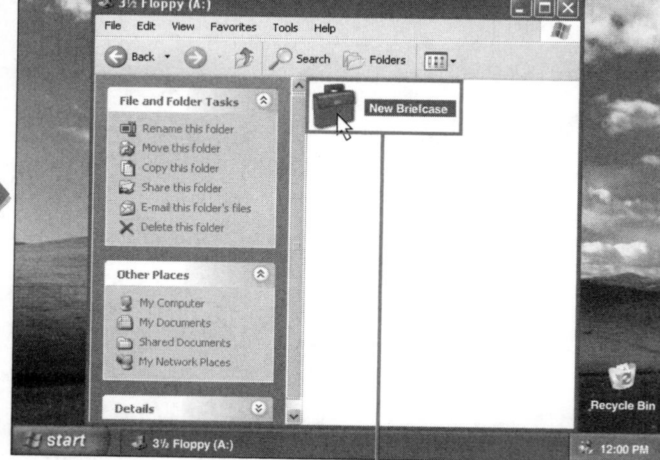

UPDATE BRIEFCASE FILES

1 When you finish working with the files on another computer, remove the disk that contains the files and then return the disk to your main computer.

2 Insert the disk into a drive on your main computer.

3 Click start.

4 Click My Computer.

■ The My Computer window appears.

5 Double-click the drive that contains the disk.

■ The contents of the disk appear.

6 Double-click the Briefcase.

How can I quickly update only some of the files in a Briefcase?

✔ In the Briefcase window, select the files you want to update. Click the Briefcase menu and then select Update Selection. You can also click [icon] to update the selected files.

Can I permanently prevent a Briefcase file from updating?

✔ In the Briefcase window, select the file you do not want to update. Click the Briefcase menu and select Split from Original. This lets you keep the changed version of the file in the Briefcase and the original file on the main computer. The file in the Briefcase is labeled an orphan file.

I created a new file in a Briefcase while working on another computer. Will the file be updated on my main computer?

✔ The file will be updated on your main computer if you created the file in an existing folder in the Briefcase. If you did not create the file in an existing folder, the file will not be updated because Windows will not know where to store the file on your main computer.

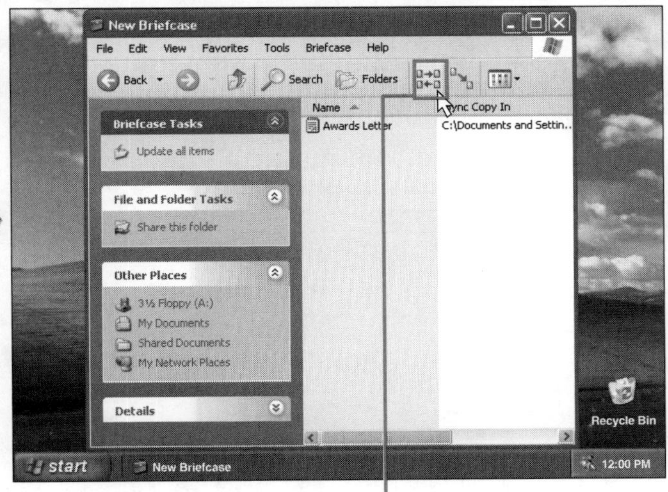

■ A window appears, displaying the contents of the Briefcase.

7 Click [icon] to update all the files.

■ The Update dialog box appears.

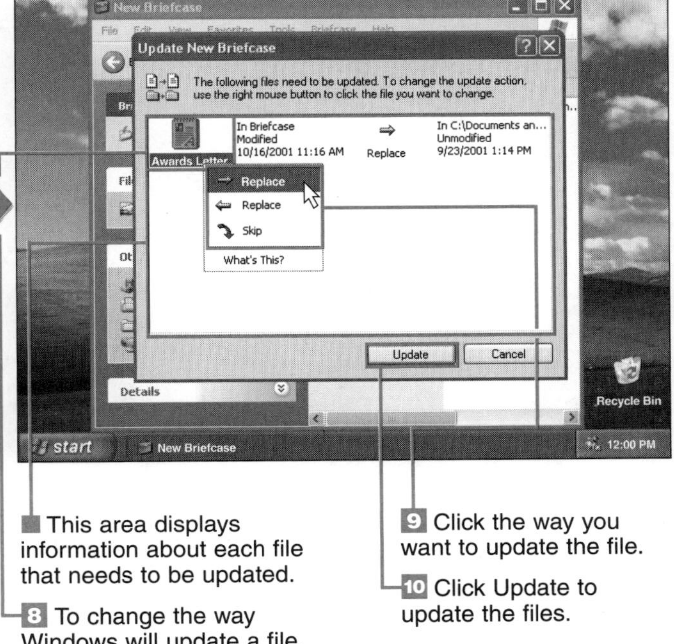

■ This area displays information about each file that needs to be updated.

8 To change the way Windows will update a file, right-click the file. A menu appears.

9 Click the way you want to update the file.

10 Click Update to update the files.

USING HYPERTERMINAL

HyperTerminal allows your computer to connect to and communicate with another computer. With HyperTerminal you can use your computer to log on to another computer, such as a Web server on the Internet, and use the computer as if you were sitting at the other computer.

HyperTerminal was originally developed to allow a computer to connect to another computer using a modem, but HyperTerminal now allows computers to communicate with each other using an Internet or network connection and a system referred to as telnet.

Before you can connect to another computer using HyperTerminal, you need to set up a connection to the computer. You must specify the address of the computer you want to connect to and the port number HyperTerminal will use to connect to the other computer.

The address and port number you enter depend on the computer you connect to. HyperTerminal allows you to enter the address as a computer name, such as telnet.abccorp.com, or as an IP (Internet Protocol) number, such as 172.20.135.71. The port number for telnet connections is 23.

USING HYPERTERMINAL

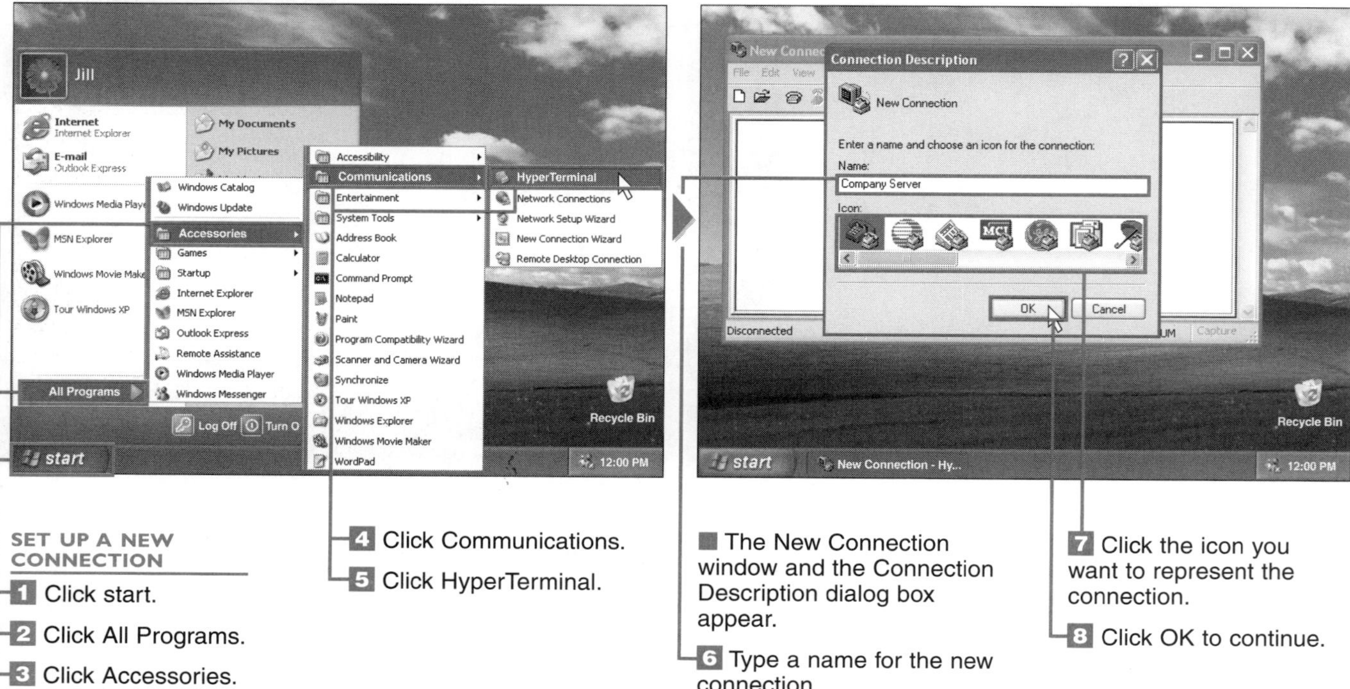

SET UP A NEW CONNECTION

1 Click start.

2 Click All Programs.

3 Click Accessories.

4 Click Communications.

5 Click HyperTerminal.

■ The New Connection window and the Connection Description dialog box appear.

6 Type a name for the new connection.

7 Click the icon you want to represent the connection.

8 Click OK to continue.

Why does a dialog box appear when I start HyperTerminal?

✔ When you start HyperTerminal, a dialog box may appear, asking you to set HyperTerminal as your default telnet program. In the dialog box, you can select the Don't ask me this question again option (☐ changes to ☑) to stop the dialog box from appearing again. To set HyperTerminal as your default telnet program, click Yes.

Where can I get the latest version of HyperTerminal?

✔ You can get an updated or more powerful version of HyperTerminal on the Web at www.hilgraeve.com.

Can I use HyperTerminal to connect to another computer using my modem?

✔ Yes. Connecting to another computer using your modem is useful if the other computer uses a modem and HyperTerminal to transfer information, such as when connecting to a Bulletin Board Service (BBS) or a friend's computer. Perform steps 1 to 8 below to display the Connect To dialog box. In the Country/region area, select your country. In the Area code and Phone number areas, type the area code and phone number of the computer you want to connect to. In the Connect using area, select the modem you want to use and then click OK. In the Connect dialog box, click the Dial button.

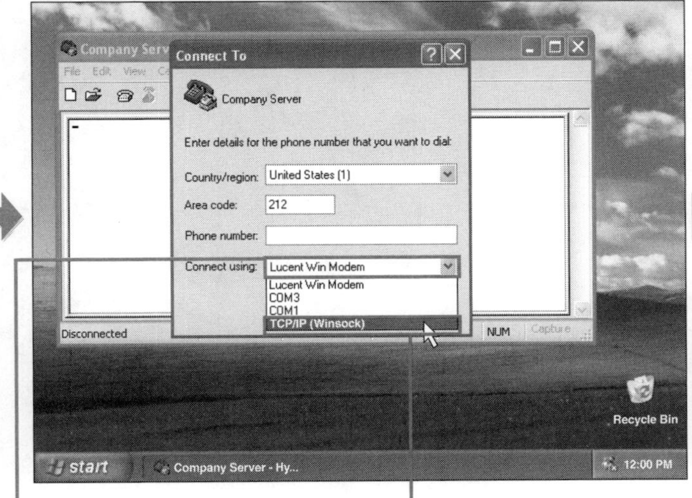

■ The Connect To dialog box appears.

9 Click this area to select the way you want to connect to the other computer.

10 Click TCP/IP (Winsock) to connect to the other computer using your Internet or network connection.

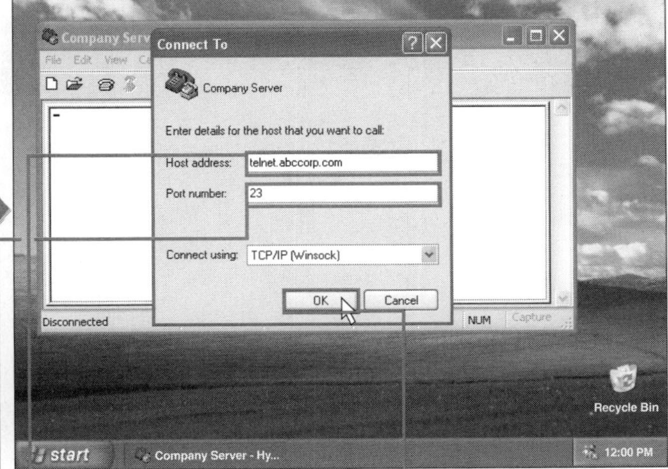

11 Click this area and type the address of the computer you want to connect to.

■ This area displays the port number HyperTerminal will use to connect to the other computer.

12 Click OK to connect to the other computer.

Note: If you are not currently connected to the Internet, a dialog box appears that allows you to connect.

CONTINUED

USING HYPERTERMINAL (CONTINUED)

When you connect to another computer using an Internet or network connection and telnet, you usually need to log on to the computer to work on the computer. To log on, you need to enter your user name and password. The password you type typically is not displayed on the screen.

Once you are connected to the other computer, you can enter commands to work with the information on the computer.

For example, entering the dir command usually allows you to list the contents of the current directory. When you enter a command, there may be a brief delay before the text is displayed on the screen.

HyperTerminal is capable of displaying only text. You will not be able to view images using HyperTerminal, but you can still perform many tasks, such as reading e-mail and accessing newsgroups.

When you are finished working with the other computer, you usually disconnect from the computer by typing the exit command.

HyperTerminal allows you to save a connection you set up. Saving the connection prevents you from having to enter the same information each time you want to connect to the computer. You can use the saved connection at any time to quickly reconnect to the computer.

USING HYPERTERMINAL (CONTINUED)

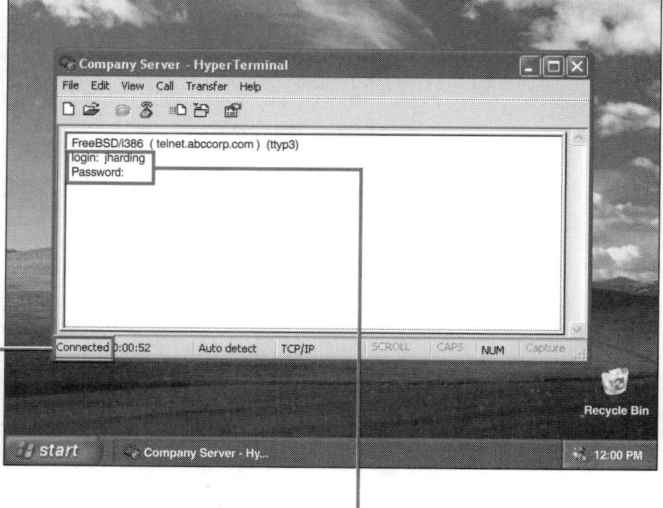

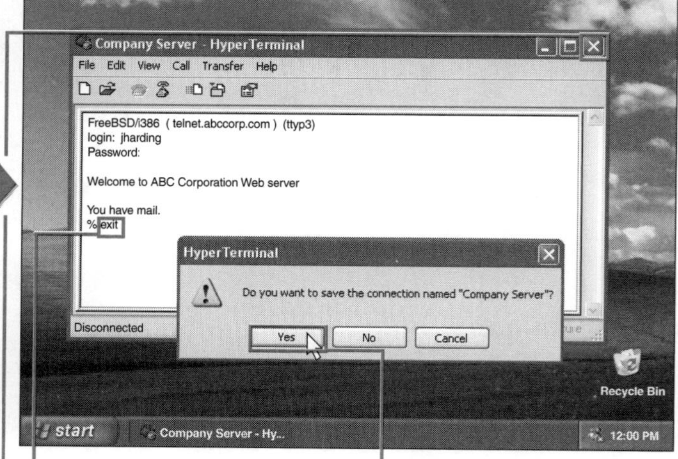

■ When you are connected to the other computer, this area displays the word "Connected."

■ Before you can work on the other computer, you may need to log on to the computer.

13 To log on to the computer, type your user name and press the Enter key.

14 Type your password and press the Enter key.

■ You can now enter commands to work on the other computer.

15 When you want to end the connection to the other computer, type the command that logs you off the computer and then press the Enter key.

16 Click ✕ to close the HyperTerminal window.

■ A message appears, asking if you want to save the information you entered for the connection.

17 Click Yes to save the connection.

Can I save the text from a HyperTerminal session?

✔ Yes. From the Transfer menu, click Capture Text. In the Capture Text dialog box, type the location and name of the file where you want to save the text. The file name should have the .txt extension so you can later work with the text in a text editor such as Notepad. Click Start to start capturing text. When you want to stop capturing text, select the Transfer menu, choose Capture Text and then click Stop.

How do I change the font of text displayed in the HyperTerminal window?

✔ From the View menu, select Font. In the Font dialog box, choose the font, style and size you want the text to display.

Can I send and receive files using HyperTerminal?

✔ You may be able to use HyperTerminal to send and receive files by clicking the Send (▭) and Receive (▭) buttons on the toolbar. You should check with the administrator of the computer you are connecting to for information about sending and receiving files using HyperTerminal.

How do I delete a saved connection?

✔ Click start, select All Programs, choose Accessories and then click Communications. Select the HyperTerminal option that displays an arrow (▸), right-click the connection you want to delete and then choose Delete from the menu that appears.

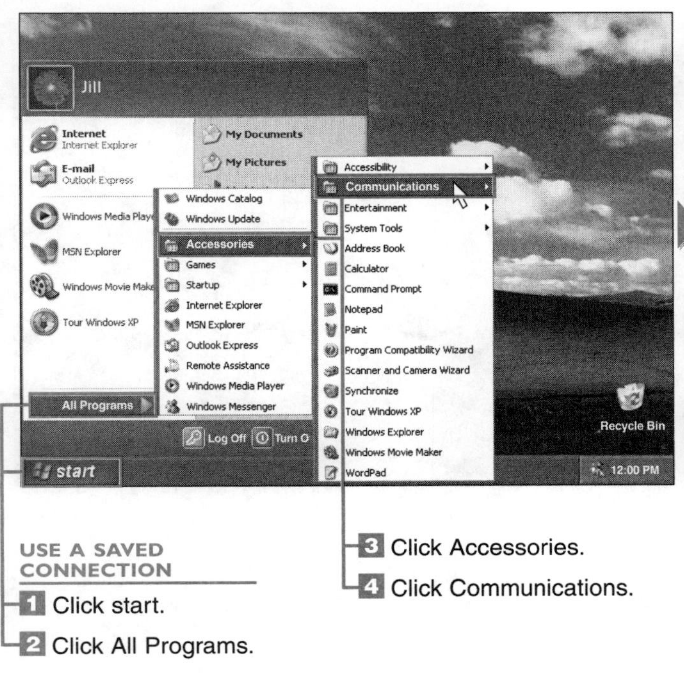

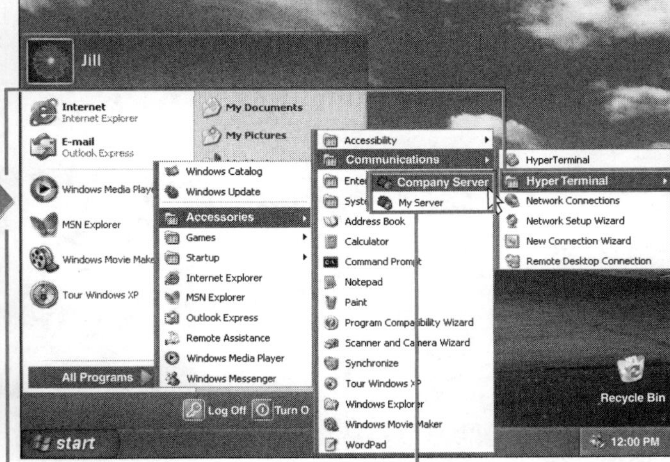

USE A SAVED CONNECTION

1 Click start.

2 Click All Programs.

3 Click Accessories.

4 Click Communications.

5 To display a list of the connections you have saved, click the HyperTerminal option that displays an arrow (▸).

6 Click the connection you want to use to connect to a computer.

■ The HyperTerminal window will appear, allowing you to work on the other computer.

USING REMOTE DESKTOP CONNECTION

You can use Remote Desktop Connection to connect to another computer on your network or the Internet so you can remotely control the computer. The computer you connect to must use Windows XP Professional.

When connecting to another computer, the computer you connect to is called the remote, or host, computer. The computer you use to connect is called the local, or client, computer.

Before you can connect to a remote computer, you must provide information about the computer, including the name or IP address of the computer and the user name and password you use to log on to the computer. The remote computer must be turned on before you can connect to the computer. If another user is already logged on to the computer, you will need to log the user off before you can connect to the computer.

Once you are connected to the remote computer, the remote desktop appears on your screen. The desktop appears as it would if you logged on to the computer directly. You can access information, programs and network resources on the computer as if you were working at the computer.

You can disconnect from the computer at any time. Any programs you have open when you disconnect will continue to run. You can later reconnect to the remote computer to continue using the programs.

CONNECT TO A REMOTE COMPUTER

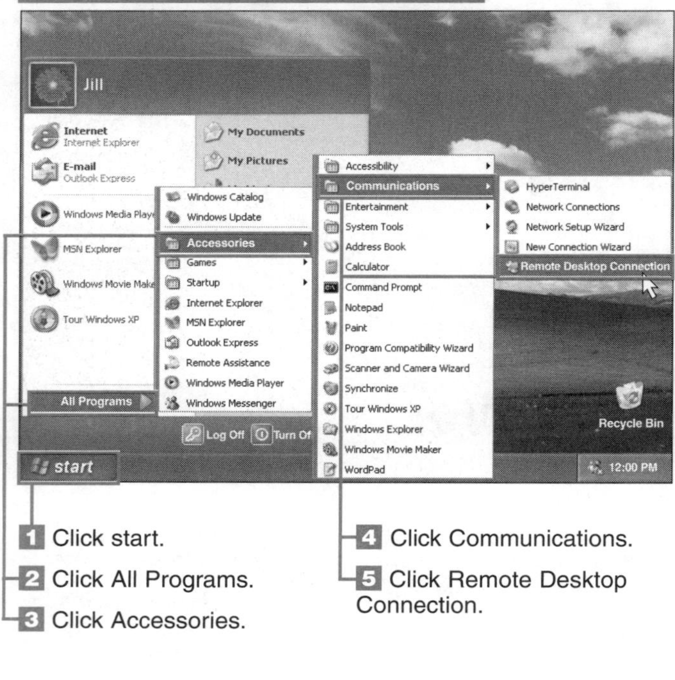

1 Click start.

2 Click All Programs.

3 Click Accessories.

4 Click Communications.

5 Click Remote Desktop Connection.

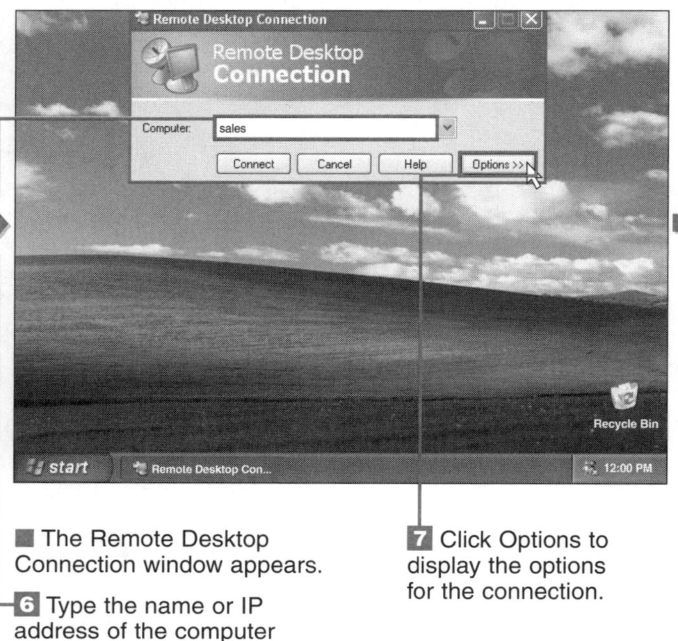

■ The Remote Desktop Connection window appears.

6 Type the name or IP address of the computer you want to connect to.

7 Click Options to display the options for the connection.

How can I change the way the remote desktop appears on my screen?

✔ When you first connect to a remote computer, the remote desktop is displayed using the entire screen. To display the remote desktop in a window, click 🗗 on the connection bar at the top of the screen. To once again view the remote desktop using the entire screen, click ▣ in the window.

Can I hide the connection bar that appears at the top of the remote desktop screen?

✔ Yes. You can click ▣ on the connection bar to hide the connection bar when you are not using it. To temporarily redisplay the connection bar, position the mouse pointer over the center of the top of the screen. To stop hiding the connection bar, click ▣ on the connection bar.

Do I need to log off the remote computer?

✔ Yes. When you close the connection to a remote computer, you are still logged on to the computer. When you are finished working with the remote computer, you must log off. On the remote desktop, click start and select Log Off. Then click the Log Off button. Windows will close any programs you have open on the remote computer before logging you off and closing the connection.

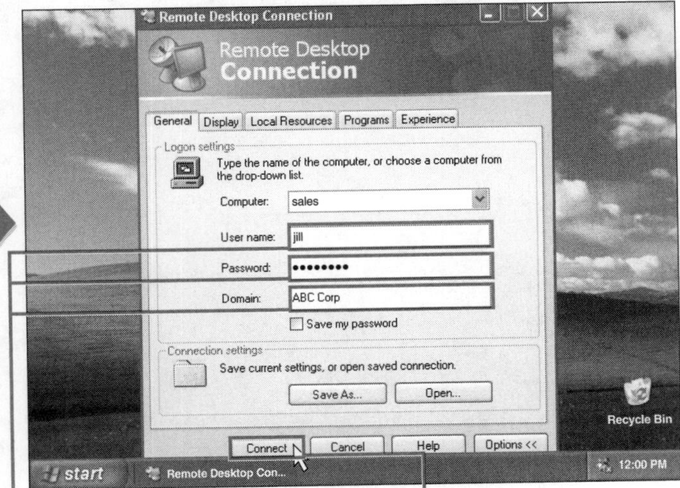

■ The options appear.

8 Double-click these areas and type your user name and password.

9 If the remote computer is connected to a network that requires you to log on to a domain, click this area and type the domain name.

10 Click Connect to connect to the other computer.

Note: If you are using a dial-up connection, a dialog box appears, allowing you to connect.

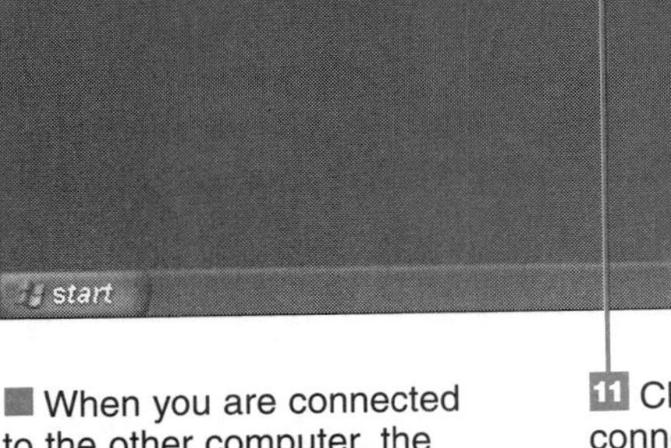

■ When you are connected to the other computer, the remote desktop appears on your screen.

■ You can now work on the other computer as if you were working directly at the computer.

11 Click X to close the connection at any time.

Note: A confirmation dialog box will appear. Click OK to close the connection to the other computer.

CONTINUED

USING REMOTE DESKTOP CONNECTION (CONTINUED)

Before connecting to a remote computer, you can customize the settings for the connection.

You can specify a size and color depth for the remote desktop. Choosing a size allows you to specify a resolution for the remote desktop or display the remote desktop using the full screen. You can also specify whether you want the connection bar to appear when the remote desktop is displayed using the full screen.

Remote Desktop Connection allows you to specify whether you want sound generated by the remote computer to play on the local computer, on the remote computer or on neither computer.

You can have shortcut keys, such as Alt+Tab, always apply to the remote computer, to the local computer or to the remote computer only when the remote desktop uses the full screen.

Remote Desktop Connection allows you to make devices on your local computer, such as disk drives, printers and serial ports, available during the remote desktop connection.

If you plan to use Remote Desktop Connection to connect to a terminal server, you can specify a program that you want to run on the terminal server when you connect.

To optimize the remote desktop connection, you can specify your connection speed.

CHANGE SETTINGS FOR A REMOTE DESKTOP CONNECTION

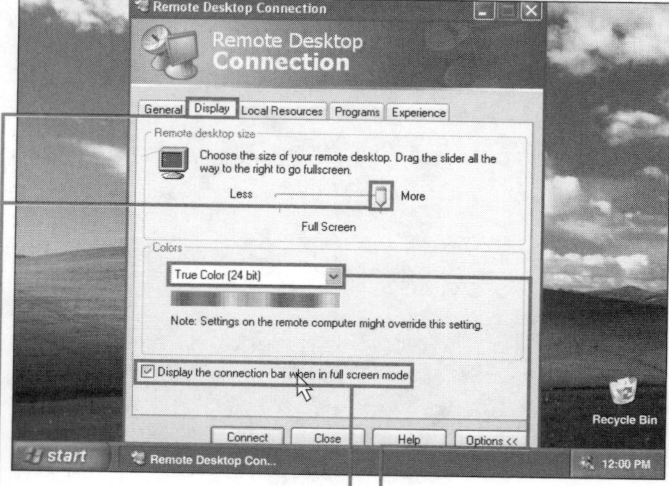

1 Perform steps 1 to 7 on page 388 to display the Remote Desktop Connection window.

2 Click the Display tab.

3 To change the screen size of the remote desktop, drag this slider ( ).

4 This area displays the color setting for the remote desktop. You can click this area to change the color setting.

5 This option displays the connection bar when in full screen mode. You can click this option to turn the option on (✓) or off ( ).

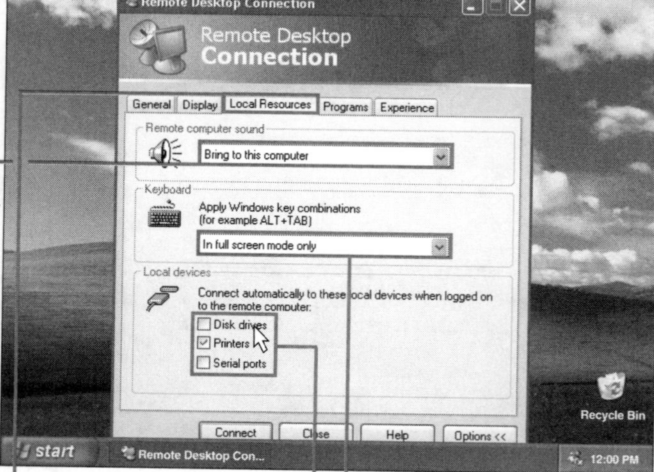

6 Click the Local Resources tab.

7 This option specifies what will occur when sound plays on the other computer. You can click this area to select a different option.

8 This option specifies how you want to apply Windows shortcut keys. You can click this area to select a different option.

9 These options allow you to make local devices available during the connection. You can click an option to turn the option on (✓) or off ( ).

How do I save the settings I customized for a remote desktop connection?

✔ To save the settings in a file, click the Save As button on the General tab and then type a name for the file. The next time you want to use the settings, you can click the Open button on the General tab and then double-click the name of the file.

How does specifying my connection speed optimize the remote desktop connection?

✔ Windows will customize the connection to suit the connection speed you specify. The connection speed determines whether items on the remote computer, such as the desktop background, window contents and animations, themes and bitmap caching, are used on the remote desktop.

What is a terminal server?

✔ A terminal server is a network computer that is dedicated to remote desktop connections. Multiple computers on a network can connect to a terminal server at the same time.

Why did a security warning appear when I tried to connect to the remote computer?

✔ If you made the disk drives or serial ports on your local computer available during the remote desktop connection, there is a chance that information on your computer could be accessed without your authorization.

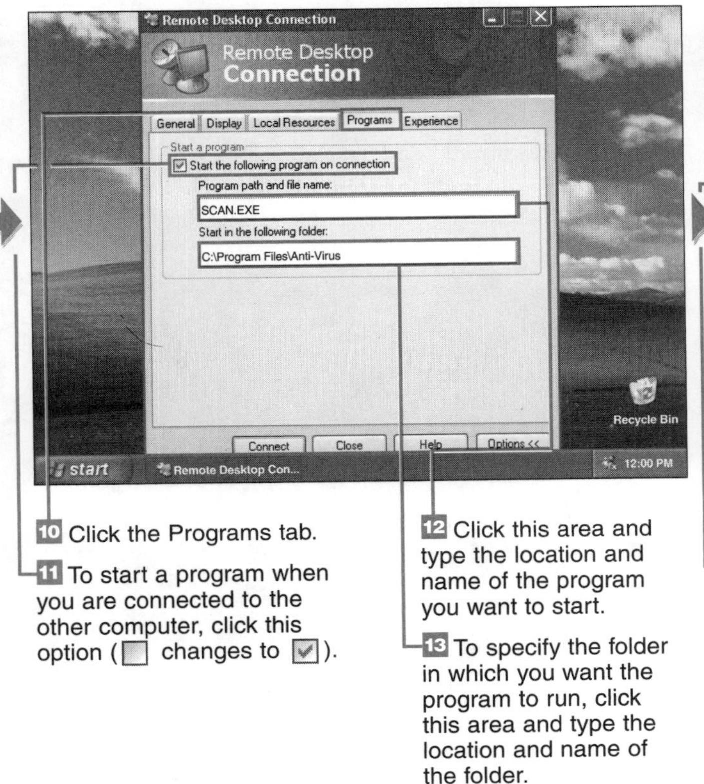

10 Click the Programs tab.

11 To start a program when you are connected to the other computer, click this option (☐ changes to ☑).

12 Click this area and type the location and name of the program you want to start.

13 To specify the folder in which you want the program to run, click this area and type the location and name of the folder.

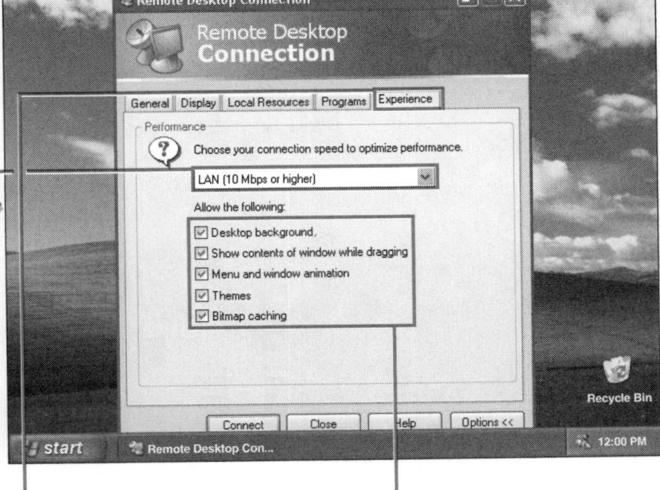

14 Click the Experience tab.

15 This area displays the speed of your connection. You can click this area to specify a different connection speed.

■ This area displays options that can be used during the connection. Each option that displays a check mark (✔) will be used. The options that display check marks depend on the connection speed you specified in step 15.

SECTION VI

18) SET UP AND MONITOR A NETWORK

19) WORK ON A NETWORK

NETWORKING

SET UP A HOME OR SMALL OFFICE NETWORK

If you have more than one computer at home or at work, you can set up a network to share information and resources, such as a printer, among the computers.

The Network Setup Wizard helps you set up a computer on your network. You must run the wizard on each computer you want to set up on the network.

If you plan to use Internet Connection Sharing (ICS), which allows a computer on your network to share its connection to the Internet with other computers on the network, you should run the wizard on the computer that shares its Internet connection first. The computer that shares its Internet connection must use Windows XP.

When you choose to share an Internet connection with other computers on your network, Windows automatically activates Internet Connection Firewall (ICF) on the computer that shares its Internet connection. Internet Connection Firewall protects your network from unauthorized access when computers on the network are connected to the Internet.

You must be logged on as a computer administrator to set up a home or small office network.

SET UP A HOME OR SMALL OFFICE NETWORK

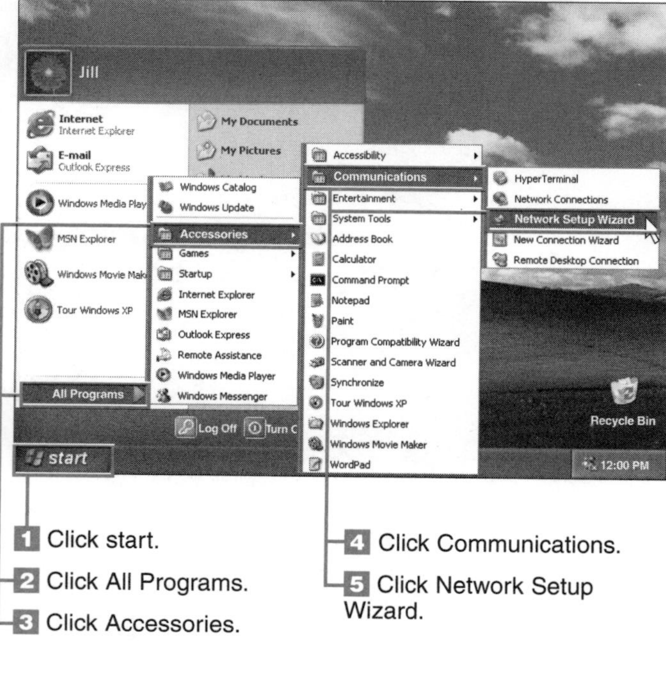

1 Click start.

2 Click All Programs.

3 Click Accessories.

4 Click Communications.

5 Click Network Setup Wizard.

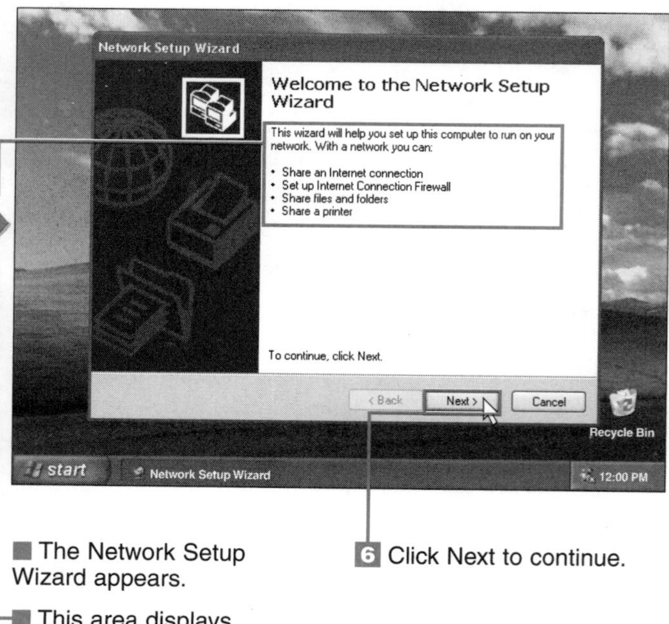

■ The Network Setup Wizard appears.

■ This area displays information about the wizard and the benefits of setting up a network.

6 Click Next to continue.

What equipment and software do I need to set up a network?

✔ Each computer you want to connect to the network must have a network or a FireWire port. Network and FireWire ports control the flow of information between the computers on a network. Cables are required to physically connect each computer to the network. Your network may also require a hub, which provides a central location where the cables on the network meet. To be able to connect to the Internet, one computer will also need an Internet connection device, such as a modem. One computer on the network must have Windows XP installed. The other computers can use Windows 98, Windows Me or Windows XP.

What should I consider when sharing an Internet connection on my network?

✔ Your Internet Service Provider (ISP) may not allow more than one computer on your network to connect to the Internet through a single Internet connection. You can contact your ISP for more information.

I am not sure which option best describes the way my computer connects to the Internet. How can I get help?

✔ In the Network Setup Wizard, click the "View an example" link below a connection method to see an illustration of the method. You can also click the "home or small office network configurations" link for more information.

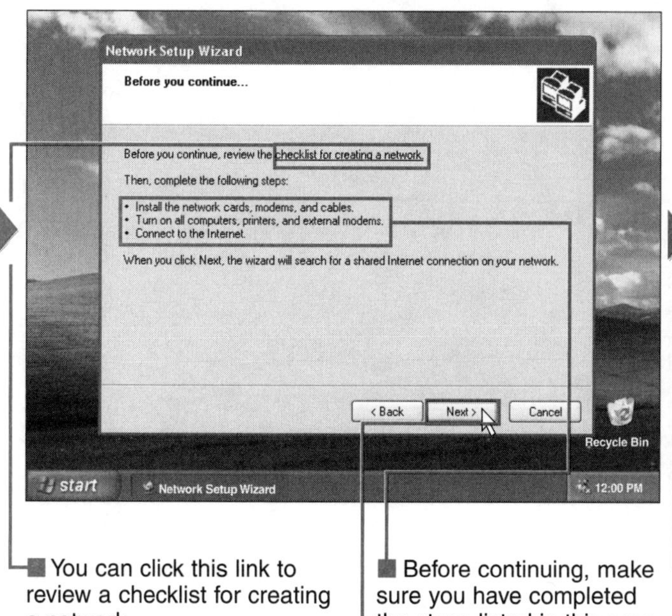

■ You can click this link to review a checklist for creating a network.

Note: If you click the link, the Help and Support Center window appears, displaying the checklist. When you finish reviewing the checklist, click ☒ to close the window.

■ Before continuing, make sure you have completed the steps listed in this area.

7 Click Next to continue.

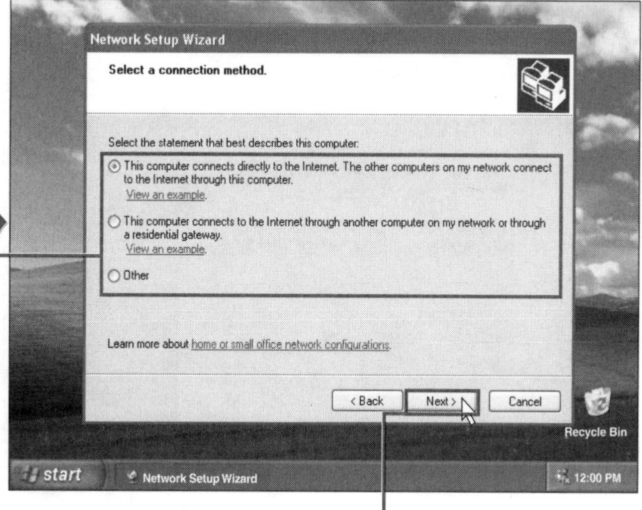

8 Click the option that best describes the way the computer connects to the Internet (○ changes to ◉).

Note: You can click Other to view additional statements if the displayed statements do not describe the computer.

9 Click Next to continue.

Note: If you selected Other in step 8, repeat steps 8 and 9.

CONTINUED

SET UP A HOME OR SMALL OFFICE NETWORK (CONTINUED)

The Network Setup Wizard may ask you to select the connection device you want to use to connect to the Internet, such as a modem.

You must specify a short description of the computer you are setting up on the network, such as "Computer in den." You must also specify a name for the computer. A computer name identifies a computer on your network and can be a location, such as "den," or a person's name, such as "Pat." Each computer on a network must have a different name. A computer name can contain up to 15 characters, but cannot contain spaces or special characters, such as ; : , " < > * + = \ | or ?. Your Internet Service Provider (ISP) may require that you use a specific name for the computer that shares its Internet connection.

You must also specify a name for the workgroup to which the computer will belong. A workgroup name identifies the group of computers on your network. Each computer on your home or small office network should have the same workgroup name.

The wizard may take a few minutes to apply the network settings. This process cannot be interrupted.

SET UP A HOME OR SMALL OFFICE NETWORK (CONTINUED)

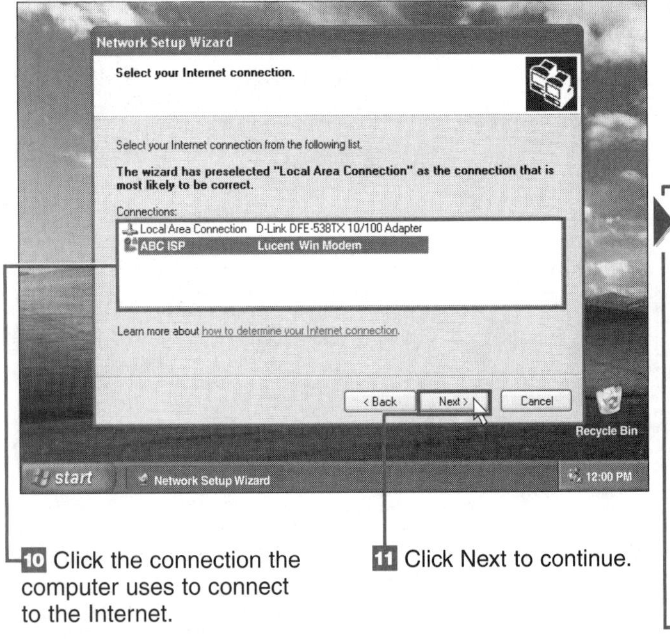

10 Click the connection the computer uses to connect to the Internet.

Note: This screen may not appear, depending on the statement you selected in step 8. If the screen does not appear, skip to step 12.

11 Click Next to continue.

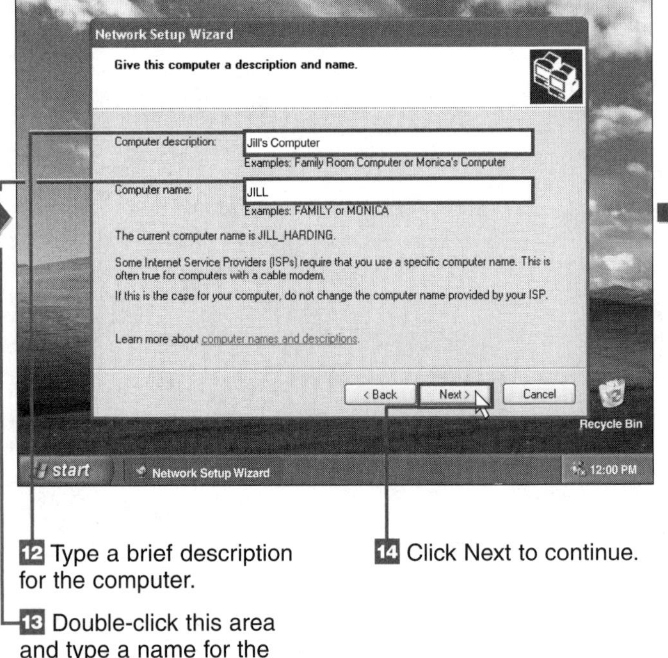

12 Type a brief description for the computer.

13 Double-click this area and type a name for the computer.

14 Click Next to continue.

How can I get help determining which Internet connection I should choose in the wizard?

✔ If you have trouble determining your Internet connection, you can click the "how to determine your Internet connection" link in the wizard for more information.

Why does a dialog box appear, stating that the wizard can bridge connections on my computer?

✔ If you have multiple network connections on your computer, the Network Setup Wizard can set up a network bridge, which helps connect different segments of your network so that all the computers on the network can communicate. You can click the "network bridging" link in the wizard for more information.

Can I later change the name or workgroup name of a computer on my network?

✔ Yes. For information about changing a computer or workgroup name, see page 418. After you change your computer or workgroup name, you should inform the people on the network who access resources on your computer of the change.

How do I view descriptions for computers on the network?

✔ Click start, select My Network Places and then click View workgroup computers to locate the computers for which you want to view descriptions. Select the View menu and then click Details.

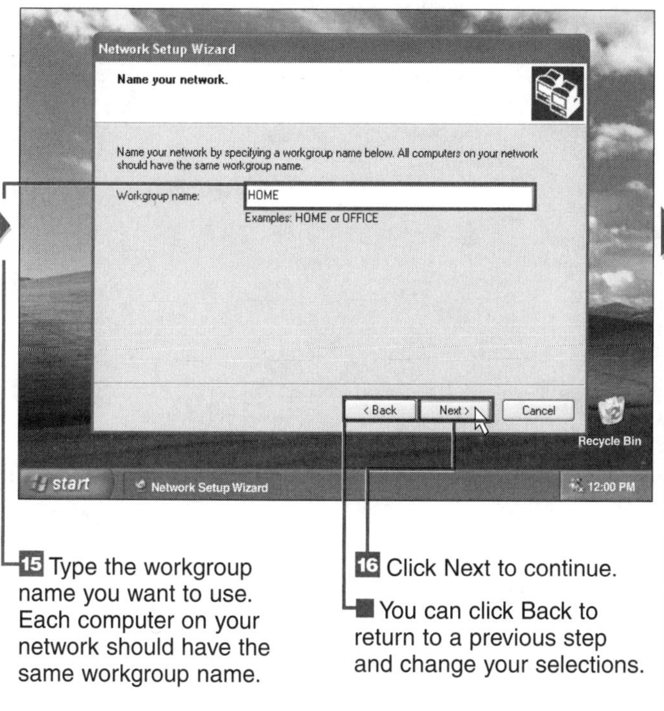

15 Type the workgroup name you want to use. Each computer on your network should have the same workgroup name.

16 Click Next to continue.

■ You can click Back to return to a previous step and change your selections.

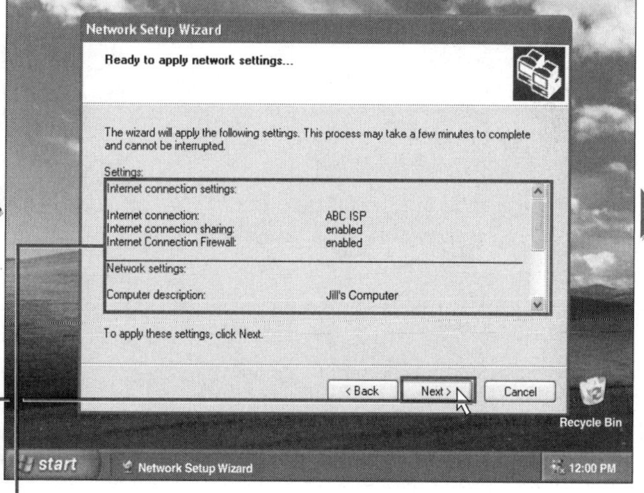

■ This area displays the network settings that the wizard will apply to the computer.

17 Click Next to apply the network settings.

■ The wizard may take a few minutes to apply the network settings. This process cannot be interrupted.

CONTINUED

SET UP A HOME OR SMALL OFFICE NETWORK (CONTINUED)

You can create a Network Setup disk or use the CD you used to install Windows XP to set up other computers that use Windows 98 or Windows Me on your home or small office network. You must run the wizard on each computer you want to set up on your network. If you do not run the wizard on every computer, the network will not work properly.

After you have completed the Network Setup Wizard, Windows may ask you to restart your computer. Restarting your computer will help ensure that the changes you specified in the wizard take effect.

If you are using Internet Connection Sharing (ICS), you may have to adjust settings in some Internet programs to ensure the programs will access the network properly.

When you set up your computer on a network, the Network Setup Wizard automatically shares your Shared Documents folder and any printers that are directly connected to your computer. For information about the Shared Documents folder, see page 190.

Once you have set up a network, you can access shared resources on the network. You can use My Network Places to see the resources shared by your computer and other computers on the network. To browse through shared resources on a network, see page 406.

SET UP A HOME OR SMALL OFFICE NETWORK (CONTINUED)

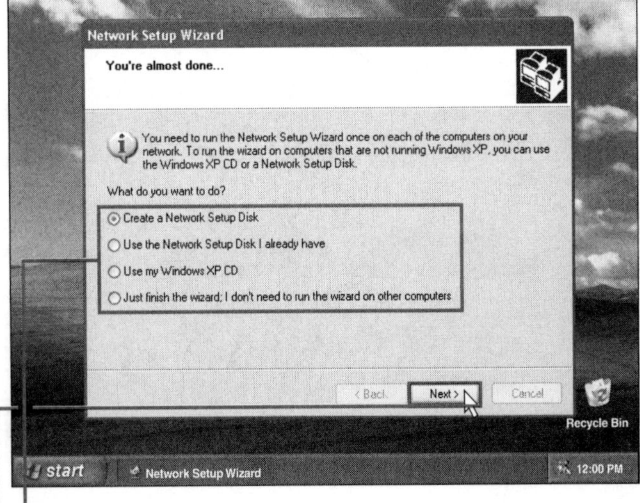

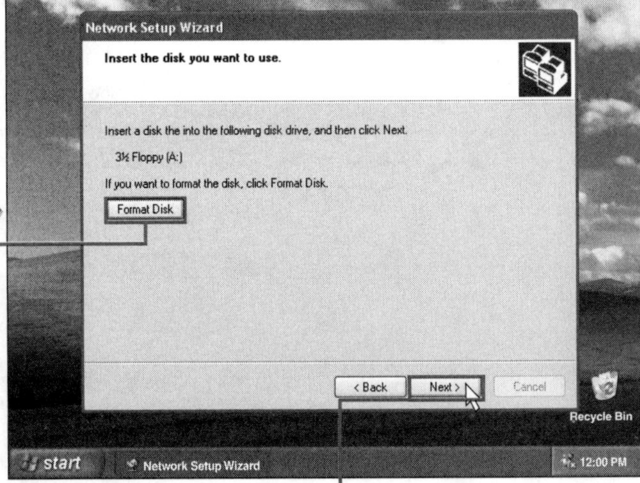

18 Click an option to specify the task you want to perform to set up other computers on your network (○ changes to ◉).

19 Click Next to continue.

Note: If you chose to use the Network Setup disk you already have or the Windows XP CD, skip to step 22. If you chose to just finish the wizard, skip to step 24.

20 Insert a formatted, blank floppy disk into the floppy drive.

■ If you are using an unformatted floppy disk or the disk contains files, you can click Format Disk to format the disk.

Note: Formatting a floppy disk will permanently remove all the information on the disk. For more information about formatting a floppy disk, see page 514.

21 Click Next to continue.

What can I do if the network I set up does not work properly?

✔ You can use the Home and Small Office Networking Troubleshooter to solve problems you may be experiencing with your network. Click start and select Help and Support. In the top left corner of the Help and Support Center window, click the area beside Search and type **networking troubleshooter**. Then press the Enter key. In the search results, click the "Home and Small Office Networking Troubleshooter" link and then follow the instructions that appear in the right side of the window.

How can I share information or my printer on the network?

✔ After you complete the Network Setup Wizard, you can share a folder or a printer attached to your computer with other people on the network. To share information, see page 410. To share a printer, see page 412.

Some Internet programs do not function properly when firewall protection is activated. Can I deactivate the firewall?

✔ Yes. Click start, select All Programs, choose Accessories, click Communications and click Network Connections. Right-click the icon for the Internet connection and click Properties on the menu that appears. Select the Advanced tab and then click the "Protect my computer and network by limiting or preventing access to this computer from the Internet" option (☑ changes to ☐).

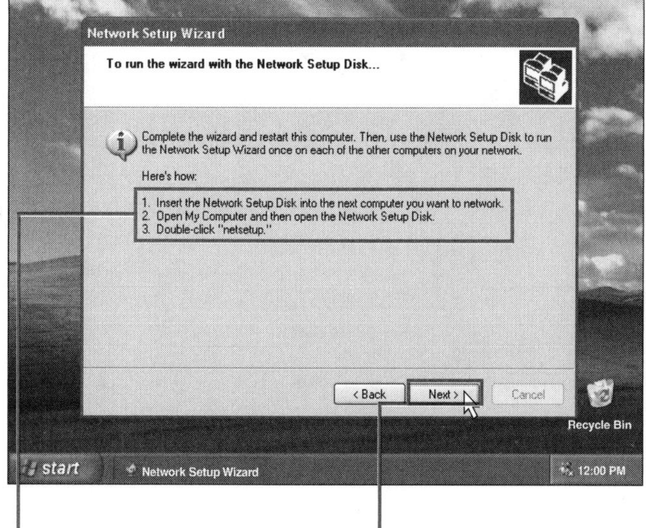

■ The wizard displays the steps you need to perform to set up other computers on your network. The displayed steps depend on the option you selected in step 18.

22 Click Next to continue.

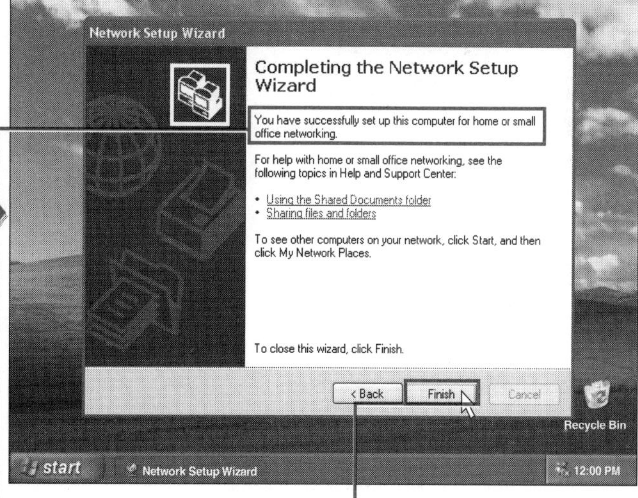

■ This message appears when you have successfully set up the computer on your network.

23 If you created a Network Setup disk, remove the floppy disk from the drive.

24 Click Finish to close the wizard.

■ A message may appear, stating that you must restart the computer before the new settings will take effect. Click Yes to restart the computer.

WORK WITH NETWORK COMPONENTS

A network component is software that allows your computer to communicate with other computers on a network. You can work with the network components for a connection on your computer to customize which components the network connection uses.

Network components include clients, services and protocols. A network client determines where information is sent on a network. For example, when you send a document to a printer, the network client determines if the document will print on a printer attached to your computer or on a printer on the network. A network service provides a particular function on a network, such as a printing service that allows you to print documents on the network. A network protocol determines how information transfers from one computer to another on a network or between different networks.

You can view the network components installed for your network connection and display descriptions of each component. You can also enable or disable components to specify which components you want the connection to use. Some network components are required to run the network and cannot be disabled.

WORK WITH NETWORK COMPONENTS

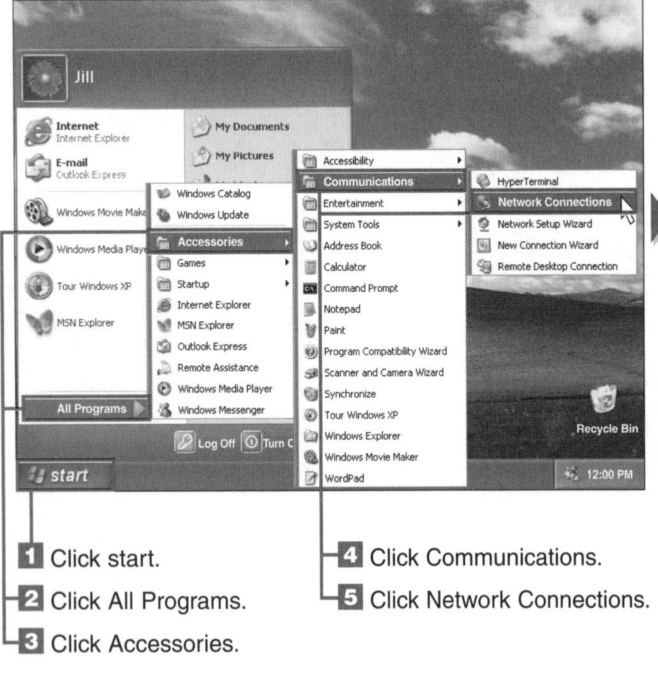

1 Click start.

2 Click All Programs.

3 Click Accessories.

4 Click Communications.

5 Click Network Connections.

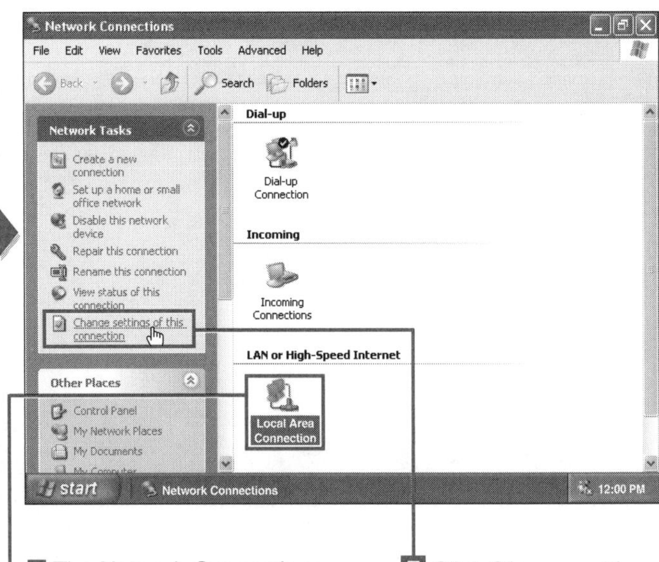

■ The Network Connections window appears, displaying the connections that are set up on your computer.

6 Click the connection that connects your computer to the network.

7 Click Change settings of this connection.

How can I change the properties for a network component?

✔ In the Properties dialog box for the connection, select the network component you want to change and click the Properties button to display the properties for the component. The properties you can change for a network component depend on the component. If the Properties button is unavailable after you select a component, you cannot change properties for the component.

Does my dial-up connection use network components?

✔ Yes. A dial-up connection can use a variety of network components. To work with the network components for a dial-up connection, select the dial-up connection in the Network Connections window and click the Change settings of this connection link. In the dialog box that appears, select the Networking tab to display the network components for the connection.

How do I remove a network component?

✔ In the Properties dialog box for the connection, click the network component you want to remove and then click the Uninstall button. Windows uninstalls the component from your computer and removes it from the list of components in the Properties dialog box. Removing unneeded components may increase the efficiency of your computer and network. If the Uninstall button is unavailable after you select a component, you cannot remove the component.

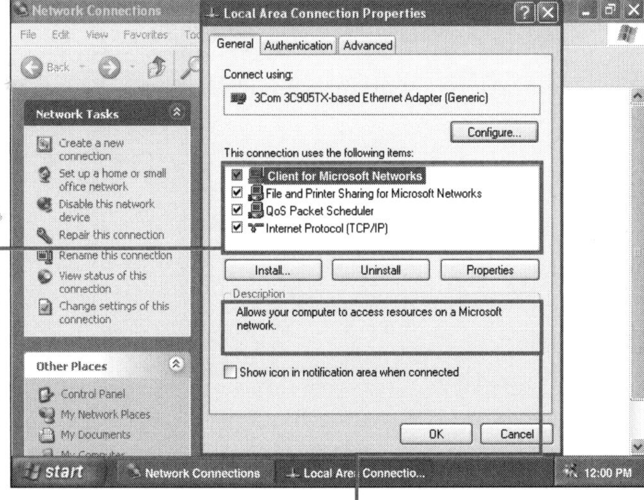

■ A Properties dialog box for the connection appears.

■ This area lists the network components installed on your computer. The icon beside a network component indicates the type of component, such as client (🖳), service (🖳) or protocol (⚟).

■ This area displays a description of the highlighted network component.

Note: To display a description of another network component, click the component.

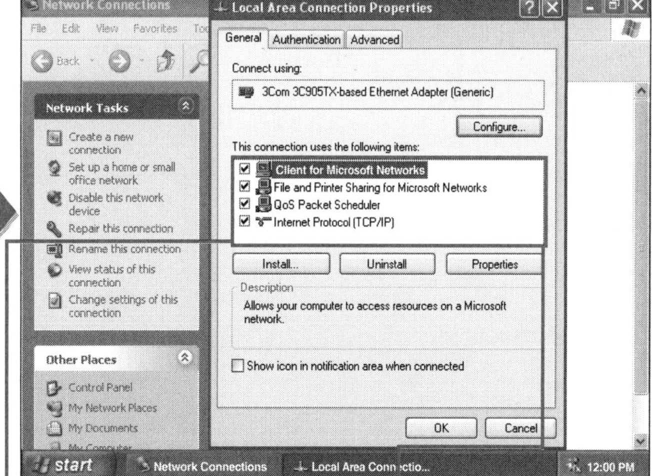

ENABLE OR DISABLE A NETWORK COMPONENT

■ A check mark (✔) appears beside each network component the connection can use.

8 To enable (☑) or disable (☐) a network component for the connection, click the box beside the component.

CONTINUED

WORK WITH NETWORK COMPONENTS (CONTINUED)

You can install a new network component on your computer to increase the capabilities and efficiency of your network connection.

Some network components are installed by default when you first set up networking on Windows XP. The File and Printer Sharing for Microsoft Networks component allows you to share information and your printer with other people on the network. The QoS (Quality of Service) Packet Scheduler component is used on large networks to regulate and monitor the flow of information on the network. The Internet Protocol (TCP/IP) component is the most popular network protocol and allows your computer to communicate with computers on your network or on the Internet.

The network components you need to install usually depend on the type of connection that will use the component. For example, a network connection that uses a network interface card to connect to a high speed device, such as a cable modem, would require different network components than a network connection that uses a FireWire port.

You will not need to install additional network components on most home networks. When connecting to a larger network, such as a company network, you should always consult the network administrator before installing network components.

WORK WITH NETWORK COMPONENTS (CONTINUED)

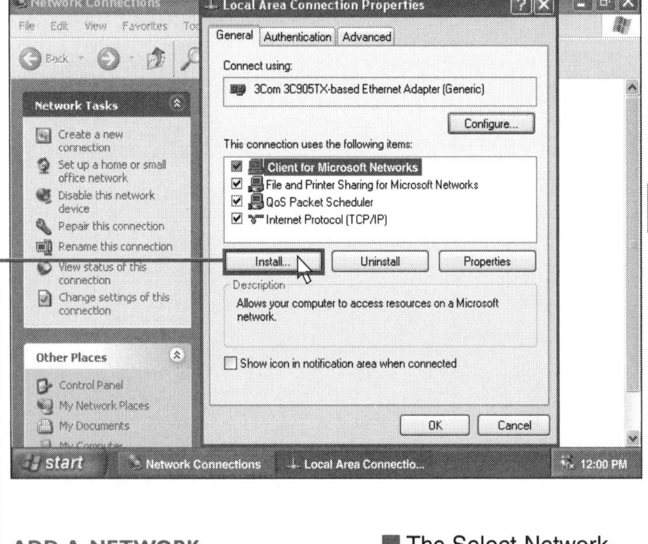

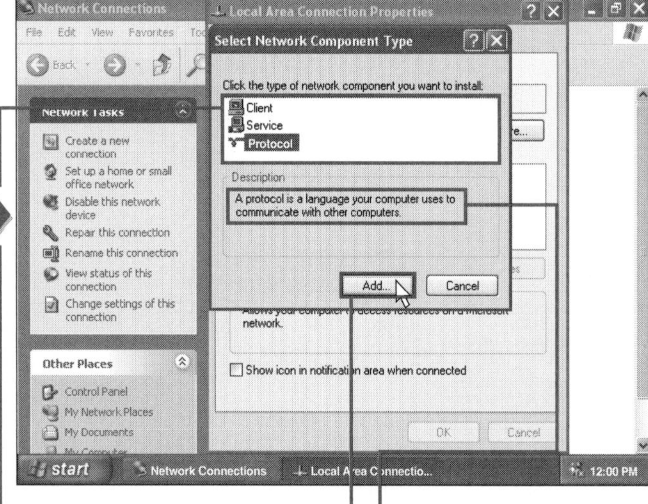

ADD A NETWORK COMPONENT

9 Click Install to add a new network component to your computer.

■ The Select Network Component Type dialog box appears.

10 Click the type of network component you want to add.

■ This area displays a description of the type of network component you selected.

11 Click Add.

How do I use an installation disk to add a network component?

✔ Insert the disk into the appropriate drive. Display the Select Network Component Type dialog box and select the component type you want to add. Click the Add button and then click the Have Disk button. In the dialog box that appears, select the drive that contains the disk and then click the Browse button to locate the installation files for the network component.

Does Windows include any other network components that I can add?

✔ Yes. In the Network Connections window, click the Advanced menu and select Optional Networking Components. Then follow the instructions in the Windows Optional Networking Components Wizard to add the network components you want.

Why is the NetBEUI protocol not in the list of protocols I can add?

✔ The NetBEUI protocol is not supported in Windows XP. If you are connecting a Windows XP computer to an older Windows network that uses the NetBEUI protocol, however, you may need to install the NetBEUI protocol on your computer to be able to communicate with the network. The NetBEUI protocol is available on your Windows XP installation CD-ROM disc. For more information, you can visit the www.microsoft.com Web site.

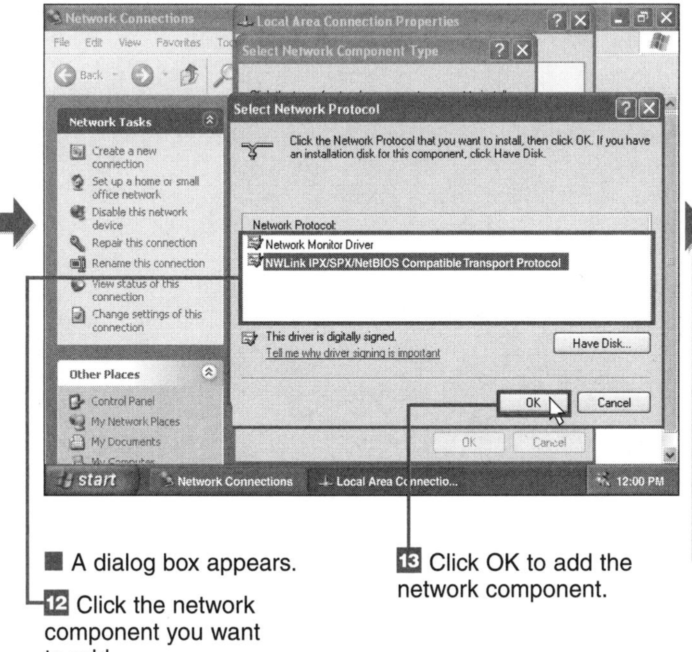

■ A dialog box appears.

12 Click the network component you want to add.

13 Click OK to add the network component.

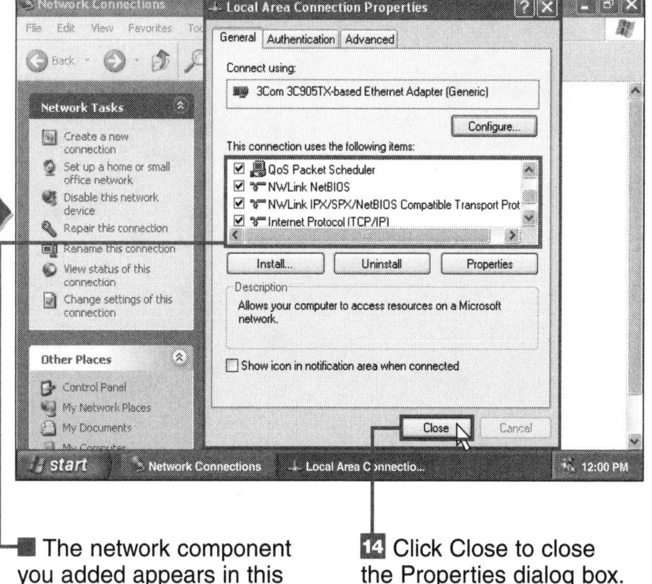

■ The network component you added appears in this area.

14 Click Close to close the Properties dialog box.

MONITOR SHARED FOLDERS

Windows allows you to monitor the folders you have shared on a network and the users connected to your shared folders. You must be logged on as a computer administrator to monitor your shared folders.

You can display the shared folders on your computer (Shares), the users currently connected to your computer (Sessions) and the files that users currently have open (Open Files).

When viewing shared folders, you can view the location of each shared folder on your computer and the number of users connected to each folder.

When viewing the users currently connected to your computer, Windows displays information such as the name of each user, the number of files each user has open and the amount of time each user has been connected.

When viewing the files that users currently have open, you can view information such as the name of each user who has opened a file and the permission each user was given when a file was opened.

Monitoring how many people access your shared folders helps you determine how sharing affects the performance of your computer. If too many people access the information on your computer, your computer may operate slower.

MONITOR SHARED FOLDERS

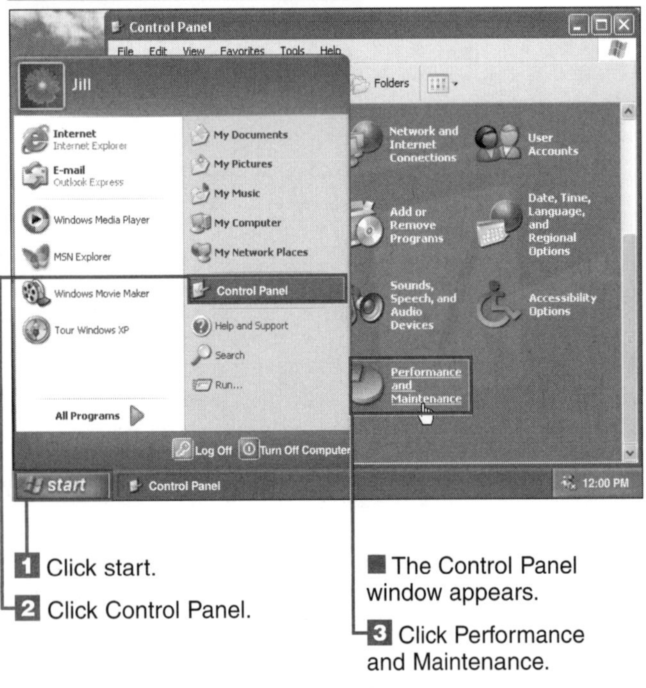

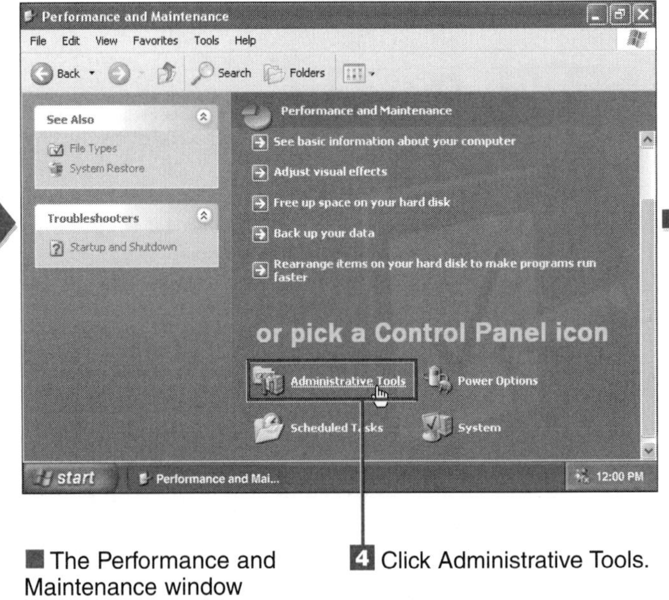

1 Click start.

2 Click Control Panel.

■ The Control Panel window appears.

3 Click Performance and Maintenance.

■ The Performance and Maintenance window appears.

4 Click Administrative Tools.

When I am viewing shared folders, why do some folders display the $ symbol?

✔ The $ symbol may indicate that a folder was shared by Windows. When you shared a folder, you may also have added the $ symbol to the end of the folder name to prevent users from seeing the shared folder on the network.

How do I disconnect a user?

✔ When viewing Sessions, you can disconnect a user by right-clicking the user's name and selecting Close Session. To disconnect all users, right-click a blank area in the right pane and select Disconnect All Sessions. You should warn users before disconnecting them to prevent them from losing data.

How do I close an open file?

✔ When viewing Open Files, you can close a file by right-clicking the file and selecting Close Open File. To close all files, right-click a blank area in the right pane and select Disconnect All Open Files. You should warn users before closing a file to prevent the users from losing data.

How do I send a message to all users accessing my shared folders?

✔ Right-click the Shares folder, select All Tasks and then choose Send Console Message. Type the message you want to send and then click the Send button.

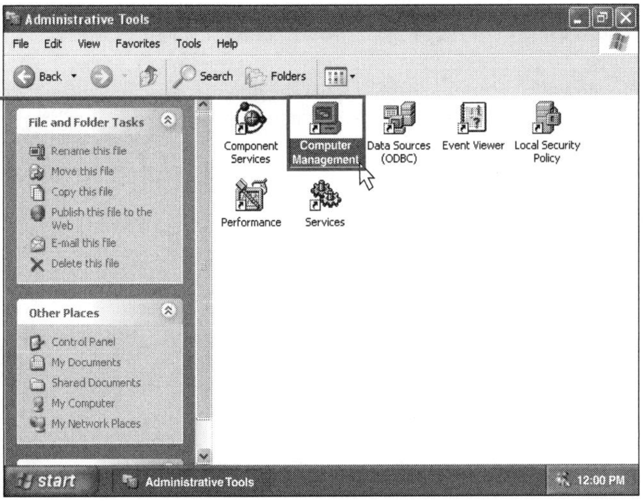

■ The Administrative Tools window appears.

5 Double-click Computer Management.

■ The Computer Management window appears.

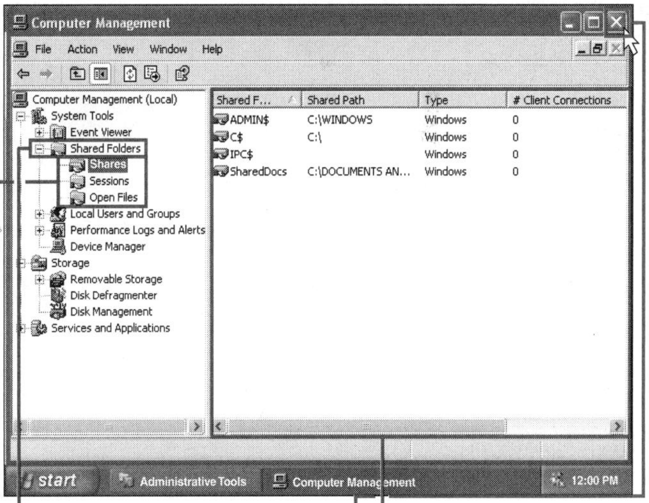

6 Click the plus sign (+) beside Shared Folders to display the contents of the folder (+ changes to −).

7 Click the type of information you want to display.

■ This area displays the information you selected.

8 When you finish reviewing the information, click ☒ to close the Computer Management window.

BROWSE THROUGH INFORMATION ON A NETWORK

You can use My Network Places to browse through the shared resources available on your network, such as files and printers. Windows automatically places shortcuts to shared folders in the My Network Places window.

Using My Network Places to locate shared resources on a network is similar to using My Computer to locate information on your own computer. You can work with the information shared on a network as you would work with information stored on your own computer.

In order to access information on a network, you may need to install the network protocol used by your network to exchange information. A network protocol is a set of rules that determines how computers on a network communicate. To install a network protocol, see page 400.

If you are unable to access a shared folder on a network, the computer that stores the folder may be turned off or the folder may no longer be shared.

BROWSE THROUGH INFORMATION ON A NETWORK

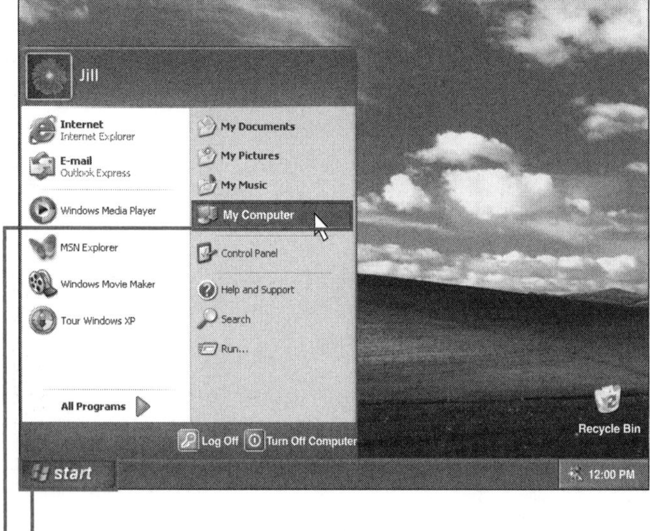

1 Click start.

2 Click My Computer.

■ If My Network Places appears on the Start menu, click My Network Places and then skip to step 4.

■ The My Computer window appears.

3 Click My Network Places to browse through the information available on your network.

Can two people on a network work on the same file at once?

✔ Most programs, such as word processors, allow only one person to make changes to a file at one time. Some programs, such as database programs, may allow several people on a network to make changes to a file at the same time.

How can I view all the computers in my workgroup?

✔ In the My Network Places window, click View workgroup computers. A window appears, displaying all the computers in your workgroup. To view or access the shared resources on a computer in your workgroup, double-click the computer.

How can I create a new shortcut to a location on my network?

✔ In the My Network Places window, click Add a network place to display the Add Network Place Wizard. You can use the wizard to create a new shortcut to a location on your network or to a Web site or FTP site. You can also use the wizard to sign up for an online file storage service, which allows you to store and share your files on the Web.

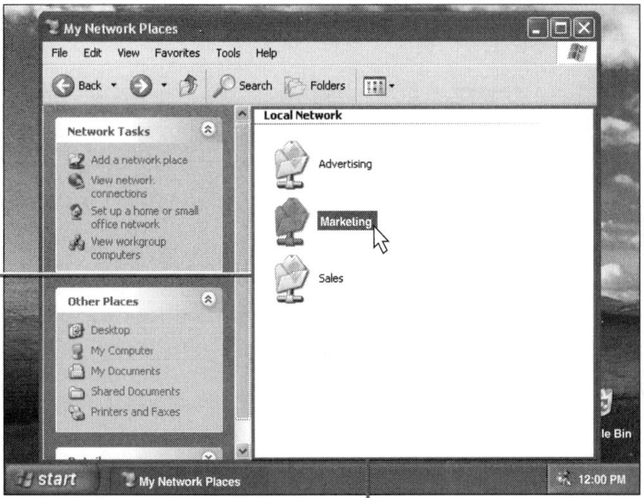

■ The My Network Places window appears.

■ This area displays the shared folders available on your network.

4 To display the contents of a folder, double-click the folder.

■ The contents of the folder appear.

■ To display the contents of a folder or file, double-click the folder or file.

■ You can click Back to return to the previous window.

5 When you finish working with information on your network, click ☒ to close the window.

SEARCH FOR A COMPUTER

You can quickly locate a computer on your network. Searching for a computer is especially useful if your network contains hundreds of computers.

If you are searching for a computer on a large network, Windows may take a while to display the names of any matching computers it finds.

You can search for a computer in your workgroup even when you know only part of the computer's name. For example, if you search for ray, Windows will find computers named Raymond and Murray.

After the search is complete, Windows displays a list of all the computers that match the name you specified. Windows also indicates the location of each computer that was found and displays a comment for each computer.

Once you find a computer, you can browse through the information and equipment shared by the computer. You can access the information stored on the computer as if the information were stored on your own computer.

SEARCH FOR A COMPUTER

1 Click start.

2 Click Search.

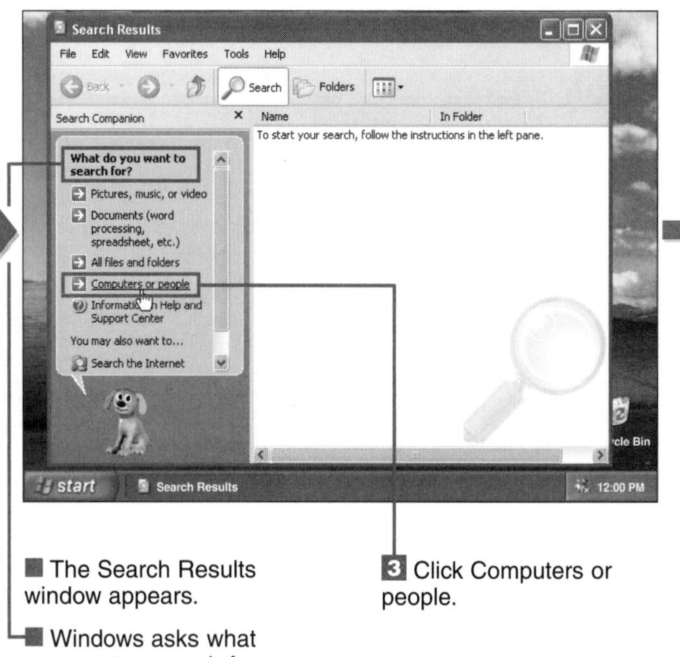

■ The Search Results window appears.

■ Windows asks what you want to search for.

3 Click Computers or people.

Can I stop a search?

✔ Yes. You can click the Stop button at any time to end a search. This is useful when the search for a computer is taking too long.

Can I search for files or folders on a computer that Windows finds?

✔ Yes. After performing a search, double-click the name of the computer you want to search and then select Search this computer for files. Choose All files and folders, type the name of the file or folder you want to find and then click the Search button.

How do I start a new search?

✔ Drag the mouse I over the text in the area below Computer name. Type the name of the computer you want to find and then click the Search button.

How can I change the order of the computers that Windows finds?

✔ You can sort the list of computers by name, location or comment. Click the heading of the column you want to use to sort the computers. Windows will sort the items alphabetically.

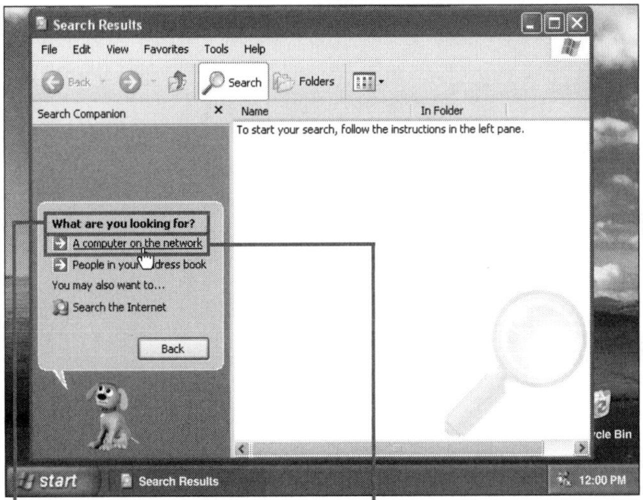

■ Windows asks what you are looking for.

4 Click this option to search for a computer on the network.

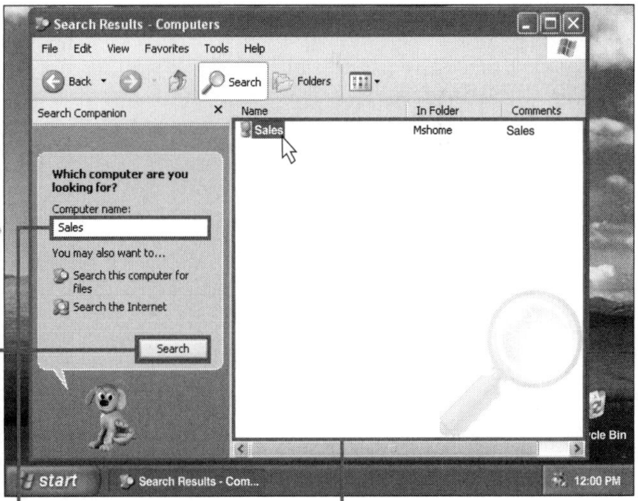

5 Type the name of the computer you want to find.

6 Click Search to start the search.

■ This area lists each computer that matches the name you specified.

■ To view the information and equipment shared by a computer, double-click the name of the computer.

SHARE INFORMATION

You can specify exactly what information on your computer you want to share with other people on a network. Sharing information is useful when people on a network are working together on a project and need to access the same files.

Before you can share information on your computer with other people on a network, your computer must be set up on the network. To set up your computer on a network, see page 394.

You can specify the name that the shared folder will display on the network. The name should not contain more than 12 characters. Specifying a name for a shared folder will not change the name of the folder on your computer.

When you share a folder on your computer, people on the network will have access to all the folders and files within the folder. They will be able to work with the files as if the files were stored on their own computers. You may want to specify that other people can only view the files, but not make changes to the files.

You cannot share some folders on your computer, such as Windows system folders and the personal folders of other users set up on your computer.

SHARE INFORMATION

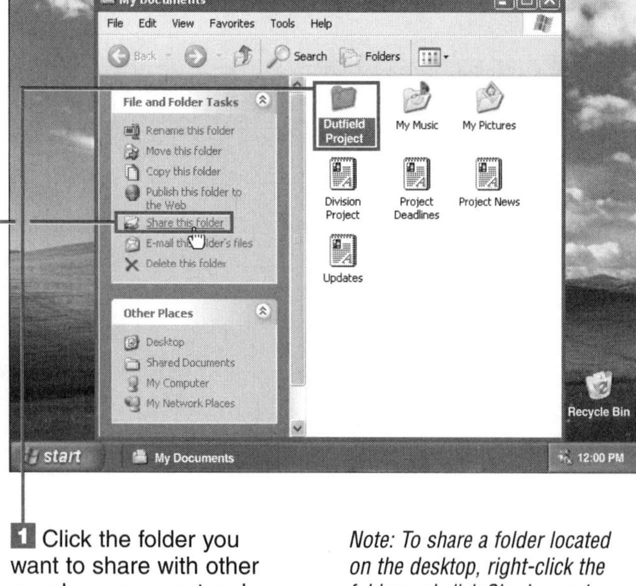

1 Click the folder you want to share with other people on your network.

2 Click Share this folder.

Note: To share a folder located on the desktop, right-click the folder and click Sharing and Security on the menu that appears instead of performing steps 1 and 2.

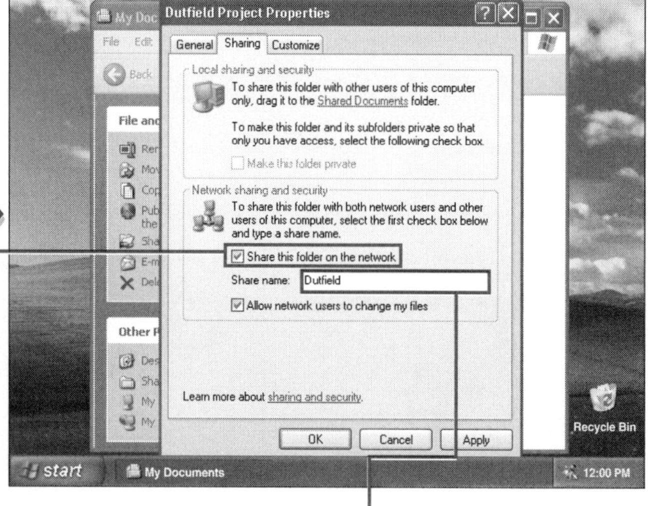

■ A Properties dialog box appears.

3 Click this option to share the folder with other people on your network (☐ changes to ☑).

4 This area displays the name of the folder people will see on the network. To change the folder name, select the current name and then type a new name.

Can I share a drive on my computer?

✔ Yes. You can share your hard drive, floppy drive or CD-ROM drive. Click start and select My Computer. Right-click the drive you want to share and select Sharing and Security from the menu that appears. Click "If you understand the risk but still want to share the root of the drive, click here" and then perform steps 3 to 6 below to share the drive.

Can I hide a shared folder from other people on the network?

✔ When sharing the folder, type a dollar sign ($) at the end of the folder's name. This will ensure that other people on the network will not see your shared folder when they browse through the information on the network. Hiding a folder is useful if you want only specific people to access the folder.

How can I view all the folders that are shared on the network?

✔ You can use My Network Places to see the folders shared by your computer and other computers on the network. To browse through shared folders on the network, see page 406.

How can I find out if people have accessed files in my shared folder?

✔ Windows allows you to view information about your shared folder, such as the name of each user who has accessed the folder. For more information, see page 404.

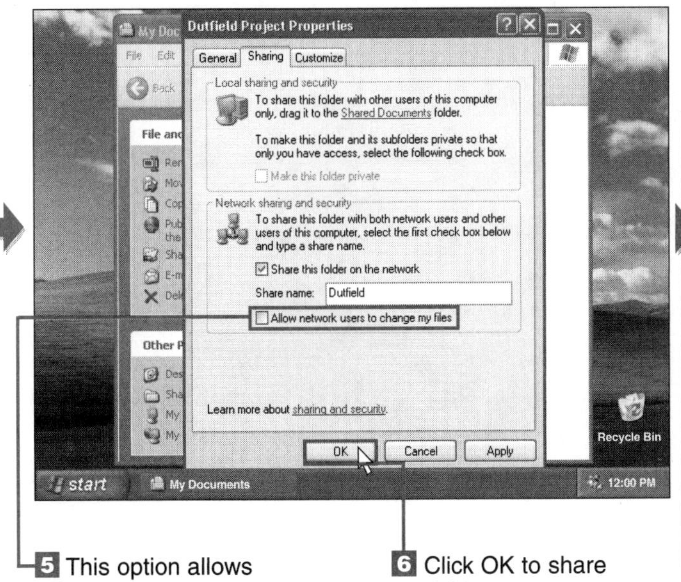

5 This option allows people on the network to make changes to files in the folder. You can click this option to turn the option on (☑) or off (☐).

6 Click OK to share the folder.

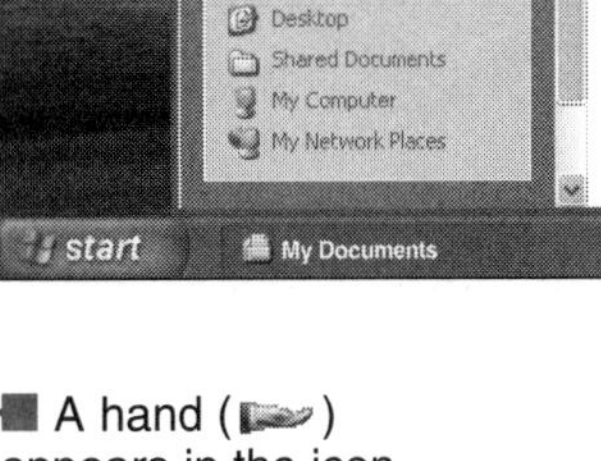

■ A hand ( ) appears in the icon for the shared folder.

■ Everyone on your network will be able to access all the files in the shared folder.

■ To stop sharing a folder, perform steps 1 to 3 (☑ changes to ☐ in step 3). Then perform step 6.

SHARE A PRINTER

You can share a printer connected to your computer with other people on a network. Sharing a printer allows others to use your printer to print documents. Using a shared printer can help individuals and companies reduce printing costs since several people on a network can use the same printer.

To share a printer, your computer must be set up on a network. To set up a computer on a network, see page 394.

When sharing a printer, you can assign a name to the printer. Other people will be able to see the name when they browse for shared printers on the network. A descriptive name helps to identify your printer if there are several printers available on the network.

After you share your printer, you must make sure that both your computer and your printer are turned on and accessible when other people need the printer.

Windows may have already shared your printer when you set up your computer on a network or installed the printer. In the Printers and Faxes window, a hand ( ) appears under the icon for a shared printer.

SHARE A PRINTER

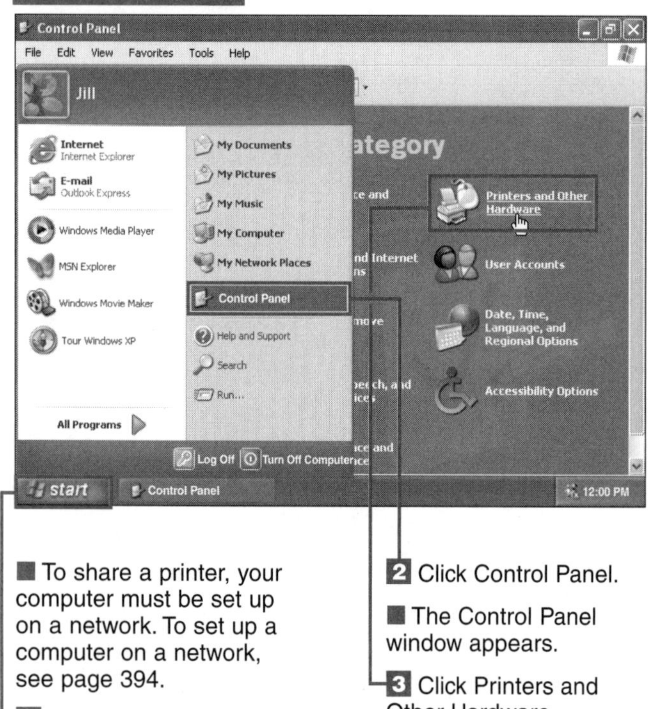

■ To share a printer, your computer must be set up on a network. To set up a computer on a network, see page 394.

1 Click start.

2 Click Control Panel.

■ The Control Panel window appears.

3 Click Printers and Other Hardware.

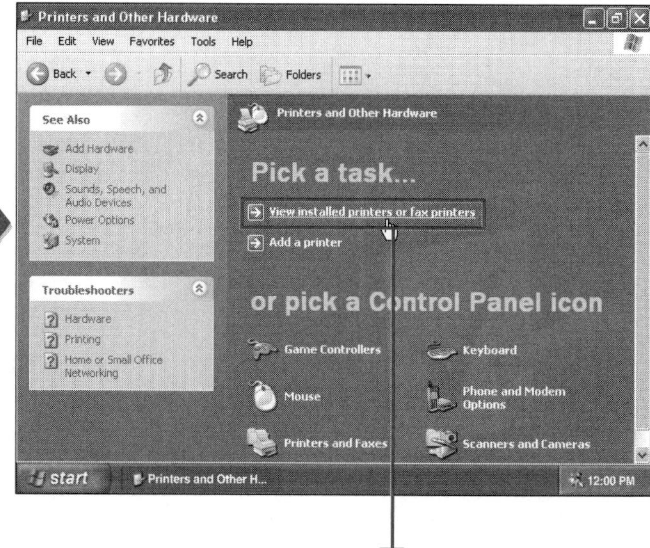

■ The Printers and Other Hardware window appears.

4 Click View installed printers or fax printers.

How do I share a printer with other people using different versions of Windows?

✔ You need to install additional drivers for the shared printer. Perform steps 1 to 6 below and then click Additional Drivers. In the dialog box that appears, select the operating environments and versions of Windows the other computers use (☐ changes to ☑) and click OK. Insert the CD-ROM disc containing the drivers you want to install into your CD-ROM drive and then click OK.

How do I stop sharing a printer?

✔ Perform steps 1 to 9 below, except select Do not share this printer in step 7 (○ changes to ◉).

How do I connect to a shared printer on the network or the Internet?

✔ Shared printers on the network usually automatically appear in the Printers and Faxes window. If the printer you want to use does not appear, perform steps 1 to 4 below to display the Printers and Faxes window. Click Add a printer and click Next. Click "A network printer, or a printer attached to another computer" (○ changes to ◉) and click Next. Click "Connect to a printer on the Internet or on a home or office network" (○ changes to ◉) and then type the location and name of the shared printer you want to connect to, followed by **/.printer**. Click Next and then follow the instructions in the wizard to finish installing the printer.

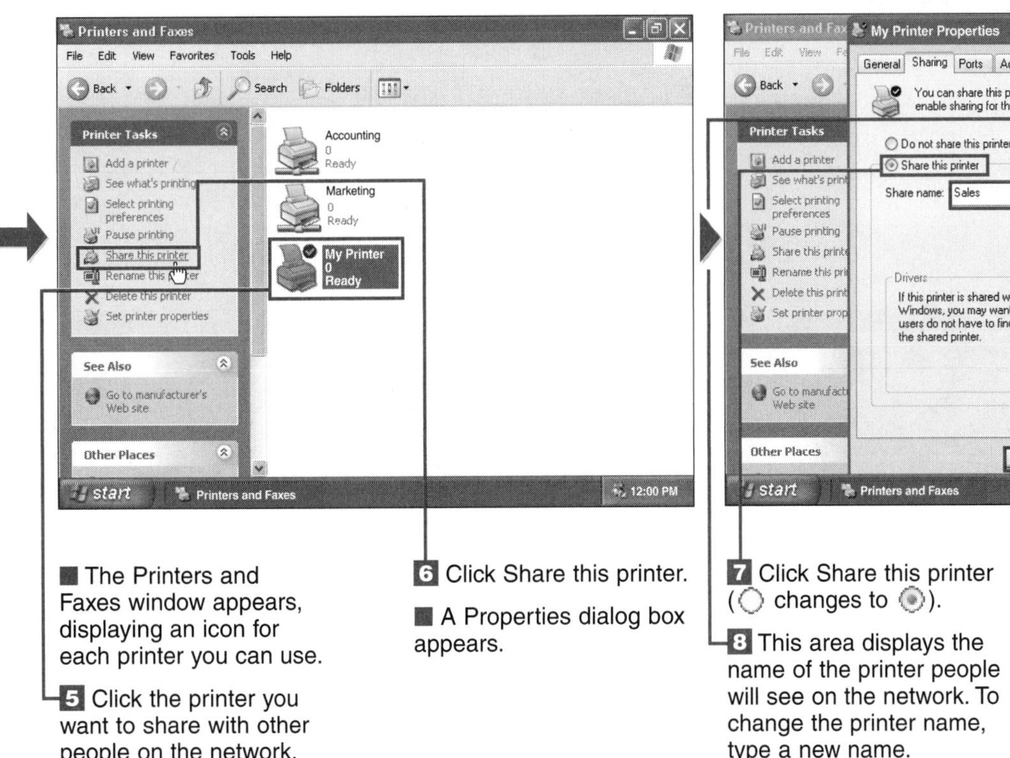

■ The Printers and Faxes window appears, displaying an icon for each printer you can use.

5 Click the printer you want to share with other people on the network.

6 Click Share this printer.

■ A Properties dialog box appears.

7 Click Share this printer (○ changes to ◉).

8 This area displays the name of the printer people will see on the network. To change the printer name, type a new name.

9 Click OK.

■ Windows will display a hand (☞) under the icon for the shared printer in the Printers and Faxes window.

ASSIGN A DRIVE LETTER TO A NETWORK FOLDER

You can assign, or map, a drive letter to a folder on the network. This provides a quick way to access information on another computer on the network. You can access a folder on the other computer as if the folder were on your own computer.

A folder you have assigned a drive letter to is often referred to as a mapped network drive.

If you frequently use information stored in a folder on another computer, assigning a drive letter to the folder can save you time, since you will not need to locate the folder on the network each time you want to use the folder.

Assigning a drive letter to a folder is also useful if you are working with MS-DOS or older Windows-based programs.

Although Windows allows you to use up to 215 characters to name a folder, older programs may not be able to read folder names that contain more than 8 characters. When you assign a drive letter to a folder, a single letter is used to represent the folder on the network, such as F:, allowing older programs to access the folder.

ASSIGN A DRIVE LETTER TO A NETWORK FOLDER

1 Click start.

2 Click My Computer.

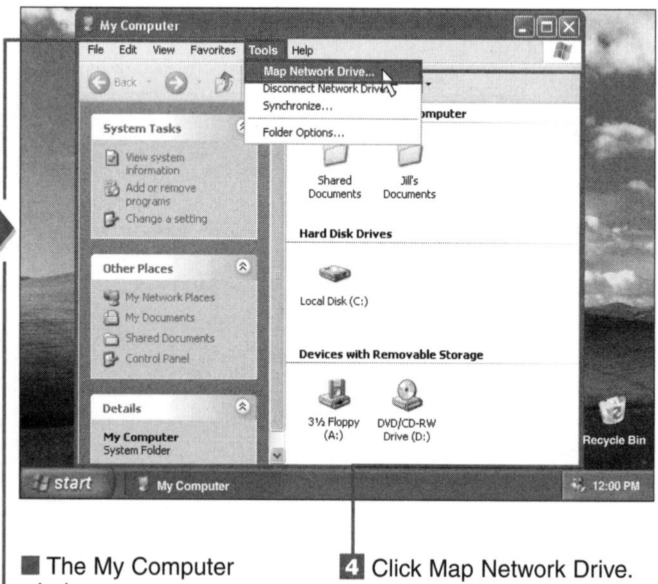

■ The My Computer window appears.

3 Click Tools.

4 Click Map Network Drive.

What drive letter should I select for a network folder?

✔ You should choose a drive letter between F and Z. You should reserve the letters A through E for your floppy drive, hard drive, CD-ROM drive and any removable drives you use on your computer.

Why do plus signs (⊞) and minus signs (⊟) appear beside items in the Browse For Folder dialog box?

✔ A plus sign indicates that an item contains hidden items. You can click the plus sign to display the items. A minus sign indicates that an item's contents are displayed. You can click the minus sign to hide the items.

Is there a quick way to specify the folder I want to assign a drive letter to?

✔ If you already know the location and name of the folder you want to assign a drive letter to, you can type the information in the Folder area instead of clicking Browse to locate the folder in step 6 below. For example, type \\JohnsComputer\StatusReports to specify a folder named StatusReports that is located on a computer named JohnsComputer. You can then skip to step 11 on page 416 to finish assigning a drive letter to the folder.

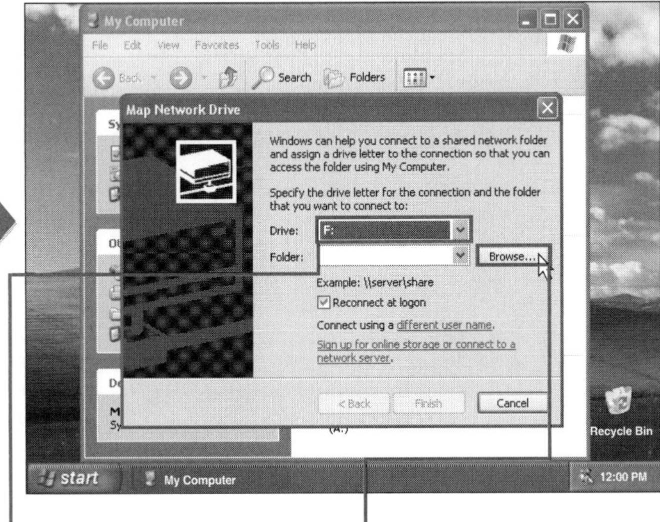

■ The Map Network Drive wizard appears.

5 This area displays the drive letter that Windows will assign to the folder. You can click this area to select a different drive letter.

6 Click Browse to locate the folder on your network that you want to assign the drive letter to.

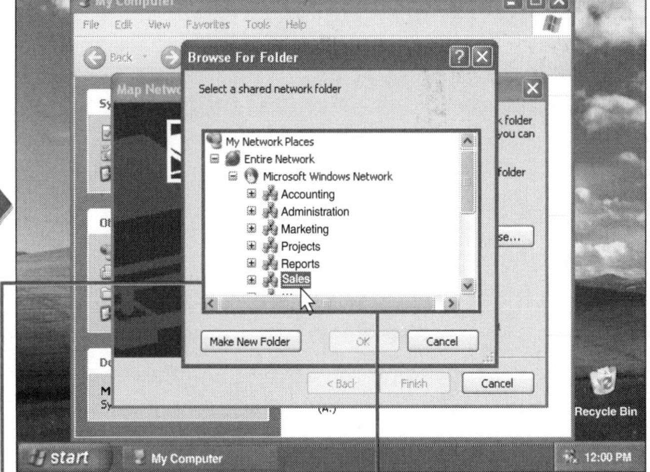

■ The Browse For Folder dialog box appears.

■ This area displays the available workgroups on your network. Windows automatically highlights the name of the workgroup that your computer belongs to.

7 Click the name of the workgroup that contains the folder you want to assign the drive letter to.

CONTINUED

ASSIGN A DRIVE LETTER TO A NETWORK FOLDER (CONTINUED)

You can browse through the computers in the workgroups on your network to locate the shared folder you want to assign a drive letter to.

Once you have located the folder to which you want to assign a drive letter, you can have Windows connect to the folder each time you start Windows. This will give you easy access to the folder every time you log on to Windows.

When you finish assigning a drive letter to a network folder, a window appears, displaying the contents of the folder. After assigning a drive letter to the folder, you will be able to easily redisplay the contents of the folder without having to locate the folder on the network.

Once you have assigned a drive letter to a network folder, the Network Drives area appears in the My Computer window. The Network Drives area displays an icon for each folder you have assigned a drive letter to. You can double-click the icon for a folder to quickly access the folder.

ASSIGN A DRIVE LETTER TO A NETWORK FOLDER (CONTINUED)

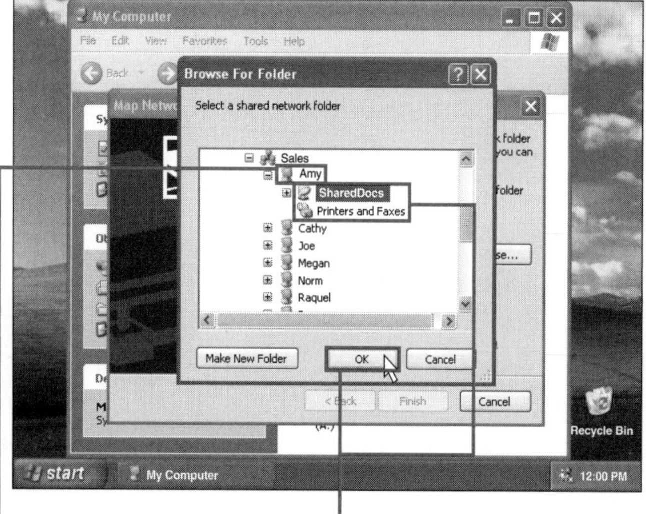

■ The computers in the workgroup you selected appear.

8 Click the name of the computer that contains the folder you want to assign the drive letter to.

■ The shared folders and printers on the computer appear.

9 Click the name of the folder you want to assign the drive letter to.

10 Click OK to confirm your selection.

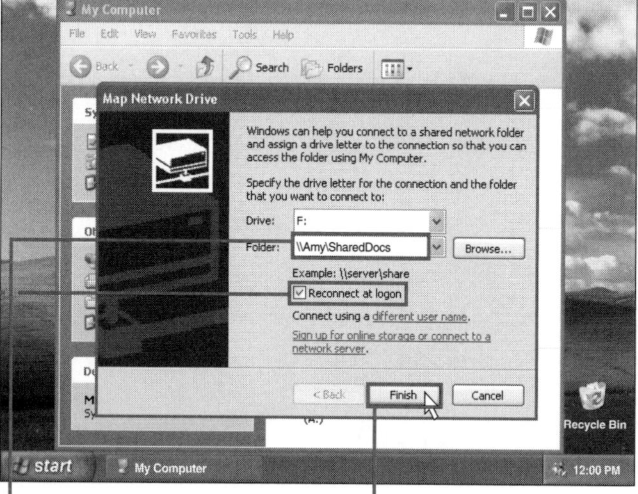

■ This area displays the location and name of the folder you selected.

11 This option indicates whether Windows will connect to the folder every time you start Windows. You can click the option to turn the option on (☑) or off (☐).

12 Click Finish to complete the wizard.

Why does an X appear on the icon for a folder I assigned a drive letter to?

✔ In the My Computer window, an X appears on the icon for a folder you assigned a drive letter to when Windows was not able to connect to the folder. Windows will notify you of the problem the next time you start Windows.

Are there any restrictions on when I can access a folder I assigned a drive letter to?

✔ The computer that shares the folder you assigned a drive letter to must be available on the network before you can access the folder.

How do I remove a drive letter from a network folder?

✔ In the My Computer window, click Tools and then select Disconnect Network Drive. In the dialog box that appears, click the icon for the folder you no longer want to be assigned a drive letter and then click OK. The folder will disappear from the Network Drives area of your My Computer window.

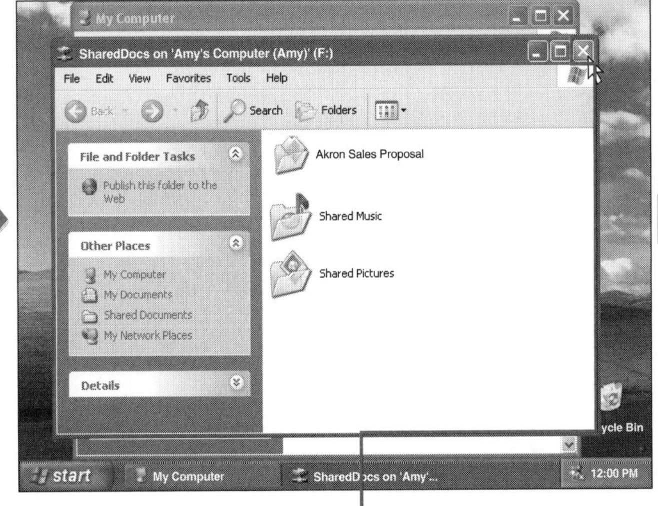

■ A window appears, displaying the contents of the folder.

13 When you finish viewing the contents of the folder, click ☒ to close the window.

■ The My Computer window reappears. The Network Drives area displays an icon for each folder on the network that you have assigned a drive letter to.

■ To display the contents of a folder, double-click its icon.

14 Click ☒ to close the My Computer window.

CHANGE COMPUTER AND WORKGROUP NAME

You can change the name of your computer and the workgroup your computer belongs to on a network. Windows uses this information to identify your computer on the network.

The computer and workgroup names are often entered when Windows is installed on a computer. On a business network, you should consult your network administrator before changing your computer or workgroup name.

Each computer on a network must have a unique name. The name of your computer cannot be the same as the name of the workgroup your computer belongs to.

You can assign your computer a description. Assigning a description gives other people on the network more detailed information about your computer, such as the computer's location. If some people on your network use computers that run operating systems other than Windows XP, such as Windows Me or Windows 98, these people may not be able to see the description you assign to your computer.

CHANGE COMPUTER AND WORKGROUP NAME

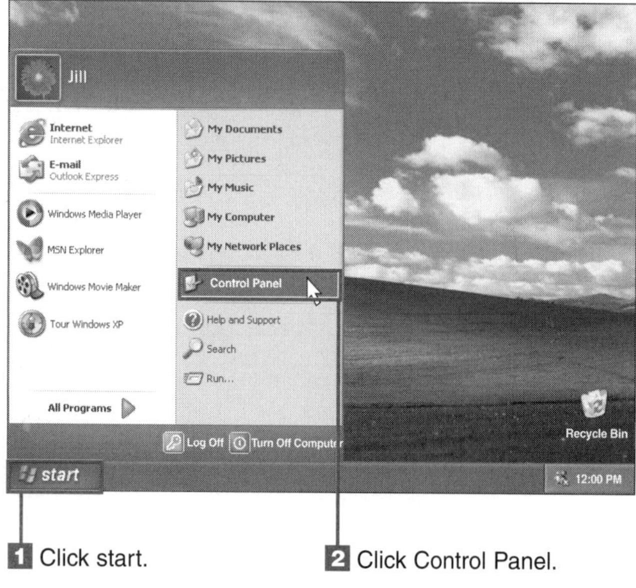

1 Click start.

2 Click Control Panel.

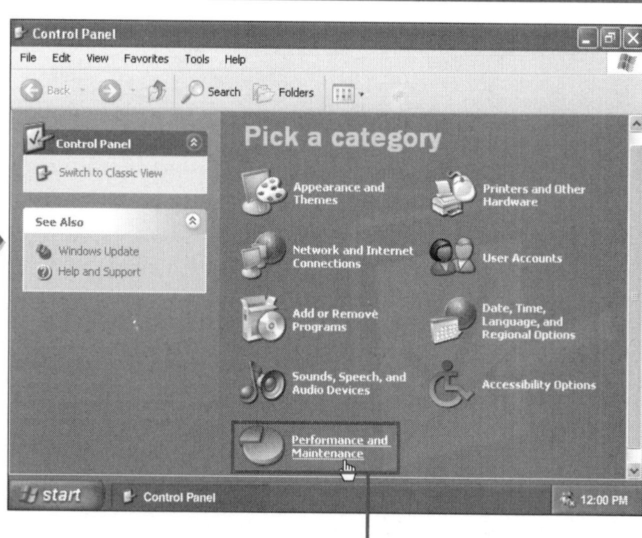

■ The Control Panel window appears.

3 Click Performance and Maintenance.

How do I view descriptions for computers on the network?

✔ Click start, select My Network Places and then locate the computers you want to view descriptions for. To quickly locate the computers in your workgroup, click View workgroup computers. Select the View menu and then click Details. Descriptions are displayed in the Comments column.

Are there any other ways to display the System Properties dialog box?

✔ Yes. To quickly display the System Properties dialog box, click start, right-click My Computer and then select Properties from the menu that appears. You can also click start, select My Computer and then click View system information to display the dialog box.

What is a workgroup?

✔ A workgroup is a group of computers that frequently share resources such as files and printers on a network. On a business network, a workgroup often consists of computers located close to each other, such as computers in the accounting or sales department. If you do not know the name of your workgroup, you can ask your network administrator. On a home network, all the computers usually belong to the same workgroup.

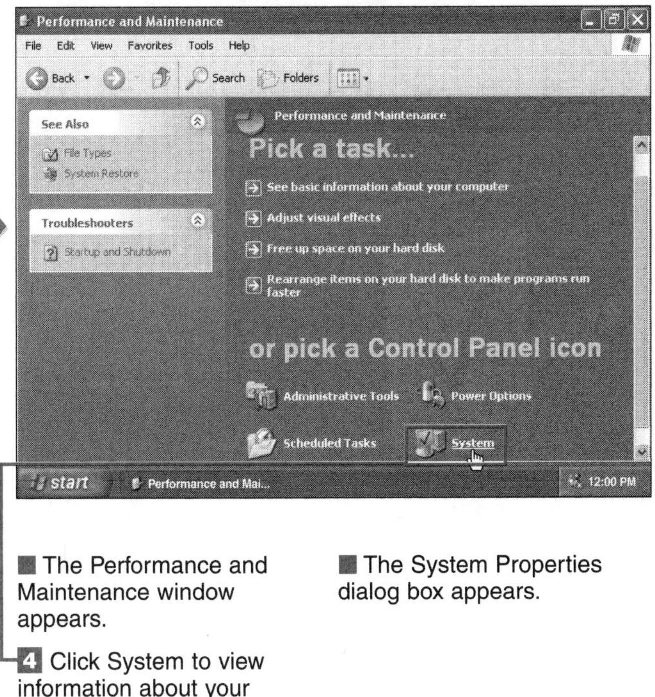

■ The Performance and Maintenance window appears.

4 Click System to view information about your computer.

■ The System Properties dialog box appears.

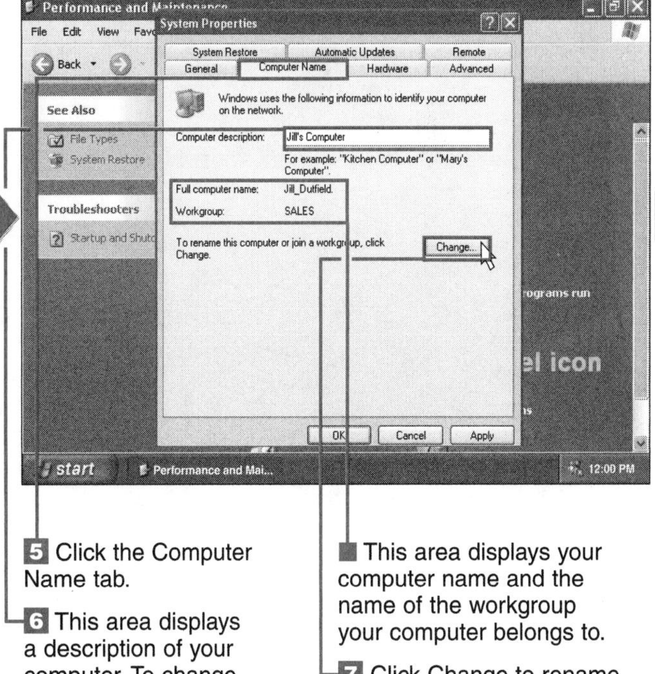

5 Click the Computer Name tab.

6 This area displays a description of your computer. To change the description, select the text and then type a new description.

■ This area displays your computer name and the name of the workgroup your computer belongs to.

7 Click Change to rename the computer or change the workgroup.

CONTINUED

CHANGE COMPUTER AND WORKGROUP NAME (CONTINUED)

When changing the name of your computer, you should use a short, descriptive name that will help other people on the network identify the computer. For example, a name such as "JohnsComputer" will make your computer easier to identify than a name such as "Computer10."

If your computer connects directly to the Internet, such as a computer that shares its Internet connection with other computers on a network, your Internet Service Provider (ISP) may require you to use a specific name for the computer.

To change the workgroup your computer belongs to, you can enter the name of the workgroup you want to join. Windows will display a message welcoming you to the workgroup.

After changing your computer or workgroup name, you will need to restart your computer before the changes will take effect. Make sure you close any open programs before restarting your computer.

After you change your computer or workgroup name, you should inform the people on the network who access resources on your computer of the change.

CHANGE COMPUTER AND WORKGROUP NAME (CONTINUED)

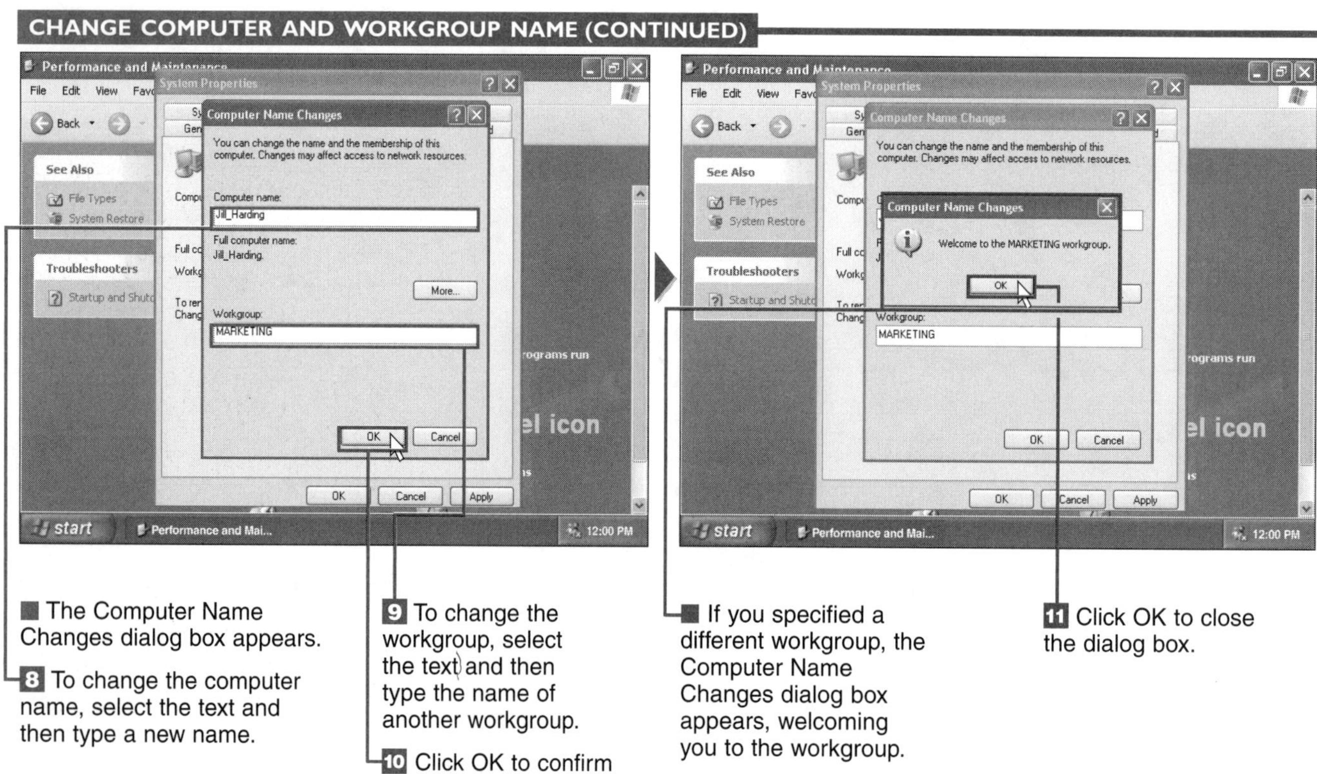

■ The Computer Name Changes dialog box appears.

8 To change the computer name, select the text and then type a new name.

9 To change the workgroup, select the text and then type the name of another workgroup.

10 Click OK to confirm your changes.

■ If you specified a different workgroup, the Computer Name Changes dialog box appears, welcoming you to the workgroup.

11 Click OK to close the dialog box.

Can I create a new workgroup on the network?

✔ Yes. In the Computer Name Changes dialog box, type a workgroup name that does not currently exist. A new workgroup with the name you specified will be created on the network. Before creating a new workgroup on a business network, you should consult your network administrator.

Are there any restrictions on computer or workgroup names?

✔ Computer and workgroup names can contain up to 15 characters, including letters and numbers, but cannot contain special characters or punctuation, such as the ; : " < > * + = \ | ? or , characters.

Will changing the name of my computer affect the resources I can access on the network?

✔ Depending on the setup of your network, changing your computer name may affect the network resources you can access. For example, access to a folder on your network may be restricted to specific computers. If you change the name of your computer, you will no longer have permission to access the folder. You should consult your network administrator to determine whether changing your computer name will affect the network resources you can access.

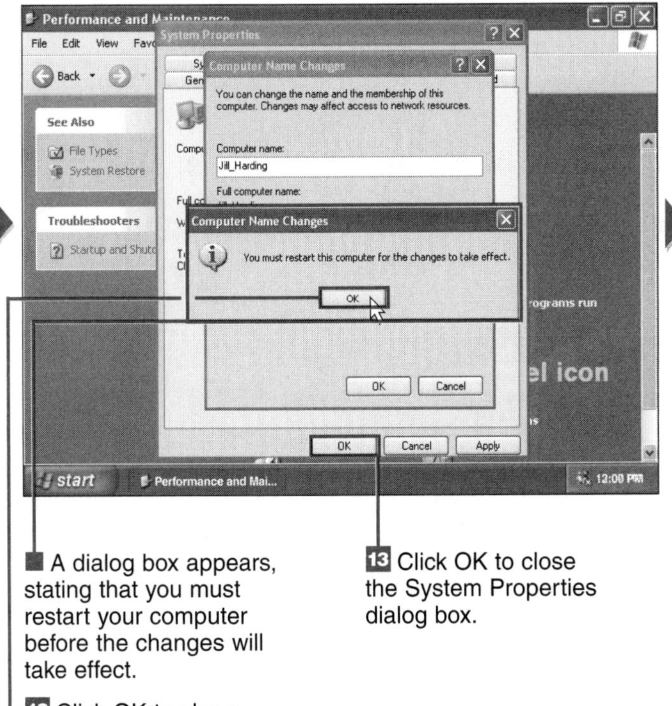

■ A dialog box appears, stating that you must restart your computer before the changes will take effect.

12 Click OK to close the dialog box.

13 Click OK to close the System Properties dialog box.

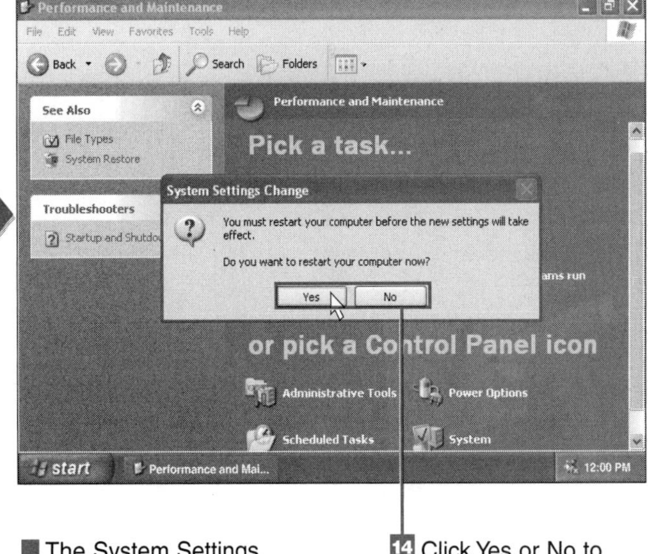

■ The System Settings Change dialog box appears, asking if you want to restart your computer now.

14 Click Yes or No to specify if you want to restart your computer.

SECTION VII

20) GET CONNECTED TO THE INTERNET

21) BROWSE THE WEB

WINDOWS XP AND THE INTERNET

22) EXCHANGE E-MAIL MESSAGES

23) USING WINDOWS MESSENGER

24) WORK WITH NEWSGROUPS

SET UP AN INTERNET CONNECTION

You can use the New Connection Wizard to set up a connection to the Internet. You only need to set up a connection to the Internet once.

If you have an account with an Internet Service Provider (ISP), you can use the New Connection Wizard to connect to the ISP using a dial-up modem, DSL or cable modem connection. An ISP is a company that provides access to the Internet.

You can access the New Connection Wizard from the Network Connections window. The Network Connections window helps you manage your network and Internet connections. The window displays an icon for each connection set up on your computer.

Once you are connected to the Internet, you will be able to access the resources available on the Internet. For example, you will be able to browse through information on the Web, exchange e-mail messages and read messages in newsgroups.

SET UP AN INTERNET CONNECTION

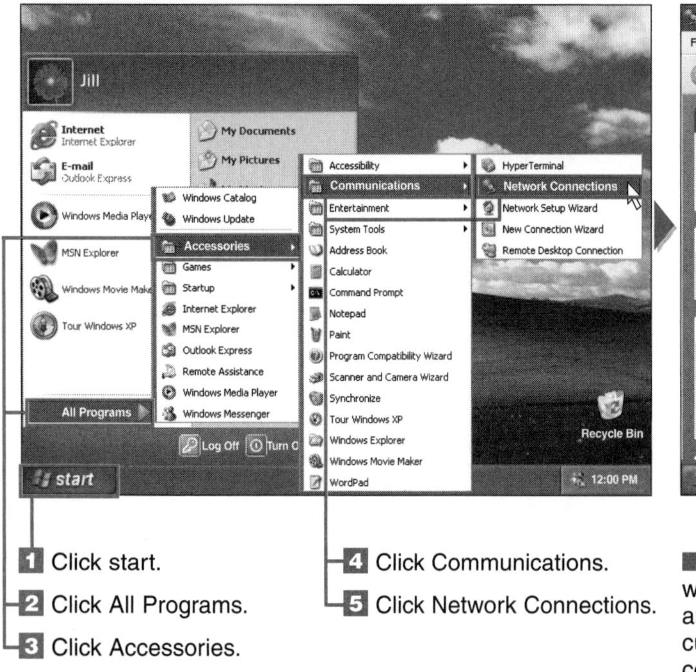

1 Click start.

2 Click All Programs.

3 Click Accessories.

4 Click Communications.

5 Click Network Connections.

■ The Network Connections window appears, displaying any connections that are currently set up on your computer.

6 Click Create a new connection.

Can I set up a connection to the Internet if I do not already have an account with an ISP?

✔ Yes. The New Connection Wizard can help you find an ISP. Perform steps 1 to 9 below and then click the Choose from a list of Internet service providers (ISPs) option. Then click Next. To use MSN as your ISP, select Get online with MSN, click Finish and then follow the instructions on your screen. To display a list of other ISPs, click Select from a list of other ISPs and click Finish. Then double-click Refer me to more Internet Service Providers and follow the instructions on your screen.

Is there another way to start the New Connection Wizard?

✔ Yes. Click start, select All Programs and choose Accessories. Click Communications and then select New Connection Wizard.

What other types of connections can I set up using the New Connection Wizard?

✔ You can use the New Connection Wizard to connect to your business network or set up a home network. For information about connecting to a business network, see page 364. To set up a home network, see page 394.

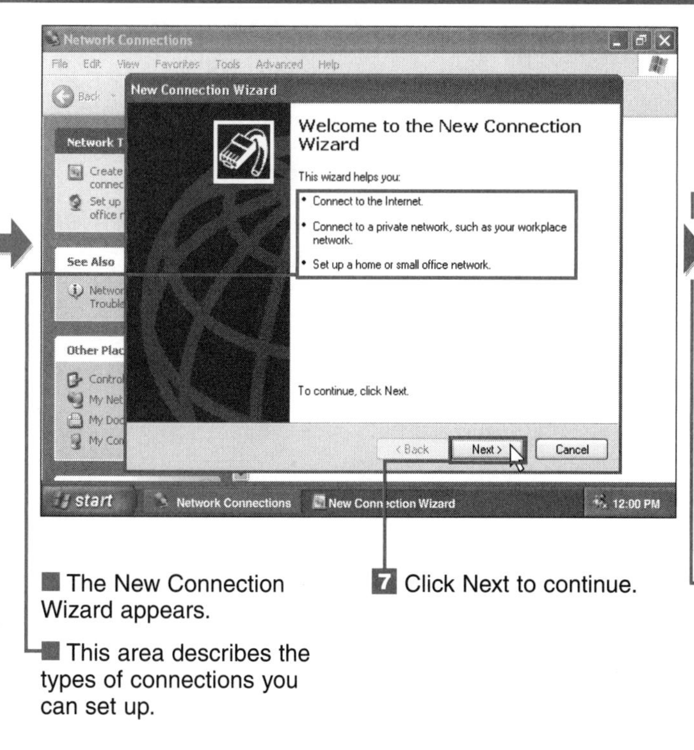

■ The New Connection Wizard appears.

■ This area describes the types of connections you can set up.

7 Click Next to continue.

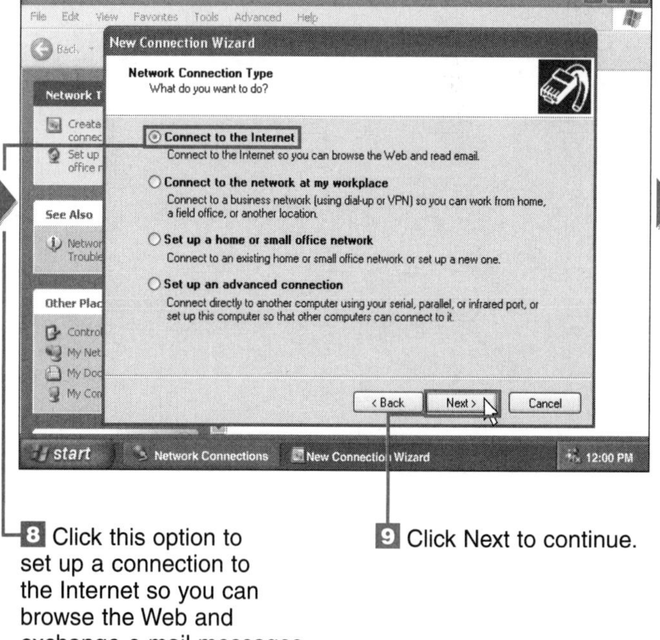

8 Click this option to set up a connection to the Internet so you can browse the Web and exchange e-mail messages (○ changes to ◉).

9 Click Next to continue.

CONTINUED

SET UP AN INTERNET CONNECTION (CONTINUED)

When setting up an Internet connection, you must specify the type of connection you will use, such as a dial-up modem connection or a broadband connection.

A dial-up modem connection uses a phone line and modem to connect to the Internet. The phone line can be a regular phone line or an ISDN phone line.

A broadband connection that requires a user name and password, sometimes called a PPPoE connection, is a high-speed connection that uses a DSL or cable modem.

A broadband connection that is always on is a high-speed connection that uses a DSL, cable modem or Local Area Network (LAN) connection. This type of connection does not require a user name or password.

You do not need to run the New Connection Wizard to set up this type of connection.

You can assign a name to the Internet connection you are setting up. An icon displaying the name for the connection will appear in the Network Connections window.

When setting up a dial-up modem connection, you must also enter the phone number of your ISP.

SET UP AN INTERNET CONNECTION (CONTINUED)

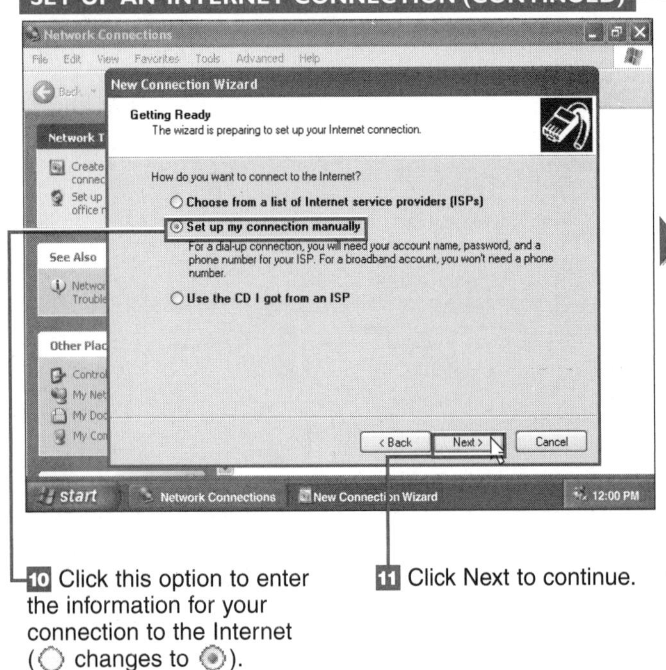

10 Click this option to enter the information for your connection to the Internet (○ changes to ◉).

11 Click Next to continue.

12 Click the option that describes the way you want to connect to the Internet (○ changes to ◉).

13 Click Next to continue.

Note: If you selected the second option in step 12, the wizard will not ask you to specify a phone number in step 16. If you selected the third option, skip to step 24.

My ISP provides a setup CD. How do I use the CD to set up my Internet connection?

✔ In step 10 below, click the Use the CD I got from an ISP option and then click Next. Click Finish to exit the New Connection Wizard and then insert the CD into your CD-ROM drive. Then follow the instructions on your screen to set up your Internet connection.

What is the difference between an ISDN phone line and a regular phone line?

✔ An ISDN line is a digital phone line offered by a telephone company. An ISDN line can transfer information faster than a regular phone line and does not tie up your telephone line while you are on the Internet. This allows you to make calls while you are connected to the Internet.

How do I set up my e-mail account?

✔ After you finish setting up your Internet connection, you can set up your e-mail account. The first time you start Outlook Express, a wizard will appear. You can follow the instructions in the wizard to set up your e-mail account. To start Outlook Express, see page 454.

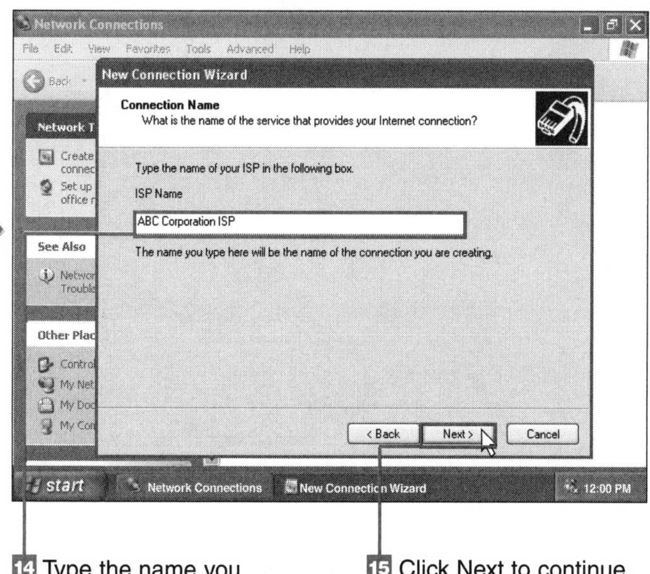

14 Type the name you want to use for the Internet connection, such as the name of your Internet service provider.

15 Click Next to continue.

16 Type the phone number you will use to connect to your Internet service provider.

Note: You may need to include a 1, the area code or both.

17 Click Next to continue.

■ You can click Back at any time to return to a previous step and change the information you have entered.

CONTINUED

SET UP AN INTERNET CONNECTION (CONTINUED)

When setting up a connection to an ISP using the New Connection Wizard, you must specify the user name and password you use to log on to your ISP. If you do not know your user name and password, contact your ISP.

You can have Windows use the user name and password you specify when other users connect to the Internet. This makes the Internet connection available to every user set up on your computer.

If you want to automatically use the Internet connection you are setting up every time you connect to the Internet, you can make the connection your default connection.

Windows allows you to turn on Internet Connection Firewall software for the Internet connection. This software will protect your computer from unauthorized access when the computer is connected to the Internet.

You can have Windows place a shortcut to the Internet connection on your desktop. This will allow you to quickly access the Internet connection.

Once your computer is set up to connect to your Internet service provider, you can connect to the Internet at any time. To connect to your Internet service provider to access the Internet, see page 430.

SET UP AN INTERNET CONNECTION (CONTINUED)

18 Type the user name for your Internet account.

19 Click this area and type the password for your Internet account.

Note: A bullet (●) appears for each character you type to prevent other people from seeing the password.

20 Click this area and type the password again to confirm the password.

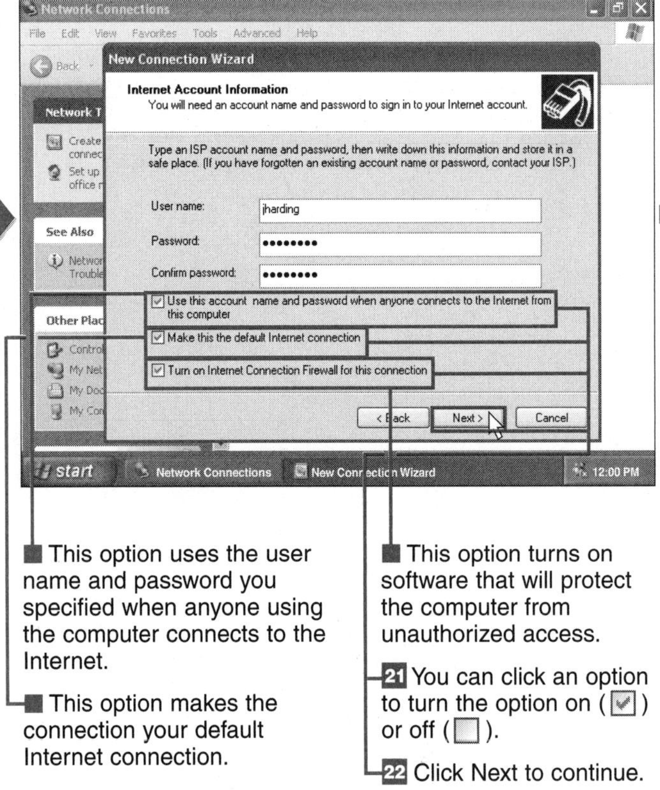

■ This option uses the user name and password you specified when anyone using the computer connects to the Internet.

■ This option makes the connection your default Internet connection.

■ This option turns on software that will protect the computer from unauthorized access.

21 You can click an option to turn the option on (☑) or off (☐).

22 Click Next to continue.

How can I change the settings for a connection I created using the New Connection Wizard?

✔ In the Network Connections window, click the connection you want to change and then click Change settings of this connection. A properties dialog box appears, displaying the settings you can change. For example, if the connection is a dial-up modem connection, you can use the General tab to change the phone number Windows will dial for the connection.

How do I delete a connection I no longer use?

✔ In the Network Connections window, click the connection you want to delete and then click Delete this connection.

My ISP provided me with an IP address I must use. How do I enter this information?

✔ In the Network Connections window, click the connection, click Change settings of this connection and then click the Networking tab. Choose the Internet Protocol (TCP/IP) option and then click Properties. Click Use the following IP address and then type the IP address in the area provided. An IP address is a number that identifies a computer on the Internet. If your ISP does not specify the IP address you must use, an address will be automatically assigned to your computer when you connect to the Internet.

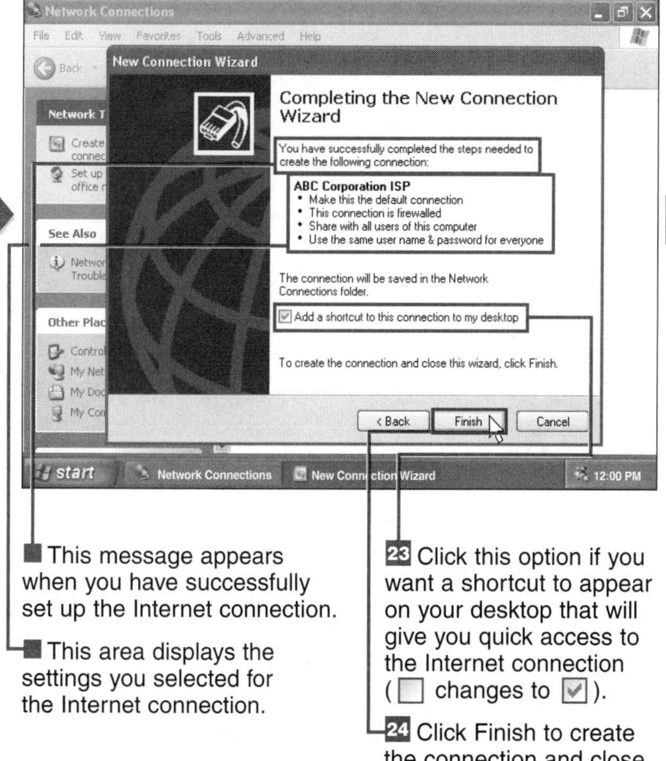

■ This message appears when you have successfully set up the Internet connection.

■ This area displays the settings you selected for the Internet connection.

23 Click this option if you want a shortcut to appear on your desktop that will give you quick access to the Internet connection (☐ changes to ☑).

24 Click Finish to create the connection and close the wizard.

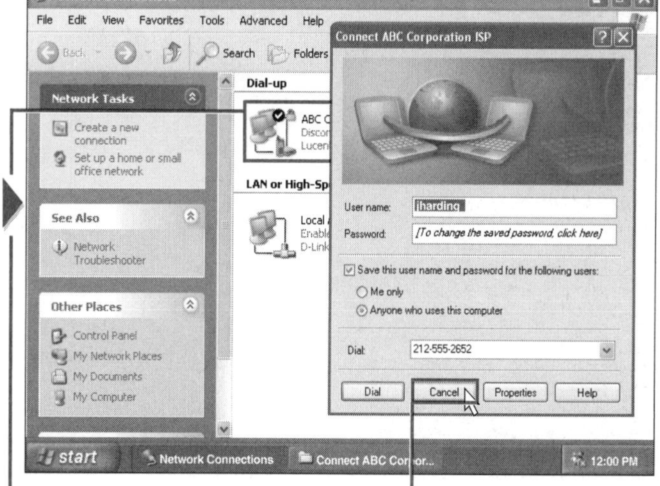

■ An icon for the Internet connection appears in the Network Connections window.

■ The Connect dialog box appears, allowing you to connect to the Internet.

25 If you do not want to connect to the Internet now, click Cancel.

Note: To connect to the Internet, see page 430.

DIAL IN TO AN INTERNET SERVICE PROVIDER

After you set up a connection to your Internet Service Provider (ISP), you can dial in to the ISP. Dialing in to an Internet service provider allows you to access the wide range of resources available on the Internet. You can browse through Web pages on various subjects, exchange electronic mail with friends and colleagues and read messages in newsgroups.

Windows displays the name of each dial-up connection you have set up on the Start menu. To set up a connection to an Internet service provider, see page 424.

Windows needs to know your user name and password to dial in to your ISP. Your service provider should have provided you with this information when you set up your account. Your user name and password are automatically saved so you do not have to enter them each time you dial in.

After your computer connects to your ISP, an icon ( ) appears on the taskbar. You can use this icon to view information about the connection or end the connection.

If you are using a high-speed connection, such as a cable modem or DSL, you probably will not need to perform the steps described below.

DIAL IN TO AN INTERNET SERVICE PROVIDER

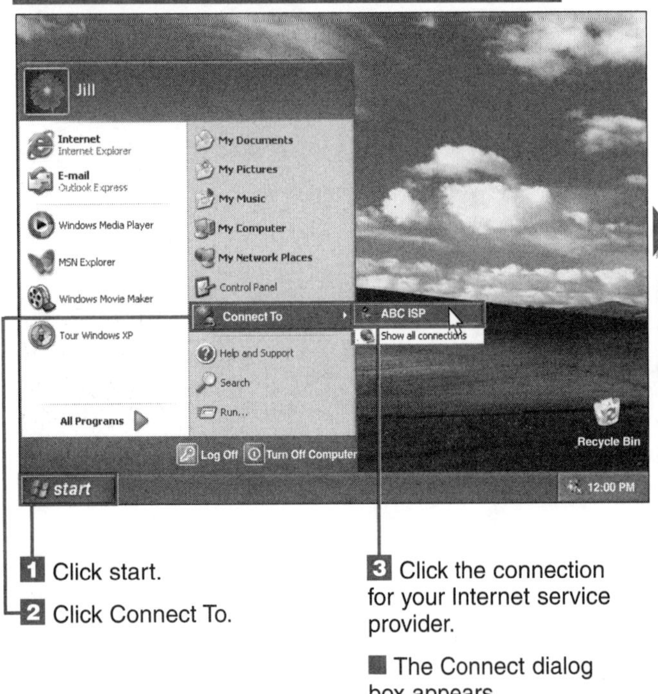

1 Click start.

2 Click Connect To.

3 Click the connection for your Internet service provider.

■ The Connect dialog box appears.

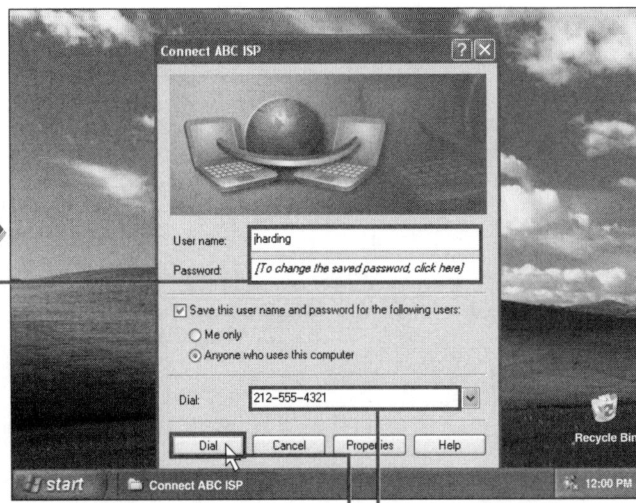

4 These areas contain the user name and password for your Internet account. To change this information, click the appropriate area and type the correct information.

5 This area displays the phone number Windows will dial. To change the number, select the current number and then type a new number.

6 Click Dial to connect to your Internet service provider.

Will other users be able to use the user name and password I entered?

✔ Yes. By default, the user name and password are saved for all users, but you can save the user name and password for your own use only. In the Connect dialog box, select the Me only option (◯ changes to ◉) and then type the password for your Internet account in the Password area. When you click the Dial button, a dialog box appears. Select Yes to delete the user name and password saved for all other users.

When I start Internet Explorer or Outlook Express, will Windows automatically dial in to my ISP?

✔ No. When you start Internet Explorer or Outlook Express, the Network Connections dialog box appears. You can choose the connection you want to use and then click the Connect button to display the Connect dialog box.

How can I test my connection to the Internet?

✔ Windows includes a program called PING that uses computer IP numbers to test connections with other computers on the Internet. Your ISP can provide you with the IP number of a computer you can use to test the connection. Open the Command Prompt window and type **ping** followed by the IP number of the computer you want to communicate with. Then press the Enter key. PING will report how long it takes to send and receive a signal between your computer and the other computer. If PING displays a message stating that the request timed out, the connection is not working. See page 170 to open the Command Prompt window.

■ When you are connected to your Internet service provider, this message and icon (🖧) appear.

■ You can now access information on the Internet.

7 To view information about the connection or to end the connection, click 🖧.

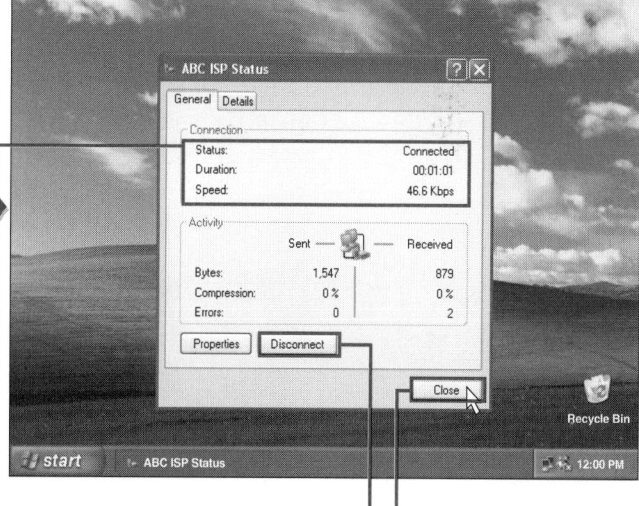

■ The Status dialog box appears.

■ This area displays information about the connection, such as the amount of time you have been connected and the speed of the connection.

8 To close the dialog box while staying connected, click Close.

■ To end the connection, click Disconnect.

START INTERNET EXPLORER AND DISPLAY WEB PAGES

You can use Internet Explorer to browse through information on the World Wide Web. The Web is part of the Internet and consists of a huge collection of documents, called Web pages, stored on computers around the world.

Web pages contain links, which are also known as hyperlinks. Links are highlighted text or images on a Web page that connect to other pages on the Web. Links allow you to easily navigate through a vast amount of information by jumping from one Web page to another.

You can display a specific Web page that you have heard or read about if you know the address of the page. Each Web page has a unique address, called a Uniform Resource Locator (URL).

Internet Explorer remembers the addresses of Web pages you have recently visited. You can select one of these addresses to quickly redisplay a Web page.

When you display a Web page, the text on the page transfers to your computer quickly so you can start reading the text right away. Images transfer more slowly, so you may have to wait a moment to clearly view the images.

START INTERNET EXPLORER AND DISPLAY WEB PAGES

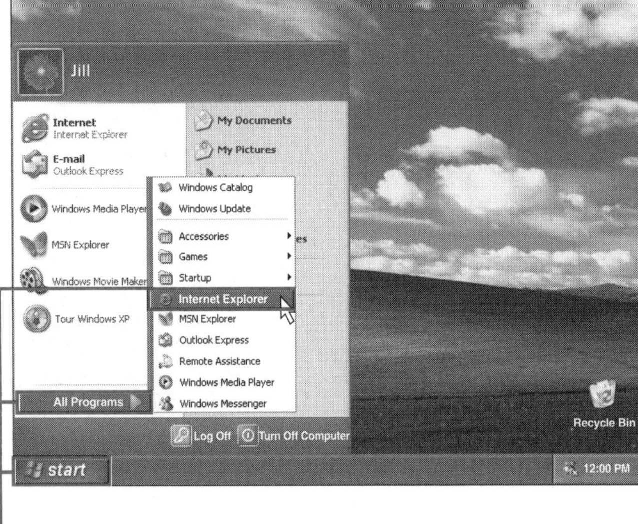

START INTERNET EXPLORER

1 Click start.

2 Click All Programs.

3 Click Internet Explorer.

■ The Microsoft Internet Explorer window appears.

Note: If you are not currently connected to the Internet, a dialog box will appear, allowing you to connect.

SELECT A LINK

1 Position the mouse over a highlighted word or image of interest. The mouse changes to a hand when over a link.

■ This area displays the address of the Web page that the link will take you to.

2 Click the word or image to display the linked Web page.

■ The linked Web page appears.

Is there a faster way to start Internet Explorer?

✔ Yes. If Internet Explorer is set as your default Web browser, you can click start and then select Internet. To change your default Web browser, see page 264.

Why does the New Connection Wizard appear when I start Internet Explorer?

✔ When you start Internet Explorer for the first time, the New Connection Wizard appears if you have not yet set up your connection to the Internet. Follow the instructions in the wizard to set up your connection. See page 424 for more information.

Can I have more than one Internet Explorer window open at a time?

✔ If you want to view two different Web pages at the same time, you can open another Internet Explorer window to view another Web page. From the File menu, select New and then choose Window.

Can I change the size of text displayed on Web pages?

✔ Yes. From the View menu, select Text Size and then choose the size you want to use. The current text size displays a dot (●).

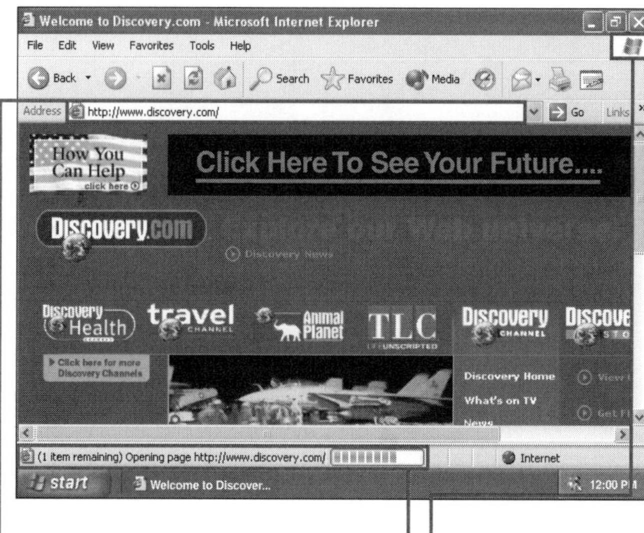

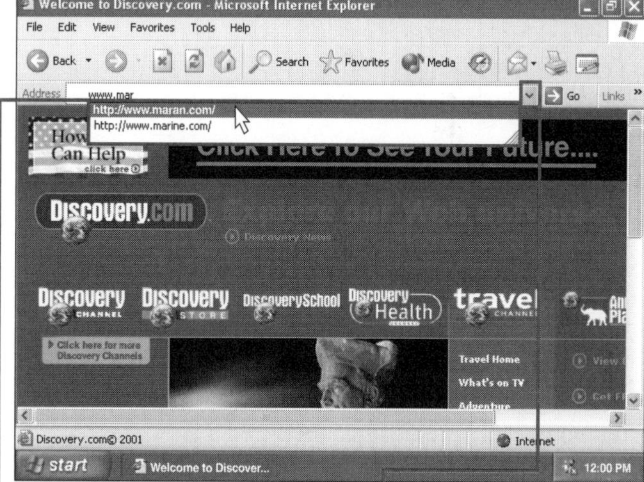

DISPLAY A SPECIFIC WEB PAGE

1 Click this area to highlight the current Web page address.

2 Type the address of the Web page you want to display and then press the Enter key.

■ The Web page appears on your screen.

■ This icon is animated as the Web page transfers to your computer.

■ This area shows the progress of the transfer.

REDISPLAY A WEB PAGE

1 When you begin typing the address of a Web page you have recently visited, a list of matching addresses appears.

2 Click the address of the Web page you want to redisplay.

■ You can also click ⌄ at any time to display a list of Web pages you have recently visited.

WORK WITH WEB PAGES

Internet Explorer provides several toolbar buttons that you can use to work with Web pages.

If a Web page is taking a long time to appear on your screen or contains information that does not interest you, you can stop the transfer of the page.

You can move back or forward through the Web pages you have viewed since you last started Internet Explorer.

Refreshing a Web page allows you to transfer a fresh copy of the page to your computer. This is useful for updating Web pages that contain constantly changing information such as news, stock market data or images from a live camera.

Internet Explorer lets you produce a paper copy of a Web page. The page number and total number of pages will appear at the top of each printed page. The Web page address and current date set in your computer appear at the bottom of each printed page.

You can display your home page at any time. The home page appears each time you start Internet Explorer.

WORK WITH WEB PAGES

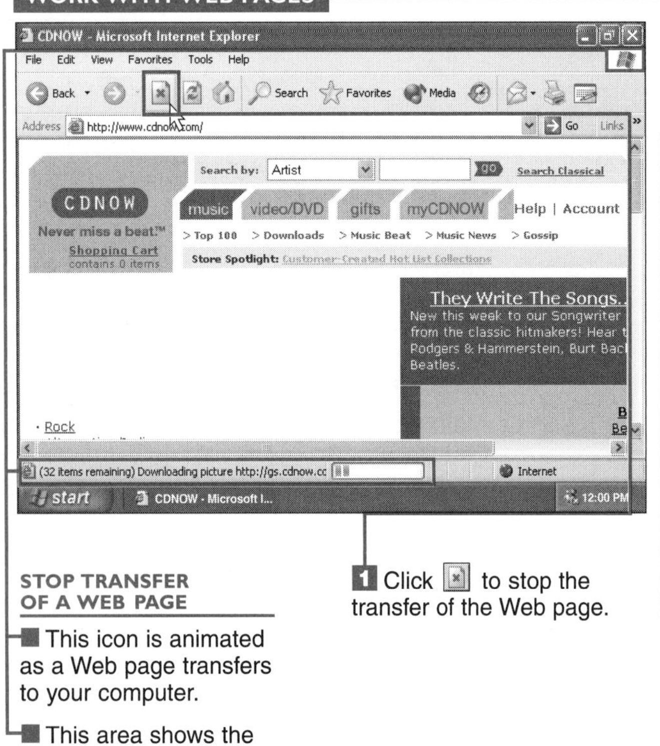

STOP TRANSFER OF A WEB PAGE

■ This icon is animated as a Web page transfers to your computer.

■ This area shows the progress of the transfer.

1 Click to stop the transfer of the Web page.

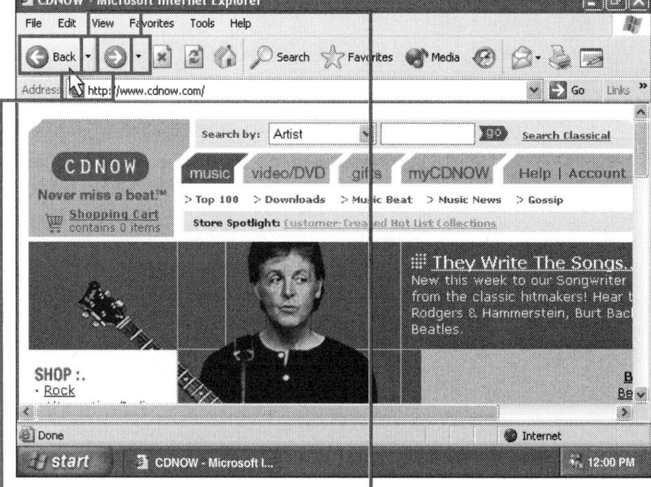

MOVE THROUGH WEB PAGES

1 Click Back or to move through the Web pages you have viewed.

Note: The button is only available after you use the Back button to return to a Web page.

■ You can also click beside Back or to display a list of Web pages you have recently viewed. You can then click the Web page you want to view again.

Can I save a Web page?

✔ From the File menu, click Save As to name and save the Web page. Windows will save the Web page in the location you specify and create a folder in the same location to store the images for the page.

Can I save an image on a Web page?

✔ To save an image, right-click the image and then select Save Picture As. Type a name for the image and then click Save.

Can I find a word on a Web page?

✔ From the Edit menu, select Find (on This Page). Type the word you want to find and then click Find Next.

Can I find out how a Web page was created?

✔ Viewing the HTML code used to create a Web page is useful if you want to find out how the effects on a Web page were created. From the View menu, select Source.

Why does a toolbar appear when I position the mouse over an image on a Web page?

✔ A toolbar appears when you position the mouse over an image that is at least 200 x 200 pixels in size. You can use the toolbar buttons to save the picture ( ), print the picture ( ), send the picture in an e-mail message ( ) or open the My Pictures folder ( ).

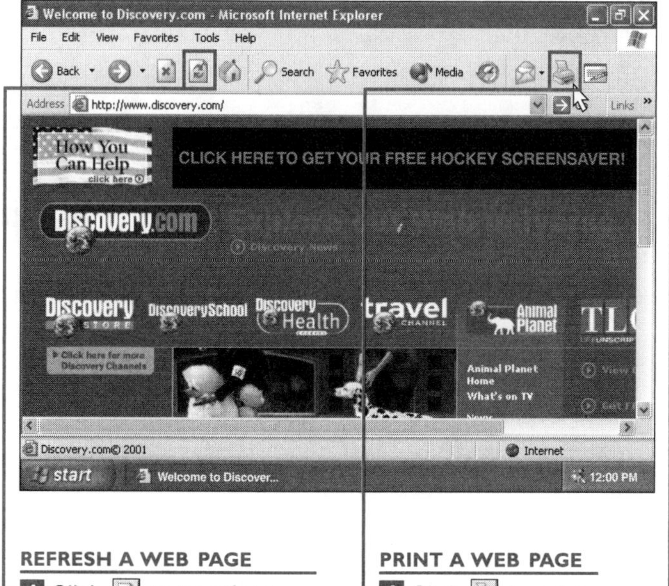

REFRESH A WEB PAGE

1 Click to transfer a fresh copy of the displayed Web page to your computer.

PRINT A WEB PAGE

1 Click to print the entire Web page.

DISPLAY YOUR HOME PAGE

1 Click to display your home page.

■ Your home page appears.

Note: Your home page may be different than the home page shown above. To change your home page, see page 439.

SEARCH THE WEB

You can use Internet Explorer's Search Companion to find Web pages that discuss topics of interest to you. You can enter a question that describes the information you want to find to display a list of matching Web pages.

By default, the Search Companion uses the MSN search tool to search for Web pages. Search tools often use software programs, called robots, to search the Web and catalog new Web pages. Many search tools also have people who review cataloged Web pages and place them in appropriate categories. When you search for Web pages about a specific topic, the MSN search tool searches its catalog for matching or related pages.

There are many other search tools available on the Web that you can use to search for Web pages. Some popular search tools include Google (www.google.com) and Yahoo! (www.yahoo.com). These search tools may allow you to perform more advanced searches.

Searching for information on the Web will give you a good starting point but will not find every page on the Web that discusses the topic. It is almost impossible to catalog every Web page because Web pages change frequently and new pages are created every day.

SEARCH THE WEB

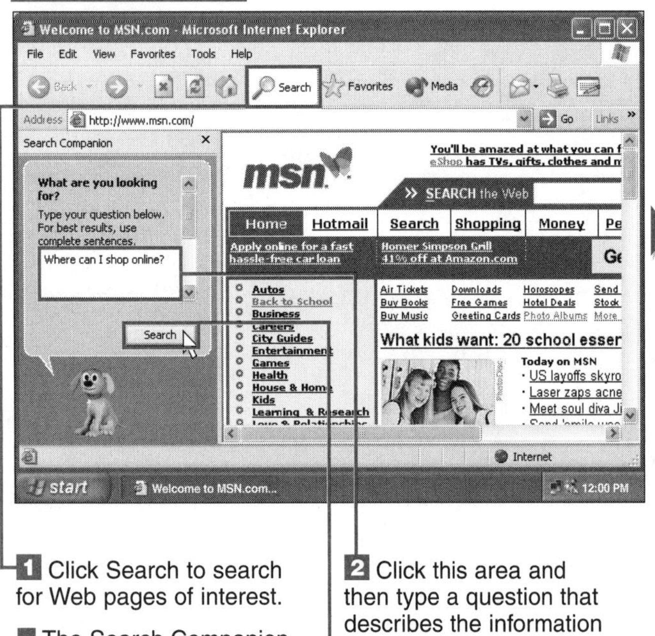

1 Click Search to search for Web pages of interest.

■ The Search Companion area appears.

2 Click this area and then type a question that describes the information you want to search for.

3 Click Search or press the Enter key to start the search.

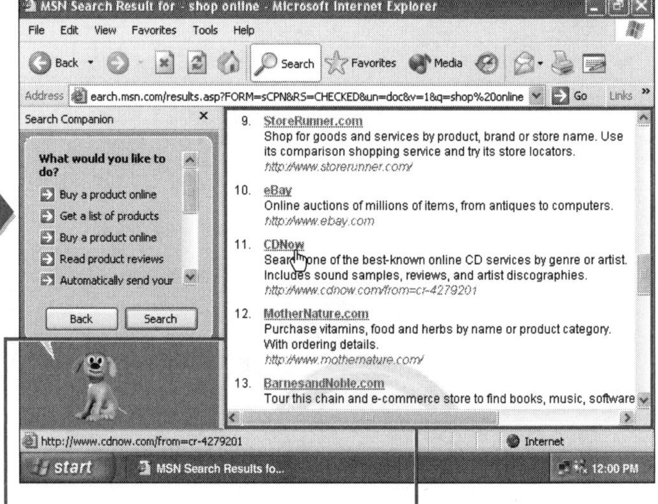

■ A list of matching Web pages and their descriptions appear in this area. You can use the scroll bar to view the entire list.

4 To display a Web page, click the Web page of interest.

Is there a quicker way to search for Web pages?

✔ In the Address bar of the Microsoft Internet Explorer window, type a question mark (?) followed by a space and the word or phrase you want to search for. Then press the Enter key. Internet Explorer will display a list of Web pages that match the word or phrase you specified.

My search results did not provide the information I expected. What can I do?

✔ You can have the Search Companion use other search engines to find the information you want by clicking Automatically send your search to other search engines. You can also modify your current search by clicking in the box below Change current search and modifying the question you entered.

How do I start a new search?

✔ You can begin a new search at any time by clicking Start a new search in the Search Companion.

Can I customize the Search Companion?

✔ Yes. Before beginning a search, you can click Change preferences in the Search Companion to display a list of options you can select to customize the Search Companion. For example, you can choose to turn off the animated screen character, change the Internet search behavior to use a different default search engine or hide the balloon tips.

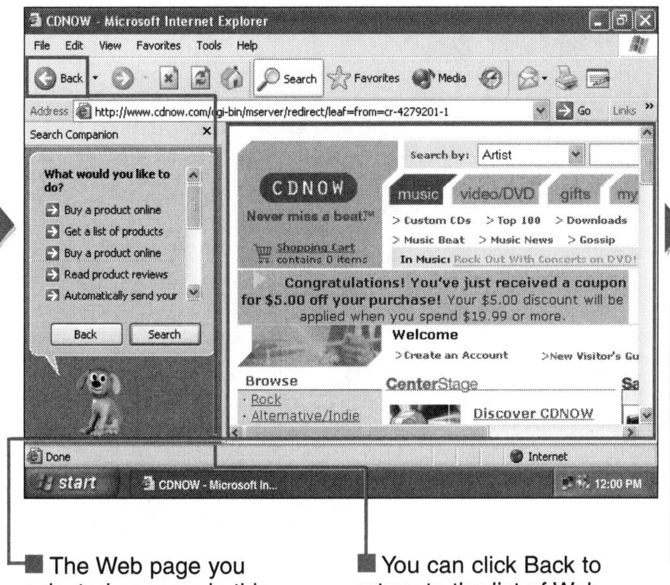

■ The Web page you selected appears in this area.

■ You can click Back to return to the list of Web pages and select another Web page.

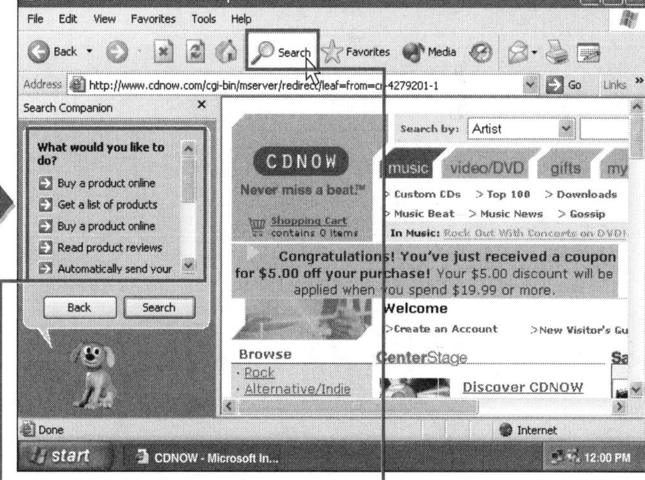

■ This area may display a list of options you can select to narrow your search. To select an option, click the option. The Search Companion will ask you questions to help you find Web pages of interest.

5 When you finish searching for Web pages, click Search to hide the Search Companion area.

FIND RELATED WEB PAGES

Internet Explorer's Related Links feature can help you quickly locate other Web pages that contain information related to the Web page you are currently viewing. Displaying related Web pages can help you quickly gather information about a topic of interest without having to return to a search tool. For example, while viewing the Web page for a university, you can display related links to find links to relevant Web pages such as Web pages for other universities and academic publications.

When you display related links, the Search Companion area appears, displaying a list of Web pages that are related to the current Web page. You can easily view a Web page displayed in the list of related links.

The Search Companion area may also display information about the current Web page, such as a traffic rating for the Web page and contact information for the Web site publisher. The traffic rating indicates the popularity of the Web page.

The related links information is provided by Alexa, which is an information service on the Web. For more information about Alexa, you can visit the www.alexa.com Web site.

FIND RELATED WEB PAGES

1 To find Web pages that are related to the Web page you are currently viewing, click Tools.

2 Click Show Related Links.

■ The Search Companion area appears, displaying a list of related Web pages and information about the Web page.

3 To view a related Web page, click the Web page.

■ The Web page you select will appear in this area.

4 When you are finished viewing the list of related Web pages, click ☒ to hide the Search Companion area.

CHANGE YOUR HOME PAGE

You can specify which Web page you want to appear each time you start Internet Explorer. This Web page is called your home page. While browsing the Web, you can use the Home button ( ) to display your home page at any time.

You can set any page on the Web as your home page. The page you choose should be a page you want to visit frequently. You may want to use a Web page that provides a good starting point for exploring the Web, such as www.yahoo.com, or a page that contains news and information related to your work or personal interests.

If you have a Web page creation program, such as FrontPage, you can design and create your own home page. You can find Web page creation programs on the Web or at computer stores.

You can reset the home page to the original home page that was set when you first started Internet Explorer at any time. You can also set a blank page as your home page. Displaying a blank page when you start Internet Explorer lets you start browsing the Web without having to wait for a home page to appear on your screen.

CHANGE YOUR HOME PAGE

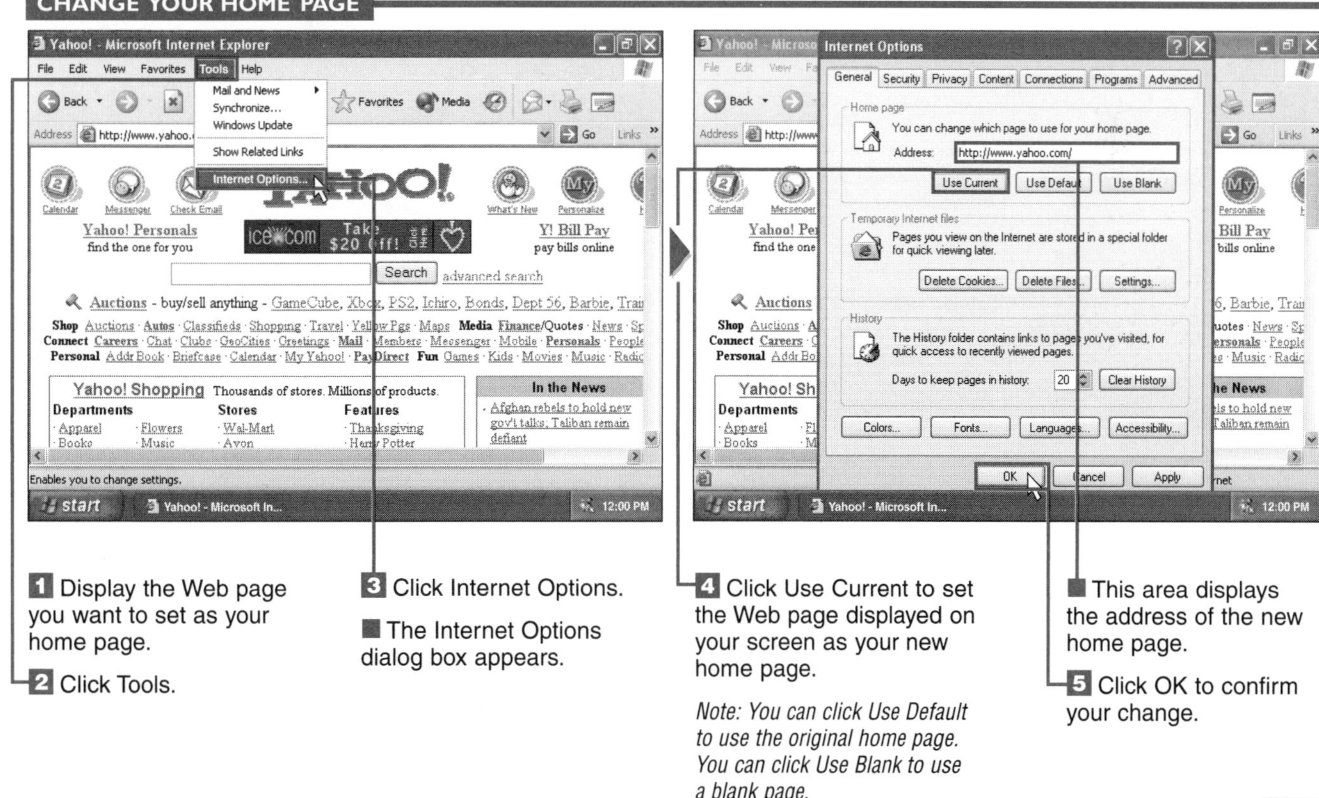

1 Display the Web page you want to set as your home page.

2 Click Tools.

3 Click Internet Options.

■ The Internet Options dialog box appears.

4 Click Use Current to set the Web page displayed on your screen as your new home page.

Note: You can click Use Default to use the original home page. You can click Use Blank to use a blank page.

■ This area displays the address of the new home page.

5 Click OK to confirm your change.

USING THE MEDIA BAR

You can use the Media bar to locate and play media files, such as music and video files, in Internet Explorer.

The Media bar displays links to media files from the WindowsMedia.com Web page. You can select a link to play a media file of interest. Each time you select a link for a new type of media file, Windows will ask if you want to play the file in Internet Explorer. Files you choose to play in Internet Explorer will play in the Media bar. Windows can remember your preferences and automatically play other media files of the same type in the Media bar.

You can use the controls in the Media bar to pause, stop and play a media file. You can also use controls to turn off the sound or adjust the volume of a media file.

If there is a Web page associated with a media file you are playing, Internet Explorer may automatically display the page on your screen. For example, when you select a link that displays a movie preview, the movie's Web page may appear.

Although most links you select in the Media bar play media files, some links connect to Web pages where you can download information, such as music files.

USING THE MEDIA BAR

1 Click Media to display the Media bar.

■ The Media bar appears, displaying links to media files from the WindowsMedia.com Web page.

2 Click the link for the media file you want to play.

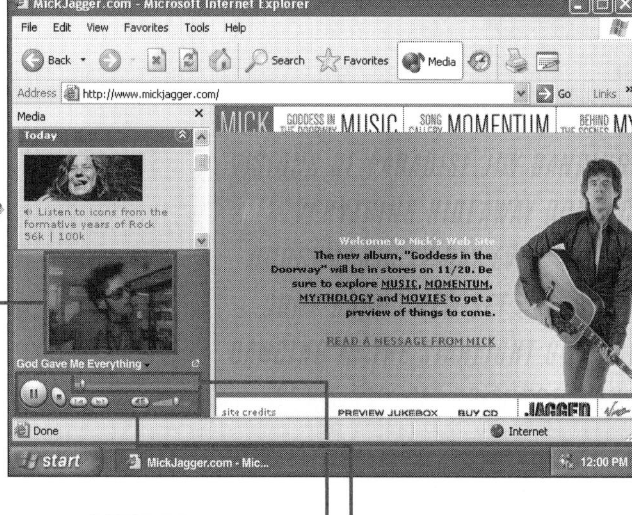

■ The media file plays.

Note: A dialog box may appear, asking how you want to play the media file. Click Yes to play the media file in the Media bar.

■ This area displays controls for playing media files.

■ This slider (▯) indicates the progress of the media file that is currently playing.

How do I browse through information in the Media bar?

✔ The media links in the Media bar are organized into categories, including Today, Music, Movies, Radio and MSN Music. The Media bar displays the links for only one category at a time. To view the links in another category, you can click the name of the category.

How can I stop Windows from playing media files in the Media bar?

✔ In the Media bar, click Media Options and then select Settings. Click Reset preferred types and then click Yes in the dialog box that appears. The next time you click the link for a media file, Windows will ask if you want to play the file in Internet Explorer. Click No to always play media files of this type in Windows Media Player.

Can I display the viewing area of the Media bar in a separate window?

✔ Yes. This is useful when you want to increase the size of the viewing area. Click ⧉ to display the viewing area in its own window. To once again display the viewing area in the Media bar, you can click ⧉.

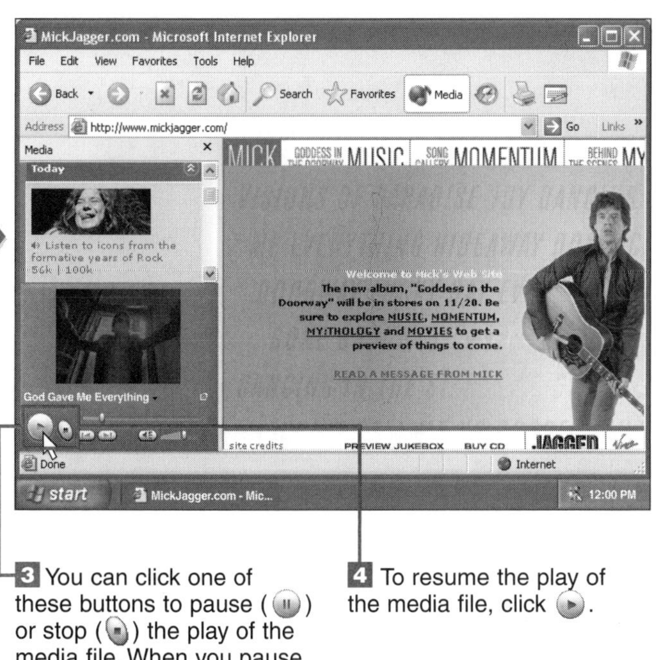

3 You can click one of these buttons to pause (⏸) or stop (■) the play of the media file. When you pause or stop the play of a media file, ⏸ changes to ▶.

4 To resume the play of the media file, click ▶.

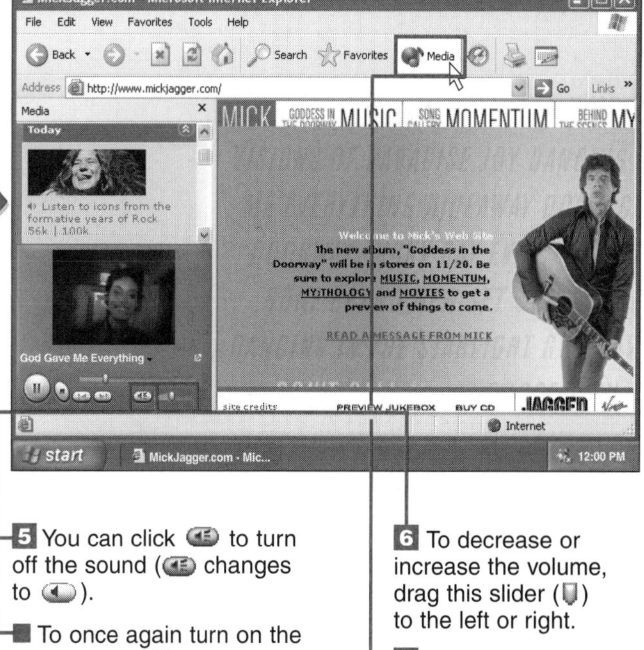

5 You can click 🔊 to turn off the sound (🔊 changes to 🔈).

■ To once again turn on the sound, click 🔈.

6 To decrease or increase the volume, drag this slider (▯) to the left or right.

7 When you finish playing media files, click Media to close the Media bar.

DISPLAY HISTORY OF VIEWED WEB PAGES

The History list keeps track of the Web pages you have recently viewed. You can select a Web page from the History list to return to the page. The History list keeps track of recently viewed Web pages even when you close Internet Explorer.

The list is organized into weeks and days so you can quickly find a Web page you viewed on a specific day. Each week and day contains an alphabetical listing of the Web sites you visited that week or day. When you select a Web site, a list of all the Web pages you visited at that site appears.

Your History list can grow quite large and may contain hundreds of Web pages. When the History list contains a large number of Web pages, Internet Explorer allows you to scroll through the list.

The History list also keeps track of any files you have recently worked with on your computer and the network.

DISPLAY HISTORY OF VIEWED WEB PAGES

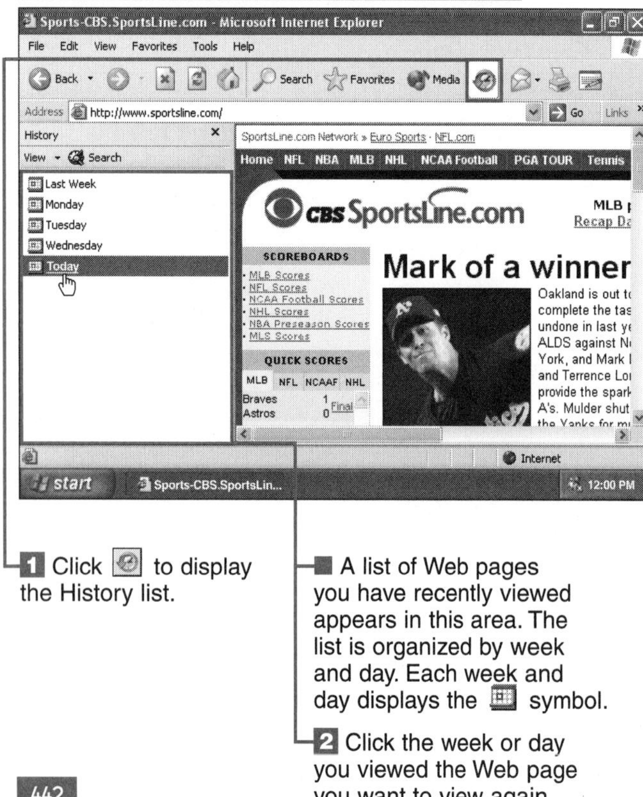

1 Click to display the History list.

■ A list of Web pages you have recently viewed appears in this area. The list is organized by week and day. Each week and day displays the symbol.

2 Click the week or day you viewed the Web page you want to view again.

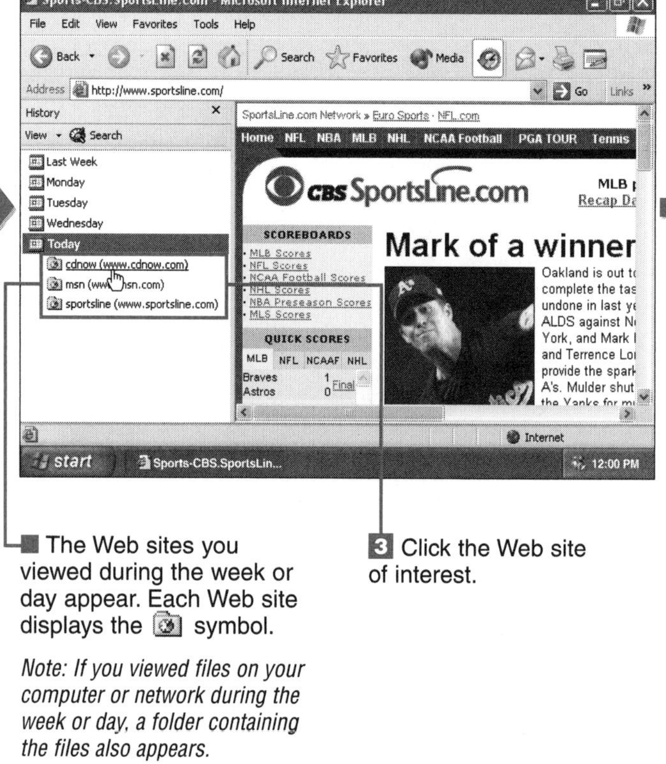

■ The Web sites you viewed during the week or day appear. Each Web site displays the symbol.

Note: If you viewed files on your computer or network during the week or day, a folder containing the files also appears.

3 Click the Web site of interest.

How long does the History list keep track of recently viewed Web pages and files?

✔ The History list keeps track of the Web pages and files you have viewed over the last 20 days. You can change the number of days by choosing the Tools menu and then selecting Internet Options. In the History area, double-click the box beside Days to keep pages in history and then type a new number.

How do I clear the History list?

✔ Select the Tools menu and then click Internet Options. In the History area, click the Clear History button. Clearing the History list frees up space on your computer.

How can I sort the items displayed in the History list?

✔ At the top of the History list, click the View button and then click the way you want to sort the items.

Can I search for a specific Web page in the History list?

✔ Yes. At the top of the History list, click the Search button. Type a word that describes the Web page you want to find and then click the Search Now button.

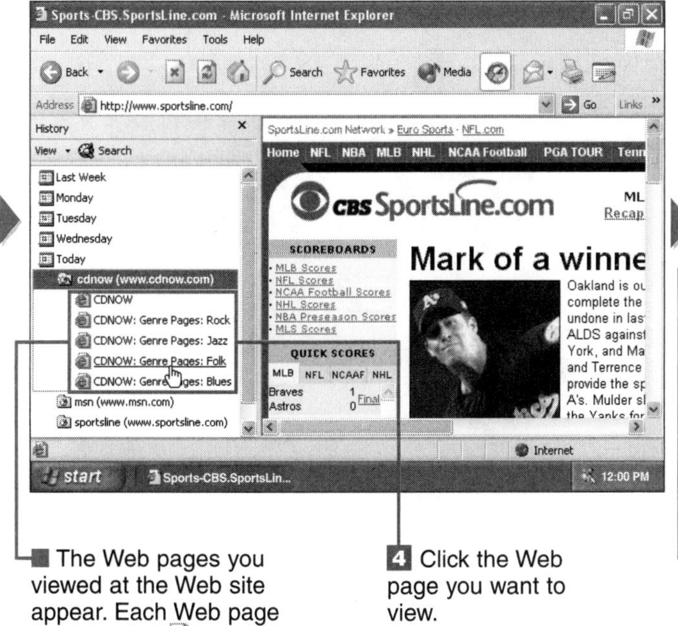

■ The Web pages you viewed at the Web site appear. Each Web page displays the symbol.

4 Click the Web page you want to view.

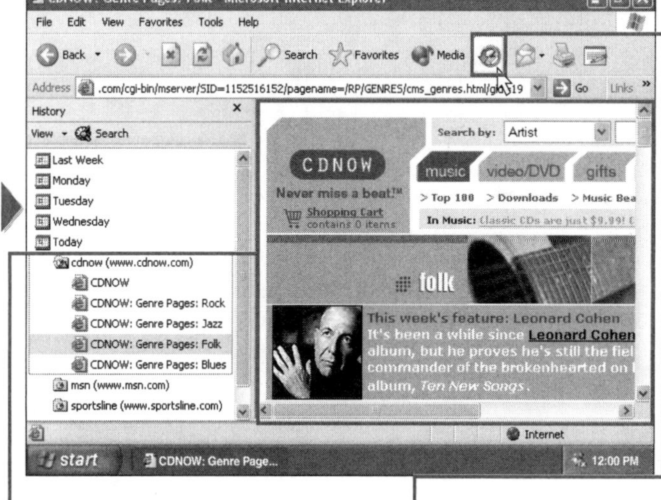

■ The Web page appears in this area.

■ You can repeat step 4 to view another Web page at the Web site.

5 When you finish displaying recently viewed Web pages, click to hide the History list.

ADD A WEB PAGE TO FAVORITES

The Favorites feature allows you to store the addresses of Web pages you frequently visit. When you know that you will be returning to a Web page, you can add the page to the Favorites list. You may return to the same Web page several times to investigate the page further or to check for new or updated information.

When you add a Web page to the Favorites list, you can give the page a new name to help you easily identify the page later.

You can quickly access a Web page in the Favorites list. Selecting Web pages from the Favorites list saves you from having to remember and constantly retype the same addresses over and over again. Using the Favorites list also eliminates the possibility that you will not be able to access a Web page because you have made a typing mistake in the address.

By default, the Favorites list includes the Links folder, which contains Web pages you may find useful and interesting. The list also includes the MSN.com and Radio Station Guide Web pages.

ADD A WEB PAGE TO FAVORITES

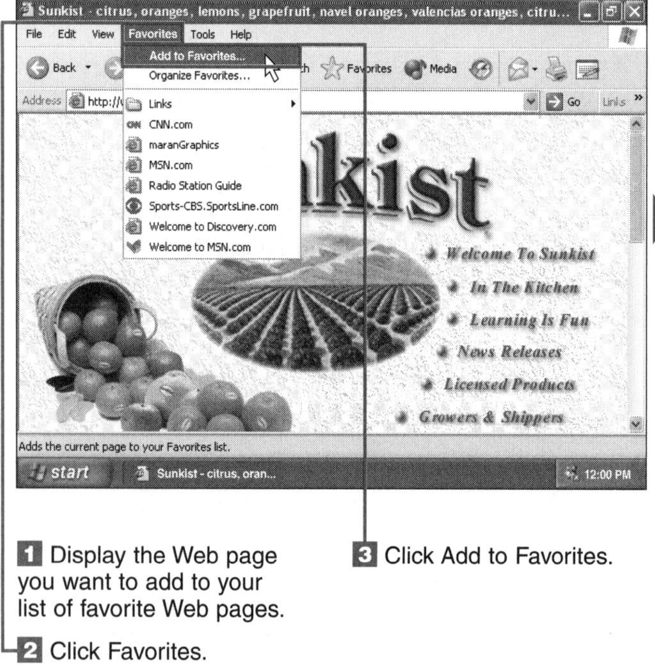

1 Display the Web page you want to add to your list of favorite Web pages.

2 Click Favorites.

3 Click Add to Favorites.

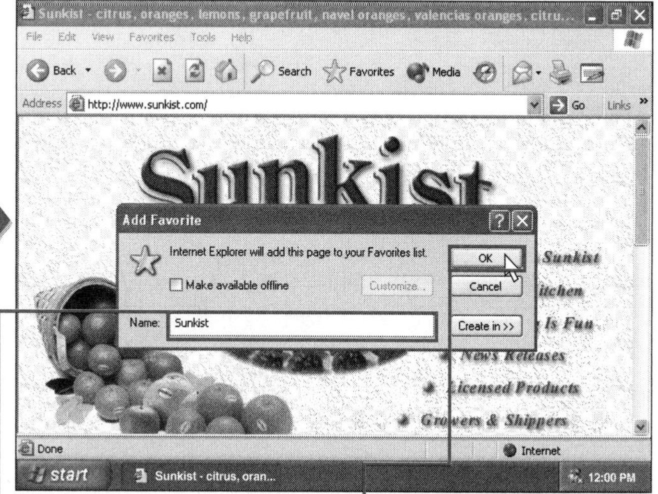

■ The Add Favorite dialog box appears.

4 This area displays the name of the Web page. To change the name, select the text and then type a new name.

5 Click OK to add the Web page to your list of favorites.

How can I make a favorite Web page available offline?

✔ Making a Web page available offline allows you to view the page even when you are not connected to the Internet. In the Add Favorite dialog box, click the Make available offline option (☐ changes to ☑) and then select the Customize button to display the Offline Favorite Wizard. You can use the wizard to specify the content you want to make available offline and to set up a schedule to automatically synchronize the Web page. Synchronizing ensures you have the most recent version of the Web page on your computer.

How do I add the currently displayed Web page to the Links folder?

✔ Drag the icon that appears beside the address of the page in the Address bar to the Links folder. Web pages you add to the Links folder are automatically added to the Links toolbar. To view the pages on the Links toolbar, click » on the Links toolbar.

Is there another way to access the Favorites list?

✔ You can select the Favorites menu to display the list of your favorite Web pages. To display the Web pages stored in a folder, click the folder.

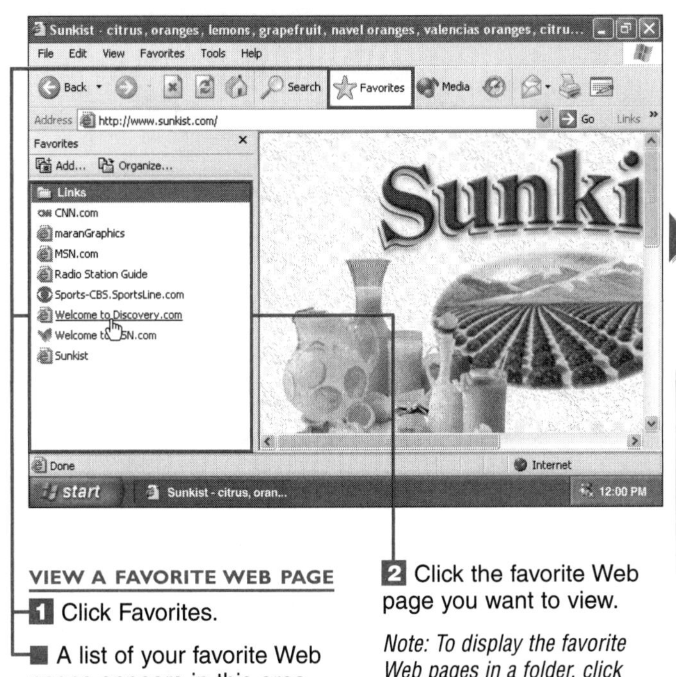

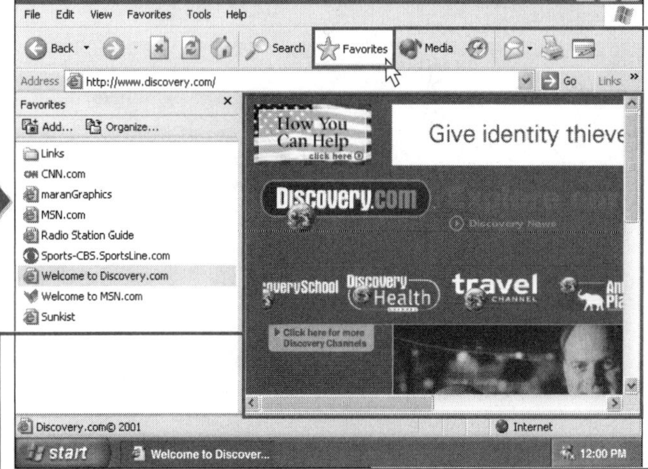

VIEW A FAVORITE WEB PAGE

1 Click Favorites.

■ A list of your favorite Web pages appears in this area.

2 Click the favorite Web page you want to view.

Note: To display the favorite Web pages in a folder, click the folder (📁).

■ The favorite Web page you selected appears in this area.

■ You can repeat step 2 to view another favorite Web page.

3 When you finish viewing your favorite Web pages, click Favorites to hide the Favorites list.

ORGANIZE FAVORITE WEB PAGES

You can organize the Web pages in the Favorites list to help make the list easier to use.

Over time, your list of favorite Web pages may become large and unmanageable. To keep your Favorites list organized, you should delete the Web pages that you no longer visit or that no longer exist.

You can create new folders to organize your favorite Web pages. For example, you can create a folder called Hobbies to keep all your favorite hobby-related Web pages together. Web pages organized into folders are easier to find. To further organize your favorite Web pages, you can create a new folder within an existing folder or move a new folder you create into another folder. A folder within another folder is called a subfolder.

You can move your favorite Web pages to a new location in the Favorites list. This is useful if you want to organize your favorite Web pages by topic. For example, you can move Web pages that cover topics such as cooking and cycling to the Hobbies folder you created.

ORGANIZE FAVORITE WEB PAGES

1 Click Favorites.

2 Click Organize Favorites.

■ The Organize Favorites dialog box appears.

DELETE A FAVORITE WEB PAGE

1 Click the favorite Web page you want to delete.

2 Click Delete.

■ A confirmation dialog box appears.

3 Click Yes to delete the favorite Web page.

How do I delete a folder from the Favorites list?

✔ In the Organize Favorites dialog box, click the folder you want to delete and then select the Delete button. Any Web pages stored in the folder will also be deleted.

I have trouble dragging favorite Web pages to folders. Is there another way to move a favorite Web page?

✔ In the Organize Favorites dialog box, select the favorite Web page you want to move and then click the Move to Folder button. Select the folder you want to move the Web page to and then click OK.

Can I change the name of a folder or favorite Web page?

✔ In the Organize Favorites dialog box, click the folder or favorite Web page you want to rename and then select the Rename button. Type a new name for the folder or Web page and press the Enter key.

Is there another way to organize the Favorites list?

✔ Click the Favorites button on the Standard Buttons toolbar to display the Favorites list. Then drag and drop Web pages to new locations in the list.

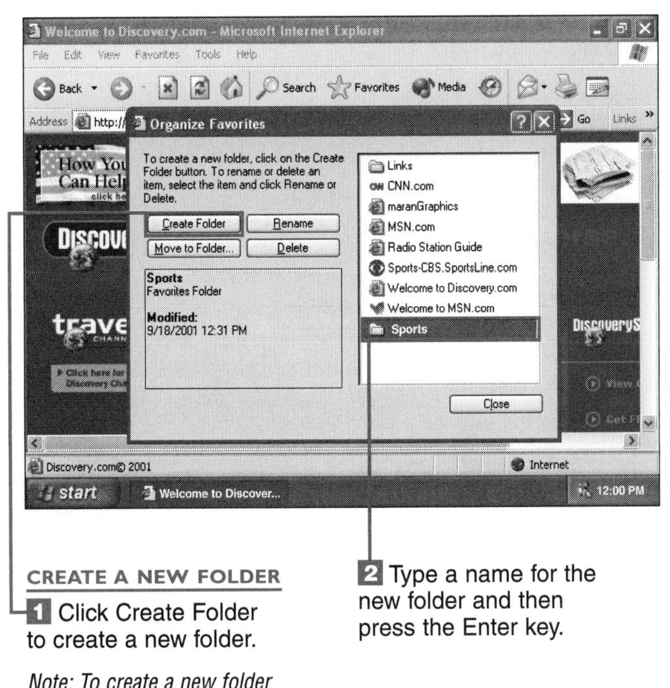

CREATE A NEW FOLDER

1 Click Create Folder to create a new folder.

Note: To create a new folder within another folder, click the folder (📁) before performing step 1.

2 Type a name for the new folder and then press the Enter key.

MOVE A FAVORITE WEB PAGE

1 Position the mouse over the favorite Web page you want to move.

Note: To display the favorite Web pages in a folder, click the folder (📁).

2 Drag the favorite Web page to a folder.

3 When you finish organizing your favorite Web pages, click Close.

SYNCHRONIZE WEB PAGES

You can use the Synchronize feature to update the Web pages on your computer that you have made available offline.

Making Web pages available offline allows you to view the Web pages when you are not connected to the Internet. You can choose to make a Web page available offline when you add the Web page to your list of Favorites. You can work with the Web pages you have made available offline the same way you work with Web pages in your Favorites list. For more information about the Favorites list, see pages 444 to 447.

Web pages you have made available offline may be frequently updated on the Web. When you are connected to the Internet, you can update, or synchronize, the Web pages to ensure that the Web pages on your computer will have the most current information when you view them offline.

By default, Windows will synchronize your current home page and every Web page you have made available offline. If you do not want to synchronize all these Web pages, you can choose the Web pages you want to synchronize.

When you synchronize Web pages, the Synchronizing window displays the progress of the synchronization and automatically disappears when the synchronization is complete.

SYNCHRONIZE WEB PAGES

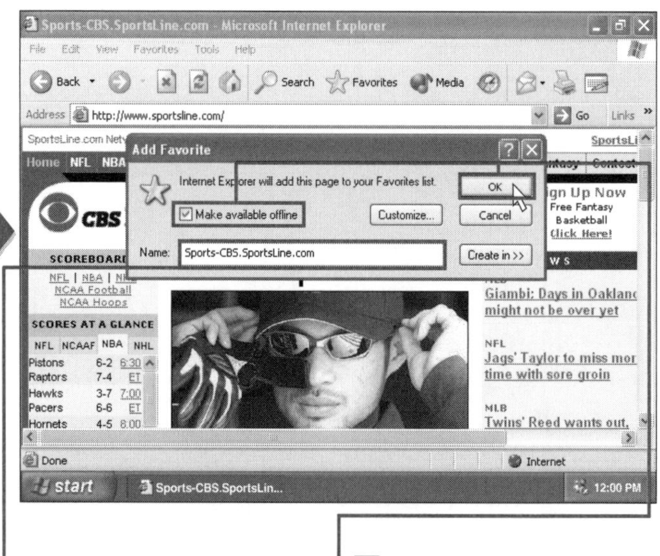

MAKE A WEB PAGE AVAILABLE OFFLINE

1 Display the Web page you want to make available offline.

2 Click Favorites.

3 Click Add to Favorites.

■ The Add Favorite dialog box appears.

4 This area displays the name of the Web page. To change the name, select the text and then type a new name.

5 Click this option to make the Web page available offline (☐ changes to ☑).

6 Click OK to confirm your changes.

Can I have Windows automatically synchronize my Web pages when I log on and off my computer?

✔ In the Items to Synchronize dialog box, click the Setup button. Select the Logon/Logoff tab. In the Synchronize the following checked items area, click the box beside each Web page you want to synchronize (☐ changes to ☑). Click the When I log on to my computer and the When I log off my computer options (☐ changes to ☑).

Can I synchronize files on my computer?

✔ Yes. If you have made files on your network available offline, the files will appear in the Items to Synchronize dialog box. To make a file available offline, right-click the file and select Make Available Offline.

Why can't I make files available offline?

✔ You can make files available offline only in the Professional version of Windows XP. You must also turn off Fast User Switching and enable offline files. To turn off Fast User Switching, click start and select Control Panel. Click User Accounts, select Change the way users log on or off and then click the Use Fast User Switching option (☑ changes to ☐). To enable offline files, click start, select Control Panel, click Appearance and Themes and choose Folder Options. Click the Offline Files tab and select the Enable Offline Files option (☐ changes to ☑).

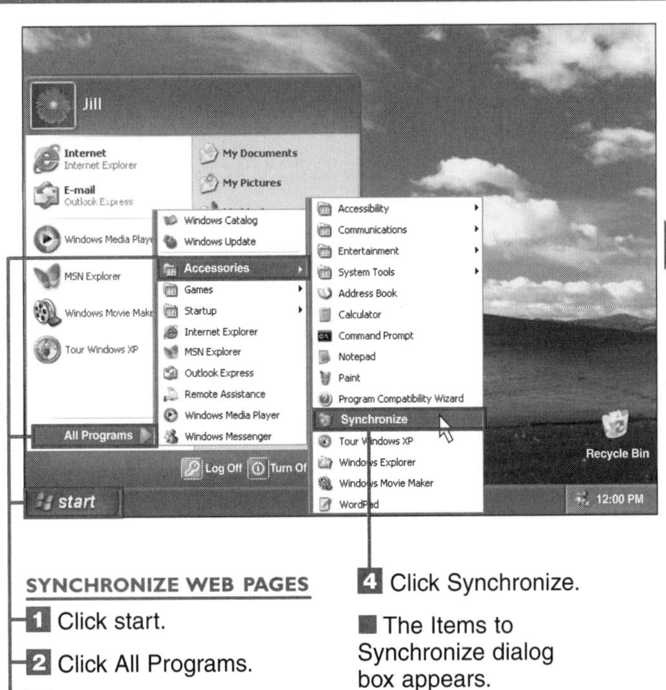

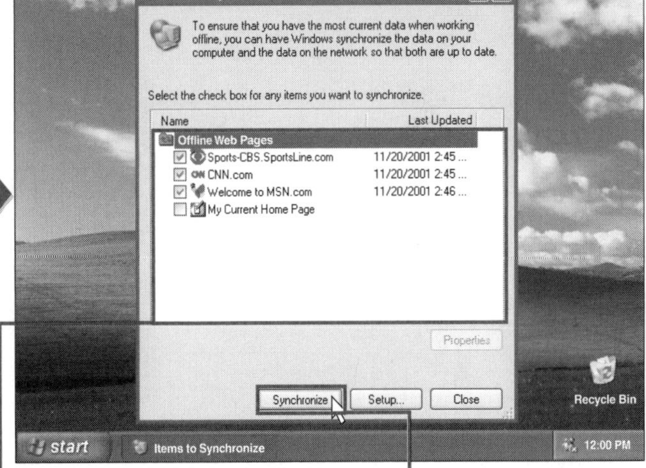

SYNCHRONIZE WEB PAGES

1 Click start.

2 Click All Programs.

3 Click Accessories.

4 Click Synchronize.

■ The Items to Synchronize dialog box appears.

■ This area displays the Web pages you have made available offline.

■ Windows will synchronize each Web page that displays a check mark (✔).

5 To add (☑) or remove (☐) a check mark beside a Web page, click the box beside the Web page.

6 Click Synchronize to update the Web pages you selected.

Note: If you are not currently connected to the Internet, a dialog box appears, allowing you to connect.

DELETE COOKIES OR TEMPORARY INTERNET FILES

You can delete cookies or temporary Internet files from your computer to free up space on your hard drive.

A cookie is a small file that a Web site uses to store information on your computer when you visit the site. For example, if you need to enter a user name to access a Web site, the Web site may store your user name in a cookie on your computer so you do not have to enter the name each time you visit the site.

Temporary Internet files are Web pages Internet Explorer stores on your hard drive while you are browsing the Web. Before transferring a Web page to your computer, Internet Explorer checks whether the page is stored on your computer. If the Web page is stored on your computer, Internet Explorer displays the stored page rather than transferring the page from the Internet again.

When you delete temporary Internet files, you can also choose to delete Web pages stored on your computer for offline viewing. For information about viewing Web pages offline, see page 448.

You can specify how often you want Internet Explorer to check for new versions of Web pages stored on your computer. You can also change the amount of disk space allotted to store temporary Internet files.

DELETE COOKIES OR TEMPORARY INTERNET FILES

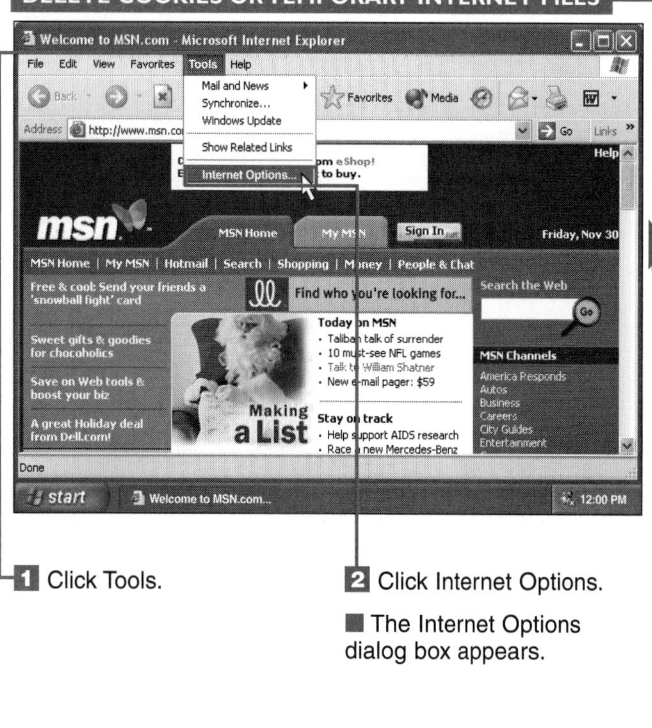

1 Click Tools.

2 Click Internet Options.

■ The Internet Options dialog box appears.

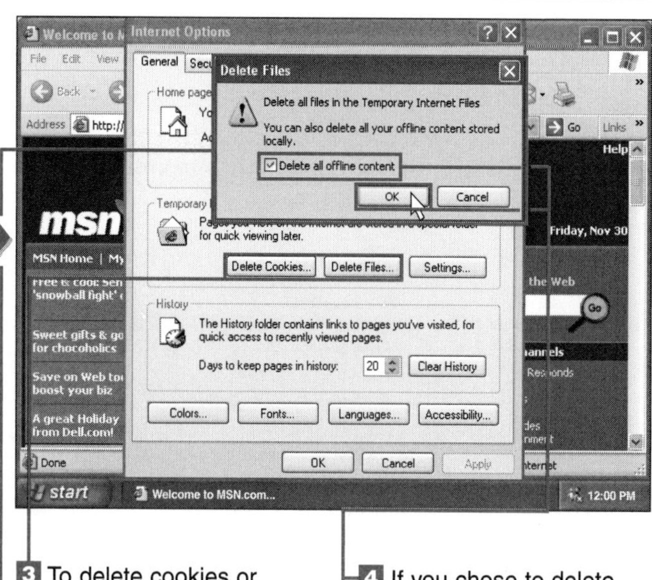

3 To delete cookies or temporary Internet files from your computer, click the appropriate button.

■ A confirmation dialog box appears.

4 If you chose to delete temporary Internet files in step 3, you can click this option to also delete all the Web pages stored on your computer for offline viewing (☐ changes to ☑).

5 Click OK to delete the cookies or files.

Can I view the cookies and temporary Internet files on my computer?

✔ Yes. In the Settings dialog box, click the View Files button to display the contents of the Temporary Internet Files folder, which contains all the cookies and temporary Internet files on your computer. The folder also displays information that can help you identify a file, such as the Internet address of the Web page that created the file.

Can I specify a new location for the Temporary Internet Files folder?

✔ In the Settings dialog box, click the Move Folder button and then select a new location for the folder. You must log off Windows and then log on again before the new location can be used.

How do I delete a single cookie or temporary Internet file?

✔ In the Settings dialog box, click the View Files button. In the list that appears, click the file you want to delete and then press the Delete key.

How do I stop Web sites from storing cookies on my computer?

✔ In the Internet Options dialog box, click the Privacy tab. In the Settings area, drag the slider (▭) to the topmost position on the bar. You may not be able to access some Web sites if you do not allow the Web sites to store cookies on your computer.

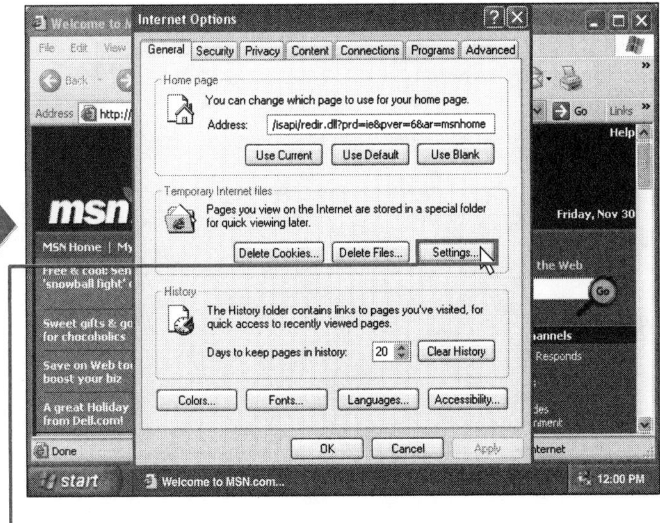

6 To change the settings for the temporary Internet files, click Settings.

■ The Settings dialog box appears.

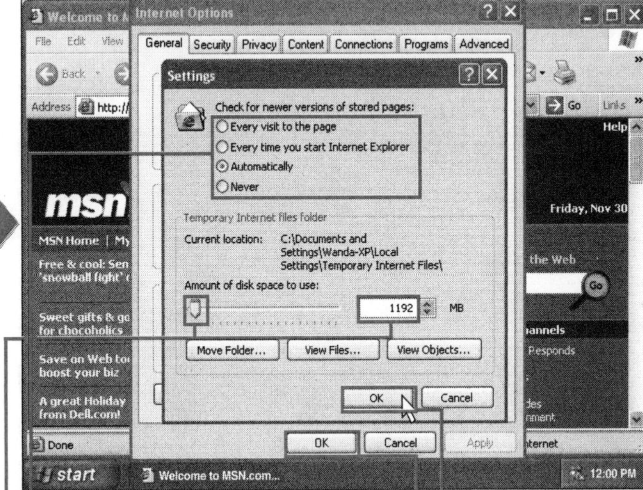

7 Click an option to specify how often Internet Explorer should check for new versions of stored Web pages (○ changes to ◉).

■ This area displays the amount of disk space allotted to temporary Internet files.

8 To change the amount of space, drag this slider (▽) to the left or right.

9 Click OK to confirm your changes.

10 Click OK to close the Internet Options dialog box.

SET UP AN E-MAIL ACCOUNT

The Internet Connection Wizard helps you set up an e-mail account on your computer. An e-mail account allows you to send and receive e-mail messages. If you have an e-mail account set up with your Internet Service Provider (ISP), the ISP will have provided you with the information you need to set up an e-mail account on your computer. If you are missing any information the wizard requires, contact your ISP.

When setting up an e-mail account, you can specify the name you want to appear in the From field of e-mail messages you send. You must also provide the wizard with your e-mail address.

You can specify the type of mail server your ISP uses to receive e-mail messages. The most common type of mail server is a POP3 server. You must also enter the addresses of the servers that receive and send your e-mail messages.

The wizard asks you to specify the account name and password that allow you to log on to your ISP's mail server. This information is usually the same as the account name and password you use to connect to the ISP. You can have Outlook Express remember your password so you do not have to type the password each time you log on to your e-mail account.

SET UP AN E-MAIL ACCOUNT

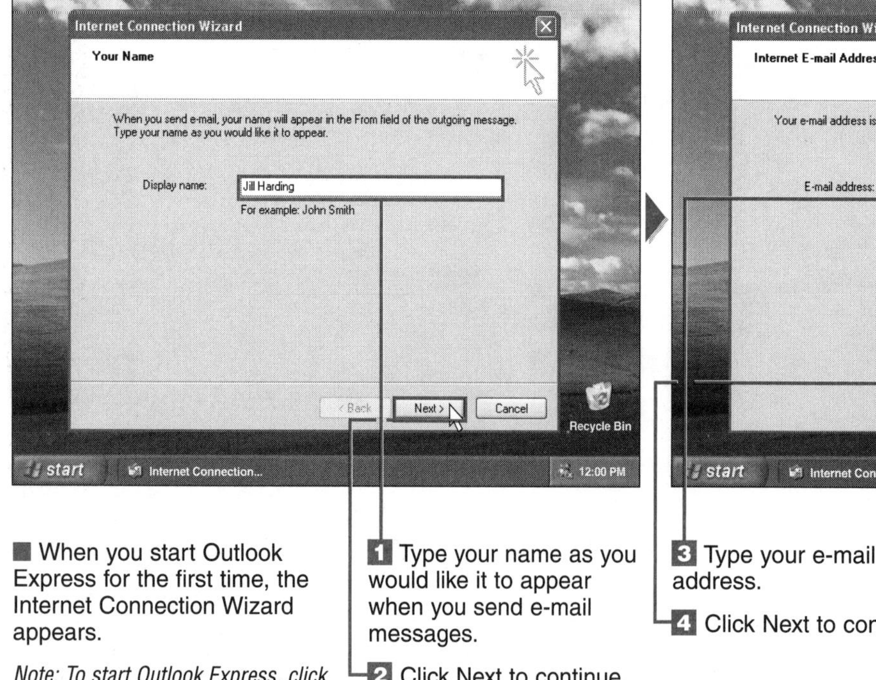

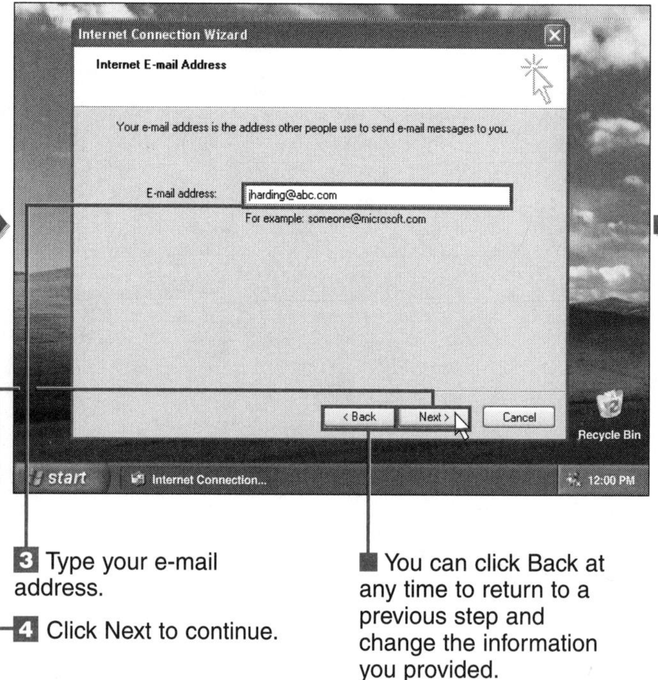

■ When you start Outlook Express for the first time, the Internet Connection Wizard appears.

Note: To start Outlook Express, click the start button, select All Programs and then click Outlook Express.

1 Type your name as you would like it to appear when you send e-mail messages.

2 Click Next to continue.

3 Type your e-mail address.

4 Click Next to continue.

■ You can click Back at any time to return to a previous step and change the information you provided.

The Internet Connection Wizard does not appear when I start Outlook Express. How do I display the wizard?

✔ In the Outlook Express window, select the Tools menu and click Accounts. Then click the Add button and select Mail.

Can I access my Hotmail e-mail account using Outlook Express?

✔ Yes. You can set up a new e-mail account in Outlook Express using your Hotmail account information. To set up a new e-mail account, display the Outlook Express window, select the Tools menu and click Accounts. Click the Add button and select Mail to start the Internet Connection Wizard. Follow the instructions in the wizard, entering the information for your Hotmail account. The mail folders for your Hotmail account will appear in the Outlook Express window.

How do I delete an e-mail account?

✔ In the Outlook Express window, select the Tools menu and click Accounts. Select the Mail tab and click the name of the e-mail account you want to delete. Then click the Remove button.

Can I later change the information for my e-mail account?

✔ Yes. In the Outlook Express window, select the Tools menu and then click Accounts. Choose the Mail tab, select the e-mail account you want to change and then click the Properties button. You can then change the information for the e-mail account.

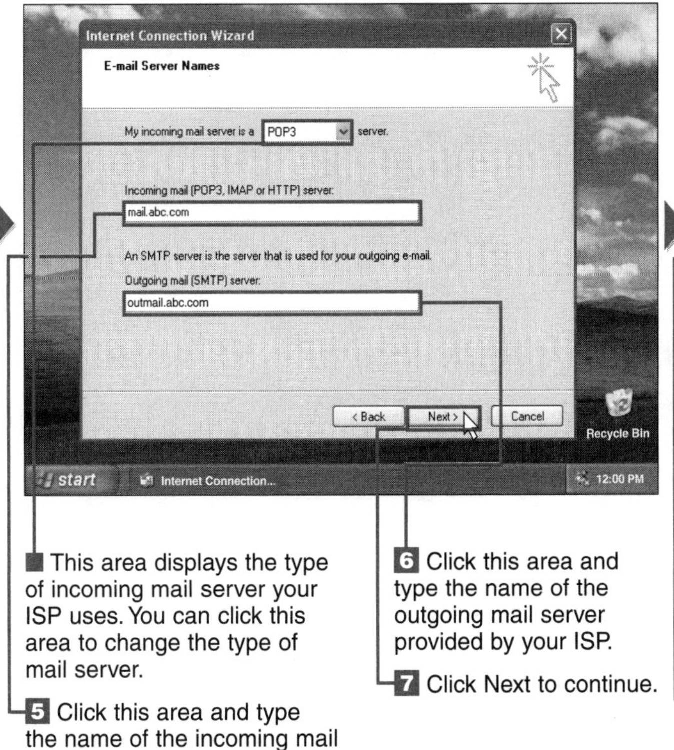

■ This area displays the type of incoming mail server your ISP uses. You can click this area to change the type of mail server.

5 Click this area and type the name of the incoming mail server provided by your ISP.

6 Click this area and type the name of the outgoing mail server provided by your ISP.

7 Click Next to continue.

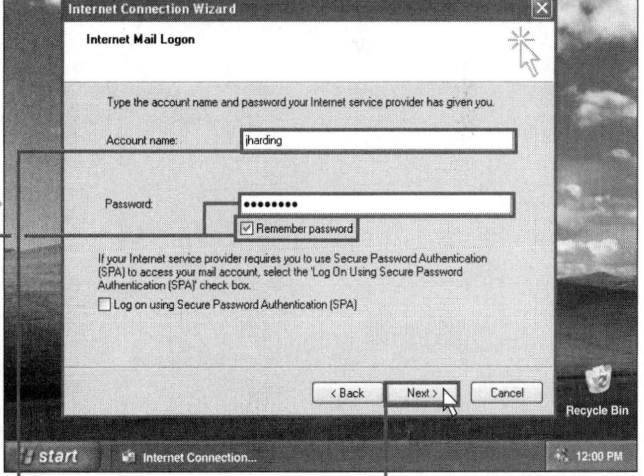

8 Type your account name provided by your ISP.

9 Click this area and type your password.

■ This option instructs Outlook Express to remember your password. You can click the option to turn the option on (☑) or off (☐).

10 Click Next to continue.

■ A message will appear, indicating that you have successfully set up your e-mail account. Click Finish to close the wizard.

START OUTLOOK EXPRESS AND READ MESSAGES

You can use Outlook Express to exchange e-mail messages with people around the world.

When you start Outlook Express, the window displays the folders that contain your messages, a list of the people in your address book and links that allow you to quickly perform common tasks.

Outlook Express has five folders to store your messages. The Inbox folder contains messages you have received. Messages waiting to be sent are held in the Outbox folder. Copies of messages you have sent are stored in the Sent Items folder. The Deleted Items folder contains any messages you have deleted. Messages you have not yet completed are stored in the Drafts folder.

If a folder contains unread messages, the name of the folder appears in bold type. A number in parentheses beside a folder name indicates how many unread messages the folder contains. Each unread message in a folder displays a closed envelope and appears in bold type. After you read a message, the message displays an open envelope and appears in regular type.

While you are connected to the Internet, Outlook Express automatically checks for new messages every 30 minutes, but you can check for new messages at any time.

START OUTLOOK EXPRESS

1 Click start.

2 Click All Programs.

3 Click Outlook Express.

■ The Outlook Express window appears.

Note: If you are not currently connected to the Internet, a dialog box will appear, allowing you to connect.

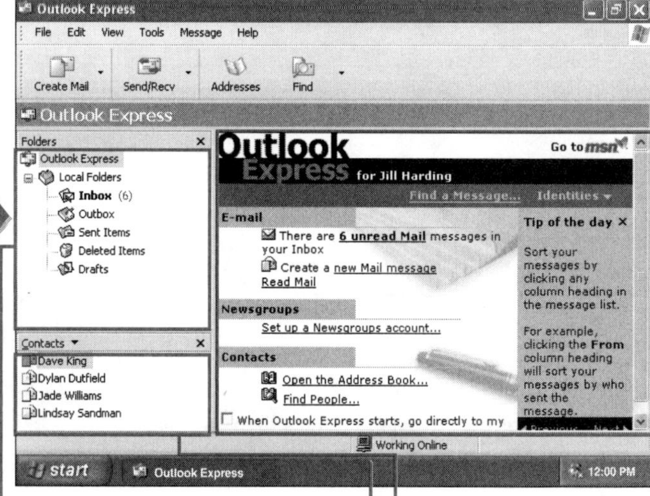

■ This area displays the folders that contain your messages.

Note: A number in parentheses beside a folder name indicates how many unread messages the folder contains. The number disappears when you have read all the messages in the folder.

■ This area displays the Contacts list, which lists each person in your address book.

■ This area displays links that allow you to perform common tasks in Outlook Express.

Is there a faster way to start Outlook Express?

✔ Yes. If Outlook Express is set as your default e-mail program, you can click start and then select E-mail. If Outlook Express is not set as your default e-mail program, you can change the default e-mail program. To change your default e-mail program, see page 264.

How can I view the contents of a message in a larger area?

✔ You can double-click a message to view its contents in a separate window.

Can I make a message appear as if I have not read it?

✔ Yes. This is useful if you want to remind yourself to review the message at a later time. Click the message you want to appear as unread. From the Edit menu, select Mark as Unread.

How can I make an important message stand out?

✔ You can flag an important message to make the message stand out. Click the message you want to flag. From the Message menu, select Flag Message. A flag icon ( ) appears beside the message.

READ MESSAGES

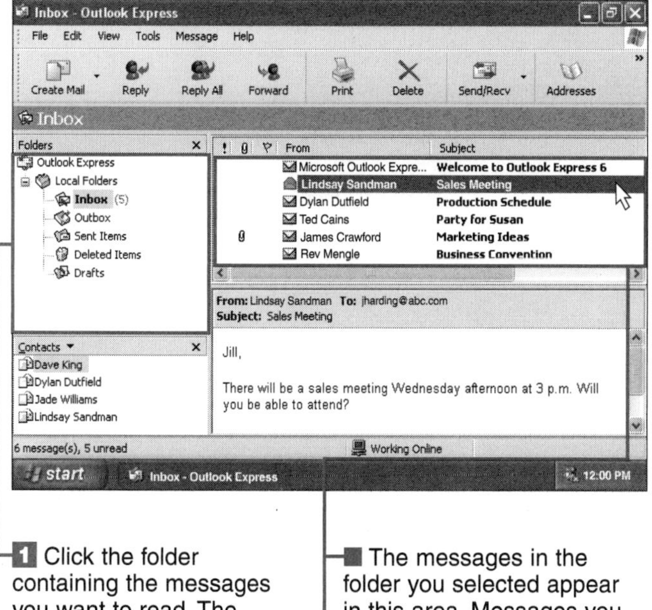

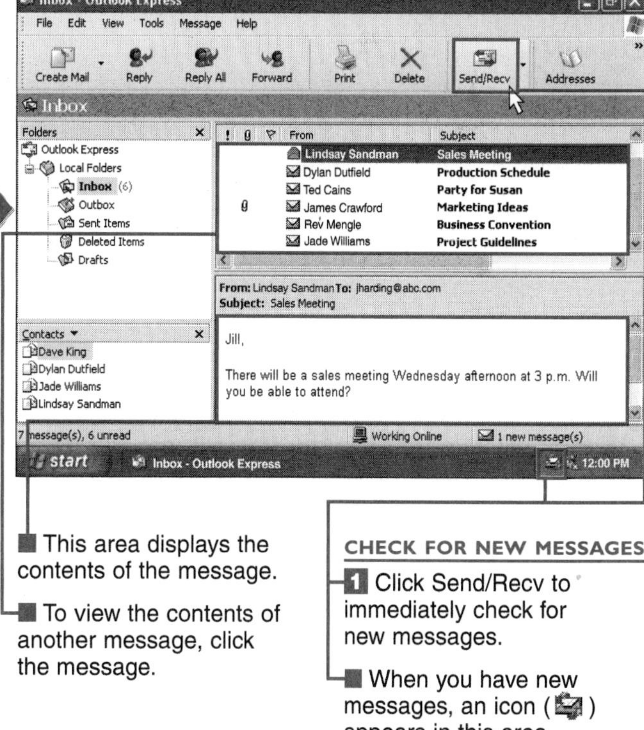

1 Click the folder containing the messages you want to read. The folder is highlighted.

■ The messages in the folder you selected appear in this area. Messages you have not read display a closed envelope ( ) and appear in bold.

2 Click a message you want to read.

■ This area displays the contents of the message.

■ To view the contents of another message, click the message.

CHECK FOR NEW MESSAGES

1 Click Send/Recv to immediately check for new messages.

■ When you have new messages, an icon ( ) appears in this area.

REPLY TO OR FORWARD A MESSAGE

You can reply to a message to answer a question, express an opinion or supply additional information.

You can send your reply to just the sender of the original message or to the sender and everyone who received the original message. When you reply to a message, a new window appears. The window displays the name of the recipients and the subject of the message you are replying to.

The reply includes the contents of the original message. This is called quoting. Including the contents of the original message helps the reader identify which message you are replying to. You can save the reader time by deleting all parts of the original message that do not directly relate to your reply.

You can also forward a message to another person. When you forward a message, you can add your own comments to the original message. Forwarding a message is useful if you know that another person would be interested in the contents of the message.

REPLY TO A MESSAGE

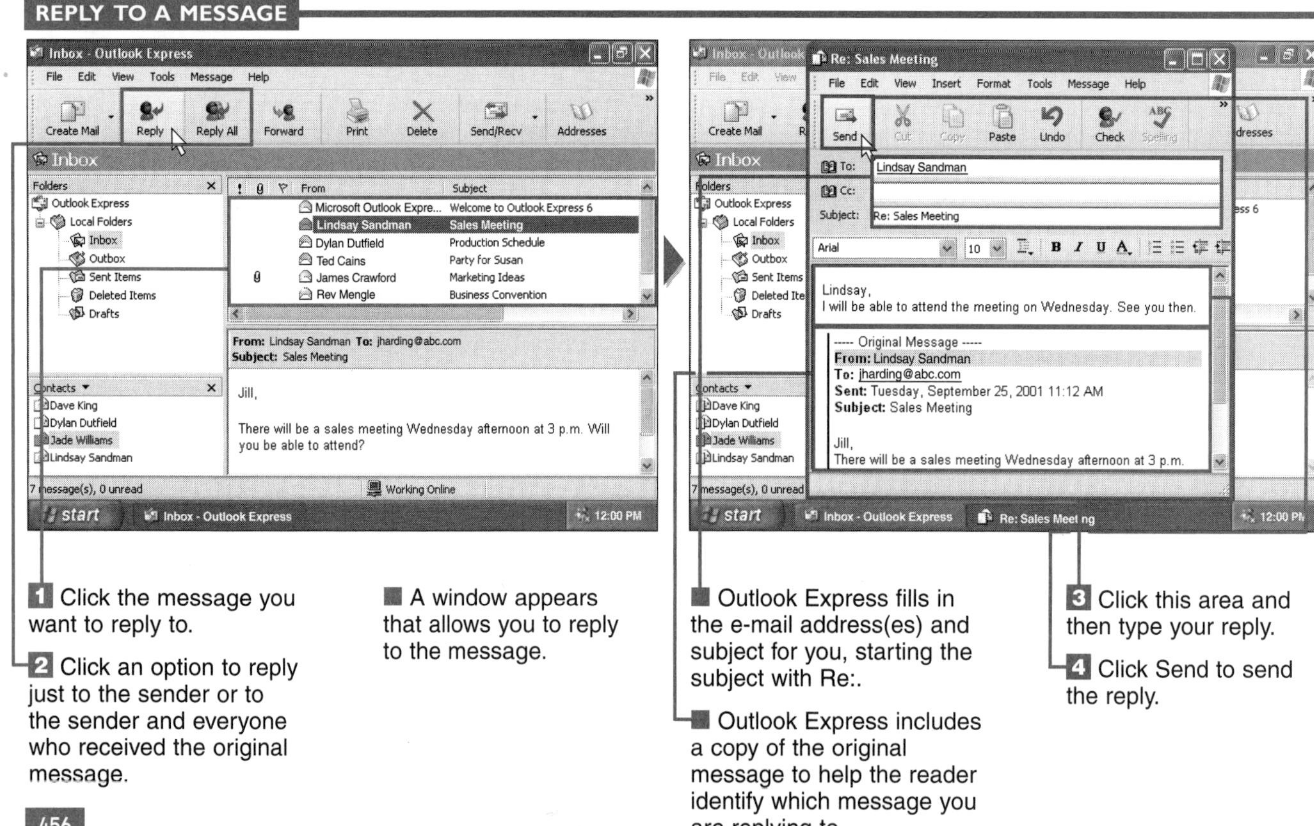

1 Click the message you want to reply to.

2 Click an option to reply just to the sender or to the sender and everyone who received the original message.

■ A window appears that allows you to reply to the message.

■ Outlook Express fills in the e-mail address(es) and subject for you, starting the subject with Re:.

■ Outlook Express includes a copy of the original message to help the reader identify which message you are replying to.

3 Click this area and then type your reply.

4 Click Send to send the reply.

How can I prevent Outlook Express from including the original message in my replies?

✔ If you do not want to include the original message in your replies, choose the Tools menu and then select Options. Select the Send tab and click the Include message in reply option (☑ changes to ☐).

Can I forward a message as an attached file?

✔ You can forward a message as an attached file instead of displaying the contents of the message. Click the message you want to forward as an attached file. From the Message menu, select Forward As Attachment.

How do I forward a message to more than one person?

✔ To forward a message to more than one person, perform steps 1 to 3 on this page. In step 3, separate each e-mail address with a semicolon (;) or a comma (,). You can also forward a message to more than one person by selecting names from the address book. To select names from the address book, see page 470.

FORWARD A MESSAGE

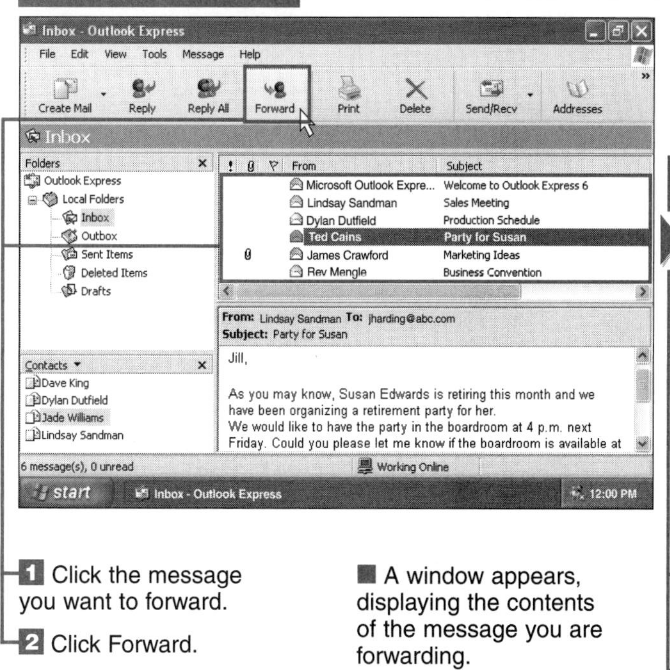

1 Click the message you want to forward.

2 Click Forward.

■ A window appears, displaying the contents of the message you are forwarding.

3 Type the e-mail address of the person you want to receive the message.

■ Outlook Express fills in the subject for you, starting the subject with Fw:.

4 Click this area and then type any comments about the message you are forwarding.

5 Click Send to forward the message.

SEND A MESSAGE

You can send an e-mail message to express an idea or request information. To practice sending a message, you can send a message to yourself.

You can address a message to more than one person. You can enter the address of each person you want to receive the message in the To: area or use the Cc: area to send a copy of the message to a person who would be interested in the message, but is not directly involved.

You should include a subject in each message you send. A descriptive subject will help the reader quickly identify the contents of your message.

When composing the content of a message, you should use both upper and lower case letters. A message written entirely in capital letters is difficult to read.

Outlook Express allows you to use the Contacts list to quickly address a message. The Contacts list displays the name of each person in your address book. For information about adding names to the address book, see page 466.

SEND A MESSAGE

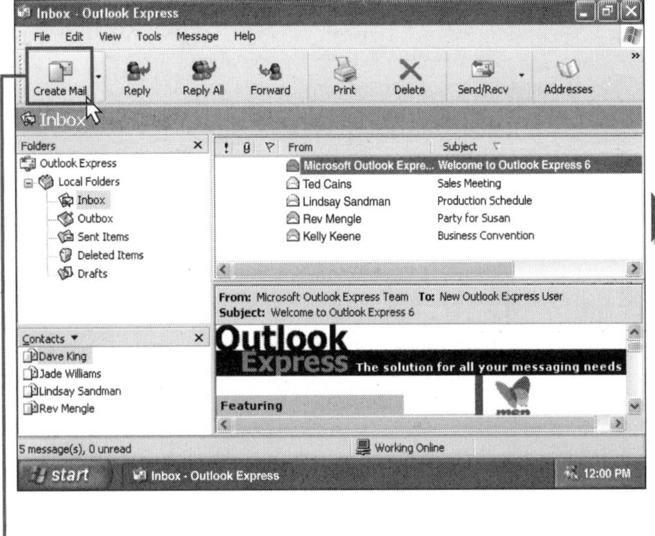

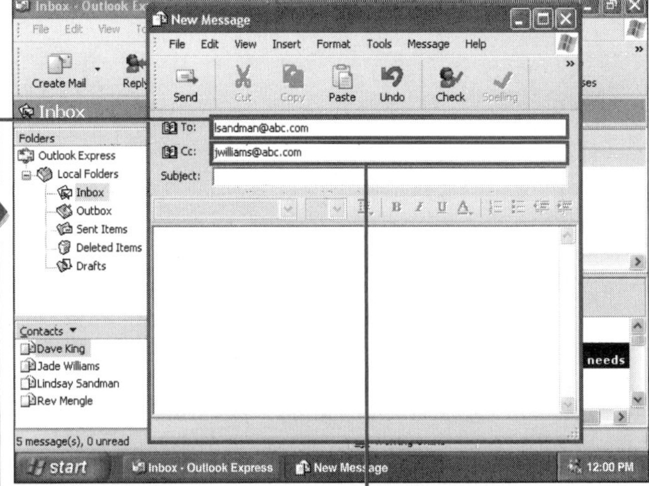

1 Click Create Mail to send a new message.

■ The New Message window appears.

2 Type the e-mail address of the person you want to receive the message.

Note: To send the message to more than one person, separate each e-mail address with a semicolon (;) or a comma (,).

3 To send a copy of the message to another person, click this area and then type the e-mail address.

Note: To select a name from the address book, see page 470.

Is there another way to send a copy of a message?

✔ In the New Message window, choose the View menu and then click All Headers. The Bcc: area appears in the window. You can type an e-mail address in this area to send someone a copy of the message without anyone else knowing that the person received the message.

Can I spell check my messages?

✔ Outlook Express uses the spell checker provided with Microsoft Office programs, such as Word and Excel. If you do not have one of these programs installed, you cannot spell check messages. To spell check a message, click the Spelling button in the New Message window.

How can I indicate the importance of a message?

✔ In the New Message window, display the Message menu and then select Set Priority. You can choose a high, normal or low priority for the message. The recipient sees an exclamation mark (!) beside high priority messages and an arrow (↓) beside low priority messages.

Can I prevent Outlook Express from storing copies of messages I send in the Sent Items folder?

✔ In the Outlook Express window, choose the Tools menu, click Options and then select the Send tab. Click the Save copy of sent messages in the 'Sent Items' folder option (☑ changes to ☐).

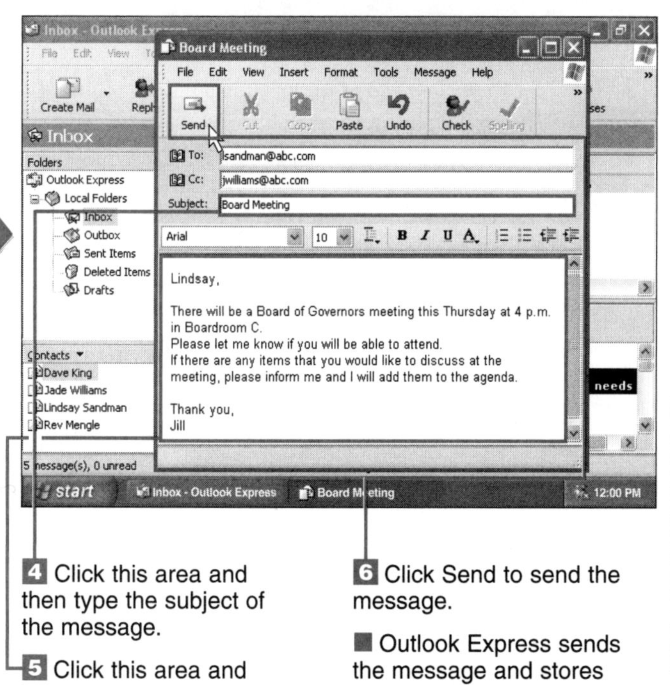

4 Click this area and then type the subject of the message.

5 Click this area and then type the message.

6 Click Send to send the message.

■ Outlook Express sends the message and stores a copy of the message in the Sent Items folder.

QUICKLY ADDRESS A MESSAGE

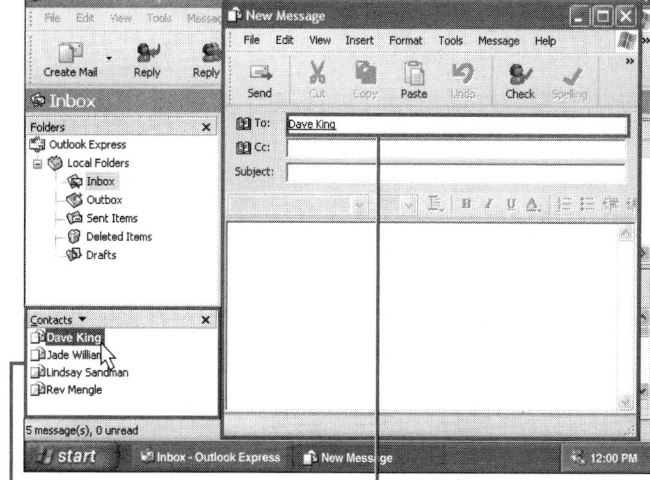

■ The Contacts list displays the name of each person in your address book.

1 To quickly send a message to a person in the Contacts list, double-click the name of the person.

■ The New Message window appears.

■ Outlook Express addresses the message for you.

2 To complete the message, perform steps 4 to 6.

SAVE A DRAFT OF A MESSAGE

You can save a draft of a message you are unable to finish composing. Saving a draft of a message allows you to complete the message at a later time. This is useful when you want to review the message again later before sending it.

When you save a draft of a message, Outlook Express stores the message in the Drafts folder until you are ready to complete and send the message.

When you want to complete a message you have saved as a draft, display the contents of the Drafts folder and double-click the message you want to complete. When you send the message, Outlook Express removes the message from the Drafts folder and places it in the Sent Items folder.

If you no longer want to complete and send a message you have saved as a draft, you can delete the message from the Drafts folder as you would delete any message. To delete a message, see page 462.

SAVE A DRAFT OF A MESSAGE

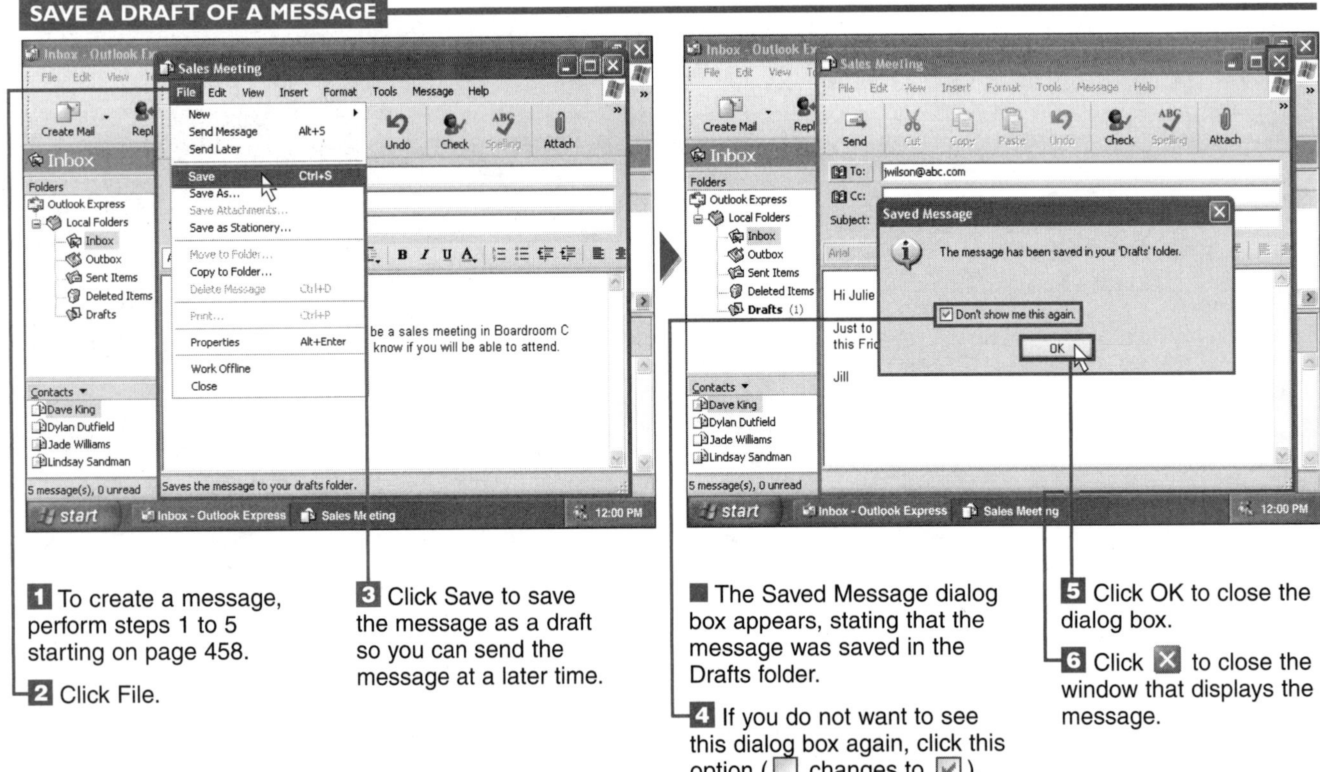

1 To create a message, perform steps 1 to 5 starting on page 458.

2 Click File.

3 Click Save to save the message as a draft so you can send the message at a later time.

■ The Saved Message dialog box appears, stating that the message was saved in the Drafts folder.

4 If you do not want to see this dialog box again, click this option (☐ changes to ☑).

5 Click OK to close the dialog box.

6 Click ☒ to close the window that displays the message.

CHECK FOR NEW MESSAGES AUTOMATICALLY

By default, Outlook Express automatically checks for new messages every 30 minutes. You can change how often Outlook Express checks for new messages. When Outlook Express checks for new messages, the new messages are transferred from the mail server at your Internet service provider to your computer.

If you have a constant connection to the Internet, you may want to have Outlook Express check for new messages as often as every few minutes. If you connect to the Internet using a modem, you may want to have Outlook Express check for new messages less frequently. Checking for messages very frequently can slow down other tasks you are performing, such as Web browsing.

If you are not connected to the Internet when Outlook Express will check for new messages, Outlook Express will not connect by default. You can specify if you want to have Outlook Express always connect to the Internet or connect only when you are not working offline.

You can click the Send/Recv button to check for new messages at any time. Clicking the Send/Recv button also immediately sends any messages stored in the Outbox folder.

CHECK FOR NEW MESSAGES AUTOMATICALLY

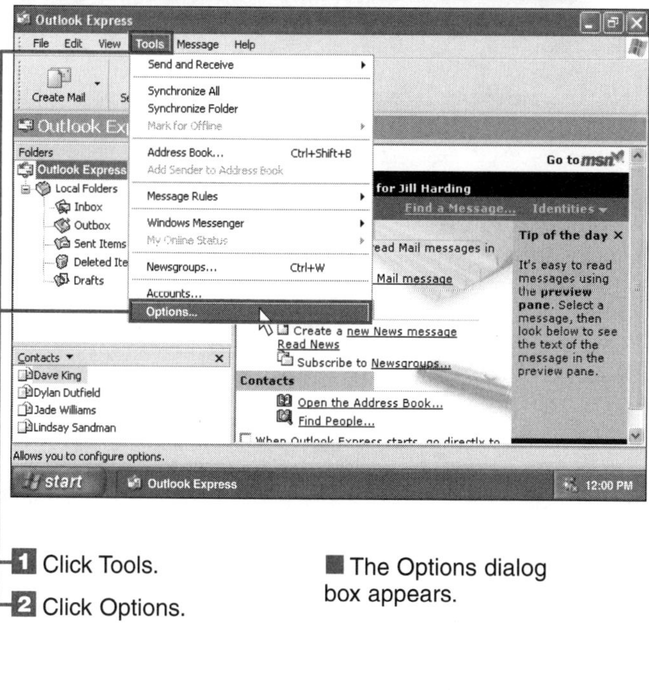

1 Click Tools.

2 Click Options.

■ The Options dialog box appears.

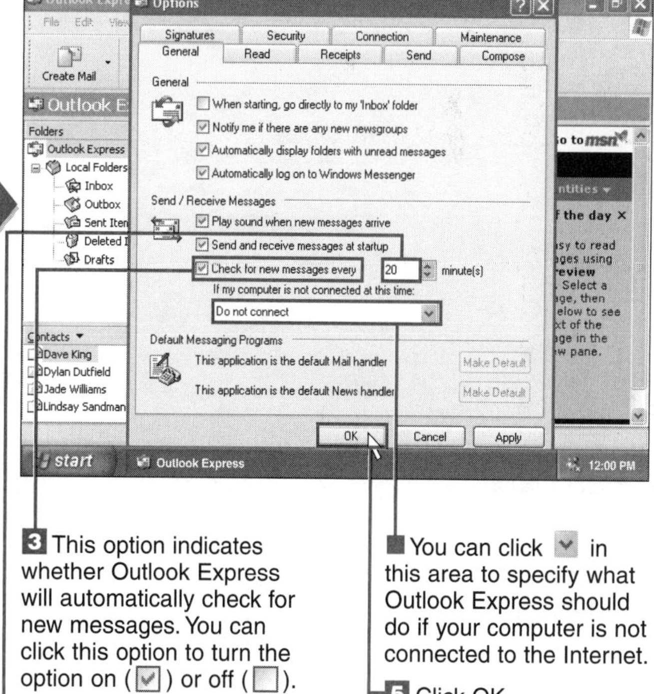

3 This option indicates whether Outlook Express will automatically check for new messages. You can click this option to turn the option on (☑) or off (☐).

4 Double-click this area and type how often you want Outlook Express to check for new messages.

■ You can click ▾ in this area to specify what Outlook Express should do if your computer is not connected to the Internet.

5 Click OK.

WORK WITH E-MAIL MESSAGES

Outlook Express allows you to organize and manage your e-mail messages.

You can sort messages in Outlook Express so they are easier to find. You can sort by the name of the person who sent or received the message, the subject of the message or the date the message was sent or received. Messages can be sorted in ascending or descending order. Messages are usually sorted by the date they were sent or received, in ascending order.

You can delete a message you no longer need. Deleting messages prevents your folders from becoming cluttered with messages. When you delete a message, Outlook Express places the deleted message in the Deleted Items folder.

You can produce a paper copy of a message. A printed message is useful when you need a reference copy of the message. When printing a message, you can specify which printer you want to use to print the message. Outlook Express prints the page number and total number of pages at the top of each page. The current date prints at the bottom of each page.

WORK WITH E-MAIL MESSAGES

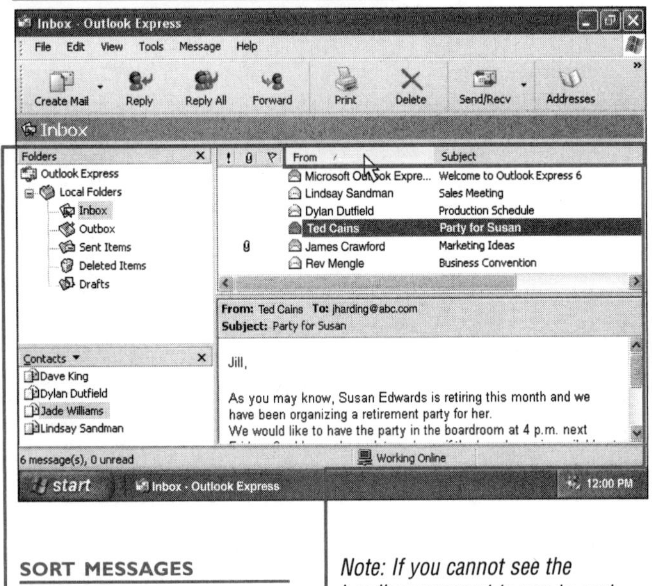

SORT MESSAGES

1 Click the heading for the column you want to use to sort the messages.

Note: If you cannot see the heading you want to use to sort the messages, use the horizontal scroll bar to display the heading.

■ You can click the heading again to sort the messages in the opposite order.

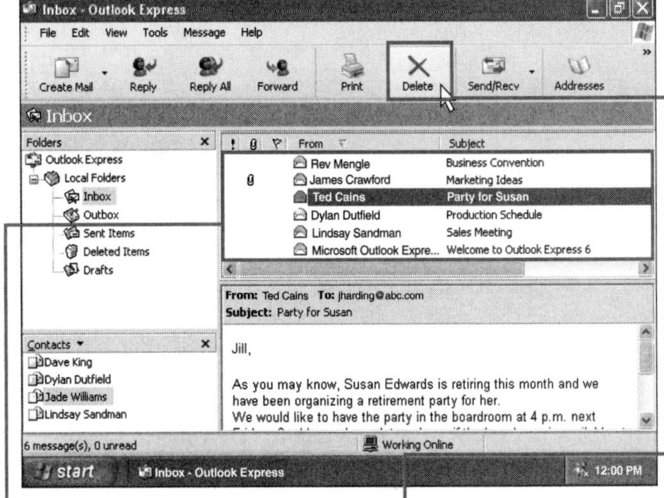

DELETE MESSAGES

1 Click the message you want to delete.

Note: To delete several messages at once, click the first message you want to delete and then hold down the Ctrl key as you click the other messages you want to delete.

2 Click Delete to delete the message.

■ Outlook Express removes the message from the current folder and places the message in the Deleted Items folder.

Can I work with a message in another program?

✔ You can save a message as a text file so you can work with the message in another program. Click the message you want to save. Choose the File menu and then select Save As. In the Save Message As dialog box, type a name for the file and then click ⌄ beside Save as type and choose Text Files (*.txt). Then click Save.

Can I permanently remove deleted messages from my computer?

✔ Yes. Right-click the Deleted Items folder and then select the Empty 'Deleted Items' Folder option.

Can Outlook Express automatically empty the Deleted Items folder?

✔ If you want the Deleted Items folder to automatically empty each time you close Outlook Express, choose the Tools menu and then click Options. Select the Maintenance tab and click the Empty messages from the 'Deleted Items' folder on exit option (☐ changes to ☑).

How do I change the width of a column?

✔ Position the mouse pointer over the right edge of the heading for the column you want to change. The mouse pointer changes to a double-headed arrow (✛). Drag the edge of the column until it displays the size you want.

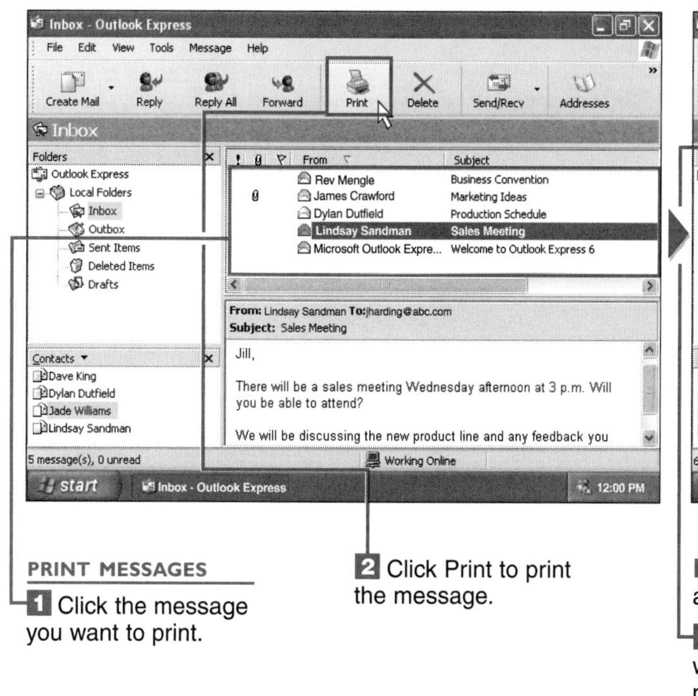

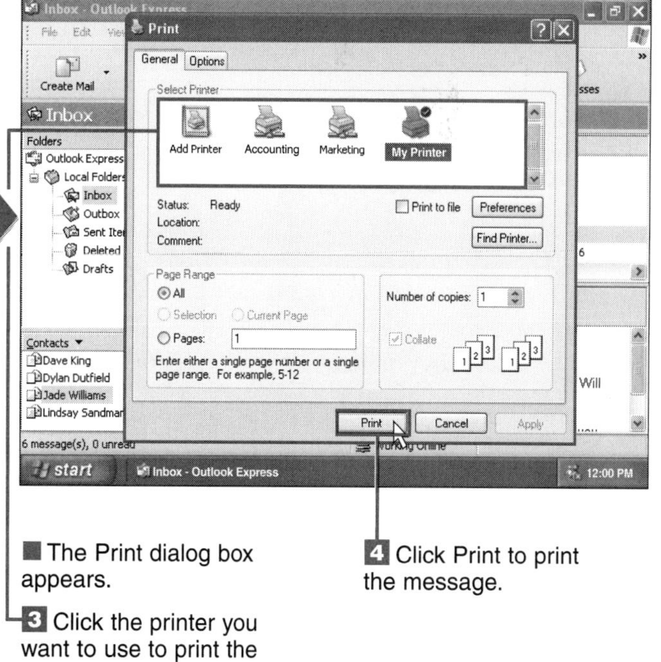

PRINT MESSAGES

1 Click the message you want to print.

2 Click Print to print the message.

■ The Print dialog box appears.

3 Click the printer you want to use to print the message.

4 Click Print to print the message.

CREATE A NEW FOLDER

You can create folders in Outlook Express to help organize your messages. Creating folders can help you keep related messages together so you will be able to find messages of interest more easily. For example, if you have many messages related to a specific project or client, you can create a folder to store all the messages in one location.

You can create a main folder that will appear with the Inbox, Outbox, Sent Items, Deleted Items and Drafts folders. You can also create a folder that will appear within an existing folder. For example, you can create a folder within the Inbox folder.

You can use descriptive names to label the folders you create, but you should try to keep the names short. Long names may not be fully displayed in the Outlook Express window.

After you create a folder, you can easily move messages into the folder.

CREATE A NEW FOLDER

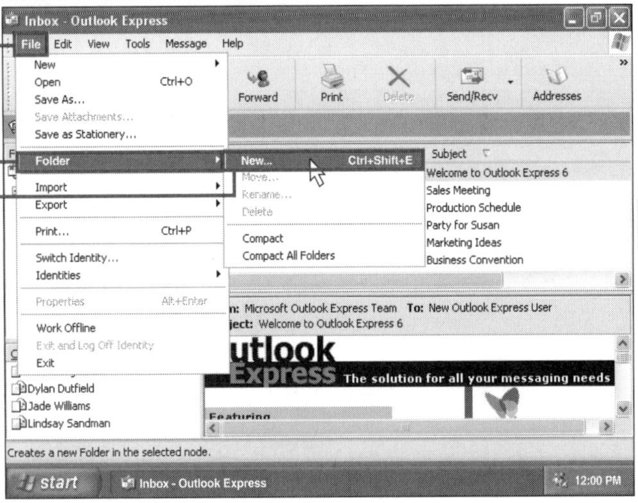

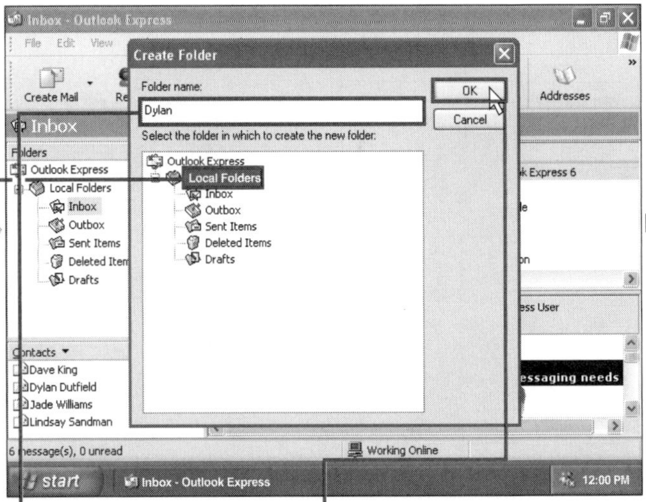

1 Click File.

2 Click Folder.

3 Click New.

Note: If the New option is not available, click a folder in the list of folders before performing step 1.

■ The Create Folder dialog box appears.

4 Type a name for the new folder.

5 Click Local Folders to create a main folder.

Note: To create a new folder within another folder, click the folder. If all the folders are not displayed, click the plus sign (+) beside Local Folders (+ changes to −).

6 Click OK to create the new folder.

Why can't I see the new folder I created?

✔ If you create a folder within another folder, the folder you created may be hidden. Click the plus sign (⊞) beside the folder that contains the folder you created (⊞ changes to ⊟).

How do I rename a folder?

✔ Right-click the folder you want to rename and then select Rename from the menu that appears. Type the new name and then press the Enter key. You can only rename folders that you have created.

How do I delete a folder I created but no longer need?

✔ Click the folder you want to delete and then press the Delete key. Outlook Express places a deleted folder in the Deleted Items folder. To permanently remove a folder from your computer, you must delete the folder from the Deleted Items folder. If you delete a folder that contains messages, the messages will also be deleted.

Can I rearrange folders I have created?

✔ Yes. Position the mouse pointer over the folder you want to move and then drag the folder to a new location.

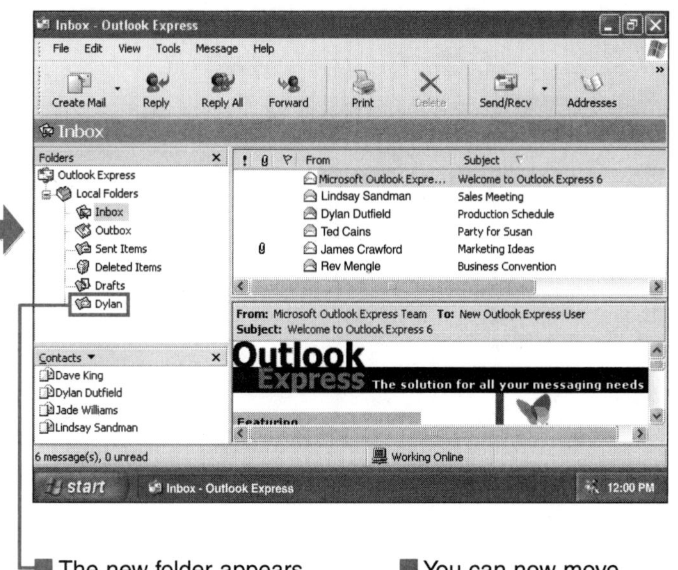

■ The new folder appears.

■ You can now move messages to the new folder.

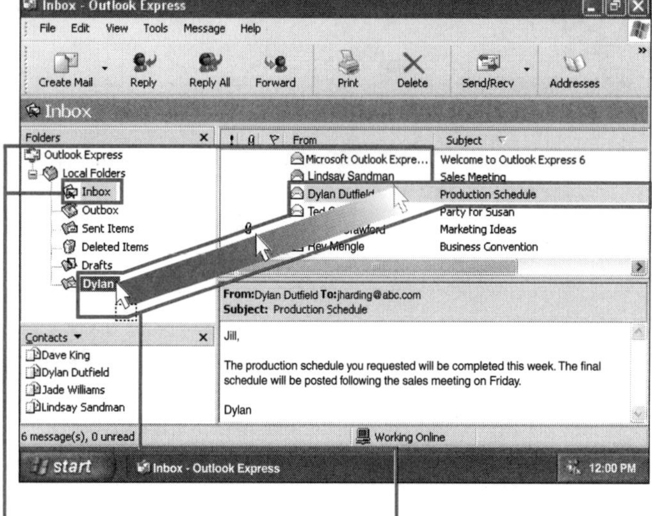

MOVE MESSAGES TO ANOTHER FOLDER

1 Click the folder that contains the message you want to move to another folder.

2 Position the mouse over the message.

3 Drag the message to the folder you want to store the message.

■ Outlook Express moves the message to the folder.

ADD A NAME TO THE ADDRESS BOOK

You can use the address book to store the names and e-mail addresses of people you frequently send messages to.

When you add a new name to the address book, you can enter the person's first, middle and last name. Outlook Express also gives you the option of entering a nickname for the person. A nickname is a name or word that describes the person. You must also enter the person's e-mail address.

When you send a message, you can select a name from the address book. You can also quickly address the message by typing the first few letters of the person's name, nickname or e-mail address. Outlook Express will automatically complete the name or e-mail address for you.

Using the address book to select names saves you from having to type the same e-mail addresses over and over. Using the address book also helps prevent typing mistakes in an address. Typing mistakes can result in a message being delivered to the wrong person or being returned to you.

Names you add to the address book also appear in the Contacts list.

ADD A NAME TO THE ADDRESS BOOK

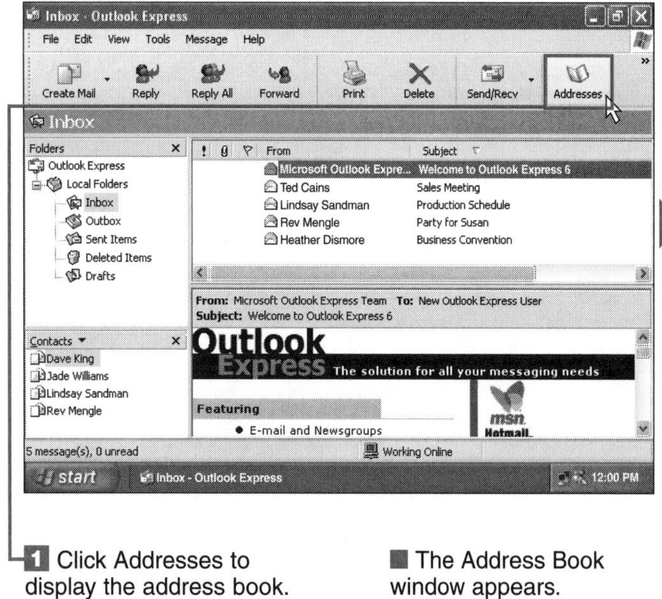

1 Click Addresses to display the address book.

■ The Address Book window appears.

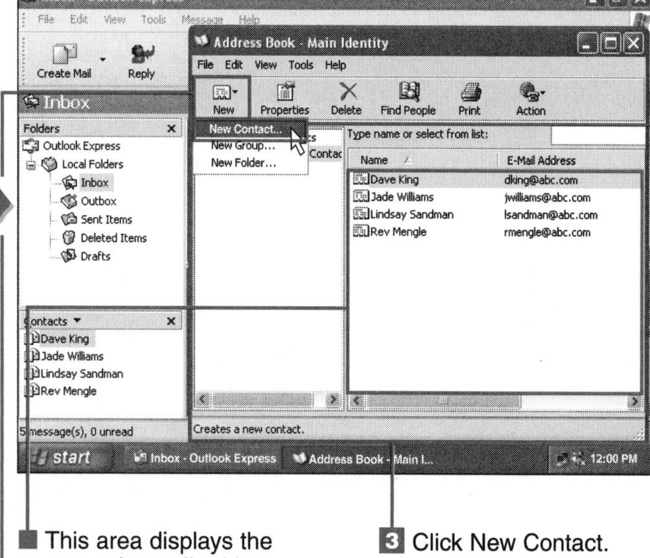

■ This area displays the name and e-mail address of each person in your address book.

2 Click New to add a name to the address book.

3 Click New Contact.

■ The Properties dialog box appears.

When I receive a message, can I add the sender to the address book?

✔ When you receive a message, you can quickly add the sender's name and e-mail address to the address book. Double-click the message and then choose the Tools menu. Select Add to Address Book and then click Sender.

Does Outlook Express automatically add names to the address book?

✔ Yes. Each time you reply to a message, the recipient's name and e-mail address are automatically added to the address book.

How do I change the information for a person in the address book?

✔ To change the information for a person in the address book, display the Address Book window and then double-click the person's name to display the information for the person. Click the Name tab and then make the changes.

How do I delete a person from the address book?

✔ To delete a person from the address book, display the Address Book window, click the person's name and then press the Delete key.

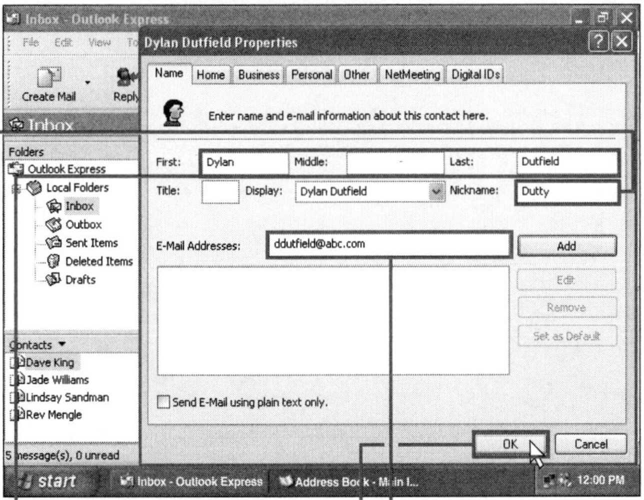

4 Click each area and type the first, middle and last name of the person. You do not have to fill in the middle name.

5 You can click this area and type a nickname. A nickname is optional.

6 Click this area and then type the e-mail address of the person.

7 Click OK to add the name to the address book.

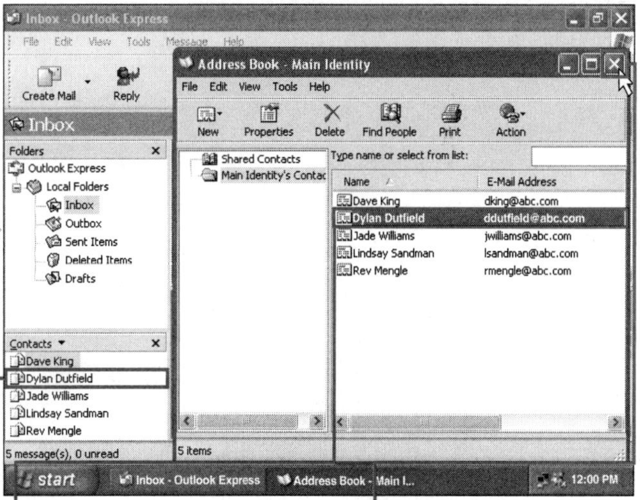

■ The name and e-mail address appear in the address book.

■ The name also appears in the Contacts list.

8 Click ☒ to close the Address Book window.

ADD A GROUP TO THE ADDRESS BOOK

You can add a group to the address book so you can quickly send the same message to every person in the group. Creating a group saves you the time of having to enter each person's e-mail address into a message. For example, if you are planning to send a message to your customers advising them of your monthly specials, you can create a group so you can send the same message to all your customers at once.

You can use the addresses in your address book to create the new group. Each group appears as a name in the address book. You can create as many groups as you need. You can also add a person to more than one group.

When composing a message you want to send to a group, you can select the name of the group from the address book. You can also type the name of the group in the New Message window. Outlook Express will send the message to everyone in the group.

Groups you add to the address book also appear in the Contacts list. This list allows you to quickly address a message.

ADD A GROUP TO THE ADDRESS BOOK

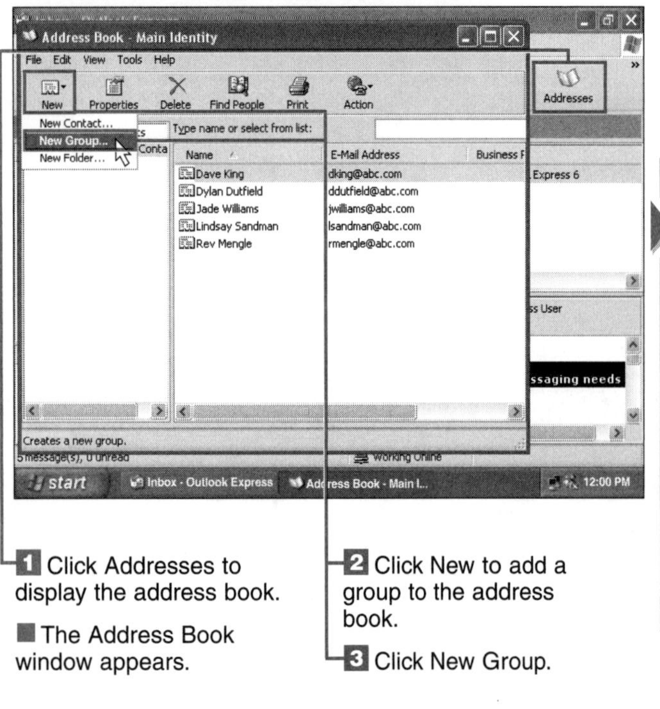

1 Click Addresses to display the address book.

■ The Address Book window appears.

2 Click New to add a group to the address book.

3 Click New Group.

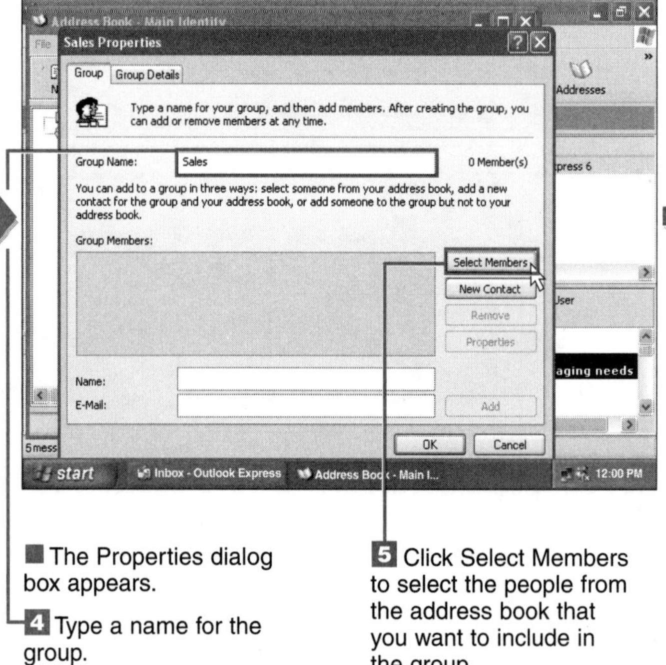

■ The Properties dialog box appears.

4 Type a name for the group.

5 Click Select Members to select the people from the address book that you want to include in the group.

How can I add a name that is not in the address book to a group?

✔ In the Address Book window, double-click the group. At the bottom of the Properties dialog box, enter the person's name and e-mail address and then click the Add button.

Can I add a name to a group and to the address book at the same time?

✔ Yes. In the Address Book window, double-click the group. In the Properties dialog box, click the New Contact button. Then perform steps 4 to 7 on page 467.

How do I remove a name from a group?

✔ In the Address Book window, double-click the group to display the list of names in the group. Select the name you want to remove from the group and then press the Delete key.

How do I remove an entire group from the address book?

✔ In the Address Book window, click the name of the group you want to remove and then press the Delete key.

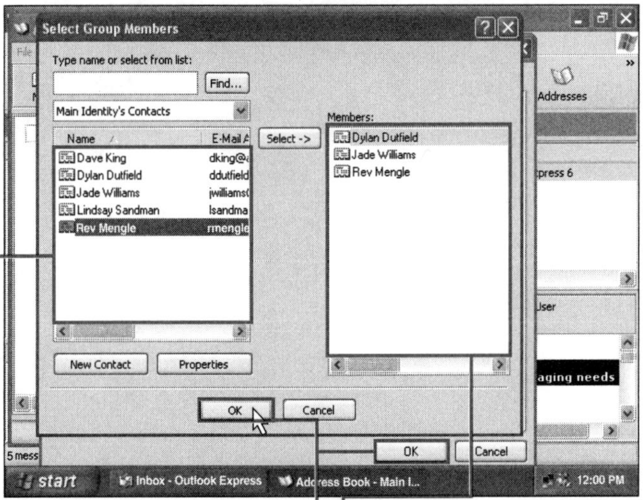

■ The Select Group Members dialog box appears.

6 Double-click the name of each person you want to include in the group.

■ The name of each person you select appears in this area.

7 Click OK when you finish selecting all the people you want to include in the group.

8 Click OK to close the Properties dialog box.

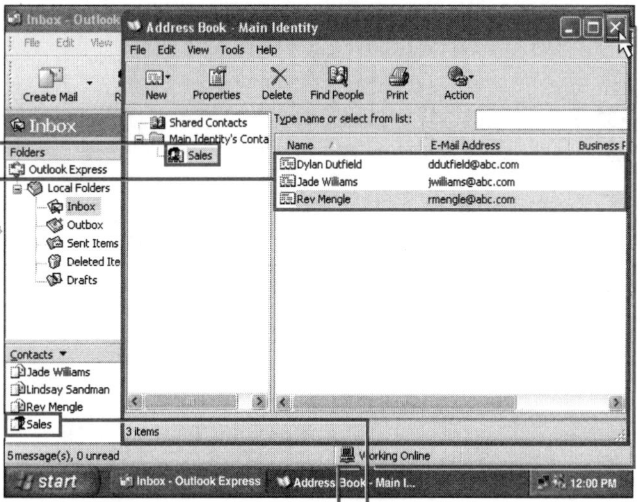

■ The group appears in the address book. A group displays the symbol.

■ This area displays each person in the group. A person displays the symbol.

■ The group also appears in the Contacts list.

9 Click ✕ to close the Address Book window.

SELECT A NAME FROM THE ADDRESS BOOK

When sending a message, you can select the name of the person you want to receive the message from the address book. Selecting names from the address book saves you from having to type e-mail addresses you often use.

The address book makes it easy to send a message when you do not remember the recipient's e-mail address. The address book also reduces the possibility that the message will be undeliverable because of a typing mistake in the address.

The address book allows you to send a message to several recipients. You can also send a copy of the message, called a carbon copy (Cc), to another person. This is useful if you want to send a copy of the message to someone who is not directly involved, but would be interested in the message.

The address book also lets you send a blind carbon copy (Bcc) of the message. A blind carbon copy is useful if you want to send a copy of the message to a person without anyone else knowing that the person received the message.

SELECT A NAME FROM THE ADDRESS BOOK

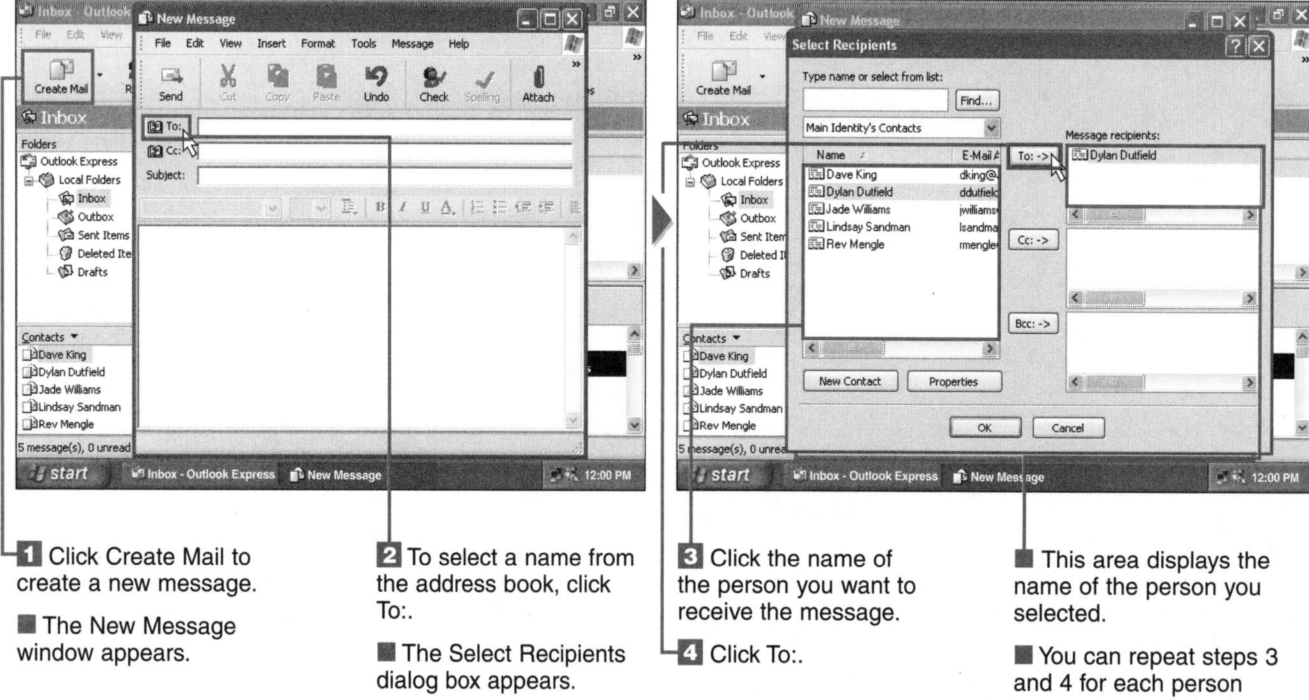

1 Click Create Mail to create a new message.

■ The New Message window appears.

2 To select a name from the address book, click To:.

■ The Select Recipients dialog box appears.

3 Click the name of the person you want to receive the message.

4 Click To:.

■ This area displays the name of the person you selected.

■ You can repeat steps 3 and 4 for each person you want to receive the message.

How do I remove a name from the To:, Cc: or Bcc: area in the Select Recipients dialog box?

✔ To remove a name, click the name and then press the Delete key.

Is there a faster way to select a name from the address book?

✔ You can quickly enter a name from the address book by typing the first few letters of a person's name, nickname or e-mail address in the To: or Cc: areas of the New Message window. Outlook Express will automatically complete the name or e-mail address for you.

Can I mix names from the address book with addresses I type?

✔ Yes. After you select a name from the address book, you can type an e-mail address. Each name and address must be separated with a comma (,) or a semicolon (;).

How do I use the Contacts list to select a name from the address book?

✔ The Contacts list appears in the bottom left corner of the Outlook Express window and displays the name of each person in your address book. To quickly send a message to a person in the Contacts list, double-click their name. The New Message window appears with the To: area addressed to the person you selected.

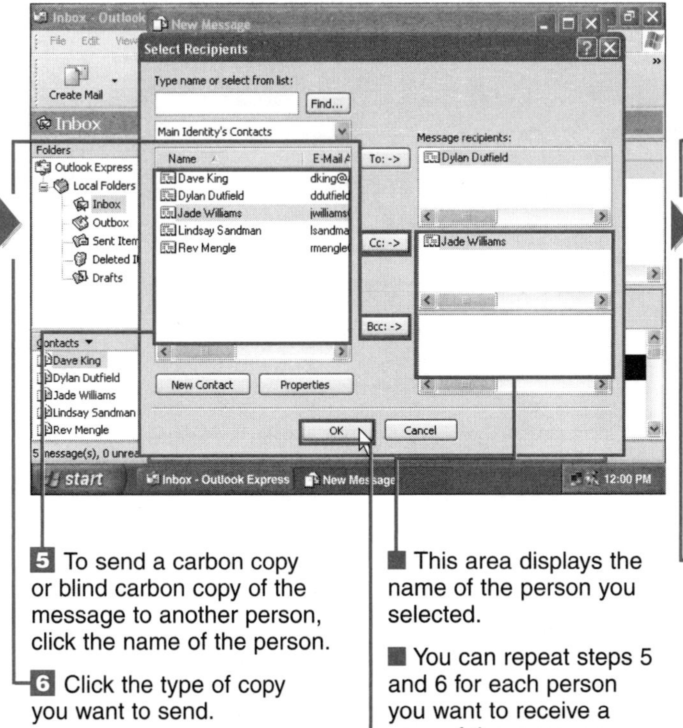

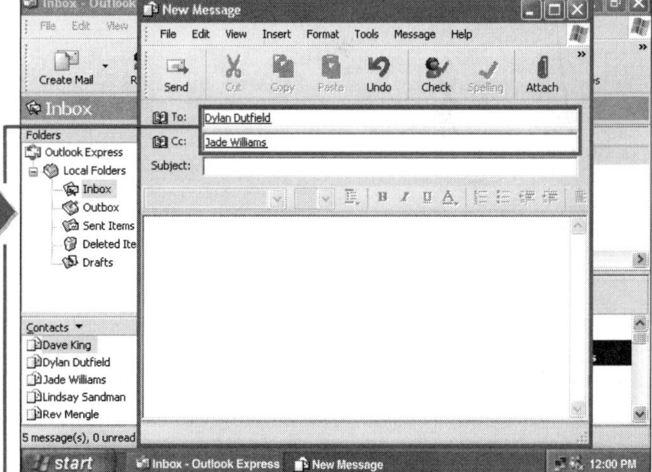

5 To send a carbon copy or blind carbon copy of the message to another person, click the name of the person.

6 Click the type of copy you want to send.

■ This area displays the name of the person you selected.

■ You can repeat steps 5 and 6 for each person you want to receive a copy of the message.

7 Click OK.

■ This area displays the name of each person you selected from the address book.

■ You can now finish composing the message.

ATTACH A FILE TO A MESSAGE

You can attach a file to a message you are sending. Attaching a file is useful when you want to include additional information with a message.

You can attach many different types of files to your messages, including document, image, program, sound and video files. The computer receiving the message must have the necessary hardware and software to display or play the file you attach.

When you receive a message with an attached file, you can open and view the file. Some files, such as program files, can contain viruses. If you open a file that contains a virus, the information on your computer could be damaged. You should make sure the files you open are from reliable sources.

When you select a file you want to open, Outlook Express may ask if you want to open or save the file. Before you open the file, you should save the file on your computer and run an anti-virus program on the file.

Some pictures, such as those in the Bitmap, GIF and JPEG formats, are displayed in the body of a message, as well as in the list of attached files.

ATTACH A FILE TO A MESSAGE

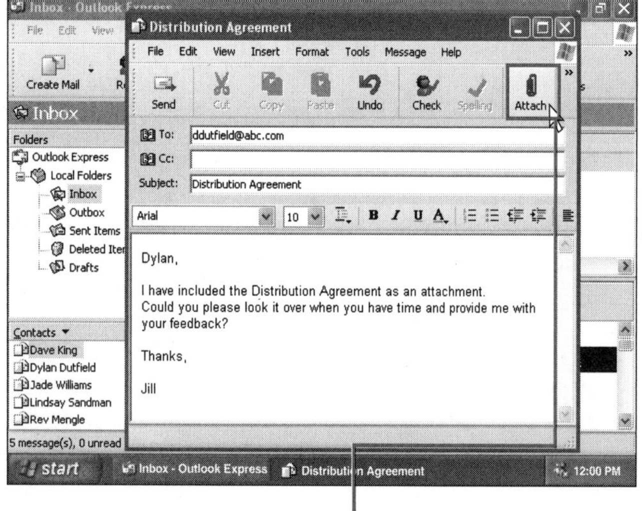

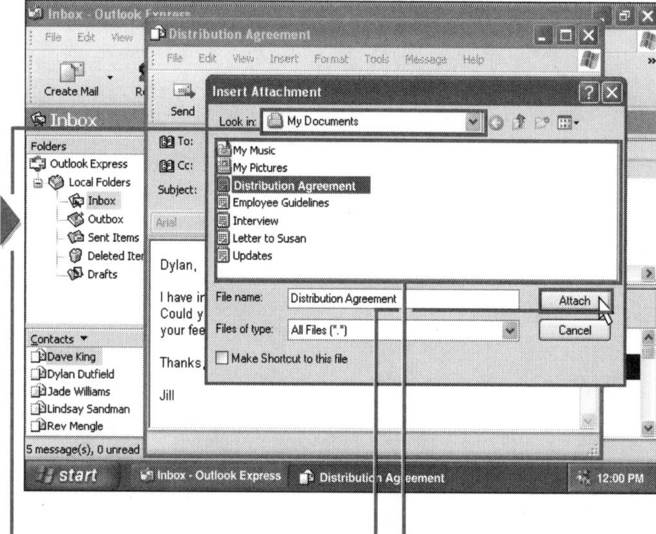

1 To create a message, perform steps 1 to 5 starting on page 458.

2 Click Attach to attach a file to the message.

Note: If the Attach button does not appear in the window, you need to enlarge the window to display the button.

■ The Insert Attachment dialog box appears.

■ This area shows the location of the displayed files. You can click this area to change the location.

3 Click the file you want to attach to the message.

4 Click Attach to attach the file to the message.

Can I drag and drop a file into a message?

✔ You can drag and drop a file from the desktop or any open window into a message. This is a quick way to attach several files to a message at once.

Instead of attaching a picture, can I send the picture as the background of a message?

✔ Yes. In the New Message window, choose the Format menu, select Background and then click Picture. In the Background Picture dialog box that appears, click the Browse button to locate the file you want to use as a background picture.

Can I send a large message with many attachments?

✔ Many mail servers cannot send and receive messages larger than 2 MB. To send a large message, you can have Outlook Express break the message into several small messages. When an e-mail program receives the group of small messages, the program will combine the messages into one large message. In the Outlook Express window, select the Tools menu and then click Accounts. Choose the Mail tab, select the Properties button and then click the Advanced tab. Select the Break apart messages larger than option (☐ changes to ☑) and then specify the maximum file size you can send.

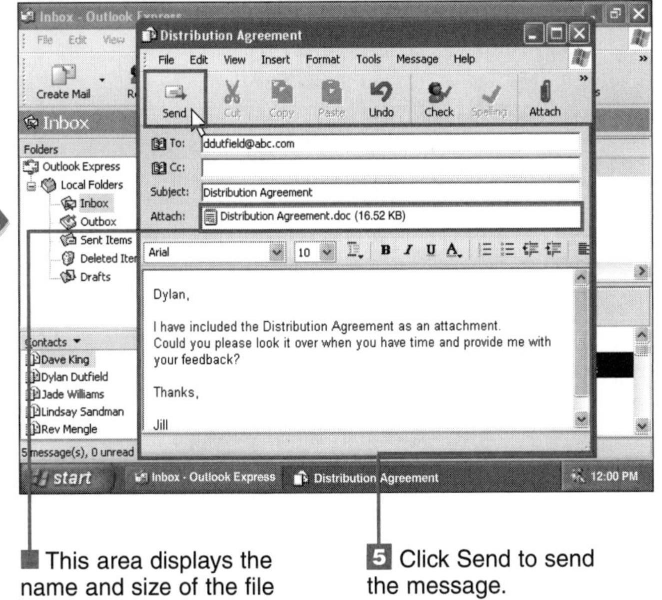

■ This area displays the name and size of the file you selected.

■ To attach additional files, repeat steps 2 to 4 for each file you want to attach to the message.

5 Click Send to send the message.

OPEN AN ATTACHED FILE

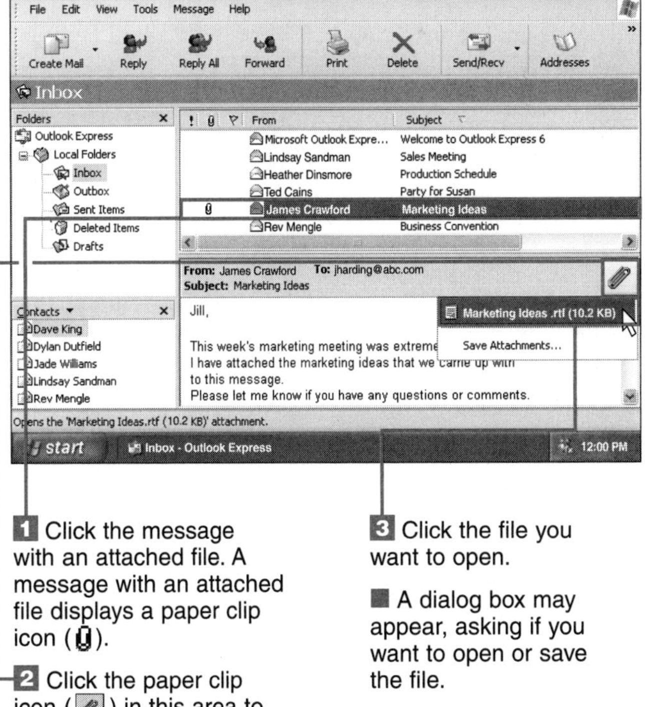

1 Click the message with an attached file. A message with an attached file displays a paper clip icon (📎).

2 Click the paper clip icon (📎) in this area to display a list of the files attached to the message.

3 Click the file you want to open.

■ A dialog box may appear, asking if you want to open or save the file.

FORMAT MESSAGES

You can format the text in a message you are composing. The formatting features found in Outlook Express are similar to those found in most word processing programs.

You can change the font and size of the text in a message. Changing the font and size of text allows you to make your messages more interesting and can help make long messages easier to read. You can use the bold, italic and underline styles to emphasize information. Changing the color of text helps draw attention to important information and can make a message more attractive.

Outlook Express uses HyperText Markup Language (HTML) to format messages. HTML is the language used to create Web pages. Most e-mail programs use HTML to format messages.

If the recipient of the message uses an e-mail program that cannot display HTML formatted text, the message will appear as plain text with no formatting. The message will include an attached file that the recipient can open in a Web browser to view the HTML formatted text.

FORMAT MESSAGES

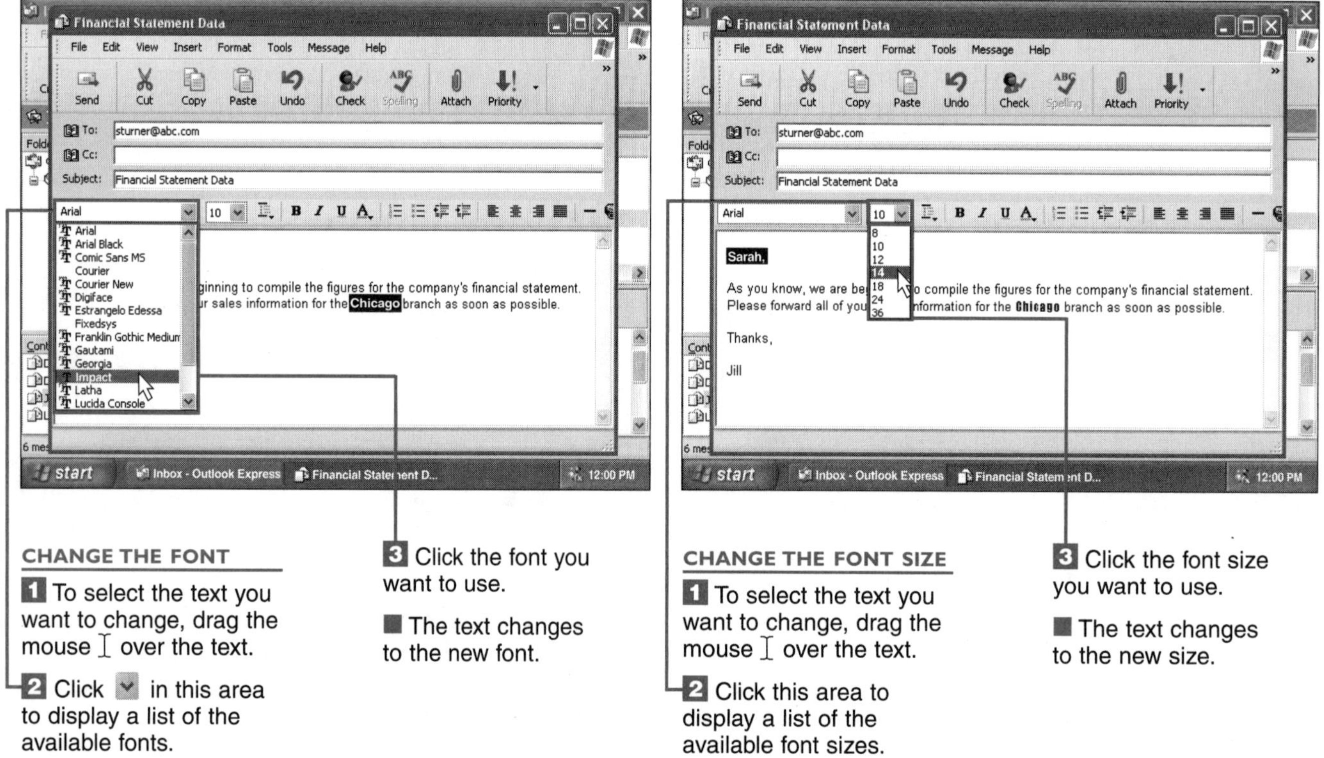

CHANGE THE FONT

1 To select the text you want to change, drag the mouse I over the text.

2 Click ▾ in this area to display a list of the available fonts.

3 Click the font you want to use.

■ The text changes to the new font.

CHANGE THE FONT SIZE

1 To select the text you want to change, drag the mouse I over the text.

2 Click this area to display a list of the available font sizes.

3 Click the font size you want to use.

■ The text changes to the new size.

Why can't I format a message?

✔ HTML formatting may be disabled. To enable HTML formatting, select the Format menu and then click Rich Text (HTML).

Does Outlook Express provide any preformatted designs I can use for my e-mail messages?

✔ Yes. Outlook Express offers several designs that have background colors and designs as well as preformatted fonts and font colors. In the Outlook Express window, click ▾ beside the Create Mail button and then select a design. The New Message window appears, displaying the design you selected.

How can I change the background color of a message?

✔ Choose the Format menu and then select Background. Click Color and then select the background color you want to use. Make sure the background color you choose works well with the text in your message. For example, red text on a blue background can be difficult to read.

Why does Outlook Express underline the e-mail and Web page addresses I type in a message?

✔ Outlook Express automatically converts any e-mail or Web page address you type to a link. The person who receives your message will be able to select the link to send a message or display the Web page.

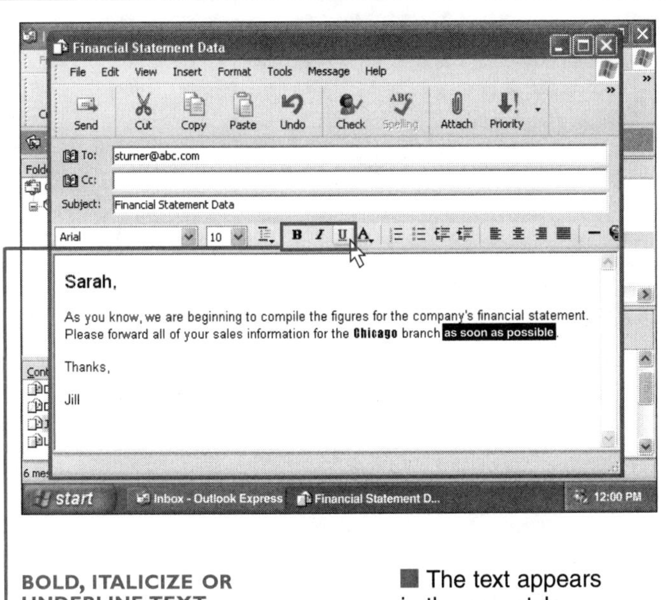

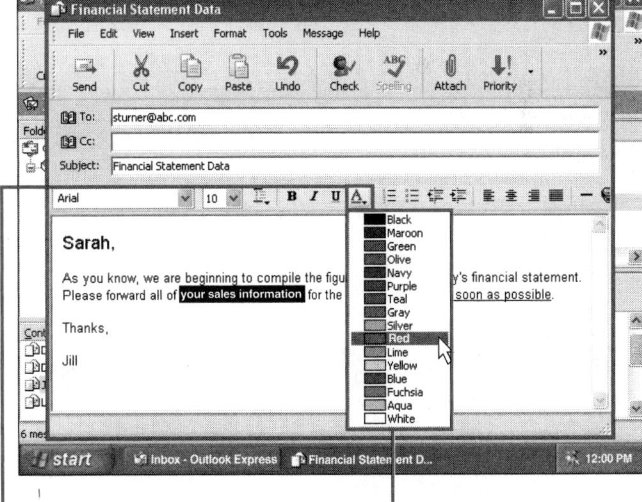

BOLD, ITALICIZE OR UNDERLINE TEXT

1 To select the text you want to change, drag the mouse I over the text.

2 Click bold (B), italic (I) or underline (U).

■ The text appears in the new style.

Note: To remove a bold, italic or underline style, repeat steps 1 and 2.

ADD COLOR

1 To select the text you want to change, drag the mouse I over the text.

2 Click A to display a list of the available colors.

3 Click the color you want to use.

■ The text appears in the color you selected.

ADD A SIGNATURE TO MESSAGES

You can have Outlook Express add information about yourself to the end of every message you send. This information is called a signature. A signature saves you from having to type the same information every time you send a message.

A signature can include information such as your name, e-mail address, occupation or Web page address.

You can also use plain characters to display simple pictures in your signature. Many people use a signature to display their favorite humorous or inspirational quotation.

You should leave a blank line at the beginning of your signature to separate the signature from the body of your message. As a courtesy to the people who will be reading your messages, you should limit your signature to four or five lines.

You can have Outlook Express add your signature to all the messages you send, reply to and forward.

ADD A SIGNATURE TO MESSAGES

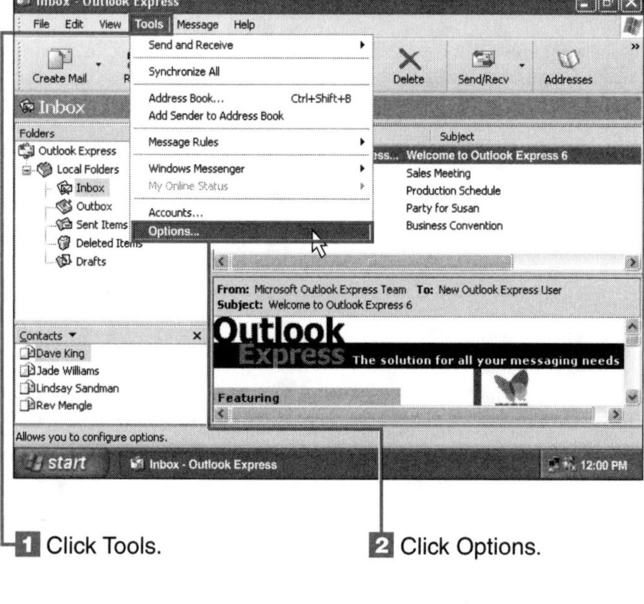

1 Click Tools.

2 Click Options.

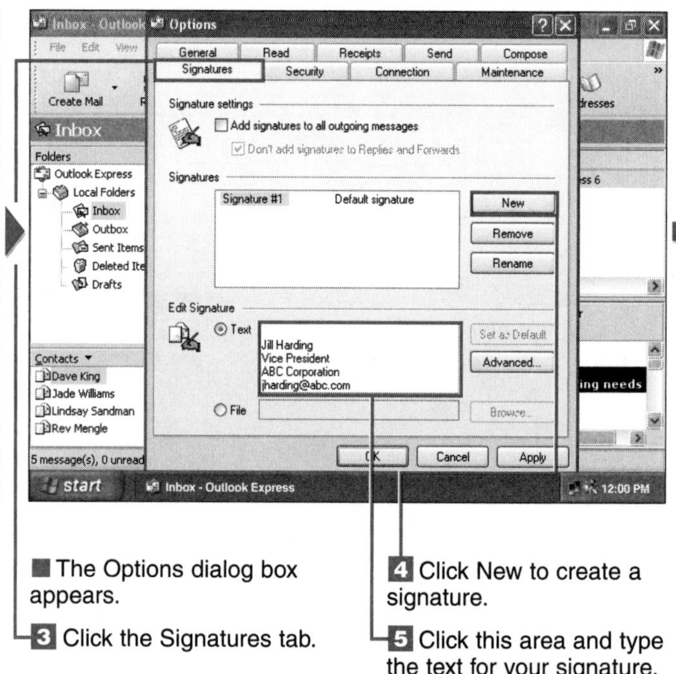

■ The Options dialog box appears.

3 Click the Signatures tab.

4 Click New to create a signature.

5 Click this area and type the text for your signature.

How can I create multiple signatures?

✔ After creating your first signature, repeat steps 4 and 5 below for each additional signature you want to create. Turn off the Add signatures to all outgoing messages option (☑ changes to ☐) and click OK. To add a signature to a message you are composing, choose the Insert menu, select Signature and click the signature you want to include.

Can I use a text file on my computer as my signature?

✔ Yes. Perform steps 1 to 4 below and then select the File option (○ changes to ◉). Click the Browse button to locate the text file and then perform steps 6 to 8.

Can I attach additional information to my messages?

✔ You can use a business card to send contact information to the recipients of your messages. To create a business card, perform steps 1 to 7 on page 466 to specify your personal information. You can use the tabs in the Properties dialog box to specify additional information. To add your business card to outgoing messages, choose the Tools menu in the Outlook Express window, select Options and click the Compose tab. In the Business Cards area, click the Mail option (☐ changes to ☑) and select your business card. A recipient can click the symbol in your message to read your contact information.

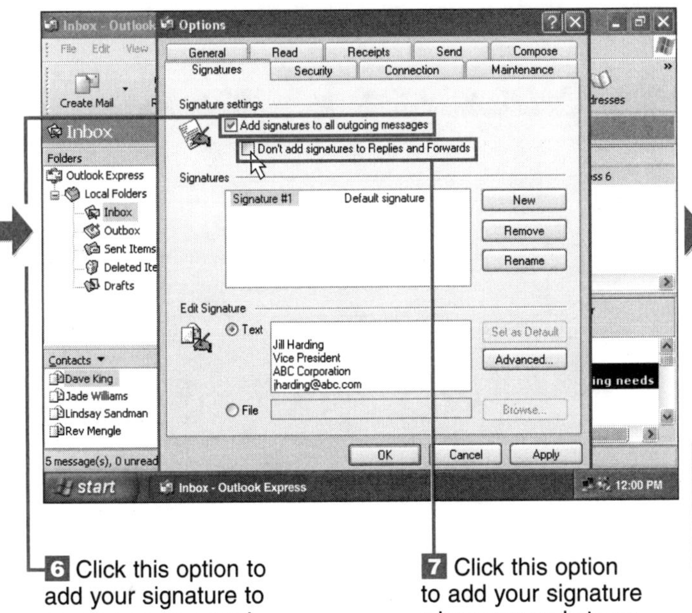

6 Click this option to add your signature to messages you send (☐ changes to ☑).

7 Click this option to add your signature when you reply to or forward a message (☑ changes to ☐).

8 Click OK to confirm your changes.

■ If you no longer want to add a signature to the messages you send, repeat steps 1 to 3. Then perform step 6 (☑ changes to ☐) and click OK.

FIND MESSAGES

If you cannot find a message you want to review, you can have Outlook Express search for the message. You should provide Outlook Express with as much information about the message as possible to help narrow your search.

If you know which folder contains the message, you can search a specific folder. You can also search all the folders for the message.

Outlook Express can search for a message you have received from a specific person. Outlook Express can also find a message you have sent to a certain person.

If you can only remember a word from the subject of the message you want to find, you can have Outlook Express search the subject area of your messages. You can also search for messages that contain specific text.

You may also want to search for messages received before or after a certain date, messages with attached files or messages you have flagged.

When the search is complete, Outlook Express displays a list of messages that match all the information you specified. You can open and read the messages.

FIND MESSAGES

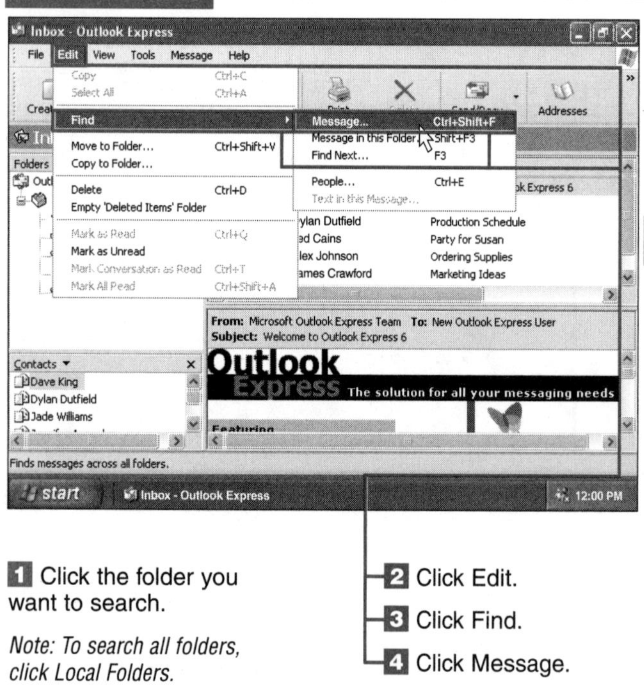

1 Click the folder you want to search.

Note: To search all folders, click Local Folders.

2 Click Edit.

3 Click Find.

4 Click Message.

■ The Find Message window appears.

5 To find messages you received from or sent to a specific person, click the appropriate area and then type the name of the person.

6 To find messages with a specific subject or that contain specific text, click the appropriate area and then type the subject or text.

Is there a faster way to open the Find Message window?

✔ Yes. You can click the Find button on the toolbar. If the Find button is not displayed, click » on the toolbar to display all the buttons.

How do I change the folder Outlook Express will search?

✔ In the Find Message window, click the Browse button to select a different folder. Outlook Express will automatically search all the subfolders within the folder you select. If you do not want to search the subfolders, click the Include subfolders option in the Find Message window to turn the option off (☑ changes to ☐).

Outlook Express didn't find the message I was looking for. What can I do?

✔ If the search did not provide the results you were expecting, you may have specified incorrect information. In the Find Message window, click the New Search button to clear the contents of the window and start a new search.

Can I search one message for specific text?

✔ If you are reviewing a message that contains a lot of text, you can use the Find feature to quickly locate a word in the message. Click anywhere in the message you want to search. From the Edit menu, select Find and then click Text in this Message. Type the text you want to find and then click Find Next.

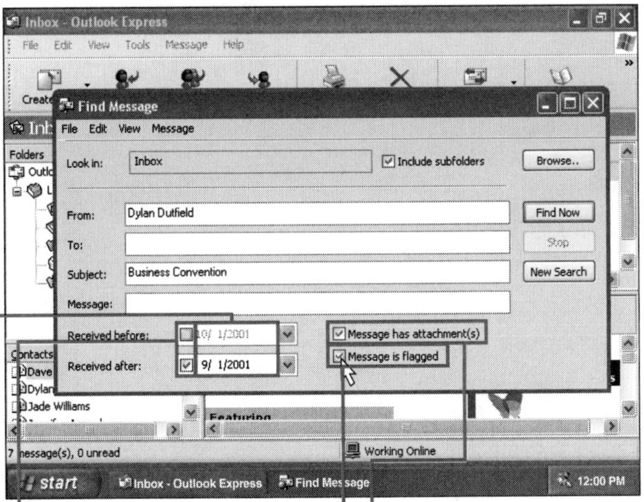

7 To find messages received before or after a certain date, click the appropriate box (☐ changes to ☑).

8 To specify the date, click the part of the date you want to change and then type a new date.

9 To find messages with attached files, click this option (☐ changes to ☑).

10 To find messages you have flagged, click this option (☐ changes to ☑).

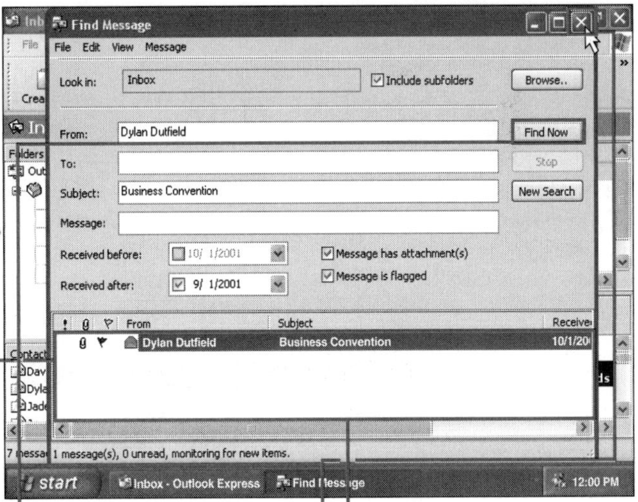

11 Click Find Now to start the search.

■ This area displays a list of the messages that match the information you specified.

■ To display the contents of a message, double-click the message.

12 When you finish reviewing the messages, click ☒ to close the Find Message window.

SORT INCOMING MESSAGES

You can have Outlook Express sort the messages you receive. This is useful if you want to organize incoming messages before you read them.

You can set up a rule to tell Outlook Express how you want to sort the messages you receive. You need to select a condition to specify which incoming messages you want Outlook Express to sort. For example, you can sort incoming messages that were sent by a specific person. You could also sort incoming messages that contain specific words in the subject or body of the message.

When setting up a rule, you will also need to specify an action you want Outlook Express to perform on messages that meet the condition you specify. Outlook Express can automatically move or copy messages to a specific folder, delete messages you do not want to read or forward messages to another e-mail address. You can even instruct Outlook Express to automatically reply to messages. Many people use automatic replies to inform people that they are on vacation.

If you use an IMAP or HTTP e-mail account, such as a Hotmail account, you cannot set up rules to sort the messages for the account.

SORT INCOMING MESSAGES

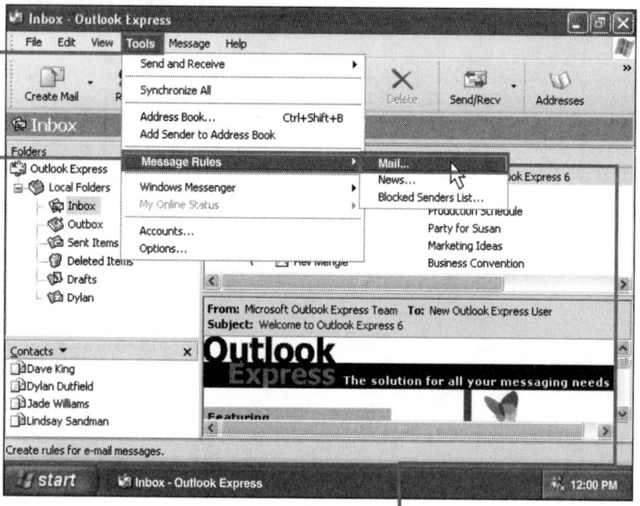

1 Click Tools.

2 Click Message Rules.

3 Click Mail.

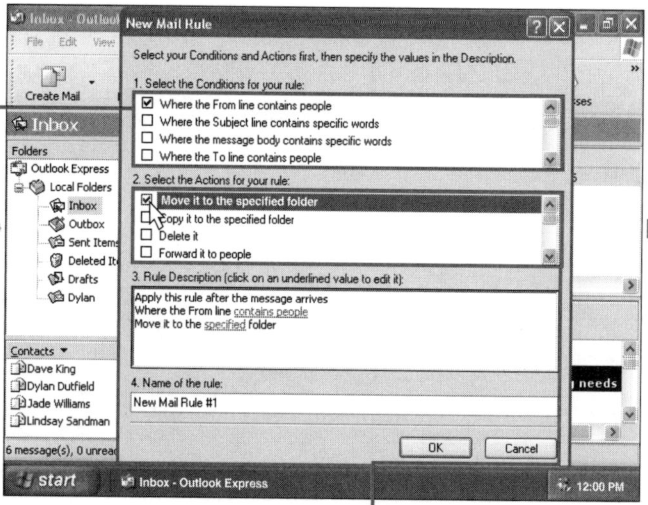

■ The New Mail Rule dialog box appears.

4 Click the box (☐) beside a condition to specify which messages you want to sort (☐ changes to ☑).

5 Click the box (☐) beside an action to specify what you want to do with messages that meet the condition you specify (☐ changes to ☑).

Why does the Message Rules dialog box appear instead of the New Mail Rule dialog box?

✔ If you have already created a rule, the New Mail Rule dialog box does not appear automatically. In the Message Rules dialog box, click the New button to display the New Mail Rule dialog box and create a new rule.

How do I quickly create a rule to sort messages from a specific person?

✔ In the Outlook Express window, select a message from the person, choose the Message menu and then click Create Rule From Message. Outlook Express automatically fills in the condition for you using the e-mail address of the person. You must specify an action for the rule.

Can I select multiple conditions and actions for a rule?

✔ Yes. Click the check box beside each condition and action you want to use (☐ changes to ☑). If you select more than one condition, Outlook Express will only sort incoming messages that meet all the conditions. To sort incoming messages that meet one or more of the conditions, click 'and' in the Rule Description area and then select the Messages match any one of the criteria option in the dialog box that appears.

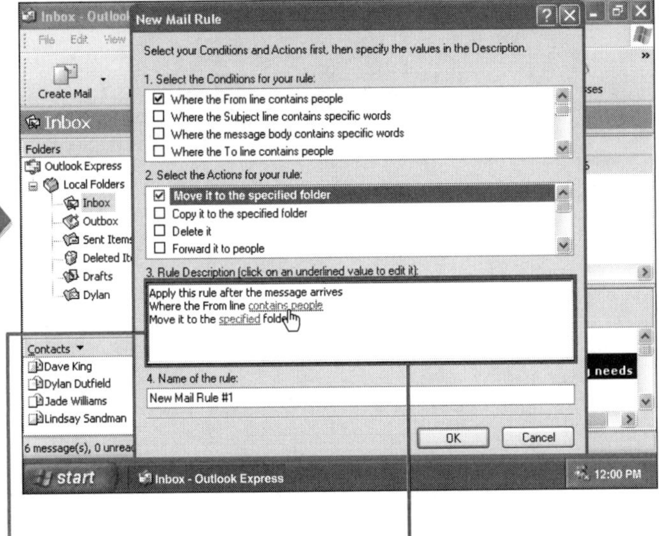

■ This area displays the condition and action you selected. You need to specify additional information for text that appears underlined and in blue.

Note: In this example, Outlook Express will move messages you receive from certain people to a specific folder.

6 Click the first instance of text that appears underlined and in blue to specify the required information.

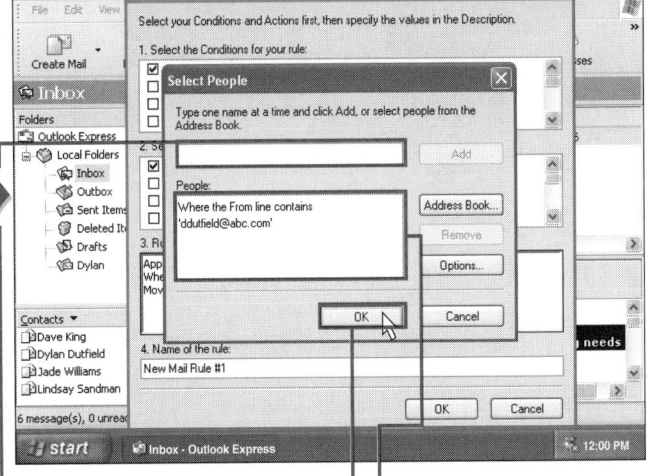

■ The Select People dialog box appears.

Note: The dialog box that appears depends on the text you selected in step 6.

7 Type an e-mail address you want to apply the rule to and then press the Enter key.

■ The e-mail address appears in this area.

8 To specify additional e-mail addresses, repeat step 7 for each address.

9 Click OK.

CONTINUED

SORT INCOMING MESSAGES (CONTINUED)

Outlook Express allows you to easily enter the information for a rule you are creating.

Once you have specified a condition and action for a rule, Outlook Express helps you complete the rule by displaying blue, underlined text to indicate where you must enter additional information. For example, when you create a rule to move messages from certain people to a specific folder, Outlook Express indicates that you must enter the e-mail addresses of people whose messages you want to move and the folder to which you want to move the messages.

You can name a rule you create. A descriptive name can help you identify the rule later, which is particularly useful if you create many rules for your e-mail messages.

Outlook Express displays rules you create in the Message Rules dialog box. You can use the Message Rules dialog box to review, modify, copy or remove the rules you create for your e-mail messages.

SORT INCOMING MESSAGES (CONTINUED)

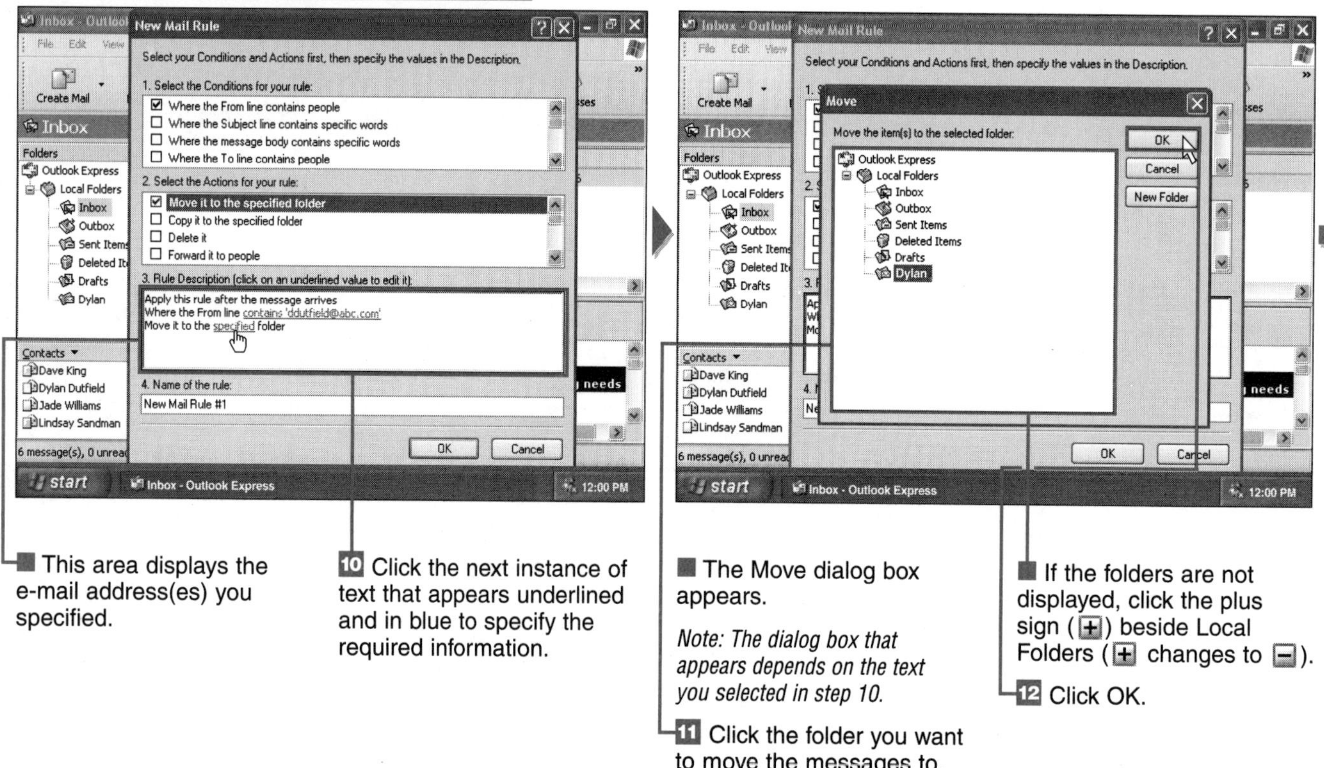

■ This area displays the e-mail address(es) you specified.

10 Click the next instance of text that appears underlined and in blue to specify the required information.

■ The Move dialog box appears.

Note: The dialog box that appears depends on the text you selected in step 10.

11 Click the folder you want to move the messages to.

■ If the folders are not displayed, click the plus sign (⊞) beside Local Folders (⊞ changes to ⊟).

12 Click OK.

Why are my messages not being sorted properly?

✔ If you are using more than one rule to sort your messages, the rules may not be affecting your messages in the proper order. The rule at the top of the Message Rules dialog box affects your messages first. To move a rule, select the rule and then click the Move Up or Move Down button.

Will a rule I create affect messages I have already received?

✔ No. A rule you create will affect only new messages you receive. To apply the rule to all the messages in your Inbox, click the Apply Now button in the Message Rules dialog box. In the dialog box that appears, click the rule and then click Apply Now.

How can I make changes to a rule I created?

✔ In the Message Rules dialog box, select the rule you want to change and then click the Modify button.

How do I remove a rule I no longer need?

✔ In the Message Rules dialog box, select the rule you no longer want to use and then click the Remove button. You can also temporarily turn off a rule by clicking the check box beside the rule in the Message Rules dialog box (☑ changes to ☐).

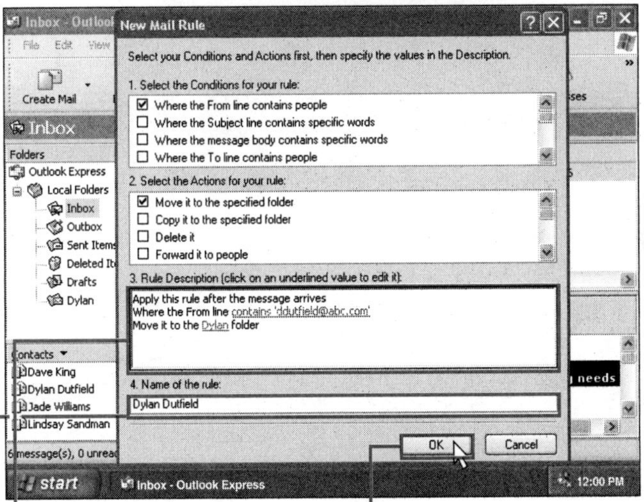

■ This area displays the name of the folder you selected.

13 To enter a name for the rule, select the text in this area and then type a name.

14 Click OK to confirm all the information you entered for the rule.

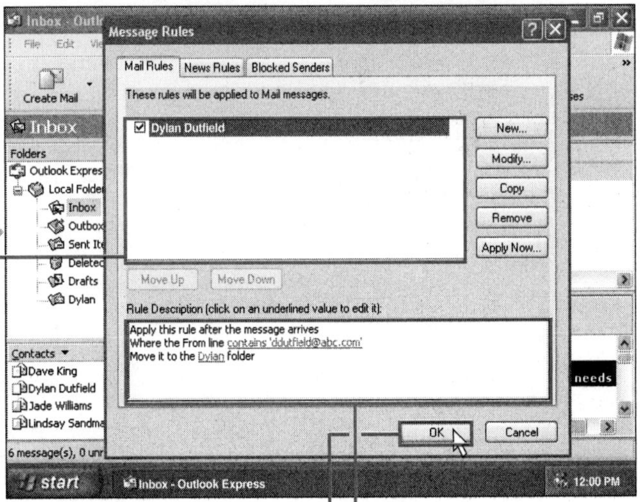

■ The Message Rules dialog box appears.

■ The name of the rule appears in this area.

■ This area displays a description of the rule.

15 Click OK to close the Message Rules dialog box.

START WINDOWS MESSENGER

You can use Windows Messenger to see when your friends are online, send instant messages, exchange files and more.

The first time you start Windows Messenger, a wizard appears, helping you to add a Passport to your user account. You must have a Passport to use Windows Messenger.

A Passport allows you to access many features and services on the Internet using a single e-mail address and password. If you have a Hotmail or MSN account, you already have a Passport. If you do not have a Passport, you can obtain one free of charge when you set up Windows Messenger.

You use your e-mail address and password to sign in to Windows Messenger. You can have Windows remember your e-mail address and password so you do not have to enter the information each time you sign in.

The Windows Messenger window displays the contacts you have added to your list and whether each contact is online or not online. The window also displays a link that you can click to check your e-mail messages.

START WINDOWS MESSENGER

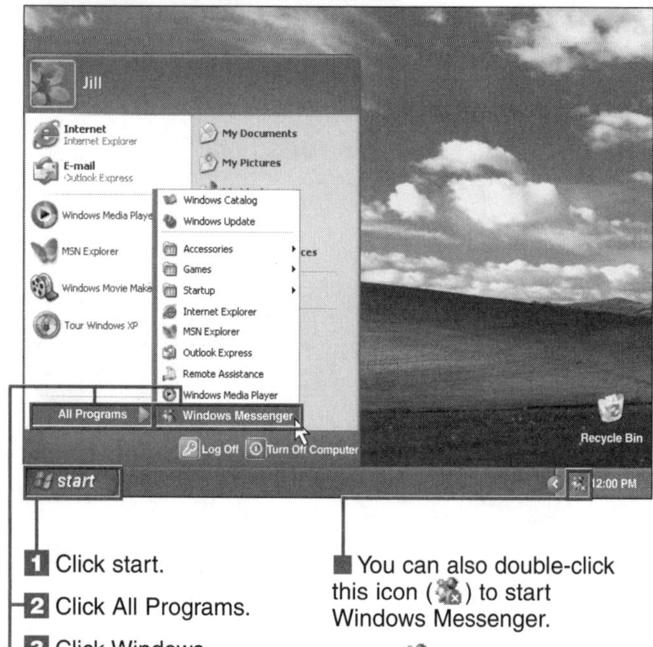

1 Click start.

2 Click All Programs.

3 Click Windows Messenger.

■ You can also double-click this icon ( ) to start Windows Messenger.

Note: If is hidden, you can click on the taskbar to display the icon.

■ The Windows Messenger window appears.

■ If you are already signed in to Windows Messenger, you do not need to perform steps 4 to 6.

4 Click this link to sign in to Windows Messenger.

■ The .NET Messenger Service dialog box appears.

I cannot sign in because I forgot my password. What can I do?

✔ If you forget your password, you can specify a new password. In the .NET Messenger Service dialog box, click the Help link. On the Web page that appears, click the I forgot my password link. Then follow the instructions on your screen to specify a new password.

How can I let others know that I am not available?

✔ In the Windows Messenger window, click your name. From the menu that appears, choose the option that best describes your status.

Can I temporarily remove the Windows Messenger window from my screen?

✔ Yes. To remove the Windows Messenger window from your screen but remain signed in, click ☒. A dialog box appears, stating that the program will continue to run.

I am finished using Windows Messenger. How do I sign out?

✔ If you no longer want to use Windows Messenger, you can sign out without disconnecting from the Internet. In the Windows Messenger window, choose the File menu and select Sign out.

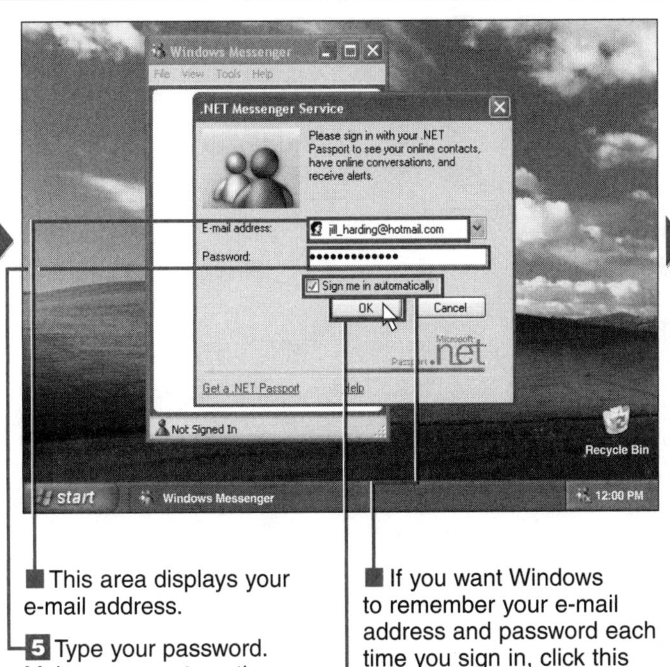

■ This area displays your e-mail address.

5 Type your password. Make sure you type the uppercase and lowercase letters exactly.

■ If you want Windows to remember your e-mail address and password each time you sign in, click this option (☐ changes to ☑).

6 Click OK.

Note: If you are not currently connected to the Internet, a dialog box may appear that allows you to connect.

■ If you have added contacts to your list, this area displays the contacts that are currently online and not online.

Note: To add contacts to your list, see page 486.

■ You can click this link to read your e-mail messages. If you have a Hotmail e-mail account, the link displays the number of new e-mail messages you have received.

ADD A CONTACT

You can add people to your contact list to see when they are online and available to exchange instant messages. Windows Messenger allows you to add up to 150 people to your contact list.

Each person you want to add to your contact list requires a Passport. When you specify the e-mail address of the person you want to add to your contact list, Windows Messenger uses the e-mail address to determine if the person has a Passport. If the person has a Passport, the name will be added to your contact list.

If the person does not have a Passport, Windows Messenger allows you to send an e-mail message inviting the person to install Windows Messenger. A Passport is obtained when Windows Messenger is set up on a computer. People using a program that is compatible with Windows Messenger can obtain a Passport at the passport.com Web site.

After you add a person to your contact list, Windows Messenger notifies the person and allows the person to choose whether or not to let you see and contact them when they are online.

ADD A CONTACT

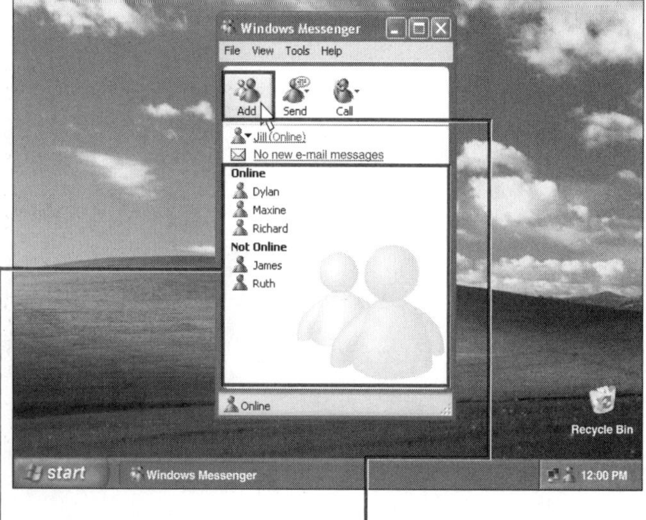

■ This area displays each person you have added to your contact list. You can see the contacts that are currently online and not online.

1 Click Add to add a person to your contact list.

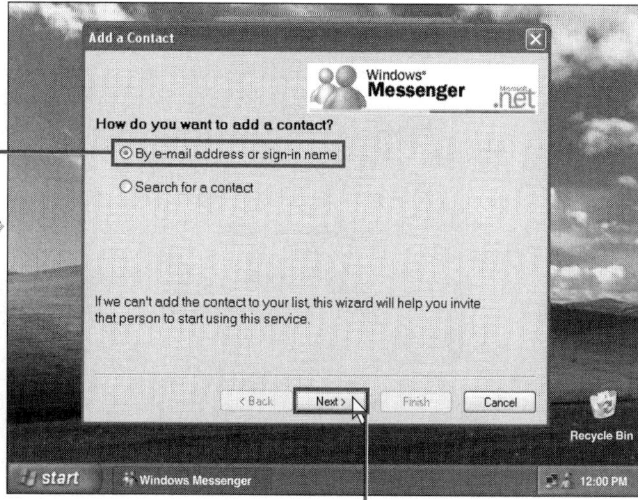

■ The Add a Contact wizard appears.

2 Click this option to add a contact by specifying the person's e-mail address (○ changes to ◉).

3 Click Next to continue.

What can I do if I don't know the e-mail address of the person I want to add to my contact list?

✔ You can have Windows Messenger search for the person. When you start the Add a Contact wizard, click the Search for a contact option and click Next. Enter the information for the person and click Next. Select the name of the person you want to add to your contact list and click Next. For privacy reasons, Windows Messenger cannot add a person it finds in the Hotmail Member Directory to your contact list. You can send the person an e-mail message that explains how to contact you.

How do I remove a person from my contact list?

✔ In the Windows Messenger window, click the name of the person you want to remove and then press the Delete key. People you remove from your list will still be able to contact you.

What can I do if the person I am adding to my contact list is not using Windows Messenger?

✔ You can send the person an e-mail message containing information on how to install Windows Messenger. When the Add a Contact wizard successfully adds a contact, click the Send Mail button in the wizard and then follow the instructions on your screen to send the person a message.

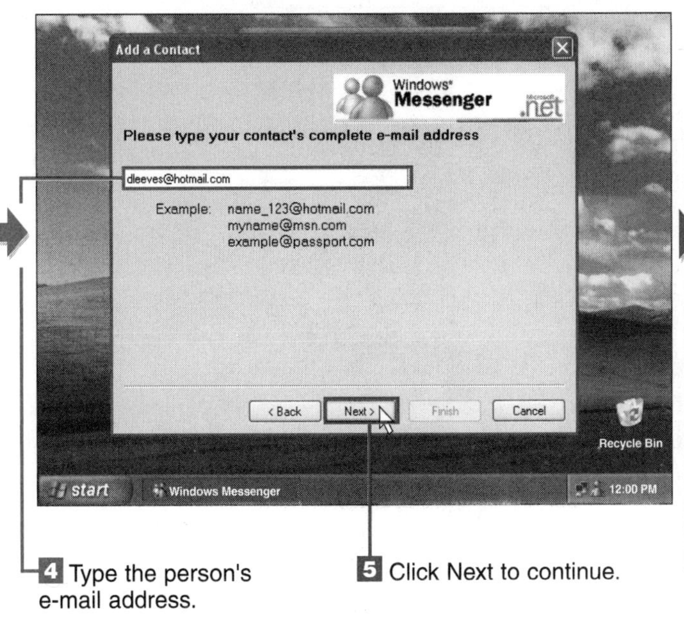

4 Type the person's e-mail address.

5 Click Next to continue.

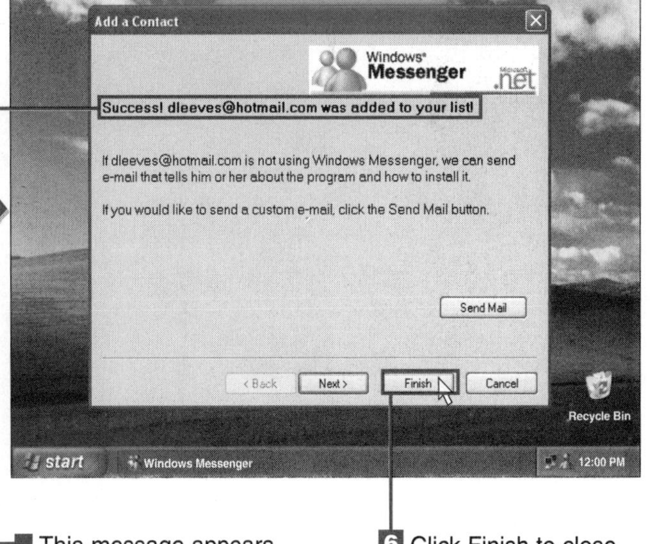

■ This message appears if the wizard added the person to your contact list.

6 Click Finish to close the wizard.

SEND AN INSTANT MESSAGE

You can send an instant message to another person who is signed in to Windows Messenger. Instant messages you send can be up to 400 characters long.

You can start a conversation with one person and then invite other people to join the conversation. Windows Messenger allows you to exchange instant messages with up to four other people at once.

You can use emoticons in your instant messages. Emoticons are characters you type to represent facial expressions such as a smile or a frown. When you send an instant message, many emoticons in the message are automatically converted to graphic images. For example, if you type :) in an instant message, Windows Messenger displays ☺ when you send the message.

The status bar at the bottom of the Conversation window displays the date and time of the last message you received or indicates when another person is typing a message.

When you receive an instant message that is not part of a conversation, your computer makes a sound and briefly displays a box containing the first part of the message. You can click the box to see the entire message.

You should never give out your password or credit card information when sending instant messages.

SEND AN INSTANT MESSAGE

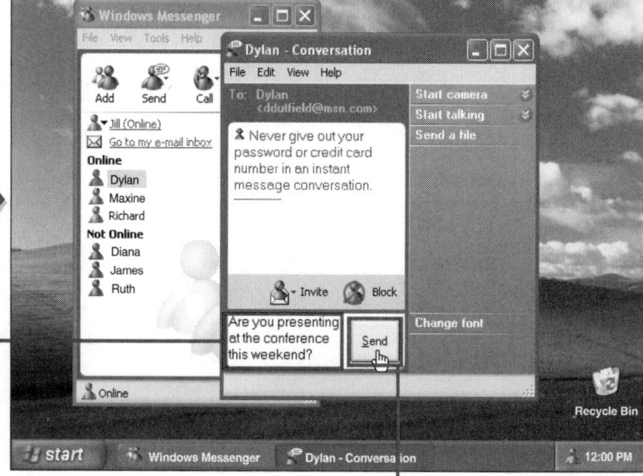

1 Double-click the name of the person you want to send an instant message to.

Note: If the person is not online, a message appears, asking if you want to send the person an e-mail message. Click Yes to send an e-mail message instead.

■ The Conversation window appears.

2 Click this area and type your message.

Note: To start a new paragraph in your message, press and hold down the Shift key as you press the Enter key.

3 Click Send to send the message.

Note: You can also press the Enter key to send the message.

How do I send an instant message to someone who is not in my contact list?

✔ In the Windows Messenger window, click the Send button and then select Other. In the Send an Instant Message dialog box, type the person's e-mail address. The person must be signed in to Windows Messenger to receive the message.

How do I prevent a contact from sending me instant messages?

✔ In the Windows Messenger window, choose the Tools menu and select Options. On the Privacy tab, select the name of the person you do not want to receive instant messages from and then click the Block button.

Can I format the text in an instant message I send?

✔ Yes. In the Conversation window, click Change font. You can add effects and change the font, font style and color of the text. You can also change the text size, but only the text displayed on your own screen will display the new size.

Can I save an instant message?

✔ You can save the text in the Conversation window as a file on your computer. In the Conversation window, click the File menu and select Save. Type a name for the file and then click the Save button.

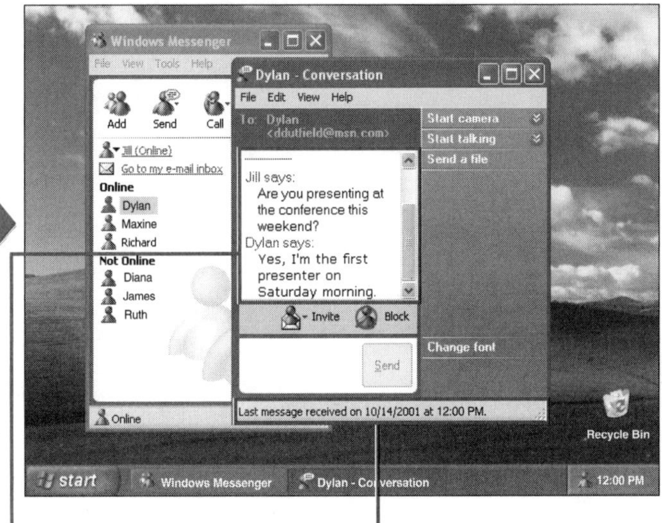

■ This area displays the message you sent and the ongoing conversation.

■ This area displays the date and time the last message was received. If the other person is typing a message, this area indicates that the person is typing.

EXCHANGE MESSAGES WITH SEVERAL PEOPLE

1 Click Invite to add a person to the conversation.

2 Click To Join This Conversation.

3 Click the name of the person you want to join the conversation.

CALL A COMPUTER

Windows Messenger allows you to call a computer to have a voice conversation with another person. Your computer and the computer you call must both have Windows Messenger installed. Both computers must also have sound capabilities and a microphone.

You can also call a computer to have a voice and video conversation. You must have a video camera to send video to the other person.

If the other person also has a video camera, you will see video from their camera during the conversation.

When you call a computer, Windows Messenger sends a message to the other person, inviting them to have a conversation with you. The other person must accept your call before you can have a conversation with the person.

The first time you call a computer, the Audio and Video Tuning Wizard appears on your screen to help you verify that your speakers, microphone and video camera are working properly.

During a call, you can control the sound level of the conversation by adjusting the speaker volume or turning off your microphone so you cannot be heard.

If your computer is connected to a network with a firewall, you may not be able to call a computer that is outside the network.

CALL A COMPUTER USING VOICE

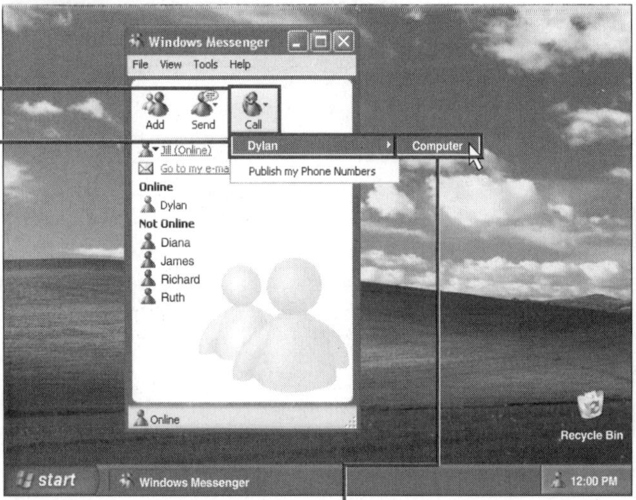

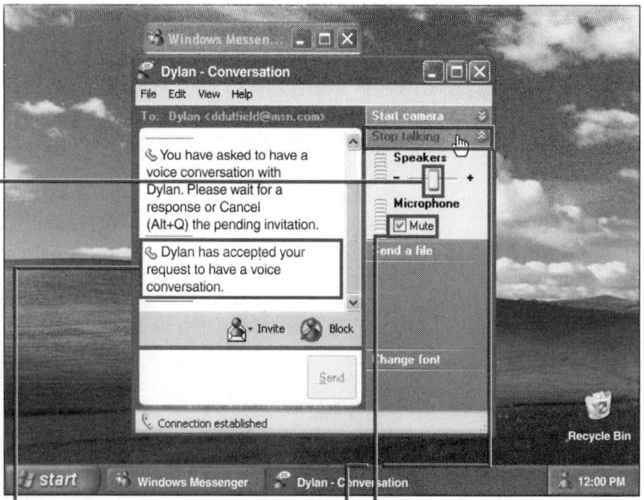

1 Click Call.

2 Click the name of the person you want to call.

3 Click Computer.

■ Windows Messenger sends a message to the other person, asking if they will accept your request to have a voice conversation.

■ This message appears when the other person accepts your request. You can use your microphone to talk to the other person.

4 To adjust the speaker volume, drag this slider ( ).

5 To temporarily turn off your microphone, click Mute (changes to).

Note: To once again turn on your microphone, click Mute again.

6 When you want to end the conversation, click Stop talking.

How can I run the Audio and Video Tuning Wizard again?

✔ In the Windows Messenger window, select the Tools menu and then click Audio and Video Tuning Wizard to start the wizard again. This is useful if you are having a problem with your microphone, speakers or video camera.

Can I stop sending video to the other person without ending the voice conversation?

✔ Yes. Below the video area, click Options and then select Stop Sending Video. Your camera will stop sending video to the other person, but the voice conversation will continue. You will also continue to receive video from the other person's camera.

How can I stop my video area from displaying a small image of the video sent by my camera?

✔ You can turn off the Picture-in-Picture option to stop the small image of the video sent by your camera from appearing in your video area. Click Options below the video area and then select Show My Video as Picture-in-Picture to turn the option off. You can repeat these steps to later turn on the Picture-in-Picture option again.

CALL A COMPUTER USING VOICE AND VIDEO

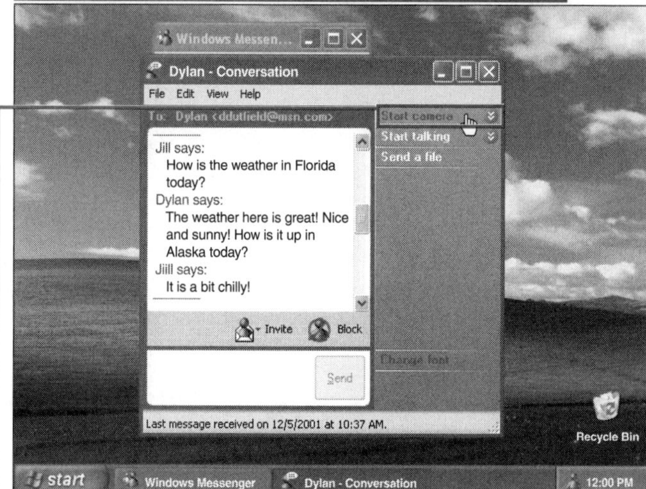

1 While exchanging instant messages with another person, click Start camera.

Note: For information about sending instant messages, see page 488.

■ Windows Messenger sends a message to the other person, asking if they will accept your request to have a voice and video conversation.

■ This message appears when the other person accepts your request. You can use your microphone to talk to the other person.

■ This area displays the video sent by the other person's camera and a smaller image of the video sent by your camera.

2 When you want to end the conversation, click Stop camera.

SEND A FILE

You can send a file to another person who is currently signed in to Windows Messenger. You can send any type of file, including a document, image, sound, video or program. The computer receiving the file must have the necessary hardware and software installed to display or play the file.

Before a file you want to send is transferred, the other person must accept the file. If you accidentally send a file, you can cancel the transfer before the other person accepts the file.

When someone sends you a file, the sender's name appears in the Conversation window, along with the name and size of the file. You can accept or decline the file.

Files you accept are automatically saved in the My Documents folder, in a subfolder called My Received Files. Windows creates this folder the first time you receive a file.

You should be very cautious of files you receive from people you do not know. When you receive a file, you should use an anti-virus program to check the file for viruses before opening the file.

If your computer is connected to a network with a firewall, you may not be able to send or receive files from contacts outside the network.

SEND A FILE

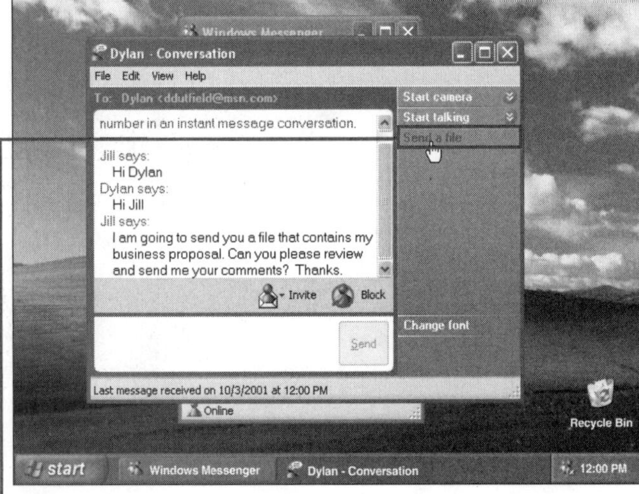

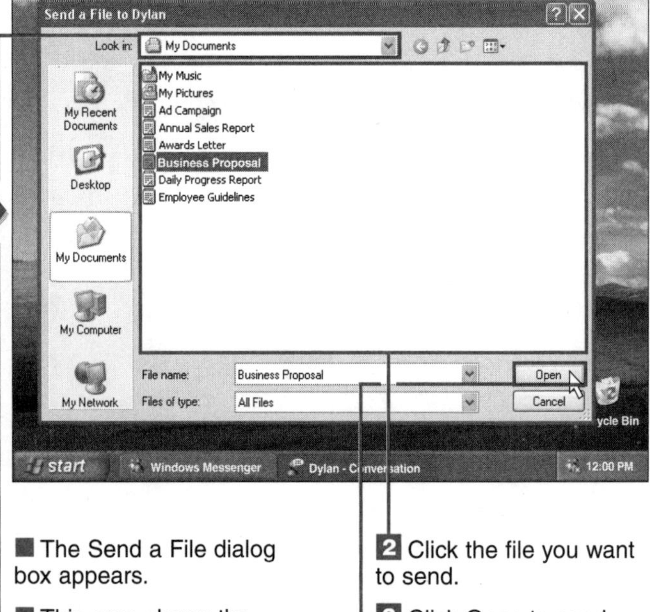

1 While exchanging instant messages with another person, click Send a file.

Note: For information on sending instant messages, see page 488.

■ The Send a File dialog box appears.

■ This area shows the location of the displayed files. You can click this area to change the location.

2 Click the file you want to send.

3 Click Open to send the file.

How do I open a file I received?

✔ After you have successfully received a file, the location and name of the file appear as a link in the Conversation window. You can click the link to open the file. To open a file later, display the Windows Messenger window, choose the File menu and select Open Received Files. Then double-click the file you want to open.

Can I change where Windows Messenger stores files I receive?

✔ Yes. In the Windows Messenger window, choose the Tools menu and click Options. In the Options dialog box, select the Preferences tab and then click the Browse button. In the Browse For Folder dialog box, select the folder where you want Windows Messenger to store files you receive.

How do I send a file when I am not in a conversation?

✔ In the Windows Messenger window, click the File menu, select Send a File To and then click the name of the contact you want to receive the file. If the person is not in your contact list, click Other, type the e-mail address of the person and click OK. Then perform steps 2 and 3 on page 492 to send the file.

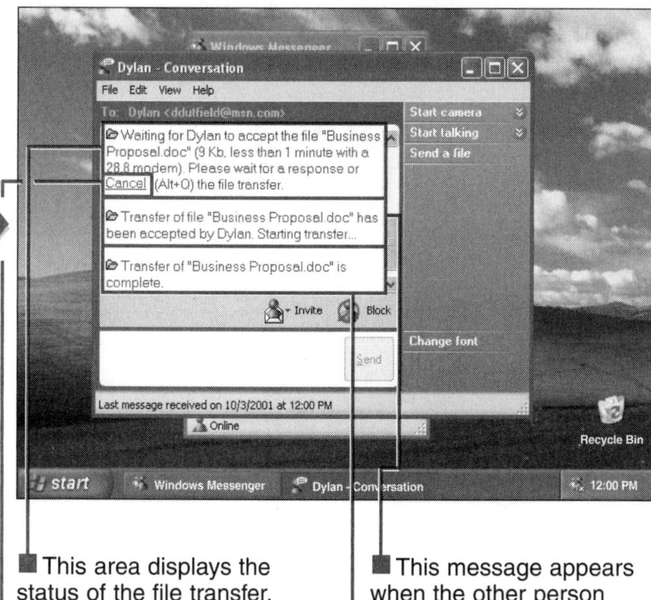

■ This area displays the status of the file transfer. The other person must accept the file before the file will transfer.

■ If you no longer want to send the file, click Cancel to stop the transfer of the file.

■ This message appears when the other person accepts the file.

■ This message appears when the file transfer is complete.

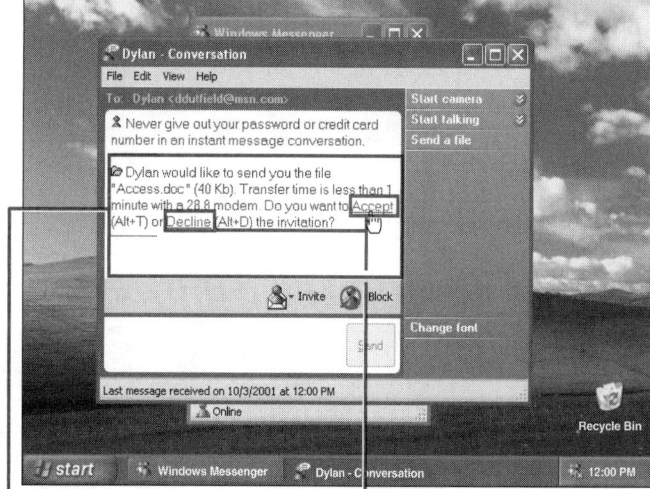

RECEIVE A FILE

■ When someone sends you a file, information about the file appears in the Conversation window.

Note: If the Conversation window is not displayed, click its button on the taskbar.

1 Click Accept or Decline to accept or decline the file.

Note: If you select Accept, a dialog box will appear, warning that some files may contain viruses. Click OK to receive the file.

USING THE WHITEBOARD

While exchanging instant messages with another person in Windows Messenger, you can invite the person to use the Whiteboard. The Whiteboard allows you to share and comment on information.

When you use the Whiteboard, both you and the other person will be able to see the comments and drawings made on the Whiteboard. The Whiteboard is useful for helping you describe, create and edit a project with another person. The Whiteboard is especially useful for displaying and discussing images and designs.

The Whiteboard tools are similar to the tools found in Microsoft Paint. Both you and the other person can use the Whiteboard tools to create lines and other basic shapes, such as rectangles and ellipses. You can both also use the tools to type text on the page and highlight information.

The Whiteboard provides a pointer tool that you and the other person can use to point out objects on the page. This allows you to easily draw attention to a specific object or an area of the page.

When you close the Whiteboard, you will be asked if you want to save the current contents of the Whiteboard.

USING THE WHITEBOARD

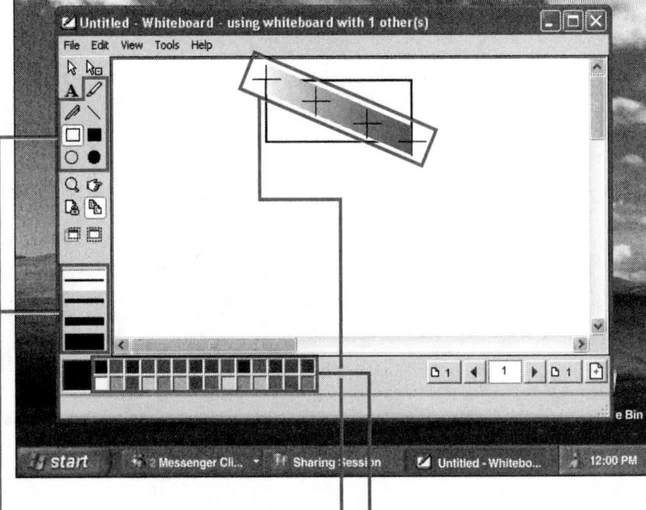

1 While exchanging instant messages with another person, click Invite.

2 Click To Start Whiteboard.

■ Windows Messenger sends a message to the other person, inviting them to use the Whiteboard. When the other person accepts the invitation, the Whiteboard window appears.

DRAW A LINE OR SHAPE

1 Click the tool for the type of object you want to draw.

2 Click a width for the object.

Note: The and tools do not provide width options.

3 Click a color for the object.

4 Position the mouse over the area where you want to begin drawing the object (changes to +, or). Then drag the mouse until the object appears the way you want.

Why did the Sharing Session toolbar appear?

✔ The Sharing Session toolbar appears when you share a program, such as the Whiteboard, with another person. The toolbar provides buttons you can use to work with programs or close a connection.

Can I add a new page to the Whiteboard?

✔ Yes. Click at the bottom of the Whiteboard window to insert a new page. You can then click the arrows (or) to move through the pages. When one person moves to another page, the other person will also see the new page.

How do I rearrange the objects on the Whiteboard?

✔ Click the Selector tool ( ) and then drag the object you want to move to a new location. To move an unfilled object, you must drag an edge of the object.

How do I delete an object on the Whiteboard?

✔ Click the Eraser tool ( ) and then click the object or text you want to delete.

Can I place a document on the Whiteboard?

✔ Yes. Open the document you want to place on the Whiteboard. In the Whiteboard window, click the Select Window tool ( ). In the dialog box that appears, click OK. Then click anywhere in the document you want to place on the Whiteboard.

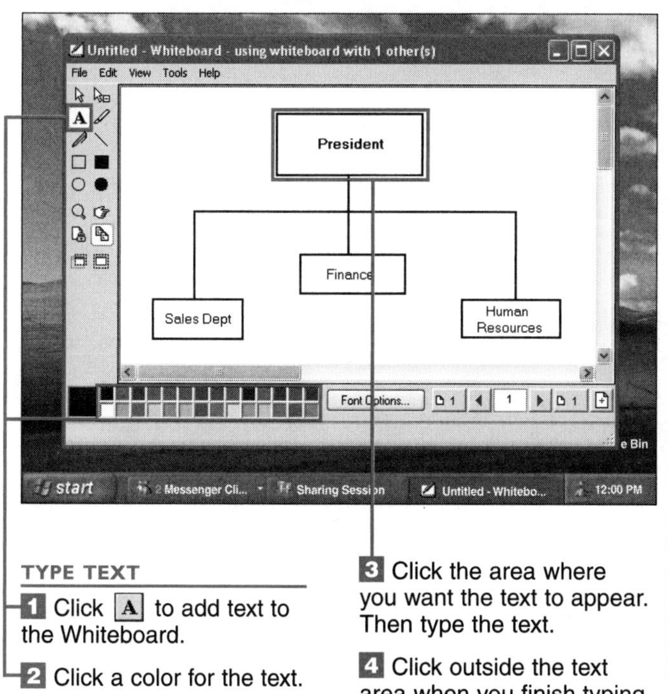

TYPE TEXT

1 Click A to add text to the Whiteboard.

2 Click a color for the text.

3 Click the area where you want the text to appear. Then type the text.

4 Click outside the text area when you finish typing the text.

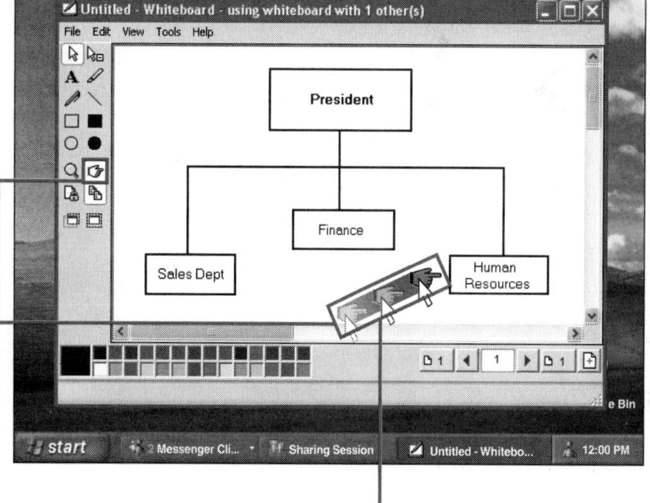

POINT TO AN OBJECT

1 Click to point to an object on the Whiteboard.

■ A hand ( ) appears on the Whiteboard.

2 Position the mouse over the hand and then drag the hand to the area you want to point out.

Note: You can repeat step 1 to hide the hand.

SHARE A PROGRAM

While exchanging instant messages with another person in Windows Messenger, you can share a program with the person. This allows you and the other person to work together.

Sharing a program is useful when you want to present a demonstration while another person watches you work. The person will be able to see the program even if they do not have the program installed on their computer. If you want the person to be able to work with the program, you can grant them control of the program.

You can also share items such as your desktop or an open folder on your computer. If you share the desktop, your entire computer will be shared. If you share a folder, My Computer window or Windows Explorer window, Windows Messenger will automatically share all the folders you have open. Windows Messenger will also share any folders and programs you open after sharing one of these items.

When you share a program, the other person cannot save or print information from the shared program on their own computer. If you want the person to have a copy of the information, you must send them the file. To send a file using Windows Messenger, see page 492.

SHARE A PROGRAM

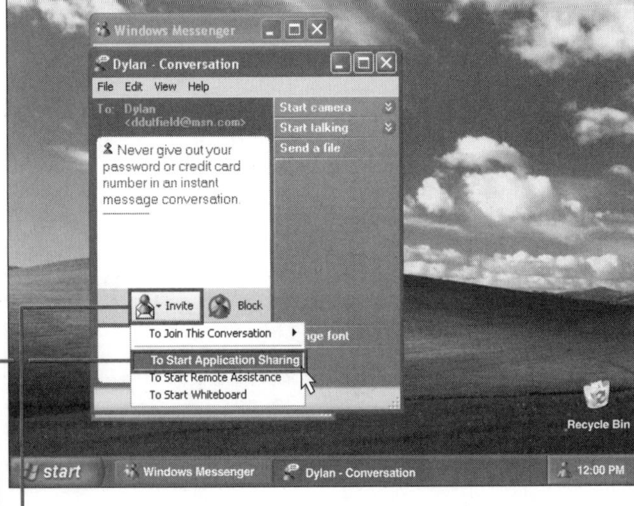

1 While exchanging instant messages with another person, click Invite.

2 Click To Start Application Sharing.

■ Windows Messenger sends a message to the other person, inviting them to start sharing programs. When the other person accepts the invitation, the Sharing window appears.

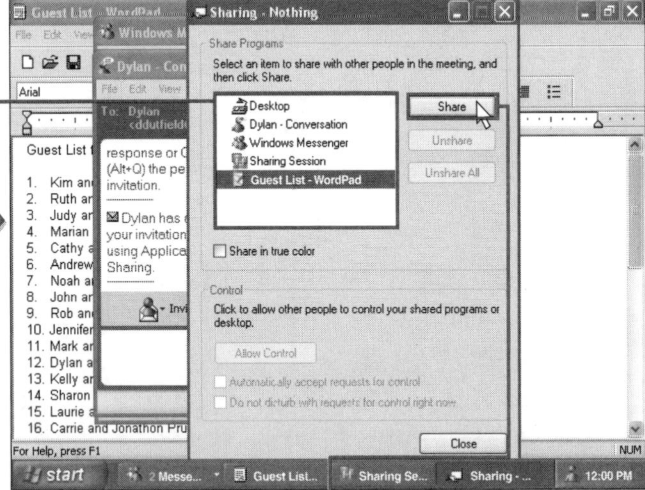

3 Start the program you want to share.

■ This area lists the programs running on your computer that you can share.

4 Click the program you want to share.

Note: You can select Desktop to share your entire computer.

5 Click Share to share the program.

Can I have Windows Messenger automatically accept requests for control of a program I shared?

✔ Yes. This is useful when you do not want a dialog box to appear each time the other person requests control. In the Sharing window, click the Automatically accept requests for control option (☐ changes to ☑).

How can I share multiple programs at the same time?

✔ You can repeat steps 3 to 5 below for each program you want to share. To quickly stop sharing all the programs, you can click the Unshare All button.

How do I work with a program another person has shared?

✔ In the window for the shared program, choose the Control menu and then click Request Control. The other person must accept your request before you can work with the program. The Request Control option is only available if the other person has chosen to allow control of the program.

A shared program is covered with a pattern of colored squares. What is wrong?

✔ The person sharing the program currently has other windows open in front of the shared program. Before you can properly view the shared program, the other person must make the shared program the active window by clicking in the program's window.

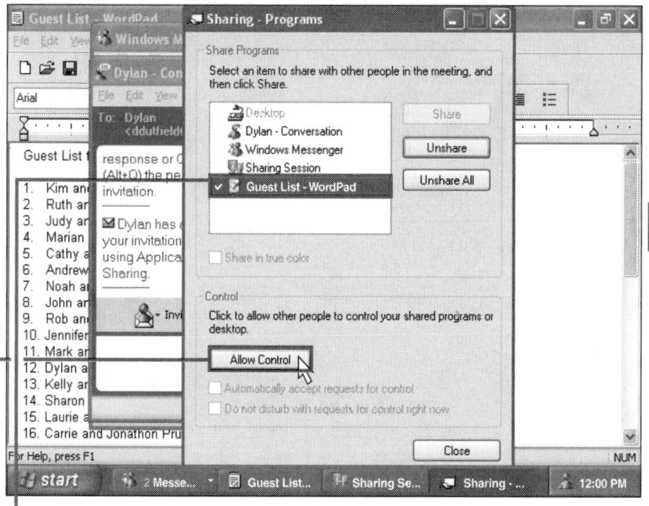

■ A check mark (✔) appears beside the program you selected to share.

6 Click Allow Control if you want the other person to be able to work with the program.

Note: When you click Allow Control, the button changes to Prevent Control. You can click Prevent Control at any time to stop allowing the other person to work with the program.

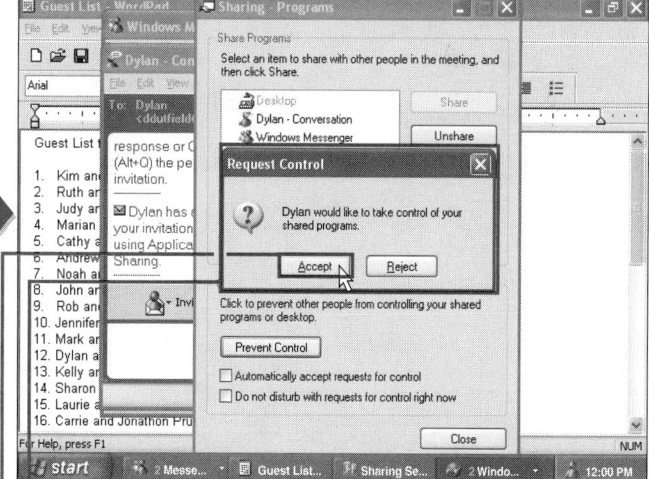

■ A dialog box appears when the other person wants to control the program.

7 Click Accept to allow the person to take control of the program and make changes.

Note: To regain control of the program at any time, click your mouse or press the Esc key.

■ To stop sharing a program, double-click the program in the Sharing window. The check mark (✔) beside the program disappears.

CHANGE WINDOWS MESSENGER OPTIONS

Windows Messenger provides a variety of options you can customize to suit your preferences.

You can change your display name to change the way your name appears to other people in Windows Messenger. People who have added you to their contact list will immediately see your new name.

You can have Windows Messenger ask for your password each time you check your Hotmail account or access Web pages that use .NET Passports. This is useful if you share your computer with other people.

You can turn emoticons on or off for instant messages. Emoticons are small graphics that are used to convey emotion. When you type certain characters, such as :) or (1), Windows Messenger can convert the characters to graphics, such as ☺ and ♥ when you send the message.

Windows Messenger also allows you to make your home, work and mobile phone numbers available to people on your contact list.

You can specify whether you want Windows Messenger to start automatically when you turn on your computer and whether you want Windows Messenger to run in the background. By default, when you close the Windows Messenger window, the program continues to run in the background. When you turn this feature off, closing the Windows Messenger window will close the program.

CHANGE WINDOWS MESSENGER OPTIONS

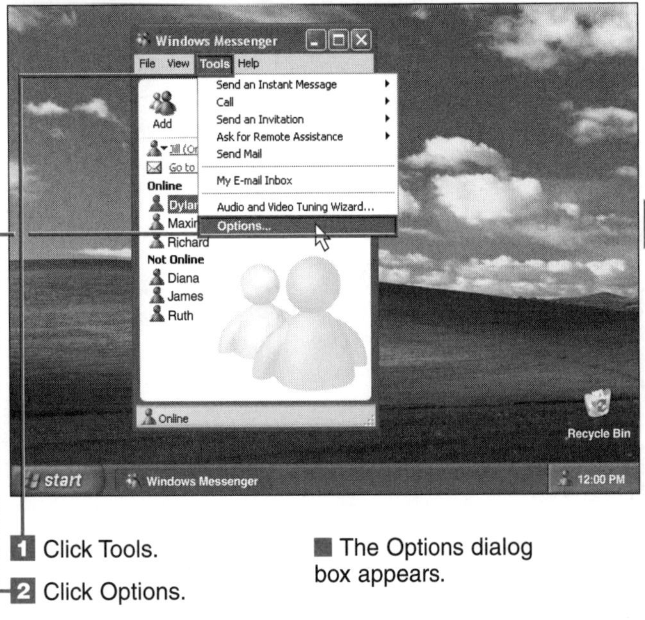

1 Click Tools.

2 Click Options.

■ The Options dialog box appears.

3 This area displays the way your name will appear to other people. To change the way your name will appear, type a new name.

■ This option instructs Windows to ask for your password when checking Hotmail or when opening Web pages that use a .NET Passport.

■ This option converts certain characters typed in instant messages to graphics.

4 To turn an option on (☑) or off (☐), click the option.

Can I change the font Windows Messenger uses for instant messages I send?

✔ Yes. On the Personal tab, click the Change Font button. In the dialog box that appears, you can select a new font, style, size and color for instant message text. When you send an instant message to another person, the person will see text with the font, style and color you specified. The person will not see changes you made to the size of text. The new text size will be displayed only in your own instant message window.

Where will the phone numbers I made available to other people appear?

✔ People who have added you to their contact list can right-click your name in the list and then select Properties to see your phone numbers.

Is there another way to make my phone numbers available?

✔ Yes. While working in the Windows Messenger window, you can click the Call button and then select Publish my Phone Numbers to quickly display the Phone tab of the Options dialog box. Type your phone numbers in the appropriate areas and then click OK.

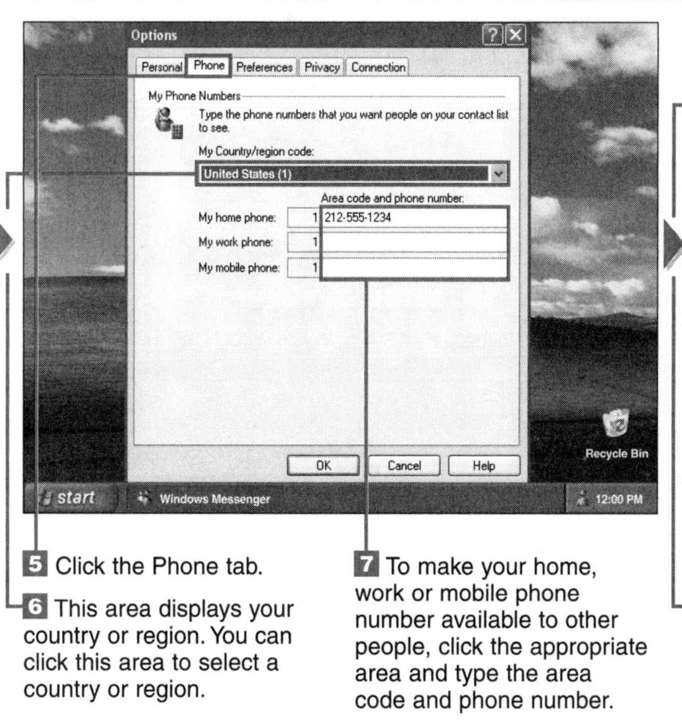

5 Click the Phone tab.

6 This area displays your country or region. You can click this area to select a country or region.

7 To make your home, work or mobile phone number available to other people, click the appropriate area and type the area code and phone number.

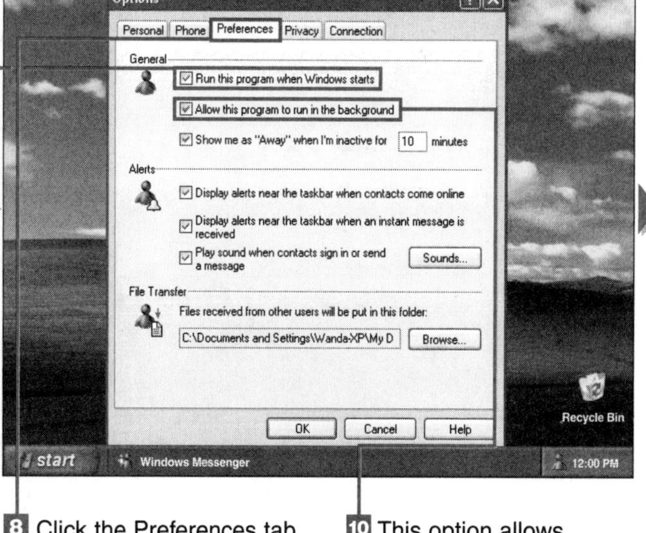

8 Click the Preferences tab.

9 This option starts Windows Messenger each time you turn on your computer. You can click the option to turn the option on (☑) or off (☐).

10 This option allows Windows Messenger to run in the background while you use other programs. You can click the option to turn the option on (☑) or off (☐).

CONTINUED

CHANGE WINDOWS MESSENGER OPTIONS (CONTINUED)

When you do not use your computer for a period of time, Windows Messenger displays your status as "Away" so that other people will know you are not available. You can specify the amount of time that you want to pass before your status will change. You can also turn this feature off to stop Windows Messenger from displaying your status as "Away."

You can specify whether you want Windows Messenger to alert you when your contacts come online or when you receive an instant message. Windows Messenger can alert you by displaying a message near your taskbar and playing a sound.

Windows Messenger provides the My Allow List and My Block List, which allow you to control who can see your online status and send you instant messages. You can add a person to your My Block List to prevent the person from seeing your status and contacting you.

When a person adds you to their contact list, Windows Messenger notifies you and allows you to specify whether you want the person to be able to see your online status and contact you. You can turn this feature off to stop Windows Messenger from notifying you each time a person adds you to their list.

CHANGE WINDOWS MESSENGER OPTIONS (CONTINUED)

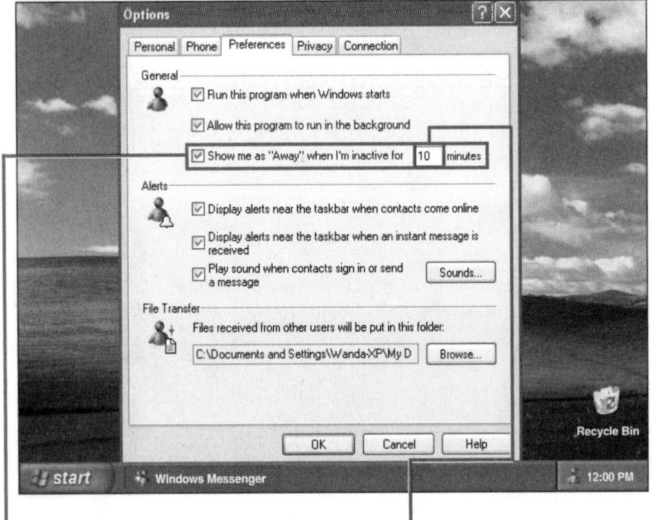

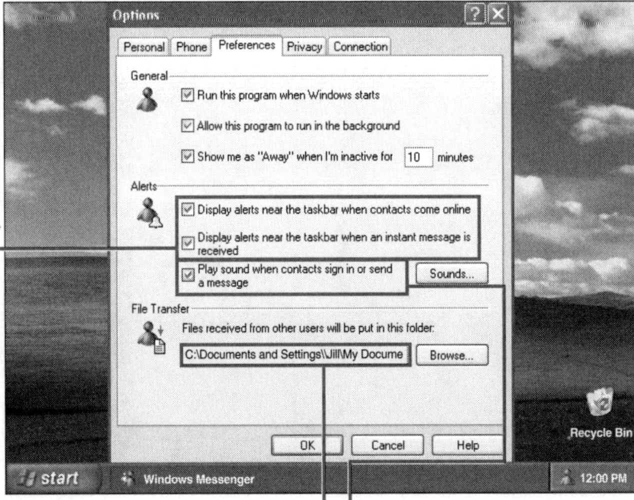

11 This option shows your status as "Away" when you do not use your computer for a certain period of time. You can click the option to turn the option on (☑) or off (☐).

12 To change the amount of time before your status changes to "Away," double-click this area and type a new number of minutes.

13 These options display an alert message when your contacts sign in or when you receive an instant message. You can click an option to turn the option on (☑) or off (☐).

14 This option plays a sound when your contacts sign in or send an instant message. You can click the option to turn the option on (☑) or off (☐).

■ Windows Messenger will store files you receive from other people in this location.

Is there another way to change my status to "Away"?

✔ Yes. You can manually set your status to "Away" when you do not want people to contact you. Click File, select My Status and then choose Away. To once again set your status to "Online," click File, select My Status and choose Online.

How can I change the location where Windows Messenger will store files I receive from other people?

✔ In the Options dialog box, choose the Preferences tab and then click the Browse button in the File Transfer area. In the dialog box that appears, select the folder where you want to store the files and then click OK. For more information about receiving files from other people, see page 492.

Can someone who does not appear in the My Allow List contact me?

✔ Yes. By default, anyone who knows your Passport e-mail address can contact you, as long as you have not added the person to your My Block List. To quickly block everyone who does not appear in your My Allow List from contacting you, choose All other users in the My Allow List and then click Block.

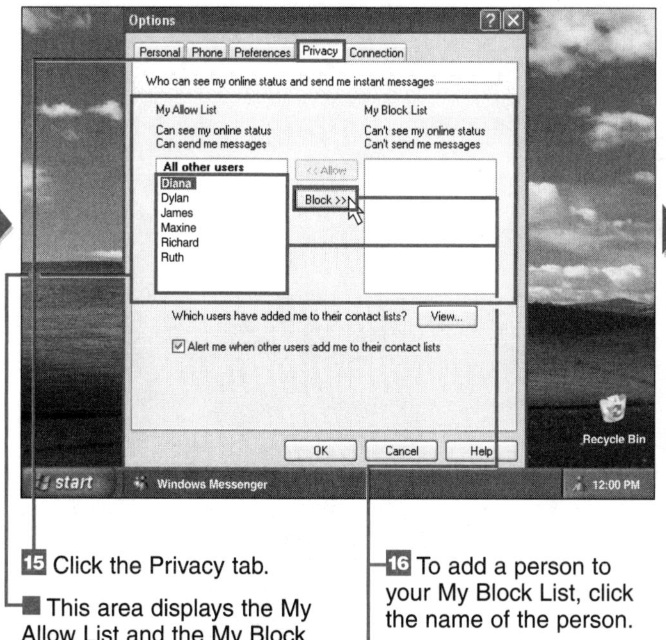

15 Click the Privacy tab.

■ This area displays the My Allow List and the My Block List, which show who can see your online status and send you instant messages.

16 To add a person to your My Block List, click the name of the person.

17 Click Block.

■ The person you selected appears in your My Block List.

Note: To return a person to your My Allow List, click the person's name and then click Allow.

18 This option alerts you when other people add you to their contacts list. You can click this option to turn the option on (☑) or off (☐).

19 Click OK to confirm all your changes.

SET UP A NEWS ACCOUNT

You must set up a news account before you can use Outlook Express to read or post messages in newsgroups. Newsgroups allow people with common interests to communicate with each other.

The Internet Connection Wizard helps you set up a news account. You must provide the wizard with information, such as your name and e-mail address. If you have already set up your e-mail account, the wizard will automatically display your name and e-mail address.

When you post a message to a newsgroup, the name you specify in the wizard will appear in the From area of the message. If a reader wants to comment on a message you post, they can send you a reply. The reply will be sent to the e-mail address you specify in the wizard.

You do not have to use your real name and e-mail address. Specifying a false e-mail address prevents junk mailers from sending you automatic messages. If you do not use your real e-mail address, remember to include your real e-mail address in the body of your message if you want other readers to be able to contact you.

SET UP A NEWS ACCOUNT

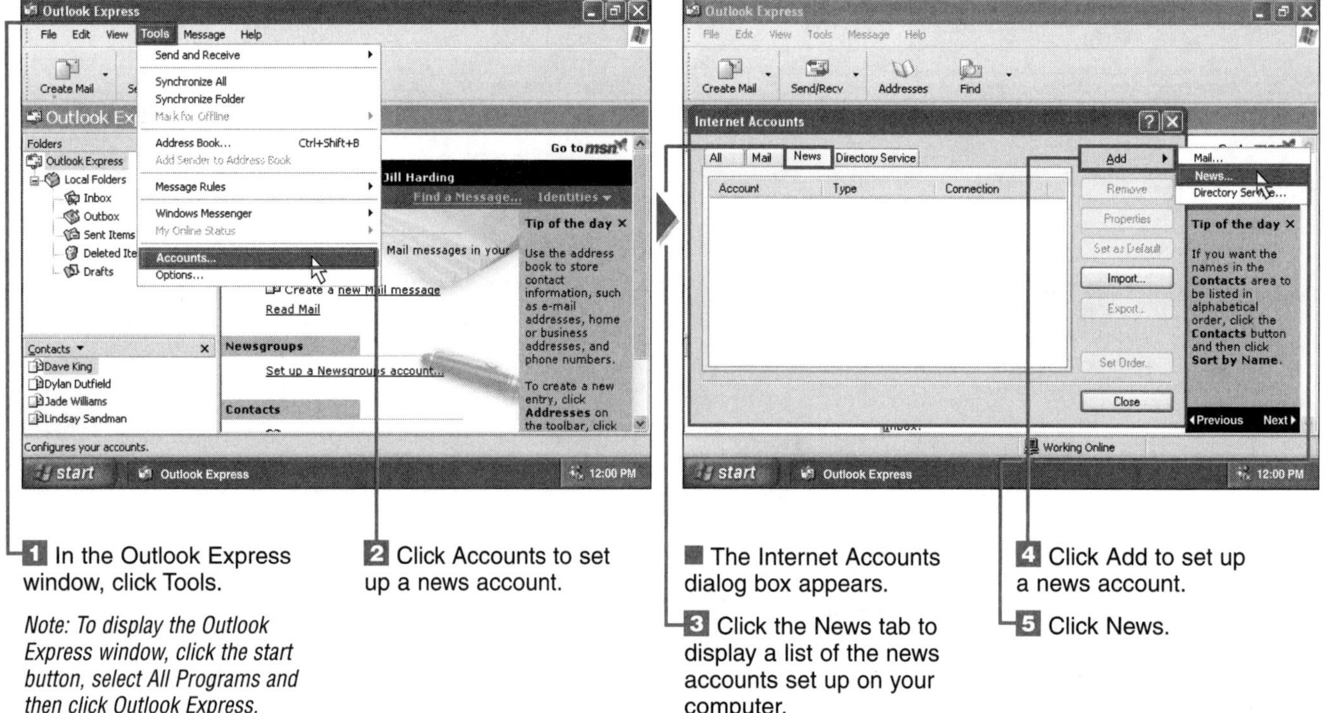

1 In the Outlook Express window, click Tools.

Note: To display the Outlook Express window, click the start button, select All Programs and then click Outlook Express.

2 Click Accounts to set up a news account.

■ The Internet Accounts dialog box appears.

3 Click the News tab to display a list of the news accounts set up on your computer.

4 Click Add to set up a news account.

5 Click News.

Can I set up more than one news account?

✔ Yes. You can set up multiple news accounts in Outlook Express. Setting up multiple news accounts allows you to access information from different news servers. For example, you could set up one news account to access newsgroups on your Internet service provider's news server and another account to access a news server set up by a company to provide product support, such as news.creativelabs.com.

Is there another way to set up a news account?

✔ Yes. In the Outlook Express window, select Outlook Express in the folders list and then click the Set up a Newsgroups account link to display the Internet Connection Wizard. This link is available only until you set up your first news account.

How do I delete a news account I no longer use?

✔ In the Internet Accounts dialog box, choose the News tab, select the news account you want to delete and then click the Remove button.

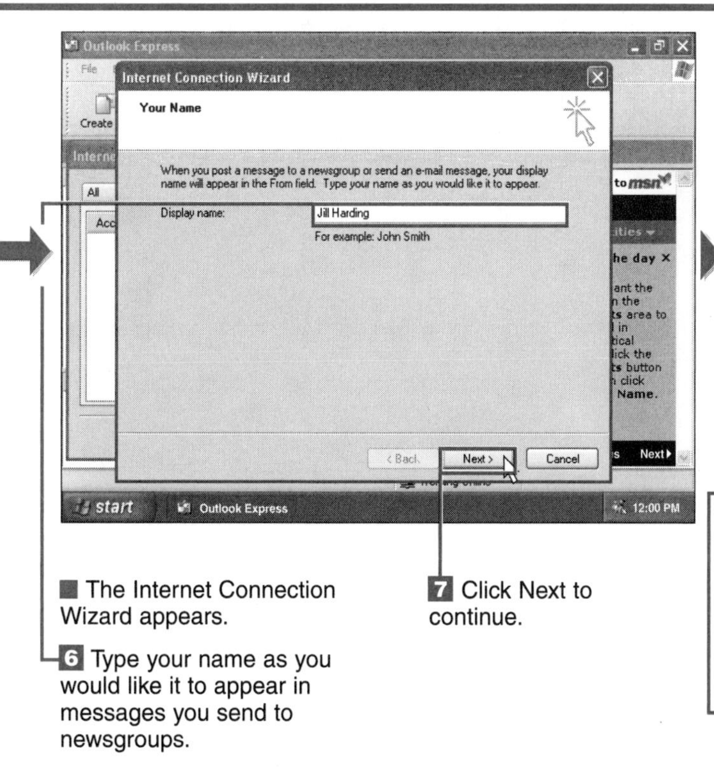

■ The Internet Connection Wizard appears.

6 Type your name as you would like it to appear in messages you send to newsgroups.

7 Click Next to continue.

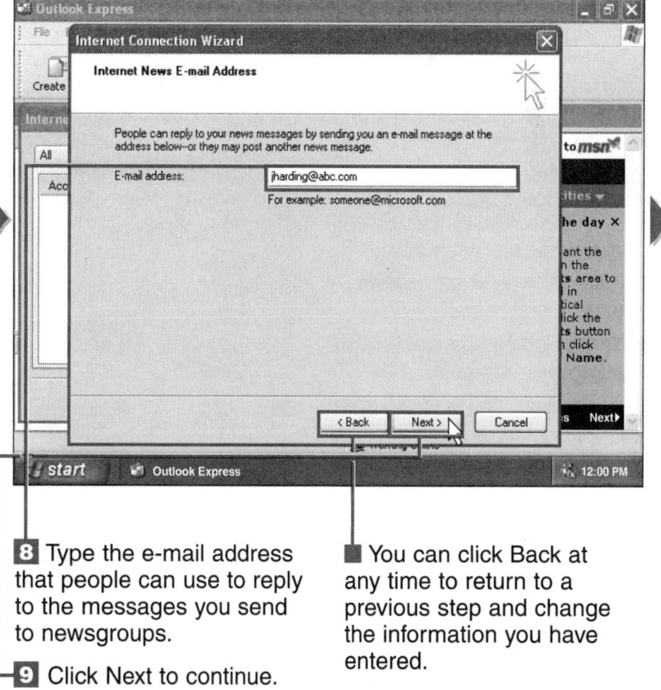

8 Type the e-mail address that people can use to reply to the messages you send to newsgroups.

9 Click Next to continue.

■ You can click Back at any time to return to a previous step and change the information you have entered.

CONTINUED

SET UP A NEWS ACCOUNT (CONTINUED)

Newsgroups are stored on computers called news servers, which are usually run and maintained by Internet service providers. When using the Internet Connection Wizard to set up a news account, you must specify the name of the news server you want to connect to. If you do not know the name of your news server, contact your Internet service provider.

Once you have set up your news account, you can have Outlook Express download a list of newsgroups from the news server. The available newsgroups that will appear in the list depend on your news server. It may take Outlook Express a few minutes to download the entire list of newsgroups. You only need to download the entire list once.

After you download the list of newsgroups to your computer, you can subscribe to newsgroups you want to read on a regular basis. For information about subscribing to newsgroups, see page 506.

The name of the news server you specified appears in the folders list in the Outlook Express window.

SET UP A NEWS ACCOUNT (CONTINUED)

10 Type the name of the news server provided by your Internet service provider.

11 Click Next to continue.

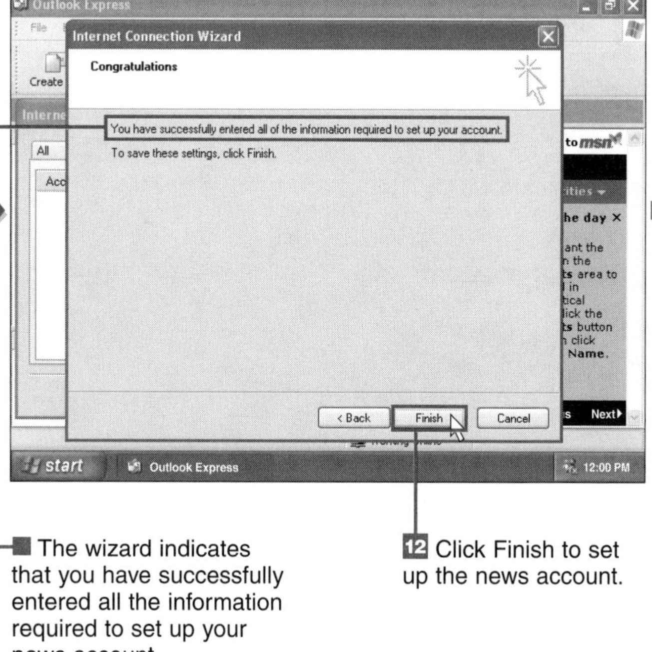

■ The wizard indicates that you have successfully entered all the information required to set up your news account.

12 Click Finish to set up the news account.

My Internet service provider gave me an account name and password to log on to the news server. Where do I enter this information?

✔ After entering the name of your news server in the Internet Connection Wizard, click the My news server requires me to log on option and then click Next. Enter your account name and password and then click Next.

Does Microsoft offer a news server with newsgroups that can help me with Windows XP?

✔ Yes. The msnews.microsoft.com news server contains hundreds of newsgroups that can help you use various Microsoft products, including Windows XP.

How do I change the settings for my news account?

✔ In the Internet Accounts dialog box, choose the News tab and then double-click the account you want to change. You can change information such as your name, e-mail address and the name of your news server.

Can I download the list of newsgroups from a news server at a later time?

✔ If you selected No in step 14 below, you can download the list of newsgroups at a later time. When you want to download the list of newsgroups, click the name of the news server in the folders list in the Outlook Express window. In the dialog box that appears, click Yes to download the list of newsgroups.

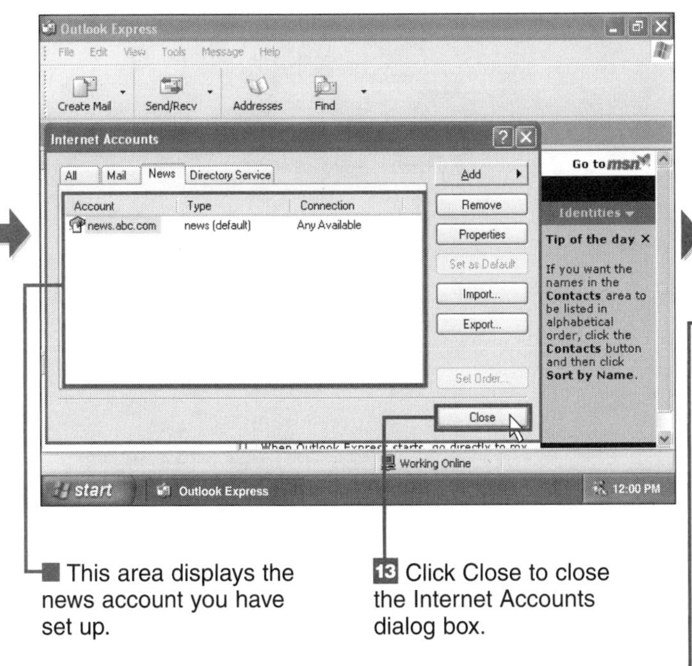

■ This area displays the news account you have set up.

13 Click Close to close the Internet Accounts dialog box.

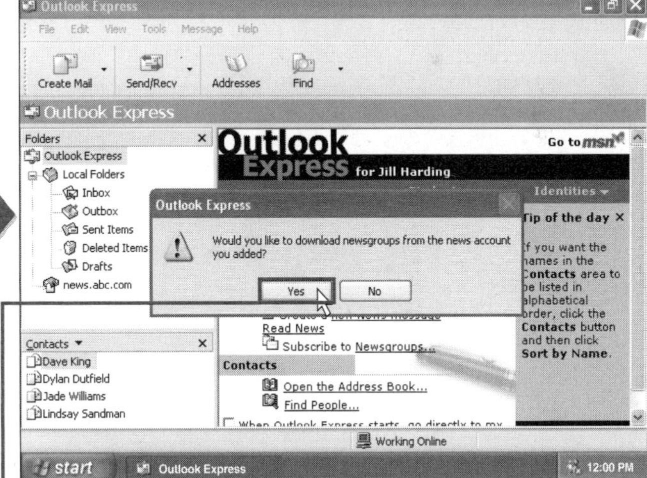

■ A dialog box appears, asking if you want to download a list of newsgroups for the news account you have set up.

14 Click Yes to download the list of newsgroups to your computer.

■ A dialog box will appear, indicating the progress of the download.

Note: When the download is complete, you can subscribe to newsgroups that you want to read on a regular basis. To subscribe to newsgroups, see page 506.

SUBSCRIBE TO NEWSGROUPS

You can use Outlook Express to subscribe to newsgroups. Newsgroups allow people with common interests to communicate with each other. Subscribing to newsgroups gives you quick access to information you want to read on a regular basis.

Newsgroups are stored on computers called news servers, which are usually run and maintained by Internet service providers. The newsgroups available to you depend on your news server. You can have Outlook Express display a list of all the newsgroups available on your news server.

There are thousands of newsgroups on every subject imaginable. The name of a newsgroup describes the type of information discussed in the newsgroup. A newsgroup name consists of two or more words, separated by dots (.). The first word describes the main topic of the newsgroup. Each of the following words narrows the topic. For example, the rec.music.folk newsgroup contains messages from folk music enthusiasts.

The main newsgroup categories include alt (alternative), biz (business), comp (computers), k12 (kindergarten to grade 12 or education related), misc (miscellaneous), news, rec (recreation), sci (science), soc (social) and talk.

SUBSCRIBE TO NEWSGROUPS

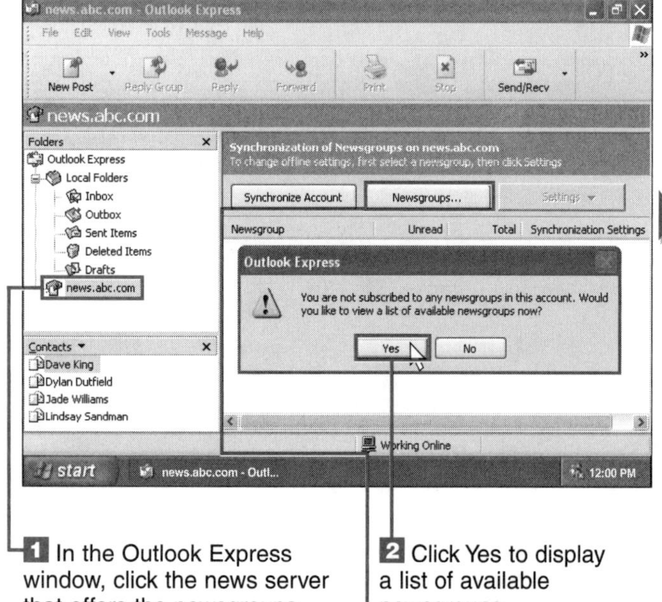

1 In the Outlook Express window, click the news server that offers the newsgroups you want to subscribe to.

■ A dialog box appears if you are not subscribed to any newsgroups.

2 Click Yes to display a list of available newsgroups.

■ If the dialog box does not appear, click Newsgroups to display a list of available newsgroups.

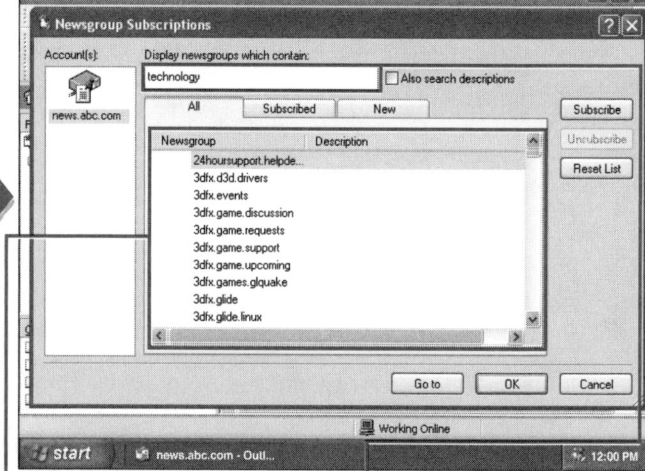

■ The Newsgroup Subscriptions dialog box appears.

■ This area displays an alphabetical list of the available newsgroups. You can use the scroll bar to browse through the list.

3 To find newsgroup names that contain a word of interest, click this area and then type the word of interest.

Are there any newsgroups designed for beginners?

✔ Yes. The news.newusers.questions newsgroup provides useful information and lets you ask questions about newsgroups.

How can I expand my search for newsgroups?

✔ Some newsgroups provide descriptions that offer information about the newsgroups. After typing a word of interest in the Newsgroup Subscriptions dialog box, select the Also search descriptions option (☐ changes to ☑) to include the descriptions of newsgroups in your search. In the dialog box that appears, click Yes to download the descriptions of newsgroups.

Can I view the messages in a newsgroup without subscribing to the newsgroup?

✔ Yes. In the Newsgroup Subscriptions dialog box, select the newsgroup that contains the messages you want to read and then click Go to.

Are there other ways to display a list of newsgroups?

✔ Yes. The Newsgroup Subscriptions dialog box has three tabs. You can click the All tab to view all the available newsgroups. You can click the Subscribed tab to view newsgroups you are subscribed to. Click the New tab to display new newsgroups that have been added since you last connected to the news server.

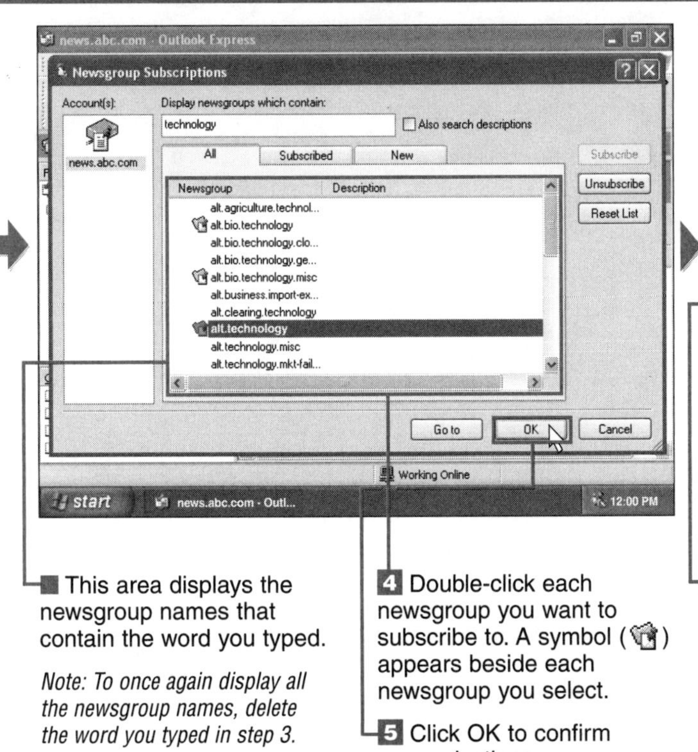

■ This area displays the newsgroup names that contain the word you typed.

Note: To once again display all the newsgroup names, delete the word you typed in step 3.

4 Double-click each newsgroup you want to subscribe to. A symbol ( ) appears beside each newsgroup you select.

5 Click OK to confirm your selections.

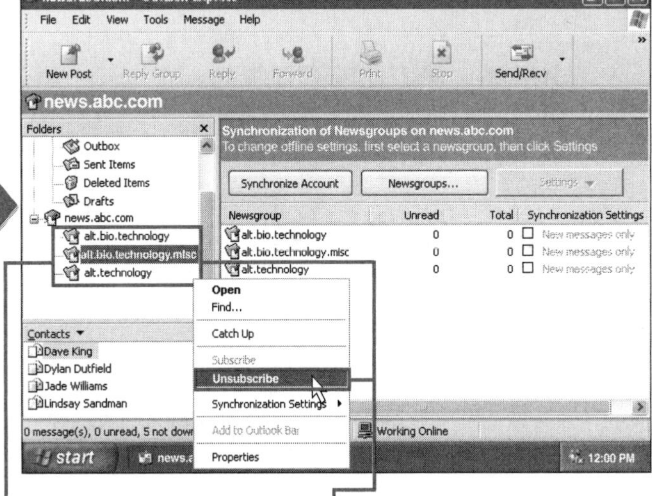

■ This area displays a list of the newsgroups you are subscribed to.

■ If you cannot see the list of newsgroups, click the plus sign (⊞) beside the news server (⊞ changes to ⊟).

UNSUBSCRIBE FROM NEWSGROUPS

1 In the Outlook Express window, right-click the newsgroup you want to unsubscribe from. A menu appears.

2 Click Unsubscribe.

READ NEWSGROUP MESSAGES

You can read the messages in a newsgroup to learn the opinions and ideas of thousands of people around the world.

Newsgroup messages that people have replied to display a plus sign (⊞). The original message and all its replies are referred to as a conversation. Outlook Express groups an original message and its replies into a conversation to help you easily keep track of related messages. For example, a message with the title "Tips for Windows XP" would be grouped with replies titled "Re: Tips for Windows XP." You can choose to view only the original message or the message and all its replies.

Some newsgroups include a message called a FAQ (Frequently Asked Questions). A FAQ normally contains a list of questions and answers that regularly appear in a newsgroup. A FAQ helps prevent new readers from posting questions that have already been answered. The news.answers newsgroup provides FAQs for a wide variety of newsgroups.

When you select a newsgroup to read, Outlook Express downloads only the first 300 messages in the newsgroup by default. If more messages are available for the newsgroup, you can download the additional messages.

READ NEWSGROUP MESSAGES

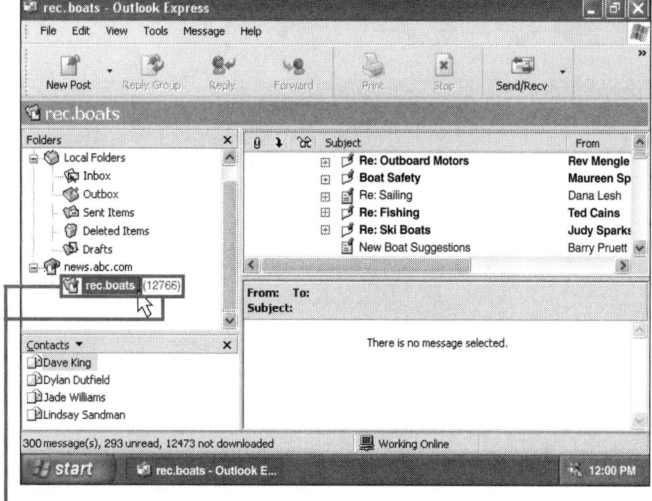

1 Click the newsgroup that contains the messages you want to read. The newsgroup is highlighted.

■ The number in parentheses beside a newsgroup indicates how many unread messages the newsgroup contains.

Note: If you cannot see the list of newsgroups you are subscribed to, click the plus sign (⊞) beside the news server (⊞ changes to ⊟).

■ This area displays the messages in the newsgroup you selected. Messages you have not read appear in bold.

2 Click a message you want to read.

■ The contents of the message appear in this area.

■ To view the contents of another message, click the message.

How do I hide the messages I have read?

✔ Click the View menu, select Current View and then choose Hide Read Messages to hide the messages you have read. You can choose Show All Messages to once again display all the messages in a newsgroup.

How do I mark a message as read without viewing it?

✔ Click the message you want to mark as read, select the Edit menu and then choose Mark as Read. You can mark an entire conversation as read by choosing Mark Conversation as Read. If you want to mark all the messages in a newsgroup as read, choose Mark All Read.

Can I search for a message of interest?

✔ Yes. You can easily find a message of interest by providing information about the message, such as the name of the sender of the message or a word that appears in the subject of the message. Click the newsgroup containing the messages you want to search and then perform steps 2 to 12 on page 478 to find the message of interest.

Can I sort newsgroup messages?

✔ Yes. Sorting messages can help you find messages on a certain subject or written by a particular person. To sort messages, click the heading for the column you want to use to sort the messages. To sort the messages in the opposite order, click the column heading again.

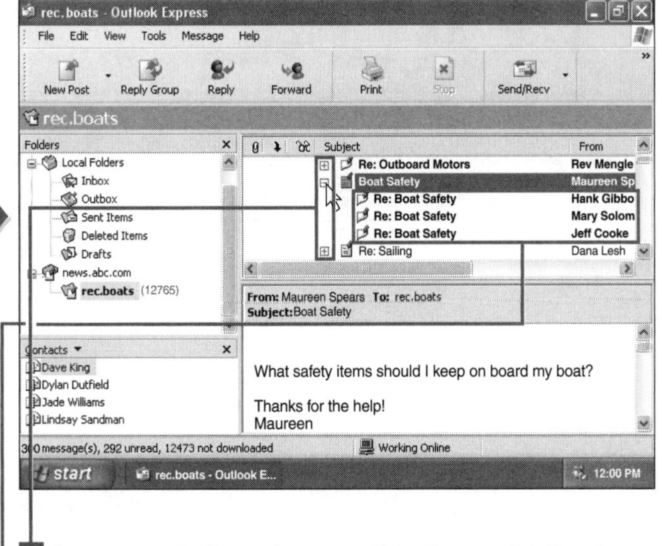

3 A message that people have replied to displays a plus sign (⊞). To display the replies to a message, click the plus sign beside the message (⊞ changes to ⊟).

■ The replies to the message appear.

Note: You can click the minus sign (⊟) beside a message to once again hide the replies to the message (⊟ changes to ⊞).

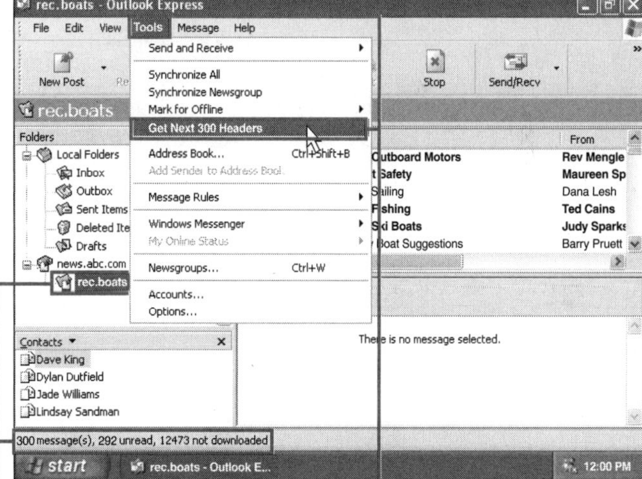

DOWNLOAD MORE MESSAGES

1 Click the newsgroup that contains additional messages you want to download.

■ This area shows the number of displayed messages, unread messages and messages you have not yet downloaded.

2 Click Tools.

3 Click Get Next 300 Headers to download more messages.

SEND A MESSAGE

You can send, or post, a new message to a newsgroup if you want to ask a question or express an opinion. Thousands of people around the world may read a message you post.

Before sending a message to a newsgroup, read the messages in the newsgroup for at least a week to learn how people in the newsgroup communicate.

When posting a message, you should include a subject. Some news servers may not accept a message that does not have a subject. A descriptive subject will help readers identify the content of the message. For example, the subject "Fishing boat for sale" is more informative than "Read this now." You should also make sure that your message is clear, concise and contains no spelling or grammar errors.

To practice sending a message, post a message to the misc.test or alt.test newsgroup. If you send a test message to other newsgroups, you may receive unwanted replies or flames.

You can reply to a newsgroup message to answer a question or supply information. You can send a reply to the entire newsgroup or only the author of the message.

When you reply to a message, Outlook Express includes a copy of the original message to help readers identify which message you are replying to. This is called quoting.

POST A NEW MESSAGE

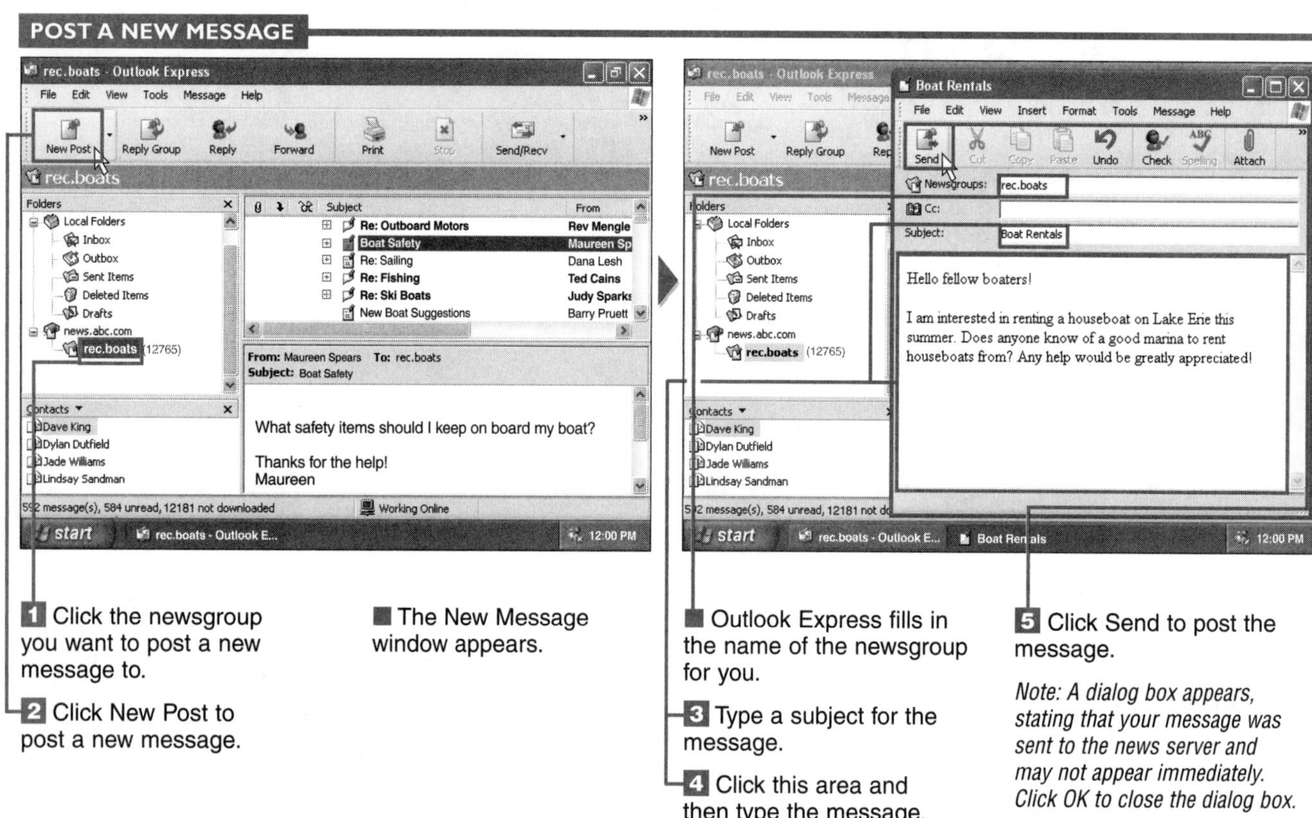

1 Click the newsgroup you want to post a new message to.

2 Click New Post to post a new message.

■ The New Message window appears.

■ Outlook Express fills in the name of the newsgroup for you.

3 Type a subject for the message.

4 Click this area and then type the message.

5 Click Send to post the message.

Note: A dialog box appears, stating that your message was sent to the news server and may not appear immediately. Click OK to close the dialog box.

Can I cancel a message I sent to a newsgroup?

✔ Yes. Select the newsgroup you sent the message to and then click the message you want to cancel. Choose the Message menu and then click Cancel Message. Keep in mind that the message may not be canceled immediately. If someone downloaded the message before you canceled it, the message will not be removed from the person's computer.

What is a flame?

✔ When other readers do not like your message, they may reply to your message in a negative or hostile manner. These rude messages are called flames. You should ignore flames.

Do I have to use my real name in my messages?

✔ No. Choose the Tools menu and then click Accounts. Select the News tab, choose the news server you use to post messages and then click the Properties button to change the name and e-mail address that appear in your messages. Changing your e-mail address prevents junk mailers from sending you automatic messages. If you want other readers to be able to contact you, remember to include your real e-mail address in the body of your message.

REPLY TO A MESSAGE

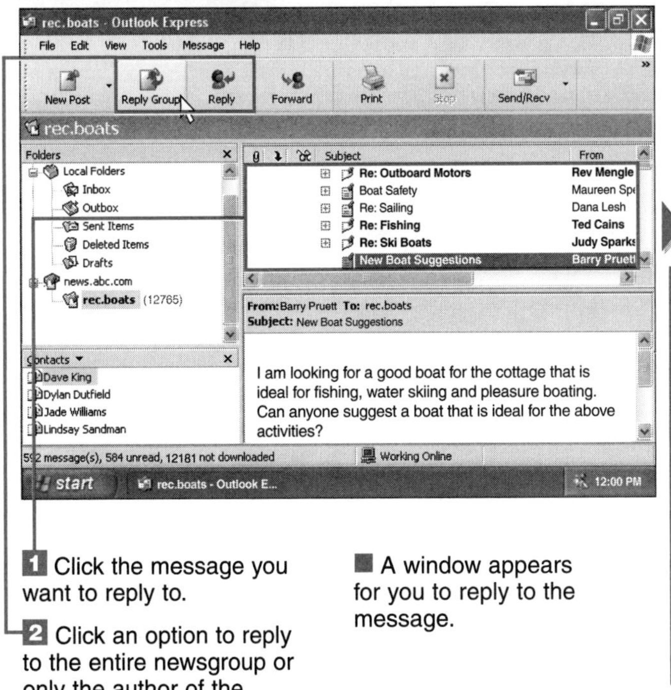

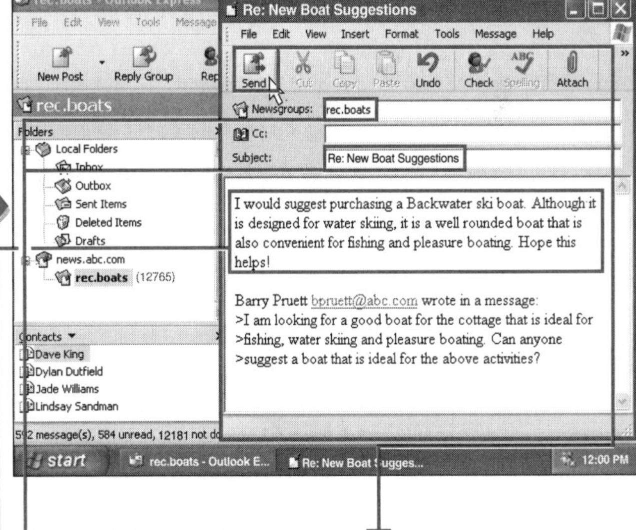

1 Click the message you want to reply to.

2 Click an option to reply to the entire newsgroup or only the author of the message.

■ A window appears for you to reply to the message.

■ Outlook Express fills in the newsgroup name or e-mail address and the subject for you.

3 Click this area and then type your reply.

4 Click Send to send the reply.

Note: A dialog box appears, stating that your message was sent to the news server and may not appear immediately. Click OK to close the dialog box.

SECTION VIII

25) DISK MANAGEMENT

26) INSTALL SOFTWARE AND HARDWARE

27) INSTALL AND UPDATE WINDOWS XP

MANAGE HARDWARE AND SOFTWARE

28) MANAGE COMPUTER AND TROUBLESHOOT PROBLEMS

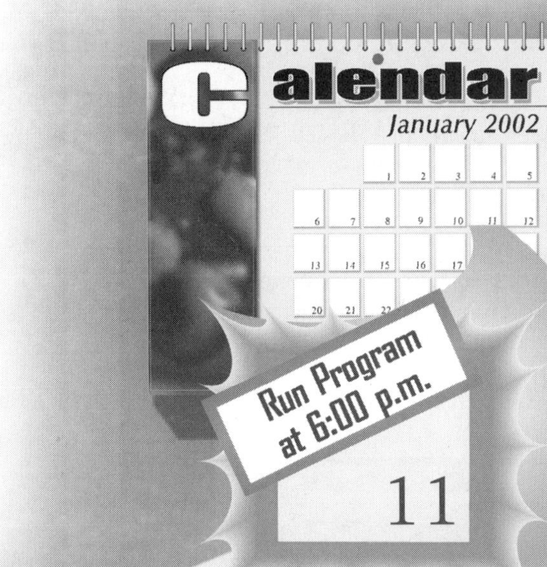

FORMAT FLOPPY DISKS

A floppy disk must be formatted before you can use it to store information. Windows can format a floppy disk with a storage capacity of 1.44 MB.

Floppy disks you buy at computer stores are usually formatted, but you may want to format a previously used floppy disk to prepare it for storing new information. When you format a floppy disk, Windows removes all the information on the disk, so you should make sure the disk does not contain information you want to keep.

Windows allows you to label the floppy disk so you can easily identify it later.

When you format a floppy disk, Windows also checks the floppy disk for damaged areas. If Windows finds damaged areas, the areas are marked so they will not be used. If you want to remove all the files from the disk but not check for damaged areas, you can select the Quick Format option. You should only use this option on a disk that was previously formatted and that you know does not have damaged areas.

When you finish formatting a floppy disk, you can format additional floppy disks. You may want to format several floppy disks at one time so you always have formatted disks available when you need them.

FORMAT FLOPPY DISKS

1 Insert the floppy disk you want to format into your floppy drive.

2 Click start.

3 Click My Computer.

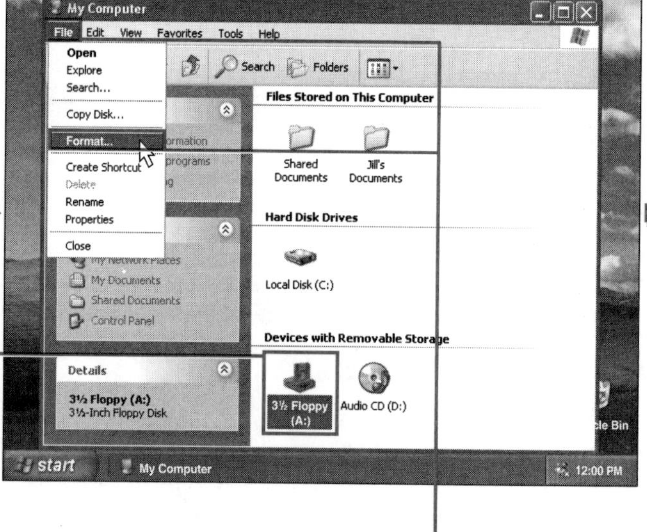

■ The My Computer window appears.

4 Click the drive that contains the floppy disk you want to format.

5 Click File.

6 Click Format.

How can I tell if a floppy disk is formatted?

✔ Windows displays an error message when you try to view the contents of a floppy disk that is not formatted. The floppy disk may never have been formatted or the disk may have been formatted on a computer that uses a different file system than Windows, such as a Macintosh computer. You cannot tell if a floppy disk is formatted by just looking at the disk. To view the contents of a floppy disk, see page 36.

Can I later re-label a floppy disk I have formatted?

✔ Yes. Insert the disk into the floppy drive. In the My Computer window, right-click the drive containing the floppy disk and then select Properties from the menu that appears. Type the new label and then press the Enter key.

I get an error message when I try to format my floppy disk. What is wrong?

✔ An error message appears if files on the floppy disk are open or if the tab on the disk is in the write-protected position. To format the floppy disk, close any open files on the disk and move the tab on the disk to the non-write-protected position.

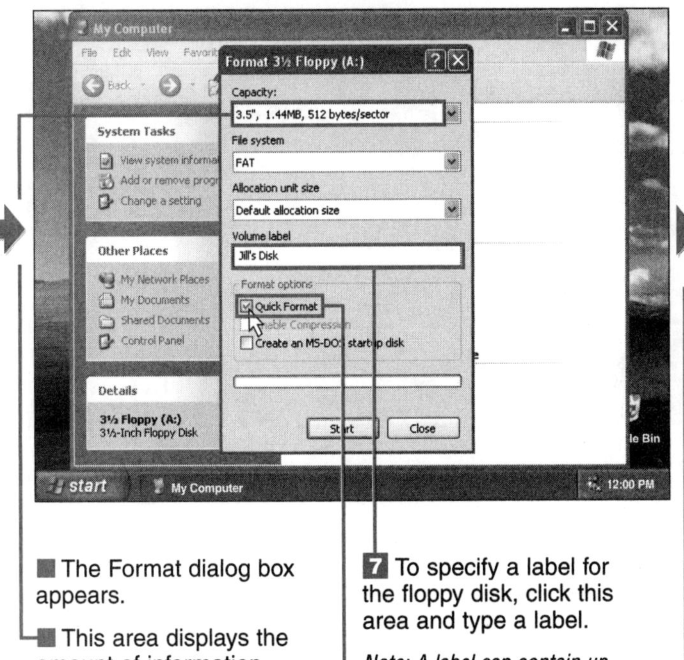

■ The Format dialog box appears.

■ This area displays the amount of information the floppy disk can store.

7 To specify a label for the floppy disk, click this area and type a label.

Note: A label can contain up to 11 characters.

8 If you want to perform a quick format, click this option (☐ changes to ☑).

9 Click Start to begin formatting the floppy disk.

■ A warning message appears, indicating that formatting the floppy disk will erase all the information on the disk.

10 Click OK to continue.

■ This area will display the progress of the format.

■ A dialog box will appear when the format is complete. Click OK to close the dialog box.

VIEW AMOUNT OF DISK SPACE

You can view the amount of used and free space on any disk, including hard disks and removable media such as floppy disks and recordable CDs.

The amount of space on a disk is measured in bytes, megabytes (MB) and gigabytes (GB). One byte equals one character. One MB equals approximately one million characters. One GB equals approximately one billion characters.

You should check the amount of available disk space on your computer at least once a month. You should also check the amount of available hard disk space before you install a new program that requires a large amount of disk space.

Your computer will operate most effectively when at least 20% of the space on your hard disk is free. For example, if you have a 20 GB hard disk, make sure you have at least 4 GB free. This will help improve virtual memory performance on your computer as well as decrease the fragmentation of your files.

You must insert a floppy disk or recordable CD into the appropriate drive on your computer before you can view the amount of space on the floppy disk or CD.

VIEW AMOUNT OF DISK SPACE

1 Click start.

2 Click My Computer.

■ The My Computer window appears.

3 To view the amount of space on a disk, click the disk.

Note: To view the amount of space on a floppy disk or recordable CD, you must insert the disk or CD into the appropriate drive before performing step 3.

4 Click File.

5 Click Properties.

How can I increase the amount of free space on my hard disk?

✔ You should delete unused files and programs from your computer. You can also use the Disk Cleanup feature to remove unnecessary files. To use Disk Cleanup, click the Disk Cleanup button in the Properties dialog box. See page 520 for more information about Disk Cleanup.

Is there a quicker way to view the amount of space on a disk?

✔ Yes. In the My Computer window, click the disk you want to check. The left side of the window may display information about the disk, such as the file system, free space and total capacity of the disk.

Can I limit the amount of hard disk space available to users to store files on my computer?

✔ Yes. The disk you want to change must use the NTFS file system and you must be logged on as a computer administrator to limit hard disk space for users. In the Properties dialog box for the disk, click the Quota tab and select the Enable quota management option (☐ changes to ☑). You can then specify the options you want to use to limit disk space.

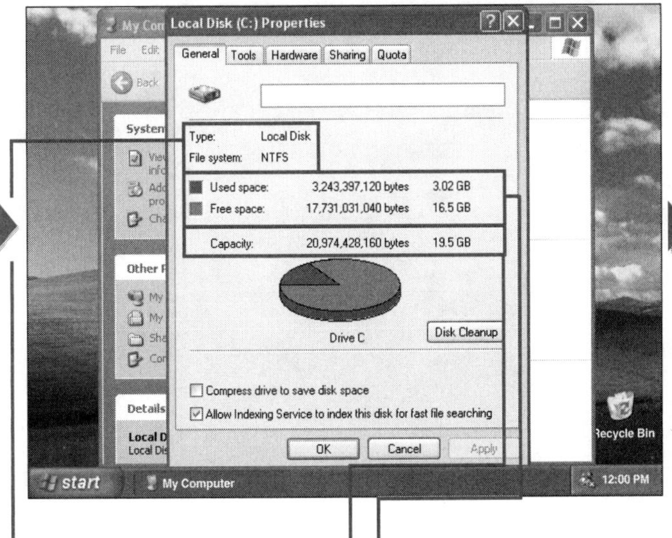

■ A Properties dialog box appears.

■ This area displays the type of disk and the file system used by the disk.

■ This area displays the amount of used and free space on the disk, in bytes and gigabytes (GB).

■ This area displays the total disk storage space, in bytes and gigabytes (GB).

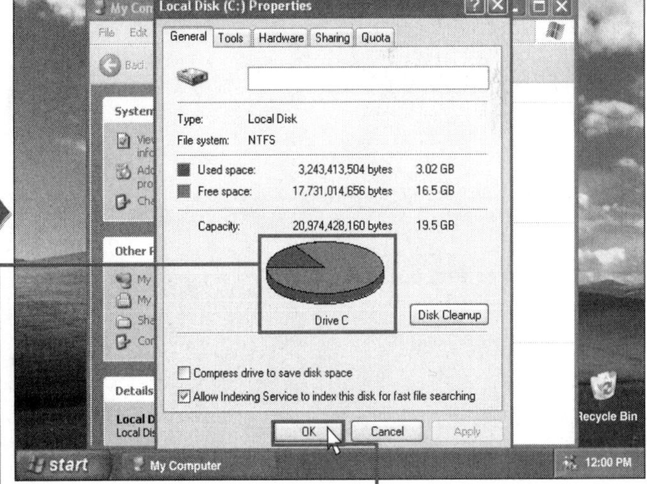

■ The pie chart displays the amount of used and free space on the disk.

6 When you finish reviewing the information, click OK to close the Properties dialog box.

VIEW GENERAL SYSTEM INFORMATION

You can find general information about Windows and your computer by displaying the System Properties dialog box.

The System Properties dialog box shows whether your computer is using Windows XP Home Edition or Windows XP Professional. Windows XP Professional has all the features of the Home Edition plus additional features, such as greater networking capabilities and file encryption, which are not available on the Home Edition.

The System Properties dialog box also displays a version number that indicates the version of Windows you are using. Over time, Microsoft will make changes and additions to Windows XP. The version number may change to reflect these changes.

You can also find registration information, such as the user name that was entered when Windows XP was installed on your computer. The last line of the registration area displays the registration number for your copy of Windows.

The System Properties dialog box also displays information about your computer's processor and the amount of memory (RAM) installed in your computer.

VIEW GENERAL SYSTEM INFORMATION

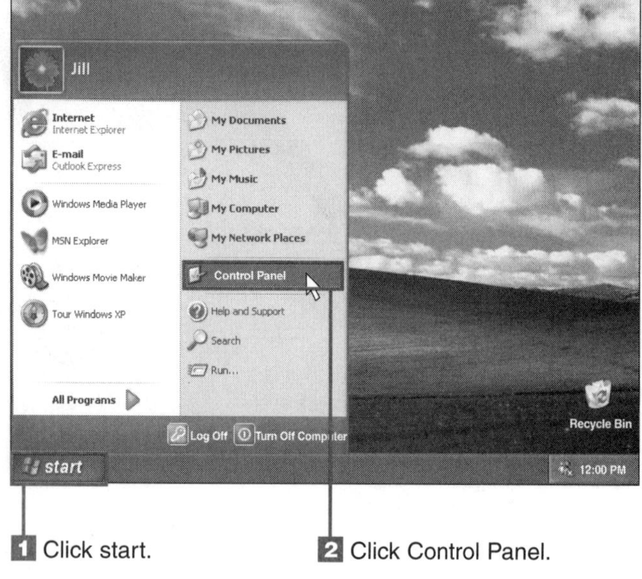

1 Click start.

2 Click Control Panel.

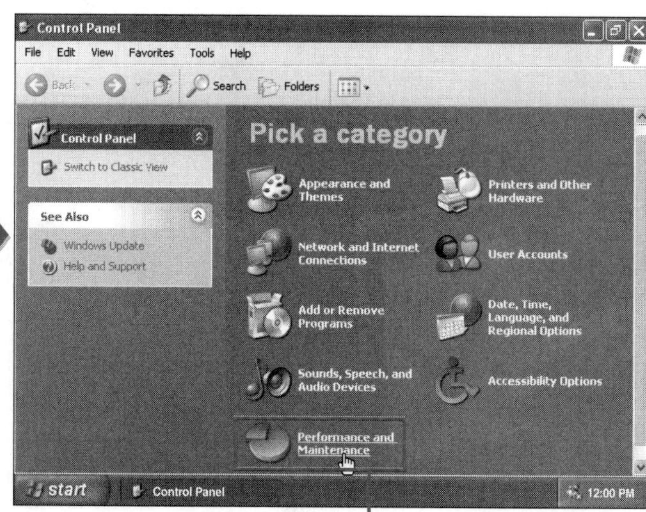

■ The Control Panel window appears.

3 Click Performance and Maintenance.

When will the system and computer information change?

✔ The system and computer information is automatically updated when you make changes to Windows or your computer. For example, after you use the Windows Update feature to install a service pack for Windows, the version number is updated to indicate that the service pack was installed. A service pack is a collection of major updates made available by Microsoft. For information about using Windows Update, see page 568. After you add more memory to your computer, the computer information will automatically display the new amount of RAM in the computer.

Is there a faster way to display the System Properties dialog box?

✔ Yes. You can click the start button and then right-click My Computer. Then click Properties on the menu that appears.

Can I change the user registration information?

✔ Yes. You can change the registration information using the Registry Editor. Click start, select Run, type **regedit** and then press the Enter key. In the Registry Editor window, display the HKEY_LOCAL_MACHINE\SOFTWARE\Microsoft\Windows NT\CurrentVersion key. You can then change the values of the RegisteredOrganization, RegisteredOwner and ProductId items. For more information about using the Registry Editor, see page 612.

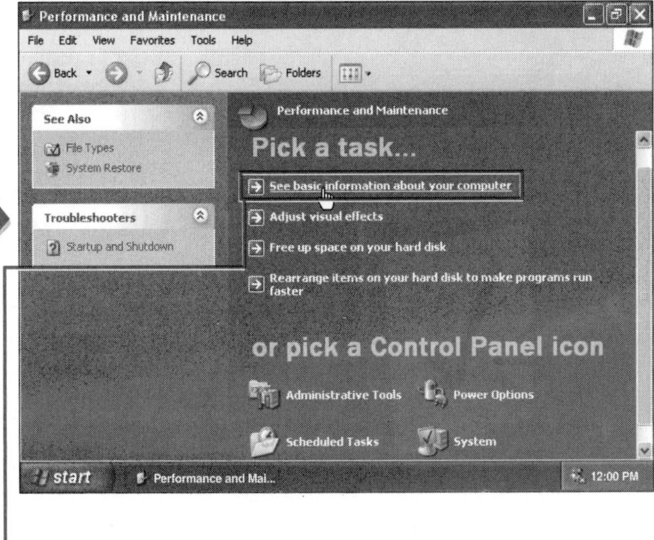

■ The Performance and Maintenance window appears.

4 Click See basic information about your computer.

■ The System Properties dialog box appears.

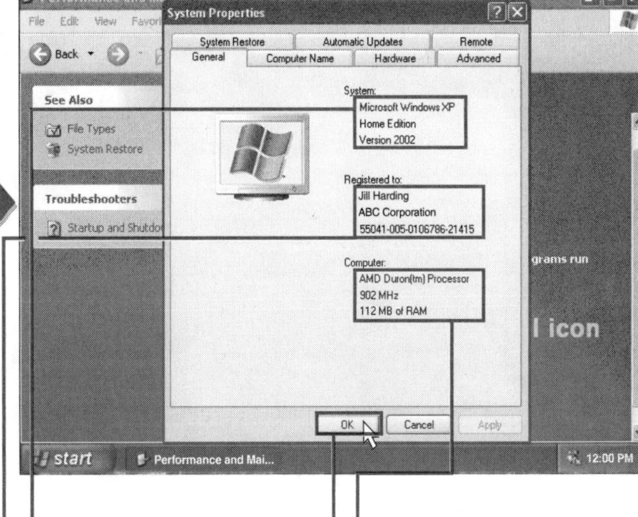

■ This area displays the edition and version of Windows you are using.

■ This area displays the name of the person who is registered to use this copy of Windows and the registration number.

■ This area displays the type and speed of processor and the amount of memory in your computer.

5 When you finish reviewing the information, click OK to close the System Properties dialog box.

USING DISK CLEANUP

You can use Disk Cleanup to remove several types of files from your computer to free up disk space. You can select the types of files you want Disk Cleanup to remove. The available file types depend on the setup of your computer.

Downloaded program files are program files that transfer to your computer automatically from the Internet when you view certain Web pages.

Temporary Internet files are Web pages that Windows stores on your hard disk while you are browsing the Web so you can quickly view the pages again.

The Recycle Bin contains files you have deleted. Selecting the Recycle Bin will permanently remove these files from your computer.

Temporary files are files stored on your hard disk when you use some programs.

WebClient/Publisher temporary files are copies of files you have recently accessed on your computer.

The Compress old files option allows you to save disk space by compressing files you have not recently used. The compressed files will not be deleted from your computer.

The Catalog files for the Content Indexer option removes index files previously used to speed up and improve file searches.

USING DISK CLEANUP

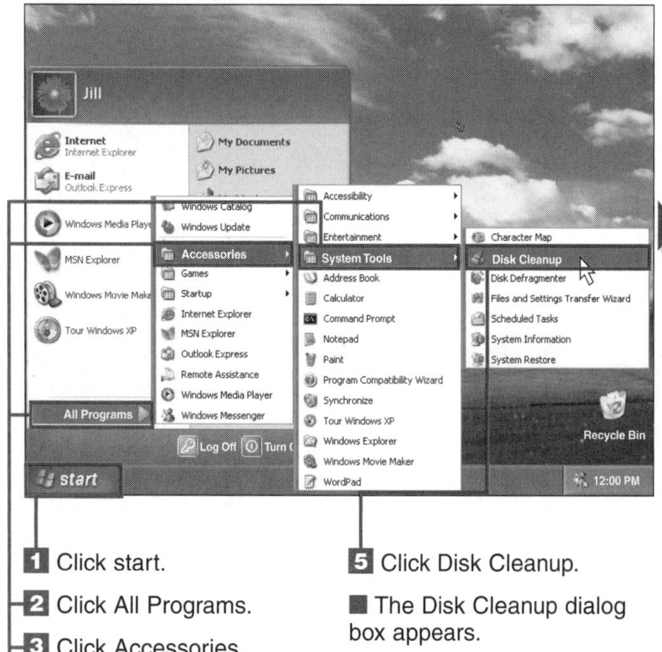

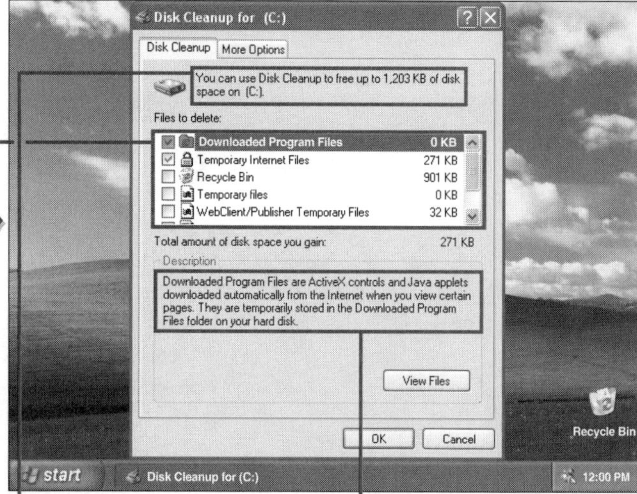

1 Click start.

2 Click All Programs.

3 Click Accessories.

4 Click System Tools.

5 Click Disk Cleanup.

■ The Disk Cleanup dialog box appears.

Note: If you have more than one drive on your computer, a dialog box may appear, asking you to select the drive to clean up. Select a drive and then click OK.

■ This area displays the total amount of disk space you can free up.

■ This area displays the types of files Windows can delete and the amount of disk space each file type uses.

■ This area displays a description of the highlighted file type.

Note: To display a description for a different file type, click the file type.

How can I see which files will be removed?

✔ In the Disk Cleanup dialog box, select a file type and then click the View Files button. A window displays the files that will be removed. Depending on the file type you select, the View Files button may display a different name or may not be available.

Can Disk Cleanup help me free up even more disk space?

✔ Yes. In the Disk Cleanup dialog box, click the More Options tab. This tab can help you remove Windows components and programs you do not use or free up disk space by reducing the amount of storage space used by System Restore.

How can I change the amount of disk space used by temporary Internet files or the Recycle Bin?

✔ Open the Internet Explorer window. To open Internet Explorer, see page 432. Click the Tools menu and then select Internet Options. On the General tab, click the Settings button. Drag the slider (▯) to change the amount of disk space used to store temporary Internet files. To change the amount of disk space used by the Recycle Bin, see page 81.

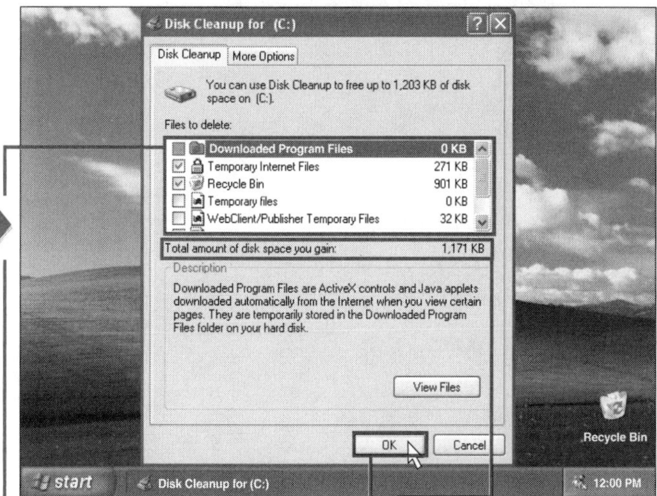

6 Windows will delete the files for each file type that displays a check mark (✔). You can click the box (☐) beside a file type to add or remove a check mark.

■ This area displays the total disk space Windows will free up by deleting the types of files you selected.

7 Click OK to confirm your selections.

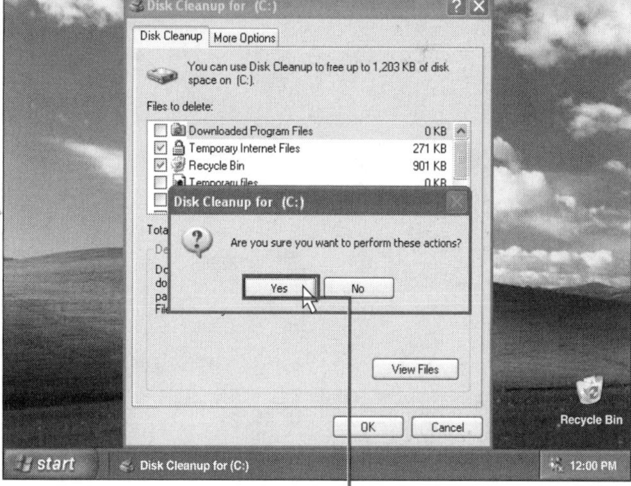

■ A dialog box appears, confirming that you want to perform the cleanup.

8 Click Yes to permanently delete the files.

DETECT AND REPAIR DISK ERRORS

Windows provides an error-checking tool that you can use to detect errors on your hard disk, including file system errors and bad sectors.

A file system error is an error that occurs in the organization of the files and folders stored on a hard disk. When checking your hard disk for errors, you can choose to have Windows automatically repair any file system errors it finds.

A bad sector is a physically damaged area that can no longer store information on a hard disk. You can have the error-checking tool detect bad sectors and attempt to recover information from the sectors. When you have Windows detect bad sectors, Windows will also automatically repair any file system errors it finds.

Using the error-checking tool is useful when you suspect that problems have developed with your hard disk. You may also want to check your hard disk for errors periodically so you can detect and repair minor problems before they become more serious.

When using the error-checking tool, keep in mind that error-checking can be time-consuming, particularly on large hard disks that store many files.

DETECT AND REPAIR DISK ERRORS

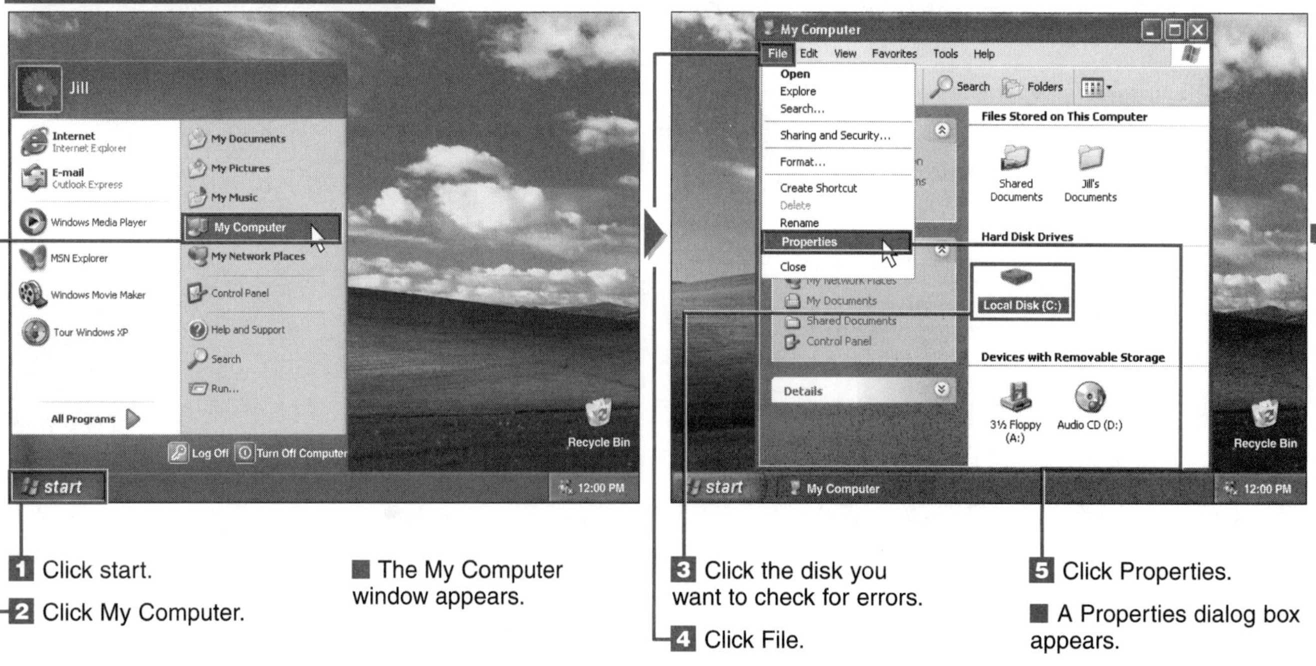

1 Click start.

2 Click My Computer.

■ The My Computer window appears.

3 Click the disk you want to check for errors.

4 Click File.

5 Click Properties.

■ A Properties dialog box appears.

Why did a dialog box appear asking if I want to schedule the disk check for the next time I start Windows?

✔ This dialog box appears when the error-checking tool cannot run while your hard disk performs other tasks. Click Yes in the dialog box to have the error-checking tool run the next time you start Windows. This will ensure that no other programs are using the hard disk while the check is being performed.

How often should I check for and repair errors?

✔ You should check your hard disk for errors approximately once a month. If you experience any problems with your hard disk, such as the inability to open or save a file, you should check for errors immediately.

Can I detect and repair errors on other types of disks?

✔ Yes. You can use Windows' error-checking tool to check for and repair errors on removable media, such as a Zip disk. You can also detect and repair errors on a floppy disk.

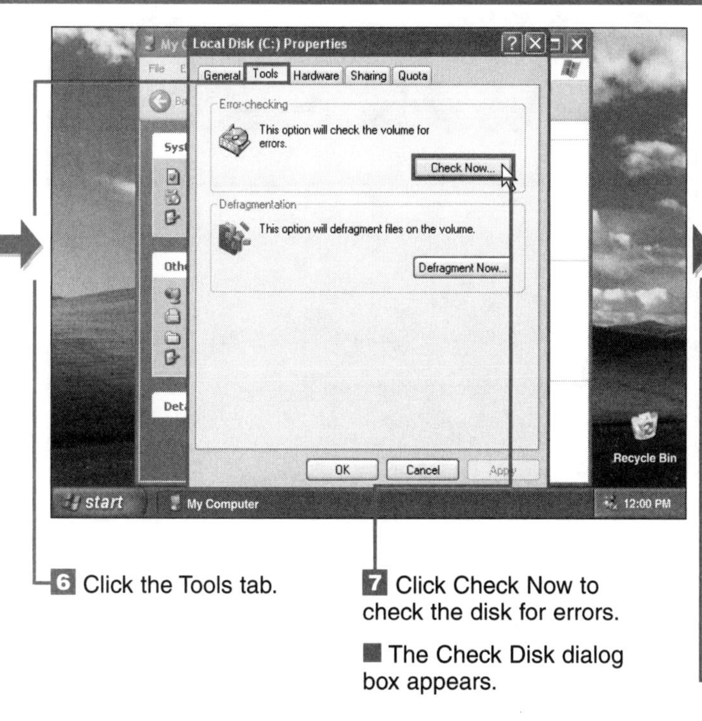

6 Click the Tools tab.

7 Click Check Now to check the disk for errors.

■ The Check Disk dialog box appears.

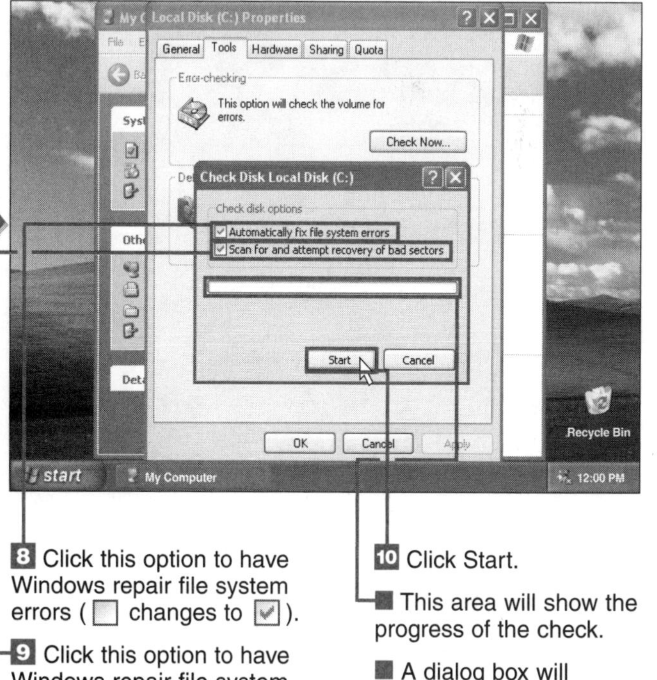

8 Click this option to have Windows repair file system errors (☐ changes to ☑).

9 Click this option to have Windows repair file system errors, locate bad sectors and recover data stored in bad sectors (☐ changes to ☑).

10 Click Start.

■ This area will show the progress of the check.

■ A dialog box will appear when the check is complete. Click OK to close the dialog box.

DEFRAGMENT A HARD DISK

You can improve the performance of your computer by defragmenting your hard disk. You cannot defragment CD-ROM discs, network drives and some removable media.

A fragmented hard disk stores parts of a file in many different locations on the disk. Your computer must search many areas on the disk to retrieve a file. Disk Defragmenter reorganizes the information on a hard disk and places all the parts of a file in one location. This reduces the time your computer will spend locating files.

Windows can analyze your hard disk to determine if you need to defragment the disk. You should have Windows analyze your hard disk at least once a week. Disk Defragmenter graphically displays the details of both the analysis and the defragmentation process.

A hard disk must have at least 15% of free space for Windows to properly defragment the disk. To view the amount of free space on a hard disk, see page 516. You must also be logged on to the computer as a computer administrator in order to run Disk Defragmenter.

Defragmenting a hard disk will not create more free space on the disk. Disk Defragmenter only reorganizes the information on the disk.

DEFRAGMENT A HARD DISK

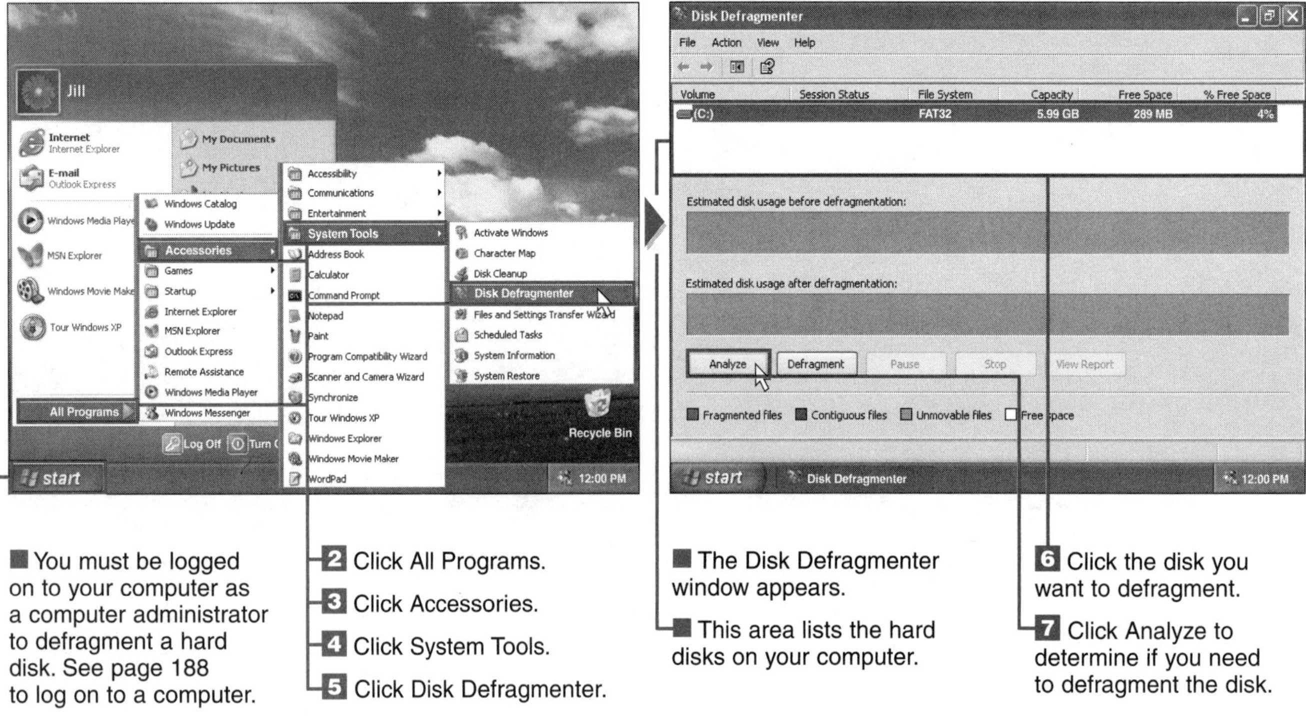

■ You must be logged on to your computer as a computer administrator to defragment a hard disk. See page 188 to log on to a computer.

1 Click start.

2 Click All Programs.

3 Click Accessories.

4 Click System Tools.

5 Click Disk Defragmenter.

■ The Disk Defragmenter window appears.

■ This area lists the hard disks on your computer.

6 Click the disk you want to defragment.

7 Click Analyze to determine if you need to defragment the disk.

How long will the defragmentation process take?

✔ The amount of time Disk Defragmenter takes to defragment a hard disk depends on several factors, including the amount of information on the disk, how fragmented the files are and whether you are working with files on your computer during the defragmentation process. It is best to defragment at a time when you are not using your computer.

Can I stop the defragmentation process?

✔ To stop defragmenting your hard disk, click the Stop button.

Can I pause the defragmentation process?

✔ To pause the defragmentation, click the Pause button. Pausing is useful if you need to finish another task immediately. When you want to continue defragmenting your drive, click the Resume button.

Can I view details about the analysis or defragmentation process?

✔ When the analysis or defragmentation is complete, click the View Report button in the Disk Defragmenter window. Windows displays information that may help a support technician determine a problem with the files on your computer.

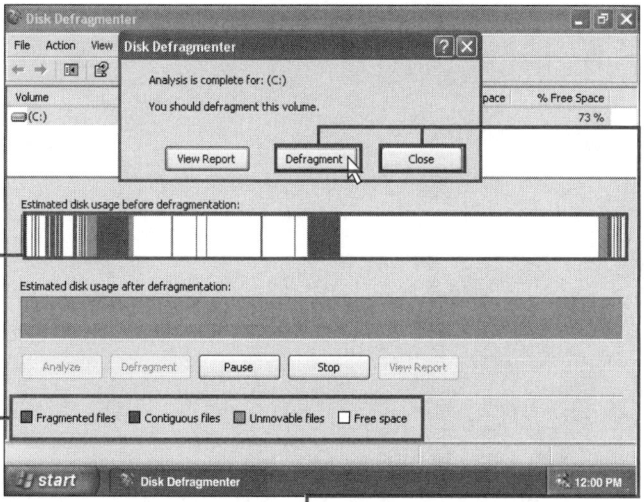

■ This area graphically displays the analysis of the disk.

■ This area displays a legend. The legend indicates what each color represents.

■ When the analysis is complete, a dialog box appears, indicating whether you should defragment the disk.

8 To defragment the disk, click Defragment.

■ If you do not want to defragment the disk, click Close.

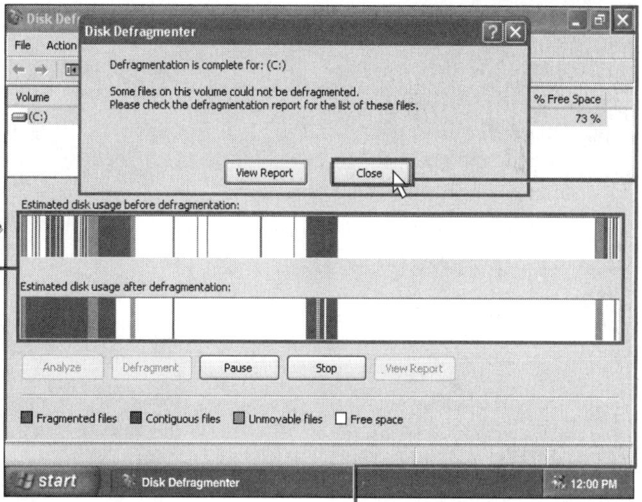

■ If you selected to defragment the disk, this area graphically displays the defragmentation process.

■ A dialog box appears when the defragmentation is complete.

9 Click Close to close the dialog box.

10 Click ☒ to close the Disk Defragmenter window.

SCHEDULE A TASK

You can use Scheduled Tasks to have Windows automatically run specific programs on a regular basis. This allows you to schedule the programs to run at times that are convenient for you.

Before scheduling a task, you must assign a password to the user account that you want to run the program, since you will need to enter the password when scheduling the task. To assign a password to a user account, see page 176.

The Scheduled Task Wizard takes you step by step through the process of scheduling a new task. You can add any program on your computer to the list of programs that Scheduled Tasks will start automatically. Scheduling a task is ideal for running computer maintenance programs, such as Disk Cleanup, on a regular basis.

Scheduled Tasks starts each time you start Windows and operates in the background.

Scheduled Tasks uses the date and time set in your computer to determine when to start scheduled tasks. You should make sure the correct date and time are set in your computer before scheduling tasks. To change the date and time, see page 194.

SCHEDULE A TASK

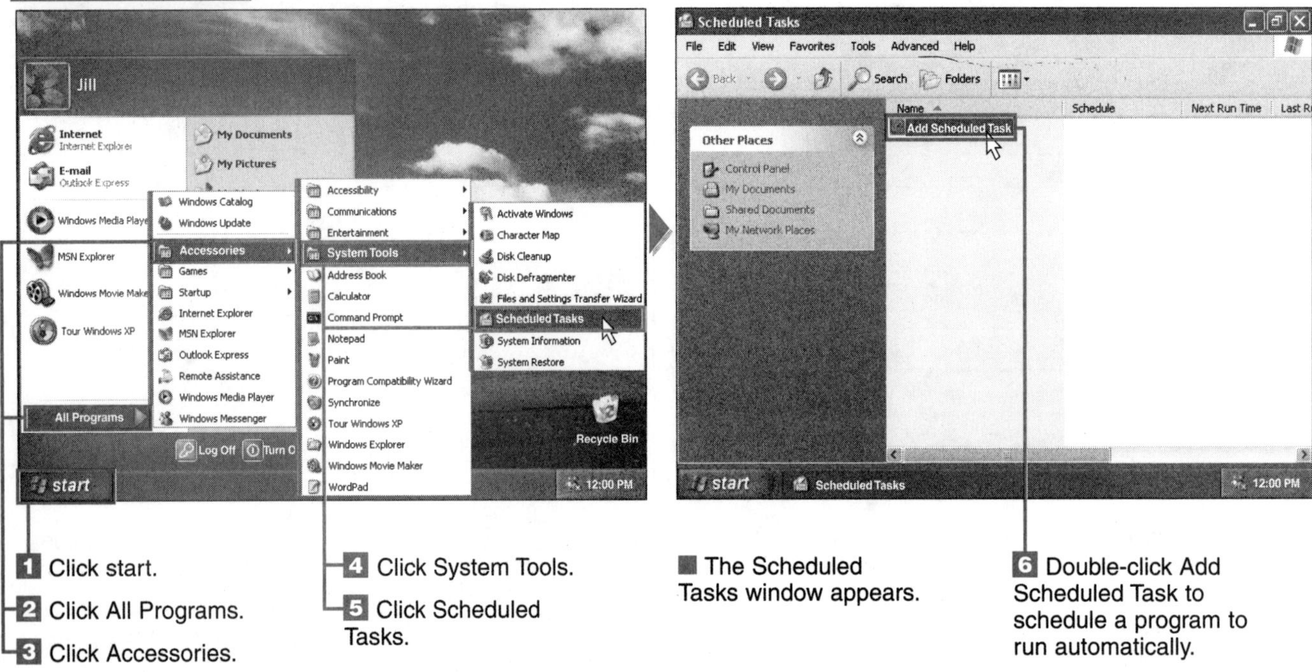

1 Click start.

2 Click All Programs.

3 Click Accessories.

4 Click System Tools.

5 Click Scheduled Tasks.

■ The Scheduled Tasks window appears.

6 Double-click Add Scheduled Task to schedule a program to run automatically.

How can I schedule a program that does not appear in the Scheduled Task Wizard?

✔ You can click the Browse button in the wizard to search for the program on your computer.

How do I turn off Scheduled Tasks?

✔ In the Scheduled Tasks window, select the Advanced menu and then click Stop Using Task Scheduler. Your scheduled tasks will not run and Scheduled Tasks will not start the next time you start Windows. To once again turn on Scheduled Tasks, select the Advanced menu and then click Start Using Task Scheduler.

Can Windows notify me of missed tasks?

✔ Yes. In the Scheduled Tasks window, select the Advanced menu and then click Notify Me of Missed Tasks. When a scheduled program is unable to run, such as when Scheduled Tasks is turned off, a notification message will appear the next time Scheduled Tasks starts.

How do I delete a scheduled task?

✔ In the Scheduled Tasks window, click the task you want to remove and then press the Delete key. Deleting a task stops the program from starting automatically but does not remove the program from your computer.

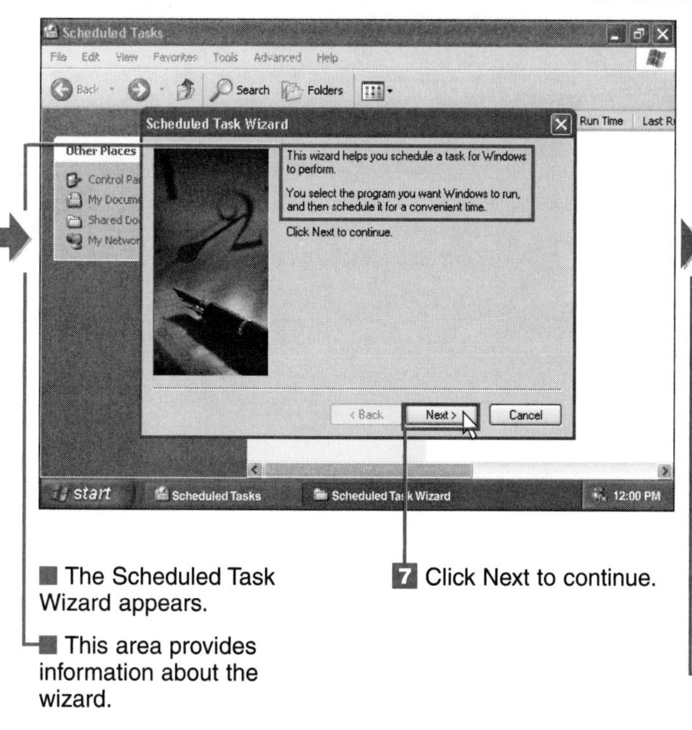

■ The Scheduled Task Wizard appears.

■ This area provides information about the wizard.

7 Click Next to continue.

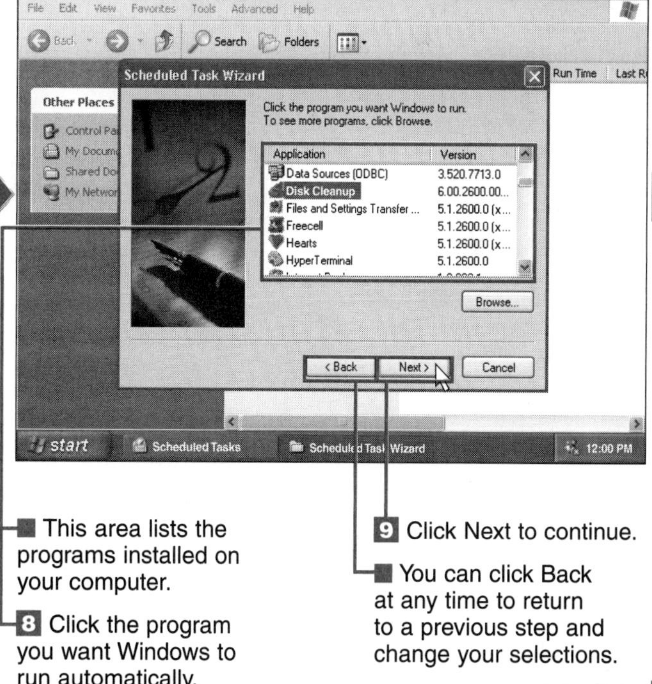

■ This area lists the programs installed on your computer.

8 Click the program you want Windows to run automatically.

9 Click Next to continue.

■ You can click Back at any time to return to a previous step and change your selections.

CONTINUED

SCHEDULE A TASK (CONTINUED)

The Scheduled Task Wizard provides a name for the program you want to start automatically. You can use a more descriptive name to help you more easily identify your scheduled tasks.

You can specify when you want a program to start. You can select a daily, weekly or monthly schedule. You can also schedule a program to start only once, start each time you turn on the computer or start each time you log on to Windows.

Depending on the schedule you choose, additional options may be available. For example, if you select a weekly schedule, you can select which days of the week you want to run the program and at what time.

You must specify the user name and password for the account on which you want the scheduled program to run. The user you specify does not have to be logged on for the task to run, but the computer must be turned on.

After you schedule a task, the task appears in the Scheduled Tasks window, which provides information about each task, such as when the task will run next and when it was run last.

SCHEDULE A TASK (CONTINUED)

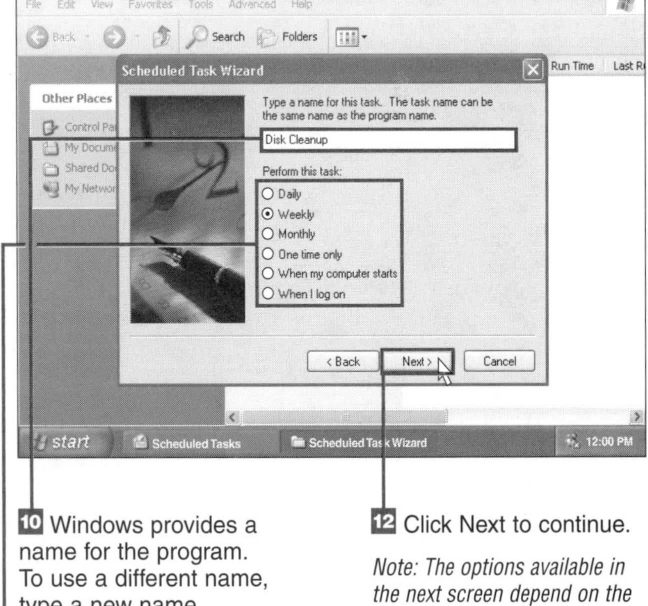

10 Windows provides a name for the program. To use a different name, type a new name.

11 Click an option to specify when you want the program to run (○ changes to ⊙).

12 Click Next to continue.

Note: The options available in the next screen depend on the option you selected in step 11.

13 To specify when you want the program to run, click the part of the time you want to change and then type a new time.

14 Windows will run the program every week. You can double-click this area and type a new number of weeks.

15 Click each day of the week you want the program to run (☐ changes to ☑).

16 Click Next to continue.

Can I stop a task while it is running?

✔ If a scheduled task begins to run at an inconvenient time, you can stop the task. Display the Scheduled Tasks window, right-click the task you want to stop and then select End Task.

Can I temporarily stop Scheduled Tasks from running all tasks?

✔ If you do not want to be interrupted while performing another task, such as when installing software, you can temporarily stop Scheduled Tasks from running all tasks. In the Scheduled Tasks window, click the Advanced menu and then select Pause Task Scheduler. To once again run all scheduled tasks, click the Advanced menu and then select Continue Task Scheduler.

Why did a scheduled task not run?

✔ You can view the Scheduled Tasks log file to find out why a scheduled task did not run. In the Scheduled Tasks window, click the Advanced menu and select View Log.

How can I immediately run a scheduled task?

✔ Display the Scheduled Tasks window and right-click the task you want to run immediately. Then click Run in the menu that appears.

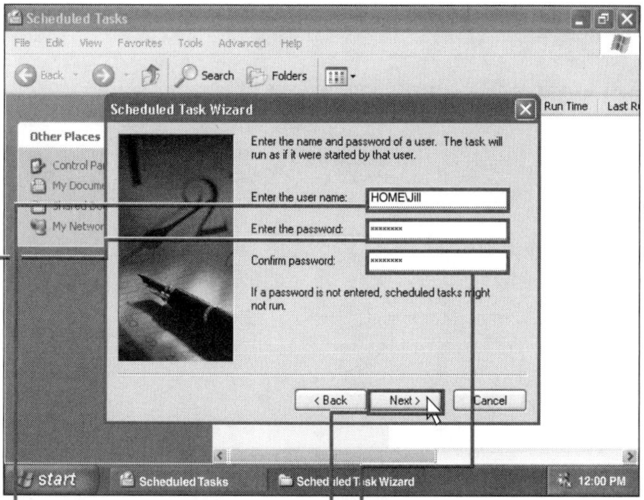

17 This area displays your computer and user name. To specify a different user, type a different user name.

18 Click this area and type the password for the user account.

19 Click this area and type the password again to confirm the password.

20 Click Next to continue.

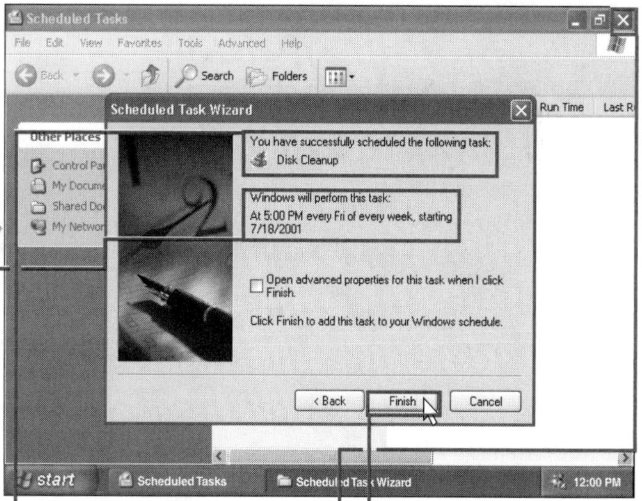

■ The wizard indicates that you have successfully scheduled the program.

■ This area indicates when Windows will run the program.

21 Click Finish.

■ The program appears in the Scheduled Tasks window.

22 Click ☒ to close the Scheduled Tasks window.

CHANGE A SCHEDULED TASK

If you find that a scheduled task does not work the way you expected, you can change the properties of the task. For example, the program you scheduled may open, but the program may not perform the action you require. Changing the properties of the task allows you to control how and when Task Scheduler performs the task.

Some programs may require certain settings, or parameters, to perform the task you want. For example, you may need to use parameters to specify exactly which backup job you want to perform for a backup program.

The program may need to access additional files stored on your computer to perform the task. If necessary, you can specify the location of the folder that contains the files. If the location includes spaces, you can place quotation marks ("") around the entire location.

Task Scheduler allows you to enter comments about a task you have scheduled. Adding comments to your tasks can help you later identify each task.

You should make sure a task is turned on to ensure that the task will run when expected. If you do not want a scheduled task to interrupt your work, you can temporarily turn off the task.

CHANGE A SCHEDULED TASK

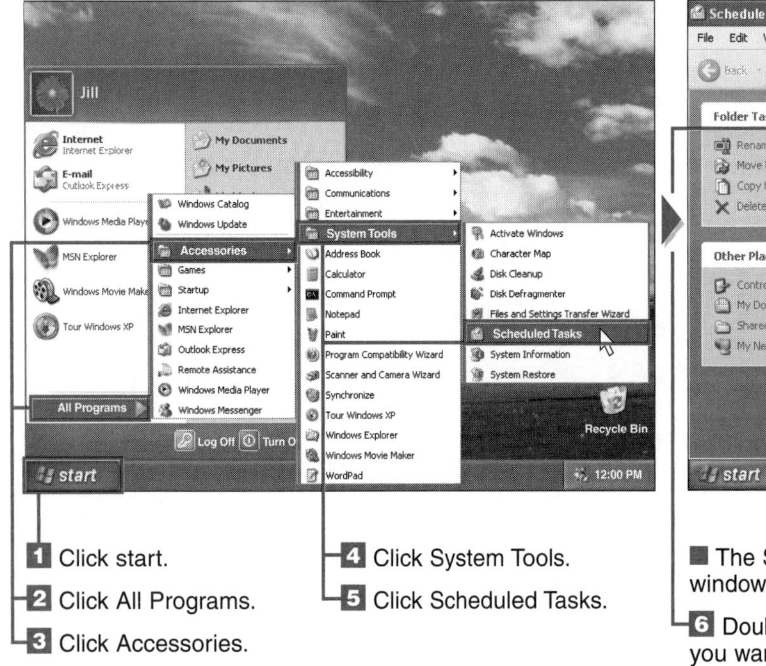

1 Click start.

2 Click All Programs.

3 Click Accessories.

4 Click System Tools.

5 Click Scheduled Tasks.

■ The Scheduled Tasks window appears.

6 Double-click the task you want to change.

■ A dialog box appears, displaying properties that you can change for the task.

How can I find out which parameters a program needs to run correctly?

✔ You may find information about the parameters a program needs to run correctly in the documentation included with the program or by using the command prompt. Click the start button and select All Programs. Choose Accessories and then click Command Prompt. At the command prompt, type the program's name followed by a space and /?. For example, type **chkdsk /?** to find the parameters you can use for the CheckDisk program.

How do I specify a different user account to run a task?

✔ When viewing the properties of a task, select the Task tab, double-click the box beside Run as and type the user account you want to run the task. Then click the Set password button to specify the password for the user account.

Can I change the program that will run for a task?

✔ Yes. When viewing the properties of a task, select the Task tab. Click the Browse button to search for the program you want to run. You can also type the location and name of the program in the Run area. After selecting the program you want to run, a dialog box appears, asking you to specify the user account that you want to run the program and the password for the user account.

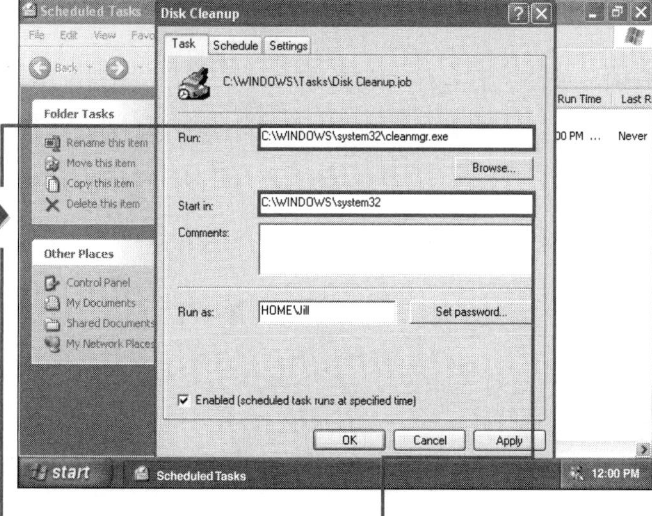

7 This area displays the location and name of the program that will run. If the program requires parameters to run, type the parameters after the program name.

8 This area displays the location and name of the folder that contains the program or related files. To change the folder, select the information and then type a new folder location and name.

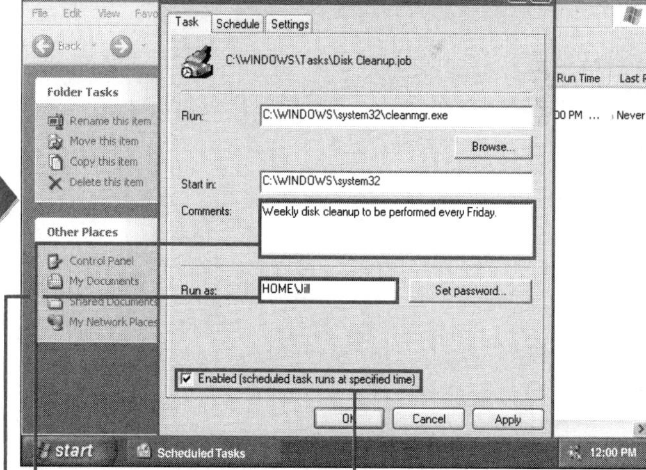

9 You can click this area and type any comments about the task.

■ This area displays the computer name followed by the user account that will run the task.

10 The task will run when a check mark (✔) appears in this area. You can click this option to temporarily turn off the task (☑ changes to ☐).

CONTINUED

CHANGE A SCHEDULED TASK (CONTINUED)

Task Scheduler allows you to change when a task will run. This is useful if a task runs at an inconvenient time or if you want to change how often the task runs.

You can have Task Scheduler delete a task when the task is not scheduled to run again. This is useful for tasks scheduled to run only once.

Task Scheduler lets you stop a task after the task has run for a certain length of time.

To prevent Task Scheduler from interrupting your work, you can have a task run only if you do not use your computer for a certain period of time. If you are using your computer when the task tries to run, Task Scheduler can continue to monitor your computer for a period of inactivity. If you start using your computer while a task is running, you can have Task Scheduler stop running the task.

You can prevent a task from starting if your computer is running on batteries. You can also stop performing a task if your computer switches to battery power. These options help conserve batteries on portable computers.

If your computer enters a sleep mode to conserve power, you can have Task Scheduler wake your computer to perform a task.

CHANGE A SCHEDULED TASK (CONTINUED)

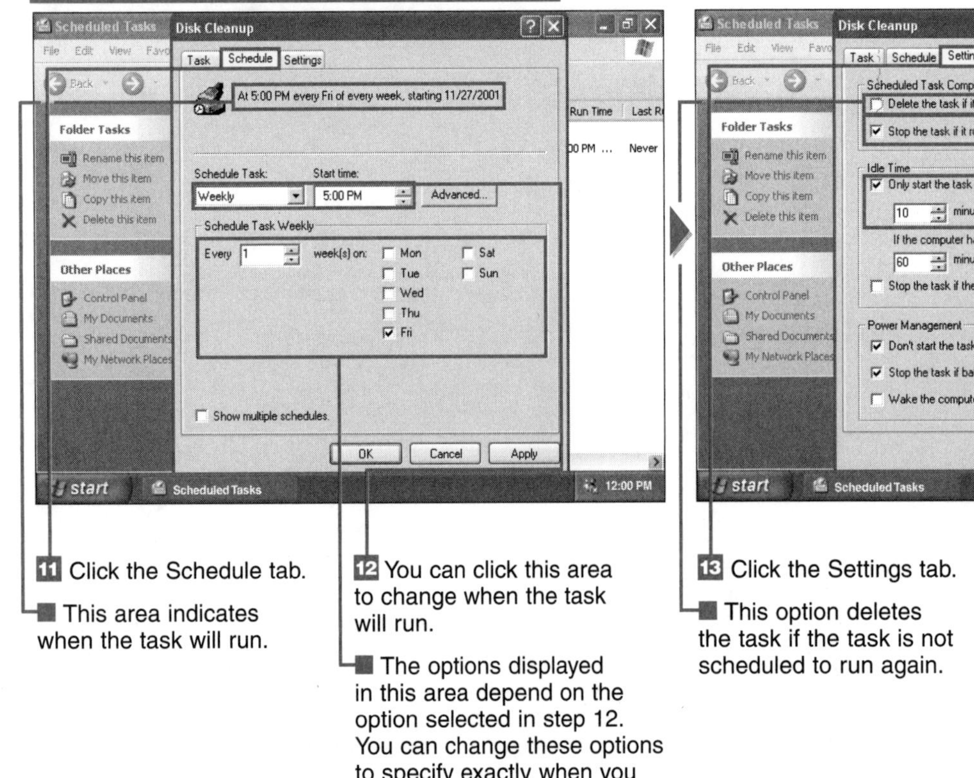

11 Click the Schedule tab.

■ This area indicates when the task will run.

12 You can click this area to change when the task will run.

■ The options displayed in this area depend on the option selected in step 12. You can change these options to specify exactly when you want the task to run.

13 Click the Settings tab.

■ This option deletes the task if the task is not scheduled to run again.

■ This option stops the task after the task runs for the time specified in this area. You can change the time.

■ This option starts the task only if you do not use your computer for the time specified in this area. You can change the time.

Can I have a task run only between certain dates?

✔ Yes. You may want to run a task only between certain dates, such as over a long weekend or while you are on vacation. When viewing the properties for a daily, weekly or monthly scheduled task, click the Schedule tab and then click the Advanced button. You can then select a start date and an end date for the task.

Why would I want to place a time limit on a task?

✔ You may want to stop running a task, such as Disk Defragmenter, if it takes a long time and interferes with your work. You may also want to use a time limit to close a program that does not close automatically when the program has finished running.

Can I have a task repeat each time it is scheduled to run?

✔ Yes. When viewing the properties for a daily, weekly or monthly scheduled task or for a task that runs only once, select the Schedule tab and click the Advanced button. In the dialog box that appears, select the Repeat task option (☐ changes to ☑). You can then specify how often you want the task to repeat each time it runs.

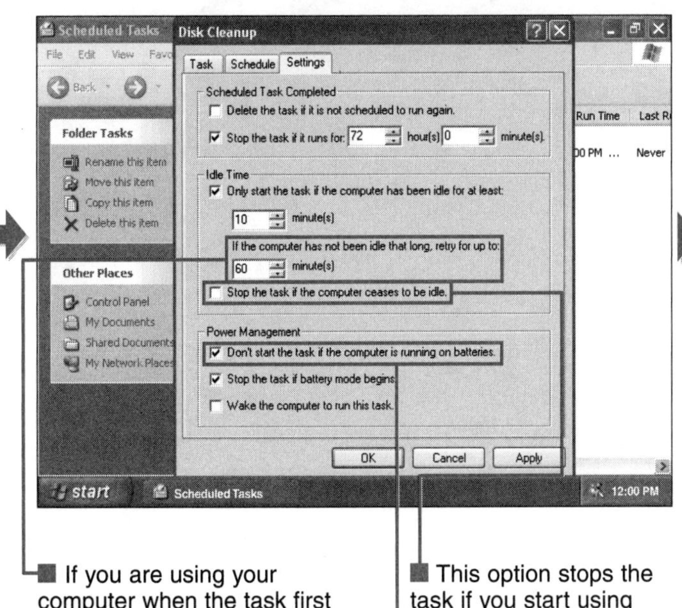

■ If you are using your computer when the task first tries to start, Task Scheduler will continue to check if you are using the computer for the time specified in this area. You can change the time.

■ This option stops the task if you start using your computer while the task is running.

■ This option prevents the task from starting if your computer is running on batteries.

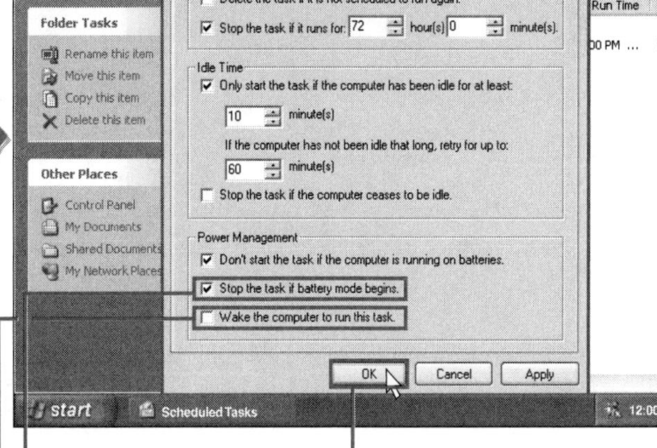

■ This option stops performing the task if your computer starts running on batteries.

■ If your computer has entered a sleep mode, this option wakes the computer to run the task.

14 Task Scheduler will use each option that displays a check mark (✔). You can click an option to turn the option on (☑) or off (☐).

15 Click OK to confirm all your changes.

CHANGE POWER OPTIONS

You can change the power options on your computer to reduce the amount of power the computer uses. This is useful if you want to reduce the energy consumption of your desktop computer or increase the battery life of your portable computer.

You can choose a power scheme, which is a collection of settings that manage the power your computer uses, for your computer.

Windows can conserve power by turning off your monitor and hard disk when your computer has been idle for a period of time. You can change the amount of time that must pass before Windows turns off these items.

Windows can also place your computer on standby, which turns off items that use power, when you do not use the computer for a period of time you specify. Windows does not automatically save your documents before going on standby. If a power outage occurs during standby, all your unsaved work will be lost.

Many computers also support the hibernate feature, which saves everything on your computer and then turns off the computer after a period of inactivity you specify. When you resume using your computer, any open programs and documents will appear as you left them on your computer.

You must be logged on to the computer as a computer administrator to change power options.

CHANGE POWER OPTIONS

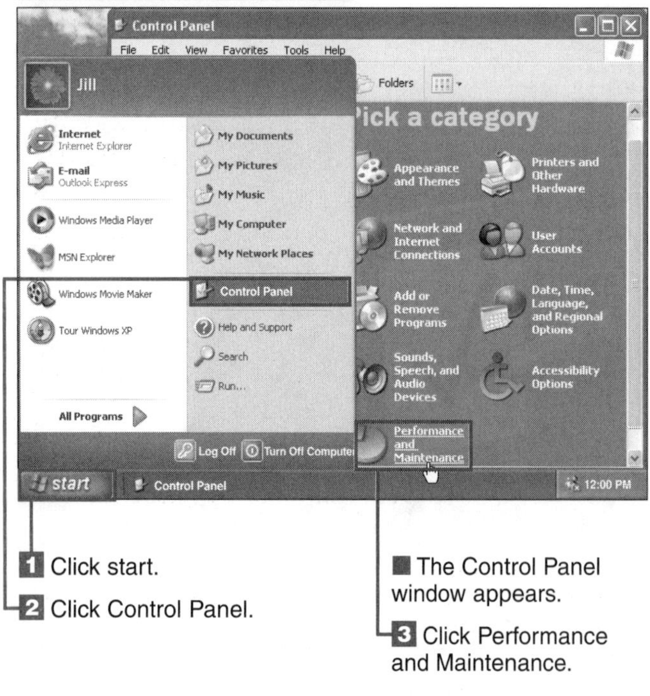

1 Click start.

2 Click Control Panel.

■ The Control Panel window appears.

3 Click Performance and Maintenance.

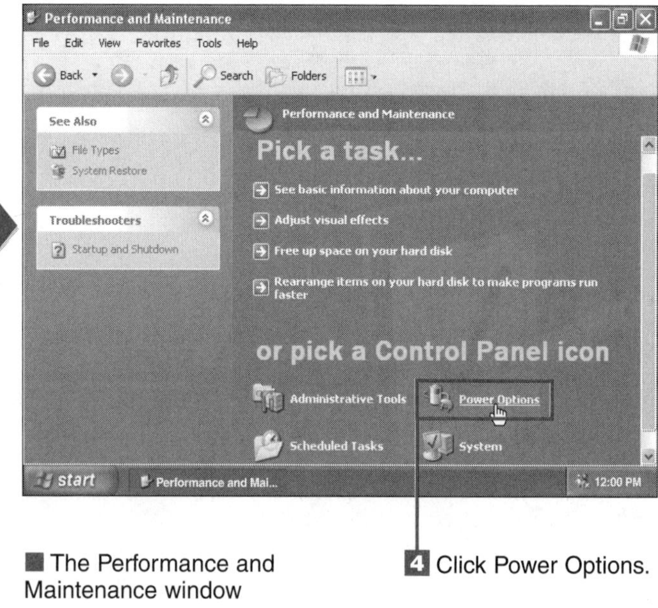

■ The Performance and Maintenance window appears.

4 Click Power Options.

Why aren't all the power options available on my computer?

✔ The available power options depend on which options are supported by the hardware installed on your computer. For example, if the option to change the amount of time that passes before your computer hibernates does not appear on the Power Schemes tab, either your hardware does not support hibernation or the hibernate feature is not enabled on your computer.

How do I create a new power scheme?

✔ In the Power Options Properties dialog box, click the Power Schemes tab and then select the options you want to use for the new power scheme. To save the new power scheme, click the Save As button. Type a name for the power scheme and press the Enter key. The new power scheme will appear in the list of power schemes.

How do I resume using my computer when it is in a power conservation mode?

✔ If your monitor or hard disk turns off or if your computer is on standby or in hibernation, you may be able to move the mouse or press a key on your keyboard to resume working. You can also press the computer's power button to bring the computer out of standby or hibernation.

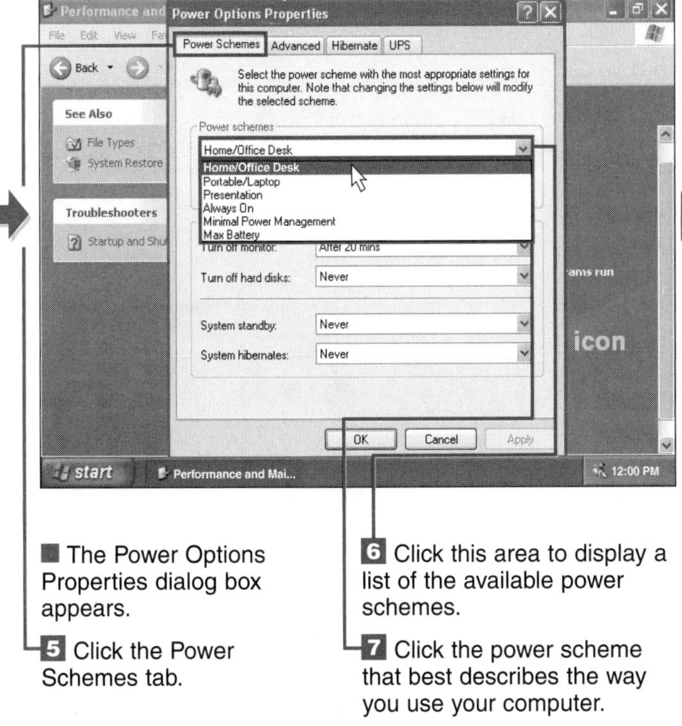

■ The Power Options Properties dialog box appears.

5 Click the Power Schemes tab.

6 Click this area to display a list of the available power schemes.

7 Click the power scheme that best describes the way you use your computer.

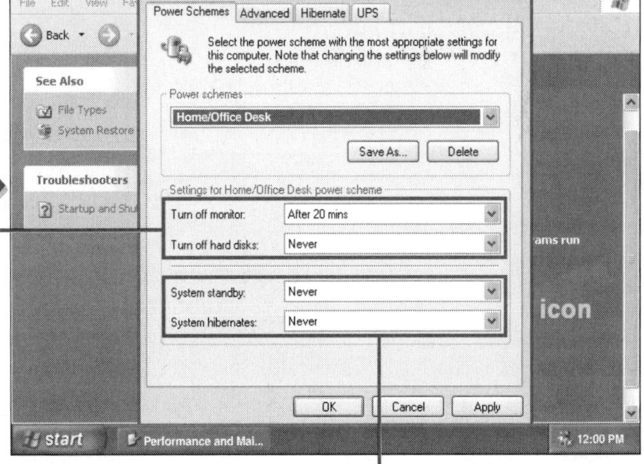

■ Windows displays the settings for the power scheme you selected.

8 These areas display the amount of time your computer must be inactive before your monitor and hard disk automatically turn off. To change the amount of time, click the appropriate area.

9 These areas display the amount of time your computer must be inactive before the computer goes on standby or hibernates. To change the amount of time, click the appropriate area.

CONTINUED

CHANGE POWER OPTIONS (CONTINUED)

You can have Windows display a power icon on the right side of the taskbar. When you double-click the icon on a desktop computer, Windows displays the Power Options Properties dialog box so you can adjust your power options. If you are using a portable computer, double-clicking the icon displays the amount of power remaining on the battery.

You can also have Windows request a password when your computer comes out of standby. A password prevents unauthorized people from using your computer when it goes on standby while you are away from your desk. The password you enter to bring the computer out of standby is the same as your logon password that you enter when you log on to Windows.

You can specify what you want the computer to do when you press the power button. You can have the computer do nothing, ask what you want to do, go on standby, hibernate or turn off. On a portable computer, you can also specify what you want to occur when you close the computer's lid or press the sleep button.

If a computer supports hibernation, you can turn on or off the option that enables hibernation. You can also view the amount of free disk space on your computer and the amount of disk space required to put your computer into hibernation.

CHANGE POWER OPTIONS (CONTINUED)

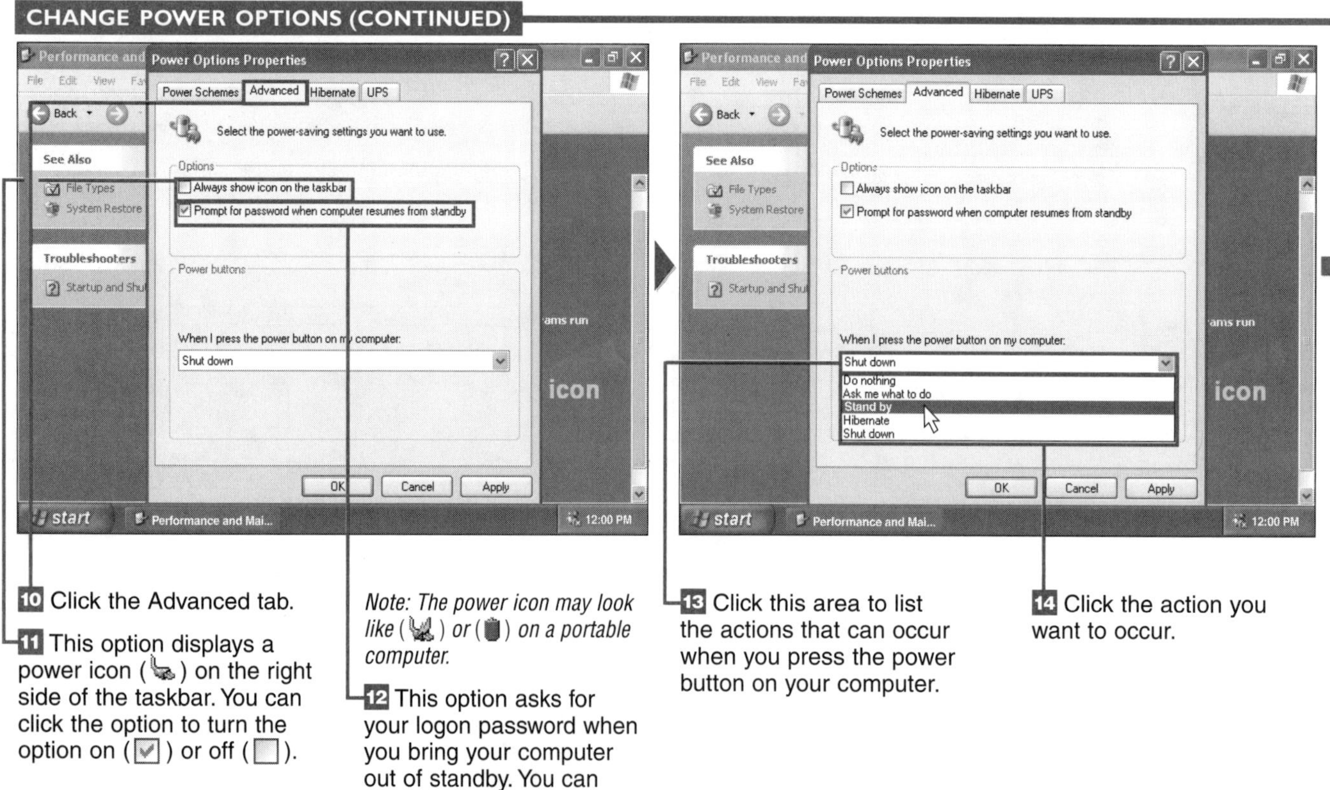

10 Click the Advanced tab.

11 This option displays a power icon ( ) on the right side of the taskbar. You can click the option to turn the option on ( ) or off ( ).

Note: The power icon may look like ( ) or ( ) on a portable computer.

12 This option asks for your logon password when you bring your computer out of standby. You can click the option to turn the option on ( ) or off ( ).

13 Click this area to list the actions that can occur when you press the power button on your computer.

14 Click the action you want to occur.

How do I change the password required to bring my computer out of standby or hibernation?

✔ You must change the password assigned to your user account. To change the password assigned to your user account, see page 179.

Will my portable computer warn me when battery power is low?

✔ If the Power Options Properties dialog box displays the Alarms tab, you can click the Alarm Action button and then select an option to have a sound or visual alarm warn you when battery power is low. You can also select the "When the alarm goes off, the computer will" option and then choose whether the computer will go on standby, hibernate or shut down when the power is low.

The power icon on my taskbar disappeared. How do I redisplay the icon?

✔ Windows may hide icons on the right side of the taskbar that have not been recently used. To redisplay the power icon, click on the taskbar.

How do I immediately put my computer on standby or into hibernation?

✔ Click the start button and then select Turn Off Computer. To put the computer on standby, click Stand By. To put the computer into hibernation, press and hold down the Shift key until the Stand By option changes to Hibernate and then click Hibernate.

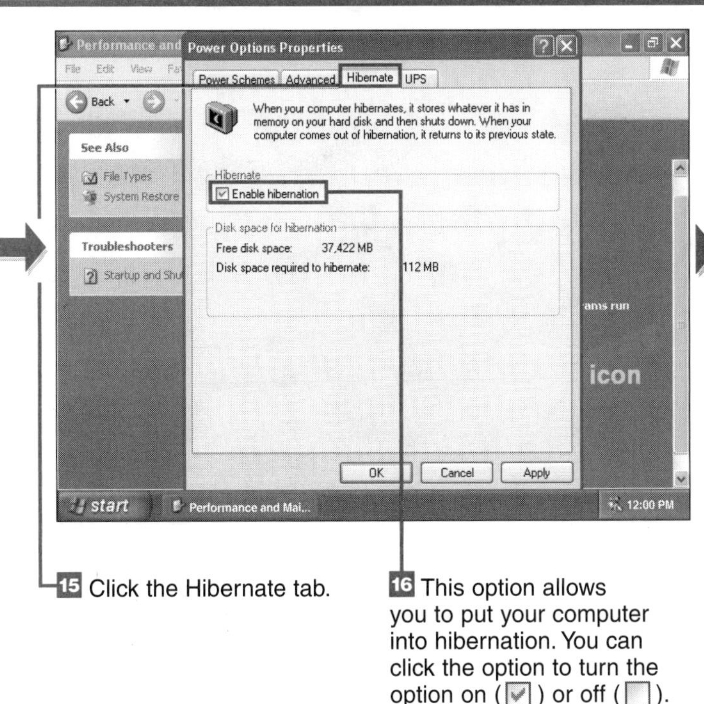

15 Click the Hibernate tab.

16 This option allows you to put your computer into hibernation. You can click the option to turn the option on (☑) or off (☐).

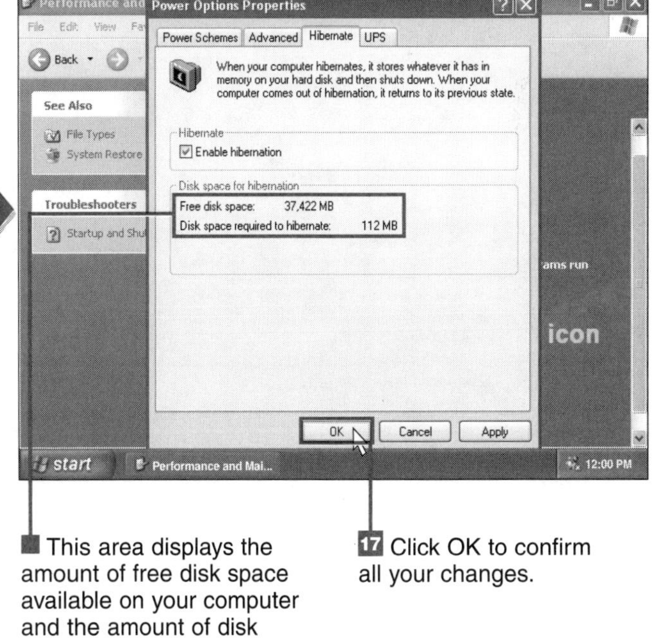

■ This area displays the amount of free disk space available on your computer and the amount of disk space required to put your computer into hibernation.

17 Click OK to confirm all your changes.

CONVERT A DRIVE TO NTFS

You can convert a drive to the NTFS file system. A file system determines the way information is stored on a hard drive.

Windows XP supports three file systems—FAT, FAT32 and NTFS. FAT is a file system used by older operating systems. FAT32 is an upgrade to FAT and improves the organization of data to reduce wasted space on hard drives larger than 512 MB.

The NTFS file system is recommended for Windows XP and offers many advantages over the FAT file systems. NTFS offers improved file security, disk compression and support for larger hard drives. Unlike the FAT file systems, NTFS can support a drive of virtually any size without compromising performance.

Before converting a drive to NTFS, you should close all open programs and files. If you are currently using the drive you want to convert, Windows will convert the drive the next time you start your computer. If you are not using the drive, Windows will convert the drive immediately.

Once you convert a drive to NTFS, you cannot convert the drive back to the previous file system.

CONVERT A DRIVE TO NTFS

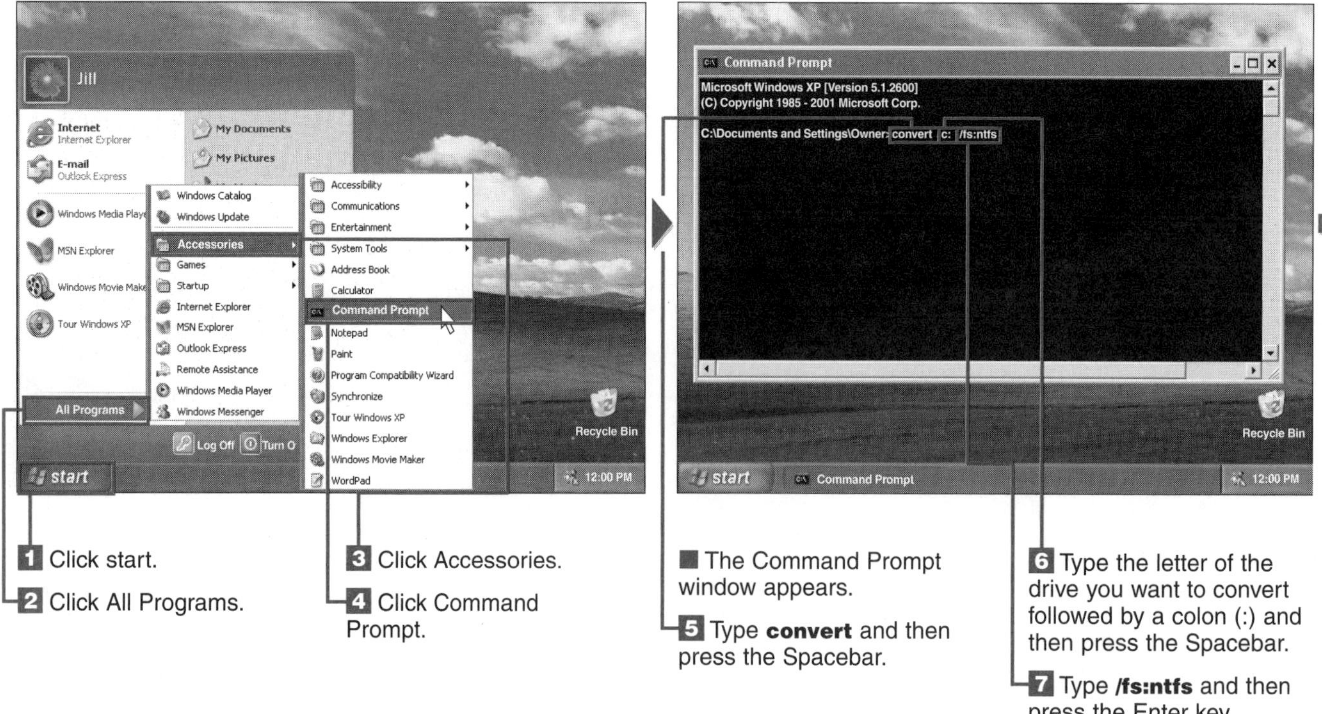

1 Click start.

2 Click All Programs.

3 Click Accessories.

4 Click Command Prompt.

■ The Command Prompt window appears.

5 Type **convert** and then press the Spacebar.

6 Type the letter of the drive you want to convert followed by a colon (:) and then press the Spacebar.

7 Type **/fs:ntfs** and then press the Enter key.

How can I tell which file system a drive is currently using?

✔ Click start and then select My Computer. In the My Computer window, right-click the drive you want to check and then select Properties. In the dialog box that appears, choose the General tab to view the file system information.

I have partitioned my hard drive. Can I convert just one partition to NTFS?

✔ Yes. Some people divide their hard drive into sections, called partitions, so they can install a different operating system on each partition. You can convert just one partition to NTFS, but you may not be able to access the files on an NTFS partition from a partition that uses another operating system, such as Windows 98 or Windows Me.

Can converting a drive to NTFS help me save disk space?

✔ Yes. You can compress an NTFS drive to save disk space. Click start and then select My Computer. In the My Computer window, right-click the NTFS drive you want to compress and then select Properties. In the dialog box that appears, choose the General tab, select the Compress drive to save disk space option (☐ changes to ☑) and then click OK. Select the Apply changes to C:\, subfolders and files option (○ changes to ◉) and then click OK.

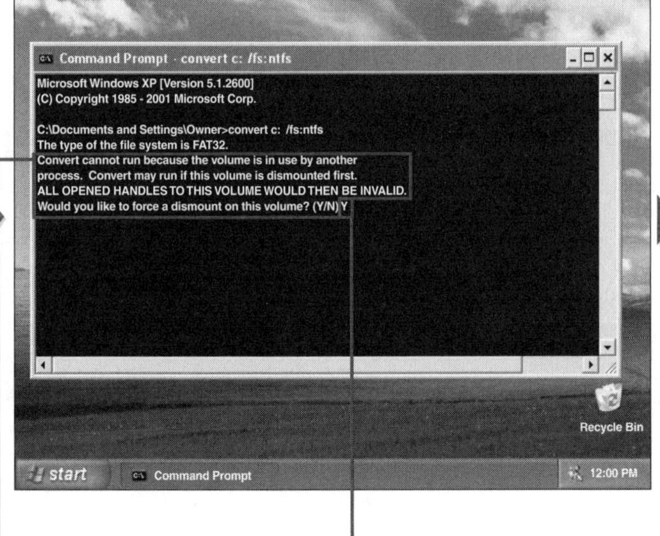

■ Windows states that it cannot convert the drive because the drive is currently in use. You must dismount the drive before you can convert the drive.

8 To dismount the drive, type **Y** (for Yes) and then press the Enter key.

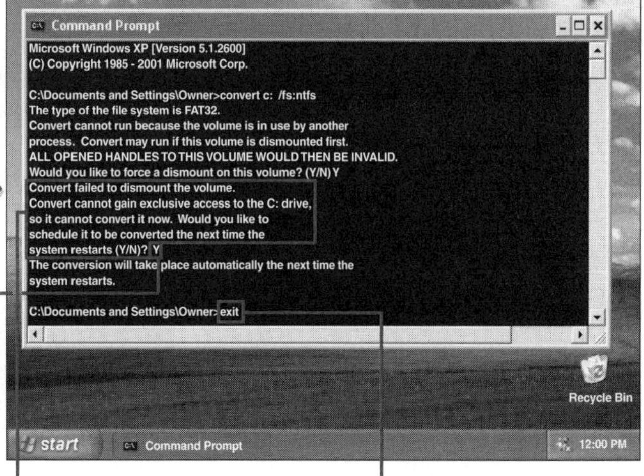

■ If Windows cannot dismount the drive now, Windows states that the drive can be converted the next time you start the computer.

9 To convert the drive the next time you start the computer, type **Y** (for Yes) and then press the Enter key.

10 To close the Command Prompt window, type **exit** and then press the Enter key.

■ When you restart your computer, Windows will convert the drive to NTFS.

ADD WINDOWS XP COMPONENTS

You can install additional Windows components to add capabilities and enhancements to your computer. The Windows Components Wizard helps you add components from the Windows XP CD-ROM disc. You must be logged on as a computer administrator in order to add Windows components.

When you install Windows, the installation program does not add all the components included with Windows to your computer. This avoids having unnecessary components that use valuable storage space and resources installed on your computer.

The wizard displays a list of components and indicates which components are installed and which are not yet installed on your computer. The wizard also displays the amount of hard disk space each component requires in megabytes (MB) and a brief description of each component.

Some components include several subcomponents. You can view the subcomponents included with a component and choose the subcomponents you want to add. The wizard uses check boxes to indicate whether all (☑), none (☐) or some (☑) of the subcomponents of a component are installed.

ADD WINDOWS XP COMPONENTS

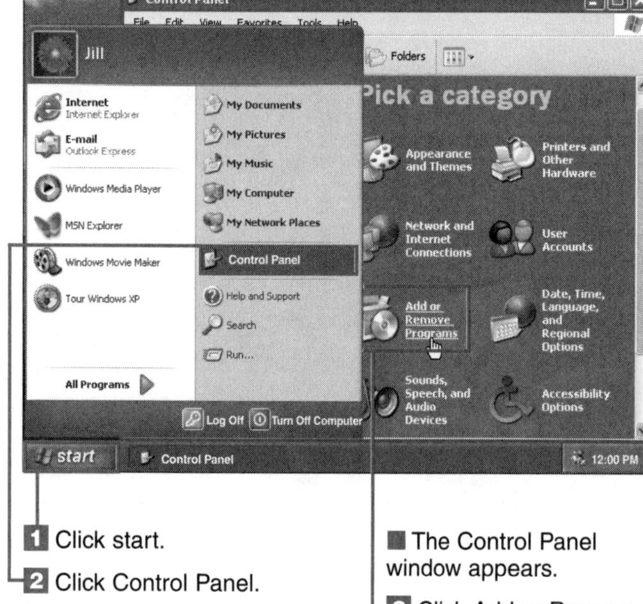

1 Click start.

2 Click Control Panel.

■ The Control Panel window appears.

3 Click Add or Remove Programs.

■ The Add or Remove Programs window appears.

4 Click Add/Remove Windows Components.

I did not receive a Windows XP CD-ROM disc when I bought my computer. How can I add Windows components?

✔ Many computer manufacturers store the contents of the Windows XP CD-ROM disc on the hard drive of a new computer or on their own CD-ROM discs that they supply with the computer. To determine how to add Windows components, you can check the instructions that came with the computer or ask the computer vendor.

Is there another way to add Windows components using the Windows XP CD-ROM disc?

✔ Yes. Insert the Windows XP CD-ROM disc into your CD-ROM drive to display the Welcome to Microsoft Windows XP screen. Then click Install optional Windows components. The Windows Components Wizard will appear, helping you to specify the components you want to add.

Is there a component that can help me set up and manage a Web site on my computer?

✔ Yes. The Internet Information Services (IIS) component allows you to set up and manage a Web site on your computer. The Internet Information Services (IIS) component is available only in the professional version of Windows XP.

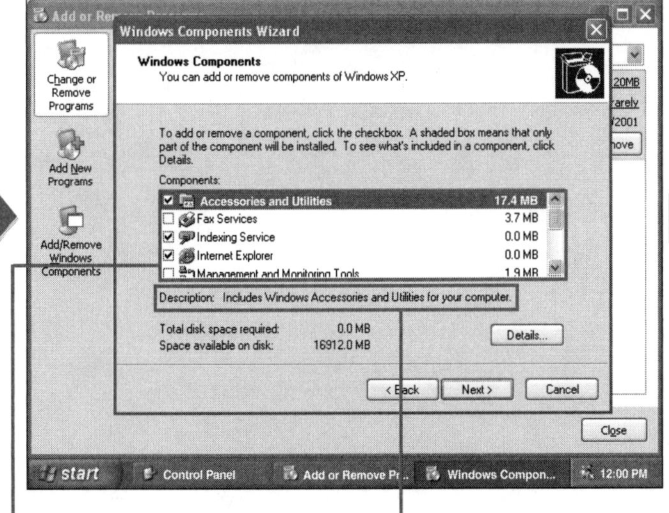

■ The Windows Components Wizard appears.

■ This area displays the components you can add to your computer and the amount of hard disk space each component requires.

■ Each component that displays a check mark (✔) is currently installed on your computer.

■ This area displays a description of the highlighted component.

Note: To display a description of another component, click the component.

5 Click the box (☐) beside each component you want to add to your computer (☐ changes to ☑).

6 Some components contain subcomponents. To display the subcomponents of a component, click the component.

7 Click Details.

Note: If the Details button is dimmed, the component does not contain any subcomponents.

CONTINUED

ADD WINDOWS XP COMPONENTS (CONTINUED)

The Windows Components Wizard displays the total amount of hard disk space required to add the components you selected. The wizard also displays the total amount of free hard disk space on your computer. These values can help you determine if you have enough space on your hard disk to add the components you selected.

There are several useful components you can add. The Fax Services component allows you to send and receive faxes using your computer. The Management and Monitoring Tools component provides tools that help you monitor and enhance the performance of your network. The Networking Services component includes services you can add to give your computer extra capabilities for sharing and accessing information on a network. The Other Network File and Print Services component allows you to add other network services, such as a print service for the Unix operating system.

When you install a component, the wizard may automatically install subcomponents of other components, since some components require subcomponents of other components to work properly.

Depending on the components you select, the installation may take several minutes.

ADD WINDOWS XP COMPONENTS (CONTINUED)

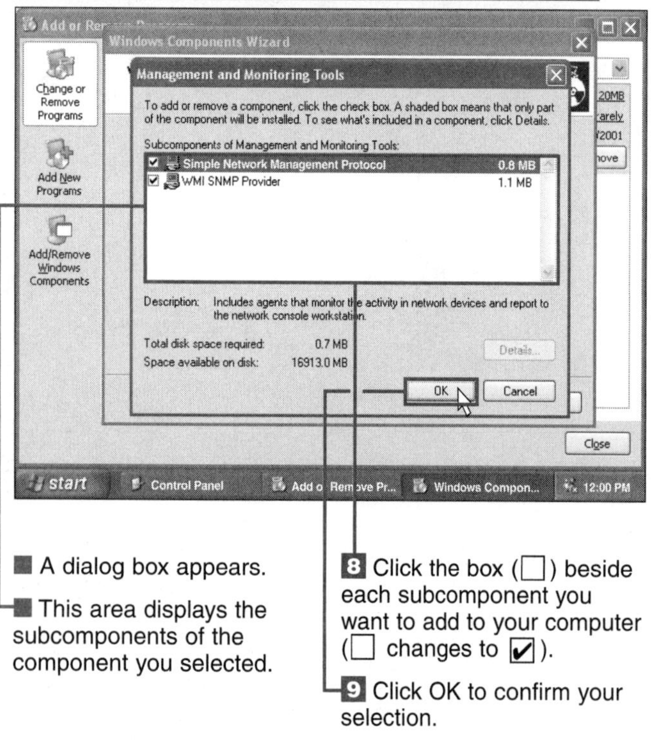

■ A dialog box appears.

■ This area displays the subcomponents of the component you selected.

8 Click the box (☐) beside each subcomponent you want to add to your computer (☐ changes to ☑).

9 Click OK to confirm your selection.

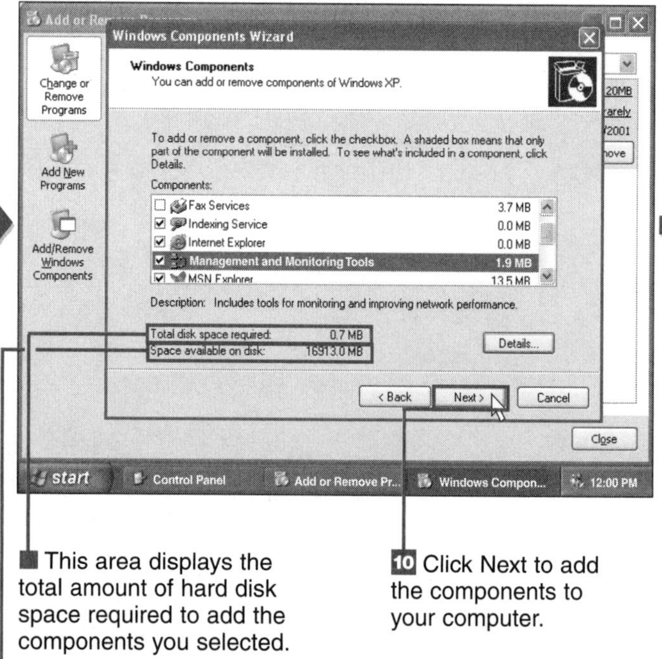

■ This area displays the total amount of hard disk space required to add the components you selected.

■ This area displays the total amount of free hard disk space on your computer.

10 Click Next to add the components to your computer.

Do subcomponents include additional components?

✔ Yes. Some subcomponents contain additional components that you can add or remove from your computer. In the dialog box that displays the subcomponents, click a subcomponent and then click the Details button to display the additional components for the subcomponent. If the Details button is dimmed, the subcomponent does not contain additional components.

How do I specify another location where Windows can copy the files needed to install a component?

✔ To have Windows copy the required files from a location other than the Windows XP CD-ROM disc, such as your hard drive or a computer on your network, click the OK button in the Insert Disk dialog box. Then click the Browse button in the Files Needed dialog box and select the location that contains the files Windows needs to copy.

How do I remove a component I no longer need?

✔ In the Windows Components Wizard, click the box beside the component you want to remove (☑ changes to ☐). Click Next and then click Finish to close the wizard. When you remove a component, Windows may ask you if you want to remove all related components.

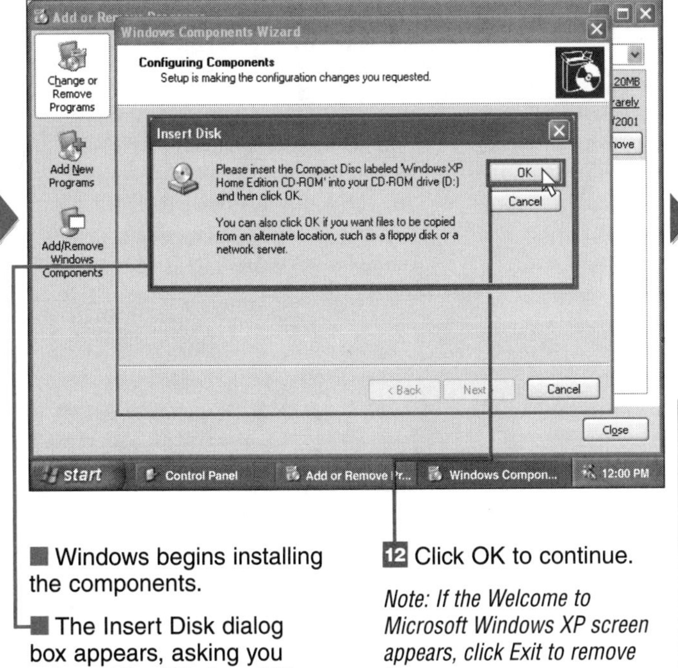

■ Windows begins installing the components.

■ The Insert Disk dialog box appears, asking you to insert the Windows XP CD-ROM disc.

11 Insert the CD-ROM disc into your CD-ROM drive.

12 Click OK to continue.

Note: If the Welcome to Microsoft Windows XP screen appears, click Exit to remove the screen.

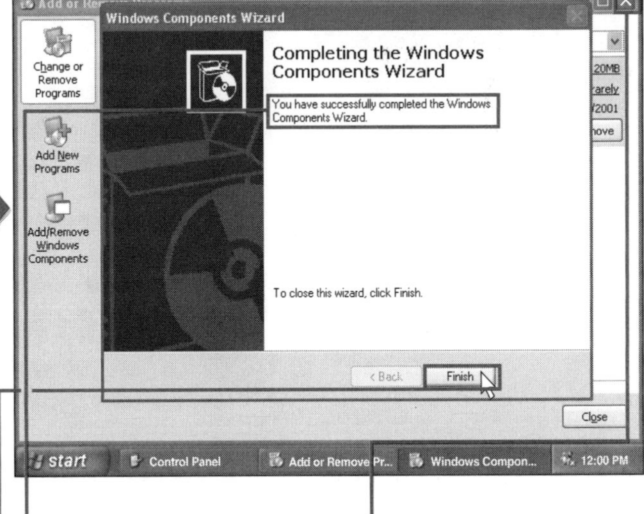

■ This message appears when you have successfully completed the wizard. The components you selected are now installed.

13 Click Finish to close the wizard.

14 Click ☒ to close the Add or Remove Programs window.

■ You can now use the components you added to your computer.

INSTALL A PROGRAM

You can install a new program on your computer. Programs are available on CD-ROM discs and floppy disks. You can use the method below only to install programs designed for Windows.

Every installation program will ask you a different set of questions. The installation program may ask you questions about your computer and how you would like to install the program. There are three common types of installations. A typical installation sets up a program with the most common components. A custom installation allows you to customize the program to suit your specific needs. A minimum installation sets up a program with a minimum number of components. A minimum installation is ideal for computers with limited disk space.

After you install a new program, make sure you keep the program's CD-ROM disc or floppy disks in a safe place. If your computer fails or you accidentally erase the program files, you may need to install the program again.

INSTALL A PROGRAM

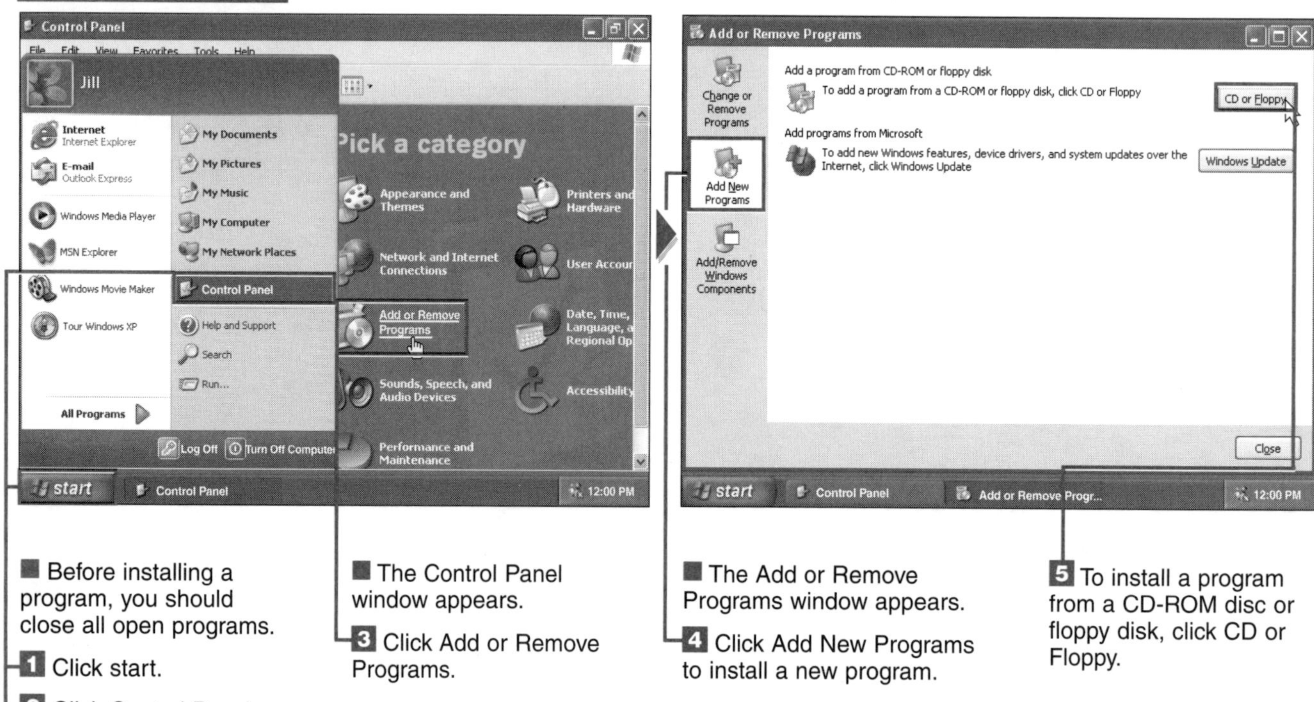

■ Before installing a program, you should close all open programs.

1 Click start.

2 Click Control Panel.

■ The Control Panel window appears.

3 Click Add or Remove Programs.

■ The Add or Remove Programs window appears.

4 Click Add New Programs to install a new program.

5 To install a program from a CD-ROM disc or floppy disk, click CD or Floppy.

Why did an installation program appear when I inserted a program's CD-ROM disc into my CD-ROM drive?

✔ Most Windows programs available on a CD-ROM disc will automatically start an installation program when you insert the disc into your CD-ROM drive. Follow the instructions on your screen to install the program.

How can I install a program if it does not have an installation program?

✔ Create a new folder on your computer and then copy all the files from the installation disk to the new folder. You can start the program from the folder.

How can I install a program I obtained on the Internet?

✔ Locate the program's files on your computer and then double-click the file that allows you to install the program. The file is usually named "install," "setup" or the name of the program.

Do I need to re-install all the programs on my computer after I upgrade to Windows XP?

✔ If you upgraded to Windows XP from a previous version of Windows, you do not need to re-install your existing programs. Some older programs may not run, however, so you may need to run the Program Compatibility Wizard or contact the program manufacturer to see if an updated version of the program is available. For information about the Program Compatibility Wizard, see page 588.

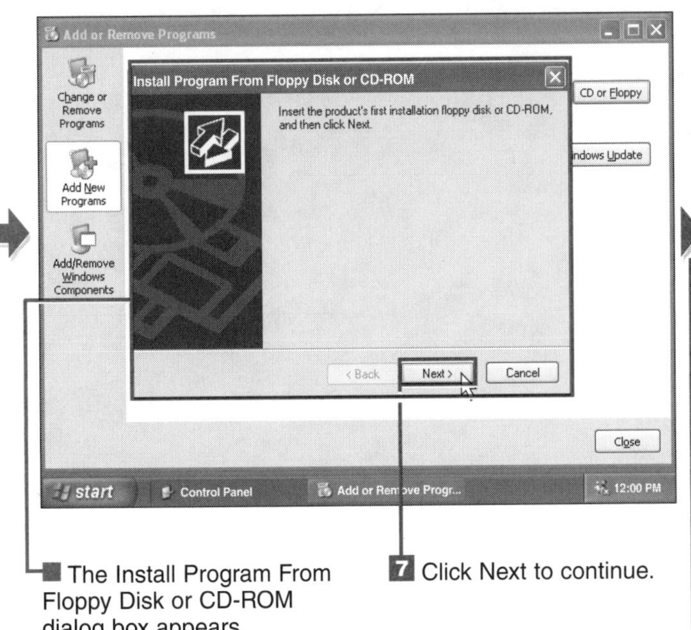

■ The Install Program From Floppy Disk or CD-ROM dialog box appears.

6 Insert the program's first installation floppy disk or CD-ROM disc into the appropriate drive on your computer.

7 Click Next to continue.

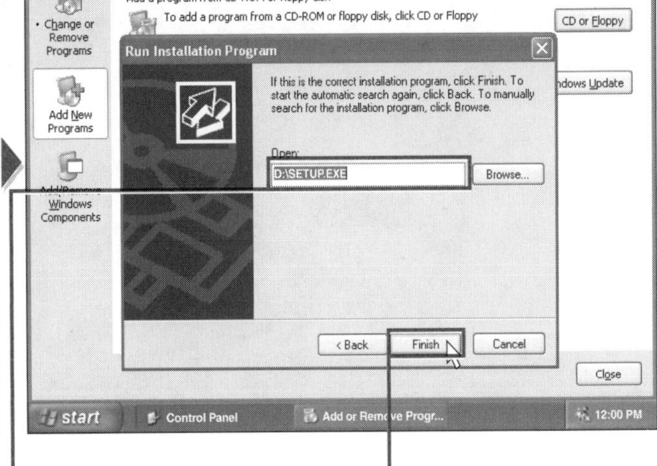

■ The Run Installation Program dialog box appears.

■ This area displays the location and name of the installation program that Windows will run to install the program.

8 Click Finish to install the program.

9 Follow the instructions on your screen. The instructions will be different for each program.

REMOVE A PROGRAM

You can remove a program you no longer use from your computer. Removing a program will free up space on your hard disk and allow you to install newer and more useful programs.

Windows keeps track of the programs you have installed on your computer. You can select the program you want to remove from a list and have Windows automatically remove the program from your computer.

When you remove a program from your computer, Windows deletes the program's files and may reverse the computer settings that were changed when the program was installed. To avoid affecting other programs, Windows may leave some of the files that other programs on your computer require to operate.

When you finish removing a program, you should restart your computer. This will ensure that any settings that were changed when the program was installed are reversed.

REMOVE A PROGRAM

1 Click start.

2 Click Control Panel.

■ The Control Panel window appears.

3 Click Add or Remove Programs.

How can I remove a program that Windows cannot automatically remove?

✔ Only programs designed for Windows will appear in the Add or Remove Programs window. For all other programs, check the documentation supplied with the program to determine how to remove the program. You can also purchase a commercial uninstall program that can help you remove unwanted programs from your computer.

How can I quickly find a program I want to remove in the Add or Remove Programs window?

✔ You can sort the programs displayed in the Add or Remove Programs window to easily locate the program you want to remove. In the Add or Remove Programs window, click the Sort by area and then click the way you want to sort the displayed programs.

The Start menu still displays a program I removed from my computer. How do I remove the program from the Start menu?

✔ On the Start menu, right-click the program you want to remove and then select Delete from the menu that appears.

How do I delete a program's shortcut from my desktop?

✔ After deleting a program, you can drag any shortcuts you no longer need to the Recycle Bin.

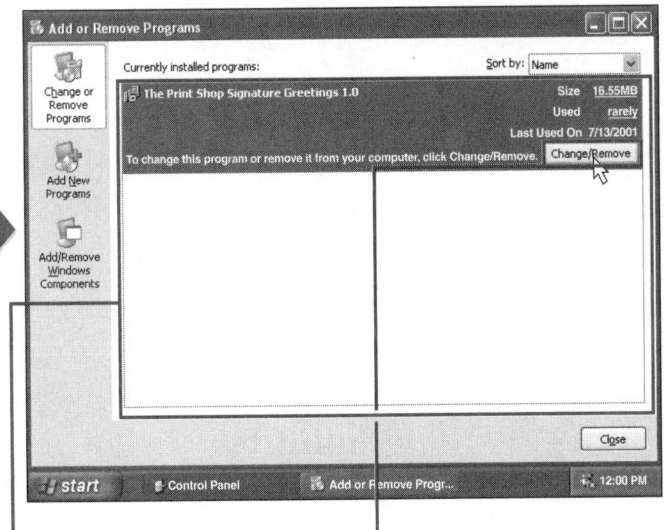

■ The Add or Remove Programs window appears.

■ This area lists the programs Windows can automatically remove from your computer.

4 Click the program you want to remove.

5 Click Change/Remove or Remove.

Note: The name of the button depends on the program you are removing.

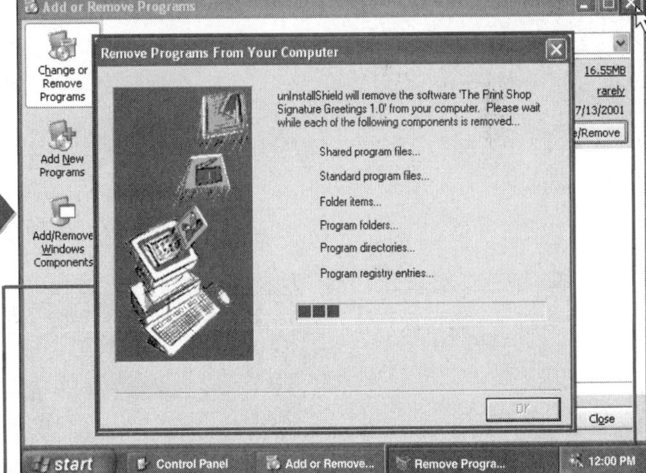

■ Windows begins the process of removing the program from your computer.

6 Follow the instructions on your screen. Every program will take you through different steps to remove the program.

7 When Windows has successfully removed the program, click ☒ to close the Add or Remove Programs window and the Control Panel window.

INSTALL NEW HARDWARE

You can install new hardware, such as a network interface card, modem or printer, on your computer. The Add Hardware Wizard guides you step by step through the installation of new hardware. You must be logged on as a computer administrator to install new hardware.

Before installing new hardware, you should read any documentation that was included with the device and connect the device to your computer. You should also close all open programs on your computer.

Windows first searches your computer for Plug and Play hardware. Plug and Play hardware uses technology that allows Windows to automatically detect the device and set up the device to work properly with your computer. This makes Plug and Play devices easy to install.

If a new Plug and Play device is attached to your computer but is not detected by Windows, the device may not be working properly. You should check to make sure the device is properly connected to your computer.

If your hardware included an installation CD-ROM disc from the manufacturer, you should use this disc to install the hardware.

INSTALL NEW HARDWARE

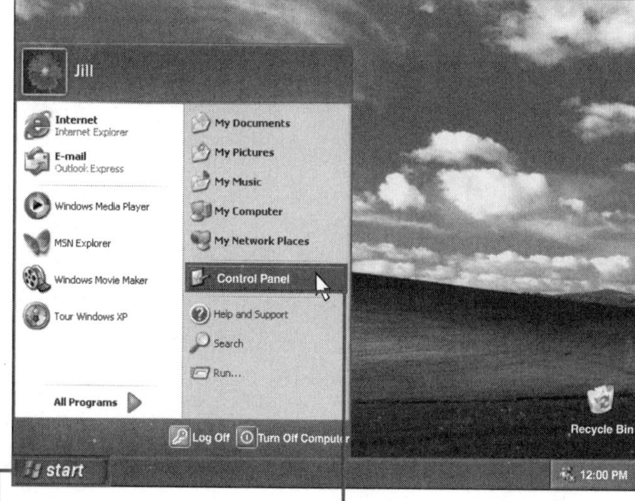

■ Before installing new hardware, make sure you connect the hardware to your computer.

1 Click start.

2 Click Control Panel.

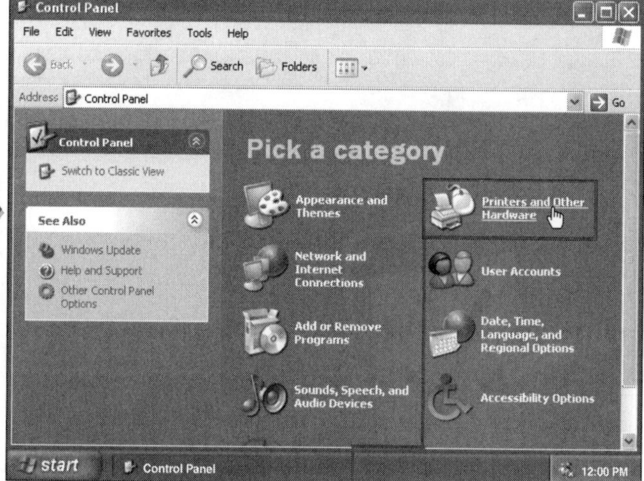

■ The Control Panel window appears.

3 Click Printers and Other Hardware.

Is there a faster way to install a new Plug and Play device?

✔ After you physically connect a Plug and Play device to your computer, Windows automatically detects the device and installs the necessary software. You may need to restart your computer before Windows can detect the device. If Windows requires information to install the device, Windows will ask you for the information.

My Plug and Play device is connected properly. Why can't Windows detect the device?

✔ The port to which the device is connected may be disabled in your computer's configuration settings. You should check your computer's settings to make sure the port is enabled. For more information about your computer's configuration settings, you can consult the documentation included with your computer.

Do I need to use the Add Hardware Wizard to install all devices?

✔ No. You can use options in the Control Panel to install specific devices. For example, to install a printer using the Add Printer Wizard, see page 130. To install a modem using the Phone and Modem Options dialog box, see page 350. To install a game controller, such as a joystick, using the Game Controllers dialog box, see page 300.

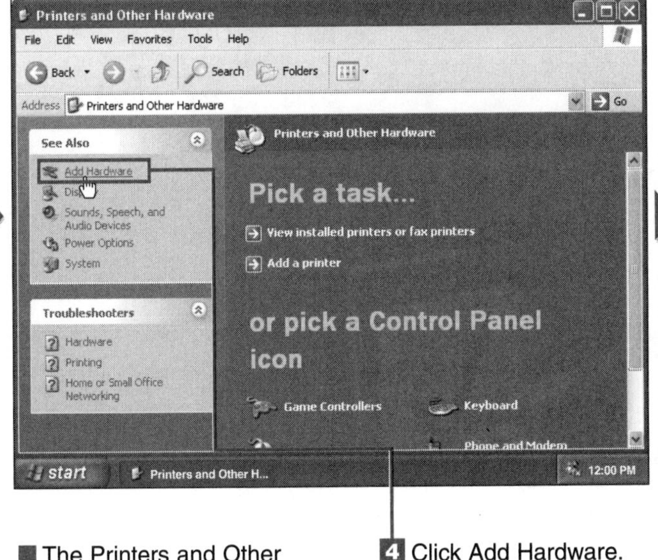

■ The Printers and Other Hardware window appears.

4 Click Add Hardware.

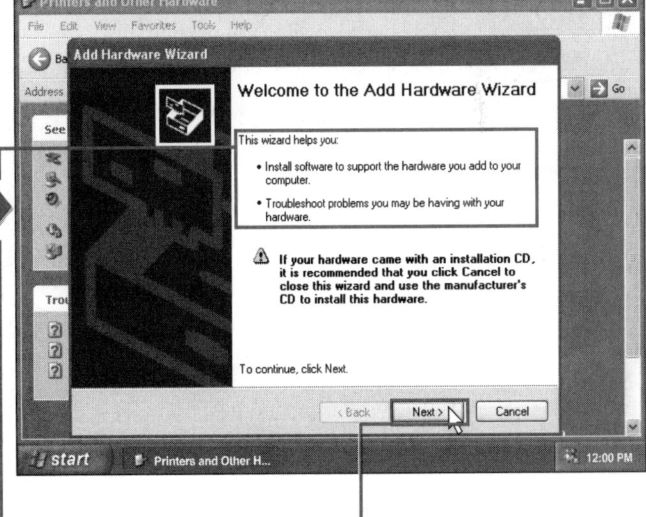

■ The Add Hardware Wizard appears.

■ This area describes the wizard.

5 Click Next to continue.

■ The wizard searches your computer for hardware you have recently connected to your computer but have not yet installed.

CONTINUED

INSTALL NEW HARDWARE (CONTINUED)

If the Add Hardware Wizard finds your new hardware device, the wizard will automatically install the hardware. If the wizard did not find your new hardware, the wizard will ask you to specify whether the hardware is connected to your computer. Before continuing, you may want to check the hardware again to make sure it is properly connected.

Windows displays a list of the hardware devices that are currently installed on your computer.

You can have Windows search your computer for new hardware that is not Plug and Play compatible. Windows may take a few minutes to search your computer. If the search stops for a long time, you should restart your computer and try installing the new hardware again.

If the Add Hardware Wizard does not find any new hardware on your computer, the wizard will allow you to select the type of hardware you want to install from a list.

INSTALL NEW HARDWARE (CONTINUED)

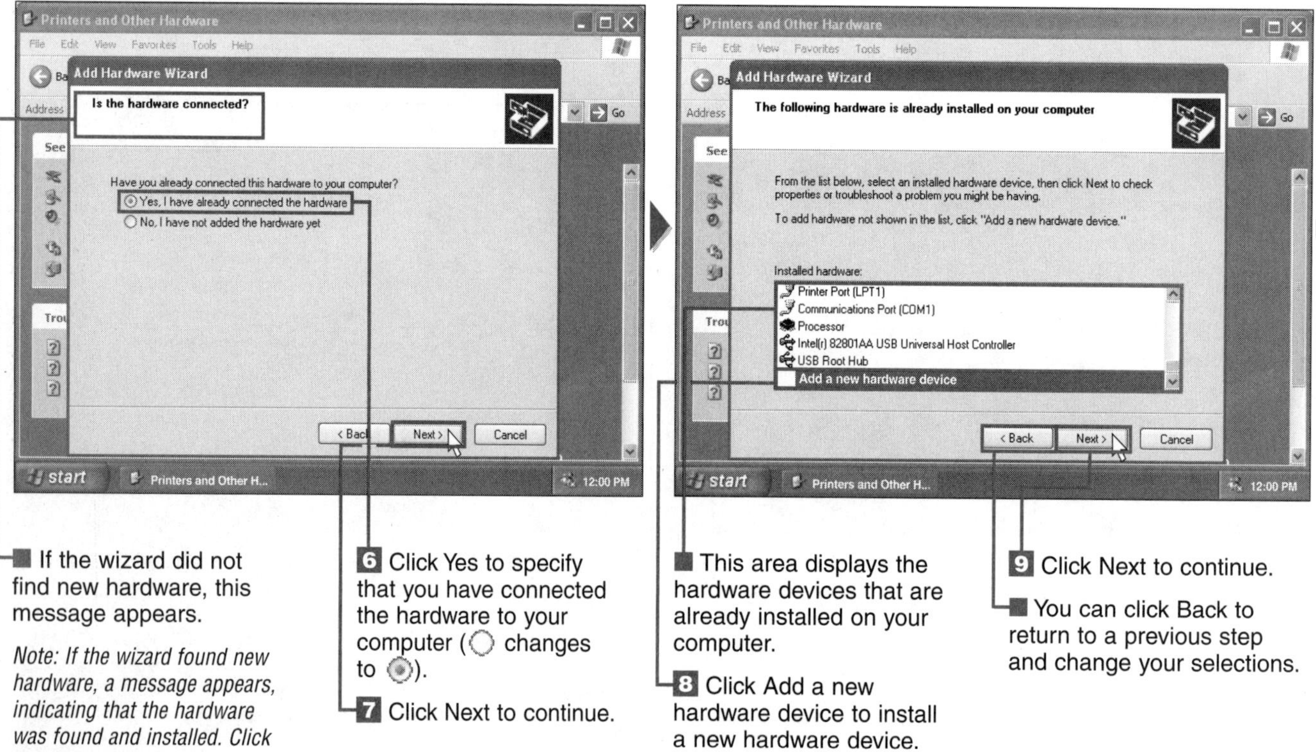

■ If the wizard did not find new hardware, this message appears.

Note: If the wizard found new hardware, a message appears, indicating that the hardware was found and installed. Click Finish to close the wizard.

6 Click Yes to specify that you have connected the hardware to your computer (○ changes to ◉).

7 Click Next to continue.

■ This area displays the hardware devices that are already installed on your computer.

8 Click Add a new hardware device to install a new hardware device.

9 Click Next to continue.

■ You can click Back to return to a previous step and change your selections.

How can I manually select my hardware instead of having Windows search for it?

✔ If you know exactly which hardware device you want to install, you can choose the "Install the hardware that I manually select from a list" option in the Add Hardware Wizard to select the hardware.

Can I troubleshoot a currently installed device using the wizard?

✔ Yes. In the list of installed hardware devices displayed in the Add Hardware Wizard, select the device you want to troubleshoot, click Next and then click Finish. The Help and Support Center window appears, displaying a troubleshooter for the device you selected. Follow the instructions on your screen to try to fix the problem.

Is there another way I can troubleshoot a device?

✔ When you finish installing a device, you can use the Hardware Troubleshooter help topic to help you solve a problem with your device. Click the start button and then click Help and Support. In the Help and Support Center window, click the Search area, type **hardware troubleshooter** and then press the Enter key. A link appears for the Hardware Troubleshooter. Click the link and then follow the instructions on your screen.

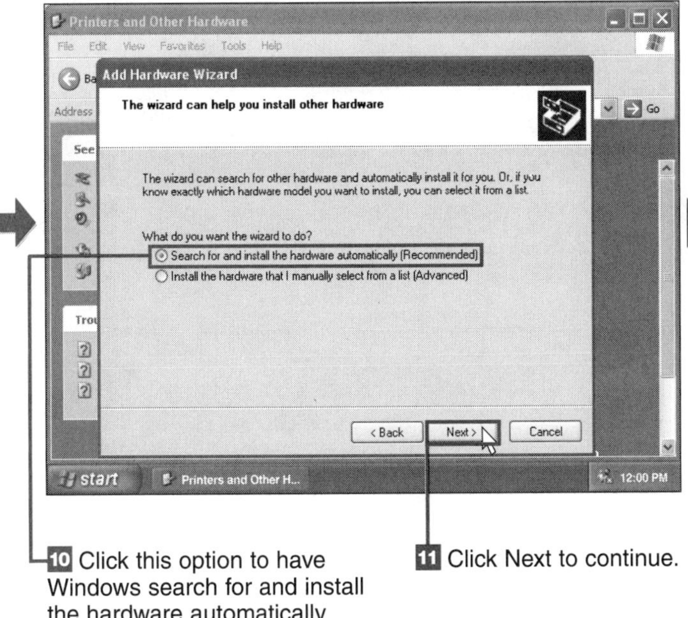

10 Click this option to have Windows search for and install the hardware automatically (○ changes to ◉).

11 Click Next to continue.

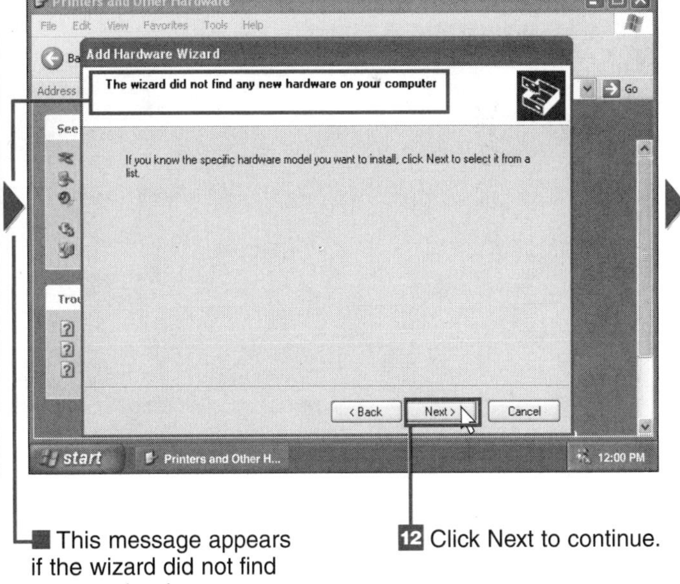

■ This message appears if the wizard did not find any new hardware on your computer.

12 Click Next to continue.

CONTINUED

INSTALL NEW HARDWARE (CONTINUED)

When installing a new hardware device, you can select the type of hardware you want to install from a list. The type of hardware you choose to install will determine what steps you need to perform to finish installing the device.

You must specify the manufacturer and model of the device. This allows Windows to select the correct driver for the device. A driver is software that enables Windows to communicate with the device.

You may need to restart your computer to complete the installation of some devices.

After you install a device, you may have to adjust the settings for the device to match the settings used by Windows. You can adjust the settings for a device by using the software that came with the device or by manually adjusting the jumpers or switches on the device. Consult the documentation that came with the device before making any adjustments. You can use Device Manager to view the settings Windows uses for the device. For information about using Device Manager, see page 580.

INSTALL NEW HARDWARE (CONTINUED)

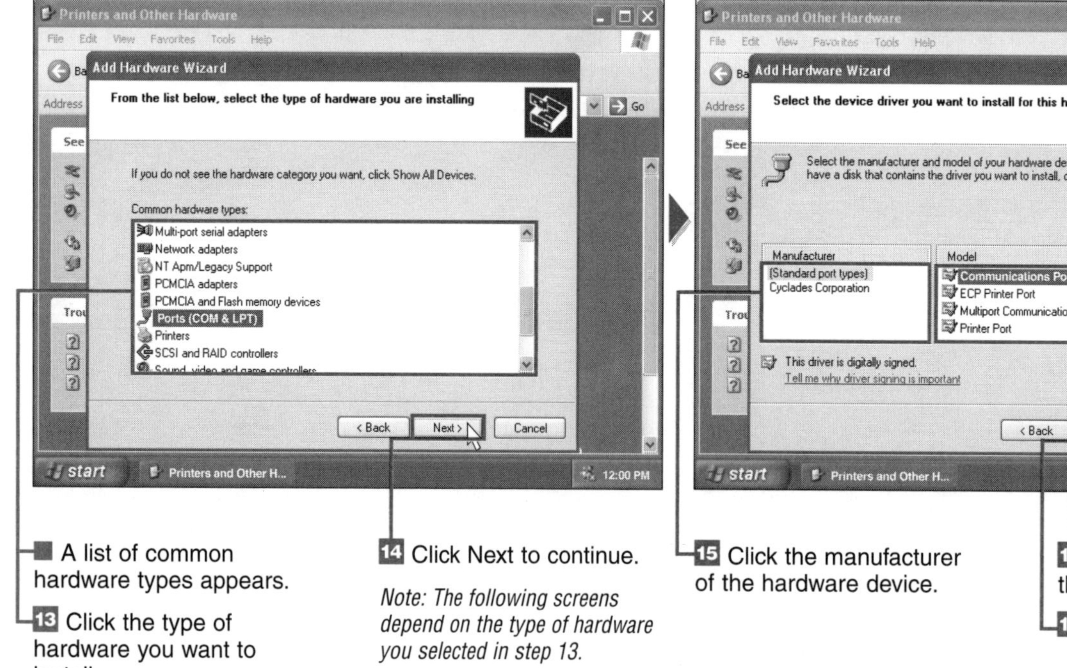

■ A list of common hardware types appears.

13 Click the type of hardware you want to install.

Note: If you do not see the type of hardware you want to install, click Show All Devices in the list.

14 Click Next to continue.

Note: The following screens depend on the type of hardware you selected in step 13.

15 Click the manufacturer of the hardware device.

16 Click the model of the hardware device.

17 Click Next to continue.

I cannot find the model of the device I want to install. What should I do?

✔ If you have a disk that contains the driver for the device, you can install the device using the disk. Insert the disk into the drive. Click the Have Disk button in the Add Hardware Wizard, select the drive that contains the disk and then press the Enter key. If you do not have a disk containing the driver for the device, try selecting a device that closely resembles the one you want to install.

Why didn't my hardware device install properly?

✔ The device you installed may not be compatible with Windows XP. To ensure your new hardware device will work with Windows XP, check the documentation that came with the device or check Microsoft's hardware compatibility list at the www.microsoft.com/hcl Web site.

How do I uninstall hardware I no longer need?

✔ You can use the Device Manager to uninstall hardware. For information about uninstalling hardware, see page 558.

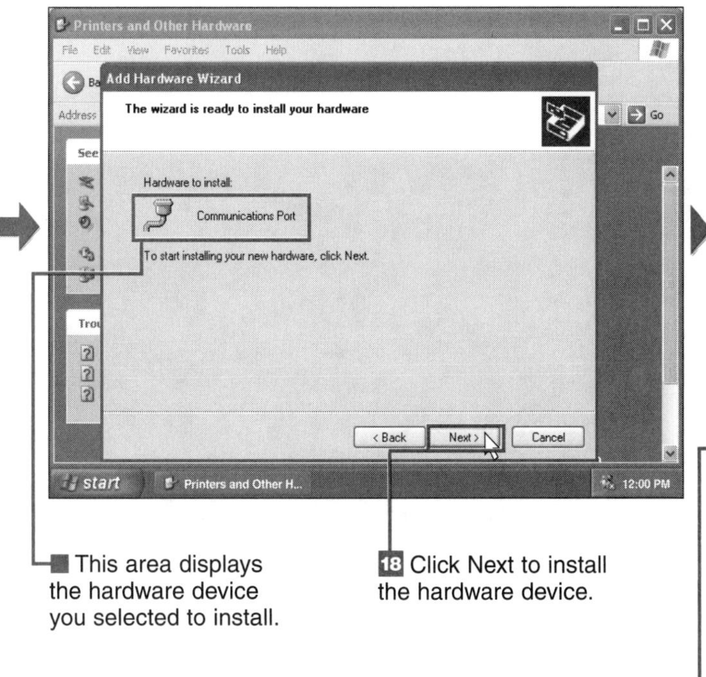

■ This area displays the hardware device you selected to install.

18 Click Next to install the hardware device.

■ This message appears when Windows has finished installing the hardware device.

19 Click Finish to close the wizard.

■ A message may appear, stating that you must restart your computer before the changes will take effect. Click Yes to restart the computer.

UPDATE DEVICE DRIVERS

Your hardware devices may work better if you are using the latest version of the software they need to operate. Hardware devices ranging from your mouse to your modem are all controlled by software, called drivers. A driver allows the computer to communicate with and control a device.

When you install a device, Windows usually automatically detects the device and then installs the appropriate driver for the device.

When you purchase a hardware device, the manufacturer may include a driver on a floppy disk or CD-ROM disc. To use the driver provided by the manufacturer instead of the driver Windows automatically installed, you will need to insert the floppy disk or CD-ROM disc when updating the driver.

You can also obtain new drivers directly from the manufacturer. Most manufacturers provide the latest drivers in the support area of their Web site. The latest driver for a device may improve the performance of the device and offer more features.

You must be logged on as a computer administrator to update device drivers on your computer.

UPDATE DEVICE DRIVERS

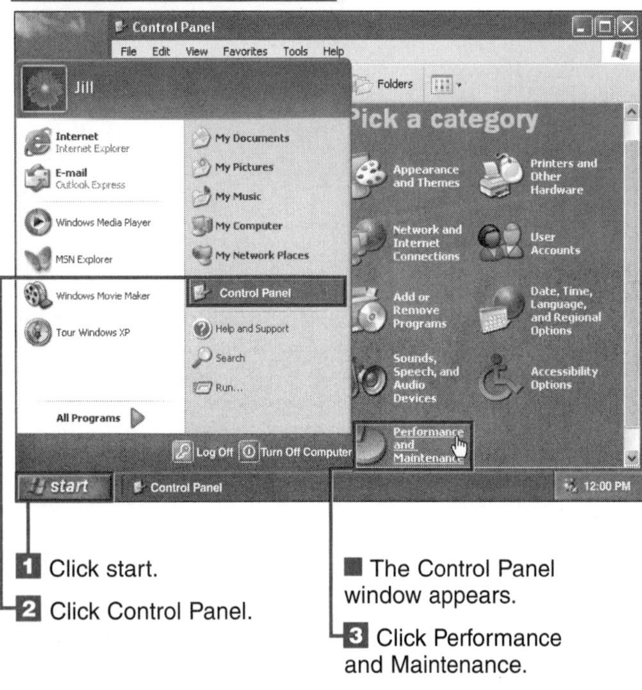

1 Click start.

2 Click Control Panel.

■ The Control Panel window appears.

3 Click Performance and Maintenance.

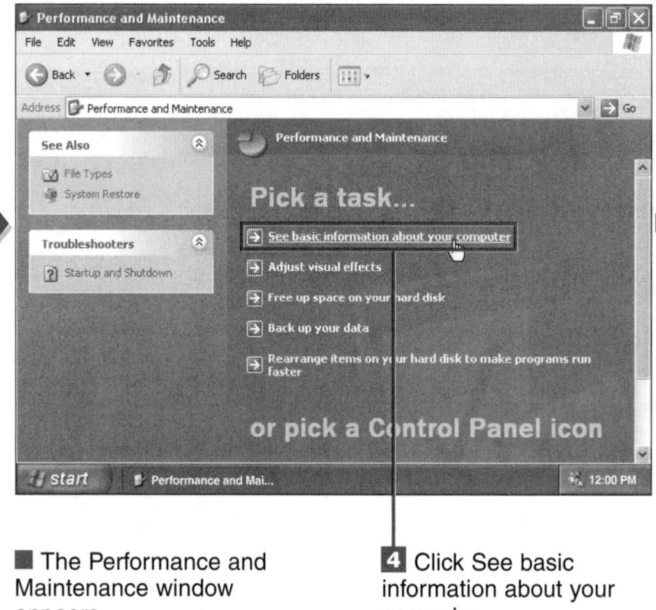

■ The Performance and Maintenance window appears.

4 Click See basic information about your computer.

Is there another way I can obtain new drivers?

✔ You can use the Windows Update feature to find new drivers on the Internet. Click the start button, select All Programs and then choose Windows Update. A Web browser window opens and displays the Windows Update Web site. Click Scan for updates and then follow the instructions on your screen.

My printer is not listed in the Device Manager window. How do I update my printer driver?

✔ Click start, select Control Panel, choose Printers and Other Hardware and then click View installed printers or fax printers. In the Printers and Faxes window, right-click the printer you want to update the driver for and then select Properties. In the dialog box that appears, choose the Advanced tab and then click the New Driver button. Then follow the instructions in the Add Printer Driver Wizard that appears.

How can I view more information about a driver?

✔ In the Properties dialog box for a device, select the Driver tab and then click the Driver Details button. The Driver File Details dialog box appears, displaying the name and location of each driver file the device may use to operate. Select a driver file to view the provider name, file version, copyright information and digital signer for the driver file.

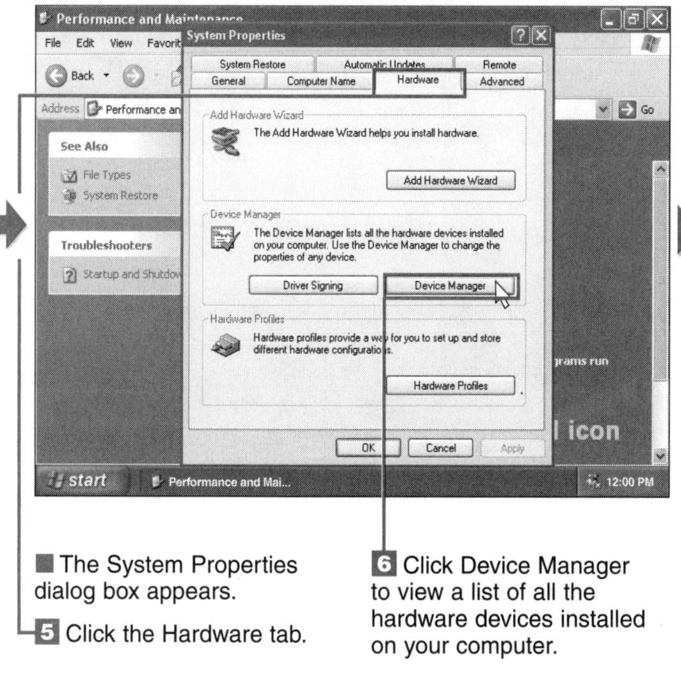

■ The System Properties dialog box appears.

5 Click the Hardware tab.

6 Click Device Manager to view a list of all the hardware devices installed on your computer.

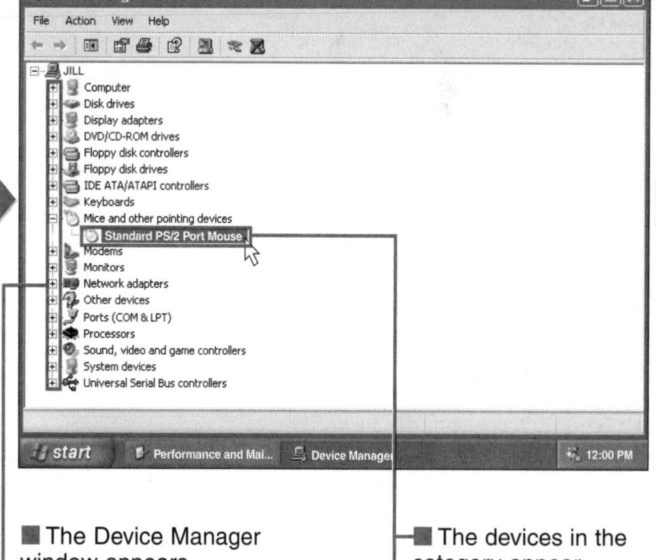

■ The Device Manager window appears.

7 Click the plus sign (⊞) beside the type of device you want to use an updated driver (⊞ changes to ⊟).

■ The devices in the category appear.

8 Double-click the device you want to use an updated driver.

CONTINUED

UPDATE DEVICE DRIVERS (CONTINUED)

When updating the driver for a device, you can have the Hardware Update Wizard automatically install the driver.

The wizard will search the Windows drivers folder on your computer for an updated driver. If you inserted a floppy disk or CD-ROM disc into a drive, Windows will search the contents of the drive for an updated driver.

When searching for an updated driver, the wizard always looks for a file with the .inf extension. The INF file contains information that tells the wizard how to install the driver. After the wizard reads the INF file, it will copy the file Windows needs and adjust any settings that are required by the device. In addition to the INF file, the wizard may need files from the Windows CD-ROM disc.

After updating the driver for a device, you may need to restart your computer before the device will function properly.

UPDATE DEVICE DRIVERS (CONTINUED)

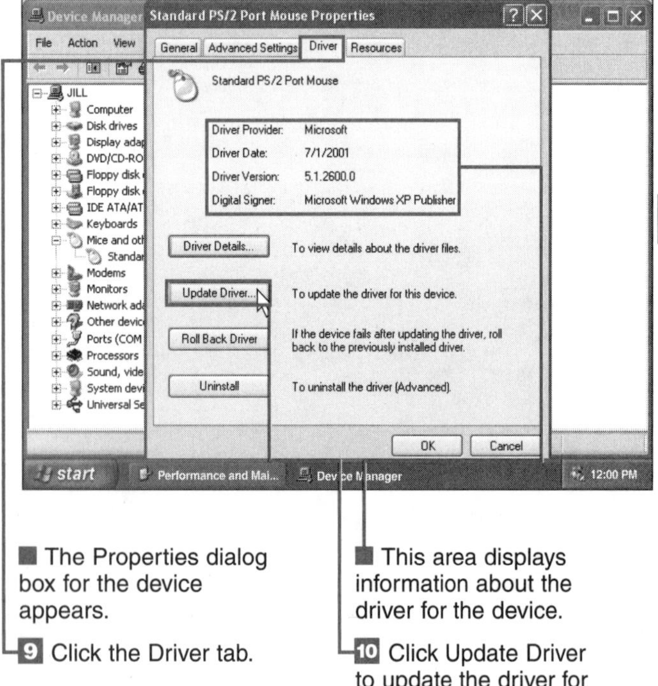

■ The Properties dialog box for the device appears.

9 Click the Driver tab.

■ This area displays information about the driver for the device.

10 Click Update Driver to update the driver for the device.

■ The Hardware Update Wizard appears.

11 If the updated driver is stored on a CD-ROM disc or floppy disk, insert the disk into the appropriate drive.

12 Click this option to have the wizard automatically install the updated driver (○ changes to ◉).

13 Click Next to continue.

Can I manually specify the location of a driver I want to install?

✔ If you know the location of the driver you want to install, you can select the Install from a list or specific location (Advanced) option in the Hardware Update Wizard and then click Next. You can then select the options that allow you to search a specific location. You can click the Browse button to choose a specific location to search. Click Next to continue installing the driver.

If a new driver is not working properly, can I reinstall the previous driver?

✔ Yes. In the Properties dialog box for the device, select the Driver tab and click the Roll Back Driver button.

How do I uninstall the driver for a device I no longer use?

✔ In the Properties dialog box for the device, select the Driver tab and then click the Uninstall button.

Why does the Confirm Device Install dialog box appear when the Hardware Update Wizard installs a driver?

✔ The Confirm Device Install dialog box appears when the wizard installs a driver that may affect other devices and drivers on your computer. To continue installing the driver, click Yes.

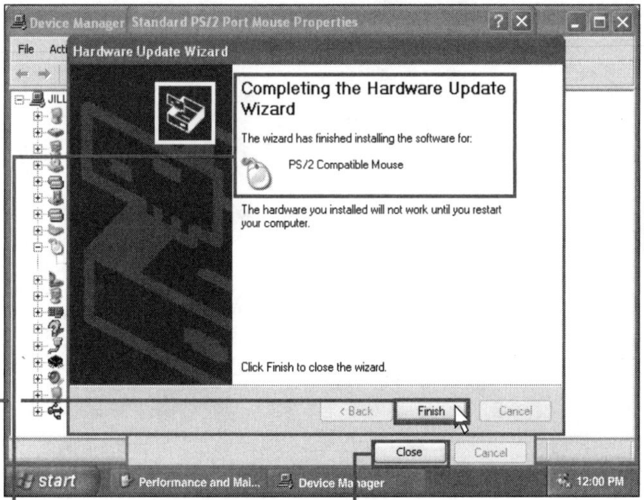

■ This message appears when the wizard has finished installing the updated driver for the device.

14 Click Finish to close the wizard.

15 Click Close to close the Properties dialog box.

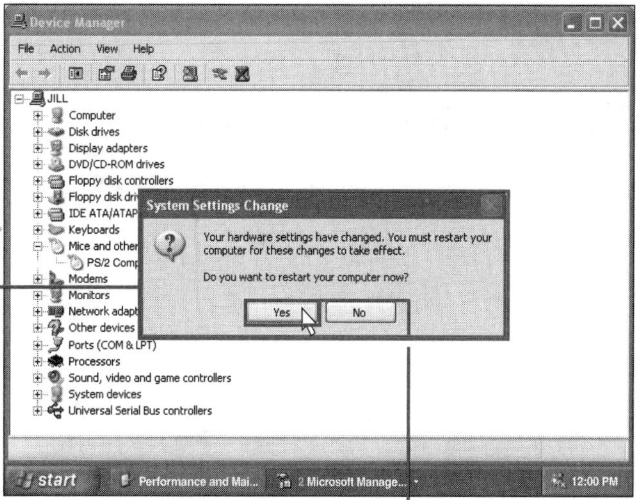

■ The System Settings Change dialog box may appear, stating that you must restart your computer for the changes to take effect.

16 Click Yes to restart your computer now.

UNINSTALL A DEVICE

You can use the Device Manager to uninstall a device on your computer. You may want to uninstall an old device to remove the device from your computer so you can install an updated version of the device.

A Plug and Play device is usually installed automatically when you connect the device to your computer and is uninstalled automatically when you physically disconnect the device. If a device is not uninstalled when you disconnect the device from the computer, you can remove the device from the Device Manager. You should always physically disconnect devices you no longer use to free up the resources used by the device and ensure that Windows will not automatically re-install a Plug and Play device.

After you uninstall a device, you should restart your computer. Restarting your computer resets the devices and software on your computer and makes sure the software for the uninstalled device is removed from memory. The software for the device may not be removed from your computer's hard disk, however.

You must be logged on as a computer administrator to uninstall a device.

UNINSTALL A DEVICE

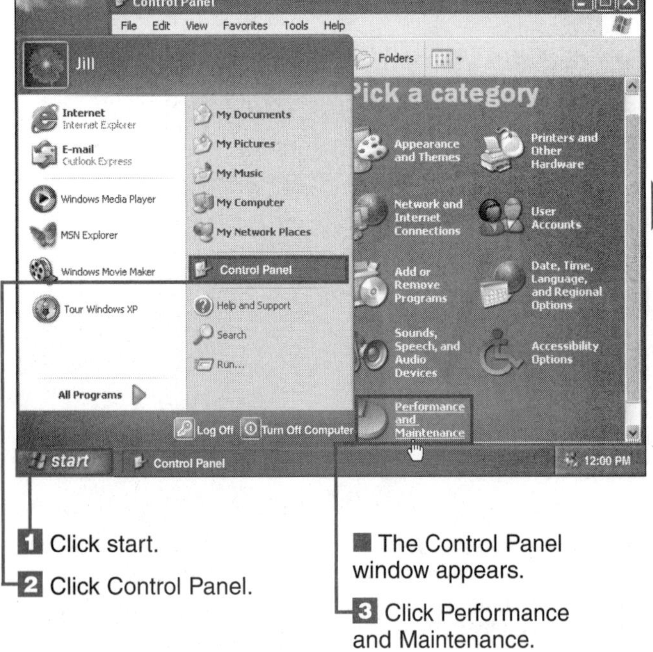

1 Click start.

2 Click Control Panel.

■ The Control Panel window appears.

3 Click Performance and Maintenance.

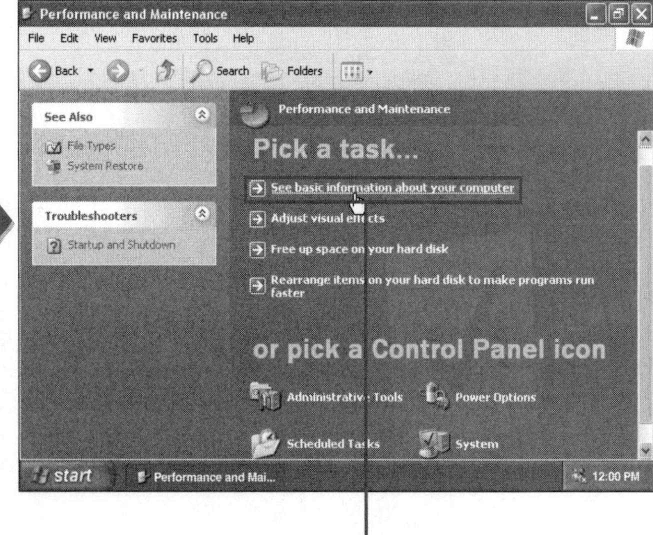

■ The Performance and Maintenance window appears.

4 Click See basic information about your computer.

Can I disable a device instead of uninstalling the device?

✔ Yes. You must be logged on as a computer administrator to disable a device. To disable a device, display the Device Manager window and then double-click the category for the device you want to disable. Click the device and then click [icon]. To later enable the device, you can click the device and then click [icon]. You should not disable a device that is required to start your computer, such as your floppy disk or CD-ROM drive. Your computer may not start if a device it requires is disabled.

How do I re-install a device on my computer?

✔ To re-install a device, turn off the computer and then reconnect the device. Windows will automatically detect a Plug and Play device when you restart your computer. If Windows does not detect the device, click the start button and select Control Panel. In the Control Panel window, click Printers and Other Hardware, click Add Hardware and then follow the instructions in the Add Hardware Wizard that appears. For more information, see page 548.

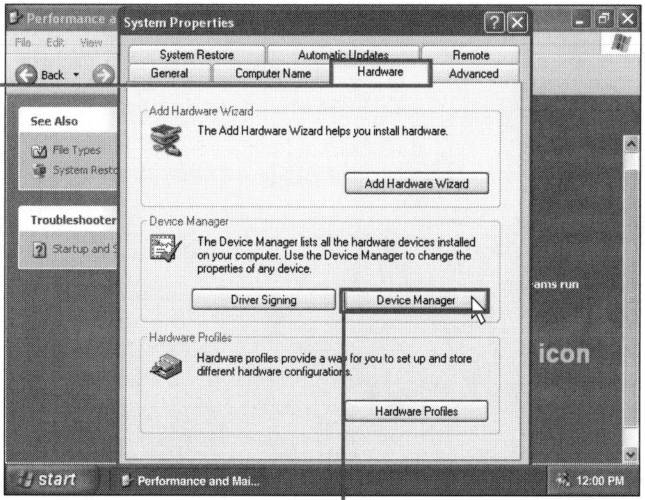

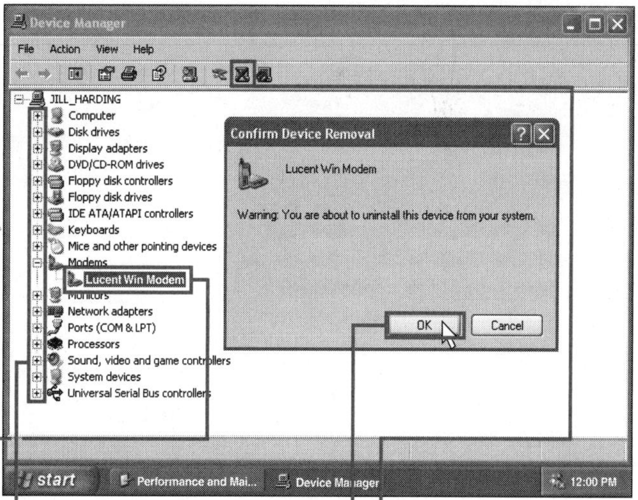

■ The System Properties dialog box appears.

5 Click the Hardware tab.

6 Click Device Manager to view a list of all the hardware devices installed on your computer.

■ The Device Manager window appears.

7 Click the plus sign (⊞) beside the type of device you want to uninstall (⊞ changes to ⊟).

■ The devices in the category appear.

8 Click the device you want to uninstall.

9 Click [icon] to uninstall the device.

■ A confirmation dialog box appears.

10 Click OK to uninstall the device.

INSTALL WINDOWS XP

You can install Windows XP Home Edition or Windows XP Professional to upgrade your computer's operating system from Windows 98 or Windows Me. If you currently have Windows 2000 or Windows NT 4.0, you can only upgrade to Windows XP Professional. The installation process for Windows XP Professional is slightly different than the process for the Home Edition.

When you upgrade to Windows XP, you replace the operating system on your computer, but you retain your settings, files and any programs you previously installed.

As a precaution, before upgrading to Windows XP, you should back up your files. You should also ensure that your computer meets the recommended hardware requirements for Windows XP. To run Windows XP Home Edition, your computer should at least have a 300 MHz Pentium or compatible processor, a Super VGA (800x600) video adapter and monitor, a CD or DVD drive, 128 MB of RAM and 1.5 GB of free hard disk space.

Windows Setup guides you step by step through the installation process. You must accept the Microsoft License Agreement before you can continue with the installation. Windows Setup also requires you to enter the 25-character product key for your copy of Windows XP. You can find the product key on the CD's packaging or documentation.

INSTALL WINDOWS XP

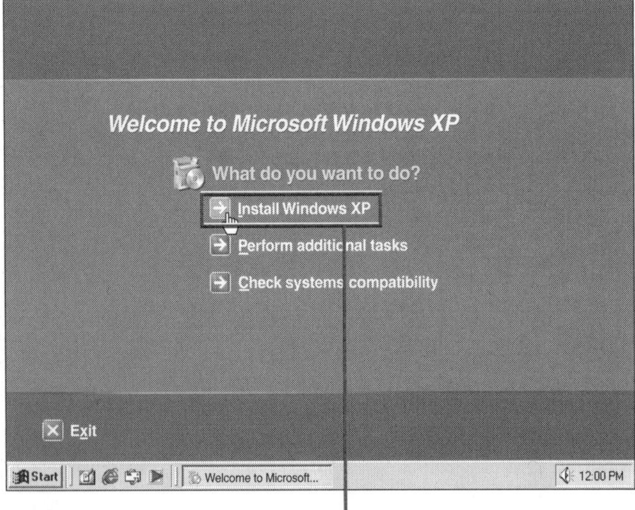

1 Insert the Windows XP installation CD into your CD drive.

■ The Welcome to Microsoft Windows XP screen appears.

2 Click Install Windows XP to upgrade your computer to Windows XP.

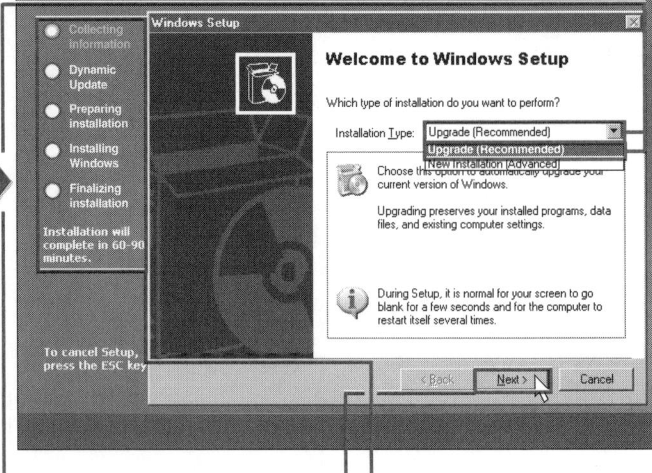

■ The Windows Setup wizard appears.

3 Click this area to select the type of installation you want to perform.

4 Click Upgrade to upgrade your computer to Windows XP.

■ This area displays the steps of the Windows XP installation and the estimated time remaining.

5 Click Next to continue.

When I inserted the installation CD, the Welcome to Microsoft Windows XP screen did not appear. What should I do?

✔ To display the Welcome to Microsoft Windows XP screen, open the My Computer window and then double-click the drive containing the CD.

Can I install Windows XP without retaining my settings, files and programs?

✔ Yes. If you want to replace the operating system on your computer without retaining your settings, files and programs, you can choose the New Installation (Advanced) installation type in the Windows Setup wizard. This option is also useful when you want to have more than one operating system installed on your computer.

How do I install Windows XP on a computer that does not have an operating system currently installed?

✔ You can use the installation CD that comes with the full version of Windows XP to install Windows on a blank hard drive. Turn on your computer and insert the Windows XP installation CD. Then follow the instructions on your screen to install Windows.

How can I cancel Windows Setup?

✔ If you do not want to proceed with the installation, you can press the Esc key to exit Windows Setup.

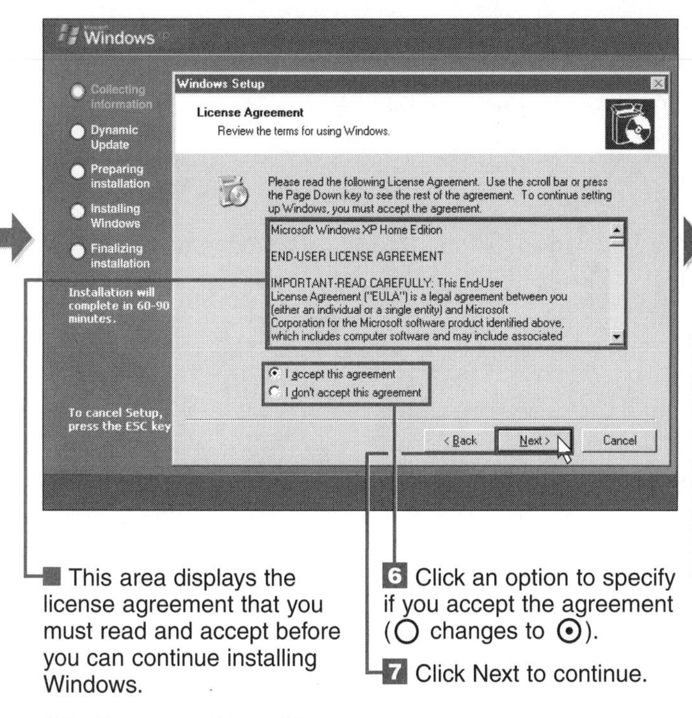

■ This area displays the license agreement that you must read and accept before you can continue installing Windows.

Note: You can use the scroll bar to browse through the agreement.

6 Click an option to specify if you accept the agreement (○ changes to ⦿).

7 Click Next to continue.

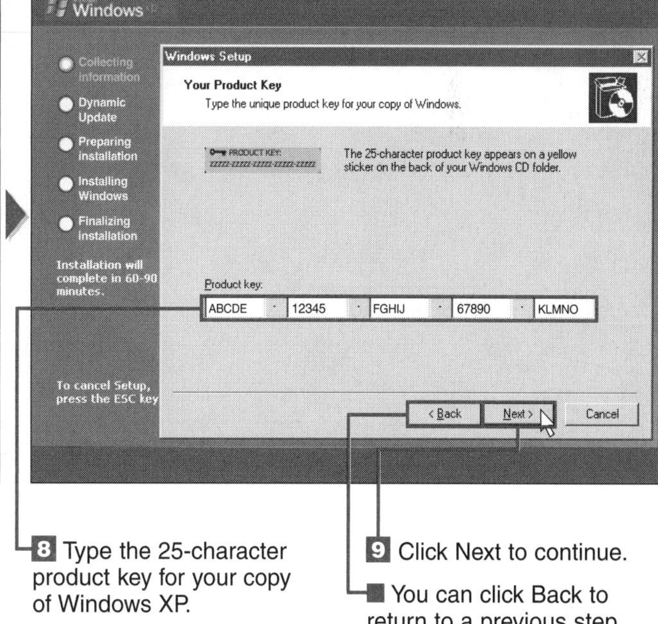

8 Type the 25-character product key for your copy of Windows XP.

9 Click Next to continue.

■ You can click Back to return to a previous step and change your selections.

CONTINUED

INSTALL WINDOWS XP (CONTINUED)

During the installation process, Windows Setup can create and save an upgrade report that describes any problems you may have with programs and hardware installed on your computer after upgrading to Windows XP. You can have Windows Setup save a limited report containing only hardware issues and some software issues, a full report, or no report.

If you have an Internet connection set up on your computer, you can use the Dynamic Update feature to obtain updated Setup files from the Microsoft Windows Update Web site. This will ensure that you are using the most recent Setup files for the installation.

Once you have finished selecting options for the installation, Windows Setup will automatically begin installing Windows XP on your computer. This process will take approximately one hour, during which time your computer may restart several times.

When the installation is complete, Windows asks if you are ready to activate your copy of Windows XP. To help reduce software piracy, you will need to activate Windows within 30 days of the installation. You do not need to give any personal information when activating Windows. If you do not want to activate Windows at this time, you can choose to activate it later. For more information, see page 566.

INSTALL WINDOWS XP (CONTINUED)

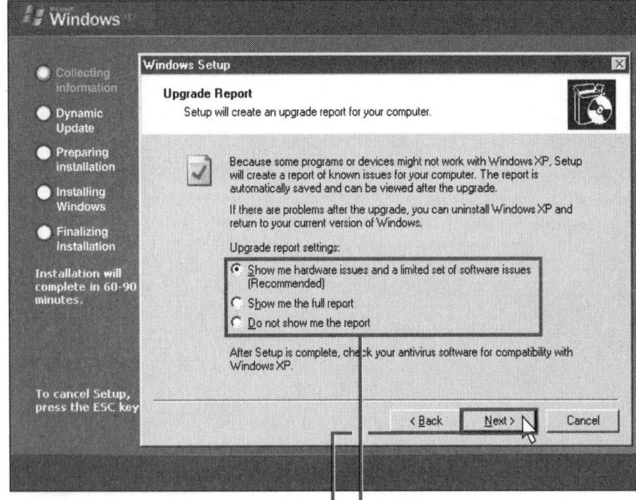

■ Windows Setup can create an upgrade report that summarizes information about hardware or software problems caused by the upgrade.

10 Click an option to specify the information you want the upgrade report to display (○ changes to ⊙).

11 Click Next to continue.

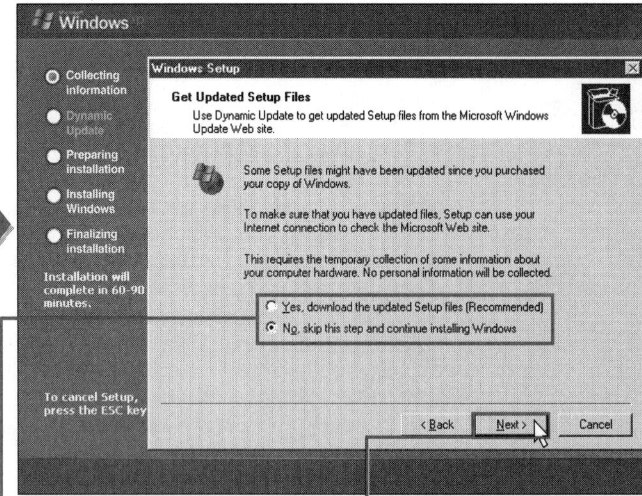

12 Click an option to specify if you want to download updated Setup files from the Microsoft Web site (○ changes to ⊙).

Note: You must have an Internet connection to download updated Setup files.

13 Click Next to continue.

Note: If you selected to download updated Setup files in step 12 and you are not currently connected to the Internet, a dialog box will appear, allowing you to connect.

Where will Windows Setup save the upgrade report it creates during the installation?

✔ If Windows Setup encounters a hardware or software problem that may affect the installation, it will display the upgrade report on your screen. You can click the Save As button to select the location where you want to save the upgrade report. If no such problems are found, Windows Setup will save the upgrade report as a text file named "upgrade" in your WINDOWS folder.

How can I display help information while setting up my computer?

✔ You can click the question mark (?) located in the bottom right corner of the Windows Setup screens to display a list of help topics about the task you are currently performing. You can then select a help topic of interest to display information about the topic.

Do I need an Internet connection to activate Windows while setting up my computer?

✔ If you do not have an Internet connection set up on your computer, you can still activate Windows if you have a modem installed. Windows will automatically search for an Internet connection that it can use to activate Windows. If no connection is found, Windows will use your modem to dial a telephone number that will activate your copy of Windows XP.

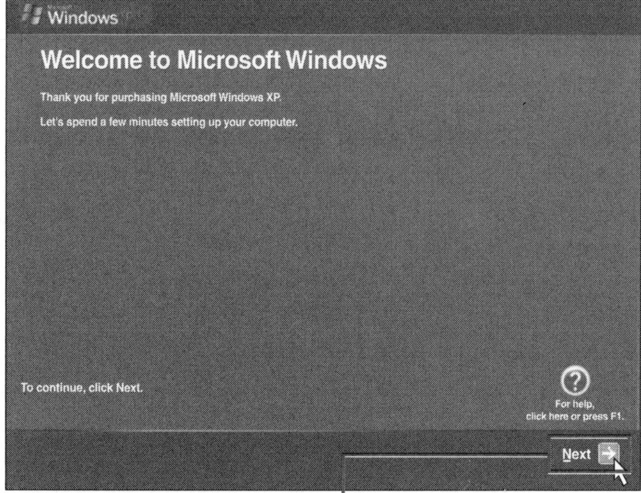

■ Windows Setup will automatically begin installing Windows XP. Your computer may restart several times before the installation is complete.

■ When the installation is complete, the Welcome to Microsoft Windows screen appears.

14 Click Next to begin setting up Windows XP.

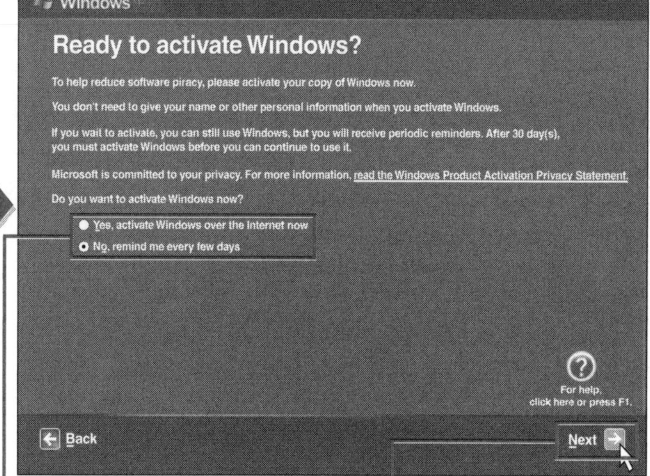

■ You will need to activate your copy of Windows to help reduce software piracy.

15 Click an option to specify whether you want to activate Windows now (○ changes to ⊙).

16 Click Next to continue.

CONTINUED

INSTALL WINDOWS XP (CONTINUED)

If you do not already have an Internet connection set up on your computer and you would like to use MSN to connect to the Internet, you can set up your Internet connection while setting up Windows XP. If you already have an Internet connection or you would prefer to use a different Internet service provider, you can choose not to set up an Internet connection at this time.

Windows asks you to enter the name of each person who will use your computer. Windows will set up a separate user account for each person you specify and will keep the personal files and settings separate for each account.

Once you have finished setting up Windows, you are ready to begin using Windows XP. If multiple users are set up on your computer, Windows will display the Welcome screen, which lists each user account. To begin using Windows, you simply select your user account from the list.

Since your settings are retained when you upgrade from an earlier version of Windows, your desktop will look slightly different than computers running the full version of Windows XP. For example, icons for items such as My Computer will appear on your desktop.

INSTALL WINDOWS XP (CONTINUED)

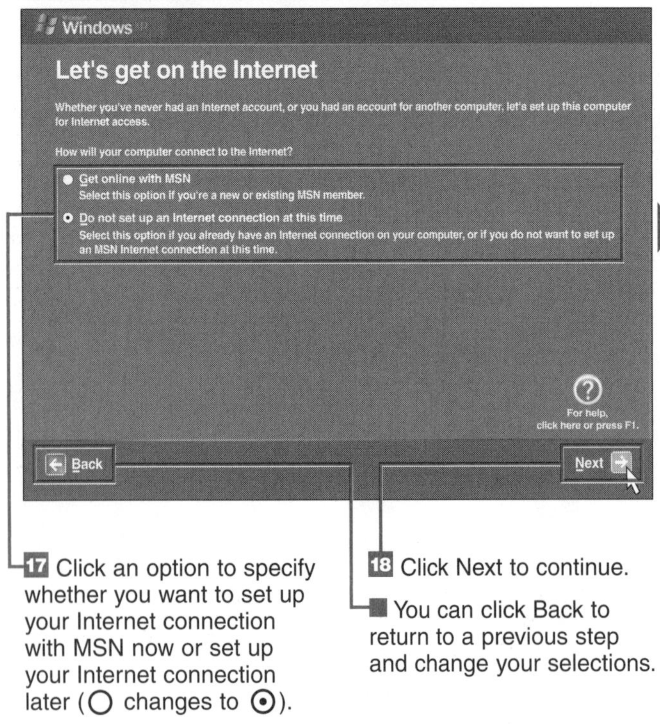

17 Click an option to specify whether you want to set up your Internet connection with MSN now or set up your Internet connection later (○ changes to ⦿).

18 Click Next to continue.

■ You can click Back to return to a previous step and change your selections.

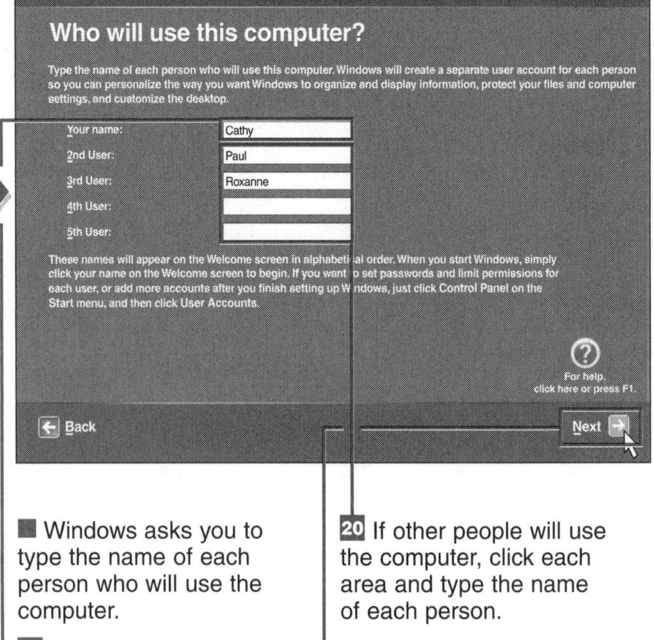

■ Windows asks you to type the name of each person who will use the computer.

19 Click this area and type your name.

20 If other people will use the computer, click each area and type the name of each person.

Note: Windows will create a separate user account for each name you specify.

21 Click Next to continue.

Can I uninstall Windows XP after upgrading from a previous version of Windows?

✔ If you experience problems after upgrading to Windows XP, you may be able to uninstall Windows XP and return to your previous version of Windows. Click the start button, select Control Panel and then click Add or Remove Programs. Select Windows XP Uninstall and then click the Change/Remove button. In the dialog box that appears, click Uninstall Windows XP and then click Continue.

Can I later make changes to the user accounts I set up during the installation?

✔ Yes. You can later assign a password to a user account, change the name of an account or change the account type. You can also add new user accounts and delete user accounts you no longer need. For more information, see pages 174 to 187.

What will happen if I choose to set up my Internet connection with MSN?

✔ If you choose the Get online with MSN option in step 17 below, Windows will use your modem to dial a phone number that will allow you to sign up for MSN Internet access. Follow the instructions on your screen to set up your Internet connection.

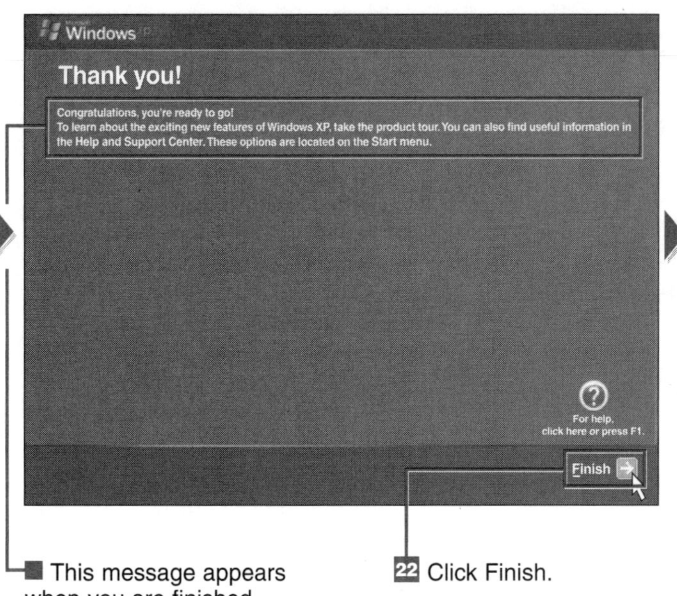

■ This message appears when you are finished setting up Windows XP.

22 Click Finish.

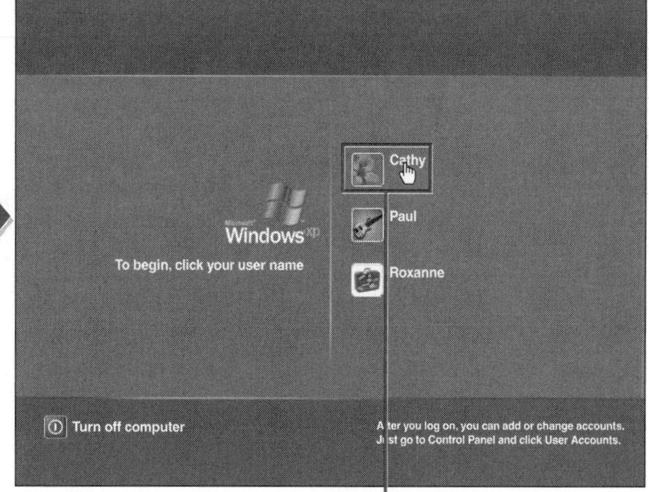

■ The Welcome screen appears, displaying the name of each person you specified in steps 19 and 20.

Note: The Welcome screen will not appear if you did not specify any additional names in step 20.

23 Click your name to begin using Windows XP.

■ Windows XP starts.

ACTIVATE WINDOWS XP

To help reduce software piracy, you must activate your copy of Windows XP within 30 days of installing the operating system. Your copy of Windows may have already been activated during the installation.

You can activate your copy of Windows XP over the Internet or over the telephone. You will not need to give any personal information when activating Windows. If you do not want to activate Windows yet, you can have Windows display a reminder message every few days.

If you plan to activate Windows XP over the Internet, you should connect to the Internet first. If you are not connected, Windows will create a modem-to-modem connection with Microsoft.

When activating Windows over the Internet, you can register your copy of Windows at the same time. Registering Windows is optional and allows you to receive information from Microsoft about products, events and special offers. You will need to provide personal information, including your name and address, to register your copy of Windows.

If you do not activate Windows XP within 30 days of the installation, you will no longer be able to use Windows until you activate your copy. An activation icon ( ) appears on your taskbar until Windows XP is activated. You can click this icon to quickly start the activation process.

ACTIVATE WINDOWS XP

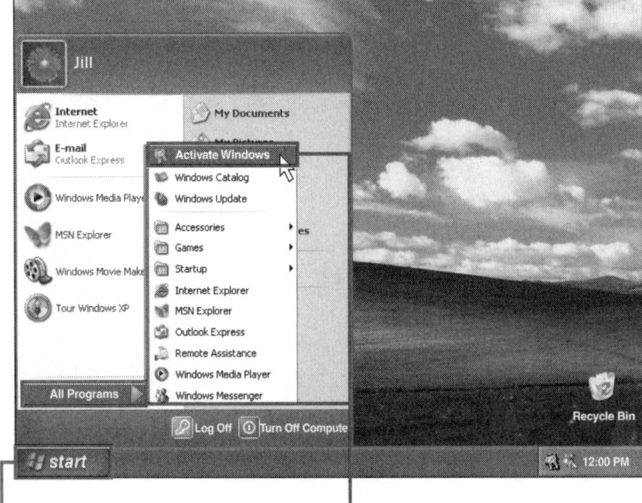

■ If you want to activate Windows over the Internet, you should connect to the Internet now. To connect to the Internet, see page 430.

1 Click start.

2 Click All Programs.

3 Click Activate Windows.

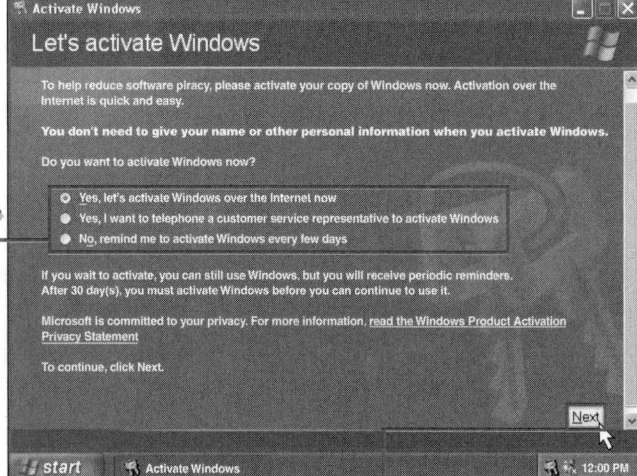

■ The Activate Windows window appears, displaying information about activating your copy of Windows.

4 Click an option to specify how you want to activate your copy of Windows (○ changes to ◉).

5 Click Next to continue.

How do I activate Windows XP over the telephone?

✔ If you chose to activate Windows by telephone in step 4 below, the Activate Windows window will display the steps for telephone activation. Click the area beside Step 1 to select your location. Then dial one of the numbers beside Step 2 to contact a customer service representative. Provide the representative with the installation ID beside Step 3 and then type the confirmation ID the representative provides in the areas beside Step 4. Then click Next to complete the activation process.

Will I ever need to activate Windows XP again?

✔ If you reinstall Windows XP on your computer or make major hardware changes to the computer, you will need to activate Windows XP again. You will not need to reactivate Windows if you make minor hardware changes, such as upgrading a device.

Can I register my copy of Windows later?

✔ Yes. You can use the Registration Wizard to later register your copy of Windows. Click start and select Run. In the dialog box that appears, type **regwiz /r** to start the wizard. Then follow the instructions on your screen to register your copy of Windows.

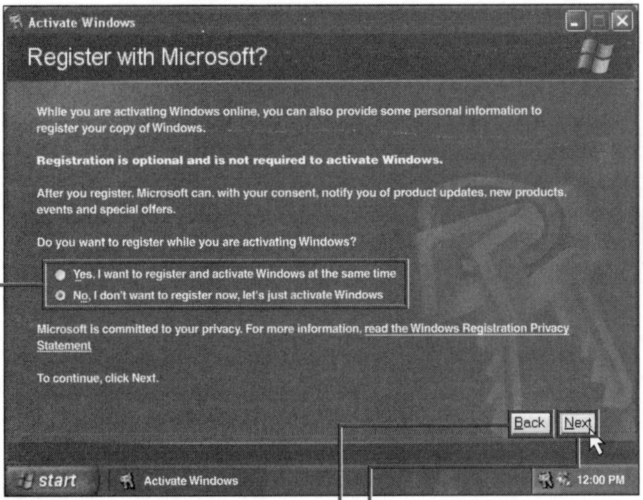

Activate Windows
Register with Microsoft?
While you are activating Windows online, you can also provide some personal information to register your copy of Windows.
Registration is optional and is not required to activate Windows.
After you register, Microsoft can, with your consent, notify you of product updates, new products, events and special offers.
Do you want to register while you are activating Windows?
Yes, I want to register and activate Windows at the same time
No, I don't want to register now, let's just activate Windows
Microsoft is committed to your privacy. For more information, read the Windows Registration Privacy Statement
To continue, click Next.
Back Next
start Activate Windows 12:00 PM

■ If you chose to activate Windows over the Internet in step 4, information about registering with Microsoft appears.

6 Click an option to specify if you want to register with Microsoft (○ changes to ◉).

7 Click Next to continue.

■ You can click Back to return to the previous screen and change your selection.

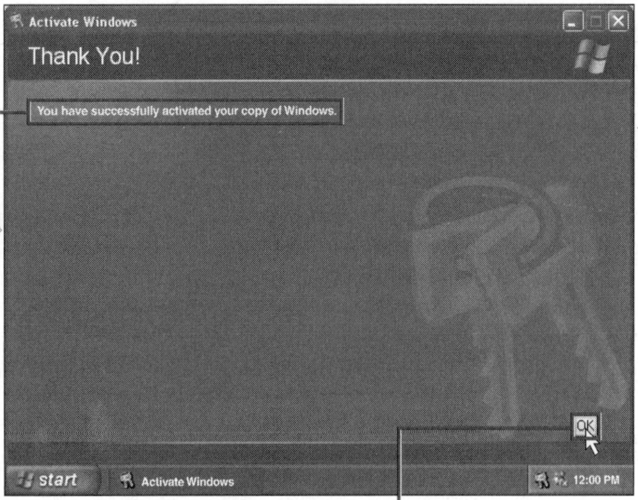

Activate Windows
Thank You!
You have successfully activated your copy of Windows.
OK
start Activate Windows 12:00 PM

■ This message appears when you have successfully activated your copy of Windows.

8 Click OK to close the Activate Windows window.

UPDATE WINDOWS XP

You can set up Windows to automatically get the latest Windows updates available on the Internet. This ensures that your computer is always up to date.

Instead of spending time manually searching for the latest updates for your computer, you can have Windows automatically search for important updates and information on the Internet. Windows will determine which updates your computer requires by comparing the software and information on your computer to the latest software and information available on the Internet. If needed, Windows can add new software, such as drivers, to your computer and fix problems with existing software to improve your computer's performance. Windows can also obtain updated help information for your computer.

When setting up automatic updates, you can choose how you want Windows to notify you when updates are available. For example, you can have Windows download the available updates automatically and notify you when they are ready to be installed.

No updates are installed at the time you set up automatic updating. If you set up Windows to automatically update your computer, Windows will check for updates when you are connected to the Internet and can download the updates so you can install them on your computer.

UPDATE WINDOWS XP

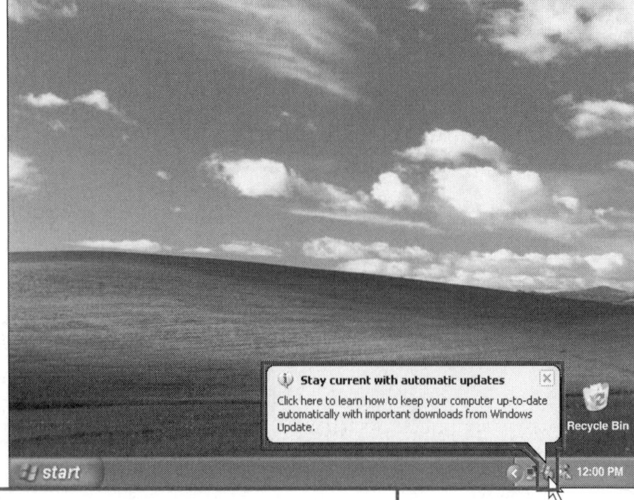

SET UP AUTOMATIC UPDATES

■ An icon and a message appear when you can set up Windows to update your computer automatically.

1 Click the icon to set up Windows to update your computer automatically.

Note: If the icon is hidden, you can click the arrow on the taskbar to display the icon.

■ The Automatic Updates Setup Wizard appears, allowing you to set up Windows to update your computer automatically.

■ This area displays information about updating your computer automatically.

2 Click Next to continue.

Will Windows collect personal information from my computer?

✔ No. Windows will not collect personal information, such as your name or e-mail address, from your computer when determining which updates are needed. Only general information about your computer, such as the version number of your operating system, will be collected. For more information, you can click the Read our privacy statement link in the Automatic Updates Setup Wizard.

Is there another way to update Windows?

✔ You can update Windows by installing specific updates from the Windows Update Web site. The Windows Update Web site can scan your computer to determine which updates you can install to update Windows. To display the Windows Update Web site, click the start button, select All Programs and then click Windows Update. Then follow the instructions on your screen.

Can I later change how I am notified when updates are available for my computer?

✔ Yes. Click the start button, select Control Panel and then click Performance and Maintenance. Click System and select the Automatic Updates tab. You can then click an option to specify how you want to be notified when updates are available for your computer (◯ changes to ◉).

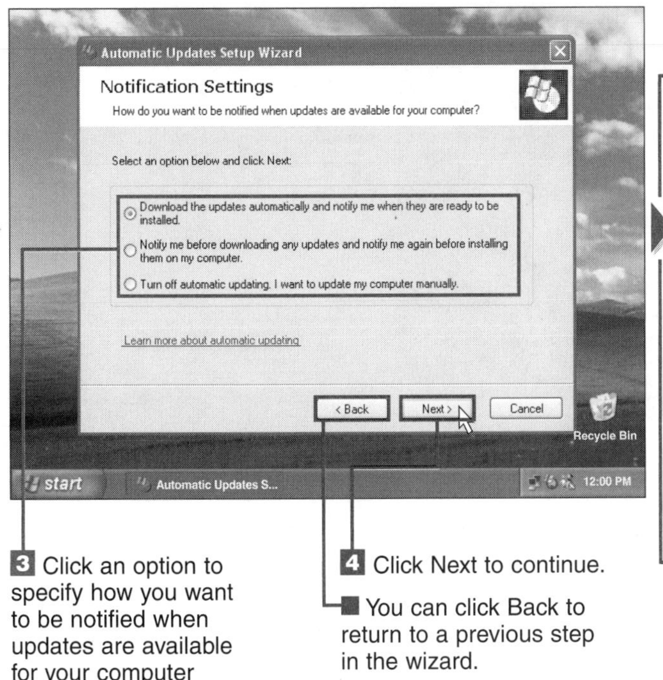

3 Click an option to specify how you want to be notified when updates are available for your computer (◯ changes to ◉).

4 Click Next to continue.

■ You can click Back to return to a previous step in the wizard.

■ This message appears when you have successfully completed the wizard.

5 Click Finish to close the wizard.

CONTINUED

UPDATE WINDOWS XP (CONTINUED)

When you are connected to the Internet, Windows will automatically check the Internet for updates that apply to your computer.

When Windows finds updates that apply to your computer, Windows may automatically download the updates to your computer or notify you before downloading the updates. The action that occurs depends on the option you chose when you set up Automatic Updates. If you selected to have Windows notify you before downloading updates, Windows will allow you to specify which updates you want to download. The updates will be downloaded without interrupting your work.

After the download is complete, Windows displays an icon on the taskbar and a message stating that the updates are ready to be installed. When you click the icon, the Automatic Updates wizard appears, allowing you to install the updates on your computer.

You can view a list of the recommended updates before installing the updates. You can also select which of the updates you want to install.

Windows may ask you to restart your computer after you install certain updates. If you do not restart your computer, your computer may not function properly.

UPDATE WINDOWS XP (CONTINUED)

INSTALL UPDATES

■ When you are connected to the Internet, an icon ( ) and a message appear when updates are ready to be installed on your computer.

1 Click the icon ( ) to install the recommended updates.

Note: If is hidden, you can click on the taskbar to display the icon.

■ The Automatic Updates wizard appears, stating that Windows is ready to install the recommended updates for your computer.

■ This area indicates that some updates require you to restart your computer. Before continuing, make sure you save your work and close any open programs.

2 Click Details to view information about the recommended updates.

Can I postpone installing updates until a more convenient time?

✔ If you do not want to install updates when Windows displays the message stating that updates are ready to be installed, you can have Windows remind you at a later time. Click on your taskbar to display the Automatic Updates wizard and then select the Remind Me Later button. A dialog box appears, allowing you to specify how long Windows should wait before reminding you.

How can I find more information about a recommended update?

✔ When viewing information about the recommended updates, you can click the Read This First link below an update to display additional information about the update.

If I choose not to install an update, can I install it later?

✔ Yes. You can have Windows offer the update again if you later change your mind. Click the start button, select Control Panel, click Performance and Maintenance and then click System. Select the Automatic Updates tab and then click the Restore Declined Updates button. Updates you have declined that still apply to your computer will appear the next time Windows notifies you of available updates.

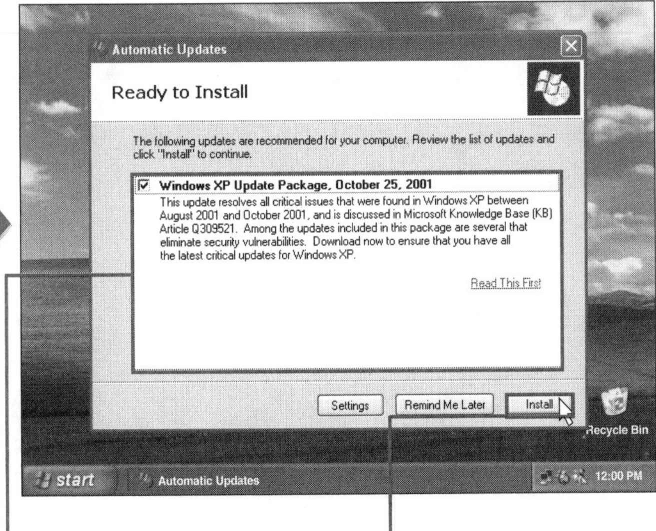

■ This area describes the recommended updates for your computer. Windows will install each update that displays a check mark (✔).

3 To add (☑) or remove (☐) a check mark for an update, click the box beside the update.

4 Click Install to install the updates.

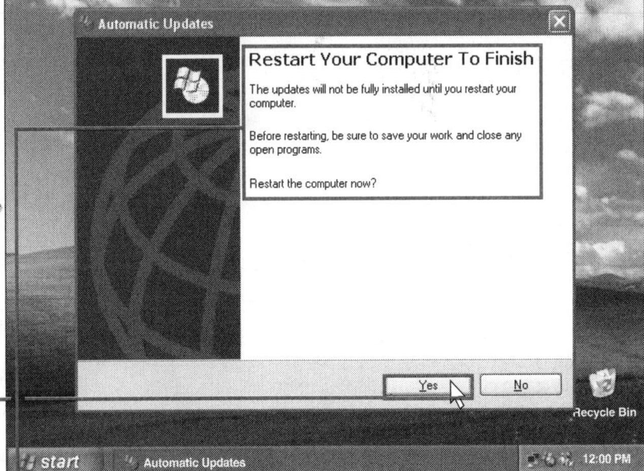

■ This message appears if you need to restart your computer to complete the installation.

5 Click Yes to restart your computer and complete the installation.

Note: If the "Installation Complete" message appears, you do not need to restart your computer. Click OK to complete the installation.

USING THE FILES AND SETTINGS TRANSFER WIZARD

You can use the Files and Settings Transfer Wizard to transfer your personal files and settings from one computer to another computer. This is useful when you want to quickly set up the same files and settings on multiple computers, set up a computer when you change computers or transfer files and settings when you upgrade to Windows XP from an older version of Windows.

You can transfer files and settings from a computer that uses Windows XP or an older version of Windows, such as Windows 95, 98, Me, NT or 2000, but the computer to which you transfer the files and settings must use Windows XP.

You should close all your open programs before using the Files and Settings Transfer Wizard.

The Files and Settings Transfer Wizard allows you to specify how you want to transfer the information to the other computer. You can use a direct cable connection, your home or small office network connection, a floppy drive or other removable media device, such as a Zip drive, or you can specify another location or drive you want to use. Using a direct cable connection or network connection is the most efficient way to transfer files and settings. If you choose to use a floppy drive, you may need a large number of floppy disks to transfer the information.

USING THE FILES AND SETTINGS TRANSFER WIZARD

ON THE OLD COMPUTER

1 On the computer that stores the files and settings you want to transfer to another computer, click start.

2 Click All Programs.

3 Click Accessories.

4 Click System Tools.

5 Click Files and Settings Transfer Wizard.

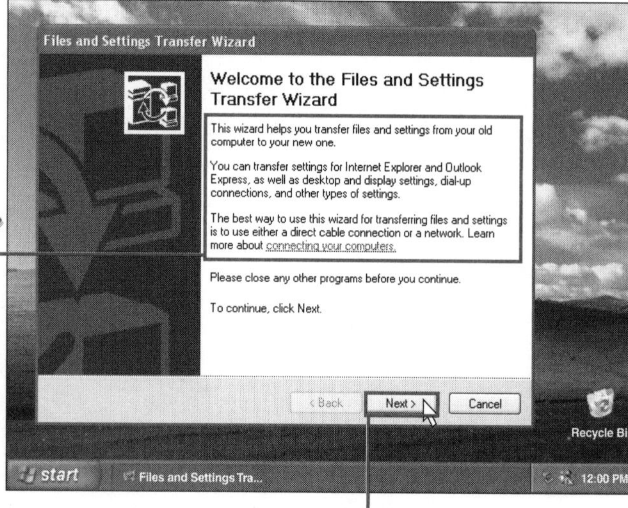

■ The Files and Settings Transfer Wizard appears.

■ This area describes the wizard.

6 Click Next to continue.

How do I start the Files and Settings Transfer Wizard on a computer running an older version of Windows?

✔ You can use the Windows XP CD-ROM disc or a Wizard Disk you create. To use the Windows XP CD-ROM disc, insert the disc into a drive on the computer. In the screen that appears, click Perform additional tasks and then select Transfer files and settings to start the wizard. To create a Wizard Disk, perform steps 15 to 22 starting on page 575. Then click I want to create a Wizard Disk in the following drive (○ changes to ◉), select the drive that contains the disk and click Next to create the disk. To use the disk to run the wizard, insert the disk into a drive on the old computer, click Start and select Run. In the Run dialog box, type **a:\fastwiz** and then press the Enter key.

Can I use a recordable CD to save the files and settings information I want to transfer?

✔ Yes. Perform steps 1 to 9 below, selecting Other in step 9. Then click the Browse button and select a location on your computer to save the information. Windows saves the information in a folder called USMT2.UNC, which you can then save to your recordable CD. For information about saving information to a recordable CD, see page 62.

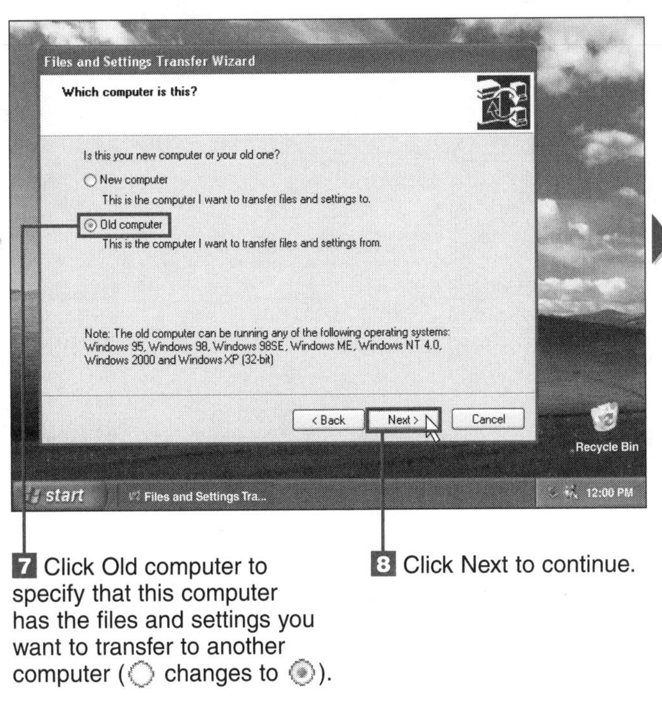

7 Click Old computer to specify that this computer has the files and settings you want to transfer to another computer (○ changes to ◉).

8 Click Next to continue.

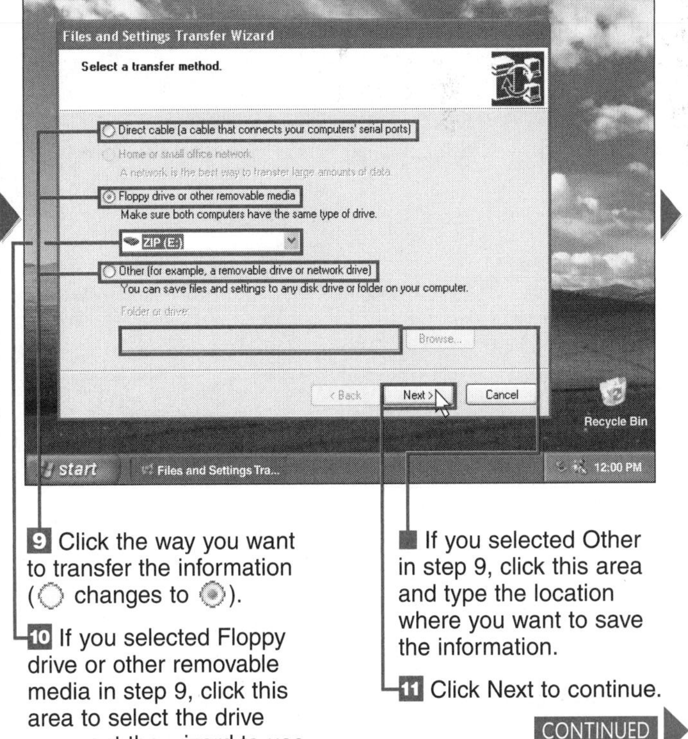

9 Click the way you want to transfer the information (○ changes to ◉).

10 If you selected Floppy drive or other removable media in step 9, click this area to select the drive you want the wizard to use.

■ If you selected Other in step 9, click this area and type the location where you want to save the information.

11 Click Next to continue.

CONTINUED

USING THE FILES AND SETTINGS TRANSFER WIZARD (CONTINUED)

The Files and Settings Transfer Wizard allows you to choose the type of information you want to transfer to the new computer. You can transfer only settings, only files or files and settings.

If you choose to store the information you want to transfer on removable media that has limited storage space, such as floppy disks, the wizard may not allow you to transfer some items. You may need to use a more efficient method, such as a direct cable connection, to transfer all the information you want.

The wizard may take a few minutes to collect the information you selected to transfer. The wizard will collect settings such as your Web browser, e-mail, network and display settings. The files in folders such as your My Documents, My Pictures and Fonts folders will also be automatically collected.

Once you have used the Files and Settings Transfer Wizard to collect the files and settings from the source computer, you can transfer the information to the other computer. You must also run the Files and Settings Transfer Wizard on the new computer to complete the transfer.

USING THE FILES AND SETTINGS TRANSFER WIZARD (CONTINUED)

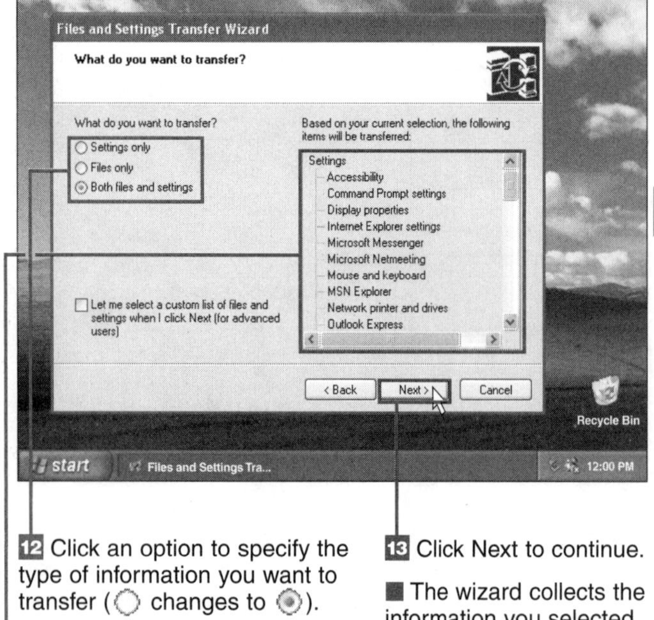

12 Click an option to specify the type of information you want to transfer (○ changes to ◉).

■ This area lists the items the wizard will transfer, based on the option you selected in step 12.

13 Click Next to continue.

■ The wizard collects the information you selected to transfer.

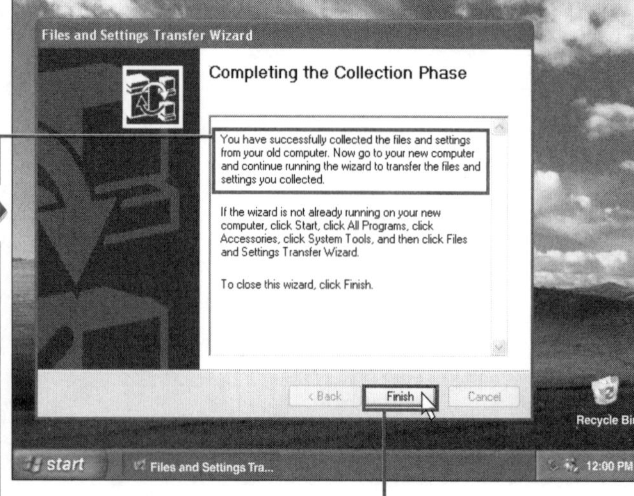

■ This message appears when the wizard has successfully collected the files and/or settings on the computer.

14 Click Finish to close the wizard.

■ You can now transfer the files and/or settings to the other computer.

Can I specify exactly which files and settings I want to transfer?

✔ Yes. In the Files and Settings Transfer Wizard, click the 'Let me select a custom list of files and settings when I click Next (for advanced users)' option (☐ changes to ☑). You can add or remove items in the list of items the wizard will copy to create a customized list of the files and settings you want to transfer. To remove an item, select the item in the list and then click the Remove button. To add an item to the list, click the appropriate button for the item you want to add and then select the item in the dialog box that appears.

How can I ensure that all my files are transferred?

✔ The Files and Settings Transfer Wizard will transfer only the most common file types. If a file uses a file extension that Windows does not recognize, you may need to add the file to the list of items the wizard will transfer.

Why does the wizard state that I should install a program on the new computer?

✔ Some programs use unique settings and options that the Files and Settings Transfer Wizard may automatically copy when copying the files for the program. The wizard may remind you to install that program on the new computer before transferring the files and settings for the program.

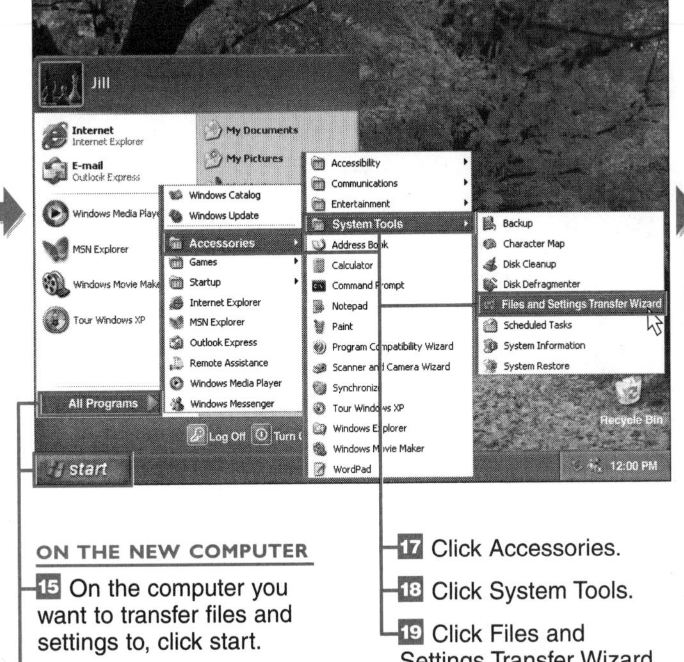

ON THE NEW COMPUTER

15 On the computer you want to transfer files and settings to, click start.

16 Click All Programs.

17 Click Accessories.

18 Click System Tools.

19 Click Files and Settings Transfer Wizard.

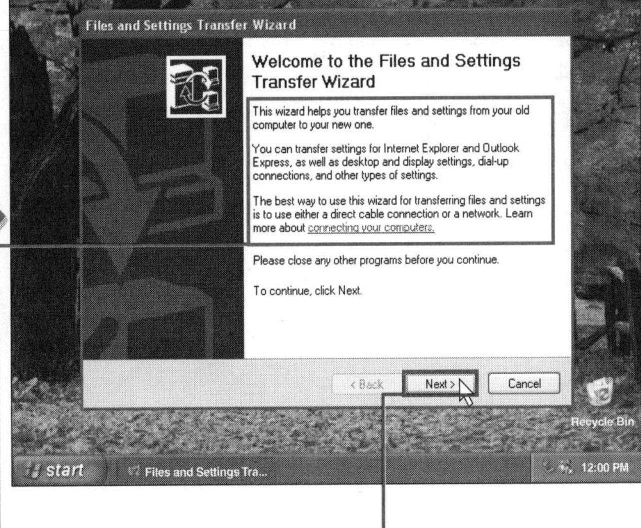

■ The Files and Settings Transfer Wizard appears.

■ This area describes the wizard.

20 Click Next to continue.

CONTINUED

USING THE FILES AND SETTINGS TRANSFER WIZARD (CONTINUED)

When using the Files and Settings Transfer Wizard, you must specify whether you are setting up the source computer or the computer to which you want to transfer the files and settings you collected. You can also specify whether you have already collected the information you want to transfer.

The wizard asks you to specify how the files and settings information collected from the other computer will be transferred to the computer that will use the information. You should use the same method you specified when you ran the wizard on the source computer.

If you saved the files and settings information to a removable media device, such as a Zip drive, you should make sure the device is connected to the computer and turned on before continuing.

The amount of time needed to transfer the files and settings to your computer depends on the speed of the transfer method you are using and the volume of information being transferred.

Once the Files and Settings Transfer Wizard has transferred the information to your computer, you may need to log off Windows or restart your computer before the new settings can take effect on the computer.

USING THE FILES AND SETTINGS TRANSFER WIZARD (CONTINUED)

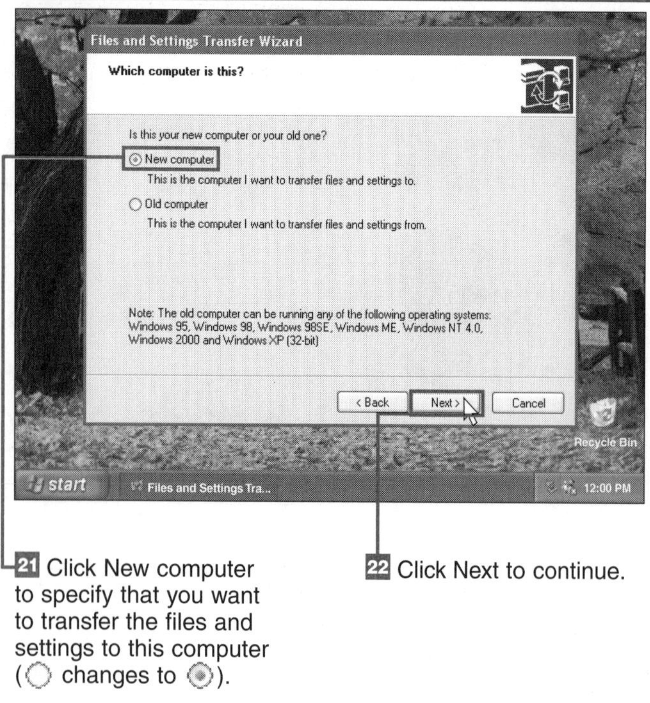

21 Click New computer to specify that you want to transfer the files and settings to this computer (◯ changes to ◉).

22 Click Next to continue.

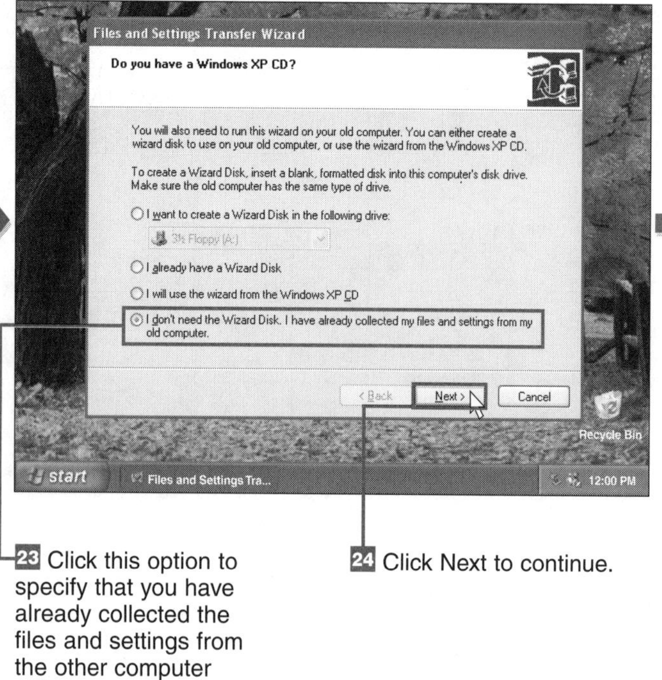

23 Click this option to specify that you have already collected the files and settings from the other computer (◯ changes to ◉).

24 Click Next to continue.

Can I use the Files and Settings Transfer Wizard to back up my files?

✔ The Files and Settings Transfer Wizard is designed to be used only to transfer your information to another computer. The wizard will copy specific files and settings, but it should not be used as your primary means of backing up the information on your computer. You should always use a backup program to back up all your files and settings.

Can I restore settings that have been changed?

✔ After you use the Files and Settings Transfer Wizard to transfer settings from another computer, the settings you transfer will replace the settings on the new computer. You cannot restore the previous settings, but you can change the settings just as you would change any settings on your computer.

I do not remember the exact location where the files and settings information is stored. How can I search for the location?

✔ In the Files and Settings Transfer Wizard, select Other in step 25 below. Then click the Browse button to search your computer for the location where the information is stored.

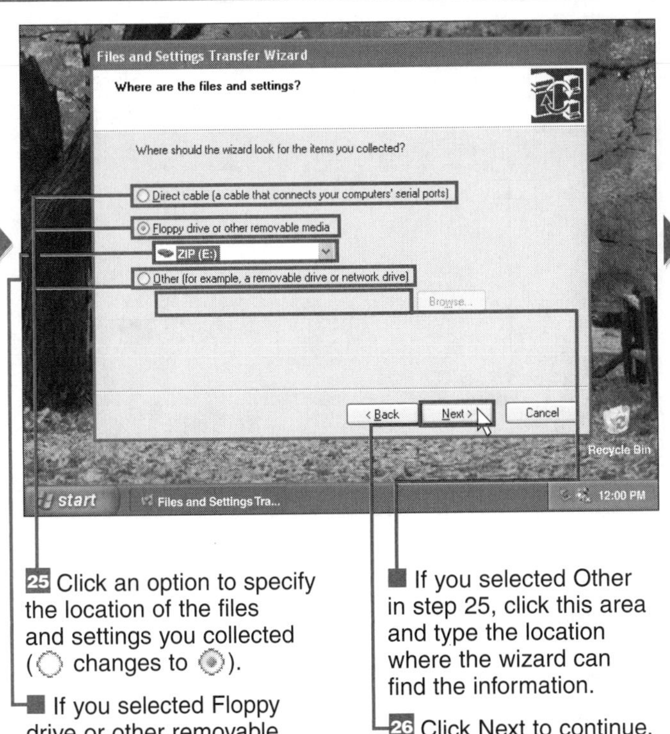

25 Click an option to specify the location of the files and settings you collected (○ changes to ◉).

■ If you selected Floppy drive or other removable media in step 25, click this area to select the drive you want to use.

■ If you selected Other in step 25, click this area and type the location where the wizard can find the information.

26 Click Next to continue.

■ This screen appears when the transfer is complete.

27 Click Finish to close the wizard.

■ A dialog box will appear, stating that you need to log off Windows for the changes to take effect. Click Yes to log off Windows.

USING WINDOWS TASK MANAGER

You can use Windows Task Manager to view the programs and processes running on your computer and to monitor CPU and memory use. You can also view information about your computer's performance.

The Applications tab allows you to view the status of each program running on your computer.

The Processes tab displays information about the processes, including services and executable programs, running on your computer. You can view information such as the amount of the CPU's time and memory that a process uses.

The Performance tab displays the CPU and page file, or virtual memory, usage on your computer. You can view graphs that show the CPU and page file usage over time. This can help you track how devices installed on your computer use the computer's resources.

The Performance tab also displays the number of handles, threads and processes running on your computer. Handles and threads are resources Windows uses when running applications. You can also view the amount of physical memory, commit charge and kernel memory on your computer in Kilobytes (K). Physical memory, commit charge and kernel memory are properties of your computer's memory used by Windows.

USING WINDOWS TASK MANAGER

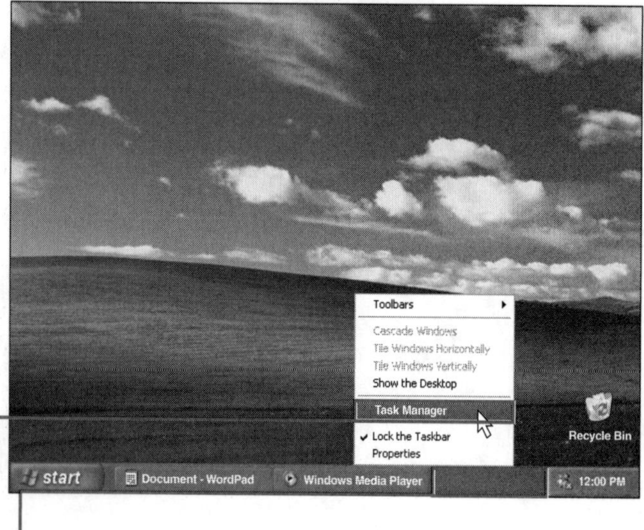

1 Right-click a blank area on the taskbar. A menu appears.

2 Click Task Manager.

■ The Windows Task Manager window appears.

Note: To quickly display the Windows Task Manager window, you can press and hold down the Ctrl and Alt keys as you press the Delete key.

APPLICATIONS

3 Click the Applications tab to view the programs that are currently running on your computer.

■ This area lists the programs that are currently running and the status of each program.

Can I use Windows Task Manager to close a program that is not responding?

✔ Yes. Select the Applications tab, click the program you want to close and click the End Task button. Then click the End Now button to close the program.

How do I identify which process runs a program?

✔ Select the Applications tab and right-click the program you want to identify the process for. Then click Go To Process.

How do I end a process displayed in Windows Task Manager?

✔ Select the Processes tab, click the process you want to close and then click the End Process button. Closing a process that Windows requires to operate may cause Windows to become unstable.

Can I change the way programs are displayed on the Applications tab?

✔ Yes. Select the View menu and then click Large Icons, Small Icons or Details.

What information can I view on the Networking tab?

✔ If your computer is connected to a network, you can click the Networking tab to view a graphical representation of the status and performance of your network.

What information can I view on the Users tab?

✔ The Users tab displays information about each user currently connected to your computer, including the user name and ID of each user.

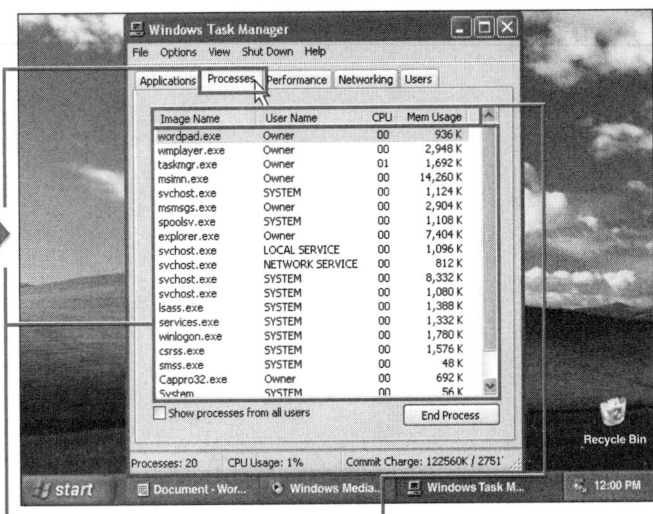

PROCESSES

4 Click the Processes tab to display the processes that are currently running on your computer.

■ This area lists the processes that are currently running and information about each process.

■ To sort the processes, click the heading for the column you want to use to sort the processes.

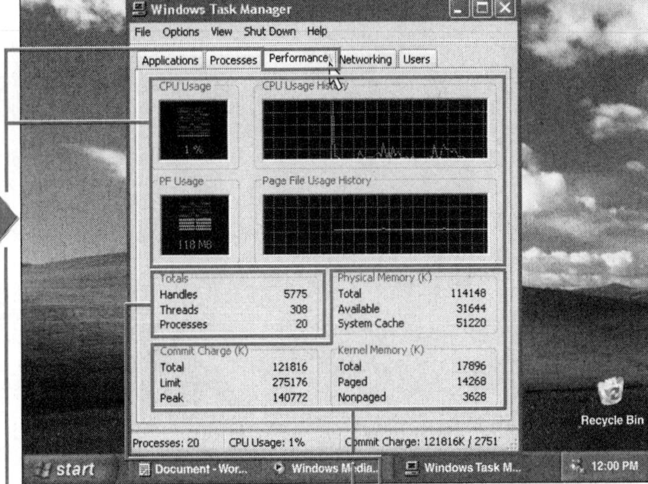

PERFORMANCE

5 Click the Performance tab to view your computer's performance.

■ These areas graphically display the CPU and page file usage. A page file is also known as virtual memory.

■ This area displays the total number of handles, threads and processes running on your computer.

■ These areas display the amount of physical memory, commit charge and kernel memory currently being used.

USING DEVICE MANAGER

If you are having trouble with your computer, the Device Manager can often help you identify the problem and find a solution.

The Device Manager organizes hardware devices into categories, such as disk drives and monitors. Each category lists the specific hardware devices installed on your computer.

If there is a problem with a hardware device, the Device Manager displays an exclamation mark (!) over the icon for the device. For example, a hardware device that was not properly installed may display an exclamation mark. A hardware device with a red X through its icon indicates the device has been disabled. These symbols can simplify the task of identifying and solving problems with your hardware.

The Device Manager information can be helpful when adding a new hardware device to your computer. You can quickly view which hardware devices are already installed on your computer.

If Windows does not start properly, you can start Windows in safe mode and use the Device Manager to determine whether a malfunctioning hardware device is causing the problem. For information about safe mode, see page 598.

USING DEVICE MANAGER

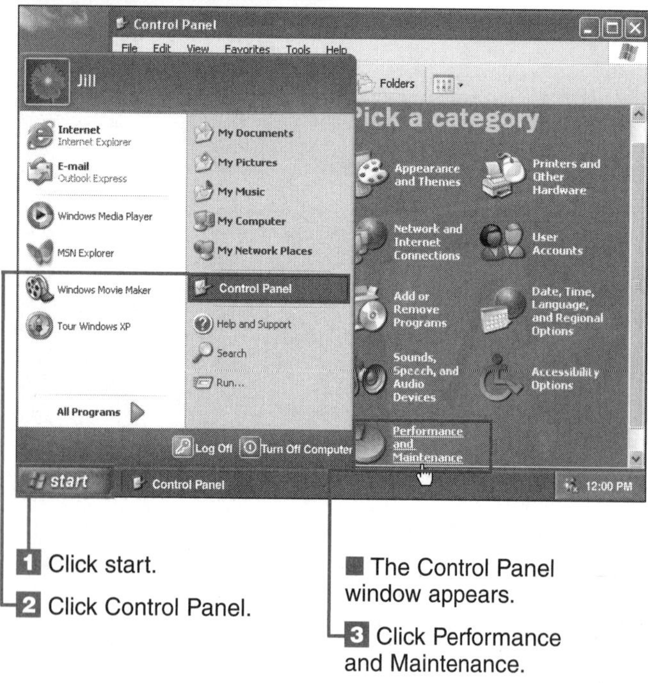

1 Click start.

2 Click Control Panel.

■ The Control Panel window appears.

3 Click Performance and Maintenance.

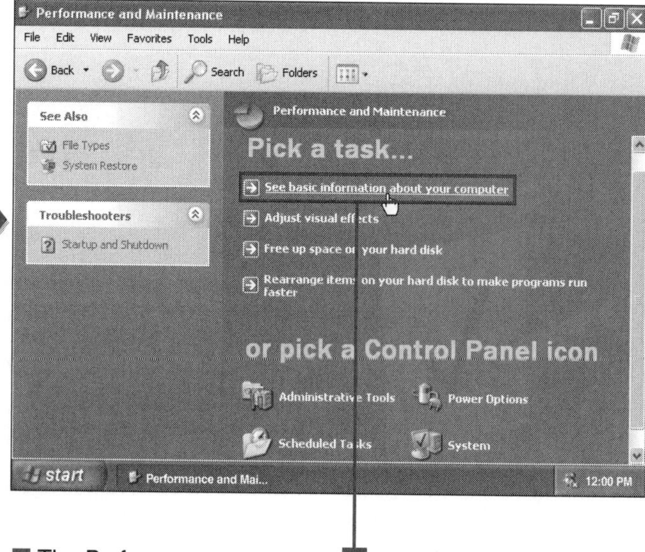

■ The Performance and Maintenance window appears.

4 Click See basic information about your computer.

How do I print information about my hardware devices?

✔ In the Device Manager window, click the device or type of device you want to print information about and then click [print icon]. In the Print dialog box, select an option for the type of information you want to print (○ changes to ◉) and then click the Print button. The System summary option prints a summary of the devices installed on your computer. The Selected class or device option prints a report for the device or type of device you selected. The All devices and system summary option prints a report about every device or hardware type and a summary of the devices installed on your computer.

How do I change the way information is displayed in the Device Manager window?

✔ In the Device Manager window, select the View menu and then click the way you want to display the information. A bullet (•) appears beside the current view. You can view devices or resources organized by type or connection.

Why doesn't the device I just connected to my computer appear in the Device Manager?

✔ After connecting a device, you may need to update the list of devices in the Device Manager. Select the Action menu and then click Scan for hardware changes.

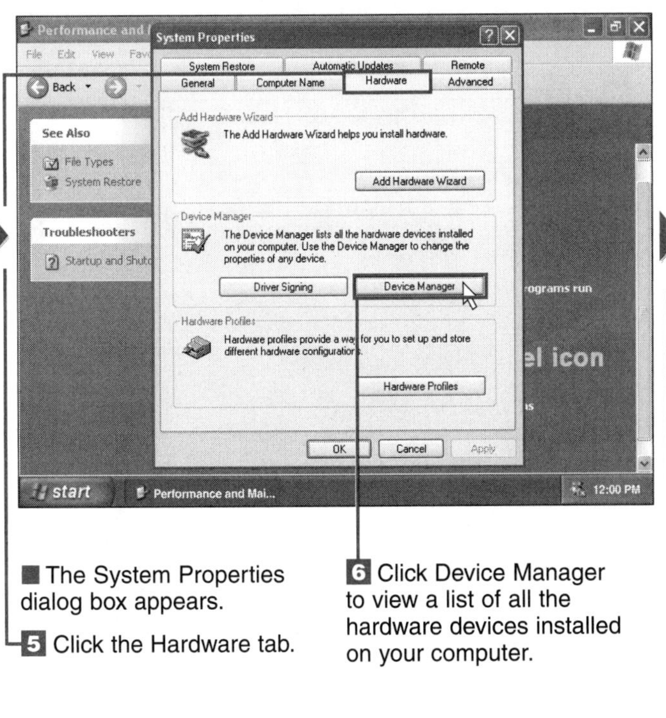

■ The System Properties dialog box appears.

5 Click the Hardware tab.

6 Click Device Manager to view a list of all the hardware devices installed on your computer.

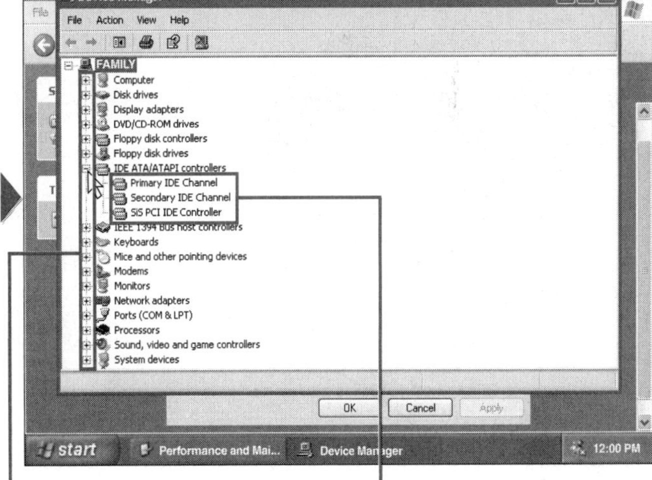

■ The Device Manager window appears, displaying the types of hardware devices installed on your computer.

7 Click the plus sign (⊞) beside a type of hardware device to see the devices in the category (⊞ changes to ⊟).

■ The devices in the category appear.

Note: You can click the minus sign (⊟) beside a type of hardware device to once again hide the devices in the category.

CONTINUED

USING DEVICE MANAGER (CONTINUED)

You can use the Device Manager to display information about a hardware device, such as the manufacturer of a device and whether a device is working properly.

You can also use the Device Manager to display information about the driver for a hardware device. A driver is software that allows the computer to communicate with a hardware device.

The Device Manager can identify which resources on your computer a hardware device uses. There are four main types of resources that control the communication between the computer and a hardware device. An Interrupt Request (IRQ) tells the computer that a device needs attention. A Direct Memory Access (DMA) channel lets a device communicate directly with your computer's memory to speed up the processing of information.

An Input/Output (I/O) Range specifies which area of memory a device uses to communicate with the computer. A Memory Range indicates which area of memory a device uses to perform functions.

You can use the Device Manager to find out if any conflicts exist that could cause problems with the operation of a hardware device. If the resource settings for a device conflict with the settings for another device, the devices may not work properly.

USING DEVICE MANAGER (CONTINUED)

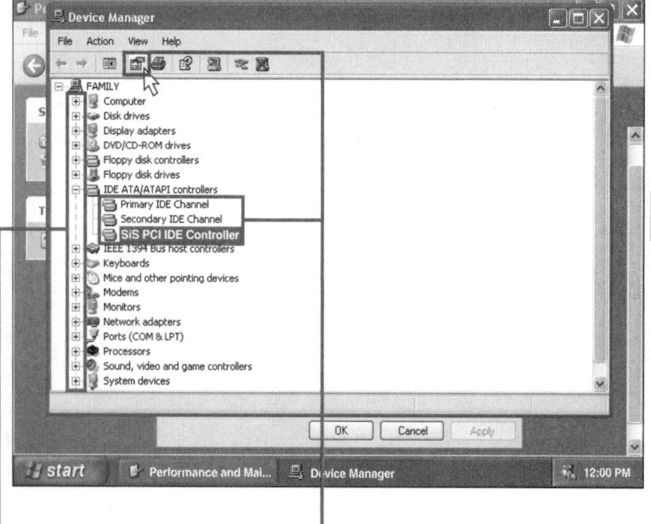

DISPLAY INFORMATION FOR A DEVICE

1 Click the plus sign (+) beside the category that contains the device of interest (+ changes to −).

■ The devices in the category appear.

2 Click the device of interest.

3 Click (properties icon) to display information about the device.

Note: You can also double-click the device instead of performing steps 2 and 3.

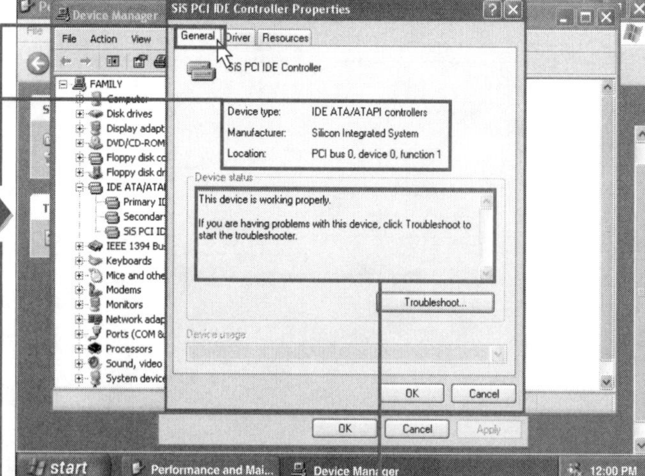

■ A Properties dialog box appears.

4 Click the General tab.

■ This area displays general information about the device, such as the manufacturer of the device.

■ This area indicates if the device is working properly. If there is a problem with the device, Windows will indicate the type of problem and a suggested solution.

The Properties dialog box displays a problem code and number. How do I use this information?

✔ When viewing the information for a device, a problem code and number may appear in the Device status area on the General tab if there is a problem with the device. If you intend to call a support line to get help for the device, this problem code and number can help a support technician identify the problem.

Why does a device display different tabs than shown below?

✔ The tabs that appear in the Properties dialog box depend on the device you selected. For example, some devices may not display a Resources tab. Additional tabs will appear if additional settings are available for the device. For example, you can use the Diagnostics tab to test your modem.

How can I resolve a hardware problem?

✔ In the Properties dialog box for the device, select the General tab and then click the Troubleshoot button. The Help and Support Center window appears, displaying a troubleshooter for the device. Follow the instructions in the troubleshooter to try to resolve the problem.

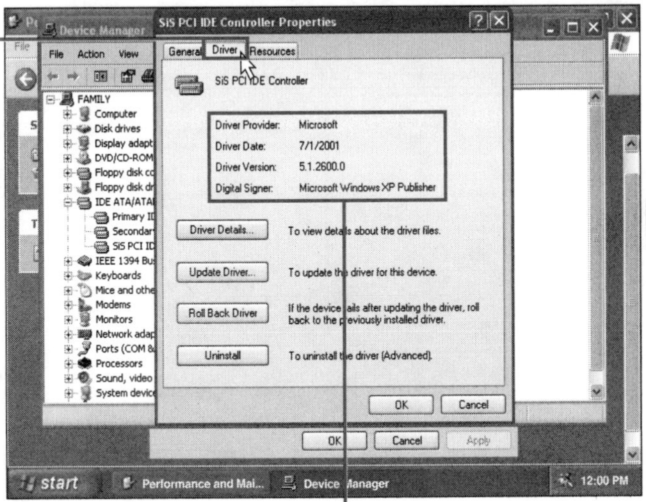

5 Click the Driver tab.

■ This area displays information about the driver the computer uses to communicate with the device.

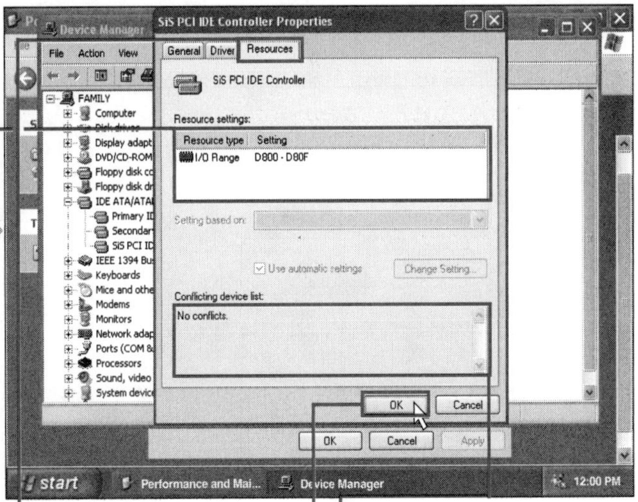

6 Click the Resources tab.

■ This area displays the resources used by the device.

■ This area indicates if any conflicts exist that could cause problems with the operation of the device.

7 When you finish reviewing information about the device, click OK to close the Properties dialog box.

RESTORE YOUR COMPUTER

If you are experiencing problems with your computer, you can use the System Restore feature to return your computer to a time before the problems occurred. For example, if you accidentally delete program files, you can restore your computer to a time before you deleted the files. Problems may also occur when you install new hardware or software or make changes to your system settings.

When you restore your computer, you return your computer to an earlier, more stable time, called a restore point. The number of available restore points primarily depends on how frequently you use your computer. Days when you do not use your computer may not have any restore points.

Windows creates different types of restore points. An initial System Checkpoint is created when you first start Windows after upgrading or installing Windows on a computer. Windows then regularly creates new System Checkpoint restore points. An Automatic Updates Install restore point is created when you install updates using the Automatic Update feature. For information about automatically updating Windows, see page 568. Windows also creates restore points when you install certain programs.

You must be logged on to the computer as a computer administrator in order to run System Restore.

RESTORE YOUR COMPUTER

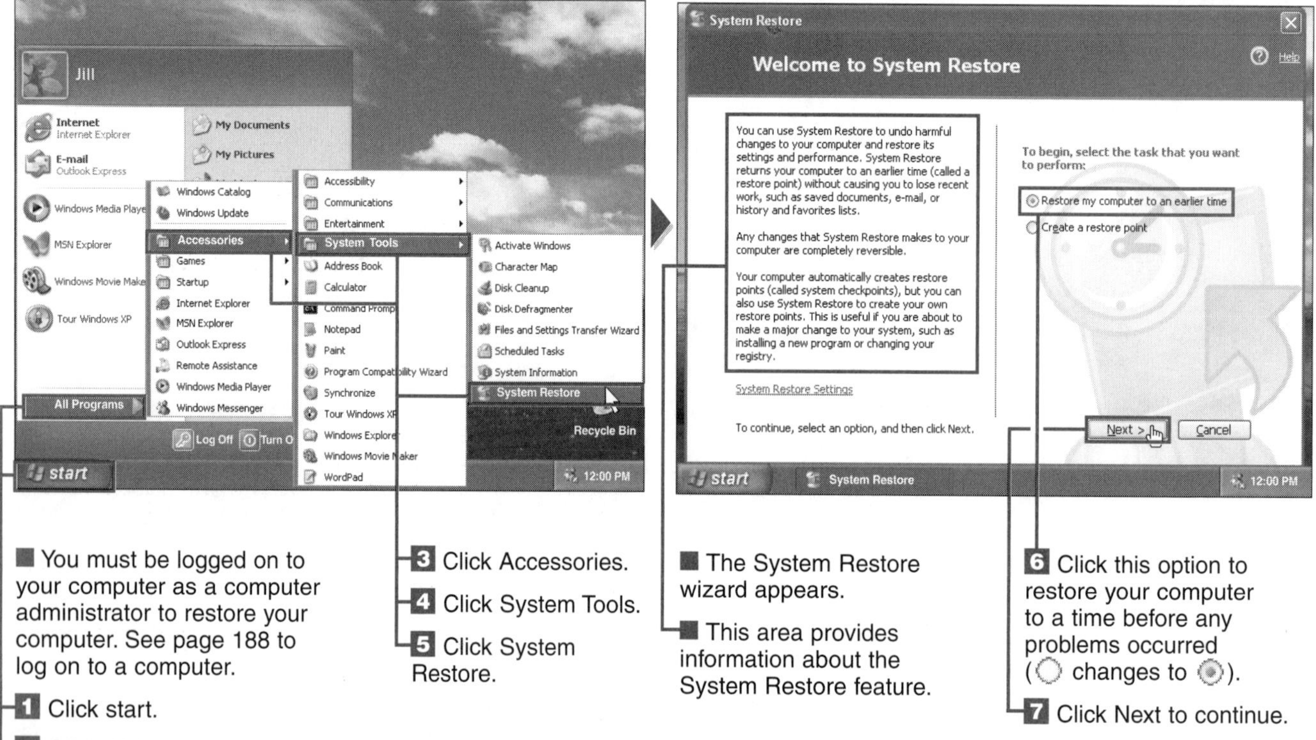

■ You must be logged on to your computer as a computer administrator to restore your computer. See page 188 to log on to a computer.

1 Click start.

2 Click All Programs.

3 Click Accessories.

4 Click System Tools.

5 Click System Restore.

■ The System Restore wizard appears.

■ This area provides information about the System Restore feature.

6 Click this option to restore your computer to a time before any problems occurred (○ changes to ◉).

7 Click Next to continue.

Why is System Restore turned off on my computer?

✔ System Restore may be turned off if you have less than 200 MB of free space on your hard drive. To turn on System Restore, you must first delete unnecessary files and programs to free up at least 200 MB of hard drive space. Then from the Start menu, select Control Panel, click Performance and Maintenance and select System to display the System Properties dialog box. Click the System Restore tab and select the Turn off System Restore option (☑ changes to ☐).

Can I create my own restore point?

✔ Yes. This is useful if you plan to make changes that could make your computer unstable, such as installing a program. Perform steps 1 to 5 below to start System Restore. Select the Create a restore point option (○ changes to ◉) and click Next. Type a description for the restore point and click Create. Click Close to complete the wizard. The restore point will appear in the System Restore wizard and will be set for the date and time the restore point was created.

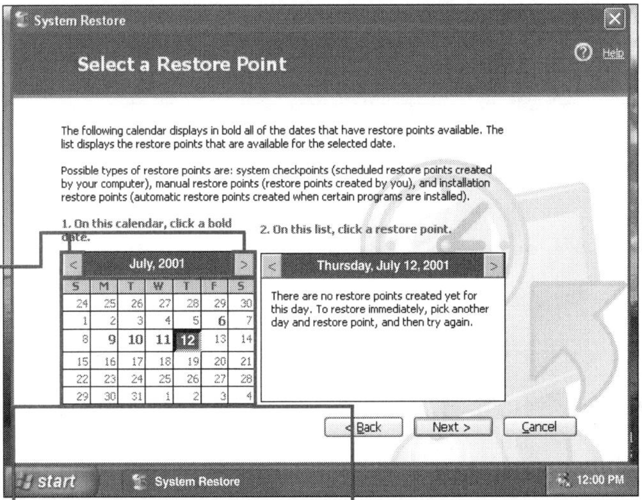

■ This area displays the days in the current month. The current day is highlighted.

■ You may be able to click < or > to display the days in the previous or next month.

■ Each day that has a restore point appears in bold.

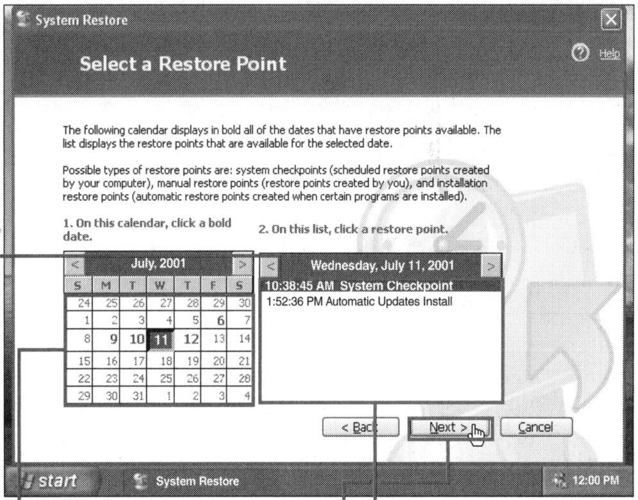

8 Click the most recent day with a restore point when your computer was working properly. The day is highlighted.

■ This area lists the restore points available for the day you selected.

9 Click the restore point you want to use.

10 Click Next to continue.

CONTINUED

RESTORE YOUR COMPUTER (CONTINUED)

Restoring your computer will not cause you to lose any common types of files, such as word processing documents or spreadsheet files. If you want to ensure a specific file is not affected by the restoration, store the file in the My Documents folder. Any documents in the My Documents folder will not be affected. System Restore will also not affect your e-mail messages or the items in your Favorites list and History list in Internet Explorer.

When you restore your computer to an earlier time, any programs you installed after that date may be uninstalled. Files you created using the program will not be deleted, but you may need to re-install the program to work with the files again.

Before restoring your computer to an earlier time, you should close all open files and programs. Your computer will automatically restart when the restoration is complete. If the restoration could not be completed, System Restore will automatically undo any changes made during the restoration.

RESTORE YOUR COMPUTER (CONTINUED)

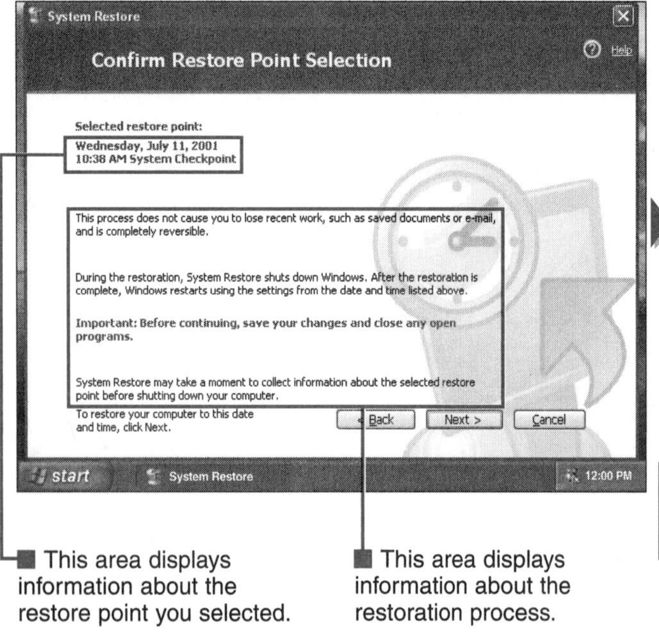

■ This area displays information about the restore point you selected.

■ This area displays information about the restoration process.

11 Click Next to restore your computer.

■ You can click Back to return to the previous screen and change the restore point you selected.

Can I reverse the changes made when I restored my computer?

✔ Yes. Any changes that System Restore makes to your computer are completely reversible. To undo the last restoration, start System Restore by performing steps 1 to 5 on page 584. In the System Restore wizard, select the Undo my last restoration option (◯ changes to ◉). Then click Next to undo the restoration.

My computer will no longer start properly. Can I run System Restore in safe mode?

✔ Windows may automatically start in safe mode if your computer cannot start properly. You can run System Restore in safe mode to return to a time when the computer started properly. For more information about working in safe mode, see page 598.

Can I use System Restore to uninstall a program?

✔ It is not recommended that you use System Restore to uninstall a program. Although System Restore may uninstall a program you installed after the date to which you restore your computer, some of the program's files may remain on your computer. For information on completely removing a program from your computer, see page 546.

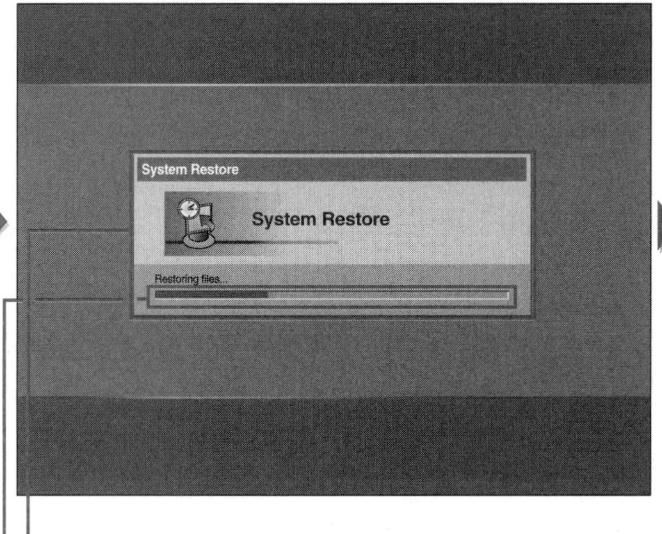

■ The System Restore dialog box appears.

■ This area shows the progress of the restoration.

■ When the restoration is complete, your computer will automatically restart.

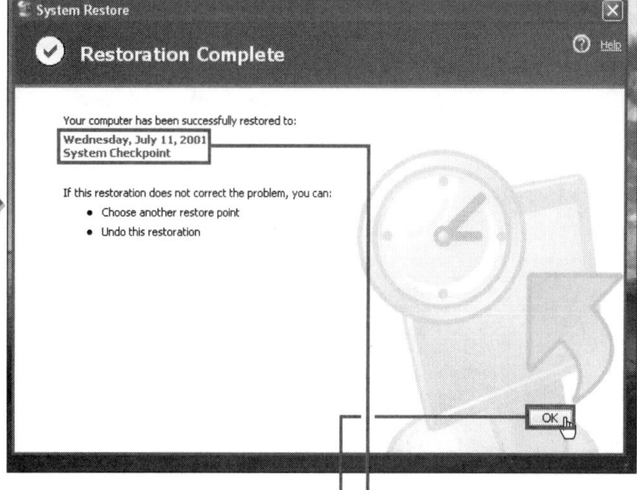

■ After your computer restarts, a dialog box appears, indicating that your computer has been successfully restored.

■ This area displays the date to which your computer was restored.

12 Click OK to close the dialog box.

USING THE PROGRAM COMPATIBILITY WIZARD

Some older programs may not work properly with Windows XP. If you are having trouble running a program that was designed for a previous version of Windows, you can use the Program Compatibility Wizard to help you solve the problem.

The Program Compatibility Wizard asks how you want to locate the program you are having problems with. If the program is installed on your computer, you can have the wizard display a list of programs you can choose from. If the program is stored on a disc in your CD-ROM drive, you can have the wizard locate the program in the drive.

You should only use the Program Compatibility Wizard when necessary. Many older programs can work with Windows XP and do not require the use of the wizard. You should not use the wizard to configure older anti-virus or backup programs. If you are having trouble using one of these types of programs with Windows XP, you should contact the manufacturer to obtain a more recent version of the program.

USING THE PROGRAM COMPATIBILITY WIZARD

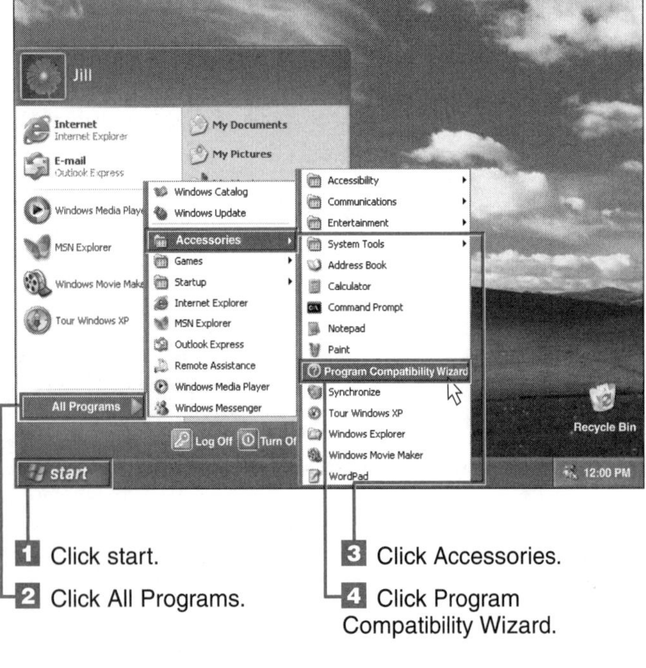

1 Click start.

2 Click All Programs.

3 Click Accessories.

4 Click Program Compatibility Wizard.

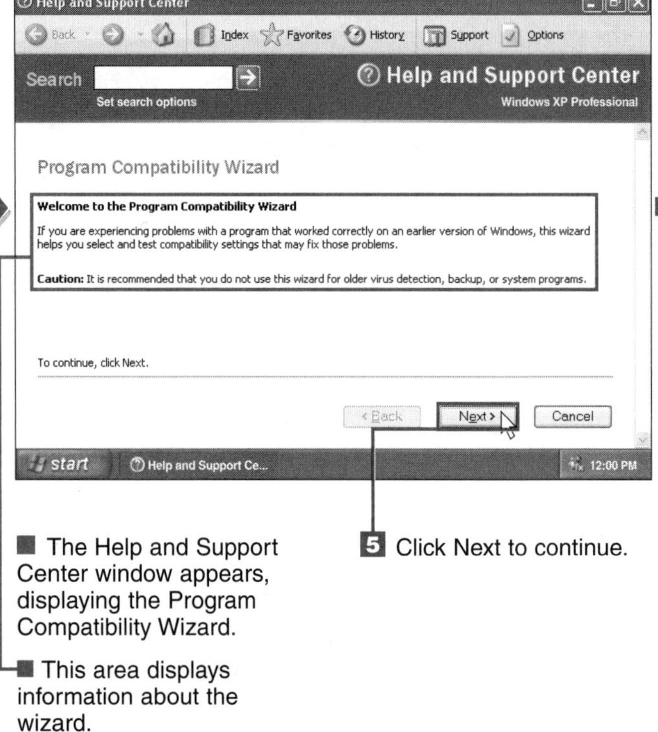

■ The Help and Support Center window appears, displaying the Program Compatibility Wizard.

■ This area displays information about the wizard.

5 Click Next to continue.

The program I want to use does not appear in the list. What should I do?

✔ You can manually locate the program on your computer. Click Back, select the I want to locate the program manually option and then click Next. Click the Browse button to locate the program on your computer. Then double-click the program in the dialog box that appears.

When would I use the Program Compatibility Wizard for a program stored on a CD?

✔ Using the wizard for a program stored on a CD is useful when you are having trouble installing the program on your computer. The wizard will locate and run the setup program on the CD using the compatibility settings you specify. You can complete the setup program in the wizard to install the program on your computer.

A dialog box appeared saying the wizard could not locate programs on my CD. What should I do?

✔ Click Cancel to close the dialog box and then click Browse in the wizard to manually locate the setup program on the CD. In the dialog box that appears, display the contents of the CD-ROM drive and then double-click the setup program for the program. The setup program will usually be named "setup" or "install."

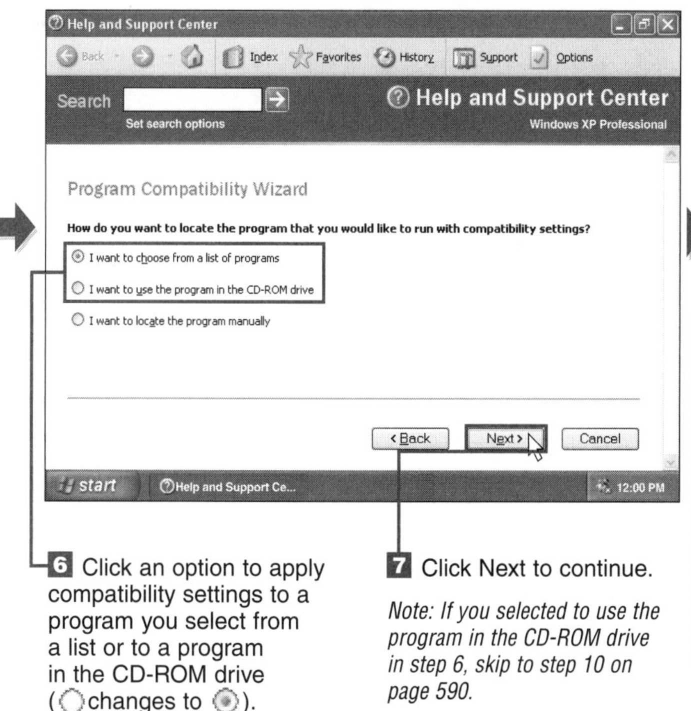

6 Click an option to apply compatibility settings to a program you select from a list or to a program in the CD-ROM drive (○ changes to ◉).

7 Click Next to continue.

Note: If you selected to use the program in the CD-ROM drive in step 6, skip to step 10 on page 590.

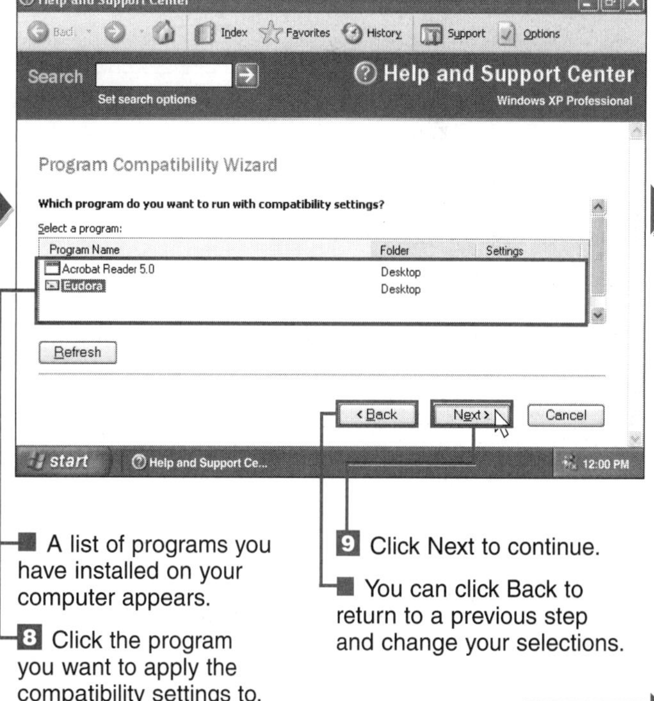

■ A list of programs you have installed on your computer appears.

8 Click the program you want to apply the compatibility settings to.

9 Click Next to continue.

■ You can click Back to return to a previous step and change your selections.

CONTINUED

USING THE PROGRAM COMPATIBILITY WIZARD (CONTINUED)

The Program Compatibility Wizard offers several compatibility modes you can choose from to run an older program. You should select the compatibility mode for the version of Windows that is recommended for the program. If you are unsure which version is recommended, you can specify the most recent version of Windows that supported the program.

You can select any recommended display settings for the program. For example, some older games and educational programs require a color setting of 256 colors or a screen resolution of 640 x 480. You can also have Windows turn off any visual themes that may interfere with the display of the program. The display settings you specify will be used only while the program is running. Once you close the program, your settings will automatically return to normal.

Once you have specified compatibility settings for a program, the wizard will start the program using the settings you specified. If the program works correctly, you can choose to have Windows use the settings each time you run the program. If the program does not work correctly, you can try again using different compatibility settings.

USING THE PROGRAM COMPATIBILITY WIZARD (CONTINUED)

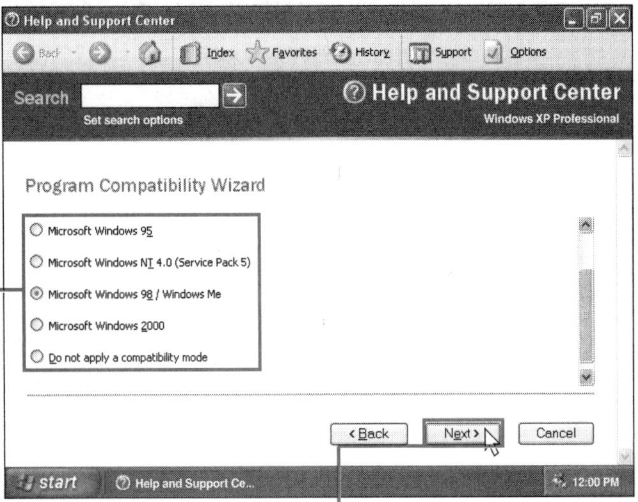

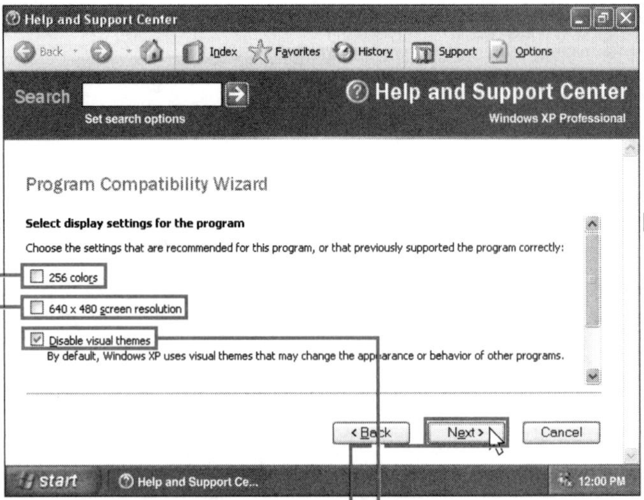

10 If the program does not run in Windows XP, click the version of Windows that can run the program successfully (○ changes to ◉).

Note: If the program runs in Windows XP but does not display correctly, select the Do not apply a compatibility mode option.

11 Click Next to continue.

12 If the program requires that the color setting be set to 256 colors, click this option (☐ changes to ☑).

13 If the program requires that the screen resolution be set to 640 x 480, click this option (☐ changes to ☑).

14 If you are experiencing problems with menus or buttons on the program's title bar, click this option (☐ changes to ☑).

15 Click Next to continue.

I am using the wizard to help me install a program from a CD. Will the wizard save the compatibility settings I specify?

✔ The wizard may not be able to save the compatibility settings you specify when installing the program. If the program does not work correctly once it is installed, you can run the Program Compatibility Wizard again for the program on your computer.

Will using compatibility settings affect the performance of a program?

✔ When you run a program using compatibility settings, the program may operate more slowly than it normally would.

Will running a program with compatibility settings affect the appearance of my other programs?

✔ If you specified display settings for the program, such as a color setting of 256 colors or a screen resolution of 640 x 480, Windows will adjust the display settings each time you start the program. If you have other programs open at the same time, these programs will also use the specified display settings. Once you close the program that uses compatibility settings, the appearance of the other programs will return to normal.

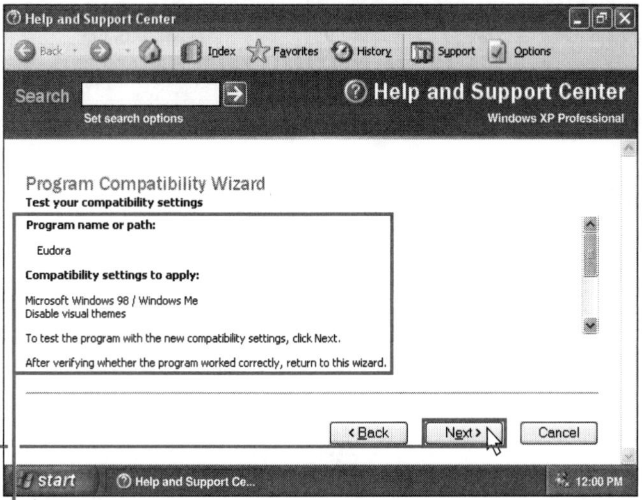

■ This area displays the name of the program and the compatibility settings you selected.

16 Click Next to test the program with the compatibility settings you selected.

17 The program will open using the compatibility settings you selected. When you finish verifying that the program works correctly, close the program to return to the wizard.

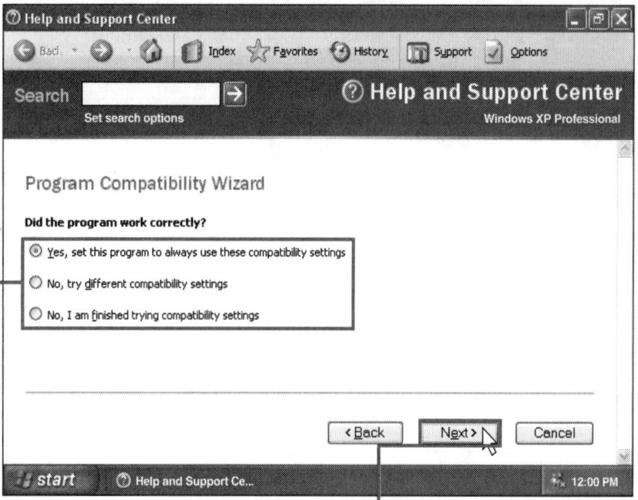

18 Click an option to specify if the program worked correctly (○ changes to ◉).

Note: If you selected to try different compatibility settings in step 18, repeat steps 10 to 18 to try different settings.

19 Click Next to continue.

CONTINUED

USING THE PROGRAM COMPATIBILITY WIZARD (CONTINUED)

The Program Compatibility Wizard creates temporary files that store information about the compatibility settings you chose for a program and whether the settings work properly. Before completing the wizard, you can choose whether you want to send these files to Microsoft. Sending the files can help Microsoft evaluate Windows XP compatibility issues and develop programs that work better with the operating system.

Once you have completed the wizard for a program, Windows will use the compatibility settings you specified each time you run the program. You can make changes to the settings at any time by running the wizard again.

You can manually change the compatibility settings for a program on your computer using the Compatibility tab of the program's Properties dialog box. This allows you to quickly adjust the compatibility settings without running the Program Compatibility Wizard.

Using the Compatibility tab allows you to adjust the same settings as the Program Compatibility Wizard, including choosing a compatibility mode and specifying recommended display settings for a program. Using the Compatibility tab does not automatically open the program using the settings you specify or allow you to send temporary files to Microsoft.

USING THE PROGRAM COMPATIBILITY WIZARD (CONTINUED)

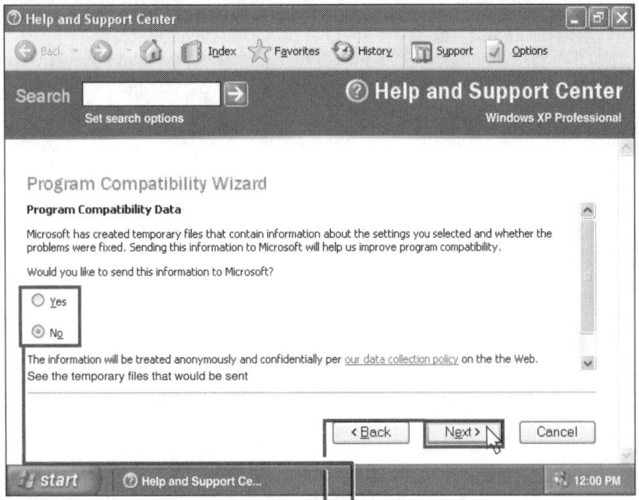

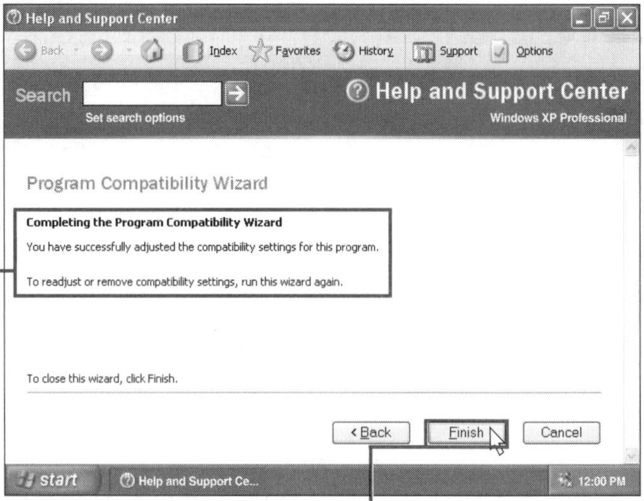

■ The wizard created files that contain information about the settings you selected and whether the problems with the program were fixed.

20 Click an option to specify if you want to send the files to Microsoft to help them improve program compatibility (○ changes to ◉).

21 Click Next to continue.

■ This message appears when you have successfully completed the Program Compatibility Wizard.

22 Click Finish to close the wizard.

How can I see the temporary files that the wizard will send to Microsoft?

✔ You can click the See the temporary files that would be sent link in the Program Compatibility Wizard. A dialog box appears, containing links to the temporary files the wizard can send. To view the contents of a file, click the link for the file.

Can I change the compatibility settings for a program using the program's shortcut on the Start menu?

✔ Yes. Right-click the program on the Start menu and then click Properties to display the Properties dialog box. Then perform steps 4 to 8 below to change the compatibility settings for the program.

My program is still not working. What can I do?

✔ Some older programs will not work with Windows XP, regardless of the compatibility settings you try. You can contact the program's manufacturer to determine if there is an updated version that is compatible with Windows XP. You can also check the Windows Update Web site to determine if there is an update to Windows that may help you use the program. To display the Windows Update Web site, click the start button, select All Programs and then click Windows Update. Then follow the instructions on your screen.

MANUALLY CHANGE THE COMPATIBILITY SETTINGS FOR A PROGRAM

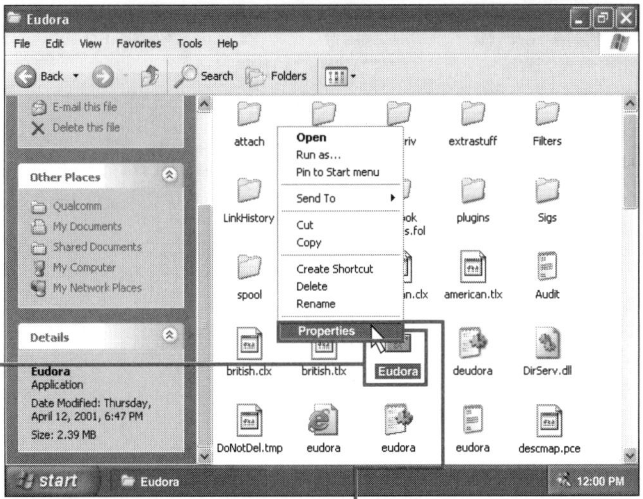

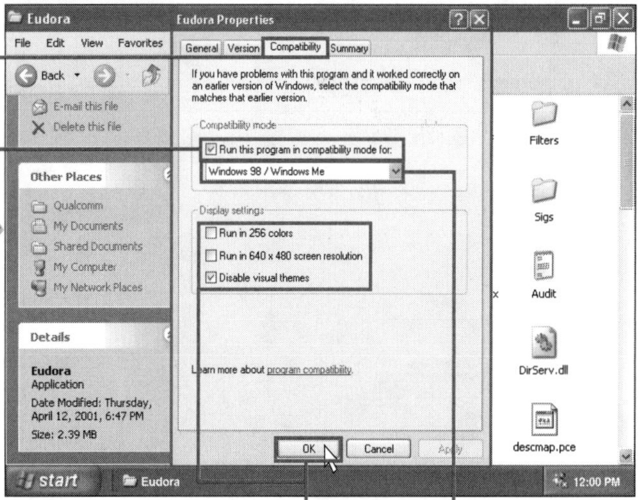

1 Locate the file on your computer that starts the program.

2 Right-click the file. A menu appears.

3 Click Properties.

■ A Properties dialog box appears.

4 Click the Compatibility tab.

5 Click this option if the program does not run in Windows XP, but did run successfully in a previous version of Windows (☐ changes to ☑).

6 Click this area to select the version of Windows that can run the program successfully.

7 Click each display setting that is required for the program (☐ changes to ☑).

8 Click OK to confirm your changes.

GET REMOTE ASSISTANCE

You can allow a person at another computer to view your computer screen and chat with you to help you solve a computer problem. With your permission, the other person can even control your computer to help you fix the problem.

To use Remote Assistance, both computers must use Windows XP and be connected to the Internet. If either computer is connected to a network, a firewall may prevent you from using Remote Assistance. A firewall protects a network from unauthorized access.

Before the other person can help you using Remote Assistance, you must send the person an invitation for Remote Assistance. You can send a Remote Assistance invitation in an e-mail message or by using Windows Messenger.

To send an invitation for Remote Assistance in an e-mail message, both computers must use an e-mail program that is compatible with Remote Assistance, such as Microsoft Outlook or Outlook Express.

To send an invitation for Remote Assistance using Windows Messenger, both computers must be signed in to Windows Messenger. The person you want to send an invitation to must also appear in your contact list in Windows Messenger. For information about Windows Messenger, see pages 484 to 501.

GET REMOTE ASSISTANCE

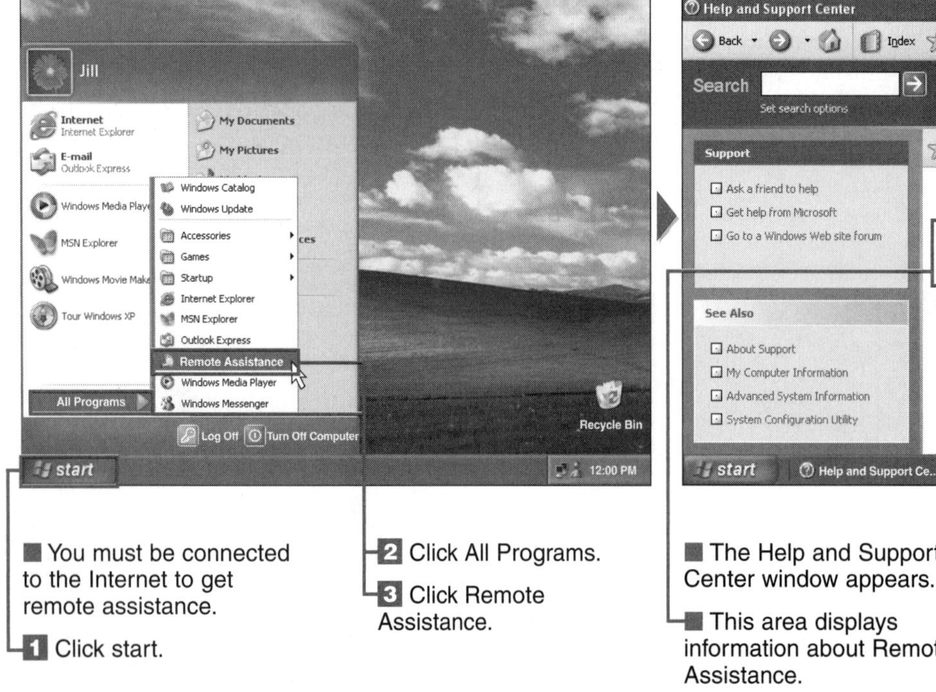

■ You must be connected to the Internet to get remote assistance.

1 Click start.

2 Click All Programs.

3 Click Remote Assistance.

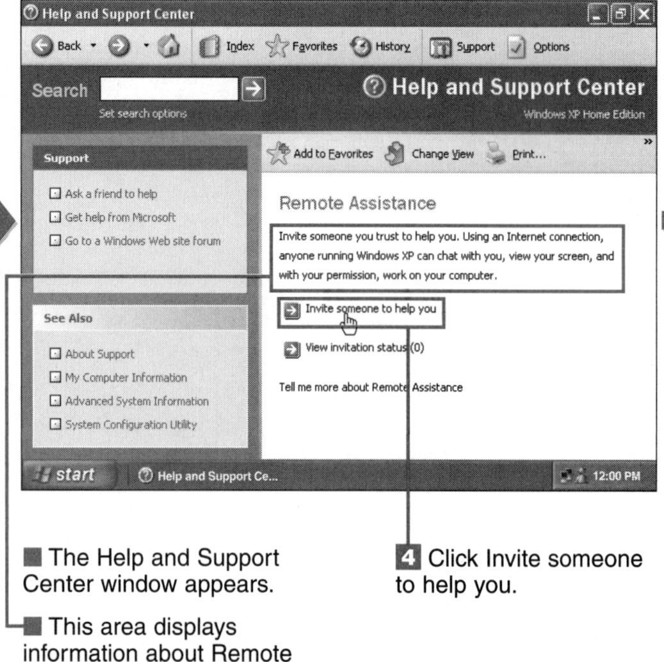

■ The Help and Support Center window appears.

■ This area displays information about Remote Assistance.

4 Click Invite someone to help you.

Is there another way to send an invitation for Remote Assistance?

✔ Yes. You can save an invitation for Remote Assistance as a file that you can transfer to another person using removable media such as a floppy disk or by placing the file on a network. Perform steps 1 to 4 below, click Save invitation as a file (Advanced) and then follow the instructions on your screen to save the invitation as a file.

Can I invite more than one person to help me?

✔ You can send multiple invitations for remote assistance, but only one person at a time can accept an invitation and use Remote Assistance to help you.

How can I change the settings for Remote Assistance?

✔ Click start, select Control Panel and choose Performance and Maintenance. Then click System to display the System Properties dialog box. Select the Remote tab and click the Advanced button. In the dialog box that appears, you can turn off the setting that allows your computer to be controlled remotely and specify a maximum amount of time that Remote Assistance invitations can remain open.

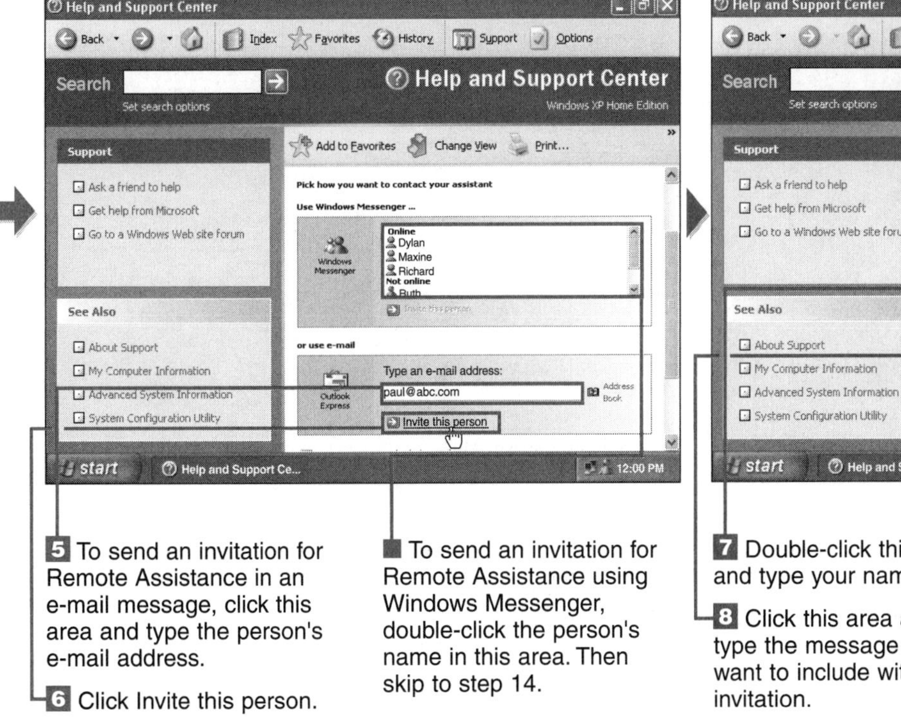

5 To send an invitation for Remote Assistance in an e-mail message, click this area and type the person's e-mail address.

6 Click Invite this person.

■ To send an invitation for Remote Assistance using Windows Messenger, double-click the person's name in this area. Then skip to step 14.

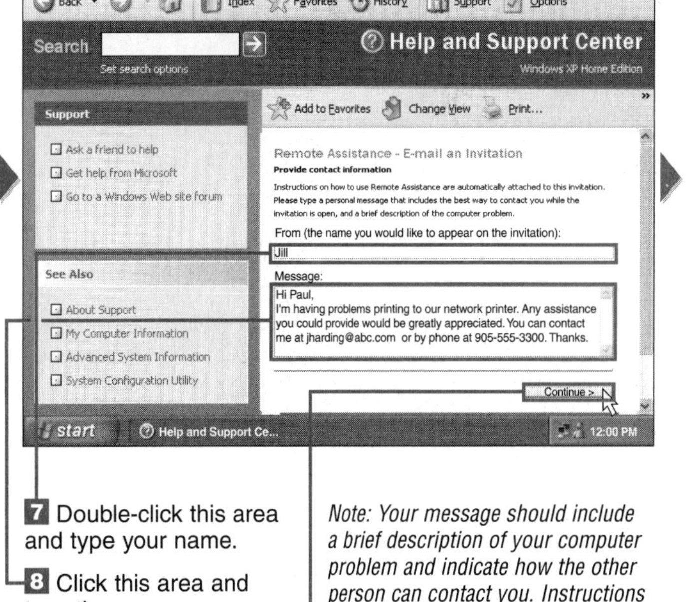

7 Double-click this area and type your name.

8 Click this area and type the message you want to include with the invitation.

Note: Your message should include a brief description of your computer problem and indicate how the other person can contact you. Instructions on how to use Remote Assistance are automatically included with the invitation.

9 Click Continue.

CONTINUED

GET REMOTE ASSISTANCE (CONTINUED)

When sending a Remote Assistance invitation in an e-mail message, you can specify when you want the invitation to expire and a password that the other person must enter to connect to your computer. Specifying an expiration time and password for an invitation protects your computer from unauthorized access.

When specifying a password, do not use your name, logon password or a common word. Make sure the password contains at least seven characters and contains letters, numbers and symbols. You must tell the other person the password you specify. You should send remote assistance invitations only to people you trust.

Once the other person has accepted your invitation for Remote Assistance, you can allow the person to view your screen and chat with you to help you solve your computer problem.

If the other person wants to control your computer to try to solve your problem, a dialog box appears allowing you to give the person permission. While the other person is controlling your computer, only one of you should use the mouse at a time, since the mouse pointer will be shared between you. You can stop the other person from controlling your computer at any time.

GET REMOTE ASSISTANCE (CONTINUED)

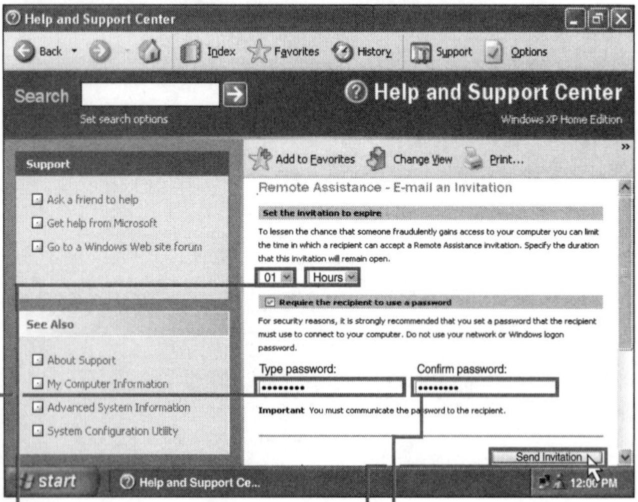

10 These areas indicate when the invitation will expire. You can click an area to change the time.

11 Click this area and type a password the other person must enter to connect to your computer.

12 Click this area and type the password again.

13 Click Send Invitation.

■ A dialog box will appear, allowing you to confirm that you want to send the message. Click Send to send the message.

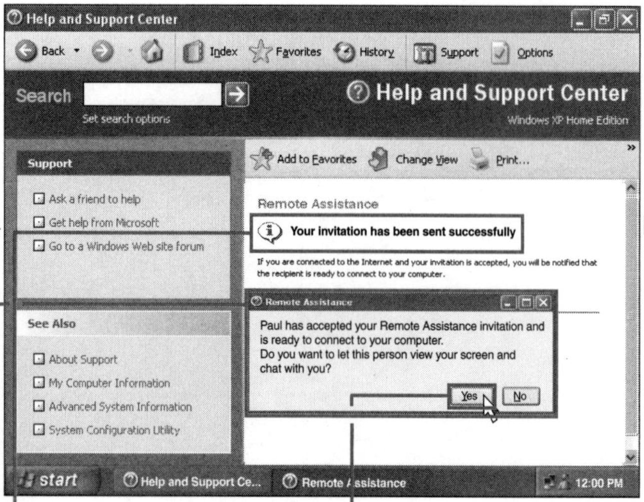

■ This message appears when your invitation has been sent successfully.

■ A dialog box appears when the other person accepts your Remote Assistance invitation.

14 Click Yes to allow the other person to view your screen and chat with you.

How can I view information about a Remote Assistance invitation I sent?

✔ Perform steps 1 to 3 on page 594 and then click View invitation status to display information about Remote Assistance invitations you have sent, including the expiration time and status of each invitation. To view more information about an invitation, click the invitation and then click the Details button.

Can I send an invitation for Remote Assistance in an e-mail message without specifying a password?

✔ Although it is recommended that you use a password for security reasons, you can click the Require the recipient to use a password option (☑ changes to ☐) to avoid having to enter a password in steps 11 and 12 below.

How can I improve the performance of Remote Assistance when using a slow Internet connection?

✔ When using Remote Assistance with a slow connection, such as a modem connection, you can improve performance by reducing the color setting and screen resolution you use. To change the color setting, see page 202. To change the screen resolution, see page 200.

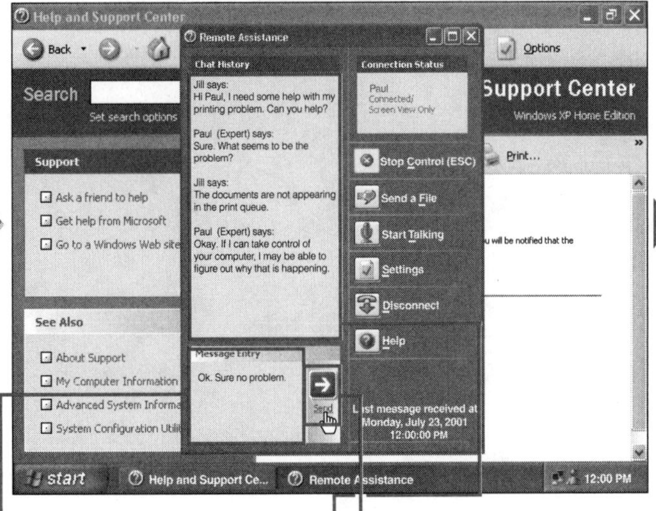

■ The Remote Assistance window appears.

15 To send a message to the other person, click this area and type a message.

16 Click Send to send the message.

Note: You can also press the Enter key to send the message.

■ This area will display the message you sent and the ongoing conversation.

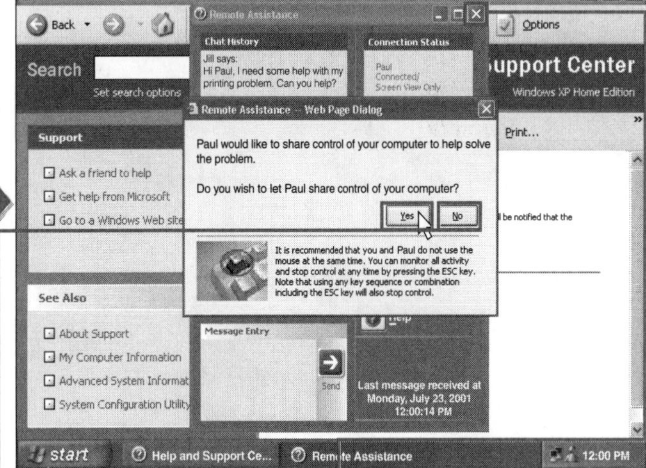

■ A dialog box appears if the other person wants to control your computer.

17 Click Yes or No to specify if you want the other person to control your computer.

■ To stop the other person from controlling your computer, press the Esc key.

Note: A message appears, indicating that the other person is no longer controlling your computer. Click OK.

18 When you finish using Remote Assistance, click  to close the window.

START WINDOWS IN SAFE MODE

You may be able to start Windows in safe mode to try to correct a problem that is preventing Windows from starting properly. For example, Windows may not start properly if you accidentally deleted important files or changed certain Windows settings.

Windows provides several safe mode options. The Safe Mode option uses the minimum capabilities required to run Windows. The Safe Mode with Networking option allows you to access your network while in safe mode. The Safe Mode with Command Prompt option starts the command prompt instead of displaying the Windows desktop. This option is useful when the other safe mode options do not work due to a problem with the computer's video setup.

To start Windows in safe mode, you must log on using a computer administrator account. Windows automatically creates an Administrator account that you can use if your computer administrator account is unavailable.

When your computer is running in safe mode, Windows displays the words "Safe Mode" in each corner of your screen. Some hardware devices, such as printers, sound cards, modems and some types of mice, are unavailable in safe mode.

When you finish fixing the problem that is preventing Windows from starting normally, you can exit safe mode and restart your computer. After restarting, your computer should function normally.

START WINDOWS IN SAFE MODE

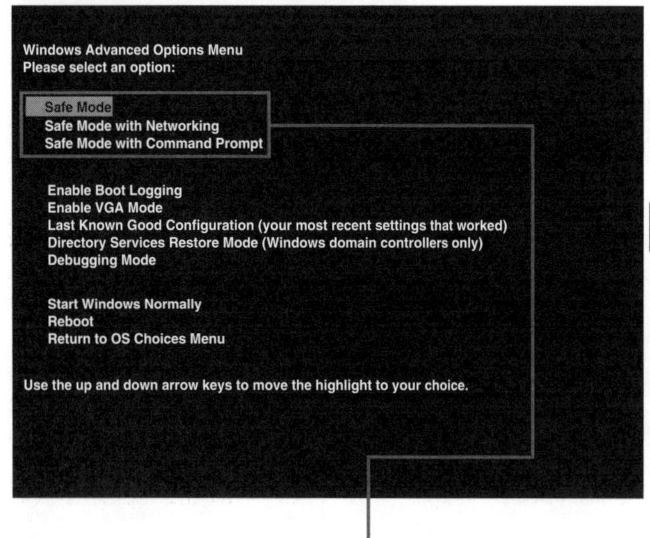

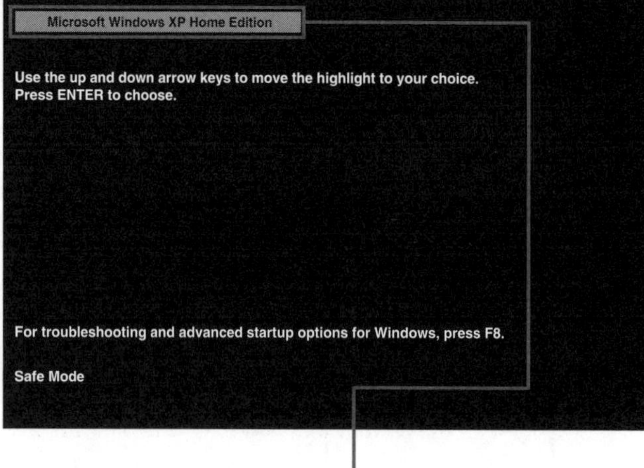

1 After you turn on your computer and monitor, press and hold down the F8 key.

■ The Windows Advanced Options Menu appears, displaying a list of options for starting Windows.

2 Press the ↓ or ↑ key until you highlight the safe mode option you want to use. Then press the Enter key.

■ Windows asks you to select the operating system you want to start.

3 Press the ↓ or ↑ key until you highlight the operating system you want to start. Then press the Enter key.

What are the other options for starting my computer?

✔ The Enable Boot Logging option records actions performed during startup in the ntbtlog.txt file stored in the WINDOWS folder. You can use this file to determine the cause of a startup problem.

The Enable VGA Mode option starts Windows using a VGA driver. This option is useful if Windows will not start due to a problem with a new video driver you installed.

The Last Known Good Configuration option allows you to restore the registry settings that were used the last time your computer started successfully. For information about the registry, see page 612.

The Directory Services Restore Mode option is useful on administrative computers or large networks that are experiencing problems.

The Debugging Mode option sends information about the computer's problems through a serial cable to another computer. Support technicians often use Debugging Mode to determine the cause of a computer problem.

How can I fix the problem that is preventing Windows from starting normally?

✔ You can reverse the action that may have caused the problem. For example, if the problem occurred when you installed a program, you can try uninstalling the program. You can also use the System Restore feature to return your computer to a time before the problem occurred. For information about System Restore, see page 584.

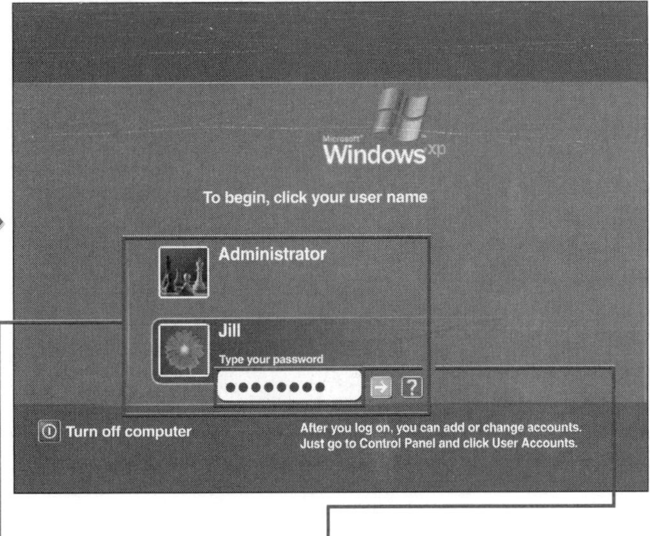

- The Welcome screen appears.
- This area displays the computer administrator accounts available on your computer.

4 Click the computer administrator account you want to use in safe mode.

- If a password is assigned to the account, a box appears that allows you to enter the password.

5 Type the password and then press the Enter key.

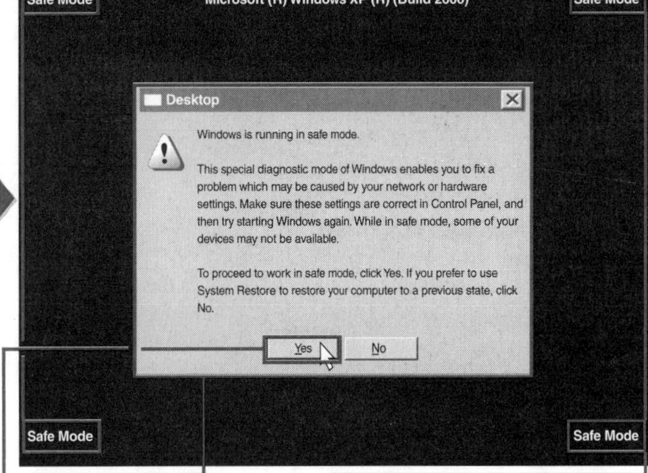

- A dialog box appears, stating that Windows is running in safe mode. The dialog box provides information about safe mode.

6 Click Yes to continue.

- Windows displays the words "Safe Mode" in each corner of your screen.
- When you finish fixing the problem that prevents Windows from starting normally, restart your computer. To restart your computer, see page 30.

USING SYSTEM INFORMATION

You can use System Information to display detailed information about the hardware and software on your computer. You can use this information to learn more about your computer or troubleshoot a problem you are experiencing. The information provided may also help a support technician identify the cause of a problem and suggest a solution.

System Information is organized into categories. The System Summary category displays general information about your computer.

The Hardware Resources category displays information about the resources on your computer and how the hardware devices installed on your computer use the resources.

The Components category contains information about your Windows setup and the hardware devices on your computer. This category is useful for determining the driver for a specific device.

The Software Environment category contains information about the software that is installed on your computer and the software that is currently running.

System Information may also display categories for some programs installed on your computer, such as Microsoft Office. These categories will display information specific to the program.

USING SYSTEM INFORMATION

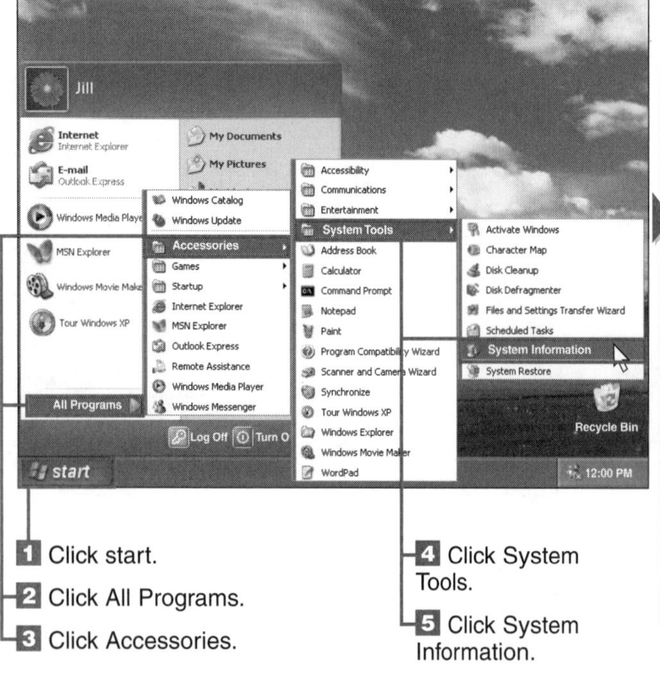

1 Click start.

2 Click All Programs.

3 Click Accessories.

4 Click System Tools.

5 Click System Information.

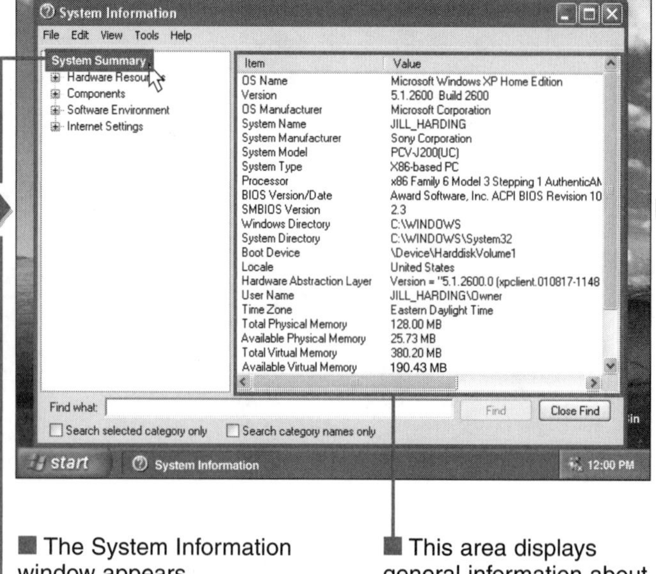

■ The System Information window appears.

6 Click System Summary to display general information about your computer.

■ This area displays general information about your computer, such as the version of Windows and the total amount of memory.

How do I print the displayed system information?

✔ Select the File menu and then click Print.

Can I save the displayed system information?

✔ Yes. Select the File menu and click Save. To later view the saved information, select the File menu and click Open. You can also choose to save the information as a text file so you can review the information in a text editor and send the information to other people by e-mail. To save the information as a text file, select the File menu and then click Export.

Can I search for specific system information?

✔ Yes. In the Find what area at the bottom of the System Information window, type the information you want to find and then click Find to start the search. Click Find Next until the information of interest appears. If the Find what area is not displayed, select the Edit menu and then click Hide Find.

Does Windows provide any tools that can help identify and solve my computer problems?

✔ Yes. Windows provides several system tools you can use. In the System Information window, select the Tools menu and click the name of the tool you want to run. Then follow the instructions displayed on your screen to use the tool.

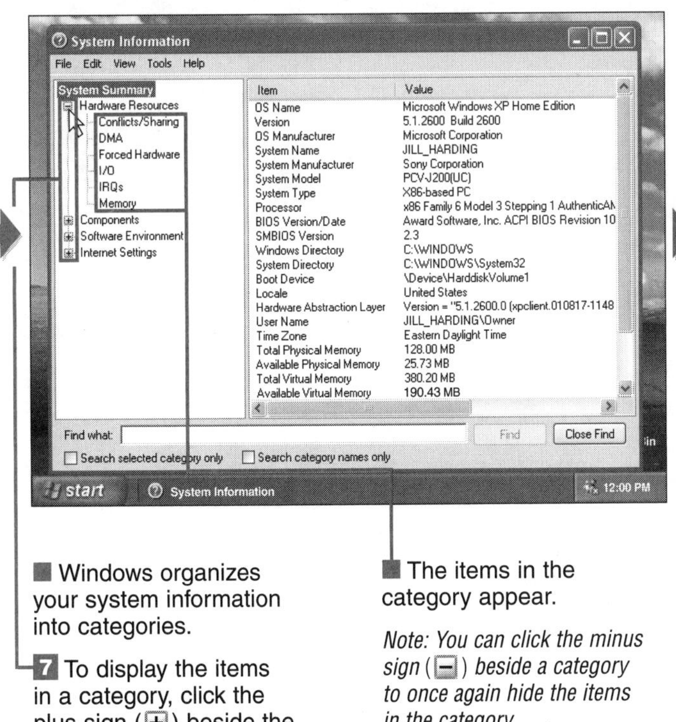

■ Windows organizes your system information into categories.

7 To display the items in a category, click the plus sign (⊞) beside the category (⊞ changes to ⊟).

■ The items in the category appear.

Note: You can click the minus sign (⊟) beside a category to once again hide the items in the category.

8 Click an item of interest.

■ This area displays information about the item you selected.

■ When you finish reviewing system information, click ☒ to close the System Information window.

USING SYSTEM MONITOR

You can use System Monitor to monitor the performance of your computer.

System Monitor is often used to monitor the speed at which parts of a computer process information. If your computer is not working properly, this information can help you determine the cause of a problem. System Monitor can also help you decide whether you need to upgrade your computer hardware.

You may want to observe and keep records of how your computer performs when there are no problems. You can use this information in a comparison later if your computer's performance starts to deteriorate. You should monitor your computer's performance over an extended period of time to get a better estimate of what normal performance is. A good way to determine if your computer is running properly is to compare it with another computer that is set up in a similar way.

By default, System Monitor monitors your computer's memory, disk and CPU usage and displays the information about your computer's performance in a graph. A legend indicates what each color in the graph represents.

USING SYSTEM MONITOR

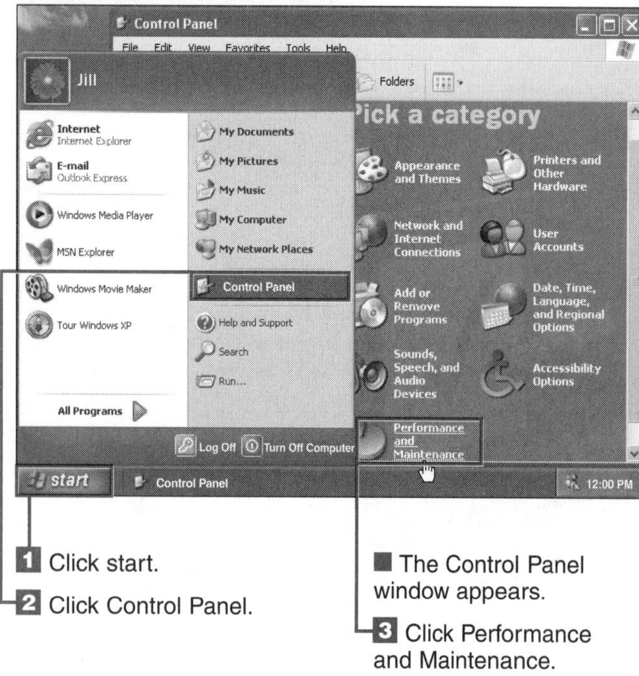

1 Click start.

2 Click Control Panel.

■ The Control Panel window appears.

3 Click Performance and Maintenance.

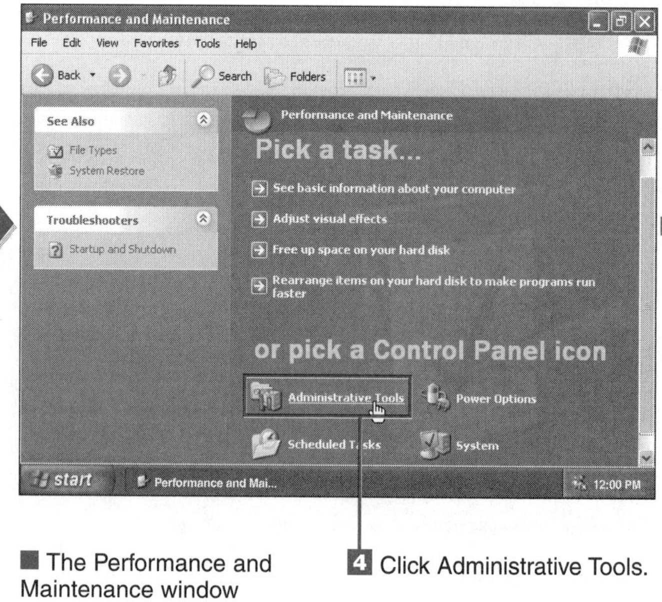

■ The Performance and Maintenance window appears.

4 Click Administrative Tools.

How do I add an item to System Monitor?

✔ In the Performance window, click [+]. In the dialog box that appears, click [▾] below Performance object and select the object you want to monitor. In the area below 'Select counters from list,' choose the counter you want to monitor. If the object you selected has more than one instance, choose the instance you want to monitor in the area below 'Select instances from list.' Then click the Add button and click Close.

How do I remove an item from System Monitor?

✔ To remove an item, click the item in the legend and then click [X]. To remove all the items at once, click [▯].

Is there another way to display the information for items in System Monitor?

✔ You can display the information in a histogram or a report. A histogram displays the value of the data using vertical bars. To change the display of the information, click graph ( ), histogram ( ) or report ( ).

Are there other ways to monitor my computer's performance?

✔ You can use counter logs to keep records of specific characteristics of your computer's performance. You can also use trace logs to record information about specific events, while an alert can notify you of a specific situation, such as low disk space. To access these additional monitoring tools, double-click Performance Logs and Alerts in the left pane of the Performance window.

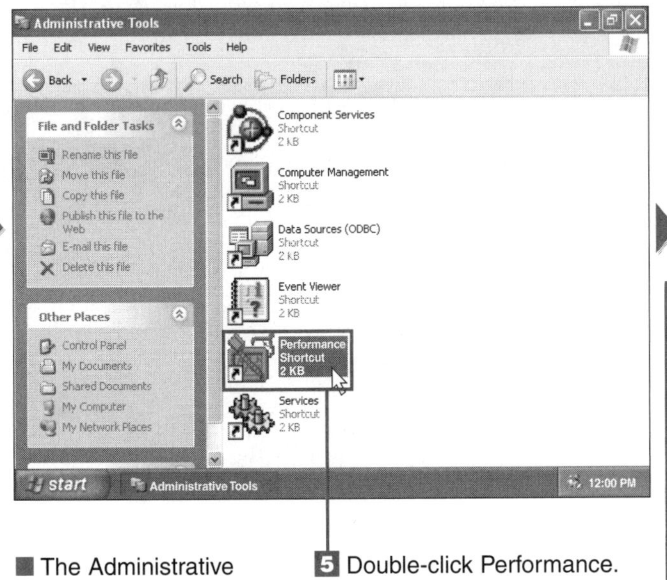

■ The Administrative Tools window appears.

5 Double-click Performance.

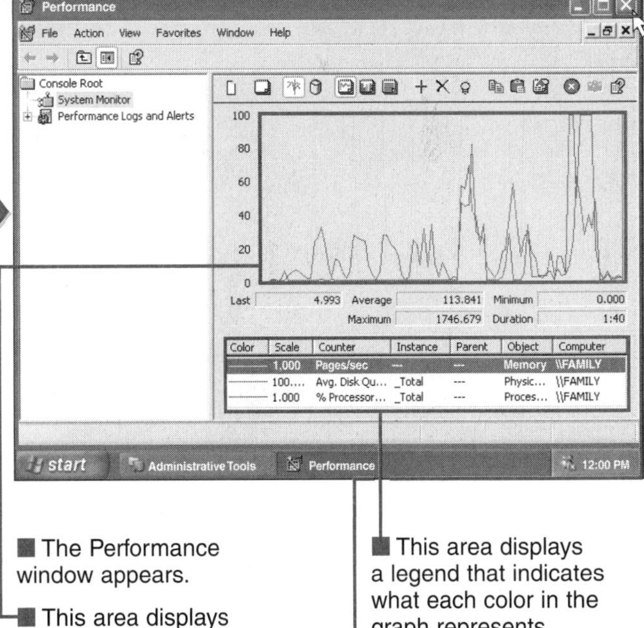

■ The Performance window appears.

■ This area displays a graph that shows the activity of each monitored item.

■ This area displays a legend that indicates what each color in the graph represents.

6 When you finish viewing the information, click [X] to close the Performance window.

USING EVENT VIEWER

You can use Event Viewer to display a list of events that have occurred on your computer.

In Event Viewer, Windows offers three logs you can display—the Application log, the System log and the Security log. The Application log displays application events, such as file errors. The System log displays system events, such as a problem with a driver for a device. The Security log displays security events, such as unsuccessful logon attempts.

All users can view the Application and System logs, but you must be logged on as a computer administrator to view the Security log.

In the Application and System logs, you can view three types of events. An Information event indicates the normal operation of hardware and software. A Warning event indicates a situation that may become a problem. An Error event signals a serious problem.

The Security log displays two types of events. A Success Audit shows a successful security access attempt, such as a user successfully logging on to Windows. A Failure Audit indicates a failed security access attempt, such a user failing to access a network drive.

USING EVENT VIEWER

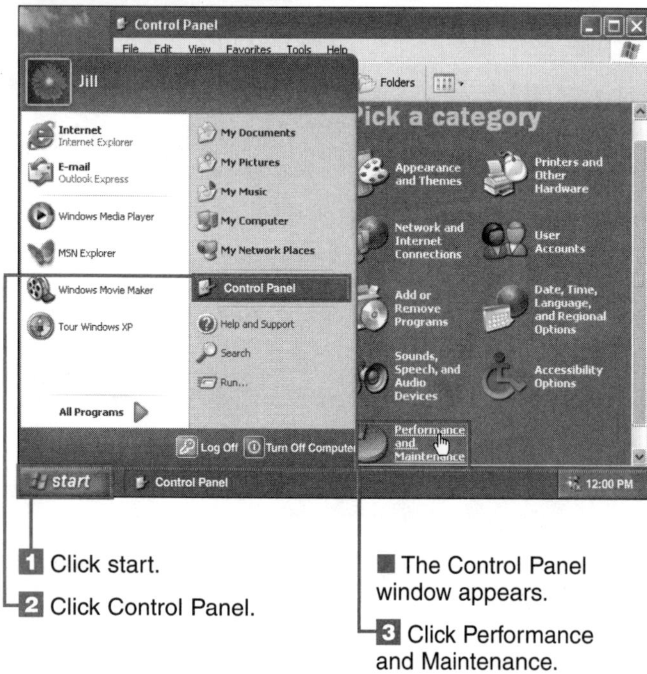

1 Click start.

2 Click Control Panel.

■ The Control Panel window appears.

3 Click Performance and Maintenance.

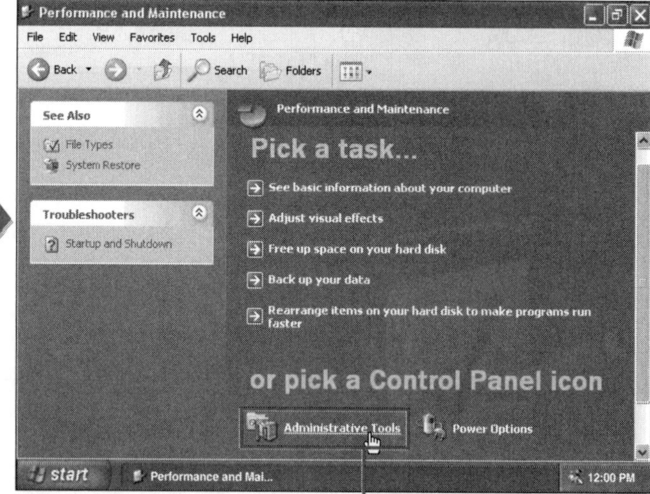

■ The Performance and Maintenance window appears.

4 Click Administrative Tools.

Can I clear an event log?

✔ Yes. Over time, an event log file can become quite large in size. You can clear an event log to remove all events from the log. Right-click the log you want to clear and then select Clear all Events. You can then save the log on your computer for future use or simply clear the log without saving it. You must be logged on as a computer administrator to clear an event log.

How do I view detailed information about an event?

✔ Double-click the event for which you want to view detailed information. In the dialog box that appears, you can click ↓ or ↑ to view detailed information about the next or previous event.

Can I copy the information about an event?

✔ Yes. Copying information about an event is useful when you want to keep a record of a single event or you want to e-mail the information to another person. Double-click the event from which you want to copy information. In the dialog box that appears, click the copy button. Then open the file on your computer where you want to place the information, select the Edit menu and click Paste.

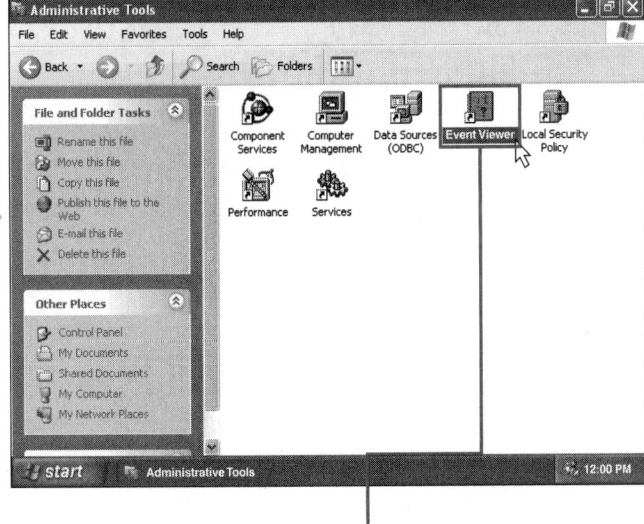

■ The Administrative Tools window appears.

5 Double-click Event Viewer.

■ The Event Viewer window appears.

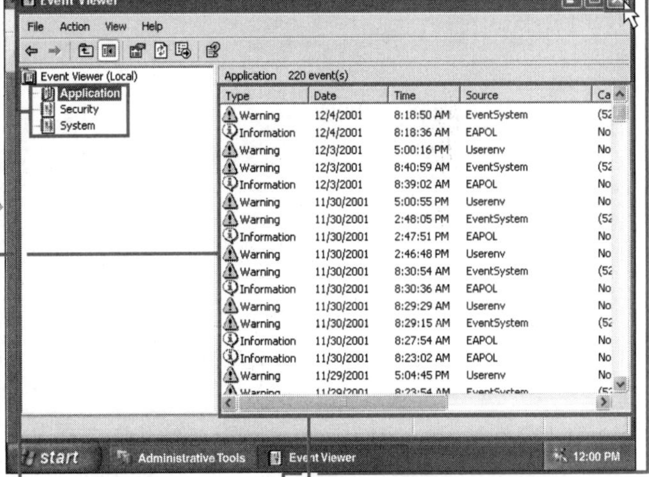

6 Click the log that records the events you want to view.

■ This area displays information about each event in the log you selected.

■ An icon appears beside each event to indicate the type of event, including Information (ⓘ), Warning (⚠), Error (⊗), Success Audit (🔑) and Failure Audit (🔒).

7 When you finish reviewing the information, click ✕ to close the Event Viewer window.

USING SERVICES

A service is a program or process that runs in the background of your computer. For example, the Themes service allows Windows to use desktop themes, while the Help and Support service makes the Help and Support Center available on your computer.

You can view information about a service on your computer, such as the name, description and status of the service. The status of a service indicates if the service has started.

Some services depend on one or more other services to operate. For example, in order for the Computer Browser service to operate, the Server and Workstation services must be running.

After you finish reviewing information about a service, you may want to make changes to the settings for the service. To change the settings for a service, you must be logged on as a computer administrator. If you make changes to the settings for a service, keep in mind that changes you make may prevent other important services from running.

USING SERVICES

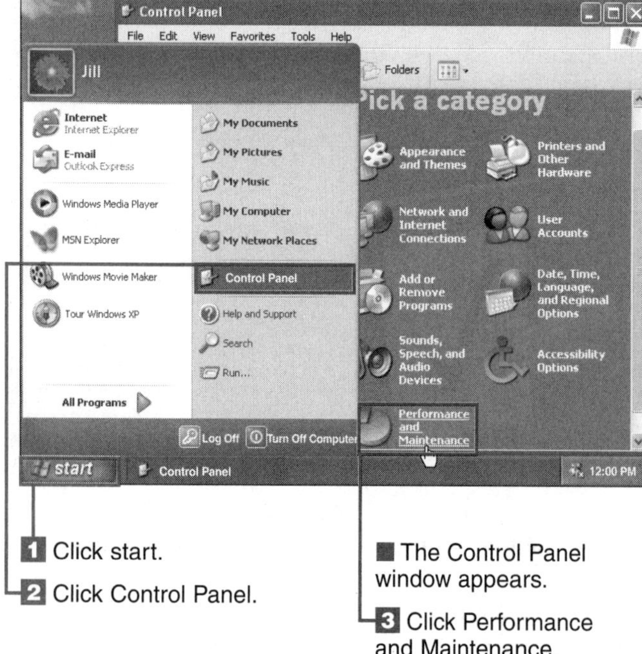

1 Click start.

2 Click Control Panel.

■ The Control Panel window appears.

3 Click Performance and Maintenance.

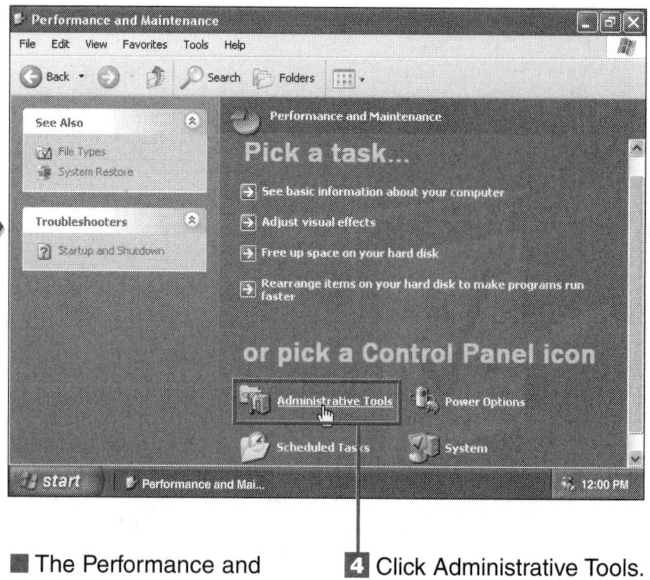

■ The Performance and Maintenance window appears.

4 Click Administrative Tools.

How do I start or stop a service?

✔ Click the service you want to start or stop and then click the Start Service (▶) or Stop Service (■) button. The status of the service changes in the Services window. To pause or restart a service, click the service and then click the Pause Service (II) or Restart Service (■▶) button.

How do I see which services depend on a service I want to change?

✔ Right-click the service you want to view dependent services for and then select Properties. In the dialog box that appears, choose the Dependencies tab. The top list shows the services that the service you selected depends on to operate. The bottom list shows the services that depend on the service you selected.

How do I change how a service is started?

✔ Right-click the service you want to change and select Properties. In the dialog box that appears, choose the General tab, click the Startup type area and then select the startup option you want to use. The Automatic option starts the service when you start your computer. If you choose the Manual option, a user or another service must start the service. If you choose the Disabled option, the service cannot be started.

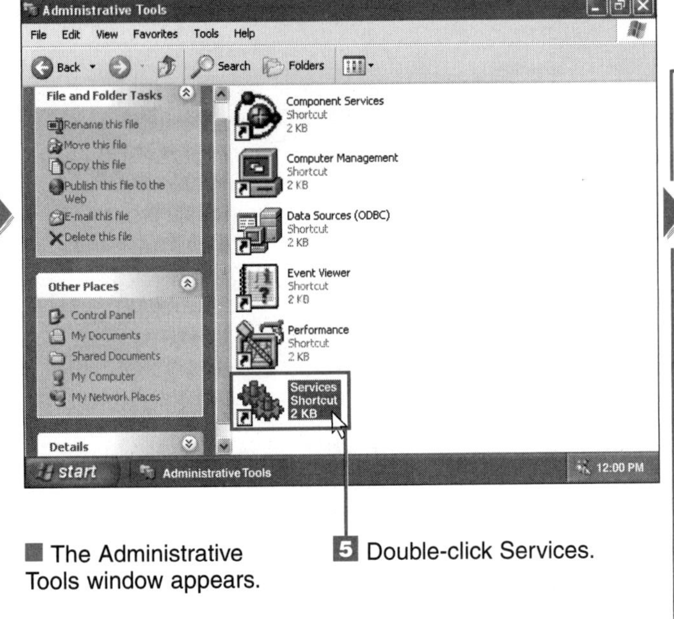

■ The Administrative Tools window appears.

5 Double-click Services.

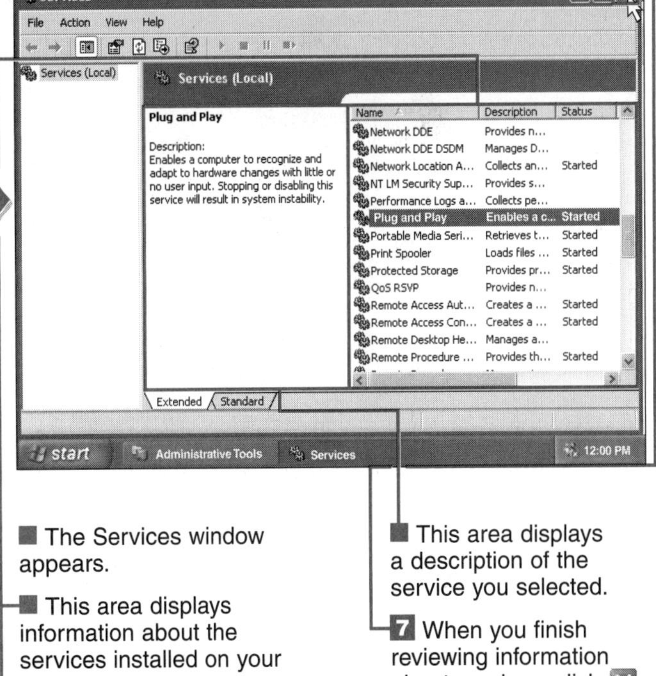

■ The Services window appears.

■ This area displays information about the services installed on your computer.

6 To view a description of a service, click the service.

■ This area displays a description of the service you selected.

7 When you finish reviewing information about services, click ☒ to close the Services window.

CREATE A HARDWARE PROFILE

You can create a new hardware profile for your computer. A hardware profile tells Windows which hardware devices are available when you start your computer. You must be logged on as a computer administrator to create a new hardware profile.

To create a new hardware profile, you copy an existing profile and then make changes to the copy.

Windows automatically creates the Docked or Undocked Profile for a portable computer. For a desktop computer, Windows automatically creates Profile 1.

A portable computer can be used in several different situations. For example, you may use the portable computer at an office where you connect to a docking station. At home, you may use the portable computer with a printer, monitor, keyboard and mouse. When traveling, you may use the portable computer without additional hardware. Each situation requires a different hardware setup. To avoid the task of having to install hardware devices on your computer each time you need to use a different hardware setup, you can save the hardware settings for each situation in a separate profile.

CREATE A HARDWARE PROFILE

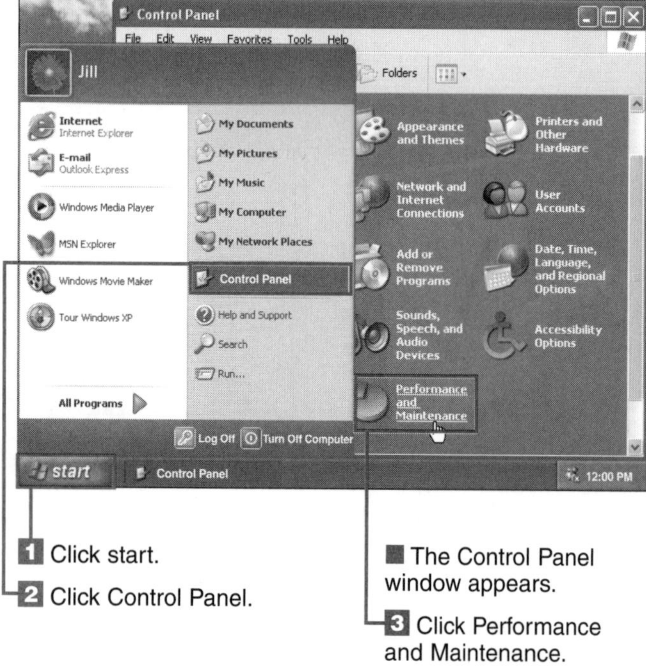

1 Click start.

2 Click Control Panel.

■ The Control Panel window appears.

3 Click Performance and Maintenance.

■ The Performance and Maintenance window appears.

4 Click See basic information about your computer.

When would I create a new hardware profile for my desktop computer?

✔ You may want to create a new profile for your desktop computer if you frequently add and remove a hardware device, such as a removable drive. Creating a profile that includes the removable drive saves you from having to install the drive each time you want to use it.

Which hardware profile should I copy as the basis for my new profile?

✔ You should choose the first hardware profile in the list of profiles in the Hardware Profiles dialog box. For portable computers, this is the profile you use when docked. For desktop computers, this is Profile 1.

How can I rename a profile I created?

✔ In the Hardware Profiles dialog box, select the profile you want to rename and click the Rename button. Then type a new name for the profile and press the Enter key.

How can I delete a profile I created?

✔ In the Hardware Profiles dialog box, select the profile you want to delete. Then click the Delete button. You cannot delete the current profile.

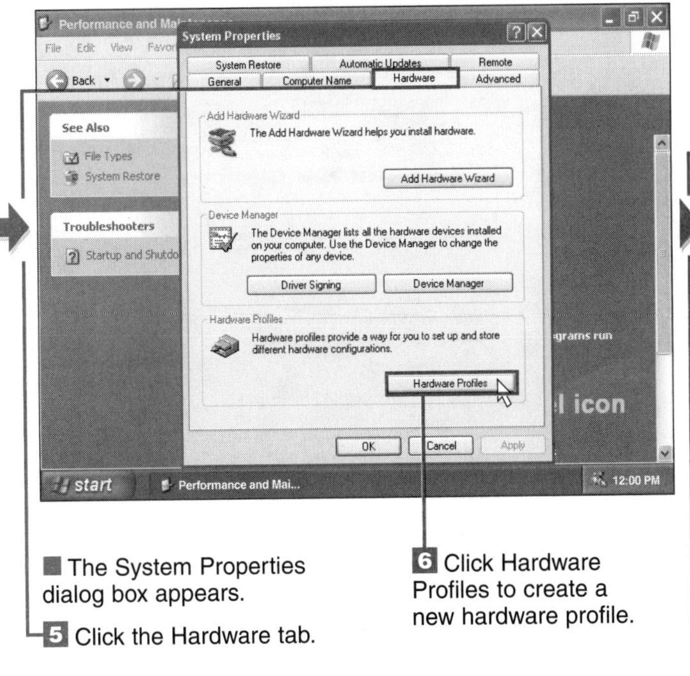

■ The System Properties dialog box appears.

5 Click the Hardware tab.

6 Click Hardware Profiles to create a new hardware profile.

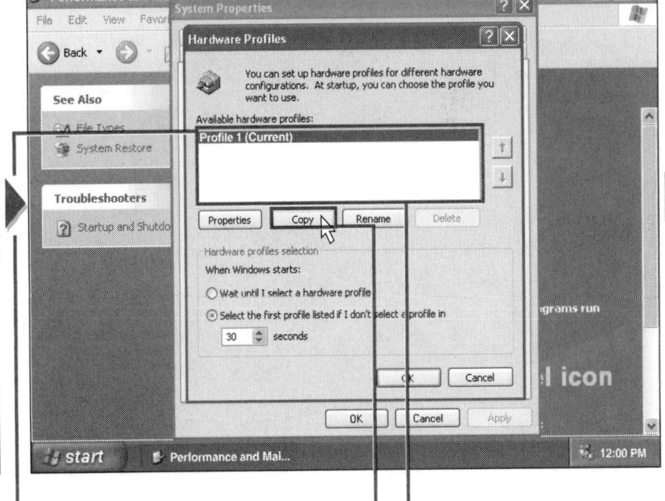

■ The Hardware Profiles dialog box appears.

■ This area displays the hardware profiles set up on your computer. The profile you are currently using displays the word "Current."

7 Click the hardware profile on which you want to base the new profile.

8 Click Copy to copy the profile.

CONTINUED

CREATE A HARDWARE PROFILE (CONTINUED)

When creating a new hardware profile, you need to name the profile you copied before customizing the profile to suit your needs. You should give the hardware profile you create a meaningful name so you will be able to recognize the profile in the future. Customizing a copied profile does not affect the other profiles on your computer.

To customize the profile you created, you must start the computer using the profile. To specify which devices should be available for the profile, you can disable each device you do not want to use in the profile. By default, all the devices installed on your computer are enabled. Disabling a device prevents Windows from loading the device's driver when you start your computer. A driver is the software Windows uses to communicate with a device. Windows displays a red X through the icon for a device you disable.

There are some devices you cannot disable, such as disk drives.

After you create a new hardware profile, Windows displays the available hardware profiles in a list when you start your computer. You can choose the profile you want to use. If you do not select a profile within 30 seconds, Windows will use the profile that is listed first in the Hardware Profiles dialog box.

CREATE A HARDWARE PROFILE (CONTINUED)

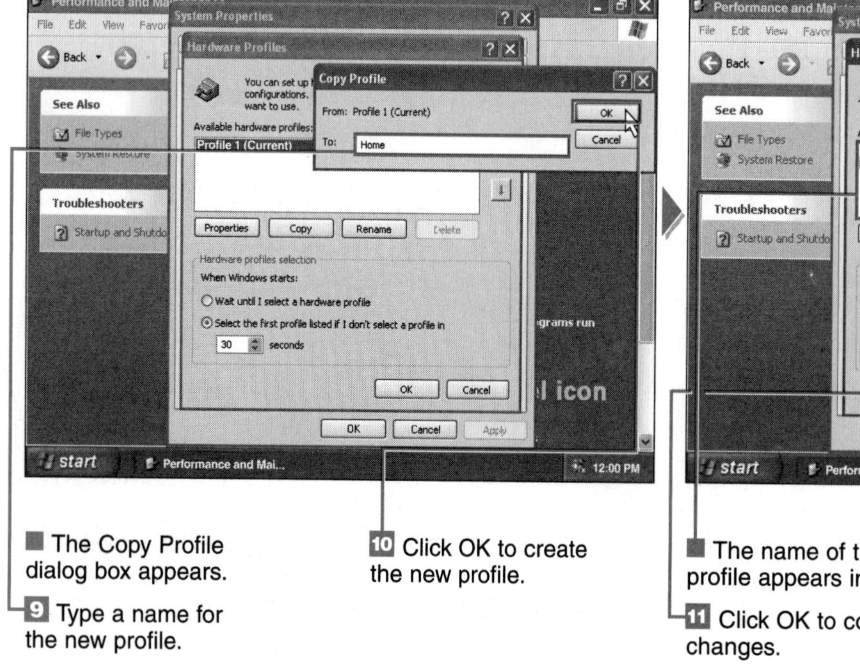

■ The Copy Profile dialog box appears.

9 Type a name for the new profile.

10 Click OK to create the new profile.

■ The name of the new profile appears in this area.

11 Click OK to confirm your changes.

12 Click OK to close the System Properties dialog box.

■ You can now customize the new hardware profile to accommodate a different situation.

How do I enable a device I disabled?

✔ In the Device Manager window, click the device you want to enable. Then click [icon]. The icon for the device will no longer display a red X. For information about using Device Manager, see page 580.

Can I change how a hardware profile is selected when Windows starts?

✔ Yes. In the Hardware Profiles dialog box, select an option to specify whether you want Windows to wait until you select a hardware profile or select the first profile listed if you don't select a profile in a certain number of seconds (○ changes to ◉). If you select the second option, double-click in the box below the option and then specify a number of seconds. You can type 0 seconds to have Windows automatically use the first profile in the list.

How do I change the order of the profiles that appear when Windows starts?

✔ The hardware profiles list displays profiles in the order in which they will appear when Windows starts. You can change the order of items in the list in the Hardware Profiles dialog box. Click the item you want to move and then click [↑] or [↓] to move the item to a new position in the list.

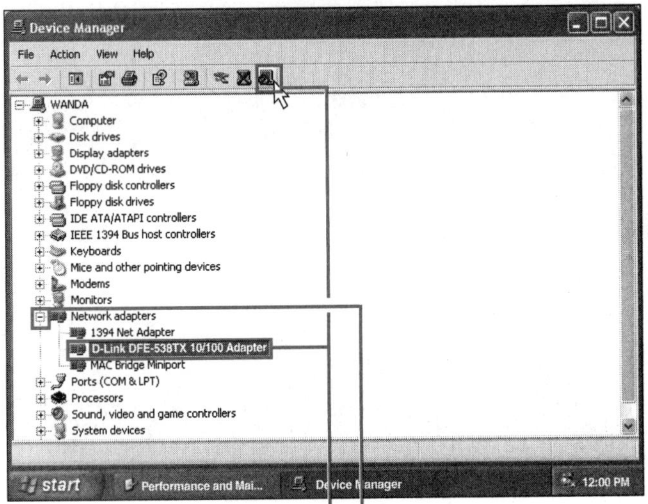

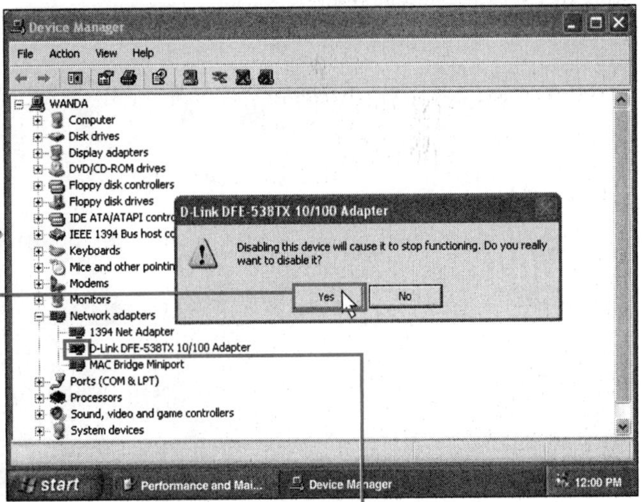

CUSTOMIZE A HARDWARE PROFILE

1 Start your computer using the hardware profile you want to customize.

2 Display the Device Manager window by performing steps 1 to 6 starting on page 580.

3 Click the plus sign (⊞) beside the type of device you want to disable.

4 Click the device you want to disable.

5 Click [icon] to disable the device.

■ A warning message appears, stating that disabling the device will cause the device to stop functioning.

6 Click Yes to disable the device for the hardware profile.

■ A red X appears through the icon for the device.

7 To disable additional devices for the hardware profile, repeat steps 3 to 6 for each device you want to disable.

WORK WITH THE REGISTRY

The Registry Editor is an advanced tool you can use to view and edit the registry. The registry contains the information Windows requires to run.

The contents of the registry are complex, so you should use the Registry Editor only when absolutely necessary. If you make a mistake while editing the registry, you could damage your system or Windows may not be able to start. Before making any changes to the registry, you should create a backup copy of the registry and make sure you know how to restore it.

The registry is made up of five main keys, also called branches. Each key can contain other keys, as well as pieces of information called values. Each value has a name and data.

The HKEY_CLASSES_ROOT key contains information about the associations between your programs and documents. HKEY_CURRENT_USER contains information specific to the current user, while HKEY_LOCAL_MACHINE contains information about your current hardware and software setup. HKEY_USERS contains information for all users and HKEY_CURRENT_CONFIG contains information about your hardware.

The Registry Editor window has two panes. The left pane displays the list of keys in the registry. The right pane displays the values, or information, for the current key.

START THE REGISTRY EDITOR

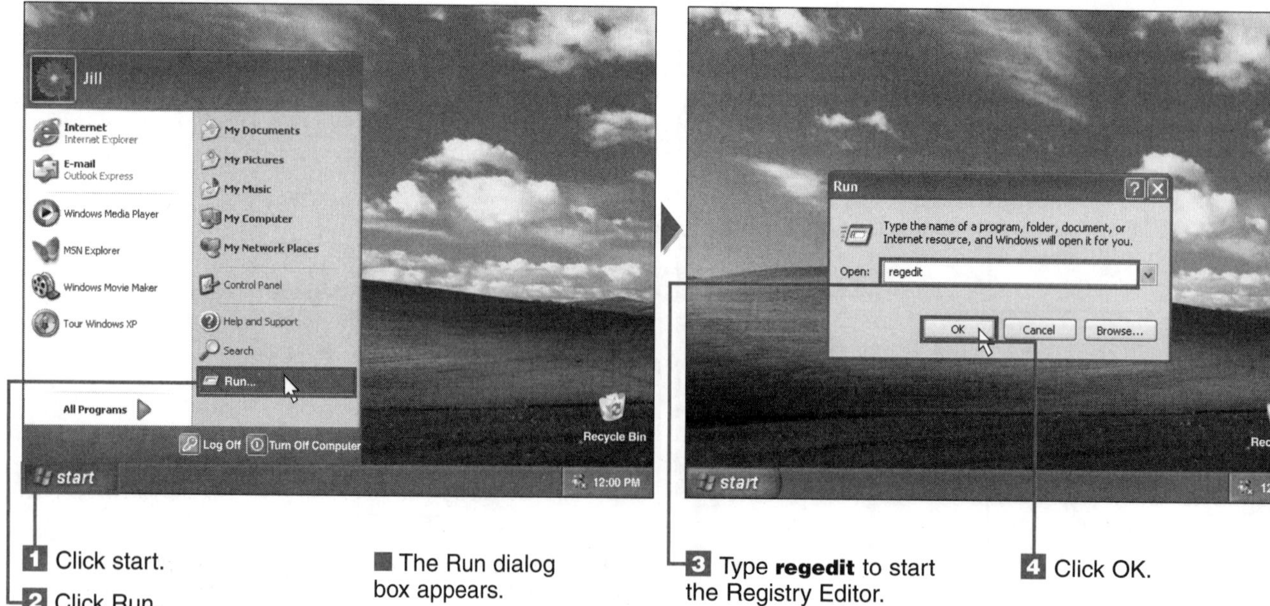

1 Click start.

2 Click Run.

■ The Run dialog box appears.

3 Type **regedit** to start the Registry Editor.

4 Click OK.

How do I back up the registry?

✔ You can create a backup copy of the registry by using a backup program designed for Windows XP. Using a backup program allows you to back up your registry onto removable media, such as a recordable CD, so you will be able to restore the registry if the registry becomes damaged.

I forgot to back up the registry! Can I still restore the registry?

✔ If you made changes to the registry and Windows will not start properly, restart the computer and hold down the F8 key. When the Windows Advanced Options Menu appears, select the Last Known Good Configuration option and then press the Enter key twice to start Windows using a previous copy of the registry.

How do I print all or part of the registry?

✔ In the left pane of the Registry Editor window, select My Computer if you want to print the entire registry or select the part of the registry you want to print. Click the File menu and choose Print. In the Print dialog box, select the printer you want to use and then click the Print button.

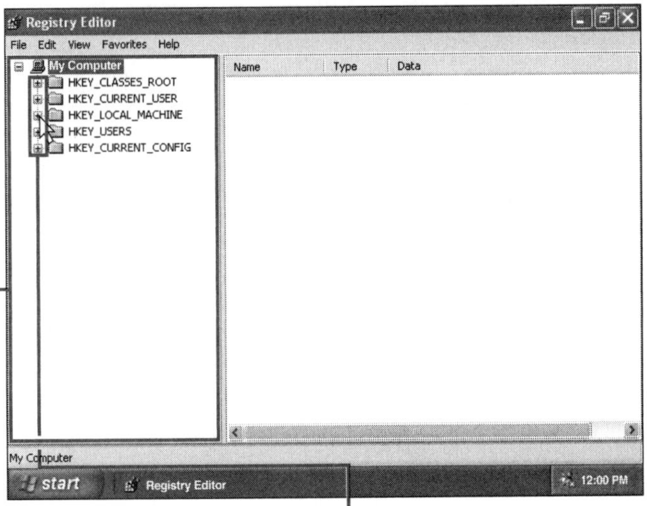

■ The Registry Editor window appears.

■ This area displays the main keys of the registry.

5 Click the plus sign (⊞) beside a key to display its contents (⊞ changes to ⊟).

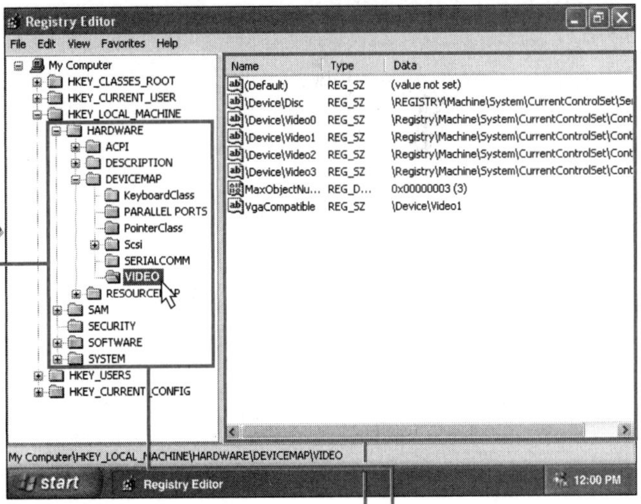

■ The contents of the key appear.

Note: You can click the minus sign (⊟) beside the key to once again hide the contents of the key.

6 Repeat step 5 until the registry item of interest appears.

7 Click the registry item to display its values.

■ This area displays the values for the registry item.

CONTINUED

WORK WITH THE REGISTRY (CONTINUED)

Looking for specific information by browsing through the Registry Editor window can be time-consuming and difficult. The Find feature can help you quickly find specific information in the registry.

Each value of a key in the registry has a name and data. By default, Windows will search all the keys, values and data in the registry for the information you specify. You can speed up the Find feature by choosing to search only keys, values or data.

You can also use the Match whole string only option to find only text that exactly matches the text you specify. For example, a search for "Directory" will not find "Download Directory."

The Find feature can only search for string data. You will not be able to search for binary or DWORD data. String data appears in quotation marks. Binary data is typically presented as pairs of hexadecimal values, while DWORD data displays 0x followed by 8 hexadecimal values and the decimal equivalent of the data in parentheses.

SEARCH THE REGISTRY

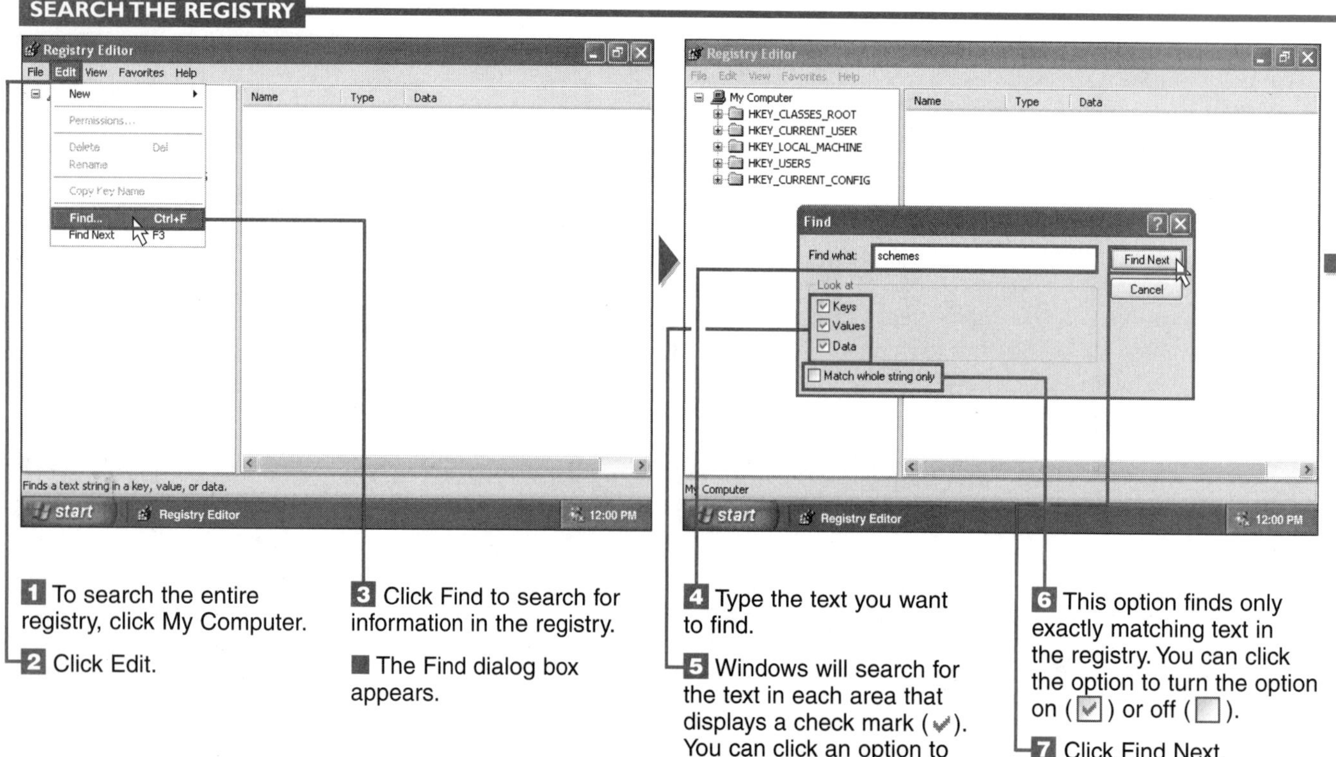

1 To search the entire registry, click My Computer.

2 Click Edit.

3 Click Find to search for information in the registry.

■ The Find dialog box appears.

4 Type the text you want to find.

5 Windows will search for the text in each area that displays a check mark (✔). You can click an option to add (☑) or remove (☐) a check mark.

6 This option finds only exactly matching text in the registry. You can click the option to turn the option on (☑) or off (☐).

7 Click Find Next.

The Registry Editor's Find feature is slow. How can I perform faster searches?

✔ You can export the entire registry to a text file and then use a word processor, such as WordPad, to search the registry. To export the registry to a text file, click the File menu and select Export. In the dialog box that appears, type a name for the file. Then click ▾ in the Save as type area and choose Text Files (*.txt) from the list that appears. In the Export range area, click All (○ changes to ◉). Then click the Save button.

How do I change a value for a registry item?

✔ In the left pane of the Registry Editor window, select the registry item that contains the value you want to change and then double-click the value you want to change in the right pane. In the dialog box that appears, select the current data and then type the new data for the value.

Are there other ways I can make changes to the registry?

✔ Yes. When you make changes to your computer settings using the tools included with Windows, such as those found in the Control Panel, Windows makes the changes to the registry for you. Whenever possible, you should use these tools to make changes to the registry.

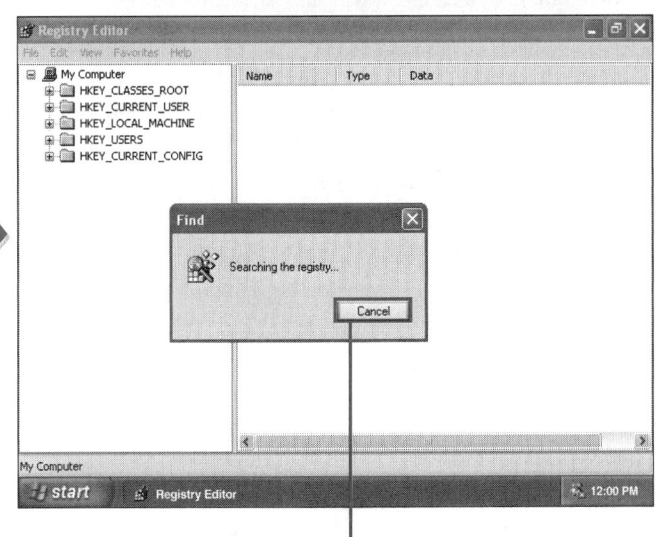

■ The Find dialog box appears while Windows searches the registry.

■ You can click Cancel to stop the search at any time.

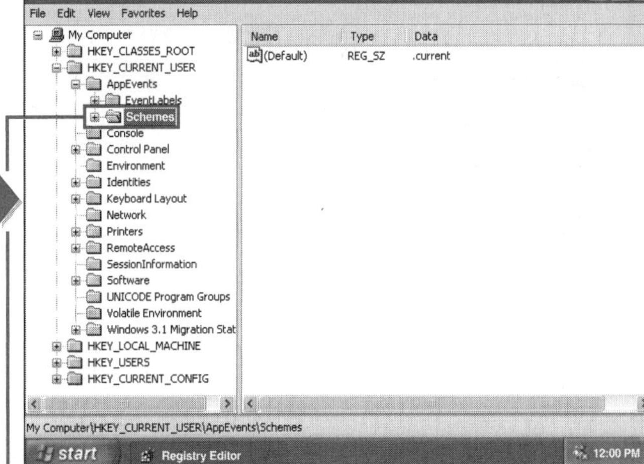

■ Windows highlights the first item that matches the text you typed.

■ You can press the F3 key to find the next instance of the text in the registry.

WHAT'S ON THE CD-ROM DISC

The CD-ROM disc included in this book contains many useful files and programs that can be used when working with Windows XP. You will find an e-version of this book, as well as several popular programs you can install and use on your computer. Before installing any of the programs on the disc, make sure a newer version of the program is not already installed on your computer. For information about installing different versions of the same program, contact the program's manufacturer.

SYSTEM REQUIREMENTS

While most programs on the CD-ROM disc have minimal system requirements, your computer should be equipped with the following hardware and software to use all the contents of the CD-ROM disc:

* A Pentium or faster processor.
* Microsoft Windows 98 or later.
* At least 64 MB of RAM.
* 180 MB of hard drive space.
* A double-speed (2x) or faster CD-ROM drive.
* A monitor capable of displaying at least 256 colors or grayscale, set to a resolution of at least 800x600.
* A modem with a speed of at least 14,400 bps.
* A sound card.

For information about the system requirements for running Windows XP, see page 560.

WEB LINKS

The CD-ROM disc contains a Web page that provides one-click access to all the Web pages and Internet references in the book. To use these links, you must have an Internet connection and a Web browser installed.

ACROBAT VERSION

The CD-ROM disc contains an e-version of this book that you can view and search using Adobe Acrobat Reader. You cannot print the pages or copy text from the Acrobat files. An evaluation version of Adobe Acrobat Reader is also included on the disc.

INSTALLING AND USING THE SOFTWARE

Before installing a program from this disc, you should exit all other programs. In order to use most of the programs, you must accept the license agreement provided with the program. Make sure you read any instruction files provided with each program.

Program Versions

Shareware programs are fully functional, trial versions of copyrighted programs. If you like a particular program, you can register with its author for a nominal fee and receive licenses, enhanced versions and technical support.

Freeware programs are free, copyrighted programs. Unlike shareware, these programs do not require a fee or provide technical support.

GNU software is governed by its own license, which is included inside the folder of the GNU software. See the GNU license for more details.

Trial, demo and evaluation versions are usually limited either by time or functionality. For example, you may not be able to save projects using these versions. Some trial versions are sensitive to system date changes. If you alter your computer's date, the programs will "time out" and will no longer be functional.

AbyssAudio Collection

For Microsoft Windows 95/98/NT/2000. Freeware version.

AbyssAudio Collection from AbyssAudio, Inc. is software that can scan your hard disk or a CD for music files and help you organize the files. You can obtain the latest version of AbyssAudio at www.abyssaudio.com.

Acrobat Reader

For Microsoft Windows 95/98/Me/NT/2000/XP. Freeware version.

Acrobat Reader from Adobe Systems, Inc. is software you can use to access and view the e-version of Master VISUALLY™ Windows® XP also included on this disc. For information about using Acrobat Reader, see page 618. You can obtain the latest version of Acrobat Reader at www.adobe.com.

FreeAmp

For Microsoft Windows 95/98/Me/NT/2000/XP. GNU version.

FreeAmp from FreeAmp.org is an audio player that you can use to play many different types of sound files and organize your audio files. For more information about FreeAmp, visit www.freeamp.org.

NameWiz

For Microsoft Windows 95/98/Me/NT/2000. Shareware version.

NameWiz from SoftByte Laboratories is a file renaming utility that allows you to change the names of a group of files quickly and easily. For more information about NameWiz, visit www.softbytelabs.com.

Paint Shop Pro

For Microsoft Windows 95/98/Me/NT/2000/XP. Evaluation version.

Paint Shop Pro from Jasc Software, Inc. is a program you can use to create and edit images. Paint Shop Pro can be used to capture and edit images from a computer screen or digital camera. You can download additional components and access technical support for Paint Shop Pro at www.jasc.com.

VirusScan

For Microsoft Windows 95/98/Me/NT/2000/XP. Internet Explorer 4.01 with Service Pack 2 or above required. Evaluation version.

VirusScan from McAfee is a program that can detect and remove computer viruses from your computer and scan incoming e-mail messages for viruses. You can find more information about VirusScan and the latest viruses at www.mcafee.com.

WinRAR

For Microsoft Windows 95/98/Me/NT/2000/XP. Trial version.

WinRAR from Softronic Oy is an archive manager, which allows you to compress your files and create archives of files you no longer use frequently. For more information about WinRAR, visit www.rarsoft.com.

WinZip

For Microsoft Windows 95/98/Me/NT/2000/XP. Shareware version.

WinZip from WinZip Computing, Inc. compresses files to make it easier and faster to transfer information from one computer to another. WinZip is commonly used to reduce the amount of disk space consumed by files and to reduce the size of files sent by e-mail. For more information about WinZip, visit www.winzip.com.

TROUBLESHOOTING

We have tried our best to compile programs that work on most computers with the minimum system requirements. Your computer, however, may differ and some programs may not work properly for some reason.

The two most likely problems are that you do not have enough memory (RAM) for the programs you want to use or you have other programs running that are affecting the installation or running of a program. If you get error messages while trying to install or use the programs on the CD-ROM disc, try one or more of the following methods and then try installing or running the software again:

* Read the ReadMe file located at the root of the CD-ROM for the latest product information at the time of publication.
* Close all running programs.
* Restart your computer.
* Turn off any anti-virus software.
* Close the CD-ROM interface and run demos or installations directly from Windows Explorer.
* Add more RAM to your computer.

If you still have trouble installing the items from the CD, please call the Hungry Minds, Inc. Customer Service phone number: 800-762-2974 (outside the U.S.: 317-572-3994). Hungry Minds will provide technical support only for installation and other general quality control items. For technical support on the applications themselves, consult the program's vendor or author.

USING THE E-VERSION OF THE BOOK

You can view *Master VISUALLY Windows XP* on your screen using the CD-ROM disc included at the back of this book. The CD-ROM disc allows you to browse through the pages of the book and search the contents of the book for a specific word or phrase. The CD-ROM disc also provides a convenient way of keeping the book handy while traveling.

You must install Adobe Acrobat Reader on your computer before you can view the book on the CD-ROM disc. This program is provided on the disc. Acrobat Reader allows you to view Portable Document Format (PDF) files, which can display books and magazines on your screen exactly as they appear in printed form.

Acrobat Reader is a popular and useful program. There are many files available on the Web that are designed to be viewed using Acrobat Reader. Look for files with the .pdf extension. For more information about Acrobat Reader, visit the Web site at www.adobe.com/products/acrobat/readermain.html.

To view the contents of the book using Acrobat Reader, display the main menu on the CD-ROM disc. Click the eBook link, select the section of the book you want to view and then click Install.

USING THE E-VERSION OF THE BOOK

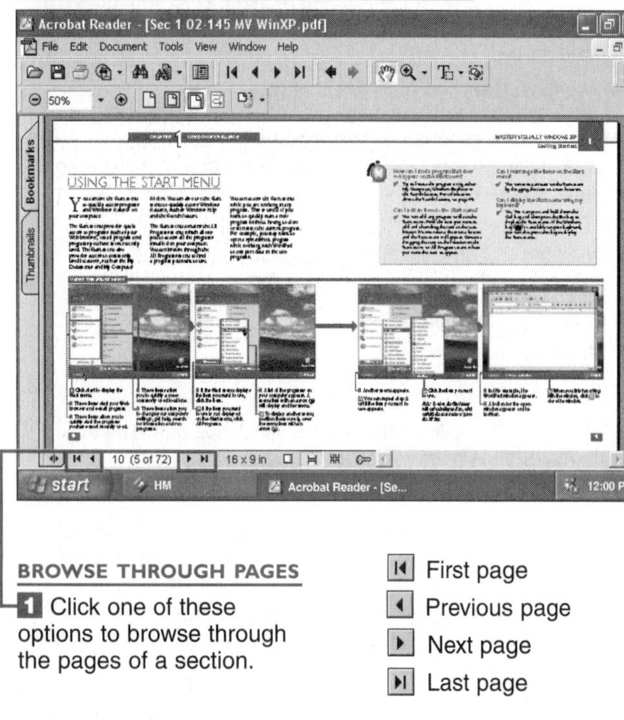

BROWSE THROUGH PAGES

1 Click one of these options to browse through the pages of a section.

- First page
- Previous page
- Next page
- Last page

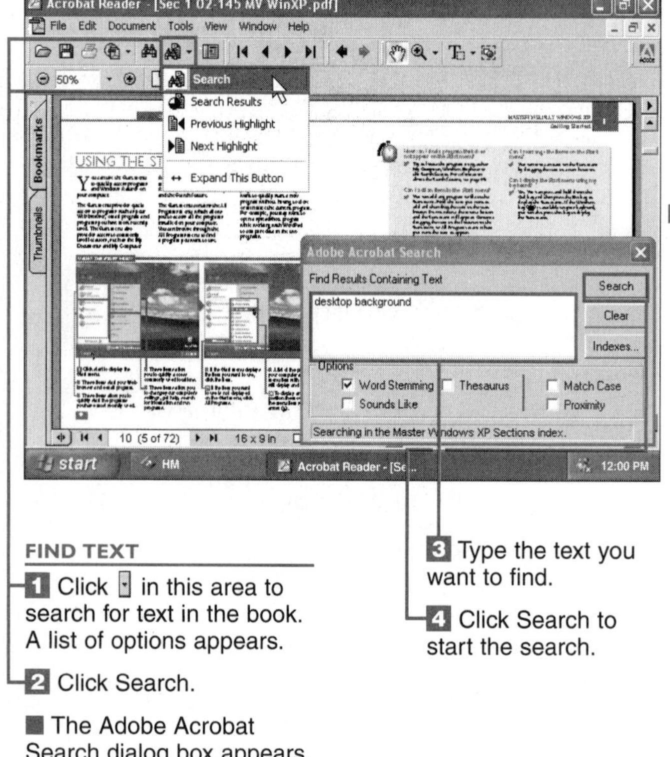

FIND TEXT

1 Click ▾ in this area to search for text in the book. A list of options appears.

2 Click Search.

■ The Adobe Acrobat Search dialog box appears.

3 Type the text you want to find.

4 Click Search to start the search.

How do I install Acrobat Reader?

✔ Display the main menu on the CD-ROM disc and click the Software link. Click Acrobat Reader, click Install and then follow the instructions on your screen.

When I search for text, the text Acrobat Reader highlights is difficult to read. How can I make highlighted text easier to read?

✔ You can turn off the font smoothing capabilities of Acrobat Reader to make highlighted text easier to read. In the Acrobat Reader window, display the Edit menu and choose Preferences. Click Display at the left side of the Preferences dialog box. In the Smoothing area, click Smooth Text (☑ changes to ☐) and then click OK.

How can I make searching the book more convenient?

✔ You can copy the PDF files to your computer. This allows you to easily access the contents of the book at any time. Display the contents of the CD-ROM disc and then copy the Book folder from the CD to your hard drive.

How can I magnify an area of the page I am viewing?

✔ In the Acrobat Reader window, click 🔍 and then click the area of the page you want to magnify until the area appears the way you want. To quickly display the page at 100% magnification, click 🗋. To once again fit the entire page inside the window, click 🗋.

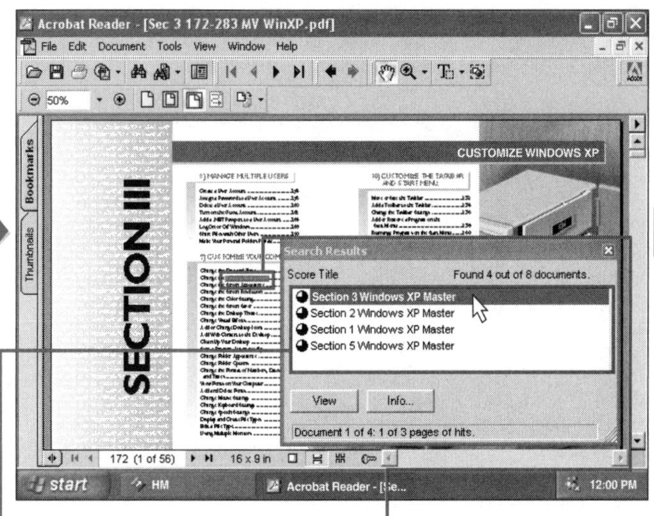

■ The Search Results dialog box appears, displaying the sections in which Acrobat Reader found the text you typed in step 3.

■ The first instance of the text in the section you selected is highlighted.

5 Double-click the section you want to view.

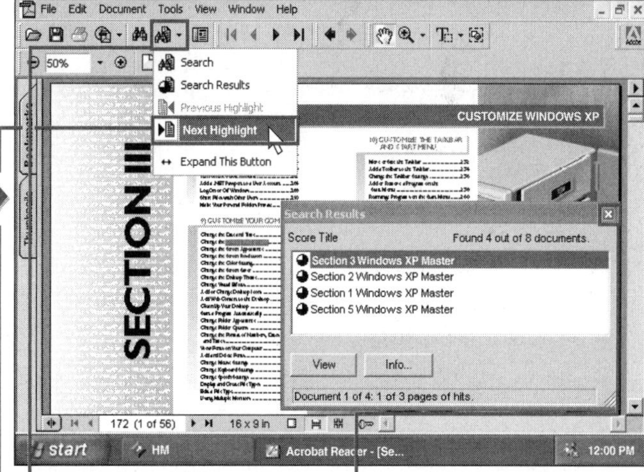

6 To find the next instance of the text, click ▾ in this area. A list of options appears.

7 Click Next Highlight.

8 Repeat steps 6 and 7 until you have viewed all the instances of the text in the section.

Note: You can repeat steps 5 to 8 to view the instances of the text found in other sections of the book.

9 Click ☒ to close the Search Results dialog box.

HUNGRY MINDS, INC.
END-USER LICENSE AGREEMENT

READ THIS. You should carefully read these terms and conditions before opening the software packet(s) included with this book ("Book"). This is a license agreement ("Agreement") between you and Hungry Minds, Inc. ("HMI"). By opening the accompanying software packet(s), you acknowledge that you have read and accept the following terms and conditions. If you do not agree and do not want to be bound by such terms and conditions, promptly return the Book and the unopened software packet(s) to the place you obtained them for a full refund.

1. License Grant. HMI grants to you (either an individual or entity) a nonexclusive license to use one copy of the enclosed software program(s) (collectively, the "Software") solely for your own personal or business purposes on a single computer (whether a standard computer or a workstation component of a multi-user network). The Software is in use on a computer when it is loaded into temporary memory (RAM) or installed into permanent memory (hard disk, CD-ROM, or other storage device). HMI reserves all rights not expressly granted herein.

2. Ownership. HMI is the owner of all right, title, and interest, including copyright, in and to the compilation of the Software recorded on the disk(s) or CD-ROM ("Software Media"). Copyright to the individual programs recorded on the Software Media is owned by the author or other authorized copyright owner of each program. Ownership of the Software and all proprietary rights relating thereto remain with HMI and its licensers.

3. Restrictions On Use and Transfer.

(a) You may only (i) make one copy of the Software for backup or archival purposes, or (ii) transfer the Software to a single hard disk, provided that you keep the original for backup or archival purposes. You may not (i) rent or lease the Software, (ii) copy or reproduce the Software through a LAN or other network system or through any computer subscriber system or bulletin-board system, or (iii) modify, adapt, or create derivative works based on the Software.

(b) You may not reverse engineer, decompile, or disassemble the Software. You may transfer the Software and user documentation on a permanent basis, provided that the transferee agrees to accept the terms and conditions of this Agreement and you retain no copies. If the Software is an update or has been updated, any transfer must include the most recent update and all prior versions.

4. Restrictions on Use of Individual Programs. You must follow the individual requirements and restrictions detailed for each individual program in What's On The CD-ROM Disc of this Book. These limitations are also contained in the individual license agreements recorded on the Software Media. These limitations may include a requirement that after using the program for a specified period of time, the user must pay a registration fee or discontinue use. By opening the Software packet(s), you will be agreeing to abide by the licenses and restrictions for these individual programs that are detailed in What's On The CD-ROM Disc and on the Software Media. None of the material on this Software Media or listed in this Book may ever be redistributed, in original or modified form, for commercial purposes.

5. Limited Warranty.

(a) HMI warrants that the Software and Software Media are free from defects in materials and workmanship under normal use for a period of sixty (60) days from the date of purchase of this Book. If HMI receives notification within the warranty period of defects in materials or workmanship, HMI will replace the defective Software Media.

(b) HMI AND THE AUTHOR OF THE BOOK DISCLAIM ALL OTHER WARRANTIES, EXPRESS OR IMPLIED, INCLUDING WITHOUT LIMITATION IMPLIED WARRANTIES OF MERCHANTABILITY AND FITNESS FOR A PARTICULAR PURPOSE, WITH RESPECT TO THE SOFTWARE, THE PROGRAMS, THE SOURCE CODE CONTAINED THEREIN, AND/OR THE TECHNIQUES DESCRIBED IN THIS BOOK. HMI DOES NOT WARRANT THAT THE FUNCTIONS CONTAINED IN THE SOFTWARE WILL MEET YOUR REQUIREMENTS OR THAT THE OPERATION OF THE SOFTWARE WILL BE ERROR FREE.

(c) This limited warranty gives you specific legal rights, and you may have other rights that vary from jurisdiction to jurisdiction.

6. Remedies.

(a) HMI's entire liability and your exclusive remedy for defects in materials and workmanship shall be limited to replacement of the Software Media, which may be returned to HMI with a copy of your receipt at the following address: Software Media Fulfillment Department, Attn.: Master VISUALLY Windows XP, Hungry Minds, Inc., 10475 Crosspoint Blvd., Indianapolis, IN 46256, or call 1-800-762-2974. Please allow four to six weeks for delivery. This Limited Warranty is void if failure of the Software Media has resulted from accident, abuse, or misapplication. Any replacement Software Media will be warranted for the remainder of the original warranty period or thirty (30) days, whichever is longer.

(b) In no event shall HMI or the author be liable for any damages whatsoever (including without limitation damages for loss of business profits, business interruption, loss of business information, or any other pecuniary loss) arising from the use of or inability to use the Book or the Software, even if HMI has been advised of the possibility of such damages.

(c) Because some jurisdictions do not allow the exclusion or limitation of liability for consequential or incidental damages, the above limitation or exclusion may not apply to you.

7. U.S. Government Restricted Rights. Use, duplication, or disclosure of the Software for or on behalf of the United States of America, its agencies and/or instrumentalities (the "U.S. Government") is subject to restrictions as stated in paragraph (c)(1)(ii) of the Rights in Technical Data and Computer Software clause of DFARS 252.227-7013, or subparagraphs (c) (1) and (2) of the Commercial Computer Software - Restricted Rights clause at FAR 52.227-19, and in similar clauses in the NASA FAR supplement, as applicable.

8. General. This Agreement constitutes the entire understanding of the parties and revokes and supersedes all prior agreements, oral or written, between them and may not be modified or amended except in a writing signed by both parties hereto that specifically refers to this Agreement. This Agreement shall take precedence over any other documents that may be in conflict herewith. If any one or more provisions contained in this Agreement are held by any court or tribunal to be invalid, illegal, or otherwise unenforceable, each and every other provision shall remain in full force and effect.

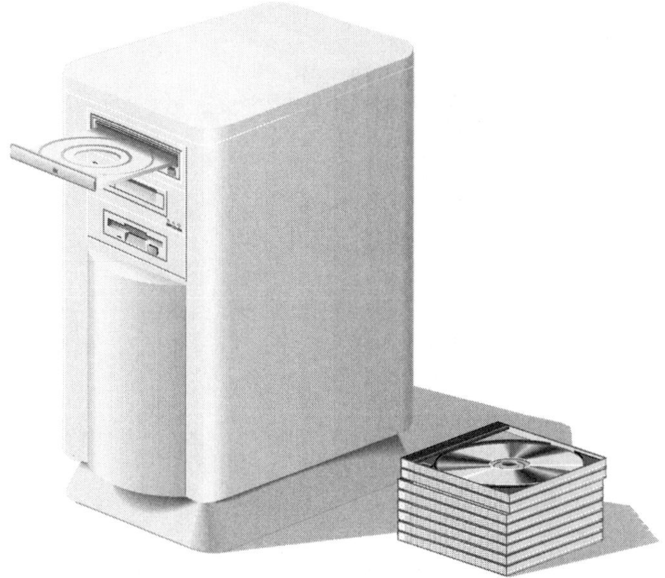

INDEX

A

B

C

D

E

F

G

H

I

J

K

L

M

N

O

P

Q

R

S

T

U

V

W

X

Z

ORDER FORM

TRADE & INDIVIDUAL ORDERS

Phone: **(800) 762-2974**
or **(317) 572-3993**
(8 a.m.–6 p.m., CST, weekdays)
FAX : **(800) 550-2747**
or **(317) 572-4002**

EDUCATIONAL ORDERS & DISCOUNTS

Phone: **(800) 434-2086**
(8:30 a.m.–5:00 p.m., CST, weekdays)
FAX : **(317) 572-4005**

CORPORATE ORDERS FOR VISUAL™ SERIES

Phone: **(800) 469-6616**
(8:30 a.m.–5 p.m., EST, weekdays)
FAX : **(905) 890-9434**

Qty	ISBN	Title	Price	Total

Shipping & Handling Charges

	Description	First book	Each add'l. book	Total
Domestic	Normal	$4.50	$1.50	$
	Two Day Air	$8.50	$2.50	$
	Overnight	$18.00	$3.00	$
International	Surface	$8.00	$8.00	$
	Airmail	$16.00	$16.00	$
	DHL Air	$17.00	$17.00	$

Subtotal ______________

CA residents add applicable sales tax ______________

IN, MA and MD residents add 5% sales tax ______________

IL residents add 6.25% sales tax ______________

RI residents add 7% sales tax ______________

TX residents add 8.25% sales tax ______________

Shipping ______________

Total ______________

Ship to:

Name ______________________________

Address ______________________________

Company ______________________________

City/State/Zip ______________________________

Daytime Phone ______________________________

Payment: ☐ Check to Hungry Minds (US Funds Only)
☐ Visa ☐ Mastercard ☐ American Express

Card # ______________ Exp. __________ Signature ______________________